CHILD DEVELOPMENT

EIGHTH EDITION

CHILD DEVELOPMENT

JOHN W. SANTROCK

UNIVERSITY OF TEXAS AT DALLAS

Boston, Massachusetts Burr Ridge, Illinois Dubuque, Iowa
Madison, Wisconsin New York, New York San Francisco, California St. Louis, Missouri

Editorial Director: Jane Vaicunas
Sponsoring Editor: Mickey Cox
Marketing Manager: James Rozsa
Project Manager: Jayne Klein
Production Supervisor: Mary E. Haas
Designer: LuAnn Schrandt
Cover credit: © Ross Whitaker/The Image Bank/Texas
Cover design: Benson Studio
Photo research coordinator: Lori Hancock
Art Editor: Joyce Watters
Compositor: GTS Graphics, Inc.
Typeface: Goudy 10/12
Printer: Quebecor Printing Book Group/Dubuque

Library of Congress Catalog Card Number: 96-78589

*With special appreciation to my wife Mary Jo, my children
Tracy and Jennifer, and my granddaughter Jordan.*

BRIEF CONTENTS

$\mathscr{C}$ONTENTS

SECTION One
The Nature of Child Development

Chapter 1
Introduction

Chapter 2
The Science of Child Development

SECTION Two
Biological Processes, Physical Development, and Perceptual Development

Chapter 3
Biological Beginnings

Chapter 4
Prenatal Development and Birth

SECTION Three

Cognition, Learning, Information Processing, and Language Development

Information Processing

(With Robert S. Siegler, Carnegie-Mellon University)

Intelligence

Language Development

SECTION Four
Socioemotional Development and the Self

Chapter 11
Attachment, Temperament, and Emotional Development

Chapter 12
The Self and Identity

SECTION Five
Social Contexts of Development

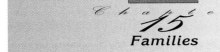

Chapter 18

Culture, Poverty, and Ethnicity

Preview   572

*Images of Children: The Cultural Conflicts of
Sonya and Michael   572*

LISTS OF FEATURES

SOCIOCULTURAL WORLDS OF CHILDREN

CRITICAL THINKING ABOUT CHILDREN'S DEVELOPMENT

PRACTICAL KNOWLEDGE ABOUT CHILDREN

PRACTICAL KNOWLEDGE ABOUT CHILDREN~CONT.

RESEARCH IN CHILD DEVELOPMENT

$\mathcal{I}$MPROVING THE LIVES OF CHILDREN

PREFACE

The first edition of *Child Development* was published in 1978. With this, the eighth edition, the book now spans more than 20 years. The child's developmental journey continues to grow in fascination for me. This is an exciting time to study and write about children's development. Scholars around the world are making new discoveries and developing new insights about virtually every domain of child development at a much faster pace than in previous decades. The field of child development is maturing to the point at which the knowledge that is being gained can be applied to children's lives to improve their adaptation, health, and well-being.

The eighth edition of *Child Development* continues to follow a topical format. The core knowledge of the field has been retained, but, as in the seventh edition, I carefully added to, subtracted from, integrated, and simplified the material for this new edition. The significant changes involved updating the research knowledge base that is the foundation of what we know about children's development and refining and applying what we know to improve the lives of children.

SUMMARY OF MAIN CHANGES IN *CHILD DEVELOPMENT*, EIGHTH EDITION

The most important changes in the eighth edition of *Child Development* are these:

1. New Explorations in Child Development chapter endpieces.
2. Extensive research updating and individual chapter content reviews by expert consultants.
3. Significant expansion and updating of the discussions of sensory and perceptual development.
4. Increased emphasis on critical thinking about children's development.

Explorations in Child Development Chapter Endpieces

The new Explorations in Child Development chapter endpieces consist of two parts: (1) Research in Child Development and (2) Improving the Lives of Children. These two parts provide students with expanded treatments of research and applications in child development.

The Research in Child Development section provides students with an opportunity to see how scientists who study child development actually conduct research studies. In the first two chapters, students learn why research in child development is important and how the journal process works. In subsequent chapters, students will read a minisimulation of a journal article that focuses on one of the chapter's topics.

The section on Improving the Lives of Children gives students an opportunity to see how information about children's development can be applied to the real worlds of children to improve their lives. The topics in this section include parenting strategies, prevention/intervention when children have problems, and better educational techniques.

Extensive Research Updating and Individual Chapter Content Reviews by Expert Consultants

Approximately 30 percent of the references in the eighth edition of *Child Development* are new. More than 300 come from 1995, 1996, 1997, and in-press sources.

The dramatic expansion of research in many areas of child development makes it virtually impossible for authors to provide a completely up-to-date rendering of content in all areas. To considerably improve the research content in many areas, the eighth edition of *Child Development* underwent the most extensive review process of all of the book's editions.

For the first time in the book's history, a different expert consultant was obtained for each chapter of *Child*

Development. The eighteen expert consultants are among the world's leading figures in their respective areas. They went over individual chapters with a fine-tooth comb, making detailed recommendations on what to add, what to delete, and how to interpret issues. The following are the leading expert consultants for the eighth edition of *Child Development:*

Chapter One: Marc Bornstein *National Institute of Child Health and Human Development*
Chapter Two: Glen Elder, Jr. *University of North Carolina*
Chapter Three: Kevin MacDonald *California State University, Long Beach*
Chapter Four: Tiffany Field *University of Miami (Florida)*
Chapter Five: Herb Pick *University of Minnesota*
Chapter Six: Cynthia Graber *Columbia University*
Chapter Seven: Mary Gauvaign *University of California, Riverside*
Chapter Eight: Deanna Kuhn *Columbia University*
Chapter Nine: Steven Ceci *Cornell University*
Chapter Ten: Nan Ratner *University of Maryland*
Chapter Eleven: Michael Lamb *National Institute of Child Health and Human Development*
Chapter Twelve: Daniel Hart *Rutgers University*
Chapter Thirteen: Janet Spence *University of Texas, Austin*
Chapter Fourteen: Lawrence Walker *University of British Columbia*
Chapter Fifteen: Dante Cicchetti *University of Rochester*
Chapter Sixteen: Janice Kupersmidt *University of North Carolina*
Chapter Seventeen: Alice Honig *Syracuse University*
Chapter Eighteen: Cynthia Garcia Coll *Wellesley College*

In addition to the eighteen expert consultants for *Child Development,* other leading researchers have also sent me valuable feedback that has influenced my thinking about material that is included in this eighth edition. These leading researchers who have served as expert consultants on my writing projects include:

Diana Baumrind *University of California, Berkeley*
Paul Baltes *Max Planck Institute, Berlin*
Florence Denmark *Pace University*
Rosalind Charlesworth *Weber State University*
Daniel Schacter *Harvard University*
Richard Brislin *University of Hawaii*
James Jones *University of Delaware*
John Harvey *University of Iowa*
Lilian Comaz-Diaz *Transcultural Institute*

Helen Tager-Flusberg *University of Massachusetts*
Sandra Graham *UCLA*

Significant Expansion and Updating of the Discussions of Perceptual and Motor Development

In the seventh edition of *Child Development,* the chapter on information processing was significantly upgraded through the efforts of one of the world's leading experts, Robert Siegler of Carnegie-Mellon University. To continue the research upgrading of *Child Development,* the material on perceptual and motor development was expanded and extensively revised. Research on perceptual and motor development in infancy has grown dramatically, and the increased space given to this important topic was needed. In addition to its increased emphasis on perceptual and motor development, chapter 6 also includes an important new section on brain development, reflecting the increased interest in this important area.

Critical Thinking About Children's Development

I continue to strive to improve the pedagogical system in *Child Development.* To this end, I have significantly expanded the critical-thinking sections of the book. To help me with this expansion, Jane Halonen of Alverno College, one of the leading experts on critical thinking in the teaching of psychology, served as an advisor and consultant.

Critical Thinking About Children's Development boxes appear twice in each chapter. Students will be encouraged to stretch their thinking about an aspect of child development related to the chapter material. In addition, the nature of critical thinking about children's development is introduced in the main body of the text toward the end of chapter 1.

STUDENT FRIENDLINESS

I remember having to read some poorly written, uninteresting textbooks when I was an undergraduate student. I have worked at length to make *Child Development,* eighth edition, a very student-friendly book. I continue to ask college students of all ages to give me feedback about which strategies for presenting material they like best and which they like least.

Student friendliness begins with writing, and students tell us that this text is written in a clear, organized manner. Examples of concepts are given at every step of the way, and the conversational writing style engages students to think about their own childhood and the lives of other children. The book also has cartoons, beautiful photographs and artpieces, and many applied features. If students enjoy this book and feel they have considerably more knowledge about both the scientific and the applied worlds of children's development upon finishing it, then I will have reached my goals for the book's eighth edition.

The book's student friendliness includes the visual preface titled **To the Student,** which follows. In this student preface, the book's learning system is visually presented along with information about how to use it effectively. Students who read the seventh edition of *Child Development* told us time after time that the learning system was extremely valuable in helping them to organize and learn about the different content domains of child development.

ANCILLARY MATERIALS

The following materials are also available. For more information please contact your local Sales Representative.

Annual Editions®

Magazines, newspapers, and journals of the public press play an important role in providing current, first-rate, relevant educational information. If in your child development course you are interested in exposing your students to a wide range of current, well-balanced, carefully selected articles from some of the most important magazines, newspapers, and journals published today, you may want to consider *Annual Editions: Child Growth and Development*, published by Dushkin/McGraw-Hill. *Annual Editions: Child Growth and Development* is a collection of over 40 articles on topics related to the latest research and thinking in child development. *Annual Editions* is updated on an annual basis, and there are a number of features designed to make it particularly useful, including a topic guide, an annotated table of contents, and unit overviews. Consult your Sales Representative for more details.

Taking Sides®

Are you interested in generating classroom discussion? In finding a tool to more fully involve your students in their experience of your course? Would you like to encourage your students to become more active learners? To develop their critical thinking skills? Lastly, are you yourself intrigued by current controversies related to issues in childhood and development? If so, you should be aware of a new publication from Dushkin/McGraw-Hill. *Taking Sides: Clashing Views on Controversial Issues in Childhood and Society*, edited by Professors Robert L. DelCampo and Diane S. DelCampo of New Mexico State University. *Taking Sides*, a reader that takes a pro/con approach to issues, is designed to introduce students to controversies in childhood and development. The readings, which represent the arguments of leading child behaviorists and social commentators, reflect a variety of viewpoints and have been selected for their liveliness, currency, and substance. Consult your Sales Representative for more details.

Primis Custom Publishing

Primis Custom Publishing allows you to create original works or tailor existing materials to suit your students' needs. All you need to do is organize chapters from your McGraw-Hill textbook to match your course syllabus. You control the number of chapters, pieces of art and end-of-chapter materials appropriate for your course. You may also include your own materials in the book. With Primis Custom Publishing all the choices are yours. In a few short weeks after consulting with us you can have a professionally printed and bound book delivered to your bookstore. Please contact your local Sales Representative for more information.

ANCILLARY MATERIALS FOR THE INSTRUCTOR

The publisher and ancillary team have worked together to produce an outstanding integrated teaching package to accompany *Child Development*. The authors of the ancillaries are all experienced teachers in the child development course. The ancillaries have been designed to make it as easy as possible to customize the entire package to meet the unique needs of professors and students.

Instructor's Manual

The key to this teaching package was created by Allen H. Keniston and Blaine F. Peden of the University of Wisconsin–Eau Claire. Allen and Blaine are both award-winning teachers and active members of The Council of Teachers of Undergraduate Psychology. This flexible manual provides a variety of useful tools to enhance your teaching efforts, reduce your workload, and increase your enjoyment. For each chapter of the text, the manual provides an outline and overview. The manual also contains lecture suggestions, classroom activities, discussion questions, integrative essay questions, a film list, and a transparency guide. It contains an abundance of handouts and exercises for stimulating classroom discussion and encouraging critical thinking.

The **Test Bank** was constructed by Lynne Blesz Vestal. This comprehensive test bank includes over 1,800 multiple-choice test questions that are keyed to the text and learning objectives. Each item is designated factual, conceptual, or applied as defined by the first three levels of Benjamin Bloom's *Taxonomy of Educational Objectives* (1956).

The questions in the Test Bank are available on **MicroTest III**, a powerful but easy-to-use test-generating program by Chariot Software Group. MicroTest is available for Windows and Macintosh. With MicroTest, you can easily select questions from the Test Bank and print a test and an answer key. You can customize questions, headings, and instructions, you can add or import questions of your own, and you can print your test in a choice of fonts if your printer supports them.

The **Student Study Guide** was created by Blaine F. Peden and Allen H. Keniston of the University of Wisconsin–Eau Claire. For each chapter of the text, the student is provided with learning objectives and key terms, a guided review, and two self-tests. One covers key terms and key persons, and the other entails multiple choice questions (with answers provided for self-testing). The study guide includes the section "How to Be a Better Student" to help students study more effectively and efficiently.

Resources for Improving Children's Development is a new course supplement that was created by author John Santrock. It includes telephone numbers, agencies, brochures, and books that can be used to improve the lives of children. This course supplement can be packaged with *Child Development*, Eighth Edition.

Guide to Life-Span Development for Future Nurses and **Guide to Life-Span Development for Future Educators** are new course supplements that help students apply the concepts of human development to the education and nursing professions. Each supplement contains information, exercises, and sample tests designed to help students prepare for certification and understand human development from these professional perspectives.

The **Human Development Transparency/Slide Set,** Second Edition, consists of 141 newly developed acetate transparencies or slides. These full-color transparencies, selected by author John Santrock and Janet Simons, include graphics from the text and various outside sources and were expressly designed to provide comprehensive coverage of all major topic areas generally covered in life-span development. A comprehensive annotated guide provides a brief description for each transparency and helpful suggestions for use in the classroom.

The **Human Development Electronic Image Bank CD-ROM** contains more than 100 useful images and a computer projection system divided into two separate programs: The Interactive Slide Show and the Slide Show Editor. The Interactive Slide Show allows you to play a preset slide show containing selected images. The Slide Show Editor allows you to customize and create your own slide show. You can add slides anywhere you like in the presentation and incorporate any audio or visual files you'd like, as well as create title screens. You also may use the CD-ROM images with your own presentation software (PowerPoint, etc.). (Images are available in both PICT and BMP formats, Macintosh and Windows compatible.)

A large selection of **Videotapes,** including *Seasons of Life*, is also available to instructors, based upon the number of textbooks ordered by your bookstore.

The **AIDS Booklet,** Third Edition, by Frank D. Cox of Santa Barbara City College, is a brief but comprehensive introduction to the Acquired Immune Deficiency Syndrome which is caused by HIV (Human Immunodeficiency Virus) and related viruses.

The **Critical Thinker,** written by Richard Mayer and Fiona Goodchild of the University of California, Santa Barbara, uses excerpts from introductory psychology textbooks to show students how to think critically about psychology. Either this or the AIDS booklet are available at no charge to first-year adopters of our textbook or can be purchased separately.

The **Human Development Interactive Videodisc Set** produced by Roger Ray of Rollins College, brings life-span development to life with instant access to over 30 brief video segments from the highly acclaimed *Seasons of Life* series. The 2-disc set can be used alone for selecting and sequencing excerpts, or in tandem with a Macintosh computer to add interactive commentary capability, as well as extra video and search options. Consult your Sales Representative for details.

ACKNOWLEDGMENTS

The eighth edition of *Child Development* benefited from the ideas of a very carefully selected group of expert consultants, who were listed earlier in this preface. In addition to those reviewers, I thank the following reviewers of previous editions:

Ruth L. Ault   *Davidson College*
William H. Barber   *Midwestern State University*
Michael Bergmire   *Jefferson College*
David Bernhardt   *Carleton University*
Kathryn Norcross Black   *Purdue University*
Elaine Blakemore   *Indiana University*
Susan Bland   *Niagara County Community College*
Maureen Callahan   *Webster University*
D. Bruce Carter   *Syracuse University*
Theodore Chandler   *Kent State University*
Audrey E. Clark   *California State University, Northridge*
Debra E. Clark   *SUNY–Cortland*
Robert C. Coon   *Louisiana State University*
Roger W. Coulson   *Iowa State University*
Fred Danner   *University of Kentucky*
Denise M. DeZolt   *Kent State University*
Daniel R. DiSalvi   *Kean College*
Diane C. Draper   *Iowa State University*
Beverly B. Dupré   *Southern University at New Orleans*
Claire Etaugh   *Bradley University*
Dennis T. Farrell   *Luzerne County Community College*
Saul Feinman   *University of Wyoming*
Jane Goins Flanagan   *Lamar University*
L. Sidney Fox   *California State University–Long Beach*
Janet Fuller   *Mansfield University*
Irma Galejs   *Iowa State University*
Colleen Gift   *Highland Community College*
Margaret S. Gill   *Kutztown State College*
Hill Goldsmith   *University of Wisconsin*
Nira Grannott   *University of Texas at Dallas*
Donald E. Guenther   *Kent State University*
Robert A. Haaf   *University of Toledo*
Elizabeth Hasson   *Westchester University*
Rebecca Heikkinen   *Kent State University*

Stanley Henson *Arkansas Technical University*
Seth Kalichman *Loyola University*
Kenneth Kallio *SUNY–Geneseo*
Daniel W. Kee *California State University,
  Fullerton*
Melvyn B. King *SUNY–Cortland*
Claire Kopp *UCLA*
John W. Kulig *Northern Illinois University*
Daniel K. Lapsley *University of Notre Dame*
Dottie McCrossen *University of Ottawa*
Sheryll Mennicke *Concordia College, St. Paul*
Carolyn Meyer *Lake Sumter Community College*
Dalton Miller-Jones *NE Foundation for Children*
Jose E. Nanes *University of Minnesota*
Sherry J. Neal *Oklahoma City Community College*
Daniel J. O'Neill *Bristol Community College*
Margaret Owen *Timberlawn Research Foundation*
Robert Pasnak *George Mason University*
Cosby Steel Rogers *Virginia Polytechnic Institute and
  State University*
Douglas B. Sawin *University of Texas, Austin*
Ed Scholwinski *Southwest Texas State University*
Dale Schunk *Purdue University*

Bill M. Seay *Louisiana State University*
Matthew J. Sharps *University of Colorado*
Marilyn Shea *University of Maine, Farmington*
Robert Siegler *Carnegie Mellon University*
Dorothy Justus Sluss *Virginia Polytechnic Institute and
  State University*
Melanie Spence *University of Texas at Dallas*
Mark S. Strauss *University of Pittsburgh*
Cherie Valeithian *Kent State University*
Kimberlee L. Whaley *Ohio State University*
Belinda M. Wholeben *Northern Illinois University*

A final note of thanks goes to my family. Mary Jo Santrock has lived through eight editions of *Child Development* and continues to provide outstanding support. When the first edition of *Child Development* was written, my daughters—Tracy and Jennifer—were young children. Through the years, they have provided me with first-hand experience in watching children develop. They have helped me render a treatment of children's development that captures its complexity, its subtlety, and its humanity.

To the Student

How the Learning System Works

This book contains a number of learning devices each of which presents the field of child development in a meaningful way. The learning devices in *Child Development* will help you learn the material more effectively.

We reach backward to our parents and forward to our children and through their children to a future we will never see, but about which we need to care.

—Carl Jung

Chapter Outline

Each chapter begins with an outline, showing the organization of topics by heading levels. The outline functions as an overview to the arrangement and structure of the chapter.

The childhood shows the man, as morning shows the day.

—Milton

IMAGES OF CHILDREN

Erikson and Piaget as Children

PREVIEW

Some individuals have difficulty thinking of child development as being a science in the same way as physics, chemistry, and biology are sciences. Can a discipline that studies how babies develop, how parents nurture children, how peers interact, and how children think be equated with disciplines that investigate how gravity works and the molecular structure of a compound? Science is defined not by *what* it investigates but by *how* it investigates. Whether you are studying photosynthesis, butterflies, Saturn's moons, or human development, it is the *way* you study that makes the approach scientific or not.

In this chapter, we will study three key ingredients of child development as a science—the scientific method, theories, and methods. You also will learn about ethics and sexism in research on child development, as well as how to be a wise consumer of information about children's development.

Imagine that you have developed a major theory of child development. What would influence someone like you to construct this theory? A person interested in developing such a theory usually goes through a long university training program that culminates in a doctoral degree. As part of the training, the future theorist is exposed to many ideas about a particular area of child development, such as biological, cognitive, or socioemotional development. Another factor that could explain why someone develops a particular theory is that person's life experiences. Two important developmental theorists, whose views we will describe later in the chapter, are Erik Erikson and Jean Piaget. Let's examine a portion of their lives as they were growing up to discover how their experiences might have contributed to the theories they developed.

Erik Homberger Erikson (1902–1994) was born near Frankfurt, Germany, to Danish parents. Before Erik was born, his parents separated and his mother left Denmark to live in Germany. At age 3, Erik became ill, and his mother took him to see a pediatrician named Homberger. Young Erik's mother fell in love with the pediatrician, married him, and named Erik after his new stepfather.

Erik attended primary school from the ages of 6 to 10 and then the gymnasium (high school) from 11 to 18. He studied art and a number of languages rather than science courses such as biology and chemistry. Erik did not like the atmosphere of formal schooling, and this was reflected in his grades. Rather than go to college at age 18, the adolescent Erikson wandered around Europe, keeping a diary about his experiences. After a year of travel through Europe, he returned to Germany and enrolled in art school, became dissatisfied, and enrolled in another. Later he traveled to Florence, Italy. Psychiatrist Robert Coles described Erikson at this time:

To the Italians he was . . . the young, tall, thin Nordic expatriate with long, blond hair. He wore a corduroy suit and was seen by his family and friends as not odd or

"sick" but as a wandering artist who was trying to come to grips with himself, a not unnatural or unusual struggle. (Coles, 1970, p.15)

The second major theorist whose life we will examine is Jean Piaget. Piaget (1896–1980) was born in Neuchâtel, Switzerland. Jean's father was an intellectual who taught young Jean to think systematically. Jean's mother was also very bright. His father had an air of detachment from his mother, whom Piaget described as prone to frequent outbursts of neurotic behavior.

In his autobiography, Piaget detailed why he chose to study cognitive development rather than social or abnormal development:

I started to forego playing for serious work very early. Indeed, I have always detested any departure from reality, an attitude which I relate to . . . my mother's poor health. It was this disturbing factor which at the beginning of my studies in psychology made me keenly interested in psychoanalytic and pathological psychology. Though this interest helped me to achieve independence and widen my cultural background, I have never since felt any desire to involve myself deeper in that particular direction, always much preferring the study of normalcy and of the workings of the intellect to that of the tricks of the unconscious. (Piaget, 1952a, p.238)

These excerpts from Erikson's and Piaget's lives illustrate how personal experiences might influence the direction in which a particular theorist goes. Erikson's own wanderings and search for self contributed to his theory of identity development, and Piaget's intellectual experiences with his parents and schooling likely contributed to his emphasis on cognitive development.

Santrock: Child Development

Images of Children

Opening each chapter is an imaginative, high-interest piece, focusing on a topic related to the chapter's content.

Preview

This brief section describes the chapter's main points.

Visual Figures

Visual figures combine a description of important content information with a photograph(s) to illustrate the content. In a number of instances, the visual figures represent summaries of key ideas in the text to enhance your retention.

Figure 1.4
One Day in the Lives of Children in the United States

1	mother dies in childbirth
3	people under 25 die from HIV
6	children and youths commit suicide
14	children and youths are murdered
16	children and youths are killed by firearms
37	children and youths die from accidents
92	babies die
144	babies are born at very low birthweight
326	children are arrested for alcohol offenses
342	children are arrested for violence crimes
359	children are arrested for drug offenses
465	babies are born to mothers who received late or no prenatal care
788	babies are born at low birthweight

1,420	babies are born to mothers younger than 20
2,444	babies are born to mothers who are not high school graduates
2,556	babies are born into poverty
3,086	public school students are corporally punished
3,356	high school students drop out*
3,533	babies are born to unmarried mothers
5,500	high school graduates do not go on to college*
6,042	children are arrested
10,829	babies are born
13,076	public school students are suspended*

*Every school day

Key Terms Definitions

Key terms appear in boldface type with their definitions immediately following in italic type. This provides you with a clear understanding of important concepts.

(following instructions, identifying letters), and spend many hours in play and with peers. First grade typically marks the end of this period.
Middle and late childhood *is the developmental period that extends from about 6 to 11 years of age, approximately corresponding to the elementary school years; sometimes this period is called the elementary school years.* Children master the fundamental skills of reading, writing, and arithmetic, and they are formally exposed to the larger world and its culture. Achievement becomes a more central theme of the child's world, and self-control increases.
Adolescence *is the developmental period of transition from childhood to early adulthood, entered at approximately 10 to 12 years of age and ending at 18 to 22 years of age.* Adolescence begins with rapid physical changes—dramatic gains in height and weight; changes in body contour; and the development of sexual characteristics such as enlargement of the breasts, development of pubic and facial hair, and deepening of the voice. At this point in development, the pursuit of independence and an identity are prominent. Thought is more logical, abstract, and idealistic. More and more time is spent outside the family during this period.

Today, developmentalists do not believe that change ends with adolescence (Baltes, Lindenberger, & Staudinger, 1997; Santrock, 1997). They describe development as a lifelong process. However, the purpose of this text is to describe the changes in development that take place from conception through adolescence.

The periods of development from conception through adolescence are shown in figure 1.6, along with the processes of development—biological, cognitive, and socioemotional. The interplay of biological, cognitive, and socioemotional processes produces the periods of development.

Developmental Issues

A number of issues generate spirited debate among developmentalists: To what extent is development influenced

by maturation and experience (nature and nurture)? To what extent is it characterized by continuity and discontinuity? To what degree does it involve early versus later experiences?

Maturation and Experience (Nature and Nurture)

We can think of development as produced not only by the interplay of biological, cognitive, and socioemotional processes but also by the interplay of maturation and experience. **Maturation** *is the orderly sequence of changes dictated by the genetic blueprint we each have.* Just as a sunflower grows in an orderly way—unless flattened by an unfriendly environment—so does a human being grow in an orderly way, according to the maturational view. The range of environments can be vast, but the maturational approach argues that the genetic blueprint produces

Figure 1.6
Processes and Periods of Development
Development moves through the prenatal, infancy, early childhood, middle and late childhood, and adolescence periods. These periods of development are the result of biological, cognitive, and socioemotional processes. Development is the creation of increasingly complex forms.

Processes of development
Biological processes
Cognitive processes
Socioemotional processes

Adolescence
Middle and late childhood
Early childhood
Infancy
Prenatal period

Critical Thinking About Children's Development Boxes

These boxes are inserted periodically in each chapter to encourage you to stretch your mind about a topic in that particular section of the chapter.

Quotations

Quotations are sprinkled through each chapter to stimulate further thought about a topic.

CRITICAL THINKING ABOUT CHILDREN'S DEVELOPMENT

Imagining What Your Development as a Child Might Have Been Like in Other Cultural Contexts

Imagine what your development as a child might have been like in a culture that offered few choices compared to the Western world—Communist China during the Cultural Revolution. Young people could not select a job or a mate in rural China. They also were not given the choice of migrating to the city.

Imagine also another cultural context, this one in the United States. Supposing that you did not grow up in such circumstances, what might your life as a child have been like if you had grown up in the inner city, where most services have moved out, schools are inferior, poverty is extreme, and crime is common? (Unfortunately, some of you did grow up in such contexts.) By imagining what your development might have been like in these cultural contexts, you are engaging in perspective taking and identifying sociohistorical and cultural factors that influence children's development.

Ethnicity (the word *ethnic* comes from the Greek word for "nation") *is based on cultural heritage, nationality characteristics, race, religion, and language.* Ethnicity is central to the development of an **ethnic identity,** *which is a sense of membership in an ethnic group based upon shared language, religion, customs, values, history, and race.* Each of you is a member of one or more ethnic groups. Your ethnic identity reflects your deliberate decision to identify with an ancestor or ancestral group. If you are of Native American and African slave ancestry, you might choose to align yourself with the traditions and history of Native Americans, although an outsider might observe that your identity is African American.

Recently, some individuals have voiced dissatisfaction with the use of the term *minority* in the phrase *ethnic minority group.* What is the nature of such dissatisfaction and objections? The term *minority* has traditionally been associated with inferiority and deficits. Further, the concept of minority implies that there is a majority. Indeed, it can be argued that there really is no majority in the United States, because Whites are actually composed of many different ethnic groups, and Whites are not a majority in the world. When we use the term ethnic minority in this text, the use is intentional. Rather than implying that ethnic minority children should be viewed as inferior or deficient in some way, we want to convey the impact that minority status has had on many ethnic minority children. The circumstances of each ethnic group are not solely a function of its own culture. Rather, many ethnic groups have experienced considerable discrimination and prejudice. For example, patterns of alcohol abuse among Native American adolescents cannot be fully understood unless the exploitation that has accompanied Native Americans' history is also considered (Sue, 1990).

Our most basic link is that we all inhabit the same planet. We all breathe the same air. We all cherish our children's future.

—John F. Kennedy

A third very important aspect of sociocultural contexts that is receiving increased attention is gender (Beal, 1994; Ruble & Martin, 1997). **Gender** *is the sociocultural dimension of being female or male.* Sex refers to the biological dimension of being female or male. Few aspects of children's development are more central to their identity and to their social relationships than their sex or gender. Society's gender attitudes are changing. But how much? Is there a limit to how much society can determine what is appropriate behavior for males and females? These are among the provocative questions about gender that we explore in *Child Development.*

Historical Accounts of Childhood

Childhood has become such a distinct period that it is hard to imagine that it was not always thought of in that way. However, in medieval times, laws generally did not distinguish between childhood and adult offenses. After analyzing samples of art along with available publications, historian Philippe Ariès (1962) concluded that European societies did not accord any special status to children prior to 1600. In the paintings, children were often dressed in smaller versions of adult clothing (see figure 1.2).

Were children actually treated as miniature adults with no special status in medieval Europe? Ariès' interpretation has been criticized. He primarily sampled aristocratic, idealized subjects, which led to the overdrawn conclusion that children were treated as miniature adults and not accorded any special status. In medieval times,

Figure–1.2

Artistic Rendition of Children as Miniature Adults
These artistic impressions show how children were viewed as miniature adults earlier in history. Artists' renditions of children as miniature adults may have been too stereotypical.

According to a report by the Children's Defense Fund (1990), the United States does not fare well in caring for children, compared with other nations. In this report, the Children's Defense Fund gave the United States an A for capacity to care for children but an F for performance on many key markers of children's well-being. Eighteen other countries have lower infant mortality rates than the United States does. An African American child born in inner-city Boston has less chance of surviving the first year of life than does a child born in Panama, North or South Korea, or Uruguay.

children did often work, and their emotional bond with parents may not have been as strong as it is for many children today. However, in medieval times, childhood probably was recognized as a distinct phase of life more than Aries believed. We know that rich conceptions of children's development were held in ancient Egypt, Greece, and Rome.

Throughout history, philosophers have speculated at length about the nature of children and how they should be reared. Three such philosophical views involve the notions of original sin, tabula rasa, and innate goodness. In the **original sin view**, *especially advocated during the Middle Ages, children were perceived as basically bad, being born into the world as evil beings.* The goal of child rearing was to provide salvation, to remove sin from the child's life. Toward the end of the seventeenth century, the **tabula rasa view** *was proposed by English philosopher John Locke. He argued that children are not innately bad but instead are like a "blank tablet," a tabula rasa.* Locke believed that childhood experiences are important in determining adult characteristics. He advised parents to spend time with their children and to help them become contributing members of society. In the eighteenth century, the **innate goodness view** *was presented by Swiss-born philosopher Jean-Jacques Rousseau, who stressed that children are inherently good.* Because children are basically good, said Rousseau, they should be permitted to grow naturally, with little parental monitoring or constraint.

In the past century and a half, our view of children has changed dramatically. We now conceive of childhood as a highly eventful and unique period of life that lays an important foundation for the adult years and is highly differentiated from them. In most approaches to childhood, distinct periods are identified, in which children master special skills and confront new life tasks.

Photographs and Legends

Special attention was given to the selection of photographs for *Child Development*. In a number of places, experts on child development sent photographs to be included in the text. Legends were carefully written to clarify and elaborate concepts.

Sociocultural Worlds of Children Boxes

Child Development gives special attention to the cultural, ethnic, and gender worlds of children. Each chapter has one or more boxed inserts that highlight the sociocultural dimensions of life-span development.

SOCIOCULTURAL
WORLDS
OF CHILDREN

The Human Species Is a Culture-Making Species
Unlike all other animal species, which evolve mainly in response to random changes in their environment, humans have more control over their own evolution. This change occurs through *cultural evolution.* For example, we've made astonishing accomplishments in the past 10,000 years or so, ever since we developed language. Biological (Darwinian) evolution continues in our species, but its rate, compared with cultural evolution, is so slow that its impact seems almost negligible. There is no evidence, for example, that brain size or structure has changed in our species since *Homo sapiens* appeared on the fossil record about 50,000 years ago.

As humans evolved, we acquired knowledge and passed it on from generation to generation. This knowledge, which originally instructed us in how to hunt, make tools, and communicate, became our culture. The accumulation of knowledge has gathered speed—from a slow swell to a meteoric rise. Hunter-gatherer tribes, characteristic of early human society, changed over thousands of years into small agricultural communities. With people rooted in one place, cities grew and flourished. Life within those cities remained relatively unchanged for generations. Then industrialization put a dizzying speed on cultural change. Now technological advances in communication and transportation—computers, fax machines, the space shuttle—transform everyday life at a staggering pace.

Whatever one generation learns, it can pass to the next through writing, word of mouth, ritual, tradition, and a host of other methods humans have developed to assure their culture's continuity (Gould, 1981). By creating cultures, humans have built, shaped, and carved out their own environments.

Evolutionists believe that humans shape culture to achieve evolutionary goals. Consider the gene for lactose tolerance. It spreads among some groups because it enables humans to eat dairy foods. This in turn has a strong effect on human culture through a shift to dairy farming and larger populations.

More than 99 percent of all humans now live in a different kind of environment from that in which the species evolved. By creating cultures, humans have, in effect, built, shaped, and carved out their own environments.

Although no dramatic evolutionary changes have occurred since *Homo sapiens* appeared on the fossil record 50,000 years ago, there have been sweeping cultural changes. Biological evolution shaped human beings into a culture-making species. More information about the human species as a culture-making species appears in Sociocultural Worlds of Children.

Sociobiology
Sociobiology *is a theory that relies on the principles of evolutionary biology to explain social behavior.* Sociobiologists believe that psychologists have a limited understanding of social behavior because they primarily study only one mammalian species—*Homo sapiens*. Sociobiology derives its information from comparisons of any among the tens of thousands of animal species that have evolved some form of social life.

According to E. O. Wilson (1975, 1995), the purpose of sociobiology is not to make crude comparisons between animal species or between animals and humans, such as simply comparing wolf and human aggression. Rather, sociobiology's purpose is to develop general laws of the evolution and biology of social behavior. The hope also is to extend the principles of sociobiology to assist in the explanation of human behavior.

Let's consider a sociobiological inquiry. In some species of birds, the young born in one year might not breed the second year, but instead help their parents

CONCEPT TABLE 1.2

The Nature of Development, Developmental Issues, Careers in Child Development, and Critical Thinking About Children's Development

Concept	Processes/ Related Ideas	Characteristics/Description
The Nature of Development	What is development?	Development is the patter of movement or change that occurs throughout the life span.
	Biological, cognitive, and socioemotional processes	Development is influenced by an interplay of biological, cognitive, and socioemotional processes.
	Periods of development	Development is commonly divided into the following periods from conception through adolescence: the prenatal period, infancy, early childhood, middle and late childhood, and adolescence.
Developmental Issues	Maturation and experience (nature and nurture)	The debate over whether development is due primarily to maturation or to experience is another version of the nature-nurture controversy.
	Continuity and discontinuity	Some developmentalists describe development as continuous (gradual, cumulative change), others as discontinuous (abrupt, sequence of stages).
	Early and later experience	This hotly debated issue focuses on whether early experiences (especially in infancy) or later experiences are more important than later experiences are.
	Evaluating the developmental issues	Most developmentalists recognize that extreme positions of the nature-nurture, continuity-discontinuity, and early-later experience issues are unwise. Despite this consensus, spirited debate still occurs on these issues.
Careers in Child Development	Their nature	A wide range of opportunities are available to individuals who want to pursue a career related to child development. These opportunities include jobs in college and university teaching, child clinical psychology and counseling, school teaching and school psychology, nursing, pediatrics, psychiatry, and social work. A special interest is the history of ethnic minority individuals in the field of child development, and the current educational status of ethnic minority individuals.
Thinking Critically About Children's Development	Its nature	Critical thinking about children's development involves such strategies as applying a developmental framework to understand behavior, making accurate observations and inferences, applying developmental concepts to enhance personal adaptation, pursing alternative explanations, evaluating the quality of conclusions and strategies, engaging in perspective taking, demonstrating an appreciation of individual differences, and developing arguments based on developmental concepts.

Concept Tables

Two times in each chapter we review what has been discussed so far in that chapter by displaying the information in concept tables. This learning device helps you get a handle on material several times a chapter so you don't wait until the end of the chapter and have too much information to digest.

Summary

At the end of each chapter, the Summary section provides you with a framework for reviewing the entire chapter. It includes a cognitive map that visually organizes the chapter's main topics.

Explorations in Child Development

Research in Child Development

This end-of-chapter feature lets you see how scientists who study children's development actually conduct their research investigations.

Improving the Lives of Children

This applied feature provides information that will help to improve the lives of children.

Key Terms

Listed and page-referenced at the end of each chapter are key terms that are defined throughout the chapter. They are listed and page-referenced again in an end-of-book glossary, where they are also defined.

Practical Knowledge About Children

These inserts appear at the end of each chapter. They consist of book recommendations that contain valuable information to help children reach their full potential.

Summary

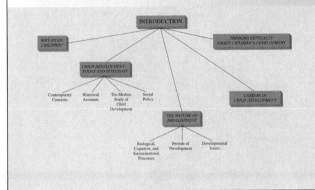

Children should have a special place in any society, for they are the society's future. An important concern is that too many children today will not reach their full potential because of inadequate rearing conditions. Far too many children live in poverty, have parents who do not adequately care for them, and go to schools where learning conditions are far from optimal.

In this chapter, you were introduced to the field of child development. You read about how today is both the best of times and the worst of times for children and why it is important to study children. You learned about the nature of child development through history, some contemporary concerns, the modern study of child development, and social policy issues. You also studied the nature of development by exploring biological, cognitive, and socioemotional processes; periods of development; and developmental issues. You read about a number of careers in child development and how to think critically about children's development.

To obtain a summary of the chapter, go back and again study the two concept tables on pages 17 and 26. In the next chapter, we will turn our attention to the field of child development as a science. You will learn about the importance of the scientific method, theories, and methods in studying children.

Key Terms

theory 35
hypotheses 35
scientific method 35
id 36
ego 36
superego 36
defense mechanisms 36
repression 37
erogenous zones 37
oral stage 37
anal stage 37
phallic stage 37
Oedipus complex 37
latency stage 38
genital stage 38
trust versus mistrust 39
autonomy versus shame and doubt 39
initiative versus guilt 39
industry versus inferiority 39
identity versus identity confusion 39
intimacy versus isolation 39
generativity versus stagnation 39
integrity versus despair 39
sensorimotor stage 42

preoperational stage 42
concrete operational stage 42
formal operational stage 42
information processing 43
classical conditioning 44
reflexes 44
unconditioned stimulus (US) 44
unconditioned response (UR) 44
conditioned stimulus (CS) 45
conditioned response (CR) 45
phobias 45
counterconditioning 46
behaviorism 46
operant conditioning 46
reinforcement 46
punishment 46
social learning theory 47
ethology 48
imprinting 48
critical period 49
ecological theory 49
microsystem 50
mesosystem 50
exosystem 50

macrosystem 50
chronosystem 50
life course theory 51
eclectic theoretical orientation 53
laboratory 56
naturalistic observation 56
questionnaire 57
case study 57
standardized tests 57
emic approach 58
etic approach 58
ethnic gloss 59
life-history records 59
correlational strategy 60
correlational coefficient 60
experimental strategy 60
random assignment 60
independent variable 61
dependent variable 61
cross-sectional approach 61
longitudinal approach 62
cohort effects 62
nomothetic research 64
idiographic needs 65

Practical Knowledge About Children

Identity: Youth and Crisis

(1968) by Erik H. Erikson, New York: W.W. Norton.

Erik Erikson was one of the leading theorists in the field of life-span development. In *Identity: Youth and Crisis*, he outlined his eight stages of life-span development and provided numerous examples from his clinical practice to illustrate the stages. This book gives special attention to the fifth stage in Erikson's theory, identity versus identity confusion. Especially worthwhile are Erikson's commentaries about identity development in different cultures.

Two other Erikson books that are excellent reading on life-span development are *Young Man Luther* and *Gandhi's Truth*.

Examining Lives in Context: Perspectives on the Ecology of Human Development

(1995) edited by Phyllis Moen, Glen H. Elder, Jr., and Kurt Luscher, Washington, DC: American Psychological Association.

In this book, more than two dozen scholars explain how Urie Bronfenbrenner's ecological theory led them to focus their own work on problems crucial to "real life." The book also highlights many concepts in Glen Elder's life course theory, such as the importance of time and place, as well as linked lives, in human development. The contributors include many leading theorists and researchers, such as Eleanor Maccoby, John Clausen, Jean Brooks-Gunn, Glen Elder, Michael Rutter, and Urie Bronfenbrenner.

Explorations in Child Development

To fully understand the field of child development today, it is important to explore both its research side and its applied side. Thus, each chapter will conclude with this endpiece, which has two parts: first a discussion of some aspect of research on child development, and second, a description of issues and programs that focus on improving the lives of children. The research discussion provides you with an opportunity to see how the scientists who study children's development actually conduct research studies. The Applications discussion will give you a sense of how professionals who work with children seek solutions to help children reach their full potential.

Research in Child Development

Why Research in Child Development Is Important

Knowledge in the field of child development rests heavily on the generation of a broad, competent research base. Over the last several decades, research in child development has grown enormously as increasing numbers of investigators have become intrigued by issues and questions that involve children's lives. The importance of research in child development is reflected in the large number of research journals in the field and the growth in the membership of the Society for Research in Child Development, the main professional organization for scholars who conduct research on children's development.

In discussing child development and social policy earlier in this chapter, we said that a current trend is to conduct research that is relevant to social policy. The question of whether child development researchers should conduct research that is relevant to social policy touches on a long-standing issue: Should research be basic or applied?

Basic research, sometimes called pure research, is the study of issues to obtain knowledge for its own sake rather than for practical applications. Basic research is often conducted to test a theory or to follow up on other research. Rarely is basic research conducted as a response to a pressing social problem. Basic research might or might not eventually be applied to social policy or practical problems. In contrast, applied research is the study of issues that have direct practical significance, often with the intent of changing behavior. Thus, social policy research is applied research, not basic research.

A developmentalist who conducts basic research might ask: How does cognitive development change during childhood? In contrast, a developmentalist who conducts applied research might ask: How can knowledge about change in children's cognitive development be used to educate them more effectively or to help them cope with stress?

Most developmentalists believe that basic and applied research are both important. Basic research can sometimes produce information that can be used to improve children's well-being, but it does not guarantee this application. Insisting that research always be relevant is like trying to grow new flowers by dealing only with the blossoms and not tending to the roots. Basic research is root research. Without the discovery of basic scientific principles, we would have little knowledge to apply. Today, research on child development includes a wealth of both basic and applied studies.

Improving the Lives of Children

Thinking About Your Future as a Parent and the Education of Your Children

Famous playwright George Bernard Shaw once commented that while parenting is a very important profession, no test of fitness for it is ever imposed. If a test were imposed, some parents would turn out to be more fit than others. Most parents do want their children to grow into socially mature individuals, but they often are not sure about what to do as a parent to help their children reach this goal (Stenhouse, 1996). One reason for parents' frustration is that they often get conflicting messages about how to deal with their children. One "expert" might urge them to be more permissive with their children; another might tell them to place stricter controls on them or they will grow up to be spoiled brats.

Most of you taking this course will be a parent someday; some of you already are. I hope that each of you will take seriously the importance of rearing your children, because they are the future of our society. Good parenting takes a considerable amount of time. If you choose to become a

---

PROLOGUE

Life for My Child Is Simple, and Is Good

Life for my child is simple, and is good.
He knows his wish. Yes, but that is not all.
Because I know mine too.
And we both want joy of undeep and unabiding things,
Like kicking over a chair or throwing blocks out of a window
Or tipping over an icebox pan
Or snatching down curtains or fingering an electric outlet
Or a journey or a friend or an illegal kiss.
No. There is more to it than that.
It is that he has never been afraid.
Rather, he reaches out and lo the chair falls with a beautiful crash,
And the blocks fall, down on the people's heads,
And the water comes slooshing sloppily out across the floor.
And so forth.
Not that success, for him, is sure, infallible.
But never has he been afraid to reach.
His lesions are legion.
But reaching is his rule.

—Gwendolyn Brooks

Gwendolyn Brooks (1917–   ) is a Pulitzer prize–winning poet and novelist. Brooks was recently awarded the highest honor given by the United States government for intellectual development in the humanities—the National Endowment for the Humanities 1994 Jefferson Lecturer. One of the most respected of contemporary poets, she is rooted in the African American experience and her childhood in Chicago, but her appeal, as this poem reveals, stretches across the full range of human experience.

The Nature of Child Development

In every child who is born, under no matter what circumstances, and of no matter what parents, the potentiality of the human race is born.

—James Agee

Examining the shape of childhood allows us to understand it better. Every childhood is distinct, the first chapter of a new biography in the world. This book is about children's development—its universal features, its individual variations, its nature as we move ever closer to the twenty-first century. Child Development is about the rhythm and meaning of children's lives, about turning mystery into understanding, and about weaving together a portrait of who each of us was, is, and will be. In Section I, you will read two chapters: "Introduction" (chapter 1) and "The Science of Child Development" (chapter 2).

Pablo Picasso
Child With a Dove detail

Chapter

1

Introduction

We reach backward to our parents and forward to our children and through their children to a future we will never see, but about which we need to care.

—Carl Jung

Chapter Outline

Chapter Boxes

Children are on a different plane. They belong to a generation and way of feeling properly their own.

—George Santayana

PREVIEW

This book is a window into the nature of children's development—your own and that of every other child of the human species. In this first chapter, you will be introduced to some ideas about why we should study children, contemporary concerns about child development, and a historical perspective on children's development. You will learn what development is and what issues are raised by a developmental perspective on children. You also will read about careers in child development and ways to think critically about children's development.

IMAGES OF CHILDREN

The Best of Times and the Worst of Times for Today's Children

It is both the best of times and the worst of times for today's children. Their world possesses powers and perspectives inconceivable 50 years ago: computers, longer life expectancies, the ability to reach out to the entire planet through television, satellites, air travel, and the Internet.

Children want to trust, but the world has become an untrustworthy place. The sometimes-fatal temptations of the adult world can descend upon children so early that their ideals become tarnished. Crack cocaine is a far more addictive and deadly substance than marijuana, the drug of an earlier generation. Strange depictions of violence and sex come flashing out of the television set and lodge in the minds of children. The messages are powerful and contradictory: Rock videos suggest orgiastic sex. Public health officials counsel safe sex. Talk show hosts conduct seminars on lesbian nuns, exotic drugs, transsexual surgery, serial murders. Television pours a bizarre version of reality into children's imaginations. In New York City, two 5-year-olds argue about whether there is a Santa Claus and what Liberace died of. In New Orleans, a first-grader shaves a piece of chalk and passes the dust around the classroom, acting as if it is cocaine.

Every stable society transmits values from one generation to the next. That is civilization's work. In today's world, the transmission of values is not easy. Parents are raising children in a world far removed from the Ozzie and Harriet era of the 1950s, when two of three American families consisted of a breadwinner (the father), a caregiver (the mother), and the children they were raising. Today fewer than one in five families fits that description. Phrases like *quality time* have found their way into the American vocabulary. A motif of absence plays in the lives of many children. It might be an absence of authority and limits or an absence of emotional commitment (Morrow, 1988).

WHY STUDY CHILDREN?

Why study children? Perhaps you are or will be a parent or teacher. Responsibility for children is or will be a part of your everyday life. The more you learn about children, the better you can deal with them. Perhaps you hope to gain some insight into your own history—as an infant, as a child, and as an adolescent. Perhaps you just stumbled onto this course thinking that it sounded interesting and that the topic of child development would raise some provocative and intriguing issues about how human beings grow and develop. Whatever your reasons, you will discover that the study of child development *is* provocative, *is* intriguing, and *is* filled with information about who we are and how we grew to be this way.

As you might imagine, understanding children's development, and our own personal journey through childhood, is a rich and complicated undertaking. You will discover that various experts approach the study of children in many different ways and ask many different questions. Amid this richness and complexity we seek a simple answer: to understand how children change as they grow up and the forces that contribute to this change.

What are some of these changes? Children grow in size and weight. They learn to stand, walk, and run. They learn to read, to write, and to solve math problems. They learn behaviors and roles that society considers acceptable for "girls," "boys," "women," and "men." They learn the necessity of curbing their will and develop an understanding of what is morally acceptable or unacceptable. They learn how to communicate and to get along with many different people. Their families—parents and siblings—are very important influences in their lives, but their growth also is shaped by successive choirs of friends, teachers, and strangers. In their most pimply and awkward moments as adolescents, they become acquainted with sex and try on one face after another, searching for an identity they can call their own. These are but a few of the fascinating changes that take place as children develop—many more await you in this text. To evaluate your own development as a child, turn to Critical Thinking About Children's Development.

In a sense, then, the modern study of child development is concerned with the same matters that we, as ordinary people, might want to understand if and when we raise our own sons and daughters, teach children in school, or try to get along with children as brothers or sisters, aunts or uncles. Whatever the context, though, it will help us immensely to understand precisely how children change.

CHILD DEVELOPMENT— TODAY AND YESTERDAY

Everywhere an individual turns in contemporary society, the development and well-being of children capture public attention, the interest of scientists, and the concern of policymakers. Throughout history, though, interest in the development of children has been uneven.

Some Contemporary Concerns

Consider some of the topics you read about in the newspapers and magazines every day: contemporary changes in the family, educational reform, sociocultural issues such as the changing status of ethnic minority groups and gender roles. What the experts are discovering is that each of these areas has direct and significant consequences for understanding children and for our decisions as a society on how children should be treated. An important theme of this textbook is to provide detailed, up-to-date coverage of the roles that family issues, education, and sociocultural contexts play in children's development. These topics are integrated into discussions throughout the book. Every chapter also includes one or more Sociocultural Worlds of Children boxes that explore how culture, ethnicity, and gender impact children's lives.

Family Issues

We hear a great deal from experts and popular writers about pressures on contemporary families. The number of families in which both parents work is increasing; at the same time, the number of one-parent families has risen over the past two decades as a result of a climbing divorce rate (Dreman, 1997; Hernandez, 1997). With more children being raised by single parents or by parents who are both working, parents have less time to spend with their children and the quality of child care is of concern to many. Are working parents making better use of the time they do have to spend with their children? Do day-care arrangements provide high-quality alternatives for parents? How troubled should we be about the increasing number of latchkey children—those at home alone after school, waiting for their parents to return from work? Answers to these questions can be formed by considering several different kinds of information obtained by experts in child development. This information comes from studies of the way working parents use their time with their children and the nature of their parenting approaches and behaviors, studies of the way various day-care arrangements influence children's social and intellectual growth compared to home-care arrangements, and examinations of the consequences of a child's being without adult supervision for hours every day after school (Clarke-Stewart, Allhusen, & Clements, 1995; Lamb, 1997).

Education

During the past several years, the American educational system has come under attack. A national commission appointed by the Office of Education concluded that our children are poorly prepared for the increasingly complex future they will be asked to face in our society. The problems are legion—declining skills of those entering

CRITICAL THINKING ABOUT CHILDREN'S DEVELOPMENT

The Importance of Asking Questions—Exploring Your Own Development as a Child

Asking questions reflects our active curiosity. Children—especially young children—are remarkable for their ability to ask question. My granddaughter, Jordan, is 3½ years old. *Why* is one of her favorite words, and she asks "Why?" relentlessly. Even though we were constantly questioning early in our lives, many of us ask far fewer questions as adults.

Asking questions can help you engage in critical thinking about children's development, including your own development as a child. As you go through this course, you might want to ask yourself questions about how you experienced a particular aspect of develop-

ment. For example, consider your experiences in your family as you were growing up. Questions you could pose to yourself might include these: "How did my parents bring me up? How did the way they reared me influence what I'm like today? How did my relationship with my brothers or sisters affect my development?" Also ask yourself about your experiences with peers and at school: "Did I have close friends while I was growing up? How much time did I spend with my peers and friends at various points in childhood and adolescence compared with the time I spent with my parents? What were the schools I attended like? How good were my teachers? How did the schools and teachers affect my achievement orientation today?"

Be curious. Ask questions. Ask your friends or classmates about their experiences as they were growing up and compare them with yours. By asking questions about your own and others' development as children, you are *applying a developmental framework to understanding behavior.*

the teaching profession, adolescents graduating from high school with primary-grade-level reading and mathematics skills, a shortage of qualified mathematics and science teachers, less time being spent by students in engaging academic work in their classrooms, an absence of any real signs of challenge and thinking required by school curricula, and a high dropout rate over the 4 years of high school. Solutions to these problems are not easy. However, in searching for solutions, policymakers repeatedly turn to experts in the field of child development, because to design an engaging curriculum, a planner must know what engages and motivates children. To improve our national effort in teaching thinking skills, planners must understand what thinking is and how it changes across the school years. To understand the roots of the social difficulties encountered by so many of today's adolescents—difficulties that lead them to drop out of school in droves—planners need to understand the socialization processes involved in the transition to adolescence and the ways in which schools fail to address them (Eccles, Wigfield, & Schiefele, 1997; Wigfield & Eccles, 1995).

Sociocultural Contexts

The tapestry of American culture has changed dramatically in recent years. Nowhere is the change more noticeable than in the increasing ethnic diversity of America's citizens (see figure 1.1). Ethnic minority groups—African American, Latino, Native American (American Indian), and Asian, for example—made up 20 percent of all children and adolescents under the age of 17 in 1989 in the

United States. Projections indicate that, by the year 2000, one-third of all school-aged children will fall into this category. This changing demographic tapestry promises not only the richness that diversity produces but also difficult challenges in extending the American dream to individuals of all ethnic groups. Historically, ethnic minorities have found themselves at the bottom of the economic and social order. They have been disproportionately represented among the poor and the inadequately educated (Edelman, 1996, 1997). Half of all African American children and one-third of all Latino children live in poverty. School dropout rates for minority youth reach an alarming 60 percent in some urban areas. These population trends and our nation's inability to prepare ethnic minority individuals for full participation in American life have produced an imperative for the social institutions that serve ethnic minorities. Schools, social services, health and mental health agencies, juvenile probation services, and other programs need to become more sensitive to ethnic issues and to provide improved services to ethnic and minority and low-income individuals (McLoyd, 1997).

An especially important idea in considering the nature of ethnic minority groups is that not only is there ethnic diversity within a culture such as the United States, but there is also considerable diversity within each ethnic group (Fisher, Jackson, & Villarvel, 1997). Not all African American children come from low-income families. Not all Latino children are members of the Catholic church. Not all Asian American children are geniuses.

Figure~1.1

Increases in Ethnic Minority Population in the United States
The percentage of African American, Latino, and Asian American individuals increased far more from 1980 to 1988 than did the percentage of Whites. Shown here are two Korean-born children on the day they became United States citizens. Asian American children are the fastest-growing group of ethnic minority children.

occurs, *a setting that is influenced by historical, economic, social, and cultural factors.* To sense how important context is in understanding children's development, consider a researcher who wants to discover whether today's children are more racially tolerant than children were a decade ago. Without reference to the historical, economic, social, and cultural aspects of race relations, the students' racial tolerance cannot be fully understood. Every child's development occurs against a cultural backdrop of contexts (McLoyd & Ceballo, 1995; Scott-Jones, 1997). These contexts or settings include homes, school, peer groups, churches, cities, neighborhoods, communities, university laboratories, the United States, China, Mexico, Japan, Egypt, and many others—each with meaningful historical, economic, social, and cultural legacies (Cole, 1997).

Three sociocultural contexts that many child development researchers believe merit special attention are culture, ethnicity, and gender. **Culture** *refers to the behavior patterns, beliefs, and all other products of a particular group of people that are passed on from generation to generation.* The products result from the interaction between groups of people and their environment over many years. A cultural group can be as large as the United States, or as small as an African hunter-gatherer group. Whatever its size, the group's culture influences the identity, learning, and social behavior of its members (Kagitcibasi, 1996; Sheweder & others, 1997). To read further about culture, turn to Critical Thinking About Children's Development.

Cross-cultural studies—*the comparison of a culture with one or more other cultures—provide information about the degree to which children's development is similar, or universal, across cultures, or to what degree it is culture-specific.* For example, the United States is an achievement-oriented culture with a strong work ethic, but recent comparisons of American and Japanese children revealed that the Japanese were better at math, spent more time working on math in school, and spent more time doing homework than the Americans did (Stevenson, 1995).

Not all Native American children drop out of school. It is easy to make the mistake of stereotyping the members of an ethnic minority group as all being the same. Keep in mind, as we describe children from ethnic groups, that each group is heterogeneous.

Sociocultural contexts of development include four important concepts: context, culture, ethnicity, and gender. These concepts are central to our discussion of children's development in this book, so we need to clearly define them. **Context** *refers to the setting in which development*

Ethnicity *(the word ethnic comes from the Greek word for "nation")* is based on cultural heritage, nationality characteristics, race, religion, and language. Ethnicity is central to the development of an **ethnic identity,** *which is a sense of membership in an ethnic group based upon shared language, religion, customs, values, history, and race.* Each of you is a member of one or more ethnic groups. Your ethnic identity reflects your deliberate decision to identify with an ancestor or ancestral group. If you are of Native American and African slave ancestry, you might choose to align yourself with the traditions and history of Native Americans, although an outsider might believe that your identity is African American.

Recently, some individuals have voiced dissatisfaction with the use of the term *minority* in the phrase *ethnic minority group.* What is the nature of such dissatisfaction and objections? The term *minority* has traditionally been associated with inferiority and deficits. Further, the concept of minority implies that there is a majority. Indeed, it can be argued that there really is no majority in the United States, because Whites are actually composed of many different ethnic groups, and Whites are not a majority in the world. When we use the term *ethnic minority* in this text, the use is intentional. Rather than implying that ethnic minority children should be viewed as inferior or deficient in some way, we want to convey the impact that minority status has had on many ethnic minority children. The circumstances of each ethnic group are not solely a function of its own culture. Rather, many ethnic groups have experienced considerable discrimination and prejudice. For example, patterns of alcohol abuse among Native American adolescents cannot be fully understood unless the exploitation that has accompanied Native Americans' history is also considered (Sue, 1990).

> *Our most basic link is that we all inhabit the same planet. We all breathe the same air. We all cherish our children's future.*
>
> —John F. Kennedy

A third very important aspect of sociocultural contexts that is receiving increased attention is gender (Beal, 1994; Ruble & Martin, 1997). **Gender** *is the sociocultural dimension of being female or male. Sex refers to the biological dimension of being female or male.* Few aspects of children's development are more central to their identity and to their social relationships than their sex or gender. Society's gender attitudes are changing. But how much? Is there a limit to how much society can determine what is appropriate behavior for males and females? These are among the provocative questions about gender that we explore in *Child Development.*

Historical Accounts of Childhood

Childhood has become such a distinct period that it is hard to imagine that it was not always thought of in that way. However, in medieval times, laws generally did not distinguish between childhood and adult offenses. After analyzing samples of art along with available publications, historian Philippe Ariès (1962) concluded that European societies did not accord any special status to children prior to 1600. In the paintings, children were often dressed in smaller versions of adult clothing (see figure 1.2).

Were children actually treated as miniature adults with no special status in medieval Europe? Ariès' interpretation has been criticized. He primarily sampled aristocratic, idealized subjects, which led to the overdrawn conclusion that children were treated as miniature adults and not accorded any special status. In medieval times,

According to a report by the Children's Defense Fund (1990), the United States does not fare well in caring for children, compared with other nations. In this report, the Children's Defense Fund gave the United States an A for capacity to care for children but an F for performance on many key markers of children's well-being. Eighteen other countries have lower infant mortality rates than the United States does. An African American child born in inner-city Boston has less chance of surviving the first year of life than does a child born in Panama, North or South Korea, or Uruguay.

children did often work, and their emotional bond with parents may not have been as strong as it is for many children today. However, in medieval times, childhood probably was recognized as a distinct phase of life more than Ariès believed. We know that rich conceptions of children's development were held in ancient Egypt, Greece, and Rome.

Figure~1.2

Artistic Rendition of Children as Miniature Adults
These artistic impressions show how children were viewed as miniature adults earlier in history. Artists' renditions of children as miniature adults may have been too stereotypical.

Throughout history, philosophers have speculated at length about the nature of children and how they should be reared. Three such philosophical views involve the notions of original sin, *tabula rasa*, and innate goodness. In the **original sin view,** *especially advocated during the Middle Ages, children were perceived as basically bad, being born into the world as evil beings.* The goal of child rearing was to provide salvation, to remove sin from the child's life. Toward the end of the seventeenth century, the **tabula rasa view** *was proposed by English philosopher John Locke. He argued that children are not innately bad but instead are like a "blank tablet," a tabula rasa.* Locke believed that childhood experiences are important in determining adult characteristics. He advised parents to spend time with their children and to help them become contributing members of society. In the eighteenth century, the **innate goodness view** *was presented by Swiss-born philosopher Jean-Jacques Rousseau, who stressed that children are inherently good.* Because children are basically good, said Rousseau, they should be permitted to grow naturally, with little parental monitoring or constraint.

In the past century and a half, our view of children has changed dramatically. We now conceive of childhood as a highly eventful and unique period of life that lays an important foundation for the adult years and is highly differentiated from them. In most approaches to childhood, distinct periods are identified, in which children master special skills and confront new life tasks.

Childhood is no longer seen as an inconvenient "waiting" period during which adults must suffer the incompetencies of the young. We now value childhood as a special time of growth and change, and we invest great resources in caring for and educating our children. We protect them from the excesses of the adult work world through tough child labor laws; we treat their crimes against society under a special system of juvenile justice; and we have governmental provisions for helping children when ordinary family support systems fail or when families seriously interfere with children's well-being.

The Modern Study of Child Development

The modern era of studying children has a history that spans only a little more than a century (Cairns, 1983, 1997). This era began with some important developments in the late 1800s and extends to the current period of the 1990s. Why is this past century so special? During the past 100 years, the study of child development has evolved into a sophisticated science. A number of major theories, along with elegant techniques and methods of study, help organize our thinking about children's development. New knowledge about children—based on direct observation and testing—is accumulating at a breathtaking pace.

During the last quarter of the nineteenth century, a major shift took place—from a strictly philosophical perspective on human psychology to a perspective that includes direct observation and experimentation. Most of the influential early psychologists were trained either in the natural sciences (such as biology or medicine) or in philosophy. In the field of child development, this was true of such influential thinkers as Charles Darwin, G. Stanley Hall, James Mark Baldwin, and Sigmund Freud. The natural scientists, even then, underscored the importance of conducting experiments and collecting reliable observations of what they studied. This approach had advanced the state of knowledge in physics, chemistry, and biology; however, these scientists were not at all sure that people, much less children or infants, could be profitably studied in this way. Their hesitation was due, in part, to a lack of examples to follow in studying children. In addition, philosophers of the time debated, on both intellectual and ethical grounds, whether the methods of science were appropriate for studying people.

The deadlock was broken when some daring and entrepreneurial thinkers began to study infants, children, and adolescents, trying new methods of study. For example, near the turn of the century, French psychologist Alfred Binet invented many tasks to study attention and memory. He used them to study his own daughters, normal children, children with mental retardation, extremely gifted children, and adults. Eventually he collaborated in the development of the first modern test of intelligence, which is named after him (the Binet). At

about the same time, G. Stanley Hall pioneered the use of questionnaires with large groups of children and popularized the findings of earlier psychologists, whom he encouraged to do likewise. In one investigation, Hall tested 400 children in the Boston schools to find out how much they "knew" about themselves and the world, asking them such questions as "Where are your ribs?"

Later, during the 1920s, a large number of child development research centers were created (White, 1995), and their professional staffs began to observe and chart a myriad of behaviors in infants and children. The centers at the Universities of Minnesota, Iowa, California at Berkeley, Columbia, and Toronto became famous for their investigations of children's play, friendship patterns, fears, aggression and conflict, and sociability. This work became closely associated with the so-called child study movement, and a new organization, the Society for Research in Child Development, was formed at about the same time.

Another ardent observer of children was Arnold Gesell. With his photographic dome, Gesell (1928) could systematically observe children's behavior without interrupting them (see figure 1.3). The direct study of children, in which investigators directly observe children's behavior, conduct experiments, or obtain information about children by questioning their parents and teachers, had an auspicious start in the work of these child study experts. The flow of information about children, based on direct study, has not slowed since that time.

Figure~1.3

Gesell's Photographic Dome
Cameras rode on metal tracks at the top of the dome and were moved as needed to record the child's activities. Others could observe from outside the dome without being seen by the child.

Gesell not only developed sophisticated observational strategies for studying children, but he also had some provocative views on the nature of children's development. He theorized that certain characteristics of children simply "bloom" with age because of a biological, maturational blueprint. Gesell strove for precision in charting what a child is like at a specific age. Gesell's views, as well as G. Stanley Hall's, were strongly influenced by Charles Darwin's evolutionary theory (Darwin had made the scientific study of children respectable when he developed a baby journal for recording systematic observations of children). Hall (1904) believed that child development follows a natural evolutionary course that can be revealed by child study. He also theorized that child development unfolds in a stagelike fashion, with distinct motives and capabilities at each stage. Hall had much to say about adolescence, arguing that it is full of "storm and stress."

Sigmund Freud's psychoanalytic theory was prominent in the early part of the twentieth century. Freud believed that children are rarely aware of the motives and reasons for their behavior and that the bulk of their mental life is unconscious. His ideas were compatible with Hall's, emphasizing conflict and biological influences on development, although Freud did stress that a child's experiences with parents in the first 5 years of life are important determinants of later personality development. Freud envisioned the child moving through a series of psychosexual stages, filled with conflict between biological urges and the environmental demands placed on the child by society. Freud's theory has had a profound influence on the study of children's personality development and socialization, especially in the areas of gender, morality, family processes, and problems and disturbances.

During the 1920s and 1930s, John Watson's (1928) theory of behaviorism influenced thinking about children. Watson proposed a view of children very different from Freud's, arguing that children can be shaped into whatever society wishes by examining and changing the environment. One element of Watson's view, and of behaviorism in general, was a strong belief in the systematic observation of children's behavior under controlled conditions. Watson had some provocative views about child rearing as well. He claimed that parents are too soft on children; quit cuddling and smiling at babies so much, he told parents.

Whereas John Watson was observing the environment's influence on children's behavior and Sigmund Freud was probing the depths of the unconscious mind to discover clues about our early experiences with our parents, others were more concerned about the development of children's conscious thoughts—that is, the thoughts of which they are aware. James Mark Baldwin was a pioneer in the study of children's thought. **Genetic epistemology** *was the term Baldwin gave to the study of how children's knowledge changes over the course of their development.* (The term *genetic* at that time was a synonym for "development," and the term *epistemology* means "the nature or study of knowledge.") Baldwin's ideas initially were proposed in the 1880s. Later, in the twentieth century, Swiss psychologist Jean Piaget adopted and elaborated on many of Baldwin's themes, keenly observing the development of thoughts in his own children and devising clever experiments to investigate how children think. Piaget became a giant in developmental psychology. Many of you, perhaps, are already familiar with his view that children pass through a series of cognitive, or thought, stages from infancy through adolescence. According to Piaget, children think in a qualitatively different manner than adults do.

Our introduction to several influential and diverse theories of children's development has been brief, designed to give you a glimpse of some of the different ways children have been viewed as the study of child development unfolded. You will read more about theoretical perspectives later in the text.

Social Policy and Children's Development

Social policy *is a national government's course of action designed to influence the welfare of its citizens.* A current trend is to conduct child development research that produces knowledge that will lead to wise and effective decision making in the area of social policy (Bridgman, 1997; Erwin, 1996; Takanishi & DeLeon, 1994). When more than 20 percent of all children and more than 40 percent of ethnic minority children are being raised in poverty, when between 40 and 50 percent of all children born in a particular era can expect to spend at least 5 years in a single-parent home, when children and young adolescents are giving birth, when the use and abuse of drugs is widespread, and when the specter and spread of AIDS is present, our nation needs revised social policy related to children (Gerry, 1997; Petersen, 1997). Figure 1.4 vividly portrays one day in the lives of children in the United States.

The shape and scope of social policy related to children is heavily influenced by our political system, which is based on negotiation and compromise (Garwood & others, 1989). The values held by individual lawmakers, the nation's economic strengths and weaknesses, and partisan politics all influence the policy agenda and whether the welfare of children will be improved. Periods of comprehensive social policy are often the outgrowth of concern over broad social issues. Child labor laws protected children and jobs for adults as well; federal day-care funding during World War II was justified by the need for women laborers in factories; and Head Start and the other War on Poverty programs in the 1960s were implemented to decrease intergenerational poverty.

Figure~1.4

One Day in the Lives of Children in the United States

1	mother dies in childbirth
3	people under 25 die from HIV
6	children and youths commit suicide
14	children and youths are murdered
16	children and youths are killed by firearms
37	children and youths die from accidents
92	babies die
144	babies are born at very low birthweight
326	children are arrested for alcohol offenses
342	children are arrested for violent crimes
359	children are arrested for drug offenses
466	babies are born to mothers who received late or no prenatal care
788	babies are born at low birthweight

1,420	babies are born to mothers younger than 20
2,444	babies are born to mothers who are not high school graduates
2,556	babies are born into poverty
3,086	public school students are corporally punished
3,356	high school students drop out*
3,533	babies are born to unmarried mothers
5,500	high school graduates do not go on to college*
6,042	children are arrested
10,829	babies are born
13,076	public school students are suspended*

*Every school day

Among the groups that have worked to improve the lives of the world's children are UNICEF in New York and the Children's Defense Fund in Washington, D.C. At a recent United Nations convention, a number of children's rights were declared (Cummings, Rebello, & Gardinier, 1995); a sampling of these rights appears in table 1.1. Marian Wright Edelman, president of the Children's Defense Fund, has been a tireless advocate for children's rights and has been instrumental in calling attention to the needs of children. Especially troubling to Edelman (1996, 1997) are the indicators of societal neglect that place the United States as one of the worst of industrialized nations in the treatment of children. Edelman says that parenting and nurturing the next generation of children is our society's most important function and that we need to take it more seriously than we have in the past. She points out that we hear a lot from politicians these days about the importance of "family values," but that when we examine our nation's policies for families, they don't reflect the politicians' words. Edelman says that we need a better health-care system for families, safer schools and neighborhoods, better parent education, and improved family support systems.

Edward Zigler (1997) has also worked extensively as a champion of children's rights, initially to urge government funding of Project Head Start and to improve the lives of children with mental retardation, and more recently to encourage the formation of a national policy on day care and schooling. Several comprehensive child-care bills recently have been proposed in Congress but have not yet been made law. One proposal places public schools at the hub of a new national system of child-care services. Before-school and after-school programs would be housed in available classrooms, with a network of family day-care providers caring for younger children. Traditional child-care services would be augmented by a home visitation program for new parents, parent education, and training for child-care staff. Another proposal, the Comprehensive Child Care bill, addresses issues that range from the licensing standards of child-care services to the upgrading of the quality and status of child-care providers.

Child developmentalists can play an important role in social policy related to children by helping develop more positive public opinion for comprehensive child welfare legislation, by contributing to and promoting research that will benefit children's welfare, and by helping provide legislators with information that will influence their support of comprehensive child welfare legislation.

As the twenty-first century approaches, the well-being of children is one of America's foremost concerns. We all cherish the future of our children, because they are the future of any society. Children who do not reach their potential, who are destined to make fewer contributions to society than it needs, and who do not take their place as productive adults diminish the power of society's future (Horowitz & O'Brien, 1989).

TABLE 1.1

A Partial Listing of the Declaration of Children's Rights Presented to the United Nations

Abuse and Neglect

The need to protect children from all forms of maltreatment by parents and others: In cases of abuse and neglect, the government is obligated to undertake preventive and treatment programs

Best Interests of the Child

The need for the best interests of children to prevail in all legal and administrative decisions, taking into account children's opinions

Child Labor

The need to protect children from economic exploitation and from engaging in work that is a threat to their health, education, and development

Children of Ethnic Minorities

The right of children from ethnic minority backgrounds to enjoy their own culture and to practice their own religion and language

Children Without Families

The right to receive special protection and assistance from the government when deprived of family support and to be provided with alternative care

Drug Abuse

The need of children to be protected from illegal drugs, including their production or distribution

Education

The right to education: The government should be obligated to provide free and compulsory education and to ensure that school discipline reflects children's human dignity

Aims of Education

Education that develops a child's personality and talents and fosters respect for human rights and for children's and others' cultural and national value

Sexual Exploitation

The right of children to be protected from sexual exploitation and abuse, including prostitution and pornography

Freedom from Discrimination

The need to protect children without exception from any form of discrimination

Handicapped Children

The right of handicapped children to special care and training designed to help them achieve self-reliance and a full, active life in society

Health and Health Services

The right to the highest standard of health and access to medical services: The government should be obligated to ensure preventive health care, health care for expectant mothers, health education, and the reduction of infant and child mortality

Leisure and Recreation

The right to leisure, play, and participation in cultural and artistic activities

Standard of Living

The right to an adequate standard of living: The government should have a responsibility to assist parents who cannot meet this responsibility

Marian Wright Edelman, president of the Children's Defense Fund (shown here interacting with a young child), has been a tireless advocate of children's rights and has been instrumental in calling attention to the needs of children.

A summary of the main ideas we have discussed so far is presented in concept table 1.1. Next, we will explore some important developmental issues in the study of children.

THE NATURE OF DEVELOPMENT

Each of us develops in certain ways like all other individuals, like some other individuals, and like no other individuals. Most of the time, our attention is directed to a person's uniqueness, but psychologists who study development are drawn to our shared as well as our unique characteristics. As humans, each of us has traveled some common paths. Each of us—Leonardo da Vinci, Joan of Arc, George Washington, Martin Luther King, Jr., you, and I—walked at about the age of 1, engaged in fantasy play as a young child, and became more independent as a youth.

What do psychologists mean when they speak of an individual's development? **Development** *is the pattern of change that begins at conception and continues through the life span.* Most development involves growth, although

it includes decay (as in death and dying). The pattern of movement is complex because it is the product of several processes—biological, cognitive, and socioemotional.

Biological, Cognitive, and Socioemotional Processes

Biological processes *involve changes in an individual's physical nature.* Genes inherited from parents, the development of the brain, height and weight gains, motor skills, and the hormonal changes of puberty all reflect the role of biological processes in development.

> *The chess-board is the world. The pieces are the phenomena of the universe. The rules of the game are what we call laws of nature.*
>
> **—Thomas Henry Huxley**

Cognitive processes *involve changes in an individual's thought, intelligence, and language.* The tasks of watching a colorful mobile swinging above a crib, putting together a two-word sentence, memorizing a poem, solving a math problem, and imagining what it would be like to be a movie star all reflect the role of cognitive processes in children's development.

> *I think, therefore I am.*
>
> **—René Descartes**

Socioemotional processes *involve changes in an individual's relationships with other people, changes in emotions, and changes in personality.* An infant's smile in response to her mother's touch, a young boy's aggressive attack on a playmate, a girl's development of assertiveness, and an adolescent's joy at the senior prom all reflect the role of social processes in children's development.

Remember as you read about biological, cognitive, and socioemotional processes that they are intricately interwoven. You will read about how socioemotional processes shape cognitive processes, how cognitive processes promote or restrict socioemotional processes, and how biological processes influence cognitive processes. Although it is helpful to study the various processes involved in children's development in separate sections of the book, keep in mind that you are studying the development of an integrated human child who has only one interdependent mind and body (see figure 1.5).

> *Man is by nature a social animal.*
>
> **—Aristotle**

Periods of Development

For the purposes of organization and understanding, we commonly describe development in terms of periods. The

ONCEPT TABLE 1.1

The Reasons for Studying Children and the History of Studying Children

Concept	Processes/Related Ideas	Characteristics/Description
Why Study Children?	Explanations	Responsibility for children is or will be a part of our everyday lives. The more we learn about children, the more we can better deal with them and assist them in becoming competent human beings.
Child Development— Today and Yesterday	Contemporary concerns	Today, the well-being of children is a prominent concern in our culture—such concerns include family processes, education, and sociocultural issues.
	Sociocultural contexts	Sociocultural contexts include the important concepts of context, culture, ethnicity, and gender. Context refers to the setting in which development occurs, a setting that is influenced by historical, economic, social, and cultural factors. Culture refers to the behavior patterns, beliefs, and all other products of a particular group of people that are passed on from generation to generation. Ethnicity is based on cultural heritage, nationality characteristics, race, religion, and language. Gender is the sociocultural definition of male or female.
	Child development and history	The history of interest in children is long and rich. In the Renaissance, philosophical views were important, including those invoking original sin, *tabula rasa,* and innate goodness. We now conceive of childhood as highly eventful. The modern era of studying children spans a little more than a century, an era in which the study of child development has developed into a sophisticated science. Methodological advances in observation and theoretical views—among them psychoanalytic, behavioral, and cognitive-developmental—characterized this scientific theme.
	Social policy research	A current trend is to conduct child development research that is relevant to the welfare of children. The shape and scope of social policy are influenced by our political system. Child developmentalists can play an important role in social policy. Improved social policy related to children is needed to help all children reach their potential.

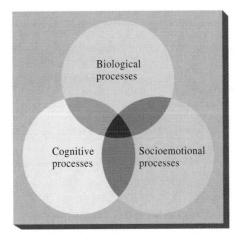

Figure~1.5

Processes of Develomental Change
Changes in development are the result of biological, cognitive, and socioemotional processes. These processes are interwoven as the child develops.

most widely used classification of developmental periods involves the following sequence: the prenatal period, infancy, early childhood, middle and late childhood, and adolescence. Approximate age bands are placed on the periods to provide a general idea of when a period first appears and when it ends.

The **prenatal period** *is the time from conception to birth.* It is a time of tremendous growth—from a single cell to an organism complete with a brain and behavioral capabilities, produced in approximately a 9-month period.

Infancy *is the developmental period that begins at birth and ends at about 18 to 24 months.* Infancy is a time of extreme dependence on adults. Many psychological activities are just beginning—language, symbolic thought, sensorimotor coordination, and social learning, for example.

Early childhood *is the developmental period that extends from the end of infancy to about 5 or 6 years of age; sometimes the period is called the preschool years.* During this time, young children learn to become more self-sufficient and to care for themselves, develop school readiness skills (following instructions, identifying letters), and spend many hours in play and with peers. First grade typically marks the end of this period.

Middle and late childhood *is the developmental period that extends from about 6 to 11 years of age, approximately corresponding to the elementary school years; sometimes this period is called the elementary school years.* Children master the fundamental skills of reading, writing, and arithmetic, and they are formally exposed to the larger world and its culture. Achievement becomes a more central theme of the child's world, and self-control increases.

Adolescence *is the developmental period of transition from childhood to early adulthood, entered at approximately 10 to 12 years of age and ending at 18 to 22 years of age.* Adolescence begins with rapid physical changes—dramatic gains in height and weight; changes in body contour; and the development of sexual characteristics such as enlargement of the breasts, development of pubic and facial hair, and deepening of the voice. At this point in development, the pursuit of independence and an identity are prominent. Thought is more logical, abstract, and idealistic. More and more time is spent outside the family during this period.

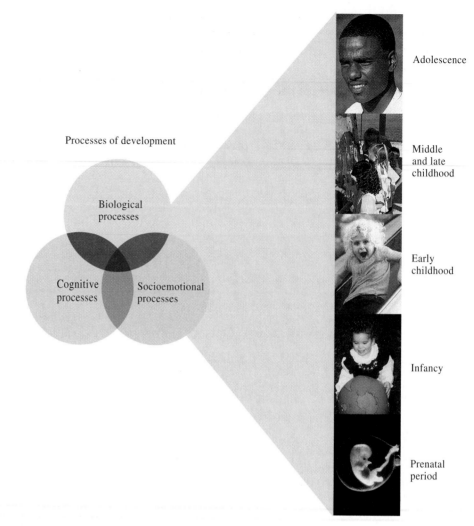

Figure~1.6

Processes and Periods of Development
Development moves through the prenatal, infancy, early childhood, middle and late childhood, and adolescence periods. These periods of development are the result of biological, cognitive, and socioemotional processes. Development is the creation of increasingly complex forms.

Today, developmentalists do not believe that change ends with adolescence (Baltes, Lindenberger, & Staudinger, 1997; Santrock, 1997). They describe development as a lifelong process. However, the purpose of this text is to describe the changes in development that take place from conception through adolescence.

The periods of development from conception through adolescence are shown in figure 1.6, along with the processes of development—biological, cognitive, and socioemotional. The interplay of biological, cognitive, and socioemotional processes produces the periods of development.

Developmental Issues

A number of issues generate spirited debate among developmentalists: To what extent is development influenced by maturation and experience (nature and nurture)? To what extent is it characterized by continuity and discontinuity? To what degree does it involve early versus later experiences?

Maturation and Experience (Nature and Nurture)

We can think of development as produced not only by the interplay of biological, cognitive, and socioemotional processes but also by the interplay of maturation and experience. **Maturation** *is the orderly sequence of changes dictated by the genetic blueprint we each have.* Just as a sunflower grows in an orderly way—unless flattened by an unfriendly environment—so does a human being grow in an orderly way, according to the maturational view. The range of environments can be vast, but the maturational approach argues that the genetic blueprint produces commonalities in our growth and development. We walk before we talk, speak one word before two words, grow rapidly in infancy and less so in early childhood, experience a rush of sexual hormones in puberty after a lull in childhood, reach the peak of our physical strength in late adolescence and early adulthood and then decline, and so on. The maturationists acknowledge that extreme environments—those that are psychologically barren or hostile—can depress development, but they believe that basic growth tendencies are genetically wired into human beings.

By contrast, other psychologists emphasize the importance of experiences in child development. Experiences run the gamut from individuals' biological environment (nutrition, medical care, drugs, and physical accidents) to their social environment (family, peers, schools, community, media, and culture).

The debate about whether development is primarily influenced by maturation or by experience has been a part of psychology since its beginning. This debate is often referred to as the **nature-nurture controversy.** *Nature refers to an organism's biological inheritance, nurture to environmental experiences. The "nature" proponents claim that biological inheritance is the most important influence on development; the "nurture" proponents claim that environmental experiences are the most important.*

Ideas about development have been like a pendulum, swinging between nature and nurture. In the 1980s, we witnessed a surge of interest in the biological underpinnings of development, probably because the pendulum previously had swung too far in the direction of thinking that development was exclusively due to environmental experiences. As we entered the 1990s, a heightened interest in sociocultural influences on development was emerging, again probably because the pendulum in the 1980s had swung so strongly toward the biological side.

Continuity and Discontinuity

Think about your development for a moment. Did you gradually grow to become the person you are, like the slow, cumulative way a seedling grows into a giant oak, or were there sudden, distinct changes in your growth, like the way a caterpillar changes into a butterfly? (See figure 1.7.) For the most part, developmentalists who emphasize experience have described development as a gradual, continuous process; those who emphasize maturation have described development as a series of distinct stages.

Some developmentalists emphasize the **continuity of development,** *the view that development involves gradual, cumulative change from conception to death.* A child's first word, while seemingly an abrupt, discontinuous event, is actually the result of months of growth and practice. Puberty, while also seemingly an abrupt, discontinuous occurrence, is actually a gradual process occurring over several years.

Other developmentalists focus on the **discontinuity of development,** *the view that development involves*

Figure~1.7

Continuity and Discontinuity in Development
Is human development like a seedling gradually growing into a giant oak? Or is it more like a caterpillar suddenly becoming a butterfly?

distinct stages in the life span. Each of us is described as passing through a sequence of stages in which change is qualitatively rather than quantitatively different. As an oak moves from seedling to giant tree, it becomes *more* oak—its development is continuous. As a caterpillar changes into a butterfly, it becomes not more caterpillar but a *different kind* of organism—its development is discontinuous. For example, at a certain point, a child moves from not being able to think abstractly about the world to being able to do so. This is a qualitative, discontinuous change in development, not a quantitative, continuous change.

Early and Later Experience

Another important developmental topic is the **early-later experience issue,** *which focuses on the degree to which early experiences (especially in infancy) or later experiences are the key determinants of the child's development.* That is, if

"If you ask me, he's come too far too fast."

Drawing by Lorenz; © 1988 The New Yorker Magazine, Inc.

How important are early experiences in development?

infants experience negative, stressful circumstances in their lives, can those experiences be overcome by later, more positive experiences? Or are the early experiences so critical, possibly because they are the infant's first, prototypical experiences, that they cannot be overridden by a later, more enriched environment?

The early-later experience issue has a long history and continues to be hotly debated among developmentalists. Some believe that unless infants experience warm, nurturant caregiving in the first year or so of life, their development will never be optimal (Bowlby, 1989; Waters & others, 1995). Plato was sure that infants who were frequently rocked became better athletes. Nineteenth-century New England ministers told parents in Sunday sermons that the way they handled their infants would determine their children's future character. The emphasis on the importance of early experience rests on the belief that each life is an unbroken trail on which a psychological quality can be traced back to its origin (Kagan, 1992).

The early-experience doctrine contrasts with the later-experience view that, rather than statuelike permanence after change in infancy, development continues to be like the ebb and flow of a river. The later-experience advocates argue that children are malleable throughout development and that later sensitive caregiving is just as important as earlier sensitive caregiving. A number of life-span developmentalists, who focus on the entire life span rather than only on child development, stress that too little attention has been given to later experiences in development (Helson, 1993). They hold that early experiences are important contributors to development, but no more important than later experiences. Jerome Kagan (1995) points out that even children who show the qualities of an inhibited

temperament, which is linked to heredity, have the capacity to change their behavior. In his research, almost one-third of a group of children who had an inhibited temperament at 2 years of age were not unusually shy or fearful when they were 4 years of age.

People in Western cultures, especially those steeped in the Freudian belief that the key experiences in development are children's relationships with their parents in the first 5 years of life, have tended to support the idea that early experiences are more important than later experiences (Lamb & Sternberg, 1992). By contrast, the majority of people in the world do not share this belief. For example, people in many Asian countries believe that experiences occurring after about 6 to 7 years of age are more important aspects of development than earlier experiences. This stance stems from the longstanding belief in Eastern cultures that children's reasoning skills begin to develop in important ways in the middle childhood years.

Evaluating the Developmental Issues

As we consider further these three salient developmental issues—nature and nurture, continuity and discontinuity, and early and later experience—it is important to realize that most developmentalists recognize that it is unwise to take an extreme position on these issues. Development is not all nature or all nurture, not all continuity or all discontinuity, and not all early or later experience. Nature and nurture, continuity and discontinuity, and early and later experience characterize our development through the human life span. For example, in considering the nature-nurture issue, the key to development is the *interaction* of nature and nurture rather than either factor alone (Plomin, 1993). An individual's cognitive development is the result of heredity-environment interaction, not heredity or environment alone, for instance. Much more about the role of heredity-environment interaction appears in chapter 3.

Nonetheless, although most developmentalists do not take extreme positions on these three important issues, this consensus has not meant the absence of spirited debate about how strongly development is influenced by each of these factors. Are girls less likely to do well in math because of their "feminine" nature or because of society's masculine bias? If, as children, adolescents experienced a world of poverty, neglect by parents, and poor schooling, can enriched experiences in adolescence remove the "deficits" they encountered earlier in their development? The answers developmentalists give to such questions depend on their stance on the issues of nature and nurture, continuity and discontinuity, and early and later experience. The answers to these questions also influence public policy decisions about children, and they influence how each of us lives through the human life span.

CAREERS IN CHILD DEVELOPMENT

A career in child development is one of the most rewarding vocational opportunities people can pursue. By choosing a career in child development, you will be able to help children who might not otherwise reach their potential as productive contributors to society develop into physically, cognitively, and socially mature individuals. Adults who work professionally with children invariably feel a sense of pride in their ability to contribute in meaningful ways to the next generation of human beings.

If you decide to pursue a career related to children's development, a number of options are available to you. College and university professors teach courses in child development, education, family development, and nursing; counselors, clinical psychologists, pediatricians, psychiatrists, school psychologists, pediatric nurses, psychiatric nurses, and social workers see children with problems and disorders or illnesses; teachers instruct children in kindergartens, elementary schools, and secondary schools. In pursuing a career related to child development, you can expand your opportunities (and income) considerably by obtaining a graduate degree, although an advanced degree is not absolutely necessary.

Most college professors in child development and its related areas of psychology, education, home economics, nursing, and social work have a master's degree and/or doctorate degree that required 2 to 5 years of academic work beyond their undergraduate degree. Becoming a child clinical psychologist or counseling psychologist requires 5 to 6 years of graduate work to obtain the necessary Ph.D.; this includes both clinical and research training. School and career counselors pursue a master's or doctorate degree in counseling, often in graduate programs in education departments; these degrees require 2 to 6 years to complete. Becoming a pediatrician or psychiatrist requires 4 years of medical school, plus an internship and a residency in pediatrics or psychiatry, respectively; this career path takes 7 to 9 years beyond a bachelor's degree. School psychologists obtain either a master's degree (approximately 2 years) or a D.Ed. degree (approximately 4 to 5 years) in school psychology. School psychologists counsel children and parents when children have problems in school, often giving psychological tests to assess children's personality and intelligence. Social work positions may be obtained with an undergraduate degree in social work or related fields, but opportunities are expanded with an M.S.W. (master's of social work) or Ph.D., which require 2 and 4 to 5 years, respectively. Pediatric and psychiatric nursing positions also can be attained with an undergraduate R.N. degree; M.A. and Ph.D. degrees in nursing, which require 2 and 4 to 5 years of graduate training, respectively, are also available. To read further about jobs and careers that involve working with children, turn to table 1.2. This list is not exhaustive but rather is meant to give you an idea of the many opportunities to pursue a rewarding career in child development and its related fields. Also keep in mind that majoring in child development or a related field can provide sound preparation for adult life.

One of our major concerns is the underrepresentation of ethnic minority individuals, not only as research subjects and the focus of developmental inquiry, but also as child developmentalists. To read about the history of ethnic minority individuals in child development and their current representation in the field of child development, turn to Sociocultural Worlds of Children.

THINKING CRITICALLY ABOUT CHILDREN'S DEVELOPMENT

What does it mean to think critically about children's development? We all use various forms of critical thinking. However, when we learn a new discipline, such as child development, we have an opportunity to refine the critical-thinking skills that the discipline emphasizes.

How should your critical-thinking skills change as a result of reading this book and taking this course on children's development? You should develop more effective critical-thinking skills in ten areas that involve children's development (see figure 1.8).

As you read this text, you will often be asked to think critically about children's development. Several times in each chapter you will read Critical Thinking About Children's Development boxes. In this chapter, you have already been asked to imagine what your development as a child would have been like if you

TABLE 1.2

Jobs and Careers in Child Development and Related Fields

Jobs/Careers	Degree	Education Required
Child clinical psychologist or counseling psychologist	Ph.D.	5–7 years postundergraduate
Child life specialist	Undergraduate degree	4 years of undergraduate study
Child psychiatrist	M.D.	7–9 years postundergraduate
Child welfare worker	Undergraduate degree is minimum	4 years minimum
College/university professor in child development, education, family development, nursing, social work	Ph.D. or master's degree	5–6 years for Ph.D. (or D.Ed.) postundergraduate; 2 years for master's degree postundergraduate
Day-care supervisor	Varies by state	Varies by state
Early childhood educator	Master's degree (minimum)	2 years of graduate work (minimum)
Elementary or secondary school teacher	Undergraduate degree (minimum)	4 years
Exceptional children teacher (special education teacher)	Undergraduate degree (minimum)	4 years or more (some states require a master's degree or passing a standardized exam to obtain a license to work with exceptional children)
Guidance counselor	Undergraduate degree (minimum); many have master's degree	4 years undergraduate; 2 years graduate
Pediatrician	M.D.	7–9 years of medical school
Pediatric nurse	R.N.	2–5 years
Preschool/kindergarten teacher	Usually undergraduate degree	4 years
Psychiatric nurse	R.N.	2–5 years
School psychologist	Master's or Ph.D.	5–6 years of graduate work for Ph.D. or D.Ed.; 2 years for master's degree

Santrock: Child Development

Nature of Training	Description of Work
Includes both clinical and research training; involves a 1-year internship in a psychiatric hospital or mental health facility.	Child clinical psychologists or counseling psychologists diagnose children's problems and disorders, administer psychological tests, and conduct psychotherapy sessions. Some work at colleges and universities where they do any combination of teaching, therapy, and research.
Many child life specialists have been trained in child development or education but undergo additional training in child life programs that includes parent education, developmental assessment, and supervised work with children and parents.	Child life specialists are employed by hospitals and work with children and their families before and after the children are admitted to the hospital. They often develop and monitor developmentally appropriate activities for child patients. They also help children adapt to their medical experiences and their stay at the hospital. Child life specialists coordinate their efforts with physicians and nurses.
Four years of medical school, plus an internship and residency in child psychiatry are required.	The role of the child psychiatrist is similar to the child clinical psychologist, but the psychiatrist can conduct biomedical therapy (for example, such as using drugs to treat clients); the child clinical or counseling psychologist cannot.
Coursework and training in social work or human services.	Child welfare workers are employed by the Child Protective Services Unit of each state to protect children's rights. They especially monitor cases of child maltreatment and abuse, and make decisions about what needs to be done to help protect the abused child from further harm and effectively cope with their prior abuse.
Take graduate courses, learn how to conduct research, attend and present papers at professional meetings.	College and university professors teach courses in child development, family development, education, or nursing; conduct research; present papers at professional meetings; write and publish articles and books; and train undergraduate and graduate students for careers in these fields.
The Department of Public Welfare in many states publishes a booklet with the requirements for a day-care supervisor.	Day-care supervisors direct day-care or preschool programs, being responsible for the operation of the center. They often make decisions about the nature of the center's curriculum, may teach in the center themselves, work with and consult with parents, and conduct workshops for staff or parents.
Coursework in early childhood education and practice in day-care or early childhood centers with supervised training.	Early childhood educators usually teach in community colleges that award associate or bachelor's degrees in early childhood education with specialization in day care. They train individuals for careers in the field of day care.
Wide range of courses with a major or concentration in education.	Elementary and secondary teachers teach one or more subjects; prepare the curriculum; give tests, assign grades, and monitor students' progress; interact with parents and school administrators; attend lectures and workshops involving curriculum planning or help on special issues; and direct extracurricular programs.
Coursework in education with a concentration in special education.	Exceptional children teachers (also called special education teachers) work with children who are educationally handicapped (those who are mentally retarded, have a physical handicap, have a learning disability, or have a behavioral disorder) or who are gifted. They develop special curricula for the exceptional children and help them to adapt to their exceptional circumstances. Special education teachers work with other school personnel and with parents to improve the adjustment of exceptional children.
Coursework in education and counseling in a school of education; counselor training practice.	The majority of guidance counselors work with secondary school students, assisting them in educational and career planning. They often give students aptitude tests and evaluate their interests, as well as their abilities. Guidance counselors also see students who are having school-related problems, including emotional problems, referring them to other professionals such as school psychologists or clinical psychologists when necessary.
Four years of medical school, plus an internship and residency in pediatrics.	Pediatricians monitor infants' and children's health and treat their diseases. They advise parents about infant and child development and the appropriate ways to deal with children.
Courses in biological sciences, nursing care, and pediatrics (often in a school of nursing); supervised clinical experiences in medical settings.	Pediatric nurses promote health in infants and children, working to prevent disease or injury, assisting children with handicaps or health problems so they can achieve optimal health, and treating children with health deviations. Some pediatric nurses specialize in certain areas (for example, the neonatal intensive care unit clinician cares exclusively for newborns; the new-parent educator helps the parents of newborns develop better parenting skills). Pediatric nurses work in a variety of medical settings.
Coursework in education with a specialization in early childhood education; state certification usually required.	Preschool teachers direct the activities of prekindergarten children, many of whom are 4-year-olds. They develop an appropriate curriculum for the age of the children that promotes their physical, cognitive, and social development in a positive atmosphere. The number of days per week and hours per day varies from one program to another. Kindergarten teachers work with young children who are between the age of preschool programs and the first year of elementary school; they primarily develop appropriate activities and curricula for 5-year-old children.
Courses in biological sciences, nursing care, and mental health in a school of nursing; supervised clinical training in child psychiatric settings.	Psychiatric nurses promote the mental health of individuals; some specialize in helping children with mental health problems and work closely with child psychiatrists to improve these children's adjustment.
Includes coursework and supervised training in school settings, usually in a department of educational psychology.	School psychologists evaluate and treat a wide range of normal and exceptional children who have school-related problems; work in a school system and see children from a number of schools; administer tests, interview and observe children, and consult with teachers, parents, and school administrators; and design programs to reduce the child's problem behavior.

SOCIOCULTURAL WORLDS OF CHILDREN

Ethnic Minorities in the Field of Child Development

Barriers have prevented the entry of African Americans, Latinos, Asian Americans, and Native Americans into the field of child development throughout most of its history. Ethnic minority individuals who obtained doctoral degrees were very dedicated and overcame extensive bias against their ethnic group. Two pioneering African American psychologists were Mamie and Kenneth Clark, who conducted research on African American children's self-conceptions and identity (Clark & Clark, 1939). In 1971, Kenneth Clark became the first African American president of the American Psychological Association. In 1932, Latino psychologist George Sanchez conducted research that demonstrated the cultural bias of intelligence tests for ethnic minority children.

In the past three decades, important movements calling for recognition of the rights and needs of ethnic minorities in higher education have surfaced. The civil rights movement has led to social change, stimulating developmentalists—especially those who also are members of ethnic minority groups—to reexamine the existing body of knowledge about children's development and to question to what degree it is relevant to ethnic minority children. This questioning has formed the basis of new areas of developmental inquiry, focusing on populations who previously were omitted from subject pools of developmental research and from the theoretical ideas of mainstream child development.

Recognizing the underrepresentation of ethnic minority individuals in psychology, the American Psychological Association (APA)—the main organization of psychologists in the United States—has formed the Board of Ethnic Minority Affairs to represent the ethnic group concerns of its members. In one survey, only 5 percent of doctoral psychologists in the developmental area, 4.7 percent in the clinical, counseling, and school areas, and 7.5 percent in the educational area were members of ethnic minority groups (Stapp, Tucker, & VandenBos, 1985). The percentage of Latino and Native American individuals with doctorates in these areas is especially low. And in nursing, the percentage of those with master's and doctoral degrees who represent ethnic minorities is equally low (for example, African Americans—5 percent; Asian Americans—2 percent; Latinos—1 percent; and Native Americans—0.2 percent).

Job opportunities are increasingly available to qualified applicants from every ethnic group. We need more qualified ethnic minority individuals in the field of child development.

George Sanchez

Mamie and Kenneth Clark conducted pioneering research on African American children's self-conceptions and identity.

Apply a developmental framework to understand behavior

Make accurate observations, descriptions, and inferences about children's development

Identify the sociohistorical, cultural contexts that influence children's development

Apply developmental concepts to enhance personal adaptation

Pursue alternative explanations to understand children's development comprehensively

Evaluate the quality of conclusions and strategies about children's development

Engage in perspective taking to better understand children's development

Use knowledge about development to improve human welfare

Demonstrate appreciation of individual differences in children's development

Create arguments based on developmental concepts

Figure~1.8

Critical Thinking About Children's Development

had grown up in a different culture, which encourages you to engage in perspective taking and identify the sociohistorical and cultural factors that influence children's development. You also asked yourself questions about your own development as a child, which helps you to apply a developmental framework to understanding behavior. In addition to the boxes on critical thinking, you will encounter many other opportunities to enhance your ability to think like a developmentalist and to improve your grasp of the concepts and principles you are learning.

At this point we have studied a number of ideas about the nature of development, developmental issues, careers in child development, and thinking critically about children's development. A summary of these ideas is presented in concept table 1.2.

The Nature of Development, Developmental Issues, Careers in Child Development, and Critical Thinking About Children's Development

Concept	Processes/ Related Ideas	Characteristics/Description
The Nature of Development	What is development?	Development is the patter of movement or change that occurs throughout the life span.
	Biological, cognitive, and socioemotional processes	Development is influenced by an interplay of biologocial, cognitive, and socioemotional processes.
	Periods of development	Development is commonly divided into the following periods from conception through adolescence: the prenatal period, infancy, early childhood, middle and late childhood, and adolescence.
Developmental Issues	Maturation and experience (nature and nurture)	The debate over whether development is due primarily to maturation or to experience is another version of the nature-nurture controversy.
	Continuity and discontinuity	Some developmentalists describe development as continuous (gradual, cumulative change), others as discontinuous (abrupt, sequence of stages).
	Early and later experience	This hotly debated issue focuses on whether early experiences (especially in infancy) are more important in development than later experiences are.
	Evaluating the developmental issues	Most developmentalists recognize that extreme positions of the nature-nurture, continuity-discontinuity, and early-later experience issues are unwise. Despite this consensus, spirited debate still occurs on these issues.
Careers in Child Development	Their nature	A wide range of opportunities are available to individuals who want to pursue a career related to child development. These opportunities include jobs in college and university teaching, child clinical psychology and counseling, school teaching and school psychology, nursing, pediatrics, psychiatry, and social work. A special interest is the history of ethnic minority individuals in the field of child development, and the current educational status of ethnic minority individuals.
Thinking Critically About Children's Development	Its nature	Critical thinking about children's development involves such strategies as applying a developmental framework to understand behavior, making accurate observations and inferences, applying developmental concepts to enhance personal adaptation, pursing alternative explanations, evaluating the quality of conclusions and strategies, engaging in perspective taking, demonstrating an appreciation of individual differences, and developing arguments based on developmental concepts.

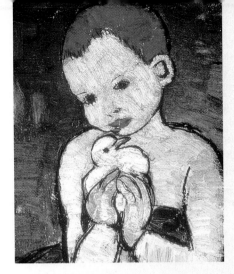

SUMMARY

Children should have a special place in any society, for they are the society's future. An important concern is that too many children today will not reach their full potential because of inadequate rearing conditions. Far too many children live in poverty, have parents who do not adequately care for them, and go to schools where learning conditions are far from optimal.

In this chapter, you were introduced to the field of child develop-ment. You read about how today is both the best of times and the worst of times for children and why it is im-portant to study children. You learned about the nature of child develop-ment through history, some contem-porary concerns, the modern study of child development, and social pol-icy issues. You also studied the nature of development by exploring biolog-ical, cognitive, and socioemotional processes; periods of development; and developmental issues. You read about a number of careers in child de-velopment and how to think critically about children's development.

To obtain a summary of the chap-ter, go back and again study the two concept tables on pages 17 and 26. In the next chapter, we will turn our attention to the field of child devel-opment as a science. You will learn about the importance of the scientific method, theories, and methods in studying children.

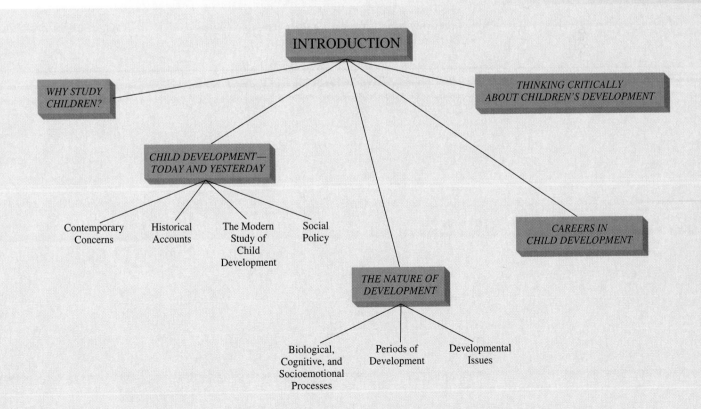

KEY TERMS

PRACTICAL KNOWLEDGE ABOUT CHILDREN

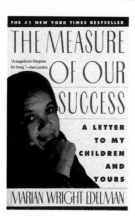

The Measure of Our Success: A Letter to My Children and Yours

(1992) by Marian Wright Edelman,
Boston: Beacon Press.

Marian Wright Edelman founded the Children's Defense Fund in 1973 and for more than two decades has been working to advance the health and well-being of America's children and parents. This slim volume begins with a message to her oldest son, Joshua, 22. In that message and throughout the book, Edelman conveys that parenting and nurturing the next generation is the most important func-tion of a society and that we need to take it more seriously than we have in the past. High on her recommended list is the belief that there is no free lunch—don't feel entitled to any-thing you don't sweat and struggle for. She warns against working only for money or for power because they won't save your soul, build a decent fam-ily, or help you sleep at night. She also tells her sons to remember that a wife is not their mother or their maid. Edelman admonishes our soci-ety for not developing better safety nets for children and not being the caring community that children and parents need.

Familyhood

(1992) by Lee Salk,
New York: Simon & Schuster.

Familyhood is about the importance of the family in children's lives and about nurturing the family values that matter. Lee Salk was a well-known clinical psychologist who championed better lives for children for many years. He died in 1992.

Salk says that though the structure of families has changed enormously in recent years because of high divorce rates, increasing numbers of stepfamilies, and huge numbers of working-mother families, the values the family cherishes most have not changed. Relying on information from a comprehensive family values survey, Salk says parents today still have the following needs, wants, and values:

- They want family members to provide emotional support for one another.
- They want children to show respect for parents.
- They believe parents should also show respect for their children.
- They think that parents should show mutual respect for each other.
- They believe that family members should take responsibility for their own actions.
- They think that family members should try to understand and listen to each other.

EXPLORATIONS IN CHILD DEVELOPMENT

To fully understand the field of child development today, it is important to explore both its research side and its applied side. Thus, each chapter will conclude with this endpiece, which has two parts: first a discussion of some aspect of research on child development, and second, a description of issues and programs that focus on improving the lives of children. The research discussion provides you with an opportunity to see how the scientists who study children's development actually conduct research studies. The Applications discussion will give you a sense of how professionals who work with children seek solutions to help children reach their full potential.

RESEARCH IN CHILD DEVELOPMENT

Why Research in Child Development Is Important

Knowledge in the field of child development rests heavily on the generation of a broad, competent research base. Over the last several decades, research in child development has grown enormously as increasing numbers of investigators have become intrigued by issues and questions that involve children's lives. The importance of research in child development is reflected in the large number of research journals in the field and the growth in the membership of the Society for Research in Child Development, the main professional organization for scholars who conduct research on children's development.

In discussing child development and social policy earlier in this chapter, we said that a current trend is to conduct research that is relevant to social policy. The question of whether child development researchers should conduct research that is relevant to social policy touches on a long-standing issue: Should research be basic or applied?

Basic research, sometimes called pure research, is the study of issues to obtain knowledge for its own sake rather than for practical applications. Basic research is often conducted to test a theory or to follow up on other research. Rarely is basic research conducted as a response to a pressing social problem. Basic research might or might not eventually be applied to social policy or practical problems. In contrast, *applied research* is the study of issues that have direct practical significance, often with the intent of changing behavior. Thus, social policy research is applied research, not basic research.

A developmentalist who conducts basic research might ask: How does cognitive development change during childhood? In contrast, a developmentalist who conducts applied research might ask: How can knowledge about change in children's cognitive development be used to educate them more effectively or to help them cope with stress?

Most developmentalists believe that basic and applied research are both important. Basic research can sometimes produce information that can be used to improve children's well-being, but it does not guarantee this application. Insisting that research always be relevant is like trying to grow new flowers by dealing only with the blossoms and not tending to the roots. Basic research is root research. Without the discovery of basic scientific principles, we would have little knowledge to apply. Today, research on child development includes a wealth of both basic and applied studies.

IMPROVING THE LIVES OF CHILDREN

Thinking About Your Future as a Parent and the Education of Your Children

Famous playwright George Bernard Shaw once commented that while parenting is a very important profession, no test of fitness for it is ever imposed. If a test were imposed, some parents would turn out to be more fit than others. Most parents do want their children to grow into socially mature individuals, but they often are not sure about what to do as a parent to help their children reach this goal (Stenhouse, 1996). One reason for parents' frustration is that they often get conflicting messages about how to deal with their children. One "expert" might urge them to be more permissive with their children; another might tell them to place stricter controls on them or they will grow up to be spoiled brats.

Most of you taking this course will be a parent someday; some of you already are. I hope that each of you will take seriously the importance of rearing your children, because they are the future of our society. Good parenting takes a considerable amount of time. If you choose to become a parent, you should be willing to commit yourself, day after day, week after week, month after month, and year after year, to providing your children with a warm, supportive, safe, and stimulating environment that will make them feel secure and allow them to reach their full potential as human beings.

Understanding the nature of children's development can help you to become a better parent. Many parents learn parenting practices and how to care for their children from their parents—they usually accept some of their parents' practices and some they discard. Unfortunately, when parenting practices and child-care strategies are passed on from one generation to the next, both desirable and undesirable ones are perpetuated. This book and your instructor's lectures in this course can help you become much more knowledgeable about the nature of children's development and to sort through which practices in your own upbringing you would like to continue with your own children and which you would like to abandon.

Like parenting, education is an extremely important dimension of children's lives. When we think of education, we usually associate it with schools. Schools are an extremely important aspect of education, but education also occurs in contexts other than schools. Children learn from their parents, from their siblings, from their peers, from books, from watching television, and from computers as well.

You can probably look back on your own education and think of ways it could have been a lot better. Some, or even most, of your school years may have been spent in classrooms in which learning was not enjoyable but boring, stressful, and rigid. Some of your teachers may have not adequately considered your own unique needs and skills. On the other hand, you probably can remember some classrooms and teachers that made learning exciting, something you looked forward to each morning you got up. You liked the teacher and the subject, and you learned.

There is widespread agreement that something needs to be done to improve the education our nation's children are receiving. What would you do to make the education of children more effective? What would you do to make schools more productive and enjoyable contexts for children's development? Would you make the school days longer or shorter? the school year longer or shorter? or keep it the same and focus more on changing the curriculum itself? Would you emphasize less memorization and give more attention to the development of children's ability to process information more efficiently? Have schools become too soft and watered-down, or should they make more demands and have higher expectations of children? Should schools focus only on developing the child's knowledge and cognitive skills, or should they pay more attention to the whole child and consider the child's socioemotional and physical development as well? Should more tax dollars be spent on schools, and should teachers be paid more to educate our nation's children? Should schools be dramatically changed so that they serve as a locus for a wide range of services, such as primary health care, child care, preschool education, parent education, recreation, and family counseling, as well as the traditional educational activity of learning in the classroom?

These are provocative questions, and how they are answered will influence your children's future. We will discuss a number of these issues later in the text in much greater detail. Good parenting and good education serve as important bases for the development of competent children.

Hayward L. Oubre
Pensive Family detail

Chapter

2

The Science
of Child
Development

*here is nothing quite so practical as a
good theory.*

—Kurt Lewin,
Psychologist, 1890–1947

The childhood shows the man, as morning shows the day.

—Milton

PREVIEW

*S*ome individuals have difficulty thinking of child development as being a science in the same way as physics, chemistry, and biology are sciences. Can a discipline that studies how babies develop, how parents nurture children, how peers interact, and how children think be equated with disciplines that investigate how gravity works and the molecular structure of a compound? Science is defined not by *what* it investigates but by *how* it investigates. Whether you are studying photosynthesis, butterflies, Saturn's moons, or human development, it is the *way* you study that makes the approach scientific or not.

In this chapter, we will study three key ingredients of child development as a science—the scientific method, theories, and methods. You also will learn about ethics and sexism in research on child development, as well as how to be a wise consumer of information about children's development.

Erikson and Piaget as Children

Imagine that you have developed a major theory of child development. What would influence someone like you to construct this theory? A person interested in developing such a theory usually goes through a long university training program that culminates in a doctoral degree. As part of the training, the future theorist is exposed to many ideas about a particular area of child development, such as biological, cognitive, or socioemotional development. Another factor that could explain why someone develops a particular theory is that person's life experiences. Two important developmental theorists, whose views we will describe later in the chapter, are Erik Erikson and Jean Piaget. Let's examine a portion of their lives as they were growing up to discover how their experiences might have contributed to the theories they developed.

Erik Homberger Erikson (1902–1994) was born near Frankfort, Germany, to Danish parents. Before Erik was born, his parents separated and his mother left Denmark to live in Germany. At age 3, Erik became ill, and his mother took him to see a pediatrician named Homberger. Young Erik's mother fell in love with the pediatrician, married him, and named Erik after his new stepfather.

Erik attended primary school from the ages of 6 to 10 and then the gymnasium (high school) from 11 to 18. He studied art and a number of languages rather than science courses such as biology and chemistry. Erik did not like the atmosphere of formal schooling, and this was reflected in his grades. Rather than go to college at age 18, the adolescent Erikson wandered around Europe, keeping a diary about his experiences. After a year of travel through Europe, he returned to Germany and enrolled in art school, became dissatisfied, and enrolled in another. Later he traveled to Florence, Italy. Psychiatrist Robert Coles described Erikson at this time:

To the Italians he was . . . the young, tall, thin Nordic expatriate with long, blond hair. He wore a corduroy suit and was seen by his family and friends as not odd or

"sick" but as a wandering artist who was trying to come to grips with himself, a not unnatural or unusual struggle. (Coles, 1970, p.15)

The second major theorist whose life we will examine is Jean Piaget. Piaget (1896–1980) was born in Neuchâtel, Switzerland. Jean's father was an intellectual who taught young Jean to think systematically. Jean's mother was also very bright. His father had an air of detachment from his mother, whom Piaget described as prone to frequent outbursts of neurotic behavior.

In his autobiography, Piaget detailed why he chose to study cognitive development rather than social or abnormal development:

I started to forego playing for serious work very early. Indeed, I have always detested any departure from reality, an attitude which I relate to . . . my mother's poor health. It was this disturbing factor which at the beginning of my studies in psychology made me keenly interested in psychoanalytic and pathological psychology. Though this interest helped me to achieve independence and widen my cultural background, I have never since felt any desire to involve myself deeper in that particular direction, always much preferring the study of normalcy and of the workings of the intellect to that of the tricks of the unconscious. (Piaget, 1952a, p.238)

These excerpts from Erikson's and Piaget's lives illustrate how personal experiences might influence the direction in which a particular theorist goes. Erikson's own wanderings and search for self contributed to his theory of identity development, and Piaget's intellectual experiences with his parents and schooling likely contributed to his emphasis on cognitive development.

THEORY AND THE SCIENTIFIC METHOD

According to nineteenth-century French mathematician Henri Poincaré, "Science is built of facts the way a house is built of bricks, but an accumulation of facts is no more science than a pile of bricks a house." Science *does* depend on the raw material of facts or data, but, as Poincaré indicated, child development's theories are more than just facts.

A **theory** *is a coherent set of ideas that helps explain data and make predictions.* A theory contains **hypotheses,** *assumptions that can be tested to determine their accuracy.* For example, a theory about children's aggression would explain our observations of aggressive children and predict why children become aggressive. We might predict that children become aggressive because of the coercive interchanges they experience and observe in their families. This prediction would help direct our observations by telling us to look for coercive interchanges in families.

The **scientific method** *is an approach that can be used to discover accurate information about behavior and development that includes the following steps: identify and analyze the problem, collect data, draw conclusions, and revise theories.* For example, you decide that you want to help aggressive children control their aggression. You *identify a problem,* which does not seem like a difficult task. However, as part of the first step, you need to go beyond a general description of the problem by isolating, analyzing, narrowing, and focusing on what you hope to investigate. What specific strategies do you want to use to reduce children's aggression? Do you want to look at only one strategy, or several strategies? What aspect of aggression do you want to study—its biological, cognitive, or socioemotional characteristics? Gerald Patterson and his colleagues (Chamberlin & Patterson, 1995; Patterson, Capaldi, & Bank, 1991) argue that parents' failure to teach reasonable levels of compliance sets in motion coercive interchanges with family members. In this first step in the scientific method, a problem is identified and analyzed.

After you have identified and analyzed the problem, the next step is to *collect information (data).* Psychologists observe behavior and draw inferences about thoughts and emotions. For example, in the investigation of children's aggression, we might observe how effectively parents teach reasonable compliance levels to their children and the extent to which coercive exchanges take place among family members.

> *Truth is arrived at by the painstaking process of eliminating the untrue.*
>
> **—Arthur Conan Doyle**

Researchers use the scientific method to obtain accurate information about children's behavior and development. Part of the scientific method is data collection, demonstrated here by a researcher conducting a study of infant development.

Once data have been collected, psychologists use *statistical procedures* to understand the meaning of quantitative data. They then try to *draw conclusions.* In the investigation of children's aggression, statistics would help us determine whether or not our observations were due to chance. After data have been collected, psychologists compare their findings with what others have discovered about the same issue.

The final step in the scientific method is *revising theory.* Psychologists have generated a number of theories about children's development; they also have theorized about why children become aggressive. Data such as those collected by Patterson and his colleagues force us to study existing theories of aggression to see if they are accurate. Over the years, some theories of children's development have been discarded and others revised. Theories are an integral part of understanding the nature of children's development. They will be woven through our discussion of children's development in the remainder of the text.

THEORIES OF CHILD DEVELOPMENT

We will briefly explore five major theoretical perspectives on child development: psychoanalytic, cognitive, behavioral/social learning, ethological, and ecological. You will read more in-depth portrayals of these theories at different points in later chapters in the book.

The diversity of theories makes understanding children's development a challenging undertaking. Just when you think one theory correctly explains children's development, another theory crops up and makes you rethink your earlier conclusion. To keep from getting frustrated, remember that children's development is a complex, multifaceted topic, and no single theory has been able to account for all its aspects. Each theory has contributed an important piece to the child development puzzle. Although the theories sometimes disagree about certain aspects of children's development, much of their information is *complementary* rather than contradictory. Together the various theories let us see the total landscape of children's development in all its richness.

Psychoanalytic Theories

For psychoanalytic theorists, development is primarily unconscious—that is, beyond awareness—and is heavily colored by emotion. Psychoanalytic theorists believe that behavior is merely a surface characteristic and that to truly understand development, we have to analyze the symbolic meanings of behavior and the deep inner workings of the mind. Psychoanalytic theorists also stress that early experiences with parents extensively shape our development. These characteristics are highlighted in the main psychoanalytic theory, that of Sigmund Freud.

> *The passions are at once tempters and chastisers. As tempters, they come with garlands of flowers on the brows of youth; as chastisers, they appear with wreaths of snakes on the forehead of deformity. They are angels of light in their delusion; they are fiends of torment in their inflictions.*
>
> —Henry Giles

Freud's Theory

Freud (1856–1939) developed his ideas about psychoanalytic theory from work with mental patients. He was a medical doctor who specialized in neurology. He spent most of his years in Vienna, though he moved to London near the end of his career because of the Nazis' anti-Semitism. Turn to Critical Thinking About Children's Development to further contemplate the setting in which Freud lived.

Freud (1917) believed that personality has three structures: the id, the ego, and the superego. The **id** *is the Freudian structure of personality that consists of instincts, which are an individual's reservoir of psychic energy.* In Freud's view, the id is totally unconscious; it has no contact with reality. As children experience the demands and constraints of reality, a new structure of personality emerges—the **ego,** *the Freudian structure of personality that deals with the demands of reality.* The ego is called the executive branch of personality because it makes rational decisions. The id and the ego have no morality. They do not take into account whether something is right or wrong. The **superego** *is the Freudian structure of personality that is the moral branch of personality.* The superego takes into

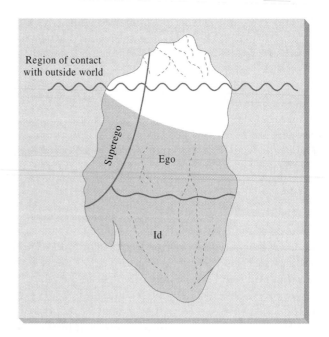

Figure~2.1

Conscious and Unconscious Processes: The Iceberg Analogy
This rather odd-looking diagram illustrates Freud's belief that most of the important personality processes occur below the level of conscious awareness. In examining people's conscious thoughts and their behaviors, we can see some reflections of the ego and the superego. Whereas the ego and superego are partly conscious and partly unconscious, the primitive id is totally unconscious, the submerged part of the iceberg.

account whether something is right or wrong. Think of the superego as what we often refer to as our "conscience." You probably are beginning to sense that both the id and the superego make life rough for the ego. Your ego might say, "I will have sex only occasionally and be sure to take the proper precautions because I don't want the intrusion of a child in the development of my career." However, your id is saying, "I want to be satisfied; sex is pleasurable." Your superego is at work too: "I feel guilty about having sex."

Remember that Freud considered personality to be like an iceberg; most of personality exists below our level of awareness, just as the massive part of an iceberg is beneath the surface of the water. Figure 2.1 illustrates this analogy.

How does the ego resolve the conflict between its demands for reality, the wishes of the id, and constraints of the superego? Through **defense mechanisms,** *the psychoanalytic term for unconscious methods, the ego distorts reality, thereby protecting it from anxiety.* In Freud's view, the conflicting demands of the personality structures produce anxiety. For example, when the ego blocks the pleasurable pursuits of the id, inner anxiety is felt. This diffuse, distressed state develops when the ego senses that the id is going to cause harm to the individual. The anxiety alerts the ego to resolve the conflict by means of defense mechanisms.

Sigmund Freud, the pioneering architect of psychoanalytic theory.

"So, Mr. Fenton . . . Let's begin with your mother."

Repression *is the most powerful and pervasive defense mechanism, according to Freud; it works to push unacceptable id impulses out of awareness and back into the unconscious mind.* Repression is the foundation from which all other defense mechanisms work; the goal of every defense mechanism is to *repress*, or push threatening impulses out of awareness. Freud said that our early childhood experiences, many of which he believed were sexually laden, are too threatening and stressful for us to deal with consciously. We reduce the anxiety of this conflict through the defense mechanism of repression.

> *They cannot scare me with their empty spaces*
> *Between stars—on stars where no human race is.*
> *I have it in me so much nearer home*
> *To scare myself with my own desert places.*
>
> —**Robert Frost**

As Freud listened to, probed, and analyzed his patients, he became convinced that their problems were the result of experiences early in life. Freud believed that we go through five stages of psychosexual development and that, at each stage of development, we experience pleasure in one part of the body more than in others. **Erogenous zones** *are, in Freud's theory, the parts of the body that have especially strong pleasure-giving qualities at each stage of development.*

Freud thought that the adult personality is determined by the way conflicts between the early sources of pleasure—the mouth, the anus, and then the genitals—

and the demands of reality are resolved. When these conflicts are not resolved, the individual may become fixated at a particular stage of development.

For example, a parent might wean a child too early, be too strict in toilet training, punish the child for masturbation, or smother the child with warmth. We will return to the idea of fixation and how it may show up in an adult's personality, but first we need to learn more about the early stages of personality development.

The **oral stage** *is the first Freudian stage of development, occurring during the first 18 months of life, in which the infant's pleasure centers around the mouth.* Chewing, sucking, and biting are the chief sources of pleasure. These actions reduce tension in the infant.

The **anal stage** *is the second Freudian stage of development, occurring between 1½ and 3 years of age, in which the child's greatest pleasure involves the anus or the eliminative functions associated with it.* In Freud's view, the exercise of anal muscles reduces tension.

The **phallic stage** *is the third Freudian stage of development, occuring between the ages of 3 and 6; its name comes from the Latin word* phallus, *which means "penis."* During the phallic stage, pleasure focuses on the genitals as the child discovers that self-manipulation is enjoyable.

In Freud's view, the phallic stage has a special importance in personality development because it is during this period that the Oedipus complex appears. This name comes from Greek mythology, in which Oedipus, the son of the King of Thebes, unwittingly kills his father and marries his mother. The **Oedipus complex** *is the Freudian concept that the young child develops an intense*

Freud and Schwarzenegger

If Sigmund Freud were alive today, what reactions do you think he might have to the violence and sexuality in contemporary action films? Conversely, how do you think Arnold Schwarzenegger might have fared in Freud's Victorian Viennese culture? Consideration of these questions sensitizes you to the importance of *identifying the sociohistorical and cultural factors that influence behavior*.

Arnold Schwarzenegger

Victorian Vienna

desire to replace the parent of the same sex and enjoy the affections of the opposite-sex parent. Freud's concept of the Oedipus complex has been criticized by some psychoanalysts and writers. To learn more about cultural- and gender-based criticisms of Freud's theory, turn to Sociocultural Worlds of Children.

How is the Oedipus complex resolved? At about 5 to 6 years of age, children recognize that their same-sex parent might punish them for their incestuous wishes. To reduce this conflict, the child identifies with the same-sex parent, striving to be like him or her. If the conflict is not resolved, though, the individual may become fixated at the phallic stage.

The **latency stage** *is the fourth Freudian stage of development, which occurs between approximately 6 years of age and puberty; the child represses all interest in sexuality and develops social and intellectual skills*. This activity channels much of the child's energy into emotionally safe areas and helps the child forget the highly stressful conflicts of the phallic stage.

The **genital stage** *is the fifth and final Freudian stage of development, occurring from puberty on. The genital stage is a time of sexual reawakening; the source of sexual pleasure*

now becomes someone outside of the family. Freud believed that unresolved conflicts with parents reemerge during adolescence. When resolved, the individual is capable of developing a mature love relationship and functioning independently as an adult.

Freud's theory has undergone significant revisions by a number of psychoanalytic theorists. Many contemporary psychoanalytic theorists place less emphasis on sexual instincts and more emphasis on cultural experiences as determinants of an individual's development. Unconscious thought remains a central theme, but most contemporary psychoanalysts believe that conscious thought makes up more of the iceberg than Freud envisioned. Next, we will explore the ideas of an important revisionist of Freud's ideas—Erik Erikson.

Erikson's Theory

Erik Erikson (1902–1994) recognized Freud's contributions but believed that Freud misjudged some important dimensions of human development. For one, Erikson (1950, 1968) says we develop in *psychosocial stages*, in contrast to Freud's psychosexual stages. For another, Erikson emphasizes developmental change throughout the

Erik Erikson with his wife, Joan, who is an artist. Erikson generated one of the most important developmental theories of the twentieth century.

human life span, whereas Freud argued that our basic personality is shaped in the first 5 years of life. In Erikson's theory, eight stages of development unfold as we go through the life span. Each stage consists of a unique developmental task that confronts individuals with a crisis that must be faced. For Erikson, this crisis is not a catastrophe but a turning point of increased vulnerability and enhanced potential. The more an individual resolves the crises successfully, the healthier development will be.

Trust versus mistrust *is Erikson's first psychosocial stage, which is experienced in the first year of life. A sense of trust requires a feeling of physical comfort and a minimal amount of fear and apprehension about the future.* Trust in infancy sets the stage for a lifelong expectation that the world will be a good and pleasant place to live.

Autonomy versus shame and doubt *is Erikson's second stage of development, occurring in late infancy and toddlerhood (1–3 years). After gaining trust in their caregivers, infants begin to discover that their behavior is their own. They start to assert their sense of independence or autonomy. They realize their will.* If infants are restrained too much or punished too harshly, they are likely to develop a sense of shame and doubt.

Initiative versus guilt *is Erikson's third stage of development, occurring during the preschool years. As preschool children encounter a widening social world, they are challenged more than when they were infants. Active, purposeful behavior is needed to cope with these challenges.* Children are asked to assume responsibility for their bodies, their behavior, their toys, and their pets. Developing a sense of responsibility increases initiative. Uncomfortable guilt feelings may arise, though, if the child is irresponsible

and is made to feel too anxious. Erikson has a positive outlook on this stage. He believes that most guilt is quickly compensated for by a sense of accomplishment.

Industry versus inferiority *is Erikson's fourth developmental stage, occurring approximately in the elementary school years. Children's initiative brings them in contact with a wealth of new experiences. As they move into middle and late childhood, they direct their energy toward mastering knowledge and intellectual skills.* At no other time is the child more enthusiastic about learning than at the end of early childhood's period of expansive imagination. The danger in the elementary school years is the development of a sense of inferiority—of feeling incompetent and unproductive. Erikson believes that teachers have a special responsibility for children's development of industry. Teachers should "mildly but firmly coerce children into the adventure of finding out that one can learn to accomplish things which one would never have thought of by oneself" (Erikson, 1968, p.127).

Identity versus identity confusion *is Erikson's fifth developmental stage, which individuals experience during the adolescent years. At this time, individuals are faced with finding out who they are, what they are all about, and where they are going in life.* Adolescents are confronted with many new roles and adult statuses—vocational and romantic, for example. Parents need to allow adolescents to explore many different roles and different paths within a particular role. If the adolescent explores such roles in a healthy manner and arrives at a positive path to follow in life, then a positive identity will be achieved. If an identity is pushed on the adolescent by parents, if the adolescent does not adequately explore many roles, and if a positive future path is not defined, then identity confusion reigns.

Intimacy versus isolation *is Erikson's sixth developmental stage, which individuals experience during the early adulthood years. At this time, individuals face the developmental task of forming intimate relationships with others.* Erikson describes intimacy as finding oneself yet losing oneself in another. If the young adult forms healthy friendships and an intimate close relationship with another individual, intimacy will be achieved; if not, isolation will result.

Generativity versus stagnation *is Erikson's seventh developmental stage, which individuals experience during middle adulthood.* A chief concern is to assist the younger generation in developing and leading useful lives—this is what Erikson means by *generativity.* The feeling of having done nothing to help the next generation is stagnation.

Integrity versus despair *is Erikson's eighth and final developmental stage, which individuals experience during late adulthood. In the later years of life, we look back and evaluate what we have done with our lives.* Through many different routes, the older person may have developed a positive outlook in most or all of the previous stages of development. If so, the retrospective glances will reveal

Culture- and Gender-Based Criticisms of Freud's Theory

Many psychologists believe Freud overemphasized behavior's biological determinants and did not give adequate attention to sociocultural influences and learning. In particular, his view on the differences between males and females, including their personality development, has a strong biological flavor, relying mainly on anatomical differences. That is, because they have a penis, boys are likely to develop a dominant, powerful personality, girls a submissive, weak personality. In basing his view of male/female differences in personality development on anatomical differences, Freud ignored the enormous impact of culture and experience in determining the personalities of the male and the female (Cloninger, 1996).

More than half a century ago, English anthropologist Bronislaw Malinowski (1927) observed the behavior of the Trobriand islanders of the Western Pacific. He found that the Oedipus complex is not universal but depends on cultural variations in families. The family pattern of the Trobriand islanders is different from that found in many cultures. In the Trobriand islands, the biological father is not the head of the household, a role reserved for the mother's brother, who acts as a disciplinarian. Thus, the Trobriand islanders tease apart the roles played by the same person in Freud's Vienna and in many other cultures. In Freud's view, this different family constellation should make no difference: the Oedipal complex should still emerge, in which the father is the young boy's hated rival for the mother's love. However, Malinowski found no indication of conflict between fathers and sons in the Trobriand islanders, though he did observe some negative feelings directed by the boy toward the maternal uncle. Thus, the young boy feared the man who was the authoritarian figure in his life, which in the Trobriand island culture was the maternal uncle, not the father. In sum, Malinowski's study documented that it was not the sexual relations within the family that created conflict and fear for a child, a damaging finding for Freud's Oedipus complex theory.

The first feminist-based criticism of Freud's theory was proposed by psychoanalytic theorist Karen Horney (1967). She developed a model of women with positive feminine qualities and self-evaluation. Her critique of Freud's theory included reference to a male-dominant society and culture. Rectification of the male bias in psychoanalytic theory continues today. For example, Nancy Chodorow (1989)

Bwaitalu village carvers in the Trobriand islands of New Guinea, with children. In the Trobriand islands, the authoritarian figure in the young boy's life is the maternal uncle, not the father. The young boys in this culture fear the maternal uncle, not the father. Thus, it is not sexual relations in a family that create conflict and fear for a child, a damaging finding for Freud's Oedipus complex theory.

Karen Horney developed the first feminist-based criticism of Freud's theory. Horney's model emphasizes women's positive qualities and self-evaluation.

Nancy Chodorow has developed an important contemporary feminist revision of psychoanalytic theory that emphasizes the meaningfulness of emotions for women.

emphasizes that many more women than men define themselves in terms of their relationships and connections to others. Her feminist revision of psychoanalytic theory also emphasizes the meaningfulness of emotions for women, as well as the belief that many men use the defense mechanism of denial in self-other connections.

a picture of a life well spent, and the person will feel a sense of satisfaction—integrity will be achieved. If the older adult resolved many of the earlier stages negatively, the retrospective glances likely will yield doubt or gloom—the despair Erikson talks about.

> *Each of us stands at the heart of the earth pierced through by a ray of sunlight: and suddenly it is evening.*
>
> —**Salvatore Quasimodo**

Erikson does not believe that the proper solution to a stage crisis is always completely positive in nature. Some exposure or commitment to the negative end of the person's bipolar conflict is sometimes inevitable—you cannot trust all people under all circumstances and survive, for example. Nonetheless, in the healthy solution to a stage crisis, the positive resolution dominates. A summary of Erikson's stages is presented in figure 2.2.

Cognitive Theories

Whereas psychoanalytic theories stress the importance of children's unconscious thoughts, cognitive theories emphasize their conscious thoughts. Two important cognitive theories are Piaget's cognitive development theory and information processing.

Erikson's stages	Developmental period	Characteristics
Trust versus mistrust	Infancy (first year)	A sense of trust requires a feeling of physical comfort and a minimal amount of fear about the future. Infants' basic needs are met by responsive, sensitive caregivers.
Autonomy versus shame and doubt	Infancy (second year)	After gaining trust in caregivers, infants start to discover that they have a will of their own. They assert their sense of autonomy, or independence. They realize their will. If infants are restrained too much or punished too harshly, they are likely to develop a sense of shame and doubt.
Initiative versus guilt	Early childhood (preschool years, ages 3–5)	As preschool children encounter a widening social world, they are challenged more and need to develop more purposeful behavior to cope with these challenges. Children are now asked to assume more responsibility. Uncomfortable guilt feelings may arise, though, if the children are irresponsible and are made to feel too anxious.
Industry versus inferiority	Middle and late childhood (elementary school years, 6 years–puberty)	At no other time are children more enthusiastic than at the end of early childhood's period of expansive imagination. As children move into the elementary school years, they direct their energy toward mastering knowledge and intellectual skills. The danger at this stage involves feeling incompetent and unproductive.

Figure~2.2

Erikson's Eight Stages of Human Development

Piaget's Theory

The famous Swiss psychologist Jean Piaget (1896–1980) stressed that children actively construct their own cognitive worlds; information is not just poured into their mind from the environment. Piaget believes that children adapt their thinking to include new ideas because additional information furthers understanding.

Piaget (1954) also believed that we go through four stages in understanding the world. Each of the stages is age related and consists of distinct ways of thinking. Remember, it is the *different* way of understanding the world that makes one stage more advanced than another; knowing *more* information does not make a child's thinking more advanced in the Piagetian view. This is what Piaget

Erikson's stages	Developmental period	Characteristics
Identity versus identity confusion	Adolescence (10 to 20 years)	Individuals are faced with finding out who they are, what they are all about, and where they are going in life. An important dimension is the exploration of alternative solutions to roles. Career exploration is important.
Intimacy versus isolation	Early adulthood (20s, 30s)	Individuals face the developmental task of forming intimate relationships with others. Erikson described intimacy as finding oneself yet losing oneself in another person.
Generativity versus stagnation	Middle adulthood (40s, 50s)	A chief concern is to assist the younger generation in developing and leading useful lives.
Integrity versus despair	Late adulthood (60s –)	Individuals look back and evaluate what they have done with their lives. The retrospective glances can either be positive (integrity) or negative (despair).

Figure~2.2—Continued

meant when he said a child's cognition is *qualitatively* different in one stage compared with another. What are Piaget's four stages of cognitive development like?

The **sensorimotor stage,** *which lasts from birth to about 2 years of age, is the first Piagetian stage. In this stage, infants construct an understanding of the world by coordinating sensory experiences (such as seeing and hearing) with physical, motoric actions—hence the term* sensorimotor. At the beginning of this stage, newborns have little more than reflexive patterns with which to work. At the end of the stage, 2-year-olds have complex sensorimotor patterns and are beginning to operate with primitive symbols.

The **preoperational stage,** *which lasts from approximately 2 to 7 years of age, is the second Piagetian stage. In this stage, children begin to represent the world with words, images, and drawings.* Symbolic thought goes beyond simple connections of sensory information and physical action. However, although preschool children can symbolically represent the world, according to Piaget, they still lack the ability to perform operations, the Piagetian term for internalized mental actions that allow children to do mentally what they previously did physically.

The **concrete operational stage,** *which lasts from approximately 7 to 11 years of age, is the third Piagetian stage. In this stage, children can perform operations, and logical reasoning replaces intuitive thought as long as reasoning can be applied to specific or concrete examples.* For instance, concrete operational thinkers cannot imagine the steps necessary to complete an algebraic equation, which is too abstract for thinking at this stage of development.

The **formal operational stage,** *which appears between the ages of 11 and 15, is the fourth and final Piagetian stage. In this stage, individuals move beyond the world of concrete experiences and think in abstract and more logical terms.* As part of thinking more abstractly, adolescents develop images of ideal circumstances. They may think about what an ideal parent is like and compare their parents with this ideal standard. They begin to entertain possibilities for the future and are fascinated with what they can be. In solving problems, formal operational thinkers are more systematic, developing hypotheses about why something is happening the way it is, then testing these hypotheses in a deductive fashion. Piaget's stages are summarized in table 2.1.

TABLE 2.1

Piaget's Four Stages of Cognitive Development

Stage	Description	Age Range
Sensorimotor	An infant progresses from reflexive, instinctual action at birth to the beginning of symbolic thought. The infant constructs an understanding of the world by coordinating sensory experiences with physical actions.	Birth to 2 years
Preoperational	The child begins to represent the world with words and images; these words and images reflect increased symbolic thinking and go beyond the connection of sensory information and physical action.	2 to 7 years
Concrete operational	The child can now reason logically about concrete events and classify objects into different sets.	7 to 11 years
Formal operational	The adolescent reasons in more abstract and logical ways. Thought is more idealistic.	11 to 15 years

Jean Piaget, the famous Swiss developmental psychologist, changed the way we think about the development of the child's mind. For Piaget, a child's mental development is continuous creation of increasingly complex forms.

Information Processing

Information processing *is concerned with how individuals process information about their world—how information enters the mind, how it is stored and transformed, and how* it is retrieved to perform such complex activities as problem solving and reasoning. *A simple model of cognition is shown in figure 2.3.

Cognition begins when children detect information from the world through their sensory and perceptual processes. Then children store, transform, and retrieve the information through the processes of memory. Notice in our model that information can flow back and forth between memory and perceptual processes. For example, children are good at remembering the faces they see, yet their memory of a person's face may differ from the way the person actually looks. Keep in mind that our information-processing model is a simple one, designed to illustrate the main cognitive processes and their interrelations. We could have drawn other arrows—between memory and language, between thinking and sensory and perceptual processes, and between language and sensory and perceptual processes, for example. Also, it is important to know that the boxes in figure 2.3 do not represent sharp, distinct stages in processing information. There is continuity and flow between the cognitive processes, as well as overlap.

Behavioral and Social Learning Theories

Behaviorists believe we should examine only what can be directly observed and measured. At approximately the same time as Freud was interpreting his patients' unconscious minds through early childhood experiences, behaviorists such as Ivan Pavlov and John B. Watson were conducting detailed observations of behavior in controlled laboratory circumstances. Out of the behavioral tradition grew the belief that development is observable behavior, learned through experience with the environment. We will study three versions of the behavioral tradition: Pavlov and classical conditioning, Skinner and operant conditioning, and Bandura and social learning theory.

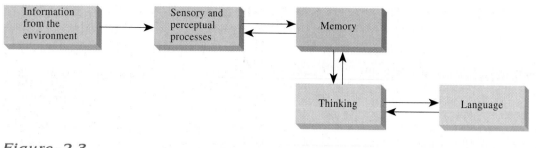

Figure~2.3

A Model of Cognition

Classical Conditioning

It is a nice spring day. A father takes his baby out for a walk. The baby reaches over to touch a pink flower and is badly stung by a bumblebee sitting on the petals. The next day, the baby's mother brings home some pink flowers. She removes a flower from the arrangement and takes it to her baby to smell. The baby cries loudly as soon as she sees the pink flower. The baby's panic at the sight of the pink flower illustrates the learning process of **classical conditioning,** *in which a neutral stimulus acquires the ability to produce a response originally produced by another stimulus.*

In the early 1900s, Russian physiologist Ivan Pavlov investigated the way the body digests food. As part of his experimentation on digestion, he routinely placed meat powder in a dog's mouth, causing the dog to salivate. Pavlov began to notice that the meat powder was not the only stimulus that caused the dog to salivate. The dog salivated in response to a number of stimuli associated with the food, such as the sight of the food dish, the sight of the individual who brought the food into the room, and the sound of the door closing when the food arrived. Pavlov recognized that the dog's association of these sights and sounds with the food was an important type of learning that came to be called classical conditioning.

Pavlov (1927) set aside his work on digestion and extensively studied the association of various stimuli with food. He wanted to know *why* the dog salivated to various sights and sounds before eating the meat powder. Pavlov observed that the dog's behavior included both learned and unlearned components. The "unlearned" part of classical conditioning is based on the fact that some stimuli automatically produced certain responses apart from any prior learning; in other words, they are inborn, or innate. **Reflexes** *are automatic stimulus-response connections.* They include salivation in response to food, nausea in response to bad food, shivering in response to low temperature, coughing in response to the throat being clogged, pupil constriction in response to light, and withdrawal in response to blows or burns. An **unconditioned stimulus (US)** *is a stimulus that produces a response without prior learning;* food was the US in Pavlov's experiments. An **unconditioned response (UR)** *is an unlearned response that is automatically associated with the US.* In Pavlov's experiments, the saliva that flowed from the dog's mouth in response to the food was the UR. In the case of the

If a bee stings this young girl while she is holding a pink flower, how would classical conditioning explain her panic at the sight of pink flowers in the future?

Cartoon by John Chase. Reprinted by permission.

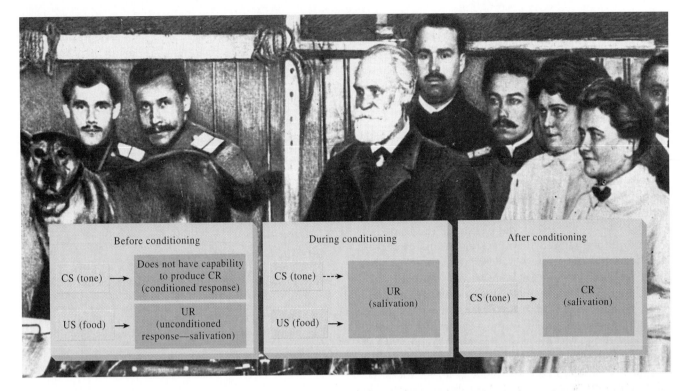

Figure~2.4

Classical Conditioning Procedure

At the start of conditioning, the US will evoke the UR, but the CS does not have this capacity. During conditioning, the CS and US are paired so that the CS comes to elicit the response. The key learning ingredient is the association of the US and CS. Pavlov (the white-bearded gentleman in the center) is shown demonstrating the nature of classical conditioning to students at the Military Medical Academy in what was then the Soviet Union.

baby and the flower, the baby's learning and experience did not cause her to cry when the bee stung her. Her crying was unlearned and occurred automatically. The bee's sting was the US and the crying was the UR.

In classical conditioning, the **conditioned stimulus (CS)** *is a previously neutral stimulus that eventually elicits the conditioned response after being paired with the unconditioned stimulus.* The **conditioned response (CR)** *is the learned response to the conditioned stimulus that occurs after CS-US pairing* (Pavlov, 1927). In studying a dog's response to various stimuli associated with meat powder, Pavlov rang a bell before giving the meat powder to the dog. Until then, ringing the bell did not have a particular effect on the dog, except perhaps to wake it from a nap; the bell was a neutral stimulus. However, the dog began to associate the sound of the bell with the food and salivated when the bell was sounded. The bell had become a conditioned (learned) stimulus (CS) and the salivation a conditioned response (CR). Before conditioning (or learning), the bell and the food were not related. After their association, however, the conditioned stimulus (the bell) produced a conditioned response (salivation). A summary of how classical conditioning works is shown in figure 2.4.

Since Pavlov's experiments, children have been conditioned in other experiments to respond to the sound

of a buzzer, a glimpse of light, or the touch of a hand. Classical conditioning has a great deal of survival value for children. Because of classical conditioning, children jerk their hands away before they are burned by fire and they move out of the way of a rapidly approaching truck before it hits them. Classical conditioning is at work in words that serve as important signals. A boy walks into an abandoned house with a friend and yells, "Snake!" His friend bolts out the door. An adolescent imagines a peaceful, tranquil scene—an abandoned beach with waves lapping onto the sand—and relaxes as if she were actually lying on the beach.

Phobias *are irrational fears.* Classical conditioning provides an explanation of these and other fears. Behaviorist John Watson conducted an investigation to demonstrate classical conditioning's role in phobias. A little boy named Albert was shown a white laboratory rat to see if he was afraid of it. He was not. As Albert played with the rat, a loud noise was sounded behind his head. As you might imagine, the noise caused little Albert to cry. After only seven pairings of the loud noise with the white rat, Albert began to fear the rat even when the noise was not sounded. Albert's fear was generalized to a rabbit, a dog, and a sealskin coat (see figure 2.5). Today, we could not ethically conduct such an experiment. Especially noteworthy is the fact that Watson did not remove Albert's fear of rats, so presumably this phobia remained with him after the experiment. Many of our fears—fear of the dentist from a painful experience, fear of driving from being in an automobile accident, fear of heights from falling off a high chair when we were infants, and fear of dogs from being bitten, for example—can be learned through classical conditioning.

If we can produce fears by classical conditioning, we should be able to eliminate them. **Counterconditioning** *is a classical conditioning procedure for weakening a CR by associating the stimuli with a new response incompatible with the CR.* Though Watson did not eliminate little Albert's fear of white rats, an associate of Watson's, Mary Cover Jones (1924), did eliminate the fears of a 3-year-old boy named Peter. Peter had many of the same fears as Albert; however, Peter's fears were not produced by Jones. Among Peter's fears were white rats, fur coats, frogs, fish, and mechanical toys. To eliminate these fears, a rabbit was brought into Peter's view but kept far enough away that it would not upset him. At the same time the rabbit was brought into view, Peter was fed crackers and milk. On each successive day, the rabbit was moved closer to Peter as he ate crackers and milk. Eventually, Peter reached the point at which he could eat the food with one hand and pet the rabbit with the other.

Some of the behaviors we associate with health problems or mental disorders can involve classical conditioning. Certain physical complaints—asthma, headaches, ulcers, and high blood pressure, for example—may partly be the products of classical conditioning. We usually say that such health problems are caused by stress, but often what has happened is that certain stimuli, such as a teacher's critical attitude or fighting by parents, are conditioned stimuli for children's physiological responses. Over time, the frequent presence of the physiological responses may produce health disorders.

Pavlov described all learning in terms of classical conditioning. In reality, children learn in many ways. Still, classical conditioning helps children learn about their environment and has been successful in eliminating children's fears. However, a view that describes children as *responding* to the environment fails to capture the *active* nature of children and their influence on the environment.

Skinner's Behaviorism

Behaviorism *emphasizes the scientific study of observable behavioral responses and their environmental determinants.* In Skinner's behaviorism, the mind, conscious or unconscious, is not needed to explain behavior and development. For him, development is behavior. For example, observations of Sam reveal that his behavior is shy, achievement oriented, and caring. Why is Sam's behavior this way? For Skinner, rewards and punishments in Sam's environment have shaped him into a

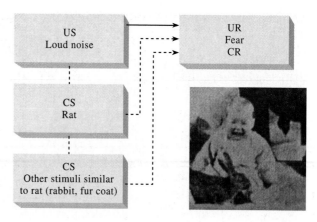

Figure~2.5

Little Albert's Generalized Fear
In 1920, to condition 9-month-old little Albert to fear a white rat, Watson paired the rat with a loud noise. When little Albert was subsequently placed with other stimuli similar to the white rat, such as the rabbit shown here with little Albert, he was afraid of them too. This illustrates the principle of stimulus generalization in classical conditioning.
Photo courtesy of Prof. Ben Harris.

shy, achievement-oriented, and caring person. Because of interactions with family members, friends, teachers, and others, Sam has *learned* to behave in this fashion.

The concept of operant conditioning was developed by American psychologist B. F. Skinner (1938). **Operant conditioning** *(or instrumental conditioning) is a form of learning in which the consequences of behavior produce changes in the probability of the behavior's occurrence.* In operant conditioning, an organism acts, or operates, on the environment to produce a change in the probability of the behavior's occurrence; Skinner chose the label *operants* for the responses that are actively emitted because of the consequences for the organism. The consequences are *contingent*, or dependent, on the organism's behavior. For example, a simple operant might be the pressing of a lever that leads to the delivery of food (the consequence); the delivery of food is contingent on pressing the lever.

Earlier we indicated that Skinner described operant conditioning as a form of learning in which the consequences of behavior lead to changes in the probability of that behavior's occurrence. The consequences—rewards or punishments—are contingent on the organism's behavior. **Reinforcement** *(or reward) is a consequence that increases the probability a behavior will occur.* By contrast, **punishment** *is a consequence that decreases the probability that a behavior will occur.* For example, if an adult smiles at a child, and the adult and child continue talking for some time, the smile reinforced the child's talking. However, if an adult meets a child and frowns at the child, and the child quickly leaves the situation, then the frown punished the child's talking with the adult.

Since behaviorists believe that development is learned and often changes according to environmental

B. F. Skinner was a tinkerer who liked to make new gadgets. The younger of his two daughters, Deborah, was raised in Skinner's enclosed Air-Crib, which he invented because he wanted to control her environment completely. The Air-Crib was soundproofed and temperature controlled. Some critics accused Skinner of monstrous experimentation with his children; however, the early controlled environment has not had any noticeable harmful effects. Debbie, shown here as a child with her parents, is currently a successful artist, is married, and lives in London (Leo, 1983).

Albert Bandura has been one of the leading architects of the contemporary version of social learning theory—cognitive social learning theory.

experiences, it follows that rearranging experiences can change development. For behaviorists, shy behavior can be transformed into outgoing behavior; aggressive behavior can be shaped into docile behavior; lethargic, boring behavior can be turned into enthusiastic, interesting behavior.

Social Learning Theory

Some psychologists believe that the behaviorists basically are right when they say development is learned and is influenced strongly by environmental experiences, but that Skinner went too far in declaring that cognition is unimportant in understanding development. **Social learning theory** *is the view of psychologists who emphasize behavior, environment, and cognition as the key factors in development.*

The social learning theorists say we are not like mindless robots, responding mechanically to others in our environment. Neither are we like weather vanes, behaving like a Communist in the presence of a Communist or like a John Bircher in the presence of a John Bircher. Rather, we think, reason, imagine, plan, expect, interpret, believe, value, and compare. When others try to control us, our values and beliefs allow us to resist their control.

American psychologists Albert Bandura (1986, 1995, 1997) and Walter Mischel (1973, 1994) are the main architects of social learning theory's contemporary version, which Mischel (1973) labeled *cognitive* social

learning theory. Both Bandura and Mischel believe that cognitive processes are important mediators of environment-behavior connections. Bandura's research program has focused heavily on observational learning, learning that occurs through observing what others do. Observational learning is also referred to as imitation or modeling. What is *cognitive* about observational learning in Bandura's view? Bandura (1925–) believes that people cognitively represent the behavior of others and then sometimes adopt this behavior themselves. For example, a young boy might observe his father's aggressive outbursts and hostile interchanges with people, and then, with his peers, display a style of interaction that is highly aggressive, showing the same characteristics as his father's behavior. A girl might adopt the dominating and sarcastic style of her teacher. When observed interacting with her younger brother, she says, "You are so slow. How can you do this work so slow?" Social learning theorists believe that children acquire a wide range of such behaviors, thoughts, and feelings through observing others' behavior. These observations form an important part of children's development.

> *We are in truth, more than half what we are by imitation.*
>
> —**Lord Chesterfield**

Social learning theories also differ from Skinner's behavioral view by emphasizing that children can regulate and control their own behavior. For example, another girl who observes her teacher behaving in a dominant and sarcastic way toward her students finds the behavior distasteful and goes out of her way to be encouraging and supportive toward her younger brother. Someone tries to persuade an adolescent to join a particular club at school. The adolescent thinks about the offer to join the club, considers her own interests and beliefs, and makes the decision not to join. The adolescent's *cognition* (thoughts) led her to control her own behavior and resist environmental influence in this instance.

Like Skinner's behavioral approach, the social learning approach emphasizes the importance of empirical research in studying children's development. This research focuses on the processes that explain children's development—the social and cognitive factors that influence what children are like (Mayer & Sutton, 1996). Bandura's (1986, 1989) most recent model of social learning involves behavior, the person (cognition), and the environment. As shown in figure 2.6, behavior, environment, and person or cognitive factors operate interactively. Behavior can influence cognition and vice versa, the child's cognitive activities can influence the environment, environmental influences can change the child's thought processes, and so on.

Let's consider how Bandura's model might work in the case of students' behavior. As students diligently study and get good grades, their behavior produces positive thoughts about their abilities. As part of their effort to make good grades, they plan a number of strategies to make studying more efficient. In these ways, their behavior has influenced their thoughts, and their thoughts have influenced their behavior. At the beginning of the school year, their counselor made a special effort to involve them in a study-skills program. Their success has stimulated the school to expand the program. In these ways, the environment influenced the behavior, and the behavior influenced the environment. The expectations of the school's counselor and principal that the program would work made it possible in the first place. The program's success has spurred expectations that this type of program could work in other schools. In these ways, cognition changed the environment, and the environment changed cognition. Expectations are important in Bandura's model.

Ethological Theories

Sensitivity to different kinds of experience varies over the life span. The presence or absence of certain experiences at particular times in the life span influences individuals well beyond the times when they first occur. Ethologists believe that most psychologists underestimate the importance of these special time frames in early

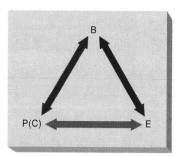

Figure~2.6

Bandura's Model of Social Learning
This is Bandura's model of reciprocal influences of behavior (B), personal and cognitive factors (P [C]), and environment (E). The arrows reflect how relations between these factors are reciprocal rather than unidirectional. Examples of personal factors include intelligence, skills, and self-control.

development and the powerful roles that evolution and biological foundations play in development (Charlesworth, 1992; Hinde, 1992).

Ethology emerged as an important view because of the work of European zoologists, especially Konrad Lorenz (1903–1989). **Ethology** *stresses that behavior is strongly influenced by biology, is tied to evolution, and is characterized by critical or sensitive periods.*

Working mostly with greylag geese, Lorenz (1965) studied a behavior pattern that was considered to be programmed within the birds' genes. A newly hatched gosling seemed to be born with the instinct to follow its mother. Observations showed that the gosling was capable of such behavior as soon as it hatched. Lorenz proved that it was incorrect to assume that such behavior was programmed in the animal. In a remarkable set of experiments, Lorenz separated the eggs laid by one goose into two groups. One group he returned to the goose to be hatched by her; the other group was hatched in an incubator. The goslings in the first group performed as predicted; they followed their mother as soon as they hatched. However, those in the second group, which saw Lorenz when they first hatched, followed him everywhere, as though he were their mother. Lorenz marked the goslings and then placed both groups under a box. Mother goose and "mother" Lorenz stood aside as the box was lifted. Each group of goslings went directly to its "mother" (see figure 2.7). Lorenz called this process **imprinting,** *the ethological concept of rapid, innate learning within a limited critical period of time that involves attachment to the first moving object seen.*

The ethological view of Lorenz and the European zoologists forced American developmental psychologists to recognize the importance of the biological basis of behavior. However, the research and theorizing of ethology still seemed to lack some ingredients that would elevate it to the ranks of the other theories discussed so far in this chapter. In particular, there was little or

Figure~2.7

Imprinting
Konrad Lorenz, a pioneering student of animal behavior, is followed through the water by three imprinted greylag geese. Lorenz described imprinting as rapid, innate learning within a critical period that involves attachment to the first moving object seen. For goslings, the critical period is the first 36 hours after birth.

nothing in the classical ethological view about the nature of social relationships across the human life span, something that any major theory of development must explain. Also, its concept of **critical period,** *a fixed time period very early in development during which certain behaviors optimally emerge,* seemed to be overdrawn. Classical ethological theory was weak in stimulating studies with humans. Recent expansion of the ethological view has improved its status as a viable developmental perspective.

Like behaviorists, ethologists are careful observers of behavior. Unlike behaviorists, ethologists believe that laboratories are not good settings for observing behavior; rather, they meticulously observe behavior in its natural surroundings, in homes, playgrounds, neighborhoods, schools, hospitals, and so on (Hinde, 1992).

Ecological, Contextual Theories

Two environmental theories that emphasize the importance of ecological, contextual factors in the adolescent's development are (1) Urie Bronfenbrenner's ecological theory and (2) Glen Elder's contextual life course theory.

Ecological Theory

Urie Bronfenbrenner (1917–) has proposed a strong environmental view of children's development that is receiving increased attention. **Ecological theory** *is Bronfenbrenner's sociocultural view of development, which consists of five environmental systems ranging from the fine-grained inputs of direct interactions with social agents to the broad-based inputs of culture. The five systems in Bronfenbrenner's*

THE FAR SIDE By GARY LARSON

When imprinting studies go awry . . .

Urie Bronfenbrenner has developed ecological theory, a perspective that is receiving increased attention. His theory emphasizes the importance of both micro and macro dimensions of the environment in which the child lives.

Glen Elder has proposed an ecological, contextual view called life course theory. What are some of the key features of Elder's theory?

ecological theory are the microsystem, mesosystem, exosystem, macrosystem, and chronosystem. Bronfenbrenner's (1986, 1995) ecological model is shown in figure 2.8.

The **microsystem** in Bronfenbrenner's ecological theory, is the setting in which an individual lives. This context includes the person's family, peers, school, and neighborhood. It is in the microsystem that most of the direct interactions with social agents take place—with parents, peers, and teachers, for example. The individual is not viewed as a passive recipient of experiences in these settings, but as someone who helps construct the settings. Bronfenbrenner points out that most of the research on sociocultural influences has focused on microsystems.

The **mesosystem** in Bronfenbrenner's ecological theory involves relationships between microsystems or connections between contexts. Examples are the relation of family experiences to school experiences, school experiences to work experiences, and family experiences to peer experiences. For instance, children whose parents have rejected them may have difficulty developing positive relations with teachers. Developmentalists increasingly believe it is important to observe behavior in multiple settings—such as family, peer, and school contexts—to obtain a more complete picture of children's development (Booth & Dunn, 1996).

The **exosystem** in Bronfenbrenner's ecological theory is involved when experiences in a social setting—in which the individual does not have an active role—influence what the individual experiences in an immediate context. For example, work experiences can affect a woman's relationship with her husband and their adolescent. The woman might receive a promotion that requires more travel, which might increase marital conflict and change patterns of parent-adolescent interaction. Another example of an exosystem is a city government, which is responsible for the quality of parks, recreation centers, and library facilities for children and adolescents.

The **macrosystem** in Bronfenbrenner's ecological theory involves the culture in which individuals live. Remember from chapter 1 that culture refers to the behavior patterns, beliefs, and all other products of a group of people that are passed on from generation to generation. Remember also that cross-cultural studies—the comparison of one culture with one or more other cultures—provide information about the universality of children's development.

The **chronosystem** in Bronfenbrenner's ecological theory involves the patterning of environmental events and transitions over the life course and sociohistorical circumstances. For example, in studying the effects of divorce

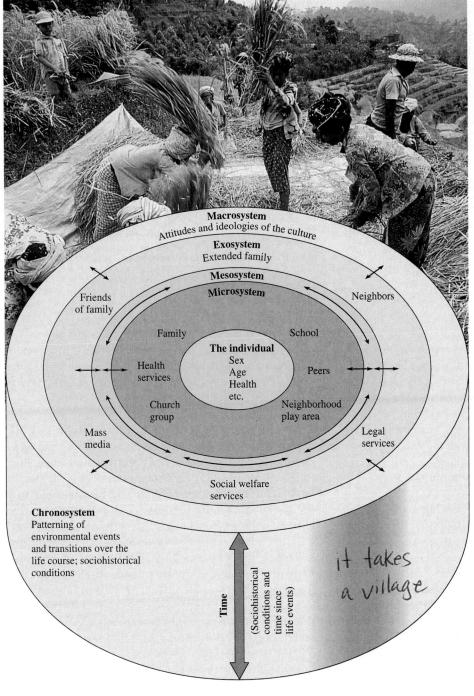

than they were 20 to 30 years ago. In ways such as these, the chronosystem has a powerful impact on children's lives.

It should be pointed out that Bronfenbrenner (1995; Bronfenbrenner & Morris, 1997) recently added biological influences to his theory and now describes it as a bioecological theory. Nonetheless, the ecological, environmental contexts still predominate in Bronfenbrenner's theory.

Life Course Theory

Although Bronfenbrenner's ecological theory strongly emphasizes environmental contexts and includes a chronosystem that involves historical time, it has not had a strong life-span developmental orientation. An environmental contextual theory that places a stronger emphasis on life-span development is **life course theory**, *Glen Elder's view that the human life span can be best understood by considering human lives in historical time and place, the timing of lives, linked or interdependent lives, and human agency and social constraints.* Elder (1995, in press) believes that the study of human development should begin with the environment of the child, adolescent, or adult and investigate the environment's developmental implications.

Figure~2.8

Bronfenbrenner's Ecological Theory of Development
Bronfenbrenner's ecological theory consists of five environmental systems: microsystem, mesosystem, exosystem, macrosystem, and chronosystem.

on children, researchers have found that the negative effects often peak in the first year after the divorce and that the effects are more negative for sons than for daughters (Hetherington, 1995). By 2 years after the divorce, family interaction is less chaotic and more stable. With regard to sociocultural circumstances, girls today are much more likely to be encouraged to pursue a career

Human Lives in Historical Time and Place
Especially in rapidly changing societies, being born at a different point in time exposes individuals to different historical circumstances. One study focused on the ways in which a drastic loss of income in the 1930s might influence children with different birthdates (Elder, 1979). Younger children (born in the early 1920s) experienced more hardships than older children (born in the late 1920s).

In John Clausen's in-depth study, which spanned nearly 50 years of his subjects' lives, planful competence in adolescence was linked with occupational and family success in the adult years.

Historical influences can be expressed in different ways in different places. In one investigation of Depression-era youth, California youth growing up in the San Francisco area managed to escape the limitations of their deprived households by joining the armed forces and using the benefits for higher education (Elder, Modell, & Parke, 1993). By contrast, college was less of an option for the working-class youth of Manchester, New Hampshire, who experienced more hardship than their California counterparts.

The Timing of Lives   Life-span development is influenced by the social timing of lives. Consider the current social timing trend of childbearing. Some individuals are waiting longer to have children, while others are having children younger. Many of those who are having children later have decided to pursue a career before marriage and children. Those who are having children earlier are adolescents. The United States has the highest adolescent pregnancy rate in the industrialized world. In most cases, adolescent childbearing is ill-timed and detrimental to both the mother and her offspring, who are at risk for a number of developmental problems.

Linked Lives   The interdependency of lives is a central concept in life course theory. Human lives are usually embedded in family relationships as well as friendships and other social relationships) throughout the life span. For example, failed marriages and careers often lead adult sons and daughters back to the parental household, a circumstance that has important implications for their parents' life plans. Thus, the misfortunes and opportunities of adult children, as well as their personal problems, become intergenerational. Consider also changes in parents' lives that can influence their children's development. Parents' economic setbacks and divorce can

impede adolescents' transition to adulthood by postponing their entrance into college, employment, and marriage. Thus, the generations are connected by fateful decisions and events in each other's life course.

Human Agency and Social Constraints   Within the constraints of their world, people are planful and make choices among options in constructing their life course. John Clausen (1993) recently conducted in-depth life history interviews with 60 male and female subjects of the Berkeley Longitudinal Study. Analyzing nearly 50 years of their lives, Clausen found that planful competence in adolescence was associated with occupational and family success in the adult years. What is planful competence? In Clausen's analysis, it consisted of three personal qualities—self-confidence, dependability, and intellectual investment. When developed by the end of the high school years, planful competence influenced the scheduling of major social roles later occupied, the stability of role performance, and the person's attainment of life satisfaction over much of the life course. Individuals high in planful competence made more realistic educational, occupational, and marital choices, whereas their counterparts who were low in planful competence found less-satisfying jobs, changed jobs and spouses more often, and experienced more pressure to change themselves during the adult years. A few adolescents who were low in planful competence became effective adults, and a few adolescents who were high in planful competence had dismal adult lives, but they were the exceptions. Clausen concluded that personality development can involve stability and change—some people have stable, continuous lives and change little, others experience recurrent crises and change a great deal over the life course.

(a)　　　　　　　　　　(b)　　　　　　　　　　(c)

Figure~2.9

Three Analogies That Have Been Used to Describe the Nature of Development
(*a*) Staircase, (*b*) seedling in a greenhouse, and, (*c*) strand of ivy in a forest.

Developmental Analogies

Different analogies, which often can be linked with theories, have been used to describe the nature of development. Three examples are the analogies of (1) a staircase, (2) a seedling in a greenhouse, and (3) a strand of ivy in a forest. The staircase analogy is directly related to the stage theories of development. Recently, cognitive developmentalist Robbie Case (1992) even titled a book *The Mind's Staircase* to emphasize the staircase-like nature of cognitive development.

The analogy of a seedling in a greenhouse has been popular for many years in developmental psychology. In this view, the individual is acted upon by the environment (according to Skinner's behavioral perspective) or the child acts on the world (in Piaget's perspective). This analogy emphasizes the child as the primary unit of development. Thus, Piaget's theory has characteristics of both the staircase analogy and the seedling analogy.

The analogy of a strand of ivy in a forest is contemporary and stresses the many different paths development can take and the importance of contextual factors in that development (Kagan, 1992). In this analogy, development is not as consistently stagelike as in the staircase analogy, and the child is not seen as a solitary young scientist as in Piaget's view. An important dimension of this analogy is its emphasis on reciprocal encounters with others and the changing symbolic construction of these relationships. The ecological, contextual perspectives of Bronfenbrenner and Elder are versions of this analogy.

Which of these analogies best reflects the way development actually occurs? As with virtually all theories and analogies, each has its adherents, although the strand-of-ivy analogy has become increasingly popular in recent years. Visual images of the three analogies are presented in figure 2.9.

An Eclectic Theoretical Orientation

An **eclectic theoretical orientation** *does not follow any one theoretical approach, but rather selects and uses whatever is considered the best in each theory.* No single theory described in this chapter is infallible or capable of explaining entirely the rich complexity of child development. Each of the theories has made important contributions to our understanding of children's development, but none provides a complete description and explanation. Psychoanalytic theory best explains the unconscious mind. Erikson's theory best describes the changes that occur in adult development. Piaget's theory is the most complete description of children's cognitive development. The behavioral and social learning, and ecological theories have been the most adept at examining the environmental determinants of development. The ethological theories have made us aware of biology's role and the importance of sensitive periods in development. It is important to recognize that, although theories are helpful guides, relying on a single theory to explain children's development is probably a mistake.

An attempt was made in this chapter to present five theoretical perspectives objectively. The same eclectic orientation will be maintained throughout the

TABLE 2.2

A Comparison of Theories and the Issues and Methods in Adolescent Development

Theory	Issues and Methods			
	Continuity/Discontinuity, Early Versus Later Experience	Biological and Environmental Factors	Importance of Cognition	Research Methods
Psychoanalytic	Discontinuity between stages—continuity between early experiences and later development; early experiences very important; later changes in development emphasized in Erikson's theory	Freud's biological determination interacting with early family experiences; Erikson's more balanced biological-cultural interaction perspective	Emphasized, but in the form of unconscious thought	Clinical interviews, unstructured personality tests, psychohistorical analyses of lives
Cognitive	Discontinuity between stages—continuity between early experiences and later development in Piaget's theory; has not been important to information-processing psychologists	Piaget's emphasis on interaction and adaptation; environment provides the setting for cognitive structures to develop; information-processing view has not addressed this issue extensively, but mainly emphasizes biological-environmental interaction	The primary determinant of behavior	Interviews and observations
Behavioral and Social Learning	Continuity (no stages); experience at all points of development important	Environment viewed as the cause of behavior in both views	Strongly deemphasized in the behavioral approach but an important mediator in social learning	Observation, especially laboratory observation
Ethological	Discontinuity but no stages; critical or sensitive periods emphasized; early experiences very important	Strong biological view	Not emphasized	Observation in natural settings
Ecological, contextual	Little attention to continuity/discontinuity in Bronfenbrenner's theory; considerable emphasis in Elder's life course theory	Very strong environmental emphasis	Not emphasized in Bronfenbrenner's view; emphasized as agency in Elder's view	Varied methods; collect data in a number of social and historical contexts; Elder stresses the importance of using life-history records

book. In this way, you can view the study of children's development as it actually exists—with different theorists making different assumptions, stressing different empirical problems, and using different strategies to discover information.

These theoretical perspectives, along with research issues that were discussed in chapter 1 and methods that will be described shortly, provide a sense of development's scientific nature. Table 2.2 compares the main theoretical perspectives in terms of how they view important developmental issues and the methods they prefer to use when they study children.

At this point we have discussed a number of ideas about the scientific method and theories of child development. A summary of these ideas is presented in concept table 2.1. Next, we will explore the methods child developmentalists use to study children, beginning with the measures they use.

Concept	Processes/ Related Ideas	Characteristics/Description
Theory and the Scientific Method	Theory	Theories are general beliefs that help us to explain what we observe and make predictions. A good theory has hypotheses, which are assumptions to be tested.
	The scientific method	The scientific method is a series of procedures (identifying and analyzing a problem, collecting data, drawing conclusions, and revising theory) to obtain accurate information.
Theories of Child Development	Psychoanalytic theories	Two important psychoanalytic theories are Freud's and Erikson's. Freud said personality is made up of three structures—id, ego, and superego—and that most of children's thoughts are unconscious. The conflicting demands of children's personality structures produce anxiety. Defense mechanisms, especially repression, protect the child's ego and reduce anxiety. Freud was convinced that problems develop because of early childhood experiences. He said individuals go through five psychosexual stages—oral, anal, phallic, latency, and genital. During the phallic stage, the Oedipus complex is a major source of conflict. Gender-based criticisms of psychoanalytic theory have been made. Erikson developed a theory that emphasizes eight psychosocial stages of development: trust versus mistrust, autonomy versus shame and doubt, initiative versus guilt, industry versus inferiority, identity versus identity confusion, intimacy versus isolation, generativity versus stagnation, and integrity versus despair.
	Cognitive theories	Two important cognitive theories are Piaget's cognitive developmental theory and information processing. Piaget said children go through four cognitive stages: sensorimotor, preoperational, concrete operational, and formal operational. Information-processing theory is concerned with how individuals process information about their world. It includes how information gets into the child's mind, how it is stored and transformed, and how it is retrieved to allow them to think and solve problems.
	Behavioral and social learning theories	Behaviorism emphasizes that cognition is not important in understanding children's behavior. Pavlov's behaviorism emphasizes classical conditioning. Development is observable behavior, which is determined by rewards and punishment in the environment, according to B. F. Skinner, a famous behaviorist. Social learning theory, developed by Alert Bandura and others, states that the environment is an important determinant of behavior but so are cognitive processes. Children have the ability to control their own behavior, in the social learning view.
	Ethological theories	Konrad Lorenz was one of the important developers of ethological theory. Ethology emphasizes the biological and evolutionary basis of development. Imprinting and critical periods are key concepts.
	Ecological, contextual theories	In Bronfenbrenner's ecological theory, five environmental systems are important: microsystem, mesosystem, exosystem, macrosystem, and chronosystem. Elder's life course theory emphasizes the study of lives in historical place and time, the timing of lives, linked lives, and human agency and social constraints.
	Developmental analogies	Three analogies with theoretical ties have been used to describe development: (1) staircase, (2) seedling in a greenhouse, and (3) strand of ivy in a forest.
	Eclectic theoretical orientation	No single theory can explain the rich, awesome complexity of children's development. Each of the theories has made a different contribution, and it probably is a wise strategy to adopt an eclectic theoretical perspective as we attempt to understand children's development.

METHODOLOGY

Remember that in addition to developing theories, a critical aspect of improving our knowledge about children's development involves conducting scientific research. In this section we will explore the methods child development researchers use when they conduct scientific research. Our discussion will cover measures, correlational and experimental strategies, and the time span of inquiry.

Measures

Systematic observations can be conducted in a number of ways. For example, we can watch behavior in a laboratory or in a more natural setting such as a school, home, or neighborhood playground. We can question children using interviews and surveys, develop and administer standardized tests, conduct case studies, examine behavior cross-culturally, or carry out physiological research. To help you understand how developmentalists use these methods, we will continue to draw examples from the study of children's aggression.

Observation

Sherlock Holmes chided Watson, "You see but you do not observe." We look at things all the time; however, casually watching a mother and her infant is not scientific observation. Unless you are a trained observer and practice your skills regularly, you might not know what to look for, you might not remember what you saw, what you are looking for might change from one moment to the next, and you might not communicate your observations effectively.

For observations to be effective, we have to know what we are looking for, who we are observing, when and where we will observe, how the observations will be made, and in what form they will be recorded. That is, our observations have to be made in a *systematic* way (Martin, 1996). Consider aggression. Do we want to study verbal or physical aggression, or both? Do we want to study younger or older children, or both? Do we want to evaluate them in a university laboratory, at school, at home, at a playground, or at all of these locations? A common way to record observations is to write them down, using shorthand or symbols. However, tape recorders, video cameras, special coding sheets, one-way mirrors, and computers are increasingly used to make observations more efficient (Rosnow & Rosenthal, 1996).

Frequently, when we observe, it is necessary to control certain factors that determine behavior but that are not the focus of our inquiry. For this reason, much psychological research is conducted in a **laboratory,** *a controlled setting in which many of the complex factors of the "real world" are removed.* For example, Albert Bandura (1965) brought children into a laboratory and had them observe an adult repeatedly hit an inflated plastic Bobo doll about 3 feet tall. Bandura wondered to what extent

Observation is an extremely valuable method for obtaining information about children's development. Here a researcher observes the social interaction of young children by using a one-way mirror through which the observer can see the children but the children cannot see the observer.

the children would copy the adult's behavior. After the children saw the adult attack the Bobo doll, they, too, aggressively hit the inflated toy (see figure 2.10). By conducting his experiment in a laboratory with adults the children did not know as models, Bandura had complete control over when the children witnessed aggression, how much aggression the children saw, and what form the aggression took. Bandura could not have had as much control in his experiment if other factors, such as parents, siblings, friends, television, and a familiar room, had been present.

Laboratory research, however, has some drawbacks. First, it is almost impossible to conduct the research without the participants' knowing they are being studied. Second, the laboratory setting might be *unnatural* and, therefore, elicit unnatural behavior from the participants. Subjects usually show less aggressive behavior in a laboratory than in a more familiar natural setting, such as in a park or at home. They also show less aggression when they are unaware they are being observed than when they are aware that an observer is studying them. Third, some aspects of child development are difficult, if not impossible, to examine in a laboratory. For instance, it would be difficult (and unethical) to recreate and study in a laboratory certain types of stress, such as the circumstances that stimulate family conflict.

Although laboratory research is a valuable tool for developmentalists, naturalistic observation provides insight we sometimes cannot achieve in a laboratory. In **naturalistic observation,** *scientists observe behavior in real-world*

Figure~2.10

Bandura's Study of Imitation and Children's Aggression
In Bandura's study, children saw an adult punch a Bobo doll.
Subsequently, the children imitated the adult's aggressive
actions.

settings and make no effort to manipulate or control the situation. Developmentalists conduct naturalistic observations at day-care centers, hospitals, schools, parks, homes, malls, dances, and other places people live in and frequent (Pellegrini, 1996). In contrast to Bandura's observations of aggression in a laboratory, naturalistic observations might include the aggression of children in nursery schools, of adolescents on street corners, and of marital partners at home.

Interviews and Questionnaires

Sometimes the best and quickest way to get information from children is to ask them for it. Psychologists use interviews and questionnaires to find out about children's experiences and attitudes. Most interviews occur face-to-face, although they can take place over the telephone.

The types of interviews range from highly unstructured to highly structured. Examples of unstructured interview questions include these: How aggressive do you see yourself as being? and How aggressive is your child? Examples of structured interview questions include these: In the last week, how often did you yell at your spouse? and How often in the last year was your child involved in fights at school? Structure is imposed by the questions themselves, or the interviewer can categorize answers by asking respondents to choose from several options. For example, in the question about your level of aggressiveness, you might be asked to choose from "highly aggressive," "moderately aggressive," "moderately unaggressive," and "highly unaggressive." In the question about how often you yelled at your spouse in the last week, you might be asked to choose among "0," "1–2," "3–5," "6–10," or "more than 10 times."

Child developmentalists also question children and adults using questionnaires or surveys. A **questionnaire** *is similar to a highly structured interview except that respondents read the questions and mark their answers on paper rather than respond verbally to the interviewer.* One major advantage of surveys and questionnaires is that they can be given to a large number of people easily. Good surveys have concrete, specific, and unambiguous questions and assessment of the authenticity of the replies.

Interviews and questionnaires are not without drawbacks. Perhaps the most critical is the "social desirability" response set, in which individuals say what they think is most socially acceptable or desirable rather than what they truly think or feel. When asked about her marital conflict, Jane might not want to disclose that arguments have been painfully tense in the past month. Her 10-year-old son might not want to divulge that he often gets into fights with his peers. Skilled interviewing techniques and questions to help eliminate such defenses are critical in obtaining accurate information. Another problem with interviews and questionnaires is that individuals also might simply lie when responding to questions.

Case Studies

A **case study** *is an in-depth look at an individual; it is used mainly by clinical psychologists when the unique aspects of a person's life cannot be duplicated, for either practical or ethical reasons.* A case study provides information about an individual's fears, hopes, fantasies, traumatic experiences, upbringing, family relationships, health, or anything that helps a psychologist understand that person's development. Some vivid case studies appear at different points in this text, among them one about a modern-day wild child named Genie, who lived in near isolation during her childhood (see chapter 10).

Although case studies provide dramatic, in-depth portrayals of people's lives, we need to exercise caution when generalizing from this information. The subject of a case study is unique, with a genetic makeup and experiences no one else shares. In addition, case studies involve judgments of unknown reliability, in that usually no check is made to see if other psychologists agree with the observations.

Standardized Tests

Standardized tests *require people to answer a series of written or oral questions. They have two distinct features. First, psychologists usually total an individual's score to yield a single score, or set of scores, that reflects something about the individual. Second, psychologists compare the individual's score to the scores of a large group of similar people to determine how the individual responded relative to others.* Scores are often described in percentiles. For example, a child who scored in the 92nd percentile of the Stanford-Binet Intelligence Test scored higher than 92 percent of the large group of children who had taken the test previously.

To continue our look at how different measures are used to evaluate aggression, consider the Minnesota Multiphasic Personality Inventory (MMPI), which includes a scale to assess delinquency or antisocial tendencies. The items on this scale ask you whether you are rebellious, impulsive, and have trouble with authority figures. This part of the MMPI might be given to adolescents to determine their delinquent and antisocial tendencies.

Cross-Cultural Research and Research with Ethnic Minority Groups

When researchers examine the behavior and mental processes of children in different cultures and different ethnic minority groups, they must follow certain strategies (Werner, 1997). When measures are used with cultural and ethnic groups with whom the researchers are unfamiliar, it is vital that they construct the measures so that they are meaningful for all of the cultural or ethnic minority groups being studied. To accomplish this objective, cross-cultural researchers do not use one culture as the sole source for developing a measure. Rather, informants from all cultures in the investigation provide information to the researchers so they can develop a meaningful measure.

In keeping with our theme of applying different ways of obtaining information about children to aggression, what have cross-cultural psychologists discovered about aggression in different cultures? They have found that aggression is a cultural universal, appearing in all cultures studied; however, the ways in which aggression is expressed may be culture-specific. For example, in the !Kung culture of southern Africa, the members actively try to dissuade individuals from behaving aggressively, whereas the members of the Yanomamo Indian culture of South America promote aggression. Yanomamo youth are told that they cannot achieve adult status unless they are capable of killing, fighting, and pummeling others.

In conducting research on cultural and ethnic minority issues, investigators distinguish between the emic approach and the etic approach (Triandis, 1994). In the **emic approach,** *the goal is to describe behavior in one culture or ethnic group in terms that are meaningful and important to the people in that culture or ethnic group, without regard to other cultures or ethnic groups.* In the **etic approach,** *the goal is to describe behavior so that generalizations can be made across cultures.* That is, the emic approach is culture-specific; the etic approach is culture-universal. If researchers construct a questionnaire in an emic fashion, their concern is only that the questions are meaningful to the particular culture or ethnic group being studied. If, however, the researchers construct a questionnaire in an etic fashion, they want to include questions that reflect concepts familiar to all cultures involved.

How might the emic and etic approaches be reflected in the study of family processes? In the emic approach,

Systematic observations in natural settings provide valuable information about behavior across cultures. For example, in one investigation, observations in different cultures revealed that American children often engage in less work and more play than do children in many other cultures (Whiting & Whiting, 1975). However, conducting cross-cultural research using such methods as systematic observation in natural settings is difficult and requires attention to a number of methodological issues.

the researchers might choose to focus only on middle-class White families, without regard for whether the information obtained in the study can be generalized or is appropriate for ethnic minority groups. In a subsequent study, the researchers may decide to adopt an etic approach by studying not only middle-class White families, but also lower-income White families, African American families, Latino families, and Asian American families. In studying ethnic minority families, the researchers would likely discover that the extended family is more frequently a support system in ethnic minority families than in White American families. If so, the emic approach would reveal a different pattern of family interaction than would the etic approach, documenting that research with middle-class White families cannot always be generalized to all ethnic groups.

In a symposium on racism in developmental research (Lee, 1992), the participants concluded that we need to include more ethnic minority children in our research. Historically, ethnic minority children have essentially been discounted from research and viewed simply as variations from the norm or average. The development of nonmainstream children has been viewed as "confounds" or "noise" in data, and consequently researchers have deliberately excluded such children from the samples they have selected (Ryan-Finn, Cauce, & Grove, 1995). Because ethnic minority children have been excluded from research for so long, there likely is more variation in children's real lives than our research data have indicated in the past (Stevenson, 1995).

Cross-cultural psychologist Joseph Trimble (1989) is especially concerned about researchers' tendencies to use ethnic gloss when they select and describe ethnic groups. By **ethnic gloss,** Trimble means *using an ethnic label, such as African, Latino, Asian, or Native American, in a superficial way that makes an ethnic group seem more homogeneous than it actually is*. For example, the following is an unsuitable description of a research sample, according to Trimble: "The subjects included 28 African Americans, 22 Latinos, and 24 Whites." An acceptable description of each of the groups requires much more detail about the participants' country of origin, socioeconomic status, language, and ethnic self-identification, such as this: "The 22 subjects were Mexican Americans from low-income neighborhoods in the southwestern area of Los Angeles. Twelve spoke Spanish in the home, while 10 spoke English; 11 were born in the United States, 11 were born in Mexico; 16 described themselves as Mexican, 3 as Chicano, 2 as American, and 1 as Latino." Trimble believes that ethnic gloss can cause researchers to obtain samples of ethnic groups and cultures that are not representative of their ethnic and cultural diversity, leading to overgeneralizations and stereotypes.

Life-History Records

Life-history records *provide information about a lifetime chronology of events and activities; they often involve a combination of data records on education, work, family, and residence*. These records might be generated by obtaining information from archival materials (public records or historical documents) or from interviews with a respondent, which might include obtaining a life calendar from the person. Life calendars record the age (year and month) at which transitions occur in a variety of activity domains and life events, thus portraying an unfolding life course. In compiling life-history records, researchers are increasingly using a wide array of materials, including written and oral reports from the subject, vital records, observation, and public documents (Clausen, 1993). An advantage of the multiple-materials approach is that information from varied sources can be compared and discrepancies can sometimes be resolved, resulting in a more accurate life-history record.

Physiological Research and Research with Animals

Two additional methods that psychologists use to gather data are physiological research and research with animals. Research on the biological basis of behavior and technological advances continue to produce remarkable insights about mind and behavior (Tomasello, 1997). For example, researchers have found that the electrical stimulation of certain areas of the brain turn docile, mild-mannered people into hostile, vicious attackers, and higher concentrations of some hormones have been associated with anger in adolescents (Susman & others, 1995).

Because much physiological research cannot be carried out with humans, psychologists sometimes use animals. Animal studies permit researchers to control their subjects' genetic background, diet, experiences during infancy, and many other factors (Drickamer, Vessey, & Miekle, 1996). In studying humans, psychologists treat these factors as random variation, or "noise," that can interfere with accurate results. In addition, animal researchers can investigate the effects of treatments (brain implants, for example) that would be unethical with humans. Moreover, it is possible to track the entire life span of some animals over a relatively short period of time. Laboratory mice, for instance, have a life span of approximately 1 year.

Multimeasure, Multisource, Multicontext Approach

The various methods have their strengths and weaknesses. Direct observations are extremely valuable tools for obtaining information about children, but there are some things we cannot observe in children—their moral thoughts, their inner feelings, the arguments of their parents, how they acquire information about sex, and so on. In such instances, other measures, such as interviews, questionnaires, and case studies, may be valuable. Because virtually every method has limitations, many investigators use multiple measures in assessing children's development. For example, a researcher studying children's aggressive behavior might interview children, check with their friends, observe them carefully at home and in their neighborhood, interview their parents, observe the children at school during recess, and ask teachers to rate the children's aggression. Researchers hope that the convergence of multimeasure, multisource, and multicontext information provides a more comprehensive and valid assessment of children's development.

Correlational and Experimental Strategies

How can we determine if a pregnant woman's cigarette smoking affects her offspring's attentional skills? How can we determine if responding nurturantly to an infant's cries increases attachment to the caregiver? How can we determine if day care is damaging to a child's development? How can we determine if listening to rock music lowers an adolescent's grades in school? When designing a research study to answer such questions, investigators must decide whether to use a correlational or an experimental strategy.

Observed correlation

Possible explanations for this correlation

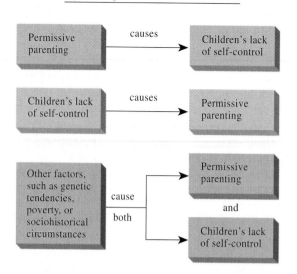

As permissive parenting increases, children's self-control decreases.

Permissive parenting → causes → Children's lack of self-control

Children's lack of self-control → causes → Permissive parenting

Other factors, such as genetic tendencies, poverty, or sociohistorical circumstances → cause both → Permissive parenting and Children's lack of self-control

Figure~2.11

Possible Explanations of Correlational Data

An observed correlation between two events cannot be used to conclude that one event causes a second event. Other possibilities are that the second event causes the first event or that a third, unkown event causes the correlation between the first two events.

Correlational Strategy

In the **correlational strategy,** *the goal is to describe the strength of the relation between two or more events or characteristics. This is a useful strategy because the more strongly events are correlated (related, or associated), the more we can predict one from the other.* For example, if we find that, as parents use more permissive ways to deal with their children, the children's self-control decreases, this does not mean that the parenting style caused the lack of self-control. It could mean that, but it also could mean that the children's lack of self-control stimulated the parents to simply throw up their arms in despair and give up trying to control the obstreperous children's behavior, or it could mean that this correlation is caused by other factors, such as genetic background, poverty, and sociohistorical conditions. (Several decades ago a permissive parenting strategy was widely advocated, but today it no longer is in vogue.) Figure 2.11 portrays these possible interpretations of correlational data.

The **correlational coefficient** *is a number based on statistical analysis that is used to describe the degree of association between two variables. The correlation coefficient ranges from −1.00 to +1.00.* A negative number means an inverse relation. For example, today we often find a *negative* correlation between permissive parenting and children's self-control, and we often find a *positive* correlation between a parent's involvement in and monitoring of a child's life and the child's self-control. The higher the correlation coefficient (whether positive or negative), the stronger the association between the two variables. A correlation of 0 means that there is no association between the two variables. A correlation of −.40 is a stronger correlation than +.20 because we disregard the negative or positive nature of the correlation in determining the correlation's magnitude.

Experimental Strategy

Whereas the correlational strategy allows us to say only that two events are related, the **experimental strategy** *allows us to precisely determine behavior's causes. Developmentalists accomplish this task by performing an experiment, which is a study done in a carefully regulated setting in which one or more of the factors believed to influence the behavior being studied is manipulated and all others are held constant.* If the behavior under study changes when a factor is manipulated, we say that the manipulated factor causes the behavior to change. Experiments establish cause and effect between events, something correlational studies cannot do. *Cause* is the event being manipulated, and *effect* is the behavior that changes because of the manipulation. Remember that, in testing correlation, nothing is manipulated; in an experiment, a researcher actively changes an event to see its effect on behavior.

The following example illustrates the nature of an experiment. The problem to be studied is whether aerobic exercise during pregnancy affects infant development. We need to have one group of pregnant women engage in aerobic exercise and the other not engage in aerobic exercise. We randomly assign our subjects to these two groups. **Random assignment** *occurs when researchers assign subjects to experimental and control conditions by chance, thus reducing the likelihood the results of the experiment will be due to preexisting differences in the two groups.* For example, random assignment greatly reduces the probability that the two groups will differ on such factors as age, social class, prior aerobic exercise, intelligence, health problems, alertness, and so on.

The **independent variable** *is the manipulated, influential, experimental factor in an experiment. The label independent is used because this variable can be changed independently of other factors.* In the aerobic exercise experiment, the amount of aerobic exercise is the independent variable. We manipulate the amount of the aerobic exercise by having the pregnant women exercise four times a week under the direction of a trained instructor. The **dependent variable** *is the factor that is measured in an experiment; it may change because of the manipulation of the independent variable. The label dependent is used because this variable depends on what happens to the subjects in the experiment.* In the aerobic exercise experiment, the dependent variable is represented by two infant measures—breathing and sleeping patterns. The subjects' responses on these measures depend on the influence of the independent variable (whether or not pregnant women engaged in aerobic exercise). An illustration of the nature of the experimental strategy, applied to the aerobic exercise study, is presented in figure 2.12. In our experiment, we test the two sets of offspring in the first week of life. We find that the experimental-group infants have more-regular breathing and sleeping patterns than do their control-group counterparts; thus, we conclude that aerobic exercise by pregnant women promotes more-regular breathing and sleeping patterns in newborn infants.

It might seem as if we should always choose an experimental strategy over a correlational strategy, since the experimental strategy gives us a better sense of the influence of one variable on another. Are there instances when a correlational strategy might be preferred? Three such instances are (1) when the focus of the investigation is so new that we have little knowledge of which variables to manipulate (as when AIDS first appeared), (2) when it is physically impossible to manipulate the variables (such as factors involved in suicide), and (3) when it is unethical to manipulate the variables (for example, in determining the association between a child's illness and exposure to dangerous chemicals).

Time Span of Inquiry

A special concern of developmentalists is the time span of a research investigation. Studies that focus on the relation of age to another variable are common in the field of child development. We have several options—we can study different children of different ages and compare them, or we can study the same individuals as they grow older.

Cross-Sectional Approach

The **cross-sectional approach** *is a research strategy in which individuals of different ages are compared all at one time.* A typical cross-sectional study might include a group of

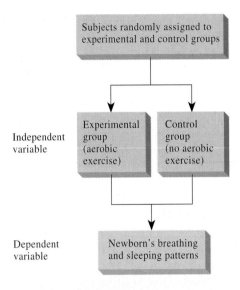

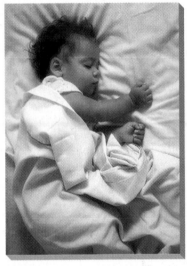

Figure~2.12

Principles of Experimental Strategy
The experimental strategy for determining the effects of aerobic exercise by pregnant women on their newborns' breathing and sleeping patterns.

5-year-olds, 8-year-olds, and 11-year-olds. The different groups can be compared with respect to a variety of dependent variables—IQ, memory, peer relations, attachment to parents, hormonal changes, and so on. All of this can be accomplished in a short time. In some studies, data are collected in a single day. Even in large-scale cross-sectional studies with hundreds of subjects, data collection usually does not take longer than several months to complete.

The main advantage of a cross-sectional study is that researchers do not have to wait for subjects to grow up. Despite its time efficiency, the cross-sectional approach has its drawbacks: It gives no information about how individuals change or about the stability of their characteristics. The increases and decreases—the hills and valleys—of growth and development can become obscured in the cross-sectional approach. Also, because the children studied are of different ages and different groups, they were born at different times; they may have experienced different types of parenting and schooling; and they may have been influenced by different trends in dress, television, and play materials.

Longitudinal Approach

The **longitudinal approach** *is a research strategy in which the same individuals are studied over a period of time, usually several years or more.* In a typical longitudinal study of the same topics we discussed regarding the cross-sectional approach, we might structure a test to administer to children once a year when they are 4, 8, and 12 years old. In this example, the same children would be studied over an 8-year time span, allowing us to examine patterns of change within each child. One of the great values of the longitudinal approach is that we can evaluate how individual children change as they grow up.

Fewer longitudinal than cross-sectional studies are conducted because they are time consuming and costly. A close examination of the longitudinal approach reveals some additional problems: (1)When children are examined over a long period of time, some drop out because they lose interest or move away and cannot be recontacted by the investigator. A fairly common finding is that the remaining children represent a slightly biased sample, in that they tend to be psychologically superior to those who dropped out on almost every dimension (intelligence, motivation, and cooperativeness, for example) that the investigator checks. (2)With repeated testing, some children may become more "testwise," which may increase their ability to perform "better" or "more maturely" the next time the investigator interacts with them. For a comparison of longitudinal and cross-sectional research designs, see figure 2.13.

Cohort Effects

Cohort effects *are those due to a subject's time of birth or generation but not actually to age.* Today's children are living a childhood of firsts (Louv, 1990). They are the first day-care generation; the first truly multicultural generation; the first generation to grow up in the electronic bubble of an environment defined by computers and new forms of media; the first post-sexual-revolution

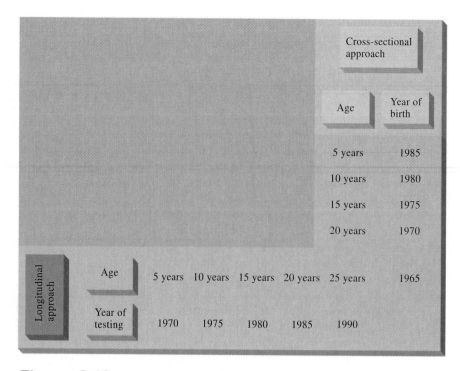

Figure~2.13

A Comparison of Cross-Sectional and Longitudinal Approaches

generation; the first generation to grow up in new kinds of dispersed, deconcentrated cities, not quite urban, rural, or suburban.

> *The mark of the historic is the nonchalance with which it picks up an individual and deposits him in a trend, like a house playfully moved in a tornado.*
>
> —**Mary McCarthy**

Cohort effects are important because they can powerfully affect the dependent measures in a study ostensibly concerned with age. Researchers have shown that cohort effects are especially important to investigate in the assessment of intelligence (Schaie, 1994). For example, individuals born at different points in time—such as 1920, 1940, and 1960—have had varying opportunities for education, with the individuals born in earlier years having less access.

RESEARCH CHALLENGES

Research on child development involves a number of challenges. Many of the research challenges involve the pursuit of research knowledge itself. Others involve the effects of the research on the participants and how consumers can improve their understanding of the information derived from research studies.

BY BILL HOEST

"That's my dad when he was 10 . . . He was in some sort of cult."

©1986; *Reprinted courtesy of Bill Hoest and* Parade Magazine

Florence Denmark (shown here talking with a group of students) has developed a number of guidelines for nonsexist research. Denmark and others believe that psychology needs to be challenged to examine the world in a new way, one that incorporates girls' and women's perspectives.

Ethics in Research on Child Development

Increasingly, child developmentalists recognize that considerable caution must be taken to ensure the well-being of children when they are involved in a research study. Today colleges and universities have review boards that evaluate the ethical nature of research conducted at their institutions. Proposed research plans must pass the scrutiny of an ethics research committee before the research can be initiated. In addition, the American Psychological Association (APA) has developed guidelines for its members' ethics.

The code of ethics adopted by the APA instructs researchers to protect their subjects from mental and physical harm. The best interests of the subjects must be kept foremost in the researcher's mind (Kimmel, 1996). All subjects, if they are old enough, must give their informed consent to participate in a research study. This requires that subjects know what their participation will entail and any risks that might develop. For example, subjects in an investigation of the effects of divorce on children should be told beforehand that interview questions might stimulate thought about issues they might not anticipate. The subjects should also be informed that in some instances a discussion of the family's experiences might improve family relationships, but in other instances it might bring up issues that bring the children unwanted stress. After informed consent is given, the subjects reserve the right to withdraw from the study at any time.

Special ethical concerns govern the conduct of research with children (Hoagwood, Jensen, & Fisher, 1996). First, if children are to be studied, informed consent from their parents or legal guardians must be obtained. Parents have the right to a complete and accurate description of what will be done with their children and may refuse to let them participate. Second, children have rights too. Psychologists are obliged to explain precisely what the children will experience. The children may refuse to participate, even after parental permission has been given. Also, if a child becomes upset during the research study, it is the psychologist's obligation to calm the child. Third, psychologists must always weigh the potential for harming children against the prospects of contributing some clear benefits to them. If there is the chance of harm—as when drugs are used, social deception takes place, or children are treated aversively (that is, punished or reprimanded)—psychologists must convince a group of peers that the benefits of the experience clearly outweigh any chance of harm. Fourth, since children are in a vulnerable position and lack power and control when facing adults, psychologists should always strive to make a professional encounter a positive and supportive experience.

Reducing Sexist Research

Traditional science is presented as being value free and, thus, a valid way of studying mental processes and behavior. However, there is a growing consensus that science in general and psychology in particular are not value free (Paludi, 1995). A special concern is that the vast majority of psychological research has been male oriented and male dominated. Some researchers believe that male-dominated sciences, such as psychology, need to be challenged to examine the world in a new way, one that incorporates girls' and women's perspectives and respects their ethnicity, sexual orientation, age, and socioeconomic status. For example, Florence Denmark and her colleagues (1988) provided the following three recommendations as guidelines for nonsexist research:

1. Research methods

   Problem: The selection of research participants is based on stereotypic assumptions and does not allow for generalizations to other groups.

Example: On the basis of stereotypes about who should be responsible for contraception, only females are studied.

Correction: Both sexes should be studied before conclusions are drawn about the factors that determine contraception use.

2. Data analysis

Problem: Gender differences are inaccurately magnified.

Example: "Whereas only 24 percent of the girls were found to . . . fully 28 percent of the boys were . . ."

Correction: The results should include extensive descriptions of the data so that differences are not exaggerated.

3. Conclusions

Problem: The title or abstract (summary) of an article makes no reference to the limitations of the study participants and implies a broader scope of the study than is warranted.

Example: A study purporting to be about "perceptions of the disabled" examines only blind White boys.

Correction: Use more-precise titles and clearly describe the sample and its selection criteria in the abstract or summary.

Being a Wise Consumer of Information About Children's Development

We live in an information society in which there is a vast amount of information about children's development available for public consumption. The information varies greatly in quality. How can you become a wise consumer of information about children's development?

Be Cautious About What Is Reported in the Media

Research and clinical findings about children's development are increasingly talked about in the media. Television, radio, newspapers, and magazines all make it a frequent practice to report on research and clinical findings involving children that are likely to be of interest to the general public. Many professional and mental health and psychological organizations regularly supply the media with information about research and clinical findings. In many cases, this information has been published in professional journals or presented at national meetings. And

most major colleges and universities have a media relations department that contacts the press about current research by their faculty.

Not all psychological and mental health information involving children that is presented for public consumption comes from professionals with excellent credentials and reputations at colleges and universities and in applied mental health settings. Journalists, television reporters, and other media personnel are not scientifically and clinically trained. It is not an easy task for them to sort through the widely varying material they come across and make a sound decision about which research and clinical information that involves children should be presented to the public.

Unfortunately, the media often focus on sensational and dramatic psychological findings. They want you to read what they have written or stay tuned and not flip to another channel. They can capture your attention and keep it by presenting dramatic, sensational, and surprising information. As a consequence, media presentations of information about children tend to go beyond what actual research articles and clinical findings really say.

Even when excellent research and clinical findings are presented to the public, it is difficult for media personnel to adequately inform people about what has been found and the implications for their lives. For example, throughout this text you will be introduced to an entirely new vocabulary. Each time we present a new concept, we precisely define it and give examples of it as well. We have an entire book to carry out our task of carefully introducing, defining, and elaborating on key concepts and issues, research, and clinical findings about children's development. However, the media do not have the luxury of time and space to go into considerable detail and specify the limitations and qualifications of research and clinical findings. They often have only a few minutes or few lines to summarize as best they can the complex findings of a study about children's development.

Among the other ways that you can think critically about the psychological information you see, hear, or read are to understand the distinction between nomothetic research and idiographic needs, to be aware of the tendency to overgeneralize from a small sample or a unique clinical sample, to know that a single study is often not the final and definitive word about an issue or topic, to be sure you understand why causal conclusions cannot be drawn from a correlational study, and to always consider the source of the information about children and evaluate its credibility.

Know How to Make a Distinction Between Nomothetic Research and Idiographic Needs

In being a wise consumer of information about children, it is important to understand the difference between nomothetic research and idiographic needs. **Nomothetic**

research *is conducted at the level of the group*. Most research on children's development is nomothetic research. Individual variations in how children respond is often not a major focus of the research. For example, if researchers are interested in the effects of divorce on children's ability to cope with stress, they might conduct a study of 50 children from divorced families and 50 children from intact, never-divorced families. They might find that children from divorced families, as a group, cope more poorly with stress than children from intact families do. That is a nomothetic finding that applies to children of divorce as a group. And that is what commonly is reported in the media. In this particular study, it likely was the case that some of the children from divorced families were coping better with stress than some of the children from intact families were—not as many, but some. Indeed, it is entirely possible that, of the 100 children in the study, the 2 or 3 children who were coping the very best with stress might have been children from divorced families and that the findings will still be reported as showing that children from divorced families (as a group) cope more poorly with stress than children from intact families do.

As a consumer of information, you want to know what the information means for you *individually*, not necessarily for a group of people. **Idiographic needs** *are needs that are important to the individual, not to the group.* The failure of the media to adequately distinguish between nomothetic research and idiographic needs is not entirely their fault. Researchers have not adequately done this either. The research they conduct too often fails to examine the overlap between groups and tends to present only the differences that are found. And when those differences are reported, too often they are reported as if there is no overlap between the groups being compared (in our example, children from divorced families and children from intact families), when in reality there is substantial overlap. If you read a study in a research journal or a media report of a study that states that children from divorced families coped more poorly with stress than did children from intact families, it does not mean that all children from divorced families coped more poorly than all children from intact families did. It simply means that as a group intact family children coped better.

Recognize How It Is Easy to Overgeneralize from a Small or Clinical Sample

There often isn't space or time in media presentations of information about children to go into details about the nature of the sample. Sometimes you will get basic information about the sample's size—whether it is based on 10 subjects, 50 subjects, or 200 subjects, for example. In many cases, small or very small samples require that care be exercised in generalizing to a larger population of individuals. For example, if a study of children from divorced families is based on only 10 or 20 such children, what is found in the study may not generalize to all divorced children, because the sample investigated may have some unique characteristics. The sample might come from families, that have substantial economic resources, are White American, live in a small southern town, and are undergoing psychotherapy. In this study, then, we clearly would be making unwarranted generalizations if we thought the findings also characterize divorced children from families who have moderate to low incomes, are from other ethnic backgrounds, live in different locations, and are not undergoing psychotherapy.

Be Aware That a Single Study Is Usually Not the Defining Word About Some Aspect of Children's Development

The media might identify an interesting piece of research or a clinical finding and claim that it is something phenomenal with far-reaching implications. While such studies and findings do occur, it is rare for a single study to provide earth-shattering and conclusive answers, especially answers that apply to all children. In fact, in most domains of children's development, where there are a large number of investigations, it is not unusual to find conflicting results about a particular topic or issue. Answers to questions about children's development usually emerge after many scientists and/or clinicians have conducted similar investigations or therapy has been practiced by a number of mental health professionals who have drawn similar conclusions. Thus, a report of one study or clinical observations by only one or two therapists should not be taken as the absolute, final answer to a problem.

In our example of divorce, if one study reports that a particular therapy conducted by a therapist has been especially effective with children of divorce, we should not conclude that the therapy will work as effectively with all such children and with other therapists until more studies are conducted.

Remember That Causal Conclusions Cannot Be Drawn from Correlational Studies

Drawing causal conclusions from correlational studies is one of the most common mistakes made by the media. In studies in which an experiment has not been conducted (remember that in an experiment, subjects are randomly assigned to treatments or experiences), two variables or factors might be related to each other. However, causal interpretations cannot be made when two or more factors are simply correlated or related to each other. We cannot say that one causes the other. In the case of divorce, a headline might read "Divorce Causes Children to Have Problems in School." We read the article and find out the headline was derived from the results of a research study. Since we obviously cannot, for ethical or practical purposes, randomly assign children to families that will become divorced or stay intact, this headline is based on a correlational study, which cannot be the basis of such causal statements. At least some of the children's problems in school probably occurred prior to the divorce of their parents. Other factors, such as poor parenting practices, low socioeconomic status, a difficult temperament, and low intelligence, may also contribute to children's problems in school and not be a direct consequence of divorce itself. What we can say in such studies, if the data warrant it, is that divorce is related to or associated with problems in school. What we cannot legitimately say in such studies is that divorce causes problems in school.

Always Consider the Source of the Information and Evaluate Its Credibility

Studies are not automatically accepted by the research community. Researchers usually have to submit their findings to a research journal, where their paper is reviewed by their colleagues, who make a decision about whether to publish it or not. While quality of research in journals is not uniform, in most cases the research has undergone far greater scrutiny and careful consideration of the quality of the work than is the case for research or any other information that has not gone through the journal process. And within the media, we can distinguish between what is presented in respected newspapers, such as the *New York Times* and *Washington Post*, as well as credible magazines, such as *Time* and *Newsweek*, and much less respected and less credible tabloids, such as the *National Enquirer* and *Star*. Refer to Critical Thinking About Children's Development to further explore reports about child development.

Since our last review, we have discussed a number of ideas about methods and how to be a wise consumer of information about children's development. A summary of these ideas is presented in concept table 2.2.

CONCEPT TABLE 2.2

Methodology and Research Challenges

Concept	Processes/ Related Ideas	Characteristics/Description
Methodology	Measures	Observation is a key ingredient in research that includes both laboratory and naturalistic observation. Interviews and questionnaires are used to assess perceptions and attitudes. Social desirability and lying can be problems for interviews and questionnaires. Case studies provide an in-depth look at an individual; caution in generalizing from these is warranted. Standardized tests are designed to assess an individual's characteristics in relation to those of a large group of similar individuals. Cross-cultural research involves etic and emic approaches. A special concern is research with ethnic minority children. Life-history records consist of information about a lifetime chronology of events and activities; they often involve a combination of data records. They might be obtained through archival materials or interviews with the person. Physiological research provides information about the biological basis of development. Animal studies can also provide information about development.
	Correlational and experimental strategies	The correlational strategy describes how strongly two or more events or characteristics are related. It does not allow causal statements. The experimental strategy involves manipulation of influential factors—independent variables—and measurement of their effect on dependent variables. Subjects are randomly assigned to experimental and control groups in many experimental studies. The experimental strategy can reveal the causes of behavior.
	Time span of inquiry	In the cross-sectional approach, individuals of different ages are compared all at one time. In the longitudinal approach, the same individuals are studied over a period of time, usually several years or more. Cohort effects are due to a subject's time of birth or generation but not to age. The study of cohort effects underscores the importance of considering the sociohistorical dimensions of development.
Research Challenges	Ethics in research on child development	Researchers must ensure the well-being of subjects in research. The risk of mental and physical harm must be reduced, and informal consent should be obtained. Special ethical considerations are involved when children are research subjects.
	Reducing sexist research	A special concern is that the vast majority of psychological research has been male oriented and male dominated. Some researchers believe that developmentalists need to be challenged to examine children's worlds in a new way, one that incorporates girls' and women's perspectives. Recommendations have been made for conducting nonsexist research.
	Being a wise consumer of information about children's development	In many instances the quality of information you read about children's development, especially in the media, varies greatly. Being a wise consumer involves understanding the distinction between nomothetic research and idiographic needs, being aware of the tendency to overgeneralize from a small sample or a unique sample, knowing that a single study is often not the defining word about an issue or problem, understanding why causal conclusions cannot be drawn from a correlational study, and always considering the source of the information and evaluating its credibility.

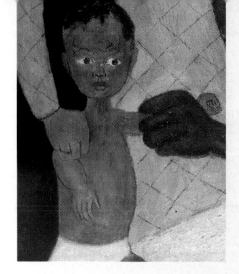

SUMMARY

A discipline that studies how babies develop, how parents nurture children, how peers interact, and how children think can be a science just as much as disciplines that investigate how gravity works and the molecular structure of a compound. That is because science is not determined by what it investigates but by how it investigates.

We began our discussion of the science of child development by evaluating the nature of theory and the scientific method. Then we turned our attention to theories of development, describing psychoanalytic theories (Freud and Erikson), cognitive theories (Piaget and information processing), behavioral and social learning theories (Pavlov, Skinner, and Bandura), ethological theories (Lorenz), and ecological, contextual theories (Bronfenbrenner and Elder), as well as developmental analogies and an eclectic theoretical orientation. Our coverage of methods focused on a number of measures that can be used to obtain information about development, strategies for setting up research studies, and the time span of inquiry. We also read about research challenges—ethical issues in research, reducing sexism in research, and being a wise consumer of information about development.

Don't forget to again study the two concept tables on pages 55 and 67, which together will provide you with a summary of the chapter's main contents. This concludes Section I of the Book. In Section II, we will explore the biological basis of children's development, their physical growth, and their perceptual development, beginning with chapter 3, "Biological Beginnings."

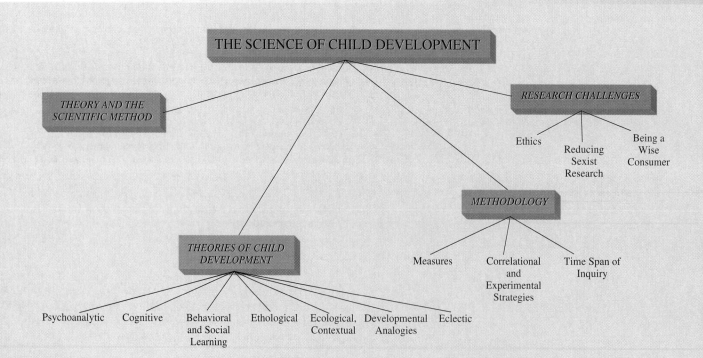

KEY TERMS

PRACTICAL KNOWLEDGE ABOUT CHILDREN

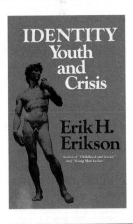

Identity: Youth and Crisis

(1968) by Erik H. Erikson, New York: W.W. Norton.

Erik Erikson was one of the leading theorists in the field of life-span development. In *Identity: Youth and Crisis*, he outlined his eight stages of life-span development and provided numerous examples from his clinical practice to illustrate the stages. This book gives special attention to the fifth stage in Erikson's theory, identity versus identity confusion. Especially worthwhile are Erikson's commentaries about identity development in different cultures.

Two other Erikson books that are excellent reading on life-span development are *Young Man Luther* and *Gandhi's Truth*.

Examining Lives in Context: Perspectives on the Ecology of Human Development

(1995) edited by Phyllis Moen, Glen H. Elder, Jr., and Kurt Luscher, Washington, DC: American Psychological Association.

In this book, more than two dozen scholars explain how Urie Bronfenbrenner's ecological theory led them to focus their own work on problems crucial to "real life." The book also highlights many concepts in Glen Elder's life course theory, such as the importance of time and place, as well as linked lives, in human development. The contributors include many leading theorists and researchers, such as Eleanor Maccoby, John Clausen, Jean Brooks-Gunn, Glen Elder, Michael Rutter, and Urie Bronfenbrenner.

EXPLORATIONS IN CHILD DEVELOPMENT

To further explore the nature of child development, we will examine the nature of research journals that include studies on child development. Then we will discuss ways to improve the lives of children by evaluating linkages between schools and families.

RESEARCH IN CHILD DEVELOPMENT

The Journal Process

At the end of chapter 1, we described why research is important in building a knowledge base about children's development. In this chapter, we described the nature of scientific research and how it is conducted—its theories, its methods, its strategies. The vast amount of research that focuses on children is presented mainly in journal articles and papers presented at scientific meetings.

Whether or not you pursue a career in child development, psychology, education, nursing, or a related field, you can benefit from learning about the journal process. As a student you might be required to look up original research in journals as part of writing a term paper; as a parent, teacher, or nurse, you might want to consult journals to obtain information that will help you understand and work more effectively with children; and as an inquiring person, you might want to look up information in journals after you have heard or read something that piqued your curiosity.

A *journal* publishes scholarly and academic information, usually in a specific domain—like physics, math, sociology, or, in the case of our interest, child development. Scholars in these fields publish most of their research in journals, which are the core source of information in virtually every academic discipline.

Journal articles are usually written for other professionals in the field of the journal's focus. Because the articles are written for other professionals, they often contain technical language and specialized terms related to a specific discipline that are difficult for nonprofessionals to understand. Most of you have already had one or more courses in psychology,

and you will be learning a great deal about the specialized field of child development in this course, which should improve your ability to understand journal articles in this field.

Many journals publish information about child development. Some are devoted exclusively to child development; others include information about other periods of the human life span as well. Among the journals devoted exclusively to child development are *Child Development* and the *Journal of Experimental Child Psychology*. Some journals, such as *Infant Behavior and Development*, even focus on a specific age period in child development. We also discuss adolescent development in this text, and a number of journals emphasize this age period—the *Journal of Research on Adolescence* and the *Journal of Research on Early Adolescence*, for example. Journals that include research on the entire human life span are *Developmental Psychology* and *Human Development*.

You also will find articles on child development in a number of journals that do not focus solely on development, such as the *Journal of Educational Psychology*, *Sex Roles*, the *Journal of Marriage and the Family*, and the *Journal of Consulting and Clinical Psychology*.

In psychology and the field of child development, most journal articles are reports of original research. Many journals also include review articles that present an overview of different studies on a particular topic—such as the effects of divorce on children's development, or some subtopic in the area of infant perception.

Many journals are very selective about what they publish. Every journal has an editorial board of experts who evaluate the articles submitted for publication. One or more of the

experts carefully examine the submitted paper and accept or reject it based on such factors as its contribution to the field, theoretical soundness, methodological excellence, and clarity of writing. Some of the most prestigious journals reject as many as 80 to 90 percent of the articles that are submitted to them because they fail to meet the journal's standards.

Where do you find journals? Your college or university library likely has some of the journals we have listed. Some public libraries also carry journals. I encourage you to look up one or more of the journals that include material on child development. Look through the issues of the last several years to get a sense of the research issues that child developmentalists are currently interested in.

To help you understand the journals, let's examine the format followed by many of them. Their organization often takes this course: abstract, introduction, method, results, discussion, and references.

The *abstract* is a brief summary that appears at the beginning of the article. The abstract lets readers quickly determine whether the article is relevant to their interests and whether they want to read the entire article. The *introduction*, as its title suggests, introduces the problem or issue that is being studied. It includes a concise review of research relevant to the topic, theoretical underpinnings, and one or more hypotheses to be tested. The *method* section consists of a clear description of the subjects evaluated in the study, the measures used, and the procedures that were followed. The method section should be sufficiently clear and detailed so that by reading it another researcher could repeat, or replicate, the study. The *results* section reports the analysis of the data that have been collected. The results section usually includes statistical analyses that are difficult for nonprofessionals to understand. The *discussion* section includes the author's conclusions, inferences, and interpretations of what was found. Statements are usually made here about whether the hypotheses presented in the introduction were supported, limitations of the study, and suggestion for future research. The *references* section is the last part of the journal article and lists every source cited in the article. The references section is often a good place to find other articles relevant to the topic you are interested in.

▮ *I*MPROVING THE LIVES OF CHILDREN

An Important Mesosystem Connection: Family and School

In Bronfenbrenner's ecological theory, the mesosystem is the system of connections between microsystems or social contexts. An important mesosystem connection is between families and schools. Researchers have consistently found that successful students often receive long-term support from parents or other adults at home, as well as strong support from teachers and others at school. Involving parents in learning activities with their children at home is one kind of parental involvement that many educators believe is an important aspect of the child's learning. Family researcher and educator Ira Gordon (1978) concluded that parents of students in the early grades can play six key roles: volunteer, paid employee, teacher at home, audience, decision maker, and adult learner. These roles likely influence not only parents' behavior and their children's schoolwork, but also the quality of schools and communities.

Today, after many decades of limited success, schools are beginning to put more thought into their communication with parents, recognizing that the initial contacts can make or break relationships and that first contacts affect later communication (Epstein, 1990, 1992). Recognizing the importance of parental involvement in education, educators are developing a number of programs to enhance communication between schools and families.

Three types of school/family programs are face-to-face meetings, technological programs, and written communication (D'Angelo & Adler, 1991). In Lima, Ohio, the main goal is for each school to establish a personal relationship with every parent. At an initial parent/teacher conference, parents are given a packet that is designed to increase their likelihood of engaging in learning activities with their children at home. Conferences, regular phone calls, and home visits establish an atmosphere of mutual understanding that makes other kinds of communication (progress reports, report cards, activity calendars, or discussions about problems that arise during the year) more welcome and successful.

Many programs are discovering new ways to use electronic communication to establish contact with a wider range of parents. In McAllen, Texas, the school district has developed a community partnership with local radio stations, and it sponsors "Discusiones Escolares," a weekly program in Spanish that encourages parents to become more involved in their children's education. Family and school relationships, parent involvement at school, preventing school dropouts, creating a learning atmosphere at home, and communicating with adolescents are some of the topics the radio programs have addressed. Parents and others in the communities may check out copies of the script or a cassette tape of each program from the parent coordinators at their schools.

In a joint effort of the New York City school system and the Children's Aid Society, Salome Urena Middle Academies have invited community organizations to provide school-based programs for 1,200 students and their families since 1992 (Carnegie Council on Adolescent Development, 1995). The school's family resource center, open from 8:30 A.M. to 8:30 P.M. is a valuable source of information and support for the community. Staffed by parents, social workers, and other volunteers, the center houses programs in adult education and drug-abuse prevention, and other activities. Because many of the families who send adolescents to the school are of Dominican origin, the school offers English As A Second Language classes for parents—400 parents are currently enrolled.

Hanshaw Middle School in California's Stanislaus County includes a resource center for students' families. Parents can take classes in parenting, computers, and other areas and they can study for their high school equivalency degree. Latino parents can get help in communicating with the school's teachers and administrators. The center also features a case management team and a referral service that is available to students and their families.

In sum, extra care in developing and maintaining channels of communication between school and families is an important aspect of children's development (Duckett, 1997; Phillips, 1997; Rosenthal & Sawyers, 1996).

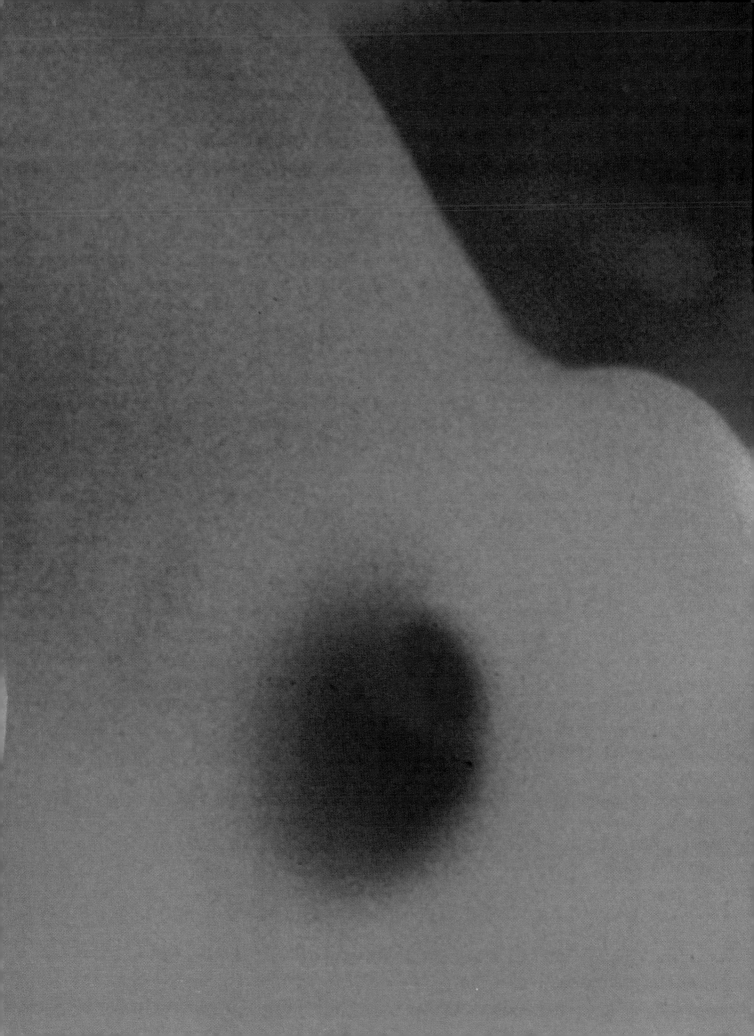

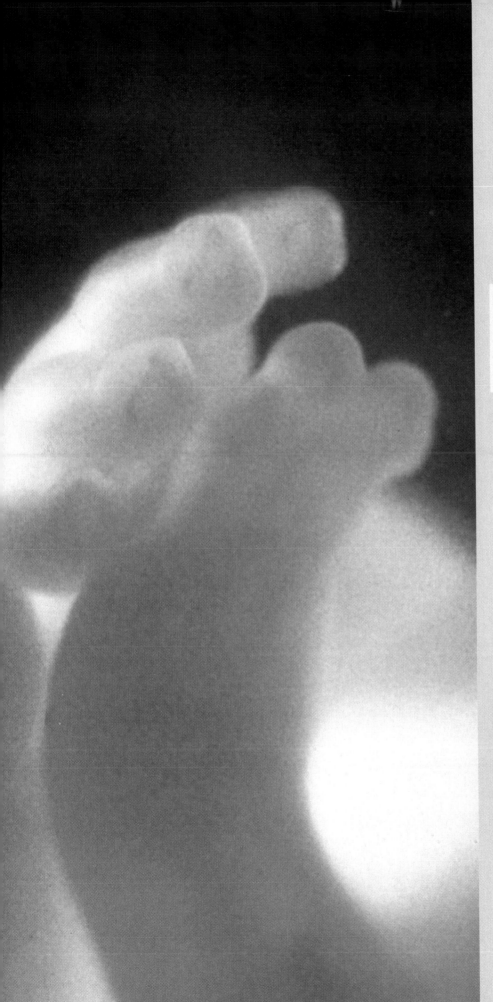

Two

Biological Processes, Physical Development, and Perceptual Development

What endless questions vex the thought, of whence and whither, when and how.

—Sir Richard Burton, Kasidah

The rhythm and meaning of life involve beginnings. Questions are raised about how from so simple a beginning endless forms develop and grow and mature. What was this organism, what is this organism, what will this organism be? In Section II you will read four chapters: "Biological Beginnings" (chapter 3), "Prenatal Development and Birth" (chapter 4), "Physical, Motor, and Perceptual Development in Infancy" (chapter 5), and "Physical Development in Childhood and Puberty" (chapter 6).

Diego Rivera
Mother and Child detail

Chapter

3

Biological Beginnings

Chapter Boxes

here are one hundred and ninety-three living species of monkeys and apes. One hundred and ninety-two of them are covered with hair. The exception is the naked ape self-named, Homo sapiens.

—Desmond Morris

> *The frightening part about*
> *heredity and environment*
> *is that we parents*
> *provide both.*
>
> —Notebook of a Printer

The Jim and Jim Twins

Jim Lewis (left) and Jim Springer (right).

PREVIEW

*T*he examples of Jim and Jim, the giggle sisters, and the identical twins who had the same nightmares stimulate us to think about our genetic heritage and the biological foundations of our existence. Organisms are not like billiard balls, moved by simple, external forces to predictable positions on life's pool table. Environmental experiences and biological foundations work together to make us who we are. Our coverage of life's biological beginnings focuses on evolution, genetics, heredity's influence on development, and the interaction of heredity and environment.

Jim Springer and Jim Lewis are identical twins. They were separated at 4 weeks of age and did not see each other again until they were 39 years old. Both worked as part-time deputy sheriffs, vacationed in Florida, drove Chevrolets, had dogs named Toy, and married and divorced women named Betty. One twin named his son James Allan, and the other named his son James Alan. The two both liked math but not spelling, enjoyed carpentry and mechanical drawing, chewed their fingernails down to the nubs, had almost identical drinking and smoking habits, had hemorrhoids, put on 10 pounds at about the same point in development, first suffered headaches at the age of 18, and had similar sleep patterns.

But Jim and Jim had some differences. One wore his hair over his forehead, the other slicked it back and had sideburns. One expressed himself best orally, the other was more proficient in writing. But for the most part, their profiles were remarkably similar.

Another pair, Daphne and Barbara, were called the "giggle sisters" because they were always making each other laugh. A thorough search of their adoptive families' histories revealed no gigglers. And the identical sisters handled stress by ignoring it, avoided conflict and controversy whenever possible, and showed no interest in politics.

Two other female identical twin sisters were separated at 6 weeks and reunited in their fifties. Both had nightmares, which they describe in hauntingly similar ways: Both dreamed of doorknobs and fishhooks in their mouths as they smothered to death! The nightmares began during early adolescence and had stopped in the last 10 to 12 years. Both women were bed wetters until about 12 or 13 years of age, and they reported educational and marital histories that were remarkably similar.

These sets of twins are part of the Minnesota Study of Twins Reared Apart, directed by Thomas Bouchard and his colleagues. They bring identical twins (identical genetically because they come from the same egg) and fraternal twins (dissimilar genetically because they come from two eggs) from all over the world to Minneapolis to investigate their lives. The twins are given a number of personality tests, and detailed medical histories are obtained, including information about diet, smoking, exercise habits, chest X-rays, heart stress tests, and EEGs (brain-wave tests). The twins are interviewed and asked more than 15,000 questions about their family and childhood environment, personal interests, vocational orientation, values, and aesthetic judgments. They also are given ability and intelligence tests (Bouchard & others, 1990).

Critics of the Minnesota identical twins study point out that some of the separated twins were together several months prior to their adoption, that some of the twins had been reunited prior to their testing (in some cases, a number of years earlier), that adoption agencies often place twins in similar homes, and that even strangers who spend several hours together and start comparing their lives are likely to come up with some coincidental similarities (Adler, 1991). Still, even in the face of such criticism, the Minnesota study of identical twins indicates how scientists have recently shown an increased interest in the genetic basis of human development, and that we need further research on genetic and environmental factors (Bouchard & others, 1996; Wilcox & Bouchard, 1996).

THE EVOLUTIONARY PERSPECTIVE

In evolutionary time, humans are relative newcomers to Earth, yet we have established ourselves as the most successful and dominant species. If we consider evolutionary time in terms of a calendar year, humans arrived here late in December (Sagan, 1977). As our earliest ancestors left the forest to feed on the savannahs, and finally to form hunting societies on the open plains, their minds and behaviors changed. How did this evolution come about?

Natural Selection and Adaptive Behavior

Natural selection *is the evolutionary process that favors individuals that are best designed to reproduce and survive.* Natural selection is a two-part process. First, variations produced by chance appear at random in the population. Second, organisms with favorable design variations are more likely to survive, reproduce, and pass their characteristics on to their offspring (Enger & others, 1996). For example, mimicry and camouflage occur by the slow accumulation over many generations of slight favorable variations, each improving the organism's ability to escape predators and to survive and leave offspring (Brower, 1996). Alfred Russell Wallace was among the individuals who called Darwin's attention to such close resemblances between animals and objects in their environment. Such resemblances, as Darwin recognized, are reinforced by the animal's patterns of behavior, also a result of natural selection (Curtis & Barnes, 1989).

Figure~3.1

Adaptation
Humans, more than any other mammal, adapt to and control most types of environments. Because of longer parental care, humans learn more complex behavior patterns, which contribute to adaptation.

> *W*hat seest thou else in the dark backward and abysm of time.
>
> **—William Shakespeare**
>
> *I* am a brother to dragons, and a companion to owls.
>
> **—Job 30:29**

The work of natural selection has resulted in the disappearing acts of moths and the quills of porcupines. Indeed, over a million species have been classified, from bacteria to blue whales, with many varieties of beetles in between. The effects of evolution can also be seen in the technological advances, intelligence, and longer parental care of human beings (see figure 3.1).

The concept of adaptive behavior is important for understanding the role of evolution in behavior (Zubay, 1996). In evolutionary conceptions of psychology, **adaptive behavior** *is behavior that promotes the organism's survival in its natural habitat.* Adaptive behavior involves the organism's modification of its behavior to increase its

likelihood of survival. All organisms must adapt to particular places, climates, food sources, and ways of life. Adaptation is natural selection for characteristics that perform a certain function. An example of adaptation is the eagle's claws, which facilitate predation. In humans, attachment has been naturally selected because the infant's closeness to the caregiver ensures feeding and protection.

Generally, evolution proceeds at a very slow pace. The lines that led to the emergence of human beings and the great apes diverged about 14 million years ago! Modern humans, *Homo sapiens*, came into existence only about 50,000 years ago. Civilization as we know it began about 10,000 years ago. No sweeping evolutionary changes in humans have occurred since then—for example, our brain is not ten times as big, we do not have a third eye in the back of our head, and we haven't learned to fly.

SOCIOCULTURAL WORLDS OF CHILDREN

The Human Species Is a Culture-Making Species

Unlike all other animal species, which evolve mainly in response to random changes in their environment, humans have more control over their own evolution. This change occurs through *cultural evolution*. For example, we've made astonishing accomplishments in the past 10,000 years or so, ever since we developed language. Biological (Darwinian) evolution continues in our species, but its rate, compared with cultural evolution, is so slow that its impact seems almost negligible. There is no evidence, for example, that brain size or structure has changed in our species since *Homo sapiens* appeared on the fossil record about 50,000 years ago.

As humans evolved, we acquired knowledge and passed it on from generation to generation. This knowledge, which originally instructed us in how to hunt, make tools, and communicate, became our culture. The accumulation of knowledge has gathered speed—from a slow swell to a meteoric rise. Hunter-gatherer tribes, characteristic of early human society, changed over thousands of years into small agricultural communities. With people rooted in one place, cities grew and flourished. Life within those cities remained relatively unchanged for generations. Then industrialization put a dizzying speed on cultural change. Now technological advances in communication and transportation—computers, fax machines, the space shuttle—transform everyday life at a staggering pace.

Whatever one generation learns, it can pass to the next through writing, word of mouth, ritual, tradition, and a host of other methods humans have developed to assure their culture's continuity (Gould, 1981). By creating cultures, humans have built, shaped, and carved out their own environments.

Evolutionists believe that humans shape culture to achieve evolutionary goals. Consider the gene for lactose tolerance. It spreads among some groups because it enables humans to eat dairy foods. This in turn has a strong effect on human culture through a shift to dairy farming and larger populations.

More than 99 percent of all humans now live in a different kind of environment from that in which the species evolved. By creating cultures, humans have, in effect, built, shaped, and carved out their own environments.

Although no dramatic evolutionary changes have occurred since *Homo sapiens* appeared on the fossil record 50,000 years ago, there have been sweeping cultural changes. Biological evolution shaped human beings into a culture-making species. More information about the human species as a culture-making species appears in Sociocultural Worlds of Children.

Sociobiology

Sociobiology *is a theory that relies on the principles of evolutionary biology to explain social behavior.* Sociobiologists believe that psychologists have a limited understanding of social behavior because they primarily study only one mammalian species—*Homo sapiens*. Sociobiology derives its information from comparisons of any among the tens of thousands of animal species that have evolved some form of social life.

According to E. O. Wilson (1975, 1995), the purpose of sociobiology is not to make crude comparisons between animal species or between animals and humans, such as simply comparing wolf and human aggression. Rather, sociobiology's purpose is to develop general laws of the evolution and biology of social behavior. The hope also is to extend the principles of sociobiology to assist in the explanation of human behavior.

Let's consider a sociobiological inquiry. In some species of birds, the young born in one year might not breed the second year, but instead help their parents rear the second year's brood, or adult birds that have lost their mates might help close relatives rear their young. These social systems that involve helping at the nest occur in Florida scrub jays (Woolfenden, 1975), African white-fronted bee-eaters (Emlen, 1984), and acorn woodpeckers in the western United States (Koenig, Mumme, & Pitelka, 1984). Nests with helpers are more successful—more young fledge. Such helping behavior appears to expend energy to benefit offspring that are not the helper's own. Sociobiologists are interested in how such helping behavior evolved and what the advantages are for helping or not helping.

Sociobiology has helped to clarify relationships between animal behavior and human behavior. It has also focused attention on the costs and benefits of behavior, directed inquiry toward individual and group differences, highlighted the role of ecology in behavior, and broadened our understanding of behavior's causes (Byrne, 1997; Crawford, 1987).

Nonetheless, sociobiology is not without its critics, especially when it is applied to human behavior. The critics argue that sociobiologists do not adequately consider human adaptability and experience, and that sociobiology describes human beings as mere automatons in thrall to their genes. The critics also say that sociobiology explains behavior after the fact, lacking the predictive ability of any good theory. Critics also argue that sociobiology promotes discrimination against women and ethnic minorities (Paludi, 1995). As you can see, when sociobiology is applied to human behavior, it is controversial.

How do sociobiologists respond to such criticisms? They argue that most psychologists have not given adequate attention to the evolutionary basis of behavior; that sociobiologists do consider both the biological and the experiential sides of behavior; that much of their work does have predictive validity; and that when sociobiology has been used to discriminate against women and ethnic minorities, it has been a misuse of sociobiological theory. An example of such a misuse of sociobiology in the past is "eugenics." Eugenicists study genetic differences in order to promote one racial group over others. Sociobiologists also claim that political and ideological issues must be clearly separated from scientific issues. That someone finds a scientific theory to be politically objectionable implies nothing about the theory's truth or falsehood.

Evolutionary Psychology

Many sociobiologists have neglected the psychological level of analysis. They argue directly from principles of evolution to patterns of social organization—such as mating systems (for instance, polygamy versus monogamy)—without investigating the psychological mechanisms involved. **Evolutionary psychology** *is a contemporary approach that emphasizes that behavior is a function of psychological mechanisms, requires input for activation, and is ultimately related to successful survival and reproduction.*

David Buss (1995) has described the basic principles of evolutionary psychology. In evolutionary psychology, psychological and physiological *mechanisms* are the product of evolution by selection. These mechanisms owe their existence to the successful solutions to adaptive problems that ancestral humans faced in their environments. Adaptive problems are numerous, and they are all related to successful survival and reproduction; reproduction is the engine that drives evolution, and survival is important because it aids reproduction. Evolutionary psychology is not about genetic determinism but rather is an interactionistic framework—no behavior can be produced without input into the evolved psychological mechanisms of humans.

The central issue for evolutionary psychologists is the nature of the psychological mechanisms created by selection and the adaptive functions they serve. According to evolutionary psychologists, human psychological mechanisms are domain-specific, or modular. Once developed, all mechanisms require particular forms of input to be activated and to function properly.

The domain-specific or modular psychological mechanisms that have been discovered include these:

- A highly patterned distribution of fears and phobias that correspond to hazards faced by humans in ancestral environments—for example, the fear of strangers that emerges between 8 and 24 months of age, as well as fear of snakes, spiders, heights, open spaces, and darkness (Marks, 1987)
- Children's imitation of high-status rather than low-status models (Bandura, 1977)
- The worldwide preference for mates who are kind, intelligent, and dependable (Buss, 1994)

According to evolutionary psychologists, research increasingly suggests that numerous mechanisms have evolved due to the diverse adaptive problems humans needed to solve in their evolutionary environments.

One of the applications of evolutionary psychology to the study of development involves the origins of attachment and warmth (Bowlby, 1989; MacDonald, 1992, 1996). For example, Kevin MacDonald (1992) argues that warmth can be viewed as a reward system that evolved to facilitate cohesive family relationships and parental investment. According to Buss (1995), other important developmental issues are the shifts from mating to parenting, and then to menopause and grandparenting. Buss asks questions like these: What psychological mechanisms are triggered by the birth of a child? Are the same psychological mechanisms in parents activated by female and male infants, or are some of the mechanisms different? Is the asymmetry between the sexes in reproductive capacity after age 50 accompanied by sex differences in effort allocation and psychological activation?

Evolutionary psychologists believe that their approach provides a much needed emphasis on the functional properties of mental processes and behavior that can help integrate the entire field of psychology. They believe that in the twenty-first century evolutionary psychology will infiltrate virtually all of psychology's domains (Barkow, Cosmides, & Tooby, 1992; Buss, 1995).

Not all psychologists agree. Many direct criticisms at evolutionary psychology that once were reserved for sociobiology—that it does not put enough emphasis on cultural diversity and that its explanations are developed after the fact, for example. Critics also argue that it is highly unlikely that one single metatheory—in this case, evolutionary psychology—will ever encompass all of psychology's complexity (Graziano, 1995). Nonetheless, the field of psychology currently benefits from the application of evolutionary psychology's principles to a number of problems regarding adaptation (Daly & Wilson, 1995; Gangestad, 1995).

Race and Ethnicity

In keeping with one of the main themes of this text—exploration of sociocultural issues—let's examine the biological concept of race and see how it has taken on elaborate, often unfortunate, social meanings. **Race** *originated as a biological concept. It refers to a system for classifying plants and animals into subcategories according to specific physical and structural characteristics.* Race is one of the most misused and misunderstood words in the English language (Atkinson, Morten, & Sue, 1993; Mays, 1991, 1993). Loosely, it has come to mean everything from a person's religion to skin color.

The three main classifications of the human race are Mongoloid, or Asian; Caucasoid, or European; and Negroid, or African. Skin color, head shape, facial features, stature, and the color and texture of body hair are the physical characteristics most widely used to determine race.

These racial classifications presumably were created to define and clarify the differences among groups of people; however, they have not been very useful. Today many people define races as groups that are socially constructed on the basis of physical differences (Van den Berghe, 1978). However, some groups, such as Native Americans, Australians, and Polynesians, do not fit into any of the three main racial categories. Also, obvious differences *within* groups are not adequately accounted for. Arabs, Hindus, and Europeans, for instance, are physically different, yet they are all called Caucasians. Although there are some physical characteristics that distinguish "racial" groups, there are, in fact, more similarities than differences among such groups.

Too often we are socialized to accept as facts many myths and stereotypes about people whose skin color, facial features, and hair texture differ from ours. For example, some people still believe that Asians are inscrutable, Jews are acquisitive, and Latinos are lazy. What people believe about race has profound social consequences. Until recently, for instance, African Americans were denied access to schools, hospitals, churches, and other social institutions attended by Whites.

Although scientists are supposed to be a fair-minded lot, some also have used racial distinctions to further their own biases. Some even claim that one racial group has a biological inheritance that gives it an adaptive advantage over other racial groups. Nineteenth-century biologist Louis Agassiz, for example, asserted that God had created Blacks and Whites as separate species. Also, in Nazi Germany, where science and death made their grisliest alliance, Jews, homosexuals, and other "undesirables" were ascribed whatever characteristics were necessary to reinforce the conclusion that "survival of the fittest" demanded their elimination.

Unfortunately, racism cloaked in science still finds champions. Recently psychologist Philipe Rushton (1985, 1988) argued that evolution accounts for racial differences in sexual practices, fertility, intelligence, and criminality. Using these traits, he ranks Asians as superior, followed by Caucasians and people of African descent. Asians, Rushton claims, are the most intelligent, most sexually restrained, most altruistic, and least criminal of the races. Rushton ascribes a similar order to social classes: Those who are impoverished resemble African Americans; those who earn high incomes resemble Asians and Whites. Rushton's theory, according to his critics, is full of "familiar vulgar stereotypes" (Weizmann & others, 1990). His notions are stitched together with frequent misinterpretations and overgeneralizations about racial differences and evolutionary history, and the data are tailored to fit his bias. Regrettably, even flimsy theories such as Rushton's provide whole cloth for anyone intent on justifying racism.

Remember that, although race is primarily a *biological* concept, ethnicity is primarily a *sociocultural* concept (Brislin, 1993). In chapter 1, you read that cultural heritage, national characteristics, religion, language, *and* race constitute *ethnicity*. Race is just one component. However, the term *race* is often mistakenly used to refer to ethnicity. Jews, for example, are thought of as a race. Most are Caucasian, but they are too diverse to group into one racial subcategory. They also share too many anatomical similarities with other Caucasians to separate them as a distinct race (Thompson & Hughes, 1958). If we think of ethnicity predominantly in terms of social and cultural heritage, then Jews constitute an ethnic group.

Although we distinguish between race and ethnicity in this book, society usually does not. *Race* is commonly used in a much broader way than many sociocultural psychologists recommend (Brislin, 1993). Social psychologist James Jones (1993) points out that thinking in racial terms has become embedded in cultures as an

Race originated as a biological concept but has unfortunately taken on a number of negative social meanings. Ethnicity is a sociocultural concept.

important factor in human interactions. For example, people often consider what race they will associate with when they decide on such things as where to live, who will make a suitable spouse, where to go to school, and what kind of job they want. Similarly, people often use race to judge whether or not another person is intelligent, competent, responsible, or socially acceptable. Children tend to adopt their parents' attitudes about race as they grow up, often perpetuating stereotypes and prejudice.

HEREDITY

Every species must have a mechanism for transmitting characteristics from one generation to the next. This mechanism is explained by the principles of genetics. Each of us carries a genetic code that we inherited from our parents. This code is located within every cell in our bodies. Our genetic codes are alike in one important way—they all contain the human genetic code. Because of the human genetic code, a fertilized human egg cannot grow into an egret, eagle, or elephant.

What Are Genes?

Each of us began life as a single cell weighing about one twenty-millionth of an ounce! This tiny piece of matter housed our entire genetic code—information about who we would become. These instructions orchestrated growth from that single cell to a person made of trillions of cells, each containing a perfect replica of the original genetic code (Miller & Harley, 1996).

> *The turtle lives twixt plated decks*
> *Which practically conceal its sex.*
> *I think it clever of the turtle*
> *In such a fix to be so fertile.*
>
> —Ogden Nash

The nucleus of each human cell contains 46 **chromosomes,** *which are threadlike structures that come in 23 pairs, one member of each pair coming from each parent. Chromosomes contain the remarkable genetic substance deoxyribonucleic acid, or DNA.* **DNA** *is a complex molecule that contains genetic information.* DNA's "double helix" shape looks like a spiral staircase (see figure 3.2.) **Genes,** *the units of hereditary information, are short segments composed of DNA. Genes act as a blueprint for cells to reproduce themselves and manufacture the proteins that maintain life.* Chromosomes, DNA, and genes can be mysterious. To help you turn mystery into understanding, refer to figure 3.3.

Reproduction

Gametes *are human reproduction cells, which are created in the testes of males and the ovaries of females.* **Meiosis** *is the process of cell doubling and separation of chromosomes, with one member of each chromosomal pair going into each gamete,*

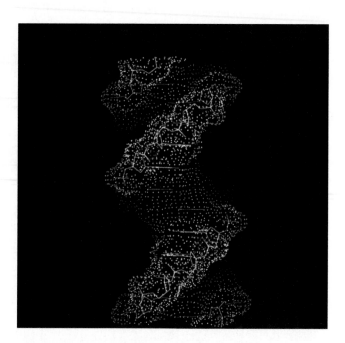

Figure~3.2

The Remarkable Substance Known as DNA
Genes are composed of DNA.

or daughter cell. Thus, each human gamete has 23 unpaired chromosomes. **Reproduction** *begins when a female gamete (ovum) is fertilized by a male gamete (sperm)* (see figure 3.4). A **zygote** *is a single cell formed through fertilization.* In the zygote, two sets of unpaired chromosomes combine to form one set of paired chromosomes—one member of each pair from the mother and the other member from the father. In this manner, each parent contributes 50 percent of the offspring's heredity.

Drawing by Ziegler, © 1985 the New Yorker Magazine, Inc.

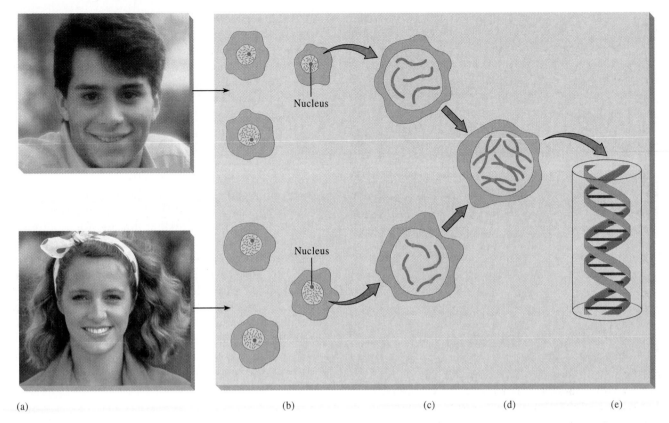

Figure~3.3

Facts About Chromosomes, DNA, and Genes

(a) The body contains billions of cells that are organized into tissue and organs. (b) Each cell contains a central structure, the nucleus, which controls reproduction. (c) Chromosomes reside in the nucleus of each cell. The male's sperm and the female's egg are specialized reproductive cells that contain chromosomes. (d) At conception the offspring receives matching chromosomes from the mother's egg and the father's sperm. (e) The chromosomes contain DNA, a chemical substance. Genes are short segments of the DNA molecule. They are the units of hereditary information that act as a blueprint for cells to reproduce themselves and manufacture the proteins that sustain life.

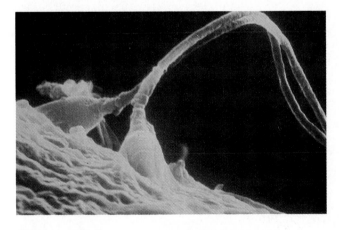

Figure~3.4

Union of Sperm and Egg

The ovum is about 90,000 times as large as a sperm. Thousands of sperm must combine to break down the ovum's membrane barrier to allow even a single sperm to penetrate the membrane barrier. Ordinarily, females have two X chromosomes and males have one X and one Y chromosome. Because the Y chromosome is smaller and lighter than the X chromosome, Y-bearing sperm can be separated from X-bearing sperm in a centrifuge. This raises the possibility that the offspring's sex can be controlled. Not only are the Y-bearing sperm lighter, but they are more likely than the X-bearing sperm to coat the ovum. This results in the conception of 120 to 150 males for every 100 females. But males are more likely to die (spontaneously abort) at every stage of prenatal development, so only about 106 are born for every 100 females.

Reproduction's fascinating moments have been made even more intriguing in recent years. **In vitro fertilization** *is conception outside the body.* Consider the following situation. The year is 1978. One of the most dazzling occurrences of the 1970s is about to unfold. Mrs. Brown is infertile, but her physician informs her of a new procedure that could enable her to have a baby. The procedure involves removing the mother's ovum surgically, fertilizing it in a laboratory medium with live sperm cells obtained from the father or another male donor

Figure~3.5

In Vitro Fertilization
Egg meets sperm in a laboratory dish.

(see figure 3.5), storing the fertilized egg in a laboratory solution that substitutes for the uterine environment, and finally implanting the egg in the mother's uterus. For Mrs. Brown, the procedure was successful, and 9 months later her daughter Louise was born.

Since the first in vitro fertilization in the 1970s, variations of the procedure have brought hope to childless couples. A woman's egg can be fertilized with the husband's sperm, or the husband and wife may contribute their sperm and egg, with the resulting embryo carried by a third party, who essentially is donating her womb.

Conception by means of the new reproductive technologies raises important questions about the psychological consequences for children. One recent study investigated the family relationships and socioemotional development of children in four types of families (Golombok & others, 1995). The two experimental groups were composed of families created by the most widely used reproductive technologies—in vitro fertilization and donor insemination; the two control groups were composed of families with a naturally conceived child and families with an adopted child. There were no differences between the four types of families on any of the measures of children's socioemotional development. The picture of the families created by the new reproductive technologies was a positive one.

It has been estimated that 10 to 15 percent of couples in the United States experience infertility, which is defined as the inability to conceive a child after 12 months of regular intercourse without contraception. The cause of infertility can rest with the woman or the man. The woman might not be ovulating, she might be producing abnormal ova, her fallopian tubes might be blocked, or she might have a disease that prevents implantation of the ova. The man might produce too few sperm, his sperm might lack motility (the ability to move adequately), or he might have a blocked passageway. In one study, longterm use of cocaine by men was related to low sperm count, low motility and a higher number of abnormally formed sperm (Bracken & others, 1990). Cocaine-related infertility appears to be reversible if users stop taking the drug for at least 1 year. In some cases of infertility, surgery might correct the problem; in others, hormonal-based drugs can improve the probability of having a child. However, in some instances fertility drugs have caused superovulation, producing as many as three or more babies at a time. A summary of some of infertility's causes and solutions in presented is table 3.1

While surgery and fertility drugs can solve the infertility problem in some cases, another choice is to adopt a child.

Adoption

Adoption is the social and legal process by which a parent-child relationship is established between a child and a person or persons who are not the child's biological parents. Researchers have found that many adopted children and adolescents show more psychological and school-related problems than nonadopted children

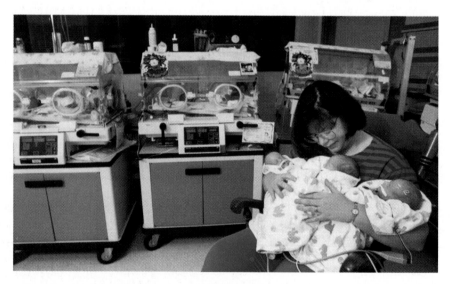

The arrival of six health babies—with the assistance of fertility technology— dramatically transformed the lives of Becky and Keith Dilley. The parents face extraordinary hardship and exhilaration, as their challenges of parenting are multiplied by six. To date, the Dilley babies continue to thrive. Not all families experiencing multiple births are so lucky. Sometimes babies born in multiple births show birth defects, and some do not survive. Thus, technological developments in childbirth have been the source of great hope and heartbreak.

TABLE 3.1

Fertility Problems and Solutions

Females

Problem	Solution
Damaged fallopian tubes	Surgery, in vitro fertilization
Abnormal ovulation	Hormone therapy, antibiotics, in vitro fertilization
Pelvic Inflammatory Disease (PID)	Antibiotics, surgery, change in birth control methods
Endometriosis*	Antibiotics, hormone therapy, surgery, artificial insemination
Damaged ovaries	Surgery, antibiotics, hormone therapy
Hostile cervical mucus	Antibiotics, artificial insemination, hormone therapy
Fibroid tumor	Surgery, antibiotics

Males

Problem	Solution
Low sperm count	Antibiotics, hormone therapy, artificial insemination, lowered testicular temperature
Dilated veins around testicle	Surgery, lowered testicular temperature, antibiotics
Damaged sperm ducts	Surgery, antibiotics
Hormone deficiency	Hormone therapy
Sperm antibodies	Antibiotics, in vitro fertilization

*Endometriosis occurs when the uterine lining grows outside of the uterus and causes bleeding, blocking, or scarring that can interfere with conception or pregnancy.
Source: Data from *The Fertility Solution*, 1991.

(Brodzinsky & others, 1984; Brodzinsky, Lang, & Smith, 1995). Adopted adolescents are referred for psychological treatment two to five times as often as their nonadopted peers (Grotevant & McRoy, 1990).

In one recent large-scale study of 4,682 adopted adolescents and the same number of nonadopted adolescents, adoptees showed somewhat poorer adjustments (Sharma, McGue, & Benson, 1996). However, adoptees showed higher levels of prosocial behavior. Also, the later the adoption occurred, the more problems the adoptees had. Infant adoptees had the fewest adjustment difficulties; those adopted after they were 10 years of age had the most. This result has policy implications, especially for the thousands of children who are relegated to the foster care system after infancy. Most often, adoptions of older children occur because of parental abuse or neglect, and parental rights are involuntarily terminated. This process can be lengthy. In the absence of other relatives, the children are turned over to the foster care system, where they must wait months or even years to be adopted. In the recent large-scale adoption study by Ann Sharma, Matthew McGue, and Peter Bensen (1996), increasingly negative effects occurred if a child was adopted after the age of 2; the effects were even more deleterious for children who were adopted after the age of 10.

A question that virtually every adoptive parent wants answered is "Should I tell my adopted child that he or she is adopted? If so, when?" Most psychologists believe that adopted children should be told that they are adopted, because they will eventually find out anyway. Many children begin to ask where they came from when they are approximately 4 to 6 years of age. This is a natural time to begin to respond in simple ways to children about their adopted status. Clinical psychologists report that one problem that sometimes surfaces is the desire of adoptive parents to make life too perfect for the adoptive child and to present a perfect image of themselves to the child. The result too often is that adopted children feel that they cannot release any angry feelings and openly discuss problems in this climate of perfection (Warshak, 1993). To think further about adoption, see Critical Thinking About Children's Development.

Abnormalities in Genes and Chromosomes

What are some abnormalities that can occur in genes and chromosomes? What tests can be used to determine the presence of these abnormalities?

Abnormalities

Geneticists and developmentalists have identified a range of problems caused by some major gene or chromosome defect (Holmes, 1992; Miller, 1992). **Phenylketonuria (PKU)** *is a genetic disorder in which the individual cannot properly metabolize an amino acid. Phenylketonuria is now easily detected, but if left untreated, mental retardation and hyperactivity result.* When detected, the disorder is treated by diet to prevent an excess accumulation of phenylalanine, an amino acid. Phenylketonuria involves a recessive gene and occurs about once in every 10,000 to 20,000 live births. Phenylketonuria accounts for about 1 percent of institutionalized mentally retarded individuals and it occurs primarily in Whites.

Down syndrome *is a common genetically transmitted form of mental retardation, caused by the presence of an extra (47th) chromosome.* An individual with Down syndrome has a round face, a flattened skull, an extra fold of skin over the eyelids, a protruding tongue, short limbs, and retardation of motor and mental abilities. It is not known why the extra chromosome is present, but the health of

Who Am I? Identity and Adoption

Most adoptive parents are given little information about the adopted child's birth parents or family history at the time of adoption. In turn, the birth parents are given little information about the adoptive parents (Brodzinsky & others, 1992). This strategy—followed by most adoption agencies—is thought to be in the best interest of both parties. A number of activist groups, such as the Adoptees Liberty Move-ment Association and Concerned United Birthmoth-ers, challenge this strategy. These groups stress that sealing records at the time of adoption violates peo-ple's basic right to know about themselves (and their offspring in the case of Concerned United Birth-mothers). They also argue that sealing records about a person's identity can set the stage for potential dif-ficulties related to the adoption experience.

Develop an argument that sealing records and giv-ing little information at the time of adoption is a wise strategy. Now argue the opposite side of this issue. By doing so, you are *creating arguments based on develop-mental concepts.*

the male sperm or female ovum may be involved (Vin-ing, 1992). Women between the ages of 18 and 38 are less likely to give birth to a Down syndrome child than are younger or older women. Down syndrome appears ap-proximately once in every 700 live births. African Amer-ican children are rarely born with Down syndrome.

Sickle-cell anemia, *which occurs most often in per-sons of African descent, is a genetic disorder affecting the red blood cells.* A red blood cell is usually shaped like a disk, but in sickle-cell anemia a change in a recessive gene modifies its shape to a hook-shaped "sickle." These cells die quickly, causing anemia and early death of the indi-vidual because of their failure to carry oxygen to the body's cells. About 1 in 400 African American babies is affected. One in 10 African Americans is a carrier, as is 1 in 20 Latinos (see figure 3.6).

(a)

(b)

Figure~3.6

Sickle-Cell Anemia
During a physical examination for a college football tryout, Jerry Hubbard, 32, learned that he carried the gene for sickle-cell anemia. Tami, 33, was also tested in college. Daughter Sara is healthy, but daughter Avery has sickle-cell anemia. The couple says that they won't try to have any more children. (*a*) The Hubbards—Jerry, Tami, Sara, and Avery. (*b*) Avery Hubbard, age 3. She is the first in a long line of carriers to develop the painful disease.

Other disorders are associated with sex-chromosome abnormalities. Remember that normal males have an X chromosome and a Y chromosome, and normal females have two X chromosomes. **Klinefelter syndrome** *is a genetic disorder in which males have an extra X chromosome, making them XXY instead of XY.* Males with this disorder have undeveloped testes, and they usually have enlarged breasts and become tall. Klinefelter syndrome occurs approximately once in every 800 live male births.

Turner syndrome *is a genetic disorder in which females are missing an X chromosome, making them XO instead of XX.* These females are short in stature and have a webbed neck. They may be mentally retarded and sexually underdeveloped. Turner syndrome occurs approximately once in every 3,000 live female births.

The **XYY syndrome** *is a genetic disorder in which the male has an extra Y chromosome. Early interest in this syndrome involved the belief that the Y chromosome found in males contributed to male aggression and violence.* It was then reasoned that if a male had an extra Y chromosome he would likely be extremely aggressive and possibly develop a violent personality. However, researchers subsequently found that XYY males were no more likely to commit crimes than were XY males (Witkin & others, 1976).

We have discussed six genetic disorders—phenylketonuria, Down syndrome, sickle-cell anemia, Klinefelter syndrome, Turner syndrome, and the XYY syndrome. A summary of these genetic disorders, as well as others, appears in table 3.2.

Each year in the United States, approximately 100,000 to 150,000 infants are born with a genetic disorder or malformation. These infants comprise about 3 to 5 percent of the 3 million births and account for at least 20 percent of infant deaths. Prospective parents increasingly are turning to genetic counseling for assistance, wanting to know their risk of having a child born with a genetic defect or malformation.

Tests to Determine Abnormalities

Scientists have developed a number of tests to determine whether the fetus is developing normally, among them amniocentesis, ultrasound sonography, the chorionic villus test, and the maternal blood test, each of which we discuss in turn.

Amniocentesis *is a prenatal medical procedure in which a sample of amniotic fluid is withdrawn by syringe and tested to discover if the fetus is suffering from any chromosomal or metabolic disorders. Amniocentesis is performed between the 12th and 16th weeks of pregnancy.* The later amniocentesis is performed, the better the diagnostic potential. The earlier it is performed, the more useful it is in deciding whether a pregnancy should be terminated (see figure 3.7).

Ultrasound sonography *is a prenatal medical procedure in which high-frequency sound waves are directed into*

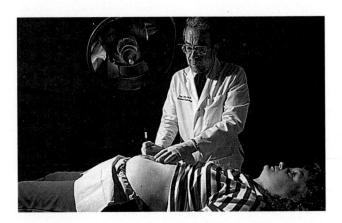

Figure~3.7

Amniocentesis Being Performed on a Pregnant Woman

the pregnant woman's abdomen. The echo from the sounds is transformed into a visual representation of the fetus's inner structures. This technique has been able to detect such disorders as microencephaly, a form of mental retardation involving an abnormally small brain. Ultrasound sonography is often used in conjunction with amniocentesis to determine the precise location of the fetus in the mother's abdomen (see figure 3.8).

As scientists have searched for more accurate, safe assessments of high-risk prenatal conditions, they have developed a new test. The **chorionic villus test** *is a prenatal medical procedure in which a small sample of the placenta is removed at some point between the 8th and 11th weeks of pregnancy.* Diagnosis takes approximately 10 days. The chorionic villus test allows a decision about abortion to be made near the end of the first trimester of pregnancy, a point when abortion is safer and less traumatic than after amniocentesis in the second trimester. These techniques provide valuable information about the presence of birth defects, but they also raise issues pertaining to whether an abortion should be obtained if birth defects are present.

The **maternal blood test** *(alpha-fetoprotein—AFP) is a prenatal diagnostic technique that is used to assess blood alphaprotein level, which is associated with neural-tube defects.* This test is administered to women 14 to 20 weeks into pregnancy only when they are at risk for bearing a child with defects in the formation of the brain and spinal cord.

So far in this chapter, we have discussed the evolutionary perspective, genes, chromosomes, reproduction, and abnormalities in genes and chromosomes. A summary of these ideas is outlined in concept table 3.1.

GENETIC PRINCIPLES AND METHODS

What are some basic genetic principles that affect children's development? What methods do behavior geneticists use

ABLE 3.2

Genetic Disorders and Conditions

Name	Description	Treatment	Incidence	Prenatal Detection	Carrier Detection
Anencephaly	Neural-tube disorder that causes brain and skull malformations; most children die at birth.	Surgery	1 in 1,000	Ultrasound, amniocentesis	None
Cystic fibrosis	Glandular dysfunction that interferes with mucus production; breathing and digestion are hampered, resulting in a shortened life span.	Physical and oxygen therapy, synthetic enzymes, and antibiotics	1 in 2,000	Amniocentesis	Family history, DNA analysis
Down syndrome	Extra or altered 21st chromosome causes mild to severe retardation and physical abnormalities.	Surgery, early intervention, infant stimulation, and special learning programs	1 in 800 women; 1 in 350 women over 35	AFP, CVS, amniocentesis	Family history, chromosomal analysis
Hemophilia	Lack of the clotting factor causes excessive internal and external bleeding.	Blood transfusions and/or injections of the clotting factor	1 in 10,000 males	CVS, amniocentesis	Family history, DNA analysis
Klinefelter syndrome	An extra X chromosome causes physical abnormalities.	Hormone therapy	1 in 800 males	CVS, amniocentesis	None
Phenylketonuria (PKU)	Metabolic disorder that, left untreated, causes mental retardation.	Special diet	1 in 14,000	CVS, amniocentesis	Family history, blood test
Pyloric stenosis	Excess muscle in upper intestine causes severe vomiting and death if not treated.	Surgery	1 male in 200; 1 female in 1,000	None	None
Sickle-cell anemia	Blood disorder that limits the body's oxygen supply. It can cause joint swelling, sickle-cell crises, heart and kidney failure.	Penicillin, medication for pain, antibiotics, and blood transfusions	1 in 400 Black children (lower among other groups)	CVS, amniocentesis	Blood test
Spina bifida	Neural tube disorder that causes brain and spine abnormalities.	Corrective surgery at birth, orthopedic devices, and physical/medical therapy	2 in 1,000	AFP, ultrasound, amniocentesis	None
Tay-Sachs disease	Deceleration of mental and physical development caused by an accumulation of lipids in the nervous system; few children live to age 5.	Medication and special diet	1 in 30 American Jews is a carrier	CVS, amniocentesis	Blood test
Thalassemia	Group of inherited blood disorders that causes anemic symptoms ranging from fatigue and weakness to liver failure.	Blood transfusions and antibiotics	1 in 400 children of Mediterranean descent	CVS, amniocentesis	Blood test
Turner syndrome	A missing or altered X chromosome may cause mental retardation and/or physical abnormalities.	Hormone therapy	1 in 3,000 females	None	Blood test

Santrock: Child Development

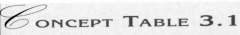

CONCEPT TABLE 3.1

The Evolutionary Perspective and Heredity

Concept	Processes/ Related Ideas	Characteristics/Description
The Evolutionary Perspective	Natural selection and adaptive behavior	Natural selection is the process that favors individuals of a species that are best adapted to survive and produce. This concept was originally proposed by Charles Darwin. Adaptive behavior is behavior that promotes the organism's behavior in its natural habitat. Although no dramatic evolutionary changes have occurred since *Homo sapiens* appeared on the fossil record 50,000 years ago, there have been sweeping cultural changes. Biological evolution shaped human beings into a culture-making species.
	Sociobiology	This approach relies on the principles of evolutionary biology to explain the social behavior of animals. Sociobiology's purpose is to develop general laws of the evolution and biology of social behavior. The hope also is that sociobiology can assist in the explanation of human behavior. Sociobiology has made important contributions to the understanding of social behavior.
	Evolutionary psychology	A contemporary approach that emphasizes that behavior is a function of mechanisms, requires input for activation, and is ultimately related to successful survival and reproduction. Psychological mechanisms are the product of evolution. The central issue for evolutionary psychologists is the nature of the psychological mechanisms created by natural selection and the adaptive functions they serve. Evolutionary psychologists believe that human psychological mechanisms are domain-specific, or modular. Evolutionary psychology can be applied to developmental psychology. Evolutionary psychologists believe their approach provides a much needed integration of psychology's disparate areas, although criticisms of the approach have been made.
	Race and ethnicity	Race is a biological concept; ethnicity is a sociocultural concept. The concept of race has taken on a number of social meanings, some of which have resulted in discrimination and prejudice. Race continues to be a misunderstood and abused concept.
Heredity	What are genes?	The nucleus of each human cell contains 46 chromosomes, which are composed of DNA. Genes are short segments of DNA and act as a blueprint for cells to reproduce and manufacture proteins that maintain life.
	Reproduction	Genes are transmitted from parents to offspring by gametes, or sex cells. Gametes are formed by the splitting of cells, a process called meiosis. Reproduction takes place when a female gamete (ovum) is fertilized by a male gamete (sperm) to create a single-celled ovum. In vitro fertilization has helped solve some infertility problems. Approximately 10 to 15 percent of couples in the United States experience infertility problems, some of which can be corrected through surgery or fertility drugs. Another choice for infertile couples is adoption.
	Adoption	Adopted children and adolescents have more problems than their nonadopted counterparts. When adoption occurs after the age of 10, it has more negative effects than when it happens in infancy.
	Abnormalities in genes and chromosomes	A range of problems is caused by major gene or chromosome defects, among them PKU, Down syndrome, sickle-cell anemia, Klinefelter syndrome, Turner syndrome, and the XYY syndrome. Genetic counseling has increased in popularity as couples desire information about their risk of having a defective child. Amniocentesis, ultrasound sonography, the chorionic villus test, and the maternal blood test are used to determine the presence of defects after pregnancy has begun.

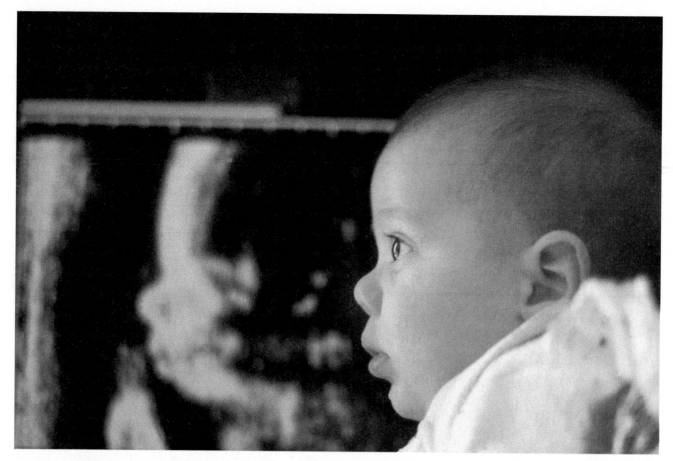

Figure~3.8

Ultrasound Sonography
A 6-month-old infant poses with the ultrasound sonography record taken 4 months into the baby's prenatal development.

to study heredity's influence? How does heredity influence such aspects of children's development as their intelligence? And how do heredity and environment interact to produce children's development?

Some Genetic Principles

Genetic determination is a complex affair, and much is unknown about the way genes work (Tamarin, 1996). But a number of genetic principles have been discovered, among them those of dominant-recessive genes, sex-linked genes, polygenically inherited characteristics, reaction range, and canalization.

According to the **dominant-recessive genes principle,** *if one gene of the pair is dominant and one is recessive, the dominant gene exerts its effect, overriding the potential influence of the recessive gene. A recessive gene exerts its influence only if the two genes of a pair are both recessive.* If you inherit a recessive gene for a trait from each of your parents, you will show the trait. If you inherit a recessive gene from only one parent, you may never know you carry the gene. Brown eyes, farsightedness, and dimples rule over blue eyes, nearsightedness, and freckles in the world of dominant-recessive genes. Can two brown-

eyed parents have a blue-eyed child? Yes. Suppose that in each parent the gene pair that governs eye color includes a dominant gene for brown eyes and a recessive gene for blue eyes. Since dominant genes override recessive genes, the parents have brown eyes. But both are carriers of blueness and pass on their recessive genes for blue eyes. With no dominant gene to override them, the recessive genes can make the child's eyes blue. Figure 3.9 illustrates the dominant-recessive genes principle.

For thousands of years, people wondered what determined whether we become male or female. Aristotle believed that the father's arousal during intercourse determined the offspring's sex. The more excited the father was, the more likely it would be a son, he reasoned. Of course, he was wrong, but it was not until the 1920s that researchers confirmed the existence of human sex chromosomes, 2 of the 46 chromosomes human beings normally carry. As we saw earlier, ordinarily females have two X chromosomes and males have an X and a Y. (Figure 3.10 shows the chromosome makeup of a male and a female.)

Genetic transmission is usually more complex than the simple examples we have examined thus far

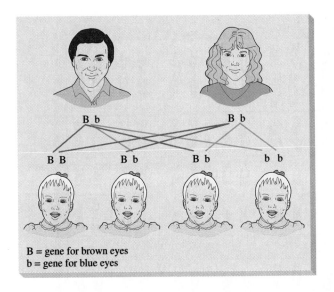

Figure~3.9

How Brown-Eyed Parents Can Have a Blue-Eyed Child
Although both parents have brown eyes, each parent can have a recessive gene for blue eyes. In this example both parents have brown eyes, but each parent carries the recessive gene for blue eyes. Therefore, the odds of their child having blue eyes is one in four—the probability the child will receive a recessive gene (b) from each parent.

(Weaver & Hedrick, 1996). **Polygenic inheritance** *is a genetic principle that the effects of many genes combine to produce a particular characteristic.* Few psychological characteristics are the result of single pairs. Most are determined by the interaction of many different genes. There are as many as 50,000 or more genes, so you can imagine that the possible combinations of these are staggering in number. Traits produced by this mixing of genes are said to be polygenically determined.

No one possesses all the characteristics that our genetic structure makes possible. **Genotype** *is the person's genetic heritage, the actual genetic material.* However, not all of this genetic material is apparent in our observed and measurable characteristics. **Phenotype** *is the way an individual's genotype is expressed in observed and measurable characteristics.* Phenotypes include physical traits (such as height, weight, eye color, and skin pigmentation) and psychological characteristics (such as intelligence, creativity, personality, and social tendencies).

> *That which comes of a cat will catch mice.*
>
> **—English proverb**

For each genotype, a range of phenotypes can be expressed. Imagine that we could identify all of the genes that would make a person introverted or extraverted. Would measured introversion-extraversion be predictable from knowledge of the specific genes? The answer is no, because even if our genetic model were adequate, introversion-extraversion is a characteristic shaped by experience throughout life. For example, parents may push an introverted child into social situations and encourage the child to become more gregarious.

To understand how introverted a person is, think about a series of genetic codes that predispose the child to develop in a particular way, and imagine environments that are responsive or unresponsive to this development. For instance, the genotype of some persons may predispose them to be introverted in an environment that promotes a turning inward of personality, yet in an environment that encourages social interaction and outgoingness, these individuals may become more extraverted. However, it would be unlikely for the individual with this introverted genotype to become a strong extravert. The term **reaction range** *is used to describe the range of possible phenotypes for each genotype, suggesting the importance of an environment's restrictiveness or enrichment* (see figure 3.11).

Sandra Scarr (1984) explains reaction range this way: Each of us has a range of potential. For example, an individual with "medium-tall" genes for height who grows up in a poor environment may be shorter than average. But in an excellent nutritional environment, the individual may grow up taller than average. However, no matter how well fed the person is, someone with "short" genes will never be taller than average. Scarr believes that characteristics such as intelligence and introversion work the same way. That is, there is a range within which the environment can modify intelligence, but intelligence is not completely malleable. Reaction range gives us an estimate of how modifiable intelligence is.

Figure~3.10

The Genetic Difference Between Males and Females
Set (a) shows the chromosome structure of a male, and set (b) shows the chromosome structure of a female. The last pair of 23 pairs of chromosomes is in the bottom right box of each set. Notice that the Y chromosome of the male is smaller than the X chromosome of the female. To obtain this kind of chromosomal picture, a cell is removed from a person's body, usually from the inside of the mouth. The chromosomes are stained by chemical treatment, magnified extensively, and then photographed.

Genotypes, in addition to producing many phenotypes, may show the opposite track for some characteristics—those that are somewhat immune to extensive changes in the environment. These characteristics seem to stay on a particular developmental course regardless of the environmental assaults on them (Waddington, 1957). **Canalization** *is the term chosen to describe the narrow path, or developmental course, that certain characteristics take. Apparently, preservative forces help to protect or buffer a person from environmental extremes.* For example, American developmental psychologist Jerome Kagan (1984) points to his research on Guatemalan infants who had experienced extreme malnutrition as infants yet showed normal social and cognitive development later in childhood. And some abused children do not grow up to be abusers themselves.

However, it is important to recognize that while the genetic influence of canalization exerts its power by keeping organisms on a particular developmental path, genes alone do not directly determine human behavior (Gottlieb, Wahlsten, & Lickliter, 1997). Developmentalist Gilbert Gottlieb (1991a) points out that genes are an integral part of the organism, but that their activity (genetic expression) can be affected by the organism's environment. For example, hormones that circulate in the blood make their way into the cell, where they influence the cell's activity. The flow of hormones themselves can be affected by environmental events such as light, day length, nutrition, and behavior.

Methods Used by Behavior Geneticists

Behavior genetics *is the study of the degree and nature of behavior's hereditary basis.* Behavior geneticists assume that behaviors are jointly determined by the interaction

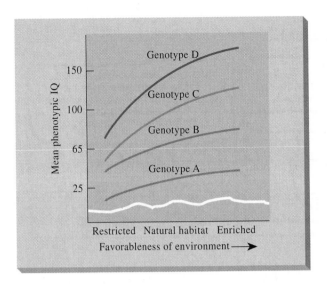

Figure~3.11

Responsiveness of Genotypes to Environmental Influences
Although each genotype responds favorably to improved
environments, some are more responsive than others to
environmental deprivation and enrichment.

Identical twins develop from a single fertilized egg that splits
into two genetically identical organisms. Twin studies
compare identical twins with fraternal twins. Fraternal twins
develop from separate fertilized eggs, making them genetically
no more similar than ordinary sisters and brothers.

of heredity and environment (Plomin & others, 1997).
To study heredity's influence on behavior, behavior
geneticists often use either twin studies or adoption studies (O'Conner, 1997; Silberg, & Rutter, 1997).

In a **twin study,** *the behavioral similarity of identical
twins is compared with the behavioral similarity of fraternal
twins.* **Identical twins** *(called monozygotic twins) develop
from a single fertilized egg that splits into two genetically identical replicas, each of which becomes a person.* **Fraternal
twins** *(called dizygotic twins) develop from separate eggs and
separate sperm, making them genetically no more similar than
ordinary siblings.* Although fraternal twins share the same
womb, they are no more alike genetically than are non-
twin brothers and sisters, and they may be of different
sexes (Scarr, 1996). By comparing groups of identical and
fraternal twins, behavior geneticists capitalize on the basic
knowledge that identical twins are more similar genetically than are fraternal twins. In one twin study, 7,000
pairs of Finnish identical and fraternal twins were compared on the personality traits of extraversion (outgoingness) and neuroticism (psychological instability) (Rose
& others, 1988). On both of these personality traits, identical twins were much more similar than fraternal twins,
suggesting the role of heredity in both traits. However,
several issues crop up as a result of twin studies. Adults
might stress the similarities of identical twins more than
those of fraternal twins, and identical twins might perceive themselves as a "set" and play together more than
fraternal twins do. If so, observed similarities in identical twins could be environmentally influenced.

In an **adoption study,** *investigators seek to discover
whether, in behavior and psychological characteristics, adopted
children are more like their adoptive parents, who provided a*
*home environment, or more like their biological parents,
who contributed their heredity. Another form of the adoption
study is to compare adoptive and biological siblings.* In one
investigation, the educational levels attained by biological parents were better predictors of adopted children's
IQ scores than were the IQs of the children's adopted parents (Scarr & Weinberg, 1983). Because of the genetic
relation between the adopted children and their biological parents, the implication is that heredity influences
children's IQ scores.

Heredity's Influence on Development

What aspects of development are influenced by genetic factors? They all are. However, behavior geneticists are interested in more precise estimates of a characteristic's
variation than can be accounted for by genetic factors. Intelligence and temperament are among the most widely investigated aspects of heredity's influence on development.

Arthur Jensen (1969) sparked a lively and, at times,
hostile debate when he presented his thesis that intelligence is primarily inherited. Jensen believes that environment and culture play only a minimal role in
intelligence. He examined several studies of intelligence,
some of which involved comparisons of identical and

THE WIZARD OF ID

By permission of Johnny Hart and Creators Syndicate, Inc.

fraternal twins. Remember that identical twins have identical genetic endowments, so their IQs should be similar. Fraternal twins and ordinary siblings are less similar genetically, so their IQs should be less similar. Jensen found support for his argument in these studies. Studies with identical twins produced an average correlation of .82; studies with ordinary siblings produced an average correlation of .50. Note the difference of .32. To show that genetic factors are more important than environmental factors, Jensen compared identical twins reared together with those reared apart; the correlation for those reared together was .89 and for those reared apart was .78 (a difference of .11). Jensen argued that, if environmental influences were more important than genetic influences, then siblings reared apart, who experienced different environments, should have IQs much farther apart.

Many scholars have criticized Jensen's work. One criticism concerns the definition of intelligence itself. Jensen believes that IQ as measured by standardized intelligence tests is a good indicator of intelligence. Critics argue that IQ tests tap only a narrow range of intelligence. Everyday problem solving, work, and social adaptability, say the critics, are important aspects of intelligence not measured by the traditional intelligence tests used in Jensen's sources. A second criticism is that most investigations of heredity and environment do not include environments that differ radically. Thus, it is not surprising that many genetic studies show environment to be a fairly weak influence on intelligence.

Intelligence is influenced by heredity, but most developmentalists have not found as strong a relationship as Jensen found in his work. Other experts estimate heredity's influence on intelligence to be in the 50 percent range (Plomin, DeFries, & McClearn, 1990). Jensen is such a strong advocate of genetic influence that he believes we can breed for intelligence.

The most recent controversy about heredity and intelligence focuses on the book *The Bell Curve: Intelligence and Class Structure in Modern Life,* in which Richard Hernstein and Charles Murray (1994) argue that America is rapidly evolving a huge underclass of intellectually deprived individuals whose cognitive abilities will never match the future needs of most employers. The authors believe that this underclass, a large proportion of which is African American, might be doomed by their shortcomings to welfare dependency, poverty, crime, and lives void of any hope of ever reaching the American dream.

Hernstein and Murray believe that IQ can be quantitatively measured and that IQ test scores vary across ethnic groups. They point out that in the United States, Asian Americans score several points higher than Whites, while African Americans score about 15 points lower than Whites. They also argue that these IQ differences are at least partly due to heredity. The authors say that government money spent on education programs such as Project Head Start is wasted, helping only the government's bloated bureaucracy.

Why do Hernstein and Murray call their book *The Bell Curve?* A bell curve is the shape of a normal distribution graph (see figure 3.12). The normal distribution graph, like a bell, bulges in the middle and thins out at the edges. This graph is used to represent large numbers of people who are sorted according to some shared characteristic, such as weight, exposure to asbestos, taste in clothing, or IQ.

Hernstein and Murray often refer to bell curves to make a point: that predictions about any individual based exclusively on the person's IQ are virtually useless. Weak correlations between intelligence and job success have predictive values only when they are applied to large groups of people. Within such large groups, say Hernstein and Murray, the pervasive influence of IQ on human society becomes apparent (Browne, 1994).

Santrock: Child Development

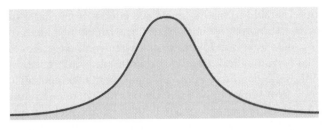

Figure~3.12

The Bell Curve
The term *bell curve* is used to describe a normal distribution graph, which looks like a bell—bulging in the middle and thinning out at the edges.

As with Jensen's work, significant criticisms have been leveled at *The Bell Curve*. Experts on intelligence generally agree that African Americans score lower than Whites on IQ tests. However, many of these experts raise serious questions about the ability of IQ tests to accurately measure a person's intelligence. Among the criticisms of IQ tests is that the tests are culturally biased against African Americans and Latinos. In 1971, the U.S. Supreme Court endorsed such criticisms and ruled that tests of general intelligence, in contrast to tests that solely measure fitness for a particular job, are discriminatory and cannot be administered as a condition of employment. Another criticism is that most investigations of heredity and environment do not include environments that differ radically, so it is not surprising that many genetic studies show environment to be a fairly weak influence on intelligence (Fraser, 1995). Cognitive psychologist Robert J. Sternberg (1994) said that using one index—IQ—for a basis of policy judgment is not only irresponsible but also dangerous.

HEREDITY-ENVIRONMENT INTERACTION AND CHILDREN'S DEVELOPMENT

A common misconception is that behavior geneticists only analyze the effects of heredity on development. While they believe heredity plays an important role in children's development, they also carve up the environment's contribution to heredity-environment interaction.

Genotype → Environment Concepts

Parents not only provide the genes for the child's biological blueprint for development, but they also play important roles in determining the types of environments their children will encounter. Behavior geneticist Sandra Scarr (1993) believes that the environments parents select for their children depend to some degree on the parents' own genotypes. Three ways behavior geneticists believe heredity and environment interact in this manner are passively, evocatively, and actively.

Passive genotype-environment interactions occur *when the biological parents, who are genetically related to the child, provide a rearing environment for the child.* For example, parents may have a genetic predisposition to be intelligent and read skillfully. Because they read well and enjoy reading, they provide their child with books to read, with the likely outcome that their children will become skilled readers who enjoy reading.

Evocative genotype-environment interactions occur *because a child's genotype elicits certain types of physical and social environments.* For example, active, smiling babies receive more social stimulation than passive, quiet babies do. Cooperative, attentive children evoke more pleasant and instructional responses from the adults around them than uncooperative, distractible children do.

Active (niche-picking) genotype-environment interactions occur *when children seek out environments they find compatible and stimulating. Niche-picking refers to finding a niche or setting that is especially suited to the child's abilities.* Children select from their surrounding environment some aspects that they respond to, learn about, or ignore. Their active selections of certain environments are related to their particular genotype. Some children, because of their genotype, have the sensorimotor skills to perform well at sports. Others, because of their genotype, may have more ability in music. Children who are athletically inclined are more likely to actively seek out sports environments in which they can perform well, while children who are musically inclined are more likely to spend time in musical environments in which they can successfully perform their skills.

Scarr (1993) believes that the relative importance of the three genotype-environment interactions changes as children develop from infancy through adolescence. In infancy, much of the environment that children experience is provided by adults. When those adults are genetically related to the child, the environment they provide is related to their own characteristics and genotypes. Although infants are active in structuring their experiences by actively attending to what is available to them, they cannot seek out and build their own environmental niches as much as older children can. Therefore, passive genotype-environment interactions are more common in the lives of infants and young children than they are for older children, who can extend their experiences beyond the family's influences and create their environments to a greater degree.

Shared and Nonshared Environmental Influences

Behavior geneticists also believe that another way the environment's role in heredity-environment interaction can be carved up is to consider the experiences that children in families have that are in common with other children living in the same home and those that are not common or shared. Behavior geneticist Robert Plomin

Sandra Scarr has developed a number of important theoretical ideas and conducted a number of research investigations on the roles of heredity and environment in children's development. She believes that the environments parents select for their children depend to some degree on the parents' own genotype. Critics argue that the environment plays a stronger role in children's development than Scarr acknowledges.

(1993) has found that common rearing, or shared environment, accounts for little of the variation in children's personality or interests. In other words, even though two children live under the same roof with the same parents, their personalities are often very different.

Shared environmental experiences *are children's common experiences, such as their parents' personalities and intellectual orientation, the family's social class, and the neighborhood in which they live.* By contrast, **nonshared environmental experiences** *are a child's own unique experiences, both within the family and outside the family, that are not shared with another sibling. Thus, experiences occurring within the family can be part of the "nonshared environment."* Parents often do interact differently with each sibling, and siblings interact differently with parents. Siblings often have different peer groups, different friends, and different teachers at school.

The Contemporary Heredity-Environment Controversy

As we have seen, Sandra Scarr (1993, 1996) believes that heredity plays a powerful role in children's development. Her theory of genotype → environment effects essentially states that genotypes drive experiences. Scarr also stresses that unless a child's family is specifically abusive or fails to provide what she calls "average expectable" conditions (conditions like those in which the species has evolved), parental differences in child-rearing styles, social class, and income have only small effects on differences in children's intelligence, personality, and interests. Scarr also has presented the provocative view that biology makes non-at-risk infants

invulnerable to lasting, negative effects of day care. In sum, Scarr stresses that, except in extreme instances of abused and at-risk children, environmental experiences play a minimal role, if any, in determining differences in children's cognitive and socioemotional development.

Not surprisingly, Scarr's beliefs have generated considerable controversy in the field of child development. Among Scarr's critics, Diana Baumrind (1993), Eleanor Maccoby (1992), and Jacquelyne Jackson (1993) point to a number of loopholes in her arguments. They conclude that Scarr has not adequately defined just what an "average expectable" environment is, that good parenting optimizes both normal and vulnerable children's development, and that Scarr's interpretations of behavior genetics studies go far beyond what is justified, given the inherent limitations of such studies.

Scarr (1993) responds to such criticisms by arguing that understanding children's development requires describing it under the umbrella of evolutionary theory and that many developmentalists do not give adequate attention to the important role that biology plays in children's development. She, like other biology-oriented theorists (Goldsmith, 1994), feels that her critics often misinterpret what she says. Scarr claims that social reformers oppose her ideas because they believe that these ideas cause pessimism about social change. She responds that she is simply motivated to discover the facts about the roles of genes and environment in determining human development. According to Scarr, all children should have an opportunity to become species-normal, culturally appropriate, and uniquely themselves—their own versions of Georgia O'Keefe and Martin Luther King; many children in today's world lack those opportunities, and their needs should be addressed. However, she concludes that humanitarian concerns should not drive developmental theory and that developmental theory must have a strong biological orientation to be accurate.

Virtually all developmentalists today are interactionists in that they believe heredity and environment interact to determine children's development (George, 1996; Kendler, 1996; Plomin, 1996). However, Scarr argues that heredity plays a powerful role in heredity-environment interaction, while Baumrind, Maccoby, and Jackson believe the environment is a much stronger influence on children's development than Scarr acknowledges. To read more about the roles of heredity and environment, turn to Critical Thinking About Children's Development.

In sum, both genes and environment are necessary for a child to even exist. Heredity and environment operate together—or cooperate—to produce a child's intelligence, temperament, height, weight, ability to pitch a baseball, reading talents, and so on (Gottlieb, 1997; Plomin & others, 1997). Without genes, there is no child; without environment, there is no child (Scarr & Weinberg, 1980). If an attractive, popular, intelligent

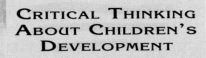

CRITICAL THINKING ABOUT CHILDREN'S DEVELOPMENT

Heredity, Environment, and You

We have concluded that every individual's development is influenced by both heredity and environment. Think about your own development for a moment—some of your most important characteristics, like your temperament, personality, and intelligence. Now think about your mother's and your father's temperament, personality, and intelligence. For example, is your mother very bright, and are you also? Is your father introverted but you are sociable? How closely do you match up with your mother's and your father's characteristics? Evaluate the extent to which you believe you inherited these characteristics or developed them through your experiences with your environment. Remember, chances are that both heredity and environment contributed to who you are today and who you were as an adolescent. And remember that determining heredity's and the environment's contributions in a scientific manner is an extremely complex undertaking. Your ability to come up with characteristics you share with one or both of your parents helps you to understand your similarities to your parents, but this does not tell you whether the characteristics are due to heredity or to environment. By thinking about heredity and environmental contributions to your own temperament, personality, and intelligence, you are learning to think critically about adolescence by *creating arguments based on developmental concepts.*

girl is elected president of her senior class in high school, should we conclude that her success is due to heredity? or to environment? Of course, the answer is both. Because the environment's influence depends on genetically endowed characteristics, we say the two factors *interact* (Mader, 1996).

A summary of the main ideas in our discussion of genetic principles and methods, heredity's influence on children's development, and how heredity and environment interact to produce development is presented in concept table 3.2.

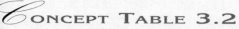

CONCEPT TABLE 3.2

Genetic Principles and Methods, Heredity's Influence, and Heredity-Environment Interaction and Children's Development

Concept	Processes/ Related Ideas	Characteristics/Description
Genetic Principles and Methods	Genetic principles	Genetic transmission is complex, but some principles have been worked out, among them, those of dominant-recessive genes, sex-linked genes, polygenic inheritance, genotype-phenotype distinction, reaction range, and canalization.
	Methods used by behavior geneticists	Behavior genetics is the field concerned with the degree and nature of behavior's hereditary basis. Among the most important methods used by behavior geneticists are twin studies and adoption studies
Heredity's Influence on Development	Its scope	All aspects of development are influenced by heredity.
	Intelligence	Jensen, and Hernstein and Murray, argue that intelligence is due primarily to heredity. This has sparked a lively, and at times bitter, debate. Intelligence is influenced by heredity, but not as strongly as Jensen, and Hernstein and Murray, envisioned.
Heredity-Environment Interaction and Children's Development	Genotype → environment concepts	Scarr believes that the environments parents select for their own children depend to some degree on the parents' genotypes. Three ways behavior geneticists believe heredity and environment interact in this manner are passively, evocatively, and actively. Passive genotype-environment interactions occur when parents, who are genetically related to the child, provide a rearing environment for the child. Evocative genotype-environment interactions occur because a child's genotype elicits certain types of physical and social environments. Active (niche-picking) genotype-environment interactions occur when children seek out environments they find compatible and stimulating. Scarr believes the relative importance of these three forms of genotype-environment interactions changes as children develop.
	Shared and nonshared environments	Shared environmental experiences are children's common experiences, such as their parents' personalities and intellectual orientation, the family's social class, and the neighborhood in which they live. Nonshared environmental experiences are the child's own unique experiences, both within a family and outside the family, that are not shared by another sibling. Plomin argues that it is nonshared environmental experiences that primarily make up the environment's contribution to why one sibling's personality is different from another's.
	The contemporary heredity-environment controversy	Scarr's genotype → environment theory has generated considerable controversy. She argues that except in extreme abusive and at-risk conditions, the environment plays a minimal role in determining differences in children's cognitive and socioemotional development. A number of criticisms of her view have been offered. In sum, without genes, there is no organism; without environment, there is no organism. Because the environment's influence depends on genetically endowed characteristics, we say that the two factors interact.

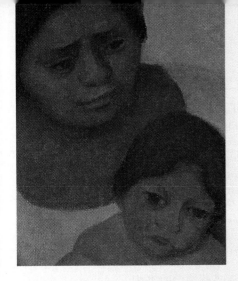

SUMMARY

Biological beginnings raise questions of how we as a species came to be, how parents' genes are shuffled to produce a particular child, and how much experience can go against the grain of heredity.

In this chapter, we studied the Jim and Jim twins; the evolutionary perspective, in which we discussed natural selection and adaptive behavior, sociobiology, evolutionary psychology, and race and ethnicity; the nature of heredity; what genes are; how reproduction takes place; adoption; some abnormalities in genes and chromosomes; genetic principles; methods used by behavior geneticists; heredity's influence on development; and what heredity-environment interaction is like. With regard to heredity-environment interaction, behavior geneticists believe that it is important to consider passive genotype-environment, evocative genotype-environment, and active genotype-environment interactions, as well as shared and nonshared environmental experiences. Scarr's biological view has recently generated considerable controversy.

Remember that you can obtain a summary of the main ideas in the entire chapter by again studying the two concept tables on pages 89 and 98. In the next chapter, we will continue our exploration of children's biological beginnings by discussing the dramatic unfolding of prenatal development.

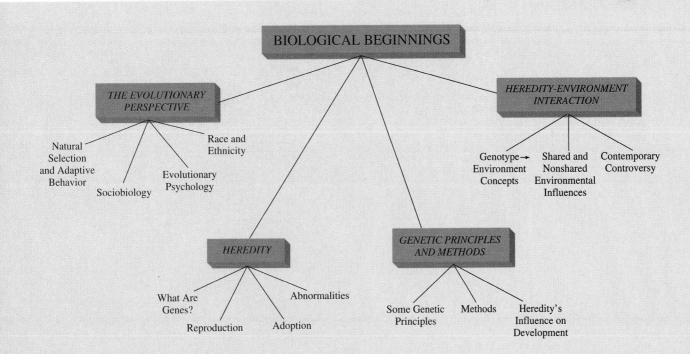

PRACTICAL KNOWLEDGE ABOUT CHILDREN

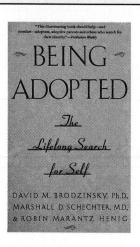

Being Adopted
(1992) by David Brodzinsky, Marshall Schechter, and Robin Henig, New York: Doubleday.

This book provides an excellent overview of how adoption influences people's lives throughout the human life span and includes a discussion of how adoption ties in with Erikson's stages of the human life cycle. The authors bring together a wide body of information to address the special hurdles that adoptees and adopters must manage. Adoptees, adoptive parents, professionals, and other interested individuals will find the book to be a rich source of information.

Prenatal Tests

(1988) by Robin J.R. Blatt,
New York: Vintage Books.

Prenatal Tests is a comprehensive guide to what prenatal tests are available, their benefits and risks, and how to decide whether to have them. The author challenges women to consider the pros and cons of various screening procedures during pregnancy. Pregnant women are encouraged to avoid the conveyor belt of routine care and make their own, informed decisions. The book also provides valuable information for the partners of pregnant women, addressing the emotional and ethical aspects of decision making that couples face when considering prenatal testing.

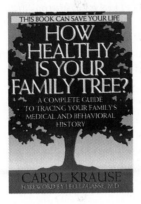

How Healthy Is Your Family Tree?

(1995) by Carol Krause,
New York: Simon & Schuster.

In this book, you will learn how to create a family medical tree. The author asks you to find out how any of your relatives died, how old they were when they died, what illnesses, health conditions, or surgeries they had had, what the exact diagnoses were, whether the person smoked, drank excessively, or took drugs, whether there was a history of mental disorders, and other information. She also suggests that once you put together a medical family tree, a specialist or genetic counselor can help you understand it.

*E*XPLORATIONS IN CHILD DEVELOPMENT

To further explore the nature of child development, we will examine a research study on whether the new reproductive technologies of in vitro fertilization and donor insemination have any negative effects on children's development, and we will discuss the nature of genetic counseling.

In this endpiece in chapters 1 and 2, we described the importance of research in advancing our knowledge about child development and the nature of journals that publish research about child development. Beginning with this chapter, the research endpieces will describe an actual research study related to the chapter's content to give you a sense of how the research process works.

In our minisimulations of journal articles, the abstracts will be omitted, and usually the results and discussion sections will be combined. In most journal articles, the results and discussion sections are presented separately. Actual journal articles are also much longer and far more detailed than our presentation. Nonetheless, the minisimulations should give you a better feel for how research in child development is conducted.

*R*ESEARCH IN CHILD DEVELOPMENT

The New Reproductive Technologies, Parenting, and Children's Development

Featured Study

Golombok, S., Cook, R., Bish, A., & Murray, C. (1995). Families created by the new reproductive technologies: Quality of parenting and social and emotional development of the children. *Child Development,* 66, 285–298.

Conception by means of the new reproductive technologies has raised important questions about the psychological consequences for children, especially when gamete donation has been used in the child's conception. It has been suggested that the missing genetic link between the child and the nongenetic parent might pose a threat to the relationship between the nongenetic parent and the child. More specifically, it has been argued that the secrecy surrounding donor insemination and egg donation can undermine family relationships, and that children conceived by gamete donation might feel confused about their identity. These children might also

feel deceived by their parents if they eventually discover the facts about their conception. The majority of children conceived by gamete donation are not told about their origins. The aim of the present study was to examine the quality of parent-child relationships and socioemotional development of children in families created by the new reproductive technologies.

Method

Forty-one families with a child conceived by in vitro fertilization and 45 families with a child conceived by donor insemination (where the child was genetically related to the mother but not to the father) were recruited through infertility clinics throughout Britain. Two control groups were also studied: 43 families with a naturally conceived child and 55 families with a child adopted at birth. These were recruited through the records of maternity wards and adoption agencies, respectively.

The parents were interviewed about their marital relationship and given measures to assess their psychiatric state; these measures included the widely used Beck Depression Inventory and Trait Anxiety Scale. The

quality of parenting was assessed with a tape-recorded maternal interview, which assessed such factors as how the parents handled problems the child displayed, pay activities, and issues related to control. A Parenting Stress Index also was filled out by both the mother and the father. The child's behavior was assessed through a maternal interview with a special focus on any problems shown by the child. The children were given the Separation Anxiety Test, which indexes secure and insecure attachment. A version of the Family Relations Test, which evaluates the child's feelings about his or her parents, was also given to the children. Each child was also administered the Pictorial Scale of Perceived Competence and Social Acceptance for Young Children, which provides scores of cognitive competence, physical competence, maternal acceptance, and peer acceptance.

Results and Discussion

Contrary to the concerns that have been raised regarding the potential negative consequences of the new reproductive technologies for family functioning and child development, the quality of parenting in families with a child conceived by assisted conception was better than that shown by families with a naturally conceived child. This finding is not surprising, given the commitment to parenting shown by many parents using the new reproductive technologies. Thus, the assisted-reproduction families were functioning very competently. The adoptive mothers and fathers were very similar in quality of parenting to the mothers and fathers of children conceived by assisted reproduction. No differences were found for any of the measures of children's development, suggesting that there were no negative effects of being born via assisted reproduction.

✐ IMPROVING THE LIVES OF CHILDREN

Genetic Counseling

In 1978, Richard Davidson was an athletic 37-year-old. A slip on an icy driveway landed him in the hospital for minor surgery for a broken foot. The day after the operation, he died. The cause was malignant hyperthermia (MH), a fatal allergy-like reaction to certain anesthetics. The condition is hereditary and preventable—if the anesthesiologist is aware of the patient's susceptibility, alternative drugs can be used. Richard's death inspired his parents, Owen and Jean Davidson, to search their family tree for others with the MH trait. They mailed 300 letters to relatives, telling them of their son's death and warning about the hereditary risk. It turned out that the gene came from Jean's side of the family. When her niece Suellen Gallamore informed the hospital where she going to have fertility surgery about the MH in her bloodline, the doctors refused to treat her. In 1981, she cofounded the Malignant Hyperthermia Association to educate medical providers about MH so that people at risk, like her sons, would not suffer as she had—or lose their lives, as her cousin Richard had (Adato, 1995).

Consider also Bob and Mary Sims, who have been married for several years. They would like to start a family, but they are frightened. The newspapers and popular magazines are full of stories about infants who are born prematurely and don't survive, infants with debilitating physical defects, and babies found to have congenital mental retardation. The Simses feel that to have such a child would create a social, economic, and psychological strain on them and on society.

Accordingly, the Simses turn to a genetic counselor for help. Genetic counselors are usually physicians or biologists who are well versed in the field of medical genetics. They are familiar with the kinds of problems that can be inherited, the odds for encountering them, and helpful measures for offsetting some of their effects. The Simses tell their counselor that there has been a history of mental retardation in Bob's family. Bob's younger sister was born with Down syndrome, a form of mental retardation. Mary's older brother has hemophilia, a condition in which bleeding is difficult to stop. They wonder what the chances are that a child of theirs might also be retarded or have hemophilia and what measures they can take to reduce their chances of having a mentally or physically defective child.

The counselor probes more deeply, because she understands that these facts in isolation do not give her a complete picture of the possibilities. She learns that no other relatives in Bob's family are retarded and that Bob's mother was in her late forties when his younger sister was born. She concludes that the retardation was probably due to the age of Bob's mother and not to some general tendency for members of his family to inherit retardation. It is well known that women over 40 have a much higher probability of giving birth to retarded children than are younger women. Apparently, in women over 40 the ova (egg cells) are not as healthy as in women under 40.

In Mary's case the counselor determines that there is a small but clear possibility that Mary might be a carrier of hemophilia and might transmit that condition to a son. Otherwise,

Malignant hyperthermia (MH) has a hereditary basis. Suellen Gallamore with her sons Scott and Greg Vincent. Suellen is the only person in her immediate family who has had the painful muscle biopsy for the MH gene. Scott and Greg assume that they carry the gene and protect against MH by alerting doctors about their family's medical history.

the counselor can find no evidence from the family history to indicate genetic problems.

The decision is then up to the Simses. In this case, the genetic problem will probably not occur, so the choice is fairly easy. But what should parents do if they face the strong probability of having a child with a major birth defect? Ultimately, the decision depends on the couple's ethical and religious beliefs.

Bertha Morisot
The Cradle detail

Chapter

4

Prenatal Development and Birth

The history of man for nine months preceding his birth would, probably, be far more interesting, and contain events of greater moment than all three score and ten years that follow it.

—Samuel Taylor Coleridge

What web is this of will be,
is, and was?

—Jorge Luis Borges

Jim and Sara, an Expectant Couple

Although Jim and Sara did not plan to have a baby, they did not take precautions to prevent it, and it was not long before Sara was pregnant. Jim and Sara read the popular pregnancy book *What to Expect When You're Expecting* (Eisenberg, Murkoff, & Hathaway, 1988). They found a nurse-midwife they liked and invented a pet name—Bibinello—for the fetus. They signed up for birth preparation classes, and each Friday night for 8 weeks they faithfully practiced simulated contractions. They drew up a birth plan that included their decisions about such matters as the type of care provider they wanted to use, the birth setting they wanted, and various aspects of labor and birth. They moved into a larger apartment so the baby could have its own room and spent weekends browsing through garage sales and secondhand stores to find good prices on baby furniture—a crib, a high chair, a stroller, a changing table, a crib mobile, a swing, a car seat.

Jim and Sara spent a lot of time talking about Sara's pregnancy, what kind of parents they wanted to be, and what their child might be like. They also discussed what changes in their lives the baby would make. One of their concerns was that Sara's maternity leave would only last 6 weeks. If she wanted to stay home longer, she would have to quit her job, something she and Jim were not sure they could afford. These are among the many questions that expectant couples face.

PREVIEW

*T*his chapter includes further information about expectant parents and chronicles the truly remarkable developments from conception through birth. Imagine . . . at one time you were an organism floating around in a sea of fluid in your mother's womb. Let's now explore what development is like from the time you were conceived through the time you were born.

PRENATAL DEVELOPMENT

Imagine how you came to be. Out of hundreds of eggs and millions of sperm, one egg and one sperm united to produce you. Remember from chapter 3 that conception occurs when a single sperm cell from the male unites with an ovum (egg) in the female's fallopian tube in a process called fertilization. Remember also that the fertilized egg is called a zygote. By the time the zygote ends its 3- to 4-day journey through the fallopian tube and reaches the uterus, it has divided into approximately 12 to 16 cells.

The Course of Prenatal Development

Prenatal development is commonly divided into three main periods: germinal, embryonic, and fetal.

The Germinal Period

The **germinal period** *is the period of prenatal development that takes place in the first 2 weeks after conception. It includes the creation of the zygote, continued cell division, and the attachment of the zygote to the uterine wall.* By approximately 1 week after conception, the zygote is composed of 100 to 150 cells. The differentiation of cells has already commenced as inner and outer layers of the organism are formed. The **blastocyst** *is the inner layer of cells that develops during the germinal period. These cells later develop into the embryo* (see figure 4.1). The **trophoblast** *is the outer layer of cells that develops during the germinal period. It later provides nutrition and support for the embryo.* **Implantation,** *the attachment of the zygote to the uterine wall,* takes place about 10 days after conception. Figure 4.2 illustrates some of the most significant developments during the germinal period.

The Embryonic Period

The **embryonic period** *is the period of prenatal development that occurs from 2 to 8 weeks after conception. During the embryonic period, the rate of cell differentiation intensifies, support systems for the cells form, and organs appear.* As the zygote attaches to the uterine wall, its cells form two layers. At this time, the name of the mass of cells changes from *zygote* to *embryo.* The embryo's **endoderm** *is the inner layer of cells, which will develop into the digestive and respiratory systems.* The outer layer of cells is divided into two parts. The **ectoderm** *is the outermost layer, which will become the nervous system, sensory receptors (ears, nose, and eyes, for example), and skin parts (hair and nails, for example).* The **mesoderm** *is the middle layer, which will become the circulatory system, bones, muscles, excretory system, and reproductive system.* Every body part eventually develops from these three layers. The endoderm primarily produces internal body parts, the mesoderm primarily produces parts that surround the internal areas, and the ectoderm primarily produces surface parts.

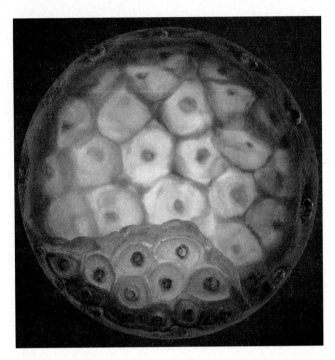

Figure~4.1

The Blastocyst

The blastocyst produces this mass of cells when the fertilized egg repeatedly divides after conception. The blastocyst is the inner layer of cells that develops during the germinal period. These cells later develop into the embryo.

*If I could have watched you grow
As a magical mother might.
If I could have seen through my magical transparent belly,
There would have been such ripening within . . .*

—Anne Sexton, *Little Girl, My String Bean, My Lovely Woman*

As the embryo's three layers form, life-support systems for the embryo mature and develop rapidly. These life-support systems include the placenta, the umbilical cord, and the amnion. The **placenta** *is a life-support system that consists of a disk-shaped group of tissues in which small blood vessels from the mother and the offspring intertwine but do not join.* The **umbilical cord** *is a life-support system, containing two arteries and one vein, that connects the baby to the placenta.* Very small molecules—oxygen, water, salt, food from the mother's blood, and carbon dioxide and digestive wastes from the embryo's blood—pass back and forth between the mother and infant. Large molecules cannot pass through the placental wall; these include red blood cells and harmful substances such as most bacteria, maternal wastes, and hormones. The mechanisms that govern the transfer of substances across the placental barrier are complex and are still not entirely understood (Rosenblith, 1992). Figure 4.3 provides an illustration of the placenta, the umbilical cord, and the

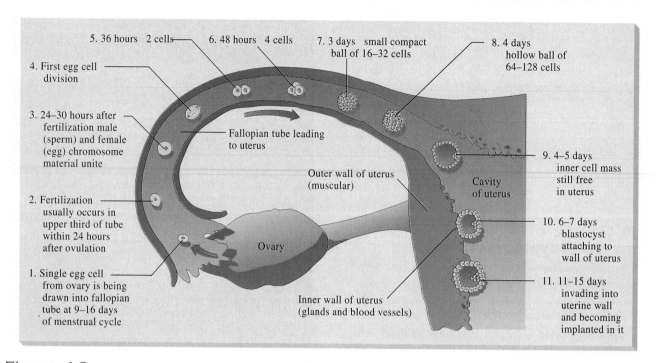

Figure~4.2

Significant Developments in the Germinal Period

The figure is labeled with the following points:

4. First egg cell division

5. 36 hours 2 cells

6. 48 hours 4 cells

7. 3 days small compact ball of 16–32 cells

8. 4 days hollow ball of 64–128 cells

3. 24–30 hours after fertilization male (sperm) and female (egg) chromosome material unite

Fallopian tube leading to uterus

Outer wall of uterus (muscular)

Cavity of uterus

9. 4–5 days inner cell mass still free in uterus

2. Fertilization usually occurs in upper third of tube within 24 hours after ovulation

Ovary

10. 6–7 days blastocyst attaching to wall of uterus

1. Single egg cell from ovary is being drawn into fallopian tube at 9–16 days of menstrual cycle

Inner wall of uterus (glands and blood vessels)

11. 11–15 days invading into uterine wall and becoming implanted in it

nature of blood flow in the expectant mother and developing child in the uterus. The **amnion,** *a bag or envelope that contains a clear fluid in which the developing embryo floats, is another important life-support system.* Like the placenta and umbilical cord, the amnion develops from the fertilized egg, not from the mother's own body. At approximately 16 weeks, the kidneys of the fetus begin to produce urine. This fetal urine remains the main source of the amniotic fluid until the third trimester, when some of the fluid is excreted from the lungs of the growing fetus. Although the volume of the amniotic fluid increases tenfold from the 12th to the 40th week of pregnancy, it is also removed in various ways. Some is swallowed by the fetus and some is absorbed through the umbilical cord and the membranes covering the placenta. The amniotic fluid is important in providing an environment that is temperature and humidity controlled, as well as shockproof.

Before most women even know they are pregnant, some important embryonic developments take place. In the third week, the neural tube that eventually becomes the spinal cord forms. At about 21 days, eyes begin to appear, and at 24 days the cells for the heart begin to differentiate. During the fourth week, the first appearance of the urogenital system is apparent, and arm and leg buds emerge. Four chambers of the heart take shape, and blood vessels surface. From the fifth to the eighth week, arms and legs differentiate further; at this time, the face starts to form but still is not very recognizable. The intestinal tract develops and the facial structures fuse. At 8 weeks, the developing organism weighs about

DENNIS THE MENACE

"My Mom says I come from Heaven. My Dad says he can't remember an' Mr. Wilson is POSITIVE I came from Mars!"

DENNIS THE MENACE® used by permission of Hank Ketcham and © by North America Syndicate.

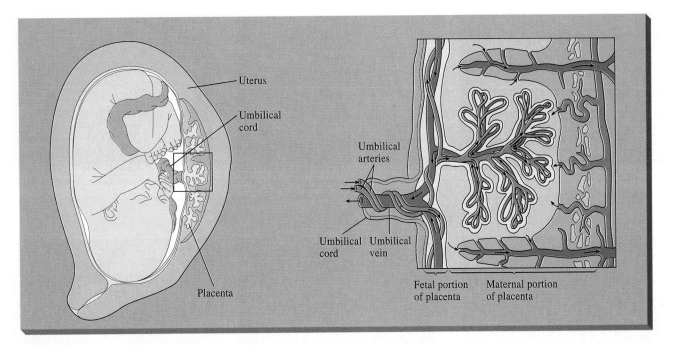

Figure~4.3

The Placenta and the Umbilical Cord
Maternal blood flows through the uterine arteries to the spaces housing the placenta and returns through the uterine veins to maternal circulation. Fetal blood flows through the umbilical arteries into the capillaries of the placenta and returns through the umbilical veins to the fetal circulation. The exchange of materials takes place across the layer separating the maternal and fetal blood supplies, so the bloods never come into contact. *Note:* The area bounded by the square is enlarged in the right half of the illustration. Arrows indicate the direction of blood flow.

one-thirtieth of an ounce and is less than 1 inch long. **Organogenesis** *is the process of organ formation that takes place during the first 2 months of prenatal development.* When organs are being formed, they are especially vulnerable to environmental changes. Later in the chapter, we will describe the environmental hazards that are harmful during organogenesis.

The Fetal Period

The **fetal period** *is the prenatal period of development that begins 2 months after conception and lasts for 7 months, on the average.* Growth and development continue their dramatic course during this time. Three months after conception, the fetus is about 3 inches long and weighs about 1 ounce. It has become active, moving its arms and legs, opening and closing its mouth, and moving its head. The face, forehead, eyelids, nose, and chin are distinguishable, as are the upper arms, lower arms, hands, and lower limbs, and the genitals can be identified as male or female. By the end of the fourth month, the fetus has grown to about 5½ inches in length and weighs about 4 ounces. At this time, a growth spurt occurs in the body's lower parts. Prenatal reflexes are stronger; arm and leg movements can be felt for the first time by the mother.

By the end of the fifth month, the fetus is about 10 to 12 inches long and weighs ½ to 1 pound. Structures of the skin—toenails and fingernails, for example—have formed. The fetus is more active, showing a preference for a particular position in the womb. By the end of the sixth month, the fetus is 11 to 14 inches long and already has gained another half pound to a pound. The eyes and eyelids are completely formed, and a fine layer of hair covers the head. A grasping reflex is present and irregular breathing occurs. By the end of the seventh month, the fetus is 14 to 17 inches long and has gained another pound, now weighing about 2½ to 3 pounds. During the eighth and ninth months, the fetus grows longer and gains substantial weight—about another 4 pounds. At birth, the average American baby weighs 7 to 7½ pounds and is about 20 inches long. In these last 2 months, fatty tissues develop and the functioning of various organ systems—heart and kidneys, for example—steps up.

We have described a number of developments in the germinal, embryonic, and fetal periods. An overview of some of the main developments we have discussed, and some more specific changes in prenatal development, are presented in figure 4.4.

Miscarriage and Abortion

A miscarriage, or spontaneous abortion, happens when pregnancy ends before the developing organism is mature enough to survive outside the womb. The embryo separates from the uterine wall and is expelled by the uterus. About 15 to 20 percent of all pregnancies end in a spontaneous abortion, most in the first 2 to 3 months. Many spontaneous abortions occur without the mother's

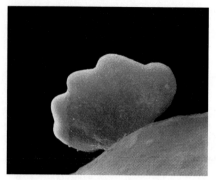

The hand of an embryo at 6 weeks.

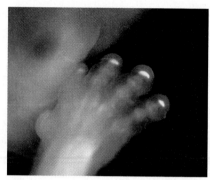

Fingers and thumb with pads seen at 8 weeks.

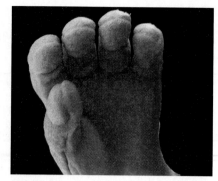

The finger pads have regressed by 13 weeks.

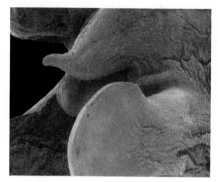

Toe ridges emerge after 7 weeks.

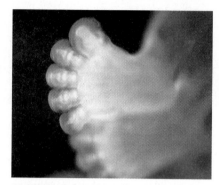

Toe pads and the emerging heel are visible by 9 weeks.

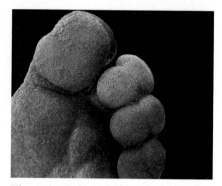

The toe pads have regressed by 13 weeks.

The fingers and toes form rapidly during the first trimester. After 13 weeks of pregnancy, the hands and feet already look remarkably similar to those of a mature human although they are still smaller than an adult's fingernail.

knowledge, and many involve an embryo or fetus that was not developing normally. Most spontaneous abortions are caused by chromosomal abnormalities.

Early in history, it was believed that a woman could be frightened into a miscarriage by loud thunder or a jolt in a carriage. Today, we recognize that this is highly unlikely; the developing organism is well protected. Abnormalities of the reproductive tract and viral or bacterial infections are more likely to cause spontaneous abortions. In some cases, severe traumas may be at fault.

Deliberate termination of pregnancy is a complex issue, medically, psychologically, socially, and legally (Schaff, 1992). Carrying a baby to term might affect a woman's health, the woman's pregnancy might have resulted from rape or incest, the woman might not be married, or perhaps she is poor or wants to continue her education. Abortion is legal in the United States. In 1973, the Supreme Court ruled that any woman can obtain an abortion during the first 6 months of pregnancy, a decision that continues to generate ethical objections from anti-abortion forces. The Supreme Court also has ruled that abortion in the first trimester is solely the decision of the mother and her doctor. Court cases also have added the point that the baby's father and the parents of minor girls do not have any say during this time frame. In the second trimester, states can legislate the time and method of abortion for protection of the mother's health. In the third trimester, the fetus's right to live is the primary concern.

What are the psychological effects of having an abortion? In 1989, a research review panel appointed by the American Psychological Association examined more than 100 investigations of the psychological effects of abortion. The panel concluded the following: Unwanted pregnancies are stressful for most women. However, it is common for women to report feelings of relief as well as feelings of guilt after an abortion. These feelings are usually mild and tend to diminish rapidly over time without adversely affecting the woman's ability to function. Abortion is more stressful for women who have a history of serious emotional problems and who are not given support by family or friends. According to the American Psychological Association report, only a small percentage of women fall into these high-risk categories. If an abortion is performed, it should involve not only competent medical care but the woman's psychological needs as well.

Maternal Characteristics

What are some maternal characteristics that affect prenatal development? They include the mother's age, nutrition, and emotional state.

Mother's Age

When the mother's age is considered in terms of possible harmful effects on the fetus and infant, two time periods are of special interest: adolescence and the thirties and beyond. Approximately 1 of every 5 births is to an adolescent; in some urban areas, the figure reaches as high as 1 in every 2 births. Infants born to adolescents are often premature. The mortality rate of infants born to adolescent mothers is double that of infants born to mothers in their twenties. Although such figures probably reflect the mother's immature reproductive system, they also can involve poor nutrition, lack of prenatal care, and low socioeconomic status. Prenatal care decreases the probability that a child born to an adolescent girl will have physical problems. However, adolescents are the least likely of women in all age groups to obtain prenatal assistance from clinics, pediatricians, and health services.

Increasingly, women are seeking to establish their careers before beginning a family, delaying childbearing until their thirties. Down syndrome, a form of mental retardation, is related to the mother's age. A baby with Down syndrome rarely is born to a mother under the age of 30, but the risk increases after the mother reaches 30. By age 40, the probability is slightly over 1 in 100, and by age 50 it is almost 1 in 10. The risk is also higher before age 18.

Women also have more difficulty becoming pregnant after the age of 30. In one study, the clients of a French fertility clinic all had husbands who were sterile (Schwartz & Mayaux, 1982). To increase their chances of having a child, they were artificially inseminated once a month for 1 year. Each woman had twelve chances to become pregnant. Seventy-five percent of the women in their twenties became pregnant, 62 percent of the women 31 to 35 years old became pregnant, and only 54 percent of the women over 35 years old became pregnant.

We still have much to learn about the role of the mother's age in pregnancy and childbirth. As women remain active, exercise regularly, and are careful about their nutrition, their reproductive systems might remain healthier at older ages than was thought possible in the past. Indeed, as we will see next, the mother's nutrition influences prenatal development.

Nutrition

A developing fetus depends completely on its mother for nutrition, which comes from the mother's blood. Nutritional status is not determined by any specific aspect of diet; among the important factors are the total number of calories and appropriate levels of protein, vitamins, and minerals. The mother's nutrition even influences her ability to reproduce. In extreme instances of malnutrition, women stop menstruating, thus precluding conception, and children born to malnourished mothers are more likely to be malformed.

One study of Iowa mothers documents the important role of nutrition in prenatal development and birth (Jeans, Smith, & Stearns, 1955). The diets of 400 pregnant women were studied and the status of their newborns was assessed. The mothers with the poorest diets were more likely to have offspring who weighed the least, had the least vitality, were born prematurely, or died. In another investigation, diet supplements given to malnourished mothers during pregnancy improved the performance of their offspring during the first 3 years of life (Werner, 1979).

Emotional States and Stress

Tales abound about the way a mother's emotional state affects the fetus. For centuries, it was thought that frightening experiences—such as a severe thunderstorm or a family member's death—would leave birthmarks on the child or affect the child in more serious ways. Today, we believe that the mother's stress can be transmitted to the fetus, but we have gone beyond thinking that this transmission is somehow magically produced. We now know that when a pregnant woman experiences intense fears, anxieties, and other emotions, she also experiences physiological changes—in respiration, and glandular secretions, for instance. Producing adrenaline in response to fear restricts blood flow to the uterine area and may deprive the fetus of adequate oxygen.

The mother's emotional state during pregnancy can influence the birth process too. An emotionally distraught mother might have irregular contractions and a more difficult labor, which can cause irregularities in the baby's oxygen supply or tend to produce irregularities after birth. Babies born after extended labor also may adjust more slowly to their world and be more irritable.

A number of researchers have found that maternal anxiety during pregnancy is related to less than optimal outcomes (Stechler & Halton, 1982). In one study, maternal anxiety during pregnancy was associated with infants who were more hyperactive and irritable and who had more feeding and sleeping problems (Stanley, Soule, & Copans, 1979). Stresses during pregnancy that have been linked with maternal anxiety include marital discord, the death of the husband, and unwanted pregnancy (Field, 1990).

In one study, Tiffany Field and her colleagues (1985) attempted to reduce anxiety about pregnancy by giving video and verbal feedback during ultrasound assessments to assure the woman of the well-being of her fetus. Compared to infants whose mothers did not receive such feedback, the infants whose mothers got the intervention were less active in utero and had higher birth weights. As newborns, they were less irritable, and on neonatal behavior assessments their performance was superior. Thus, reassuring the mother of fetal well-being had positive outcomes for the infants in this study.

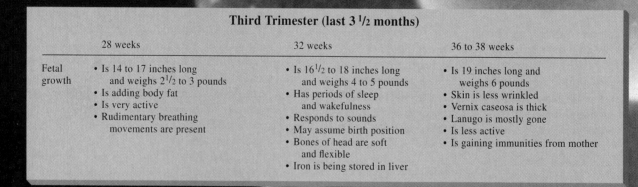

First Trimester (first 3 months)

	Conception to 4 weeks	8 weeks	12 weeks
Fetal growth	• Is less than 1/10 inch long • Beginning development of spinal cord, nervous system, gastrointestinal system, heart, and lungs • Amniotic sac envelops the preliminary tissues of entire body • Is called an "ovum"	• Is less than 1 inch long • Face is forming with rudimentary eyes, ears, mouth, and tooth buds • Arms and legs are moving • Brain is forming • Fetal heartbeat is detectable with ultrasound • Is called an "embryo"	• Is about 3 inches long and weighs about 1 ounce • Can move arms, legs, fingers, and toes • Fingerprints are present • Can smile, frown, suck, and swallow • Sex is distinguishable • Can urinate • Is called a "fetus"

Second Trimester (middle 3 months)

	16 weeks	20 weeks	24 weeks
Fetal growth	• Is about 5 1/2 inches long and weighs about 4 ounces • Heartbeat is strong • Skin is thin, transparent • Downy hair (lanugo) covers body • Fingernails and toenails are forming • Has coordinated movements; is able to roll over in amniotic fluid	• Is 10 to 12 inches long and weighs 1/2 to 1 pound • Heartbeat is audible with ordinary stethoscope • Sucks thumb • Hiccups • Hair, eyelashes, eyebrows are present	• Is 11 to 14 inches long and weighs 1 to 1 1/2 pounds • Skin is wrinkled and covered with protective coating (vernix caseosa) • Eyes are open • Meconium is collecting in bowel • Has strong grip

Third Trimester (last 3 1/2 months)

	28 weeks	32 weeks	36 to 38 weeks
Fetal growth	• Is 14 to 17 inches long and weighs 2 1/2 to 3 pounds • Is adding body fat • Is very active • Rudimentary breathing movements are present	• Is 16 1/2 to 18 inches long and weighs 4 to 5 pounds • Has periods of sleep and wakefulness • Responds to sounds • May assume birth position • Bones of head are soft and flexible • Iron is being stored in liver	• Is 19 inches long and weighs 6 pounds • Skin is less wrinkled • Vernix caseosa is thick • Lanugo is mostly gone • Is less active • Is gaining immunities from mother

Figure~4.4

The Three Trimesters of Prenatal Development

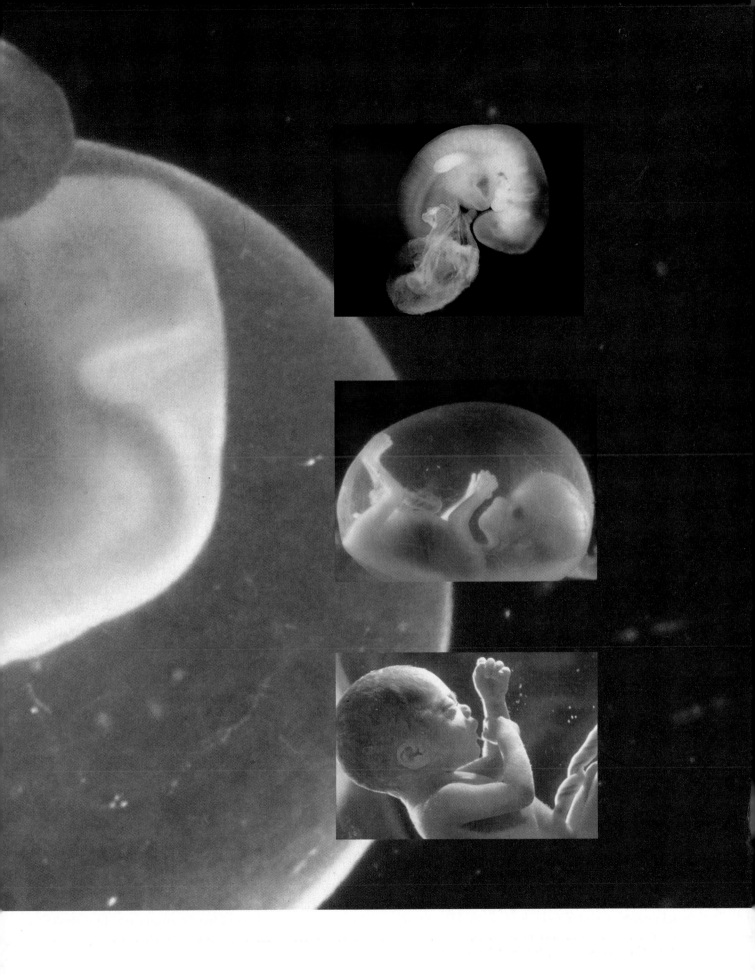

Teratology and Hazards to Prenatal Development

Some expectant mothers carefully tiptoe about in the belief that everything they do and feel has a direct effect on their unborn child. Others behave casually, assuming that their experiences will have little effect. The truth lies somewhere between these two extremes. Although living in a protected, comfortable environment, the fetus is not totally immune to the larger world surrounding the mother (McFarlane, Parker, & Soeken, 1996). The environment can affect the child in many well-documented ways. Thousands of babies born deformed or mentally retarded every year are the result of events that occurred in the mother's life, as early as 1 or 2 months before conception.

Teratology

A **teratogen** *(from the Greek word* tera *meaning "monster")* *is any agent that causes a birth defect. The field of study that investigates the causes of birth defects is called teratology.* A specific teratogen (such as a drug) usually does not cause a specific birth defect (such as malformation of the legs). So many teratogens exist that practically every fetus is exposed to at least some of them. For this reason, it is difficult to determine which teratogen causes which birth defect. In addition, it may take a long time for the effects of a teratogen to show up; only about half of all potential effects appear at birth.

Despite the many unknowns about teratogens, scientists have discovered the identity of some of these hazards to prenatal development and the particular point of fetal development at which they do their greatest damage. As figure 4.5 shows, sensitivity to teratogens begins about 3 weeks after conception. The probability of a structural defect is greatest early in the embryonic period, because this is when organs are being formed. After organogenesis is complete, teratogens are less likely to cause anatomical defects. Exposure later, during the fetal period, is more likely to stunt growth or to create problems in the way organs function. The precision of organogenesis is evident; teratologists point out that the brain is most vulnerable at 15 to 25 days after conception, the eyes at 24 to 40 days, the heart at 20 to 40 days, and the legs at 24 to 36 days.

Maternal Diseases and Conditions

Maternal diseases or infections can produce defects by crossing the placental barrier, or they can cause damage during the birth process itself. Rubella (German measles) is a maternal disease that can damage prenatal development. A rubella outbreak in 1964–1965 resulted in 30,000 prenatal and neonatal (newborn) deaths, and more than 20,000 infants were born with malformations, including mental retardation, blindness, deafness, and heart problems. The greatest damage occurs when mothers contract rubella in the third and fourth weeks of pregnancy, although infection during the second month is also damaging. Elaborate preventive efforts ensure that rubella will never again have the disastrous effects it had in the mid 1960s. A vaccine that prevents German measles is routinely administered to children, and women who plan to have children should have a blood test before they become pregnant to determine if they are immune to the disease.

Syphilis (a sexually transmitted disease) is more damaging later in prenatal development—4 months or more after conception. Rather than affecting organogenesis, as rubella does, syphilis damages organs after they have formed. Damage includes eye lesions, which can cause blindness, and skin lesions. When syphilis is present at birth, other problems involving the central nervous system and gastrointestinal tract can develop. Most states require that pregnant women be given a blood test to detect the presence of syphilis.

Another infection that has received widespread attention recently is genital herpes. Newborns contract this virus when they are delivered through the birth canal of a mother with genital herpes. About one-third of babies delivered through an infected birth canal die; another one-fourth become brain damaged. If a pregnant woman detects an active case of genital herpes close to her delivery date, a cesarean section can be performed (in which the infant is delivered through the mother's abdomen) to keep the virus from infecting the newborn.

AIDS

The importance of women's health to the health of their offspring is nowhere better exemplified than when the mother has acquired immune deficiency syndrome (AIDS). As the number of women with HIV (human immunodeficiency virus) grows, more children are born exposed to and infected with HIV (Cohen & others, 1996). Through the end of 1991, there were 3,123 children younger than 13 who had been diagnosed with AIDS. The number of pediatric AIDS cases does not include as many as 10,000 children infected with HIV who have not yet suffered the full effects of AIDS. African American and Latino children make up 83 percent of all pediatric AIDS cases. The majority of mothers who transmit HIV to their offspring were infected through intravenous drug use or heterosexual contact with injecting drug users.

There are three ways a mother with AIDS can infect her offspring: (1) during gestation across the placenta, (2) during delivery through contact with maternal blood or fluids, and (3) postpartum through breast-feeding. Approximately one-third of infants born to infected mothers will ultimately become infected with HIV themselves (Caldwell & Rogers, 1991). Babies born to AIDS-infected mothers can be (1) infected and symptomatic (show AIDS symptoms), (2) infected but asymptomatic (not show AIDS symptoms), and (3) not infected at all. An infant who is infected and asymptomatic may still develop AIDS

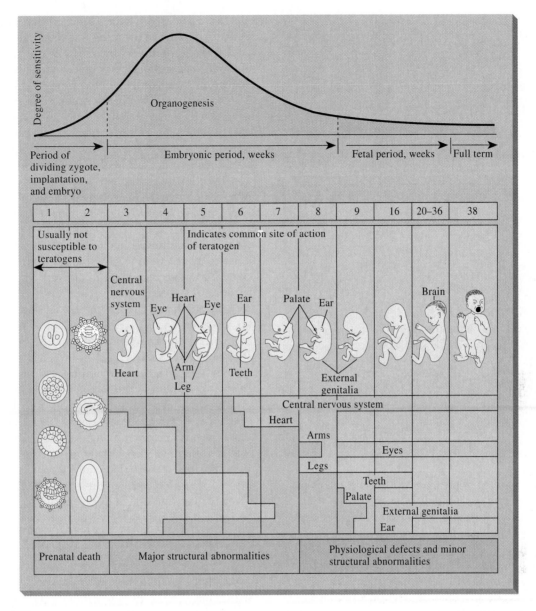

Figure~4.5

Teratogens and the Timing of Their Effects on Prenatal Development
The danger of structural defects caused by teratogens is greatest early in embryonic development. This is the period of organogenesis, and it lasts for several months. Damage caused by teratogens during this period is represented by the dark-colored bars. Later assaults by teratogens typically occur during the fetal period and, instead of causing structural damage, are more likely to stunt growth or cause problems of organ function.

symptoms up until 15 months of age. One recent study documented the rare case of HIV disappearing in an infant who had been born with it (Bryon & others, 1995). This may represent an unusual transient or defective form of HIV.

Drugs

How do drugs affect prenatal development? Some pregnant women take drugs, smoke tobacco, and drink alcohol without thinking about the possible effects on the fetus. Occasionally, a rash of deformed babies are born, bringing to light the damage drugs can have on a developing fetus. This happened in 1961, when many pregnant women took a popular tranquilizer, thalidomide, to alleviate their morning sickness. In adults, the effects of thalidomide are mild; in embryos, however, they are devastating. Not all infants were affected in the same way. If the mother took thalidomide on day 26 (probably before she knew she was pregnant), an arm might not grow. If she took the drug 2 days later, the arm might not grow past the elbow. The thalidomide tragedy shocked the medical community and parents into the stark realization that the mother does not have to be a chronic drug user for the fetus to be harmed. Taking the wrong drug at the wrong time is enough to physically handicap the offspring for life.

She has
her father's
eyes and her
mother's smile.
She also
has AIDS.

Reduce your risk of getting
or giving the AIDS virus.

DON'T SHOOT DRUGS.
IF YOU MUST SHOOT DRUGS,
DON'T SHARE YOUR WORKS.
HAVE SAFE SEX OR
NONE AT ALL.
IF YOU THINK YOU HAVE
THE AIDS VIRUS,
DON'T GET PREGNANT.
IT'S YOUR CHOICE.
IT COULD BE
YOUR CHILD'S LIFE.

EarthTide, Inc. Baltimore, Maryland
Call: (301)-225-9635

Heavy drinking by pregnant women can also be dev-astating to offspring (Janzen & Nanson, 1993; Olson & Burgess, 1996). **Fetal alcohol syndrome (FAS)** *is a clus-ter of abnormalities that appears in the offspring of mothers who drink alcohol heavily during pregnancy.* The abnor-malities include facial deformities and defective limbs, face, and heart. Most of these children are below aver-age in intelligence and some are mentally retarded. Al-though many mothers of FAS infants are heavy drinkers, many mothers who are heavy drinkers do not have children with FAS, or might have one child with FAS and other children who do not have it. While no serious malformations such as those produced by FAS are found in infants born to mothers who are moderate drinkers, in one investigation, infants whose mothers drank mod-erately during pregnancy (for example, one to two drinks a day) were less attentive and less alert, with the effects still present at 4 years of age (Streissguth & oth-ers, 1984).

Expectant mothers are becoming more aware that alcohol and pregnancy do not mix. In one recent study of 1,712 pregnant women in twenty-one states, the preva-lence of alcohol consumption by pregnant women de-clined from 32 percent in 1985 to 20 percent in 1988 (Serdula & others, 1991). The declines in drinking were greatest among the oldest and most educated pregnant women—19 percent of pregnant college graduates drank

in 1988, a decline from the 41 percent rate in 1985. How-ever, no decline in drinking was found among the least educated and youngest pregnant women. The proportion of drinkers among pregnant women with only a high school education stayed at 23 percent from 1985 to 1988.

Cigarette smoking by pregnant women can also adversely influence prenatal development, birth, and post-natal development (Johnson & others, 1993). Fetal and neonatal deaths are higher among smoking mothers; also prevalent are a higher incidence of preterm births and lower birthweights (see figure 4.6). In one study, pre-natal exposure to cigarette smoking was related to poorer language and cognitive development at 4 years of age (Fried & Watkinson, 1990). In another study, mothers who smoked during pregnancy had infants who were awake more on a consistent basis—a finding one might expect, since the active ingredient in cigarettes is the stimulant nicotine (Landesman-Dwyer & Sackett, 1983). Respira-tory problems and sudden infant death syndrome (also known as crib death) are also more common among the offspring of mothers who smoked during pregnancy (Schoendorf & Kiely, 1992). Intervention programs de-signed to get pregnant women to stop smoking are suc-cessful in reducing some of smoking's negative effects on offspring, especially in raising their birthweights (Chemitz, Cheung, & Lieberman, 1995). To further ex-plore pregnancy and smoking, turn to Critical Thinking About Children's Development.

Marijuana use by pregnant women also has detri-mental effects on a developing child. Marijuana use by pregnant mothers is associated with increased tremors and startles among newborns and poorer verbal and mem-ory development at 4 years of age (Fried & Watkinson, 1990).

It is well documented that infants whose mothers are addicted to heroin show several behavioral difficul-ties (Hans, 1989). The young infants of these mothers are addicted and show withdrawal symptoms characteristic of opiate abstinence, such as tremors, irritability, abnor-mal crying, disturbed sleep, and impaired motor control. Behavioral problems are still often present at the first birthday, and attention deficits may appear later in the child's development. The treatment most often used for heroin addicts—methadone—is associated with very se-vere withdrawal symptoms in newborns.

With the increased use of cocaine in the United States, there is growing concern about its effects on the embryos, fetuses, and infants of pregnant cocaine users (Dow-Edwards, 1995; Mayes & Bornstein, 1995). Cocaine use during pregnancy has recently attracted consider-able attention because of concerns about possible harm to the developing embryo and fetus (Wooten & Miller, 1994). The most consistent finding is that infants born to cocaine abusers have reduced birth weight and length (Chasnoff & others, 1992). There are increased frequencies of congenital abnormalities in the offspring of cocaine

Intervention to Stop Pregnant Women from Smoking

Scientists have known for more than three decades about the negative consequences of smoking, but they have made little progress in promoting effective interventions to help pregnant women quit smoking or to keep young women from becoming addicted. What needs to be done to get pregnant women to not smoke? Consider the role of health-care providers and their training, the role of insurance companies, and specific programs targeted at pregnant women. By considering ways to intervene in the lives of pregnant women to get them to stop smoking, you are learning to think critically by *using knowledge to improve human welfare*.

users during pregnancy, but other factors in the drug addict's lifestyle, such as malnutrition and other substance abuse, may be responsible for the congenital abnormalities (Eyler, Behnke, & Stewart, 1990). For example, cocaine users are more likely to smoke cigarettes and marijuana, drink alcohol, and take amphetamines than are cocaine nonusers. Teasing apart these potential influences from the effects of cocaine use itself has not yet been adequately accomplished (Lester, Freier, & LaGasse, 1995). Obtaining valid information about the frequency and type of drug use by mothers is also complicated, since many mothers fear prosecution or loss of custody because of their drug use. A list of the effects of cocaine, and of various other drugs, on offspring are presented in table 4.1.

Environmental Hazards

Radiation, chemicals, and other hazards in our modern industrial world can endanger the fetus. For instance, radiation can cause a gene mutation, an abrupt but permanent change in genetic material. Chromosomal abnormalities are higher among the offspring of fathers exposed to high levels of radiation in their occupations (Schrag & Dixon, 1985). Radiation from X rays also can affect the developing embryo and fetus, with the most dangerous time being the first several weeks after conception, when women do not yet know they are pregnant. It is important for women and their physicians to weigh the risk of an X ray when an actual or potential pregnancy is involved.

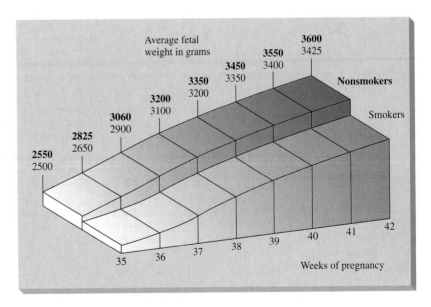

Figure~4.6

The Effects of Smoking by Expectant Mothers on Fetal Weight
Throughout prenatal development, the fetuses of expectant mothers who smoke weigh less than the fetuses of expectant mothers who do not smoke.

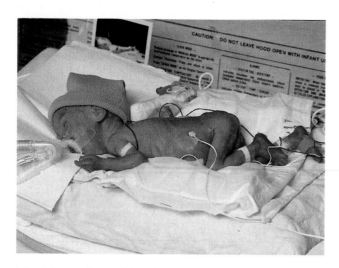

This baby was born addicted to cocaine because its mother was a cocaine addict. Researchers have found that the offspring of women who use cocaine during pregnancy often have hypertension and heart damage. Many of these infants face a childhood full of medical problems.

Environmental pollutants and toxic wastes are also sources of danger to unborn children. Researchers have found that various hazardous wastes and pesticides cause defects in animals exposed to high doses. Among the dangerous pollutants and wastes are carbon monoxide, mercury, and lead. Some children are exposed to lead because they live in houses where lead-based paint flakes off the walls or near busy highways, where there are heavy automobile emissions from leaded gasoline. Researchers believe that early exposure to lead affects children's mental development. For example, in one investigation, 2-year-old infants who prenatally had high levels of lead in their umbilical cord blood performed poorly on a test of mental development (Bellinger & others, 1987).

Researchers also have found that the manufacturing chemicals known as PCBs are harmful to prenatal development. In one investigation, the extent to which pregnant women ate PCB-polluted fish from Lake Michigan was examined, and subsequently their newborns were observed (Jacobson & others, 1984). Women who had eaten more PCB-polluted fish were more likely to have smaller, preterm infants who were more likely to react slowly to stimuli. And in one study, prenatal exposure to PCBs was associated with problems in visual discrimination and short-term memory in 4-year-old children (Jacobson & others, 1992).

A recent environmental concern involves women who spend long hours in front of a video display terminal. The fear is that low levels of electromagnetic radiation from the video display terminal adversely affect their offspring. In one investigation, 2,430 telephone operators were studied (Schnorr & others, 1991). Half of the women worked at video display terminals, half did not. During the 4 years of the study, 730 women became pregnant, some more than once, for a total of 876 pregnancies. Over the 4 years, there was no significant difference in miscarriage rates between the two groups. The researchers concluded that working at a video display terminal does not increase miscarriage risk. Critics point out that there was no check for early fetal loss and that all of the women were younger than 34 years of age, so whether the findings hold for early fetal loss and older women will have to await further research. In this study, miscarriages were higher among women who had more than eight alcoholic drinks per month or smoked more than twenty cigarettes a day. While video display terminals might not be related to miscarriage, they are associated with an increase in a variety of problems involving eye strain and the musculoskeletal system of female workers.

TABLE 4.1

Drug Use During Pregnancy

Drug	Effects on Fetus and Offspring
Alcohol	Small amounts increase risk of spontaneous abortion. Moderate amounts (1-2 drinks a day) are associated with poor attention in infancy. Heavy drinking can lead to fetal alcohol syndrome. Some experts believe that even low to moderate amounts, especially in the first 3 months of pregnancy, increase the risk of FAS.
Nicotine	Heavy smoking is associated with low-birthweight babies, which means the babies may have more health problems than other infants do. Smoking may be especially harmful in the second half of pregnancy.
Tranquilizers	Taken during the first 3 months of pregnancy, they may cause cleft palate or other congenital malformations.
Barbiturates	Mothers who take large doses may have babies who are addicted. Babies may have tremors, restlessness, and irritability.
Amphetamines	They may cause birth defects.
Cocaine	Cocaine may cause drug dependency and withdrawal symptoms at birth, as well as physical and mental problems, especially if the mother uses cocaine in the first three months of pregnancy. There is a higher risk of hypertension, heart problems, developmental retardation, and learning difficulties.
Marijuana	It may cause a variety of birth defects and is associated with low birthweight and height.

Source: Modified from the National Institute on Drug Abuse.

Another environmental concern is **toxoplasmosis,** *a mild infection that causes coldlike symptoms or no apparent illness in adults. However, toxoplasmosis can be a teratogen for the unborn baby, causing possible eye defects, brain defects, and premature birth.* Cats are common carriers of toxoplasmosis, especially outdoor cats who eat raw meat, such as rats and mice. The toxoplasmosis organism passes from the cat in its feces and lives up to 1 year. The expectant mother can pick up these organisms by handling cats or cat litter boxes, or by working in soil where cats have buried their feces. Eating raw or uncooked meat is another way of acquiring the disease. To avoid getting toxoplasmosis, expectant mothers need to wash their hands after handling cats, litter boxes, and raw meat. In addition, pregnant women should make sure that all meats are thoroughly cooked before eating them.

Yet another recent environmental concern for expectant mothers is prolonged exposure to heat in saunas or hot tubs, which can raise the mother's body temperature, creating a fever that endangers the fetus. The high temperature of a fever can interfere with cell division and can cause birth defects or even fetal death if the fever occurs repeatedly for prolonged periods of time. If the expectant mother wants to take a sauna or bathe in a hot tub, prenatal experts recommend that she take her oral temperature while she is exposed to the heat. When the expectant mother's body temperature rises a degree or more, she should get out and cool down. Ten minutes is a reasonable length of time for expectant mothers to spend in a sauna or a hot tub, since the body temperature does not usually rise in this length of time. If the expectant mother feels uncomfortably hot in a sauna or a hot tub, she should get out even if she has only been there for a short time.

Prenatal Care

Prenatal care varies enormously but usually involves a package of medical care services in a defined schedule of visits. In addition to medical care, prenatal care programs often include comprehensive educational, social, and nutritional services (Shiono & Behrman, 1995).

Prenatal care usually includes screening that can reveal manageable conditions and/or treatable diseases that could affect both the baby's life and the mother's. The education the mother receives about pregnancy, labor and delivery, and caring for the newborn can be extremely valuable, especially for first-time mothers. Prenatal care is also very important for women in poverty, because it links them with other social services. The legacy of prenatal care continues after the birth, because women who receive this type of care are more likely to get preventive care for their infants (Bates & others, 1994).

Inadequate prenatal care can be due to the nature of the health-care system, provider practices, or the pregnant woman's own individual and social characteristics (Alexander & Korenbrot, 1995). In one national study,

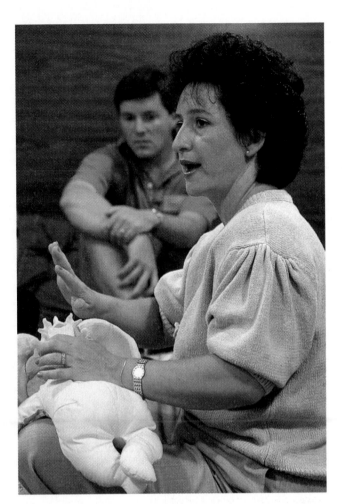

Early prenatal education classes focus on such topics as changes in the development of the fetus, while later classes often focus on preparation for the birth and care of the newborn.

71 percent of low-income women experienced a problem in getting prenatal care (U.S. General Accounting Office, 1987). They cited problems with finances, transportation, and child care as barriers. Motivating positive attitudes toward pregnancy is also important. A woman who does not want her pregnancy, who has a negative attitude about being pregnant, or who became pregnant unintentionally is more likely to delay prenatal care or to miss appointments (Joseph, 1989).

At this point we have discussed a number of ideas about the course of prenatal development, miscarriage and abortion, and teratology and hazards to prenatal development. A summary of these ideas is presented in concept table 4.1.

BIRTH

After the long journey of prenatal development, birth takes place. Among the important topics related to birth that we explore are stages of birth, delivery complications, and the use of drugs during childbirth; childbirth strategies; preterm infants; and measures of neonatal health and responsiveness.

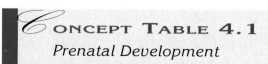

CONCEPT TABLE 4.1

Prenatal Development

Concept	Processes/ Related Ideas	Characteristics/Description
The Course of Prenatal Development	Germinal period	This period is from conception to about 10 to 14 days later. A fertilized egg is called a zygote. The period ends when the zygote attaches to the uterine wall.
	Embryonic period	The embryonic period lasts from about 2 to 8 weeks after conception. The embryo differentiates into three layers, life-support systems develop, and organ systems form (organogenesis).
	Fetal period	The fetal period lasts from about 2 months after conception until 9 months or when the infant is born. Growth and development continue their dramatic course and organ systems mature to the point where life can be sustained outside the womb.
Miscarriage and Abortion	Their nature and ethical issues	A miscarriage, or spontaneous abortion, happens when pregnancy ends before the developing organism is mature enough to survive outside the womb. Estimates indicate that about 15 to 20 percent of all pregnancies end this way, many without the mother's knowledge. Induced abortion is a complex issue—medically, psychologically, socially, and legally. An unwanted pregnancy is stressful for the woman regardless of how it is resolved. A recent ethical issue focuses on the use of fetal tissue in transplant operations.
Maternal Characteristics	Mother's age	Two time periods increase risks: adolescence and the thirties and beyond.
	Nutrition	Important factors include the total number of calories and appropriate levels of proteins, minerals, and vitamins.
	Emotional states and stress	The mother's emotional state during pregnancy can influence prenatal development and birth.
Teratology and Hazards to Prenatal Development	Teratology	This field investigates the causes of congenital (birth) defects. Any agent that causes birth defects is called a teratogen.
	Maternal diseases and conditions	Maternal diseases and infections can cause damage by crossing the placental barrier, or they can be destructive during the birth process. Among the maternal diseases and conditions believed to be involved in possible birth defects are rubella, syphilis, and genital herpes.
	AIDS	A mother with AIDS can infect her offspring.
	Drugs	Thalidomide was a tranquilizer given to pregnant women in the early 1960s to alleviate their morning sickness. Thousands of babies were malformed as a consequence of their mother having taken this drug. Alcohol, tobacco, marijuana, heroin, and cocaine are other drugs that can adversely affect prenatal and infant development.
	Environmental hazards	Among the environmental hazards that can endanger the fetus are radiation in occupations and X rays, environmental pollutants, toxic wastes, toxoplasmosis, and prolonged exposure to heat in saunas and hot tubs.
Prenatal Care	Its nature	Prenatal care varies extensively but usually involves medical care services with a defined schedule of visits. Prenatal care programs also often include comprehensive educational, social, and nutritional services. Inadequate prenatal care can be due to the nature of the health-care system, provider practices, and individual and social characteristics of the pregnant woman.

Stages of Birth

The birth process occurs in three stages. For a woman having her first child, the first stage lasts an average of 12 to 24 hours; it is the longest of the three stages. In the first stage, uterine contractions are 15 to 20 minutes apart at the beginning and last up to a minute. These contractions cause the woman's cervix to stretch and open. As the first stage progresses, the contractions come closer together, appearing every 2 to 5 minutes. Their intensity increases too. By the end of the first birth stage, contractions dilate the cervix to an opening of about 4 inches so that the baby can move from the uterus to the birth canal.

The second birth stage begins when the baby's head starts to move through the cervix and the birth canal. It terminates when the baby completely emerges from the mother's body. This stage lasts approximately 1½ hours. With each contraction, the mother bears down hard to push the baby out of her body. By the time the baby's head is out of the mother's body, the contractions come almost every minute and last for about a minute.

Afterbirth *is the third stage, at which time the placenta, umbilical cord, and other membranes are detached and expelled.* This final stage is the shortest of the three birth stages, lasting only minutes.

Delivery Complications

Complications can accompany the baby's delivery. A **precipitate delivery** *is a delivery that takes place too rapidly. A precipitate delivery is one in which the baby takes less than 10 minutes to be squeezed through the birth canal.* This deviation in delivery can disturb the infant's normal flow of blood, and the pressure on the infant's head can cause hemorrhaging. On the other hand, **anoxia,** *the insufficient supply of oxygen to the infant,* can develop if the delivery takes too long. Anoxia can cause brain damage.

The **breech position** *is the baby's position in the uterus that causes the buttocks to be the first part to emerge from the vagina.* Normally, the crown of the baby's head comes through the vagina first, but in 1 of every 25 babies, the head does not come through first. Breech babies' heads are still in the uterus when the rest of their bodies are out, which can cause respiratory problems. Some breech babies cannot be passed through the cervix and must be delivered by cesarean section.

A **cesarean section** *is the surgical removal of the baby from the uterus.* A cesarean section is usually performed if the baby is in a breech position, if it is lying crosswise in the uterus, if the baby's head is too large to pass through the mother's pelvis, if the baby develops complications, or if the mother is bleeding vaginally. The cesarean section rate often increases as postterm, postmature babies are being born.

The benefits and risks of cesarean section delivery are debated. Cesarean section deliveries are safer than breech deliveries, but a higher infection rate, a longer hospital stay, greater expense, and the stress that accompanies any surgery characterize cesarean section deliveries. Some critics believe that, in the United States, too many babies are delivered by cesarean section. More cesarean sections are performed in the United States than

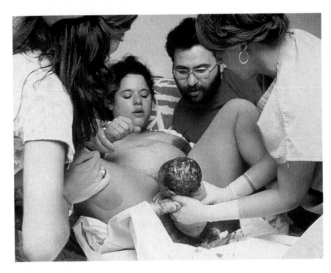

After the long journey of prenatal development, birth takes place, at which time the baby is on a threshold, between two worlds.

in any other industrialized nation. From 1979 to 1987, the cesarean section rate increased almost 50 percent in the United States alone, to an annual rate of 24 percent. However, a growing use of vaginal birth after a previous cesarean, greater public awareness, and peer pressure in the medical community are beginning to slow the rate of increase.

The Use of Drugs During Childbirth

Drugs can be used to relieve pain and anxiety and to speed delivery during the birth process. The most common use of drugs during delivery is to relieve the expectant mother's pain or anxiety. A wide variety of tranquilizers, sedatives, and analgesics are used for this purpose. Researchers are interested in the effects of these drugs because they can cross the placental barrier, and because their use is so widespread. One survey of hospitals found that only 5 percent of deliveries involve no anesthesia (Brackbill, 1979).

Oxytocin, *a hormone that stimulates and regulates the rhythmicity of uterine contractions,* has been widely used as a drug to speed delivery. Controversy surrounds the use of this drug. Some physicians argue that it can save the mother's life or keep the infant from being damaged. They also stress that using the drug allows the mother to be well rested and prepared for the birth process. Critics argue that babies born to mothers who have taken oxytocin are more likely to have jaundice; that induced labor requires more painkilling drugs; and that greater medical care is required after the birth, resulting in the separation of the infant and mother.

Recently prostaglandins have been used both to replace oxytocin and to precede its use. An accumulation of research suggests that prostaglandins are as effective as, or more effective than, oxytocin. They also are more acceptable to women and easier for hospital personnel to administer.

The following conclusions can be reached, based on research about the influence of drugs during delivery (Rosenblith, 1992):

1. Few research studies have been done, and many that have been completed have had methodological problems. However, not all drugs have similar effects. Some—tranquilizers, sedatives, and analgesics, for example—do not seem to have long-term effects. Other drugs—oxytocin, for example—are suspected of having long-term effects.

2. The degree to which a drug influences the infant is usually small. Birth weight and social class, for instance, are more powerful predictors of infant difficulties than drugs are.

3. A specific drug may affect some infants but not others. In some cases, the drug may have a beneficial effect, whereas in others it may be harmful.

4. The overall amount of medication may be an important factor in understanding drug effects on delivery.

Next, we will discuss a number of the increasing variety of childbirth strategies. In the last several decades, more expectant mothers have chosen to have a prepared, or natural, childbirth. One aspect of prepared childbirth is an attempt to minimize the use of medication.

Childbirth Strategies

In the past two decades, the nature of childbirth has changed considerably. Where heavy medication was once the norm, now natural, or prepared, childbirth has become increasingly popular. Today, husbands much more frequently participate in childbirth. Alternative birthing centers and birthing rooms have become standard in many maternity units, and the acceptance of midwives has increased. Before we examine some of these contemporary trends in childbirth strategies, let's explore the nature of standard childbirth.

Standard Childbirth

In the standard childbirth procedure that has been practiced for many years—and the way many of you probably were delivered—the expectant mother is taken to a hospital, where a doctor is responsible for the baby's delivery. Hospital staff prepare the pregnant woman for surgery by shaving her pubic hair and giving her an enema. She then is placed in a labor room, which often is filled with other pregnant women, some of whom are screaming. When she is ready to deliver, she is taken to the delivery room, which looks like an operating room. She is laid on the table with her legs in the air, and the physician, along with an anesthetist and a nurse, delivers the baby.

What could be wrong with this procedure? Critics list three things: (1) Important individuals related to the mother are excluded from the birth process. (2) The mother is separated from her infant in the first minutes and hours after birth. (3) Giving birth is treated like a disease, and a woman is thought of as a sick patient (Rosenblith, 1992). As we will see next, some alternatives differ radically from this standard procedure.

The Leboyer Method

The **Leboyer method,** *developed by French obstetrician Frederick Leboyer, intends to make the birth process less stressful for infants. Leboyer's procedure is referred to as "birth without violence."* He describes standard childbirth as torture (Leboyer, 1975). He vehemently objects to holding newborns upside down and slapping or spanking them, putting silver nitrite into their eyes, separating them immediately from their mothers, and scaring them with bright lights and harsh noises in the delivery room. Leboyer also criticizes the traditional habit of cutting the umbilical cord as soon as the infant is born; this forces the infant to immediately take in oxygen from the air to breathe. Leboyer believes that the umbilical cord should be left intact for several minutes to allow the newborn a chance to adjust to a world of breathing air. In the Leboyer method, the baby is placed on the mother's stomach immediately after birth so the mother can caress the infant. Then the infant is placed in a bath of warm water to relax. Although most hospitals do not use the soft lights and warm baths that Leboyer suggests, they sometimes do place the newborn on the mother's stomach immediately after birth, believing that it will stimulate mother-infant bonding.

> *We must respect this instant of birth, this fragile moment. The baby is between two worlds, on a threshold, hesitating, . . .*
>
> —Frederick Leboyer, **Birth Without Violence**

Prepared, or Natural, Childbirth

Prepared, or natural, childbirth *includes being informed about what will happen during the procedure, knowing about comfort measures for childbirth, anticipating that little or no medication will be used, and if complications arise, expecting to participate in decisions made to resolve the problems.* Medical treatment is used when there is a reason to, but it should always be done with care and concern for the expectant mother and the offspring. Prepared childbirth assumes the presence and support of a partner or friend, and in some cases, a labor-support person identified through local childbirth education groups. At least two persons, including the laboring woman, are needed to work with each contraction.

Prepared childbirth includes a number of variations. Consider the following three instances of prepared childbirth. The first woman in labor lies awake under light medication with an intravenous needle in her arm into which a nearby pump introduces a labor stimulant. She is attached to electronic monitoring devices and confined to the bed. A second woman is wearing her own clothes, sitting in a rocking chair in a birthing room, relaxing, attending to her breathing, and sipping a glass of cider with none of the above medications or equipment being used. At her infant's birth there will be no gowns or masks, and she will give birth in the birthing room instead of being moved to the delivery room. An older child who has learned about childbirth may even be in the room, preparing to welcome the new sibling. The third woman and her husband are "prepared" parents, who may or may not have attended cesarean preparation classes, but agree that cesarean birth is required. Both parents are in the delivery room and she is awake. Despite obvious involvement of the couple in the decision to have the cesarean birth, no one has yet described a cesarean birth as a natural one.

A basic philosophy of prepared childbirth is that information and teaching methods should support parent confidence, provide the knowledge required to carry out normal childbirth, and explain how the medical system functions in childbirth. Professional disciplines involved in childbirth now go beyond obstetrics (with its main emphasis on pathology rather than normal birth) and also include nursing, public health, education, physical therapy, psychology, sociology, and physiology. Each of these areas has contributed to teaching programs and provided increased knowledge about childbirth. But never to be overlooked is the input to health professionals from parents themselves.

The **Lamaze method** *has become a widely used childbirth strategy; it is a form of prepared or natural childbirth developed by Fernand Lamaze, a pioneering French obstetrician. It has become widely accepted by the medical profession and involves helping the expectant mother to cope actively with the pain of childbirth and to avoid or reduce medication.* Lamaze training for parents is available on a widespread basis in the United States and usually consists of six weekly classes. In these classes, the pregnant woman learns about the birth process and is trained in breathing and relaxation exercises. As the Lamaze method has grown in popularity, it has become more common for the father to participate in the exercises and to assist in the birth process.

Lamaze exercises and breathing have much in common with the other methods of prepared childbirth, with the exception that breathing techniques are more central to the method; Lamaze breathing is very active. Whatever the method of prepared childbirth that expectant couples choose, each will provide information about birth, ways of relaxing and releasing muscle tension, breathing patterns to relieve anxiety and bring adequate oxygen to the contracting uterine muscle, ways to avoid hyperventilation (overbreathing), and basic physical conditioning exercises.

The Doula

Doula is a Greek word that means "a woman who helps other women." In contemporary perinatal care, a **doula** *is a caregiver who provides continuous physical, emotional, and educational support to the mother before, during, and just after childbirth.* Doulas remain with the mother throughout labor, assessing and responding to her needs. In one recent study, mothers who received doula support reported less labor pain than mothers who did not receive doula support (Klaus, Kennell, & Klaus, 1993).

A doula is a layperson, usually a woman, who understands the biological and medical processes involved in labor and obstetrics, and who usually has assisted in at least five or six deliveries supervised by another doula. Doulas typically function as part of a "birthing team," serving as an adjunct to the midwife or the hospital obstetric staff.

In the United States, most doulas work as independent providers hired by the expectant woman. Managed care organizations are increasingly offering doula support as part of regular obstetric care. In some European countries, doula support is offered as standard care by midwives or nursing students. In many cultures, the practice of having a knowledgeable woman help a mother in labor is not officially labeled as "doula" support but is simply an ingrained, centuries-old custom.

Childbirth Today

Among the current changes in childbirth are shifts in emphasis, new choices, and an understanding of obstetrical terminology (Tappero, 1996). And an increasing number of instructors report that they are now using a more eclectic approach to childbirth, drawing information from several different methods (Bean, 1990). Let's examine some of these trends in more detail:

- Breathing methods continue to be important but are more flexible in accord with the individual needs of the expectant mother. In general, breathing is becoming less active and less vigorous, with more attention given to other methods of providing comfort. However, some prepared-childbirth instructors believe that the importance of breathing should not be downplayed too much.
- New ways of teaching relaxation are offered, including guided mental imagery, massage, and meditation.
- The use of warm water for comfort is recognized, and many hospitals have showers in their labor and delivery areas. Some hospitals have introduced Jacuzzis.
- A more homelike institutional environment is believed to be important.
- Stress from intense lighting and an intrusive environment can inhibit uterine contraction,

possibly slowing labor and even making the introduction of medication necessary. Hospitals are moving in the direction of having most nonsurgical births, including anesthetized births, in homelike birthing rooms that are quiet, peaceful, and less intensely lit.

- Walking during labor and the use of varied body positions during labor and birth are encouraged. For many women, the squatting position is the most comfortable and effective position.
- The "nothing by mouth" policy during labor is being seriously questioned and reexamined. Light food was initially introduced in home birth and freestanding birthing centers. It is now beginning to be offered in some hospitals.
- The use of midwife-assisted birth is becoming more widespread, allowing longer and more informative prenatal visits, labor support, and less use of medication.
- Parent-infant bonding, which we will discuss later in the chapter, is widely available and encouraged. Even if the baby is premature or ill, parents go to the intensive care nursery to see, touch, and talk to their newborn.
- Siblings and grandparents are welcome to touch and hold the baby in the hospital.
- Hospital stays have been shortened to 3 days or less, mainly because of recent government reimbursement regulations. Approximately 5 days are allowed for cesarean births.
- Increased amounts of time are spent discussing the pros and cons of various obstetrical and birthing options.

To further explore birth strategies, turn to Critical Thinking About Children's Development.

> *The strongest principle of human growth lies in human choice.*
>
> —Alexander Chase, *Perspectives*, 1966

The Father's Participation

In the past several decades, fathers increasingly have participated in childbirth. Fathers-to-be are now more likely to go to at least one meeting with the obstetrician or caregiver during the pregnancy, attend childbirth preparation classes, learn about labor and birth, and be more involved in the care of the young infant. The change is consistent with our culture's movement toward less rigid concepts of "masculine" and "feminine."

For many expectant couples today, the father is trained to be the expectant mother's coach during labor, helping her to learn relaxation methods and special breathing techniques for labor and birth. Most health

How is the scene above in a hospital recovery room in the 1990s different from the childbirth that took place earlier in this century?

professionals now believe that, just as with pregnancy, childbirth should be an intimate, shared moment between a man and a woman who are creating a new life together. Nonetheless, some men do not want to participate in prepared childbirth, and some women also still prefer that they not have a very active role. In such cases, other people can provide support for childbirth—mother, sister, friend, midwife, or physician, for example.

Husbands who are motivated to participate in childbirth have an important role at their wives' side. In the long stretches when there is no staff attendant present, a husband can provide companionship, support, and encouragement. In difficult moments of examination or medication, he can be comforting. Initially, he may feel embarrassed to use the breathing techniques he learned in preparation classes, but he usually begins to feel more at home when he realizes he is performing a necessary function for his wife during each contraction.

Some individuals question whether the father is the best coach during labor. He may be nervous and feel uncomfortable in the hospital, and, never having gone through labor himself, he might not understand the expectant mother's needs as well as another woman. There is no universal answer to this issue. Some laboring women want to depend on another woman, someone who has been through labor herself; others want their husbands to intimately share the childbirth experience. Many cultures exclude men from births, just as the American culture did until the last several decades. In some cultures, the woman's mother, or occasionally a daughter, serves as her assistant.

Siblings

If parents have a child and are expecting another, it is important for them to prepare the older child for the birth of a sibling. Sibling preparation includes providing the child with information about pregnancy, birth, and life with a newborn that is realistic and appropriate for the child's age.

CRITICAL THINKING ABOUT CHILDREN'S DEVELOPMENT

Birth Strategies

There are many birth strategies available to parents today. Among the strategies we discussed are standard childbirth, the Leboyer method, prepared or natural childbirth, and the Lamaze method. Which method do you think is best—for the mother, the father, and the offspring? Might there be individual differences in what works best? Evaluating different birth strategies encourages you to think critically about children's development by *using knowledge about development to improve human welfare.*

Parents can prepare their older child for the approaching birth at any time during pregnancy. The expectant mother might announce the pregnancy early to explain her tiredness and vomiting. If the child is young and unable to understand waiting, parents may want to delay announcing the pregnancy until later, when the expectant mother's pregnancy becomes obvious and she begins to look "fat" to the child.

Parents may want to consider having the child present at the birth. Many family-centered hospitals, birth centers, and home births make this option available. Some parents wish to minimize or avoid separation from the older child, so they choose to give birth where sibling involvement is possible. These parents feel that if there is no separation, the child will not develop separation anxiety and will not see the new baby as someone who took the mother away. Sibling involvement in the childbirth may enhance the attachment between the older child and the new baby. On the other hand, some children might not want to participate in the birthing process and should not be forced into it. Some preschool children might be overwhelmed by the whole process, and other children might feel embarrassed.

To help the child cope with the arrival of the new baby, parents can do the following:

- Before and after the birth, read books to the child about living with a new baby.
- Plan for time alone with the older child and do what he or she wants to do.
- Use the time when the baby is asleep and the parent is rested to give special attention to the older child.
- Give a gift to the older child in the hospital or at home.
- "Tell" the baby about her or his special brother or sister when the older sibling is listening.

Preterm Infants and Age-Weight Considerations

How can we distinguish between a preterm infant and a low-birthweight infant? What are the developmental outcomes for low-birthweight infants? Do preterm infants have a different profile than that of full-term infants? What conclusions can we reach about preterm infants?

An infant is full-term when it has grown in the womb for the full 38 to 42 weeks between conception and delivery. A **preterm infant** *(also called a premature infant) is one who is born prior to 38 weeks after conception.* **Low-birthweight infants** *are infants born after a regular gestation period (the length of time between conception and birth) of 38 to 42 weeks, but who weigh less than 5½ pounds. Both preterm and low-birthweight infants are considered high-risk infants* (Smith, Ulvund, & Lindemann, 1994).

A short gestation period does not necessarily harm an infant (Kopp, 1983). The neurological development of a short-gestation infant continues after birth on approximately the same timetable as if the infant still were in the womb. For example, consider an infant born after a gestation period of 30 weeks. At 38 weeks, approximately 2 months after birth, this infant shows the same level of brain development as a 38-week fetus who is yet to be born.

Some infants are born very early and have a precariously low birth weight. "Kilogram kids" weigh less than 2.3 pounds (which is 1 kilogram, or 1,000 grams) and are very premature. The task of saving such a baby is not easy. At the Stanford University Medical Center in Palo Alto, California, 98 percent of the preterm babies survive; however, 32 percent of those between 750 and 1,000 grams do not, and 76 percent of those below 750 grams do not. Approximately 250,000 preterm babies are born in the United States each year, and more than 15,000 of these weigh less than 1,000 grams.

Equal opportunity for life is an American ideal that is not fulfilled at birth (Paneth, 1995). African American babies are twice as likely as White babies to be born low in birth weight, to be born preterm, and to die at birth. Seventeen percent of all births are to African American families, yet 33 percent of all low-birthweight births and 38 percent of all very low-birthweight births are to African American families.

Although a large majority of low-birthweight infants are normal and healthy, as a group they have more

When parents have a child and are expecting another, they can provide the child with information about pregnancy, birth, and life with a newborn that is realistic and appropriate for the child's age. This information helps the child cope with the birth of a sibling. As part of the sibling preparation process, some parents choose to have the child present at the sibling's birth.

health and developmental problems than their normal-birthweight counterparts (Hack, Klein, & Taylor, 1995). The number and severity of these problems increase as birth weight decreases. With the improved survival of more infants who are born very early and very small comes increased numbers of children with severe brain damage. Cerebral palsy and other forms of brain injury are highly correlated with brain weight—the lower the brain weight, the greater the likelihood of brain injury. Approximately 7 percent of moderately low-birthweight infants (3 pounds 5 ounces to 5 pounds 8 ounces) have brain injuries. This figure increases to 20 percent for the smallest newborns (1 pound 2 ounces to 3 pounds 5 ounces). Low-birthweight infants are also more likely than normal-birthweight infants to have lung or liver diseases.

At school age, children who were born low in birth weight are more likely than their normal-birth-weight counterparts to have a learning disability, attention deficit disorder, and breathing problems such as asthma (Taylor, Klein, & Hack, 1994). Children born very low in birth weight have more learning problems and lower levels of achievement in reading and math than moderately low-birthweight children. These problems are reflected in much higher proportions of low-birthweight children enrolled in special education programs. Approximately one-half of all low-birthweight children enroll in special education programs.

It should be noted that not all of these adverse consequences can be attributed solely to being born low in birth weight. Some of the less severe but more common developmental and physical delays are a consequence of a disproportionate number of low-birthweight children coming from disadvantaged environments.

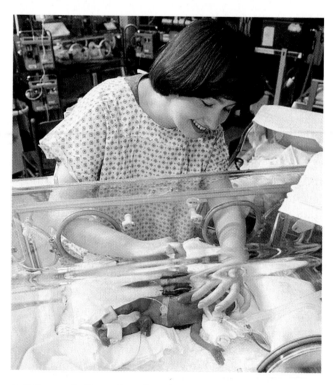

A "kilogram kid" weighing less than 2.3 pounds at birth. In the neonatal intensive care unit, banks of flashing lights, blinking numbers, and beeping alarms stand guard over kilogram kids, who are extreme preterm infants. They often lie on a water bed that gently undulates; the water bed is in an incubator that is controlled for temperature and humidity by the baby's own body. Such vital signs as brain waves, heartbeat, blood gases, and respiratory rate are constantly monitored. All of this care can be very expensive. Though the cost can usually be kept within five figures, 5 or 6 months of neonatal intensive care can result in expenses of as much as $1 million or more.

Some of the devastating effects of being born low in birth weight can be reversed (Blair & Ramey, 1996; Shiono & Behrman, 1995). Intensive enrichment programs that provide medical and educational services for both the parents and the child have been shown to improve short-term developmental outcomes for low-birthweight children. Federal laws mandate that services for school-age disabled children (which include medical, educational, psychological, occupational, and physical care) be expanded to include family-based care for infants. At present, these services are aimed at children born with severe congenital disabilities. The availability of services for moderately low-birthweight children who do not have severe physical problems varies from state to state, but generally these services are not available.

Despite the advances made in prenatal care and technology in the United States, the availability of high-quality medical and educational services still needs much improvement (Brooks-Gunn, McCarton, & Tonascia, 1992). In some countries, especially in Scandinavia and Western Europe, more consistent, higher-quality prenatal care is provided than in the United States. To read further about the nature of prenatal care in different countries, turn to Sociocultural Worlds of Children.

Measures of Neonatal Health and Responsiveness

The **Apgar scale** *is a method widely used to assess the health of newborns at 1 and 5 minutes after birth. The Apgar scale evaluates infants' heart rate, respiratory effort, muscle tone, body color, and reflex irritability.* An obstetrician or nurse does the evaluation and gives the newborn a score, or reading, of 0, 1, or 2 on each of these five health signs (see figure 4.6). A total score of 7 to 10 indicates that the newborn's condition is good, a score of 5 indicates there may be developmental difficulties, and a score of 3 or below signals an emergency and indicates that the baby's survival may be in doubt.

Whereas the Apgar scale is used immediately after birth to identify high-risk infants who need resuscitation, the **Brazelton Neonatal Behavioral Assessment Scale** *is given shortly after birth to assess the newborn's neurological development, reflexes, and reactions to people* (Brazelton, 1973). Twenty reflexes are assessed, along with reactions to circumstances, such as the infant's reaction to a rattle. The examiner rates the newborn, or neonate, on each of 27 categories (table 4.2). As an indication of how detailed the ratings are, consider item 15: "cuddliness." Nine categories are involved in assessing this item, with infant behavior scored on a continuum that ranges from the infant's being very resistant to being held to the infant's being extremely cuddly and clinging. The Brazelton scale not only is used as a sensitive index of neurological competence in the week after birth, but it

also is used widely as a measure in many research studies on infant development. In recent versions of scoring on the Brazelton scale, Brazelton and his colleagues (1987) categorize the 27 items into four categories—physiological, motoric, state, and interaction. They also classify the baby in global terms, such as *worrisome*, *normal*, or *superior*, based on these categories.

A very low Brazelton score can indicate brain damage, or it might reflect stress to the brain that might heal in time. If an infant merely seems sluggish in responding to social circumstances, parents are encouraged to give the infant attention and become more sensitive to the infant's needs. Parents are shown how the newborn can respond to people and how to stimulate such responses. Researchers have found that the social interaction skills of both high-risk infants and healthy, responsive infants can be improved through such communication with parents (Widmayer & Field, 1980).

THE POSTPARTUM PERIOD

Many health professionals believe that the best postpartum care is family centered, using the family's resources to support an early and smooth adjustment to the newborn by all family members. What is the postpartum period? What physical changes does it involve? What emotional and psychological changes are encountered?

The Nature of the Postpartum Period

The **postpartum period** *is the period after childbirth or delivery. It is a time when the woman's body adjusts, both physically and psychologically, to having completed the process of childbearing. It lasts for about 6 weeks or until the body has completed its adjustment and has returned to a near prepregnant state.* Some health professionals refer to the postpartum period as the "fourth trimester." While the time span of the postpartum period does not necessarily cover 3 months, the terminology of "fourth trimester" demonstrates the idea of continuity and the importance of the first several months after birth for the mother.

The postpartum period is influenced by what preceded it. During pregnancy the woman's body gradually adjusted to physical changes, but now it is forced to respond quickly. The method of delivery and circumstances surrounding the delivery affect the speed with which the woman's body readjusts during the postpartum period.

The postpartum period involves a great deal of adjustment and adaptation. The baby has to be cared for; the mother has to recover from childbirth; the mother has to learn how to take care of the baby; the mother needs to learn to feel good about herself as a mother; the father needs to learn how to take care of his recovering wife; the father needs to learn how to take care of the baby; and the father needs to learn how to feel good about himself as a father.

Prenatal Care in the United States and Around the World

As advanced as the United States has become economically and technologically, it still has more low-birthweight infants than a number of other countries (Grant, 1996). As indicated in table 4.A, only 4 percent of the infants born in Sweden, Finland, the Netherlands, and Norway are low in birth weight, and only 5 percent of those born in New Zealand, Australia, France, and Japan are low in birth weight. Also, as indicated in table 4.A, in some developing countries, such as Bangladesh, where poverty is rampant and the health and nutrition of mothers is poor, the percentage of low-birthweight infants reaches as high as 50 percent of all infants.

In the United States, there also are discrepancies in prenatal development and birth between African American infants and White infants. African American infants are twice as likely to be born prematurely, have low birth weight, and have mothers who received late or no prenatal care; are three times as likely to have their mothers die in childbirth; and are five times as likely to be born to unmarried teenage mothers (Edelman, 1996).

In many of the countries with a lower percentage of low-birthweight infants than the United States, either free or very low-cost prenatal and postnatal care is available to mothers. This care includes paid maternity leave from work that ranges from 9 to 40 weeks. In Norway and the Netherlands, prenatal care is coordinated with a general practitioner, an obstetrician, and a midwife.

Pregnant women in the United States do not receive the uniform prenatal care that women in many Scandinavian and Western European countries receive. The United States does not have a national policy of health care that assures high-quality assistance for pregnant women. The cost of giving birth is approximately $4,000 in the United States (more than $5,000 for a cesarean birth), and more than 25 percent of all American women of prime childbearing age do not have insurance that will pay for hospital costs. More than one-fifth of all White mothers and one-third of all African American mothers do not receive prenatal care in the first trimester of their pregnancy. Five percent of White mothers and 10 percent of African American mothers receive no prenatal care at all. Many infant-development researchers believe that the United States needs more comprehensive medical and educational services to improve the quality of prenatal care and reduce the percentage of low-birth-weight infants.

TABLE 4.A

Percentage of Low-Birthweight Infants

Country	Low-Birthweight Infants (Percentage)
Bangladesh	50
India	30
Guatemala	18
Iran	14
Mexico	12
USSR	9
United States, Great Britain, Israel, Egypt	7
Canada, China	6
New Zealand, Australia, France, Japan	5
Sweden, Finland, the Netherlands, Norway	4

Source: Data from J. Grant, *State of the World's Children*, 1986.

The 27 Categories on the Brazelton Neonatal Behavioral Assessment Scale (NBAS)

1. Response decrement to repeated visual stimuli
2. Response decrement to rattle
3. Response decrement to bell

4. Response decrement to pinprick
5. Orienting response to inanimate visual stimuli
6. Orienting response to inanimate auditory stimuli

7. Orienting response to inanimate visual and auditory stimuli
8. Orienting response to animate visual stimuli—examiner's face
9. Orienting response to animate auditory stimuli—examiner's voice

10. Orienting response to animate visual and auditory stimuli
11. Quality and duration of alert periods
12. General muscle tone—in resting and in response to being handled, passive, and active

13. Motor activity
14. Traction responses as the infant is pulled to sit
15. Cuddliness—responses to being cuddled by examiner

16. Defensive movements—reactions to a cloth over the infant's face
17. Consolability with intervention by examiner
18. Peak of excitement and capacity to control self

19. Rapidity of buildup to crying state
20. Irritability during the examination
21. General assessment of kind and degree of activity

22. Tremulousness
23. Amount of startling
24. Lability of skin color—measuring autonomic lability

25. Lability of states during entire examination
26. Self-quieting activity—attempts to console self and control state
27. Hand-to-mouth activity

Physical Adjustments

The woman's body makes numerous physical adjustments in the first days and weeks after childbirth. She may have a great deal of energy or feel exhausted and let down. Most new mothers feel tired and need rest. While these changes are normal, the fatigue can undermine the new mother's sense of well-being and confidence in her ability to cope with a new baby and a new family life.

Involution is *the process by which the uterus returns to its prepregnant size 5 or 6 weeks after birth.* Immediately following birth, the uterus weighs 2 to 3 pounds and the fundus can be felt midway between the naval and the pubic bone. By the end of 5 or 6 weeks, the uterus weighs 2 to 3½ ounces and it has returned to its prepregnancy size. Nursing the baby helps to contract the uterus at a rapid rate.

After delivery, a woman's body undergoes sudden and dramatic changes in hormone production. When the placenta is delivered, estrogen and progesterone levels drop steeply and remain low until the ovaries start producing hormones again. The woman will probably begin menstruating again in 4 to 8 weeks if she is not breast-feeding. If she is breast-feeding, she might not menstruate for several months, though ovulation can occur during this time. The first several menstrual periods following delivery may be heavier than usual, but periods soon return to normal.

Some women and men want to resume sexual intercourse as soon as possible after the birth. Others feel constrained or afraid. A sore perineum (the area between the anus and vagina in the female), a demanding baby, lack of help, and extreme fatigue affect a woman's ability to relax and to enjoy making love. Physicians often recommend that women refrain from having sexual intercourse for approximately 6 weeks following the birth of the baby. However, it is probably safe to have sexual intercourse when the stitches heal, vaginal discharge stops, and the woman feels like it.

If the woman regularly engaged in conditioning exercises during pregnancy, exercise will help her to recover her former body contour and strength during the postpartum period. With a caregiver's approval, the woman can begin some exercises as soon as 1 hour after delivery. In addition to recommending exercise in the postpartum period for women, health professionals also increasingly recommend that women practice the relaxation techniques they used during pregnancy and childbirth. Five minutes of slow breathing on a stressful day in the postpartum period can relax and refresh the new mother as well as the new baby.

Emotional and Psychological Adjustments

Emotional fluctuations are common on the part of the mother in the postpartum period. These emotional fluctuations can be due to any of a number of factors: hormonal changes, fatigue, inexperience or lack of confidence with newborn babies, or the extensive time and demands involved in caring for a newborn. For some women, the emotional fluctuations decrease within several weeks after the delivery and are a minor aspect of their motherhood. For others, they are longer lasting and can produce feelings of anxiety, depression, and difficulty in coping with stress. Mothers who have such feelings, even when they are getting adequate rest, may benefit from professional help in dealing with their problems. Following are some of the signs that may indicate a need for professional counseling about postpartum adaptation:

- Excessive worrying
- Depression
- Extreme changes in appetite
- Crying spells
- Inability to sleep

Postpartum depression affects as many as 70 percent of women (Field, 1995). The effect of postpartum depression on the infant can be considerable, with delays in growth and development if the mother continues to be depressed when the infant is 6 months of age. Postpartum depression is also a primary consideration regarding a return to work (Campbell, Cohn, & Meyers, 1995; Field, 1995). Some experts believe that the mother who stays at home and becomes depressed is probably doing her infant a greater disservice than if she went to work and the infant was cared for by someone who was not depressed.

Another adjustment for the mother and for the father is the time and thought that go into being a competent parent of a young infant. It is important for both the mother and the father to become aware of the young infant's developmental needs—physically, psychologically, and emotionally. Both the mother and the father need to develop a comfortable relationship with the young infant.

A special aspect of the parent-infant relationships is **bonding,** *the occurrence of close contact, especially physical, between parents and newborn in the period shortly after birth.* Some physicians believe that this period shortly after birth is critical in development; during this time, the parents and child need to form an important emotional attachment that provides a foundation for optimal development in years to come. Special interest in bonding came about when some pediatricians argued that the circumstances surrounding delivery often separate mothers and their infants, preventing or making difficult the development of a bond. The pediatricians further argued that giving the mother drugs to make her

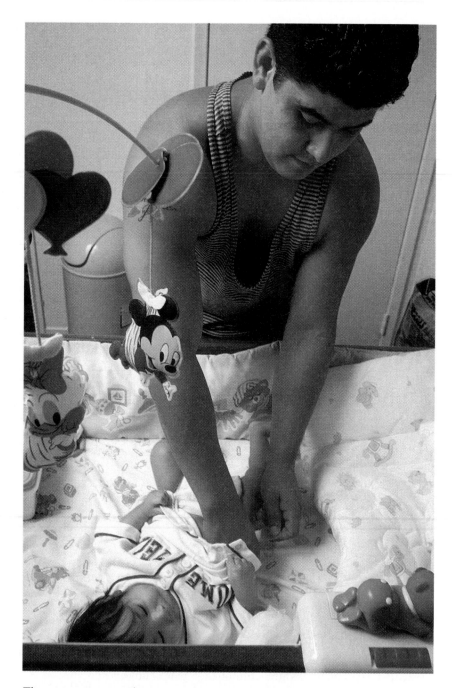

The postpartum period is a time of considerable adjustment and adaptation for both the mother and the father. Fathers can provide an important support system for mothers, especially in helping mothers care for young infants.

delivery less painful may contribute to the lack of bonding. The drugs may make the mother drowsy, thus interfering with her ability to respond to and stimulate the newborn. Advocates of bonding also assert that preterm infants are isolated from their mothers to an even greater degree than full-term infants, thereby increasing their difficulty in bonding.

Is there evidence that such close contact between mothers and newborns is absolutely critical for optimal development later in life? Although some research supports the bonding hypothesis (Klaus & Kennell, 1976), a growing body of research challenges the significance of the first few days of life as a critical period (Bakeman & Brown, 1980). Indeed, the extreme form of the bonding hypothesis—that the newborn must have close contact with the mother in the first few days of life to develop optimally—simply is not true (Lamb, 1994).

Nonetheless, the weakness of the maternal-infant bonding research should not be used as an excuse to keep motivated mothers from interacting with their infants in the postpartum period, because such contact brings pleasure to many mothers. In some mother-infant pairs—including preterm infants, adolescent mothers, or mothers from disadvantaged circumstances—the practice of bonding may set in motion a climate for improved interaction after the mother and infant leave the hospital.

The new baby also changes a mother's and father's relationship with each other. Among the questions that have to be dealt with are these: How will we share the housework and baby care? How can we find enough time for each other when the baby takes up so much of our time? How can we arrange to get out of the house so we can enjoy some of the things we did before the baby came? At some point, new parents have to figure out which of their commitments are the most important, and which have to get less time, or be dropped. Support from relatives, friends, and baby-sitters can help new parents find time to renew some of these activities they enjoyed earlier.

A special concern of many new mothers is whether they should stay home with the baby or go back to work. Some mothers want to return to work as soon as possible after the infant is born, others want to stay home with the infant for several months, then return to work, others want to stay home for a year before they return to work, and yet others, of course, did not work prior to the baby's arrival and do not plan to do so in the future.

At this point we have discussed a number of ideas about birth and the postpartum period. A summary of these ideas is presented in concept table 4.2.

CONCEPT TABLE 4.2

Birth and the Postpartum Period

Concept	Processes/ Related Ideas	Characteristics/Description
Birth	Stages of birth	Three stages of birth have been defined. The first lasts about 12 to 24 hours for a woman having her first child. The cervix dilates to about 4 inches. The second stage begins when the baby's head moves through the cervix and ends with the baby's complete emergence. The third stage is afterbirth.
	Delivery complications	A baby can move through the birth canal too rapidly or too slowly. A delivery that is too fast is called precipitate; when delivery is too slow, anoxia may result. A cesarean section is the surgical removal of the baby from the uterus.
	The use of drugs during childbirth	A wide variety of tranquilizers, sedatives, and analgesics are used to relieve the expectant mother's pain and anxiety, and oxytocin is used to speed delivery. Birthweight and social class are more powerful predictors of problems than are drugs. A drug can have mixed effects and the overall amount of medication needs to be considered.
	Childbirth strategies	In standard childbirth, the expectant mother is taken to the hospital, where a doctor is responsible for the baby's delivery. The birth takes place in a delivery room, which looks like an operating room, and medication is used in the procedure. Criticisms of the standard childbirth procedure have been made. The Leboyer method and prepared, or natural, childbirth are alternatives to standard childbirth. A widely practiced form of natural childbirth is the Lamaze method. The doula is a caregiver who provides support for the mother before, during, and after birth. Among the current changes in childbirth are shifts in emphases, new choices, and an understanding of obstetrical terminology. In the past several decades, fathers have increasingly participated in childbirth. Another special concern is the sibling's role in childbirth.
	Preterm infants and age-weight considerations	Preterm infants are those born after an abnormally short time period in the womb. Infants who are born after a regular gestation period of 38 to 42 weeks but who weigh less than 5½ pounds are called low-birth-weight infants. Whether a preterm infant will have developmental problems is a complex issue. Although a large majority of low-birthweight infants are normal and healthy, as a group they have more health and developmental problems than their normal-birthweight counterparts. The number and severity of the problems increase as birth weight decreases.
	Measures of neonatal health and responsiveness	For many years the Apgar scale has been used to assess the newborn's health. A more recently developed test—the Brazelton Neonatal Behavioral Assessment Scale—is used for long-term neurological assessment. It assesses not only the newborn's neurological integrity but also its social responsiveness.
The Postpartum Period	Its nature	The postpartum period is the period after childbirth or delivery. It is a time when the woman's body adjusts, both physically and psychologically, to the process of childbearing. It lasts for about 6 weeks or until her body has completed its adjustment.
	Physical adjustments	These include fatigue, involution (the process by which the uterus returns to its prepregnant size 5 or 6 weeks after birth), hormone changes that include a dramatic drop in estrogen and progesterone, consideration of when to resume sexual intercourse, and participation in exercises to recover former body contour and strength.
	Emotional and psychological adjustments	Emotional fluctuations on the part of the mother are common in the postpartum period. They may be due to hormonal changes, fatigue, inexperience or lack of confidence with newborn babies, or the extensive time and other demands involved in caring for a newborn. For some, the emotional fluctuations are minimal and disappear in several weeks; for others, they are more long-lasting. Another adjustment for both the mother and the father is the time and thought that go into being a competent parent of a young infant. A special interest in parent-infant relationships is bonding, which has not been found to be critical in the development of a competent infant or child, but which may stimulate positive interaction between some mother-infant pairs. The new baby also changes the mother's and father's relationship with each other.

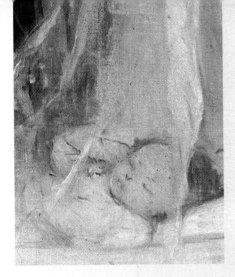

SUMMARY

When a species reproduces itself, life comes from life. Much of this chapter was about becoming. Pregnancy is a state of becoming. An unborn baby is becoming a person capable of life outside the mother's body, and a man and a woman are becoming parents.

In this chapter, you read about the course of prenatal development and its three main periods—germinal, embryonic, and fetal, as well as about miscarriage and abortion, maternal characteristics, teratology and hazards to prenatal development, such as the mother's use of drugs, and prenatal care. You also read about birth, including childbirth strategies, preterm infants, and age-weight considerations. And you studied the postpartum period and its physical and psychological adjustments.

Don't forget that you can obtain a summary of the entire chapter by again studying the two concept tables on pages 120 and 132. In the next chapter, we will continue the early aspects of the child's development, focusing on physical, motor, and perceptual development in infancy.

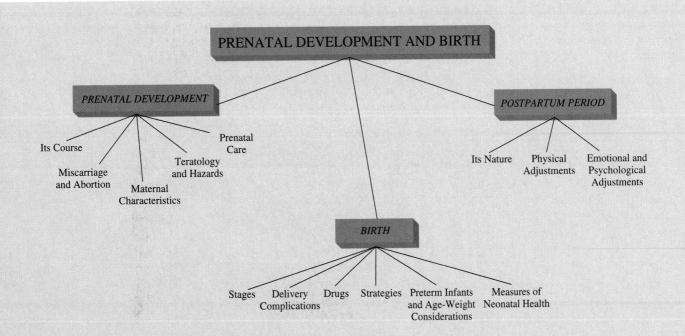

PRACTICAL KNOWLEDGE ABOUT CHILDREN

What to Expect When You're Expecting

(1991) by Arlene Eisenberg, Heidi E. Murkoff, and Sandee E. Hathaway, New York: Workman.

What to Expect When You're Expecting is a month-by-month, step-by-step comprehensive guide to pregnancy and childbirth.

This is an excellent book for expectant parents. It is reassuring and thorough, and filled with charts and lists that make understanding pregnancy an easier task. One of the book's enthusiasts said that it is like having an experienced mother nearby whom you can always call with questions like, "Hey, did you get leg cramps in the fifth month of pregnancy?"

Will It Hurt the Baby?

(1990) by Richard Abrams, Reading, MA: Addison-Wesley.

Will It Hurt the Baby? examines the safe use of medication during pregnancy and breast-feeding. The author is a professor of medicine and pediatrics at the University of Colorado School of Medicine. Abrams describes the trend in eliminating medicine during pregnancy, but believes that in some cases a drug's benefits outweigh its risks. He discusses fifteen common medical problems women face during pregnancy, their symptoms, and special concerns about them. He also describes nine environmental and occupational hazards during pregnancy, such as food additives, pesticides, and physical exertion. In a final section of almost three hundred pages, hundreds of drugs, from acetaminophen (Tylenol) to zidovudine (AZT), are evaluated.

This is a good reference guide for expectant mothers and breast-feeding mothers. Respected pediatrician T. Berry Brazelton (1990) commented that the book is very timely and useful.

Methods of Childbirth

(1990, rev. ed.) by Constance Bean, New York: Quill.

Methods of Childbirth is a comprehensive guide to prepared childbirth, including discussion of the Lamaze, Bradley, Dick-Read, Kitzinger, and other methods. Also covered are topics such as conditioning exercises, the pros and cons of medication, fitness, how to reduce the chance of having a cesarean section, working and breast-feeding, home birth, alternative birth centers, midwives, and how to have a meaningful dialogue with a doctor and hospital staff.

This is a good resource for learning about a wide variety of childbirth methods and for information about how to make a baby's birth as safe and worry-free as possible.

EXPLORATIONS IN CHILD DEVELOPMENT

To further explore the nature of child development, we will examine a research study involving an intervention program for low-birthweight infants, and we will discuss the role of touch and massage in development.

RESEARCH IN CHILD DEVELOPMENT

Evaluation of an Intervention Program for Low-Birthweight Infants

Featured Study
Achenbach, T. M., Phares, V., Howell, C. T., Rauh, V. A., & Nurcombe, B. (1990). Seven-year outcome of the Vermont Intervention Program for Low-Birthweight Infants. *Child Development, 61,* 1672–1681.

An important task is to find ways to effectively intervene in the lives of low-birthweight infants who are at risk for developmental problems. The intervention used in this investigation was designated as the Mother-Infant Transaction Program. This program was developed to improve the mother's adjustment to caring for a low-birthweight infant by (a) enabling the mother to appreciate her baby's specific behavioral and temperamental characteristics, (b) sensitizing her to the baby's cues, especially those that signal stimulus overload, distress, and readiness for interaction, and (c) teaching her to

respond appropriately to those cues in order to facilitate mutually satisfying interactions.

The Mother-Infant Transaction Program was implemented by a neonatal intensive care nurse who worked with the mother and infant in seven daily sessions during the week prior to the infant's discharge from the hospital and four home sessions at 3, 14, 30, and 90 days after discharge. The purpose of the present study was to assess the long-term effects of the Mother-Infant Transaction Program by evaluating early-school-age children's cognitive skills.

Method
The subjects weighed less than 2,250 grams at birth and were free of congenital abnormalities and severe neurological defects. They were randomly assigned to an experimental group (the Mother-Infant Transaction Program) or to a control group (who did not get the intervention program). Also a normal-birthweight comparison group (weighing more than 2,800 grams at birth and born after more than 37 weeks' gestation) was recruited for study from babies

after each low-birthweight baby in the control group.

Cognitive tests were administered to 24 experimental-group children, 32 control-group children, and 37 normal-birthweight children in the summer of their seventh birthday. The tests used were (a) the Kaufman Assessment Battery for Children, which included cognitive scales and an achievement scale, and (b) the Peabody Picture Vocabulary Test.

Results and Discussion
At age 7, the low-birthweight children whose mothers had participated in the early intervention program scored higher than the control group of low-birthweight children on a number of the cognitive, information-processing measures in the Kaufman Battery. Further, the cognitive scores of the low-birthweight children in the program intervention group were very similar to those of the normal-birthweight children. The findings revealed that the intervention prevented cognitive lags in the low-birthweight children.

IMPROVING THE LIVES OF CHILDREN

The Power of Touch and Massage in Development

Interest has surged in the roles of touch and massage in improving the growth, health, and well-being of infants and children. The interest has especially been stimulated by a number of

research investigations by Tiffany Field, director of the Touch Research Institute at the University of Miami School of Medicine. In one investigation, 40 preterm infants who had just been released from an intensive care unit and placed in a transitional nursery were studied (Field, Scafidi, & Schanberg, 1987). Twenty

of the preterm babies were given special stimulation with massage and exercise for three 15-minute periods at the beginning of 3 consecutive hours every morning for 10 weekdays. For example, each infant was placed on its stomach and gently stroked. The massage began with the head and neck and moved downward to the feet.

It also moved from the shoulders down to the hands. The infant was then rolled over. Each arm and leg was flexed and extended; then both legs were flexed and extended. Next, the massage was repeated.

The massaged and exercised preterm babies gained 47 percent more weight than their preterm counterparts who were not massaged and exercised, even though both groups had the same number of feedings per day and averaged the same intake of formula. The increased activity of the massaged, exercised infants would seem to work against weight gain. However, similar findings have been discovered with animals. The increased activity may increase gastrointestinal and metabolic efficiency. The massaged infants were more active and alert, and they performed better on developmental tests. Also, their hospital stay was about 6 days shorter than that of the non-massaged, nonexercised group, which saved about $3,000 per preterm infant. Field (1992) has recently replicated these findings with preterm infants in another study.

In a recent study, Field (1992) gave the same kind of massage (firm stroking with the palms of the hands) to preterm infants who were exposed to cocaine in utero. The infants also showed significant weight gain and improved scores on developmental tests. Currently, Field is using massage therapy with HIV-exposed preterm infants with the hope that their immune system functioning will be improved. Others she has targeted include infants of depressed mothers, infants with colic, infants and children with sleep problems, as well as children who have diabetes, asthma, and juvenile arthritis.

In one recent study, Field and her colleagues (in press) investigated 1- to 3-month old infants born to depressed adolescent mothers. The infants were given 15 minutes of either massage or rocking for 2 days per week for a 6-week period (Field & others, in press). Infants who received massage therapy were calmer and gained more weight than the rocked infants.

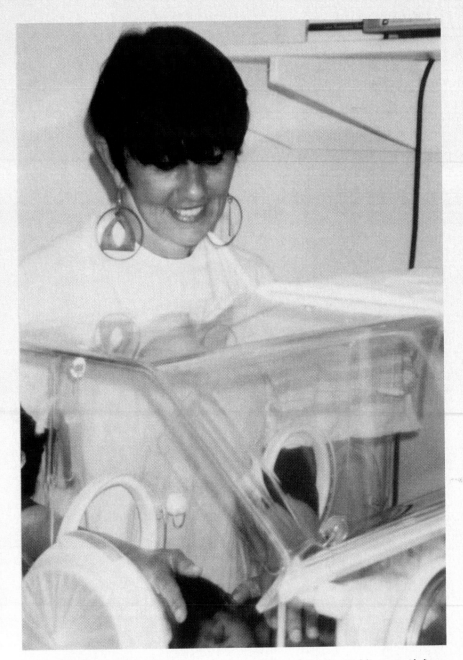

Shown here is Dr. Tiffany Field massaging a newborn infant. Dr. Field's research has clearly demonstrated the power of massage in improving the developmental outcome of at-risk infants. Under her direction the Touch Research Institute in Miami, Florida, was recently developed to investigate the role of touch in a number of domains of health and well-being.

Field (1995) also reports that touch has been helpful with children and adolescents who have touch aversions, such as children who have been sexually abused, autistic children, and adolescents with eating disorders. Field also is studying the amount of touch a child normally receives during school activities. She hopes that positive forms of touch will return to school systems where touching has been outlawed because of potential sexual-abuse lawsuits.

Thomas Eakins
Baby at Play, 1876, detail

Chapter

5

Physical, Motor, and Perceptual Development in Infancy

Systematic reasoning is something we could not, as a species of individuals, do without. But neither, if we are to remain sane, can we do without direct perception . . . of the inner and outer world into which we have been born.

—Aldous Huxley

> *A baby is the most complicated object made by unskilled labor.*
>
> —Anonymous

Studying Newborns

PREVIEW

𝒜mong the first things developmentalists were able to demonstrate was that infants have highly developed perceptual motor systems. Until recently, even some nurses in maternity hospitals believed that newborns are blind at birth, and they told this to mothers. Most parents also were told that their newborns could not taste, smell, or feel pain. As you will discover later in this chapter, we now know that newborns can see (albeit fuzzily), taste, smell, and feel pain. Before we turn to the fascinating world of infant perception, we will discuss a number of ideas about the infants' physical growth, the brain and its development, and motor development.

The creature has poor motor coordination and can move itself only with great difficulty. Its general behavior appears to be disorganized, and, although it cries when uncomfortable, it uses few other vocalizations. In fact, it sleeps most of the time, about 16 to 17 hours a day. You are curious about this creature and want to know more about what it can do. You think to yourself, "I wonder if it can see. How could I find out?"

You obviously have a communication problem with the creature. You must devise a way that will allow the creature to "tell" you that it can see. While examining the creature one day, you make an interesting discovery. When you move a large object toward it, it moves its head backward, as if to avoid a collision with the object. The creature's head movement suggests that it has at least some vision.

In case you haven't already guessed, the creature you have been reading about is the human infant, and the role you played is that of a developmentalist interested in devising techniques to learn about the infant's visual perception. After years of work, scientists have developed research tools and methods sophisticated enough to examine the subtle abilities of infants and to interpret their complex actions. Videotape equipment allows researchers to investigate elusive behaviors, and high-speed computers make it possible to perform complex data analysis in minutes instead of months and years. Other sophisticated equipment is used to closely monitor respiration, heart rate, body movement, visual fixation, and sucking behavior, which provide clues to what is going on inside the infant.

PHYSICAL GROWTH AND DEVELOPMENT

Infants' physical development in the first 2 years of life is extensive. We will begin our evaluation of these changes by examining some general growth patterns.

Cephalocaudal and Proximodistal Sequences

The **cephalocaudal pattern** *is the sequence in which the greatest growth always occurs at the top—the head—with physical growth in size, weight, and feature differentiation gradually working its way down from top to bottom (for example, neck, shoulders, middle trunk, and so on).* This same pattern occurs in the head area, because the top parts of the head—the eyes and brain—grow faster than the lower parts, such as the jaw. An extraordinary proportion of the total body is occupied by the head during prenatal development and early infancy (see figure 5.1).

The **proximodistal pattern** *is the sequence in which growth starts at the center of the body and moves toward the extremities.* An example of this is the early maturation of muscular control of the trunk and arms as compared with that of the hands and fingers.

Height and Weight

The average North American newborn is 20 inches long and weighs 7½ pounds. Ninety-five percent of full-term newborns are 18 to 22 inches long and weigh between 5½ and 10 pounds. In the first several days of life, most newborns lose 5 to 7 percent of their body weight before they learn to adjust to neonatal feeding. Once infants adjust to sucking, swallowing, and digesting they grow rapidly, gaining an average of 5 to 6 ounces per week during the first month. They have doubled their birthweight by the age of 4 months and nearly tripled it by their first birthday.

Infants grow about 1 inch per month during the first year, reaching approximately 1½ times their birth length by their first birthday.

Infants' rate of growth is considerably slower in the second year of life. By 2 years of age, infants weigh approximately 26 to 32 pounds, having gained a quarter to half a pound per month during the second year; now they have reached about one-fifth of their adult weight. At 2 years of age, the average infant is 32 to 35 inches in height, which is nearly one-half of their adult height.

Infant States

Developmentalists do not only chart infants' height and weight patterns; they also examine the infant's states. *States* is an abbreviation for *states of consciousness,* which refers to an individual's level of awareness. One classification scheme describes seven infant states (Thoman & others, 1981):

1. *No REM sleep.* The infant's eyes are closed and still, and there is no motor activity other than occasional startle, rhythmic mouthing, or slight limb movement.

2. *Active sleep without REM.* The infant's eyes are closed and still, and motor activity is present.

3. *REM sleep.* The infant's eyes are closed, although they might open briefly. Rapid eye movements can be detected through closed eyelids, and motor activity might or might not be present.

4. *Indeterminate sleep.* This category is reserved for all transitional sleep states that cannot fit the above codes.

5. *Drowsy.* The infant's eyes might be opening and closing, but they have a dull, glazed appearance. Motor activity is minimal.

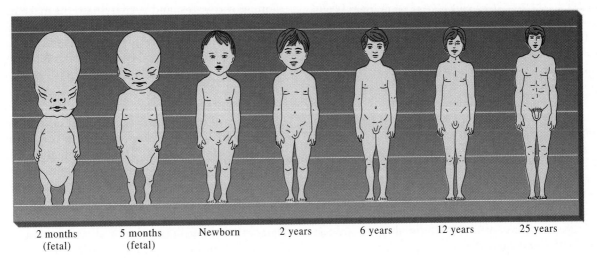

| 2 months (fetal) | 5 months (fetal) | Newborn | 2 years | 6 years | 12 years | 25 years |

Figure~5.1

Changes in Body Form and Proportion During Prenatal and Postnatal Growth
Note the changes in body proportions from 2 months into fetal development to 25 years of age and the "large" head of the newborn.

6. *Inactive alert.* The infant is relatively inactive, although there might be occasional limb movements. The eyes are wide open and bright and shiny.

7. *Active awake.* The infant's eyes are open, and there is motor activity.

8. *Crying.* The infant's eyes can be open or closed, and motor activity is present. Agitated vocalizations are also present.

Using classification schemes such as the one just described, researchers have identified many different aspects of infant development. One such aspect is the sleeping-waking cycle. When we were infants, sleep consumed more of our time than it does now. Newborns sleep for 16 to 17 hours a day, although some sleep more and others less. The range is from a low of about 10 hours to a high of about 21 hours. The longest period of sleep is not always between 11 P.M. and 7 A.M. Although total sleep remains somewhat consistent for young infants, their sleep during the day does not always follow a rhythmic pattern. An infant might change from sleeping several long bouts of 7 or 8 hours to three or four shorter sessions only a few hours in duration. By about 1 month of age, most infants have begun to sleep longer at night, and by about 4 months of age they usually have moved closer to adultlike sleep patterns, spending their longest span of sleep at night and their longest span of waking during the day.

> *S*leep that knits up the ravelled sleave of care. . . .
> Balm of hurt minds, nature's second course.
> Chief nourishers in life's feast.
> —**William Shakespeare**

Researchers are intrigued by the various forms of infant sleep. They are especially interested in **REM (rapid eye movement) sleep,** *a recurring sleep stage during which vivid dreams commonly occur.* Most adults spend about one-fifth of their night in REM sleep, and REM sleep usually appears about 1 hour after non-REM sleep. However, about one-half of an infant's sleep is REM sleep, and infants often begin their sleep cycle with REM sleep rather than non-REM sleep. By the time infants reach 3 months of age, the percentage of time spent in REM sleep falls to about 40 percent and no longer does REM sleep begin the sleep cycle. The large amount of REM sleep may provide infants with added self-stimulation, since they spend less time awake than do older children. REM sleep also may promote the brain's development.

A special concern about infant sleep is **sudden infant death syndrome (SIDS),** *a condition that occurs when an infant stops breathing, usually during the night, and suddenly dies without apparent cause.* Approximately 13 percent of infant deaths are due to SIDS; between 10 days after birth and 1 year of age, SIDS results in more deaths than any other factor. While we do not know exactly what causes SIDS, infants who die from the condition reveal biological vulnerabilities early in their development, including a greater incidence of prematurity, a low birthweight, low Apgar scores, and respiratory problems (Woolsey, 1992). In one recent study, the greater the total number of cigarettes the infant was passively exposed to after birth from all adults, the higher was the infant's risk of SIDS (Klonoff-Cohen & others, 1995). Lying in a prone position and having an elevated fetal hemoglobin have also been found to be risk factors in SIDS. Researchers now believe that SIDS is caused by multiple factors.

Nutrition

Four-month-old Robert lives in Bloomington, Indiana, with his middle-class parents. He is well nourished and healthy. By contrast, 4-month-old Nikita lives in Ethiopia. Nikita and his parents live in impoverished conditions. Nikita is so poorly nourished that he has become emaciated and lies near death. The lives of Robert and Nikita reveal the vast diversity of nutritional status among today's children. Our coverage of infant nutrition begins with information about nutritional needs and eating behavior, then turns to the issue of breast- versus bottle-feeding, and concludes with an overview of malnutrition.

Nutritional Needs and Eating Behavior

The importance of adequate energy and nutrient intake consumed in a loving and supportive environment during the infant years cannot be overstated (Grantham-McGregor, 1995; Yip, 1995). From birth to 1 year of age, human infants triple their weight and increase their length by 50 percent. Individual differences among infants in terms of their nutrient reserves, body composition, growth rates, and activity patterns make defining actual nutrient needs difficult. However, because parents need guidelines, nutritionists recommend that infants consume approximately 50 calories per day for each pound they weigh—more than twice an adult's requirement per pound.

Parents often want to know when to introduce new types of food. In the second half of the first year, human milk or formula continues to be the infant's primary nutritional source. The major change in feeding habits is the addition of solid foods to the infant's diet. The one generally accepted rule is to introduce infant cereal as the first food because of its high iron content. Because of its benefit as a source of iron, infant cereal should be continued until the infant is about 18 months of age. The addition of other foods is arbitrary. A common sequence is strained fruits, followed by vegetables, and finally meats. At 6 months, foods such as a cracker or zwieback can be offered as a type of finger and teething food.

Weaning—the process of giving up one method of feeding for another—usually refers to relinquishing the breast or bottle for a cup. In Western cultures, this is often regarded as an important task for infants, being psychologically significant because the infant has to give up a major source of oral pleasure. There is no one time for weaning that is best for every infant, but most infants show signs of being ready for weaning in the second half of the first year. Weaning should be gradual, by replacing one bottle- or breast-feeding at a time.

Some years ago, controversy surrounded the issue of whether a baby should be fed on demand or on a regular schedule. The famous behaviorist John Watson (1928) argued that scheduled feeding was superior because it increased the child's orderliness. An example of a recommended schedule for newborns was 4 ounces of formula every 6 hours. In recent years, demand feeding—which the timing and amount of feeding are determined by the infant—has become more popular.

In the 1990s, we have become extremely nutrition-conscious. Does the same type of nutrition that makes us healthy adults also make young infants healthy? Some affluent, well-educated parents almost starve their babies by feeding them the low-fat, low-calorie diet they eat themselves. Diets designed for adult weight loss and prevention of heart disease may actually retard growth and development in babies. Fat is very important for babies. Nature's food—the mother's breast milk—is not low in fat or calories. No child under the age of 2 should be consuming skim milk.

In one investigation, seven cases were documented in which babies 7 to 22 months of age were unwittingly undernourished by their health-conscious parents (Lifshitz & others, 1987). In some instances, the parents had been fat themselves and were determined that their child was not going to be. The well-meaning parents substituted vegetables, skim milk, and other low-fat foods for what they called junk food. However, for infants, broccoli is not always a good substitute for a cookie. For growing infants, high-calorie, high-energy foods are part of a balanced diet.

Breast- Versus Bottle-Feeding

Human milk, or an alternative formula, is the baby's source of nutrients and energy for the first 4 to 6 months. For years, developmentalists and nutritionists have debated whether breast-feeding an infant has substantial benefits over bottle-feeding. The growing consensus is that breast-feeding is better for the baby's health (Eiger, 1992). Breast-feeding provides milk that is clean and digestible and helps immunize the newborn from disease (Newman, 1995). Breast-fed babies gain weight more rapidly than do bottle-fed babies. However, only about one-half of mothers nurse newborns, and even fewer continue to nurse their infants after several months. Mothers who work outside the home find it impossible to breast-feed their young

Human milk, or an alternative formula, is a baby's source of nutrients for the first 4 to 6 months. The growing consensus is that breast-feeding is better for the baby's health, although controversy still swirls about the issue of breast- versus bottle-feeding.

infants for many months. Even though breast-feeding provides more ideal nutrition, some researchers argue that there is no long-term evidence of physiological or psychological harm to American infants when they are bottle-fed (Ferguson, Harwood, & Shannon, 1987). Despite these researchers' claims that no long-term negative consequences of bottle-feeding have been documented in American children, the American Academy of Pediatrics, the majority of physicians and nurses, and two leading publications for parents—the *Infant Care Manual* and *Parents* magazine—endorse breast-feeding as having physiological and psychological benefits (Young, 1990).

There is a consensus among experts that breast-feeding is the preferred practice, especially in developing countries where inadequate nutrition and poverty are common. In 1991, the Institute of Medicine, part of the National Academy of Sciences, issued a report that women should be encouraged to breast-feed their infants exclusively for the first 4 to 6 months of life. According to the report, the benefits of breast-feeding are protection against some gastrointestinal infections and food allergies for infants, and possible reduction of osteoporosis and breast cancer for mothers. Nonetheless, while the majority of experts recommend breast-feeding, the issue of breast- versus bottle-feeding continues to be hotly debated. Many parents, especially working mothers, are now following a sequence of breast-feeding in the first several months and bottle-feeding thereafter. This strategy allows the mother's natural milk to provide nutritional benefits to the infant early in development and permits mothers to return to work after several months. Working mothers are also increasingly using "pumping," in which they use a pump to extract breast milk that can be stored for later feeding of the infant when the mother is not present.

Malnutrition in Infancy

Marasmus *is a wasting away of body tissues in the infant's first year, caused by severe protein-calorie deficiency*. The infant becomes grossly underweight and its muscles atrophy. The main cause of marasmus is early weaning from breast milk to inadequate nutrients such as unsuitable and unsanitary cow's milk formula. Something that looks like milk, but is not, usually a form of tapioca or rice, also might be used. In many of the world's developing countries, mothers used to breast-feed their infants for at least 2 years. To become more modern, they stopped breast-feeding much earlier and replaced it with bottle-feeding. Comparisons of breast-fed and bottle-fed infants in such countries as Afghanistan, Haiti, Ghana, and Chile document that the death rate of bottle-fed infants is up to five times greater than that of breast-fed infants (Grant, 1996).

Even if not fatal, severe and lengthy malnutrition is detrimental to physical, cognitive, and social development (Mortimer, 1992). In some cases, even moderate malnutrition can produce subtle difficulties in development. In one investigation, two groups of extremely malnourished 1-year-old South African infants were studied (Bayley, 1970). The children in one group were given adequate nourishment during the next 6 years; no intervention took place in the lives of the other group. After the seventh year, the poorly nourished group of children performed much worse on tests of intelligence than did the adequately nourished group. In yet another investigation, the diets of rural Guatemalan infants were associated with their social development at the time they entered elementary school (Barrett, Radke-Yarrow, & Klein, 1982). Children whose mothers had been given nutritious supplements during pregnancy and who themselves had been given more nutritious, high-calorie foods in their first 2 years of life were more active, more involved, more helpful with their peers, less anxious, and happier than their counterparts, who were not given nutritional supplements. The undernourished Guatemalan infants were only mildly undernourished in infancy, suggesting how important it is for parents to be attentive to the nutritional needs of their infants.

In the most recent research on early supplementary feeding and children's cognitive development, Ernesto Pollitt and his colleagues (1993) conducted a longitudinal investigation over two decades in rural Guatemala. They found that early nutritional supplements in the form of protein and increased calories can have positive long-term consequences for cognitive development. The researchers also found that the relation of nutrition to cognitive performance was moderated both by the time period during which the supplement was given and by the sociodemographic context. For example, children in the lowest socioeconomic groups benefited more than did children in the higher socioeconomic groups. And although there still was a positive nutritional influence when supplementation began after 2 years of age, the effect on cognitive development was less powerful.

Much of our discussion of malnutrition has focused on developing countries, but hunger is also a problem in some areas of the United States. To read about children living hungry in America, turn to Sociocultural Worlds of Children.

Toilet Training

Being toilet trained is a physical and motor skill that is expected in the North American culture to be attained by 3 years of age (Charlesworth, 1987). By the age of 3, 84 percent of children are dry throughout the day and 66 percent are dry throughout the night. The ability to control elimination depends both on muscular maturation and on motivation. Children must be able to control their muscles to eliminate at the appropriate time and they must also want to eliminate in the toilet or potty rather than in their pants.

In actuality, there are literally no data on the optimal time for toilet training. However, developmentalists argue that, whenever it is initiated, it should be accomplished in a warm, relaxed, supportive manner. Many of today's parents begin toilet-training their infants between 20 months and 2 years of age.

One reason to avoid late toilet training, it is sometimes argued, is the "terrible twos." The 2-year-old's strong push for autonomy can lead to confrontations and battles for parents who are trying to toilet train the 2-year-old. Late toilet training can become such a battleground that it extends to 4 or 5 years of age. Another argument against late toilet training is that many toddlers go to day care and a child in diapers or training pants can be stigmatized by peers.

At this point, we have seen that there is extensive physical growth and development during infancy. As we will see next, the infant's brain plays important roles in this growth.

THE BRAIN

As an infant walks, talks, runs, shakes a rattle, smiles, or frowns, the infant's brain is involved. Let's first explore some basic aspects of the brain and then turn to the brain's development.

The Brain's Makeup

The brain is organized at macro and micro levels. At the macro level, the brain consists of the hindbrain, the midbrain, and the forebrain. The **hindbrain**, *located at the skull's rear, is the lowest portion of the brain.* One of the hindbrain's structures is the cerebellum, which plays an important role in motor development and control. The **midbrain**, *located*

Children Living Hungry in America

Harlingen, Texas, is a heavily Chicano city of approximately 40,000 near the Rio Grande. At Su Clinica ("Your Clinic"), which serves many Chicano residents, poverty and unemployment are evident in the waiting list of 800 families needing low-cost care. Many of the Chicanos working in Texas agriculture receive no health-care benefits, and few make even the minimum wage. Farm workers usually get less than $1.50 an hour for working long days in the pesticide-infested fields. The infant mortality rate for the region is listed as good by the U.S. government, but this description is wrong. Many of the deaths are not counted. A baby dies and is buried. People outside the family seldom know. Many infants and young children experience growth problems because they do not get enough to eat. This is not unique to Harlingen, Texas; many other locations in the United States have their share of impoverished families who have difficulty making ends meet and putting food on the table. Hunger and poverty are seen in the children of poor Mississippi tenant farmers, in the children of laid-off coal miners in West Virginia, in neglected children in the ghettos of New York and Chicago, and in the increasing number of homeless families across the nation. In many instances, these children are the victims of silent undernutrition—less dramatic than in Africa or Bangladesh, but no less real.

Many locations in the United States, including the ghettos of many large American cities, have impoverished families that have difficulty making ends meet and putting food on the table.

between the hindbrain and forebrain, is where many fibers ascend and descend, connecting higher and lower portions of the brain. In particular, the midbrain relays information between the brain and the eyes and ears. The infant's ability to attend to an object visually, for example, is linked to a bundle of fibers in the midbrain. The **forebrain** consists of a number of structures, including the cerebrum, the most recently evolved part of the brain. The cerebrum makes up about 80 percent of the brain's volume and covers the lower portions of the brain like a large cap. The cerebrum plays critical roles in many important human functions, such as perception, language, and thinking. Figure 5.2 shows an image of the brain and a description of the location of the major brain levels.

The cerebrum is divided into four main areas called lobes. The **occipital lobe** is involved in vision; the **temporal lobe** is involved in hearing; the **frontal lobe** is involved in the control of voluntary muscles and intelligence; and the **parietal lobe** is involved in processing bodily sensations, such as touch (see figure 5.3).

At the micro level, the brain is made up of cells. **Neurons** are nerve cells that handle information processing at the cellular level. The mature human brain has about 100 billion neuros. The average neuron is as complex as a small computer, with as many as 15,000 connections

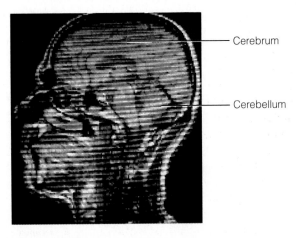

— Cerebrum

— Cerebellum

Figure~5.2

Levels and Structures in the Human Brain
This image of the human brain reveals some of the brain's most important levels and structures. The hindbrain is the lowest portion of the brain; the cerebellum is part of the hindbrain. The midbrain's ascending and descending fibers cannot be seen in this image—the midbrain is between the hindbrain and forebrain. The highest area of the human brain is the forebrain; the cerebrum is a part of the forebrain.

to other cells. Neurons are like every other cell in that they have a nucleus and a cell body. However, due to their specialized information processing in the brain, neurons also have connecting parts extending out from the cell body. The **dendrite** *is the receiving part of the neuron, collecting information and routing it to the cell body. The* **axon** *is the part of the neuron that carries information away from the cell body to other cells.* Figure 5.4 shows the makeup of a neuron. The axon is typically much thinner and longer than a dendrite and looks like an ultrathin cylindrical tube. The axon of a single neuron can extend all the way from the top of the brain to the base of the spinal cord. A **myelin sheath,** *a layer of fat cells, encases most axons. The myelin sheath not only insulates nerve cells but also helps nerve impulses travel faster.*

The Brain's Development

As the human embryo develops inside the womb, the central nervous system begins as a long, hollow tube on the embryo's back. At 3 weeks or so after conception, the brain forms into a large mass of neurons and loses its tubular appearance, developing into the three major divisions of the brain (hindbrain, midbrain, and forebrain) (see figure 5.5).

Scientists have identified three processes in the development of neurons: cell production, cell migration, and cell elaboration. Most neurons are produced between 10 and 26 weeks after conception. Somewhat amazingly, this means that cells are being generated at about 250,000 per minute in the fetal brain. At birth, the infant probably has all of the neurons it is going to have in its entire life. The second stage of neuron development involves cell migration, which involves the movement of neurons from near the center of the brain, where they are produced, to their appropriate locations. The migration of neurons is completed by 7 months after conception. The third stage of neuron development involves cell elaboration, which begins after cell migration. During cell elaboration, axons and dendrites grow and form connections

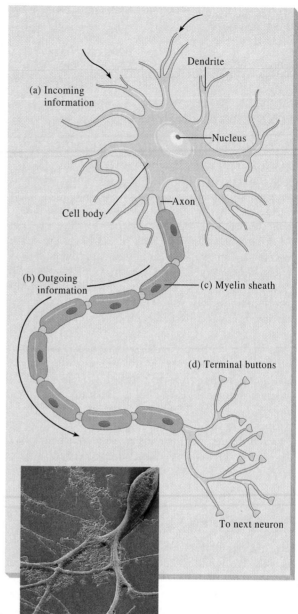

Figure~5.4

The Neuron
(*a*) The dendrites of the cell body receive information from other neurons, muscles, or glands through the axon. (*b*) Axons transmit information away from the cell body. (*c*) A myelin sheath covers most axons and speeds information transmission. (*d*) As it ends, the axon branches out into terminal buttons. Shown in the insert is a photograph of a neuron. Notice the branching dendrites at the bottom and the cell body at the top right.

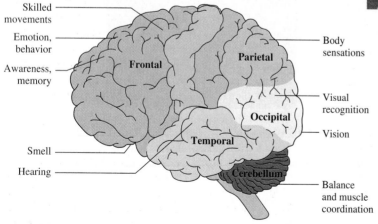

Figure~5.3

The Brain's Four Lobes
Shown here are the locations of the brain's four lobes: occipital, temporal, frontal, and parietal.

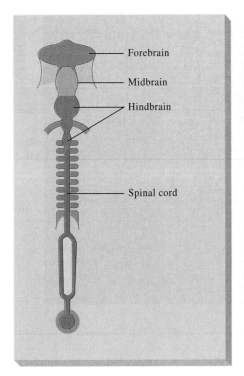

Forebrain
Midbrain
Hindbrain
Spinal cord

Figure~5.5

Embryological Development of the Nervous System
In the photograph on the right, you can see the primitive, tubular appearance of the nervous system at 6 weeks in the human embryo. The drawing shows the major brain regions and spinal cord as they appear early in the development of a human embryo.

reflexes and rhythmic movements, then turn our attention to gross and fine motor skills. To conclude, we will cover the fascinating field of developmental biodynamics, which is responsible for the awakened interest in how infants acquire motor skills.

Reflexes and Rhythmic Motor Behavior

The newborn is not an empty-headed organism. Among other things, it has some basic reflexes that are genetically carried survival mechanisms. For example, the newborn has no fear of water; when submerged, it naturally holds its breath and contracts its throat to keep water out. Reflexes and rhythmic movements can be important building blocks for subsequent purposeful motor activity.

with other cells. Cell elaboration continues for years after birth. During infancy, the increase in dendritic branching is extensive (see figure 5.6).

Myelination begins prenatally but continues after birth. Myelination for visual pathways proceeds rapidly after birth and is completed sometime during the first 6 months. Although prenatal myelination begins earlier for auditory pathways than for visual pathways, the completion of auditory myelination occurs later, not until 4 or 5 years of age. Some myelination continues into adolescence; this includes the myelination of some large bundles of fibers that connect the brain's two hemispheres.

At birth, the newborn's brain is about 25 percent of its adult weight, and by the second birthday it is about 75 percent of its adult weight. The brain's areas do not mature uniformly. For instance, the primary motor areas develop earlier than the primary sensory areas.

At this point we have discussed a number of ideas about the infant's physical growth and brain development. A summary of these ideas is presented in concept table 5.1.

MOTOR DEVELOPMENT

There has been a renaissance in the study of motor development in the last decade. New discoveries are being made about how infants acquire motor skills. We will begin our exploration of motor development by examining

Reflexes

Reflexes govern the newborn's movements, which are automatic and beyond the newborn's control. They are built-in reactions to certain stimuli. In these reflexes infants have adaptive responses to their environment before they have had the opportunity to learn. The **sucking reflex** *occurs when newborns automatically suck an object placed in their mouth. The sucking reflex enables newborns to get nourishment before they have associated a nipple with food.* The sucking reflex is an example of a reflex that is present at birth but later disappears. The **rooting reflex** *occurs when the infant's cheek is stroked or the side of the mouth is touched. In response, the infant turns its head toward the side that was touched, in an apparent effort to find something to suck.* The sucking and rooting reflexes disappear when the infant is about 3 to 4 months old. They are replaced by the infant's voluntary eating. The sucking and rooting reflexes have survival value for newborn mammals, who must find the mother's breast to obtain nourishment.

The **Moro reflex** *is a neonatal startle response that occurs in reaction to a sudden, intense noise or movement. When startled, the newborn arches its back, throws its head back, and flings out its arms and legs. Then the newborn rapidly closes its arms and legs to the center of the body.* The Moro reflex is a vestige from our primate ancestry, and it too has survival value. This reflex, which is normal in all newborns, also tends to disappear at 3 to 4 months of age.

...like Piaget, believe that we can directly perceive information that exists in the world around us. We do not have to build up representations of the world in our mind; information about the world is available out there in the environment. According to the **ecological view,** *perception has the functional purposes of bringing the organism into contact with the environment and increasing its adaptation.* A key aspect of this perceptual adaptation is to detect perceptual invariants—features of perception that remain—in a constantly changing world. A significant feature of the ecological view is the claim that even complex things (such as a spatial layout) can be perceived directly without constructive activity.

The Gibsons believe that if complex things can be perceived directly, perhaps they can be perceived even by young infants. Thus, the ecological view has inspired investigators to search for the competencies that young infants possess (Bower, 1989). Of course, ecological theorists do not deny that perception develops as infants and children develop. In fact, the ecological theorists stress that as the child's perceptual processes mature, the child becomes more efficient at discovering the invariant properties of objects available to the senses.

For the Gibsons, all objects have many **affordances**—*opportunities for interaction offered by an object that are necessary to perform functional activities.* For example, adults immediately know when a chair is appropriate for sitting, a surface is appropriate for walking, or an object is within reach. We directly and accurately preceive these affordances by sensing information from the environment—the light or sound reflecting from the surfaces of the world—and from our own bodies through muscle receptors, joint receptors, and skin receptors, for example. The developmental question, though, is how these affordances are acquired. In one investigation, infants who were crawlers or walkers recognized the action-specific properties of surfaces (Gibson & others, 1987). When faced with a rigid plywood surface or a squishy waterbed, crawlers crossed both without hesitating. The toddlers, however, first stopped and explored the waterbed, then chose to crawl rather than walk across it.

Visual Perception

How do we see? Anyone who has ever taken pictures while on vacation appreciates the miracle of perception. The camera is no match for it. Consider a favorite spot that you visited and photographed sometime in the past. Compare your memory of this spot with the snapshot. Although your memory might be faulty, there is little doubt that the richness of your perceptual experience is not captured by the photograph. The sense of depth that you felt at this spot probably is not conveyed by the snapshot. Neither is the subtlety of the colors you perceived or the intricacies of textures and shapes. Human vision is complex, and so is its development (Kellman & Banks, 1997). To evaluate how visual perception and other areas of perception might be measured in infancy, turn to Critical Thinking About Children's Development.

Visual Acuity and Color

Psychologist William James (1890/1950) called the newborn's perceptual world a "blooming, buzzing confusion." Was James right? A century later we can safely say that he was wrong. The infant's perception of visual information is far more advanced than was previously thought.

Just how well can infants see? The newborn's vision is estimated to be 20/400 to 20/800 on the well-known Snellan chart that you are tested with when you have your eyes examined (Haith, 1991). This is about 10 to 30 times lower than normal adult vision (20/20). By 6 months of age, though, vision is 20/100 or better, and by about 1 year of age the infant's vision approximates that of an adult (Banks & Salapatek, 1983). Figure 5.12 shows a computer estimation of what a picture of a face looks like to 1-month-old, 2-month-old, and 3-month-old infants, and to a 12-month-old infant and an adult, from a distance of about 6 inches.

Figure~5.12

Visual Acuity During the First Months of Life
The four photographs represent a computer estimation of what a picture of a face looks like to a 1-month-old, 2-month-old, 3-month-old, and 1-year old (which approximates that of an adult).

Measuring Infant Perception

Because young infants are preverbal and have limited motor skills, it is a challenge to measure their perceptual development. At the beginning of this chapter you read about how moving a large object toward an infant's head is a technique for determining whether a newborn can see. The infant's head movement suggests that it has at least some vision.

Can you think of other techniques that could be used to study the young infant's perception? One simple method is to look for evidence that an infant prefers one stimulus to another. If you are studying visual stimulation, you might place two visual stimuli in front of an infant and determine which stimulus the infant looks at more. If you have a question about smell, you might place a different odorous substance on each side of the infant's head and see if the infant turns more toward one side than toward the other. To test for auditory perception, you might use a "conditioned head-turning procedure": An infant sits on its mother's lap and a sound comes out of a speaker. If the infant turns toward the speaker, she sees a colorful mechanical toy in motion (the toy is switched on if the infant turns toward the sound). This is rewarding, and the infant soon learns to look at the speaker whenever she hears a sound coming from it. If you are interested in determining the infant's threshold for hearing, you might manipulate the loudness of the sound. Can you think of yet other ways the young infant's perception could be explored?

By evaluating the ways infant perception can be measured, you are learning to think critically about children's development by *making accurate observations, descriptions, and inferences about children's development.*

Can newborns see color? At birth, babies can distinguish between green and red (Adams, 1989). And adult-like functioning in all three types (red, blue, green) of color-sensitive receptors (cones) is present by 2 months of age.

Visual Preferences

Robert Fantz (1963), an important pioneer in the study of visual perception in infants, made an important discovery that advanced the ability of researchers to investigate infants' visual perception: Infants look at different things for different lengths of time. Fantz placed infants in a "looking chamber," which had two visual displays on the ceiling above the infant's head. An experimenter viewed the infant's eyes by looking through a peephole. If the infant was fixating on one of the displays, the experimenter could see the display's reflection in the infant's eyes. This allowed the experimenter to determine how long the infant looked at each display. In figure 5.13 you can see Fantz's looking chamber and the results of his experiment. The infants preferred to look at patterns rather than at color or brightness. For example, they preferred to look at a face, a piece of printed matter, or a bull's-eye longer than at red, yellow, or white discs. In another experiment, Fantz found that younger infants—only 2 days old—looked longer at patterned stimuli, such as faces and concentric circles, than at red, white, or yellow discs. Based on these results, it is likely that pattern perception has an innate basis, or at least is acquired after only minimal environmental experience. The newborn's visual world is not the blooming, buzzing confusion William James imagined.

Perception of Faces

The human face is perhaps the most important visual pattern for the newborn to perceive. The infant masters a sequence of steps in progressing toward full perceptual appreciation of the face (Gibson, 1969). At about 3½ weeks, the infant is fascinated with the eyes, perhaps because the infant notices simple perceptual features such as dots, angles, and circles. At 1 to 2 months of age, the infant notices and perceives contour. At 2 months of age and older, the infant begins to differentiate facial features—it distinguishes eyes from other parts of the face, notices the mouth, and pays attention to movements of the mouth. By 5 months of age, the infant has detected other features of the face—its plasticity, its solid, three-dimensional surface, the oval shape of the head, and the orientation of the eyes and the mouth. Beyond 6 months of age, the infant distiguishes familiar faces from unfamiliar faces—mother from stranger, masks from real faces, and so on.

How do young infants scan the human face? In one study, researchers showed human faces to 1- and 2-month-old infants (Maurer & Salapatek, 1976). By use of a special mirror arrangement, the faces were projected as images in front of the infant's eyes so that the infant's eye movements could be photographed. Figure 5.14 shows the plotting of the eye fixations of a 1-month-old and a

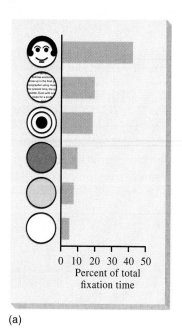

(a)

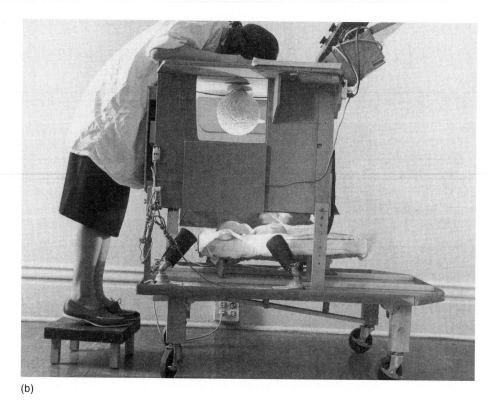

(b)

Figure~5.13

Fantz's Experiment on Infants' Visual Perception
(a) Infants 2 to 3 months old preferred to look at some stimuli more than others. In Fantz's experiment, infants preferred to look at patterns rather than at color or brightness. For example, they looked longer at a face, a piece of printed matter, or a bull's-eye than at red, yellow, or white discs. (b) Fantz used a "looking chamber" to study infants' perception of stimuli.

Adapted from "The Origin of Form Perception" by R. L. Fantz. Copyright © 1961 by Scientific American, Inc. All rights reserved.

Figure~5.14

How 1- and 2-Month Old Infants Scan the Human Face

2-month-old infant. Notice that the 1-month-old scanned only a few portions of the entire face—a narrow segment of the chin and two spots on the head. The 2-month-old scanned a much wider area of the figure—the mouth, the eyes, and a large portion of the head. The older infant spent more time examining the internal details of the face, while the younger infant concentrated on areas on the outer contour of the face.

Perceptual Constancy

Some perceptual accomplishments are especially intriguing because they seem to indicate that an infant's perception is better than it ought to be on the basis of sensory information. Such is the case for perceptual constancy, in which the sensory stimulation is changing but our perception (like the world) remains constant. Let's explore three types of perceptual constancy: size constancy, shape constancy, and brightness constancy.

Size constancy *is the recognition that an object remains the same size even though the retinal image of the object changes.* The size of an object on the retina is not sufficient to determine its actual size. The farther away from us an object is, the smaller its image is on our eyes. For example, a bicycle standing right in front of a child appears smaller than a car parked across the street, even though the bicycle casts a larger image on the child's eyes than the car does.

But what about babies? Do they have size constancy? Researchers have found that size constancy is not present prior to 3 months of age, that some size constancy appears in 5- to 7-month-old infants, and that size constancy improves at least through 10 to 11 months of age (Day, 1987).

Shape constancy *is the recognition that an object remains the same shape even though its orientation to us changes.* Look around the room while you are reading this book. You probably see objects of various shapes—chairs and tables, for example. If you walk around the room, you will see these objects from different sides and angles. Even though your retinal images of the objects change as you walk, you still perceive the objects as remaining the same shape.

Do babies have shape constancy? As with size constancy, researchers have found that babies as young as 3 months of age have shape constancy, at least for regularly shaped objects like toy blocks (Bower, 1966; Day & McKenzie, 1973). Three-month-old infants, however, do not seem to have shape constancy for irregularly shaped objects, such as those with tilted planes (Cook & Birch, 1984).

Brightness constancy *is the recognition that an object retains the same degree of brightness even though different amounts of light fall on it*. For example, regardless of whether you are reading this book indoors or outdoors, the white pages and black print do not look any different to you in terms of their whiteness or blackness.

Do babies have brightness constancy? Researchers have found that infants as young as 7 weeks old may have brightness constancy (Dannemiller, 1985).

Why is it important for infants to develop these perceptual constancies early in their lives? If infants did not develop perceptual constancy, each time they saw an object at a different distance, in a different orientation, or at a different level of brightness, they would perceive it as a different object. Thus, the development of perceptual constancy allows the infant to perceive its world as stable.

Depth Perception

Earlier we indicated that some perceptual accomplishments are especially intriguing because they seem to indicate that an infant's perception is better than it ought to be on the basis of sensory information. Such was the case in our discussion of perceptual constancy, and so it also is for depth perception, in which the sensory stimulation is two-dimensional but we perceive a three-dimensional world.

How early can infants perceive depth? To investigate this question, infant perception researchers Eleanor Gibson and Richard Walk (1960) conducted a classic experiment. They constructed a miniature cliff with a drop-off covered by glass. The motivation for this experiment arose when Gibson was eating a picnic lunch on the edge of the Grand Canyon. She wondered whether an infant looking over the canyon's rim would perceive the dangerous dropoff and back up. In their laboratory, Gibson and Walk placed infants on the edge of a visual cliff and had their mothers coax them to crawl onto the glass (see figure 5.15). Most infants would not crawl out on the glass, choosing instead to remain on the shallow side, indicating that they could perceive depth. However, because the 6- to 14-month-old infants had extensive visual experience, this research did not answer the question of whether depth perception is innate.

Figure~5.15

Examining Infants' Depth Perception on the Visual Cliff
The apparatus consists of a board laid across a sheet of heavy glass, with a patterned material directly beneath the glass on one side and several feet below it on the other. Placed on the center board, the child crawls to its mother across the "shallow" side. Called from the "deep" side, the child pats the glass but, despite this tactual evidence that the cliff is a solid surface, the child refuses to cross over to the mother.

Exactly how early in life does depth perception develop? Since younger infants do not crawl, this question is difficult to answer. Research with 2- to 4-month-old infants shows differences in heart rate when they are placed directly on the deep side of the visual cliff instead of on the shallow side (Campos, Langer, & Krowitz, 1970). However, an alternative interpretation is that young infants respond to differences in some visual characteristics of the deep and shallow cliffs, with no actual knowledge of depth.

Visual Expectations

Infants not only see forms and figures at an early age, they also develop expectations about future events in their world by the time they are 3 months of age. Marshall Haith and his colleagues (Canfield & Haith, 1991; Haith, Hazen, & Goodman, 1988) studied whether babies would form expectations about where an interesting picture

Figure~5.16

The Infant's Visual Expectations
A 4-month-old in Elizabeth Spelke's infant perception laboratory is tested to determine if it knows that an object in motion will not stop in midair. She measured babies' looking time and found longer looking intervals for unexpected events than for expected events.

would appear. The pictures were presented to the infants in either a regular alternating sequence (such as left, right, left, right) or in an unpredictable sequence (such as right, right, left, right). When the sequence was predictable, the 3-month-old infants began to anticipate the location of the picture, looking to the side on which it would next appear in the sequence. The young infants formed this visual expectation in less than a minute. However, younger infants did not develop expectations about where a picture would be presented.

Elizabeth Spelke (1988, 1991) also has demonstrated that young infants form visual expectations. She placed babies before a puppet stage and showed them a series of unexpected actions—for example, a ball seems to roll through a solid barrier, another seems to leap between two platforms, and a third appears to hang in midair (Spelke, 1979) (see figure 5.16). Spelke measured the babies' looking time and recorded longer intervals for unexpected actions than for expected actions. She concluded that by 4 months of age, even though infants do not yet have the ability to talk about objects, move around objects, manipulate objects, or even see objects with high resolution, they can recognize where a moving object is when it has left their visual field and make inferences about where it should be when it comes into their sight again.

Other Senses

Considerable development also takes place in other sensory systems. We will explore development in hearing, touch and pain, smell, and taste.

Hearing

What is the nature of hearing in newborns? Can the fetus hear? What types of auditory stimulation should be used with infants at different points in the first year? We examine each of these questions.

Immediately after birth, infants can hear, although their sensory thresholds are somewhat higher than those of adults (Werner & Marean, 1996). That is, a stimulus must be louder to be heard by a newborn than by an adult. Also, in one study, as infants aged from 8 to 28 weeks, they became more proficient at localizing sounds

(Morrongiello, Fenwick, & Chance, 1990). Not only can newborns hear, but the possibility has been raised that the fetus can hear as it nestles within its mother's womb. Let's examine this possibility further.

In the last few months of pregnancy, the fetus can hear sounds: the mother's voice, music, and so on (Kisilevsky, 1995; Lecanuet, Granier-Deferre, & Busnel, 1995). Given that the fetus can hear sounds, two psychologists wanted to find out if listening to Dr. Seuss' classic story *The Cat in the Hat*, while still in the mother's womb, would produce a preference for hearing the story after birth (DeCasper & Spence, 1986). Sixteen pregnant women read *The Cat in the Hat* to their fetuses twice a day over the last 6 weeks of their pregnancies. When the babies were born, their nonnutritive sucking behavior was studied while they listened to each of two recordings: one of their mothers reading *The Cat in the Hat*, the other of their mothers reading *The King, the Mice and the Cheese*, a story with a different rhyme and pace. The newborns preferred listening to *The Cat in the Hat*, which they had heard frequently as a fetus (see figure 5.17).

Two important conclusions can be drawn from this investigation. First, it reveals how ingenious scientists have become at assessing the development not only of infants but of fetuses as well, in this case discovering a way to "interview" newborn babies who cannot yet talk. Second, it reveals the remarkable ability of an infant's brain to learn even before birth.

Babies are born into the world prepared to respond to the sounds of any human language. Even very young infants can discriminate subtle phonetic differences, such as those between the speech sounds of *ba* and *ga* (Aslin, Jusczyk, & Pisoni, 1997). Young infants also will suck more on a nipple to hear a recording of their mother's voice than they will to hear the voice of an unfamiliar woman, and they will suck more to listen to their mother's native language than they will to listen to a foreign language (Mehler & others, 1988; Spence & DeCasper, 1987). And an interesting developmental change occurs during the first year: Six-month-old infants can discriminate phonetic contrasts from languages to which they have never been exposed, but they lose this discriminative ability by their first birthday, demonstrating that experience with a specific language is necessary for maintaining this ability (Werker & LaLonde, 1988).

Touch and Pain

Do newborns respond to touch? What activities can adults engage in that involve tactile (touch) stimulation at various points in the infant's development? Can newborns feel pain?

Touch in the Newborn   Newborns do respond to touch. A touch to the cheek produces a turning of the head, whereas a touch to the lips produces sucking movements. An important ability that develops in infancy

(a)

(b)

Figure~5.17

Prenatal Auditory Perception

(*a*) Pregnant mothers read *The Cat in the Hat* to their fetuses during the last few months of pregnancy. (*b*) When they were born, the babies preferred listening to a recording of their mothers reading *The Cat in the Hat*, as evidenced by their sucking on a nipple that produced this recording.

is to connect information about vision with information about touch. One-year-olds clearly can do this, and it appears that 6-month-olds can too (Acredolo & Hake, 1982). Whether still younger infants can coordinate vision and touch is yet to be determined. To further evaluate the nature of touch in development, turn to Critical Thinking About Children's Development.

Devising Age-Appropriate Activities to Stimulate Infants' Sensory Modalities

Devise a list of age-appropriate activities for the two sensory modalities we have just discussed—hearing and touch. For each modality, think about stimulation in the first 6 months and from 6 months to 1 year. Hints: Think about auditory activities like listening to music boxes, musical mobiles, talking animals and dolls, and records, as well as about tactile activities like touching stuffed animals and books with textures.

By developing lists of age-appropriate activities to stimulate infants' different sensory modalities, you are learning to think critically by *creating arguments based on developmental concepts*.

Pain If and when you have a son and need to consider whether he should be circumcised, the issue of an infant's pain perception probably will become important to you. Circumcision is usually performed on young boys about the third day after birth. Will your young son experience pain if he is circumcised when he is 3 days old? Increased crying and fussing occur during the circumcision procedure, suggesting that 3-day-old infants experience pain (Gunnar, Malone, & Fisch, 1987).

In the investigation by Megan Gunnar and her colleagues (Gunnar, Malone, & Fisch, 1987), the healthy newborn's ability to cope with stress was evaluated. The newborn infant males cried intensely during the circumcision, indicating that it was stressful. The researchers pointed out that it is rather remarkable that the newborn infant does not suffer serious consequences from the surgery. Rather, the circumcised infant displays amazing resiliency and ability to cope. Within several minutes after the surgery, the infant can nurse and interact in a normal manner with his mother. And, if allowed

to, the newly circumcised newborn drifts into a deep sleep that seems to serve as a coping mechanism. In this experiment, the time spent in deep sleep was greater in the 60 to 240 minutes after the circumcision than before it.

For many years, doctors have performed operations on newborns without anesthesia. The accepted medical practice was followed because of the dangers of anesthesia and the supposition that newborns do not feel pain. Recently, as researchers have convincingly demonstrated that newborns can feel pain, the long-standing practice of operating on newborns without anesthesia is being challenged.

Smell

Newborn infants can differentiate odors. For example, by the expressions on their faces, they seem to indicate that they like the way vanilla and strawberry smell but do not like the way rotten eggs and fish smell (Steiner, 1979). In one investigation, young infants who were breast-fed showed a clear preference for smelling their

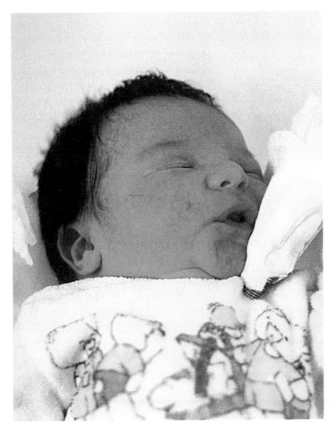

Figure~5.18

Newborns' Preference for the Smell of Their Mother's Breast Pad
In the experiment by MacFarlane (1975), 6-day-old infants preferred to smell their mother's breast pad over a clean one that had never been used, but 2-day-old infants did not show this preference, indicating that this odor preference requires several days of experience to develop.

mother's breast pad when they were 6 days old (Mac-Farlane, 1975) (see figure 5.18). However, when they were 2 days old, they did not show this preference (compared to a clean breast pad), indicating that they require several days of experience to recognize this odor.

Taste

Sensitivity to taste might be present before birth. When saccharin was added to the amniotic fluid of a near-term fetus, increased swallowing was observed (Windle, 1940). In one study, even at only 2 hours of age, babies made different facial expressions when they tasted sweet, sour, and bitter solutions (Rosenstein & Oster, 1988) (see figure 5.19). At about 4 months of age, infants begin to prefer salty tastes, which as newborns they were averse to (Harris, Thomas, & Booth, 1990).

Intermodal Perception

Are young infants so competent that they can relate and integrate information from several senses? Imagine yourself playing basketball or tennis. You are experienc-

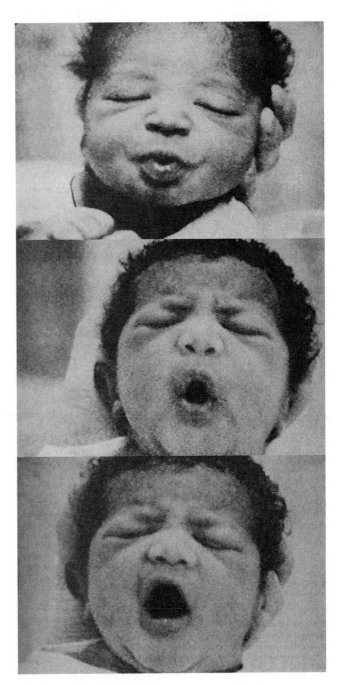

Figure~5.19

Facial Responses of Newborns to Basic Tastes
Facial expressions elicited by (*top*) a sweet solution, (*center*) a sour solution, and (*bottom*) a bitter solution in babies only 2 hours old.

ing many visual inputs: the ball coming and going, other players moving around, and so on. You are also experiencing many auditory inputs, such as the sound of the ball bouncing or being hit and the player's grunts and groans. There is good correspondence between much of the visual and auditory information: When you see the ball bounce, you hear it bounce; when a player stretches to hit a ball, you hear a groan.

We live in a world of objects and events that can be seen, heard, and felt. When mature observers simultaneously watch and listen to an event, they experience a unitary episode. All of this is so commonplace that it scarcely seems worth mentioning. But consider the task of very young infants with little practice at perceiving. Can they put vision and sound together as precisely as adults can?

Intermodal perception *is the ability to relate and integrate information from two or more sensory modalities, such as vision and hearing.* The two main theories we described earlier address the question of whether young infants develop intermodal perception. The ecological view argues that infants have intermodal perception capabilities very early in infancy. In this view, infants only have to attend to the appropriate sensory information, they do not have to build up an internal representation of the information through months of sensorimotor experiences. In contrast, the contructivist view advocated by Piaget stresses that perceptual abilities such as vision, hearing, and touch are not coordinated early in infancy, and that therefore young infants do not have intermodal perception. According to Piaget, only through months of sensorimotor interaction with the world is intermodal perception possible. For example, infants can coordinate touch and vision only when they learn to look at objects as their hand grasps them. Let's explore the research on the issue of whether young infants have intermodal perception.

Auditory-Visual Intermodal Perception

To test intermodal perception, Elizabeth Spelke (1979) showed 4-month-old infants two films simultaneously. In each film a puppet jumped up and down, but in one of the films a sound track matched the puppet's dancing movements, in the other film it did not. By measuring the infants' gazes, Spelke found that the infants looked more at the puppet whose actions were synchronized with the sound track, suggesting that they recognized the visual-auditory correspondence. Young infants can also coordinate visual-auditory information involving people. In one study, as early as 3½ months of age, infants looked more at their mother when they heard her voice and longer at their father when they heard his voice (Spelke & Owsley, 1979).

Might auditory-visual relations even be coordinated in newborns? Newborns do turn their eyes and head toward the sound of a voice or rattle when the sound is maintained for several seconds (Clifton & others, 1981). But the newborn can only localize a sound and look at an object in a crude way (Bechtold, Busnell, & Salapatek, 1979). Improved accuracy at auditory-visual coordination likely requires a sharpening through experience with visual and auditory stimuli. Nonetheless, at a crude level, auditory-visual intermodal perception appears to be present at birth, likely having evolutionary value.

Haptic-Visual Intermodal Perception

The word *haptic* refers to exploration through the sensory modality of touch, as when a baby manipulates a rattle. Six- to 12-month-old babies can recognize objects visually that they previously explored only with their hands, but whether this ability is present in the first 6 months of life is questionable (Rose & Ruff, 1987; Streri & Pecheux, 1986). Infants can't competently grasp objects, such a rattles, before 4 or 5 months of age, but soon after they are born they move their arms in the direction of objects they see (Spelke, 1987).

Conclusions

Crude exploratory forms of intermodal perception exist in newborns. These become sharpened with experience in the first year of life. In the first 6 months, infants have difficulty forming mental representations that connect sensory input from different modes, but in the second half of the first year they show an increased ability to make this connection mentally. Thus, babies are born into the world with some innate abilities to perceive relations among sensory modalities, but their intermodal abilities improve considerably through experience. As with all aspects of development, nature and nurture interact or cooperate.

Perceptual-Motor Coupling and Unification

The main thrust of research in the Gibsonian tradition has been to discover how perception guides action. A less well studied but equally important issue is how action shapes perception. Motor activities might be crucial, because they provide the means for exploring the world and learning about its properties. Only by moving one's eyes and head, hands and arms, and traversing from one location to another can individuals fully experience their environment and learn to effectively adapt to it.

Distinguishing between perceiving and doing has been a time-honored tradition in psychology. But Esther Thelen (1995) questions whether this distinction is real. She argues that individuals perceive in order to move and move in order to perceive. Thus, there is an increasing belief that perceptual and motor development do not develop in isolation from one other, but rather are coupled. Babies are continually coordinating their movements with concurrent perceptual information to learn how to maintain balance, reach for objects in space, and locomote across various surfaces and terrains (Bertenthal & Clifton, 1997).

At this point we have discussed many ideas about motor, sensory, and peceptual development. A summary of these ideas is presented in concept table 5.2.

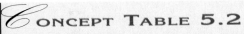

CONCEPT TABLE 5.2

Motor, Sensory, and Perceptual Development

Concept	Processes/ Related Ideas	Characteristics/Description
Motor Development	Reflexes and rhythmic motor behavior	The newborn is no longer viewed as a passive, empty-headed organism. Reflexes—automatic movements—govern the newborn's behavior. For infants, sucking is an important means of obtaining nutrition. Nonnutritive sucking is of interest to researchers, especially as a means of assessing attention. Thelen argues that rhythmic motor behavior has an important adaptative function in the first year of life as a transition between uncoordinated activity and complex coordinated behavior.
	Gross and fine motor skills	Gross motor skills involve large-muscle activities such as moving one's arms and walking. A number of gross motor milestones occur in infancy. Fine motor skills involve more finely tuned movements than gross motor skills do. A number of fine motor milestones also occur in infancy.
	Developmental biodynamics	This approach seeks to explain how motor behaviors are assembled for perceiving and acting. It emphasizes the importance of exploration and selection in finding solutions to new task demands. A key theme is that perception and action are coupled when new skills are learned.
Sensory and Perceptual Development	What are sensation and perception?	Sensation occurs when information interacts with sensory receptors—the eyes, ears, tongue, nostrils, and skin. Perception is the interpretation of what is sensed.
	Theories of perceptual development	The constructivist view, advocated by Piaget and information-processing psychologists, states that perception is a cognitive construction based on sensory input plus information retrieved from memory. The ecological view, developed by the Gibsons, states that perception has a functional purpose of bringing the organism into contact with the environment and increasing its adaptation. A key aspect of the ecological approach involves perceptual invariants. For the Gibsons, all objects have affordances.
	Visual perception	William James was wrong—the newborn's visual world is not a "blooming, buzzing confusion." Newborns can see and can distinguish greens and reds. In Fantz's pioneering research, infants only 2 days old looked longer at patterned stimuli, such as faces, than at single colored discs. The human face is an important visual pattern for the newborn, and the infant gradually masters a sequence of steps in perceiving it. Three types of perceptual constancies are size, shape, and brightness. All three are present in infants by 3 months of age. A classic study of Gibson and Walk demonstrated through the use of a visual cliff that infants as young as 6 months of age have depth perception. Infants develop expectations about future events in their world by the time they are 3 months of age.
	Other senses	The fetus can hear several weeks before birth. Newborns respond to touch and they can feel pain. Both smell and taste are present in the newborn.
	Intermodal perception	Intermodal perception is the ability to relate and integrate information about two or more sensory modalities, such as vision and hearing. The ecological view argues that young infants have intermodal perception; the constructivist view states that sensory modalities are not coordinated early in infancy. Spelke's research demonstrated that infants as young as 3 months of age can connect visual and auditory stimuli. Six-month-old babies can recognize objects visually that they previously only explored with their hands. Crude exploratory forms of intermodal perception are present in newborns and become sharpened in the first year of life. Infants have difficulty forming mental images that connect sensory input from different modes in the first 6 months of life, but increase their ability to make this connection in the second 6 months.
	Perceptual-motor coupling and unification	Thelen argues that perceptual and motor development are coupled and unified. She says that individuals perceive in order to move and move in order to perceive.

SUMMARY

It once was believed that the newborn is an empty-headed organism that experiences the world as a "blooming, buzzing confusion." Today, developmentalists believe that the young infant has far more advanced capabilities. Infants assemble their motor and perceptual skills to adapt to their world.

Our coverage of physical growth and development focused on cephalocaudal and proximodistal sequences, height and weight, infant states, nutrition, and toilet training. We evaluated the brain including its makeup and development. We also discussed motor development—reflexes and rhythmic motor behavior, gross and fine motor skills, and developmental biodynamics. And we examined the following topics in sensory and perceptual development: the nature of sensation and perception, theories of perceptual development, visual perception, other senses, intermodal perception, and perceptual-motor coupling and unification.

Remember that you can obtain an overall summary of the chapter by again studying the two concept tables on pages 149 and 165. Physical development, of course, is not confined to infancy. In the next chapter, we will explore physical development in childhood and adolescence.

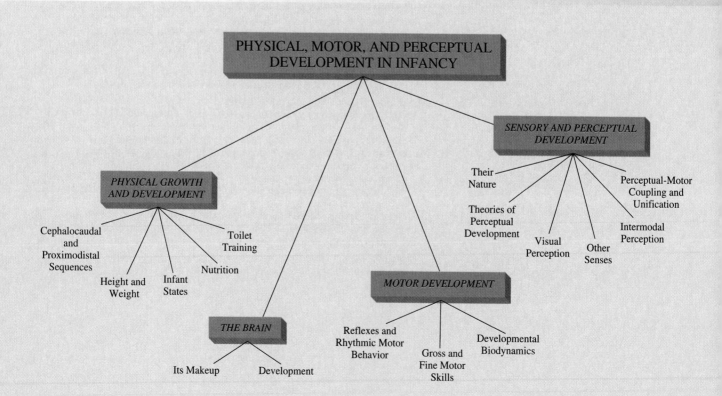

PRACTICAL KNOWLEDGE ABOUT CHILDREN

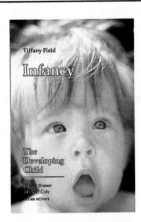

Infancy

(1990) by Tiffany Field,
Cambridge, MA: Harvard
University Press.

This outstanding book on infant development is written by one of the world's leading researchers on the topic. The book accurately captures the infant's experiences as an active learner and shows infants to be far more competent than once was believed. Chapters focus on how infants are studied before and after birth, emotions and attachment, peer interactions and day care, and infants and risk. The chapter on infants at risk provides an excellent overview of intervention strategies.

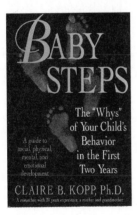

Baby Steps

(1994) by Claire Kopp,
New York: W.H. Freeman.

Baby Steps is a guide to physical, cognitive, and socioemotional development in the first 2 years of life. The author, Claire Kopp, is a leading researcher in prenatal and infant development. The book is organized developmentally, with major sections divided into birth through 3 months, 4 through 7 months, 8 through 12 months, and the second year. Within each of these major sections, precise descriptions and explanations of infant behavior are provided for even smaller time frames. For example, in the first section, birth through 3 months, separate chapters describe what development is like at each month. This well-written book more closely meshes with the way development is presented in most child development texts than most other popular books on infancy do. It provides an excellent overview of development in the first 2 years of life.

EXPLORATIONS IN CHILD DEVELOPMENT

To further explore the nature of child development, we will examine a research study on the perception of auditory-visual distance relations in young infants, and then we will discuss what the right stimulation is for infants.

RESEARCH IN CHILD DEVELOPMENT

Perception of Auditory-Visual Distance Relations in Young Infants

Featured Study
Pickens, J. (1994). Perception of auditory-visual distance relations by 5-month-olds. *Developmental Psychology, 30,* 537–544.

Adults use acoustic and visual cues to judge an object's distance and direction of motion. However, little is known about the emergence and development of the infant's capacity in this realm. The purpose of the present study was to determine whether, and on what basis, 5-month-old infants perceive auditory-visual distance relations.

Method
The subjects were 64 infants whose mean age was 5 months. They were placed in an infant seat about 80 centimeters away from two side-by-side 19-inch color telelvision monitors. Observers monitored infants' visual fixations from openings in an opaque screen surrounding the monitors. Side-by-side videotaped events (such as an approaching toy train on one screen and a retreating toy train on the other) were displayed simultaneously with sound (that of a lawnmower engine) corresponding to one of the two events presented from a centrally located speaker. The videos showed pairs of toy trains (a) approaching/retreating across a naturalistic landscape, (b) expanding/contracting against a black background, (c) increasing/ decreasing in brightness against a black background, and (d) moving up/down against a black background.

Results and Discussion
The 5-month-olds were sensitive to auditory-visual distance relations, and size changes were an important depth cue. Infants did not show evidence of matching in other conditions in which the sound tracks were paired with videos depicting shifts in the train's luminance or showing the train moving vertically with no change in size. The infants' matching performance suggested that 5-month-olds respond to invariant auditory-visual relations that specify meaningful spatial properties.

The Right Stimulation

Some parents don't interact with their infants often enough and don't provide them with adequate experiences to stimulate their senses. Other well-meaning parents may actually overstimulate their baby.

Infants do need a certain amount of stimulation to develop their perceptual skills. Infants should not be unattended for long stretches of time in barren environments. Many babies born into impoverished families, as well as babies in day-care centers that are like "warehouses" where there are many babies per caregiver and an absence of appropriate stimuli and toys, are at risk for receiving inadequate sensory stimulation.

Caregivers should play with infants, give them toys, and periodically provide them with undivided attention during the course of a day. Some infant experts, however, worry that parents who want to have a "superbaby" may give their infant too much stimulation, which can cause the infant to become confused, irritated, or withdrawn (Bower, 1977). Such parents

What is the right amount of stimulation for babies?

likely place too much pressure on the infant's developing sensory systems and cause more damage than good.

In thinking about the "right" amount and type of stimulation, it is important to recognize that what is "right" may differ from one baby to another. Some infants have a low threshold for sensory stimulation—that is, they can't handle a heavy load of stimulation. They become overwhelmed and cry and fuss when they are frequently exposed to sensory stimulation. Other infants have a high threshold for sensory stimulation—that is, they like a lot of

sensory stimulation and can benefit from it (Zuckerman, 1979).

Another important point about sensory stimulation is that when infants can control a display, they gain more pleasure from it and show more persistence in using it. That is, infants should be active rather than passive participants while observing and manipulating displays.

In sum, it is important for parents to be sensitive to their infant's stimulation needs and monitor when the infant "senses" too little or too much stimulation.

Carl Larsson
In the Hawthorn Hedge

Chapter

6

Physical Development in Childhood and Puberty

*T*hat energy which makes a child hard to manage is the energy which afterward makes him a manager of life.

—Henry Ward Beecher,
Proverbs from Plymouth Pulpit, 1887

Chapter Outline

Chapter Boxes

IMAGES OF CHILDREN

Training Children for the Olympics in China

Standing on the balance beam at a sports school in Beijing, China, 6-year-old Zhang Liyin stretches her arms outward as she gets ready to perform a backflip. She wears the bright-red gymnastic suit of the elite—a suit given to only the best ten girls in her class of 6- to 8-year-olds. But her face wears a dreadful expression; she can't drum up enough confidence to do the flip. Maybe it is because she has had a rough week; a purple bruise decorates one leg, and a nasty gash disfigures the other. Her coach, a woman in her twenties, makes Zhang jump from the beam and escorts her to the high bar, where she is instructed to hang for 3 minutes. If Zhang falls, she must pick herself up and try again. But she does not fall, and she is escorted back to the beam, where her coach puts her through another tedious routine.

Zhang attends the sports school in the afternoon. The sports school is a privilege given to only 260,000 of China's 200 million students of elementary to college age. The Communist party has decided that sports is one avenue China can pursue to prove that China has arrived in the modern world. The sports schools designed to produce Olympic champions were the reason for China's success in recent Olympics. These schools are the only road

to Olympic stardom in China. There are precious few neighborhood playgrounds. And for every 3.5 million people, there is only one gymnasium.

Many of the students who attend the sports schools in the afternoon live and study at the schools as well. Only a few attend a normal school and then come to a sports school in the afternoon. Because of her young age, Zhang stays at home during the mornings and goes to the sports school from noon until 6 P.M. A part-timer like Zhang can stay enrolled until she no longer shows potential to move up to the next step. Any child who seems to lack potential is asked to leave.

Zhang was playing in a kindergarten class when a coach from a sports school spotted her. She was selected because of her broad shoulders, narrow hips, straight legs, symmetrical limbs, open-minded attitude, vivaciousness, and outgoing personality. If Zhang continues to show progress, she could be asked to move to full-time next year. At age 7, she would then go to school there and live in a dorm 6 days a week. If she becomes extremely competent at gymnastics, Zhang could be moved to Shishahai, where the elite gymnasts train and compete (Reilly, 1988).

PREVIEW

*L*ater in the chapter, we will further discuss children's sports and physical fitness in middle and late childhood. Our coverage of children's development in this chapter will also focus on physical development in early childhood; physical development in middle and late childhood; children's health, nutrition, and exercise; puberty; adolescent sexuality; and some adolescent problems and disorders.

The training of future Olympians in the sports schools of China. Six-year-old Zhang Liyin (*third from the left*) hopes someday to become an Olympic gymnastics champion. Attending the sports school is considered an outstanding privilege; only 260,000 of China's 200 million children are given this opportunity.

PHYSICAL DEVELOPMENT IN EARLY CHILDHOOD

Remember from chapter 5 that an infant's growth in the first year is extremely rapid and follows cephalocaudal and proximodistal patterns. At a point around their first birthday, most infants begin to walk. During an infant's second year, the growth rate begins to slow down, but both gross and fine motor skills progress rapidly. The infant develops a sense of mastery through increased proficiency in walking and running. Improvement in fine motor skills—such as being able to turn the pages of a book one at a time—also contributes to the infant's sense of mastery in the second year. The growth rate continues to slow down in early childhood; otherwise, we would be a species of giants.

Height and Weight

The average child grows 2½ inches in height and gains between 5 and 7 pounds a year during early childhood. As the preschool child grows older, the percentage of increase in height and weight decreases with each additional year. Figure 6.1 shows the average height and weight of children as they age from 2 to 6 years. Girls are only slightly smaller and lighter than boys during these years, a difference that continues until puberty. During the preschool years, both boys and girls slim down as the trunk of their bodies lengthens. Although their heads are still somewhat large for their bodies, by the end of the preschool

years most children have lost their top-heavy look. Body fat also shows a slow, steady decline during the preschool years, so that the chubby baby often looks much leaner by the end of early childhood. Girls have more fatty tissue than boys, and boys have more muscle tissue.

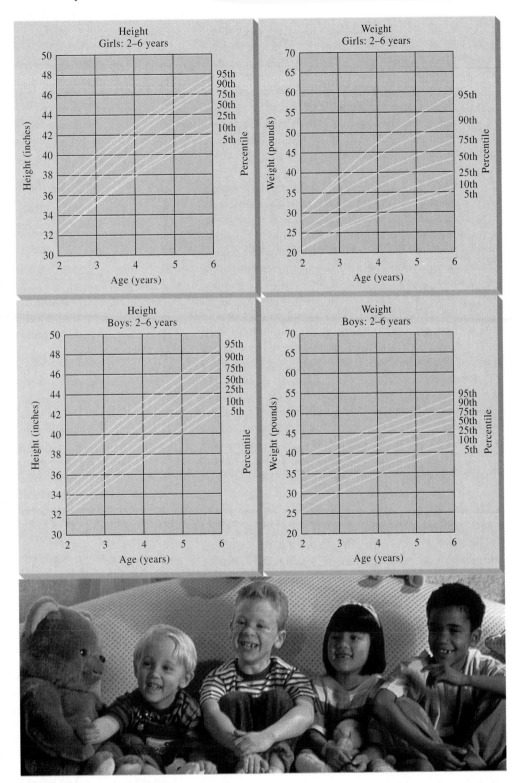

Figure 6.1

Average Height and Weight of Girls and Boys from 2 to 6 Years of Age

Growth patterns vary individually. Think back to your preschool years. This was probably the first time you noticed that some children were taller than you, some shorter; that some were fatter, some thinner; that some were stronger, some weaker. Much of the variation is due to heredity, but environmental experiences are involved to some extent. A review of the heights and weights of children around the world concluded that the two most important contributors to height differences are ethnic origin and nutrition (Meredith, 1978). Urban, middle-class, and firstborn children were taller than rural, lower-class, and later-born children. Children whose mothers smoked during pregnancy were half an inch shorter than children whose mothers did not smoke during pregnancy. In the United States, African American children are taller than White children.

Why are some children unusually short? The culprits are congenital factors (genetic or prenatal problems), a physical problem that develops in childhood, or an emotional difficulty. In many cases, children with congenital growth problems can be treated with hormones. Usually this treatment is directed at the pituitary, the body's master gland, located at the base of the brain. This gland secretes growth-related hormones. With regard to physical problems that develop during childhood, malnutrition and chronic infections can stunt growth, although if the problems are properly treated, normal growth usually is attained. **Deprivation dwarfism** *is a type of growth retardation caused by emotional deprivation; when children are deprived of affection, they experience stress, which alters the release of hormones by the pituitary gland.* Some children who are not dwarfs may also show the effects of an impoverished emotional environment, although most parents of these children say they are small and weak because they have a poor body structure or constitution (Gardner, 1972).

The Brain

One of the most important physical developments during early childhood is the continuing development of the brain and nervous system (Johnston, 1997). While the brain continues to grow in early childhood, it does not grow as rapidly as in infancy. By the time children have reached 3 years of age, the brain is three-quarters of its adult size. By age 5, the brain has reached about nine-tenths its adult size.

The brain and the head grow more rapidly than any other part of the body. The top parts of the head, the eyes, and the brain grow faster than the lower portions, such as the jaw. Figure 6.2 reveals how the growth curve for the head and brain advances more rapidly than the growth curve for height and weight. At 5 years of age, when the brain has attained approximately 90 percent of its adult weight, the 5-year-old's total body weight is only about one-third of what it will be when the child reaches adulthood.

Some of the brain's increase in size is due to the increase in the number and size of nerve endings within and between areas of the brain. These nerve endings

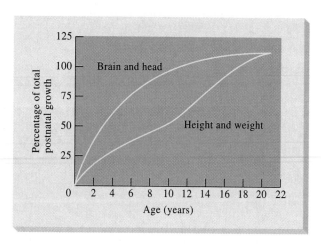

Figure~6.2

Growth Curves for the Head and Brain and for Height and Weight
The more rapid growth of the brain and head can be easily seen. Height and weight advance more gradually over the first two decades of life.

continue to grow at least until adolescence. Some of the brain's increase in size also is due to the increase in **myelination,** *a process in which nerve cells are covered and insulated with a layer of fat cells. This process has the effect of increasing the speed at which information travels through the nervous system.* Some developmentalists believe myelination is important in the maturation of a number of children's abilities. For example, myelination in the areas of the brain related to hand-eye coordination is not complete until about 4 years of age. Myelination in the areas of the brain related to focusing attention is not complete until the end of late childhood (Tanner, 1978).

The increasing maturation of the brain, combined with opportunities to experience a widening world, contribute enormously to children's emerging cognitive abilities. Consider a child who is learning to read and is asked by the teacher to read aloud to the class. Input from the child's eyes is transmitted to the child's brain, then passed through many brain systems, which translate (process) the patterns of black and white into codes for letters, words, and associations. The output occurs in the form of messages to the child's lips and tongue. The child's own gift of speech is possible because brain systems are organized in ways that permit language processing.

> *Swiftly the brain becomes an enchanted loom, where millions of flashing shuttles weave a dissolving pattern—always a meaningful pattern—though never an abiding one.*
>
> —**Sir Charles Sherrington, 1906**

Motor Development

Running as fast as you can, falling down, getting right back up and running just as fast as you can . . . building

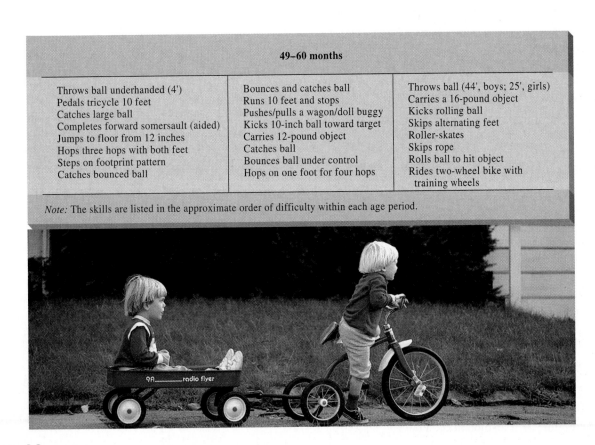

49–60 months		
Throws ball underhanded (4')	Bounces and catches ball	Throws ball (44', boys; 25', girls)
Pedals tricycle 10 feet	Runs 10 feet and stops	Carries a 16-pound object
Catches large ball	Pushes/pulls a wagon/doll buggy	Kicks rolling ball
Completes forward somersault (aided)	Kicks 10-inch ball toward target	Skips alternating feet
Jumps to floor from 12 inches	Carries 12-pound object	Roller-skates
Hops three hops with both feet	Catches ball	Skips rope
Steps on footprint pattern	Bounces ball under control	Rolls ball to hit object
Catches bounced ball	Hops on one foot for four hops	Rides two-wheel bike with training wheels

Note: The skills are listed in the approximate order of difficulty within each age period.

Figure 6.3

The Development of Gross Motor Skills in Early Childhood

towers with blocks . . . scribbling, scribbling, and more scribbling . . . cutting paper with scissors. During your preschool years you probably developed the ability to perform all of these activities.

Gross Motor Skills

The preschool child no longer has to make an effort simply to stay upright and to move around. As children move their legs with more confidence and carry themselves more purposefully, the process of moving around in the environment becomes more automatic (Poest & others, 1990).

At 3 years of age, children are still enjoying simple movements such as hopping, jumping, and running back and forth, just for the sheer delight of performing these activities. They take considerable pride in showing how they can run across a room and jump all of 6 inches. The run-and-jump will win no Olympic gold medals, but for the 3-year-old the activity is a source of considerable pride and accomplishment.

By 4 years of age, children are still enjoying the same kinds of activities, but they have become more adventurous. They scramble over low jungle gyms as they display their athletic prowess. Although they have been able to climb stairs with one foot on each step for some time now, they are just beginning to be able to come down the same way. They still often revert to marking time on each step.

By 5 years of age, children are even more adventuresome than when they were 4. Five-year-olds run hard and enjoy races with each other and their parents. A summary of development in gross motor skills during early childhood is shown in figure 6.3.

You probably have arrived at one important conclusion about preschool children: They are very, very active. Indeed, researchers have found that 3-year-old children have the highest activity level of any age in the entire human life span. They fidget when they watch television. They fidget when they sit at the dinner table. Even when they sleep, they move around quite a bit. Because of their activity level and the development of large muscles, especially in the arms and legs, preschool children need daily exercise. To further evaluate preschool children's development, turn to Critical Thinking About Children's Development.

Fine Motor Skills

At 3 years of age, children are still emerging from the infant ability to place and handle things. Although they have had the ability to pick up the tiniest objects between their thumb and forefinger for some time now, they are still somewhat clumsy at it. Three-year-olds can build surprisingly high block towers, each block being placed with intense concentration but often not in a completely straight line. When 3-year-olds play with a form board or a simple jigsaw puzzle, they are rather rough in placing the

pieces. Even when they recognize the hole a piece fits into, they are not very precise in positioning the piece. They often try to force the piece in the hole or pat it vigorously.

At 4 years of age, children's fine motor coordination has improved substantially and becomes much more precise. Sometimes 4-year-old children have trouble building high towers with blocks because in their desire to place each of the blocks perfectly they might upset those already stacked. By age 5, children's fine motor coordination has improved further. Hand, arm, and body all move together under better command of the eye. Mere towers no longer interest the 5-year-old, who now wants to build a house or a church complete with steeple, though adults may still need to be told what each finished project is meant to be. A summary of the development of fine motor skills in early childhood is shown in figure 6.4.

Handedness

For centuries left-handers have suffered unfair discrimination in a world designed for the right-hander. Even the devil himself was portrayed as a left-hander. For many years, teachers forced all children to write with their right hand even if they had a left-hand tendency. Fortunately, today most teachers let children write with the hand they favor.

37–48 months

Approximates circle
Cuts paper
Pastes using pointer finger
Builds three-block bridge
Builds eight-block tower
Draws *0* and *+*
Dresses and undresses doll
Pours from pitcher without spilling

49–60 months

Strings and laces shoelace
Cuts following line
Strings ten beads
Copies figure *X*
Opens and places clothespins
 (one-handed)
Builds a five-block bridge
Pours from various containers
Prints first name

61–72 months

Folds paper into halves and quarters
Traces around hand
Draws rectangle, circle, square, and
 triangle
Cuts interior piece from paper
Uses crayons appropriately
Makes clay object with two small parts
Reproduces letters
Copies two short words

Note: The skills are listed in the approximate order of difficulty within each age period.

Figure~6.4

The Development of Fine Motor Skills in Early Childhood

Some children are still discouraged from using their left hand, even though many left-handed individuals have become very successful. Their ranks include Leonardo da Vinci, Benjamin Franklin, and Pablo Picasso. Each of these famous men was known for his imagination of spatial layouts, which may be stronger in left-handed individuals. Left-handed athletes also are often successful; since there are fewer left-handed athletes, the opposition is not as accustomed to the style and approach of "lefties." Their tennis serve spins in the opposite direction, their curve ball in baseball swerves the opposite way, and

Today, most teachers let children write with the hand they favor.

their left foot in soccer is not the one children are used to defending against. Left-handed individuals also do well intellectually. In an analysis of the Scholastic Aptitude Test (SAT) scores of more than 100,000 students, 20 percent of the top-scoring group was left-handed, which is twice the rate of left-handedness found in the general population (Bower, 1985). Quite clearly, many left-handed people are competent in a wide variety of human activities, ranging from athletic skills to intellectual accomplishments.

When does hand preference develop? Adults usually notice a child's hand preference during early childhood, but researchers have found handedness tendencies in the infant years. Even newborns have some preference for one side of their body over the other. In one research investigation, 65 percent of infants turned their head to the right when they were lying on their stomachs in the crib. Fifteen percent preferred to face toward the left. These preferences for the right or left were related to later handedness (Michel, 1981). By about 7 months of age, infants prefer grabbing with one hand or the other, and this is also related to later handedness. By 2 years of age, about 10 percent of children favor their left hand. Many preschool children, though, use both hands, with a clear hand preference not completely distinguished until later in development. Some children use one hand for writing and drawing, and the other for throwing a ball. My oldest daughter, Tracy, confuses the issue even further. She writes left-handed and plays tennis left-handed, but she plays golf right-handed. During her early childhood, her handedness was still somewhat in doubt. My youngest daughter, Jennifer, was left-handed from early in infancy. Their left-handed orientation has not handicapped them in their athletic and academic pursuits, although Tracy once asked me if I would buy her a pair of left-handed scissors.

PHYSICAL DEVELOPMENT IN MIDDLE AND LATE CHILDHOOD

The period of middle and late childhood involves slow, consistent growth. This is a period of calm before the rapid growth spurt of adolescence. Among the important aspects of body change in this developmental period are those involving the skeletal system, the muscular system, and motor skills.

As children move through the elementary school years, they gain greater control over their bodies. Physical action is essential for them to refine their developing skills.

TABLE 6.1

Changes in Height and Weight in Middle and Late Childhood

Height (inches)

Age	Female Percentiles			Male Percentiles		
	25th	50th	75th	25th	50th	75th
6	43.75	45.00	46.50	44.25	45.75	47.00
7	46.00	47.50	49.00	46.25	48.00	49.25
8	48.00	49.75	51.50	48.50	50.00	51.50
9	50.25	53.00	53.75	50.50	52.00	53.50
10	52.50	54.50	56.25	52.50	54.25	55.75
11	55.00	57.00	58.75	54.50	55.75	57.25

Weight (pounds)

Age						
6	39.25	43.00	47.25	42.00	45.50	49.50
7	43.50	48.50	53.25	46.25	50.25	55.00
8	49.00	54.75	61.50	51.00	55.75	61.50
9	55.75	62.75	71.50	56.00	62.00	69.25
10	63.25	71.75	82.75	62.00	69.25	78.50
11	71.75	81.25	94.25	69.00	77.75	89.00

Note: The percentile tells how the child compares to other children of the same age. The 50th percentile tells us that half of the children of a particular age are taller (heavier) or shorter (lighter). The 25th percentile tells us that 25 percent of the children of that age are shorter (lighter) and 75 percent are taller (heavier).

Source: Data from R. E. Behman and V. C. Vaughan (eds.), *Nelson Textbook of Pediatrics*, W. B. Saunders, Philadelphia, PA, 1987.

The Skeletal and Muscular Systems

During the elementary school years, children grow an average of 2 to 3 inches a year until, at the age of 11, the average girl is 4 feet 10¾ inches tall and the average boy is 4 feet 9 inches tall. Children's legs become longer and their trunks slimmer. During the middle and late childhood years, children gain about 5 to 7 pounds a year. The weight increase is due mainly to increases in the size of the skeleton and muscular systems, as well as the size of some body organs. Muscle mass and strength gradually increase as "baby fat" decreases. The loose movements and knock-knees of early childhood give way to improved muscle tone. The increase in muscular strength is due to heredity and to exercise. Children double their strength capabilities during these years. Because of their greater number of muscle cells, boys are usually stronger than girls. A summary of changes in height and weight in middle and late childhood appears in table 6.1.

Motor Skills

During middle and late childhood, children's motor development becomes much smoother and more coordinated than it was in early childhood. For example, only one child in a thousand can hit a tennis ball over the net at the age of 3, yet by the age of 10 or 11 most children can learn to play the sport. Running, climbing, skipping rope, swimming, bicycle riding, and skating are just a few of the many physical skills elementary school children can master. And when mastered, these physical skills are a source of great pleasure and accomplishment for children. In gross motor skills involving large muscle activity, boys usually outperform girls rather handily.

As children move through the elementary school years, they gain greater control over their bodies and can sit and attend for longer periods of time. However, elementary school children are far from having physical maturity, and they need to be active. Elementary school children become more fatigued by long periods of sitting than by running, jumping, or bicycling. Physical action is essential for these children to refine their developing skills, such as batting a ball, skipping rope, or balancing on a beam. An important principle of practice for elementary school children, therefore, is that they should be engaged in *active*, rather than passive, activities (Katz & Chard, 1989).

Increased myelinization of the central nervous system is reflected in the improvement of fine motor skills during middle and late childhood. Children's hands are used more adroitly as tools. Six-year-olds can hammer, paste, tie shoes, and fasten clothes. By 7 years of age, children's hands become steadier. At this age, children prefer a pencil to a crayon for printing, and reversal of letters is less common. Printing becomes smaller. Between 8 to 10 years of age, the hands can be used independently with more ease and precision. Fine motor coordination develops to the point where children can write rather than print words. Letter size becomes smaller and more even. By 10 to 12 years of age, children begin to show manipulative skills similar to the abilities of adults. The complex, intricate, and rapid movements

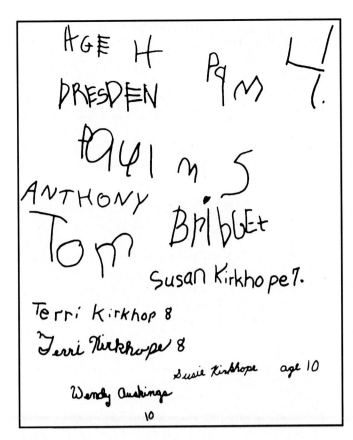

Figure~6.5

Improvement in Fine Motor Control
Improvement of fine motor control is evidenced by changes in handwriting. These children were asked to write their names on a blank piece of paper. As the children increase in age, their writing becomes smaller, and the evenness and the uniformity of letter configurations improve. Females generally exhibit more highly developed fine motor skills during these years because of advanced neurological development. Note the immaturity in discrimination as well as coordination of the 4-year-olds; the reversal of letters of a 6-year-old (Bridget); the mixture of upper-and-lowercase letters of the 6-year-olds; and the letter dropping of the 8-year-old. All are common for the ages of the children.

needed to produce fine-quality crafts or play a difficult piece on a musical instrument can be mastered. Figure 6.5 reflects the improvement in children's fine motor skills as they move through the elementary school years. One final point: Girls usually outperform boys in fine motor skills.

HEALTH, NUTRITION, AND EXERCISE

Although we have become a health-conscious nation, aware of the importance of nutrition and exercise in our lives, many of us still eat junk food, have extra flab hanging around our middles, and spend too much time as couch potatoes. All too often, this description fits children as well as adults.

A Developmental Perspective on Children's Health

Although there has been great national interest in the psychological aspects of adult health, only recently has a developmental perspective on the psychological aspects of children's health been proposed (Tinsley, 1992). The uniqueness of young children's health-care needs is evident when we consider their motor, cognitive, and social development (Maddux & others, 1986). For example, think about the infant's and preschool child's motor development—it is inadequate to ensure personal safety while riding in an automobile. Adults must take preventive measures to restrain infants and young children in car seats. Young children might lack the intellectual skills—including reading ability—to discriminate between safe and unsafe household substances, and they might lack the impulse control to keep them from running out into a busy street while chasing after a ball or toy.

Playgrounds for young children need to be designed with their safety in mind (Frost & Wortham, 1988). The initial step in ensuring children's safety is to walk with children through the existing playground or the site where the playground is to be developed, talking with them about possible safety hazards, letting them assist in identifying hazards, and indicating how they can use the playground safely. The outdoor play environment should enhance children's motor, cognitive, and social development.

Health education programs for preschool children need to be cognitively simple. There are three simple but important goals for health education programs for preschool children (Parcel & others, 1979): (1) to help children identify feelings of wellness and illness and be able to express them to adults, (2) to help children identify appropriate sources of assistance for health-related problems, and (3) to help children independently initiate the use of sources of assistance for health problems.

Caregivers have an important health role for young children (Farmer, Peterson, & Kashani, 1989). For example, by controlling the speed of the vehicles they drive, by decreasing their drinking, and by not smoking around children, caregivers enhance children's health. In one investigation, it was found that if a mother smokes, her children are twice as likely to have respiratory ailments (Etzel, 1988). The young children of single, unemployed, smoking mothers are also three times more likely to be injured. Smoking may serve as a marker to identify mothers less able to supervise young children. In sum, caregivers can actively affect young children's health and safety by training them and monitoring their recreational safety, self-protection skills, proper nutrition, and dental hygiene.

Illnesses, especially those that are not life threatening, provide an excellent opportunity for young children to expand their development. The preschool period is a peak time for such illnesses as respiratory infections (colds, flu) and gastrointestinal upsets (nausea, diarrhea). The illnesses usually are of short duration and are often handled outside the medical community, through the family, day care, or school. Such minor illnesses can increase the young child's knowledge of health and illness and sense of empathy (Parmalee, 1986). Young children might confuse such terms as *feel bad* with bad behavior and *feel good* with good behavior. Examples include:

"I feel bad. I want aspirin."

"I feel bad. My tummy hurts."

"Bobby hurt me."

"I bad girl. I wet my pants."

"Me can do it. Me good girl."

"I'm hurting your feeling, 'cause I was mean to you."

"Stop; it doesn't feel good."

Young children often attribute their illness to what they view as a transgression, such as having eaten the wrong food or playing outdoors in the cold when told not to. In illness and wellness situations, adults have the potential to help children sort out distressed feelings resulting from emotional upsets from those caused by physical illness. For example, a mother might say to her young daughter, "I know you feel bad because you are sick like your sister was last week, but you will be well soon, just as she is now," or a father might comment, "I know you feel bad because I am going on a trip and I can't take you with me, but I will be back in a few days" (Parmalee, 1986).

Poverty and Children's Health

A special concern is the health of children in poverty (Huston, McLoyd, & Coll, 1994). Poor children are at risk for health and nutritional problems, and these problems can have a negative influence on their development. Too often we assume that health conditions in the United States are not sufficiently severe for concern. In many cases, children living in poverty have inadequate health knowledge. In one recent study of low-income Mexican American children's understanding of health in three areas, the children knew more about safety and hygiene than they did about food consumption and their health (Olvera-Ezzell & others, 1994). Lack of adequate health knowledge can mediate negative health outcomes for children living in poverty.

Illness and Health in the World's Children

A special concern is children's illness and health in developing countries around the world. One death of every three in the world is the death of a child under the age of 5 (Grant, 1996). Every week, more than a quarter of a million children die in developing countries in a quiet carnage of infection and undernutrition. The leading cause of childhood death in the world is dehydration and malnutrition as a result of diarrhea. Approximately

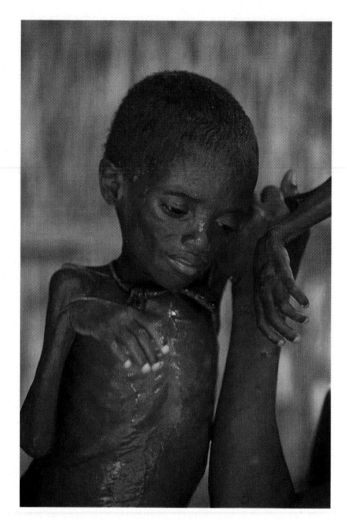

The crisis in Somalia brought to light how extensive malnutrition is in some developing countries.

70 percent of the more than 40 million children killed by diarrhea in 1989 could have been saved if parents had available a low-cost breakthrough known as **oral rehydration therapy (ORT),** *a treatment involving a range of techniques designed to prevent dehydration during episodes of diarrhea by giving the child fluids by mouth.*

Most child malnutrition and deaths could now be prevented by parental actions that are almost universally affordable and based on knowledge that is already available. Making sure that parents know they can improve their children's health by adequate birth spacing, care during pregnancy, breast-feeding, immunization, special feeding before and after illness, and regular monitoring of the children's weight can overcome many causes of malnutrition and poor growth.

> *A simple child,*
> *That lightly draws its breath,*
> *What should it know of death?*
>
> —**William Wordsworth**

Among the nations with the highest mortality rates for children under age 5 are Asian nations, such as Afghanistan, and African nations, such as Ethiopia (Grant, 1996). In Afghanistan, in 1986, for every 1,000 children born alive, 325 died before the age of 5; in Ethiopia, the figure was 255 per 1,000. Among the countries with the lowest mortality rate under age 5 are Scandinavian countries, such as Sweden and Finland, where only 7 of every 1,000 children born died before the age of 5 in 1986. The United States mortality rate under age 5 is better than that of most countries, but, of 131 countries for which figures were available in 1986, 20 countries had better rates than the United States. In 1986, for every 1,000 children born alive in the United States, 13 died before the age of 5.

Nutrition and Children's Obesity

In the middle and late childhood years, children's average body weight doubles. And children exert considerable energy as they engage in many different motor activities. To support their growth and active lives, children need to consume more food than they did in the early childhood years. From 1 to 3 years of age, infants and toddlers only need to consume 1,300 calories per day on the average and only 1,700 calories per day at 4 to 6 years of age. However, at 7 to 10 years of age, children need to consume 2,400 calories per day on the average (the range being 1,650 to 3,300 calories, depending on the child's size) (Pipes, 1988).

A special concern during middle and late childhood is the development of **obesity,** *weighing 20 percent or more above the ideal weight for a particular age, taking both height and sex into account.* Some obese children do not become obese adolescents and adults, but approximately 40 percent of children who are obese at age 7 also are obese as adults. Understanding why children become obese is complex, involving genetic inheritance, physiological mechanisms, cognitive factors, and environmental influences (Muecke & others, 1992). Some children inherit a tendency to be overweight. Only 10 percent of children who do not have obese parents become overweight themselves, whereas 40 percent of children who have one obese parent become obese, and 70 percent of children who have two obese parents become obese. The extent to which this is due to genes or experience with parents cannot be determined in research with humans, but animals can be bred to have a propensity for fatness.

Another factor in the weight of children is **set point,** *the weight maintained when no effort is made to gain or lose weight.* Exercise can lower the body's set point for weight, making it much easier to maintain a lower weight. Indeed, exercise is an important aspect of helping overweight children lose weight and maintain weight loss.

A child's insulin level is another important factor in eating behavior and obesity. American health psychology researcher Judy Rodin (1992) argues that what children eat influences their insulin levels. When children eat complex carbohydrates like cereals, bread, and pasta, insulin levels rise and fall gradually. When children consume simple sugars like candy bars and Cokes, insulin levels rise and then fall sharply—producing the sugar low with which many of us are all too familiar. Glucose levels in the blood are affected by these complex carbohydrates and simple sugars. Children are more likely to eat within the next several hours after eating simple sugars than they are after eating complex carbohydrates. And the food children eat at one meal influences what they will eat at the next meal. So consuming doughnuts and candy bars, in addition to providing minimal nutritional value, sets up an ongoing sequence of what and how much children crave the next time they eat.

Obesity is related to children's self-esteem. In one study, obese children in the third, fourth, and fifth grades had more-negative self-concepts than those of average-weight children (Sallade, 1973).

What can parents do if their child is obese? A medical checkup is the first step to determine if the child has a metabolic disorder. If a metabolic disorder is present, the physician may be able to effectively treat the disorder with a revised diet or drugs. Next, parents need to ensure that the child is getting a well-balanced diet that especially includes complex carbohydrates, such as pasta, potatoes, and cereals. A regular program of physical exercise should be part of the weight loss plan. And every effort should be made to encourage the children's motivation to lose weight so that they feel they are responsible for their weight loss rather than that the parents have imposed the weight loss program on them and are controlling their activity.

Exercise

Many of our patterns of health and illness are long-standing. Our experiences as children contribute to our health practices as adults. Did your parents seek medical help at your first sniffle, or did they wait until your temperature reached 104 degrees? Did they feed you heavy doses of red meat and sugar or a more rounded diet with vegetables and fruit? Did they get you involved in sports or exercise programs, or did you lie around watching television all the time?

Are children getting enough exercise? The 1985 School Fitness Survey tested 18,857 children aged 6 to 17 on nine fitness tasks. Compared to a similar survey in 1975, there was virtually no improvement on the tasks. For example, 40 percent of the boys 6 to 12 years of age could not do more than one pull-up, and a full 25 percent could not do any. Fifty percent of the girls aged 6 to 17, and 30 percent of the boys aged 6 to 12, could not run a mile in less than 10 minutes. In the 50-yard dash, the adolescent girls in 1975 were faster than the adolescent girls in 1985.

Exercise is an important component of children's lives. Everything we know about children's development suggests that children's lives should be active and involve a number of physical activities.

The quality of life is determined by its activities.
—Aristotle, 4th century B.C.

Some experts suggest that television is at least partially to blame for the poor physical condition of our nation's children. In one investigation, children who watched little television were significantly more physically fit than were children who watched a great deal of television (Tucker, 1987). The more children watch television, the more likely they are to be overweight. No one is quite sure whether this is because children spend their leisure time in front of the television set instead of chasing each other around the neighborhood or whether they tend to eat a lot of junk food they see advertised on television.

Some of the blame also falls on the nation's schools, many of which fail to provide physical education classes on a daily basis (Schlicker, Borra, & Regan, 1994). In the 1985 School Fitness Survey, 37 percent of the children in the first through the fourth grades took gym classes only once or twice a week. The investigation also revealed that parents are poor role models when it comes to physical

fitness. Less than 30 percent of the parents of children in grades 1 through 4 exercised 3 days a week. Roughly half said they never get any vigorous exercise. In another study, observations of children's behavior in physical education classes at four elementary schools revealed how little vigorous exercise is done in these classes (Parcel & others, 1987). Children moved through space only 50 percent of the time they were in the class, and they moved continuously an average of only 2.2 minutes. In summary, not only do children's school weeks not include adequate physical education classes, but the majority of children do not exercise vigorously even when they are in such classes. Furthermore, most children's parents are poor role models for vigorous physical exercise.

Does it make a difference if we push children to exercise more vigorously in elementary school? One investigation says yes (Tuckman & Hinkle, 1988). One hundred fifty-four elementary schoolchildren were randomly assigned either to three 30-minute running programs per week or to regular attendance in physical education classes. Although the results sometimes varied according to sex, for the most part the cardiovascular health and the creativity of children in the running program were enhanced. For example, the boys in this program had less body fat and the girls had more creative involvement in their classrooms.

In addition to the school, the family plays an important role in a child's exercise program. A wise strategy is for the family to take up activities involving vigorous physical exercise that parents and children can enjoy together. Running, swimming, cycling, and hiking are especially recommended. In encouraging children to exercise more, parents should not push them beyond their physical limits or expose them to competitive pressures that take the fun out of sports and exercise. For example, long-distance running may be too strenuous for young children and could result in bone injuries. Recently, there has been an increase in the number of children competing in strenuous athletic events such as marathons and triathalons. Doctors are beginning to see some injuries in children that they previously saw only in adults. Some injuries, such as stress fractures and tendinitis, stem from the overuse of young, still-growing bodies. If left to their own devices, how many 8-year-old children would want to prepare for a marathon? It is recommended that parents downplay cutthroat striving and encourage healthy sports that children can enjoy, a topic we discuss further in our examination of children's competitive sports.

We are underexercised as a nation. We look instead of play. We ride instead of walk. Our existence deprives us of the minimum of physical activity essential for healthy living.
—John F. Kennedy, 1961

Sports

Sports have become an increasingly integral part of American culture. Thus, it is not surprising that more and more children become involved in sports every year. Both in public schools and in community agencies, children's sports programs that involve baseball, soccer, football, basketball, swimming, gymnastics, and other activities have grown to the extent that they have changed the shape of many children's lives.

Participation in sports can have both positive and negative consequences for children. Children's participation in sports can provide exercise, opportunities to learn how to compete, increased self-esteem, and a setting for developing peer relations and friendships. However, sports also can have negative outcomes for children: too much pressure to achieve and win, physical injuries, a distraction from academic work, and unrealistic expectations for success as an athlete. Few people challenge the value of sports for children when conducted as part of a school physical education or intramural program, but some question the appropriateness of highly competitive, win-oriented sports teams in schools and community agencies.

There is a special concern for children in "high-pressure" sports settings involving championship play with accompanying media publicity. Some clinicians and child developmentalists believe such activities not only put undue stress on the participants, but also teach children the wrong values, namely a "win-at-all-costs" philosophy. The possibility of exploiting children through highly organized, win-oriented sports programs is an ever-present danger. Overly ambitious parents, coaches, and community boosters can unintentionally create a highly stressful atmosphere in children's sports. When parental, agency, or community prestige becomes the central focus of the child's participation in sports, the danger of exploitation is clearly present. Programs oriented toward such purposes often require long and arduous training sessions over many months and years, frequently leading to sports specialization at too early an age. In such circumstances, adults often transmit a distorted view of the role of the sport in the child's life, communicating to the child that the sport is the most important aspect of the child's existence.

At this point, we have discussed a number of ideas about children's physical growth, health, nutrition, and exercise. A summary of these ideas is presented in concept table 6.1. Now we will turn our attention to the nature of pubertal changes.

PUBERTY AND ADOLESCENCE

After the slow, methodical growth of middle and late childhood, children encounter more-rapid growth during pubertal change. In this section we explore the nature of pubertal change as well as some important dimensions of adolescent development.

Children's participation in sports can have both positive and negative consequences. On the positive side, sports can provide children with exercise, opportunities to learn how to compete, increased self-esteem, and a setting for developing peer relations and friendships. However, on the negative side, sports sometimes involve too much pressure to achieve and win, physical injuries, distractions from academic work, and unrealistic expectations for success as an athlete.

Puberty

Imagine a toddler displaying all features of puberty. Think about a 3-year-old girl with fully developed breasts or a boy just slightly older with a deep male voice. That is what we would see by the year 2250 if the age at which puberty arrives were to continue to decrease at its present pace (Petersen, 1979).

In Norway, **menarche,** *first menstruation,* now occurs at just over 13 years of age, as opposed to 17 years of age in the 1840s. In the United States—where children mature up to a year earlier than do children in European countries—the average age of menarche has declined from 14.2 years of age in 1900 to about 12.45 years of age today. The age of menarche has been declining at an average of about 4 months per decade for the past century (see figure 6.6).

Fortunately, however, we are unlikely to see pubescent toddlers, since what has characterized the past century is special—most likely, a higher level of nutrition and health. The available information suggests that menarche began to occur earlier at about the time of the Industrial Revolution, a period associated with increased standards of living and advances in medical science.

Menarche is one event that characterizes puberty, but there are others. What are puberty's markers? What are the psychological accompaniments of puberty's changes? What health-care issues are raised by early and late maturation?

Pubertal Change

Puberty *is a period of rapid skeletal and sexual maturation that occurs mainly in early adolescence.* However, puberty is not a single, sudden event. It is part of a gradual process. We know when a young person is going through puberty,

Physical Development in Early and Middle and Late Childhood, and Health, Nutrition, and Exercise

Concept	Processes/Related Ideas	Characteristics/Description
Physical Development in Early Childhood	Height and weight	The average child grows 2½ inches in height and gains between 5 and 7 pounds a year during early childhood. Growth patterns vary individually, though. Some children are unusually short because of congenital problems, a physical problem that develops in childhood, or emotional problems.
	The brain	The brain is a key aspect of growth. By age 5, the brain has reached nine-tenths of its adult size. Some of its increase in size is due to increases in the number and size of nerve endings, some to myelination. Increasing brain maturation contributes to improved cognitive abilities.
	Motor development	They increase dramatically during early childhood. Children become increasingly adventuresome as their gross motor skills improve. Young children's lives are extremely active, more active than at any other point in the life span. Rough-and-tumble play often occurs, especially in boys, and it can serve positive educational and developmental functions. Developmentally appropriate activities for young children's gross motor skills include such activities as fundamental movement, daily fitness, and perceptual-motor opportunities. Fine motor skills also improve substantially during early childhood.
	Handedness	At one point, all children were taught to be right-handed. In today's world, the strategy is to allow children to use the hand they favor. Left-handed children are as competent in motor skills and intellect as right-handed children are. Both genetic and environmental explanations of handedness have been given.
Physical Development in Middle and Late Childhood	The skeletal and muscular systems	During the elementary school years, children grow an average of 2 to 3 inches a year. Muscle mass and strength gradually increase. Legs lengthen and trunks slim down as "baby fat" decreases. Growth is slow and consistent.
	Motor skills	During the middle and late childhood years, children's motor development becomes much smoother and more coordinated. Children gain greater control over their bodies and can sit and attend for longer frames of time. However, their lives should be activity oriented and very active. Increased myelinization of the central nervous system is reflected in improved fine motor skills. Improved fine motor development is reflected in children's handwriting skills over the course of middle and late childhood. Boys are usually better at gross motor skills, girls at fine motor skills.
Health, Nutrition, and Exercise	A developmental perspective on children's health	Only recently have researchers applied a developmental perspective to children's health. Children's health-care needs involve their motor, cognitive, and social development.
	Poverty and children's health	Poor children are at risk for health and nutritional problems. A lack of adequate health knowledge might result in negative health outcomes for children in poverty.
	The state of illness and health in the world's children	One death of every three in the world is the death of a child under age 5. The main causes of death and child malnutrition in the world are diarrhea, measles, tetanus, whooping cough, acute respiratory infections (mainly pneumonias), and undernutrition. Contributing factors include the timing of births and hygiene. Most child malnutrition and child deaths could be prevented by parental actions that are affordable and based on knowledge that is available today. The United States has a relatively low rate of child deaths compared to other countries, although the Scandinavian countries have the lowest rate.
	Nutrition and children's obesity	In the middle and late childhood years, children's average body weight doubles, and children exert considerable energy as they engage in different motor activities. To support their growth and active lives, children need to consume more food than they did in the early childhood years. However, a special concern during the middle and late childhood years is the development of obesity. Why children become obese is complex, involving genetic inheritance, physiological mechanisms, cognitive factors, and environmental influences.
	Exercise and sports	Every indication suggests that our nation's children are not getting enough exercise. Television viewing, parents being poor role models for exercise, and the lack of adequate physical education classes in schools may be the culprits. Children's participation in sports can have both positive and negative consequences.

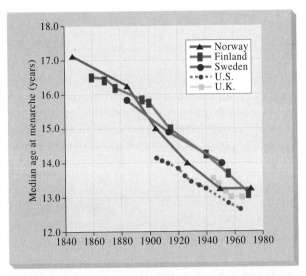

Figure~6.6

Median Ages at Menarche
This graph shows median ages at menarche in selected
northern European countries and the United States from 1845
to 1969. Notice the steep decline in the age at which girls
experienced menarche in five different countries. Recently the
age at which girls experience menarche has been leveling off.

but pinpointing its beginning and its end is difficult.
Except for menarche, which occurs rather late in puberty,
no single marker heralds puberty (Brooks-Gunn, 1991). *foreshadow*
For boys, the first whisker and first wet dream are events
that could mark its appearance, but both might go
unnoticed.

Behind the first whisker in boys and widening of
hips in girls is a flood of hormones, powerful chemical
substances secreted by the endocrine glands and carried
through the body by the bloodstream. The concentrations of certain hormones increase dramatically during
adolescence. **Testosterone** *is a hormone associated in boys
with the development of genitals, an increase in height, and
a change in voice.* **Estradiol** *is a hormone associated in girls*

Puberty involves a dramatic upheaval in bodily change. Young
adolescents develop an acute concern about their bodies.
Columnist Bob Greene (1988) dialed a party line in Chicago,
called *Connections*, to discover what young adolescents were
saying to each other. The first things the boys and girls asked
for—after first names—were physical descriptions. The
idealism of the callers was apparent. Most of the girls described
themselves as having long blond hair, being 5 feet 5 inches
tall, and weighing about 110 pounds. Most of the boys said
they had brown hair, lifted weights, were 6 feet tall, and
weighed about 170 pounds.

with breast, uterine, and skeletal development. In one investigation, testosterone levels increased eighteenfold in
boys but only twofold in girls during puberty; estradiol
increased eightfold in girls but only twofold in boys (Nottelmann & others, 1987).

> *What is formed for long duration arrives slowly to
> its maturity.*
>
> —**Samuel Johnson, *The Rambler*, 1750**

The same influx of hormones that puts hair on a
male's chest and imparts curvature to a female's breast *middelar*
may contribute to psychological development in adolescence (Dorn & Lucas, 1995; Susman & others, 1995).
In one study of 108 normal boys and girls ranging in age
from 9 to 14, a higher concentration of testosterone was
present in boys who rated themselves as more socially
competent (Nottelmann & others, 1987). In another
investigation of 60 normal boys and girls in the same
age range, girls with higher estradiol levels expressed more
anger and aggression (Inoff-Germain & others, 1988).
However, hormonal effects by themselves may account
for only a small portion of the variance in adolescent
development. For example, in one study, social factors
accounted for two to four times as much variance as hormonal factors did in young adolescent girls' depression
and anger (Brooks-Gunn & Warren, 1989).

These hormonal and body changes occur, on the
average, about 2 years earlier in females (10½ years of
age) than in males (12½ years of age) (see figure 6.7).

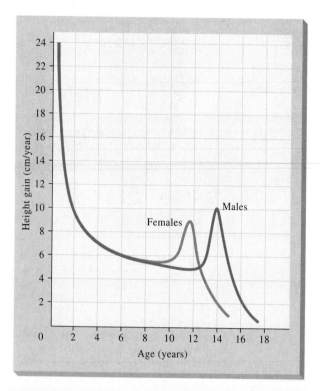

Figure~6.7

Pubertal Growth Spurt
On the average, the growth spurt that characterizes pubertal change occurs 2 years earlier for girls (10½) than for boys (12½).

Four of the most noticeable areas of body change in females are height spurt, menarche, breast growth, and growth of pubic hair; four of the most noticeable areas of body change in males are height spurt, penile growth, testes growth, and growth of pubic hair. The normal range and average age of these characteristics are shown in figure 6.8. Among the most remarkable variations is that, of two boys (or two girls) of the same chronological age, one might complete the pubertal sequence before the other has begun it. For girls, the first menstrual period might occur as early as the age of 10 or as late as the age of 15½ and still be considered normal, for example.

Puberty is not simply an environmental accident; genetic factors are also involved. As indicated earlier,

although nutrition, health, and other factors affect puberty's timing and variations in its makeup, the basic genetic program is wired into the nature of the species (Scarr & Kidd, 1983).

Another key factor in puberty's occurrence is body mass. For example, menarche occurs at a relatively consistent weight in girls. A body weight of approximately 103 to 109 pounds signals menarche and the end of the adolescent growth spurt. For menarche to begin and continue, fat must make up 17 percent of a girl's total body weight.

One thing is certain about the psychological aspects of physical change in adolescence: Adolescents are preoccupied with their bodies and develop individual images of what their bodies are like. Perhaps you looked in the mirror daily or even hourly to see if you could detect anything different about your changing body. Preoccupation with one's body image is strong throughout adolescence, but it is especially acute during puberty, a time when adolescents are more dissatisfied with their bodies than they are in late adolescence.

Psychological Accompaniments of Pubertal Change

A host of psychological changes accompanies an adolescent's physical development (Graber, Petersen & Brooks-Gunn, 1996). Imagine yourself as you were beginning puberty. Not only did you probably think about yourself differently, but your parents and peers probably began acting differently toward you. Maybe you were proud of your changing body even though you were perplexed about what was happening. Perhaps your parents no longer perceived you as someone with whom they could sit in bed and watch television or as someone who should be kissed goodnight.

Being physically attractive and having a positive body image are associated with an overall positive conception of oneself. In one investigation, girls who were judged as being physically attractive and who generally had a positive body image had higher opinions of themselves in general (Lerner & Karabenick, 1974). In another investigation, breast growth in girls 9 to 11 years old was associated with a positive body image, positive peer relationships, and superior adjustment (Brooks-Gunn & Warren, 1989).

Some of you entered puberty early, others late, and yet others on time. When adolescents mature earlier or later than their peers, might they perceive themselves differently? Some years ago, in the Berkeley Longitudinal Study, early-maturing boys perceived themselves more positively, and had more-successful peer relations, than did their late-maturing counterparts (Jones, 1965). The findings for early-maturing girls were similar but not as strong as for boys. When the late-maturing boys were in their thirties, however, they had developed a stronger sense of identity than the early-maturing boys

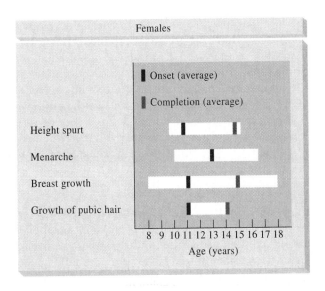

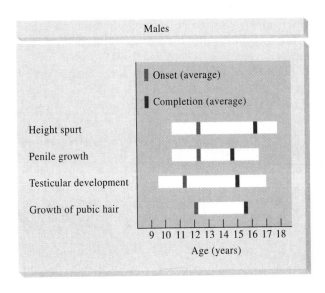

Figure~6.8

Normal Range and Average Development of Sexual Characteristics in Females and Males

Adapted from "Growing Up" by J. M. Tanner. Copyright © 1973 by Scientific American, Inc. All rights reserved.

had (Peskin, 1967). Possibly this occurred because the late-maturing boys had more time to explore life's options or because the early-maturing boys continued to focus on their advantageous physical status instead of on career development and achievement.

More-recent research confirms, though, that at least during adolescence it is advantageous to be an early-maturing rather than a late-maturing boy (Simmons & Blyth, 1987). The more recent findings for girls suggest that early maturation is a mixed blessing: These girls experience more problems in school but also more independence and popularity with boys. The time when maturation is assessed also is a factor. In the sixth grade, early-maturing girls showed greater satisfaction with their figures than did late-maturing girls, but by the tenth grade late-maturing girls were more satisfied. The reason for this is that, by late adolescence, early-maturing girls are

shorter and stockier, whereas late-maturing girls are taller and thinner. Late-maturing girls in late adolescence have bodies that more closely approximate the current American ideal of feminine beauty—tall and thin.

In the last decade an increasing number of researchers have found that early maturation increases girls' vulnerability to a number of problems (Brooks-Gunn & Paikoff, 1993). Early-maturing girls are more likely to smoke, drink, be depressed, have an eating disorder, request earlier independence from their parents, and have older friends; and their bodies are likely to elicit responses from males that lead to earlier dating and earlier sexual experiences (Magnusson, Stattin, & Allen, 1985). In one study, early-maturing girls had lower educational and occupational attainment in adulthood (Stattin & Magnusson, 1990). Apparently as a result of their social and cognitive immaturity, combined with early physical development,

early-maturing girls are easily lured into problem behaviors, not recognizing the possible long-term effects of these on their development (Petersen, 1993).

Some researchers now question whether the effects of puberty are as strong as once believed (Petersen, 1993). Puberty affects some adolescents more strongly than others and some behaviors more strongly than others. Body image, dating interest, and sexual behavior are affected by pubertal change. The recent questioning of puberty's effects suggests that if we look at overall development and adjustment in the human life span, pubertal variations (such as early and late maturation) are less dramatic than is commonly thought. In thinking about puberty's effects, keep in mind that an adolescent's world involves cognitive and social changes as well as physical changes. As with all periods of development, these processes work in concert to produce who we are in adolescence.

Models of Pubertal Change and Behavior

We have just seen that puberty's effects are complex. Given this complexity, it is not surprising that a number of models have been proposed to explain the linkages between pubertal change and behavior. The possible links include (1) direct hormonal effects on behavior, (2) indirect effects of hormones on behavior via secondary sexual characteristics, (3) connections of pubertal change with social events, and (4) the roles of puberty and social events in setting adolescents on a particular developmental trajectory (Brooks-Gunn, Graber, & Paikoff, 1994).
path/course

Direct Hormonal Effects   This is the most simplistic model of links between pubertal change and behavior. There has been some support for a link between androgens and aggressive affect in adolescent boys (Olweus & others, 1988; Susman & others, 1987) but less so for girls (Brooks-Gunn & Warren, 1989). Less clear-cut evidence exists for links between pubertal hormones and depressive affect than for aggressive behavior and affect. Many developmentalists believe that more complex models than the direct hormonal effects model are needed to explain links between pubertal change and behavior.

Indirect Effects via Secondary Sexual Characteristics
The timing of pubertal development, assessed by hormonal and secondary sex characteristics change, is a candidate for explaining behavioral and affective changes in early adolescence, especially for girls. For example, early maturation in girls has been associated with depressive affect, while late maturation has acted as a buffer against depression (Baydar, Brooks-Gunn, & Warren, 1992; Petersen, Sarigiani, & Kennedy, 1991).

Connections with Social Events   Another model emphasizes the possibility that social events or contexts link pubertal change and behavior. This model underscores

the fact that biological and psychological development take place within a social context (Bronfenbrenner, 1995). One study investigated the influence of hormonal functioning, pubertal development (status and timing), and life events on depressive and aggressive affect (Brooks-Gunn & Warren, 1989). Social events (such as life events that occurred at school, at home, and in peer relations) were associated with negative affect to a much greater degree than hormonal changes were. Social events and hormonal change together predicted negative affect better than hormonal change alone did.

Puberty, Social Events, and Developmental Trajectories
Another model suggests that puberty and social events are linked with each other and contribute to negative affect. The assumption is that experiences during puberty set the individual on a trajectory of either high or low levels of affective expression over the course of the adolescent years. In one longitudinal study, initial hormonal changes (in estradiol, for example) were associated with depressive and aggressive affect in girls when initially assessed and 1 year later (Paikoff, Brooks-Gunn, & Warren, 1991). The linkages remained even when the researchers controlled for such factors as prior affective expression, physical maturation, and physical timing.

Similar links have been found in the development of eating behavior problems across the adolescent years. One study found that initial associations between pubertal status, social relationships, and eating problems set the individual on longer-term trajectories, so that girls who had recurring eating problems matured earlier than other girls (Graber & others, 1994). Puberty played a key role during the early adolescent years in determining the particular trajectory that would appear in the late adolescent and young adult years.

Other models of links between pubertal change and behavior have been proposed, but the four models described here provide a sense of the different explanations that are being developed. A summary of the four models in presented in figure 6.9. To fully document which of these models presents the most accurate portrayal of connections between pubertal change and behavior will require more intensive longitudinal studies of hormonal system, social/contextual factors, and behavior.

Sexuality

I am 16 years old and I really like this one girl. She wants to be a virgin until she marries. We went out last night and she let me go pretty far, but not all the way. I know she really likes me too, but she always stops me when things start getting hot and heavy. It is getting hard for me to handle. She doesn't know it but I'm a virgin too. I feel I am ready to have sex. I have to admit I think about having sex with other girls too. Maybe I should be dating other girls.

—Frank C.

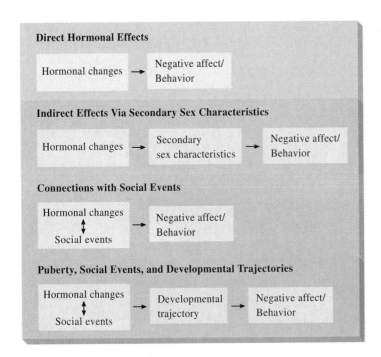

Direct Hormonal Effects

Hormonal changes → Negative affect/Behavior

Indirect Effects Via Secondary Sex Characteristics

Hormonal changes → Secondary sex characteristics → Negative affect/Behavior

Connections with Social Events

Hormonal changes ↕ Social events → Negative affect/Behavior

Puberty, Social Events, and Developmental Trajectories

Hormonal changes ↕ Social events → Developmental trajectory → Negative affect/Behavior

Figure~6.9

Models of Pubertal Change and Behavior

I'm 14 years old. I have a lot of sexy thoughts. Sometimes just before I drift off to sleep at night I think about this hunk who is 16 years old and plays on the football team. He is so gorgeous and I can feel him holding me in his arms and kissing and hugging me. When I'm walking down the hall between classes at school, I sometimes start daydreaming about guys I have met, and wonder what it would be like to have sex with them. Last year I had this crush on the men's track coach. I'm on the girls' track team so I saw him a lot during the year. He hardly knew I thought about him the way I did, although I tried to flirt with him several times.

—Amy S.

If we listen to boys and girls at the very moment they seem most pimply, awkward and disagreeable, we can partly penetrate a mystery most of us once felt heavily within us, and have now forgotten. This mystery is the very process of creation of man and woman.

—Colin Macinnes, *The World of Children*

During adolescence, the lives of males and females become wrapped in sexuality (Brooks-Gunn & Paikoff, in press). Adolescence is a time of sexual exploration and experimentation, of sexual fantasies and sexual realities, of incorporating sexuality into one's identity. At a time when sexual identity is an important developmental task of adolescence, the adolescent is confronted with conflicting sexual values and messages. The majority of adolescents eventually manage to develop a mature sexual identity, but most have periods of vulnerability and confusion along life's sexual journey (Miller, Christopherson, & King, 1993). Our coverage of adolescent sexuality focuses on sexual attitudes and behavior, sexually transmitted diseases, and adolescent pregnancy.

Sexual Attitudes and Behavior

How extensively have heterosexual attitudes and behaviors changed in the twentieth century? What sexual scripts do adolescents follow? How extensive is homosexual behavior in adolescence? We will consider each of these questions in turn.

Adolescent Heterosexual Behavior—Trends and Incidence

Had you been in high school or college in 1940, you probably would have had a different attitude toward many aspects of sexuality that you do today, especially if you are a female. A review of students' sexual practices and attitudes from 1900 to 1980 revealed two important trends (Darling, Kallen, & VanDusen, 1984). First, the percentage of youth reporting that they had had sexual intercourse increased dramatically. Second, the percentage of females reporting that they had had sexual intercourse increased more rapidly than did the percentage of males, although the initial base for males was greater. These changes suggest movement away from a double standard that says it is more appropriate for males than for females to have sexual intercourse.

Large numbers of American adolescents are sexually active (Crump & others, 1996). Figure 6.10 reveals that by age 17, 66 percent of males and 50 percent of females have had sexual intercourse; by age 19, 86 percent of males and 75 percent of females have had sexual intercourse (Alan Guttmacher Institute, 1990). According to the Alan Guttmacher Institute, which periodically surveys adolescent sexual behavior, sexual intercourse among adolescents is increasing, with fewer youth saving sex for adulthood, much less marriage. Among the other findings recently reported by the institute:

- Both males and females report dramatic increases in condom use, undoubtedly due to AIDS education. However, only one-third of male adolescents use condoms all of the time.

- Nearly two-thirds of the sexually experienced girls have had at least two partners; the average sexually active 17- to 19-year old urban male claims he has had six partners.

- An adolescent girl having sex in 1988 was less likely to get pregnant than one having sex in 1982, probably due to increased use of contraceptives. However, because a larger number of girls had sex in 1988, overall

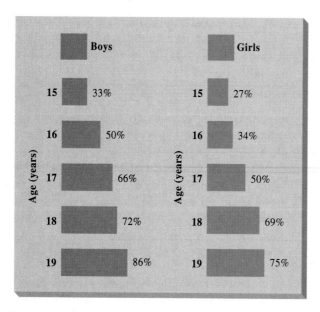

Figure~6.10

Adolescent Sexual Intercourse
Percentage of U.S. adolescents (by sex and age) who say they have had sexual intercourse.

A sexual script is a stereotyped pattern of role prescriptions for how individuals should behave sexually. How do female and male sexual scripts differ?

pregnancy rates remained constant at 127 per 1,000 girls each year—a level far above that of other industrialized countries.

Recent data indicate that, in some areas of the country, sexual experiences of young adolescents may be even greater in number than these figures suggest (Forrest, 1990). In inner-city Baltimore, 81 percent of 14-year-old males said they had already engaged in sexual intercourse. Other surveys in inner-city, low-income areas also reveal a high incidence of early sexual intercourse (Clark, Zabin, & Hardy, 1984).

Adolescent Sexual Scripts   As adolescents explore their sexual identities, they engage in sexual scripts (Bancroft, 1990). A **sexual script** is a stereotyped pattern of role prescriptions for how individuals should behave sexually. Differences in the way females and males are socialized are wrapped up in the sexual scripts adolescents follow. Discrepancies in male/female scripting can cause problems and confusion for adolescents as they work out their sexual identities. Adolescent girls have learned to link sexual intercourse with love. Female adolescents often rationalize their sexual behavior by telling themselves that they were swept away by love. A number of investigators have reported that adolescent females, more than adolescent males, report being in love as the main reason for being sexually active (Cassell, 1984). Far more females than males have intercourse with partners they love and would like to marry. Other reasons for females having sexual intercourse include giving in to male pressure, gambling that sex is a way to get a boyfriend,

curiosity, and sexual desire unrelated to loving and caring. In one recent study, adolescent males said that boys do expect sex from girls (Crump & others, 1996). They also said that the typical adolescent male does not force sex but does put pressure on females to have sex. Adolescent males might be aware that their female counterparts have been socialized into a love ethic. They also might understand the pressure many of them feel to have a boyfriend. A classic male line shows how males understand female thinking about sex and love: "If you really loved me, you would have sex with me." The female adolescent who says "If you really loved me, you would not put so much pressure on me" reflects her insight about male sexual motivation.

Homosexual Attitudes and Behavior   Both the early (Kinsey) and more recent (Hunt) surveys indicated that about 4 percent of males and 3 percent of females are exclusively homosexual (Hunt, 1974; Kinsey, Pomeroy, & Martin, 1948). In a recent national survey, the percentage of individuals who reported being active homosexuals was 2.7 percent for males and 1.3 percent for females (Michael & others, 1994).

Why are some individuals homosexual and others heterosexual? Speculation about this question has been extensive, but no firm answers are available. Homosexual and heterosexual males and females have similar physiological responses during sexual arousal and seem to be aroused by the same types of tactile stimulation. Investigators find that, in terms of a wide range of attitudes, behaviors, and adjustments, there are no differences between homosexuals and heterosexuals (Bell, Weinberg, & Mammersmith, 1981). Recognizing that homosexuality is not a form of mental illness, the American Psychiatric Association discontinued its classification of homosexuality as a disorder, except in those cases where the individuals themselves consider the sexual orientation to be abnormal.

An individual's sexual orientation—heterosexual, bisexual, or homosexual—is most likely determined by a combination of genetic, hormonal, and environmental factors (Savin-Williams & Rodriguez, 1993). Most experts on homosexuality believe that no one factor alone causes homosexuality and that the relative weight of each factor may vary from one individual to the next. In truth, no one knows *exactly* what causes an individual to be a homosexual. Scientists have a clearer picture of what does *not* cause homosexuality. For example, children raised by gay or lesbian parents or couples are no more likely to be homosexual than are children raised by heterosexual parents (Golombok & Tasker, 1996; Patterson, 1995). There also is no evidence that male homosexuality is caused by a dominant mother or a weak father, or that female homosexuality is caused by girls choosing male role models. Among the biological factors believed to be involved in homosexuality are prenatal hormone conditions (Ellis & Ames, 1987). In the second to fifth months after conception, exposure to hormone levels characteristic of females is speculated to cause an individual (male or female) to become attracted to males. If this "prenatal critical-period hypothesis" turns out to be correct, it would explain why researchers and clinicians have found it difficult to modify a homosexual orientation.

Adolescence may play an important role in the development of homosexuality (Gruskin, 1994). In one investigation, participation in homosexual behavior and sexual arousal by same-sex peers in adolescence was strongly related to an adult homosexual orientation (Bell, Weinberg, & Mammersmith, 1981). An adolescent whose interest in the same sex is intense and compelling often experiences severe conflict. American culture stigmatizes homosexuality; negative labels, such as *fag* and *queer*, are given to male homosexuals, and *lezzie* and *dyke* to female homosexuals. The sexual socialization of adolescent homosexuals becomes a process of learning to hide (Herdt, 1988). Some gay males wait out their entire adolescence, hoping that heterosexual feelings will develop. Many female adolescent homosexuals have similar experiences. Many adult females who identify themselves as homosexuals considered themselves predominantly heterosexual during adolescence (Bell, Weinberg, & Mammersmith, 1981).

Sexually Transmitted Diseases

Tammy, age 15, has just finished listening to a lecture in her health class. We overhear her talking to one of her girlfriends as she walks down the school corridor. "That was a disgusting lecture. I can't believe all the diseases you can get by having sex. I think she was probably trying to scare us. She spent a lot of time talking about AIDS, which I've heard that normal people don't get. Right? I've heard that only homosexuals and drug addicts get AIDS, and I've also heard that gonorrhea and most other sexual diseases can be cured, so what's the big deal if you get something like that?" Tammy's view of sexually transmitted diseases (formerly called venereal disease, or VD) is common among adolescents. Teenagers tend to believe that sexually transmitted diseases always happen to someone else, can be easily cured without any harm done, and are too disgusting for a nice young person to even hear about, let alone get. This view is wrong. Adolescents who are having sex *do* run a risk of getting sexually transmitted diseases. Sexually transmitted diseases are common among today's adolescents (Nevid & Gottfried, 1995).

Chlamydia Sexually transmitted diseases are primarily transmitted through sexual intercourse, although they can be transmitted orally. **Chlamydia** *is a sexually transmitted disease named for the bacteria that cause it*. Chlamydia affects as many as 10 percent of all college males and females. Males experience a burning sensation during urination and a mucoid discharge. Females experience painful urination or a vaginal discharge. These signs often mimic gonorrhea. However, when penicillin is prescribed for gonorrhealike symptoms, the problem does not go away as it would if gonorrhea were the culprit. If left untreated, the disease can affect the entire reproductive tract. This can lead to problems left by scar tissue, which can prevent the female from becoming pregnant. Effective drugs are available to treat this common sexually transmitted disease.

Herpes Simplex Virus II An alarming increase in another sexually transmitted disease, herpes simplex virus II, has occurred in recent years. **Herpes simplex virus II** *is a sexually transmitted disease whose symptoms include irregular cycles of sores and blisters in the genital area*. Although this disease is more common among young adults (estimates range as high as 1 in 5 sexually active adults), as many as 1 in 35 adolescents have genital herpes. The herpes virus is potentially dangerous. If babies are exposed to the active virus during birth, they are vulnerable to brain damage or even death, and women with herpes are eight times more likely than unaffected women to develop cervical cancer. At present, herpes is incurable.

Syphilis Sexual problems have plagued human beings throughout history. Hippocrates wrote about syphilis in 460 B.C. The first major recorded epidemic of syphilis appeared in Naples, Italy, 2 years after Columbus' first

This AIDS advertisement indicates how vulnerable our nation's population is to the epidemic of AIDS, and the disease's lethal consequences.

return. It is believed that millions of people died of the disease, which is sexually transmitted through intercourse, kissing, or intimate body contact. The cause of syphilis is a tiny bacterium that requires warm, moist surfaces to penetrate the body. It was not until 400 years after the Italian outbreak that penicillin, a successful treatment for syphilis, was discovered.

AIDS   Today, we harbor the same fear of sexually transmitted disease as people had in Columbus's time, but instead of syphilis it is AIDS, a major sex-related problem, that has generated considerable fear in today's world (Cox, 1994). **AIDS (acquired immune deficiency syndrome)** *is caused by a virus (HIV) that destroys the body's immune system. Consequently, many germs that usually do not harm someone with a normal immune system produce devastating results, and even death, in a person infected with this virus.*

In 1981, when AIDS was first recognized in the United States, there were fewer than 60 reported cases. Beginning in 1990, we began losing as many Americans each year to AIDS as died in the Vietnam War, almost 60,000 people. According to federal health officials, 1 to 1.5 million Americans are now asymptomatic carriers of AIDS—they are infected with the virus and presumably capable of infecting others but show no clinical symptoms of AIDS. In 1989, the first attempt to assess AIDS among college students was made. Testing of 16,861 students found 30 students infected with the virus (American College Health Association, 1989). If the 12.5 million students attending college in 1989 were infected at the same rate, 25,000 of those students would have had the AIDS virus.

Experts say that AIDS can be transmitted only through sexual contact, shared needles, blood transfusion, or other exchange of bodily fluids (Kalichman, 1996). Although in the United States 90 percent of all AIDS

ABLE 6.2

Understanding AIDS: What's Risky, What's Not

The AIDS virus is not transmitted like colds or the flu, but by an exchange of infected blood, semen, or vaginal fluids. This usually occurs during sexual intercourse, in sharing drug needles, or to babies infected before or during birth.

You Won't Get AIDS From:

- Everyday contact with individuals around you in school, stores, the workplace, at parties, or child-care centers.
- Swimming in a pool, even if someone in the pool has the AIDS virus.
- A mosquito bite, bedbugs, lice, flies, or other insects.
- Saliva, sweat, tears, urine, or a bowel movement.
- A kiss.
- Clothes, telephones, or toilet seats.
- Using a glass or eating utensils that someone else has used.
- Being on a bus, train, or crowded elevator with an individual who is infected with the virus, or who has AIDS.

Blood Donations and Transfusions:

- You will not come into contact with the AIDS virus by donating blood at a blood bank.
- The risk of getting AIDS from a blood transfusion has been greatly reduced. Donors are screened for risk factors and donated blood is tested.

Risky Behavior:

- Having a number of sex partners.
- Sharing drug needles and syringes.
- Engaging in anal sex with or without a condom.
- Performing vaginal or oral sex with someone who shoots drugs or engages in anal sex.
- Engaging in sex with someone you don't know well or with someone who has several sex partners.
- Engaging in unprotected sex (without a condom) with an infected individual.

Safe Behavior:

- Not having sex.
- Having sex with one mutually faithful, uninfected partner.
- Not shooting drugs.

Source: America Responds to AIDS, U.S. government educational pamphlet, 1988.

cases continue to occur among homosexual males and intravenous drug users, a disproportionate increase among females who are heterosexual partners of bisexual males or of intravenous drug users has been recently noted: This increase suggests that the risk of AIDS might be increasing among heterosexual individuals who have multiple sex partners (Jones, 1996). Table 6.2 describes what's risky and what's not, regarding AIDS.

Because it is possible, and even probable among high-risk groups, to have more than one STD at a time, efforts to prevent one disease help reduce the prevalence of other diseases. Efforts to prevent AIDS can also help prevent adolescent pregnancy and other sex-related problems. Because of the high rate of sexually transmitted diseases, it is crucial that both teenagers and adults understand these diseases.

One recent study evaluated 37 AIDS prevention projects (Janz & others, 1996). Small-group discussions, outreach to populations engaged in high-risk behaviors, and training peers and volunteers were the activities rated the most effective. Small-group discussions, with an emphasis on open communication and repetition of messages, are excellent opportunities for adolescents to learn and share information about AIDS. The best outreach programs are culturally tailored and include incentives *Sperre/Shmulans* to participate. Outreach workers who are familiar and respected might be able to break through the barriers of fear and mistrust to ensure that appropriate messages are heard and heeded. For incentives to work, they also must be tailored for specific populations. School-age children might be attracted by academic credit or a stipend. Food, shelter, and a safe place to congregate might attract participants who inject drugs. Child care and an opportunity to spend time with other adults might draw working women. The use of peer educators is often an effective strategy. As role models, peers can mirror healthy lifestyles for the target population as well as provide reinforcement and shape group norms that support behavior change. Peer educators often are effective in getting adolescents involved in AIDS prevention projects.

Adolescent Pregnancy

Angela is 15 years old and pregnant. She reflects, "I'm 3 months pregnant. This could ruin my whole life. I've made all of these plans for the future and now they are down the drain. I don't have anybody to talk to about my problem. I can't talk to my parents. There is no way they can understand." Pregnant adolescents were once practically invisible and unmentionable, but yesterday's secret has become today's national dilemma.

Incidence and Nature of Adolescent Pregnancy   The adolescent pregnancy rate in the United States is much higher than in other industrialized countries (East & Felice, 1996). It is more than twice as high as the rates in England, France, and Canada, almost three times as high as the rate in Sweden, and seven times as high as the rate in the Netherlands (Child Trends, 1996; Jones & others, 1985). Though American adolescents are no more sexually active than their counterparts in these other countries, they are many more times likely to become pregnant. To read further about sexuality in the lives of adolescents in Holland and Sweden, turn to Sociocultural Worlds of Children.

Each year more than 500,000 American teenagers become pregnant, and more than 70 percent of them are unmarried (Child Trends, 1996). They represent a flaw in America's social fabric. Like Angela, far too many become pregnant in their early or middle adolescent years. More than 200,000 females in the United States have a child before their eighteenth birthday. As one 17-year-old Los Angeles mother of a 1-year-old son said, "We are children having children." The only bright spot in adolescent pregnancy statistics is that small declines in the teenage birth rate began to appear in 1992 and 1993; the rate rose by one-fourth between 1986 and 1991.

Despite the rise in the teenage birth rate in the late 1980s, the rate is lower now than it was in the 1950s and 1960s. What is different now, though, is the steady rise in nonmarital teenage birth (see figure 6.11). In the last three decades, American culture has been swept with changes in sexual attitudes and social morals (Rubert & Robovits, 1997). As shown in figure 6.11, adolescents gave birth at a higher rate in 1950 than they do today; but that was a time of early marriage when the overwhelming majority of births to adolescent mothers occurred within a marriage and involved females 17 years of age and older. Two or three decades ago, many unwed adolescent girls who became pregnant were swiftly married off in a "shotgun wedding." If marriage was impractical, the girl would discreetly disappear, the child would be put up for adoption, and the predicament would never be discussed again. Abortion was not a real option for most adolescent females until 1973, when the Supreme Court ruled that it could not be outlawed.

In today's world, if the pregnant adolescent girl does not choose to have an abortion (almost 40 percent do), she usually keeps the baby and raises it without the traditional involvement of marriage. Because the stigma of illegitimacy is less severe today, adolescent girls are less likely to give up their babies for adoption. Fewer than 5 percent do, compared with approximately 35 percent in the early 1960s. But even though the stigma of illegitimacy has lessened, the lives of most pregnant adolescent females are anything but rosy. Let's now explore the consequences of adolescent pregnancy.

Adolescent Pregnancy: Consequences and Social Policy
The consequences of our nation's high adolescent pregnancy rate are of great concern (Brooks-Gunn & Chase-Lansdale, 1995; Luster & others, 1995). Pregnancy in adolescence increases the health risks to both the child and the mother. Infants born to adolescent mothers are more likely to have low birth weights (a prominent cause of infant mortality), as well as neurological problems and childhood illnesses (Furstenberg, Brooks-Gunn, & Chase-Lansdale, 1989). Adolescent mothers often drop out of school, fail to gain employment, and become dependent on welfare. Although many adolescent mothers resume

Sex is less mystified and dramatized in Sweden than in the United States, and adolescent pregnancy rates are much lower in Sweden than in the United States.

Sex Education and Attitudes Among Adolescents in Holland and Sweden

In Holland and Sweden, sex does not carry the mystery and conflict it does in American society. Holland does not have a mandated sex-education program, but adolescents can obtain contraceptive counseling at government-sponsored clinics for a small fee. The Dutch media also have played an important role in educating the public about sex through frequent broadcasts focused on birth control, abortion, and related matters. Most Dutch adolescents do not consider having sex without birth control.

Swedish adolescents are sexually active at an earlier age than are American adolescents, and they are exposed to even more explicit sex on television. However, the Swedish National Board of Education has developed a curriculum that ensures that every child in the country, beginning at age 7, will experience a thorough grounding in reproductive biology and, by the age of 10 or 12, will have been introduced to information about various forms of contraception. Teachers are expected to handle the subject of sex whenever it becomes relevant, regardless of the subject they are teaching. The idea is to dedramatize and demystify sex so that familiarity will make students less vulnerable to unwanted pregnancy and sexually transmitted diseases. American society is not nearly so open about sex education.

their education later in life, they generally do not catch up with women who postpone childbearing. In the National Longitudinal Survey of Work Experience of Youth, it was found that only half of the women 20 to 26 years old who first gave birth at age 17 had completed high school by their twenties. The percentage was even lower for those who gave birth at a younger age (Mott & Marsiglio, 1985). By contrast, among females who waited until age 20 to have a baby, more than 90 percent had obtained a high school education. Among the younger adolescent mothers, almost half had obtained a general equivalency diploma (GED), which rarely opens up good employment opportunities.

These educational deficits have negative consequences for the young women themselves and for their children. Adolescent parents are more likely than those who delay childbearing to have low-paying, low-status jobs or to be unemployed. The mean family income of White females who gave birth before age 17 is approximately half that of families in which the mother delays birth until her mid or late twenties.

Serious, extensive efforts need to be developed to help pregnant adolescents and young mothers enhance their educational and occupational opportunities (Murray, 1996). Adolescent mothers also need extensive help in obtaining competent day care and in planning for

the future. Experts recommend that, to reduce the high rate of teen pregnancy, adolescents need improved sex education and family-planning information, greater access to contraception, and broad community involvement and support (Crockett & Chopak, 1993). Another very important consideration, especially for young adolescents, is abstinence, which is increasingly being included as a theme in sex-education classes.

Following are some of the policy implications that could improve the lives of adolescent mothers (Chase-Lansdale & Brooks-Gunn, 1994). First, the diversity in the life courses of adolescent mothers suggests that no single service delivery program is universally applicable. Rather, different types of programs should be developed for different types of adolescent mothers. For example, adolescent mothers who drop out of school either before or after pregnancy need different services than adolescent mothers who graduate from high school and are employed. Second, services should be expanded to include elementary-age children. Despite the fact that most studies show more negative consequences for older children than for younger children, the majority of child-oriented services target infants and preschool children.

Two other policy implications involve the coordination of services and family systems. Better coordination of services for mothers and children is needed.

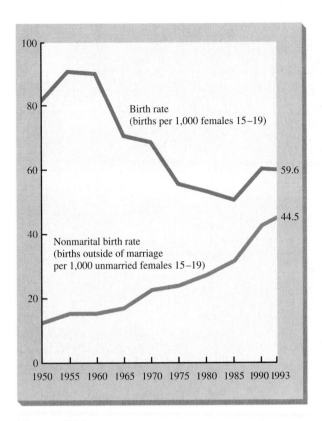

Figure~6.11

Trends in the Teenage Birth Rate and the Nonmarital Teenage Birth Rate, 1950–1993

Historically, programs have targeted either mothers (emphasizing work training) or children (emphasizing early enrichment) but have not linked the lives of mothers and their children. Also, a family systems perspective is missing from policy perspectives. Grandmothers often are significant members of teenage mothers' families, and service programs need to take this fact into account. Virtually no programs target grandmothers themselves. In addition, the family system can help or hinder the young mother's efforts to be an effective parent or to achieve economic security.

Some Adolescent Problems and Disorders

In addition to the increase in adolescent pregnancy, other problems that may arise in adolescence are drug abuse, juvenile delinquency, suicide, and eating disorders, each of which we will discuss in turn.

Drugs

The 1960s and 1970s were a time of marked increase in the use of illicit drugs. During the social and political unrest of those years, many youth turned to marijuana, stimulants, and hallucinogens. Increases in alcohol consumption by adolescents also were noted (Robinson & Greene, 1988). More-precise data about drug use by adolescents have been collected in recent years. Each year since 1975, Lloyd Johnston, Patrick O'Malley, and Gerald

Bachman (1996), working at the Institute of Social Research at the University of Michigan, have carefully monitored drug use by America's high school seniors in a wide range of public and private high schools. From time to time, they also sample the drug use of younger adolescents and adults.

In the 1993 survey, drug use among American youth increased for the first time in a number of years. A sharp rise in the use of marijuana, as well as increases in the use of stimulants, LSD, and inhalants, occurred among high school students in 1993. Johnston, Bachman, and O'-Malley (1996) concluded that there had recently been a decrease in knowledge about the dangers associated with these drugs; when such knowledge decreases, an increase in drug use usually occurs. In addition, of the world's industrialized nations, the United States has the highest rate of drug use by adolescents. In 1996, 40 percent of the nation's high school seniors tried an illicit drug, up from 27 percent in 1992. The rise in illicit drug use has been especially pronounced for marijuana. From 1991 to 1996, annual use of marijuana (any use during the 12 months prior to the survey), tripled among eighth graders (to 18 percent), doubled among tenth graders (to 34 percent), and increased by 50 percent among high school seniors (to 36 percent).

According to Lloyd Johnston and his colleagues, considerable progress was made in the 1980s in reducing the number of adolescents who use drugs—in particular marijuana and cocaine. However, we may now be in danger of losing some of the hard-won ground as a new, more naive generation of children enters adolescence and as society decreases its communication to adolescents about the danger of drugs.

Alcohol   Some mornings, 15-year-old Annie was too drunk to go to school. Other days, she'd stop for a couple of beers or a screwdriver on the way to school. She was tall, blonde, and good looking, and no one who sold her liquor, even at 8 A.M., questioned her age. Where did she get her money? She got it from baby-sitting and from what her mother gave her to buy lunch. Annie used to be a cheerleader, but no longer; she was kicked off the squad for missing practice so often. Soon, she and several of her peers were drinking almost every morning. Sometimes, they skipped school and went to the woods to drink. Annie's whole life began to revolve around her drinking. This routine went on for 2 years. After a while, Annie's parents discovered her problem. Even though they punished her, it did not stop her drinking. Finally, this year, Annie started dating a boy she really liked who would not put up with her drinking. She agreed to go to Alcoholics Anonymous and has just successfully completed treatment. She has been off alcohol for 4 consecutive months now, and she hopes that her abstinence will continue.

Alcohol is the drug most widely used by adolescents in our society. For them, it has produced many enjoyable moments and many sad ones as well. Alcoholism is the third-leading killer in the United States, with more than 13 million people classified as alcoholics, many of whom established their drinking habits during adolescence. Each year, approximately 25,000 people are killed and 1.5 million injured by drunk drivers. In 65 percent of the aggressive male acts against females, the offender is under the influence of alcohol. In numerous instances of drunken driving and assaults on females, the offenders are adolescents.

How extensive is alcohol use by adolescents? Alcohol use by high school seniors has gradually declined. Monthly use declined from 72 percent in 1980 to 51 percent in 1996. The prevalence of drinking five or more drinks in a row in a 2-week interval fell from 41 percent in 1980 to 31 percent in 1996. There remains a substantial gender difference in heavy adolescent drinking: 20 percent for females versus 36 percent for males in 1992, although the gender difference was much greater before the 1980s. There has been much less change in binge drinking among college students. In 1992, 41 percent of college students reported that they engaged in binge drinking, about the same percentage as in 1980 (Johnston, O'Malley, & Bachman, 1993).

Cocaine   Did you know that cocaine was once an ingredient in Coca-Cola? Of course, it has long since been

What is the pattern of alcohol consumption among adolescents?

removed from the soft drink. Cocaine comes from the coca plant, native to Bolivia and Peru. For many years, Bolivians and Peruvians chewed the plant to increase their stamina. Today, cocaine is usually snorted, smoked, or injected in the form of crystals or powder. The effect is a rush of euphoric feelings, which eventually wear off, followed by depressive feelings, lethargy, insomnia, and irritability.

Cocaine is a highly controversial drug. Users claim it is exciting, makes them feel good, and increases their confidence. It is clear, however, that cocaine has potent cardiovascular effects and is potentially addictive. When the drug's effects are extreme, it can produce a heart attack, stroke, or brain seizure. The increase in cocaine-related deaths is traced to very pure or tainted forms of the drug.

In the late 1980s and early 1990s, adolescents' use of crack declined (from 4.1 percent in 1986 to 1.5 percent in 1993—for use in the last year). However, in 1996 adolescents' use of crack had increased to 2.1 percent (Johnston, Bachman, & O'Malley, 1996).

Suicide

Suicide is a common problem in our society. Its rate has tripled in the past 30 years in the United States; each year, about 25,000 people take their own lives. Beginning with the 15-year-old age group or so, the suicide rate begins to rise rapidly. Suicide accounts for about 12 percent of the mortality in the adolescent and young adult age group. Males are about three times as likely to commit suicide as females are; this may be because of their more

TABLE 6.3

What to Do and What Not to Do When You Suspect Someone Is Likely to Commit Suicide

What to Do

1. Ask direct, straightforward questions in a calm manner: "Are you thinking about hurting yourself?"
2. Assess the seriousness of the suicidal intent by asking questions about feelings, important relationships, others with whom the person has talked, and the amount of thought given to the means to be employed. If a gun, pills, rope, or other means has been obtained and a specific plan has been developed, the situation is very dangerous. Stay with the person until help arrives.
3. Listen and be supportive, without giving false reassurances.
4. Encourage the young person to get professional help and provide assistance.

What Not to Do

1. Do not ignore warning signs.
2. Do not refuse to talk about suicide if a young person approaches you.
3. Do not react with horror, disapproval, or repulsion.
4. Do not offer false reassurances ("Everything is going to be all right.") or platitudes and simple answers ("You should be thankful for. . . .").
5. Do not abandon the young person after the crisis has passed or after professional counseling has begun.

From: *Living with 10- to 15-Year-Olds: A Parent Education Curriculum.* Copyright 1992 by the Center for Early Adolescence, University of North Carolina at Chapel Hill, D-2 Carr Mill Town Center, Carrboro, NC 27510.

active methods for attempting suicide—shooting, for example. By contrast, females are more likely to use passive methods, such as sleeping pills, which are less likely to produce death. Although males commit suicide more frequently, females attempt it more frequently (Forshaun, 1996).

Estimates indicate that, for every successful suicide in the general population, 6 to 10 attempts are made. For adolescents, the figure is as high as 50 attempts for every life taken. As many as two in every three college students has thought about suicide on at least one occasion; their methods range from overdosing on drugs to crashing into the White House in an airplane.

Why do adolescents attempt suicide? There is no simple answer to this important question (Maris, Silverman, & Canetto, 1997). It is helpful to think of suicide in terms of proximal and distal factors. Proximal, or immediate, factors can trigger a suicide attempt. Highly stressful circumstances, such as the loss of a boyfriend or girlfriend, poor grades at school, or an unwanted pregnancy, can trigger a suicide attempt. Drugs have been involved more often in recent suicide attempts than in attempts in the past (Wagner, Cole, & Schwartzman, 1993).

Distal, or earlier, experiences often are involved in suicide attempts as well. A long-standing history of family instability and unhappiness may be present (Reinherz & others, 1994). Just as a lack of affection and emotional support, high control, and pressure for achievement by parents during childhood are related to adolescent depression, so are such combinations of family experiences likely to show up as distal factors in suicide attempts. Lack of supportive friendships also may be present (Rubenstein & others, 1989). In an investigation of suicide among gifted women, previous suicide attempts, anxiety, conspicuous instability in work and in relationships, depression, or alcoholism also were present in the women's lives (Tomlinson-Keasey, Warren, & Elliot, 1986). These factors are similar to those found to predict suicide among gifted men (Schneidman, 1971).

Just as genetic factors are associated with depression, so are they associated with suicide. The closer the genetic relationship a person has to someone who has committed suicide, the more likely that person is to commit suicide (Wender & others, 1986).

What is the psychological profile of the suicidal adolescent like? Suicidal adolescents often have depressive symptoms (Gadpaille, 1996). Although not all depressed adolescents are suicidal, depression is the most frequently cited factor associated with adolescent suicide. A sense of hopelessness, low self-esteem, and high self-blame are also associated with adolescent suicide (Harter & Marold, 1992; Shagle & Barber, 1994).

Table 6.3 provides valuable information about what to do and what not to do when you suspect someone is contemplating suicide.

Eating Disorders

Fifteen-year-old Jane gradually eliminated foods from her diet to the point where she subsisted by eating *only* applesauce and eggnog. She spent hours observing her body, wrapping her fingers around her waist to see if it was getting any thinner. She fantasized about becoming a beautiful fashion model who would wear designer bathing suits. Even when she reached 85 pounds, Jane still felt fat. She continued to lose weight, eventually emaciating herself. She was hospitalized and treated for **anorexia nervosa,** *an eating disorder that involves the relentless pursuit of thinness through starvation.* Eventually, anorexia nervosa can lead to death, as it did for popular singer Karen Carpenter.

Anorexia nervosa afflicts primarily females during adolescence and early adulthood (only about 5 percent of anorexics are male) (Worrell & Todd, 1996). Most individuals with this disorder are White and from well-educated, middle- and upper-income families. Although anorexics avoid eating, they have an intense interest in food; they cook for others, they talk about food, and they insist on watching others eat. Anorexics have a distorted body image, perceiving that they will look better even if they become skeletal (Stormer & Thompson, 1996; Thompson, 1996). As self-starvation continues and the fat content of the body drops to a bare minimum, menstruation usually stops and behavior often becomes hyperactive.

Numerous causes of anorexia nervosa have been proposed (Garner & Garfinkel, 1997). They include societal, psychological, and physiological factors (Striegel-Moore & others, 1993). The societal factor most often held responsible is the current fashion of thinness. Psychological factors include a motivation to get attention, a desire for individuality, a denial of sexuality, and a way of coping with overcontrolling parents. Anorexics sometimes have parents who place high demands for achievement on them. Unable to meet their parents' high standards, anorexics feel unable to control their own lives. By limiting their food intake, anorexics gain a sense of self-control. Physiological causes focus on the hypothalamus, which becomes abnormal in a number of ways when an individual becomes anorexic. At this time, however, we are not exactly certain what causes anorexia nervosa.

Bulimia *is an eating disorder that involves a binge-and-purge sequence on a regular basis.* Bulimics binge on large amounts of food and then purge by self-induced vomiting or the use of a laxative. The binges sometimes alternate with fasting; at other times, they alternate with normal eating behavior. Like anorexia nervosa, bulimia is primarily a female disorder, and it has become prevalent among college women. Some estimates suggest that 50 percent of college women binge and purge at least some of the time. However, recent estimates suggest that true bulimics—those who binge and purge on a regular basis—make up less than 2 percent of the college female population (Stunkard, 1987). Whereas anorexics can control their eating, bulimics can not. Depression is a common characteristic of bulimics. Many of the same causes proposed for anorexia nervosa are offered for bulimia (Pomeroy, 1996).

Anorexia nervosa has become prominent in adolescent females.

The Interrelation of Problems, and Programs That Prevent or Reduce Adolescent Problems

So far we have described some of the major problems adolescents are at risk for developing. In many instances, adolescents have more than one problem. Researchers are increasingly finding that problem behaviors in adolescence are interrelated (Tubman, Windle, & Windle, 1996). For example, heavy substance abuse is related to early sexual activity, lower grades, dropping out of school, and delinquency. Early initiation of sexual activity is associated with the use of cigarettes and alcohol, use of marijuana and other illicit drugs, lower grades, dropping out of school, and delinquency. Delinquency is related to early sexual activity, early pregnancy, substance abuse, and dropping out of school. As many as 10 percent of the adolescent population in the United States have serious multiple-problem behaviors (adolescents who have dropped out of school, or are behind in their grade level, are users of heavy drugs, regularly use cigarettes and marijuana, and are sexually active but do not use contraception). Many, but not all, of these very high-risk

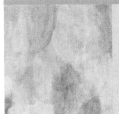

CRITICAL THINKING ABOUT CHILDREN'S DEVELOPMENT

Why Is a Course of Risk Taking in Adolescence Likely to Have More Serious Consequences Today Than in the Past

The world is a dangerous place for too many of America's teenagers, especially those who live in low-income families, neighborhoods, and school districts. Many adolescents are resilient and cope with the challenges of adolescence without too many setbacks, but other adolescents struggle unsuccessfully to find jobs, are written off as losses by their schools, become pregnant before they are ready to become parents, or risk their health through drug abuse. Adolescents in virtually every era have been risk takers, testing limits and making short sighted judgments. But why are the consequences of choosing a course of risk taking possible more serious today than they have ever been before? By evaluating the consequences of pursuing a course of risk taking today, you are learning to think critically by *identifying the sociocultural, historical contexts of development*.

youth "do it all." Another 15 percent of adolescents participate in many of these same behaviors but with slightly lower frequency and less-deleterious consequences. These high-risk youth often engage in two or three problem behaviors (Dryfoos, 1990). To further evaluate adolescent problems, turn to Critical Thinking About Children's Development.

> *There is no easy path leading out of life, and few are the easy ones that lie within it.*
>
> —Walter Savage Landor,
> *Conversations*, 1824

In addition to understanding that many adolescents engage in multiple problem behaviors, it also is important to develop programs that reduce adolescent problems. In a recent review of the programs that have been successful in preventing or reducing adolescent problems, adolescent researcher Joy Dryfoos (1990) described the common components of these successful programs. The common components include these:

1. *Intensive individualized attention.* In successful programs, high-risk children are attached to a responsible adult who gives the child attention and deals with the child's specific needs. This theme occurred in a number of different programs. In a successful substance-abuse program, a student assistance counselor was available full-time for individual counseling and referral for treatment.

2. *Community-wide multiagency collaborative approaches.* The basic philosophy of community-wide programs is that a number of different programs and services have to be in place. In one successful substance-abuse program, a community-wide health promotion campaign was implemented that used local media and community education in concert with a substance-abuse curriculum in the schools.

3. *Early identification and intervention.* Reaching children and their families before children develop problems, or at the beginning of their problems, is a successful strategy. One preschool program serves as an excellent model for the prevention of delinquency, pregnancy, substance abuse, and dropping out of school. Operated by the High Scope Foundation in Ypsilanti, Michigan, the Perry Preschool has had a long-term positive impact on its students (Berrueta-Clement & others, 1986). This enrichment program, directed by David Weikart, services disadvantaged African American children. They attend a high-quality 2-year preschool program and receive weekly home visits from program personnel. Based on official police records, by age 19 individuals who had attended the Perry Preschool program were less likely to have been arrested and reported fewer adult offenses than a control group. The Perry Preschool students also were less likely to drop out of school, and teachers rated their social behavior as more competent than that of a control group who did not receive the enriched preschool experience.

Stereotyping Adolescents and the Complexity of Adolescence

Have the problems of adolescents been overdramatized? Are many adolescents unfortunately stereotyped? How complex is adolescent development? Let's examine these questions.

In the study by Daniel Offer and his colleagues (1988), a healthy self-image characterized at least 73 percent of the adolescents studied around the world, including adolescents from Japan and Turkey (*inset*).

Stereotyping Adolescents

It is easy to stereotype a person, groups of people, or classes of people. A **stereotype** *is a broad category that reflects our impressions and beliefs about people. All stereotypes refer to an image of what the typical member of a particular group is like.* We live in a complex world and want to simplify this complexity. Stereotyping people is one way we do this. We simply assign a label to a group of people—for example, we label youths as "promiscuous." Then we have much less to consider when we think about this set of people. Once we assign the labels, though, it is difficult to abandon them, even in the face of contradictory evidence.

Stereotypes about adolescents are plentiful: "They say they want a job, but when they get one, they don't want to work"; "They are all lazy"; "They are all sex fiends"; "They are all into drugs, every last one of them"; "Kids today don't have the moral fiber of my generation"; "The problem with adolescents today is that they all have it too easy"; "They are a bunch of egotistical, smart-alecks"; and so it goes.

Two studies illustrate just how widespread the stereotyping of adolescents is. In the first study, pollster Daniel Yankelovich (1974) compared the attitudes of adolescents with those of their parents about various values, lifestyles, and codes of personal conduct. There was little or no difference between the attitudes of the adolescents and their parents toward self-control, hard work, saving money, competition, compromise, legal authority, and private property. There was a substantial difference, however, between the adolescents and their parents when

their attitudes toward religion were sampled (89 percent of the parents said that religion was important to them, compared to only 66 percent of the adolescents). Note, though, that a majority of the adolescents still subscribed to the belief that religion is important.

A second study, which documents the stereotypical view of adolescents as highly stressful and disturbed, was conducted by adolescence researcher Daniel Offer and his colleagues (1988). The self-images of adolescents around the world were sampled—in the United States, Australia, Bangladesh, Hungary, Israel, Italy, Japan, Taiwan, Turkey, and West Germany. At least 73 percent of the adolescents studied had a healthy self-image. They appeared to be moving toward adulthood with a healthy integration of previous experiences, self-confidence, and optimism about the future. Although there were some differences among the adolescents, they were happy most of the time, they enjoyed life, they perceived themselves as able to exercise self-control, they valued work and school, they expressed confidence about their sexual selves, they expressed positive feelings toward their families, and they felt they had the capability to cope with life's stresses: not exactly a storm-and-stress portrayal of adolescence.

Beginning with G. Stanley Hall's (1904) portrayal of adolescence as a period of storm and stress, for much of this century in the United States and other Western cultures, adolescence has unfortunately been perceived as a problematic period of the human life cycle that youths,

Increasingly, as researchers carefully examine adolescents' lives, they recognize the complexity of adolescent development. Because of this complexity, no single model fits all adolescents. Too often, today's young people receive ambivalent messages about such topics as sexuality, drugs, and learning.

their families, and society had to endure. As we just saw in two studies, however, a large majority of adolescents do not seem to be nearly as disturbed and troubled as the popular stereotype of adolescence suggests. According to adolescence researchers Shirley Feldman and Glen Elliott (1990), public attitudes about adolescence emerge from a combination of personal experience and media portrayals, neither of which produce an objective picture of how normal adolescents develop. Some of the readiness to assume the worst about adolescents likely involves the short memories of adults. Many adults measure their current perceptions of adolescents by their memories of their own adolescence. Adults may portray today's adolescents as more troubled, less respectful, more self-centered, more assertive, and more adventurous than they were.

However, in matters of taste and manners, the young people of every generation have seemed radical, unnerving, and different from adults—different in how they look, in how they behave, in the music they enjoy, in their hairstyles, and in the clothing they choose. It is an enormous error, though, to confuse adolescents' enthusiasm for trying on new identities and enjoying moderate amounts of outrageous behavior with hostility toward parental and societal standards. Acting out and boundary testing are time-honored ways in which adolescents move toward accepting, rather than rejecting, parental values.

Stereotypes of adolescents are also generated by media portrayals. The media often present sensational and "newsworthy" material, which means that they are far more likely to focus on troubled adolescents than on normal adolescents. The impact of such media coverage conveys the impression that a majority of young people

engage in deviant behaviors, when in fact only a small minority recurrently do. As we will see next in our consideration of today's adolescents, not only do the messages of the media convey an image of adolescents as highly troubled, but the messages to adolescents from both adults and the media are often ambivalent.

The Complexity of Adolescent Development

As researchers more carefully examine the lives of adolescents, they are recognizing that a single developmental model might not accurately characterize all adolescents (Galambos & Tilton-Weaver, 1996). The most widely described general model of adolescent development states that adolescence is a transition from childhood to adulthood during which individuals explore alternatives and experiment with choices as part of developing an identity. Although this model may accurately fit many White middle-class adolescents, it is less well suited to adolescents from low-income families, school dropouts, and unemployed adolescents (Carnegie Council on Adolescent Development, 1995). For many of these youths, development often is more chaotic and restricted. For them, social and racial barriers too frequently signal the presence of discrimination and prejudice (McLoyd & Ceballo, 1995).

At this point we have discussed a number of ideas about puberty and adolescence. A summary of these ideas is presented in concept table 6.2. In the next section of the book, we will turn our attention to children's cognition, beginning with chapter 7, "Cognitive Development and Piaget's Theory."

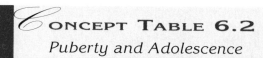

CONCEPT TABLE 6.2
Puberty and Adolescence

Concept	Processes/ Related Ideas	Characteristics/Description
Puberty	Pubertal change	Puberty is a period of rapid skeletal and sexual maturation that occurs mainly in early adolescence. Testosterone plays an important role in male pubertal development, estradiol in female pubertal development. The growth spurt occurs about 2 years later for boys than for girls; 12½ is the average age of onset for boys, 10½ for girls. Individual maturation in pubertal change is extensive.
	Psychological accompaniments of pubertal change	Adolescents show a heightened interest in their body image. Early maturation favors boys, at least during adolescence. As adults, though, late-maturing boys achieve more competent identities than early-maturing boys do. Researchers are increasingly finding that early-maturing girls are vulnerable to a number of problems.
	Models of pubertal change and behavior	Four models that have been proposed are direct hormonal effects; indirect effects via secondary sex characteristics; social events; and developmental trajectory.
Sexuality	Heterosexual attitudes and behavior	In the twentieth century, there has been a major increase in the number of adolescents reporting intercourse. The number of females reporting intercourse has increased more rapidly than the proportion of males. As we develop our sexual attitudes, we follow certain sexual scripts, which often are different for females and males.
	Homosexual attitudes and behavior	Rates of homosexuality have remained constant in the twentieth century. Homosexuality is no longer classified as a disorder. No definitive conclusions about the causes of homosexuality have been reached.
	Sexually transmitted diseases	Any adolescent who has sex runs the risk of getting a sexually transmitted disease, formerly called venereal disease, although many adolescents underestimate their own risk. Among the sexually transmitted diseases adolescents may get are chlamydia, herpes simplex virus II, syphilis, and AIDS.
	Adolescent pregnancy	More than 1 million American adolescents become pregnant each year. The U.S. adolescent pregnancy rate is the highest in the Western world. The consequences of adolescent pregnancy include health risks for the mother and the offspring. There is a special interest in adolescent mothers and social policy.
Adolescent Problems and Disorders	Drugs and alcohol	The United States has the highest adolescent drug-use rate of any industrialized nation. The 1960s and 1970s were times of marked increase in adolescent drug use. An increase in drug use by high school seniors occurred in 1993; this was the first such increase in a number of years. Alcohol is the drug most widely used by adolescents; alcohol abuse by adolescents is a major problem.
	Suicide	The rate of suicide has increased. The suicide rate increases dramatically at about the age of 15. Both proximal and distal factors are involved in suicide's causes.
	Eating disorders	Anorexia nervosa and bulimia increasingly have become problems for adolescent females. Societal, psychological, and physiological causes of these disorders have been proposed.
	Interrelation of problems, and programs that prevent or reduce adolescent problems	At-risk adolescents often have more than one problem. Common components of successful programs designed to prevent or reduce these problems include community-wide intervention, individualized attention, and early identification and intervention.
Stereotyping Adolescents and the Complexity of Adolescent Development	Stereotyping adolescents	Many stereotypes about adolescence are inaccurate. Many adolescents today are successfully negotiating the path to adulthood, but too many youth are not provided with adequate support. Adolescents are a heterogeneous group.
	The complexity of adolescent development	As researchers carefully examine adolescents' lives, they recognize the complexity of adolescent development. Because of this complexity, no single developmental model fits all adolescents.

Santrock: Child Development

Summary

Growth in childhood slows down from its rapid rate in infancy, otherwise we would be a species of giants. After slow growth in childhood, however, the rapid maturational changes of puberty arrive.

In this chapter, we began by discussing physical development in early childhood and in middle and late childhood, evaluating changes in a number of areas such as gross and fine motor skills. Then we studied children's health, nutrition, and exercise.

The last half of the chapter was devoted to pubertal change, including its psychological accompaniments, sexuality, and the adolescent problems of drug use, suicide, and eating disorders. We also discussed the interrelation of problems, programs that prevent or reduce adolescent problems, and the roles of parents and education in drug use, and we evaluated the stereotyping of adolescents and the complexity of adolescent development.

Don't forget to again study the two concept tables on pages 184 and 202, which together will provide you with a summary of the chapter's contents. This concludes Section II. In Section III, we will study the nature of children's cognition, learning, information processing, and language development, beginning with chapter 7, "Cognitive Development and Piaget's Theory."

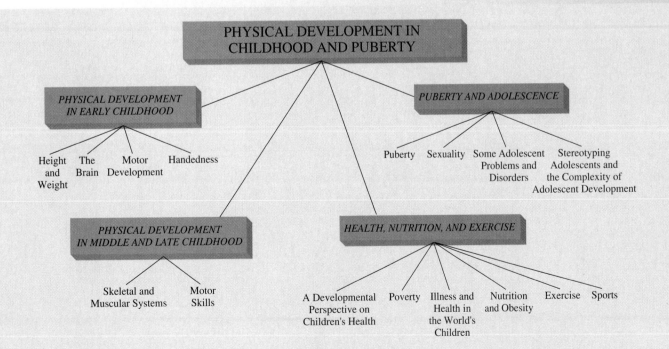

KEY TERMS

deprivation dwarfism   174
myelination   174
oral rehydration therapy (ORT)   180
obesity   181
set point   181
menarche   183

puberty   183
testosterone   185
estradiol   185
sexual script   190
chlamydia   191
herpes simplex virus II   191

AIDS (Acquired Immune Deficiency
   Syndrome)   192
anorexia nervosa   198
bulimia   198
stereotype   200

PRACTICAL KNOWLEDGE ABOUT CHILDREN

To Listen to a Child
(1984) by T. Berry Brazelton, Reading, MA: Addison-Wesley.

The focus in *To Listen to a Child* is primarily on problematic events that arise in children's lives. Fears, feeding problems, sleeping problems, stomachaches, and asthma are among the normal problems of growing that Brazelton evaluates. He assures parents that it is only when parents let their own anxieties interfere that these problems (such as bed-wetting) become chronic and guilt-laden. Each chapter closes with practical guidelines for parents. A final chapter focuses on the hospitalized child, including how to prepare the child for a hospital stay and how to interact with the child at the hospital. *To Listen to a Child* includes clearly explained examples and is warm, personal, and entertaining. It is a good resource book for parents to hold on to as their child ages through the childhood years and to consult when physical problems develop.

Kid Fitness

(1992) by Kenneth Cooper, New York: Random House.

Author Kenneth Cooper developed the concept of aerobic fitness. In this book he adapts to children his ideas that have helped millions of adults become more physically fit. Cooper describes a total program of diet and exercise designed to improve children's physical fitness and foster healthy eating habits. Customized programs are presented for children of all fitness levels, from the physically unfit to the average child to the athletically gifted. The book includes a comprehensive checklist of tests to help gauge the child's level of physical fitness. Standard fitness levels for children and adolescents from 5 to 16+ are provided. This is an excellent book for improving children's physical fitness and eating habits.

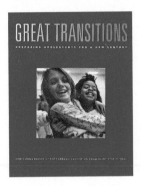

Great Transitions

(1995) by the Carnegie Council of Adolescent Development, New York: Carnegie Foundation.

This recent report by the Carnegie Council on Adolescent Development covers a wide range of topics. Part 1 focuses on transitions, with a special emphasis on early adolescence. A number of discussions evaluate ways to reduce adolescent risk and enhance opportunities. Part 2 emphasizes preparing adolescents for the new century. Topics discussed in this section include reengaging families with their adolescents, education adolescents for a changing world, promoting adolescent health, strengthening communities with adolescents, and redirecting the pervasive power of the media. This is an excellent resource book for improving the lives of adolescents.

EXPLORATIONS IN CHILD DEVELOPMENT

To further explore the nature of child development, we will examine a research study on the antecedents of menarcheal age, and then we will discuss ways to improve the balance between risk and opportunity for youth.

RESEARCH IN CHILD DEVELOPMENT

The Antecedents of Menarcheal Age

Featured Study

Graber, J. A., Brooks-Gunn, J., & Warren, M. P. (1995). The antecedents of menarcheal age: Heredity, family environment, and stressful life events. *Child Development, 66,* 346–359.

Variations in pubertal development have been linked with several hereditary and environmental antecedents. Researchers recently have evaluated a broad range of environmental stressors and their influence on the development of the reproductive system. The purpose of the present study was to evaluate which of a number of antecedents influence pubertal timing, as indexed by menarche.

Menarche is one of the most studied pubertal events because it not only signals the beginning of reproductive ability but also has psychological significance in the family, peer relations, and society. With regard to genetic influences, variations in age at menarche have been assessed by studying associations between maternal and daughter age at menarche; the results reveal a moderately significant correlation (approximately .30). With regard to environmental influences, physical stressors such as exercise, nutrition, and weight have been associated with pubertal timing. Psychosocial stressors linked with

pubertal change include stressful life events and family factors.

Method

The subjects were 75 premenarcheal, White, middle-class girls between the ages of 10 and 14 drawn from a larger longitudinal study of female adolescent development. They completed questionnaires about various aspects of their psychological functioning and development. Physical examinations also were conducted at a hospital laboratory in the community.

Girls provided reports of their age at menarche during interviews. Because the subsample of girls in this part of the larger longitudinal study were premenarcheal, their age at menarche was obtained from subsequent times of assessment. Their breast development was rated on a 5-point scale (1=beginning breast development, 5=mature adult stage). Weight, height, and body fat were measured during the hospital lab visit. Maternal age at menarche was used as an index of hereditary transmission, although it does contain environmental contributions. A measure of life events was administered. Examples of negative life events include breaking up with a boyfriend and parents becoming separated or divorced. Determination of exposure to an adult male was based on girls' reports of who lived in their home. Parental approval and warmth, as well as conflict with

parents, were assessed with a Family Relations Scale given to the girls. Depressive affect was evaluated by asking the girls to respond to the Depressive Withdrawal Scale, which includes items such as "I am unhappy, sad, or depressed."

Results

Breast development, weight, family relations, and depressive affect predicted age at menarche. More-advanced breast development and heavier weights were associated with younger ages at menarche. Better family relations (such as high warmth and low conflict) and lower depressive affect were linked with later ages of menarche. In this study, body fat, the presence of an adult male in the household, and stressful life events did not predict age at menarche. There was a tendency for the mother's age at menarche to be associated with the daughter's age at menarche.

Discussion

The results of this study demonstrate the complexity of the linkages among biological and psychological aspects of development. They also document that the young adolescent's physiological system is responsive to social factors. At this time, the research literature on the antecedents of pubertal timing has focused primarily on girls. Whether such factors as depressed affective states influence pubertal timing in boys is not known.

Improving the Balance Between Risk and Opportunity

Today's world holds experiences for adolescents unlike those encountered by their parents and grandparents. Today's adolescents face greater risks to their health than ever before. Drug and alcohol abuse, depression, violence, pregnancy, sexually transmitted diseases, and school-related problems place far too many of today's adolescents at risk for not reaching their full potential. Recent estimates suggest that as many as one-fourth of American adolescents are in the high-risk category.

Adolescent expert Ruby Takanishi (1993) recently described the importance of improving the opportunity side of the adolescent risk-opportunity equation. Increased clinical and research knowledge suggests a viable approach away from remediation of single problems, such as drug abuse or delinquency or adolescent pregnancy, to the promotion of adolescent health or a cluster of health-enhancing behaviors. This approach recognizes that targeting only one problem behavior, such as drug abuse, may overlook its link to other problems, such as school failure or delinquency.

Because the adolescent interventions of the past have been so targeted, we are only beginning to unravel the clues to multiple adolescent problems that characterize many at-risk youth. For example, does improving peer resistance skills to combat smoking or other drug abuse also reduce at-risk sexual behavior in adolescents?

A special concern is that just providing information and teaching skills to adolescents is not sufficient to improve their health and well-being. Like people at other points in the human life span, adolescents have to be motivated to use information, skills, and services.

Networks of support from families, peers, and caring adults are crucial for improving the lives of at-risk youth. And social policymakers need to target improved economic opportunities for youth and their families.

Each of us who comes in contact with adolescents—as adults, parent, youth workers, professionals, and

Ruby Takanishi (*right*) has worked diligently to improve the adolescent-risk-opportunity equation.

educators—can help to make a difference in improving their health and well-being.

SECTION
Three

Cognition, Learning, Information Processing, and Language Development

Learning is an Ornament in Prosperity, a Refuge in Adversity.

—Aristotle

Children thirst to know and understand. In their effort to know and understand, they construct their own ideas about the world around them. They are remarkable for their curiosity and their intelligence. In Section III, you will read four chapters: "Cognitive Development and Piaget's Theory" (chapter 7), "Information Processing" (chapter 8), "Intelligence" (chapter 9), and "Language Development (chapter 10).

Paul Klee
The Gifted Boy detail

Chapter

7

Cognitive Development and Piaget's Theory

We are born capable of learning.

—Jean-Jacques Rousseau

Piaget's Observations of His Children

I wish I could travel by the road that crosses the baby's mind, and out beyond all bounds; where messengers run errands for no cause between the kingdoms of kings of no history; where Reason makes kites of her laws and flies them, and Truth sets Fact free from its fetters.

—Rabindranoth Tagore, 1913

PREVIEW

We will spend most of this chapter examining Piaget's theory of cognitive development. Piaget's four main stages of cognitive development will be examined in depth, applications of his theory to education will be presented, and contributions and criticisms of his theory will be outlined. Then we will consider a provocative theory of children's cognitive development that has recently been given a great deal of attention, that of Russian psychologist Lev Vygotsky.

Jean Piaget, the famous Swiss psychologist, was a meticulous observer of his three children—Lucienne, Jacqueline, and Laurent. His books on cognitive development are filled with these observations. The following selections provide a glimpse into Piaget's observations of his children's cognitive development in infancy (Piaget, 1952):

- At 21 days of age, Laurent finds his thumb after three attempts; once he finds his thumb, he begins prolonged sucking. But when he is placed on his back, he doesn't know how to coordinate his arm movements with his mouth movements; his hands draw back even when his lips seek them.

- During his third month, thumb sucking becomes less important to Laurent because he has new visual and auditory interests. But when he cries, his thumb goes to the rescue.

- Toward the end of her fourth month, Lucienne is lying in her crib. Piaget hangs a doll above her feet. Lucienne thrusts her feet at the doll and makes it move. Afterward she looks at her motionless foot for a second, then kicks at the doll again, She has no visual control of her foot, because her movements are the same whether the doll is over her feet or her head. By contrast, she has tactile control of her foot, because when she tries to kick the doll and misses, she slows her foot movements to improve her aim.

- At 11 months, while seated Jacqueline shakes a little bell. She then pauses abruptly so she can delicately place the bell in front of her right foot; then she kicks the bell hard. Unable to recapture it, she grasps a ball and places it in the same location where the bell was. She gives the ball a firm kick.

- At 1 year, 2 months, Jacqueline holds in her hands an object that is new to her: a round, flat box that she turns over and shakes, then rubs against her crib. She lets it go and tries to pick it up. She succeeds in touching it only with her index finger, being unable to fully reach and grasp it. She keeps trying to grasp it and presses to the edge of her crib. She makes the box tilt up but it nonetheless falls again. Jacqueline shows an interest in this result and studies the fallen box.

- At 1 year, 8 months, Jacqueline arrives at a closed door with a blade of grass in each hand. She stretches her right hand toward the doorknob but detects that she cannot turn it without letting go of the grass. So she puts the grass on the floor, opens the door, picks up the grass again, and then enters. But when she wants to leave the room, things get complicated. She puts the grass on the floor and grasps the doorknob. Then she perceives that by pulling the door toward her, she simultaneously blows away the grass that she had placed between the door and the threshold. So she picks up the grass and places it out of the door's range of movement.

For Piaget, these observations reflect important changes in the infant's cognitive development. Later in this chapter, you will learn that Piaget believed that infants go through six substages of infant cognitive development, and that the observations you have just read about are characteristics of those substages.

PIAGET'S COGNITIVE DEVELOPMENTAL THEORY

What is Piaget's place in developmental psychology? What is the basic nature of his theory?

Jean Piaget and His Place in Developmental Psychology

In discussing Sigmund Freud's contribution to psychology, Edwin Boring (1950) remarked that it is not likely that a history of experimental psychology could be written in the next three centuries without mention of Freud's name and still claim to be a general history of psychology. Indeed, the best criterion of greatness might be posthumous fame. Four decades after Boring published his book, it seems likely that his judgment was accurate—Freud is still a dominating presence in psychology. However, Jean Piaget's contribution to developmental psychology may be as important as Freud's contribution to personality and abnormal behavior. Piaget's death was rather recent (he died in 1980), so it may be too early to judge, but Piaget's contributions will be strongly felt for the foreseeable future. He truly is a giant in the field of developmental psychology.

Shortly after Piaget's death, John Flavell (1980), a leading Piagetian scholar, described what we owe Piaget:

> First, we owe him a host of insightful concepts of
> enduring power and fascination . . . concepts of object
> permanence, conservation, assimilation,
> accommodation, and decentration, for example.
> Second, we owe him a vast conceptual framework that
> has highlighted key issues and problems in human
> cognitive development. This framework is the now-
> familiar vision of the developing child, who, through
> its own active and creative commerce with its
> environment, builds an orderly succession of
> cognitive structures en route to intellectual maturity.
> These two debts add up to a third, more general one:
> We owe him the present field of cognitive
> development . . . Our task is now to extend and go
> beyond what he began so well. (p.1)

Cognitive Developmental Theory and Processes

What is the basic nature of cognitive developmental theory? What cognitive processes are responsible for changes in a child's development?

Piaget stressed that children actively construct their own cognitive worlds; information is not just poured into their minds from the environment. Two processes underlie an individual's construction of the world: organization and adaptation. To make sense of our world, we organize our experiences. For example, we separate important ideas from less important ideas. We connect one

Jean Piaget, the famous Swiss developmental psychologist, dramatically changed the way we think about children's cognitive development.

idea to another. We not only organize our observations and experiences, however, we also *adapt* our thinking to include new ideas because additional information furthers understanding. Piaget (1954) believed that we adapt in two ways: through assimilation and accommodation.

Assimilation *occurs when children incorporate new information into their existing knowledge.* **Accommodation** *occurs when children adjust to new information.* Consider a circumstance in which an 8-year-old girl is given a hammer and nails to hang a picture on the wall. She has never used a hammer, but from experience and observation she realizes that a hammer is an object to be held, that it is swung by the handle to hit the nail, and that it is usually swung a number of times. Recognizing each of these things, she fits her behavior into information she already has (assimilation). However, the hammer is heavy, so she holds it near the top. She swings too hard and the nail bends, so she adjusts the pressure of her strikes. These adjustments reveal her ability to alter her conception of the world slightly (accommodation).

Piaget thought that assimilation and accommodation operate even in a very young infant's life. Newborns reflexively suck everything that touches their lips; by sucking different objects, infants learn about the nature of these objects—their taste, texture, shape, and so on (assimilation). After several months of experience, though, they construct their understanding of the world differently. Some objects, such as fingers and the mother's breast, can be sucked, and others, such as fuzzy blankets, should not be sucked (accommodation).

Piaget also emphasized that, to make sense out of their world, children cognitively organize their experiences. **Organization** *is Piaget's concept of grouping isolated behaviors into a higher-order, more smoothly functioning cognitive system. Every level of thought is organized.* Continual refinement of this organization is an inherent part of development. A boy who has only a vague idea about how to use a hammer may also have a vague idea about how to use other tools. After learning how to use each one, he must interrelate these uses, or organize his knowledge, if he is to become skilled in using tools. In the same way, children continually integrate and coordinate the many other branches of knowledge that often develop independently. Organization occurs within stages of development as well as across them.

Equilibration *is a mechanism in Piaget's theory invoked to explain how children shift from one stage of thought to the next. The shift occurs as children experience cognitive conflict or a disequilibrium in trying to understand the world. Eventually, the child resolves the conflict and reaches a balance, or equilibrium, of thought.* Piaget believed there is considerable movement between states of cognitive equilibrium and disequilibrium as assimilation and accommodation work in concert to produce cognitive change. For example, if a child believes that an amount of liquid changes simply because it is poured into a container with a different shape (from a container that is short and wide into a container that is tall and narrow), she might be puzzled by such issues as where the "extra" liquid came from and whether there is actually more liquid to drink. The child will eventually resolve these puzzles as her thought becomes more advanced. In the everyday world, the child is constantly faced with such counterexamples and inconsistencies.

Piaget also believed that we go through four stages in understanding the world. Each of the stages is age related and consists of distinct ways of thinking. Remember, it is the *different* way of understanding the world that makes one stage more advanced than another; knowing *more* information does not make a child's thinking more advanced, in the Piagetian view. This is what Piaget meant when he said a child's cognition is *qualitatively* different in one stage compared with another. Let's now examine Piaget's first stage of cognitive development.

PIAGET'S STAGES OF COGNITIVE DEVELOPMENT

Piaget proposed that cognitive development consists of four main stages: sensorimotor, preoperational, concrete operational, and formal operational.

Sensorimotor Thought

Poet Nora Perry asked, "Who knows the thoughts of the child?" As much as anyone, Piaget knew. Through careful, inquisitive interviews and observations of his own three children—Laurent, Lucienne, and Jacqueline—Piaget changed our perceptions of the way infants think about their world. Two of the most important features of sensorimotor thought involve the child's coordination of sensation and action and the nonsymbolic aspects of the period.

The sensorimotor stage lasts from birth to about 2 years of age, corresponding to the period known as infancy. During this time, infants develop the ability to organize and coordinate their sensations and perceptions with their physical movements and actions. This coordination of sensation with action is the source of the term *sensorimotor*. The stage begins with the newborn, who has little more than reflexes to coordinate senses with actions. The stage ends with the 2-year-old, who has complex sensorimotor patterns and is beginning to adopt a primitive symbol system. For example, a 2-year-old can imagine looking at a toy and manipulating it with her hands before she actually does so. The child can also use simple sentences—such as, *Mommy jump*—to represent a sensorimotor event that has just occurred.

Nonsymbolic, sensorimotor intelligence is what Piaget claimed the very young infant has up until about 1½ years of age. Thus, the most critical aspect of Piaget's sensorimotor stage is that it is nonsymbolic throughout most of its duration.

One argument for the nonsymbolic nature of thought in early infancy concerns the solving of problems through internal reflection or insight. Problem solving occurs quite early in life, perhaps by 12 months of age; however, Piaget claimed that, until about 1½ to 2 years of age, this problem solving is of the trial-and-error variety, devoid of an internal, symbolic component. For example, one of Piaget's daughters insightfully discovered how to get a matchbox open; looking at the slightly open matchbox, she began opening and closing her mouth. Only after making a few such movements did she reach for the matchbox and pull out its drawer with her hands. Piaget interpreted the moving-mouth behavior as reflecting internal, symbolic operations, which emerge only at the end of the sensorimotor stage.

The Substages of Sensorimotor Thought

The sensorimotor stage is divided into six substages, which involve qualitative changes in sensorimotor organization. Within a given substage, there may be different schemes—sucking, rooting, and blinking in substage 1, for example. The term **scheme** *refers to the basic unit of an organized pattern of sensorimotor functioning.* In substage 1, schemes are basically reflexive. From substage to substage, the organization of the schemes changes. The six substages of sensorimotor development are (1) simple reflexes; (2) first habits and primary circular reactions; (3) secondary circular reactions; (4) coordination of secondary circular reactions; (5) tertiary circular reactions, novelty, and curiosity; and (6) internalization of schemes (see figure 7.1).

Simple reflexes *is Piaget's first sensorimotor substage, which corresponds to the first month after birth. In this substage, the basic means of coordinating sensation and action is through reflexive behaviors, such as rooting and sucking, which the infant has at birth.* In substage 1, the infant exercises these reflexes. More important, the infant develops an ability to produce behaviors that resemble reflexes in the absence of obvious reflexive stimuli. A newborn might suck when a bottle or nipple is only nearby, for example. When the baby was just born, the bottle or nipple would have produced the sucking pattern only when placed directly in the newborn's mouth or touched to the lips. Reflex-like actions in the absence of a triggering stimulus are evidence that the infant is initiating action and is actively structuring experiences in the first month of life.

First habits and primary circular reactions *is Piaget's second sensorimotor substage, which develops between 1 and 4 months of age. In this substage, infants learn to coordinate sensation and types of schemes or structures—that is, habits and primary circular reactions.* A *habit* is a scheme based on a simple reflex, such as sucking, that has become completely divorced from its eliciting stimulus. For example, an infant in substage 1 might suck when orally stimulated by a bottle or when visually shown the bottle, but an infant in substage 2 might exercise the sucking scheme even when no bottle is present.

Primary circular reactions *are schemes based on the infant's attempt to reproduce an interesting or pleasurable event that initially occurred by chance.* In a popular Piagetian example, a child accidentally sucks his fingers when they are placed near his mouth; later, he searches for his fingers to suck them again, but the fingers do not cooperate in the search because the infant cannot coordinate visual and manual actions. Habits and circular reactions are stereotyped in that the infant repeats them. The infant's own body remains the center of attention; there is no outward pull by environmental events.

Secondary circular reactions *are Piaget's third sensorimotor substage, which develops between 4 and 8 months of age. In this substage, infants become more object oriented or focused on the world, moving beyond preoccupation with the self in sensorimotor interactions.* The chance shaking of a rattle, for example, may fascinate the infant, and the infant will repeat this action for the sake of experiencing fascination. The infant imitates some simple actions of others, such as the baby talk or burbling of adults, and some physical gestures. However, these imitations are limited to actions the infant is already able to produce. Although directed toward objects in the world, the infant's schemes lack an intentional, goal-directed quality.

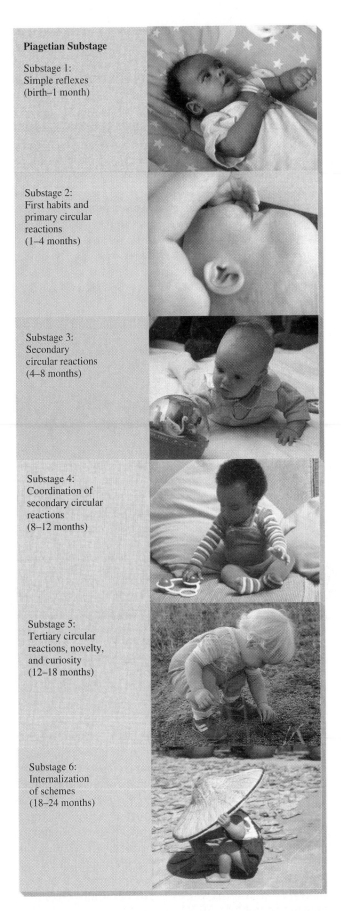

Piagetian Substage

Substage 1:
Simple reflexes
(birth–1 month)

Substage 2:
First habits and
primary circular
reactions
(1–4 months)

Substage 3:
Secondary
circular reactions
(4–8 months)

Substage 4:
Coordination of
secondary circular
reactions
(8–12 months)

Substage 5:
Tertiary circular
reactions, novelty,
and curiosity
(12–18 months)

Substage 6:
Internalization
of schemes
(18–24 months)

Figure~7.1

Piaget's Substages of Sensorimotor Development

Coordination of secondary circular reactions *is Piaget's fourth sensorimotor substage, which develops between 8 and 12 months of age. In this substage, several significant changes take place involving the coordination of schemes and intentionality.* Infants readily combine and recombine previously learned schemes in a *coordinated* way. They may look at an object and grasp it simultaneously or visually inspect a toy, such as a rattle, and finger it simultaneously in obvious tactile exploration. Actions are even more outwardly directed than before. Related to this coordination is the second achievement—the development of *intentionality* (the separation of means and goals in accomplishing simple feats). For example, infants might manipulate a stick (the means) to bring a desired toy within reach (the goal). They may knock over one block in order to reach another to play with.

Tertiary circular reactions, novelty, and curiosity *is Piaget's fifth sensorimotor substage, which develops between 12 and 18 months of age. In this substage, infants become intrigued by the variety of properties that objects possess and by the multiplicity of things they can make happen to objects.* A block can be made to fall, spin, hit another object, slide across the ground, and so on. **Tertiary circular reactions** *are schemes in which the infant purposely explores new possibilities with objects, continually changing what is done to them and exploring the results.* Piaget said that this stage marks the developmental starting point for human curiosity and interest in novelty. Previous circular reactions have been devoted exclusively to reproducing former events, with the exception of imitation of novel acts, which occurs as early as substage 4. The tertiary circular act is the first to be concerned with novelty.

Internalization of schemes *is Piaget's sixth sensorimotor substage, which develops between 18 and 24 months of age. In this substage, infants' mental functioning shifts from a purely sensorimotor plane to a symbolic plane, and they develop the ability to use primitive symbols.* According to Piaget, a symbol is an internalized sensory image or word that represents an event. Primitive symbols permit the infant to think about concrete events without directly acting them out or perceiving them. Moreover, symbols allow the infant to manipulate and transform the represented events in simple ways. In the Piagetian example mentioned earlier, Piaget's young daughter saw a matchbox being opened and closed; sometime later, she mimicked the event by opening and closing her mouth. This was an obvious expression of her image of the event. In another example, a child opened a door slowly to avoid disturbing a piece of paper lying on the floor on the other side. The child had an image of the unseen paper at that time and of what would happen to it if the door opened quickly. Developmentalists have debated whether 2-year-olds really have such representations of action sequences at their command, however (Corrigan, 1981).

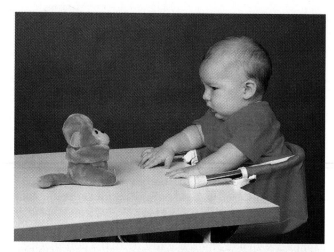
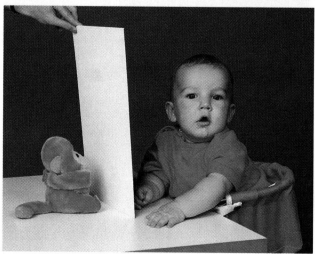

Figure 7.2

Object Permanence

Piaget thought that object permanence was one of infancy's landmark cognitive accomplishments. For this 5-month-old boy, "out of sight" is literally out of mind. The infant looks at the toy monkey (*top*), but, when his view of the toy is blocked (*bottom*), he does not search for it. Eventually, he will search for the hidden toy monkey, reflecting the presence of object permanence.

Object Permanence

Imagine what thought would be like if you could not distinguish between yourself and your world. Your thought would be chaotic, disorganized, and unpredictable. This is what the mental life of the newborn is like, according to Piaget. There is no self-world differentiation and no sense of object permanence (Piaget, 1952). By the end of the sensorimotor period, however, both are present.

Object permanence *is the Piagetian term for one of an infant's most important accomplishments: understanding that objects and events continue to exist even when they cannot directly be seen, heard, or touched.*

The principal way that object permanence is studied is by watching infants' reactions when an attractive object or event disappears (see figure 7.2). If they show

Santrock: Child Development

no reaction, it is assumed they believe the object no longer exists. By contrast, if they are surprised at the disappearance and search for the object, it is assumed they believe it continues to exist. According to Piaget, object permanence develops in a series of substages that correspond to the six substages of sensorimotor development. Table 7.1 shows how the six substages of object permanence reflect Piaget's substages of sensorimotor development.

Although Piaget's stage sequence is the best summary of what might happen as an infant fathoms the permanence of things in the world, some contradictory findings have emerged (Baillargeon, 1995; Xu & Carey, 1995). Piaget's stages broadly describe the interesting changes reasonably well, but an infant's life is not neatly packaged into distinct areas of organization as Piaget believed. Some of Piaget's explanations for the causes of change are debated.

For example, Piaget claimed that certain processes are crucial in stage transitions. The data do not always support his explanations, however. According to Piaget, the critical requirement for an infant to progress into sensorimotor substage 4 is the coordination of vision and the sense of touch, or hand-eye coordination. Another important feature in the progression into substage 4 is an infant's inclination to search for an object hidden in a familiar location rather than to look for the object in a new location. The **A̅B̅ error** *is the Piagetian object-permanence concept in which an infant progressing into substage 4 makes frequent mistakes, selecting the familiar hiding place (A) rather than new hiding places (B̅).* Researchers have found, however that the A̅B̅ error does not show up consistently (Corrigan, 1981; Sophian, 1985). There is also accumulating evidence that A̅B̅ errors are sensitive to the delay between hiding an object at B̅ and the infant's attempt to find it (Diamond, 1985). Thus, the A̅B̅ error might be partly due to the failure of memory. And the A̅B̅ error might be due to a lack of maturation of the frontal cortex of the brain (Diamond, 1995; Diamond & Goldman-Rakic, 1989).

> *There was a child who went forth every day. And the first object he looked upon, that object he became. And that object became part of him for the day, or a certain part of the day, or for many years, or stretching cycles of years.*
>
> —**Walt Whitman**

At this point, we have discussed a number of characteristics of Piaget's stage of sensorimotor thought. To help you remember Piaget's description of the main characteristics of sensorimotor thought, turn to figure 7.3.

A New Perspective on Cognitive Development in Infancy

In the past decade, a new understanding of infant cognitive development has been taking place. For many years,

TABLE 7.1

The Six Substages of Object Permanence

Sensorimotor Stage	Behavior
Substage 1	There is no apparent object permanence. When a spot of light moves across the visual field, an infant follows it but quickly ignores its disappearance.
Substage 2	A primitive form of object permanence develops. Given the same experience, the infant looks briefly at the spot where the light disappeared, with an expression of passive expectancy.
Substage 3	The infant's sense of object permanence undergoes further development. With the newfound ability to coordinate simple schemes, the infant shows clear patterns of searching for a missing object, with sustained visual and manual examination of the spot where the object apparently disappeared.
Substage 4	The infant actively searches for a missing object in the spot where it disappeared, with new actions to achieve the goal of searching effectively. For example, if an attractive toy has been hidden behind a screen, the child may look at the screen and try to push it away with a hand. If the screen is too heavy to move or is permanently fixed, the child readily substitutes a secondary scheme—for example, crawling around it or kicking it. These new actions signal that the infant's belief in the continued existence of the missing object is strengthening.
Substage 5	The infant now is able to track an object that disappears and reappears in several locations in rapid succession. For example, a toy may be hidden under different boxes in succession in front of the infant, who succeeds in finding it. The infant is apparently able to hold an image of the missing object in mind longer than before.
Substage 6	The infant can search for a missing object that disappeared and reappeared in several locations in succession, as before. In addition, the infant searches in the appropriate place even when the object has been hidden from view as it is being moved. This activity indicates that the infant is able to "imagine" the missing object and to follow the image from one location to the next.

Ability to
organize and
coordinate
sensations
with physical
movements

Is nonsymbolic
through most
of its duration

Consists of
six substages
of cognitive
development

Object
permanence
develops

Figure~7.3

*Piaget's Description of the Main Characteristics of
Sensorimotor Thought*

Piaget's ideas were so widely known and respected that,
to many psychologists, one aspect of development seemed
certain: Human infants go through a long, protracted
period during which they cannot think (Mandler,
1990). They can learn to recognize things and smile at
them, to crawl, and to manipulate objects, but they do
not yet have concepts and ideas. Piaget believed that only
near the end of the sensorimotor stage of development,
at about 1½ to 2 years of age, do infants learn how to represent the world in a symbolic, conceptual manner.

Piaget constructed his view of infancy mainly by
observing the development of his own three children.
Very few laboratory techniques were available at that
time. Recently, however, sophisticated experimental techniques have been devised to study infants, and a large
number of research studies on infant cognitive development have accumulated. Much of the new research suggests that Piaget's theory of sensorimotor development
will have to be modified substantially (Gounin-Decarie,
1996).

Piaget's theory of sensorimotor development has
been attacked from two sources. First, extensive research in the area of infant perceptual development suggests that a stable and differentiated perceptual world is

established much earlier in infancy than Piaget envisioned. Second, researchers recently have found that memory and other forms of symbolic activity occur by at least
the second half of the first year (Gelman & Au, 1996).

Perceptual Development   In chapter 5, we described research on infants' perceptual development, indicating
that a number of theorists, such as Eleanor Gibson (1989),
Elizabeth Spelke (1991, 1997), and Tom Bower (1989,
1996), believe that infants' perceptual abilities are highly
developed very early in development. For example, Spelke
has demonstrated that infants as young as 4 months of
age have intermodal perception—the ability to coordinate information from two or more sensory modalities,
such as vision and audition. Other research by Spelke
(1988) and by Renée Baillargeon (1987, 1995) documents
that infants as young as 4 months expect objects to be
substantial (in the sense that the objects cannot move
through other objects, and other objects cannot move
through them) and permanent (in the sense that the objects are assumed to continue to exist when hidden). In
sum, the perceptual development researchers believe that
infants see objects as bounded, unitary, solid, and separate from their background, possibly at birth or shortly
thereafter, but definitely by 3 to 4 months of age. Young
infants still have much to learn about objects, but the
world appears both stable and orderly to them and, thus,
capable of being conceptualized.

Conceptual Development   It is more difficult to study
what infants are thinking about than what they see. Still,
researchers have devised ways to assess whether or not
infants are thinking. One strategy is to look for symbolic
activity, such as using a gesture to refer to something.
Piaget (1952) used this strategy to document infants'
motor recognition. For example, he observed his 6-month-
old daughter make a gesture when she saw a familiar toy
in a new location. She was used to kicking at the toy in
her crib. When she saw it across the room, she made a
brief kicking motion. However, Piaget did not consider
this to be true symbolic activity, because it was a motor
movement, not a purely mental act. Nonetheless, Piaget
suggested that his daughter was referring to, or classifying, the toy through her actions (Mandler, 1990, 1997).
In a similar way, infants whose parents use sign language
have been observed to start using conventional signs at
about 6 to 7 months of age (Bonvillian, Orlansky, &
Novack, 1983).

Another type of evidence for conceptual functioning is the recall of absent objects or events. Piaget considered recall to be evidence of conceptual representation.
Imagery or other symbolic means must be involved. We
usually associate recall with the verbal re-creation of
the past, and, as Piaget observed, this does not usually
take place until about 18 months of age or older. However, recall does not have to be verbal, as we will see next.

To demonstrate recall, a researcher needs to see a baby do something such as find a hidden object after a delay or imitate a previously observed event. Andrew Meltzoff (1988) showed that 9-month-old infants can imitate actions they saw performed 24 hours earlier. This is approximately 9 months earlier than Piaget believed possible. In another experiment (Baillargeon, DeVos, & Graber, 1989), 8-month-olds searched for an object behind a screen 70 seconds after the object was hidden. In yet another experiment, 4-to-5-month-olds recalled an object's location 8 to 12 seconds later (Baillargeon, DeVos, & Graber, 1989). These performances of infants 9 months of age and younger reflect a representational ability that cannot be attributed to sensorimotor schemes.

In summary, the recent research on infants' perceptual and conceptual development suggests that infants have more-sophisticated perceptual abilities and can begin to think earlier than Piaget envisioned. These researchers believe that infants either are born with these abilities or acquire them early in their development (Mandler, 1990, 1997).

Preoperational Thought

The cognitive world of the preschool child is creative, free, and fanciful. The imagination of preschool children works overtime and their mental grasp of the world improves. When Piaget described the preschool child's cognition as *preoperational*, what did he mean?

The Nature of Preoperational Thought

Since this stage of thought is called *preoperational*, it would seem that not much of importance occurs until full-fledged operational thought appears. Not so. The preoperational stage stretches from approximately the age of 2 to the age of 7. It is a time when stable concepts are formed, mental reasoning emerges, egocentrism begins strongly and then weakens, and imaginary beliefs are constructed. Preoperational thought is anything but a convenient waiting period for concrete operational thought, although the label *preoperational* emphasizes that the child at this stage does not yet think in an operational way.

What are operations? **Operations** *are internalized sets of actions that allow children to do mentally what before they had done physically.* Operations are highly organized and conform to certain rules and principles of logic. The operations appear in one form in concrete operational thought and in another form in formal operational thought. Thought in the preoperational stage is still flawed and not well organized. Preoperational thought is the beginning of the ability to reconstruct at the level of thought what has been established in behavior. Preoperational thought also involves a transition from primitive to more sophisticated use of symbols.

"Mrs. Hammond! I'd know you anywhere from little Billy's portrait of you."

Drawing by Frascino; © 1988 The New Yorker Magazine, Inc.

The Substages of Preoperational Thought

Preoperational thought can be subdivided into two substages: the symbolic function substage and the intuitive thought substage.

Symbolic Function Substage The **symbolic function substage** *is the first substage of preoperational thought, occurring roughly between the ages of 2 and 4. In this substage, the young child gains the ability to mentally represent an object that is not present.* The ability to engage in such symbolic thought is called symbolic function, and it vastly expands the child's mental world.

Possibly because preschool children are not very concerned about reality, their drawings are fanciful and inventive. Suns are blue, skies are yellow, and cars float on clouds in their symbolic, imaginative world. One 3½-year-old child looked at the scribble he had just drawn and said it was a pelican kissing a seal (figure 7.4a). The symbolism is simple but strong, like the abstractions found in some modern art. As Picasso commented, "I used to draw like Raphael but it has taken me a lifetime to learn to draw like young children." In the elementary school years, a child's drawings become more realistic, neat, and precise (see figure 7.4b). Suns are yellow, skies are blue, and cars travel on roads (Winner, 1986).

Other examples of symbolism in early childhood are the prevalence of pretend play (to be discussed in chapter 16) and language (to be discussed in chapter 10). In sum, the ability to think symbolically and represent the world mentally predominates in this early substage of preoperational thought. However, although young children make distinct progress during this substage, their thought still has several important limitations, two of which are egocentrism and animism.

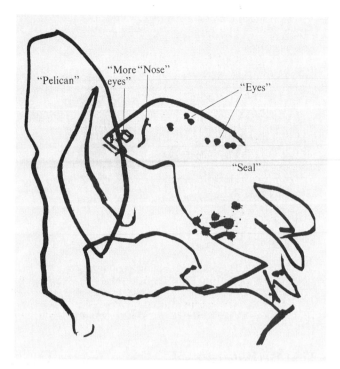

A 3½-Year-Old's Symbolic Drawing
Halfway into this drawing, the 3½-year-old artist said it was "a pelican kissing a seal."

An 11-Year-Old's Drawing
An 11-year-old's drawing is neater and more realistic but also less inventive.

Figure~7.4

Developmental Changes in Children's Drawings

Egocentrism *is a salient feature of preoperational thought. It is the inability to distinguish between one's own perspective and someone else's perspective.* The following telephone conversation between 4-year-old Mary, who is at home, and her father, who is at work, typifies Mary's egocentric thought:

Father: Mary, are you doing OK?
Mary: (Silently nods)
Father: Mary, are you there?
Mary: (Nods again silently)

Mary's response is egocentric in that she fails to consider her father's perspective before replying. A nonegocentric thinker would have responded verbally.

Piaget and Barbel Inhelder (1969) initially studied young children's egocentrism by devising the three mountains task (see figure 7.5). The child walks around the model of the mountains and becomes familiar with what the mountains look like from different perspectives and can see that there are different objects on the mountains. The child is then seated on one side of the table on which the mountains are placed. The experimenter moves a doll to different locations around the table, at each location asking the child to select, from a series of photos, the one photo that most accurately reflects the view the doll is seeing. Children in the preoperational stage often pick their view from where they are sitting rather than the

doll's view. Perspective taking does not seem to develop uniformly in preschool children, who frequently show perspective skills on some tasks but not others.

> *False would be a picture which insisted on the brutal egocentrism of the child, and ignored the physical beauty which softens it.*
>
> —A. A. Milne

Animism, *another facet of preoperational thought, is the belief that inanimate objects have "lifelike" qualities and are capable of action.* A young child might show animism by saying, "That tree pushed the leaf off, and it fell down" or "The sidewalk made me mad; it made me fall down." A young child who uses animism fails to distinguish the appropriate occasions for using human and nonhuman perspectives. Some developmentalists, though, believe that animism represents incomplete knowledge and understanding, not a general conception of the world (Dolgin & Behrend, 1984).

Intuitive Thought Substage Tommy is 4 years old. Although he is starting to develop his own ideas about the world he lives in, they are still simple and he is not very good at thinking things out. He has difficulty understanding events he knows are taking place but

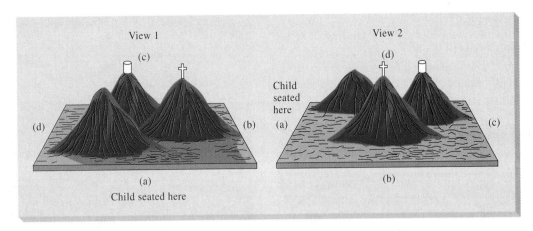

Figure~7.5

The Three Mountains Task

View 1 shows the child's perspective from where he or she is sitting. View 2 is an example of the photograph the child would be shown mixed in with others from different perspectives. To correctly identify this view, the child has to take the perspective of a person sitting at spot (b). Invariably, a preschool child who thinks in a preoperational way cannot perform this task. When asked what a view of the mountains looks like from position (b), the child selects a photograph taken from location (a), the child's view at the time.

cannot see. He has little control over reality, to which his fantasized thoughts bear little resemblance. He cannot yet reliably answer the question "What if?" For example, he has only a vague idea of what would happen if a car were to hit him. He also has difficulty negotiating traffic because he cannot do the mental calculations necessary to estimate whether an approaching car will hit him when he crosses the road.

The **intuitive thought substage** *is the second substage of preoperational thought, occurring approximately between 4 and 7 years of age. In this substage, children begin to use primitive reasoning and want to know the answers to all sorts of questions.* Piaget called this time period *intuitive* because, on one hand, young children seem sure about their knowledge and understanding yet are unaware of how they know what they know. That is, they say they know something but know it without the use of rational thinking.

An example of young children's reasoning ability is the difficulty they have putting things into their correct classes. Faced with a random collection of objects that can be grouped together on the basis of two or more properties, a preoperational child is seldom capable of using these properties consistently to sort the objects into appropriate categories. Look at the collection of objects in figure 7.6a. You would respond to the direction "Put the things together

that you believe belong together" by sorting them by size and shape. Your sorting might look something like that shown in figure 7.6b. The young child in the intuitive thought substage cannot do this correct sorting. In the social realm, a 4-year-old girl might be given the task of dividing her peers into groups according to whether they are friends and whether they are boys or girls. She would be unlikely to arrive at the following classification: friendly boys, friendly girls, unfriendly boys, unfriendly

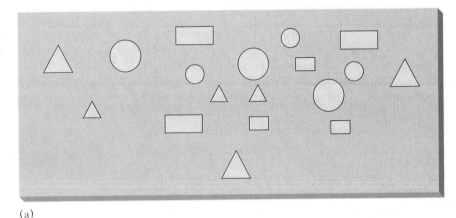

(a)

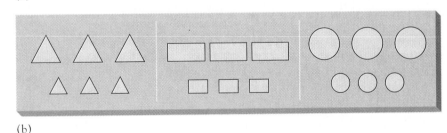

(b)

Figure~7.6

(a) A Random Array of Objects. (b) An Ordered Array of Objects

girls. Another example of classification shortcomings involves the preoperational child's understanding of religious concepts (Elkind, 1976). When asked "Can you be a Protestant and an American at the same time?" 6- and 7-year-olds usually say no; 9-year-olds are likely to say yes, understanding that objects can be cross-classified simultaneously.

Many of these examples show a characteristic of preoperational thought called **centration,** *the focusing, or centering, of attention on one characteristic to the exclusion of all others*. Centration is most clearly evidenced in young children's lack of **conservation,** *the idea that an amount stays the same regardless of how its container changes*. To adults, it is obvious that a certain amount of liquid stays the same regardless of a container's shape, but this is not obvious at all to young children; instead, they are struck by the height of the liquid in the container. In the liquid conservation task—Piaget's most famous—a child is presented with two identical beakers, each filled to the same level with liquid (see figure 7.7). The child is asked if the beakers have the same amount of liquid, and she usually says yes. Then the liquid from one beaker is poured into a third beaker, which is taller and thinner than the first two. The child is then asked if the amount of liquid in the tall, thin beaker is equal to that which remains in one of the original beakers. If the child is younger than 7 or 8 years old, she usually says no and justifies her answer in terms of the differing height or width of the beakers. Older children usually answer yes and justify their answers appropriately ("If you poured the milk back, the amount would still be the same"). The older child can mentally reverse actions; the preoperational child cannot.

In Piaget's theory, failing the conservation of liquid task is a sign that children are at the preoperational stage of cognitive development, whereas passing this test is a sign that they are at the concrete operational stage. In Piaget's view, preoperational children fail to show conservation not only of liquid but also of number, matter, length, volume, and area (see figure 7.8).

Some developmentalists do not believe Piaget was entirely correct in his estimate of when children's conservation skills emerge. For example, Rochel Gelman (1969; Gelman & Baillargeon, 1983) has shown that, when an experimenter instructs a child to attend to relevant aspects of the conservation task, the child is more likely to conserve. Gelman has also demonstrated that attentional training on one type of task, such as numbers, improves the preschool child's performance on another type of task, such as mass. Thus, Gelman believes that conservation appears earlier than Piaget thought and that the process of attention is especially important in explaining conservation.

Yet another characteristic of preoperational children is that they ask a barrage of questions. Children's earliest questions appear around the age of 3, and by the

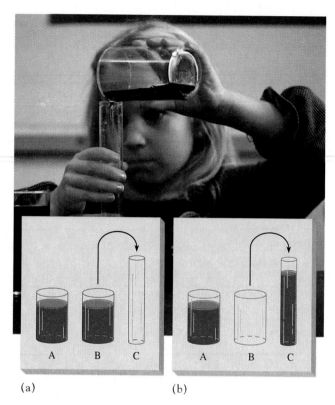

(a)   (b)

Figure~7.7

Piaget's Conservation Task

The beaker test is a well-known Piagetian test to determine whether a child can think operationally—that is, can mentally reverse actions and show conservation of the substance. (*a*) Two identical beakers are presented to the child. Then, the experimenter pours the liquid from B into C, which is taller and thinner than A or B. (*b*) The child is asked if these beakers (A and C) have the same amount of liquid. The preoperational child says no. When asked to point to the beaker that has more liquid, the preoperational child points to the tall, thin beaker.

age of 5 they have just about exhausted the adults around them with "why" questions. Their questions yield clues about their mental development and reflect intellectual curiosity. These questions signal the emergence of children's interest in reasoning and figuring out why things are the way they are. Some samples of the questions children ask during the questioning period of 4 to 6 years of age are the following (Elkind, 1976):

"What makes you grow up?"

"What makes you stop growing?"

"Why does a lady have to be married to have a baby?"

"Who was the mother when everybody was a baby?"

"Why do leaves fall?"

"Why does the sun shine?"

At this point, we have discussed a number of preoperational thought's characteristics. To help you remember these characteristics, refer to figure 7.9. We also have discussed a number of ideas about Piaget and

Type of conservation	Initial presentation	Manipulation	Preoperational child's answer
Number	Two identical rows of objects are shown to the child, who agrees they have the same number.	One row is lengthened and the child is asked whether one row now has more objects.	Yes, the longer row.
Matter	Two identical balls of clay are shown to the child. The child agrees that they are equal.	The experimenter changes the shape of one of the balls and asks the child whether they still contain equal amounts of clay.	No, the longer one has more.
Length	Two sticks are aligned in front of the child. The child agrees that they are the same length.	The experimenter moves one stick to the right, then asks the child if they are equal in length.	No, the one on the top is longer.
Volume	Two balls are placed in two identical glasses with an equal amount of water. The child sees the balls displace equal amounts of water.	The experimenter changes the shape of one of the balls and asks the child if it still will displace the same amount of water.	No, the longer one on the right displaces more.
Area	Two identical sheets of cardboard have wooden blocks placed on them in identical positions. The child agrees that the same amount of space is left on each piece of cardboard.	The experimenter scatters the blocks on one piece of cardboard and then asks the child if one of the cardboard pieces has more space covered.	Yes, the one on the right has more space covered up.

Figure 7.8

Conservation

Some dimensions of conservation: number, matter, length, volume, and area.

his place in child psychology, cognitive developmental theory, cognitive processes, sensorimotor thought, and preoperational thought. A summary of these ideas is presented in concept table 7.1.

Concrete Operational Thought

In the well-known test of reversibility of thought involving conservation of matter, a child is presented with two identical balls of clay. An experimenter rolls one ball into a long, thin shape; the other remains in its original ball shape. The child is then asked if there is more clay in the ball or in the long, thin piece of clay. By the time children reach the age of 7 or 8, most answer that the amount of clay is the same. To answer this problem correctly, children have to imagine that the clay ball is rolled out into a long, thin strip and then returned to its original round shape—imagination that involves a reversible mental action. Thus, a concrete operation is a reversible mental action on real, concrete objects. Concrete operations allow children to coordinate several

Figure~7.9

Characteristics of Preoperational Thought

characteristics rather than focus on a single property of an object. In the clay example, a preoperational child is likely to focus on height or width; a concrete operational child coordinates information about both dimensions. We can get a better understanding of concrete operational thought by considering further ideas about conservation and the nature of classification.

Conservation

We already have highlighted some of Piaget's basic ideas on conservation in our discussion of preoperational children's failure to answer questions correctly about such circumstances as the beaker task. Remember that conservation involves the recognition that the length, number, mass, quantity, area, weight, and volume of objects and substances do not change by transformations that alter their appearance. An important point that needs to be made about conservation is that children do not conserve all quantities or on all tasks simultaneously. The order of their mastery is number, length, liquid quantity, mass, weight, and volume. **Horizontal décalage** *is Piaget's concept that similar abilities do not appear at the same time within a stage of development.* As we have just seen, during the concrete operational stage, conservation of number usually appears first and conservation of volume last. Also, an 8-year-old child may know that a long stick of clay can be rolled back into a ball but not understand that the ball and the stick weigh the same. At about 9 years of age, the child recognizes that they weigh the same,

and eventually, at about 11 to 12 years of age, the child understands that the clay's volume is unchanged by rearranging it. Children initially master tasks in which the dimensions are more salient and visible, only later mastering those not as visually apparent, such as volume.

Do children in all cultures acquire conservation skills at about the same age? To learn the answer to this question, turn to Sociocultural Worlds of Children.

Classification

Many of the concrete operations identified by Piaget involve the ways children reason about the properties of objects. One important skill that characterizes concrete operational children is the ability to classify or divide things into sets or subsets and to consider their interrelationships. An example of concrete operational classification skills involves a family tree of four generations (Furth & Wachs, 1975) (see figure 7.10). This family tree suggests that the grandfather (A) has three children (B, C, and D), each of whom has two children (E through J), and that one of these children (J) has three children (K, L, and M). The concrete operational child understands that person J can, at the same time, be father, brother, and grandson. A child who comprehends this classification system can move up and down a level (vertically), across a level (horizontally), and up and down and across (obliquely) within the system.

Although concrete operational thought is more advanced than preoperational thought, it has its limitations.

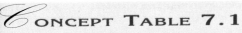

CONCEPT TABLE 7.1

Piaget's Place in Developmental Psychology, Cognitive Developmental Theory, Cognitive Processes, Sensorimotor Thought, and Preoperational Thought

Concept	Processes/Related Ideas	Characteristics/Description
Piaget's Place in Developmental Psychology and Cognitive Developmental Theory	Piaget's giant <u>stature</u>	Piaget's contribution to developmental psychology may be as important as Freud's contribution to personality and abnormal psychology. We owe him the present field of cognitive development.
	Cognitive developmental theory	The developing child's rational thinking and stages of thought are emphasized. Thoughts are the central focus of development, the primary determinants of children's action.
Cognitive Processes in Piaget's Theory	Adaptation	Piaget developed this concept of the child's effective interaction with the environment. The interaction is a cognitive one that involves assimilation and accommodation.
	Assimilation and accommodation	Assimilation occurs when children incorporate new information into their existing knowledge. Accommodation occurs when children adjust to new information.
	Organization	Organization is Piaget's concept of grouping isolated behaviors into a higher-order, more smoothly functioning cognitive system. Every level of thought is organized.
	Equilibration	Equilibration is a mechanism in Piaget's theory that explains how children shift from one stage of thought to the next. The shift occurs as the child experiences cognitive conflict or a disequilibrium in trying to understand the world. Eventually, the child resolves the conflict and reaches a balance, or equilibrium, of thought. Piaget believed there is considerable movement between states of cognitive equilibrium and disequilibrium as assimilation and accommodation work in concert to produce cognitive change.
Sensorimotor Thought	Basic features	The infant is able to organize and coordinate sensations with physical movements. The stage lasts from birth to about 2 years of age and is nonsymbolic through most of its duration.
	Substages of sensorimotor thought	Sensorimotor thought has six substages: simple reflexes; first habits and primary circular reactions; secondary circular reactions; coordination of secondary circular reactions; tertiary circular reactions, novelty, and curiosity; and internalization of schemes.
	Object permanence	The term *object permanence* refers to the ability to understand that objects and events continue to exist even though the infant no longer is in contact with them. Piaget believed that this ability develops over the course of the six substages of sensorimotor thought.
	A new perspective on cognitive development in infancy	In the past decade, a new understanding of infants' cognitive development has been occurring. Piaget's theory has been attacked from two sources. First, extensive research in perceptual development suggests that a stable and differentiated perceptual world is established much earlier than Piaget envisioned. Second, researchers recently have found that memory and other forms of symbolic activity occur by at least the second half of the first year.
Preoperational Thought	Its nature	It is the beginning of the ability to reconstruct at the level of thought what has been established in behavior, and a transition from primitive to more sophisticated use of symbols. The child does not yet think in an operational way.
	Symbolic function substage	This substage occurs roughly between 2 and 4 years of age and is characterized by symbolic thought, egocentrism, and animism.
	Intuitive thought substage	This substage stretches from approximately 4 to 7 years of age and is called intuitive because children seem sure about their knowledge, yet they are unaware of how they know what they know. The preoperational child lacks conservation and asks a barrage of questions.

SOCIOCULTURAL WORLDS OF CHILDREN

Conservation Skills Around the World

Psychologist Patricia Greenfield (1966) conducted a series of studies among Wolof children in the West African nation of Senegal to see if Piaget's theory of concrete operational thought is universal. Using Piaget's beaker tasks, she found that only 50 percent of the 10- to 13-year-olds understood the principle of conservation. Comparable studies among cultures in central Australia, New Guinea (an island north of Australia), the Amazon jungle region of Brazil, and rural Sardinia (an island off the coast of Italy) yielded strongly similar results (Dasen, 1977). These findings suggested that adults in some cultures do not reach the stage of concrete operational thought. However, if this were so, such adults would be severely handicapped in everyday life. Like preschool children, they would be unable

The age at which individuals acquire conservation skills is related to the extent to which the culture provides practice relevant to the concept of conservation. The children shown here live in Nepal, and they have extensive experience as potters. They gain an understanding of the concept of conservation of quantity earlier than children the same age who do not have experience manipulating a material like clay.

to think through the implications of their actions and would be unable to coordinate various kinds of information about objects. They also would be incapable of going beyond an egocentric perspective to understand another person's point of view.

Some researchers believe that the failure to find concrete operational thought in various cultures is due to inadequate communication between the experimenter and the children. For example, in one study of two cultural groups from Cape Breton, Nova Scotia— one English-speaking European, the other Micmac Indian—no difference in conservation abilities appeared between the groups of 10- to 11-year-olds when they were interviewed in their native languages (Nyiti, 1982). The Micmac children all spoke their ancestral tongue at home but had also spoken English since the first grade. However, when the Micmac children were interviewed in English, they understood the concept of conservation only half as well as the English-speaking children of European descent did. This study illustrates the importance of communication between the experimenter and the research participants in cross-cultural studies.

Researchers have also investigated whether or not a child's ability to use the concept of conservation can improve if the child comes from a culture in which conservation is not widely practiced. In one study, rural aboriginal Australian children performed some exercises similar to Piaget's beaker task (Dasen, Ngini, & Lavaleé, 1979). This "training" improved their performance on the beaker task. Even so, their grasp of the conservation concept lagged behind that of children from the Australian city of Canberra by approximately 3 years. These findings suggest that the aboriginal culture does not provide practice that is relevant to the conservation concept.

In sum, the age at which individuals acquire conservation skills is associated with the degree to which their culture provides relevant practice. However, such cross-cultural differences tend to disappear when the studies are conducted by experimenters who are familiar with the language of the people being studied or when the participants receive special training (Cole & Cole, 1993).

Logical reasoning replaces intuitive thought as long as the principles can be applied to specific or *concrete* examples. For example, a concrete operational child cannot imagine the steps necessary to complete an algebraic equation, which is too abstract for thinking at this stage of cognitive development. A summary of the characteristics of concrete operational thought is shown in

figure 7.11. To evaluate the nature of transitions in Piaget's stages, turn to Critical Thinking About Children's Development.

Application of Piaget's Ideas to Education

Piaget was not an educator, but he did provide a sound

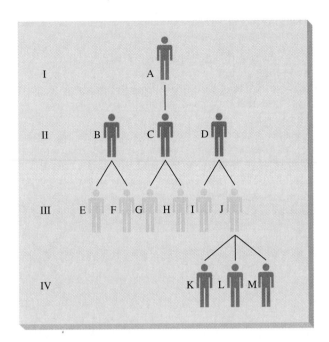

Figure~7.10

Classification

Classification is an important ability in concrete operational thought. When shown a family tree of four generations (I to IV), the preoperational child has trouble classifying the members of the four generations; the concrete operational child can classify the members vertically, horizontally, and obliquely (up and down and across).

conceptual framework from which to view educational problems. What are some of the principles in Piaget's theory of cognitive development that can be applied to children's education? David Elkind (1976) describes three. First, the foremost issue in education is *communication*. In Piaget's theory, a child's mind is not a blank slate; to the contrary, the child has a host of ideas about the physical and natural world, but these ideas differ from those of adults. Adults must learn to comprehend what children are saying and to respond in the same mode of discourse that children use. Second, the child is always unlearning and relearning in addition to acquiring knowledge. Children come to school with their own ideas about space, time, causality, quantity, and number. Third, the child is a knowing creature, motivated to acquire knowledge. The best way to nurture this motivation for knowledge is to allow the child to interact spontaneously with the environment; education needs to ensure that it does not dull the child's eagerness to know by providing an overly rigid curriculum that disrupts the child's rhythm and pace of learning.

Formal Operational Thought

Adolescents' developing power of thought opens up new cognitive and social horizons. Their thought becomes more abstract, logical, and idealistic. Adolescents are more capable of examining their own thoughts, others' thoughts, and what others are thinking about them, and more likely to interpret and monitor the social world.

Characteristics of Formal Operational Thought

Piaget believed that formal operational thought comes into play between the ages of 11 and 15. Formal operational thought is more *abstract* than a child's thinking.

Can use operations, mentally reversing action; shows conservation skills

Logical reasoning replaces intuitive reasoning, but only in concrete circumstances

Not abstract (can't imagine steps in algebraic equation, for example)

Classification skills—can divide things into sets and subsets and reason about their interrelations

Figure~7.11

Characteristics of Concrete Operational Thought

Evaluating Transitions in Piaget's Stages

Piaget was especially intrigued with the points of transition in children's cognitive development as children improve their ability to understand principles in the physical world. For example, when on a trip with the family that involves crossing the "state line," preop- erational children may literally expect a line to be observable on the ground. They discover that the line is an abstract concept rather than a physical descriptor. Can you think of examples from your past or from your interactions with children that could also signal a shift from the preoperational to the concrete operational stage? For example, consider superstitions held by children or cultural rituals that involve magical forces. By evaluating transitions in Piaget's stages, you are learning to think critically by *applying a developmental perspective to understand behavior.*

Adolescents are no longer limited to concrete experience as the anchor of thought. Instead, they may conjure up make-believe situations, hypothetical possibilities, or purely abstract propositions and reason about them. Adolescents increasingly think about thought itself. One adolescent pondered, "I began thinking about why I was thinking what I was. Then I began thinking about why I was thinking about why I was thinking about what I was." If this sounds abstract, it is, and it characterizes adolescents' increased interest in thought itself and the abstractness of thought.

Accompanying the abstract nature of adolescent thought is the quality of idealism. Adolescents begin to think about ideal characteristics for themselves and others and to compare themselves and others to these ideal standards. In contrast, children think more in terms of what is real and what is limited. During adolescence, thoughts often take fantasy flights into the future. It is not unusual for adolescents to become impatient with these newfound ideal standards and to be perplexed about which of many ideal standards to adopt.

At the same time as adolescents begin to think more abstractly and idealistically, they also begin to think more logically. Adolescents begin to think more as a scientist thinks, devising plans to solve problems and systematically testing solutions. This type of problem solving has an imposing name. **Hypothetical-deductive reasoning** *is Piaget's formal operational concept that adolescents have the cognitive ability to develop hypotheses, or best guesses, about ways to solve problems, such as an algebraic equation. They then systematically deduce or conclude which is the best path to follow in solving the problem.* By contrast, children are more likely to solve problems in a trial-and-error fashion. An example of a hypothetical-deductive reasoning problem is presented in table 7.2 and a summary of the main features of formal operational thought is shown in figure 7.12. To further evaluate the nature of formal operational thought, turn to Critical Thinking About Children's Development.

> *The error of youth is to believe that intelligence is a substitute for experience, while the error of age is to believe that experience is a substitute for intelligence.*
>
> —Slyman Bryson

Adolescent Egocentrism

Another characteristic of adolescent thought is adolescent egocentrism. David Elkind (1978) believes that **adolescent egocentrism** *has two parts: an imaginary audience and a personal fable.* An **imaginary audience** *is an adolescent's belief that others are as preoccupied with her as she is.* Attention-getting behavior, common in adolescence, reflects egocentrism and the desire to be on-stage, noticed, and visible. Imagine an eighth-grade boy who thinks he is an actor and all others the audience as he stares at the small spot on his trousers. Imagine the seventh-grade girl who thinks that all eyes are riveted on her complexion because of the tiny blemish she has. Current controversy about the nature of egocentrism focuses on whether it emerges because of formal operational thought or because of perspective taking and interpersonal understanding (Lapsley & Murphy, 1985).

Jennifer talks with her best friend, Anne, about something she has just heard. "Anne, did you hear about Barbara? You know she fools around a lot. Well, the word is that she is pregnant. Can you believe it? That would never happen to me." Later in the conversation, Anne tells Jennifer, "I really like Bob, but sometimes he's a jerk. He just can't understand me. He has no clue about what my personal feelings are." A **personal fable** *is an adolescent's sense of personal uniqueness and indestructibility.* In their efforts to maintain a sense of uniqueness and indestructibility, adolescents sometimes create fictitious stories, or fables. Imagine a girl who is having difficulty getting a date. She might develop a fictitious account of a handsome young man living in another part of the country who is madly in love with her.

TABLE 7.2

An Example of Hypothetical-Deductive Reasoning

A common task for all of us is to determine what can be inferred logically from a statement made by someone else. Young children are often told by teachers that, if they work hard, they will receive good grades. Regardless of the empirical truth of the claim, the children may believe that good grades are the result of hard work and that, if they do not get good grades, they did not work hard enough. (Establishing the direction of the relationship between variables is an important issue.)

Children in the late concrete operational stage, too, are concerned with understanding the relations between their behavior and their teachers' grading practices. However, they are beginning to question the "truths" of their childhood. First, they now know that there are four possible combinations if two variables are dichotomized (work hard–not work hard; good grades–not good grades):

Behavior	Consequences
1 Work hard	Good grades
2 Work hard	Not good grades
3 Not work hard	Good grades
4 Not work hard	Not good grades

Two combinations are consistent with the hypothesis that hard work is necessarily related to good grades: (1) students work hard and get good grades and (4) they do not work hard and do not get good grades. When the presumed "cause" is present, the effect is present; when the cause is absent, the effect is absent. There are also two combinations that do not fit the hypothesis of a direct relation between hard work and good grades: (2) students work hard and do not get good grades and (3) they get good grades without working hard.

An adolescent's notion of possibility allows him or her to take this analysis of combinations one important step further. Each of the four basic combinations of binary variables may be true or it may not. If 1, 2, 3, or 4 is true alone or is true in combination, there are 16 possible patterns of truth values:

1 or 2 or 3 or 4 is true	4 patterns
1-2 or 1-3 or 1-4 or 2-3 or 2-4 or 3-4 are true	6 patterns
1-2-3 or 1-2-4 or 1-3-4 or 2-3-4 are true	4 patterns
All (1-2-3-4) are true	1 pattern
All are false	1 pattern
Total	16 patterns

The list is critically important because each pattern leads to a different conclusion about the possible relation between two variables.

Excerpt from *Piaget: With Feeling* by Philip A. Cowan, copyright © 1978 by Holt, Rinehart and Winston, Inc., reprinted by permission of the publisher.

". . . and give me good abstract-reasoning ability, interpersonal skills, cultural perspective, linguistic comprehension, and a high sociodynamic potential."

Drawing by Ed Fisher, © 1981 The New Yorker Magazine, Inc.

ability to think hypothetically produces unconstrained thoughts with unlimited possibilities. This early formal operational thought submerges reality (Broughton, 1983). Reality is overwhelmed. Idealism and possibility dominate. During the middle years of adolescence, an intellectual balance is restored; adolescents test the products of their reasoning against experience and develop a consolidation of formal operational thought.

Piaget's (1952) early writings seemed to indicate that the onset and consolidation of formal operational thought is completed during early adolescence, from about 12 to 15 years of age. Later, Piaget (1972) concluded that formal operational thought is not achieved until later in adolescence, between approximately 15 and 20 years of age.

Piaget's concepts of assimilation and accommodation help us understand the two phases of formal operational thought. Remember that *assimilation* occurs when adolescents incorporate new information into their existing knowledge; *accommodation* occurs when adolescents adjust to new information. During early adolescence, there is an excess of assimilation as the world is perceived too subjectively and idealistically. In the middle years of adolescence, an intellectual balance is restored, as the individual accommodates to the cognitive upheaval that has taken place. In this view, the assimilation of formal operational thought marks the transition to adolescence; accommodation marks a later consolidation of thought (Lapsley, 1989).

Variations in Adolescent Cognition

Piaget's theory emphasizes universal and consistent patterns of formal operational thought; his theory does not adequately account for the unique differences that characterize the cognitive development of adolescents. These individual variations in adolescents' cognitive development have been documented in a number of investigations (Neimark, 1982).

Early and Late Formal Operational Thought

Formal operational thought has been conceptualized as occurring in two phases. In the first phase, the increased

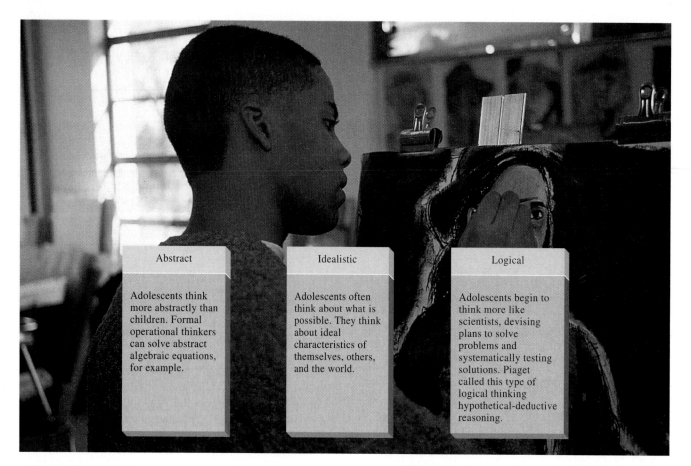

Abstract

Adolescents think more abstractly than children. Formal operational thinkers can solve abstract algebraic equations, for example.

Idealistic

Adolescents often think about what is possible. They think about ideal characteristics of themselves, others, and the world.

Logical

Adolescents begin to think more like scientists, devising plans to solve problems and systematically testing solutions. Piaget called this type of logical thinking hypothetical-deductive reasoning.

Figure~7.12

Characteristics of Formal Operational Thought

Adolescents begin to think more as scientists think, devising plans to solve problems and systematically testing solutions. Piaget gave this type of thinking the imposing name *hypothetical-deductive reasoning.* In addition to thinking more logically, adolescents also think more abstractly and idealistically.

CRITICAL THINKING ABOUT CHILDREN'S DEVELOPMENT

Formal Operational Thought, Politics, and Ideology

The development of formal operational thought expands adolescents' worlds by allowing them to consider possibilities, to conduct experiments and test hypotheses, and to think about thoughts. Part of the cognitive expansion of their worlds involves constructing theories about politics and ideology. It is during adolescence that for the first time individuals become adept at generating ideas about the world as it *could* be. In the realm of moral development, adolescents often quickly make the leap from how the world could be to how it *should* be. And many adolescents believe the world *should* be transformed in the direction of some utopian ideal.

Examine what we have said about Piaget's stages of cognitive development. How might movement into the formal operational stage be reflected in the way adolescents view politics and ideology? For example, how might an 8-year-old and a 16-year-old differ in their evaluations of the statements of presidential candidates? By thinking about the influence of formal operational thought on adolescents' examination of politics and ideology, you are learning to think critically by *creating arguments based on developmental concepts.*

Santrock: Child Development

Some individuals in early adolescence are formal operational thinkers; others are not. A review of formal operational thought investigations revealed that only about one of every three eighth-grade students is a formal operational thinker (Strahan, 1983). Some investigators have found that formal operational thought increases with age in adolescence (Martorano, 1977); others have not (Strahan, 1987). Many college students and adults do not think in formal operational ways, either. For example, investigators have found that from 17 percent to 67 percent of all college students think in formal operational ways (Elkind, 1961; Tomlinson-Keasey, 1972).

Many young adolescents are at the point of consolidating their concrete operational thought, using it more consistently than in childhood. At the same time, many young adolescents are just beginning to think in a formal operational manner. By late adolescence, many adolescents have begun to consolidate their formal operational thought, using it more consistently, and there often is variation across the content areas of formal operational thought, just as there is in concrete operational thought in childhood. A 14-year-old might reason at the formal operational level when it comes to analyzing algebraic equations but not do so with verbal problem solving or when reasoning about interpersonal relations.

Formal operational thought is more likely to be used in areas in which adolescents have the most experience and knowledge (Carey, 1988). Children and adolescents gradually build up elaborate knowledge through extensive experience and practice in various sports, games, hobbies, and school subjects such as math, English, and science. The development of expertise in different domains of life may make possible high-level, developmentally mature-looking thought. In some instances, the sophisticated reasoning of formal operational thought may be responsible. In other instances, however, the thought may be largely due to the accumulation of knowledge that allows more automatic, memory-based processes to function. Some developmentalists wonder if the acquisition of knowledge accounts for all cognitive growth. Most, however, argue that *both* cognitive changes in such areas as concrete and formal operational thought *and* the development of expertise through experience are at work in understanding the adolescent's cognitive world. More about the role of knowledge in the adolescent's thinking appears in the next chapter.

Beyond Formal Operational Thought

Some critics of Piaget's theory argue that specialized thinking about a specific skill represents a higher stage of thought than formal operational thought. Piaget did not believe that this was so. For him, the change to reasoning about a special skill (such as the kind of thinking engaged in by a nuclear physicist or a medical researcher) is no

(a)

(b)

(c)

(a) Adolescents' thoughts are more abstract and idealistic than children's thoughts are. (b) Young adults' thoughts are more pragmatic, specialized, and multiple (less dualistic) than adolescents' thoughts are. (c) Older adults may not be as quick with their thoughts as younger adults are, but they may have more general knowledge and wisdom. This elderly woman shares the wisdom of her experiences with a classroom of children.

more than window dressing. According to Piaget, a nuclear physicist may think in ways that an adolescent cannot think, but the adolescent and the nuclear physicist differ only in their familiarity with an academic field of inquiry. They differ in the content of their thought, not in the operations they bring to bear on the content (Piaget, 1970).

Some developmentalists believe that the absolutist nature of adolescent logic and buoyant optimism diminish in early adulthood. According to Gisela Labouvie-Vief (1982, 1986), a new integration of thought takes place in early adulthood. She thinks that the adult years produce pragmatic constraints that require an adaptive strategy of less reliance on logical analysis in solving problems. Commitment, specialization, and channeling energy into finding one's niche in complex social and work systems replace the youth's fascination with idealized logic. If we assume that logical thought and buoyant optimism are the criteria for cognitive maturity, we would have to admit that the cognitive activity of adults is too concrete and pragmatic. But from Labouvie-Vief's view, the adult's understanding of reality's constraints reflects maturity, not immaturity.

Even Piaget (1967) detected that formal operational thought may have its hazards:

> With the advent of formal intelligence, thinking takes wings and it is not surprising that at first this unexpected power is both used and abused. . . . Each new mental ability starts off by incorporating the world in a process of egocentric assimilation. Adolescent egocentricity is manifested by a belief in the omnipotence of reflection, as though the world should submit itself to idealistic schemes rather than to systems of reality. (pp. 63–64)

Our cognitive abilities are very strong in early adulthood, and they do show adaptation to life's pragmatic concerns (Moshman, 1997). Less clear is whether our logical skills actually decline. Competence as a young adult probably requires doses of both logical thinking skills and pragmatic adaptation to reality. For example, when architects design a building, they logically analyze and plan the structure but understand the cost constraints, environmental concerns, and the time it will take to get the job done effectively.

William Perry (1981) also has charted some important ways in which young adults' thinking differs from adolescents' thinking. He believes that adolescents often view the world in a basic dualistic fashion of polarities, such as right/wrong, black/white, we/they, or good/bad. As youths mature and move into the adulthood years, they gradually become aware of the diversity of opinion and the multiple perspectives that others hold, which shakes their dualistic perceptions. Their *dualistic thinking* gives way to *multiple thinking,* as they come to understand that authorities may not have all of the answers. They begin to carve out their own territory of individualistic thinking, often believing that everyone is entitled to their own opinion and that one's personal opinion is as good as anyone else's. As these personal opinions become challenged by others, multiple thinking yields to

relative subordinate thinking, in which an analytical, evaluative approach to knowledge is consciously and actively pursued. Only in the shift to *full relativism* does the adult completely comprehend that truth is relative, that the meaning of an event is related to the context in which that event occurs and on the framework that the knower uses to understand that event. In full relativism, the adult recognizes that relativism pervades all aspects of life, not just the academic world. And in full relativism, the adult understands that knowledge is constructed, not given; contextual, not absolute. Perry's ideas, which are oriented toward well-educated, bright individuals, have been widely used by educators and counselors in working with young adults in academic settings.

Another candidate for thought that is more advanced than formal operational thought is wisdom, which, like good wine, may get better with age. What is this thing we call wisdom? **Wisdom** *is expert knowledge about the practical aspects of life* (Baltes, in press; Baltes & others, 1995). This practical knowledge involves exceptional insight into human development and life matters, good judgment, and an understanding of how to cope with difficult life problems. Thus, wisdom, more than standard conceptions of intelligence, focuses on life's pragmatic concerns and human conditions. This practical knowledge system takes many years to acquire, accumulating through intentional, planned experiences and through incidental experiences. Of course, not all older adults solve practical problems in wise ways. In one recent investigation, only 5 percent of adults' responses to life-planning problems were considered wise, and these wise responses were equally distributed across the early, middle, and late adulthood years (Smith & Baltes, in press).

What does the possibility that older adults are as wise or wiser than younger adults mean in terms of the basic issue of intellectual decline in adulthood? Remember that intelligence comes in different forms. In many instances, older adults are not as intelligent as younger adults when speed of processing is involved, and this probably harms their performance on many traditional school-related tasks and standardized intelligence tests. But consideration of general knowledge and something we call wisdom may result in an entirely different interpretation.

Now that we have considered many different ideas about Piaget's theory of adolescent cognition, including the issue of whether there are forms of thought more advanced than formal operational thinking, we turn our attention to evaluating Piagetian contributions and criticisms.

PIAGETIAN CONTRIBUTIONS AND CRITICISMS

We have spent considerable time outlining Piaget's theory of cognitive development. Let's briefly summarize some of Piaget's main contributions, and then enumerate criticisms of his theory.

Piaget, shown sitting on a bench, was a genius at observing children. By carefully observing and interviewing children, Piaget constructed his comprehensive theory of children's cognitive development.

Contributions

To restate what we said at the beginning of the chapter, we owe Piaget the present field of cognitive development. We owe him a long list of masterful concepts of enduring power and fascination, such as object permanence, conservation, assimilation, and accommodation. We also owe Piaget the currently accepted vision of children as active, constructive thinkers who, through their commerce with the environment, are manufacturers of their own development (Flavell, 1992; Lourenco & Machado, 1996).

Piaget was a genius when it came to observing children; his astute observations showed us inventive ways to discover how children, and even infants, act on and adapt to their world. Piaget showed us some important things to look for in children's cognitive development, including the shift from preoperational to concrete operational thought. He also showed us how we must make experiences fit our cognitive framework yet simultaneously adapt our cognitive orientation to experience. Piaget also revealed how cognitive change is likely to occur if the situation is structured to allow gradual movement to the next-higher level.

Criticisms

Piaget's theory has not gone unchallenged, however (Bjorklund, 1997). Questions are raised about the following areas: estimates of the child's competence at different developmental levels; stages; training of children to reason at higher levels; and culture and education.

Estimates of Children's Competence

Some cognitive abilities emerge earlier than Piaget thought, and their subsequent development is more prolonged than he believed. As we saw earlier in the chapter, some aspects of object permanence emerge much earlier in infancy than Piaget believed. Even 2-year-olds are nonegocentric in some contexts—when they realize that another person will not see an object they see if the person is blindfolded or is looking in a different direction (Lempers, Flavell, & Flavell, 1977). Conservation of number has been demonstrated in children as young as 3 years of age, although Piaget did not think it came about until 7 years of age. Young children are not as "pre-" this and "pre-" that (precausal, preoperational) as Piaget thought (Flavell, 1992). Some aspects of formal operational thinking that involve abstract reasoning do not consistently emerge in early adolescence as Piaget envisioned. And adults often reason in far more irrational ways than Piaget believed (Siegler, 1995). In sum, recent trends highlight the cognitive competencies of infants and young children and the cognitive shortcomings of adolescents and adults.

Stages

Piaget conceived of stages as unitary structures of thought, so his theory assumes synchrony in development. That is, various aspects of a stage should emerge at about the same time. However, several concrete operational concepts do not appear in synchrony. For example, children do not learn to conserve at the same time as they learn to cross-classify.

Most contemporary developmentalists agree that children's cognitive development is not as grand-stage-like as Piaget thought. **Neo-Piagetians** *are developmentalists who have elaborated on Piaget's theory, believing children's cognitive development is more specific in many respects than he thought.* Neo-Piagetians don't believe that all of Piaget's ideas should be junked. However, they argue that a more accurate vision of the child's cognitive development involves fewer references to grand stages and more emphasis on the roles of strategies, skills, how fast and automatically children can process information, the task-specific nature of children's cognition, and the importance of dividing cognitive problems into smaller, more precise steps (Case, 1992; Pascual-Leone, 1987).

Neo-Piagetians still believe that children's cognitive development contains some general properties (Flavell, 1992). They stress that there is a regular, maturation-based increase with age in some aspects of the child's information-processing capacity, such as how fast or efficiently the child processes information (Fischer & Bidell, 1997). As the child's information-processing capacity increases with increasing age, new and more-complex forms of cognition in all content domains are possible because the child can now hold in mind and think about more things at once. For example, Canadian

An outstanding teacher and education in the logic of science and mathematics are important cultural experiences that promote the development of concrete and formal operational thought. Schooling and education likely play more important roles in the development of formal operational thought than Piaget envisioned.

developmentalist Robbie Case (1985) argues that adolescents have increasingly more available cognitive resources than they did as children because they can process information more automatically, they have more information-processing capacity, and they are more familiar with a range of content knowledge.

In Case's most recent formulation (Case, 1996, 1997; Case & Okamoto, 1996), he argues that Piaget's notion of a general cognitive structure has been abandoned prematurely and that what is needed is to rework it. He says that in moving beyond the notion of centrality toward modularity, specificity, and relativity as the keys to understanding cognitive development, the field has lost sight of the unifying nature of general structural change.

Training Children to Reason at a Higher Level

Children who are at one cognitive stage (such as preoperational thought) can be trained to reason at a higher cognitive stage (such as concrete operational thought). This poses a problem for Piaget, who argued that such training works only on a superficial level and is ineffective unless the child is at a point of transition from one stage to the next (Gelman & Williams, 1997).

Culture and Education

Culture and education exert stronger influences on children's development than Piaget believed. Earlier in the chapter, we studied how the age at which individuals acquire conservation skills is associated to some extent

with the degree to which their culture provides relevant practice. And in many developing countries, formal operational thought is a rare occurrence. As you will learn shortly, there has been a wave of interest in how children's cognitive development progresses through interaction with skilled adults and peers, and how the children's embeddedness in a culture influences their cognitive growth. Such views stand in stark contrast to Piaget's view of the child as a solitary young scientist.

VYGOTSKY'S THEORY OF COGNITIVE DEVELOPMENT

Children's cognitive development does not occur in a social vacuum. Lev Vygotsky (1896–1934), a Russian psychologist, recognized this important point about children's minds more than half a century ago. Vygotsky's theory is increasingly receiving attention as we move toward the close of the twentieth century (Light & Butterworth, 1993; Rogoff, 1997; Rogoff & Morelli, 1989). Before we turn to Vygotsky's ideas on language and thought and culture and society, let's examine his important concept of the zone of proximal development.

The Zone of Proximal Development

Zone of proximal development (ZPD) *is Vygotsky's term for the range of tasks too difficult for children to master alone but that can be mastered with the guidance and assistance of adults or more highly skilled children.* Thus, the lower

Lev Vygotsky (1896–1934), shown here with his daughter, believed that children's cognitive development is advanced through social interaction with skilled individuals embedded in a sociocultural backdrop.

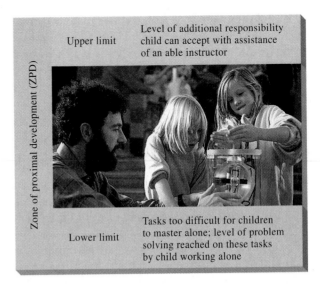

Upper limit — Level of additional responsibility child can accept with assistance of an able instructor

Zone of proximal development (ZPD)

Lower limit — Tasks too difficult for children to master alone; level of problem solving reached on these tasks by child working alone

Figure~7.13

Vygotsky's Zone of Proximal Development

Vygotsky's zone of proximal development has a lower limit and an upper limit. Tasks in the ZPD are too difficult for the child to perform alone. They require assistance from an adult or a skilled child. As children experience the verbal instruction or demonstration, they organize the information in their existing mental structures so they can eventually perform the skill or task alone.

limit of the ZPD is the level of problem solving reached by a child working independently. The upper limit is the level of additional responsibility the child can accept with the assistance of an able instructor (see figure 7.13). Vygotsky's emphasis on ZPD underscored his belief in the importance of social influences on cognitive development and the role of instruction in children's development. As children experience verbal instruction or demonstration, they organize information into their existing mental structures so they can eventually perform the skill or task without assistance (Vygotsky, 1962).

The zone of proximal development is conceptualized as a measure of learning potential. IQ, or intelligence quotient, also is a measure of learning potential. However, IQ emphasizes that intelligence is a property of the child, whereas ZPD emphasizes that learning is interpersonal, a dynamic social event that depends on a minimum of two minds, one better informed or more drilled than the other. Rather than having a ZPD, the child *shares* a ZPD with an instructor.

The practical teaching involved in the ZPD begins toward the zone's upper limit, where the child is able to reach a goal only through close collaboration with an instructor. With adequate continuing instruction and practice, the child organizes and masters the behavioral sequences necessary to perform the target skill (DiPardo, 1996). As the instruction continues, the performance transfers from the instructor to the child as the teacher gradually reduces the explanations, hints, and demonstrations until the child is able to perform adequately alone. Once the goal is achieved, it may become the foundation for the development of a new ZPD.

Learning by toddlers provides an example of how the zone of proximal development works. Toddlers have to be motivated and must be involved in activities that involve skill at a reasonably high level of difficulty—that is, toward the zone's upper end. The teacher must have the know-how to exercise the target skill at any level required by the activity, and the teacher must be able to locate and stay in the zone. The teacher and the child also must adapt to each other's requirements. The reciprocal relationship between the toddler and the teacher adjusts dynamically as the division of labor is negotiated and aimed at increasing the weaker partner's share of the goal attainment. Vygotsky's concept of the zone of proximal development is also being effectively applied to teaching children reading, writing, and math (Glassman, 1995; Steward, 1995).

Language and Thought

In Vygotsky's view, a child's mental or cognitive structures are made of relations between mental functions. The relation between language and thought is believed to be especially important in this regard (Vygotsky, 1962). Vygotsky said that language and thought initially develop independently of each other but eventually merge.

Two principles govern the merging of thought and language. First, all mental functions have external or social origins. Children must use language and communicate with others before they focus inward on their own mental processes. Second, children must communicate externally and use language for a long period of time before the transition from external to internal speech takes place. This transition period occurs between 3 and 7 years of age and involves talking to oneself. After a while, the self-talk becomes second nature to children and they can act without verbalizing. When this occurs, children have internalized their egocentric speech in the form of inner speech, which becomes their thoughts. Vygotsky believed that children who engage in a large amount of private speech are more socially competent than those who do not use it extensively. He argued that private speech represents an early transition in becoming more socially communicative.

Vygotsky's theory challenges Piaget's ideas on language and thought. Vygotsky argued that language, even in its earliest forms, is socially based, whereas Piaget emphasized young children's egocentric and nonsocially oriented speech. According to Vygotsky, young children talk to themselves to govern their behavior and to guide themselves. In contrast, Piaget stressed that young children's egocentric speech reflects social and cognitive immaturity.

Culture and Society

Many developmentalists who work in the field of culture and development are comfortable with Vygotsky's theory, which focuses on the sociocultural context of development (Gauvain, 1995). Vygotsky's theory offers a portrayal of human development that is inseparable from social and cultural activities. Vygotsky emphasized how the development of higher mental processes, such as memory, attention, and reasoning, involve learning to use the inventions of society such as language, mathematical systems, and memory devices. He also emphasized how children are aided in development by the guidance of individuals who are already skilled in these tools. Vygotsky's emphasis on the role of culture in cognitive development and society contrasts with Piaget's description of the solitary little scientist.

Vygotsky stressed both the institutional and the interpersonal levels of social contexts. At the institutional level, cultural history provides organizations and tools useful to cognitive activity through such institutions as schools and such inventions as the computer and literacy. Institutional interaction gives children broad behavioral and societal norms to guide their lives. The interpersonal level has a more direct influence on a child's mental functioning. According to Vygotsky (1962), skills in mental functioning develop through immediate social interaction. Information about cognitive tools, skills, and interpersonal relations are transmitted through direct interaction with people. Through the organization of these social interactional experiences embedded in a cultural backdrop, children's mental development matures.

At this point, we have discussed a number of ideas about concrete operational thought, formal operational thought, the contributions and criticisms of Piaget's theory, and Vygotsky's theory of cognitive development. A summary of these ideas is presented in concept table 7.2. In the next chapter, we will turn our attention to two other important views of children's development—learning and information processing.

Concrete Operational Thought, Formal Operational Thought, Piagetian Contributions and Criticisms, and Vygotsky's Theory of Cognitive Development

Concept	Processes/ Related Ideas	Characteristics/Description
Concrete Operational Thought	Its nature	It is made up of operations, mental actions that are reversible. The concrete operational child shows conservation and classification skills. Conservation involves a horizontal décalage. Concrete operational thought is limited by the inability to reason about abstract matters. Piaget's ideas have been widely applied to children's education. Emphasis is on communication and the belief that the child has many ideas about the world, that the child is by nature a knowing creature.
Formal Operational Thought	Its nature	Piaget believed that formal operational thought comes into play between 11 and 15 years of age. Formal operational thought is more abstract, idealistic, and logical than concrete operational thought. Piaget believed that adolescents become capable of using hypothetical-deductive reasoning.
	Adolescent egocentrism	Adolescents develop a special type of egocentrism that involves an imaginary audience and a personal fable about being unique and indestructible.
	Early and late formal operational thought and individual variation	Formal operational thought has two phases—an assimilation phase in which reality is overwhelmed (early adolescence) and an accommodation phase in which intellectual balance is restored through a consolidation of formal operational thought (middle years of adolescence). Individual variation in formal operational thought is extensive. Piaget did not give adequate consideration to individual variation. Many young adolescents are not formal operational thinkers but, rather, are consolidating their concrete operational thought.
	Beyond formal operational thought	Many life-span developmentalists believe that Piaget was incorrect in assuming that formal operational thought is the highest form of cognition. They argue that more pragmatic, specialized, and multiple (less dualistic) thought takes place in early adulthood and that wisdom may increase throughout the adult years.
Piagetian Contributions and Criticisms	Contributions	Piaget was a genius at observing children. He showed us some important things to look for and mapped out some general cognitive changes.
	Criticisms	Criticisms focus on such matters as estimates of children's competence, stages (neo-Piagetians offer more precise views and information-processing explanations), training children to reason at a higher level, and culture and education.
Vygotsky's Theory of Cognitive Development	Zone of proximal development	ZPD is Vygotsky's term for tasks too difficult for children to master alone but can be mastered with the guidance and assistance of adults or more highly skilled children.
	Language and thought	Language and thought develop independently and then merge. The merging of language and thought takes place between 3 and 7 years of age and involves talking to oneself.
	Culture and society	Vygotsky's theory stresses how the child's mind develops in the context of the sociocultural world. Cognitive skills develop through social interaction embedded in a cultural backdrop.

SUMMARY

The child is a thinking child, and this thinking translates into adaptation. As their thinking develops, children construct all sorts of ideas about what is happening in their world. With cognitive growth, children refine their thinking and move through a number of cognitive milestones.

In this chapter, we began by providing a glimpse of Piaget's observations of his own children. Next we studied some basic ideas about Piaget's stages and cognitive processes and then explored each of his four stages—sensorimotor, preoperational, concrete operational and formal operational—in depth. His contributions and criticisms of his work were noted. Vygotsky's theory, which is receiving increased attention, was outlined.

You can obtain a much more detailed summary of the entire chapter by again studying the two concept tables on pages 225 and 237. One criticism of cognitive developmental theory is that it pays little attention to the specific ways children process information. In the next chapter, we will turn our attention to the study of children's information processing.

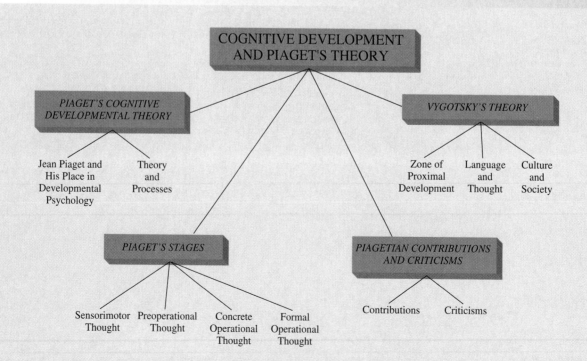

KEY TERMS

PRACTICAL KNOWLEDGE ABOUT CHILDREN

The Hurried Child
(1988, rev. ed.)
by David Elkind, Reading, MA: Addison-Wesley.

The Hurried Child describes a pervasive and harmful circumstance that all too many American children face—that of growing up too fast and too soon. Author David Elkind is an expert on children's and adolescents' lives. Elkind says that today's American parents too often push their children to be "superkids" who are competent to deal with all of life's ups and downs. He doesn't just fault parents; he also points the finger of blame at schools and the media. According to Elkind, many parents' expectations for their children—regarding not just their children's academic journeys, but also their athletic accomplishments—are unrealistic. Elkind recommends that parents respect children's own developmental timetables and needs, encourage children to play and fantasize, and make sure that their expectations and support are in reasonable balance.

EXPLORATIONS IN CHILD DEVELOPMENT

To further examine the nature of child development, we will examine a research study on object permanence in infancy, and we will then discuss apprenticeship thinking.

RESEARCH IN CHILD DEVELOPMENT

Objective Permanence in Infancy

Featured Study

Baillargeon, R. (1986). Representing the existence and the location of hidden objects: Object permanence in 6- and 8-month-old infants. *Cognition, 23,* 21–41.

What do infants know about the existence and properties of hidden objects? To find out, Renée Baillargeon devised a study to evaluate two aspects of object permanence in infants: (1) the ability to represent the existence and the location of a hidden stationary object, and (2) the ability to represent the existence and the trajectory of a moving object.

Method

The subjects were twenty-six 6- and 8-month-old infants, who sat in front of a screen. An inclined ramp was to the left of the screen. The infants watched the following event: The screen was raised and then lowered again, and then a toy car rolled down the ramp, passed behind the screen, and exited the apparatus to the right. After the infants habituated to this event (quit looking at it), they saw two test events (figure 7.14 shows the habituation event). These were identical to the habituation event, except that a box was placed behind the screen. In one event (the possible event), the box was set back from the car's tracks and did not block its path; in the other (the impossible event), the box sat on top of the tracks, blocking the car's path (a researcher moved the box off the tracks after the screen was lowered, so that the car could roll down the tracks).

Results and Discussion

Infants looked longer at the impossible event than at the possible event, suggesting that they were surprised to see the car reappear from behind the screen when the box stood in its path. A control experiment in which the box was placed in front (possible event) or on top (impossible event) of the car's tracks yielded similar results. The results of the experiments indicate that the infants believed that (1) the box continued to exist, in its same location, after it was occluded by the screen; (2) the car continued to exist, pursuing its trajectory, after it disappeared behind the screen; and (3) the car could not roll through the space occupied by the box.

The results of this study underscore that infants are far more competent than Piaget's account of object permanence suggests. By 6 months of age, infants represent the existence and location of stationary objects, and they represent the existence and trajectory of hidden moving objects. Furthermore, they are able to use such representations to reason about simple occlusion events involving hidden objects.

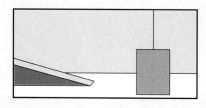 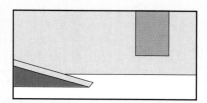 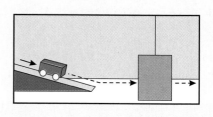

Figure~7.14

The Habituation Event Used in Experiment 1 in Baillargeon's Study of Object Permanence in Infancy

Apprenticeship Training

Barbara Rogoff (1990) believes that children's cognitive development is an apprenticeship that occurs through participation in social activity, guided by companions who stretch and support children's understanding of and skill in using the "tools" of the culture. Some of the technologies that are important tools for handling information in a culture are (1) language systems that organize categories of reality and structure ways of approaching situations, (2) literate practices to record information and transform it through written exercises, (3) mathematical systems that handle numerical and spatial problems, and (4) memory strategies to preserve information in memory over time. Some of these technologies have material supports, such as pencil and paper, word-processing programs, alphabets, calculators, abacus and slide rule, notches on sticks, and knots on ropes. These tools provide a mechanism for transmitting information from one generation to the next.

In presenting her ideas on apprenticeship in thinking, Rogoff draws heavily on Vygotsky's theory. Rogoff argues that guided participation is widely used around the world, but with important variations in activities for and communication with children in different cultures. The most salient differences focus on the goals of development—what lessons are to be learned—and the means available for children either to observe and participate in culturally important activities or to receive instruction outside the context of skilled activity (Morelli, Rogoff, & Angelillo, 1992).

The general processes of guided participation appear around the world. Caregivers and children arrange children's activities and revise children's responsibilities as they gain skill and knowledge. With guidance, children participate in cultural activities that socialize them into skilled activities. For example, Mayan mothers in Guatemala help their daughters learn to weave in a process of guided par-

At about 7 years of age, Mayan girls in Guatemala are assisted in beginning to learn to weave a simple belt, with the loom already set up for them. The young girl shown here is American developmental psychologist Barbara Rogoff's daughter, being taught to weave by a Mayan woman.

ticipation. In the United States and in many other nations, the development of prominent and creative thinkers is promoted through interaction with a knowledgeable person rather than by studying books or by attending classes and exhibits.

Children begin to practice the skills for using cultural tools, such as literacy, even before the children have contact with the technology. For example, most middle-class American parents involve their children in extensive conversation long before they go to kindergarten or elementary school, and they provide their young children with picture books and read stories to them at bedtime as part of their daily routine. Most middle-class American parents embed their children in a way of life in which reading and writing are integral parts of communication, recreation, and livelihood (Rogoff, 1990).

By contrast, consider the practices of two communities whose children have trouble reading (Heath, 1989). Parents in an Appalachian mill town taught their children respect for

the written word but did not involve book characters or information in the children's everyday lives. Their children did well in the first several years of learning to read but had difficulty when required to use these literate skills to express themselves or interpret text. Children of rural origin in another mill town learned the skillful and creative use of language but were not taught about books or the style of communication and language used in school. These children had difficulty learning to read, which kept them from using their creative skills with language in the school setting. Early childhood in both of these communities did not include school-style reading and writing in the context of daily life and, not surprisingly, the children experienced difficulties with literacy in school.

In sum, Rogoff argues that guided participation—the participation of children in skilled cultural activities with other people of varying levels of skill and status—is an important aspect of children's development.

Pierre Auguste Renoir
Young Girls at the Piano detail

Chapter

8

Information
Processing

(With Robert S. Siegler, Carnegie-Mellon University)

Our life is what our thoughts make it.

—Marcus Aurelius

Chapter Boxes

The mind is an enchanting thing.

—Marianne Moore

Reading Bridge to Terabithia

Sam Winters, a fifth-grade student, leaves his book on the dining room table and goes off to school. It is a popular novel, written for 9- to-12-year-olds, describing how two children strike up a friendship in a rural elementary school in contemporary Maryland. The book is entitled *Bridge to Terabithia*; the author, Katherine Paterson, won a Newbery Medal for one of her novels for children in 1981.

Sam's 3-year-old sister Nancy spies the inviting cover of the book shortly after Sam has left, swoops the book up, and heads to her room to "read" it. Nancy stares at the book's cover drawing of two children for a while and then turns the book upside down to contemplate what the drawing looks like from that perspective. A few moments later, Nancy is poring over the story. A quick "reader," Nancy finishes the entire 128-page book in about 6 minutes. In that 6 minutes, she studies each of the twelve drawings in the book and thinks to herself what each drawing represents. Nancy also picks out several capital letters she knows (B, A, D, Z, M, N, C, Y) and spots some familiar numbers on different pages (0, 1, 3, 6). She returns the book to the dining room table when she has finished.

Sam comes home from school at noon to have lunch. After wolfing down his hamburger, he decides to spend a little time reading and picks up *Bridge to Terabithia*. He sits quietly for 15 minutes and reads the eight pages of chapter 2, which introduces a new character, Leslie—a bright 11-year-old girl. A few of the words in the chapter are unfamiliar, but Sam gets the idea that Leslie looks like a boy, she says whatever she pleases, and she knows a lot about everything. The other character in the story, Jess, sort of likes her, and Sam figures that the rest of the book will be about the two of them.

Nancy, still eating lunch, hollers over to Sam, "Did you finish the book? I did!"

Sam smiles. "You can't read this book, Nancy. You're just a little kid."

Their mother intervenes to prevent a predictable fight. "Well, tell us what you read, Nancy."

"A boy . . . um . . . a girl . . . a little dog house . . . a B, a 6."

Sam laughs and Mrs. Winters compliments Nancy for reading so well. After Sam has gone back to school and Nancy is occupied with her crayons and coloring book, Mrs. Winters sits down with *Bridge to Terabithia* to see what she can learn about the novel. She skims the book in 20 minutes, forming a general idea of the plot outline. As she reads, she makes some mental notes about words and concepts she would discuss at a later time with Sam, because she is fairly certain he doesn't know them. She also considers whether the book is a good selection for Sam. Is the book's difficulty level about right, given her assessment of his reading skills, and will Sam assimilate the moral lessons the author is trying to communicate?

PREVIEW

When we read, we process information and interpret it; thus, reading serves as a practical example of information processing in childhood, the focus of this chapter. To begin, we will learn about the nature of the information-processing approach. Then we will turn our attention to a number of areas of children's thinking: memory, conceptual development, problem solving, and academic skills.

THE INFORMATION-PROCESSING APPROACH

Georgie (a 2-year-old) wants to throw rocks out of the kitchen window. The lawn mower is outside. Dad says that Georgie can't throw rocks out the window because he'll break the lawn mower with the rocks. Georgie says, "I got an idea." He goes outside, brings in some green peaches that he had been playing with, and says, "They won't break the lawn mower" (Waters, 1989, p. 7).

The information-processing approach represents an attempt to characterize the type of active thinking and problem solving that this example illustrates. It is based on a flattering, almost heroic, depiction of children's thinking. The depiction speaks to the essential tension within cognitive development, the tension produced by the fact that children are severely limited in what they can do, yet constantly strive to find ways of overcoming these limitations.

To surmount these constraints, children use a variety of *strategies* (Siegler, 1995). They draw analogies to related problems (for example, substituting peaches for rocks when parents forbid them to throw rocks—note that Georgie was only 2 years when he drew the analogy). They use memory strategies such as rehearsal (repeating material over and over before recalling it, as when trying to remember a phone number) to overcome their limited memory capacity. They use external memory aids such as books to overcome their limited knowledge. The challenges raised by the need to devise strategies that allow them to overcome barriers and reach goals provide some of the most dramatic moments in the development of children's thinking.

Defining the Information-Processing Approach

There is no single information-processing theory of development, but rather a large number of particular theories of different aspects of development. However, all of these information-processing theories share certain fundamental assumptions. The basic assumption is that *thinking is information processing*. Information-processing theories do not usually describe children as being in one stage at one age and in a different stage at a different age. Instead, they focus on the processes involved in thinking: how children remember, form concepts, and solve problems in particular contexts (Klahr & MacWhinney, 1997).

A second defining characteristic of information-processing theories of development is an emphasis on *precise analysis of change mechanisms*. Two critical goals are to identify the mechanisms that contribute most to cognitive development and to specify exactly how these change mechanisms operate. Information-processing theories also attempt to identify the cognitive limits that prevent development from occurring more rapidly than

it does. Thus, such theories attempt to explain both how children of each age can think as well as they can, and why they cannot think better.

A third defining characteristic is that careful *task analyses* are viewed as crucial for understanding children's thinking. The reason is that people's representations and processing of information are in large part attributable to the task they are trying to perform. Consider the following description:

> We watch an ant make his laborious way across a wind-and-wave-molded beach. He moves ahead, angles to the right to ease his climb up a steep dunelet, detours around a pebble, stops for a moment to exchange information with a compatriot. Thus he makes his weaving, halting way back to his home. So as not to anthropomorphize about his purposes, I sketch the path on a piece of paper. . . .
>
> Viewed as a geometric figure, the ant's path is irregular, complex, hard to describe. But its complexity is really a complexity in the surface of the beach, not a complexity in the ant. On that same beach another small creature with a home at the same place as the ant might well follow a very similar path. (Simon, 1981, pp. 63–64)

As in the ant's journey across the beach, much of the complexity in people's thinking reflects the complexity of the environment they are thinking about, rather than any special characteristics of the people themselves. Only through a detailed analysis of the demands of particular tasks can cognitive activity be understood, since so much of thinking is determined by what task the individual is trying to do. In situations where people cannot solve problems effectively, task analyses play a different but equally important role. By indicating what processing is required, such task analyses provide a background against which to evaluate exactly where the processing difficulty lies. Thus, task analyses can help distinguish actions that people take because the actions are adaptive for that task, from actions that they take because of the inadequacy of their information-processing capabilities.

In summary, the **information-processing approach** *emphasizes that thinking is information processing, stresses the processes involved in thinking (such as memory, concept formation, and problem solving in particular contexts), focuses on precise analysis of change mechanisms, and advocates careful task analyses.*

Comparing the Information-Processing and Piagetian Approaches

What is the relation of the information-processing approach to the Piagetian approach? The two approaches have quite a bit in common. Both try to identify children's cognitive capabilities and limits at various points in development. Both try to describe the ways in which children do and do not understand important concepts at different points in life and try to explain how later, more-advanced understandings grow out of earlier, more-primitive ones. Both emphasize the impact that existing understandings can have on children's ability to acquire new understandings.

The two approaches also differ in important ways, though. Information-processing theories place greater emphasis on the role of processing limitations, strategies for overcoming the limitations, and knowledge about specific content. They also focus more on precise analyses of change and on the contribution of ongoing cognitive activity to that change. These differences have led to a greater use of formal descriptions, such as computer simulations and flow diagrams, that allow information-processing theorists to model in detail how thinking proceeds.

Recent studies that have explored particular cognitive changes in precise ways converge on several conclusions (Kuhn, 1995; Siegler, 1991, 1996): Individual children often think about a given phenomenon in multiple ways. They inconsistently apply new ways of thinking, even when they have previously applied the new way of thinking successfully on an identical problem. The child's discovery of new ways of thinking is a frequent rather than a rare event.

A final difference is that information-processing theories assume that our understanding of how children think can be greatly enriched by knowledge of how adults think. The underlying belief is that just as we can more deeply understand our own adult thinking when we appreciate how it developed during childhood, we also can better understand the development of children's thinking when we know where the development is heading.

Information-processing analyses have been applied to numerous areas of children's thinking. Among the most prominent are memory, conceptual development, problem solving, and academic skills such as reading and mathematics. Below we discuss some of the key findings in each of these areas of children's thinking.

MEMORY

Our discussion of memory in children's development includes the following topics: the nature of memory, time frames of memory, schemas, basic processes, memory strategies, metacognitive knowledge, and content knowledge.

What Is Memory?

There are few moments when children's lives are not steeped in memory. Memory is at work with each step children take, each thought they think, and each word they utter. Without memory, virtually all learning and thinking would be impossible. **Memory** *is the retention of information over time. It is central to information processing.* It is no accident that so many popular stories focus on

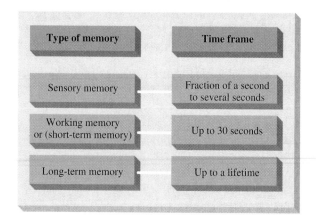

Figure~8.1

Time Frames of Memory

amnesiacs, people who have lost their memories. If people cannot remember their past, they don't know who they are. Lose your memory and you lose your identity!

> *Life is all memory, except for the one present moment that goes by you so quick you hardly catch it going.*
>
> —Tennessee Williams,
> **The Milk Train Doesn't Stop Here Anymore, 1963**

Time Frames of Memory

We remember some information for less than a second, some for half a minute, and other information for minutes, hours, years, even a lifetime. In terms of time frames, there are three types of memory: *sensory memory* (with time frames of a fraction of a second to several seconds), *working memory* (often called short-term memory—with time frames of up to about 30 seconds), and *long-term memory* (with time frames of up to a lifetime) (see figure 8.1).

Sensory Memory

Sensory memory *holds information from the world in its original sensory form for only an instant, not much longer than the information is exposed to the visual, auditory, and other senses.* Sensory memory is rich and detailed, but the information in it is quickly lost unless certain processes are engaged that transfer it into working or long-term memory.

Stimulation from the outside environment first enters the cognitive system through the senses. For example, when a child reads a word, a pattern of horizontal, vertical, and oblique lines and curves enter the child's sensory memory. The sensory memories of children as young as 5 years old have the same capacity as those of adults (Morrison, Holmes, & Haith, 1974). However, young children form sensory-level representations at a slower speed than adults do. Under ideal viewing conditions, adults can represent objects at a sensory level for 1/10 of a second, while 7-year-olds take about 1/7 of a second to form similar representations (Hoving & others, 1978). Although this difference is small, when multiplied by the huge amount of sensory-level processing that people do every day, the differences likely have large cumulative effects.

Working Memory (Short-Term Memory) and Long-Term Memory

Working memory (short-term memory) *is a limited-capacity memory system in which information is retained for as long as 30 seconds, unless the information is rehearsed, in which case it can be retained longer.* **Long-term memory** *is a relatively permanent type of memory that holds huge amounts of information for a long period of time.*

Working memory and long-term memory develop differently. The capacity of long-term memory seems to be unlimited throughout development. By contrast, as children develop, they become able to hold increasing amounts of information in working memory.

One way to illustrate the growth of working, or short-term, memory is to present children of different ages with memory tasks. If you have taken an intelligence test, you probably were exposed to one of these tasks. A short list of stimuli, usually digits, is presented at a rapid pace (for example, one item per second). Using this type of memory-span task, researchers have found that short-term memory increases over time in childhood (Case, 1985; Dempster, 1981). The increase is from about two digits in 2- to 3-year-old children, to about five digits in 7-year-old children, to about seven digits in 12- to 13-year-old children. Not every child of a given age has the same short-term memory capacity, however, which is why these items are often used on intelligence tests. In general, children who have larger short-term memory spans do better in school than do their counterparts of the same age who have smaller spans (Siegler, 1991).

Just as the capacity of short-term memory increases with age, so does the speed of processing (Pressley & Schneider, 1997). This has been the finding with virtually every task that has been used to study memory. For example, children are sometimes shown two shapes, such as those in figure 8.2, and asked whether the shape on the left is just a rotated form of the shape on the right or whether they are different shapes. For children and adults of all ages, the greater the amount of rotation, the longer it takes to tell that the shapes are the same (on trials in which they are the same). However, the rate of rotation is slower for younger children and gradually increases with age, reaching adultlike levels only at about 15 years of age.

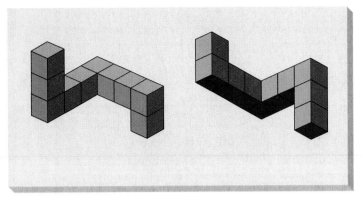

Figure~8.2

Cubes Used to Study Mental Rotation Abilities
Both children and adults attempt to determine whether the Lego-like figures are identical by rotating one of them into the same orientation as the other. For all age groups, the more discrepant the initial position of the two figures, the longer this rotation process takes. However, from age 5 to adulthood, the older the individual, the faster their rate of mental rotation.

Because the growth of processing speed is similar on many different tasks, some investigators have concluded that the speedup reflects a basic maturation of the central nervous system (Hale, 1990; Kail, 1993). Other researchers have reviewed the same data and concluded that they reflect the greater amount of practice that older children engage in, rather than changes in physiological maturation (Stigler, Nusbaum, & Chalip, 1988).

Developmental changes in processing speed are intertwined with changes in processing capacity. For example, in one study, the faster that 6-year-olds repeated auditorially presented words, the longer their memory spans for those words were (Case, Kurland, & Goldberg, 1982). When speed of word presentation was controlled, though, the memory spans of the 6-year-olds were equal to those of young adults. Thus, the greater memory spans usually observed in older children might be due in large part to the fact that older children can process the material more quickly.

Schemas

Although the capacity of long-term memory does not seem to develop, substantial development occurs in the contents of memories. These contents are organized entities rather than isolated bits of information. Much of the information is organized into **schemas**—*concepts and knowledge about events that influence how an individual interprets new information.* For example, someone who has a restaurant schema knows that, at most restaurants, a diner goes to a certain location in the front of the restaurant and waits for a host or hostess to lead the diner to a seat, the diner is then brought a menu, the diner looks at the menu and selects what to eat, next a waiter or waitress comes to take the order, and so on. Without such schemas, individuals would have little idea of what to

Setting	1	Once there was a big gray fish named Albert.
	2	He lived in a pond near the edge of a forest.
Initiating event	3	One day Albert was swimming around the pond.
	4	Then he spotted a big juicy worm on top of the water.
Internal response	5	Albert knew how delicious worms tasted.
	6	He wanted to eat that one for his dinner.
Attempt	7	So he swam very close to the worm.
	8	Then he bit into him.
Consequence	9	Suddenly, Albert was pulled through the water into a boat.
	10	He had been caught by a fisherman.
Reaction	11	Albert felt sad.
	12	He wished he had been more careful.

Figure~8.3

"Albert, the Fish," a Representative Story

Simple stories have structure; after reading or hearing about enough stories, children develop a strong expectation about what kind of information will be contained in a story. That expectation is a story schema.

do in a restaurant or in other contexts, and would not be able to accurately anticipate the sequence of events and prepare for them.

Schemas influence the way children encode, make inferences about, and retrieve information from memory. Children have schemas for stories, scenes, spatial layouts (a bathroom or a park, for example), and common events (such as going to a restaurant, playing with toys, or practicing the piano), and for sociocultural dimensions such as gender and ethnicity (Levy & Katz, 1993).

What experiences lead children to form schemas? Some schemas come from everyday experience, especially experience in which the same basic events recur in different contexts. Others come from the stories children are told and that they read. Simple stories have a structure; after hearing enough stories, children develop a strong expectation about what kind of information will be contained in a story. This expectation is called a *story schema.* For example, a story tells about what happens in a particular place and time. The context is called the setting. A story has at least one main character, the protagonist, who attempts to achieve a purposeful goal for a clear reason. The protagonist's actions are usually captured in one or more episodes of the story, which can be further broken down and distilled into a fairly simple, one-episode story (see figure 8.3).

From a very young age, children are able to use structures like these to fill in information, remember better, and tell relatively coherent stories (Ackerman, 1988). Changes

occur throughout childhood, though, in children's ability to identify salient events in stories, to unscramble mixed-up stories, and to keep multiple plot lines straight in their minds when they face complex stories that have several episodes and more than one major character. Thus, a substantial part of the changes that occur with age in the contents of a long-term memory involve elaborations of existing schemas and the addition of new ones.

A **script** *is a schema that focuses on the order of a predictable series of events.* The series of restaurant events described earlier is an example of a script. Children's first scripts appear very early in development, perhaps as early as the first year of life. Children clearly have scripts by the time they enter school (Gomez & Thompson, 1993).

As children develop, their scripts become more sophisticated. For example, a 4-year-old's script for a restaurant might include only information about sitting down and eating food. In middle and late childhood, the child adds information to the restaurant script about the types of people who serve food, about paying the cashier, and so on. The process of elaborating this type of information in long-term memory continues throughout life.

In addition to these general characteristics of working (or short-term) and long-term memory, memory development includes a number of more-specific processes. These processes can be divided into the following types: basic processes, strategies, metacognitive knowledge, and content knowledge.

Basic Processes—Habituation, Automaticity, and Attention

Basic processes are the building blocks upon which all of the rest of memory is based. These basic processes tend to be present from the first days of infancy and to be used in a wide range of activities involved in learning and remembering. Among the most important basic processes are habituation, automaticity, and attention.

Habituation

Studying the memory processes of infants poses special problems. Unlike older individuals, infants cannot tell us what they remember, cannot follow task instructions, and in the first 6 months cannot even sit up unaided. Thus, for a long time little was known about their memories.

Although infants cannot do many things, they can do one seemingly unimportant thing that has proved to have important consequences—they can get bored. In particular, like all of us, they become bored if they are presented the same stimulus over and over, and show renewed interest if the situation changes. Thus, if a stimulus involving a sight or a sound is presented to an infant several times in a row, the infant usually pays less attention to it each time. This is the process of **habituation,** *the repeated presentation of a stimulus that causes reduced attention to the stimulus.* **Dishabituation** *is renewed interest in a stimulus.* If infants do not recognize the difference in stimuli, they will not show any renewed interest. Thus, if infants can code and remember an aspect of a situation that is being repeated, they will look at it for less and less time. Such decreased looking time is evidence that they coded and remembered the repeated aspect of the situation.

The usefulness of the habituation paradigm for studying infant memory is evident in studies of individual differences in infants. Infants who are destined to have higher IQs when they are 6 to 9 years of age habituate more rapidly as 6-month-olds, and dishabituate more completely in response to new stimuli, than do infants destined to have lower IQs (Bornstein & Sigman, 1986). This link might reflect more-intelligent infants' encoding stimuli more effectively and thus recognizing earlier that they have seen a certain stimulus but that they have not seen the new, somewhat different stimulus presented in the dishabituation trials.

Newborn infants can habituate to repetitive stimulation in every stimulus modality: vision, audition, touch, and so on (Rovee-Collier, 1987). However, habituation becomes more acute during the first 3 months of life. The extensive assessment of habituation in recent years has resulted in its use as a measure of an infant's maturity and well-being. Infants who have brain damage or have suffered birth traumas, such as lack of oxygen, do not habituate well and later may have developmental and learning problems.

A knowledge of habituation and dishabituation can also benefit parent-infant interaction. Infants respond to changes in stimulation. If a parent repeats a stimulation often, the infant's response will decrease to the point that the infant no longer responds to the parent. In parent-infant interaction, it is important for parents to do novel things and to repeat them until the infant grows less interested. The wise parent senses when the infant shows an interest and realizes that many repetitions of the stimulus may be necessary for the infant to process the information. The parent stops or changes behaviors when the infant redirects her attention (Rosenblith, 1992).

Until as recently as a decade ago, it was widely believed that infants and children younger than 3 years of age could not recall events that occurred earlier in their lives. Several developments, including findings of representational competence in infants in the first year of life and evidence of long-term recall abilities in children as young as 3, have led to revision of this assumption (Bauer, 1996).

Before we leave our discussion of infant memory, a few comments about some of the ingenious ways researchers study infant memory are in order. In Patricia Bauer's research (Bauer & Dow, 1994; Bauer & Hertsgaard, 1993), a technique called "elicited imitation" is used to assess infant memory. In this technique, props are used to produce a specific event that the child then is given the opportunity to imitate. Children's nonverbal reproduction of the event, rather than their verbal description of it, serves as the measure of recall. Using this technique, it has been found that 13-month-old infants remember specific events over the very short term (immediately after seeing them modeled) and after a 1-week delay. Also, 21-month-old infants remember events from 8 months earlier.

In her study of habituation, Carolyn Rovee-Collier (1987) placed a baby in a crib underneath an elaborate mobile, tied one of the baby's ankles to the mobile with a ribbon, then observed as the baby kicked to make the mobile move. Weeks later, the baby was returned to the crib, under the mobile, but its foot was not tied to the mobile. The baby tried to move the mobile again by kicking its foot, apparently remembering the earlier effects of its kicking (see figure 8.4). However, if the mobile's makeup is changed even slightly, the baby does not kick at it. Then as soon as the familiar and expected are brought back into the context, the baby remembers and begins kicking.

In another study, infants were laid in large black boxes where they looked up at television screens and viewed a sequence of colorful objects (Canfield & Haith, 1991). The babies' eye movements were monitored with an infrared camera linked to a computer. After only five tries the babies anticipated where the next object would appear. With just a little more practice, they predicted a four-step sequence, and most could remember it up to 2 weeks later!

In sum, the capacity for memory appears much earlier in infancy than was once believed, and it is also more precise than earlier conclusions suggested. Figure 8.5 shows another strategy contemporary researchers are using to assess infants' memories.

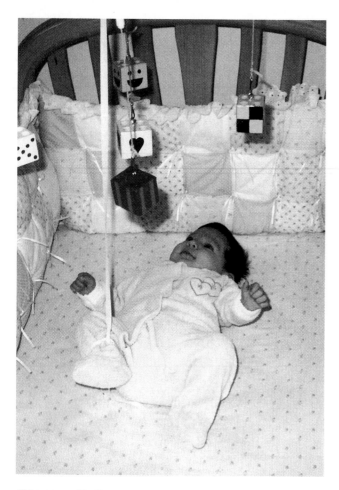

Figure~8.4

The Technique Used in Rovee-Collier's Investigation of Infant Memory
The mobile is connected to the infant's ankle by the ribbon and moves in direct proportion to the frequency and vigor of the infant's kicks.

Automaticity

Automaticity *is the ability to process information with little or no effort.* It is evident when a bright 4-year-old, while thinking about his teddy bear rather than about taking off and putting on clothing, takes off his pajamas in the morning and puts on the clothes his mother laid out for him. It is also present when an able 10-year-old zips through a practice list of single-digit addition problems (for example, 5 + 8) with little conscious effort.

By comparison, if each of these activities had been done by younger and less experienced children, they would have demanded more careful attention and conscious control. For any given task, such as calculating, reading, or writing, *automaticity* improves dramatically as children get older (Keating, 1990; Siegler, 1991). Automaticity is linked to speed and processing capacity; as an activity is completed faster, it requires less processing capacity. As processing capacity increases, it becomes easier to complete tasks that were previously considered to be difficult.

Attention

Although children can perform some activities automatically, many others require them to pay **attention,** *which means concentrating and focusing mental resources.* One quality that is critical is the successful deployment of attention selectivity. **Selective attention** *is the ability to focus mental effort on the stimuli that are important in a particular situation (such as test questions) while excluding other stimuli (such as other children throwing erasers at each other).* When selective attention fails, children have difficulty ignoring information that is irrelevant to their interests or goals (Posner & Rothbart, 1989). For example, if a television set or stereo is blaring while a child is studying, the child may have difficulty concentrating.

Effective deployment of attention requires not only selectivity but also *flexibility.* If a teacher asks students a new question, they must shift their attention from where it was before to the new question. An external stimulus is not necessary to elicit a shift in attention. At any moment children can shift their attention from one topic to another, virtually at will. They might think about the last time they played basketball, then think about the last time they took a test, then think about the upcoming piano lesson, and so on.

How does ability to effectively deploy attention develop? Attention is clearly related to habituation. Thus, when an infant habituates to a stimulus, it is stopping paying attention to it, and when the infant dishabituates, it is showing renewed attention. Although the infant's attention has important implications for later cognitive development, significant changes also take place well beyond infancy (Pillow, 1988; Ruff & Lawson, 1990). The toddler wanders around, shifting attention from one activity to another, usually seeming to spend little time focused on any one object or event. By comparison, the preschool child might be observed watching "Barney" or "Sesame Street" for a half hour or more at a time.

Although preschool children's ability to pay attention exceeds that of infants, it is still quite fragile. One particular problem during the preschool years concerns the ability to focus on the aspects of a situation that are important, rather than those that are attention-grabbing. For example, a problem might have a flashy, attractive clown that presents the directions for solving the problem. Preschool children are influenced strongly by the features of the task that stand out, such as the flashy, attractive clown. They might focus on the clown to the exclusion of the instructions the clown is giving. This is a particular problem in teaching preschoolers and early elementary children to read in books with attractive pictures—they often pay attention to the pictures to the exclusion of the written material. After the age of 6 or 7, children attend more efficiently to the dimensions of the task that are

Figure~8.5

A Research Technique to Study Infant Memory
In researcher Mark Johnson's laboratory at Carnegie Mellon University, babies have shown an ability to organize their world and to anticipate future events by learning and remembering sequences of colorful images on TV monitors.

relevant, such as the directions for solving a problem. Developmentalists believe that this change reflects a shift to cognitive control of attention so that children act less precipitously and reflect more (Paris & Lindauer, 1982).

Ability to deploy attention selectively and flexibly continues to improve well into the elementary school years. In the classroom, children are able to observe the teacher for increasing lengths of time, and they become able to pore over their books for longer periods of independent study. These feats exceed what could be expected of preschoolers. The changes in durability of attention have a dramatic influence on children's learning. For example, learning to write good stories requires ability to effectively shift attention among the competing goals of forming the letters, grammar and punctuation, paragraph structure, and conveying the story as a whole. As children develop, they become increasingly able to shift attention effectively among these competing goals (Beal, 1990).

Memory Strategies

Strategies *are cognitive processes that do not occur automatically but require work and effort. They are under the learner's conscious control and can be used to improve memory*

(Intons-Peterson, 1996). Four important strategies that improve children's memory are rehearsal, organization, elaboration, and imagery.

Rehearsal

Rehearsal *is extended repetition of material after it has been presented.* If someone tells a child to remember a phone number, how might the child remember it more effectively? A classic study by John Flavell and his colleagues (Flavell, Beach, & Chinsky, 1966) illustrates the importance of rehearsal and developmental changes in its use. Children from 5 to 10 years old were given the task of remembering the names of a set of two to five pictures for 15 seconds. The novel feature of the experiment was that the experimenter was a trained lip-reader. Although not many children said anything aloud, a number of children made lip movements that indicated rehearsal of names and pictures. The percentage of children making lip movements increased with age: 10 percent of the 5-year-olds, 60 percent of the 7-year-olds, and 85 percent of the 10-year-olds made lip movements. In a later study of 6-year-olds, the research team found that children who rehearsed showed better recall than those who did not. When nonrehearsers were taught to rehearse, their performance rivaled that of the spontaneous rehearsers (Keeney, Cannizzo, & Flavell, 1967).

Cognitive developmentalist John Flavell has been a pioneer in providing insights into the ways in which children think.

My thoughts are my company; I can bring them together, select them, detain them, dismiss them.

—**Walter Savage Landor**

Subsequent investigations made the interesting point that rudimentary, rehearsal-like processes begin to appear at very young ages (DeLoache, Cassidy, & Brown, 1985). In one study, 3- and 4-year-old children watched a toy dog being hidden under one of three cups. Instructed to remember where the dog was hidden, the children looked at, pointed to, and touched the appropriate cup (Wellman, Ritter, & Flavell, 1985). Even 1½-year-olds, under certain circumstances, use rehearsal—when they see an object hidden in a room, they will point to it, touch it, and repeat its name while they wait to be able to retrieve it (DeLoache, 1984).

If using rehearsal is so helpful in remembering, why do young children so often not rehearse? One simple reason is that young children both benefit less and incur greater costs by using the strategy than do older children. When children begin to use rehearsal (and other new strategies), executing the new strategy requires greater mental resources than it will later (Kee & Howell, 1988). Similarly, when the experimental procedure makes it easier to execute the strategy, the difference between the performances produced by older and younger children's use of the strategy decreases (DeMarie-Dreblow & Miller, 1988). The point is that children need a reasonable amount of experience with a strategy before they can gain the full potential benefit from using it.

A second reason why young children tend not to rehearse, even when they have been taught to do so and have benefited from doing so, is that they often attribute their success to other factors—luck, greater effort, or being smart. Those children who attribute their success to the new strategy they used tend to use it again in the future, but those who think other factors were responsible tend not to use the new approach again (Fabricius & Hagen, 1984).

Organization

Organization *is the grouping or arranging of items into categories. The use of organization improves long-term memory.* Children show increased organization in middle and late childhood. In one investigation, children were presented with a circular array of pictures from four categories: clothing, furniture, animals, and vehicles (Moely & others, 1969). The children were told to study the pictures so that later they could say their names back to the experimenter. They also were told they could move the pictures around to remember them better. The 10- and 11-year-olds performed such groupings; the younger children did not. When younger children were put through a brief training procedure that encouraged grouping, they were able to follow this strategy, and their memory for the pictures improved.

The development of organizational strategies in many ways parallels that of rehearsal. Organization is used far less often by 5- and 6-year-olds than by 9- and 10-year-olds and older children. The quality of the younger children's execution of the strategy is also lower than that of older ones. Executing the strategy also requires more of the younger children's cognitive resources, so it often yields poorer recall among younger than among older children (Bjorklund & Harnishfeger, 1987). Thus, it is not altogether surprising that young children use these strategies less often than older children do—they have more difficulty executing the strategies, and realize smaller benefits from using them.

Elaboration

Elaboration *involves going beyond the information given in order to make information more memorable.* Good students often use elaboration when they study for a test. For instance, they read examples in physics books, and then explain to themselves in a more elaborate way what they have read (Chi & others, 1989). Such elaborations frequently will involve relating the examples to material presented earlier in the textbook, commonsense reasoning, and other attempts to make sense of the material. Students who engage in such active elaboration remember more of the material and do better on subsequent tests than do students who read the material and just try to remember it verbatim (Chi, Slotta, & de Leeuw, 1994).

Self-reference in which people relate a word to a context that is meaningful within their own lives, is another effective way of using elaboration to enhance memory. For example, if the word *win* is on a list of words that children need to remember, they might think of the last time they won a bicycle race with a friend. If the word *cook* appears, they might imagine the last time their father cooked dinner. In general, elaboration is an excellent way to remember.

One reason why elaboration enhances memory is that it adds to the distinctiveness of the memory code (Ellis, 1987). To remember a piece of information, such as a name, an experience, or a fact about geography, a child needs to search for the code that contains this information among the mass of codes in the child's long-term memory. The search process is easier if the code is somehow unique. The situation is like that of a child searching for a friend in a crowded park. If the child's friend has a highly distinctive appearance, the child will more easily find the friend in the park. Similarly, highly distinctive memory codes are more easily differentiated from other memory codes.

As children get older, they are more likely to use elaboration without being instructed to do so (Schneider & Bjorklund, 1997). There are especially impressive increases in the use of elaboration from late childhood to late adolescence (Schneider & Pressley, 1989). Elementary-school-age children are less likely to use elaboration spontaneously, but they benefit considerably from being taught to use it to remember.

Imagery

Imagine walking up the sidewalk to your house, opening the door, and going inside. What do you see when you are standing inside the door? Now mentally walk through the house to a room in the back and form a picture of what this room is like. Now picture your bedroom in the house. Where is your bed in relation to the door? Imagining these things is reasonably easy for most adults and children.

Imagery *involves sensations without the presence of corresponding external stimuli. Imagery is another strategy that helps individuals to improve their memory.* The **keyword method** *is an imagery strategy that uses vivid imagery of important words, or keywords, to improve memory.* This method has been used to practical advantage in teaching children how to rapidly master new information, such as foreign vocabulary words, the states and capitals of the United States, and the names of presidents of the United States. For example, in teaching children that Annapolis is the capital of Maryland, instructors taught the children the keywords for the states, such that when a state (Maryland) was given, the children could supply the keyword (*marry*). Then, children were given the reverse type of keyword practice with the capitals. That is, they had to respond with the capital (Annapolis) when given a keyword (*apple*). Finally, an illustration was provided (see figure 8.6). The

Figure~8.6

The Keyword Method
To help children remember the state capitals, the keyword method was used. A special component of the keyword method is the use of mental imagery, which was stimulated by presenting the children with a vivid visual image, such as two apples being married. The strategy is to help the children associate *apple* with Annapolis and *marry* with Maryland.

keyword strategy's use of vivid mental imagery, such as the image in figure 8.6, was effective in increasing children's memory of state capitals. Developmentalists today encourage the use of imagery in our nation's schools, believing it helps increase children's memory (McDaniel & Pressley, 1987). To further evaluate memory strategies, turn to Critical Thinking About Children's Development.

Metacognitive Knowledge

Metacognitive knowledge *is knowledge about how the human mind works.* Metacognitive knowledge can be subdivided roughly into knowledge about *persons* (oneself as well as other human beings), *tasks*, and *strategies*.

Metacognitive knowledge about *persons* includes such insights as the following (Yussen & Levy, 1975):

1. People, including me, have limits to the amount of information they can process. It is not possible to deal with all of the information that comes my way. If I worry too much about this, I will feel the stress of information overload.

2. I am better at doing some things than at other things (for example, I am better at reading than arithmetic, and better at verbalizing than imaging events).

3. I can handle information better in some states (for example, when I am relaxed, rested, or happy) than in others (for example, when I am anxious, tired, or sad).

Metacognitive knowledge about *tasks* includes such insights as the following:

1. Some conditions always make it harder or easier to solve a problem or complete a task. For example, the more time available to solve a problem, the better I do. The smaller the number of items to be processed (that is, attended to, remembered, perceived, and so on), the easier it is for me to do.

2. Some tasks are harder than others. It is easier to understand what someone says than to explain the same message to someone else. It is easier to read something than to explain the main ideas contained in the reading. Tests of recall (for example, retrieving previously learned information, as on an essay test) are more difficult than tests of recognition (for example, merely identifying, or "recognizing," previously learned items, as on a multiple-choice test.

3. I cannot complete some tasks. For example, the tasks might require knowledge that I do not have and cannot obtain, or the tasks might require a highly developed skill that I have not yet mastered (such as a different language, use of a tool or social skill).

Metacognitive knowledge about *strategies* includes such insights as the following:

1. Some cognitive steps will be useful across a wide range of cognitive tasks (remembering, communicating, reading, and so on). Among these are some aspects of problem solving, such as establishing goals, planning one's approach, and monitoring the progress one is making.

2. Particular cognitive tasks require specific strategies, in addition to the general steps, if a person is to maximize performance. Thus, to remember something, the strategies of rehearsal,

organization, elaboration, and imagery are often very helpful. However, to communicate adequately, it might be more important to state the message in several different ways to the listener and to focus on the listener's signals of comprehension or miscomprehension.

3. Some strategies are more effective than others with a particular task. For example, it generally is easier to master a lengthy list of names by using the imagery keyword method than by rehearsing the names using simple repetition (Levin, 1980). Also, one studies more effectively for a test by focusing only on the material to be included on it than by reviewing everything covered in the course.

Many developmentalists believe that metacognitive knowledge is beneficial in school learning and that this knowledge possibly can be taught to students (especially younger ones) who are deficient in it (Slawinski & Best, 1995). Several researchers have developed school programs to impart metacognitive knowledge to children in the areas of reading comprehension, writing, and mathematics.

Content Knowledge

Children's ability to remember new information about a subject depends extensively on what they already know about it (Albro, 1993). For example, if a girl makes a trip to a toy store, her ability to recount what she saw is largely governed by what she already knows about toy stores and the things found there. With little knowledge about what is usually found in a toy store, the child would have a much harder time recounting what was there.

The contribution of content knowledge to memory is especially evident in examining the memory of experts, people who have unusually great knowledge about a topic. These experts often demonstrate especially impressive memory in their areas of expertise. One reason why children generally remember less than adults do is that they are far less expert in most areas. This has led to

Although in some ways children are universal novices, some children have high levels of skill in chess.

their being referred to as "universal novices" (Brown & DeLoache, 1978). A novice is the opposite of an expert, someone who is just beginning to learn about an area.

> *Knowledge is power.*
> —**Francis Bacon**

In those areas where children are experts, their memory is often extremely good. In fact, it often exceeds that of adults who are novices in that content domain. One memorable example was provided in a study of 10-year-old chess experts (Chi, 1978). These children were strong chess players, but were not especially brilliant in other ways. When their memory spans for digits were contrasted with those of adults, they, like most 10-year-olds, remembered fewer of the numbers. However, when they were presented chess boards, they remembered the configurations far better than the adults who were novices at chess did.

Similar results have been obtained with German children who were more or less expert at soccer. Young experts with relatively low IQs remembered more about stories about hypothetical soccer games than did children who were not soccer experts and who were older or peers with higher IQs (Schneider, Korkel, & Weinart, 1989). Older children and children with higher IQs may become experts more quickly, but once expertise is acquired, even younger and lower-IQ children remember material in that area extremely well.

What is it that makes experts' memory for new material so good? Schneider's study of the soccer experts provides a strong clue. It is not that the children have high IQs or generally superior memory skills—remember that the low-IQ soccer experts remembered more about the soccer stories than did the high-IQ nonexperts. Nor is it anything else having to do with general developmental level; if it were, the older children would have done better than the younger children did. Instead, the key factor was knowledge about the content of the particular domain. These children knew a lot about soccer. This told them that they should remember the game in terms of the two halves, that there would be relatively few goals, that players playing certain positions were the ones most likely to make the goals, and other key information that allowed much easier remembering.

Is there certain content knowledge that people should know? In some cultures, children are required to

The ability to remember new information about a subject depends extensively on what children already know about it. In the study of German children's memory for soccer information, the children already knew a lot about soccer.

CONCEPT TABLE 8.1

The Information-Processing Approach and Memory

Concept	Processes/ Related Ideas	Characteristics/Description
The Information-Processing Approach	Its nature	This approach emphasizes that thinking is information processing. The processes involved in thinking include memory, concept formation, and problem solving. This approach emphasizes analysis of change mechanisms and careful task analyses.
	Comparison with the Piagetian approach	Both the information-processing approach and the Piagetian approach try to identify children's cognitive capacities and limits at various points in development. The two approaches also have other similarities. However, the information-processing approach places more importance than Piaget's approach does on processing limitations, strategies for overcoming limitations, and knowledge about specific content. It also focuses more on precise analyses of change than Piaget's approach does.
Memory	What is memory?	Memory is the retention of information over time. It is central to information processing.
	Time frames of memory	Sensory memory holds information in its original sensory form for only an instant. Working memory (also called short-term memory) is a limited-capacity memory system in which information is retained as long as 30 seconds unless the information is rehearsed, in which case it can be retained longer. Long-term memory is a relatively permanent type of memory that holds huge amounts of information for a long period of time. Working memory and long-term memory differ in their development. The capacity of long-term memory seems to be unlimited throughout development. By contrast, as children develop, they become able to hold increasing amounts of information in working memory. Just as the capacity of short-term memory increases, so does the speed of processing.
	Schemas	Schemas are concepts and knowledge about events that influence how an individual interprets information. A script is a schema that focuses on the order of a predictable series of events. As children develop, their schemas and scripts become more sophisticated.
	Basic processes	Among the important basic processes that serve as building blocks for memory are habituation, automaticity, and attention. Habituation is the repeated presentation of a stimulus that causes reduced attention to the stimulus (by contrast, dishabituation is renewed interest in a stimulus). Newborn infants can habituate. Automaticity is the ability to process information with little or no effort. Automaticity improves dramatically as children get older. Attention means concentrating and focusing mental resources. Selective attention is the ability to focus mental effort on stimuli that are important in a particular situation while excluding other stimuli. Effective deployment of attention requires not only selectivity but also flexibility. Ability to deploy attention selectively and flexibly continues to improve well into the elementary school years.
	Memory strategies	Strategies are cognitive processes that do not occur automatically but require work and effort. They are under the learner's conscious control and can be used to improve memory. Four important strategies that can improve children's memory are rehearsal, organization, elaboration, and imagery.
	Metacognitive knowledge	Metacognitive knowledge is knowledge about how the human mind works. It can roughly be subdivided into knowledge about persons, tasks, and strategies.
	Content knowledge	Children's ability to remember new information about a subject depends extensively on what they already know about it. The contribution of content knowledge is especially evident in the memory of experts, who have unusually great knowledge about a topic.

memorize huge amounts of information. For example, in Iran children must memorize large blocks of cultural and religious texts. Iranians are often surprised at how little Americans seem to know.

At this point we have discussed a number of ideas about the nature of the information-processing approach and memory. A summary of these ideas is presented in concept table 8.1.

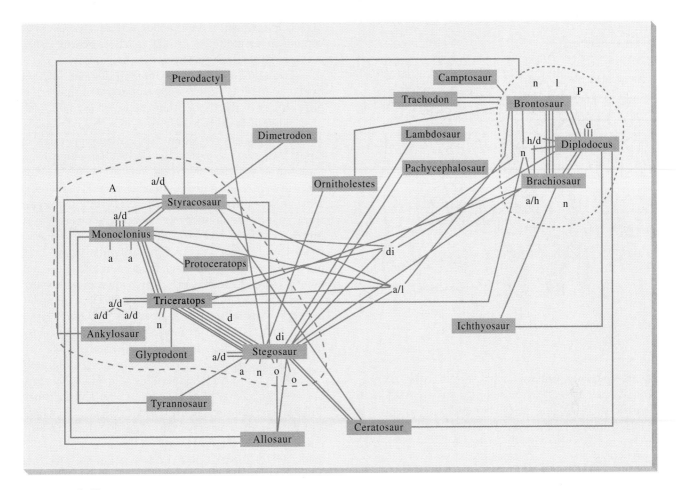

Figure~8.7

A 4-Year-Old Expert's Semantic Network for Dinosaurs

CONCEPTUAL DEVELOPMENT

The expertise that allows child experts often to remember better than adult novices is based in large part on sophisticated understanding of key concepts in a domain. This conceptual understanding was evident in an investigation of a 4-year-old dinosaur expert (Chi & Koeske, 1983). Like many children his age, this young boy enjoyed hearing stories about dinosaurs and examining picture books of dinosaurs. Unlike most children, however, he was able to name at least forty-six dinosaurs and could identify at least one, and often many, features of each (for example, whether it ate plants or flew).

Figure 8.7 shows a mapping of the boy's knowledge about dinosaurs. This type of diagram is called a **semantic network**—*the network of relations among the key concepts in an individual's representation of a domain.* Although the figure is complicated, some simple points can be gleaned from it. Each line represents a conceptual link, each circled letter represents a dinosaur attribute, and the individual dinosaur names/concepts are included in the boxes. Notice, first, that some dinosaurs are not linked to many others. This is true of Dimetrodon and Pterodactyl.

We would not expect these dinosaurs to be as easily remembered or compared with others by this child, because they are isolated from the others in the semantic network. Notice also that, among the dinosaurs that are linked, some have more links (for example, Styracosaur has more links than Ornitholestes); the dinosaurs with the most links to other information are the ones that represent the child's deepest understanding. In general, the more linkages among a child's concepts, the deeper the child's understanding of the concepts.

Concepts as Implicit Theories

Many of children's concepts embody implicit theories about the world (Carey & Gelman, 1991). Children often are not able to state these theories explicitly, but their use of the concepts shows many of the features characteristic of concepts within the theories of adult scientists.

Frank Keil (1989) proposed an intriguing set of ideas regarding the resemblances between children's concepts and the theories formed by scientists. He suggested that most concepts are partial theories, in the sense that they include explanations of relations among their parts and of their relations to other concepts. Cause-effect relations

Drawing by Koren; © 1986 The New Yorker Magazine, Inc.

play an especially prominent role within children's theories, as they do within those of scientists. Also as in scientific theories, information in children's theories is organized into hierarchies, in which the most general concepts organize somewhat less general ones, which in turn organize yet less general ideas.

These ideas about concepts as implicit theories can be illustrated with a hypothetical example (Siegler, 1991). Suppose a girl who knows nothing about yaks other than that they are animals is asked, "Why do yaks have four legs rather than three or five?" She might think about how other four-legged large animals, such as horses and cows, run and then answer that four legs can be moved in pairs, which allows yaks to run quickly yet still maintain their balance. This answer would illustrate that the child had a theory that emphasized the causal relation between the number of legs that an animal has and the ways in which it can move. The answer also illustrates the hierarchical organization of the child's conceptual understanding. Despite not knowing anything in particular about yaks except that they are animals, she can reason that number of legs affects movements in all animals, and therefore that it must in yaks as well.

Theoretical understanding of concepts helps young children see deep similarities that go beyond superficial appearances. For example, when 3- and 4-year-olds are told a fact that they previously did not know, their theoretical knowledge leads them to generalize the information to members of the same category rather than to objects that just share similar appearances (Gelman & Markman, 1987). Thus, when told that brown oil floats to the top when put into water, preschoolers expect other types of oil that look different to react in the same way, but expect different substances that look like the brown

oil (such as brown honey) to act differently. Such conceptual understanding is critical in helping children draw accurate generalizations from their experience.

Even infants might form implicit theories. Elizabeth Spelke and her colleagues (1992) proposed that infants begin life with the theory that the world is composed of physical objects that are cohesive, have boundaries, and continue to exist even when they can no longer be seen. One source of evidence for this view is that 4-month-olds look for a long time when an object appears to move through a space occupied by another object (Baillargeon, 1987). This does not mean that infants know everything there is to know about the objects; clearly, learning about objects, like other types of concept formation, is a lifelong process. Spelke's point is that in this and a number of other fundamental domains, infants have rudimentary understandings that provide a platform from which they can build further knowledge. Thus, for Spelke, conceptual development is a process of theory enrichment, in which the basic theories with which infants begin life are gradually fleshed out and enriched.

Just as scientific theories are organized hierarchically, with some applying very broadly and others more narrowly, so might children's theories be. Thus, although children might possess many specific theories, they might also possess a few very general ones that apply to broad ranges of phenomena. Henry Wellman and Susan Gelman (1992) proposed that children begin life with three grand theories—a theory of the mind (naive psychology), a theory of the physical world (naive physics), and a theory of living things (naive biology). They further proposed that much of early conceptual development involves elaborating these three theories. Let's now further explore these theories.

Concepts of the Mind

From early in infancy, children interact differently with people than with animals, plants, or inanimate objects in their environment (DelCielo & others, 1993). This suggests that just as they have some theoretical understanding of the properties of physical objects, they might also have an emerging understanding of the human mind (Ritblatt, 1995; Slaughter, 1995). As might be expected, however, their conceptual understanding increases considerably as they develop (Gopnik, 1997).

One of the most basic understandings relevant to the mind is that of **agency,** *the idea that people cause events to happen through motivation that is entirely internal.* Even infants in their first year of life appear to understand that people are agents of their own actions (Poulin-Dubois & Shultz, 1988). This makes them different from inanimate objects such as tables, cars, or plants. The very different ways in which infants interact with people, compared with how they interact with other animals, also suggest that they have implicit knowledge that people differ from other animals.

Henry Wellman (*right*) has significantly improved our knowledge of the young child's understanding of the human mind.

Children's understanding of the human mind grows extensively in the first few years (Wellman, 1997). By the age of 3, children turn some of their thoughts inward and understand that they and others have internal mental states (Flavell, Green, & Flavell, 1995). Beginning at about 3 years of age, children also show an understanding that the internal beliefs and desires of a person are connected to that person's actions (Wellman & Gelman, 1992).

How do children come to have this understanding of their own minds and those of other people? Henry Wellman (1990) proposed that from about 3 years of age children have a naive theory of how the mind works. He labeled this the belief-desire theory. He classified it as a theory because it divides the world into coherent categories, because it explains why events occur, and because it identifies the causal relations between mental states and actions.

In particular, Wellman proposed that from age 3 onward, children have four types of understanding that provide a foundation for their theory of mind:

1. Understanding that minds are different from other objects in the world
2. Understanding that the mind generates both beliefs and desires
3. Understanding of how different types of mental states are related
4. Understanding that the mind is used to represent external reality

Regarding the first point, Wellman demonstrated that most 3-year-olds understand that thoughts, memories, and dreams differ from physical objects and from other insubstantial entities such as smoke and sounds. When 3-year-olds were asked to explain why they could not touch their thoughts, they often advanced explanations such as "Because it's in my mind." They did not explain the difficulty of touching sounds or smoke in this way. The 3-year-olds also knew that beliefs and desires were motivators of action, and that they could lead people to act even when they were incorrect (Wellman & Bartsch, 1988). They also knew that mental entities such as images usually corresponded to an external reality that could be touched, even though the images themselves could not be.

This belief-desire theory of mind appears to develop from an earlier understanding of desire without an understanding of belief. Two-year-olds know that desires influence what people do, but they do not understand that having a belief can lead to an action even when the belief is mistaken (Wellman & Wooley, 1990).

Development of the child's theory of mind also continues beyond 3 years of age (Wellman & Gelman, 1997). One of the most interesting later developments involves children's coming to distinguish between appearance and reality, that is, between what seems to be true and what really is true. In one study, 3- to 5-year-olds were shown sponge-like objects that looked like rocks; then they were encouraged to play with them so that they knew that the sponge rocks were not actual rocks (Flavell, Flavell, & Green, 1983). The preschoolers were then asked what the object looked like and what it "really, really was," and also what the object would look like to another child and what it would "really, really be."

In a series of recent studies, 3- to 5-year old children could distinguish thinking from seeing, talking, touching, and knowing (Flavell, Green, & Flavell, 1995). The young children appear to know that thinking is an internal, mental activity that can refer to either real or imagined objects or events.

Most 4- and 5-year-olds could distinguish between appearances and reality regarding the objects. They knew that the object looked like a rock to them, that it was not really a rock, and that another child who had not played with it would think it was a rock because it looked like one. In contrast, most 3-year-olds confused the appearance with the reality, regarding the rock and other objects that were presented in the same way. For example, they often claimed that a model of an orange that smelled like an orange "really, really" was an orange. Many 3-year-olds also claim that the images on television represent real objects inside the television rather than transmitted images.

What difference does it make how well people understand their own minds and those of other people? Considering the way we play games can help illustrate just how important it is. Regardless of whether we are playing chess, football, poker, or tennis, we analyze our opponents' intentions and beliefs, and vary our own behavior to take advantage of their expectations. Of course, they are doing the same with us, which is what makes playing such games so challenging. Without a theory not only of how minds in general work, but of how the minds of particular opponents work, such games would not be nearly as interesting, and probably would not be played at all.

Biological Concepts

Children of all ages are fascinated by living things. Such words as *doggie* and *kitty* regularly are among the first words that they learn. Even before they learn language, infants will intently watch people and other animals. Part of this is due to their general interest in things that move. However, even compared with inanimate moving things, such as cars and trucks, children appear to be especially interested in things that move and that are living as well. Already during the first year of life, infants distinguish between the types of motion that biological entities tend to make and the types of motion characteristic of things that are not alive; they show special interest in the biological motion (Bertenthal, 1993).

Biological knowledge is complex, and young children have a great deal to learn about it. One key characteristic is growth—unlike nonliving things, biological entities often grow in size in regular, predictable ways. Another key characteristic is consumption of food; all living beings must ingest nutrients in order to produce energy. Another is that despite massive changes in appearance, biological entities keep their identity; the caterpillar before the metamorphosis is the same thing as the butterfly after it. Still another is the consistency of the innards of biological entities; two sofas may have within them entirely different materials, but two cats always have the same basic things inside them.

Even 3- and 4-year-olds have fairly sophisticated biological concepts. They in general realize that plants and animals grow and that other things do not (Inagaki, 1995). They also know that living things inherit many of their properties from their parents, and that subsequent environmental events that alter their appearance do not change these basic properties (Keil, 1989). They also know that animals and plants always have offspring that are of the same species—dogs always have puppies and never kittens. These offspring retain their basic characteristics even if they are raised by another type of animal. For example, 3- and 4-year-olds believe that a rabbit raised by a monkey family will still prefer lettuce rather than bananas (Springer & Keil, 1991).

A great deal of conceptual development occurs beyond this initial understanding of biology. For example, until the early years of schooling, many children do not know that plants as well as animals are living things. The age at which children realize which types of objects are living and which are not depends greatly on the particular culture in which they grow up. Somewhat surprisingly,

in light of the generally poor performance of children in the United States in cross-national comparisons of scientific knowledge, a recent study of kindergartners, second-graders, and fourth-graders in the United States, Israel, and Japan showed that the children in the United States were the most advanced in their understanding of this aspect of biology (Hatano & others, 1993). That is, children from the United States more consistently knew that plants were living things and that impressive, old, inanimate objects such as mountains and rivers were not.

The reasons for the differences among children in the three countries appeared to reside in differences in the three cultures. Israeli children were by far the latest to understand that plants were alive; even Israeli fourth-graders often did not know this. The fact that the Hebrew word for "animal" is almost identical to that for "living thing," whereas the word for "plant" is unrelated, might have been related to these children not knowing that plants as well as animals are living things. Similarly, the strength within Japan of the Buddhist tradition, which ascribes properties of living things to all objects, might have been related to Japanese children's being more likely than Israeli or U.S. children to say that inanimate objects were alive. These differences, together with the higher degree of exposure in the United States to nature-oriented shows on television, may have produced the differences in biological knowledge among children in the three societies.

Physical Concepts

Infants' understanding of key properties of physical objects was described earlier. They know (by some measures) not only that objects continue to exist even when they cannot be seen, but also that all parts of an object move together, that solid objects cannot pass through each other, and that objects do not spontaneously move without being acted on by some external force (Spelke, 1988).

Understanding of the physical world, of course, goes well beyond understanding of the properties of objects. Another important type of understanding involves knowledge of space. We live in a world of locations and distances, paths and barriers, enclosed and open space. Our ability to move around in this world and to pursue our goals depends critically on our ability to represent such spatial information accurately.

Like their understanding of the human mind, older children's understanding of space builds on rudimentary early understanding. Even infants have some understanding of space, largely in relation to themselves. As time passes, they represent space in an increasingly objective way that is decreasingly dependent on where they themselves are within the space. They come to form at least three types of spatial representations: egocentric, landmark-based, and allocentric.

Egocentric Representations

Perhaps the earliest way of representing space is in terms of the relation between our own location and that of other objects. Thus, an object's position might be represented as "a few steps to my left."

Piaget (1971) suggested that before infants are 1 year old, they form only egocentric representations, and thus can represent locations of objects only in relation to themselves. Consistent with Piaget's hypothesis, 6- and 11-month-olds frequently fail to compensate for changes in their own spatial position (Acredolo, 1978). If they have previously found an object when they turned in a particular direction, and then moved so that turning in that direction no longer leads them to the object, they continue to turn in the direction that previously was successful. Not until 16 months of age do they compensate for the change in their position relative to the target.

Although infants often form egocentric representations of space, this has proved not to be the only type of spatial representation that they can form. Their difficulty in adjusting to changes in spatial position can be mitigated if cues to the object's location are provided by either distinctive landmarks or gravity (Rieser, 1979). Under such conditions, 6-month-olds usually turn in the appropriate direction, even when it differs from the direction that previously led to the object.

Experience in moving around in the environment seems to be one critical influence that helps infants to overcome this early spatial egocentrism. Eight-month-olds who can crawl or who have extensive experience in a walker succeed more often in locating objects' spatial positions than do infants of the same age who neither crawl well nor have experience with walkers (Bertenthal, Campos, & Barrett, 1984). The longer children have been locomoting, the greater their advantage (Kermoian & Campos, 1988).

The source of locomotion also matters. Just as it is easier for adults to learn a spatial layout when they drive rather than are driven, infants learn spatial layouts more effectively when they crawl or walk around them than when they are carried. The reason seems to involve differences in attention. When 12-month-olds walk to the other side of a layout and have the opportunity to look at all times at the point where a prize has been hidden, they both look at it more than do children who are carried and subsequently do better in turning toward the object from the new position. In contrast, when they cannot see the prize as they walk from one position to the other, they subsequently are no better in turning toward it than are children who were carried (Acredolo, Adams, & Goodwyn, 1984). Thus, one benefit of self-produced motion is that it leads to more-effective deployment of visual attention.

Landmark-Based Representations

We often give directions in terms of landmarks, as in "You go north on Reading Avenue until you pass the Stop and Go, where you turn left, and then you go until the third stoplight and turn right." We do this because landmarks provide a way of dividing the physical environment into more-manageable segments. In a sense, landmarks allow people to apply a divide-and-conquer strategy to solving the perennial problem of how to get from here to there.

Representation of spatial locations in terms of landmarks begins in the first year after birth. As noted previously, 6-month-olds' representations of an object's position survive a change in perspective if a distinctive landmark is near the object (Rieser, 1979). People as well as objects can provide such landmarks; 9-month-olds at times use their mother's location as a landmark for locating interesting objects near her (Presson & Ihrig, 1982).

The use of landmarks appears to undergo considerable refinement beyond this initial period (Huttenlocher & Newcombe, 1984). Before a child's first birthday, only landmarks immediately adjacent to the target usually lead to accurate location of targets. By about 2 years of age, a child is also helped by landmarks that are more distant from the target. By age 5, children can represent an object's position relative to multiple landmarks, a much more powerful procedure for establishing exact locations.

Allocentric Representations

Frequently, we can neither see nor go directly from here to there. Such situations demand integration of spatial information from multiple perspectives into a common abstract representation. Such representations are perhaps the most purely spatial codes of the three types. Egocentric and landmark-based representations can be reduced to a verbal form relatively easily (for example, "The hotel is two blocks to my left"; "The hotel is one block north of the Empire State Building"). In contrast, **allocentric representations,** *which include all relations among the entities within the space,* cannot easily be reduced to verbal form.

Most 4- to 6-year-olds can form allocentric representations, though the precision of the representations increases considerably with development. In one study, 4- to 6-year-olds, 8- and 9-year-olds, and adults who lived in a housing complex in identical two-story townhouses were asked to shine a light pen to indicate the location of a target relative to their own position within such a townhouse (Lockman & Pick, 1984). For example, children might stand in the kitchen and be asked to point to their bedroom on the second floor. The target's location could never be seen; it was always hidden behind a wall, floor, or ceiling. When the question involved rooms on the same floor, performance was very accurate at all ages. When the question involved rooms on a different floor, there was substantial improvement with age. Even the 4- to 6-year-olds were reasonably accurate, though. This ability to estimate hidden positions in three-dimensional space without direct routes to link the locations suggests that 4- to 6-year-olds can form allocentric representations.

How does the capacity to form such representations develop? Some experts claim that children innately represent spatial layouts, along with information about distances among landmarks, in terms of an abstract reference system (Landau, Spelke, & Gleitman, 1984). However, some recent, striking data on the spatial representations of visually impaired people render this claim questionable (Rieser & others, 1989). The spatial representations of adults who had developed severe visual impairments either early in life (before age 3, almost always before birth) or later in life (after age 5, usually after age 10) were contrasted. The task was to imagine standing at a particular landmark facing in a particular direction in a familiar part of one's neighborhood and point toward where the other imagined landmarks would be. Those whose visual impairments began early in life and included difficulties with peripheral vision represented the spatial layout much less accurately than did those whose impairments started later or whose peripheral vision was intact. If space were innately represented in a geometric form, there would be no reason to expect these differences within the visually impaired population. Instead, the finding appeared to be due to early perceptual learning before the onset of visual impairment; this suggests that such learning is critical for geometrically accurate spatial representations.

Researchers are interested in infants' knowledge of numbers. Using Mickey Mouse dolls, a researcher in Karen Wynn's lab creates an equation of 2 + 1 = 2 for a baby. Two dolls dance across a stage and disappear behind a screen. Then a third doll dances across and disappears behind the screen. The researcher then whisks away one doll just before the screen is removed. The baby expects to see three dolls, but only two appear.

Number

Another critical concept for understanding the physical world is number. An understanding of numbers involves knowledge of two basic kinds of numerical properties: cardinality and ordinality. **Cardinality** *is absolute numerical size.* A common property of people's arms, legs, eyes, and feet is that there are two of them. The cardinal property of two-ness is what these sets share. **Ordinality** *is the property of numerical relation. Ordinal properties are numerical relations among things.* That someone is the third-prettiest girl in the class and that 5 is the fifth number of the counting string are ordinal properties.

An understanding of cardinality begins surprisingly early in infancy. By the age of 2 months, infants can discriminate one object from two, and two objects from three (Antell & Keating, 1983; Wynn, 1992). This was learned through the use of the habituation paradigm. Infants were shown sets of objects that differed in a variety of ways but that all had the same number of objects (for instance, two objects). Once the infants habituated to displays with this number of objects, they were shown a set with a different number. Their renewed looking testified that they had abstracted the number of objects in the previous sets.

Discriminating among larger numbers of objects poses greater difficulty for infants. Those below 1 year of age do not appear to discriminate four objects from five or six (Strauss & Curtis, 1984). This finding suggests that infants identify cardinalities through *subitizing,* a quick and effortless perceptual process that people can apply only to sets of one, two, three, and maybe four objects. When we see a row of between one and four objects, we feel as if we immediately know how many there are; in contrast, with larger numbers of objects we usually feel less sure.

Between 2 and 4 years of age, children become proficient in another means of establishing how many objects there are that can deal with these larger sets—*counting*. Some developmentalists point to the rapidity with which children learn to count and hypothesize that the rapid learning is possible because it is guided by knowledge of *counting principles* (Gelman & Gallistel, 1978; Sophian, Wood, & Vong, 1995). In particular, even before age 2, children know these principles:

1. The *one-one principle*: Assign one and only one number word to each object.

2. The *stable-order principle*: Always assign the numbers in the same order.

3. The *cardinality principle*: The last number assigned indicates the number of objects in the set.

4. The *abstraction principle*: The other principles apply to any set of objects.

5. The *order irrelevance principle*: The order in which objects are counted is irrelevant.

Several types of evidence suggest that children understand all of these principles by age 5, and most of them by age 3 or 4. Even when children err in their counting, they show knowledge of the one-one principle, since they assign exactly one number word to most of the objects. For instance, they might count all but one object once, either skipping or counting twice the single miscounted object. These errors seem to be ones of execution rather than of misguided intent. Children demonstrate knowledge of the stable-order principle by almost always saying the number words in a constant order. Usually this is the conventional order, but occasionally it is an idiosyncratic order such as "1, 3, 6." Even when children use an idiosyncratic order, they use the same idiosyncratic order on each count. Preschoolers demonstrate knowledge of the cardinality principle by saying the last number with special emphasis. They show understanding of the abstraction principle by not hesitating to count sets that include different types of objects. Finally, the order irrelevance principle seems to be the most difficult, but even here 5-year-olds demonstrate understanding. Many of them recognize that counting could start in the middle row of objects, as long as each object is eventually counted. Although few children can state the principles, their counting suggests that they understand and use them.

Just as children show substantial understanding of cardinal properties of numbers, they also show an understanding of ordinal properties. These ordinal properties involve the relative positions or magnitudes of numbers. A number might be first or second in an order, or it might be greater or less than another number. Mastery of ordinal properties of numbers, like mastery of cardinal properties, begins in infancy. However, it seems to begin later, between 12 and 18 months.

The most basic ordinal concepts are *more than* and *less than*. To test when infants understand these concepts as they apply to numbers, researchers repeatedly presented 16- to 18-month-olds with two squares—one containing one dot, the other containing two dots (Strauss & Curtis, 1984). They then presented two new squares (such as squares with four dots and three dots). The babies more often chose the set of dots that maintained the "larger than" relation, thus indicating understanding of this ordinal property.

In the preschool period, children learn to compare numbers apart from the objects they represent. For example, they learn to solve such problems as "Which is bigger, 6 or 3?" To study the process by which they do so, researchers asked 3-, 4-, and 5-year-olds to compare the magnitudes of all 36 possible pairs of numbers 1 through 9 (Siegler & Robinson, 1982). The 3-year-olds' performance was at chance level, whereas both 4- and 5-year-olds were correct on more than 80 percent of trials. Also, the 3-year-olds' errors were evenly distributed among problems, whereas those of the older children were concentrated on problems with the larger numbers and relatively small differences between them (such as 8 versus 7). Interestingly, these are the same kinds of problems adults find most difficult (for instance, adults take more time to discriminate 8 from 7 dots than they do to discriminate either 8 from 2 dots or 4 from 3 dots). In sum, substantial progress is made between ages 3 and 5 in understanding both cardinal and ordinal properties of numbers.

PROBLEM SOLVING

As noted at the beginning of the chapter, **problem solving** *is an attempt to find an appropriate way of attaining a goal when barriers prevent its immediate attainment.* As adults, we face many problems in our everyday lives—trying to figure out why our car won't start, how to get enough money to buy a stereo, or what our chances are of winning the lottery, for instance. Children also face many problems in their everyday lives—such as working a jigsaw puzzle, doing math homework, or getting a purse that is out of reach.

Although problem solving is a common and important activity in the lives of adults, it is even more central in the lives of children. As we mentioned earlier, children have been referred to as "universal novices" (Brown & DeLoache, 1978). Because they lack experience in many areas, they are constantly being forced to confront new problems. Tasks such as walking home from the drugstore, which are not problems for adults who have walked the same route many times and have a good general representation of space, constitute genuine problems for children who might not have walked the route previously and whose concepts of space might be less advanced.

Much of information-processing research on problem solving has been aimed at identifying the rules children use to solve problems. The balance scale problem is useful for illustrating this research. The type of balance scale that has been used to examine children's understanding is shown in figure 8.8. The scale includes a fulcrum and an arm that can rotate around it. The arm can tip left or right or remain level, depending on how weights (metal disks with holes in the center) are arranged on the pegs on each side of the fulcrum. The child's task is to look at the configuration of weights on the pegs on each problem and then predict whether the left side will go down, the right side will go down, or the arm will balance.

Robert Siegler (1976) hypothesized that children would use one of the four rules depicted in figure 8.9.

Rule I. If the weight is the same on both sides, predict that the scale will balance. If the weight differs, predict that the side with more weight will go down.

Rule II. If the weight is greater on one side, say that that side will go down. If the weights on the two sides are equal, choose the side on which the weight is farther from the fulcrum.

Rule III. Act as in Rule II, except that if one side has more weight and the weight on the other side is farther from the fulcrum, then guess.

Rule IV. Proceed as in Rule III, unless one side has more weight and the other more distance. In that case, calculate torques by multiplying weight times distance on each side. Then predict that the side with the greater torque will go down.

But how could it be determined which rule, if any, a given child was using? Siegler reasoned that presenting problems on which different rules would generate different outcomes would allow assessment of each child's rules. For example, suppose there were four weights on the third peg to the left of the fulcrum and three weights on the fourth peg to the right of the fulcrum. A child using Rule I or Rule II would say that the left side will go down, because it has more weight; a child using Rule III would guess and therefore sometimes say one answer and sometimes another; and a child using Rule IV would compute torques and realize that the two sides would balance. Through a child's pattern of correct answers and errors on a set of such problems, that child's underlying rule could be inferred.

This *rule assessment approach* demonstrated that almost 90 percent of children aged 5 to 17 years used one of the four rules. Almost all 5-year-olds used Rule I, almost all 9-year-olds used either Rule II or Rule III, and

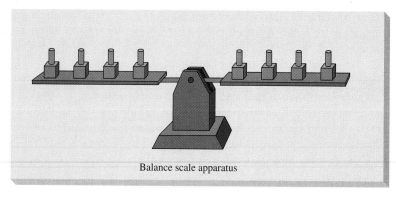

Balance scale apparatus

Figure~8.8

The Type of Balance Scale Used by Siegler (1976)
Weights could be placed on pegs on each side of the fulcrum; the torque (the weight on each side times the distance of that weight from the fulcrum) determined which side would go down.

both 13-year-olds and 17-year-olds generally used Rule III. Interestingly, despite the 17-year-olds' having studied balance scales in their physics course, almost none of them used the only rule that generated consistently correct answers, Rule IV. Discussions with their teachers revealed why; the balance scale the students had studied was a pan balance, on which small pans could be hung

Problem solving is a central activity in the lives of children. Think back to your own childhood and the problems you encountered and how you tried to solve them. Do you solve problems differently as an adult than you did as a child?

Santrock: Child Development

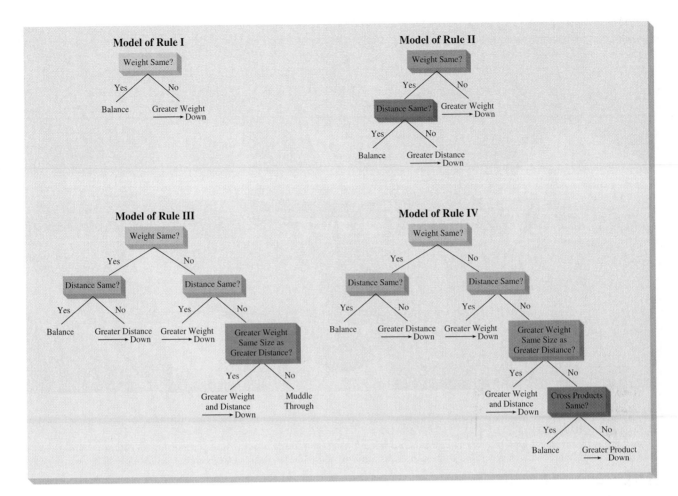

Figure~8.9

Four Rules for Solving the Balance Scale Task

Children following Rule I would always pick the side with more weight as the one that would go down, and would say that the scale would balance whenever the two sides had the same amount of weight. Children using Rule II would do the same, except that if the two sides had the same amount of weight, they would base their judgments on the distance of the weights from the fulcrum. Children using Rule III would always consider both weight and distance, and would respond correctly if one or both were equal. However, they would muddle through or guess if one side had more weight and the other had its weight farther from the fulcrum. Finally, children using Rule IV would act the same as those using Rule III, except that they would compute torques when one side had more weight and the other had its weight farther from the fulcrum.

from various locations along the arm, rather than an arm balance, with pegs extending upward. Retesting the children showed that most could consistently solve the problems when the familiar pan balance was used. The example illustrates a set of lessons that frequently has emerged from studies of problem solving—learning is often quite narrow, generalization beyond one's existing knowledge is difficult, and even analogies that seem straightforward are often missed.

The development of problem solving does not start at age 5. Certain basic problem-solving abilities are already present in infancy. Below we consider some of these, as well as the subsequent development of a number of other key problem-solving capabilities.

Infant Imitation

One of the most important ways to solve problems is to imitate the actions of more-knowledgeable others

who are confronted with similar problems (Call, 1995). This is especially true for young children, who have less experience solving problems and fewer general problem-solving strategies than older individuals have. Copying its mother's problem-solving strategies has, clearly, survival value for an infant. Thus, it is not surprising that basic imitative abilities are present from early in life.

Just how early certain imitative capacities are present became apparent in an intriguing experiment conducted by Tiffany Field and her colleagues (1982). They examined the capabilities of newborns within 36 hours of their birth. An adult held each newborn in front of her, with its head upright, 10 inches from herself. With her face she expressed one of the three emotions: happiness, sadness, or surprise. Infants were most likely to imitate the model's display of surprise by widely opening their mouths. When the infants observed a happy

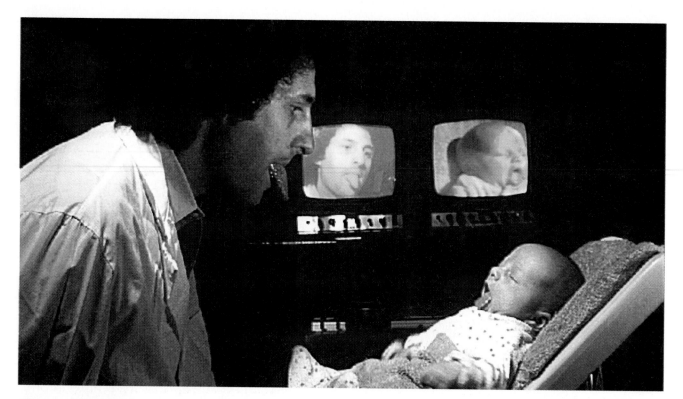

Figure~8.10

Infants' Ability to Imitate
Shown here is infant development researcher Andrew Meltzoff displaying tongue protrusion, prompting an infant to imitate his behavior. Researchers have demonstrated that infants can imitate adults' behavior far earlier than traditionally believed.

expression, they frequently widened their lips. When the adult's face looked sad, the infant's lips moved into a pouting expression.

> *Children need models more than they need critics.*
> —Joseph Joubert

Infant development researcher Andrew Meltzoff (1990) has conducted numerous studies of infants' imitative abilities. He believes that these abilities are biologically based, because infants can imitate a facial expression within the first few days after birth, before they have had the opportunity to observe social agents in their environment engage in tongue protrusion and other behaviors. He also believes that infants' imitative abilities do not fit the ethologists' concept of a hardwired, reflexive, innate releasing mechanism, but rather that these abilities are flexible and adaptable to the demands of particular situations. In Meltzoff's observations of infants in the first 72 hours of life, the infants gradually displayed a full imitative response to an adult's facial expressions, such as tongue protrusion or a wide opening of the mouth (see figure 8.10). Initially, a young infant might only get its tongue to the edge of its lips, but after a number of attempts and observations of adult behavior, the infant displays a more full-blown imitation.

Meltzoff also has studied deferred imitation, imitation that occurs hours or days after the original event. In one investigation, Meltzoff (1988) demonstrated that 9-month-old infants can imitate actions they saw performed 24 hours earlier. Each action consisted of an unusual gesture, such as pushing a recessed button in a box (which produced a beeping sound). Piaget had concluded that deferred imitation was impossible until about 18 months of age, because he believed that until then infants lacked basic representational abilities needed to maintain the memory of the earlier event. Meltzoff's research suggests that infants can form such representations much earlier in development.

> *We are in truth, more than half what we are by imitation.*
> —Lord Chesterfield

Means-Ends Analysis and Plans

Infants' problem solving extends beyond imitation to a capability called **means-ends analysis,** *which involves examining one's current situation, as well as one's current goal, and how to get from the current situation to the goal.* Infants less than 1 year of age exhibit such means-ends analysis in some situations. For example, in one study 9-month-olds were presented with a foam-rubber barrier, behind which was hidden a cloth (Willatts, 1990). Some of the babies saw a small toy on the far end of the cloth, others saw the toy beside, rather than on top of, the cloth. When the toy was on the cloth rather than beside it, the 9-month-olds were much more likely to knock down the barrier and pull the cloth to them.

Means-ends analysis later is extended to much more complex situations, involving more numerous and complex subgoals and requiring the discipline to resist the lure of short-term goals to pursue longer-term ones. These changes can be seen in 3- to 6-year-olds' approaches to the Tower of Hanoi task (see figure 8.11). The goal of this game is to place one's own cans in the same configuration as the adult's in as few moves as possible. At the beginning, the child has three cans on a single peg, with the smallest on the bottom and the largest on the top. At the end, the child wants to duplicate the configuration on the experimenter's side, where the three cans are in the same configuration but on a different peg. The only rules are that a smaller can may not be placed on top of a larger one; and one, and only one, can may be moved at a time. The game sounds easy, but it quickly becomes quite complex. To appreciate the complexity, try to imagine the seven moves by which the child's configuration in figure 8.11 can be transformed into the adult's configuration.

It should be no surprise that older children can solve problems requiring more moves than the number of moves in the problems that can be solved by younger children. Few 3-year-olds can solve problems requiring more than 2 moves; most 4-year-olds can solve 4-move problems; most 6-year-olds can solve 5- or 6-move problems. What is perhaps more surprising is that the number of moves is not the key source of difficulty. What is really hard for children is to make moves that in the short run appear to take you farther from the goal but in the long run are essential to getting there. For example, to transform the child's configuration in figure 8.11 into that of the adult, it is essential to first move the largest can to the

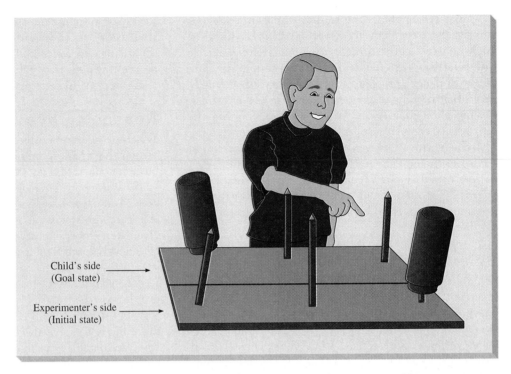

Figure~8.11

A Child Trying to Solve the Tower of Hanoi Task
The child's goal is to make his tower look like that of the experimenter while adhering to the rules of the game. The quickest solution requires seven moves; can you find it?

Child's side (Goal state)

Experimenter's side (Initial state)

peg where it will ultimately go, and then later to move it to the other peg that started out empty. Realizing that you need to go away from the goal in the short run to get there in the long run is what makes the Tower of Hanoi problem truly challenging.

Planning continues to be an important determinant of problem-solving ability well beyond early childhood. It is one of the central distinguishing characteristics of experts; relative to other individuals, experts spend far more time doing problem solving during initial planning (Berg & Sansone, 1991; Friedman, 1991; Trabasso, 1991). Present a problem to an expert, and the expert spends more time, relative to the total time needed to complete the task, than a novice or less experienced person would spend in thinking about how to solve the problem or complete the task. Expert writers spend a great deal of time thinking about what they want to communicate, how to communicate it, and what the parts or units of their written product will be. Expert computer programmers spend a considerable amount of time, before they write any code at all, describing to themselves what their finished program will accomplish and the form their program will take. Expert athletes spend a great deal of effort planning their approach to conditioning, polishing skills, and choosing competition. Novices, on the other hand, often leap right in. They might not have the skill to plan effectively, or they might not realize the value of initial planning.

Experts' emphasis on planning often surprises people, because a common stereotype of experts is that they know how to do everything in their domain of expertise with relatively little effort. In fact, if a task is straightforward and not a problem to solve, experts are extremely fast. Their performances seem automatic and effortless. Having planned an essay, an expert writer might dash off pages of print in just several hours. The contrasting performance of a novice is one of sluggish fits and starts, conscious thought about what to do, and great effort. Acquiring expertise often requires years of experience, but once it is acquired, it can lead to superior ability to plan solutions for novel problems, as well as ability to solve familiar ones.

Scientific Reasoning

Children's problem solving is often compared to that of scientists. Both children and scientists ask fundamental questions about the nature of reality. Both also seek answers to problems that seem utterly trivial or unanswerable to other people (such as, Why is the sky blue?). Both also are granted by society the time and freedom to pursue answers to the problems they find interesting. This "child as scientist" metaphor has led researchers to ask whether children generate hypotheses, perform experiments, and reach conclusions concerning the meaning of their data in ways resembling those of scientists (Clinchy, Mansfield, & Schott, 1995).

Scientific reasoning often is aimed at identifying causal relations. In some ways, children's causal inferences are similar to those of scientists. For example, like scientists, they place a great deal of emphasis on causal mechanisms (Frye & others, 1996). Their understanding of how events are caused weighs more heavily in their causal inferences than do even such strong influences as whether the cause happened immediately before the effect (Shultz & others, 1986).

There also are important differences between the reasoning of children and the reasoning of scientists, however. This is true even of preadolescents who have had some instruction in school regarding the scientific method. One difference comes in the preadolescents' much greater difficulty in separating their prior theories from the evidence that they have obtained. Often, when they try to learn about new phenomena, they maintain their old theories regardless of the evidence (Kuhn, Schauble, & Garcia-Mila, 1992). Another difference is that they are more influenced by happenstance events than by the overall pattern of occurrences (Kuhn, Amsel, & O'Laughlin, 1988). They also have difficulty designing new experiments that can distinguish conclusively among alternative causes. Instead, they tend to bias the experiments in favor of whichever hypothesis they began with, and sometimes they will see the results as supporting their original hypothesis even when the results directly contradict it (Schauble, 1990). Thus, although there are important similarities between children and scientists, in their basic curiosity and in the kinds of questions they ask, there are also important differences in their ability to design conclusive experiments and in the degree to which they can separate theory and evidence (Schauble, 1996).

Reasoning by Analogy

When people encounter new problems, often they interpret them with reference to better-understood, previously encountered ones. For example, in one study college students were presented with a problem in which a physician needed to destroy a patient's tumor, and the only way to do so was with massive amounts of radiation (Duncker, 1945). However, the amount of radiation was sufficiently large that it would also destroy healthy tissue on the way to the tumor. Half the dosage of radiation would not kill the healthy tissue, though it also would not destroy the tumor. What should the physician do?

Most people find this problem difficult. They are more likely to solve it, however, if they first learn the solution to another problem in which an attacking army cannot travel in one large group, because the attack route is too narrow, but instead must divide into separate units, come from different directions, and converge at a central location. This suggests to many the idea of sending half the desired amount of radiation from each of two directions, with the two converging at the site of the tumor. Such extrapolation from better-understood to less-understood problems is the key to analogical problem solving.

The development of analogical problem solving resembles that of scientific reasoning. Even very young children can draw reasonable analogies under some circumstances and use them to solve problems (Freeman & Gehl, 1995). Under other circumstances, even college students fail to draw seemingly obvious analogies (as in the example of the high school students' difficulty in extrapolating from the familiar pan balance to the unfamiliar arm balance, described earlier). This resemblance is not coincidental, since scientific reasoning often depends on drawing useful analogies.

Ann Brown and her collaborators (Brown, 1990; Brown, Kane, & Echols, 1986) have demonstrated some of the types of analogical reasoning that occur at ages 1 through 5 years. When 1- and 2-year-olds are shown that a curved stick can be used as a tool to pull in a toy that is too far away to be reached unaided, they draw the correct analogy in choosing which stick to use the next time. They do not choose sticks on the basis of their being of the same color as the stick they used before. They also do not just choose objects that look exactly like the tool they saw demonstrated to be effective (such as a curved cane); instead they identify the essential property and will choose whichever objects have it (they will choose a straight rake as well as the curved cane). The 2-year-olds were more likely than the 1-year-olds to learn the

What was the source of the 2½-year-olds' difficulty on the task? It was not inability to understand how any type of symbol could represent another situation. Shown line drawings or photographs of the larger room, 2½-year-olds had no difficulty finding the object. Instead, the difficulty seemed to come from the toddlers' simultaneously viewing the scale model as a symbol of the larger room and as an object in itself. Surprising consequences followed from this insight. Allowing children to play with the scale model before using it as a symbol worsened their performance, presumably because playing with it made them think of it more as an object in itself. Conversely, putting the scale model in a glass case, where the children could not handle it at all, resulted in the children's more often being able to use it successfully to find the object hidden in the larger room. The general lesson is that young children can use a variety of tools to draw analogies, but they easily can forget that an object is being used as a symbol of something else and instead take it as being of interest as an object in its own right.

Judy DeLoache (*left*) has conducted research that focuses on young children's developing cognitive abilities. She has demonstrated that children's symbolic representation between 2½ and 3 years of age enables them to find a toy in a real room that is a much bigger version of the scale model.

initial task without any help, but once they learned the task, both 1- and 2-year-olds drew the right analogy to new problems.

Successful analogical problem solving often involves tools more abstract than curved sticks for hauling in objects that are beyond one's reach. Maps and verbal descriptions of routes, for example, often help us to figure out how to get where we want to go (DeLoache, Miller, & Pierroutakos, 1997). Recent studies of toddlers' abilities to use scale models to guide their problem-solving activities show that dramatic developments occur in such tool use quite early in development.

Judy DeLoache (1989) created a situation in which 2½- and 3-year-olds were shown a small toy hidden within a scale model of a room. The child was then asked to find the toy in a real room that was a bigger version of the scale model. If the toy was hidden under the armchair in the scale model, it was also hidden under the armchair in the real room. Considerable development occurred between 2½ and 3 years on this task. Thirty-month-old children rarely could solve the problem; by 36 months they generally could.

Problem Solving in Social Contexts

Children's problem-solving skills do not develop in a vacuum. Instead, they evolve in a rich context of social interactions. The social environment influences both what problems children attempt to solve and how they attempt to solve them.

Influences on What Problems Children Solve

The nature of the social and physical environment in which children develop profoundly influences what problems they attempt to solve. Consider Aboriginal children in the Australian desert. Much of Aboriginal life is a series of treks between widely spaced wells and creeks. Few obvious landmarks exist in the stony desert to indicate where the water is, and shifting rainfall patterns create continuing needs to approach sources of water from new directions.

One researcher hypothesized that these children's need to think a great deal about large spaces might create distinctive competencies in solving spatial problems (Kearins, 1981). She therefore contrasted the spatial capabilities of Aboriginal children with those of white

Australian children raised in the city. Children were presented with twenty objects arranged in a 5 × 4 rectangle. After they observed the objects for 30 seconds, the experimenter picked the objects up and asked the children to rearrange them as the objects had been previously.

The Aboriginal children, who had never received any formal schooling, consistently showed superior spatial problem-solving abilities relative to the city-raised children, who attended conventional schools. Regardless of whether the objects were familiar or unfamiliar, the Aboriginal children did well, whereas the city-raised children did well only when they were familiar with the objects. The Aboriginal children's approach was to study the objects in silence and try to think about how they looked, whereas the city-raised children named the objects and tried to remember them in a list. Thus, it appears that continuing experience in thinking about space leads children to develop superior skills for solving spatial problems.

Influences on How Children Solve Problems

Cultures differ not only in which problems they emphasize but also in the tools they provide for solving the problems. These tools can greatly influence how children solve problems. Acquisition of expertise in using abacuses to solve arithmetic problems illustrates this influence. Abacuses are frequently used in East Asia to solve such problems, though they are much less common elsewhere in the world. Even though the widespread availability of cheap and powerful calculators and computers might be expected to have made abacuses obsolete, they are still widely used by both children and adults in East Asian societies.

Children and adults who have become abacus experts tend to be exceptionally good at mental arithmetic, even when they are not using the abacuses (Stigler, 1984). For example, 11-year-old abacus experts can quickly and accurately add four four-digit numbers.

How do they attain such expertise? It appears that they form an image of how the problem would look on the abacus, then imagine solving the problem on the abacus, and then advance the answer. This analysis is supported by the fact that the types of errors made by the young abacus experts were ones that could easily arise on an abacus but that would not arise ordinarily. For example, because only a single 5s bead distinguishes the abacus representation of numbers that differ by 5, it is quite common for abacus experts to make such errors as substituting an answer of 67,391 for 67,891. People who are not accustomed to using an abacus do not often make this kind of error. Similarly, interfering with the ability to visualize the problem interfered with abacus experts' efforts to solve complex arithmetic problems but did not interfere with other people's efforts, whereas interfering with efforts to verbally keep track of the running

sum interfered with other people's efforts on the addition problems but did not interfere with the efforts of the abacus experts.

In our own society, technological change is continually modifying the ways in which children and adults solve problems. Calculators, computers, spell checkers, and text-editing systems are just a few of the mechanisms that have changed how we solve a wide range of problems. Some hard-won problem-solving skills become obsolete—for example, generations of students spent long periods mastering slide rules and algorithms for obtaining square roots, both of which became irrelevant when calculators became available. The rapid pace of technological change is one reason why many authorities emphasize the importance of obtaining general problem-solving skills rather than just focusing on ways of solving specific problems.

ACADEMIC SKILLS

Many of the most important aspects of cognitive development occur in the classroom. Children learn not only mathematics, reading, and writing but also more-general thinking skills. The goal is for them not only to learn specific content but also to "learn to learn." In this concluding section of the chapter, we consider how children acquire specific competencies in mathematics and reading, how they acquire more-general thinking skills, and how individual and cultural differences influence their acquisition of both specific and general information.

Mathematics

As noted in the earlier section on the development of numerical concepts, children already have a substantial understanding of numbers before they enter first grade. Most middle-class kindergartners can count past 20, and often as high as 100 or more; can accurately count the number of objects in a set; can solve small-number addition and subtraction problems (such as 3 + 2); and know the relative magnitudes of single-digit numbers (such as, Which is bigger, 8 or 6?) (Siegler & Robinson, 1982).

When they go to school, children learn many more-advanced kinds of numerical skills (Ginsburg, Klein, & Starkey, 1997). People often think that children just either learn or fail to learn what they are taught. In fact, what they learn often reflects their own thinking as much as anything they are taught. This is true even in the case of basic addition and subtraction, which might be thought to involve only the simplest of learning procedures, memorization.

Arithmetic

In most instruction aimed at helping children learn basic arithmetic facts (such as, How much is 3 plus 9?), the goal is to teach children how to retrieve the answer from memory. For a period of several years after they enter school, however, children use a mix of strategies, including ones that no one ever taught them. Thus, on a problem such as 3 + 9, some first-, second-, and third-graders will retrieve the answer from memory, some will count from 1, some will count from 9, and some will reason that 9 is 1 less than 10, that 3 + 10 is 13, and therefore 3 + 9 must be 12. These last two strategies are rarely taught by teachers or parents, yet children frequently use them anyway.

The fact that first-, second-, and third-graders use all of these arithmetic strategies to solve single-digit problems does not mean that no development occurs over the period. Children become both much faster and more accurate, in part because they increasingly use the faster and more accurate strategies, such as retrieval, and in part because they execute each of the strategies more quickly and accurately. Eventually, they solve all of these problems consistently, correctly, and very quickly.

As they move toward the end of the elementary school period, children learn to solve multidigit arithmetic problems and problems involving fractions. Much of what's involved in learning these more advanced arithmetic skills is overcoming misconceptions. For example, in learning multidigit subtraction, children need to overcome "buggy" rules (named for the "bugs" that appear in faulty computer programs). Suppose a third-grader is given the following four problems and generates the answers shown here:

306	453	204	370
−43	−274	−177	−89
343	179	177	281

Can you figure out what the student was doing wrong?

Analysis of the problems indicates that the child was following a "buggy" rule, similar to the partially correct balance scale rules discussed earlier (figure 8.9). The difficulty with these subtraction problems arose only when the problem involved borrowing across a zero; the child answered correctly on the problem that did not involve a zero and on the problem in which the zero was in the rightmost column. When it was necessary to borrow across a zero, the child proceeded in a consistent, but wrong, way that involved subtracting the zero from the number beneath it, rather than the reverse, and then not decrementing the number next to the zero (presumably because nothing had been borrowed from it). Such buggy algorithms are quite common in third-, fourth-, and fifth-graders' subtraction (VanLehn, 1986).

Making teachers aware of the bugs that interfere with their students' learning can lead to better mathematics instruction. For example, in one study a group of student teachers were taught how to design problems that would tell them the precise nature of the bugs in each student's performance (since different children show different bugs) (Brown & Burton, 1978). The precise assessment of children's difficulties promises to allow us to

go well beyond standard written comr ̲ ̲ ̲ correct—You can do better!") to ? ̲ ̲ to the needs of individual childr ̲ ̲

Algebra

Children develop far more powerful mathe ̲ ̲ soning when they learn algebra. A single equati ̲ ̲ represent an infinite variety of situations. Even many s ̲ dents who get A's and B's in algebra classes, however, do so without understanding what they are learning— they simply memorize the equations. This approach might work well in the classroom, but it limits these students' ability to use algebra in real-world contexts.

This difficulty does not affect just junior high and high school students getting their first exposure to algebra—it also extends to the college level. Fewer than 30 percent of engineering students at a high-quality state university correctly solved the following problem:

> Write an equation using the variables C and S to represent the following statement: "At Mindy's restaurant, for every four people who order cheesecake, there are five people who order strudel." Let C represent the number of cheesecakes and S the number of strudels. (Clement, Lockhead, & Soloway, 1979, p. 46)

Most of the students represented this problem as $4C = 5S$. Although this might initially seem logical, this equation says that multiplying two smaller quantities (4 and the number of people ordering cheesecake) yields a result equal to multiplying two larger quantities (5 and the number of people ordering strudel). The underlying difficulty is that even college students at fine universities often do not connect their mathematical equations to what the equations mean. Without such connections, algebra becomes a meaningless exercise in symbol manipulation. Clearly, successful instruction in algebra, as in other areas of mathematics, requires not only teaching students how to solve problems, but also leading students to a deeper understanding of how the solution procedures yield the solutions.

Reading

Learning to read is one of the central rites of passage in our society. It separates young children from the world of older children and adults. At a general level, the development of reading skills can be viewed as occurring in five stages (Chall, 1979). The age boundaries are approximate and do not apply to every child—for example, some children learn to read quite fluently before they begin school. Nonetheless, the stages convey a general sense of major developments in reading and about when they usually occur.

Stage 0. In this stage, lasting from birth to the beginning of first grade, children master several prerequisites for reading. Many learn to identify the letters of the alphabet, quite a few learn to write their names (more or less correctly), some learn to read a few words that appear on signs. Due to shows like "Sesame Street," children today tend to have considerably greater knowledge of reading during this period than did their counterparts in the past.

Stage 1. In first and second grade, children acquire the ability to sound out words, that is, to translate letters into sounds and to blend the sounds into words. They also complete their learning of letter names and sounds during this stage.

Stage 2. In second and third grade, children learn to retrieve individual words and to read somewhat more fluently. However, at this stage, reading is still not used much for learning. The demands of the mechanics of reading on children's processing resources are great enough that they do not have much left over for processing the content.

Stage 3. In fourth through eighth grade, children become increasingly able to obtain new information from print. As Chall puts it, "In the primary grades, children learn to read; in the higher grades, they read to learn" (Chall, 1979, p. 46). They still are limited in the degree to which they can do this, however. For example, they still have difficulty understanding information presented from multiple perspectives within the same story.

Stage 4. During the high school years, children become fully competent readers. Their ability to understand material told from many perspectives makes possible much more sophisticated discussions of literary works, as well as discussions of history, economics, and politics, than previously. It is no accident that great novels are presented for the first time in high school. This is partly due to the fact that adolescents' increasing life experience makes it possible for them to understand the themes of such works more deeply than they could have earlier, but it is also partly due to their increasingly advanced reading comprehension.

Why does this development of reading take as long as it does? The basic translation of letters into sounds is mastered fairly quickly, but developing advanced reading comprehension skills takes much longer. Part of the reason has to do with memory capacity; as children become better able to hold longer passages in short-term memory, they become better able to integrate previous and new ideas and to infer connections among them (Perfetti, 1984). Also, as in oral contexts, knowledge of causal relations is especially important in reading comprehension.

A further important influence on reading comprehension is the ability to monitor one's own comprehension. Older readers, and better readers at any given age, are generally better at knowing when they understand

and when they do not (Baker & Brown, 1984). Finally, development of more-flexible strategies helps older children read more effectively. For example, between 10 and 14 years of age, children become increasingly likely to skim material when they need only the gist or a particular fact, and to read more slowly and carefully when they need detailed understanding (Kobasigawa, Ransom, & Holland, 1980).

In recent years, researchers have increasingly turned to the question of how reading comprehension can be improved. The kinds of research you have read about in this chapter have provided a guide to the kinds of instructional techniques that can be effective. One method that has proved to be important is to ensure that children understand the background assumptions of stories before they read them. That is, they must have the relevant content knowledge. As noted previously, incomplete or erroneous prior knowledge often leads children to make incorrect assumptions and thus to misunderstand new material. In the context of reading, this often leads them to misunderstand what the author means, and thus misconstrue the point of the story. Providing relevant background knowledge that addresses likely misconceptions can enhance comprehension of stories.

This point was illustrated compellingly in a study of a story in a second-grade reader called "The Raccoon and Mrs. McGinnis" (Beck & McKeown, 1984). Mrs. McGinnis was a poor but good-hearted farmer who was in danger of losing her farm. She wished upon a star that she could get the money she needed to buy a barn for her animals. Later that night, bandits came and stole the animals. A raccoon, who came to Mrs. McGinnis' doorstep each night to get food, came, saw the bandits, and followed them. The bandits saw the raccoon's masked face, thought it was another bandit, and became frightened and ran away, leaving not only the animals but a bag of money they had stolen from someone else. The raccoon picked up the bag of money, returned to Mrs. McGinnis' to get more food, and dropped the bag of money on her doorstep. Mrs. McGinnis found the money the next morning, thought her wish had come true, and thanked her lucky star.

Although adults find this story quite charming, many of the second-graders for whom it was written found it difficult to understand. They often concluded that the raccoon had purposefully followed the bandits to get the money and that it was the raccoon's heroism, rather than lucky coincidences, that had led to the outcome. Based on these observations, researchers taught children two concepts before the story was presented: the concepts of coincidence and habit (Beck & McKeown, 1984). They explained that coincidences involve events that just happen to occur together, with neither causing the other, and that habits often lead people and animals to engage in the same activities repeatedly. They also told children several useful background facts: that the dark circles around a raccoon's eyes look like a mask, that raccoons habitually hunt for food at night, and that raccoons often pick up objects and carry them to other locations.

Children who understood these background concepts and facts had much greater comprehension of the story. They understood that the raccoon had not tried to help Mrs. McGinnis, despite things having worked out that way, and realized that Mrs. McGinnis drew the wrong conclusion from the events. These findings led the researchers to recommend that teachers not just introduce stories in general terms, as had been recommended in the teacher's manual that accompanied the reader, but that they analyze the background knowledge needed to understand the stories, find out if the children possess this knowledge, and provide them with the relevant information if they do not. More information about reading appears in chapter 10.

General Thinking Skills—Critical Thinking and Cognitive Monitoring

The idea of education is not just to teach children specific skills in reading, writing, and mathematics. It is also to help them learn to think more clearly, evaluate claims that they encounter, and learn how to learn more than they already know.

Unfortunately, it is easier to describe such goals than to achieve them. Virtually no researchers think that we are doing a good job in inculcating such skills, which are essential for citizenship as well as for occupational success. Some students achieve them, but too many do not.

Critical Thinking

The gap between the importance of the goal of teaching students to think critically and the severely limited success in achieving it has led a number of psychologists and educators to study the acquisition of critical-thinking skills (Halonen, 1995). The goal is not a new one. Educator John Dewey (1933) was working with a similar concept when he contrasted reflective thinking with nonreflective thinking in the use of formulas or rules to achieve goals. So was Gestalt psychologist Max Wertheimer (1945) when he distinguished between productive thinking and blind induction. Although today's definitions vary, they all have in common the notion that **critical thinking** *involves grasping the deeper meaning of problems, keeping an open mind about different approaches and perspectives, not accepting on faith what other people and books tell you, and thinking reflectively rather than accepting the first idea that comes to mind.* Another, often implicit, assumption is that critical thinking is an important aspect of everyday reasoning (Galotti, 1989). Critical thinking can and should be used not just in the classroom, but outside it as well.

How can we cultivate in children the ability to think critically and clearly? According to leading cognitive psychologist Robert Sternberg (1987), we need to teach children to use the right thinking processes, develop problem-solving strategies, improve their mental representations, expand their knowledge base, and become motivated to use their newly learned thinking skills.

To think critically or to solve any problem or learn any new knowledge, children need to take an active role in learning. This means that children need to call on a variety of active thinking processes, such as these:

- Listening carefully
- Identifying or formulating questions
- Organizing their thoughts
- Noting similarities and differences
- Deducing (reasoning from the general to the specific)
- Distinguishing between logically valid and invalid inferences

Children also need to learn how to ask questions of clarification, such as *What is the main point? What do you mean by that?* and *Why?*

Good thinkers do more than just choose the right thinking process from among the approaches they have used in the past. They also know how to combine processes into new strategies for solving problems. Rarely can a problem be solved by a single type of thought process used in isolation. Critical thinking involves combining thought processes in a way that makes sense, not just jumbling them together.

Critical thinking also requires seeing things from multiple points of view. If children cannot interpret information from more than one viewpoint, they might rely on inadequate information. In particular, if they are not encouraged to seek alternative explanations and interpretations of problems and issues, their conclusions might be based solely on their own expectations, prejudices, stereotypes, and personal experiences, which can lead to erroneous conclusions.

It is important to keep in mind that thinking does not occur in the absence of knowledge. Children need something to think about. It is a mistake, however, to concentrate only on specific knowledge to the exclusion of more-general thinking skills. The consequence of doing so would likely be to produce individuals who have a lot of knowledge but who are unable to evaluate and apply it. It would be an equally serious mistake to concentrate only on thinking skills, because children might then become individuals who know how to think but have nothing to think about.

Researchers are increasingly finding that critical-thinking programs are more effective when they are domain-specific rather than domain-general (Resnick, 1987). For example, if the goal is to reduce teenage pregnancy, decision-making skills should be taught using teenage pregnancy as the content. This strategy will be more effective at reducing teenage pregnancy than will teaching general logic skills (Brynes, 1993).

CRITICAL THINKING ABOUT CHILDREN'S DEVELOPMENT

Developing a Critical-Thinking Attitude

Scientists often have a healthy skepticism about accepting theoretical and research conclusions. Researchers know how difficult it is to identify all of the causes of development. Thus, they argue that their conclusions are often tentative rather than definite. Psychologists often begin their answers to queries about behavior with the phrase *It depends on* as a reflection of their tentativeness. This response can be frustrating until you recognize that this tentative approach is a hallmark of psychological ways of thinking. Psychologists challenge the positions of others, whether to seek clarification, suggest improvements, identify inadequacies in stated positions, or propose alternatives.

Consider the following statement: *The best way for children to learn to think critically is by observing competent critical-thinking models.* Do you accept the conclusion? Or do you quickly think, *It depends on . . . .* Might simply observing competent critical-thinking models keep children from generating their own critical-thinking skills? Might discovery materials that challenge children to think critically possibly work as well or better? Possibly because of individual differences in children, some critical-thinking contexts might work best for some children but be less effective for other children.

By developing a critical-thinking attitude through such strategies as having a healthy skepticism and accepting many conclusions as tentative rather than definite, you are learning to think critically by *evaluating the quality of conclusions about children's development.*

Finally, all of the thinking skills children could possibly master would be irrelevant if they were not actually put to use. Critical thinking is both a matter for academic study and a part of living. Children need to be motivated to put their critical-thinking skills to practical use and given practice in doing so. To read further about critical thinking, turn to Critical Thinking About Children's Development.

Cognitive Monitoring

Another very general thinking skill that is critical for academic success is **cognitive monitoring**—*the process of taking stock of what you are currently doing, what you will do next, and how effectively the mental activity is unfolding.* When children engage in an activity like reading, writing, or solving a math problem, they are repeatedly called on to figure out what they are doing and what they plan to do next (Brown & Palincsar, 1989). For example, when children begin to solve a math problem—especially one that might take a while to finish—they must decide what kind of problem they are working on and what would be a good approach to solving it. Once they undertake a problem solution, it is helpful for them to check on whether the solution strategy seems to be working or whether another approach would be better.

The source of much cognitive monitoring for young children is other people, especially parents and teachers. Adults provide a lot of guidance and direction for children's activities, and they tell children what specific strategies to use to complete various cognitive tasks. They suggest when children should start an activity, they

intervene at points when they think children might encounter difficulty (for instance, to explain difficult words, how to get started writing on a topic, how to look at math problems, or how to study), and they check children's progress and understanding (for instance, giving oral spelling quizzes, asking for explanations, or holding discussions). As children become better able to monitor their own performance, they operate increasingly independently of this social support.

Instructional programs in reading comprehension, writing, and mathematics have been designed to foster the development of cognitive monitoring. Developmental psychologists Ann Brown and Annemarie Palincsar's (1984, 1989) program for reading comprehension is an excellent example of an instructional program that emphasizes cognitive monitoring.

Brown and Palincsar's program uses reciprocal teaching techniques to develop cognitive monitoring skills. Such reciprocal instruction requires students to take turns in leading a study group in the use of strategies for comprehending and remembering text content. The instruction involves a small group of students, often working with an adult leader, actively discussing a short text, with the goal of summarizing it, asking questions to promote understanding, offering clarifying statements for difficult or confusing words and ideas, and predicting what will come next. The procedure actively involves children, it teaches them techniques for thinking about their own understanding, and the group interaction is highly motivating and engaging. The program has proven effective not only for increasing reading comprehension but also for increasing performance on tests of science and social studies proficiency (which also require good reading comprehension skills).

Programs like Brown and Palincsar's reciprocal teaching approach are not the only ones in which collaborative learning has been shown to be effective. A flurry of recent research has documented the power of peer collaboration in learning and problem solving (Ayman-Nolley & Church, 1993; Tudge & Winterhoff, 1993). Working with other children, rather than individually, seems to increase learning, not only because it increases the probability that someone will generate a good idea, but also because it is highly motivating and because being exposed to other people's thinking stimulates new ideas in each participant.

Individual and Cultural Differences

Children are far from identical in the ways they learn. Some differences are attributable to individual talents, aptitudes, and proclivities; some are due to differences in the families in which children grow up; some are due to characteristics of the cultures into which they are born. Below we examine some of the individual, family, and cultural differences that influence the learning of academic materials.

Individual Differences

Although most children do not learn to read until they go to school, a few 2- and 3-year-olds manage to do so. How does such precocious reading ability develop in these children, and why them rather than their peers?

As a group, precocious readers tend to have above-average IQs, though their scores are not in general exceptional. The most important difference between precocious readers and others appears to be interest, not general intellectual factors. This includes both the children's interest and that of their families. Both parents of precocious readers and parents of other children report that their children were interested in reading before they entered school. The parents of the precocious readers, however, more often report that reading materials and blackboards are present in the homes, and that children are unusually interested in word meanings. The parents of the precocious readers also appear to read to their children unusually often, presumably because both they and the children are interested in the activity.

What happens to precocious readers later? Contrary to the fears of some educators, they remain excellent readers at least through sixth grade. They do not all maintain their superiority, but they continue to do much better than average.

Not all individual differences in children involve differences in knowledge or ability; some involve differences in cognitive style. One such difference in style involves impulsivity and reflectivity. **Impulsivity** *is a cognitive style in which individuals act before they think.* If fine discriminations of information are required, this style often leads to errors. **Reflection** *is a cognitive style in which individuals think before they act, usually scanning information carefully and slowly.* This style leads to fewer errors when fine discriminations of information are required. Impulsivity is not always disadvantageous; impulsive students usually finish objective tests quickly, whereas reflective students sometimes are still contemplating their answers when the exam period is almost over.

> *As many men, so many minds; every one his own way.*
>
> —Terence

The test most often used to measure individual differences in impulsivity/reflection is the Matching Familiar Figures Test (Kagan, 1965) (see figure 8.12). On this test, children are presented with a series of pictures in which they must select the one picture of the six at the bottom that exactly matches the picture at the top. Impulsive children typically scan the six options quickly, often making a choice that is inaccurate. By contrast, reflective children carefully examine each of the six pictures and choose slowly, more often making a choice that is correct.

Much learning that takes place in classrooms requires reflection rather than impulsivity. To do well on many school tasks, children must carefully examine the details of information, reflect on what the best answer is, and evaluate their errors after they have failed at a task (Pascual-Leone & Shafrir, 1991). Researchers have trained impulsive children to become more reflective by improving their scanning strategies, teaching them to take more time, and instructing them to talk to themselves to control their behavior (Meichenbaum & Goodman, 1971). Even with reflection training, though, impulsive children rarely attain the careful examination of information that characterizes their reflective counterparts. Also, it is important to keep in mind that not all cognitive tasks require extensive examination of the fine details of information. Sometimes a quick scan of information is all that is needed to discover the information one needs. If a child wakes up in the morning, looks out the window, and sees it is raining, she does not have to reflect at length when she looks in her closet to determine what type of coat she will wear to school. She only has to quickly pick out her raincoat.

Individual differences in academic tasks often involve a combination of differences in knowledge and differences in cognitive style. Consider a study of first-graders' performance in addition, subtraction, and reading (Siegler, 1988). Analysis of the children's performance revealed three subgroups: good students, not-so-good students, and perfectionists. The not-so-good students had a relatively poor knowledge of the subject matter and an

Figure~8.12

Two Sample Items from the Matching Familiar Figures Test
The child is asked to find the object in the six items at the bottom of each card that is identical to the object at the top of the card.

impulsive cognitive style. They frequently quickly advanced answers to problems even when they did not know the answers. The good students had a high level of knowledge and a fairly reflective style. On the relatively easy problems, they generally stated the answer quickly and accurately; on the harder problems, they used slower approaches that yielded high degrees of accuracy on those problems. The perfectionists had as high a level of knowledge as the good students did, but were more reflective. They rarely answered quickly, even though they were almost always correct when they did so. These differences among children predict future placements into special education classes and retention in the same grade, hold stable over at least a 1-year period, and apply to both lower- and middle-income students (Kerkman & Siegler, 1993; Siegler & Campbell, 1989). The same types of differences have been found to apply to both arithmetic and reading, and individual children tend to show the same patterns in both areas.

Cultural Differences

Most psychologists agree that the cognitive processes by which children remember, form concepts, and learn are the same all over the world. However, the particular content that they learn and how well they learn it are greatly influenced by the culture in which they grow up (see Sociocultural Worlds of Children). The types of

cultural differences that have recently been found in academic areas have not been ones to make citizens of the United States especially proud.

In the last decade, the poor performance of American children in math and science has become all too clear. For example, in one recent cross-national comparison of the math and science achievement of 9- to 13-year-old students, the United States finished 13th (out of 15) in science and 15th (out of 16) in math achievement (Educational Testing Service, 1992). Korean and Taiwanese students placed first and second, respectively.

Reasons for the superior performance of Asian students have been documented in research conducted by Harold Stevenson and his colleagues (Hofer, Carlson, & Stevenson, 1996; Stevenson, 1992, 1995; Stevenson, Chen, & Lee, 1993). Over the past 15 years, they have conducted a series of cross-national studies of children's learning and achievement in Japan, Taiwan, mainland China, and the United States. Rather than just describing the deficiencies of American children's achievement in comparison to children from other nations, they have sought to answer the all-important question: Why?

Their findings are intriguing. Contrary to popular stereotypes, Asian children's high level of achievement does not result from rote learning and repeated drilling in tension-filled schools. Rather, the children are highly motivated to learn, and teaching is innovative and interesting in many

Learning Math in New Guinea and Brazil

Children's math learning depends not only on their innate ability to handle abstractions and adult efforts to teach math concepts, but also on the adults' own knowledge about numbers, which in turn depends on their cultural heritage (Cole & Cole, 1993). Children growing up among the Oksapmin of New Guinea seem to have the same ability to grasp basic number concepts as children growing up in Tokyo or Los Angeles have. However, the counting system used in the Oksapmin culture—counting by body parts—does not support the more sophisticated development of algebraic thinking (Saxe, 1981). The Oksapmin use 29 body parts in their system of counting (see figure 8.A). In America it is not unusual for children to use their fingers to keep track of numbers early in their math learning, but because of American schooling they go far beyond Oksapmin children in learning math.

Although schooling often helps with learning math, in some cultures children who do not attend school learn math as part of their everyday experience. For example, whereas most Brazilian children attend school, Brazilian market children do not, yet they learn remarkable math skills in the context of everyday buying and selling. However, when presented with the same math problems in a school-like format, they have difficulty (Carraher & Carraher, 1981). Another example is that many high school students in the United States can solve certain physics problems, which they consider elementary, that baffled the brilliant Greek philosopher Aristotle in ancient times. In each of these instances, culture has shaped the course of learning.

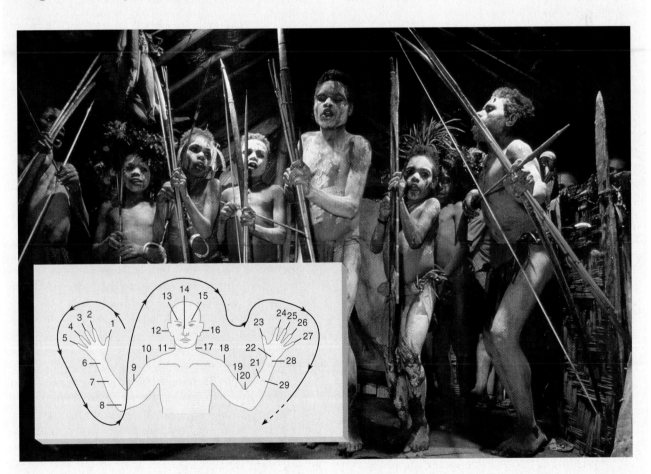

Figure~8.A

The Counting System of the Oksapmin of New Guinea
The arithmetic counting of the Oksapmin of New Guinea is based on 29 numbers that correspond to a sequence of body parts.

Asian schools, particularly those in Japan. Knowledge is not force-fed to children; rather, children are encouraged to construct their own ways of representing the knowledge. Asian children have many more school days per year than children in the United States do, but their school days are punctuated often by exercise and recess periods. Asian schools embrace many of the ideals Americans have for their own schools, but are more successful in implementing them in interesting and productive ways that make learning more enjoyable for children.

Not all of the achievement differences between Asian and U.S. children can be ascribed to Asian schools' being superior to those in the United States. Children in Asian societies might know more about math even before they enter school. For example, preschool children in mainland China have been found to know more about arithmetic than U.S. preschoolers do (Geary & others, 1993). In general, Asian cultures seem to place greater emphasis on mathematical understanding. However, schools are a large contributor to the cultural differences; the longer Asian and American children are in school, the wider the gap between their math scores becomes.

Many Asian grade schools intersperse studying with frequent periods of activities. This approach helps children maintain their attention and likely makes learning more enjoyable. Shown here are Japanese fourth-graders making wearable masks.

To learn more about the ways in which schools, families, and the general culture contribute to these large cross-cultural differences in achievement, Stevenson and his colleagues (Stevenson, Chen, & Lee, 1993) have spent hundreds of hours observing classrooms; interviewing teachers, children, and mothers; and giving questionnaires to the fathers. They have found that American parents are more satisfied with their children's educational achievement than are Asian parents, even though the Asian children are achieving far more. Perhaps related to this difference in evaluation, American parents believe that their children's math achievement is primarily determined by innate ability, whereas Asian parents believe their children's math achievement is mainly the result of effort and training. If you believe that math achievement is largely determined by biological factors beyond anyone's control, then there is no point in being dissatisfied with your child's achievement in the subject. On the other hand, if you believe that math achievement is mainly a product of effort and training, then shortcomings in your child's performance are reasons for dissatisfaction.

In 1990, former president Bush and the nation's governors adopted a well-publicized goal: to change

American education in ways that will help U.S. students to lead the world in math achievement by the year 2000. Stevenson and his colleague James Stigler (1992) say that is unlikely to happen. American standards and expectations for children's math achievement are simply too low by international standards to make such a large change so quickly.

While Asian students are doing so well in math achievement, might there be a dark underside of too much stress and tension in the students and their schools? Stevenson and his colleagues (Stevenson, Chen, & Lee, 1993) have not found that to be the case. They asked eleventh-grade students in Japan and the United States how often in the past month they had experienced feelings of stress, depression, aggression, and other problems, such as not being able to sleep well. They also asked the students how often they felt nervous when they took tests. On all of these characteristics, the Japanese students reported less stress and fewer problems than did the American students. Such findings do not support the Western stereotype that Asian students are tense, wired individuals driven by relentless pressures for academic excellence.

Critics of cross-national studies say that such comparisons are flawed because countries differ greatly in the percentage of their children who go to school and in the nature of their curricula. Even in the face of such criticisms,

Concept	Processes/ Related Ideas	Characteristics/Description
Conceptual Development	Concepts as implicit theories	Many of children's concepts embody implicit theories about the world. Such theories are organized hierarchically, with some applying broadly, others more narrowly.
	Concepts of the mind	Children's understanding of the human mind grows extensively in the first few years. Wellman proposed that from about 3 years of age children have a naive theory of how the mind works—he labeled it the belief-desire theory.
	Biological concepts	Even 3- and 4-year-olds have fairly sophisticated biological concepts.
	Physical concepts	Older children's understanding of space builds on rudimentary early understanding. As they develop, children come to form at least three types of spatial representations: egocentric, landmark-based, and allocentric. Another key concept for understanding the physical world is number.
Problem Solving	Its nature	Problem solving is a central activity of children's lives. Much of information-processing research on problem solving has been aimed at identifying the rules children use to solve problems.
	Infant imitation	Infants can imitate facial expressions in the first few days of life. Meltzoff has demonstrated that deferred imitation occurs at about 9 months of age, much earlier than Piaget believed.
	Means-ends analysis and plans	Infants less than 1 year of age show means-ends analysis in some situations. Means-ends analysis is later extended to much more complex situations. Planning is an important determinant of problem-solving ability throughout the childhood years.
	Scientific reasoning	Children's problem solving shares certain characteristics with that of scientists, but also differs in some ways.
	Reasoning by analogy	Even very young children can draw reasonable analogies under some circumstances and use them to solve problems.
	Problem solving in social contexts	Children's problem-solving skills do not develop in a vacuum—rather, they evolve in a rich context of social interactions.
Academic Skills	Mathematics	Children already have a substantial understanding of numerical concepts before they enter the first grade. When they go to school, children learn many more-advanced kinds of numerical skills.
	Reading	Children develop through a number of stages in learning to read. Memory capacity, monitoring one's own comprehension, and having relevant content knowledge are important in the development of reading comprehension.
	General thinking skills	To think critically, children need to take an active role in learning. Children also need to ask questions for clarification. Critical-thinking programs usually are more effective when they are domain-specific rather than domain-general. Another excellent thinking skill is cognitive monitoring—the process of taking stock of what you are currently doing, what you will do next, and how effectively the mental activity is unfolding.
	Individual and cultural differences	Individual differences include differences in learning to read. Most children do not learn to read until they go to school, but some precocious readers learn to read at 2 to 3 years of age. One important individual difference involves impulsivity versus reflection. Much learning that takes place in classrooms involves reflection. There are also cultural differences in children's academic skills. Developmentalists have shown a strong interest in the high achievement levels of Japanese, Chinese, and other Asian children.

there is a growing consensus, based on information collected by different research teams, that American children's achievement is very low, that American educators' and parents' expectations for children's math achievement are too low, and that American schools are long overdue for an extensive overhaul. Perhaps if we incorporate the lessons of research on how children remember, form concepts, solve problems, and acquire academic skills, we will be able to provide better education in the future.

At this point we have studied a number of ideas about conceptual development, problem solving, and academic skills. A summary of these ideas is presented in concept table 8.2.

As children develop and learn, they process information. And they do this in many different ways.

We began the chapter by exploring the nature of the information-processing approach, defining it and comparing it with the Piagetian approach. Then we studied a process that is central to information processing—memory, including what memory is, time frames of memory, schemas, basic processes, strategies, metacognitive knowledge, and content knowledge. Next, we examined children's conceptual development, including concepts as implicit theories, as well as children's concepts of mind and their biological and physical concepts. Our coverage of children's problem solving focused on infant imitation, means-ends analysis and plans, scientific reasoning, reasoning by analogy, and problem solving in social contexts. We also read about children's academic skills—mathematics, reading, general thinking skills, and individual and cultural differences in academic skills.

Don't forget to again study the concept tables on pages 256 and 279 to obtain an overall summary of the chapter. So far in this section of the book we have studied the nature of cognitive development and Piaget's theory and information processing. In the next chapter we will turn our attention to yet another approach to children's cognition, that of individual differences and intelligence.

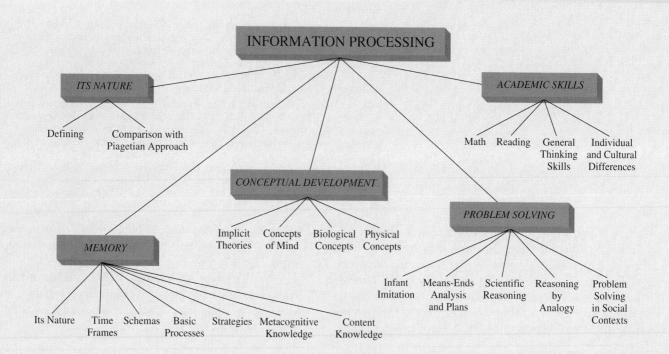

PRACTICAL KNOWLEDGE ABOUT CHILDREN

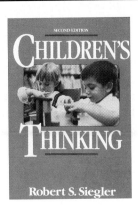

Children's Thinking
(1991, 2nd Ed.) by Robert S. Siegler, Englewood Cliffs, NJ: Prentice Hall.

Siegler, one of the world's leading authorities on children's thinking, provides a comprehensive overview of how children think. This is an up-to-date treatment of key issues in children's thinking, information-processing theories of development, and specific aspects of children's thinking such as perceptual development, language development, memory development, conceptual development, and problem solving. Siegler also discusses how children learn reading, writing, and mathematical skills, as well as the learning abilities of blind, deaf, gifted, and mentally retarded children.

EXPLORATIONS IN CHILD DEVELOPMENT

To further explore the nature of child development, we will examine a research study on young children's knowledge about thinking, and then we will discuss the nature of repressed memories and child abuse.

RESEARCH IN CHILD DEVELOPMENT

Young Children's Knowledge About Thinking

Featured Study

Flavell, J. H., Green, F. L., & Flavell, E. R. (1955). Young children's knowledge about thinking. *Monographs of the Society for Research in Child Development, 60(1).*

What do preschoolers know and not know about thinking? Answering this question was the goal of the research described in this monograph, which reports the results of fourteen studies focused on young children's knowledge about their thinking. A monograph differs in certain ways from a typical article in a research journal. A monograph is much longer than a typical journal article; a monograph might run anywhere from 75 to over 200 typed double-spaced pages, whereas a journal article usually is in the range of 15 to 20 double-spaced typed pages. A monograph is intended as an outlet for major reports of research that generate authoritative new findings and use these to foster a fresh or better-integrated perspective on a conceptually significant issue or controversy.

Note that in the monograph being described here, fourteen studies were conducted. Space limitations obviously keep us from describing all of these studies. To help you get a

sense of how researchers study young children's knowledge about thinking, we will describe the first of the fourteen studies. The purpose of this study was to find out how easily young children could (with the experimenter's help) learn to distinguish what a depicted child was thinking about (as portrayed in a "thought bubble") from what the child was looking at or doing.

Method

Three groups of children (mean ages of 3 years, 3 months; 3 years, 10 months; and 4 years, 8 months) were tested; there were 8 girls and 8 boys in each group. The female experimenter began by modeling thinking for the children. She gave the topic of what she would think about, such as her bedroom, and described some of its contents. The subject was encouraged to do the same. The task stimuli were six drawings of children. In each drawing a child was doing one thing (such as looking at her mother or riding a bicycle) while thinking about something else (such as her teddy bear or kicking a football); the thoughts were illustrated in a thought bubble over the character's head. Two of the six bubbles were used in pretraining to explain the idea of thought bubbles.

Four test pictures were presented. In two of the pictures, characters were shown looking at one object but think-

ing of another. For example, in one a girl was depicted looking at her mother while thinking about her teddy bear: "Here's Sally and her mom. Sally is really *doing* something right now. Is she really looking at her mom? Sally is *thinking* about something right now. Is she thinking about her mom?" These questions were asked about the perceived object. In the other picture depicting "looking at," the questions were asked about the object in the thought bubble. Thus, the yes/no questions were framed so that within each block the correct answer to one "think" question ("Is she thinking about . . . ?") was yes and to the other it was no.

Results and Discussion

Even the young 3-year-olds understood that thinking was an activity different from looking and overt motor actions. They appeared to understand the experimenter's initial examples of thinking and to follow her brief explanation of the thought bubbles fairly well (although some of the youngest children incorrectly said yes in the pretraining when asked if a child was also thinking about an object not shown in the thought bubble). They were then able to use that information to map thinking onto what was inside the bubbles. And the young children understood that looking and acting were outside the thought bubbles.

Repressed Memories, Child Abuse, and Reality

Discussions of the abilities of adults to remember early experiences, especially those involving childhood abuse, have become very heated (Ornstein, 1995). Arguments concerning the recovery of repressed memories and the creation of memories have polarized the clinical and research communities, as well as the general public. Recently, developmental psychologists have shown an increasing interest in exploring the developing memory system in terms of its implications for this debate (Fivush, 1995; Howe, 1995; Stein, 1995).

Repression is one of psychology's most controversial concepts. Long the province of clinical psychology, repression of threatening, anxiety-laden unconscious thoughts has caught the eye of memory researchers in cognitive psychology. Memory researcher Elizabeth Loftus (1993) recently analyzed the reality of repressed memories.

Repression takes place when something shocking happens and the mind pushes the person's memory of the occurrence into some inaccessible part of the unconscious mind. At some later point in time, the memory might emerge into consciousness. Repression is one of the foundations on which the field of psychoanalysis rests.

Recently there has been a dramatic increase in reported memories of childhood sexual abuse that were allegedly repressed for many years. With recent changes in legislation, people with recently discovered memories are suing alleged perpetrators for events that occurred 20, 30, even 40 or more years earlier.

In 1991, popular actress Roseanne's story was a cover story of *People* magazine. She reported that her mother had abused her from the time she was an infant until she was 6 or 7 years of age and that she became aware of the abuse only recently during therapy. Other highly publicized cases of repressed memories of child abuse coming into awareness during therapy dot the pages of large numbers of popular magazines, and many self-help books encourage readers to uncover repressed memories of childhood abuse.

There is little doubt that actual childhood abuse is tragically too common. Loftus and others (Ceci & Bruck, 1993) don't dispute that child abuse is a serious social problem. What Loftus does take issue with is how the abuse is recalled in the minds of adults. Despite the belief on the part of many in the therapeutic community that childhood repression of abuse is very common, few research studies provide evidence about the extent to which repression occurs. At present, there aren't any completely satisfying methods for discovering the answer to how common repressed abuse is. Repression researchers are in the unenviable position of asking people about a memory for a forgotten memory (Ceci & Bruck, 1997). In the studies that have been conducted, from 18 to 59 percent of therapists' clients have reported having become aware of repressed memories of child abuse as an adult. As Loftus points out, this is a large range and hardly suggestive of an accurate, agreed-upon incidence of repressed memories of child abuse.

Repressed memories of abuse often return in therapy, in some cases after suggestive probing by the therapist. The media (television, self-help books, magazines) are full of reports that can also be a source of suggestion, resulting in memories that often seem detailed and confidently held. Despite an absence of corroboration, some of the recollections could be authentic, while others might not be.

According to Loftus, psychotherapists, counselors, social service agencies, and law enforcement personnel need to be careful about probing for horrors on the other side of some amnesiac barrier. They should be cautious in their interpretation of uncorroborated repressed memories that return. Clarification, compassion, and gentle confrontation along with a demonstration of empathy are techniques that can be used to help individuals in their painful struggle to come to grips with their personal truths.

One final tragic risk of suggestive probing and uncritical acceptance of all allegations made by clients is that these activities lead to an increased likelihood that society in general will disbelieve the actual cases of child abuse that deserve extensive attention and evaluation.

Diego Rivera
Delfina Flores detail

The thirst to know and understand . . . these are the goods in life's rich hand.

—Sir William Watson, 1905

Children are remarkable for their intelligence and ardor, for their curiosity, their intolerance of shams, the clarity of their vision.

—Aldous Huxley

PREVIEW

*T*he topic of children's intelligence includes a number of controversies, such as the use of intelligence tests to place children in EMR classes and the Escondido sperm bank. In this chapter we also will explore other controversies in children's intelligence, examine how to measure their intelligence, describe the extremes of intelligence — mental retardation and giftedness — and discuss children's creativity. But to begin with, we need to determine just what intelligence is.

Information about children's intelligence and intelligence tests frequently makes the news. The following two stories appeared in the *Los Angeles Times:*

> IQ testing that leads to the placement of an unusually large number of black children in so-called mentally retarded classes has been ruled unconstitutional by a federal judge. On behalf of five African American children, Chief District Court Judge Robert Peckham said the use of standardized IQ tests to place children in educable mentally retarded (EMR) classes violated recently enacted federal laws and the state and federal constitutions. . . . Peckham said the history of IQ testing and special education in California "revealed an unlawful discriminatory intent . . . not necessarily to hurt African American children, but it was an intent to assign a grossly disproportionate number of black children to the special, inferior and dead-end EMR classes." (October 18, 1979)
>
> A controversial Escondido sperm bank for superbrains has produced its first baby—a healthy, nine-pound girl born to a woman identified only as a small-town resident in "a sparsely populated state." . . . Founded by inventor Robert K. Graham of Escondido in 1979, the facility contains sperm donated by at least three Nobel Prize winners, plus other prominent researchers. . . . The sperm bank was founded to breed children of higher intelligence. The goal has been denounced by many critics, who say that a child's intelligence is not determined so much by his genes as by his upbringing and environment. (May 25, 1982)

As you might expect, these stories sparked impassioned debate (Kail & Pellegrino, 1985). Some arguments focus on the ethical and moral implications of selective breeding of bright children and selective placement of children in special classes. Other arguments concern the statistical basis of conclusions of intelligence tests, such as whether the tests are really biased if the data are analyzed properly. What you hear *less* often but should hear *more* often is a discussion of the construct of intelligence itself (Sternberg, 1990). That is, what is intelligence? How should it be conceptualized?

THE NATURE OF INTELLIGENCE AND ITS MEASUREMENT

What is intelligence? How are tests, such as intelligence tests, constructed and evaluated?

What Is Intelligence?

Intelligence is a possession most of us value highly, yet its concept is abstract, with few agreed-upon referents. We all would agree on referents for such characteristics as children's height, weight, and age, but there is less certainty about the referents for a child's size. Size is more *abstract* than height or weight. Also, size is more difficult to measure directly. We can only estimate size from a set of empirical measures of height and weight. Measuring intelligence is much the same as measuring size, though intelligence is *much more* abstract. That is, we believe children's intelligence exists, but we do not measure their intelligence directly. We cannot peel back a child's scalp and observe her intellectual processes in action. We can study those intellectual processes only *indirectly*, by evaluating the intelligent acts that children generate. For the most part, psychologists have relied on intelligence tests to provide an estimate of children's intellectual processes.

While many psychologists and laypeople equate intelligence with verbal ability and problem-solving skills, others prefer to define it as the individual's ability to learn from and adapt to the experiences of everyday life. If we were to settle on a definition of intelligence based on these criteria, it would be that **intelligence** is *verbal ability, problem-solving skills, and the ability to learn from and adapt to the experiences of everyday life* (see figure 9.1).

> *What a piece of work is a man! How noble in reason! how infinite in faculty! in form, in moving, how express and admirable! in action how like an angel! in apprehension how like a god!*
>
> **—William Shakespeare**

Although we have just defined general intelligence, keep in mind that the way intelligence is expressed in behavior may vary from culture to culture (Lonner, 1990). For example, in most Western cultures, people are considered intelligent if they are both smart (have considerable knowledge and can solve verbal problems) and fast (can process information quickly). On the other hand, in the Buganda culture in Uganda, people who are wise, slow in thought, and say the socially correct thing are considered intelligent (Wober, 1974).

The components of intelligence are very close to the information-processing skills we discussed in chapter 8. The difference between how we discussed information-processing skills and how we will discuss intelligence lies in the concepts of individual differences and assessment. **Individual differences** *are the stable, consistent ways in which people are different from each other*. The history of the study of intelligence has focused extensively on individual differences (Cohen, Swerdlik, & Phillips, 1996). We can talk about individual differences in personality or in any other domain of development, but it is in the area of intelligence that the most attention is given to individual differences. For example, an intelligence test tells us whether a child can reason better than most others who have taken the test. **Psychometrics** *is the field that involves the assessment of individual differences*. We will examine several of the tests most widely used to assess children's intelligence, but first we need to know something very important in psychometrics—how tests are constructed and evaluated.

> *As many men, as many minds; everyone his own way.*
>
> **—Terence**

How Tests Are Constructed and Evaluated

The first evidence of formal tests comes from China. In 2200 B.C. the emperor Ta Yu conducted a series of three oral "competency tests" for government officials; based on the results, they were either promoted or fired (Sax, 1989). Numerous variations on those early exams have been causing anxiety for employees and students ever since. Any good test must meet three criteria—it must be reliable, it must be valid, and it must be standardized. With a reliable test, scores will not fluctuate significantly as a result of chance factors, such as how much sleep the test taker got the night before, who the examiner is, or what the temperature is in the testing room. **Reliability** *is the extent to which a test yields a consistent, reproducible measure of performance.* One method of assessing reliability is **test-retest reliability,** *which is the extent to which a test yields the same measure of performance when an individual is given the same test on two different occasions.* For example, a reliable test would be one on which the same students who score high one day also score high 6 months later. One drawback of test-retest reliability is that people sometimes do better the second time they take the test because they are familiar with it.

Another way in which consistency can be deceptive is that a test may or may not measure the attribute we seek. For example, let's say we want to measure intelligence but the test design is flawed and we actually measure something else, such as anxiety. The test might

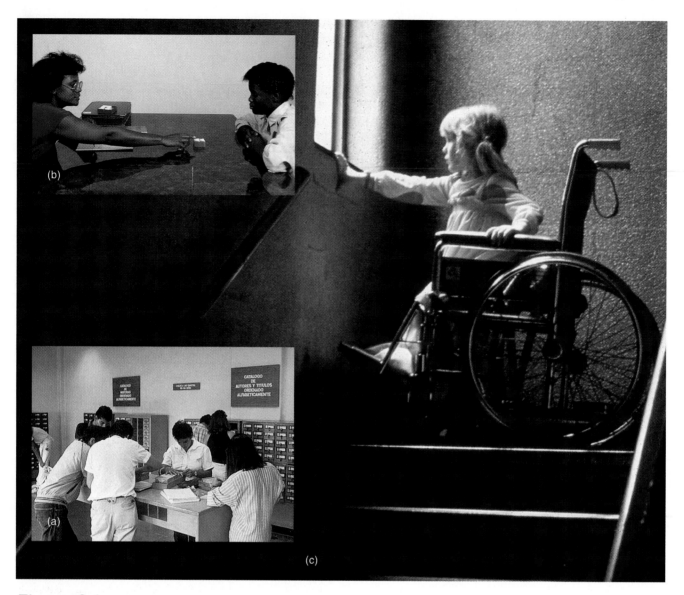

Figure~9.1

Defining Intelligence
Intelligence is an abstract concept that has been defined in various ways. The three most commonly agreed-upon aspects of intelligence are the following: (a) verbal ability, as reflected in the verbal skills of these students searching for library books; (b) problem-solving skills, as reflected in the ability of this girl to solve the design problem presented her; and (c) ability to learn from and adapt to experiences of everyday life, as reflected in this handicapped child's adaptation to her inability to walk.

consistently measure how anxious the subjects are, and thus have high reliability, but fail to measure intelligence. **Validity** *is the extent to which a test measures what it is intended to measure.* Two important forms of validity are content validity and criterion validity.

Content validity *is a test's ability to test a broad range of the content that is to be measured.* For example, if your instructor for this class plans a comprehensive final exam, it will probably cover topics from each of the chapters rather than from just two or three chapters. If an intelligence test purports to measure both verbal ability and problem-solving ability, the test should include a liberal sampling of items testing each. The

test would not have high content validity if it asked you to define several vocabulary items (one measure of verbal ability) and did not require you to use reason in solving a number of problems.

Criterion validity *is a test's ability to predict an individual's performance when measured by other measures, or criteria, of an attribute.* For example, rather than relying solely on the results of one intelligence test to assess a person's intelligence, a psychologist might also ask that person's employer how he or she performs at work. The employer's perceptions would be another criterion for assessing intelligence. Using additional measures—by, for instance, administering a different intelligence test, soliciting an employer's perception of intelligence, and observing a person's problem-solving ability—is a good strategy for establishing criterion validity.

Good tests are not only reliable and valid, but they also are standardized. **Standardization** *involves developing uniform procedures for administering and scoring a test, and it also involves developing norms for the test.* Uniform testing procedures require that the testing environment be as similar as possible for everyone who takes the test. For example, the test directions and the amount of time allowed to complete the test should be uniform. **Norms** *are established standards of performance for a test. Norms are arrived at by giving the test to a large group of people who represent the target population. This allows the researcher to determine the distribution of test scores. Norms inform us which scores are considered high, low, or average.* For example, a score of 120 on an intelligence test has little meaning alone. The score takes on meaning when we compare it with other scores. If only 20 percent of the standardized group scores above 120, then we can interpret that score as high, rather than average or low. Many tests of intelligence are designed for people from diverse groups. So that the tests will be applicable to such different groups, many tests have norms—that is, established standards of performance for people of different ages.

> *No man is smart, except by comparison with others who know less.*
>
> —Edgar Watson Howe

Although there has been some effort to standardize intelligence tests for African Americans and Latinos, little has been done to standardize tests for people from other ethnic minorities. Psychologists need to ensure that the tests are standardized for a person's particular ethnic group and to put the test results in an appropriate cultural context (Sue, 1990). Otherwise they must use caution interpreting the test's results.

Children's Intelligence Tests

Robert J. Sternberg recalls being terrified of taking IQ tests as a child. He literally froze, he says, when the time came to take such tests. Even as an adult, Sternberg stings with humiliation when he recalls being in sixth grade and taking an IQ test with the fifth-graders. Sternberg finally overcame his anxieties about IQ tests and not only performed much better on them, but at age 13 he even devised his own IQ test and began assessing his classmates—until the school psychologist found out and scolded him. In fact, Sternberg became so fascinated with the topic that he's made it a lifelong pursuit. Sternberg's theory of intelligence, which we will discuss later in the chapter, has received considerable attention

recently. We will begin at the beginning, with the first intelligence test, in our discussion of the measurement and nature of intelligence.

The Binet Tests

In 1904 the French Ministry of Education asked psychologist Alfred Binet to devise a method of identifying children who were unable to learn in school. School officials wanted to reduce crowding by placing into special schools those who did not benefit from regular classroom teaching. Binet and his student Theophile Simon developed an intelligence test to meet this request. The test is referred to as the 1905 Scale and consisted of thirty questions, ranging from the ability to touch one's nose or ear when asked to the ability to draw designs from memory and define abstract concepts.

Binet developed the concept of **mental age (MA),** *which is an individual's level of mental development relative to others.* Binet reasoned that a child with mental retardation would perform like a normal child of a younger age. He developed averages for intelligence by testing 50 normal children from 3 to 11 years of age. Children who were thought to be mentally retarded also were tested. Their scores were then compared with the scores of normal children of the same chronological age. Average mental-age scores (MA) correspond to chronological age (CA), which is age from birth. A bright child has an MA above CA; a dull child has an MA below CA.

The term **intelligence quotient (IQ)** *was devised in 1912 by William Stern. IQ consists of a person's mental age divided by chronological age, multiplied by 100:*

$$IQ = MA/CA \times 100$$

If mental age is the same as chronological age, then the person's IQ is 100; if mental age is above chronological age, then IQ is more than 100; if mental age is below chronological age, then IQ is less than 100. Scores noticeably above 100 are considered above average, and scores noticeably below 100 are considered below average. For example, a 6-year-old child with a mental age of 8 would have an IQ of 133, whereas a 6-year-old child with a mental age of 5 would have an IQ of 83.

The Binet test has been revised many times to incorporate advances in the understanding of intelligence and intelligence testing. These revisions are called the Stanford-Binet tests (Stanford University is where the revisions were done). Many of the revisions were carried out by Lewis Terman, who applied Stern's IQ concept to the test, developed extensive norms, and provided detailed, clear instructions for each problem on the test.

In an extensive effort to standardize the Stanford-Binet test, it has been given to thousands of children and adults of different ages, selected at random from various parts of the United States. By administering the test to large numbers of people and recording the results, researchers have found that intelligence measured

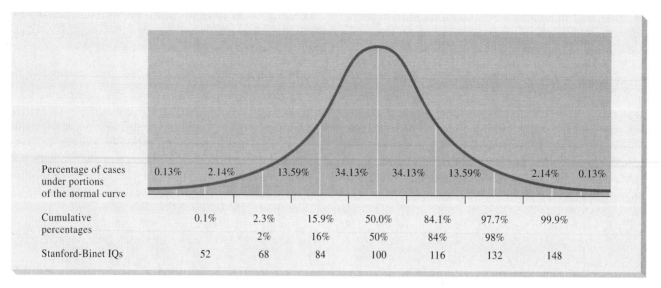

Percentage of cases under portions of the normal curve	0.13%	2.14%	13.59%	34.13%	34.13%	13.59%	2.14%	0.13%
Cumulative percentages	0.1%	2.3%	15.9%	50.0%	84.1%	97.7%	99.9%	
		2%	16%	50%	84%	98%		
Stanford-Binet IQs	52	68	84	100	116	132	148	

Figure~9.2

The Normal Curve and the Stanford-Binet IQ Scores
The distribution of IQ scores approximates a normal curve. Most of the population falls in the middle range of scores. Notice that extremely high and extremely low scores are very rare. Slightly more than two-thirds of the scores fall between 84 and 116. Only about 1 in 50 individuals has an IQ of more than 132 and only about 1 in 50 individuals has an IQ of less than 68.

by the Stanford-Binet approximates a normal distribution (see figure 9.2). A **normal distribution** *is symmetrical, with a majority of cases falling in the middle of the possible range of scores and few scores appearing toward the extremes of the range.*

The current Stanford-Binet is given to individuals from the age of 2 through adulthood. It includes a wide variety of items, some requiring verbal responses, others nonverbal responses. For example, items that characterize a 6-year-old's performance on the test include the verbal ability to define at least six words, such as *orange* and *envelope*, and the nonverbal ability to trace a path through a maze. Items that reflect an average adult's intelligence include defining such words as *disproportionate* and *regard*, explaining a proverb, and comparing idleness and laziness.

The fourth edition of the Stanford-Binet was published in 1985 (Thorndike, Hagan, & Sattler, 1985). One important addition to this version is the analysis of the individual's responses in terms of four content areas: verbal reasoning, quantitative reasoning, abstract/visual reasoning, and short-term memory. A general composite score also is obtained to reflect overall intelligence. The Stanford-Binet continues to be one of the most widely used individual tests of intelligence.

The Wechsler Scales

Besides the Stanford-Binet, the other widely used intelligence tests are the Wechsler scales, developed by David Wechsler. They include the Wechsler Adult Intelligence Scale–Revised (WAIS-R); the Wechsler Intelligence Scale for Children–Revised (WISC-R), to test children between the ages of 6 and 16; and the Wechsler Preschool and Primary Scale of Intelligence (WPPSI), to test children from the ages of 4 to 6½.

Not only do the Wechsler scales provide an overall IQ score, but the items are grouped according to 11 subscales, of which 6 are verbal and 5 nonverbal (performance). This allows an examiner to obtain separate verbal and nonverbal IQ scores and to see quickly the areas of mental performance in which a tested individual is below average, average, or above average. The inclusion of a number of nonverbal subscales makes the Wechsler test more representative of verbal and nonverbal intelligence; the Stanford-Binet test includes some nonverbal items, but not as many as the Wechsler scales. Several of the Wechsler subscales are shown in figure 9.3.

Does Intelligence Have a Single Nature?

Is it more appropriate to think of a child's intelligence as a general ability or as a number of specific abilities? Psychologists were debating the nature of the components of intelligence long before David Wechsler analyzed intelligence in terms of general and specific abilities (giving a child an overall IQ but also providing information about specific subcomponents of intelligence).

Early Factor Approaches

Charles Spearman (1927) proposed that intelligence has two factors. **Two-factor theory** *is Spearman's theory that children have both general intelligence, which he called g, and a number of specific types of intelligence, which he called s.* Spearman believed that these two factors account for a child's performance on an intelligence test.

VERBAL SUBSCALES

Similarities

An individual must think logically and abstractly to answer a number of questions about how things might be similar.

For example, "In what ways are boats and trains the same?"

Comprehension

This subtest is designed to measure an individual's judgment and common sense.

For example, "Why do individuals buy automobile insurance?"

PERFORMANCE SUBSCALES

Picture arrangement

A series of pictures out of sequence is shown to an individual, who is asked to place them in their proper order to tell an appropriate story. This subtest evaluates how individuals integrate information to make it logical and meaningful.

For example, "The pictures below need to be placed in an appropriate order to tell a story."

Block design

An individual must assemble a set of multicolored blocks to match designs that the examiner shows. Visual-motor coordination, perceptual organization, and the ability to visualize spatially are assessed.

For example, "Use the four blocks on the left to make the pattern at the right."

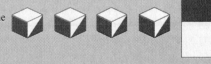

Remember that the Wechsler includes 11 subscales, 6 verbal and 5 nonverbal. Four of the subscales are shown here.

Figure~9.3

Sample Subscales of the Wechsler Intelligence Scale for Children, Revised

Simulated items similar to those in the Wechsler Intelligence Scales for Adults and Children. Copyright © 1994 by The Psychological Corporation. Reproduced by permission. All rights reserved.

However, some factor approaches abandoned the idea of general intelligence and searched for specific factors only. **Multiple-factor theory** *is L. L. Thurstone's (1938) theory that intelligence consists of seven primary abilities: verbal comprehension, number ability, word fluency, spatial visualization, associative memory, reasoning, and perceptual speed.*

Gardner's Seven Frames of Mind

A more recent attempt to classify intelligence, developed by Howard Gardner (1983, 1989), includes seven components, which he calls *frames of mind*, although they are not the same as Thurstone's seven factors. For example, the talents of Michael Jordan and Ludwig von Beethoven

Howard Gardner, here working with a young child, developed the view that intelligence comes in seven different forms: verbal skills, mathematical skills, ability to spatially analyze the world, movement skills, insightful skills for analyzing ourselves, insightful skills for analyzing others, and musical skills.

reflect the diversity of Gardner's concept of intelligence. Jordan and Beethoven are two different types of individuals, with different types of abilities. Jordan, the 6-foot-6-inch superstar of the Chicago Bulls, springs into motion. Grabbing a rebound off the defensive board, he quickly moves across two-thirds of the 94-foot basketball court, all the while processing the whereabouts of his five opponents and four teammates. As the crowd screams, Jordan calmly looks left, finesses his way past a defender, and whirls a behind-the-back pass to a fast-breaking teammate, who dunks the ball for two points. Is there specific intelligence in Jordan's movement and perception of the basketball court's spatial layout? Now we turn the clock back 200 years. A tiny boy just 4 years old is standing on a footstool in front of a piano keyboard, practicing. At the age of 6, the boy is given the honor of playing concertos and trios at a concert. Beethoven's musical genius was evident at a young age. Did Beethoven have a specific type of intelligence, one we might call musical intelligence?

Gardner argues that Jordan's talent reflects his movement intelligence and his ability to analyze the world spatially, and that Beethoven's talent reflects his

musical intelligence. Beyond these three forms of intelligence, Gardner believes there are four other main forms of intelligence: verbal intelligence, mathematical intelligence, insightful skills for analyzing ourselves, and insightful skills for analyzing others.

Gardner believes that each of the seven intelligences can be destroyed by brain damage, that each involves unique cognitive skills, and that each shows up in exaggerated fashion in both the gifted and *idiots savants* (individuals who are mentally retarded but who have unbelievable skill in a particular domain, such as drawing, music, or computing).

Gardner is especially interested in musical intelligence, particularly when it is exhibited at an early age. He points out that musically inclined preschool children not only have the remarkable ability to learn musical patterns easily, but also rarely forget them. He recounts a story about Stravinsky, who as an adult could still remember the musical patterns of the tuba, drums, and piccolos of the fife-and-drum band that marched outside his window when he was a young child.

To measure musical intelligence in young children, Gardner might ask a child to listen to a melody and then ask the child to recreate the tune on some bells he provides. He believes that such evaluations can be used to develop a profile of a child's intelligence. He also believes that it is during this early time in life that parents can make an important difference in how a child's intelligence develops.

Critics of Gardner's approach point out that there are geniuses in many domains other than music. There are outstanding chess players, prize-fighters, writers, politicians, physicians, lawyers, preachers, and poets, for example, yet we do not refer to chess intelligence, prize-fighter intelligence, and so on. Another criticism of Gardner's theory is that he has never provided evidence for the independence of the seven types of intelligence (Ceci, 1996).

Sternberg's Triarchic Theory of Intelligence

Robert J. Sternberg (1986) developed a theory that intelligence has three factors. **Triarchic theory** is *Sternberg's theory that intelligence consists of componential intelligence, experiential intelligence, and contextual intelligence.* Consider Ann, who scores high on traditional intelligence tests, such as the Stanford-Binet, and is a star analytical thinker. Consider Todd, who does not have the best test scores but has an insightful and creative mind. Consider Art, a street-smart child who has learned to deal in practical ways with his world, although his scores on traditional IQ tests are low.

Sternberg calls Ann's analytical thinking and abstract reasoning *componential intelligence;* it is the closest to what we call intelligence in this chapter and what is commonly measured by intelligence tests. Sternberg

CRITICAL THINKING ABOUT CHILDREN'S DEVELOPMENT

Triangulating and Framing Your Own Intelligence

Both Sternberg and Gardner have proposed interesting theories to explain human intelligence. If you adopt Sternberg's triarchic model, which aspect of the triangle would you consider to be your relative strength—the componential (analytic and abstract reasoning), the experiential (insightful and creative thinking), or the contextual (practical intelligence or street smarts)? Which would be your relative weakness?

If you adopt Gardner's approach, in which of the seven frames of intelligence do your intellectual strengths mostly clearly lie? Which of these frames is least comfortable for you?

- Are you mathematically inclined?
- Do you seem to have special gifts in understanding spatial relations?
- Do you show comfort and confidence in moving your body through space?
- Do you have special artistic talents?
- Are words and languages your forte?
- Do you have special abilities in relating to other people?
- Do you show unusual insights into what makes people tick?

Now that you have applied two theoretical frameworks to your own abilities, which framework do you prefer? Why does this framework appeal more to you? Your ability to *apply these developmental concepts to enhance personal adaptation* may have some implications for the course of study you select and the future career path you choose.

calls Todd's insightful and creative thinking *experiential intelligence*, and Art's street smarts and practical know-how *contextual intelligence*.

In Sternberg's view, the basic unit of intelligence is a *component*, simply defined as a basic unit of information processing. Sternberg believes that such components include the ability to acquire or store information, to retain or retrieve information, to transfer information, to plan, to make decisions, to solve problems, and to translate thought into performance.

The second part of Sternberg's model focuses on experience. According to Sternberg, intelligent individuals have the ability to solve new problems quickly, but they also learn how to solve familiar problems in an automatic, rote way so that their minds are free to handle other problems that require insight and creativity.

The third part of Sternberg's (1997) model involves practical intelligence—such as how to get out of trouble, how to replace a fuse, and how to get along with people. Sternberg describes this practical, or contextual, intelligence as all of the important information about getting along in the real world that you are not taught in school. He believes that contextual intelligence is sometimes more important than the "book knowledge" that is taught in school (Ferrari & Sternberg, 1997). To further evaluate the components of intelligence turn to Critical Thinking About Children's Development.

Why Are There So Many Different Theories of the Components of Intelligence?

As we discussed different approaches to intelligence, you probably noticed that theorists often disagree about the definition of intelligence. There are two reasons for this disagreement (Kail & Pellegrino, 1985). First, the

"You're wise, but you lack tree smarts."

Drawing by D. Reilly, © 1988 The New Yorker Magazine, Inc.

same data can be analyzed in many ways. Different apparent solutions, which produce different psychological interpretations, can be obtained from the same data. Second, the data obtained in separate studies differ. The critical data for interpretations of whether intelligence is a general ability or a cluster of specific abilities involves correlations (recall our discussion of this in chapter 2). The pattern of correlations depends on the group tested (schoolchildren, armed-services recruits, or criminals, for example), the total number of tests administered, and the specific tests that are included in the battery (Meehl, 1990). The outcome of such studies is that the abilities thought to make up the core of intelligence can vary across investigations. Despite these inconsistencies, evidence suggests that intelligence is *both* a general ability and a number of specific abilities.

Daniel Keating (1997, in press-a, in press-b) argues that early approaches to intelligence focused on the question of who had more or less intellectual capacity. He believes we need to move toward a new developmental model with different questions, such as these: How are the universal human capacities—for language, social interaction, planning, and abstract thinking—translated into attained capacities? How can we arrange the human social environment to maximize competence, maintain the valuable diversity of domains of expertise, and create the social frameworks that facilitate productive networks for collaborative learning?

INFANT INTELLIGENCE AND THE STABILITY OF INTELLIGENCE

Many standardized intelligence tests do not assess infant intelligence. Intelligence tests that have been created for infants are often called *developmental scales*. What are these tests like? Can we predict a child's or an adolescent's intelligence from the individual's scores on an infant intelligence test? How much do intelligence test scores change as children grow and develop?

Infant Intelligence Tests

In chapter 4, we discussed the Brazelton Neonatal Behavioral Assessment Scale, which is widely used to evaluate newborns. Developmentalists want to know how development proceeds during the course of infancy as well. If an infant advances at an especially slow rate, then enrichment may be necessary. If an infant develops at an advanced pace, parents may be advised to provide toys that stimulate cognitive growth in slightly older infants.

The infant-testing movement grew out of the tradition of IQ testing with older children. However, the measures that assess infants are necessarily less verbal than IQ tests that assess the intelligence of older children. The infant

developmental scales contain far more items related to perceptual motor development. They also include measures of social interaction.

The most important early contributor to the developmental testing of infants was Arnold Gesell (1934). He developed a measure that served as a clinical tool to help sort out potentially normal babies from abnormal ones. This was especially useful to adoption agencies, which had large numbers of babies awaiting placement. Gesell's examination was used widely for many years and still is frequently employed by pediatricians in their assessment of normal and abnormal infants. The current version of the Gesell test has four categories of behavior: motor, language, adaptive, and personal-social. The **developmental quotient (DQ)** *is an overall developmental score that combines subscores in the motor, language, adaptive, and personal-social domains in the Gesell assessment of infants.* Overall scores on such tests as the Gesell do not correlate highly with IQ scores obtained later in childhood. This is not surprising, since the nature of the items on the developmental scales is considerably less verbal than the items on intelligence tests given to older children.

The **Bayley Scales of Infant Development,** *developed by Nancy Bayley (1969), are widely used in the assessment of infant development. The current version has three components: a Mental scale, a Motor scale, and an Infant Behavior Profile.* Unlike Gesell, whose scales were clinically motivated, Bayley wanted to develop scales that could document infant behavior and predict later development. The early version of the Bayley scales covered only the first year of development; in the 1950s, the scales were extended to assess older infants.

According to the Bayley scales, at approximately 6 months of age an average baby should be able to do the following:

1. Accept a second cube—the baby holds the first cube, while the examiner places the second cube within easy reach of the infant
2. Grasp the edge of a piece of paper when it is presented
3. Vocalize pleasure and displeasure
4. Persistently reach for objects placed just out of immediate reach
5. Turn his or her head toward a spoon the experimenter suddenly drops on the floor
6. Approach a mirror when the examiner places it in front of the infant

At approximately 12 months of age, an average baby should be able to do the following:

1. Inhibit behavior when commanded to do so—for example, when the infant puts a block in his or her mouth and the examiner says, "No, no," the infant should cease the activity
2. Repeat an action if he or she is laughed at

3. Imitate words the experimenter says, such as *mama* and *dada*

4. Imitate the experimenter's actions—for example, if the experimenter rattles a spoon in a cup, the infant should imitate this action

5. Respond to simple requests, such as "Take a drink"

The Stability of Intelligence

In one study conducted by Nancy Bayley, no relation was found between the Bayley scales and intelligence as measured by the Stanford-Binet at the ages of 6 and 7 (Bayley, 1943). Another investigation found correlations of only .01 between intelligence measured at 3 months and at 5 years of age and .05 between measurements at 1 year and at 5 years (Anderson, 1939). These findings indicate virtually no relation between infant development scales and intelligence at 5 years of age. Again, it should be remembered that one of the reasons for this finding is that the components of intelligence tested in infancy are not the same as the components of intelligence tested at the age of 5.

There is a strong relation between IQ scores obtained at the ages of 6, 8, and 9 and IQ scores obtained at the age of 10. For example, in one study, the correlation between IQ at the age of 8 and IQ at the age of 10 was .88. The correlation between IQ at the age of 9 and IQ at the age of 10 was .90. These figures show a very high relation between IQ scores obtained in these years. The correlation of IQ in the preadolescent years and IQ at the age of 18 is slightly less but still statistically significant. For example, the correlation between IQ at the age of 10 and IQ at the age of 18 was .70 in one study (Honzik, MacFarlane, & Allen, 1948).

What has been said so far about the stability of intelligence has been based on measures of groups of individuals. The stability of intelligence also can be evaluated through studies of individuals. As we will see next, there can be considerable variability in an individual's scores on IQ tests.

Let's look at an example of the absence of a relation between intelligence in infancy and intelligence in later years for two children in the same family. The first child learned to speak at a very early age. She displayed the characteristics of an extravert, and her advanced motor coordination was indicated by her ability to walk at a very early age. The second child learned speech very late, saying very few words until she was 2½ years old. Both children were given standardized tests of intelligence during infancy and then later, during the elementary school years. In the earlier test, the first child's scores were higher than her sister's. In the later test, their scores were reversed. What are some of the possible reasons for the reversal in the IQ scores of the two girls? When the second child did begin to speak, she did so prolifically, and the complexity of her language increased rapidly, undoubtedly

as a result of her biological readiness to talk. Her sensorimotor coordination had never been as competent as the first child's, perhaps also accounting in part for her lower scores on the infant intelligence tests. The parents recognized that they had initially given the first child extensive amounts of their time. They were not able to give the second child as much of their time, but when the second child was about 3 years old, they made every opportunity to involve her in physical and academic activities. They put her in a Montessori preschool program, gave her dancing and swimming lessons, and frequently invited other children of her age in to play with her. There may have been other reasons as well for the changes in scores, but these demonstrate that infant intelligence tests may not be good predictors of intelligence in later years.

Robert McCall and his associates (McCall, Applebaum, & Hogarty, 1973) studied 140 children between the ages of 2½ and 17. They found that the average range of IQ scores was more than 28 points. The scores of one out of three children changed by as much as 30 points and one out of seven by as much as 40 points. These data suggest that intelligence test scores can fluctuate dramatically across the childhood years and that intelligence is not as stable as the original intelligence theorists envisioned.

The Use of Information-Processing Tasks in Infancy to Predict Intelligence

The explosion of interest in infant development has produced many new measures, especially tasks that evaluate the ways infants process information (Rose, Feldman, & Wallace, 1992). Evidence is accumulating that measures of habituation and dishabituation predict intelligence in childhood (Bornstein, 1989; Bornstein & Sigman, 1986). Quicker decays or less cumulative looking in the habituation situation and greater amounts of looking in the dishabituation situation reflect more-efficient information processing. Both types of attention—decrement and recovery—when measured in the first 6 months of infancy, are related to higher IQ scores on standardized intelligence tests given at various times between infancy and adolescence. In sum, more-precise assessment of infant cognition with information-processing tasks involving attention has led to the conclusion that continuity between infant and childhood intelligence is greater than was previously believed (Bornstein & Krasnegor, 1989).

What can we conclude about the nature of stability and change in childhood intelligence? Children are adaptive beings. They have the capacity for intellectual changes but they do not become entirely new intelligent beings. In a sense, children's intelligence changes but has connections to earlier points in development—amid intellectual changes is some underlying coherence and continuity.

CONCEPT TABLE 9.1

Intelligence, Test Construction, and Intelligence Tests

Concept	Processes/ Related Ideas	Characteristics/Description
What Is Intelligence?	Its nature	The concept of intelligence is abstract, and intelligence is measured indirectly. Psychologists rely on intelligence tests to estimate intellectual processes. Verbal ability and problem-solving skills are included in a definition of intelligence. Some psychologists believe intelligence includes an ability to learn from and adapt to everyday life. Extensive effort is given to assessing individual differences in intelligence; this is called psychometrics.
How Tests Are Constructed and Evaluated	Reliability	Reliability is the consistency with which a test measures performance. One form of reliability is test-retest.
	Validity	Validity is the extent to which a test measures what it is intended to measure. Validity can be assessed by determining content validity and criterion validity.
	Standardization	Standardization involves uniform procedures for administering and scoring a test; it also involves norms.
Children's Intelligence Tests	Alfred Binet and the Binet tests	Alfred Binet developed the first intelligence test, known as the 1905 Scale. He developed the concept of mental age, whereas William Stern developed the concept of IQ. The Binet has been standardized and revised a number of times. The many revisions are called the Stanford-Binet tests. The test approximates a normal distribution. The current test is given to individuals from the age of 2 through adulthood.
	The Wechsler scales	Besides the Binet, the Wechsler scales are the most widely used intelligence tests. They include the WAIS-R, the WISC-R, and the WPPSI. These tests produce an overall IQ, verbal and performance IQ, and information about subtests.
	Does intelligence have a single nature?	Psychologists debate whether intelligence is a general ability or a number of specific abilities. Spearman's two-factor theory and Thurstone's multiple-factor theory state that a number of specific factors are involved. Current thinking suggests that Spearman's conceptualization of intelligence as both a set of specific abilities and a general ability was right. Gardner's seven frames of mind and Sternberg's triarchic theory—of componential, experiential, and contextual intelligence—are contemporary efforts to determine the components of intelligence.
Infant Intelligence and the Stability of Intelligence	Infant intelligence tests	Many standardized intelligence tests do not assess infant intelligence. Intelligence tests designed to assess infant intelligence are often referred to as developmental scales, the most widely used being the Bayley scales. Gesell was an important early contributor to the developmental testing of infants. The developmental quotient (DQ) is an overall score in the Gesell assessment of infants.
	The stability of intelligence	Although intelligence is more stable across the childhood years than many other attributes are, many children's scores on intelligence tests fluctuate considerably.
	The use of information-processing tasks in infancy to predict intelligence	Recently, developmentalists have found that infant information-processing tasks that involve attention—especially habituation and dishabituation—are related to scores on standardized tests in childhood.

At this point, we have discussed many ideas about the nature of intelligence, test construction, and intelligence tests. A summary of these ideas is presented in concept table 9.1. Now we will turn our attention to some controversies and issues in intelligence.

CONTROVERSIES AND ISSUES IN INTELLIGENCE

Intelligence has been one of psychology's concepts that seem to attract controversy. Among the most controver-

CRITICAL THINKING ABOUT CHILDREN'S DEVELOPMENT

Exploring IQ and Inheritance

Consider Jensen's controversial conclusion that intelligence is largely a matter of inheritance. What are various reasons children from different cultural backgrounds might score poorly on standardized tests? In what way do the specific aspects of the testing context contribute to relatively poorer performance? What could be some explanations of why such children do poorly in school? Your consideration of the full array of factors that influence intellectual performance demonstrates your ability to *consider alternative explanations to explain development comprehensively*.

---

sial issues about intelligence are those related to hereditary-environmental determination, cultural and ethnic differences, and the use and misuse of intelligence tests.

The Heredity-Environment Controversy

Arthur Jensen (1969) sparked lively and at times hostile debate when he stated his theory that intelligence is primarily inherited and that environment and culture play only a minimal role in intelligence. In one of his most provocative statements, Jensen claimed that genetics accounts for clear-cut differences in the average intelligence among races, nationalities, and social classes. When Jensen published an article in the *Harvard Educational Review* stating that lower intelligence probably is the reason why African Americans do not perform as well in school as Whites do, he was called naive and racist. He received hate mail by the bushel, and police had to escort him to his classes at the University of California at Berkeley.

Jensen reviewed the research on intelligence, much of which involved comparisons of identical and fraternal twins. Remember that identical twins have exactly the same genetic makeup. If intelligence is genetically determined, Jensen reasoned, identical twins' IQs should be similar. Fraternal twins and ordinary siblings are less similar genetically, so their IQs should be less similar. Jensen found support for his argument. The studies on intelligence in identical twins that Jensen examined showed an average correlation between IQs of .82, a very high positive association. Investigations of fraternal twins, however, produced an average correlation of .50, a moderately high positive correlation. Note the substantial difference of .32. To show that genetic factors are more important than environmental factors, Jensen compared the intelligence of identical twins reared together with that of those reared apart. The correlation for those reared together was .89 and for those reared apart it was .78, a difference of .11. Jensen argued that if environmental factors are more important than genetic factors, siblings reared apart, who experience different environments, should have IQs that differ more than .11. Jensen places heredity's influence on intelligence at about 80 percent.

Scientists generally agree that even if differences *within* each of two groups (such as identical vs. fraternal twins, or persons in two different racial groups) are due, in part, to heredity, this does not mean that differences *between* the two groups also are due to heredity. Imagine planting two strains of corn in two very different soil environments. Strain A is planted in a desert, strain B in a fertile farm field in Iowa. Even if all of the differences in the height of cornstalks *within* each environment were due solely to heredity, this says nothing about the basis of average height differences *between* the fields. The desert environment might have stunted the growth of the corn planted there, independently of heredity. We just cannot assume that high heritabilities within a group implies that differences between groups are due to heredity (Ceci, 1996).

Today most researchers agree that genetics does not determine intelligence to the extent Jensen envisioned. Their estimates fall more in the 50/50 range—50 percent genetic makeup, 50 percent environmental factors (Plomin, 1993). For most people, this means that modifying their environment can change their IQ scores considerably (Weinberg, 1989). It also means that programs designed to enrich a person's environment can have a considerable impact, improving school achievement and the acquisition of skills needed for employability.

Keep in mind, though, that environmental influences are complex. Growing up with "all the advantages," for example, does not necessarily guarantee success. Children from wealthy families may have easy access to excellent schools, books, travel, and tutoring, but they may take such opportunities for granted and fail to develop the motivation to learn and achieve. In the same way, being "poor" or "disadvantaged" does not automatically mean that one is "doomed." To further evaluate the heredity-environment controversy, turn to Critical Thinking About Children's Development.

Some years ago, I (your author) knocked on the door of a house in a low-income area of a large city. The father came to the door and invited me into the living room. Even though it was getting dark outside, no lights were on inside the house. The father excused himself, then returned with a light bulb, which he screwed into a lamp socket. He said he could barely pay his monthly mortgage and the electric company had threatened to turn off the electricity, so he was carefully monitoring how much electricity his family used. There were seven children in the family, ranging in age from 2 to 16 years old. Neither parent had completed high school. The father worked as a bricklayer when he could find work, and the mother ironed clothes in a laundry. The parents wanted their children to pursue education and to have more opportunities in life than they had had. The children from the inner-city family were exposed to both positive and negative influences. On the one hand, they were growing up in an intact family in which education was encouraged, and their parents provided a model of the work ethic. On the other hand, they were being short-changed by society and had few opportunities to develop their intellectual abilities.

Researchers increasingly are interested in manipulating the early environment of children who are at risk for impoverished intelligence. The emphasis is on prevention rather than remediation (Garwood & others, 1989). Many low-income parents have difficulty providing an intellectually stimulating environment for their children. Programs that educate parents to be more sensitive caregivers and that train them to be better teachers, as well as support services such as Head Start, can make a difference in a child's intellectual development.

One research program demonstrates the effect of environmental change on intelligence: the Carolina Abecedarian Project conducted by Craig Ramey and Frances Campbell (Campbell & Ramey, 1994). They intervened in the lives of young children living in poverty by changing parental adaptive and responsive functioning and/or providing competent educational day care. Positive effects on intellectual development were maintained through age 12. More about this research study is provided at the end of this chapter in Explorations in Child Development.

In another recent study, 483 low-birthweight premature White and African American children were assessed with the Wechsler Preschool and Primary Scale of Intelligence when they reached 5 years of age (Brooks-Gunn, Klebanov, & Duncan, 1996). These children had been followed since birth, and information about their neighborhood and family income, family structure, family resources, maternal characteristics, and home environment had been obtained over the first 5 years of their lives. The African American children's IQ scores were one standard deviation lower than those of the White children. Adjustments for economic and social differences

in the lives of the African American and White children virtually eliminated differences in the IQ scores of the two groups. Especially powerful in reducing the group IQ differences between African American and White children were adjustments for poverty, maternal education, and home environment.

Although environmental factors contribute substantially to the development of intelligence, we do not completely understand which environmental factors are the most important or how they work (Neisser & others, 1996). Schooling is definitely related to individual differences in intelligence, but we still do not know which aspects of schooling are critical.

Culture and Ethnicity

Are there cultural and ethnic differences in intelligence? How does adaptation affect the role culture plays in understanding intelligence? Are standard intelligence tests biased? If so, can we develop tests that are fair?

Cultural and Ethnic Comparisons

In the United States, children from African American and Latino families score below children from White families on standardized intelligence tests. On the average, African American schoolchildren score 10 to 15 points lower on standardized intelligence tests than White American schoolchildren do (Anastasi, 1988). We are talking about average scores, though. Estimates also indicate that 15 to 25 percent of all African American schoolchildren score higher than half of all White schoolchildren do, and many Whites score lower than most African Americans. This is because the distributions of the scores for African Americans and Whites overlap.

How extensively are ethnic differences in intelligence influenced by heredity and environment? There is no evidence to support a genetic interpretation (Neisser & others, 1996). For example, as African Americans have gained social, economic, and educational opportunities, the gap between African American and White children on standardized intelligence tests has begun to narrow. Also, when children from disadvantaged African American families are adopted into more-advantaged middle-class families, their scores on intelligence tests more closely resemble national averages for middle-class children than for lower-class children (Scarr, 1989; Scarr & Weinberg, 1976).

Culture, Intelligence, and Adaptation

People adapt to their environment, and what's appropriate in one environment may not be appropriate in another. As mentioned earlier in the chapter, intelligence is expressed differently in different cultures. In one study, the researcher asked members of the Kpelle

"You can't build a hut, you don't know how to find edible roots and you know nothing about predicting the weather. In other words, you do terribly on our IQ test."

© 1991 Sidney Harris

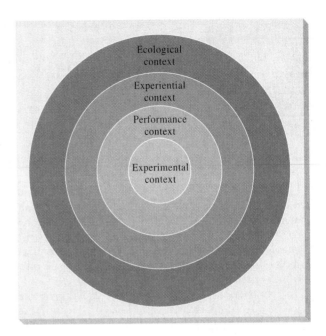

Figure~9.4

Berry's Model of the Contexts of Intelligence
In Berry's model of the contexts of intelligence, there is much more to consider than the actual context in which a test is being administered (the experimental context). In addition, it is also important to consider three other contextual levels—the performance context, experiential context, and ecological context.

in Liberia (located on the western coast of Africa) to sort twenty objects (Glick, 1975). Rather than sort the objects into the "appropriate" categories the researcher had predicted, the Kpelle sorted the objects into functional groups—for instance, putting a knife with an apple and a potato with a hoe. Surprised by the answers, the researcher asked the Kpelle to explain their reasoning. The Kpelle responded that that was the way a wise person would group things. When the researcher asked how a fool would classify the objects, the Kpelle answered that four neat piles of food in one category, four tools in another category, and so on was the fool's way. The Kpelle were not lacking in intelligence; the researcher lacked an understanding of the Kpelle culture. The Kpelle sorted the items in ways that were adaptive for their culture.

Another example of human adaptability involves spatial ability. One study showed that people who live in hunter-gatherer societies score higher on spatial ability tests than do people from industrialized societies (Berry, 1971). People who must hunt to eat depend on their spatial skills for survival.

Few of us will ever have first-hand experience with hunter-gatherer societies, but many of us know people who are adaptable, savvy, and successful yet do not score correspondingly high on intelligence tests. Canadian cross-cultural psychologist John Berry (1983) has an explanation for this gap between intelligence exhibited in one's own culture and intelligence displayed in a formal testing situation. He describes people as being embedded in four levels of environmental contexts.

Level 1, the ecological context, is an individual's natural habitat. Level 2, the experiential context, is the pattern of recurring experiences from which the individual regularly learns. Level 3, the performance context, is the limited set of circumstances in which the individual's natural behavior is observed. Level 4, the experimental context, is the set of environmental circumstances under which test scores are actually generated (Berry's model is presented in figure 9.4).

When the experimental context differs considerably from the ecological or experiential context, Berry says, the individuals being tested are at a disadvantage. Presumably, the greater the difference, the greater the disadvantage. However, relations among contexts change. If an individual has been given the same test previously, some of the gap between the experiential and the experimental contexts closes, resulting in higher test scores.

Another contextual view of intelligence has been proposed by Steven Ceci (1990; Ceci & Barnett, 1997). Ceci's view builds on Sternberg's triarchic framework of exploring internal processing mechanisms, experience, and context. However, Ceci's view examines context in greater depth than Sternberg's. For Ceci, context includes the domain of knowledge in which one thinks, institutions such as schools, and the historical era in which a person lives. Two other emphases are linked

SOCIOCULTURAL WORLDS OF CHILDREN

Larry P., Intelligent but Not on Intelligence Tests

Larry P. is African American and poor. When he was 6 years old, he was placed in a class for the "educable mentally retarded" (EMR), which to school psychologists means that Larry learns much more slowly than average children. The primary reason Larry was placed in the EMR class was his very low score of 64 on an intelligence test.

Is there a possibility that the intelligence test Larry was given is culturally biased? Psychologists still debate this issue. The controversy has been the target of a major class action suit challenging the use of standardized IQ tests to place African American elementary school students in EMR classes. The initial lawsuit, filed on behalf of Larry P., claimed that the IQ test he took underestimated his true learning ability. The lawyers for Larry P. argued that IQ tests place too much emphasis on verbal skills and fail to account for the backgrounds of African American children. Therefore, it was argued, Larry was incorrectly labeled mentally retarded and may forever be saddled with that stigma.

As part of the lengthy court battle involving Larry P., six African American EMR students were independently retested by members of the Bay Association of Black Psychologists in California. The psychologists made sure they established good rapport with the students and made special efforts to overcome the students' defeatism and distraction. For example, items were rewarded in terms more consistent with the children's social background, and recognition was given to nonstandard answers that showed a logical, intelligent approach to problems. This testing approach produced scores of 79 to 104—17 to 38 points higher than the scores the students received when initially tested by school psychologists. In every case, the retest scores were above the ceiling for placement in an EMR class.

In Larry's case, the judge ruled that IQ tests are biased and that their use discriminates against African Americans and other ethnic minorities. IQ tests cannot be used now in California to place children in EMR classes. During the Larry P. trial, it was revealed that 66 percent of the elementary school students in EMR classes in San Francisco were African American, whereas African Americans make up only 28.5 percent of the San Francisco school population.

What was the state's argument for using intelligence tests as one criterion for placing children in EMR classes? In the Larry P. case, there was extensive testimony by Nadine Lambert and Jerome Saddler, supporting the predictive validity of IQ for different ethnic groups. Indeed, the bulk of the state of California's case centered on the validity of IQ tests and the assertion that they are equally predictive for all ethnic groups.

The decision in favor of Larry P. was upheld by a three-judge appeals panel in 1984. However, in another court case, *Pase v. Hannon* in Illinois, a judge was unconvinced by the same arguments and ruled that IQ tests are not culturally biased.

with context. Ceci says that intelligence also rests on multiple cognitive potentials rather than on a single general capacity for abstract problem solving (*g*). Furthermore, in Ceci's scheme, knowledge is critical for intelligence. Ceci believes that highly elaborated and organized bases of knowledge, not general abstract problem-solving ability, allow an individual to carry out complex intellectual activities. Cognitive complexity—the ability to use one's knowledge bases flexibly and efficiently—is a more accurate marker of intelligence in real life than an IQ score, he says.

Cultural Biases and Culture-Fair Tests

Many of the early intelligence tests were culturally biased, favoring people from urban rather than rural environments, middle-class rather than lower-class people, and Whites rather than African Americans (Miller-Jones, 1989). For example, a question on an early test asked what should be done if you find a 3-year-old child in the street. The correct answer was "call the police"; however, children from inner-city families who perceive the police as adversaries are unlikely to choose this answer. Similarly, children from rural areas might not choose this answer if there is no police force nearby. Such questions clearly do not measure the knowledge necessary to adapt to one's environment or to be "intelligent" in an inner-city neighborhood or in rural America (Scarr, 1984). Also, members of minority groups often do not speak English or might speak nonstandard English. Consequently, they may be at a disadvantage in trying to understand verbal questions framed in standard English, even if the content of the test is appropriate (Gibbs & Huang, 1989). More information about cultural bias in intelligence testing appears in Sociocultural Worlds of Children, where you will read

Figure~9.5

Iatmul and Caroline Islander Intelligence
(a) The intelligence of the Iatmul people of Papua, New Guinea, involves the ability to remember the names of many clans.
(b) The Caroline Islands number 680 in the Pacific Ocean east of the Philippines. The intelligence of their inhabitants includes the ability to navigate by the stars.

about a widely publicized case in which a 6-year-old African American boy was classified as mentally retarded.

Cultures also vary in the way they define intelligence (Rogoff, 1990). Most European Americans, for example, think of intelligence in terms of technical skills, but people in Kenya consider responsible participation in family and social life an integral part of intelligence. Similarly, an intelligent person in Uganda is someone who knows what to do and then follows through with appropriate action. Intelligence to the Iatmul people of Papua, New Guinea, involves the ability to remember the names of 10,000 to 20,000 clans, and the islanders in the widely dispersed Caroline Islands incorporate the talent of navigating by the stars into their definition of intelligence (see figure 9.5).

Another example of possible cultural bias in intelligence tests can be seen in the life of Gregory Ochoa. When Gregory was a high school student, he and his classmates took an IQ test. When Gregory looked at the test questions, he understood only a few words, since he did not speak English very well and spoke Spanish at home. Several weeks later, Gregory was placed in a special class for mentally retarded students. Many of the students in the special class, it turns out, had last names such as

Ramirez and Gonzales. Gregory lost interest in school, dropped out, and eventually joined the Navy. In the Navy, Gregory took high school courses and earned enough credits to attend college later. He graduated from San Jose City College as an honors student, continued his education, and became a professor of social work at the University of Washington in Seattle.

As a result of such cases, researchers have tried to develop tests that accurately reflect a person's intelligence. **Culture-fair tests** *are intelligence tests that are intended to not be culturally biased.* Two types of culture-fair tests have been devised. The first includes questions that are familiar to people from all socioeconomic and ethnic backgrounds. For example, a child might be asked how a bird and a dog are different, on the assumption that virtually all children are familiar with birds and dogs. The second type of culture-fair test removes all verbal questions. Figure 9.6 shows a sample question from the Raven Progressive Matrices Test. Even though such tests as the Raven Progressive Matrices are designed to be culture-fair, people with more education still score higher than those with less education do.

One test that takes into account the socioeconomic background of children is the SOMPA, which stands for System of Multicultural Pluralistic Assessment

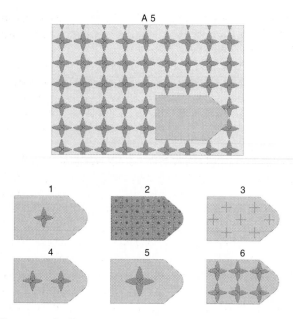

Figure~9.6

Sample Item from the Raven Progressive Matrices Test
Individuals are presented with a matrix arrangement of
symbols, such as the one at the top of this figure and must
then complete the matrix by selecting the appropriate missing
symbol from a group of symbols.

(Mercer & Lewis, 1978). This test can be given to children from 5 to 11 years of age and was especially designed for children from low-income families. Instead of relying on a single test, SOMPA is based on information from four areas of a child's life: (1) verbal and nonverbal intelligence, assessed by the WISC-R; (2) social and economic background, obtained through a 1-hour parent interview; (3) social adjustment to school, determined through a questionnaire that parents complete; and (4) physical health, assessed by a medical examination.

The Kaufman Assessment Battery for Children (K-ABC) has been trumpeted as an improvement over other culture-fair tests (Kaufman & Kaufman, 1983). The test is based on a more representative sample, which includes a greater number of minority and handicapped children. The intelligence portion focuses less on language than the Stanford-Binet does, and the K-ABC includes an achievement section, with subtests for arithmetic and reading. However, the K-ABC, like other culture-fair tests, has its detractors. Based on the three main criteria for evaluating tests, the K-ABC fares well on reliability and standardization, but not as well on validity.

While some people believe that intelligence tests are culturally biased, many experts on intelligence testing believe they are not. The conclusion that IQ tests are not culturally biased was recently reached by a task force established by the American Psychological Association (Neisser & others, 1996).

The Use and Misuse of Intelligence Tests

Psychological tests are tools. Like all tools, their effectiveness depends on the knowledge, skill, and integrity of the user. A hammer can be used to build a beautiful kitchen cabinet or it can be used as a weapon of assault. Like a hammer, psychological tests can be used for positive purposes or they can be badly abused. It is important for both the test constructor and the test examiner to be familiar with the current state of scientific knowledge about intelligence and intelligence tests (Reynolds & Kamphaus, 1990).

Even though they have limitations, tests of intelligence are among psychology's most widely used tools. To be effective, though, intelligence tests must be viewed realistically. They should not be thought of as unchanging indicators of intelligence. They should be used in conjunction with other information about an individual, not relied on as the sole indicator of intelligence. For example, an intelligence test should not solely determine whether a child is placed in a special education or gifted class. The child's developmental history, medical background, performance in school, social competencies, and family experiences should be taken into account too.

The single number provided by many IQ tests can easily lead to stereotypes and expectations about an individual (Rosnow & Rosenthal, 1997). Many people do not know how to interpret the results of intelligence tests, and sweeping generalizations are too often made on the basis of an IQ score. For example, imagine that you are a teacher in the teacher's lounge the day after school has started in the fall. You mention a student—Johnny Jones—and a fellow teacher remarks that she had Johnny in class last year; she comments that he was a real dunce and points out that his IQ is 78. You cannot help but remember this information, and it might lead to thoughts that Johnny Jones is not very bright so it is useless to spend much time teaching him. In this way, IQ scores are misused and stereotypes are formed (Rosenthal & Jacobsen, 1968).

Ability tests can help a teacher group together children who function at roughly the same level in math or reading so they can be taught the same concepts together. However, when children are placed in tracks, such as "advanced," "intermediate," and "low," extreme caution needs to be taken. Periodic assessment of the groups is needed, especially with the "low" group. Ability tests measure *current* performance, and maturational changes or enriched environmental experiences may advance a child's intelligence, requiring that she be moved to a higher group.

Despite their limitations, when used judiciously by a competent examiner, intelligence tests provide valuable information about individuals. There are not many alternatives to these tests. Subjective judgments about individuals simply reintroduce the bias the tests were designed to eliminate.

However, most experts agree that standardized tests do not sample all forms of intelligence (Neisser & others, 1996). Aspects of intelligence not sampled by standardized tests include creativity, wisdom, practical sense, and social sensitivity. Despite the importance of these abilities, we know little about them—how they develop, what factors influence their development, and how they are related to traditional measures of intelligence.

Comparison of Approaches to Children's Learning, Cognitive Development, and Intelligence

In chapters 2, 7, 8, and so far in this chapter, we have studied a number of different approaches to children's learning, cognitive development, and intelligence. This is a good time to review some of the basic ideas of these approaches to get a feel for how they conceptualize children's development. So far we have examined six different approaches to children's learning, cognitive development, and intelligence: Piaget's cognitive developmental theory, Vygotsky's theory, learning theory, social learning theory, information-processing theory, and psychometrics. Let's explore how these approaches view some important aspects of children's development—maturation/environmental influences, stages, individual differences, cognitive processes/mechanisms—and their models of the child.

With regard to maturation/environmental influences, Piaget's theory is the strongest maturational approach; Vygotsky's theory also emphasizes maturation but to a lesser degree. Both Piaget's and Vygotsky's theories are interactionist in the sense that they emphasize maturation-environment interaction. The psychometric approach doesn't deal with this issue extensively, but its age-related emphasis implies a maturational underpinning. The information-processing approach also does not focus on this issue to any degree, but it is also best conceptualized as interactionist. The learning and cognitive social learning views are primarily environmental.

With regard to stages, only the Piagetian cognitive view has a strong stage emphasis. Indeed, stages of cognitive development—sensorimotor, preoperational, concrete operational, and formal operational—are at the heart of Piaget's theory. The neo-Piagetians, who combine some of Piaget's ideas with an emphasis on more-precise aspects of information processing, place some emphasis on age-related changes in cognition. The Vygotskian, learning, social learning, and psychometric approaches do not emphasize stages at all.

With regard to individual differences, only the psychometric approach and Vygotsky's theory emphasize them. In this chapter we have seen that individual differences are at the heart of the psychometric approach. Vygotsky's concept of the zone of proximal development also addresses individual differences. Recently, some information-processing researchers have begun to study individual differences in information processing, but the information-processing approach does not give individual differences a high priority. The Piagetian learning and social learning approaches do not emphasize individual differences.

With regard to cognitive processes/mechanisms, Piaget's cognitive developmental approach stresses the importance of assimilation, accommodation, equilibration, organization, conservation, and hypothetical-deductive reasoning. Vygotsky's theory stresses the importance of discussion and reasoning through interaction with skilled others. The learning approach does not emphasize cognitive processes/mechanisms at all, but rather the environmental processes of reinforcement, punishment, and classical conditioning. The cognitive social learning approach places importance on the cognitive processes of attention, memory, plans, expectancies, problem-solving skills, and self-efficacy. The information-processing approach emphasizes a large number of cognitive processes/mechanisms, including processing speed, capacity, and automaticity; attention; memory; problem solving; cognitive monitoring; critical thinking; and knowledge and expertise. The psychometric approach focuses on general intelligence and/or a number of specific forms of intelligence, such as Sternberg's three forms—componential, experiential, and contextual.

With regard to conceptualization of the basic nature of the child or a model of how the child develops, Piagetian theory emphasizes a model of the child as active, cognitive constructivist, and a solitary young scientist. Vygotsky's theory describes the child as active, interactive, and sociocultural constructivist. The learning approach focuses on the child as passive, environmentally determined, and an empty vessel. Cognitive social learning portrays the child as interactive and reciprocal determinist (behavior, cognition, and environment reciprocally interact). The information-processing approach conceptualizes the child as cognitive constructivist, and the psychometric approach in terms of individual differences.

A summary of how the six different approaches we have discussed in the last three chapters portray children's development is presented in table 9.1. So far in this chapter we have focused mainly on the psychometric approach that emphasizes individual differences and the assessment of intelligence through intelligence tests. Next, we continue our discussion of intelligence and its related dimensions by examining the extremes of intelligence.

THE EXTREMES OF INTELLIGENCE AND CREATIVITY

Intelligence tests have been used to discover indications of mental retardation or intellectual giftedness, the extremes of intelligence. At times intelligence tests have been misused for this purpose. Keep in mind the theme

Comparison of Approaches to Children's Learning, Cognitive Development, and Intelligence

	Piagetian/ Cognitive Development	Vygotsky's Theory	Learning	Cognitive Social Learning
Maturation/environment	Strong maturational view, but maturation does interact with environmental experiences	Interactionist, but much stronger role for culture than in Piaget's view; interaction with skilled people	Strong emphasis on environment; little contribution by heredity/maturation	Strong environmental emphasis
Stages	Strong emphasis; cognitive stages are core of this approach	No stages emphasized	No stages	No stages
Individual differences	No emphasis	Moderately strong emphasis	No emphasis	No emphasis
Cognitive processes/mechanism	Assimilation, accommodation, equilibration, organization, conservation, and hypothetical-deductive reasoning skills	Discussion and reasoning through social interaction with skilled others	None	Attention, memory, plans, expectancies, problem solving skills; self-efficacy, imitation
Model of child	Active, cognitive constructivist, solitary little scientist	Active, interactive, sociocultural constructivist	Passive, environmental determinist; empty vessel	Interactive, reciprocal determinist

that an intelligence test should not be used as the sole indicator of mental retardation or giftedness as we explore the nature of these intellectual extremes.

Mental Retardation

The most distinctive feature of mental retardation is inadequate intellectual functioning. Long before formal tests were developed to assess intelligence, the individuals with mental retardation were identified by a lack of age-appropriate skills in learning and caring for themselves. Once intelligence tests were developed, numbers were assigned to indicate degrees of mental retardation. It is not unusual to find that, of two individuals with mental retardation with the same low IQ, one is married, employed, and involved in the community and the other requires constant supervision in an institution. These differences in social competence led psychologists to include deficits in adaptive behavior in their definition of mental retardation. **Mental retardation** *is a condition of limited mental ability in which an individual has a low IQ, usually below 70 on a traditional intelligence test, has difficulty adapting to everyday life, and has an onset of these characteristics during the so-called developmental period—by age 18.* The reason for including developmental period in the definition of mental retardation is that we don't usually think of a college student who suffers

massive brain damage in a car accident, resulting in an IQ of 60 as "mentally retarded." The low IQ and low adaptiveness should be evident in childhood, not following a long period of normal functioning that is interrupted by an insult of some form. About 5 million Americans fit this definition of mental retardation.

There are several classifications of mental retardation. About 89 percent of individuals with mental retardation fall into the mild category, with IQs of 55 to 70. About 6 percent are classified as moderately retarded, with IQs of 40 to 54; these people can attain a second-grade level of skills and may be able to support themselves as adults through some type of labor. About 3.5 percent of the individuals with mental retardation are in the severe category, with IQs of 25 to 39; these individuals learn to talk and engage in very simple tasks but require extensive supervision. Less than 1 percent have IQs below 25; they fall into the profoundly mentally retarded classification and are in constant need of supervision.

Mental retardation can have an organic cause, or it can be social and cultural in origin. **Organic retardation** *is mental retardation caused by a genetic disorder or by brain damage; organic refers to the tissues or organs of the body, so there is some physical damage in organic retardation.* Down syndrome, one form of organic mental retardation, occurs when an extra chromosome is present in an

Information Processing	Psychometric
Interactionist, but little attention given to this, except by neo-Piagetians who emphasize age-related changes	Little attention to this issue, although age-related emphasis implies maturational emphasis
No stages	No stages
No emphasis, although recently some information-processing researchers have started to investigate	Strong emphasis; at core of the approach
Processing speed, capacity, and automaticity; attention; memory; problem solving, cognitive monitoring; critical thinking; knowledge and expertise	General intelligence and a number of specific forms of intelligence that vary with the theory
Cognitive constructivist	Individual difference

Figure~9.7

A Child with Down Syndrome
What causes a child to develop Down syndrome? In what major classification of mental retardation does the condition fall?

individual's genetic makeup (see figure 9.7). It is not known why the extra chromosome is present, but it might involve the health or age of the female ovum or male sperm. Most people who suffer from organic retardation have IQs that range between 0 and 50.

Cultural-familial retardation *is a mental deficit in which no evidence of organic brain damage can be found; individuals' IQs range from 55 to 70.* Psychologists suspect that such mental deficits result from the normal variation that distributes people along the range of intelligence scores above 55, combined with growing up in a below-average intellectual environment. As children, those who are familially retarded can be detected in schools, where they often fail, need tangible rewards (candy rather than praise), and are highly sensitive to what others—both peers and adults—want from them (Feldman, 1996). However, as adults the familially retarded are usually invisible, perhaps because adult settings don't tax their cognitive skills as sorely. It may also be that the familially retarded increase their intelligence as they move toward adulthood (Sattler, 1988).

Giftedness

There have always been people whose abilities and accomplishments outshine others'—the whiz kid in class, the star athlete, the natural musician. People who are **gifted** *have above-average intelligence (an IQ of 120 or higher) and/or superior talent for something.* When it comes to programs for the gifted, most school systems select children who have intellectual superiority and academic aptitude. Children who are talented in the visual and performing arts (arts, drama, dance), athletics, or other special aptitudes tend to be overlooked.

> *Never to be cast away are the gifts of the gods, magnificent.*
>
> —**Homer, *The Iliad*, 9th Century B.C.**

Until recently giftedness and emotional distress were thought to go hand in hand. English novelist Virgina Woolf suffered from severe depression, for example, and eventually committed suicide. Sir Isaac Newton, Vincent van Gogh, Ann Sexton, Socrates, and Sylvia Plath all had emotional problems. However, these are the exception rather than the rule; in general, no relation between giftedness and mental disorder has been found. Recent studies support the conclusion that gifted people tend to be more mature, have fewer emotional problems than others, and grow up in a positive family climate (Draper & others, 1993; Feldman & Piirto, 1995).

Characteristics of Gifted Children

Ellen Winner (1996) recently described three criteria that characterize gifted children, whether in art, music, or academic domains:

1. *Precocity.* Gifted children are precocious. They begin to master an area earlier than their peers. Learning in their domain is more effortless for them than for ordinary children. In most instances, these gifted children are precocious because they have an inborn high ability in a particular domain or domains.

2. *Marching to their own drummer.* Gifted children learn in a qualitatively different way than ordinary children. One way that they march to a different drummer is that they need minimal help, or scaffolding, from adults to learn. In many instances, they resist any kind of explicit instruction. They also often make discoveries on their own and solve problems in unique ways.

3. *A passion to master.* Gifted children are driven to understand the domain in which they have high ability. They display an intense, obsessive interest and an ability to focus. They are not children who need to be pushed by their parents. They motivate themselves, says Winner.

Ten-year-old Alexandra Nechita has recently burst onto the child prodigy scene. She paints quickly and impulsively on large canvases, some as large as 5 feet by 9 feet. It is not unusual for her to complete several of these large paintings in a week's time. Her paintings—in the modernist tradition—sell for up to $80,000 apiece. When she was only 2 years of age, Alexandra colored in coloring books for hours. She has no interest in dolls or friends. Once she started school, she would start painting as soon as she got home. And she continues to paint—relentlessly and passionately. It is, she says, what she loves to do.

The Terman Gifted Children

Lewis Terman (1925) has followed the lives of approximately 1,500 children whose Stanford-Binet IQs averaged 150 into adulthood; the study will not be complete until the year 2010. Terman has found that this remarkable group is an accomplished lot: Of the 800 males, 78 have obtained doctorates (they include two past presidents of the American Psychological Association), 48 have earned M.D.'s, and 85 have been granted law degrees. Most of these figures are 10 to 30 times greater than those found among the 800 men of the same age chosen randomly as a comparison group. These findings challenge the commonly held belief that the intellectually gifted are emotionally disordered or socially maladjusted.

The 672 gifted women studied by Terman (Terman & Oden, 1959) underscore the importance of relationships and intimacy in women's lives. Two-thirds of these exceptional women graduated from college in the

Ten-year-old Alexandra Nechita is a gifted child in the domain of art. She is precocious, marches to the tune of a different drummer, and has a passion to master her domain.

1930s, and one-fourth attended graduate school. Despite their impressive educational achievements, when asked to order their life's priorities, the gifted women placed families first, friendships second, and careers last. For these women, having a career often meant not having children. Of the 30 most successful women, 25 did not have any children. Such undivided commitments to the family are less true of women today. Many of the highly gifted women in Terman's study questioned their intelligence and concluded that their cognitive skills had waned in adulthood. Studies of gifted women today reveal that they have a stronger confidence in their cognitive skills and intellectual abilities than did the gifted women in Terman's study (Tomlinson-Keasey, 1990). Terman's gifted women represented a cohort who reached midlife prior to the women's movement and the pervasiveness of the dual-career couple and the single-parent family (Tomlinson-Keasey, 1993, 1997).

In the most recent analysis of Terman's gifted children, two factors predicted longevity: personality and family stability (Friedman & others, 1995). With regard to personality, children who were conscientious and less impulsive lived significantly longer. With regard to family stability, children whose parents divorced before the children reached age 21 faced a one-third greater mortality risk than their counterparts whose parents did not divorce. Individuals who became divorced themselves also faced a shorter life. And not marriage itself, but rather a stable marriage history, was linked with increased longevity.

One assertion that has come out of the Terman gifted study is that the high achievements of the "Termites" (the label given to Terman's subjects) was due to their high IQs. However, Steven Ceci (1990) cautioned that it is important to remember that factors such as socioeconomic status and job opportunities also influence achievement. Nearly all of the Termites who came from upper-income families went on to become the most successful adults. However, a few of the most successful adults came from low-income families. And the Termites who became adults during the Great Depression turned out to be less successful than those who became adults later, when there were more job opportunities.

Gifted Disadvantaged Children

Disadvantaged children in the United States come from diverse cultural backgrounds and are often the victims of social discrimination (Ogbu, 1989). These children live in environments that fail to challenge their creativity and do not provide them with the resources needed to develop their creativity.

When gifted disadvantaged children learn to adapt their behavior to the values and demands of school, they begin to accomplish required tasks successfully, their achievements start to attract teachers' attention, and more opportunities are made available to them. This "snowball effect" has crucial implications for the child's personal and motivational development (Arroyo & Sternberg, 1993).

Parents in low-income families can help their children develop the self-management skills required to function well in a school setting, but in many instances they do not. For gifted disadvantaged children, teachers and other influential persons within the school can compensate for the lack of appropriate direction these children have received at home. Alternative socialization agents can expose gifted disadvantaged children to wide-ranging experiences that influence their emerging view of themselves and their future.

Especially important in the case of gifted disadvantaged children is the development of measures to identify who they are. Traditionally, giftedness has been assessed in one dimension—intellectual superiority. However, to adequately identify gifted disadvantaged children, it is necessary to widen the assessment procedure to include not only intellectual abilities but also behavior, motivation, and personality attributes. Researchers have found that high-achieving disadvantaged children are self-confident, industrious, tough-minded, and individualistic (Comer, 1988). These same characteristics often appear in children high in creativity who come from advantaged backgrounds.

The behaviors of the gifted disadvantaged are often motivated by the desire to transform their social and economic conditions. Because this goal requires long-range planning and self-management, giftedness among disadvantaged children needs to be assessed over time.

Creativity

Most of us would like to be both gifted and creative. Why was Thomas Edison able to invent so many things? Was he simply more intelligent than most people? Did he spend long hours toiling away in private? Surprisingly, when Edison was a young boy, his teacher told him he was too dumb to learn anything. Other famous people whose creative genius went unnoticed when they were young include Walt Disney, who was fired from a newspaper job because he did not have any good ideas; Enrico Caruso, whose music teacher told him that his voice was terrible; and Winston Churchill, who failed 1 year of secondary school.

Disney, Edison, Caruso, and Churchill were intelligent and creative men; however, experts on creativity believe that intelligence is not the same as creativity. One common distinction is between **convergent thinking,** *which produces one correct answer and is characteristic of the kind of thinking on standardized intelligence tests* and **divergent thinking,** *which produces many answers to the same question and is more characteristic of creativity* (Guilford, 1967). For example, the following is a typical problem on an intelligence test that requires convergent thinking: "How many quarters will you get in return for 60 dimes?" The following question, though, has many possible answers: "What image comes to mind when you hear the phrase 'sitting alone in a dark room'?" (Barron, 1989). Such responses as "the sound of a violin with no strings" and "patience" are considered creative answers. Conversely, common answers, such as "a person in a crowd" or "insomnia" are not very creative.

Creativity *is the ability to think about something in novel and unusual ways and to come up with unique solutions to problems.* When creative people, such as artists and scientists, are asked what enables them to solve problems in novel ways, they say that the ability to find affinities between seemingly unrelated elements plays a key role. They also say they have the time and independence in an enjoyable setting to entertain a wide range of possible solutions to a problem. How strongly is creativity related to intelligence? Although most creative people are quite intelligent, the reverse is not necessarily true. Many highly intelligent people (as measured by IQ tests) are not very creative.

Some experts remain skeptical that we will ever fully understand the creative process. Others believe that a psychology of creativity is in reach. Most experts agree, however, that the concept of creativity as spontaneously bubbling up from a magical well is a myth. Momentary flashes of insight, accompanied by images, make up only a small part of the creative process. At the heart of the creative process are ability and experience that shape an individual's intentional and sustained effort, often over the

Controversies and Issues in Intelligence, Different Approaches,
the Extremes of Intelligence, and Creativity

Concept	Processes/ Related Ideas	Characteristics/Description
Controversies and Issues	The heredity-environment controversy	In the late 1960s, Jensen argued that intelligence is approximately 80 percent hereditary and that genetic differences exist in the average intelligence of ethnic groups and social classes. Intelligence is influenced by heredity, but not as strongly as Jensen believed. The environments we provide children do make a difference.
	Culture and ethnicity	There are cultural and ethnic differences on intelligence tests, but the evidence suggests they are not genetically based. In recent decades, the gap between African Americans and Whites on intelligence test scores has diminished as African Americans have experienced more socioeconomic opportunities. To understand intelligence within a given culture, the adaptive requirements of the culture must be known. Ceci has proposed a contextual view of intelligence. Early intelligence tests favored White, middle-class, urban individuals. Current tests try to reduce this bias. Culture-fair tests are an alternative to traditional tests; most psychologists believe they cannot completely replace the traditional tests.
	The use and misuse of intelligence tests	Despite limitations, when used by a judicious examiner, tests are valuable tools for determining individual differences in children's intelligence. The tests should be used with other information about the children who are being tested. IQ scores can produce unfortunate stereotypes and expectations. Ability tests can help teachers sort children into homogeneous groups. However, periodic testing should be done. Intelligence or a high IQ is not necessarily the ultimate human value.
Different Approaches to Children's Learning, Cognitive Development, and Intelligence	The nature of the differences	We compared six different approaches to children's learning, cognitive development, and intelligence in the following areas: maturation/environment interaction, stages, individual differences, and cognitive processes/mechanisms, and model of the child. The approaches we evaluated were Piaget's (chapter 7), Vygotsky's (chapter 7), learning (chapter 8), cognitive social learning (chapter 8), information processing (chapter 8), and psychometric (this chapter). For example, only Piaget's approach is a strong maturational approach and a strong stage theory, while the psychometric approach and Vygotsky's theory are the only approaches that underscore the importance of individual differences.
The Extremes of Intelligence	Mental retardation	A child with mental retardation has a low IQ, usually below 70 on a traditional IQ test, and has difficulty adapting to everyday life. Classifications of mental retardation have been made. The two main types of retardation are organic and cultural-familial.
	Giftedness	A gifted child has above-average intelligence (an IQ of 120 or more) and/or superior talent for something. Three characteristics of gifted children are precocity, individuality, and a passion to master. The Terman gifted children have provided insights about the nature of giftedness. There is a special concern for gifted disadvantaged children.
Creativity	Its nature	Creativity is the ability to think about something in a novel or unusual way and to come up with unique solutions to problems.

course of a lifetime (Curran, 1997). As we learn more about creativity, we come to understand how important it is as a human resource and as truly one of life's wondrous gifts.

> *The artist finds a greater pleasure in painting than in having completed the picture.*
>
> —Seneca

At this point, we have discussed a number of ideas about controversies and issues in intelligence, different approaches to children's learning, cognitive development, and intelligence, and about the extremes of intelligence. A summary of these ideas is presented in concept table 9.2.

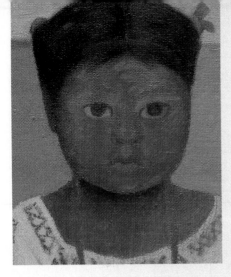

Summary

The study of children's intelligence has historically focused on the assessment of children's intelligence through intelligence tests and the nature of individual differences. There also has been a special interest in what intelligence is, including debate about its components.

In this chapter, we began by briefly discussing several issues that often incite inflammatory debate—the use of IQ tests to place children in special classes and sperm banks designed to genetically engineer children's intelligence. Then we evaluated what intelligence is and how it is measured, infant intelligence and the stability of intelligence, and controversies and issues in intelligence. Among the issues and controversies are the degree intelligence is due to heredity or to environment, cultural and ethnic influences on intelligence, cultural biases and culture-fair tests, and the use and misuse of intelligence tests. We also reviewed and compared different approaches to children's learning, cognitive development, and intelligence, and studied the extremes of intelligence—mental retardation and giftedness—and creativity.

Remember that you can obtain a summary of the chapter by again studying the two concept tables on pages 296 and 308. In the next chapter, we will evaluate another very important part of children's development—language.

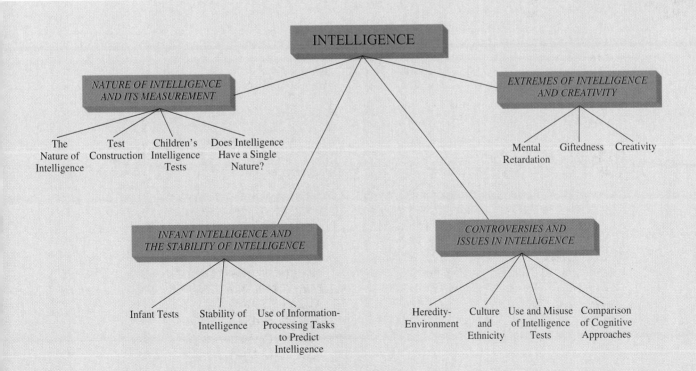

KEY TERMS

PRACTICAL KNOWLEDGE ABOUT CHILDREN

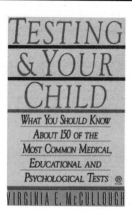

Testing and Your Child
(1992) by Virginia McCullough, New York: Plume.

Written for parents, this book describes 150 of the most common educational, psychological, and medical tests. This comprehensive guide explains who administers the tests, what the tests test for, what they cannot reveal, what preparation is required, what influences scoring, and what follow-up testing might be recommended. What the tests test for ranges from intelligence to giftedness to achievement to personality.

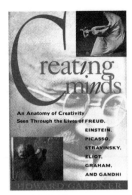

Creating Minds

(1993) by Howard Gardner, New York: Basic Books.

Building on his framework of seven intelligences, ranging from musical intelligence to intelligence involved in understanding oneself, Gardner explores the lives of seven extraordinary individuals—Sigmund Freud, Albert Einstein, Pablo Picasso, Igor Stravinsky, T. S. Eliot, Martha Graham, and Mahatma Gandhi—each an outstanding exemplar of one kind of intelligence. In analyzing their lives, Gardner describes patterns crucial to understanding how people can become more creative. He believes it takes at least 10 years to make the initial creative breakthrough and another 10 years for subsequent breakthroughs. Gardner argues that an essential element in the creative process is the support of caring individuals who believe in the revolutionary ideas of their creators.

Gifted Children: Myths and Realities

(1996) by Ellen Winner, New York: Basic Books.

Ellen Winner has studied gifted children for many years. In this recent book, she sorts out the myths and realities of gifted children, examining gifted children's distinctive abilities and their intellectual and social lives.

Winner also evaluates the school's role in gifted children's lives and discusses how our society has largely failed to identify and nurture children with exceptional abilities.

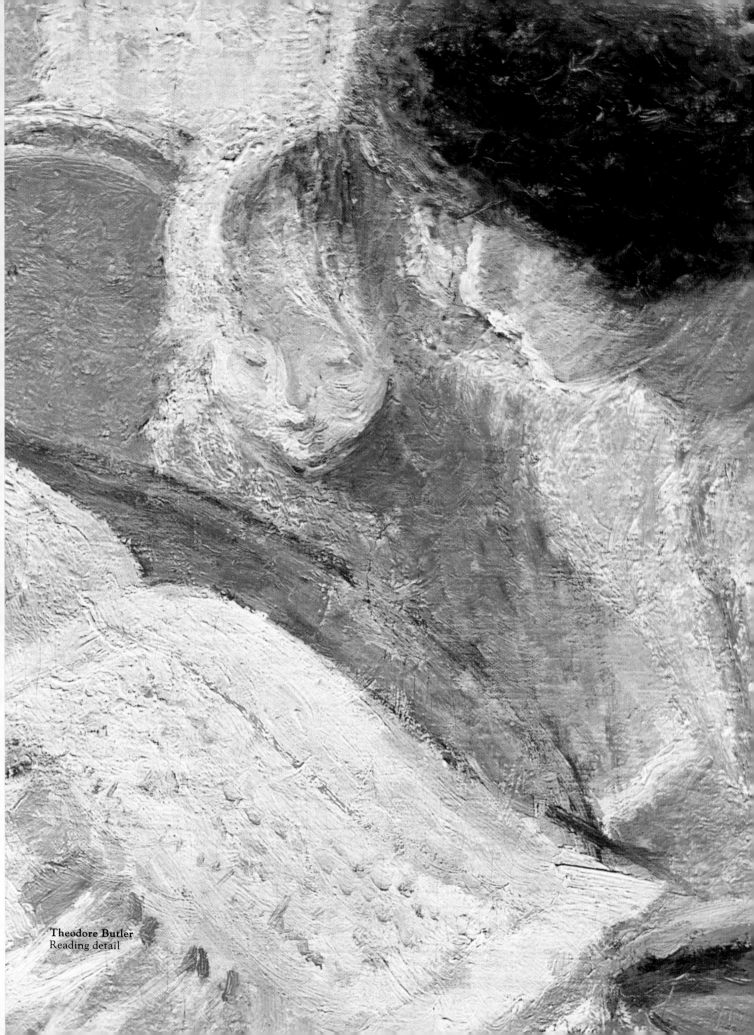

Theodore Butler
Reading detail

Chapter 10

Language Development

Words not only affect us temporarily; they change us, they socialize us, and they unsocialize us.

—David Riesman

Chapter Outline

Chapter Boxes

Children pick up words as pigeons pick up peas.

—John Ray

The Language Worlds of Helen Keller

One of the most stunning portrayals of children isolated from the mainstream of language is the case of Helen Keller (1880–1968). At 18 months of age, Helen was an intelligent toddler in the process of learning her first words. Then she developed an illness that left her both deaf and blind, suffering the double affliction of sudden darkness and silence. For the next 5 years she lived in a world she learned to fear because she could not see or hear.

Even with her fears, Helen spontaneously invented a number of gestures to reflect her wants and needs. For example, when she wanted ice cream, she turned toward the freezer and shivered. When she wanted bread and butter, she imitated the motions of cutting and spreading. But this homemade language system severely limited her ability to communicate with the surrounding community, who did not understand her idiosyncratic gestures.

Alexander Graham Bell, the famous inventor of the telephone, suggested to her parents that they hire a tutor named Anne Sullivan to help Helen overcome her fears. By using sign language, Anne was able to teach Helen to communicate. Anne realized that language learning needs to occur naturally, so she did not force Helen to memorize words out of context as in the drill methods that were in vogue at the time. Sullivan's success depended not only on the child's natural ability to organize language according to form and meaning but also on introducing language in the context of communicating about objects events, and feelings about others.

Helen Keller eventually graduated from Radcliffe with honors, became a very successful educator, and crafted books about her life and experiences. She had this to say about language: "Whatever the process, the result is wonderful. Gradually from naming an object we advance step by step until we have traversed the vast distance between our first stammered syllable and the sweep of thought in a line of Shakespeare."

PREVIEW

In this chapter, we will tell the elegant story of children's language development. The questions we will explore include the following: What is language? What are language's rule systems? What is language's biological heritage (including the question of whether chimpanzees can learn language)? What is language's environmental heritage? What is cognition's role in language? What is the course of children's language development? How should reading be taught to children? What issues are involved in bilingualism?

What Is Language?

Every human society has language. There are thousands of human languages, and they differ so dramatically that many individuals despair of ever mastering more than one. However, all human languages have some common characteristics.

First, language consists of a sequence of words (Miller, 1981). This description ascribes to language two parts—the presence of words and sequencing. It might seem obvious that all languages have words, but think for a moment about what words are. We produce and perceive words every day—yet words have an almost magical quality. They stand for, or symbolize, things. We use words to refer to objects, people, actions, events, and even abstract ideas. What a word refers to is arbitrary, in the sense that it is based on convention; a word symbolizes whatever a group of language users agree that it symbolizes. To understand this point, consider that different languages have different names for the same thing. What we call a "house" is called "casa" in Spanish and "maison" in French. Since different languages have different words, we are forced to conclude that words are linked arbitrarily and by convention to their referents.

Although words are important in language, the mere presence of words is not enough to make a language. Sequencing of the words is also required. Can you imagine a language with one-word utterances? A 13-month-old infant might use one-word utterances, but, as we will see later in the chapter, experts stress that the infant has whole sentences in mind when uttering a single word.

Why is sequencing important for language? The answer leads to another important characteristic of language—**infinite generativity,** *an individual's ability to generate an infinite number of meaningful sentences using a finite set of words and rules, which makes language a highly creative enterprise.* It is possible for us to say things never before said by anyone else.

> *T**he maker of a sentence launches out into the infinite and builds a road into chaos and old night, and is followed by those who hear him with something of a wild, creative light.*
>
> —Ralph Waldo Emerson

Yet another characteristic of language is **displacement,** *the use of language to communicate information about another place and time,* although we also use language to describe what is currently happening in our immediate environment. Anyone who reads fiction can attest to the power of displacement in language. However, reading fiction is just one example of how language gives second-hand experience. Consider the everyday experience of being told what happened elsewhere or what someone else said.

Language contributes to the transmission of knowledge, not only from one individual to another but also from one generation to the next.

Language's role in communication needs to be underscored. Indeed, above all else, language enables humans to communicate. We speak to others, listen to others, and write something that others will read, all as part of using language to communicate.

Another property of language is *signal simultaneity and overlap.* Unlike simple signaling systems (such as a traffic signal or a telephone bell), language transmits several aspects of information simultaneously. Each bit of language is packed with information about word- and sentence-level meaning, as well as speaker identity and emotion. In addition, language is not discrete and sequential like beads on a string, but instead is compressed and overlapped. For example, try saying the words *see* and *sue.* Notice that the *s* portion of the word *see* already sounds higher and more *ee*-like than the *s* of *sue.* In other words, part of the vowel sound is already present in the consonant part of the word. This type of signal overlap is common in language.

A final important aspect of language is that it is characterized by rule systems, which involve phonology, morphology, syntax, semantics, and pragmatics. We will discuss these rule systems shortly.

In summary, we can define **language** *as a system of symbols, or word sequences, that is used to communicate with others and that involves infinite generativity, displacement, signal simultaneity and overlap, and rule systems.* One of the truly remarkable aspects of language is that children not only can acquire such a complex system, but can acquire it so quickly. Let's now explore the important rule systems of language.

Language's Rule Systems

When nineteenth-century American writer Ralph Waldo Emerson said, "The world was built in order and the atoms march in tune," he must have had language in mind. The truly elegant system of language is highly ordered and organized. What are this order and organization like? The order and organization of language involve five rule systems: phonology, morphology, syntax, semantics, and pragmatics (see figure 10.1).

Phonology

Language is made up of basic sounds, or *phonemes.* In the English language, there are approximately thirty-six phonemes. **Phonology** *is the study of a language's sound system.* Phonological rules ensure that certain sound sequences (such as *sp, ba,* or *ar*) occur and others do not. **Phonotactics** *is the term given to allowable sound sequences; that is, certain sounds cannot appear in certain sequences within words or in certain positions within words.* For example, *ft* cannot appear as the first two sounds in an English word. Likewise, *zks* cannot appear as the first three sounds in an English word, nor can *kwp.*

Figure~10.1

Language's Rule Systems

Imagine what language would be like if there were no phonology. Each word in the language would have to be represented by a signal—a sound, for example—that differed from the signals of all other words. The obvious consequence is that the number of words could be no larger than the number of different signals that an individual could efficiently produce and perceive. We do not know precisely what that number is, but we do know that it is very small, especially in the case of speech, in contrast to the hundreds of thousands of words that commonly constitute a language. An increasing number of researchers believe that speech is an infant's gateway to language (Eimas, 1995; Morgan & Demuth, 1995). In their speech perception and processing, infants find cues in the speech stream that allow them to abstract out irregularities in words and how words are combined (Ratner, 1996).

What phonology does is provide a basis for constructing a large and expandable set of words—all that are or ever will be in that language—out of two or three dozen phonemes. We do not need 500,000, we need only two or three dozen.

Patricia Kuhl's (1993a, 1993b) research reveals that, long before they actually begin to learn words, infants can sort through a number of spoken sounds in search of the ones that have meaning. Kuhl argues that from birth to about 4 months of age, infants are "universal linguists" who are capable of distinguishing each of the 150 sounds that make up human speech. But by about 6 months of age, they have started to specialize in the speech sounds of their native language.

In one experiment, babies listened to a tape-recorded voice that repeated vowel and consonant combinations (see figure 10.2). Each time the sounds changed from *ah* to *oooh*, for instance, a toy bear in a box lit up and danced. The babies quickly learned to look at the bear when they heard sounds that were new to them. When Kuhl studied American and Swedish 6-month-old babies, she found that they ignored subtle variations in the pronunciation of their own language's sounds, but they heard similar variations in a foreign language as separate sounds. The implication of this research is that 6-month-old infants can already distinguish the sounds they will need for later speech.

By 8 to 9 months of age, comprehension is more noticeable. For example, babies look at a ball when their mothers say "ball." Language experts say that it is impossible to determine how many words babies understand at this point, but research with only slightly older children

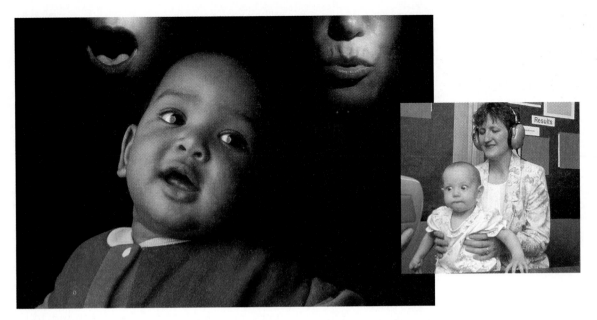

Figure~10.2

Infants' Recognition of Speech Sounds
In Patricia Kuhl's research, babies at 7 months *(left)* show an ability to read lips, connecting vowel sounds with lip movements. In the insert, a 6-month-old baby is being tested in Kuhl's laboratory to determine if she recognizes the sounds of her native language.

suggests that comprehension might outpace expression by a factor of as much as one hundred to one. Researchers have found that although some babies are slow in beginning to talk, comprehension is often about equal between the early and late talkers (Bates & Thal, 1991).

Morphology

Morphology *is the study of what language users know about the units of meaning and the rules for combining morphemes.* A morpheme *is a meaningful string of phonemes (sounds) that has no smaller meaningful parts.* Every word in the English language is made up of one or more morphemes. Some words consist of a single morpheme (for example, *help*), whereas others are made up of more than one morpheme (for example, *helper*, which has two morphemes, *help + -er*, with the morpheme *-er* meaning "one who"—in this case "one who helps"). However, not all morphemes are words (for example, *pre-*, *-tion*, and *ing*). Just as the rules that govern phonemes ensure that certain sound sequences occur, the rules that govern morphemes ensure that certain strings of sounds occur in meaningful sequences. For example, we would not reorder *helper* as *erhelp*.

What are called *bound* morphemes by their very nature attach to members of another group of morphemes, called *free* morphemes (which can stand alone). Thus *cats* consists of one free morpheme (*cat*) and one bound morpheme (*-s*). Bound morphemes in English convey certain grammatical concepts, such as tense, number agreement on verbs, plurality, and possession. Other types of bound morphemes (such as *pre-* and *-tion*) can change the meanings of root words.

Syntax

Syntax *involves the ways words are combined to form acceptable phrases and sentences.* For example, *He didn't stay, did he?* is a grammatical sentence, but *He didn't stay, didn't he?* is unacceptable. Similarly, if I say to you, "Bob slugged Tom" and "Bob was slugged by Tom," you know who did the slugging and who was slugged in each case because we share the same syntactic understanding of sentence structure. This concept of "who does what to whom" is called *grammatical relations*, and it is an important type of syntactic information.

> *The adjective is the banana peel of the parts of speech.*
>
> —Clifton Fadiman

If you learn another language, it will soon be clear to you that your English syntax will not get you very far. For example, in English an adjective usually precedes a noun (as in *blue sky*), whereas in Spanish the adjective follows the noun (*cielo azul*). In fact, the difficulty of learning new syntactic patterns is one of the main complaints of a second-language learner. Despite the differences in their syntactic structures, however, the world's languages have much in common. For example, consider the following short sentences:

The cat killed the mouse.
The mouse ate the cheese.
The farmer chased the cat.

"If you don't mind my asking, how much does a sentence diagrammer pull down a year?"

© Bob Thaves.

In many languages it is possible to combine these sentences into more-complex sentences. For example:

The farmer chased the cat that killed the mouse.
The mouse the cat killed ate the cheese.

However, no language in the world permits sentences like the following one:

The mouse the cat the farmer chased killed ate the cheese.

Can you make sense of this sentence? If you can, you probably can do it only after wrestling with it for several minutes. You likely could not understand it at all if someone uttered it during a real conversation. It appears that language users cannot process subjects and objects arranged in too complex a fashion in a sentence. That is good news for language learners, because it means there is some common ground that all syntactic systems adhere to. Such findings are also considered important by researchers who are interested in the universal properties of syntax (Maratos, 1997).

Semantics

The term **semantics** *refers to the meanings of words and sentences.* Every word has a set of semantic features. *Girl* and *woman*, for example, share some of the semantic features of the words *female* and *human* but differ in their meanings regarding age. Words have semantic restrictions on how they can be used in sentences. The sentence *The bicycle talked the boy into buying a candy bar* is syntactically correct but semantically incorrect. The sentence violates our semantic knowledge—bicycles do not talk.

> *A person gets from a symbol the meaning he puts into it, and what is one man's comfort and inspiration is another's jest and scorn.*
>
> **—Justice Robert Jackson**

Pragmatics

A final set of language rules involves **pragmatics,** *the use of appropriate conversation and knowledge underlying the use of language in context.* The domain of pragmatics is broad, covering such circumstances as (a) taking turns in discussions instead of everyone talking at once; (b) using questions to convey commands ("Why is it so noisy in here?" "What is this, Grand Central Station?"); (c) using words like *the* and *a* in a way that enhances understanding ("I read *a* book last night. *The* plot was boring"); (d) using polite language in appropriate situations (for example, when talking to one's teacher); and (e) telling stories that are interesting, jokes that are funny, and lies that convince.

Pragmatic rules can be complex and differ from one culture to another. If you were to study the Japanese language, you would come face-to-face with countless pragmatic rules about conversing with individuals of various social levels and with various relationships to you. Some of these pragmatic rules concern the ways of saying thank you. Indeed, the pragmatics of saying thank you are complex even in our own culture. Preschoolers' use of the phrase *thank you* varies with sex, socioeconomic status, and the age of the individual they are addressing. Through pragmatics, children learn to convey meaning with words, phrases, and sentences. Pragmatics helps children communicate more smoothly with others (Didow, 1993).

Is this ability to generate rule systems for language and then use them to create an almost infinite number of words the product of biology and evolution, or is it learned?

LANGUAGE'S BIOLOGICAL AND SOCIOCULTURAL/ ENVIRONMENTAL HERITAGES

To what extent is language rooted in biology and evolution? How much of language is due to sociocultural/ environmental influences?

Biological Influences

The strongest evidence for the biological basis of language is that children all over the world reach language milestones at about the same time developmentally and in about the same order, despite the vast variation in the language input they receive. For example, in some cultures adults never talk to children under 1 year of age, yet these infants still acquire language. Also, there is no other convincing way to explain how *quickly* children learn language than through biological foundations.

With these thoughts in mind, let's now explore these questions about biological influences on language: How strongly is language influenced by biological evolution? What is the brain's role in language? Do animals have language? Is there a critical period for language acquisition? Are children biologically prewired to learn language?

Biological Evolution

A number of experts on language stress its biological basis (Chomsky, 1957; Maratsos, 1989). They believe that human infants are not unlike newborn birds, who come into the world biologically prepared to sing the song of their species. These language experts believe that biological evolution shaped humans into linguistic creatures (Scott, 1997). In terms of biological evolution, the brain, nervous system, and vocal system changed over hundreds of thousands of years. Prior to *Homo sapiens*, the physical equipment to produce language did not exist; *Homo sapiens* went beyond the groans and shrieks of their predecessors to develop abstract speech. Estimates vary as to how long ago humans acquired language—from about 20,000 to 70,000 years ago. In evolutionary time, then, language is a very recent acquisition.

The Brain's Role in Language

Another aspect of biology's role in language involves the accumulating evidence that a substantial portion of language processing occurs in the brain's left hemisphere (Gazzaniga, 1986). Studies of language in brain-damaged individuals have pinpointed two areas of the left hemisphere that are especially critical. In 1861, a patient of Paul Broca, a French surgeon and anthropologist, received an injury to the left side of his brain. The patient became known as Tan, because that was the only word he could speak after his brain injury. Tan suffered from **aphasia,** *a language disorder, resulting from brain damage, that involves a loss of the ability to articulate and/or comprehend ideas.* Tan died several days after Broca evaluated him, and an autopsy revealed the location of the injury. Today, we refer to the part of the brain in which Broca's patient was injured as **Broca's area,** *an area of the left frontal lobe of the brain that directs the muscle movements involved in speech production.* Another place in the brain where an injury can seriously impair language is **Wernicke's area,** *an area of the brain's left hemisphere involved in language comprehension.* Individuals with damage to Wernicke's area often babble words in a meaningless way. The locations of Broca's area and Wernicke's area are shown in figure 10.3.

Although the brain's left hemisphere is especially important in language, keep in mind that in most activities there is an interplay between the brain's two hemispheres (Hellige, 1990). For example, in reading, the left hemisphere comprehends syntax and grammar, which the right hemisphere does not. However, the right hemisphere is better at understanding a story's intonation and emotion.

Do Animals Have Language?

Many animal species have complex and ingenious ways to signal danger and to communicate about basic needs, such as food and sex. For example, in one species of firefly, the females have learned to imitate the flashing

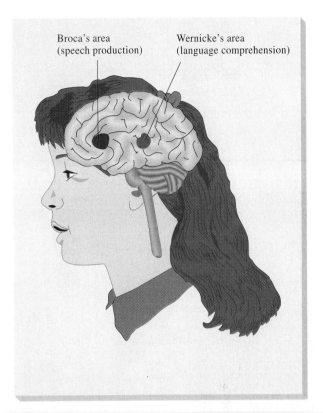

Figure~10.3

Broca's Area and Wernicke's Area
Damage to Broca's area often causes problems in speech production, whereas damage to Wernicke's area often causes problems in language comprehension. These areas are in the left hemisphere of the brain.

signal of another species to lure the aliens into their territory. Then they eat the aliens. However, is this language in the human sense? What about higher animals, such as apes? Is ape language similar to human language? Can we teach language to them?

Some researchers believe that apes can learn language. One simian celebrity in this field is a chimp named Washoe, who was adopted when she was about 10 months old (Gardner & Gardner, 1971). Since apes do not have the vocal apparatus to speak, the researchers tried to teach Washoe American Sign Language, which is one of the sign languages of the deaf. Washoe used sign language during everyday activities, such as meals, play, and car rides. In 2 years, Washoe learned 38 signs, and by the age of 5 she had a vocabulary of 160 signs. Washoe learned how to put signs together in novel ways, such as "you drink" and "you me tickle." A number of other efforts to teach language to chimps have had similar results (Premack, 1986).

The debate about chimpanzees' ability to use language focuses on two key issues. Can apes understand the meaning of symbols (that is, can they comprehend that one thing stands for another), and can apes learn syntax (that is, can they learn the mechanics and rules

Figure~10.4

Do Chimps Have Language?
Sue Savage-Rumbaugh is shown with a chimp in front of a board with language-like visual geometric symbols. The Rumbaughs (Sue and Duane) claim that these pygmy chimpanzees have a communication system in which they can come up with novel combinations of words.

that give human language its creative productivity)? The first of these issues may have been settled by Duane Rumbaugh and Sue Savage-Rumbaugh (Rumbaugh & Rumbaugh, 1990). They claim that pygmy chimpanzees they are working with have learned a communication system that combines a set of visual geometric symbols and responses to spoken English words (see figure 10.4). These animals, they say, often come up with novel combinations of words and have language knowledge that is broader than that of common chimpanzees.

Although there still is no strong evidence that chimps can learn syntax, perhaps other animals can. Ron Schusterman has worked with a sea lion named Rocky, teaching him to follow such commands as "Ball fetch" and "Disc ball fetch." The first command means that Rocky should take a disc to a ball in his tank. The second command means that Rocky should take the ball to the disc. Although Rocky and other sea lions make some errors in decoding these complex commands, their performance is much better than chance, indicating they

"Letter from Lonso...and he sounds pretty lonely."

have learned rules that link the ordering of symbols to abstract meanings. Such rules are either syntax or something close to it.

The debate over whether or not animals can use language to express thoughts is far from resolved. Researchers agree that animals can communicate with each other and that some can be trained to manipulate language-like symbols. However, although such accomplishments might be remarkable, they fall far short of human language, with its infinite number of novel phrases to convey the richness and subtleties of meaning that are the foundation of human relationships.

Is There a Critical Period for Learning Language?

Almost all children learn one or more languages during their early years of development, so it is difficult to determine whether there is a critical period for language development (Obler, 1993). In the 1960s, Eric Lenneberg (1967) proposed a biological theory of language acquisition. He said that language is a maturational process and that there is a critical period, between about 18 months of age and puberty, during which a first language can be acquired. Central to Lenneberg's thesis is the idea that language develops rapidly and with ease during the preschool years as a result of maturation. Lenneberg provided support for the critical-period concept from studies of several atypical populations, including children with damage in the left hemisphere of the brain, deaf children, and children with mental retardation (Tager-Flusberg, 1994). With regard to brain damage, Lenneberg believed that adults had already passed the critical period during which plasticity of brain functioning allows reassignment and relearning of language skills.

The stunted language development of a modern "wild child" also supports the idea of a critical period for language acquisition. In 1970 a California social worker made a routine visit to the home of a partially blind woman who had applied for public assistance. The social worker discovered that the woman and her husband had kept their 13-year-old daughter Genie locked away from the world (see figure 10.5). Kept in almost total isolation during childhood, Genie could not speak or stand erect. During the day, she was left to sit naked on a child's potty seat, restrained by a harness her father had made—she could move only her hands and feet. At night she was placed in a kind of straitjacket and caged in a crib with wire mesh sides and a cover. Whenever Genie made a noise, her father beat her. He never communicated with her in words but growled and barked at her instead.

Genie spent a number of years in extensive rehabilitation programs, such as speech and physical therapy (Curtiss, 1977; Rymer, 1992). She eventually learned to walk with a jerky motion and to use the toilet. Genie also learned to recognize many words and to speak in rudimentary sentences. At first she spoke in one-word utterances. Later she was able to string together two-word combinations, such as *big teeth*, *little marble*, and *two hand*. Consistent with the language development of most children, three-word combinations followed—for example, *small two cup*. Unlike normal children, however, Genie did not learn how to ask questions or to understand grammar. Genie is not able to distinguish between pronouns or passive and active verbs. Four years after she began stringing words together, her speech still sounded like a garbled telegram. As an adult she speaks in short, mangled sentences, such as *father hit leg*, *big wood*, and *Genie hurt*.

Second-language acquisition is another independent source of evidence for the critical-period concept. Some language experts argue that children who are exposed to two languages have little difficulty acquiring both languages and eventually speak each with little or no interference from the other. They point out that when children are exposed to a new language later in their development (such as late childhood), they have more difficulty learning it. At some point (as yet not pinpointed) in late childhood, there is a critical-period cutoff for learning to speak a new language without an accent (Obler, 1993).

In sum, many researchers have proposed that the infant and preschool years (until about age 5) might be

Figure~10.5

Genie
What was the nature of Genie's experiences, and what implications do her experiences have for language acquisition?

a critical period for language acquisition. Evidence for this notion comes from studies of brain development in young children and from the amount of language learned by young children. However, other evidence suggests that there is no such critical period. Although much language learning takes place during the infant and preschool years, learning continues well into the later child and adult years. Also, with respect to second-language learning, adults can do as well as or better than young children, provided they are motivated and spend an equivalent amount of time learning the second language. In other words, some language experts now believe that young children's language proficiency, while impressive, does not involve a biologically salient period that has already passed in older children and adults. The issue of whether there is a critical period for learning language continues to be controversial.

LAD (Language Acquisition Device)

Famous linguist Noam Chomsky (1957) believes that humans are biologically prewired to learn language at a certain time and in a certain way. He also argues that children are born into the world with a **language acquisition device (LAD),** *a biological prewiring that enables children to detect certain language categories, such as phonology, syntax, and semantics. The LAD is an innate grammatical ability that underlies all human languages.* The LAD is a theoretical construct that flows from evidence about the biological basis of language.

Is there evidence for the existence of the LAD? Supporters of the LAD concept cite the uniformity of language milestones across languages and cultures, biological substrates for language, and evidence that children create language even in the absence of well-formed input. With regard to the last argument, most deaf children are the offspring of hearing parents (Sachs, 1993). Some of these parents choose not to expose their deaf child to sign language, in order to motivate the child to learn speech while providing the child with a supportive social environment. Susan Goldin-Meadow (1977) has found that these children develop spontaneous gestures that are not based on their parents' gestures.

Sociocultural and Environmental Influences

In 1799, a nude boy was observed running through the woods of France. The boy was captured when he was approximately 11 years old. It was believed he had lived in the wild for at least 6 years. He was given the name Victor and was called the Wild Boy of Aveyron (Lane, 1976). When the boy was found, he made no effort to communicate. Even after a number of years, he could not communicate effectively. His social isolation likely contributed to his language inadequacies, just as Genie's social isolation did. We do not learn language in a social vacuum. Most of us are bathed in language from a very early age. We need this early exposure to language to acquire competent language skills.

Cultural Change and the Sociocultural Context of Language

In our discussion of biological evolution, we indicated that, prior to *Homo sapiens,* the physical equipment to produce speech did not exist. Anthropologists speculate about the social conditions that led to the development of language. Social forces may have pushed humans to develop abstract reasoning and to create an economical system for communicating with others (Crick, 1977). For example, humans probably developed complex plans and strategies for obtaining food and finding shelter, and they may have been motivated to develop language to reach a higher level of competence.

Today, most language acquisition researchers believe that children from a wide variety of cultural contexts acquire their native language without explicit teaching, in some cases without apparent encouragement. Thus, the necessary aspects of learning a language seem to be quite minimal. However, the facilitative effects usually require more support and involvement on the part of caregivers and teachers. Of special concern are children who grow up in poverty and are not exposed to guided participation in language. In Sociocultural Worlds of Children, you can read about how the rich language traditions of African Americans are disappearing in such poverty conditions.

Social Supports for Language

What are some of the social supports that provide infants and children with a rich language-learning environment? They include the parental simplification and framing of language through motherese, recasting, echoing, expanding, labeling, modeling, and corrective feedback.

One intriguing element of the environment in a young child's language acquisition is **motherese,** *talk to babies using higher-than-normal pitch, more extreme intonation contours, simpler, more repetitive vocabulary, shorter utterances, and concentration on "here and now" communication.* It is hard to talk in motherese when not in the presence of a baby, but as soon as you start talking to a baby, you immediately shift into motherese. Much of this is automatic and something most parents are not aware that they are doing. Motherese has the important functions of capturing the infant's attention and maintaining communication. When parents are asked why they use motherese, they point out that it is designed to teach their baby to talk. Older peers also talk motherese to infants (Dunn & Kendrick, 1982).

Other than motherese, are there other strategies adults use to enhance the child's acquisition of language? Four candidates are recasting, echoing, expanding, and labeling. **Recasting** *is phrasing the same or a similar meaning of a sentence in a different way, perhaps turning it into a question.* For example, if a child says, "The dog was barking," the adult can respond by asking, "When was the dog barking?" Letting a child initially indicate an interest and then proceeding to elaborate on that interest—commenting, demonstrating, and explaining—may enhance communication and help language acquisition. In contrast, an overly active, directive approach to communicating with the child may be harmful (Rice, 1989). **Echoing** *is repeating what the child says to you, especially if it is an incomplete phrase or sentence.* **Expanding** *is restating what the child has said in a linguistically sophisticated form.* **Labeling** *is giving the names of objects.* Young children are forever being asked to give the names of objects. Roger Brown (1986) identified this as the great word game and claimed that much of the early vocabulary acquired by children is motivated by this adult pressure to identify the words associated with objects.

African American Language Traditions and Urban Poverty

Shirley Brice Heath (1989) examined the language traditions of African Americans from low-income backgrounds. She traced some aspects of African American English to the time of slavery. Heath also examined how those speech patterns have carried over into African American English today. She found that agricultural areas in the southern United States have an especially rich oral tradition.

Specifically she found that adults do not simplify or edit their talk for children, in essence challenging the children to be highly active listeners. Also, adults ask only "real questions" of children—that is, questions for which the adult does not already know the answer. Adults also engage in a type of teasing with children, encouraging them to use their wits in communication. For example, a grandmother might pretend that she wants to take a child's hat and then starts a lively exchange in which the child must understand many subtleties of argument, mood, and humor—does Grandma really want my hat? Is she mad at me? Is she making a joke? Can I persuade her to give it back to me? Finally, there is an appreciation of wit and flexibility in how language is used, as well as an acknowledgment of individual differences—one person might be respected for recounting stories, another for negotiating and peacemaking skills.

Heath argues that the language tradition she describes is richly varied, cognitively demanding, and well suited to many real-life situations. She says that the oral and literary traditions among poor African Americans in the cities are well suited for many job situations. Years ago many inner-city jobs required only that a person follow directions in order to perform repetitious tasks. Today many positions require continuous interactions involving considerable flexibility in language, such as the ability to persuade co-workers or to express dissatisfaction, in a subtle way, for example.

Despite its utility in many job situations, the rich language tradition possessed by low-income African Americans does not meet with the educational priorities of our nation's schools. Too often schools stress rote memorization, minimizing group interaction and discouraging individual variations in communicative style. Also, the language tradition of African American culture is rapidly dying in the face of current life among poor African Americans, where the structure of low-income, frequently single-parent families often provides little verbal stimulation for children.

One mother agreed to let Heath tape-record her interactions with her children over a 2-year period and to write notes about her activities with them. In the interactions recorded in 500 hours of tape and more than a thousand lines of notes, the mother initiated talk with her three preschool children on only eighteen occasions (other than giving them a brief directive or asking a quick question). Few of the mother's conversations involved either planning or executing actions with or for her children.

Heath (1989) points out that the lack of family and community supports is widespread in urban housing projects, especially among African Americans. The deteriorating, impoverished conditions of these inner-city areas severely impede the ability of young children to develop the cognitive and social skills they need to function competently.

The strategies we have just described—recasting, echoing, expanding, and labeling—are used naturally and in meaningful conversations. Parents do not (and should not) use any deliberate method to teach their children to talk. Even for children who are slow in learning language, the experts agree that intervention should occur in natural ways, with the goal of being able to convey meaning.

It is important to recognize that children vary in their ability to acquire language and that this variation cannot be readily explained by differences in environmental input alone (Rice, 1996). For children who are slow in developing language skills, opportunities to talk and be talked with are important, but remember that encouragement of language development is the key, not drill and practice (de Villiers,

1996; Nelson, 1997; Snow, 1996). Language development is not a simple matter of imitation and reinforcement, a fact acknowledged even by most behaviorists today.

The Behavioral View

Behaviorists view language as just another behavior, like sitting, walking, or running. They argue that children's language is acquired through the learning process of reinforcement (Skinner, 1957) and imitation (Bandura, 1977). However, many of the sentences children produce are novel, in the sense that they have not previously heard them. For example, children might hear the sentence *The plate fell on the floor* and then say, "My mirror fell on the blanket," after they drop the mirror on the blanket. The

---

CRITICAL THINKING ABOUT CHILDREN'S DEVELOPMENT

Parental Strategies in Promoting Children's Language Development

How should parents respond to children's grammatical mistakes in conversation? Should parents allow the mistakes to continue and assume that their young children will grow out of them, or should they closely monitor their children's grammar and correct mistakes whenever they hear them?

Should you also as a parent:
- Be an active conversation partner with your infant or child?
- Talk as if the infant understands what you are saying?
- Use a language style with which you feel comfortable?

Some answers to these questions appear at the end of this chapter in Improving the Lives of Children, but before you read that section jot down your own answers to these questions. By evaluating how parents should interact with their children to promote their language development, you are learning to think critically by *applying a developmental framework to understand behavior*.

Children who grow up in low-income, poverty-ridden neighborhoods of large cities often experience a lack of family and community support, which can seriously undermine the development of their language skills.

behavioral mechanisms of reinforcement (smiles, hugs, pats on the back, corrective feedback) and imitation (modeling of words and syntax) cannot completely explain this utterance.

While spending long hours observing parents and their young children, American pioneer in language research Roger Brown (1973) searched for evidence that parents reinforce their children for speaking grammatically. He found that parents sometimes smiled and praised their children for sentences they liked, but that they also reinforced sentences that were ungrammatical. Brown concluded that no evidence exists to document that reinforcement is responsible for language's rule systems. However, recently, some researchers have found evidence that many parents provide more corrective feedback for children's ungrammatical utterances than Brown originally thought (Penner, 1987). To further evaluate the parent's role in children's language development, turn to Critical Thinking About Children's Development.

An Interactionist View of Language

We have seen that language has very strong biological foundations. The view that language has a biological base was especially promoted by Chomsky (1957), who, as we have noted, proposed the existence of a language acquisition device (LAD) to account for the complexity and speed of young children's understanding of grammar. We have also seen that children all over the world acquire language milestones at about the same time developmentally and in about the same order, despite the vast variation in language input they receive, which is also evidence for a strong biological influence in language development.

However, children do not learn language in a social vacuum. American psychologist Jerome Bruner (1983, 1989, 1997) recognized this important point when he proposed that the sociocultural context is extremely important in understanding children's language development. Like Vygotsky, Bruner stresses the role of parents and teachers in constructing a child's communication environment. Bruner developed the concept of a language acquisition support system (LASS) to describe the behaviors of a language-skilled individual, especially a parent, in structuring and supporting the child's language development. Bruner's concept has much in common with Vygotsky's concept of a zone of proximal development, which was discussed in chapter 7. Thus, language development requires social involvement as well as a child's natural, biological propensity to learn language (Bloom, 1997; Snow, 1997).

The importance of the language environment was recently underscored in a longitudinal study conducted by Betty Hart and Todd Risley (1995). They observed the language environments of 42 children—13 with parents classified as professionals, 23 with parents described as working-class, and 6 with parents on welfare. They found that all the children developed normally in terms of learning to talk and acquiring all the forms and patterns of English and basic vocabulary. However, there were enormous differences in the sheer amount of language to which the children were exposed and the level of language development the children achieved. For example, in a typical hour, professional parents spent almost twice as much time interacting with their children as welfare parents did with their children. The children of professional parents heard about 2,100 words per hour, whereas their child counterparts in welfare families heard only about 600 words per hour.

The researchers estimated that by the age of 4 the average child in a welfare family would have 13 million fewer words of cumulative language experience than the average child in a working-class family. Somewhat amazingly, they found that the average 3-year-old *child* from a professional family had a recorded vocabulary that exceeded the recorded vocabulary size of the average welfare *parent*.

In sum, all of the children heard all of the basic forms and functions of English. Furthermore, all of the children acquired the basic forms and functions of the English language and the universals of language. But there was great variation in the amount of language they were exposed to and the level of language development attained.

In the interactionist view, the language acquisition device (LAD) interacts with the language acquisition support system (LASS) to make the language system function (see figure 10.6). John Locke (1993) argued that one reason why social interactionist aspects have been underplayed recently in explaining language

development is that linguists concentrate on language's complex, structural properties, especially the acquisition of grammar, and give inadequate attention to the communicative aspects of language. Locke reminds us that language learning occurs in the very real context of physical and social maturation, and that children are neither exclusively young biological linguists nor exclusively social beings (Ratner, 1993b). An interactionist view emphasizes the contributions of both biology and experience in language—that is, that children are biologically prepared to learn language as they and their caregivers interact (Nelson & Réger, 1995).

At this point we have discussed a number of ideas about what language is, language's rule systems, biological influences, and cultural, social, and behavioral influences. A summary of these ideas is presented in concept table 10.1.

THE ROLE OF COGNITION IN LANGUAGE

There are essentially two basic and separate issues involved in exploring connections between language and cognition. The first is, Is cognition necessary for language? Although some researchers have noted that certain aspects of language development typically follow mastery of selected cognitive skills in both normally developing children and children with mental retardation (Mundy, Seibert, & Hogan, 1984), it is not clear that language development depends upon any specific aspect of cognitive abilities (Lenneberg, 1967). Some experts believe that it is more likely that language and cognitive development occur in parallel but dissociated fashions (Cromer, 1987; Ratner, 1993a). Thus, based on research and experts' judgments, cognition is not necessary for language development.

The second issue is this: Is language necessary for (or important to) cognition? This issue is addressed by studies of deaf children. On a variety of thinking and problem-solving skills, deaf children perform at the same level as children of the same age who have no hearing problems. Some of the deaf children in these studies do not even have command of written or sign language (Furth, 1973). Thus, based on studies of deaf children, language is not necessary for cognitive development.

HOW LANGUAGE DEVELOPS

In the thirteenth century, the Holy Roman Emperor Frederick II had a cruel idea. He wanted to know what language children would speak if no one talked to them. He selected several newborns and threatened their caregivers with death if they ever talked to the infants. Frederick never found out what language the children spoke because they all died. As we move toward the twenty-first century, we are still curious about infants' development

Language
Acquisition
Device (LAD)

Biological
prewiring for
language

✕

Language
Acquisition
Support System
(LASS)

Sociocultural
structuring and
support

=

Children's
language
acquisition

Figure~10.6

An Interactionist View of Language: Chomsky's LAD and Bruner's LASS
In the interactionist view, language acquisition involves the child's natural propensity to learn language (described by Chomsky as the language acquisition device [LAD]) and social involvement (described by Bruner as the language acquisition support system [LASS]).

of language, although our experiments and observations are, to say the least, far more humane than the evil Frederick's.

Language Development in Infancy

When does an infant utter her first word? This event usually occurs at about 10 to 13 months of age, though some infants wait longer. Many parents view the onset of language development as coincident with this first word, but some significant accomplishments are attained earlier. Before babies say words, they babble, emitting such vocalizations as "goo-goo" and "ga-ga." Babbling starts at about 3 to 6 months of age. The start is determined by biological maturation, not reinforcement or the ability to hear (Locke & others, 1991). Even deaf babies babble for a time (Lenneberg, Rebelsky, & Nichols, 1965). Babbling exercises the baby's vocal apparatus and facilitates the development of articulation skills that are useful in later speech. The purpose of a baby's earliest communication, however, is to attract attention from parents and others in the environment. Infants engage the attention of others by making or breaking eye contact, by vocalizing sounds, and by performing manual actions such as pointing. All of those behaviors involve pragmatics.

A child's first words include those that name important people (*dada*), familiar animals (*kitty*), vehicles (*car*), toys (*ball*), food (*milk*), body parts (*eye*), clothes (*hat*), household items (*clock*), or greeting terms (*bye*). These were the first words of babies 50 years ago and they are the first words of babies today (Clark, 1983). At times, it is hard to tell what these one-word utterances mean. One possibility is that they stand for an entire sentence in the infant's mind. Because of the infant's limited cognitive or linguistic skills, possibly only one word comes out instead of the whole sentence. The **holophrase hypothesis** *is the theory that, in infants' first words, a single word is used to imply a complete sentence.*

Children sometimes overextend or underextend the meanings of the words they use (Woodward & Markman, 1997). **Overextension** *is the tendency of children to misuse words by extending one word's meaning to include objects that are not related to, or are inappropriate for, the word's meaning.* For example, when children learn to say the word *dada* for "father," they often apply the word beyond the individual it was intended to represent, using it for other men, strangers, or boys. With time, such overextensions decrease and eventually disappear. **Underextension** *occurs when children fail to use a noun to name a relevant*

What Is Language, Language's Rule Systems, and Language's Biological and Sociocultural/Environmental Heritages

Concept	Processes/ Related Ideas	Characteristics/Description
What Is Language?	Its nature	Language is a system of symbols, or word sequences, used to communicate with others, that involves infinite generativity, displacement, signal simultaneity and overlap, and rule systems.
Language's Rule Systems	Phonology	Phonology governs the sequencing of phonemes (basic sounds that differ in their distinctive features).
	Morphology	Morphology governs the sequencing of morphemes (the smallest units of language that carry meaning).
	Syntax	Syntax governs the ordering of words within sentences or phrases. These rules apply to deep and surface structures.
	Semantics	Semantics places restrictions on how words must be used to make meaningful sentences.
	Pragmatics	Pragmatics facilitates good communication and good social relations among language users.
Biological Influences	Strongest evidence	Children all over the world acquire language milestones at about the same time developmentally and in about the same order, despite the vast variation in input they receive.
	Biological evolution	The fact that biological evolution shaped humans into linguistic creatures is undeniable.
	The brain's role in language	The brain's left hemisphere plays an important role in language. Damage to Broca's area affects speech production, whereas damage to Wernicke's area affects language comprehension. Although the left hemisphere has a powerful influence on language, keep in mind that, in most activities, there is an interplay between the brain's two hemispheres.
	Do animals have language?	Animals can communicate, and pygmy chimpanzees can be taught to use symbols. Whether animal communication has all of the properties of human language is debated.
	Is there a critical period for learning language?	Based on observations of brain injury effects on language at different points in development, Lenneberg argued that a critical period for language acquisition ends at puberty. The experiences of Genie and other children also suggest that the early childhood years are a crucial period in language acquisition. And observations about second-language acquisition, especially speaking with or without an accent, provide evidence for a critical period. However, some language experts argue that there is evidence against a critical period.
	Biological prewiring—LAD	Linguist Noam Chomsky believes that humans are prewired to learn language. He said children are born with a language acquisition device (LAD), a biological prewiring, or innate grammatical ability, that enables a child to detect certain language categories.
Sociocultural and Environmental Influences	Cultural change and the sociocultural context of language	Sociocultural conditions might have pushed humans to develop abstract reasoning and to create an economical system for communicating with others. Among the social supports that contribute to children's language are parental simplification and framing of language through motherese, recasting, echoing, expanding, and labeling.
	The behavioral view	Behaviorists view language as just another behavior, like sitting, walking, or running. They argue that children's language is acquired through reinforcement and imitation. Chomsky believes that the behavioral view is wrong.
An Interactionist View of Language	Its nature	One interactionist view proposes that Chomsky's biological language acquisition device (LAD) interacts with Bruner's language acquisition support system (LASS). An interactionist view emphasizes the contributions of both biology and experience in language—that is, that children are biologically prepared to learn language as they and their caregivers interact.

event or object. For example, a child might learn to use the word *boy* to describe a 5-year-old neighbor but not apply the word to a male infant or a 9-year-old male.

By the time children are 18 to 24 months of age, they usually have begun to utter two-word statements. During this two-word stage, they quickly grasp the importance of expressing concepts and the role that language plays in communicating with others. To convey meaning with two-word utterances, the child relies heavily on gesture, tone, and context. The many kinds of meaning children can communicate with a two-word utterance include these:

> *Identification:* See doggie.
> *Location:* Book there.
> *Repetition:* More milk.
> *Nonexistence:* Allgone thing.
> *Negation:* Not wolf.
> *Possession:* My candy.
> *Attribution:* Big car.
> *Agent-action:* Mama walk.
> *Action-direct-object:* Hit you.
> *Action-indirect-object:* Give papa.
> *Action-instrument:* Cut knife.
> *Question:* Where ball? (Slobin, 1972)

One of the most striking aspects of this list is that these meanings are expressed by children all over the world. The examples are taken from utterances in English, German, Russian, Finnish, Turkish, Samoan, and Luo.

Telegraphic speech *is the use of short, precise words to communicate; it is characteristic of young children's two-word utterances.* When we write telegrams, we try to be terse, excluding any unnecessary words. As indicated in the examples, in the list above, of telegraphic speech from children from around the world, articles, auxiliary verbs, and other connectives usually are omitted. Of course, telegraphic speech is not limited to two-word utterances. "Mommy give ice cream" and "Mommy give Tommy ice cream" also are examples of telegraphic speech.

In expanding this concept of classifying children's language development in terms of number of utterances, Roger Brown (1973) has proposed that **mean length of utterance (MLU),** *an index of language development based on the number of morphemes per sentence a child produces in a sample of about 50 to 100 sentences,* is a good index of language maturity. Brown identified five stages based on MLU:

Stage	MLU
1	1+ to 2.0
2	2.5
3	3.0
4	3.5
5	4.0

Around the world, young children learn to speak in two-word utterances, in most cases at about 18 to 24 months of age.

The first stage begins when a child generates sentences consisting of more than one morpheme, such as the examples of two-morpheme utterances mentioned earlier. The 1+ designation suggests that the average number of morphemes in each utterance is greater than one but not yet two, because some of the child's utterances are still holophrases. This stage continues until the child averages two morphemes per utterance. Subsequent stages are marked by increments of .5 in mean length of utterance. Brown's stages are shown in figure 10.7.

Brown's stages are important for several reasons. First, children who differ in chronological age by as much as ½ to ¾ year still have similar speech patterns. Second, children with similar mean lengths of utterance seem to have similar rule systems that characterize their language. In some ways, then, MLU is a better indicator of language development than is chronological age. Figure 10.8 shows the individual variation in chronological age that characterizes children's MLU. In one recent study of communicative development from 8 to 30 months of age, there was extensive variability in the rate of lexical, gestural, and grammatical development, which challenged the concept of the modal child (Fenson & others, 1994).

Language Development in Early Childhood

Young children's understanding sometimes gets way ahead of their speech. One 3-year-old, laughing with delight as an abrupt summer breeze stirred his hair and tickled his skin, commented, "It did winding me!" Adults would be understandably perplexed if a young child ventured, "Anything is not to break, only plates and glasses," when she meant, "Nothing is breaking except plates and glasses." Many of the oddities of young children's language sound like mistakes to adult listeners. From the children's point of view, however, they are not

Stage	Age Range (months)	Mean Length of Utterance (average number of morphemes per sentence)	Characteristics	Typical Sentences
1	12–26	1.00–2.00	Vocabulary consists mainly of nouns and verbs with a few adjectives and adverbs; word order is preserved	Baby bath.
2	27–30	2.00–2.50	Correct use of plurals; use of past tense, use of *be*, definite and nondefinite articles, some prepositions	Cars go fast.
3	31–34	2.50–3.00	Use of yes-no questions, *wh*-questions (who, what, where); use of negatives and imperatives	Put the baby down.
4	35–40	3.00–3.75	Embedding one sentence within another	That's the truck mommy buyed me.
5	41–46	3.75–4.50	Coordination of simple sentences and propositional relations	Jenny and Cindy are sisters.

Figure~10.7

Brown's Stages of Language Development

mistakes; they represent the way young children perceive and understand their world at that point in their development. Among the important issues in language during the early childhood years are those involving developmental changes in language's rule systems.

What kinds of changes occur in language development during early childhood? Language continues to obey certain principles, following the rules of phonology, morphology, syntax, semantics, and pragmatics.

Regarding phonology, some preschool children have difficulty producing consonant clusters (for example, *str* as in *string*). Pronouncing some of the more difficult phonemes—*r*, for example—is still problematic and can continue to be a problem up to about 7 or 8 years of age. Also, some of the phonological rules for pronouncing word endings (in the past tense, for example) are not mastered until children are 6 to 8 years of age.

Regarding morphology, there is clear evidence that, as they move beyond two-word utterances, children know morphological rules. Children begin using the plural and possessive forms of nouns (*dogs* and *dog's*); putting appropriate endings on verbs (*-s* when the subject is third-person singular, *-ed* for the past tense, and *-ing* for the present progressive tense); and using prepositions (*in* and *on*), articles (*a* and *the*), and various forms of the verb *to be* ("I *was going* to the store"). Some of the best evidence for morphological rules appears in the form of *overgeneralizations* of these rules. Have you ever heard a preschool child say

"foots" instead of "feet" or "goed" instead of "went"? If you do not remember having heard such things, talk to some parents who have young children or to the young children themselves. You will hear some interesting errors in the use of morphological rule endings.

In a classic experiment, children's language researcher Jean Berko (1958) presented preschool and first-grade children with cards such as the one shown in figure 10.9. Children were asked to look at the card while the experimenter read the words on it aloud. Then the children were asked to supply the missing word. This might sound easy, but Berko was interested not just in the children's ability to recall the right word but also in their ability to say it "correctly" (with the ending that was dictated by morphological rules). *Wugs* would be the correct response for the card in figure 10.9. Although the children were not perfectly accurate, they were much better than chance would dictate. Moreover, they demonstrated their knowledge of morphological rules not only with the plural forms of nouns ("There are two wugs") but also with possessive forms of nouns and with the third-person singular and past-tense forms of verbs. And Berko's study demonstrated not only that the children relied on rules, but also that they had *abstracted* the rules from what they had heard and could apply them to novel situations. What makes Berko's study impressive is that all of the words were fictional; they were created especially for the experiment. Thus, the children could not base their responses on remembering past instances of hearing the words. It seems, instead, that they were forced to rely on *rules*. Their performance suggested that they did so successfully.

Similar evidence that children learn and actively apply rules can be found at the level of syntax (Budwig, 1993). After advancing beyond two-word utterances, the child speaks word sequences that show a growing mastery of complex rules for how words should be ordered. Consider the case of *wh-* questions: "Where is Daddy going?" and "What is that boy doing?" for example. To ask these questions properly, the child has to know two important differences between *wh-* questions and simple affirmative statements (for instance, "Daddy is going to work" and "That boy is waiting on the school bus"). First, a *wh-* word must be added at the beginning of the sentence. Second, the auxiliary verb must be "inverted"—that is, exchanged with the subject of the sentence. Young children learn quite early where to put the *wh-* word, but they take much longer to learn the auxiliary-inversion rule. Thus, it is common to hear preschool children asking such questions as "Where daddy is going?" and "What that boy is doing?"

As children move into the elementary school years, they become skilled at using syntactical rules to construct lengthy and complex sentences. Utterances such as "The man who fixed the house went home" and "I don't want you to use my bike" are impressive demonstrations of how the child can use syntax to combine ideas into a single sentence. Just how a young child achieves the mastery of such complex rules, while at the same time she may be struggling with relatively simple arithmetic rules, is a mystery we have yet to solve.

Regarding semantics, as children move beyond the two-word stage, their knowledge of meanings also rapidly advances. The speaking vocabulary of a 6-year-old child ranges from 8,000 to 14,000 words (Carey, 1977). Assuming that word learning began when the child was 12 months old, this translates into a rate for new word meanings of 5 to 8 words a day between the ages of 1 and 6. After 5 years of word learning, the 6-year-old child does not slow down. According to some estimates, the average child of this age is moving along at the awe-inspiring rate of 22 words a day (Miller, 1981). How would you fare if you were given the task of learning 22 new words every day? It is truly miraculous how quickly children learn language (Fenson & others, 1994).

Figure~10.8

Roger Brown and His Examination of MLU in Three Children
The graph shows the average length of utterances by three children ranging in age from $1\frac{1}{2}$ to just over 4 years. The photograph shows Roger Brown talking with a young girl. Brown has been a pioneer in providing rich insights about children's language development. Among his contributions is the concept of MLU, or mean length of utterance, which has been documented as a good index of a child's language maturity.

Changes in pragmatics also characterize young children's language development (Ninio & Snow, 1996). A 6-year-old is simply a much better conversationalist than a 2-year-old is. What are some of the improvements in pragmatics that are made in the preschool years? At about 3 years of age, children improve in their ability to talk about things that are not physically present; that is, they improve their command of the characteristic of language known as *displacement*. One way displacement is revealed is in games of pretend. Although a 2-year-old might know the word *table*, he is unlikely to use this word to refer to an imaginary table that he pretends is standing in front of him. A child over 3 years of age probably has this ability, though, even if she does not always use it. There are large individual differences in preschoolers' talk about imaginary people and things.

Somewhat later in the preschool years—at about 4 years of age—children develop a remarkable sensitivity to the needs of others in conversation. One way in which they show such sensitivity is their use of the articles *the* and *an* (or *a*). When adults tell a story or describe an event, they

Figure~10.9

Stimuli in Berko's Study of Young Children's Understanding of Morphological Rules

In Jean Berko's (1958) study, young children were presented cards such as this one with a "wug" on it. Then the children were asked to supply the missing word and say it correctly. "Wugs" is the correct response here.

"No, Timmy, not 'I sawed the chair.' It's 'I saw the chair' or 'I have seen the chair.'"

© Glenn Bernhardt.

generally use *an* (or *a*) when they first refer to an animal or an object, and then use *the* when referring to it later (for example, "Two boys were walking through the jungle when *a* fierce lion appeared. *The* lion lunged at one boy while the other ran for cover."). Even 3-year-olds follow part of this rule (they consistently use the word *the* when referring to previously mentioned things). However, the use of the word *a* when something is initially mentioned develops more slowly. Although 5-year-old children follow this rule on some occasions, they fail to follow it on others.

Another pragmatic ability that appears around 4 to 5 years of age involves speech style. As adults, we have the ability to change our speech style in accordance with social situations and persons with whom we are speaking. An obvious example is that adults speak in a simpler way to a 2-year-old child than to an older child or to an adult. Interestingly, even 4-year-old children speak differently to a 2-year-old than to a same-aged peer (they "talk down" to the 2-year-old, using shorter utterance lengths). They also speak differently to an adult than to a same-aged peer, using more polite and formal language with the adult (Shatz & Gelman, 1973).

Language Development in Middle and Late Childhood

As children develop during middle and late childhood, changes in their vocabulary and grammar take place. Reading assumes a prominent role in their language world, as do writing and the importance of literacy. An increasingly important consideration is bilingualism.

Vocabulary and Grammar

During middle and late childhood, a change occurs in the way children think about words. They become less tied to the actions and perceptual dimensions associated with words, and they become more analytical in their approach to words. For example, when asked to say the first thing that comes to mind when they hear a word, such as *dog*, preschool children often respond with a word related to the immediate context of a dog. A child might associate *dog* with a word that indicates its appearance (*black, big*) or to an action associated with it (*bark, sit*). Older children more frequently respond to dog by associating it with an appropriate category (*animal*) or to information that intelligently expands the context (*cat, veterinarian*). The increasing ability of elementary school children to analyze words helps them understand words that have no direct relation to their personal experiences. This allows children to add more abstract words to their vocabulary. For example, *precious stones* can be understood by understanding the common characteristics of *diamonds* and *emeralds*. Also, children's increasing analytical abilities allow them to distinguish between such similar words as *cousin* and *nephew*, or *city, village,* and *suburb.*

Children make similar advances in grammar. The elementary school child's improvement in logical reasoning and analytical skills helps in the understanding of such constructions as the appropriate use of comparatives

As children develop, they become much better conversationalists. At about 4 years of age, children become more sensitive to the needs of others in conversation.

Reading is more than the sum of whole-word and phonics methods. Information-processing skills are involved in successful reading. When children read, they process information and interpret it.

(*shorter, deeper*) and subjunctives ("*If* I *were* president, . . ."). By the end of the elementary school years, children can usually apply most of the appropriate rules of grammar.

Reading

Reading is a complex ability that involves a number of different processes. What are the main ways that children are taught to read? How is development involved in children's reading?

Approaches to Teaching Reading Education and language experts continue to debate how children should be taught to read. The debate focuses on the whole-language approach versus the basic-skills-and-phonetics approach. The **whole-language approach** *stresses that reading instruction should parallel children's natural language learning. Reading materials should be whole and meaningful.* That is, in early reading instruction, children should be presented with materials in their complete form, such as stories and poems. In this way, say the whole-language enthusiasts, children can appreciate language's communicative function. By contrast, the **basic-skills-and-phonetics approach** *advocates that reading instruction should stress phonetics and its basic rules for translating written symbols into sounds. Early reading instruction should involve simplified materials.* Only after they have learned phonological rules should children be given complex reading material such as books and poems.

Which approach is best? Researchers have not been able to successfully document that one approach is superior to the other. Some language experts believe that a combination of the two approaches should be followed—an approach advocated in the following developmental description of learning to read.

A Developmental Information-Processing Approach to Reading Following is a summary of a comprehensive developmental information-processing approach to reading proposed by Louise Spear-Swerling and Robert J. Sternberg (1994). The model involves this sequence: visual-cue recognition, phonetic-cue word recognition, automatic word recognition, strategic reading, and proficient adult reading. In this model, reading is viewed as a developmental process in which the nature of reading changes with development; the cognitive processes implicated in reading are not the same in a 6-year-old beginning reader as they are in a proficient adult reader.

Normal reading acquisition begins with a phase of paired-associate learning, in which children do not make use of letter-sound correspondences. In this early phase of learning to read, children use salient visual cues, such as colors or distinctive logos, to recognize words. An example of visual-cue recognition would be recognizing the MacDonald's restaurant sign on the basis of the red and yellow colors but not recognizing the letters if they were printed in a different context—for instance, when printed in plain black letters on a piece of white paper. Visual-cue recognition characterizes many preschool children who are just starting to recognize words.

In the second phase of reading, children begin to use phonetic cues to recognize words, although their use of these cues is not complete and frequently involves only the first or last letters of a word. For example, a child might recognize the word *house* primarily on the basis of the *h* and the final *se*, but might confuse the words *house* and *mouse* in this phase. Thus, children in the phonetic-cue word recognition phase are not fully capable of decoding words.

To reach the phonetic-cue word recognition phase, children must have at least a rudimentary level of phonological awareness, must know at least some letter-sound correspondences, and must have discovered the alphabetic principle that letters and sounds map onto each other in a systematic manner (this is often referred to as "alphabetic insight"). Some children, especially those who come from highly literate families, may enter school already in the phonetic-cue word recognition phase. Children who have been exposed to word games, letters, and books might attain alphabetic insight outside of school and apply it in learning to recognize words. For many children, though, alphabetic insight only develops through formal schooling.

The third phase of reading in Spear-Swerling and Sternberg's (1994) model involves achieving automatic word recognition. In this phase, children have fully attained word-decoding skills. In recognizing the word *house*, they use the *ou*, as well as the *h* and *se*, and thus do not confuse *house* with similarly spelled words. Automatization of word recognition sets the stage for increasing reading comprehension, because children can now devote their mental resources to understanding the meaning of the text rather than to recognizing words. Some researchers believe that many children begin to acquire automatization between the first and second grade, although it might continue to develop through adulthood (Perfetti, 1992).

In the automatic word recognition phase, children do not make efficient, routine use of strategies to aid comprehension. But with developing metacognitive abilities, with reading experience, with an increasing knowledge base, and with automatic word recognition skills, children become more capable of acquiring strategies to increase their comprehension. When they begin to routinely use a number of these strategies, they are in the phase of strategic reading. For example, when children fail to comprehend what they have just read, they have available a number of "fix-up" strategies, such as rereading, reading ahead to see if an inconsistency is resolved, or looking up an unfamiliar word in the dictionary. Researchers have found that many children begin to use strategies in the middle and late elementary school years (Myers & Paris, 1978).

Although many older elementary-school-age children use strategies to aid their reading comprehension, they are not as proficient at reading as a college student is. What is the difference in their reading skills? The defining feature of proficient reading is highly developed comprehension abilities. Highly proficient readers are insightful, reflective, and analytical. Strategic readers lack these higher-order skills. A summary of the phases in the developmental information-processing approach to reading is presented in figure 10.10, along with the developmental timetable for their normal occurrence.

Phase	Normal Age of Achievement
Visual cue recognition	Preschool, kindergarten
Phonetic cue recognition	Kindergarten, first grade
Automatic word recognition	Between first and second grade
Strategic reading	Middle to late elementary school years
Proficient adult reading	Adolescence, adulthood

Figure~10.10

A Developmental Information-Processing Model of Reading

Early intervention is important for children who develop reading problems. Once children have developed negative expectations, lowered motivation, and lowered levels of practice, it is increasingly difficult to get them back on track to becoming a proficient reader. Mainstream reading approaches that have a strong decoding component in the early grades should benefit children with reading problems.

There is an age-old controversy in reading instruction between the advocates of phonics instruction (an approach that emphasizes the sounds that letters make when in words—such sounds differ from the names of

The devl and the babe goste

A DEVL NAPD IN THE BRITE SUNLITE he SED IT IS HOLOWENE I HAV to GeT UP AND GeT. reDE to SCer The littL CHILJRIN WeN THAEGO to CHRICOR CHRETE FRST He MADE A JACAL ETRN He PUT 2 CEDIS IN it to RELE SCer THem TYN He MADE A COL JRIN to CAST SPELS ON The CHIL JRIN.

Figure~10.11

The Devl and Babe Goste
This story was written by a 6-year-old first-grade girl, Anna Mudd. What aspects of literacy does it reflect?

these letters, as when the sound of the letter *c* is not found in *cat*) and the advocates of the whole-language approach to teaching reading. Spear-Swerling and Sternberg (1994) believe that this debate is over the wrong question. Their model emphasizes that, although decoding is important in early reading acquisition, a competent reading program should emphasize *both* fluent decoding and good comprehension. A reading program that has children complete endless phonic exercises and do little else is likely to be as flawed as one that fails to teach decoding at all (a characteristic of some whole-language programs). Reading instruction that does not foster higher-level comprehension skills not only might result in impaired comprehension, but also might negatively influence children's motivation for reading.

In Spear-Swerling and Sternberg's view, a combination of whole-language techniques and a strong decoding program is likely to benefit children with reading problems, and would probably benefit many nondisabled readers as well. They also point out that the aspects of the whole-language approach that are likely to benefit children with reading problems are its emphases on early writing, on integrating reading with other subject areas, and on motivational reading materials.

Literacy   Reading is essentially the act of understanding language on paper. **Literacy** *is the ability to read and write.* Anna Mudd is the 6-year-old, first-grade author of "The Devl and the Babe Goste," shown in figure 10.11. Anna has been writing stories for at least 2 years. Her story includes poetic images, sophisticated syntax, and vocabulary that reflects advances in her oral language and the fact that her written language now has a life of its own—one that will in turn influence her oral language, reading, and future writing. Anna's example reveals the interconnection of early oral language, emergent literacy, and writing development. During the elementary school years, most children move from a world of predominantly oral language to a world in which written language is stressed and oral language becomes more complex (Adams, Treiman, & Pressley, 1997).

Emergent literacy *is the term given to circumstances in which children begin constructing knowledge about the uses of and nature of written language long before they begin decoding familiar words and writing in conventional ways.* Emergent literacy is a long, gradual process for children in most cultures. It starts in infancy with the child's first baby book and is elaborated on by parents, siblings, and caregivers as they share books and tell stories. Emergent literacy is also influenced by daily routines such as watching television programs like "Reading Rainbow" and "Sesame Street."

Unfortunately, in the push to develop a nation of literate people by emphasizing the early development of reading and writing skills, some dangers have emerged (Early Childhood and Literacy Development Committee, 1986). Too many young children have been subjected to rigid, formal prereading programs with expectations and experiences that are too advanced for children at their level of development.

What should a literacy program for young children be like? Instruction should be built on what children already know about oral language, reading, and writing. All young children should experience feelings of success and pride in their early reading and writing exercises. Teachers and parents need to help young children perceive themselves as people who enjoy exploring oral and written language. Reading should be integrated into the entire broad communication process, which includes speaking, listening, and writing, as well as other communication systems such as art, music, and math. Children's early writing attempts should be encouraged without concern for proper formation of letters or correct conventional spelling. Children should be encouraged to take risks in reading and writing; errors should be viewed as a natural part of the child's development. Teachers and parents should regularly take time to read to children from a wide variety of poetry, fiction, and nonfiction. Teachers and parents should present models for young children to emulate by using language appropriately, listening and responding to children's talk, and engaging in their own reading and writing (Whitehurst,

1997). Children should also be encouraged to be active, rather than passive, participants in the learning process. Parents and teachers can accomplish this by using activities that stimulate children's experimentation with talking, listening, writing, and reading.

Bilingualism

Octavio's Mexican parents moved to the United States 1 year before Octavio was born. They do not speak English fluently and have always spoken to Octavio in Spanish. At 6 years of age, Octavio has just entered the first grade at an elementary school in San Antonio, Texas, and he speaks no English. What is the best way to teach Octavio? How much easier would elementary school be for Octavio if his parents had been able to speak to him in Spanish *and* English when he was an infant?

Well over 6 million children in the United States come from homes in which English is not the primary language. Often, like Octavio, they live in a community in which English as a second language is the main means of communication. These children face a more difficult task than most of us: They must master the native tongue of their family to communicate effectively at home, and they must also master English to make their way in the larger society. The number of bilingual children is increasing at such a rapid rate in our country that they constitute an important subgroup of language learners that society must deal with. Although the education of such children in the public schools has a long history, only recently has a national policy evolved to guarantee a high-quality language experience for them (National Association for the Education of Young Children, 1996).

Bilingual education *is programs for students with limited proficiency in English that instruct students in their own language part of the time while they learn English.* The rationale for bilingual education was provided by the U.S. Commission on Civil Rights (1975): Lack of English proficiency is the main reason language minority students do poorly in school; bilingual education should keep students from falling far behind in a subject while they are learning English. Bilingual programs vary extensively in content and quality. At a minimum, they include instruction in English as a second language for students with limited English proficiency. Bilingual programs often include some instruction in Spanish as well. The largest number of bilingual programs in the United States are in Spanish, so our examples refer to Spanish, although the principles also apply to bilingual programs in other languages. Bilingual programs differ in the extent to which the Latino culture is taught to all students, and some bilingual programs teach Spanish to all students, regardless of whether their primary language is Spanish.

Most bilingual education programs are simply transitional programs developed to support students in Spanish until they can understand English well enough to function in the regular classroom, which is taught in English. A typical bilingual program begins teaching students with limited English proficiency in their primary language in kindergarten and then changes to English-only classes at the end of the first or second grade (Slavin, 1988).

Research evaluation of bilingualism has led to the conclusion that bilingualism does not interfere with performance in either language (Hakuta & Garcia, 1989). There is no evidence that the native language should be eliminated as early as possible because it might interfere with learning a second language. Instead, higher degrees of bilingualism are associated with cognitive flexibility and improved concept formation (Diaz, 1983). These findings are based primarily on research in additive bilingual settings—that is, in settings where the second language is added as an enrichment to the native language and not at its expense. Causal relations between bilingualism and cognitive or language competence are difficult to establish, but, in general, positive outcomes are often noted in communities where bilingualism is not socially stigmatized.

In one recent study, Kimbrough Oller (1995) compared a group of children from bilingual families, where they grew up speaking both English and Spanish, with a group of children from families that spoke only English. As infants, both groups began making simple speech sounds, such as "da" and "ba," at about the same age. At 3 years of age, the bilingual children performed as well in Spanish as the children who spoke only that language. The results apply only to children who learn English and Spanish simultaneously from a young age. Latino children who begin learning English in kindergarten might be handicapped in school because they have not yet developed fundamental English skills.

In another investigation, Grace Yeni-Komshian (1995) studied individuals who had moved from Korea to the United States at between 2 and 24 years of age. She found that those who began speaking English at about 6 to 8 years of age were proficient in neither Korean nor English. One recommendation regarding kindergarten and school-age children living in the United States who have not yet learned English is a two-way program in which bilingual children learn in their native language for half of the day and in English the other half. There are about 200 two-way programs in the United States; these usually continue through elementary school.

Increasingly, researchers are recognizing the complexity of bilingualism's effects (Ellis & Laporte, 1997; Segalowitz, 1997). For example, as indicated earlier, bilingualism programs vary enormously. Some are of excellent quality; others are of poor quality. Some teachers in bilingual education programs are completely bilingual; others are not. Some programs begin in kindergarten, others in elementary school. Some programs end in the first or second grade; others continue through the fifth

Bilingual Education and Learning a Second Language

Bilingualism is a complex concept, and some programs are more effective than others. As we indicated in the text, some programs begin in kindergarten, others in elementary school; some end in the first or second grade, others continue through the fifth or sixth grade. Some include instruction in the culture of a language, others focus exclusively on language instruction.

We also mentioned that the United States is one of the few countries in which most students graduate from high school knowing only one language.

Assume that you have taken a position as director of language instruction for elementary schools in a large school system in a major U.S. city. What policy on bilingual education would you try to get enacted? What would your stance be on encouraging all elementary school children to learn a second language, such as French or Spanish? By arriving at a policy on bilingual education and learning a second language, you are learning to think critically by *creating arguments based on developmental concepts.*

What are the arguments for and against bilingual education?

or sixth grade. Some include instruction in the Latino culture; others focus only on language instruction. Some researchers select outcome measures that include only proficiency in English; others focus on cognitive variables such as cognitive flexibility and concept formation; and still others include more social variables such as integration into the school, self-esteem, and attitude toward school. In sum, there is more to development of bilingual education than simple language proficiency (Hakuta & Garcia, 1989).

The National Association for the Education of Young Children (1996) recently developed recommendations for responding to linguistic and cultural diversity. The association stresses that early childhood educators can help linguistic and culturally diverse children and their families by acknowledging the importance of and respecting the child's home language and culture. It also emphasizes that administrative support for bilingualism should be a goal within the educational setting. Educational practices should focus on educating children to flourish in the "school culture" while preserving and respecting the diversity of the home language and culture that each child brings to the early-learning setting.

One final point about bilingualism deserves attention. The United States is one of the few countries in the world in which most students graduate from high school knowing only their own language. For example, in Russia, schools have ten grades, called forms, which correspond roughly to the twelve grades in American schools. Children begin school at age 7. In the third form, Russian students begin learning English. Because of the emphasis on teaching English in their schools, most Russian citizens today under the age of 35 speak at least some English (Cameron, 1988). To further evaluate bilingualism and learning a second language, turn to Critical Thinking About Children's Development.

At this point, we have discussed a number of ideas about the role of cognition in language and the development of language. A summary of these ideas is presented in concept table 10.2.

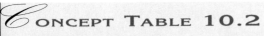

Concept	Processes/ Related Ideas	Characteristics/Description
The Role of Cognition	Its nature	Two basic and separate issues are involved in language/cognition connections: (1) Is cognition necessary for language? (2) Is language necessary for cognition? Most language experts argue that the answer is no to both questions and believe that cognitive and language development likely have independent paths of development.
Language Development in Infancy and Early Childhood	Infancy	Vocalization begins with babbling at about 3 to 6 months of age. A baby's earliest communication skills are pragmatic. One-word utterances occur at about 10 to 13 months; the holophrase hypothesis has been applied to this. By 18 to 24 months, most infants have begun to use two-word utterances. Language at this point is referred to as telegraphic. Brown developed the idea of mean length of utterance (MLU). Five stages of MLU have been identified, providing a valuable indicator of language maturity.
	Early childhood	Advances in phonology, morphology, syntax, semantics, and pragmatics continue in early childhood.
Language Development in Middle and Late Childhood	Vocabulary and grammar	In middle and late childhood, children become more analytical and logical in their approach to words and grammar.
	Reading	Educational experts debate whether to teach reading by a whole-language approach or a basic-skills-and-phonetics approach. A developmental information-processing approach to reading emphasizes that normal reading develops in the following sequence: visual-cue recognition, phonetic-cue recognition, automatic word recognition, strategic reading, and proficient adult reading.
	Literacy	Literacy is the ability to read and write. Early oral language, emergent literacy, and writing development are interconnected. During the elementary school years, children move from a world of predominantly oral language to a world of written language and more-complex oral language. *Emergent literacy* is the term given to children's beginning to construct knowledge about the uses and nature of written language long before they begin decoding familiar words and writing in conventional ways. In the push to teach young children to read and write, unfortunately, there have been some dangers—rigid, intense programs too advanced for children's developmental level. Young children need to develop positive feelings about their reading and writing skills. Children should be active participants, and immersed, in a wide range of interesting and enjoyable listening, talking, writing, and reading experiences.
	Bilingualism	This has become a major issue in our nation's schools, with debate raging over the best way to conduct bilingual education. No negative effects of bilingualism have been found, and bilingual education is often associated with positive outcomes, although causal relations are difficult to establish. Increasingly, researchers are recognizing the complexity of bilingual education.

Summary

Children's language development has some magnificent moments and milestones—from first babbles and words to the development of a sophisticated vocabulary utterance of complex sentences. Language is a wonderful tool that helps children in their adaptation to the world.

In this chapter we began by reading about Helen Keller's remarkable life, and then we discussed what language is and language's important rule systems—phonology, morphology, syntax, semantics, and pragmatics. Then we explored language's biological and sociocultural/environmental heritages, the role of cognition in language development, and how language develops in infancy, early childhood, and middle and late childhood.

Don't forget that you can obtain a summary of the chapter by studying the two concept tables on pages 329 and 339. This chapter concludes Section III. In Section IV we will turn our attention to the nature of children's socioemotional development and the self, beginning with chapter 11, "Attachment, Temperament, and Emotional Development."

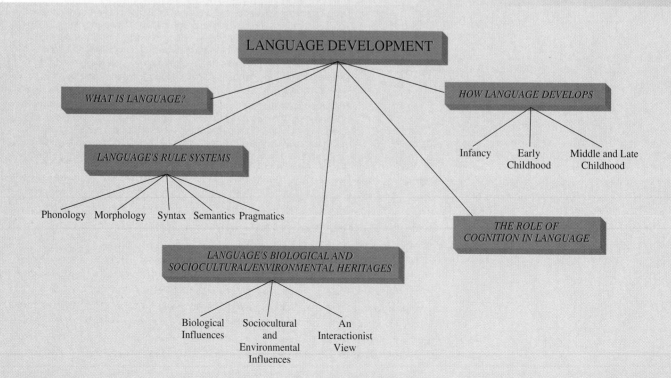

PRACTICAL KNOWLEDGE ABOUT CHILDREN

Growing Up with Language
(1992) by Naomi Baron, Reading, MA: Addison-Wesley.

Dr. Naomi Baron is a professor of linguistics at American University in Washington, D.C. In this book, she presents an excellent portrayal of the appropriate role of parents in children's language development. Baron focuses on three representative children and their families, exploring how children put their first words together, how they struggle to understand meaning, and how they come to use language as a creative tool. She shows parents how their own attitudes about language are extremely important in the child's language development. Baron especially advocates that parents need to instill an enduring love of language in children by asking them interactive questions, using humor in conversation, and engaging them in conversation and other aspects of language through the use of books, computers, and even television. Concerns about gender differences, birth order, raising bilingual children, and adults' use of baby talk are evaluated. Katherine Nelson, an expert in language development, commented that Baron's book provides an insightful analysis of how children become skilled language users.

The New York Times Parent's Guide to the Best Books for Children
(1991) by Eden Lipson, New York: Random House.

This revised and updated edition includes book recommendations for children of all ages. More than 1,700 titles are evaluated. The six sections are organized according to reading level: wordless, picture, story, early reading, middle reading, and young adult. Each entry provides the essential information needed to become acquainted with the book's content and where to find it in a local library or bookstore. More than 55 indexes make it easy to match the right book to the right child. This is an extensive, thorough, competent guide to selecting children's books.

EXPLORATIONS IN CHILD DEVELOPMENT

To further explore the nature of child development, we will examine a research study on children's songs to infant siblings, and then we will discuss the parent's role in the child's language development.

RESEARCH IN CHILD DEVELOPMENT

Children's Songs to Infant Siblings

Featured Study

Trehub, S. E., Unyk, A. M., & Henderson, J. L. (1994). Children's songs to infant siblings: Parallels with speech. *Journal of Child Language, 21,* 735–744.

Mothers are not the only ones who alter their speech substantially when interacting with their infants; children also modify their speech when they talk to infant siblings. Modifications in older siblings' speech to infant siblings include raised pitch, exaggerated intonation, repetition, and mimicry. These adjustments are evident in older siblings as young as 2 years of age.

Infant-directed vocal adjustments are not limited just to speech. Caregivers around the world often use a special musical fare, the lullaby, for soothing infants and bringing on sleep. Characteristic features of adults' lullabies are low pitch and smooth, falling pitch contours. Given that children show infant-directed adjustments in speech, might they also demonstrate adjustments when singing a lullaby to an infant sibling?

Method

The singers were 42 musically untrained children, ranging in age from 2 years, 6 months, to 8 years, 3 months, with a mean age of 4 years, 9 months. Their lullabies were recorded with an audiocassette player and lapel microphone in their own homes as they sang in two contexts: (1) while interacting with their infant sibling (infants' ages ranged from 5 months to 1 year, 2 months, with a mean age of 9 months); and (2) when the infant was not in the singer's view. Children chose their own songs with or without prompting from their mother.

Twenty-five adults 18 to 26 years of age with varying musical experience listened to the tape recordings of the songs and were asked to judge which excerpt of the pair had been sung to the infant. They were also asked to judge whether the infant-directed song was more smoothing or playful than the other song.

Results

The listeners identified the infant-directed lullaby at above-chance levels, and the identification was unrelated to the listener's musical background. However, the identification was below what would be expected for mothers singing lullabies in similar circumstances. In an attempt to identify the features that might underlie the distinctiveness of children's infant-directed adjustments, a musicologist blind to the contexts of the songs (infant-directed or not) measured the songs' pitch level. The children altered their singing style in the infant's presence by singing at a higher pitch level—which was expected, given the children's excitement. The children also sang to their infant sibling in a more soothing and smiling way.

Discussion

Children sang in a perceptibly different manner in the presence of their infant sibling compared to when the infant was out of view. Their infant-directed singing showed features that have been associated with children's infant-directed speech.

IMPROVING THE LIVES OF CHILDREN

The Parent's Role in the Child's Language Development

In *Growing Up with Language,* linguist Naomi Baron (1992) provides a number of helpful ideas about ways that parents can facilitate their child's language development. A summary of her ideas follows:

Infants

• *Be an active conversational partner.* Initiate conversation with the infant.

If the infant is in a daylong child-care program, ensure that the baby gets adequate language stimulation from adults.

• *Talk as if the infant understands what you are saying.* Parents can generate self-fulfilling prophecies by addressing their young children as if they understand what is being said. The process may take 4 to 5 years, but children gradually rise to match the language model presented to them.

• *Use a language style with which you feel comfortable.* Don't worry about how you sound to other adults when you talk with your child. Your effect, not your content, is more important when talking with an infant. Use whatever type of baby talk you feel comfortable with.

Toddlers

• *Continue to be an active conversational partner.* Engaging toddlers in conversation, even one-sided conversation, is the most important thing a parent can do to nourish a child linguistically.

• *Remember to listen.* Since toddlers' speech is often slow and laborious, parents are often tempted to supply words and thoughts for them. Be patient and let toddlers express themselves, no matter how painstaking the process is or how great a hurry you are in.

• *Use a language style with which you are comfortable,* but consider ways of expanding your child's language abilities and horizons. For example, using long sentences need not be problematic; don't be afraid to use ungrammatical language to imitate the toddler's novel forms (such as "No eat"); use rhymes; ask questions that encourage answers other than "Yes"; actively repeat, expand, and recast the child's utterances; introduce new topics; and use humor in your conversation.

• *Adjust to your child's idiosyncrasies instead of working against them.* Many toddlers have difficulty pronouncing words and making themselves understood. Whenever possible, make toddlers feel that they are being understood.

• *Avoid sexual stereotypes.* Don't let the toddler's sex unwittingly determine your amount or style of conversation. Many American mothers are more linguistically supportive of girls than of boys, and many fathers talk less with their children than mothers do. Active and cognitively enriching initiatives from both mothers and fathers benefit both boys and girls.

• *Resist making normative comparisons.* Be aware of the ages at which your child reaches specific milestones (first word, first fifty words, first grammatical combination), but be careful not to measure this development rigidly against children of neighbors or friends. Such social comparisons can bring about unnecessary anxiety.

Preschool Children

• *Become aware of the grammatical features of the baby talk you use with your child that produce unusual or ungrammatical language.* As preschoolers expand their grammatical skills, they increasingly benefit from hearing standard grammar modeled. Many baby-talk characteristics that were initially used to enhance social rapport or facilitate communication should now be dropped.

• *Reinforce, build on, and correct your preschool child's grammatical efforts.* Actively model the kind of grammar you want your children to be learning. Repetitions, expansions, and recastings provide a natural way of advancing the child's language.

• *Encourage entire sentences (not single words) in requests and in answers to questions.* Encourage children to exercise their growing grammatical knowledge.

• *Use a conversational style appropriate to a budding conversational partner.* Emphasize interactive rather than directive language.

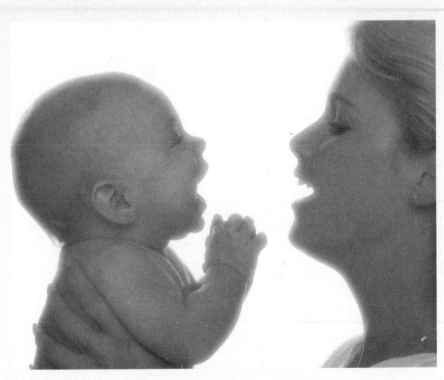

With infants, parents should be active conversational partners, talk as if the infant understands what they are saying, and use a language style they feel comfortable with.

SECTION

Four

Socioemotional Development and the Self

*T*he thoughts of youth are
l thoughts.

—Henry Wadsworth

As children develop, they need
the meeting eyes of love. They
split the universe into two halves:
"me" and "not me." They juggle
the need to curb their own will
with becoming what they can
will freely. They also want to
fly but discover that first they
have to learn to stand and walk
and climb and dance. As they
become adolescents, they try
on one face after another, looking for a face of their own. In Section IV you will read four chapters:
"Attachment, Temperament, and
Emotional Development" (chapter 11), "The Self and Identity"
(chapter 12), "Gender" (chapter
13), and "Moral Development"
(chapter 14).

Gustave Klimt
Three Ages of Woman detail

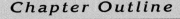

Chapter

Attachment, Temperament, and Emotional Development

Blossoms are scattered by the wind
And the wind cares nothing, but
The blossoms of the heart
No wind can touch.

—Youshida Kenko

IMAGES OF CHILDREN

The Newborn Opossum, Wildebeest, and Human

The newborns of some species function independently in the world; other species are not so independent. At birth, the opossum is still considered fetal and is capable of finding its way around only in its mother's pouch, where it attaches itself to her nipple and continues to develop. This protective environment is similar to the uterus. By contrast, the newborn wildebeest must run with the herd moments after birth. This behavior is far more adult than the opossum's, although the wildebeest does have to obtain food through suckling. The maturation of the human infant lies somewhere between these two extremes; much learning and development must take place before the human infant can sustain itself (Maccoby, 1980).

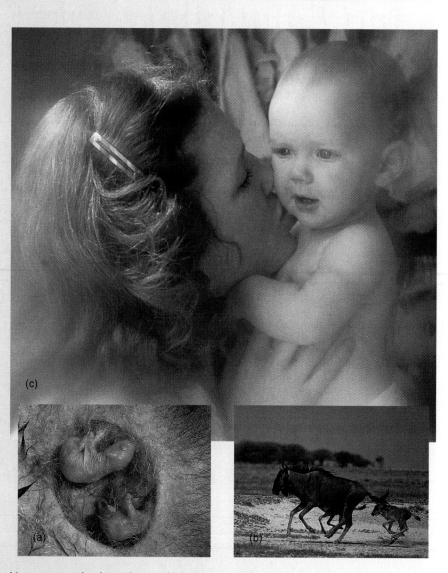

Variations in the dependency of newborns of different species. (*a*) The newborn opossum is fetal, capable of finding its way around only in its mother's pouch, where it attaches itself to her nipple and continues to develop. (*b*) In contrast, the wildebeest runs with the herd moments after birth. (*c*) The human newborn's maturation lies somewhere in between that of the opossum and that of the wildebeest.

PREVIEW

*B*ecause it cannot sustain itself, the human infant requires extensive care. What kind of care is needed, and how does the infant start down the road to social maturity? Much of the interest in infant care focuses on attachment and parent-infant interaction, although the role of day care and temperament in infant development also are important considerations. Recently, child developmentalists have also shown increased interest in children's emotional development.

ATTACHMENT

A small curly-haired girl named Danielle, age 11 months, begins to whimper when her mother leaves the room. After a few seconds, she begins to wail. The psychologist observing Danielle is conducting a research study on the nature of attachment between infants and their mothers. Subsequently, the mother reenters the room, and Danielle's crying ceases. Quickly Danielle crawls over to where her mother is seated and reaches out to be held. This scenario is one of the main ways that psychologists study the nature of attachment during infancy.

What Is Attachment?

In everyday language, *attachment* refers to a relationship between two individuals who feel strongly about each other and do a number of things to continue the relationship. Different pairs of people are attached, such as relatives and lovers. In the language of developmental psychology, though, attachment is often restricted to a relationship between particular social figures and a particular phenomenon that is thought to reflect unique characteristics of the relationship. In this case, the developmental period is infancy, the social figures are the infant and one or more adult caregivers, and the phenomenon is a bond (Bowlby, 1969, 1989). To summarize, **attachment** *is a close emotional bond between the infant and the caregiver*.

There is no shortage of theories about infant attachment. Freud believed that infants become attached to the person or object that provides oral satisfaction; for most infants, this is the mother, since she is most likely to feed the infant.

However, is feeding as important as Freud thought? A classic study by Harry Harlow and Robert Zimmerman (1959) suggests that the answer is no. These researchers evaluated whether feeding or contact comfort was more important to infant attachment. Infant monkeys were removed from their mothers at birth and reared for 6 months by surrogate (substitute) "mothers." As shown in figure 11.1, one of the mothers was made of wire, the other of cloth. Half of the infant monkeys were fed by the wire mother, half by the cloth mother. Periodically, the amount of time the infant monkeys spent with either the wire or the cloth monkey was computed. Regardless of whether they were fed by the wire or the cloth mother, the infant monkeys spent far more time with the cloth mother. This study clearly demonstrated that feeding is not the crucial element in the attachment process and that contact comfort is important.

Most toddlers develop a strong attachment to a favorite soft toy or a particular blanket. Toddlers might carry the toy or blanket with them everywhere they go, just as Linus does in the "Peanuts" cartoon strip, or they might run for the toy or blanket only in moments of crisis, such as after an argument or a fall. By the time they

Figure~11.1

Harlow's Classic "Contact Comfort" Study
Regardless of whether they were fed by a wire mother or by a cloth mother, the infant monkeys overwhelmingly preferred to be in contact with the cloth mother, demonstrating the importance of contact comfort in attachment.

have outgrown the security object, all that might be left is a small fragment of the blanket, or an animal that is hardly recognizable, having had a couple of new faces and all its seams resewn half a dozen times. If parents try to replace the security object with something newer, the toddler will resist. There is nothing abnormal about a toddler carrying around a security blanket. Children know that the blanket or teddy bear is not their mother, and yet they react affectively to these objects and derive comfort from them as if they were their mother. Eventually, they abandon the security object as they grow up and become more sure of themselves.

Might familiarity breed attachment? The famous study by ethologist Konrad Lorenz (1965) suggests that the answer is yes. Remember from our description of this study in chapter 2 that newborn goslings became attached to "father" Lorenz rather than to their mother because he was the first moving object they saw. The time period during which familiarity is important for goslings is the first 36 hours after birth; for human beings, it is more on the order of the first year of life.

Erik Erikson (1968) believed that the first year of life is the key time frame for the development of attachment. Recall his proposal—also discussed in chapter 2—that the first year of life represents the stage of trust versus mistrust. A sense of trust requires a feeling of physical comfort and a minimal amount of fear and apprehension

Mary Ainsworth (*above*) believes that the caregiver's sensitivity to the infant's signals increases secure attachment.

infant responds positively to being picked up by others and, when put back down, freely moves away to play. An insecurely attached infant, by contrast, avoids the mother or is ambivalent toward her, fears strangers, and is upset by minor, everyday separations.

Ainsworth believes that insecurely attached infants can be classified as either anxious-avoidant or anxious-resistant, making three main attachment categories: secure (type B), anxious-avoidant (type A), and anxious-resistant (type C). **Type B babies** *use the caregiver as a secure base from which to explore the environment.* **Type A babies** *exhibit insecurity by avoiding the mother (for example, ignoring her, avoiding her gaze, and failing to seek proximity).* **Type C babies** *exhibit insecurity by resisting the mother (for example, clinging to her but at the same time fighting against the closeness, perhaps by kicking and pushing away).*

> *A child forsaken, waking suddenly,*
> *Whose gaze affeard on all things round doth rove,*
> *And seeth only that it cannot see*
> *The meeting eyes of love.*
>
> —George Eliot

about the future. Trust in infancy sets the stage for a lifelong expectation that the world will be a good and pleasant place to be. Erikson also believed that responsive, sensitive parenting contributes to an infant's sense of trust.

The ethological perspective of British psychiatrist John Bowlby (1969, 1989) also stresses the importance of attachment in the first year of life and the responsiveness of the caregiver. Bowlby believes that an infant and its mother instinctively form an attachment. He argues that the newborn is biologically equipped to elicit the mother's attachment behavior. The baby cries, clings, coos, and smiles. Later, the infant crawls, walks, and follows the mother. The infant's goal is to keep the mother nearby. Research on attachment supports Bowlby's view that, at about 6 to 7 months of age, the infant's attachment to the caregiver intensifies (Sroufe, 1985).

Individual Differences

Although attachment to a caregiver intensifies midway through the first year, isn't it likely that some babies have a more positive attachment experience than others? Mary Ainsworth (1979) thinks so and says that, in **secure attachment,** *infants use the caregiver, usually the mother, as a secure base from which to explore the environment. Ainsworth believes that secure attachment in the first year of life provides an important foundation for psychological development later in life.* The caregiver's sensitivity to the infant's signals increases secure attachment. The securely attached infant moves freely away from the mother but processes her location through periodic glances. The securely attached

Why are some infants securely attached and others insecurely attached? Following Bowlby's lead, Ainsworth believes that attachment security depends on how sensitive and responsive a caregiver is to an infant's signals. For example, infants who are securely attached are more likely to have mothers who are more sensitive, accepting, and expressive of affection toward them than those who are insecurely attached (Coffman, Levitt, & Guacci-Franco, 1996; Pederson & others, 1989).

The mothers of Type A babies are insensitive to their infant's signals, rarely have close body contact with the infant, and, rather than being affectionate, interact with the infant in an angry and irritable manner. The mothers of Type C babies are insensitive and awkward in their interaction with their infants, and they are low in affection but not as rejecting as the Type A "avoidant" mothers.

If early attachment to a caregiver is important, it should be related to a child's social behavior later in development (Bretherton, 1996; Teti & Teti, 1996). Research by Alan Sroufe (1985; Hiester, Carlson, & Sroufe, 1993) documents this connection. In one investigation, infants who were securely attached to their mothers early in infancy were less frustrated and happier at 2 years of age than were their insecurely attached counterparts (Matas, Arend, & Sroufe, 1978). In another longitudinal investigation, securely attached infants were more socially competent and had better grades in the third grade (Egeland, 1989). Linkages between secure attachment and many other aspects of children's competence have been found (Gruys, 1993; Waters, 1997).

(a)

(b)

The attachment theorists argue that early experience plays an important role in the child's social behavior later in development. (a) Secure attachment to the mother in infancy was related to (b) the preschool child's social competence as reflected in more happy feelings and less frustration in one investigation.

Sroufe's current research includes following a group of 180 disadvantaged children—now age 19—since before birth, examining the mother-infant attachment and social competence in children and youth (Ostoja & others, 1995). He has found that even though these children have had unstable lives, those who have had a secure mother-infant attachment are likely to be self-reliant in adolescence, have fewer problems, enjoy successful peer relations, and do well in school. Sroufe also has found that anxious, poorly attached infants can become more secure if their mothers enter stable love relationships or alleviate their symptoms of depression.

Megan Gunnar and her colleagues (1996) found that secure infant attachment is related to coping with stress by buffering physiological reactions to novel or unexpected events. She exposed children to mildly stressful events and measured changes in their stress-related hormones. Seventy-seven 18-month-old children were exposed to three stimuli that they could choose to approach or avoid: a live clown, a robot clown, and a puppet show. After the experiment, the researchers measured the children's cortisol levels (an increase in cortisol indicates an extreme stress reaction); a week later they assessed infant-mother attachment using the Ainsworth Strange Situation. As expected, no increase in cortisol occurred for children who approached the stimuli without fear. However, for children who appeared scared and would not approach the stimuli, cortisol levels varied depending on the children's attachment to their mothers. Inhibited children who had secure attachments showed no increase in cortisol; those with insecure attachments showed an increase.

Measuring Attachment

Much of the early research on attachment relied on impressions of caregivers rather than on direct observation of caregivers interacting with their infant. However, interview data may be flawed and unreliably related to what actually takes place when parents interact with their infant. In the last several decades, researchers have increasingly observed infants with their caregivers. The main setting that has been used to observe attachment in infancy is the Strange Situation developed by attachment researcher Mary Ainsworth (1967). The **Strange Situation** *is an observational measure of infant attachment that requires the infant to move through a series of introductions, separations, and reunions with the caregiver and an adult stranger in a prescribed order* (see figure 11.2).

Although the Strange Situation has been used in a large number of studies of infant attachment, some critics believe the isolated, controlled events of the setting might not necessarily reflect what would actually happen if infants were observed with their caregiver in a natural environment. The issue of using controlled, laboratory assessments versus naturalistic observations is widely debated in child development circles.

Attachment, Temperament, and the Wider Social World

Not all developmentalists believe that a secure attachment in infancy is the only path to competence in life. Indeed, some developmentalists believe that too much emphasis is placed on the importance of the attachment bond in infancy. Jerome Kagan (1987, 1989), for example,

Episode	Persons Present	Duration of Episode	Description of Setting
1	Caregiver, baby, and observer	30 seconds	Observer introduces caregiver and baby to experimental room, then leaves. (Room contains many appealing toys scattered about.)
2	Caregiver and baby	3 minutes	Caregiver is nonparticipant while baby explores; if necessary, play is stimulated after 2 minutes.
3	Stranger, caregiver, and baby	3 minutes	Stranger enters. First minute: stranger is silent. Second minute: stranger converses with caregiver. Third minute: stranger approaches baby. After 3 minutes caregiver leaves unobstrusively.
4	Stranger and baby	3 minutes or less	First separation episode. Stranger's behavior is geared to that of baby.
5	Caregiver and baby	3 minutes or more	First reunion episode. Caregiver greets and/or comforts baby, then tries to settle the baby again in play. Caregiver then leaves, saying "bye-bye."
6	Baby alone	3 minutes or less	Second separation episode.
7	Stranger and baby	3 minutes or less	Continuation of second separation. Stranger enters and gears behavior to that of baby.
8	Caregiver and baby	3 minutes	Second reunion episode. Caregiver enters, greets baby, then picks baby up. Meanwhile stranger leaves unobtrusively.

Figure~11.2

The Ainsworth Strange Situation

believes that infants are highly resilient and adaptive; he argues that they are evolutionarily equipped to stay on a positive developmental course even in the face of wide variations in parenting. Kagan and others stress that genetic and temperament characteristics play more important roles in a child's social competence than the attachment theorists, such as Bowlby, Ainsworth, and Sroufe, are willing to acknowledge (Calkins & Fox, 1992; DiBiase, 1993; Young & Shahinfar, 1995). For example, infants may have inherited a low tolerance for stress; this, rather than an insecure attachment bond, may be responsible for their inability to get along with peers.

Another criticism of attachment theory is that it ignores the diversity of socializing agents and contexts that exist in an infant's world (Thompson, 1991). In some cultures, infants show attachments to many people. In the Hausa culture in Nigeria, both grandmothers and siblings provide a significant amount of care to infants (Super, 1980). Infants in agricultural societies tend to form attachments to older siblings, who are assigned a major responsibility for younger siblings' care. The attachments formed by infants in group care in Israeli kibbutzim provide another challenge to the singular attachment thesis.

Researchers recognize the importance of competent, nurturant caregivers in an infant's development—at issue, though, is whether or not secure attachment, especially to a single caregiver, is critical.

Fathers as Caregivers for Infants

Can fathers take care of infants as competently as mothers can? Observations of fathers and their infants suggest that fathers have the ability to act sensitively and responsively with their infants (McHale & others, 1995;

In the Hausa culture, siblings, as well as grandmothers, provide a significant amount of care to infants, and infants show strong attachments to them.

Parke & Sawin, 1980). Probably the strongest evidence of the plasticity of male caregiving abilities is derived from information about male primates who are notoriously low in their interest in offspring but are forced to live with infants whose female caregivers are absent. Under these circumstances, the adult male competently rears the infants. Remember, however, that, although fathers can be active, nurturant, involved caregivers with their infants, too many fathers choose not to follow this pattern.

Do fathers behave differently toward infants than mothers do? Whereas maternal interactions usually center around child-care activities—feeding, changing diapers, bathing—paternal interactions are more likely to include play. Fathers engage in more rough-and-tumble play, bouncing their infants, throwing them up in the air, tickling them, and so on (Lamb, 1986). Mothers do play with infants, but their play is less physical and arousing than that of fathers.

In stressful circumstances, do infants prefer their mother or father? In one investigation, twenty 12-month-olds were observed interacting with their parents (Lamb, 1977). With both parents present, the infants preferred neither their mother nor their father. The same was true when the infants were alone with the mother or the father. However, the entrance of a stranger, combined with boredom and fatigue, produced a shift in the infants' social behavior toward the mother. In stressful circumstances, then, infants show a stronger attachment to the mother.

Might the nature of parent-infant interaction be different in families that adopt nontraditional gender roles? This question was investigated by Michael Lamb and his colleagues (1982). They studied Swedish families in which the fathers were the primary caregivers of their firstborn, 8-month-old infants. The mothers were working full time. In all observations, the mothers were more likely to discipline, hold, soothe, kiss, and talk to the infants than were the fathers. These mothers and fathers dealt with their infants differently, along the lines of American fathers and mothers following traditional gender roles. Having fathers assume the primary caregiving role did not seem to alter substantially the way they interacted with their infants. This may be for biological reasons or because of deeply ingrained socialization patterns in cultures.

In Sweden, mothers or fathers are given paid maternity or paternity leave for up to 9 months. Sweden and many other European countries have well-developed child-care policies. To learn about these policies, turn to Sociocultural Worlds of Children. In Sweden, day care for infants under 1 year of age is usually not a major concern because one parent is on paid leave for child care. As we will see, since the United States does not have a policy of paid leave for child care, day care in the United States has become a major national concern.

Day Care

Each weekday at 8 A.M., Ellen Smith takes her 1-year-old daughter Tanya to the day-care center at Brookhaven College in Dallas. Then Mrs. Smith goes to work and

Can fathers take care of infants as competently as mothers can? Do fathers interact with infants in the same way as mothers do?

returns in the afternoon to take Tanya home. After 3 years, Mrs. Smith reports that her daughter is adventuresome and interacts confidently with peers and adults. Mrs. Smith believes that day care has been a wonderful way to raise Tanya.

In Los Angeles, however, day care has been a series of horror stories for Barbara Jones. After 2 years of unpleasant experiences with sitters, day-care centers, and day-care homes, Mrs. Jones has quit her job as a successful real estate agent to stay home and take care of her 2½-year-old daughter, Gretchen. "I didn't want to sacrifice my baby for my job," said Mrs. Jones, who was unable to find good substitute care in day-care homes. When she put Gretchen into a day-care center, she said that she felt her daughter was being treated like a piece of merchandise—dropped off and picked up.

Many parents worry whether day care will <u>adversely</u> affect their children. They fear that day care will reduce their infants' emotional attachment to them, retard the infants' cognitive development, fail to teach them how to control anger, and allow them to be <u>unduly</u> influenced by their peers. How extensive is day care? Are the worries of these parents justified?

In the 1990s, far more young children are in day care than at any other time in history; about 2 million children currently receive formal, licensed day care, and

SOCIOCULTURAL WORLDS OF CHILDREN

Child-Care Policy Around the World

Sheila Kamerman (1989) surveyed child-care policies around the world with special attention given to European countries. Maternity and paternity policies for working parents include paid, job-protected leaves, which are sometimes supplemented by additional unpaid, job-protected leaves. Child-care policy packages also often include full health insurance. An effective child-care policy is designed to get an infant off to a competent start in life and to protect maternal health while maintaining income. More than a hundred countries around the world have such child-care policies, including all of Europe, Canada, Israel, and many developing countries (Kamerman & Kahn, 1988). Infants are assured of at least 2 to 3 months of maternal/paternal care, and in most European countries 5 to 6 months.

The maternity policy as now implemented in several countries involves a paid maternity leave that begins 2 to 6 weeks prior to expected childbirth and lasts from 8 to 20 or even 24 weeks after birth. This traditional maternal policy stems from an effort to protect the health of pregnant working women, new mothers, and their infants. Only since the 1960s has the

maternity policy's link with employment become strong. A second child-care policy emphasizes the importance of parenting and recognizes the potential of fathers as well as mothers to care for their infants. In Sweden a parent insurance benefit provides protection to the new mother before birth and for 6 to 12 weeks after birth but then allows the father to participate in the postchildbirth leave. Approximately one-fourth of Swedish fathers take at least part of the postchildbirth leave, in addition to the 2 weeks of paid leave all fathers are entitled to at the time of childbirth. In a typical pattern in Sweden, the working mother might take off 3 months, after which she and her husband might share child care between them, each working half-time for 6 months. In addition, Swedish parents have the option of taking an unpaid but fully protected job leave until their child is 18 months old and working a 6-hour day (without a reduction in pay) from the end of the parental leave until their child is 8 years old.

In sum, almost all the industrialized countries have recognized the importance of developing maternity/paternity policies that allow working parents some time off after childbirth to physically recover, to adapt to parenting, and to improve the well-being of the infant. These policies are designed to let parents take maternity/paternity leave without losing employment or income.

more than 5 million children attend kindergarten. Also, uncounted millions of children are cared for by unlicensed baby-sitters. Day care clearly has become a basic need of the American family.

The type of day care that young children receive varies extensively. Many day-care centers house large groups of children and have elaborate facilities. Some are commercial operations, others are nonprofit centers run by churches, civic groups, and employers. Child care is frequently provided in private homes, at times by child-care professionals, at others by mothers who want to earn extra money.

A special contemporary interest of researchers who study day care is the role that poverty plays (Huston, McLoyd, & Coll, 1994). In one study, day-care centers that served high-income children delivered better-quality care than did centers that served middle- and low-income children (Phillips & others, 1994). The indices of quality (such as teacher-child ratios) in subsidized centers for the poor were fairly good, but the quality of observed teacher-child interaction was lower than in high-income centers.

The quality of care children experience in day care varies extensively (Burchinal & others, 1996). Some caregivers have no training, others have extensive training; some day-care centers have a low caregiver-child ratio, others have a high caregiver-child ratio. Some experts have recently argued that the quality of day care most children receive in the United States is poor. Infant researcher Jay Belsky (1989, 1992) not only believes that the quality of day care children experience is generally poor, but he also believes this translates into negative developmental outcomes for children. Belsky concludes that extensive day-care experience during the first 12 months of life—as typically experienced in the United States—is associated with insecure attachment as well as increased aggression, noncompliance, and possibly social withdrawal during the preschool and early elementary school years.

One study supports Belsky's beliefs (Vandell & Corasaniti, 1988). Extensive day care in the first year of life was associated with long-term negative outcomes. In contrast to children who began full-time day care later, children who began full-time day care (defined as more

Provision of day care in most developing countries has improved, but this often has been in a form that denies access to the poorest children. In some locations in India, mobile day-care centers have provided intensive integrated child services to younger children in slum settlements within large cities and rural villages.

is a problem because of the different types of day care children experience and the different measures used to assess outcome (Honig, 1995; Park & Honig, 1991). Belsky's analysis does suggest that parents should be very careful about the quality of day care they select for their infants, especially those 1 year of age or less. Even Belsky agrees, though, that day care itself is not the culprit; rather, it is the quality of day care that is problematic in this country. Belsky acknowledges that no evidence exists to show that children in high-quality day care are at risk in any way.

What constitutes a high-quality day-care program for infants? The demonstration program developed by Jerome Kagan and his colleagues (Kagan, Kearsley, & Zelazo, 1978) at Harvard University is exemplary. The day-care center included a pediatrician, a nonteaching director, and an infant-teacher ratio of 3 to 1. Teachers' aides assisted at the center. The teachers and aides were trained to smile frequently, to talk with the infants, and to provide them with a safe environment that included many stimulating toys. No adverse effects of day care were observed in this project. More information about what to look for in a quality day-care center is presented in table 11.1. Using such criteria, Carolee Howes (1988) discovered that children who entered low-quality child care as infants were least likely to be socially competent in early childhood (less compliant, less self-controlled, less task-oriented, more hostile, and having more problems in peer interaction). Unfortunately, children who come from families with few resources (psychological, social, and economic) are more likely to experience poor-quality day care than are children from more-advantaged backgrounds (Lamb, 1994).

In the next decade, we should learn considerably more about the effects of day care on children's development from several large-scale studies already in progress (Clarke-Stewart, Allhusen, & Clements, 1995). In one of these—the NICHD study of early child care—children are being studied from birth until 7 years of age. They are observed periodically at home and in any day-care settings in which they regularly spend at least 10 hours per week. Their experiences at home and in day care will be studied for possible linkages to their cognitive and socioemotional development. Thirteen hundred infants from a wide variety of family backgrounds are being evaluated at ten sites across the United States.

In a recent evaluation in the NICHD study, day care itself did not weaken infants' attachments to their mothers (NICHD Early Child Care Research Network, 1996). Infant day care led to weak ties only if the mother was insensitive to the infant's cues—such as behavior that is detached or too intrusive—and the infant was either in poor-quality care, spending more than 10 hours a week at day care, or switched from one caregiver to another several times in the first 15 months of life.

than 30 hours per week) as infants were rated by parents and teachers as being less compliant and as having poorer peer relations. In the first grade, they received lower grades and had poor work habits by comparison.

Belsky's conclusions about day care are controversial. Other respected researchers have arrived at a different conclusion; their review of the day-care research suggests no ill effects of day care (Clarke-Stewart, Allhusen, & Clements, 1995; Scarr, Lande, & McCartney, 1989).

Some researchers have found that the attachments children form with their primary caregivers (such as their day-care providers and early childhood teachers) are remarkably similar to the attachments they form with their mothers (Howes & Hamilton, 1992). However, secure attachments occurred only with 50 percent of the teachers compared with 70 percent of mothers. The lower rate of secure attachment likely reflects the lower quality and level of closeness of the relationship between the nonmaternal caregiver and the child. Howes also found that, among 4-year-olds, secure attachment to a teacher was linked with more competent social behavior (less aggressiveness, more sociable peer relations, for example) than insecure attachment to a teacher.

What can we conclude? Does day care have adverse effects on children's development? Trying to combine the results into an overall conclusion about day-care effects

BAD EVENTS

Pessimistic	Optimistic
• Teachers are unfair.	• Mrs. Carmine is unfair.
• I'm a total clod at sports.	• I stink at kickball.
• Tony hates me and will never hang out with me again.	• Tony is mad at me today.
• Nobody will ever want to be friends with me here.	• It takes time to make a new best friend when you're at a new school.
• I got grounded because I'm a bad kid.	• I got grounded because I hit Michelle.
• I got a C because I'm stupid.	• I got a C because I didn't study enough.

GOOD EVENTS

Pessimistic	Optimistic
• I'm smart at math.	• I'm smart.
• I was voted safety patrol captain because the other kids wanted to do a nice thing for me.	• I was voted safety patrol captain because the other kids like me.
• Dad is spending time with me because he's in a good mood.	• Dad loves to spend time with me.
• The only reason I won the spelling bee is because I practiced hard this time.	• I won because I'm a hard worker and I study my lessons.

Figure~11.5

Optimistic and Pessimistic Children's Interpretation of Bad and Good Events

Recently, psychologists have emphasized that life's daily experiences as well as life's major events may be the culprits in stress (Crnic, 1996; Sorensen, 1993). Enduring a tense family life and living in poverty do not show up on scales of major life events in children's development, yet the everyday pounding children take from these living conditions can add up to a highly stressful life and, eventually, psychological disorders or physical illnesses. (Compas, 1989; Creasy & others, 1993; Folkman & Lazarus, 1991; Pillow, Zautra, & Sandler, 1996).

> *It's not the large things that send a man to the madhouse. . . . No, it's the continuing series of small tragedies that send a man to the madhouse. . . . Not the death of his love but a shoelace that snaps with no time left.*
>
> —Charles Bukowski

Sociocultural Factors

Among the sociocultural factors involved in stress are acculturative stress, socioeconomic status, and the feminization of poverty.

Acculturative Stress *Acculturation is cultural change that results from continuous, firsthand contact between two distinctive cultural groups. Acculturative stress is the negative consequence of acculturation.* Members of ethnic minority groups have historically encountered hostility,

prejudice, and lack of effective support during crises, which contributes to alienation, social isolation, and heightened stress (Huang & Gibbs, 1989). As upwardly mobile ethnic minority families have attempted to penetrate all-White neighborhoods, interracial tensions often mount. Similarly, racial tensions and hostility often emerge among the various ethnic minorities as they each struggle for limited housing and employment opportunities, seeking a fair share of a limited market. Clashes become inevitable as Latino family markets spring up in African American urban neighborhoods; as Vietnamese extended families displace Puerto Rican apartment dwellers; as the increasing enrollment of Asian students on college campuses is perceived as a threat to affirmative action policies by other non-White ethnic minority students. While race relations in the United States have historically been conceptualized as Black/White, this is no longer the only combination producing ethnic animosity.

As the number of Latinos and Asians has increased dramatically, and as Native Americans have crossed the boundaries of their reservations, the visibility of these groups has brought them in contact not only with the mainstream White society, but with one another as well. Depending on the circumstances, this contact has been sometimes harmonious, sometimes antagonistic.

Although the dominant White society has tried, on many occasions, to enslave or dispossess entire populations, these ethnic minority groups have survived and flourished. In the face of severe stress, these ethnic minority groups have shown remarkable

To help buffer the stress in their lives, many ethnic minority groups have developed their own social structures, which include the African American church, Mexican American kin systems, Chinese American family associations, and Native American tribal associations.

resilience and adaptation (Chen & Yu, 1997; Markstrom & Tryon, 1997; Root, 1992). Confronted with overt or covert attempts at segregation, they have developed their own communities and social structures, which include African American churches, Vietnamese mutual assistance associations, Chinese American family associations, Japanese-language schools, Indian "bands" and tribal associations, and Mexican American kin systems; at the same time they have learned to negotiate with the dominant White culture in America. They essentially have mastered two cultures and have developed impressive competencies and coping strategies for adapting to life in America. The resilience and adaptation shown by ethnic minority groups can teach us much about coping and survival in the face of overwhelming adversity (Ceballo & Olson, 1993).

Socioeconomic Status Poverty imposes considerable stress on children and their families (Aber, 1993; McLoyd, 1993). Chronic life conditions such as inadequate housing, dangerous neighborhoods, burdensome responsibilities, and economic uncertainties are potent stressors in the lives of the poor (Brooks-Gunn, Klebanov, & McCarton, 1997; Sameroff & Bartko, 1997). The incidence of poverty is especially pronounced among ethnic minority children and their families (Braham, Rattansi, & Skellington, 1992). For example, African American women heading families face a risk of poverty that is more than 10 times that of White men heading families. Puerto Rican female family heads face a poverty rate that is almost 15 times that found among White male family heads (National Advisory Council on Economic Opportunity, 1980). Many individuals who become poor during their lives remain poor for 1 or 2 years. However, African Americans and female family heads are at risk for experiencing persistent poverty. The average poor African American child experiences poverty that will last almost 20 years (Wilson & Neckerman, 1986).

Poverty is related to threatening and uncontrollable events in children's lives (Russo, 1990). For example, poor females are more likely to experience crime and violence than middle-class females are. Poverty also undermines sources of social support that play a role in buffering the effects of stress.

Poverty is related to threatening and uncontrollable events in children's lives. Poverty also undermines sources of social support that play a role in buffering the effects of stress.

Social scientist Deborah Belle, shown here interviewing a young girl, has demonstrated how poverty imposes considerable stress on children. Chronic living conditions, such as inadequate housing, dangerous neighborhoods, burdensome responsibilities, and economic uncertainties, are potent stressors in the lives of the poor.

Sometimes just one person can make a difference in children's lives in low-income neighborhoods. One such person is Madeline Cartwright. When she became principal of the James G. Blaine public school, in a North Philadelphia neighborhood enshrouded in poverty and rocked by violence, she was determined to make a difference.

The most important thing Cartwright did when she became the principal was to, as she said, "browbeat" parents into getting involved in the school. She told them that she came from the same circumstances they did and that, at Blaine school, the children were going to get a better education and have a better life than most children who attended her elementary school when she was growing up. But she told the parents that this was going to happen only if they worked with her and became partners with the school in educating and socializing the children.

When she came to Blaine school, she told the parents, "This place is dirty! How can your kids go to school in a place like this!" One of the parents commented, "You must think you are in the suburbs." The parent expected the neighborhood and the school to be dirty. Cartwright told the parent, "The dirt in the suburbs is the same as the dirt in North Philadelphia—if you don't *move* it. And the same detergents work here." Cartwright rounded up eighteen parents and scrubbed the building until it was clean.

Blaine school's auditorium overflowed with parents when parent meetings were scheduled. Cartwright made children bring their parents to the meetings. She told the children, "Your parents need to know what we are doing in school." She gave the children a doughnut or a pretzel the next day if one of their parents came. She told the parents they could come to her if they had problems—that she could direct them to places and people who would help them solve their problems. Because of Cartwright's efforts, parents now feel comfortable at Blaine school.

Cartwright believes that a very important aspect of intervening in the lives of children who come from low-income families is increasing the positive role models they see and with whom they can interact. She wants the state of Pennsylvania to set up "mentor houses," into which salvageable families can be moved. These vacant houses are located in better neighborhoods, and a family with positive values is appointed or paid to be a mentor or role model for the family. Says Cartwright, "I would like to be a mentor."

Some people would say that Cartwright's dreams are naive, but maybe not. One safe and clean school, one set of clean clothes, one clean toilet, one safe house—and then another safe school, and another, and another. Concludes Cartwright, "I'm telling you; there are things you can do!" (Louv, 1990).

Resilience

Even when children are faced with adverse conditions, such as poverty, are there characteristics they can have that make them resilient and help buffer them against negative developmental outcomes? Some children do triumph over life's adversities (Masten & Hubbard, 1995). Norman Garmezy (1985, 1993) has studied resilience amid diversity and disadvantage for a number of years. He concludes that three factors often appear to help children become resilient to stress, adversity, and disadvantage: (1) reflectiveness, cognitive skills (including

Madeline Cartwright is an elementary school principal who has made a powerful difference in many impoverished children's lives. Especially important is Cartwright's persistence in getting parents more involved in their children's education.

attention), and positive responsiveness to others; (2) a family, even if one in poverty, marked by warmth, cohesion, and the presence of some caring adult, such as a grandparent, who takes responsibility in the absence of responsive parents or in the presence of intense marital discord; and (3) the presence of some source of external support, such as a strong maternal substitute in the form of a teacher, a neighbor, parents of peers, or even an institutional structure such as a caring agency or a church. These three factors characterized the developmental course of resilient individuals in a longitudinal study in Kuaia (Werner, 1989).

Garmezy (1993) describes a setting in a Harlem neighborhood of New York City to illustrate resilience. In the foyer of a walkup apartment building, on a wall in the entranceway, is a large picture frame holding photographs of the children who live in the building and a written request that if anyone sees any of the children endangered on the street, they bring the children back to the apartment house. Garmezy says this is an excellent example of adult competence and concern for the safety and well-being of children.

At this point we have discussed a number of ideas about emotional development. A summary of these ideas is presented in concept table 11.2.

Concept	Processes/ Related Ideas	Characteristics/Description
The Nature of Children's Emotions	What is emotion?	Emotion is feeling or affect that involves a mixture of physiological arousal and overt behavior. Emotions can be classified in terms of positive affectivity and negative affectivity.
	Functions of emotions in children's development	The three main functions are adaptation and survival, regulation, and communication.
	Affect in parent-child relationships	Emotions are the first language that parents and infants communicate with before the infant acquires speech. Infant and adult affective communicative capacities make possible coordinated infant-adult interaction.
Emotional Development in Infancy	Developmental timetable of emotions	Izard developed the Maximally Discriminative Facial Coding System (called MAX) for coding infants' expression of emotions. Based on this coding system, interest, distress, and disgust are present at birth; a social smile appears at about 4–6 weeks; anger, surprise, and sadness emerge at about 3–4 months; fear is displayed at about 5–7 months; shame and shyness emerge at about 6–8 months; and contempt and guilt appear at about 2 years of age.
	Crying	Crying is the most important mechanism newborns have for communicating with their world. Babies have at least three types of cries—basic, anger, and pain. Most parents, and adults in general, can tell whether an infant's cries signify anger or pain. Controversy still swirls about whether babies should be soothed when they cry. An increasing number of developmentalists support Ainsworth and Bowlby's idea that infant crying should be responded to immediately in the first year of life.
	Smiling	Smiling is an important communicative affective behavior of the infant. Two types of smiling can be distinguished in infants: reflexive and social.
The New Functionalism in Emotion	Its nature	The new functionalist view emphasizes that emotion is relational rather than intrapsychic, that there is a close link between emotion and the person's goals and effort, that emotional expressions can serve as social signals, and that the physiology of emotion is much more than homeostasis and the person's interior—it also includes the ability to regulate and be regulated by social processes.
Children's Depression and Depressed Parents	Children's depression	Depression is a mood disorder in which the individual is unhappy, demoralized, self-derogatory, and bored. In childhood, the features of depression are often mixed with a broader array of behaviors than in adulthood. Depression is more likely to occur in adolescence than in childhood, and is more frequent among females than males. Bowlby's developmental view, Beck's cognitive view, and Seligman's learned helplessness view are three perspectives on children's depression.
	Depressed parents	Depression is especially prominent in women of child-bearing age. Depression in parents is associated with problems of adjustment and disorders, especially depression, in their children.
	Depression in adolescence	Increasingly distinctions are being made among depressed mood, depressive syndromes, and clinical depression (major depressive disorder and dysthymia). Female adolescents are more likely to have mood and depressive disorders than males are.
Stress	What is stress?	Stress is the response of individuals to the circumstances and events, called stressors, that threaten them and tax their coping abilities.
	Cognitive factors in stress	Lazarus believes that children's stress depends on how they cognitively appraise and interpret events. Cognitive appraisal is the term Lazarus uses to describe individuals' interpretation of events in their lives as harmful, threatening, or challenging (primary appraisal), and their determination of whether they have the resources to effectively cope with the event (secondary appraisal). Seligman distinguishes between optimistic and pessimistic children, and believes young pessimists can be turned into optimists.
	Life events and daily hassles	Both life events (such as divorce, incest, death of a parent) and daily hassles (such as living in an impoverished world) can cause stress.
	Sociocultural influences	Acculturation is cultural change that results from continuous, first-hand contact between two distinctive cultural groups. Acculturative stress refers to the negative consequences of acculturation. Members of ethnic minority groups have historically encountered hostility, prejudice, and lack of effective support during crises, which contribute to alienation, social isolation, and heightened stress. Poverty also imposes considerable stress on children and their families. Chronic life conditions such as inadequate housing, dangerous neighborhoods, burdensome responsibilities, and economic uncertainties are potent stresses in the lives of the poor. The incidence of poverty is especially pronounced among ethnic minority children and their families.
	Resilience	Garmezy concludes that three sets of characteristics are reflected in the lives of children who show resilience amid adversity and disadvantage: (1) temperament factors; (2) families marked by warmth, cohesion, and the presence of a caring adult; and (3) a source of external support.

*S*UMMARY

Babies are wrapped in a socioemotional world with their caregivers from birth. Babies and their caregivers communicate with each other through their emotions, their senses, and their words. Through interaction with their caregivers, infants learn to adapt to their world.

We began this chapter by briefly examining how the human infant cannot sustain itself, and therefore requires extensive care. Much of the interest in the infant's social world has focused on attachment. We considered what attachment is, individual differences in attachment (secure and insecure), measuring attachment, and attachment, temperament, and the wider social world. We evaluated fathers as caregivers of infants and the role of day care in children's lives and how it affects their development. We learned that temperament is an important aspect of the infant's development, studying temperament's nature and parenting and the child's temperament. We also discussed many different facets of children's emotional development, including the nature of children's emotions, emotional development in infancy, the new functionalism in emotion, children's depression and depressed parents, depression in adolescence, and stress.

Don't forget to again study the two concept tables on pages 361 and 372, which together will provide you with a summary of the chapter. In the next chapter, we will turn our attention to the self and identity development. Some theorists, especially Ainsworth and Bowlby, believe that secure attachment provides an important foundation for the development of a positive sense of self.

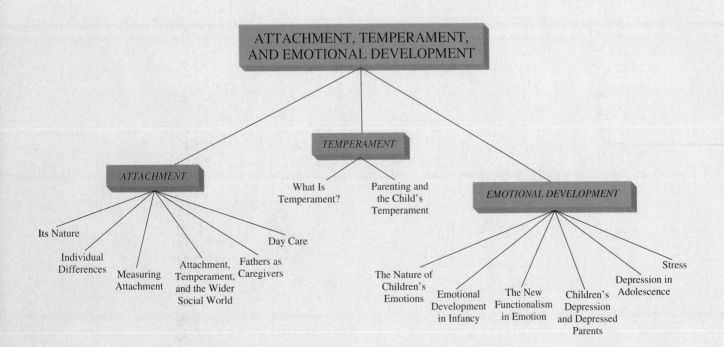

PRACTICAL KNOWLEDGE ABOUT CHILDREN

Daycare

(revised edition, 1993) by Alison Clarke-Stewart, Cambridge, MA: Harvard University Press.

This book draws on extensive research to survey the social, political, and economic contexts of day care. Evaluation of options and consequences allows parents to make informed choices. The author provides a broad overview of day care's role in contemporary society and evaluates the emergence and current state of institutional day care in schools and businesses. A checklist parents can use to assess their own arrangements is included.

Touchpoints

(1992) by T. Berry Brazelton, Reading, MA: Addison-Wesley.

Touchpoints is highly respected pediatrician T. Berry Brazelton's most recent book, covering the child's development from pregnancy through first grade. Brazelton focuses on the concerns and questions that parents have about the child's feelings, behavior, and development. The title *Touchpoints* derives from Brazelton's belief that there are universal spurts of development, and the trying times of adaptation that accompany them, throughout childhood. Section 1 describes development from pregnancy through 3 years, section 2 describes a number of challenges to development—from allergies to toilet training—and section 3 focuses on important figures in the child's development, such as father, mother, grandparents, friends, caregivers, and the child's doctor.

The Optimistic Child

(1995) by Martin Seligman, Boston: Houghton Mifflin.

Seligman believes it is important to distinguish between children who are optimists and those who are pessimists. Pessimistic children have many more difficulties in life than optimistic children do. Pessimistic children's attitudes make them feel so hopeless that they often see no point in trying, whether the challenge is academic or social. Seligman believes that optimistic children interpret events far more positively than pessimistic children do. The book describes a number of strategies adults can use to help turn young pessimists into optimists.

Grace Carpenter Hudson
Indian Girl with Kachina detail

Chapter

12

The Self and
Identity

*Explore thyself. Herein are demanded the
eye and the nerve.*

—Henry David Thoreau

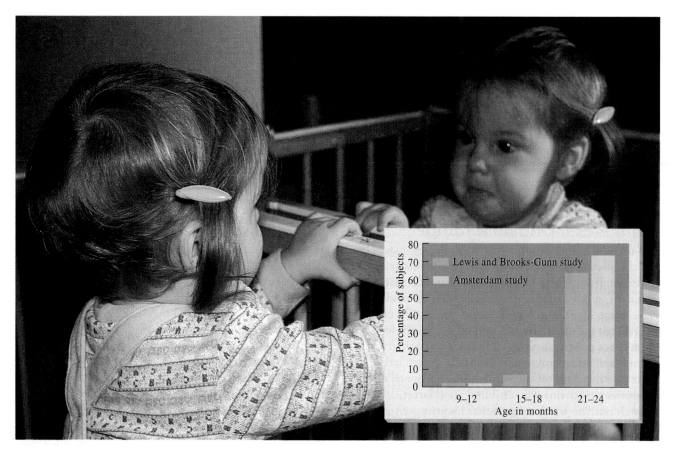

Figure~12.1

The Development of Self-Recognition in Infancy
The graph gives the findings of two studies in which infants of different ages showed recognition of rouge by touching, wiping, or verbally referring to it. Notice that self-recognition did not occur extensively until the second half of the second year of life.

Early Childhood

Because children can verbally communicate their ideas, research on self-understanding in childhood is not limited to visual self-recognition, as it is during infancy. Mainly through interviews, researchers have probed children's conceptions of many aspects of self-understanding, including mind and body, self in relation to others, and pride and shame in self. In early childhood, children usually conceive of the self in physical terms. Most young children conceive of the self as part of the body, which usually means the head. Young children generally confuse self, mind, and body (Broughton, 1978). For them, because the self is a body part, it can be described along many material dimensions, such as size, shape, and color. Young children distinguish themselves from others through many different physical and material attributes. Says 4-year-old Sandra, "I'm different from Jennifer because I have brown hair and she has blonde hair." Says 4-year-old Ralph, "I am different from Hank because I am taller and I am different from my sister because I have a bicycle."

Researchers also believe that the *active dimension* is a central component of the self in early childhood

(Keller, Ford, & Meacham, 1978). If we define the category "physical" broadly enough, we can include physical actions as well as body image and material possessions. For example, preschool children often describe themselves in terms of activities such as play. In sum, in early childhood, children often describe themselves in terms of a physical self or an active self.

Middle and Late Childhood

In middle and late childhood, self-understanding increasingly shifts from defining oneself through external characteristics to defining oneself through internal characteristics. Also, elementary-school-age children are more likely to define themselves in terms of social characteristics and social comparison.

In middle and late childhood, children not only recognize differences between inner and outer states, but they are also more likely to include subjective inner states in their definition of self. In one investigation, second-grade children were much more likely than younger children to name psychological characteristics (such as preferences or personality traits) in their self-definition and less likely to name physical characteristics (such as eye color or possessions) (Aboud & Skerry, 1983). For example, 8-year-old Todd includes in his self-description, "I am smart and I am popular." Ten-year-old Tina says about herself, "I am pretty good about not worrying most of the time. I used to lose my temper but I'm better about that now. I also feel proud when I do well in school."

In addition to the increase of psychological characteristics in self-definition during the elementary school years, the *social aspects* of the self also increase at this point in development. In one investigation, elementary school children included references to social groups in their self-description (Livesly & Bromley, 1973). For example, some children referred to themselves as Girl Scouts, as Catholics, or as someone who has two close friends.

Children's self-understanding in the elementary school years also includes increasing reference to *social comparison*. At this point in development, children are more likely to distinguish themselves from others in comparative rather than in absolute terms. That is, elementary-school-age children are no longer as likely to think about what I do or do not do, but are more likely to think about what I can do *in comparison with others*. This developmental shift provides an increased tendency of establishing one's differences as an individual apart from others. In a series of studies, Diane Ruble (1983) investigated children's use of social comparison in their self-evaluations. Children were given a difficult task and then offered feedback on their performance, as well as information about the performances of other children their age. The children were then asked for self-evaluations. Children younger than 7 made virtually no reference to the information about other children's performances. However, many children older than 7 included socially comparative information in their self-descriptions.

Adolescence

The development of self-understanding in adolescence is complex and involves a number of aspects of the self. Let's examine how the adolescent's self-understanding differs from the child's.

Abstract and Idealistic   Remember from our discussion of Piaget's theory of cognitive development in chapters 2 and 7 that many adolescents begin to think in more *abstract* and *idealistic* ways. When asked to describe themselves, adolescents are more likely than children to use abstract and idealistic labels. Consider 14-year-old Laurie's abstract description of herself: "I am a human being. I am indecisive. I don't know who I am." Also consider her idealistic description of herself: "I am a naturally sensitive person who really cares about people's feelings. I think I'm pretty good-looking."

Differentiated   Adolescents' self-understanding becomes increasingly *differentiated*. Adolescents are more likely

than children to describe the self with contextual or situational variations. For example, 15-year-old Amy describes herself with one set of characteristics in her relationship with her family and another set of characteristics in her relationship with peers and friends. Yet another set of characteristics appears in her description of her romantic relationship. In sum, adolescents are more likely than children to understand that one possesses different selves, depending on one's role or particular context (Harter, 1990a, 1997).

Contradictions Within the Self   After adolescence ushers in the need to differentiate the self into multiple roles in different relational contexts, there naturally arise potential contradictions between these differentiated selves. In one study, Susan Harter (1986) asked seventh-, ninth-, and eleventh-graders to describe themselves. She found that the number of contradictory ways in which adolescents described themselves (as moody *and* understanding, ugly *and* attractive, bored *and* inquisitive, caring *and* uncaring, introverted *and* fun-loving, and so on) dramatically increased between the seventh and ninth grades. The contradictory self-descriptions declined in the eleventh grade but still were higher than in the seventh grade. Adolescents develop the cognitive ability to detect these inconsistencies in the self as they strive to construct a general theory of the self or of their personality (Damon, 1991; Harter & Monsour, 1992).

The Fluctuating Self   Given the contradictory nature of the self in adolescence, it is not surprising that the self fluctuates across situations and across time (Harter, 1990a, 1997). The 15-year-old girl quoted at the beginning of the chapter in the "Images of Children" section remarked that she could not understand how she could switch so fast—from being cheerful one moment, to anxious the next, and then sarcastic a short time later. One researcher described the fluctuating nature of the adolescent's self with the metaphor of "the barometric self" (Rosenberg, 1986). The adolescent's self continues to be characterized by instability until the adolescent constructs a more unified theory of self, usually not until late adolescence or even early adulthood.

Real and Ideal, True and False Selves   The adolescent's emerging ability to construct ideal selves in addition to actual ones can be perplexing to the adolescent. The capacity to recognize a discrepancy between *real* and *ideal* selves represents a cognitive advance, but humanistic theorist Carl Rogers (1950) believed that when the real and ideal selves are too discrepant, it is a sign of maladjustment. Depression may result from a substantial discrepancy between one's actual self and one's ideal self (the person one wants to be), because an awareness of this discrepancy can produce a sense of failure and self-criticism (Hart & others, in press).

CRITICAL THINKING
ABOUT CHILDREN'S
DEVELOPMENT

*Examining Possibilities for
Your Future Selves*

For this exercise, recruit two friends to help. Conduct a conversation in which each of you describes two of

your possible future selves. What do you envision will make you happiest about the self that you aspire to become? What prospect about a potential negative possibility in the future fills you with dread? By determining in what ways your visions of the future are alike and in what ways they are different, you and your friends are learning to think critically by *demonstrating individual differences*.

Researchers have found that the discrepancy between the real self and the ideal self is greater in middle adolescence than in early or late adolescence (Strachen & Jones, 1982). While, as just mentioned, some theorists consider a strong discrepancy between the ideal and real selves as maladaptive, others argue that this is not always true, especially in adolescence. For example, in one view, an important aspect of the ideal or imagined self is the **possible self,** *what individuals might become, what they would like to become, and what they are afraid of becoming* (Markus & Nurius, 1986). Thus, adolescents' possible selves include both what adolescents hope to be as well as what they dread they will become. In this view, the presence of both hoped-for as well as dreaded selves is psychologically healthy, providing a balance between positive, expected selves and negative, feared selves. The attributes of future positive selves (getting into a good college, being admired, having a successful career) can direct future positive states, while attributes of future negative selves (being unemployed, being lonely, not getting into a good college) can identify what is to be avoided in the future (Martin, 1997).

Can adolescents distinguish between their true and false selves? In one research study, they could (Harter & Lee, 1989). Adolescents are most likely to show their false self in romantic or dating situations, and with classmates; they are least likely to show their false self with close friends. Adolescents display a false self to impress others, to try out new behaviors or roles, because others force them to behave in false ways, and because others do not understand their true self (Harter, 1990b). Some adolescents report that they do not like their false-self behavior, but others say that it does not bother them. Harter and her colleagues (in press) found that experienced authenticity of the self is highest among adolescents who say they receive support from their parents.

To further reflect on possible future selves, turn to Critical Thinking About Children's Development.

Social Comparison Some developmentalists believe that adolescents are more likely than children to use *social*

comparison to evaluate themselves (Ruble & others, 1980). However, adolescents' willingness to *admit* that they engage in social comparison to evaluate themselves declines in adolescence because they view social comparison as socially undesirable. They think that acknowledging their social comparison motives will endanger their popularity (Harter, 1990a). Relying on social comparison information in adolescence may be confusing because of the large number of reference groups. For example, should adolescents compare themselves to classmates in general? to friends? to others of their own gender? to popular adolescents? to good-looking adolescents? to athletic adolescents? Simultaneously considering all of these social comparison groups can get perplexing for adolescents.

Self-Conscious Adolescents are more likely than children to be *self-conscious* about and *preoccupied* with their self-understanding. As part of their self-conscious and preoccupied self-exploration, adolescents become more introspective. However, the introspection is not always done in social isolation. Sometimes, adolescents turn to their friends for support and self-clarification, obtaining their friends' opinions of an emerging self-definition. As one researcher on self-development commented, adolescents' friends are often the main source of reflected self-appraisals, becoming the social mirror into which adolescents anxiously stare (Rosenberg, 1979). This self-consciousness and self-preoccupation reflect adolescent egocentrism, which we discussed in chapter 4.

Self-Protective Adolescents' self-understanding includes more mechanisms to *protect the self* (Harter, 1990a). Although adolescents often display a sense of confusion and conflict stimulated by introspective efforts to understand the self, they also call on mechanisms to protect and enhance the self. In protecting the self, adolescents are prone to denying their negative characteristics. For example, in Harter's investigation of self-understanding, positive self-descriptions, such as *attractive, fun-loving, sensitive, affectionate,* and *inquisitive,* were more likely to be placed at the core of the self, indicating more importance, whereas negative self-descriptions, such as *ugly, mediocre, depressed, selfish,* and *nervous,* were more likely to be placed at the periphery of the self, indicating less importance (Harter, 1986). Adolescents' tendency to protect themselves fits with the earlier description of adolescents' tendency to describe themselves in idealistic ways.

Unconscious Adolescents' self-understanding involves greater recognition that the self includes *unconscious,* as well as conscious, components, a recognition not likely to occur until late adolescence (Selman, 1980). That is, older adolescents are more likely than younger adolescents to believe that certain aspects of their mental experience are beyond their awareness or control.

Self-Integration Adolescents' self-understanding becomes more *integrative,* with the disparate parts of the self more systematically pieced together, especially in late adolescence. Older adolescents are more likely to detect inconsistencies in their earlier self-descriptions as they attempt to construct a general theory of self, an integrated sense of identity (Harter, 1990b; Selman, 1980).

Because the adolescent creates multiple self-concepts, the task of integrating these varying self-conceptions becomes problematic. At the same time that adolescents are faced with pressures to differentiate the self into multiple roles, the emergence of formal operational thought presses for *integration* and the development of a consistent, coherent theory of self (Harter, 1990b). These budding formal operational skills initially present a liability because they first allow adolescents to *detect* inconsistencies in the self across varying roles, only later providing the cognitive capacity to *integrate* such apparent contradictions. In the "Images of Children" narrative that opened the chapter, the 15-year-old girl could not understand how she could be cheerful yet depressed and sarcastic, wondering "which is the real me." Researchers have found not only that 14- to 15-year-olds detect inconsistencies across their various roles (with parents, friends, and romantic partners, for example) but that they are much more troubled by these contradictions than younger (11- to 12-year-old) and older (17- to 18-year-old) adolescents are (Damon & Hart, 1988; Harter, 1986).

> *The living self has one purpose only: to come into its own fullness of being, as a tree comes into full blossom, or a bird into spring beauty, or a tiger into lustre.*
>
> —**D. H. Lawrence**

Conclusions As we have seen, the development of self-understanding in adolescence is complex and involves a number of aspects of the self. Rapid changes that occur in the transition from childhood to adolescence result in heightened self-awareness and self-consciousness. This heightened self-focus leads to consideration of the self and the many changes that are occurring in it, which can produce doubt about who one is and which facets of the self are "real" (Hart, 1996).

James Marcia (1996) believes that changes in the self in adolescence can best be understood by dividing them up into early (deconstruction), middle (reconstruction), and late (consolidation) phases. That is, the adolescent is initially confronted by contradictory self-descriptions, followed by attempts to resolve those contradictions, and then subsequently develops a more integrated self-theory (identity).

At this point, we have discussed a number of characteristics of adolescents' self-understanding. A summary of these characteristics is presented in figure 12.2.

Further Developmental Considerations in Self-Understanding

In the developmental sequence of self-understanding just outlined, we presented the emergence of various self-dimensions. It is important to keep in mind that just because a particular dimension of the self is listed in a particular period, the dimension does not occur exclusively in that period. For example, early childhood is described as the time period for the emergence of a physical and active self; however, many elementary school children also describe themselves in terms of physical characteristics and various activities. We described middle and late childhood as the time period when the internal self, social self, and social comparative self become more prominent. These characteristics of the self also are very important in adolescent self-understanding and, in many cases, are more prevalent in adolescents' self-description than in children's self-description. However, these characteristics were discussed in relation to the middle and late childhood period because that is the time when many developmentalists believe they emerge to become important self-dimensions.

The Role of Perspective Taking in Self-Understanding

Many child developmentalists believe that perspective taking plays an important role in self-understanding. As you learned earlier, perspective taking is the ability to assume another person's perspective and understand his or her thoughts and feelings. Robert Selman (1980) has proposed a developmental theory of perspective taking that has been given considerable attention. He believes that perspective taking involves a series of five stages, ranging from 3 years of age through adolescence (see table 12.1). These stages begin with the egocentric viewpoint in early childhood and end with in-depth perspective taking in adolescence.

Abstract and idealistic

Differentiated

Contradictions within the self

Fluctuating

Real and ideal,
true and false selves

Social comparison

Self-conscious

Self-protective

Integrative

Figure~12.2

Characteristics of Adolescents' Self-Understanding

To study children's perspective taking, Selman interviews individual children, asking them to comment on such dilemmas as the following:

Holly is an 8-year-old girl who likes to climb trees. She is the best tree climber in the neighborhood. One day while climbing down from a tall tree, she falls, . . . but does not hurt herself. Her father sees her fall. He is upset and asks her to promise not to climb trees anymore. Holly promises.

Later that day, Holly and her friends meet Shawn. Shawn's kitten is caught in a tree and can't get down.

Something has to be done right away or the kitten may fall. Holly is the only one who climbs trees well enough to reach the kitten and get it down but she remembers her promise to her father. (Selman, 1976, p. 302)

Subsequently, Selman asks each child a series of questions about the dilemma, such as the following:

- Does Holly know how Shawn feels about the kitten?
- How will Holly's father feel if he finds out she climbed the tree?

TABLE 12.1

Selman's Stages of Perspective Taking

Stage	Perspective-Taking Stage	Ages	Description
0	Egocentric viewpoint	3–6	Child has a sense of differentiation of self and others but fails to distinguish between the social perspective (thoughts, feelings) of other and self. Child can label other's overt feelings but does not see the cause-and-effect relation of reasons to social actions.
1	Social-informational perspective taking	6–8	Child is aware that other has a social perspective based on other's own reasoning, which may or may not be similar to child's. However, child tends to focus on one perspective rather than coordinating viewpoints.
2	Self-reflective perspective taking	8–10	Child is conscious that each individual is aware of the other's perspective and that this awareness influences self and other's view of each other. Putting self in other's place is a way of judging other's intentions, purposes, and actions. Child can form a coordinated chain of perspectives but cannot yet abstract from this process to the level of simultaneous mutuality.
3	Mutual perspective taking	10–12	Adolescent realizes that both self and other can view each other mutually and simultaneously as subjects. Adolescent can step outside the two-person dyad and view the interaction from a third-person perspective.
4	Social and conventional system perspective taking	12–15	Adolescent realizes mutual perspective taking does not always lead to complete understanding. Social conventions are seen as necessary because they are understood by all members of the group (the generalized other), regardless of their position, role, or experience.

- What does Holly think her father will do if he finds out she climbed the tree?
- What would you do in this situation?

By analyzing children's responses to these dilemmas, Selman (1980) concluded that children's perspective taking follows the developmental sequence described in table 12.1.

Children's perspective taking not only can increase their self-understanding, but it can also improve their peer group status and the quality of their friendships. For example, one investigation found that the most popular children in the third and eighth grades had competent perspective-taking skills (Kurdek & Krile, 1982). Children who are competent at perspective taking are better at understanding the needs of their companions, so they likely can communicate more effectively with them (Hudson, Forman, & Brion-Meisels, 1982).

At this point, we have studied a number of developmental changes in self-understanding. Remember from our introduction to the self that self-conception involves not only self-understanding but also self-esteem and self-concept. That is, not only do children try to define and describe attributes of the self (self-understanding), but they also evaluate these attributes (self-esteem and self-concept).

Self-Esteem and Self-Concept

What are self-esteem and self-concept? How are they measured? How do parent-child relationships contribute to self-esteem? How is group identity involved in children's self-esteem? What are the consequences of children's low self-esteem? And how can children's self-esteem be enhanced?

What Are Self-Esteem and Self-Concept?

Self-esteem *is the global evaluative dimension of the self. Self-esteem is also referred to as self-worth or self-image.* For example, a child might perceive that she is not merely a person but a *good* person. Of course, not all children have an overall positive image of themselves. **Self-concept** *refers to domain-specific evaluations of the self.* Children can make self-evaluations in many domains of their lives—academic, athletic, physical appearance, and so on. In sum, self-esteem refers to global self-evaluations, self-concept to more domain-specific evaluations.

> *It is difficult to make people miserable when they feel worthy of themselves.*
>
> —**Abraham Lincoln**

Investigators have not always made clear distinctions between self-esteem and self-concept, sometimes using the terms interchangeably or not precisely defining them. As you read the remaining discussion of self-esteem and self-concept, the distinction between self-esteem as global self-evaluation and self-concept as domain-specific self-evaluation should help you to keep the terms straight.

Measuring Self-Esteem and Self-Concept

Measuring self-esteem and self-concept hasn't always been easy, especially when assessing adolescents (Wylie, 1979). Recently, different measures have been developed to assess children and adolescents.

Susan Harter's (1985) Self-Perception Profile for Children is a revision of her original instrument, the Perceived Competence Scale for Children (Harter, 1982). The Self-Perception Profile for Children taps five specific domains of self-concept—scholastic competence, athletic competence, social acceptance, physical appearance, and behavioral conduct—plus general self-worth. Harter's scale does an excellent job of separating children's self-evaluations in different skill domains, and when general self-worth is assessed, questions focus on the overall self-evaluations rather than on specific skill domains.

The Self-Perception Profile for Children is designed to be used with third-grade through sixth-grade children. Harter also has developed a separate scale for adolescents, recognizing important developmental changes in self-perceptions. The Self-Perception Profile for Adolescents (Harter, 1989) taps eight domains—scholastic competence, athletic competence, social acceptance, physical appearance, behavioral conduct, close friendship, romantic appeal, and job competence—plus global self-worth. Thus the adolescent version has three skill domains not present in the children's version—job competence, romantic appeal, and close friendship.

Some assessment experts believe that a combination of several methods should be used to measure children's self-esteem. In addition to self-report scales, ratings of a child's self-esteem by others and observations of the child's behavior in various settings may provide a more comprehensive portrait of self-esteem. Children's facial expressions and the extent to which they congratulate or condemn themselves are also good indicators of self-esteem. For example, children who rarely smile or act happy reveal something about their self-esteem. By referring to figure 12.3, you can examine the behavioral categories that were used to measure self-esteem in one investigation (Savin-Williams & Demo, 1983).

Parent-Child Relationships and Self-Esteem

In the most extensive investigation of parent-child relationships and self-esteem, a measure of self-esteem was given to elementary school boys, and the boys and their mothers were interviewed about their family relationships (Coopersmith, 1967). Based on these assessments, the following parenting attributes were associated with boys' high self-esteem:

- Expression of affection
- Concern about the child's problems
- Harmony in the home
- Participation in joint family activities
- Availability to give competent, organized help to the boys when they need it
- Setting clear and fair rules
- Abiding by these rules
- Allowing the children freedom within well-prescribed limits

Remember that these findings are correlational, and so, we cannot say that these parenting attributes *cause* children's high self-esteem. Such factors as parental acceptance and allowing children freedom within well-prescribed limits probably are important determinants of children's self-esteem, but we still must say that they *are related* to rather than that they *cause* children's self-esteem, based on the available research data.

Group Identity and Self-Esteem

Children's group identity is also related to their self-esteem. **Social identity theory** *is social psychologist Henry Tajfel's (1978) theory that, when individuals are assigned to a group, they invariably think of that group as an ingroup for them. This occurs because individuals want to have a positive self-image.* According to Tajfel, self-image consists of both a personal identity and many different social identities. Tajfel argues that individuals can improve their self-image by enhancing either their personal or their social identity. Tajfel believes that social identity is especially important. When children or adults compare the social identity of their group with the social identity of another group, they often maximize the distinctions between the two groups. For example, think of an adolescent's identity with the school's football or basketball team. When the school's teams win, students' self-images are enhanced, regardless of whether

Behavioral Indicators of Self-Esteem	
Positive Indicators	**Negative Indicators**
1. Gives others directives or commands	1. Puts down others by teasing, name-calling, or gossiping
2. Uses voice quality appropriate for situation	2. Uses gestures that are dramatic or out of context
3. Expresses opinions	3. Engages in inappropriate touching or avoids physical contact
4. Sits with others during social activities	4. Gives excuses for failures
5. Works cooperatively in a group	5. Glances around to monitor others
6. Faces others when speaking or being spoken to	6. Brags excessively about achievements, skills, appearance
7. Maintains eye contact during conversation	7. Verbally puts self down; self-depreciation
8. Initiates friendly contact with others	8. Speaks too loudly, abruptly, or in a dogmatic tone
9. Maintains comfortable space between self and others	9. Does not express views or opinions, especially when asked
10. Little hesitation in speech, speaks fluently	10. Assumes a submissive stance

Figure~12.3

Behavioral Indicators of Self-Esteem

they play on the teams or not. Why? Because they have a social identity with the school and the school's teams.

As children and adults strive to promote their social identities, it is not long before proud, self-congratulatory remarks are interspersed with nasty comments about the opposing group(s). In a capsule, the theme becomes, "My group is good and I am good. Your group is bad and you are bad." So it goes with the sexes, ethnic groups, teams, social classes, religions, and countless other groups, all seeking to improve their respective self-images through social identity with the group and comparison of the group with other groups. These comparisons can easily lead to competition, conflict, and even a perception that discrimination against other groups is legitimate.

Tajfel showed that it does not take much to get children or adults to think in terms of "we" and "they," or in-group and out-group. He assigned children to two groups based on a trivial task. For example, one individual was assigned to one group because she overestimated the number of dots on a screen and another individual was assigned to another group because he underestimated the number. Once assigned to the two groups, the members were asked to award amounts of money to pairs of other subjects. Those eligible to receive the money were anonymous except for their membership in one of the two groups Tajfel created. Invariably, the children acted favorably toward (awarded money to) members of their own group. It is no wonder, then, that if we favor our own group based on such trivial criteria, we will show intense in-group favoritism when differences are not as trivial.

Closely related to group identity and self-esteem is **ethnocentrism,** *the tendency to favor one's own group over other groups.* Ethnocentrism's positive side appears in the sense of in-group pride that fulfills our strong urge to attain and maintain a positive self-image. In-group pride has mushroomed as we approach the end of the twentieth century. Children observe and listen to their parents speak about African American pride, Latino pride,

Native American pride, Irish pride, Italian pride, and so on. Unfortunately, sometimes prejudice develops. **Prejudice** *is an unjustified negative attitude toward an individual because of that person's membership in a group.* People can be prejudiced against groups of people made up of a particular ethnic group, sex, age, religion, or other detectable difference.

Also related to group identity and self-esteem is the self-esteem of various ethnic minority groups. To learn more about self-esteem in ethnic-minority-group children, turn to Sociocultural Worlds of Children.

Consequences of Low Self-Esteem

For most children and adolescents, low self-esteem results only in temporary emotional discomfort (Damon, 1991). But in some children and adolescents, low self-esteem can translate into other problems (DuBois, Felner, & Brand, 1997). It has been implicated in depression, suicide, anorexia nervosa, and delinquency (Harter & Marold, 1992). The seriousness of the problem depends not only on the nature of the child's and adolescent's low self-esteem but on other conditions as well. When low self-esteem is compounded by difficult school transitions or family life, or by other stressful events, the child's problems can intensify (Rutter & Garmezy, 1983).

Increasing Children's Self-Esteem

Four ways children's self-esteem can be improved are through (1) identifying the causes of low self-esteem and the domains of competence important to the self, (2) emotional support and social approval, (3) achievement, and (4) coping (see figure 12.4).

Identifying children's sources of self-esteem—that is, competence in domains important to the self—is critical to improving self-esteem. Self-esteem theorist and researcher Susan Harter (1990b) points out that the self-esteem enhancement programs of the 1960s, in which self-esteem itself was the target and individuals were encouraged to simply feel good about themselves, were

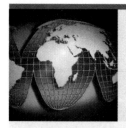

Ethnicity, Self, and Self-Esteem

Many of the early attempts to assess the nature of self-esteem in various ethnic groups compared African American and White individuals (Clark & Clark, 1939; Coopersmith, 1967; Deutsch, 1967). The early reports indicated that African American individuals, especially African American children, have less self-esteem than White individuals. However, more recent research suggests that African American, Mexican American, and Puerto Rican American children and adults report self-esteem that is equal to, if not higher than, that reported by children and adults from other ethnic groups, such as Anglo-American children and adults (Allen & Majidi-Ahi, 1989; Powell & Fuller, 1972).

A generation of ethnic awareness and pride appears to have advanced the self-esteem of ethnic minority groups (Garbarino, 1980). Ethnic pride based on success within a subgroup has both costs and benefits for individuals. An obvious benefit is that their cultural roles are more clearly defined by the subgroup (such as African American, Latino, or Native American) and that they know what they must do to become competent people in the subculture. In these usually tight-knit neighborhoods, there is a feeling of closeness and support among neighbors. Thus, individuals from the ethnic group can obtain help and learn strategies for coping with problems, which makes developing a positive sense of self somewhat easier. An ethnic-group individual gains a sense of rootedness and acceptance.

However, there is no indication that the distribution of self-acceptance in a group is related to the social prestige of the group in American society at large (Rosenberg, 1965). Thus, there may be a negative reality in the social environment beyond the ethnic-group neighborhood with which individuals must eventually come to terms if they are to succeed in the larger society. The ethnic-group neighborhood's beliefs, values, morals, and behaviors may not be accepted by the society as a whole, which can impede the development of social competence in the mainstream of society.

A discussion of ethnicity and self-esteem raises the fundamental question, "What kind of people does the world need?" (Garbarino, 1980). There is a growing recognition of the need for individuals to develop more harmonious, cooperative relationships if the quality of life on this planet is to be enhanced. Such a society needs persons to define themselves in new ways that deemphasize competition, achievement, and materialism in favor of cooperation, connectedness with others, empathy, and spiritual development. We need to ask whether we are socializing children to develop the kind of self that is needed to create a competent, caring, sustainable society.

ineffective. Harter believes, rather, that intervention must occur at the level of the causes of self-esteem if the individual's self-esteem is to improve significantly.

Children have the highest self-esteem when they perform competently in domains important to the self. Therefore, children should be encouraged to identify and value areas of competence. Emotional support and social approval in the form of confirmation from others also powerfully influence children's self-esteem (Harter, 1990b). Some children with low self-esteem come from conflicted families or conditions in which they experience abuse or neglect—situations in which support is unavailable. In some cases, alternative sources of support can be implemented, either informally through the encouragement of a teacher, a coach, or another significant adult, or more formally through programs such as Big Brothers and Big Sisters. While peer approval becomes increasingly important during adolescence, both adult and peer support are important influences on the adolescent's self-esteem. In one recent study, both parental and peer support were related to the adolescent's general self-worth (Robinson, 1995).

Achievement also can improve children's self-esteem (Bednar, Wells, & Peterson, 1995). For example, the straightforward teaching of real skills to children often results in increased achievement and, thus, in enhanced self-esteem. Children develop higher self-esteem because they know the important tasks to achieve goals, and they have experienced performing them or similar behaviors. The emphasis on the importance of achievement in improving self-esteem has much in common with Bandura's cognitive social learning concept of *self-efficacy*, which refers to individuals' beliefs that they can master a situation and produce positive outcomes.

Self-esteem also is often increased when children face a problem and try to cope with it rather than avoid it (Bednar, Wells, & Peterson, 1995). If coping

Figure~12.4

Four Key Aspects of Improving Self-Esteem

Identifying the causes of low self-esteem and which domains of competence are important to the self

Emotional support and social approval

Achievement

Coping

rather than avoidance prevails, children often face problems realistically, honestly, and nondefensively. This produces favorable self-evaluative thoughts, which lead to the self-generated approval that raises self-esteem. The converse is true of low self-esteem. Unfavorable self-evaluations trigger denial, deception, and avoidance in an attempt to disavow that which has already been glimpsed as true. This process leads to self-generated disapproval as a form of feedback to the self about personal adequacy.

At this point, we have discussed a number of ideas about the self in adolescence, including information about self-understanding and self-esteem. A summary of these ideas is presented in concept table 12.1. Next, we turn our attention to an important concept related to the self—identity.

IDENTITY

By far the most comprehensive and provocative theory of identity development is Erik Erikson's. Some experts on adolescence consider Erikson's ideas to be the single most influential theory of adolescent development. Erikson's theory was introduced in chapter 2. Here that introduction is expanded, beginning with reanalysis of his ideas on identity. Then we examine some contemporary

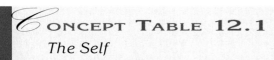
Concept	Processes/Related Ideas	Characteristics/Description
Self-Understanding	What is it?	It is a child's cognitive representation of self, the substance and content of the child's self-conceptions. Self-understanding provides the rational underpinnings of personal identity.
	Infancy	Watson's research demonstrates that self-awareness emerges very early in infancy and develops over the first 3 to 4 months. Infants develop a rudimentary form of self-recognition at approximately 18 months of age.
	Early childhood	The physical and active self becomes a part of self-understanding as young children often describe themselves in physical or active terms.
	Middle and late childhood	The internal self, the social self, and the socially comparative self become more prominent in self-understanding. Elementary-school-age children increasingly describe themselves with internal, psychological characteristics. They also are more likely to define themselves in terms of social characteristics and social comparison.
	Adolescence	Dimensions of adolescents' self-understanding include abstract and idealistic; construction of ideal and real, true and false selves; differentiated; contradictions within the self; self-conscious; self-protective; recognition that the self includes an unconscious dimension; social comparison; fluctuating and integrative.
	Further developmental considerations	Once the characteristics emerge as a part of self-understanding, they continue to be part of self-understanding, although they may wax and wane in varying degrees as development proceeds. For example, although the internal self is described as becoming more prominent in middle and late childhood, the internal self continues to be an integral part of self-understanding in adolescence. The physical self continues to be a part of self-description in adolescence, but it is often less central in self-description than in early childhood.
	Perspective taking	It is the ability to assume another person's perspective and understand his or her thoughts and feelings. Selman proposed a developmental theory of perspective taking with five stages, ranging from 3 years of age through adolescence, beginning with the egocentric viewpoint in early childhood and ending with the in-depth perspective taking of adolescence.
Self-Esteem and Self-Concept	What are they?	Self-esteem is the global evaluative dimension of the self. Self-esteem is also referred to as self-worth or self-image. Self-concept refers to domain-specific evaluations of the self.
	Measuring self-esteem and self-concept	Researchers such as Susan Harter have constructed various measures for children and adolescents. Harter's measures assess self-evaluations in different skill domains as well as general self-worth. Some assessment experts believe that several methods, including observations of behavior, should be used to measure children's self-esteem.
	Parent-child relationships and self-esteem	In Coopersmith's study, children's self-esteem was associated with such parenting attributes as parental acceptance and allowing children freedom within well-prescribed limits. It is important to remember that these associations are correlational.
	Group identity and self-esteem	Social identity theory is Tajfel's theory that, when individuals are assigned to a group, they invariably think of the group as an in-group for them. This occurs because they want to have a positive self-image. Tajfel believes self-image consists of a personal *and* many different social identities related to group membership and identity. Group identity often leads to competitiveness, and sometimes conflict, between groups. Closely related to group identity and self-esteem is ethnocentrism, the tendency to favor one's own group over other groups. The positive side of ethnocentrism is the sense of in-group pride, but sometimes a negative side—prejudice—develops. A special concern is the self-esteem of ethnic minority children.
	Consequences of low self-esteem	For most children and adolescents, low self-esteem only translates into temporary emotional discomfort, but for others, low self-esteem can result in depression, suicide, eating disorders, and delinquency.
	Increasing children's self-esteem	Four ways to increase children's self-esteem involve (1) identifying the causes of adolescents' low self-esteem and which domains of competence are important to the self, (2) emotional support and social approval, (3) achievement, and (4) coping.

thoughts on identity, the four statuses of identity, developmental changes, family influences on identity, cultural and ethnic aspects of identity, and gender and identity development.

Erikson's Ideas on Identity

Who am I? What am I all about? What am I going to do with my life? What is different about me? How can I make it on my own? Not usually considered during childhood, these questions surface as common, virtually universal, concerns during adolescence. Adolescents clamor for solutions to these questions that revolve around the concept of identity, and it was Erik Erikson who first understood how central such questions are to understanding adolescent development. That today identity is believed to be a key concept in adolescent development is a result of Erikson's masterful thinking and analysis.

Revisiting Erikson's Views on Identity and the Human Life Span

Identity versus identity confusion *is Erikson's fifth developmental stage, which individuals experience during the adolescent years. At this time, adolescents face finding out who they are, what they are all about, and where they are going in life.* Adolescents are confronted with many new roles, such as vocational and romantic roles. **Psychosocial moratorium** *is Erikson's term for the gap between childhood security and adult autonomy that adolescents experience as part of their identity exploration.* As adolescents explore and search their culture's identity files, they often experiment with different roles. Youth who successfully cope with these conflicting identities emerge with a new sense of self that is both refreshing and acceptable. Adolescents who do not successfully resolve this identity crisis suffer what Erikson calls identity confusion. The confusion takes one of two courses: Individuals withdraw, isolating themselves from peers and family, or they immerse themselves in the world of peers and lose their identity in the crowd.

Erikson's ideas about adolescent identity development reveal rich insights into adolescents' thoughts and feelings, and reading one or more of his original writings is worthwhile. A good starting point is *Identity: Youth and Crisis* (1968). Other works that portray identity development are *Young Man Luther* (1962) and *Gandhi's Truth* (1969)—the latter won a Pulitzer Prize.

> " *Who are you?*" said the caterpillar. Alice replied rather shyly, "I—I hardly know; sir, just at present— at least I know who I was when I got up this morning, but I must have changed several times since then."
>
> —Lewis Carroll
> **Alice in Wonderland, 1865**

Mahatma Gandhi was the spiritual leader of India in the middle of the twentieth century. In his Pulitzer Prize-winning novel on Gandhi's life, Erikson describes the personality formation of Gandhi during his youth:

> Straight and yet not stiff; shy and yet not withdrawn; intelligent and yet not bookish; willful and yet not stubborn; sensual and yet not soft . . . We must try to reflect on the relation of such a youth to his father because the Mahatma places service to the father and the crushing guilt of failing in such service in the center of his adolescent turbulence. Some historians and political scientists seem to find it easy to interpret this account in psychoanalytic terms; I do not. For the question is not how a particular version of the Oedipal complex "causes" a man to be both great and neurotic in a particular way, but rather how such a young person . . . manages the complexes which constrict other men. (Erikson, 1969, p. 113)

Personality and Role Experimentation

Two core ingredients in Erikson's theory of identity development are personality and role experimentation. As indicated earlier, Erikson believes that adolescents face an overwhelming number of choices and at some point during youth enter a period of psychological moratorium. During this moratorium, they try out different roles and personalities before they reach a stable sense of self. They may be argumentative one moment, cooperative the next. They may dress neatly one day, sloppily the next day. They may like a particular friend one week, despise the friend the next week. This personality experimentation is a deliberate effort on the part of adolescents to find out where they fit in the world.

As they gradually come to realize that they will be responsible for themselves and their own lives, adolescents search for what those lives are going to be. Many parents and other adults, accustomed to having children go along with what they say, may be bewildered or incensed by the wisecracks, the rebelliousness, and the rapid mood changes that accompany adolescence. It is important for adults to give adolescents the time and opportunities to explore roles and personalities. In turn, most adolescents eventually discard undesirable roles.

There are literally hundreds of roles for adolescents to try out, and probably just as many ways to pursue each role. Erickson believes that, by late adolescence, vocational roles are central to identity's development, especially in a highly technological society such as the United States. Youth who have been well trained to enter a workforce that offers the potential of reasonably high self-esteem will experience the least stress during the development of identity. Some youth have rejected jobs offering good pay and traditionally high social status, choosing instead to work in situations that allow them to be more genuinely helpful to their fellow humans, such as in the Peace Corps, in mental health clinics, or in schools for children from low-income backgrounds. Some youth prefer unemployment to the prospect of working at a job they feel they would be unable to perform well or at which they would feel useless. To Erikson, this attitude reflects the desire to achieve a meaningful identity through being true to oneself, rather than burying one's identity in that of the larger society.

Some Contemporary Thoughts About Identity

Contemporary views of identity development suggest several important considerations. First, identity development is a lengthy process; in many instances it is a more gradual, less cataclysmic transition than Erikson's term *crisis* implies. Second, identity development is extraordinarily complex (Marcia, 1980, 1987). Identity formation neither begins nor ends with adolescence. It begins with the appearance of attachment, the development of a sense of self, and the emergence of independence in infancy, and reaches its final phase with a life review and integration in old age. What is important about identity in adolescence, especially late adolescence, is that for the first time physical development, cognitive development, and social development advance to the point at which the individual can sort through and synthesize childhood identities and identifications to construct a viable pathway toward adult maturity. Resolution of the identity issue at adolescence does not mean identity will be stable through the remainder of one's life. A person who develops a healthy identity is flexible, adaptive, and open to changes in society, in relationships, and in careers. This openness assures numerous reorganizations of identity features throughout the life of the person who has achieved identity.

Identity formation does not happen neatly, and it usually does not happen cataclysmically. At the bare minimum, it involves commitment to a vocational direction, an ideological stance, and a sexual orientation. Synthesizing the identify components can be a long, drawn-out process with many negations and affirmations of various roles and faces. Identities are developed in bits and pieces. Decisions are not made once and for all, but have to be made again and again. And the decisions may seem

"Do you have any idea who I am?"

Drawing by Koren; ©1988 The New Yorker Magazine, Inc.

trivial at the time: whom to date, whether or not to break up, whether or not to have intercourse, whether or not to take drugs, whether to go to college after high school or get a job, which major to choose, whether to study or whether to play, whether or not to be politically active, and so on. Over the years of adolescence, the decisions begin to form a core of what the individual is all about as a person—what is called identity (Archer, 1989).

> *As long as one keeps searching, the answers come.*
>
> —Joan Baez

The Four Statuses of Identity

Eriksonian researcher James Marcia (1980, 1994) believes that Erikson's theory of identity development can be understood in terms of four statuses of identity, or ways of resolving the identity crisis: identity diffusion, identity foreclosure, identity moratorium, and identity achievement. The extent of an adolescent's crisis and commitment is used to classify the individual according to one of the four identity statuses. **Crisis** *is defined as a period of identity development during which the adolescent is choosing among meaningful alternatives.* Most researchers use the term exploration rather than crisis, although, in the spirit of Marcia's formulation, the term crisis is used here. **Commitment** *is part of identity development in which adolescents show a personal investment in what they are going to do.*

Identity diffusion *is Marcia's term for the status of adolescents who have not yet experienced a crisis (that is, they have not yet explored meaningful alternatives) or made any commitments.* Not only are they undecided about occupational and ideological choices, they are also likely to show little interest in such matters. **Identity foreclosure** *is Marcia's term for the status of adolescents who have made a commitment but have not exprienced a crisis.* This occurs most often when parents hand down commitments

James Marcia, shown talking with college students, developed the concept of identity status. Over three decades, Marcia has greatly advanced our understanding of identity development.

to their adolescents, usually in an authoritarian way. In these circumstances, adolescents have not had adequate opportunities to explore different approaches, ideologies, and vocations on their own. **Identity moratorium** *is Marcia's term for the status of adolescents who are in the midst of a crisis but whose commitments are either absent or only vaguely defined.* **Identity achievement** *is Marcia's term for the status of adolescents who have undergone a crisis and have made a commitment.*

Developmental Changes

Young adolescents are primarily in Marcia's identity statuses of diffusion, foreclosure, or moratorium. At least three aspects of the young adolescent's development are important in identity formation (Marcia, 1987, 1996): Young adolescents must be confident in having parental support, have an established sense of industry, and be able to adopt a self-reflective stance toward the future. Marcia's four statuses of identity development are summarized in figure 12.5.

The identity status approach has been sharply criticized by some researchers and theoreticians (Blasi, 1988; Cote & Levine, 1988; Lapsley & Power, 1988). They believe that the identity status approach distorts and trivializes Erikson's notions of crisis and commitment. For example, concerning crisis, Erikson emphasized the youth's questioning of the perceptions and expectations of one's culture and developing an autonomous position with regard to one's society. In the identity status approach, these complex questions are dealt with by simply evaluating whether a youth has thought about certain issues and considered alternatives. Erikson's idea of commitment loses the meaning of investing one's own self in certain lifelong projects and is interpreted simply as having made a firm decision or not. Others still believe that the identity status approach is a valuable contribution to understanding identity (Archer, 1989; Waterman, 1989).

Some researchers believe the most important identity changes take place in youth rather than earlier in adolescence. For example, Alan Waterman (1985, 1992) has found that, from the years preceding high school through the last few years of college, there is an increase in the number of individuals who are identity achieved, along with a decrease in those who are identity diffused. College upperclassmen are more likely to be identity achieved than are college freshmen or high school students. Many young adolescents are identity diffused. These developmental changes are especially true for vocational choice. For religious beliefs and political ideology, fewer college students have reached the identity-achieved status, with a substantial number characterized by foreclosure and diffusion. Thus, the timing of identity may depend on the particular life area involved and many college students are still wrestling with ideological commitments (Arehart & Smith, 1990).

Many identity status researchers believe that a common pattern of individuals who develop positive identities is to follow what are called "MAMA" cycles of moratorium–achievement–moratorium–achievement (Archer, 1989). These cycles may be repeated throughout life (Francis, Fraser, & Marcia, 1989). Personal, family, and societal changes are inevitable, and as they occur, the flexibility and skill required to explore new alternatives and develop new commitments are likely to facilitate an individual's coping skills. Regarding commitment, Marcia (1996) believes that the first identity is just that—it is not, and should not be expected to be, the final product.

Family Influences on Identity

Parents are important figures in the adolescent's development of identity. In studies that relate identity development to parenting styles, democratic parents, who encourage adolescents to participate in family decision making, foster identity achievement. Autocratic parents, who control the adolescent's behavior without giving the adolescent an opportunity to express opinions, encourage identity foreclosure. Permissive parents, who provide little guidance to adolescents and allow them to make their own decisions, promote identity diffusion (Enright & others, 1980).

In addition to studies on parenting styles, researchers have also examined the role of individuality and connectedness in the development of identity. Developmentalist Catherine Cooper and her colleagues (Cooper & Grotevant, 1989; Cooper & others, 1982; Grotevant & Cooper, in press) believe that the presence of a family atmosphere that promotes both individuality and connectedness are important in the adolescent's identity development. **Individuality** *consists of two dimensions: self-assertion, the ability to have and communicate a point of view; and separateness, the use of communication patterns to express how one is different from others.* **Connectedness** *also consists of two dimensions: mutuality, sensitivity to and respect for others' views; and permeability, openness to others' views.* In general, Cooper's research findings reveal that identity formation is enhanced by family relationships that are both individuated, which encourages adolescents to develop their own point of view, and connected, which provides a secure base from which to explore the widening social worlds of adolescence. However, when connectedness is strong and individuation weak, adolescents often have an identity foreclosure status; by contrast, when connectedness is weak, adolescents often reveal an identity confusion status (Archer & Waterman, 1994).

In sum, family interaction styles that give the adolescent the right to question and to be different, within a context of support and mutuality, foster healthy patterns of identity development.

Cultural and Ethnic Aspects of Identity

Erikson is especially sensitive to the role of culture in identity development. He points out that, throughout the world, ethnic minority groups have struggled to maintain their cultural identities while blending into the dominant culture (Erikson, 1968). Erikson says that this struggle for an inclusive identity, or identity within the larger culture, has been the driving force in the founding of churches, empires, and revolutions throughout history.

Adolescence is often a special juncture in development for ethnic minority individuals (Dreyer & others, 1994; Kurtz, Cantu & Phinney, 1996; Markstrom-Adams & Spencer, 1994; Phinney & others, 1994; Spencer

"While we're at supper, Billy, you'd make Daddy and Mommy very happy if you'd remove your hat, your sunglasses, and your earring."

Drawing by Ziegler; ©1985 The New Yorker Magazine, Inc.

& Dornbusch, 1990). Although children are aware of some ethnic and cultural differences, most ethnic minority individuals consciously confront their ethnicity for the first time in adolescence. In contrast to children, adolescents have the ability to interpret ethnic and cultural information, to reflect on the past, and to speculate about the future (Harter, 1990a). As they cognitively mature, ethnic minority adolescents become acutely aware of the evaluations of their ethnic group by the majority White culture (Ogbu, 1989). As one researcher commented, the young African American child may learn that Black is beautiful, but conclude as an adolescent that White is powerful (Semaj, 1985).

Ethnic minority youth's awareness of negative appraisals, conflicting values, and restricted occupational opportunities can influence life choices and plans for the

Position on occupation and ideology	Identity status			
	Identity moratorium	Identity foreclosure	Identity diffusion	Identity achievement
Crisis	Present	Absent	Absent	Present
Commitment	Absent	Present	Absent	Present

Figure~12.5

Marcia's Four Statuses of Identity

Margaret Beale Spencer, shown here talking with adolescents, believes that adolescence is often a critical juncture in the identity development of ethnic minority individuals. Most ethnic minority individuals consciously confront their ethnicity for the first time in adolescence.

The Native American adolescent's quest for identity involves a cultural meshing of tribal customs and the technological, educational demands of modern society. The following poem by a young Native American vividly captures some important ingredients of adolescents' interest in a peaceful identity:

> Rivers flow.   A small pebble
> The sea sings.   On a giant shore;
> Oceans roar.   Who am I
> Tides rise.   To ask who I am?
> Who am I?   Isn't it enough to be?

future (Spencer & Dornbusch, 1990). As one ethnic minority youth stated, "The future seems shut off, closed. Why dream? You can't reach your dreams. Why set goals? At least if you don't set any goals, you don't fail."

For many ethnic minority youth, a lack of successful ethnic minority role models with whom to identify is a special concern (Blash & Unger, 1992). The problem is especially acute for inner-city ethnic minority youth. Because of the lack of adult ethnic minority role models, some ethnic minority youth may conform to middle-class White values and identify with successful White role models. However, for many adolescents, their ethnicity and skin color limit their acceptance by the White culture. Thus, many ethnic minority adolescents have a difficult task: negotiating two value systems—that of their own ethnic group and that of the White society. Some adolescents reject the mainstream, foregoing the rewards controlled by White Americans; others adopt the values and standards of the majority White culture; and yet others take the difficult path of biculturalism (Hiraga & others, 1993).

In one investigation, ethnic identity exploration was higher among ethnic minority than among White American college students (Phinney & Alipura, 1990). In this same investigation, ethnic minority college students who had thought about and resolved issues involving their ethnicity had higher self-esteem than did their

ethnic minority counterparts who had not. In another investigation, the ethnic identity development of Asian American, African American, Latino, and White American tenth-grade students in Los Angeles was studied (Phinney, 1989). Adolescents from each of the three ethnic minority groups faced a similar need to deal with their ethnic-group identification in a predominantly White American culture. In some instances, the adolescents from the three ethnic minority groups perceived different issues to be important in their resolution of ethnic identity. For Asian American adolescents, pressures to achieve academically and concerns about quotas that make it difficult to get into good colleges were salient issues. Many African American adolescent females discussed their realization that White American standards of beauty (especially hair and skin color) did not apply to them; African American adolescent males were concerned with possible job discrimination and the need to distinguish themselves from a negative societal image of

Exploring Your Identity Development

Now that you have read about various aspects of identity development, this is a good time to explore your own identity development. How can you gain insight into your personal self or identity? One way is to list adjectives that describe yourself. You also could ask people who know you well, such as family members and/or friends, to tell you how they honestly would describe you. How well does their perception of you match your self-perception? Consider also your interests, attitudes, and hobbies. How did you develop your personal characteristics and interests? Try to trace their origins. Tracing the development of aspects of yourself can help you gain insight into your own identity formation. By exploring your identity development, you are learning to think critically by *applying developmental concepts to enhance personal adaptation.*

African American male adolescents. For Latino adolescents, prejudice was a recurrent theme, as was conflicting values between their Latino culture heritage and the majority culture.

Identity development is influenced by the contexts in which young people live (Stanton-Salazar & Dornbusch, in press). Many ethnic minority youth in the United States live in low-income urban settings where support for developing a positive identity is absent (Bat-Chava & others, 1997). Many of these youth live in pockets of poverty, are exposed to drugs, gangs, and criminal activities, and interact with other youth and adults who have dropped out of school or are unemployed. In such settings, effective organizations and programs for youth can make important contributions to developing a positive identity (Cooper & others, 1996).

Shirley Heath and Milbrey McLaughlin (1993) studied sixty youth organizations that involved 24,000 adolescents over a period of 5 years. They found that these organizations were especially good at building a sense of pride in inner-city ethnic youth. Heath and McLaughlin believe that many inner-city youth have too much time on their hands, too little to do, and too few places to go. Inner-city youth want to participate in organizations that nurture them and respond positively to their needs and interests. Organizations that perceive youth as fearful, vulnerable, and lonely, but also frame them as capable, worthy, and eager to have a healthy and productive life, contribute in positive ways to the identity development of ethnic minority youth.

Gender and Identity Development

In Erikson's (1968) classic presentation of identity development, the division of labor between the sexes was reflected in his assertion that males' aspirations were mainly oriented toward career and ideological commitments, while females' were centered around marriage and childbearing. In the 1960s and 1970s researchers found support for Erikson's assertion about gender differences in identity. For example, vocational concerns were more central to the identity of males, and affiliative concerns were more important in the identity of females (La Voie, 1976). However, in the last decade, as females have developed stronger vocational interests, gender differences are turning into gender similarities (Waterman, 1985).

Some investigators believe the order of stages proposed by Erikson is different for females and males. One view is that, for males, identity formation precedes the stage of intimacy, while for females intimacy precedes identity (Douvan & Adelson, 1966). These ideas are consistent with the belief that relationships and emotional bonds are more important concerns for females, while autonomy and achievement are more important concerns for males (Gilligan, 1990). In one study, the development of a clear sense of self by adolescent girls was related to their concerns about care and response in relationships (Rogers, 1987). In another investigation, a strong sense of self in college women was associated with their ability to solve problems of care in relationships while staying connected with both self and others (Skoe & Marcia, 1988). Indeed, conceptualization and measurement of identity development in females should include interpersonal content (Patterson, Sochting, & Marcia, 1992).

The task of identity exploration may be more complex for females than for males, in that females may try to establish identities in more domains than males do. In today's world, the options for females have increased and thus can at times be confusing and conflicting, especially for females who hope to successfully integrate family and career roles (Archer, 1994; Gilligan, 1990; Josselson, 1994). To think further about identity turn to Critical Thinking About Children's Development.

At this point we have discussed many different ideas about culture and identity in adolescence. A summary of these ideas is presented in concept table 12.2.

CONCEPT TABLE 12.2

Identity

Concept	Processes/Related Ideas	Characteristics/Description
Erikson's Ideas on Identity	Their nature	Erikson argues that identity versus identity confusion is the fifth stage in the human life span, occurring at about the time of adolescence, a time when individuals enter a psychosocial moratorium between the security of childhood and the autonomy of adulthood.
	Personality and role experimentation	Personality exploration and the exploration of roles are two important ingredients of identity development. In technological societies like the United States, the vocational role is especially important.
	Some contemporary thoughts about identity	Identity development is a lengthy process, in many cases more gradual than Erikson implied. Identity development is extraordinarily complex. Identity development is done in bits and pieces. For the first time in development, individuals during adolescence are physically, cognitively, and socially mature enough to synthesize their lives and pursue a viable path toward adult maturity.
	The four statuses of identity	Marcia proposed four identity statuses—identity diffusion, identity foreclosure, identity moratorium, and identity achievement—that are based on crisis (exploration) and commitment. Some experts believe that the identity status approach oversimplifies Erikson's ideas.
Developmental Changes	Their nature	Some experts believe that the main identity changes take place in youth rather than earlier in adolescence. College juniors and seniors are more likely to be identity achieved than freshmen or high school students, although many college students are still wrestling with the ideological commitments. Individuals often follow "moratorium-achievement-moratorium-achievement" cycles throughout life.
Family Influences, Cultural and Ethic Aspects, and Gender	Family influences on identity	Parents are important figures in adolescents' identity development. Democratic parenting facilitates identity development in adolescence; autocratic and permissive parenting do not. Cooper and her colleagues have shown that both individuality and connectedness in family relations are important contributors to adolescent identity development. Hauser has shown that enabling behaviors promote identity development more than constraining behaviors.
	Cultural and ethnic aspects of identity	Erikson is especially sensitive to the role of culture in identity development, underscoring how, throughout the world, ethnic minority groups have struggled to maintain their cultural identities while blending into dominant cultures. Adolescence is often a special juncture in the identity development of ethnic minority individuals because for the first time they consciously confront their ethnic identity. Although children are aware of some ethnic and cultural differences, most individuals first consciously confront their ethnicity in adolescence. A problem for many ethnic minority youth is the lack of successful ethnic minority role models with whom to identify. For inner-city ethnic minority adolescents, youth organizations can provide support for the positive development of identity.
	Gender and identity development	Erikson's classical theory argued that gender differences in identity development exist, with adolescent males having a stronger interest in vocational roles, adolescent females a stronger interest in marriage and family roles. More recent studies have revealed that, as females have developed stronger vocational interests, gender differences in identity have turned into similarities. However, others argue that relationships and emotional bonds are more central to the identity development of females than of males and that female identity development is more complex than male identity development.

SUMMARY

This chapter on the self and identity has been about how children perceive themselves, evaluate themselves, feel about themselves, and explore who they are.

We began this chapter by examining a 15-year-old girl's complex self-description and then studied three important aspects of the self—self-understanding, self-esteem, and self-concept. In reading about self-understanding, we learned what self-understanding is, its developmental course, and the role of perspective taking in self-understanding. In reading about self-esteem and self-concept, we learned what they are, how they can be measured, the role of parenting in children's self-esteem, how group identity is related to self-esteem, the consequences of low self-esteem, and how children's self-esteem can be improved. Our exploration of identity focused on Erikson's ideas about identity, some contemporary thoughts about identity, the four statuses of identity, family influences on identity, cultural and ethnic aspects of identity, and the relation of gender to identity development.

By again studying the two concept tables on pages 392 and 399 you can obtain a summary of this chapter. Although in this chapter we only briefly studied gender development—exploring gender's role in identity development—in the next chapter we will extensively examine the role of gender in children's development.

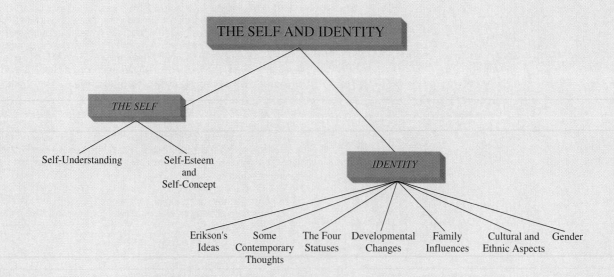

THE SELF AND IDENTITY

THE SELF

Self-Understanding

Self-Esteem and Self-Concept

IDENTITY

Erikson's Ideas

Some Contemporary Thoughts

The Four Statuses

Developmental Changes

Family Influences

Cultural and Ethnic Aspects

Gender

PRACTICAL KNOWLEDGE ABOUT CHILDREN

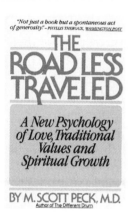

"Not just a book but a spontaneous act of generosity." – PHYLLIS THEROUX, WASHINGTON POST

THE ROAD LESS TRAVELED

A New Psychology of Love, Traditional Values and Spiritual Growth

BY M. SCOTT PECK, M.D.
Author of The Different Drum

The Road Less Traveled
(1978) by M. Scott Peck,
New York: Simon & Schuster.

The Road Less Traveled presents an approach to self-fulfillment based on spirituality and emotion. Peck begins by stating that life is difficult and that we all suffer pain and disappointment. He believes we should face up to life's difficulties and not be lazy. Indeed, Peck equates laziness with the original sin, going on to say that people's tendency to avoid problems and emotional suffering is the root of mental disorders. Peck also believes that people are thirsting for integrity in their lives. They are not happy with a country that has "In God we trust" as one of its main emblems and at the same time still leads the world's arms race. They also can't tolerate being just Sunday-morning Christians, he says. To achieve integrity, Peck believes, people need to move spirituality into all phases of their lives.

The Road Less Traveled has been an immensely popular book, on the *New York Times* best-sellers list for more than a year. Peck has developed a cult-like following, especially among young people. The book's enthusiasts say that Peck recognized some important voids in people's lives, especially the need for an integrated, spiritually-based existence. Some critics say that Peck's ideas are not new and that his thoughts are occasionally fuzzy, especially when he arrives at the meeting point between God and man, and unconscious and conscious selves.

DAVID ELKIND
Author of *The Hurried Child*

All Grown Up & No Place to Go

Teenagers in Crisis

All Grown Up and No Place to Go: Teenagers in Crisis
(1984) by David Elkind,
Reading, MA: Addison-Wesley.

Elkind believes that raising teenagers in today's world is more difficult than ever. He argues that teenagers are expected to confront adult challenges too early in their development. By being pressured into adult roles too soon, today's youth are all grown up with no place to go, hence the title of the book. Elkind believes that the main reason teenagers are pressed into adult roles too early is that parents are more committed to their own self-fulfillment than to their adolescents'. These parents of the "me" generation are often too quick to accept their teenagers' outward sophistication as a sign of emotional maturity. Teens' emotional needs are also neglected by a school system that is up-to-date in computer gadgetry but is bankrupt in responding to adolescents' emotional needs and individual differences, says Elkind. He also believes the media exploit adolescents by appealing to their vulnerability to peer pressure.

EXPLORATIONS IN CHILD DEVELOPMENT

To further explore the nature of child development, we will examine a research study on perceived support and its relation to adolescents' self-worth, and we will discuss the nature of education, work, and identity development.

RESEARCH IN CHILD DEVELOPMENT

Perceived Support and Adolescents' Self-Worth

Featured Study

Robinson, N. S. (1995). Evaluating the nature of perceived support and its relation to perceived self-worth in adolescents. *Journal of Research on Adolescence,* 5, 253–280.

The purpose of this study was to better understand the link between adolescents' perceptions of global self-worth and their perceptions of various types of support—approval, emotional support, and instrumental aid. It was hypothesized that positive regard or approval from others—especially approval from peers, because they represent such an important reference group for adolescents—would be most strongly related to self-worth.

Method

The subjects were 370 seventh- and eighth-grade students from two middle schools and 189 ninth- to twelfth-graders from one high school. Both females and males were studied, and the schools served primarily White middle-class adolescents.

The main measures included the Perceived Social Support Scale and the Self-Perception Profile. A revised version of Harter's Social Support Scale for Children was administered. Separate subscales tapped emotional support (such as "perceptions of how much people in their lives care about their feelings or listen to them when they are upset"), approval (such as the extent to which people "praise them or say nice things about them," "are really proud of them," or "like most of the things they do"), and instrumental aid (such as the level of assistance or aid provided along the lines of "helping them do the things they cannot do themselves" or "teaching them about the things they want to know"). The adolescents were asked the extent to which each of the three types of support was being provided by five sources: mother, father, best friend, classmates, and teacher. For high school students, a sixth source was added: a person in whom they were romantically interested. Modified versions of Harter's Self-Perception Profile were given to the adolescents—a shortened version of the Self-Perception Profile for Children was given to the middle school students, and a shortened version of the Self-Perception Profile for Adolescents was given to the high school students. Both measures assessed students' perceptions of their competence in four domains (academic, social, physical appearance, and behavior/conduct), as well as their perceptions of global self-worth. The items on the global self-worth scale (the only part of this measure of interest in this study) asked to what extent individuals were happy or pleased with themselves, liked the way they were carrying out their lives, liked who they are, and thought that the way they do things is fine.

Results and Discussion

Perceptions of approval from others, especially from a peer reference group such as classmates, was more strongly related to general self-worth than were perceptions of emotional support or instrumental aid. Females consistently reported higher levels of approval, emotional support, and instrumental aid from their best friends than did males. Parental support and peer support were acknowledged as being important throughout adolescence.

IMPROVING THE LIVES OF CHILDREN

Education, Work, and Identity Development

Susan Harter (1990a, 1990b) addressed the importance of developing programs for youth that promote the *active* and *realistic* exploration of broad identity goals, such as educational and occupational choices. Such programs may take the form of on-the-job experiences, as occurs in the Boston Compact Youth Incentive Program, which provides students with well-paying summer jobs if they maintain a good record of school attendance and performance. Another program strengthens the link between high school activities and the world of work

Daniel Garber
Tanis, 1915, detail

and provides opportunities for exploring alternatives (Lang & Rivera, 1987). This program emphasizes adolescents' choice of areas in which they are both interested and competent, letting them choose educational opportunities that further their development in these domains. This strategy is consistent with Harter's conclusion that the highest levels of self-esteem are found in individuals who are performing competently in domains that are important to the self.

One strategy is to encourage society to recognize the positive benefits of competence in many different domains, not just academic competence. Another strategy is to acknowledge that education is the primary means for achieving success, and to provide individuals with poor academic skills and low self-esteem better support and more individualized attention. The inspiration of Latino high school teacher Jaime Escalante, documented in the movie *Stand and Deliver,* reflects this latter strategy. Escalante was a California high school teacher who spent many evenings and weekends tutoring Latino students in math, in addition to effectively teaching the students math in the classroom. Escalante's commitment and motivation were transferred to the Latino high school students, many of whom obtained college scholarships and passed advanced placement tests in calculus. Insisting that high school and college athletes maintain a respectable grade point average is a policy that endorses the importance of academic achievement and competence in other domains, as is the requirement that students maintain respectable grades to participate in jobs programs.

One program in Washington, D.C., has helped many ethnic minority adolescents do better in school. In 1983, Dr. Henry Gaskins began an after-school tutorial program for ethnic minority students. For 4 hours every weeknight and all day Saturday, 80 students receive one-on-one assistance from Gaskins and his wife, two adult volunteers, and academically talented peers. Those who can afford it contribute $5 to cover the cost of school supplies. In addition to tutoring in specific subjects, Gaskins' home-based academy helps students set personal goals and commit to a desire to succeed. Many of his students come from families in which the parents are high school dropouts and either can't or are not motivated to help their adolescent sons and daughters achieve in school. In addition, the academy prepares students to qualify for scholarships and college entrance exams. Gaskins recently received the President's Volunteer Action Award at the White House.

Shown here is a scene from the movie *Stand and Deliver,* in which Latino High school teacher Jaime Escalante (played by James Olmos, in the center with a cap) spent many evenings and weekends tutoring Latino students in math in addition to effectively teaching the students math in the classroom. Escalante's commitment and motivation was transferred to the students, many of whom obtained college scholarships and passed advanced placement tests in calculus.

Dr. Henry Gaskins, here talking with three high school students, began an after-school tutorial program for ethnic minority students in 1983 in Washington, D.C. Volunteers like Dr. Gaskins can be especially helpful in developing a stronger sense of the importance of education in ethnic minority adolescents.

Chapter

13

Gender

*I*t is fatal to be man or woman pure and simple; one must be woman-manly or man-womanly.

—Virginia Woolf

What are little boys made of?
Frogs and snails
And puppy dogs' tails.
What are little girls made of?
Sugar and spice
And all that's nice.

—J. O. Halliwell,
Nursery Rhymes of England, 1844

PREVIEW

*T*he famous quotation above describes the behavior of boys and girls as being different—boys are made of frogs and snails and puppy dogs' tails, girls of sugar and spice and all that's nice. In this chapter we will tackle the question of how different or similar boys and girls really are, as well as gender stereotypes. We will also study biological, social, and cognitive influences on gender, how gender roles are classified, developmental windows of gender opportunity and asymmetric gender socialization, women's and men's issues, as well as ethnicity and gender. But to begin, we first need to define gender.

IMAGES OF CHILDREN

Tomorrow's Gender Worlds of Today's Children

Controversial currents swirl around today's females and males. Females increasingly struggle to gain influence and change the worlds of business, politics, and relationships with males. The changes are far from complete, but social reformers hope that, a generation from now, the struggles of the last decades of the twentieth century will have generated more freedom, influence, and flexibility for females. Possibly a decade or two from now today's children will live in a world in which equal pay, child care, abortion, rape, and domestic violence will be discussed no longer as "women's issues" but rather as economic issues, family issues, and ethical issues—reflecting equal concern of females and males. Possibly a 10-year-old girl today will head a major corporation in 30 years and the circumstance will not make headlines by virtue of her gender. Half the presidential candidates may be women and nobody will notice.

What would it take to get from here to there? The choices are not simple ones. When Barbara Bush went to Wellesley College to celebrate motherhood and wifely virtues, she stimulated a national debate on what it means to be a successful woman. The debate was further fueled by TV anchorwoman Connie Chung's announcement that she would abandon the fast track at CBS in a final drive to become a mother at 44. At the same time, children's male role models are also in a state of flux. Wall Street star Peter Lynch, the head of Fidelity Investment's leading mutual fund, resigned to have more time with his family and pursue humanitarian projects.

When asked to sketch their futures, many of today's college students say they want good careers, good marriages, and two or three children, but they don't want their children to be raised by strangers (Spade & Reese, 1991). Idealistic? Maybe. Some of you will reach these goals, while others of you will make other choices. Some women will choose to remain single as they pursue their career goals, others will become married but not have children, and yet others will balance the demands of family and work. In a word, not all females have the same goals; neither do all males. What is important for us is to develop a society free of barriers and discrimination, one that allows today's children—whether female or male—to choose freely, to meet their expectations, and to fulfill their potential.

WHAT IS GENDER?

What exactly is meant by gender? **Gender** *refers to the sociocultural dimension of being female or male.* Two aspects of gender bear special mention: gender identity and gender role. **Gender identity** *is the sense of being female or male, which most children acquire by the time they are 3 years old.* A **gender role** *is a set of expectations that prescribes how females and males should think, act, and feel.*

BIOLOGICAL, SOCIAL, AND COGNITIVE INFLUENCES ON GENDER

How strong is biology's influence on gender? How extensively do children's social experiences shape their gender development? How do cognitive factors influence gender development?

Biological Influences

It was not until the 1920s that researchers confirmed the existence of human sex chromosomes, the genetic material that determines our sex. In chapter 3, you learned that humans normally have 46 chromosomes, arranged in pairs. The 23rd pair may have two X-shaped chromosomes to produce a female, or it may have an X-shaped and a Y-shaped chromosome to produce a male.

In the first few weeks of gestation, female and male embryos look alike. Male sex organs start to differ from female sex organs when XY chromosomes in the male embryo trigger the secretion of **androgen,** *the main class of male sex hormones.* Low levels of androgen in a female embryo allow the normal development of female sex organs.

Although rare, an imbalance in this system of hormone secretion can occur during fetal development. If there is insufficient androgen in a male embryo or an excess of androgen in a female embryo, the result is an individual with both male and female sex organs, a hermaphrodite. When genetically female (XX-chromosome) infants are born with masculine-looking genitals, surgery at birth can achieve a genital/genetic match. **Estrogen** *is the main class of female sex hormones.* At puberty, the production of estrogen begins to influence both physical development and behavior, but before then these females often behave in a "tomboyish" manner, acting more aggressively than most girls. They also dress and play in ways that are more characteristic of boys than girls (Ehrhardt, 1987).

Is the behavior of these surgically corrected girls due to their prenatal hormones, or is it the result of their social experiences? Experiments with various animal species reveal that, when male hormones are injected into female embryos, the females develop masculine physical traits and behave more aggressively (Hines, 1982). However, in humans, hormones exert less control over behavior. Perhaps, because these girls look more masculine, they are treated more like boys and so adopt their boyish ways.

Although prenatal hormones may or may not influence gender behavior, psychoanalytic theorists, such as Sigmund Freud and Erik Erikson, have argued that an individual's genitals do play a pivotal role. Freud argued that human behavior and history are directly influenced by sexual drives and suggested that gender and sexual behavior are essentially unlearned and instinctual. Erikson went even further: He argued that, because of genital structure, males are more intrusive and aggressive, females more inclusive and passive. Erikson's critics contend that he has not given enough credit to experience, and they argue that women and men are more free to choose their behavior than Erikson allowed. In response, Erikson clarified his view, pointing out that he never said that biology is the sole determinant of differences between the sexes. Biology, he said, interacts with both cultural and psychological factors to produce behavior.

No one argues about the presence of genetic, biochemical, and anatomical differences between the sexes. Even child developmentalists with a strong environmental orientation acknowledge that boys and girls are treated differently because of their physical differences and their different roles in reproduction. The importance of biological factors is not at issue. What is at issue is the directness or indirectness of their effects on social behavior (Huston, 1983; Rose, 1997). For example, if a high androgen level directly influences the central nervous system, which in turn increases activity level, then the biological effect on behavior is direct. By contrast, if a child's high level of androgen produces strong muscle development, which in turn causes others to expect the child to be a good athlete and, in turn, leads the child to participate in sports, then the biological effect on behavior is indirect.

Although virtually everyone thinks that children's behavior as males or females is due to an interaction of biological and environmental factors, an interactionist position means different things to different people (Maccoby, 1997). For some, it suggests that certain environmental conditions are required before preprogrammed dispositions appear. For others, it suggests that a particular environment will have different effects, depending on the child's predispositions. For still others, it means that children shape their environments, including their interpersonal environment, and vice versa. The processes of influence and counterinfluence unfold over time. Throughout development, males and females actively construct their own versions of acceptable masculine and feminine behavior patterns.

Social Influences

Once the label *girl* or *boy* is assigned by the obstetrician, virtually everyone, from parents to siblings to strangers, begins treating the infant differently (Matlin, 1993). Look at the photograph of the baby in figure 13.1. Imagine that

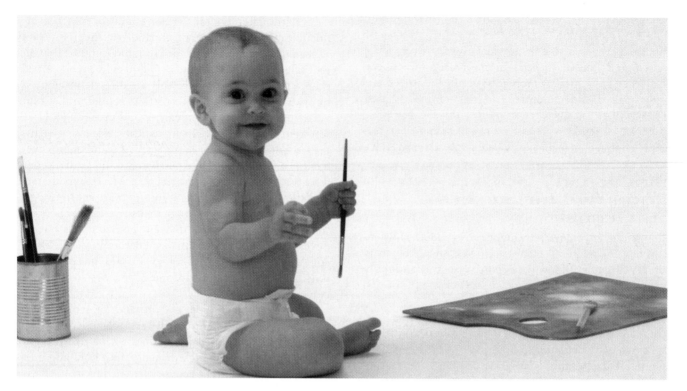

Figure~13.1

Gender Expectations
First imagine that this is a photograph of a baby girl. What expectations would you have for her? Then imagine that this is a photograph of a baby boy. What expectations would you have for him?

the baby is a girl. What characteristics would you attribute to the baby because it is a girl? What expectations might you have for her? Now replace the image of the baby as a girl with an image of the baby as a boy. What characteristics do you attribute to the baby boy? What expectations do you have for him? Probably very different ones. Possibly you said that the baby girl is soft, nice, and very cuddly, and that the baby boy is strong, solid, and will be adventuresome.

In one study, an infant girl, Avery, was dressed in a neutral outfit of overalls and a T-shirt (Brooks-Gunn & Matthews, 1979). People responded to her differently if they thought she was a girl rather than a boy. People who thought she was a girl made comments like "Isn't she cute. What a sweet little, innocent thing." By contrast, people who thought the baby was a boy made remarks like "I bet he is a tough little customer. He will be running around all over the place and causing trouble in no time."

In general, parents even hope that their offspring will be a boy. In one investigation in the 1970s, 90 percent of the men and 92 percent of the women wanted their firstborn child to be a boy (Peterson & Peterson, 1973). In a more recent study, parents still preferred a boy as the firstborn child—75 percent of the men and 79 percent of the women had that preference (Hamilton, 1991).

In some countries, a male child is so preferred over a female child that many mothers will abort a female fetus after fetal testing procedures, such as amniocentesis and sonograms, that reveal the fetus' sex. For example, in South Korea, where fetal testing to determine sex is common, male births exceed female births by 14 percent, in contrast to a worldwide average of 5 percent. To help counteract this trend, Asian nations designated 1990 as the Year of the Girl Child.

In recent years, the idea that parents are the critical socializing agents in gender-role development has come under fire (Huston, 1983). Parents are only one of many sources through which the individual learns gender roles. Culture, schools, peers, the media, and other family members are others. Yet it is important to guard against swinging too far in this direction because—especially in the early years of development—parents are important influences on gender development.

Identification and Social Learning Theories

Two prominent theories address the way children acquire masculine and feminine attitudes and behaviors from their parents. **Identification theory** *stems from Freud's view that the preschool child develops a sexual attraction to the opposite-sex parent, then by approximately 5 or 6 years of age*

Theory	Processes	Outcome
Freud's identification theory	Sexual attraction to opposite-sex parent at 3 to 5 years of age; anxiety about sexual attraction and subsequent identification with same-sex parent at 5 to 6 years of age	Gender behavior similar to that of same-sex parent
Social learning theory	Rewards and punishments of gender-appropriate and inappropriate behavior by adults and peers; observation and imitation of models' masculine and feminine behavior	Gender behavior

Figure~13.2

Identification and Social Learning Theories of Gender

renounces this attraction because of anxious feelings, and subsequently identifies with the same-sex parent, unconsciously adopting the same-sex parent's characteristics. However, today many child developmentalists do not believe that gender development proceeds on the basis of identification, at least in terms of Freud's emphasis on childhood sexual attraction. Children become gender-typed much earlier than 5 or 6 years of age, and they become masculine or feminine even when the same-sex parent is not present in the family.

Children need models rather than critics.

—Joseph Joubert

The **social learning theory of gender** *emphasizes that children's gender development occurs through observation and imitation of gender behavior, and through the rewards and punishments children experience for gender-appropriate and -inappropriate behavior.* Unlike identification theory, social learning theory argues that sexual attraction to parents is not involved in gender development. (A comparison of identification and social learning views is presented in figure 13.2.) Parents often use rewards and punishments to teach their daughters to be feminine ("Karen, you are being a good girl when you play gently with your doll") and masculine ("Keith, a boy as big as you is not supposed to cry"). Peers also extensively reward and punish gender behavior. And by observing adults and peers at home,

at school, in the neighborhood, and on television, children are widely exposed to a myriad of models who display masculine and feminine behavior. Critics of the social learning view argue that gender development is not as passively acquired as it indicates. Later we will discuss the cognitive views of gender development, which stress that children actively construct their gender world.

Parental Influences

Parents, by action and example, influence their children's gender development (Winstead, Derlega, & Rose, 1997). Both mothers and fathers are psychologically important in children's gender development. Mothers are more consistently given responsibility for nurturance and physical care; fathers are more likely to engage in playful interaction and be given responsibility for ensuring that boys and girls conform to existing cultural norms. And whether or not they have more influence on them, fathers are more involved in socializing their sons than in socializing their daughters (Lamb, 1986). Fathers seem to play an especially important part in gender-role development—they are more likely to act differently toward sons and daughters than mothers are, and thus contribute more to distinctions between the genders (Huston, 1983).

Many parents encourage boys and girls to engage in different types of play and activities (Fagot, 1995; Fisher-Thompson & others, 1993). Girls are more likely to be given dolls to play with during childhood and, when old enough, are more likely to be assigned baby-sitting

As reflected in this tug-of-war battle between boys and girls, the playground in elementary school is like going to "gender school." Elementary school children show a clear preference for being with and liking same-sex peers. Eleanor Maccoby (at right) has studied children's gender development for many years. She believes peers play especially strong roles in socializing each other about gender roles.

duties. Girls are encouraged to be more nurturant and emotional than boys, and their fathers are more likely to engage in aggressive play with their sons than with their daughters. As adolescents increase in age, parents permit boys more freedom than girls, allowing them to be away from home and stay out later without supervision. When parents place severe restrictions on their adolescent sons, it has been found to be especially disruptive to the sons' development (Baumrind, 1989).

Peer Influences

Parents provide the earliest discrimination of gender roles in development, but before long, peers join the societal process of responding to and modeling masculine and feminine behavior. Children who play in sex-appropriate activities tend to be rewarded for doing so by their peers. Those who play in cross-sexed activities tend to be criticized by their peers or left to play alone. Children show a clear preference for being with and liking same-sex peers (Buhrmester, 1993; Maccoby, 1993), and this tendency usually becomes stronger during the middle and late childhood years (Hayden-Thomson, Rubin, & Hymel, 1987). After extensive observations of elementary school playgrounds, two researchers characterized the play settings as "gender school," pointing out that boys teach one another the required masculine behavior and enforce it strictly (Luria & Herzog, 1985). Girls also pass on the female culture and mainly congregate with one another. Individual "tomboy" girls can join boys' activities without losing their status in the girls' groups, but the reverse is not true for boys, reflecting our society's greater sex-typing pressure for boys.

Peer demands for conformity to gender role become especially intense during adolescence. While there is greater social mixing of males and females during early adolescence, in both formal groups and in dating, peer pressure is strong for the adolescent boy to be the very best male possible and for the adolescent girl to be the very best female possible.

School and Teacher Influences

In certain ways, both girls and boys might receive an education that is not fair (Sadker & Sadker, 1994). For example:

- Girls' learning problems are not identified as often as boys' are.
- Boys are given the lion's share of attention in schools.
- Girls start school testing higher than boys in every academic subject, yet they graduate from high school scoring lower on the SAT exam.
- Boys are most often at the top of their classes, but they also are most often at the bottom as well— more likely to fail a class, miss promotion, or drop out of school.
- Pressure to achieve is more likely to be heaped on boys than on girls.

Consider the following research study (Sadker & Sadker, 1986). Observers were trained to collect data in more than 100 fourth-, sixth-, and eighth-grade classrooms. At all three grade levels, male students were involved in more interactions than female students were, and male students were given more attention than female students were. Male students were also given more re-mediation, more criticism, and more praise than female students. It has also been found that girls with strong math abilities are given lower-quality instruction than their male counterparts are (Eccles, 1993).

Myra and David Sadker (1994), who have been studying gender discrimination in schools for more than two decades, believe that many educators are unaware of the subtle ways in which gender infiltrates the school's environment. Their hope is that sexism can be eradicated in the nation's schools.

Gender and the Media

Children encounter masculine and feminine roles in their everyday interactions with parents, peers, and teachers. The messages carried by the media about what is appropriate or inappropriate for males and for females are important influences on gender development as well.

A special concern is the way females are pictured on television. In the 1970s, it became apparent that television was portraying females as less competent than males. For example, about 70 percent of the prime-time characters were males, men were more likely to be shown in the workforce, women were more likely to be shown as housewives and in romantic roles, men were more likely to appear in higher-status jobs and in a greater diversity of occupations, and men were presented as more aggressive and constructive (Sternglanz & Serbin, 1974).

In the 1980s, television networks became more sensitive to how males and females were portrayed on television shows. Consequently, many programs now focus on divorced families, cohabitation, and women in high-status roles. Even with the onset of this type of programming, researchers continue to find that television portrays males as more competent than females (Durkin, 1985). In one investigation, young adolescent girls indicated that television occupations are more extremely stereotyped than real-life occupations are (Wroblewski & Huston, 1987).

Television directed at adolescents might be the most extreme in its portrayal of the sexes, especially of teenage girls (Beal, 1994). In one study, teenage girls were shown as primarily concerned with dating, shopping, and their appearance (Campbell, 1988). They were rarely depicted as interested in school or career plans. Attractive girls were often portrayed as "airheads" and intelligent girls as unattractive.

Another highly stereotyped form of programming specifically targeted for teenage viewers is rock music videos. What adolescents see on MTV and rock music videos is highly stereotyped and slanted toward a male audience (for example, the "Beavis and Butt-Head" and "Wayne and Garth" shows). In music videos, females are twice as likely as in prime-time programming to be dressed provocatively, and aggressive acts are often perpetrated by females; for example, in one scene a woman pushes a

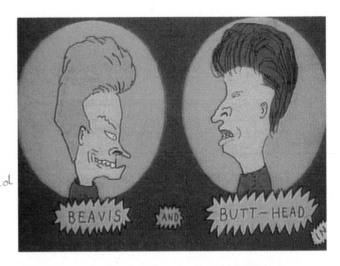

"Beavis and Butt-Head" is the most popular MTV program. What kind of models do these characters provide for adolescents? They torture animals, harass girls, and sniff paint thinner. They like to burn things. And they emit an insidious laugh: "Huh-huh, huh-huh, huh-huh." They were initially created by a beginner animator for a festival of "sick and twisted" cartoons, but quickly gained fame—their own nightly MTV program, T-shirts, dolls, a book, a comic book, a movie, CDs (including one with Cher), and a Christmas special. What age group are Beavis and Butt-Head most likely to appeal to? Why? Are some adolescents more likely to be attracted to them than others?

man to the ground, holds him down, and kisses him. MTV has been described as a teenage boy's "dreamworld," filled with beautiful, aroused women who outnumber men, who seek out and even assault men to have sex, and who always mean yes even when they say no.

If television can communicate sexist messages and influence adolescents' gender behavior, might nonstereotyped gender messages on television reduce sexist behavior? One major effort to reduce gender stereotyping was the television series "Freestyle" (Johnston, Etteman, & Davidson, 1980; Williams, LaRose, & Frost, 1981). The series was designed to counteract career stereotypes in 9- to 12-year-olds. After watching "Freestyle," both girls and boys were more open to nontraditional career possibilities. The benefits of "Freestyle" were greatest for students who viewed the TV series in the classroom and who participated in discussion groups about the show led by their teacher. Classroom discussion was especially helpful in altering boys' beliefs, which were initially more stereotyped than girls'.

However, in one study with young adolescents 12 to 13 years of age, the strategy of showing nonstereotyped television programming backfired (Durkin & Hutchins, 1984). The young adolescents watched sketches that portrayed people with nontraditional jobs, such as a male secretary, a male nurse, and a female plumber. After viewing the series, the adolescents still held traditional views about careers, and in some cases were more disapproving of the alternative careers than they had been before watching the TV series. Thus, once stereotypes are strongly in place, they are difficult to change.

Gender stereotyping also appears in the print media. In magazine advertising, females are shown more often in advertisements for beauty products, cleaning products, and home appliances, while males are shown more often in advertisements for cars, liquor, and travel. As with television programs, advertisements now portray women as more competent than they did in the past, but advertisers have not yet given them equal status with males.

How are females and males portrayed in children's books? The problem of gender bias in children's books first began receiving widespread attention in the early 1970s. In 1972, a report on 134 elementary school textbooks indicated that girls and women were more invisible, compared to boys and men (Women on Words & Images, 1974). In the real world, less than 50 percent of the population are males, but of the characters in the children's readers, more than 70 percent were males. Not only were females underrepresented in the books, but they also were misrepresented. Few women were portrayed doing work outside of the home; those who were, were shown in traditionally female occupations.

Females and males are portrayed with different personalities, and perform different tasks, in children's books (Matlin, 1993). Males are described and pictured as clever, industrious, and brave. They acquire skills, earn fame and fortune, and explore. By contrast, females tend to be passive, dependent, and kind. They cook and clean up (Bordelon, 1985; Marten & Matlin, 1976).

The biased presentation of females is not confined to English-language books. In an analysis of textbooks used in Puerto Rico and in bilingual programs in the United States, girls were generally portrayed as passive, weak, and dependent, boys as courageous, creative, and persistent (Picó, 1983).

Are children's books becoming less biased than they were a decade or two ago? There are some reasons for optimism (Matlin, 1993). An analysis of the winners of the prestigious Newbery Medal for children's books revealed several examples of competent, nonstereotypical girls (Kinman & Henderson, 1985). Further, an interview with a 10-year-old African American girl indicated that on her own she had been able to find and read a number of books about African American girls (Sims, 1983). One of her favorites is shown in figure 13.3.

In one recent study, 150 children's books were analyzed for gender-role content (Kortenhaus & Demarest, 1993). It was found that the frequency with which females and males are depicted in the stories has become more equal over the past 50 years. The roles played by females and males in the books have changed in a more subtle way. Girls are now being pictured in more instrumental activities (behavior that is instrumental in attaining a goal), but in the portrayals they are as

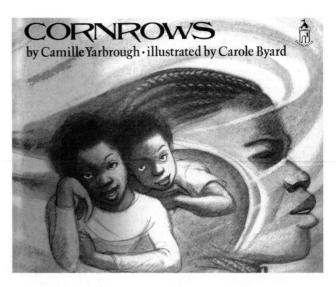

Figure~13.3

Race- and Gender-Appropriate Imagery
Camille Yarbrough's book *Cornrows* includes appropriate images of people of color and females.

passive and dependent as they were depicted as being 50 years ago! Boys are occasionally shown as passive and dependent today, but the activities they are pictured in are no less instrumental than they were 50 years ago.

Today, with effort, parents and teachers can locate interesting books in which girls and women are presented as appropriate models. And it is worth the effort (Matlin, 1993).

Cognitive Influences

What is the cognitive developmental view of gender? What is the gender schema theory of gender development? What role does language play in gender development? We consider each of these questions in turn.

Cognitive Developmental Theory

In the **cognitive developmental theory of gender,** *children's gender typing occurs after they have developed a concept of gender. Once they consistently conceive of themselves as male or female, children often organize their world on the basis of gender.* Initially developed by psychologist Lawrence Kohlberg (1966), this theory argues that gender development proceeds in the following way: A child realizes, "I am a girl; I want to do girl things; therefore, the opportunity to do girl things is rewarding." Having acquired the ability to categorize, children then strive toward consistency in the use of categories and behavior. Kohlberg based his ideas on Piaget's cognitive developmental theory. As children's cognitive development matures, so does their understanding of gender. Although 2-year-olds can apply the labels *boy* and *girl* correctly to themselves and others, their concept of gender is simple and concrete. Preschool children rely on physical features, such as dress and hairstyle, to decide who falls into which category. Girls are people with long hair, they think, whereas boys are people who never wear dresses. Many preschool children believe that people can change their own gender at will by getting a haircut or a new outfit. They do not yet have the cognitive machinery to think of gender as adults do. According to Kohlberg, all the reinforcement in the world won't modify that fact. However, by the concrete operational stage (the third stage in Piaget's theory, entered at about 6 or 7 years of age), children understand gender constancy—that a male is still a male regardless of whether he wears pants or a skirt, or his hair is short or long (Tavris & Wade, 1984). When their concept of gender constancy is clearly established, children are then motivated to become a competent, or "proper," girl or boy. Consequently, she or he finds female or male activities rewarding and imitates the behavior of same-sex models.

> *Childhood decides.*
>
> —Jean-Paul Sartre

Gender Schema Theory

A **schema** *is a cognitive structure, or network of associations, that organizes and guides an individual's perceptions. A* **gender schema** *organizes the world in terms of female and male.* **Gender schema theory** *states that an individual's attention and behavior are guided by an internal motivation to conform to gender-based sociocultural standards and stereotypes* (Bem, 1981; Levy & Carter, 1989; Liben & Signorella, 1993; Rose & Martin, 1993). Gender schema theory suggests that "gender typing" occurs when individuals are ready to encode and organize information along the lines of what is considered appropriate or typical for males and females in a society. Whereas Kohlberg's cognitive developmental theory argues that a particular cognitive prerequisite—gender constancy—is necessary for gender typing, gender schema theory states that a general readiness to respond to and categorize information on the basis of culturally defined gender roles fuels children's gender-typing activities. A comparison of the cognitive developmental and gender schema theories is presented in figure 13.4.

While researchers have shown that the appearance of gender constancy in children is related to their level of cognitive development, especially the acquisition of conservation skills (which supports the cognitive developmental theory of gender) (Serbin & Sprafkin, 1986), they have also shown that young children who are pre-gender-constant have more gender-role knowledge than the cognitive developmental theory of gender predicts (which supports gender schema theory) (Carter & Levy, 1988).

Theory	Processes	Outcome
Cognitive developmental theory	Development of gender constancy, especially around 6 to 7 years of age, when conservation skills develop; after children develop ability to consistently conceive of themselves as male or female, children often organize their world on the basis of gender, such as selecting same-sex models to imitate	Gender-typed behavior
Gender schema theory	Sociocultural emphasis on gender-based standards and stereotypes; children's attention and behavior are guided by an internal motivation to conform to these gender-based standards and stereotypes, allowing children to interpret the world through a network of gender-organized thoughts	Gender-typed behavior

Figure~13.4

A Comparison of Cognitive Developmental and Gender Schema Theories of Gender Development

The Role of Language in Gender Development

Gender is present in the language children use and encounter (Hort & Leinbach, 1993). The nature of the language children hear most of the time is sexist. That is, the English language contains gender bias, especially through the use of *he* and *man* to refer to everyone. For example, in one investigation, mothers and their 1- to 3-year-old children looked at popular children's books, such as *The Three Bears*, together (DeLoache, Cassidy, & Carpenter, 1987). The three bears were almost always referred to as boys: 95 percent of all characters of indeterminate gender were referred to by mothers as males.

GENDER STEREOTYPES, SIMILARITIES, AND DIFFERENCES

How pervasive is gender stereotyping? What are the real differences between boys and girls?

Gender Stereotyping

Gender stereotypes *are broad categories that reflect our impressions and beliefs about what behavior is appropriate for females and males.* All stereotypes, whether they are based on gender, ethnicity, or other groupings, refer to an image of what the typical member of a particular social category is like. The world is extremely complex. Every day we are confronted with thousands of different stimuli. The use of stereotypes is one way we simplify this complexity. If we simply assign a label (such as *soft*) to someone, we then have much less to consider when we think about the individual. However, once labels are assigned they are remarkably difficult to abandon, even in the face of contradictory evidence.

Many stereotypes are so general they are very ambiguous. Consider the stereotypes for "masculine" and "feminine." Diverse behaviors can be called on to support each stereotype, such as scoring a touchdown or growing facial hair for "masculine" and playing with dolls or wearing lipstick for "feminine." The stereotype may be modified in the face of cultural change. At one point in history, muscular development may be thought of as masculine; at another point, masculinity might be associated with a more lithe, slender physique. The behaviors popularly agreed upon as reflecting a stereotype may also fluctuate according to socioeconomic circumstances. For example, lower socioeconomic groups might be more likely than higher socioeconomic groups to include "rough and tough" as part of a masculine stereotype.

> *If you are going to generalize about women, you will find yourself up to here in exceptions.*
>
> —**Dolores Hitchens, *In a House Unknown***

Even though the behaviors that are supposed to fit the stereotype often do not, the label itself can have significant consequences for the individual. Labeling a male "feminine" and a female "masculine" can produce significant social reactions to the individuals in terms of status and acceptance in groups, for example.

How widespread is feminine and masculine stereotyping? According to a far-ranging study of college students in thirty countries, stereotyping of females and males is pervasive (Williams & Best, 1982). Males were widely believed to be dominant, independent, aggressive, achievement oriented, and enduring, while females were widely believed to be nurturant, affiliative, less esteemed, and more helpful in times of distress.

In a more recent investigation, women and men who lived in more highly developed countries perceived themselves as being more similar to each other than did women and men who lived in less-developed countries (Williams & Best, 1989). In the more highly developed countries, women were more likely to attend college and be gainfully employed. Thus, as sexual equality increases, male and female stereotypes, as well as actual behavioral differences, may diminish. In this investigation, women were more likely to perceive similarity between the sexes than men were (Williams & Best, 1989). And the sexes were perceived more similarly in Christian than in Muslim societies.

Gender stereotyping also changes developmentally. Stereotypic gender beliefs increase during the preschool years, peak in the early elementary school years, and then decrease in the middle and late elementary school years (Bigler, Liben, & Yekel, 1992). In one recent study, age-related decreases in gender stereotyping were related to the acquisition of cognitive skills (Bigler & Liben, in press). Next, we go beyond stereotyping and examine the similarities and differences between the sexes.

Gender Similarities and Differences

Let's now examine some of the differences between the sexes, keeping in mind the following: (a) The differences are averages—not all females versus all males; (b) even when differences are reported, there is considerable overlap between the sexes; and (c) the differences may be due primarily to biological factors, sociocultural factors, or both.

> *There is more difference within the sexes than between them.*
>
> —**Ivy Compton-Burnett**

Physical/Biological

From conception on, females are less likely than males to die, and females are less likely than males to develop

"So according to the stereotype, you can put two and two together, but I can read the handwriting on the wall."

physical or mental disorders. Estrogen strengthens the immune system, making females more resistant to infection, for example. Female hormones also signal the liver to produce more "good" cholesterol, which makes their blood vessels more elastic than males'. Testosterone triggers the production of low-density lipoprotein, which clogs blood vessels. Males have twice the risk of coronary disease as females. Higher levels of stress hormones cause faster clotting in males, but also higher blood pressure than in females. Adult females have about twice the body fat of their male counterparts, most concentrated around breasts and hips. In males, fat is more likely to go to the abdomen. On the average, males grow to be 10 percent taller than females. Male hormones promote the growth of long bones; female hormones stop such growth at puberty.

In one recent study, there was both similarity and dissimilarity in the metabolic activity of the brains of females and males (Gur & others, 1995). On many analyses, the only differences in metabolic activity between female and male brains are in the areas of the brain involved with emotional expression (more active in females) and physical expression (more active in males). In sum, though, there are many physical differences in females and males. Are there as many cognitive differences?

Cognitive

In their classic review of gender differences, Eleanor Maccoby and Carol Jacklin (1974) concluded that males have better math skills and better visuospatial abilities (the kind of skills an architect needs to design a building's angles and dimensions), while females have better verbal abilities. More recently, Maccoby (1987) revised her conclusions about several gender dimensions. She said that the accumulation of research evidence now suggests that verbal differences between females and males have

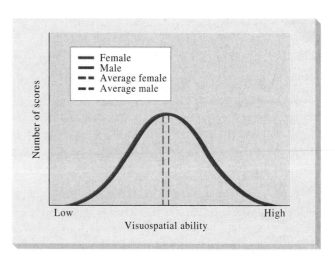

Figure~13.5

Visuospatial Ability of Males and Females
Notice that although an average male's visuospatial ability is higher than an average female's, the overlap between the sexes is substantial. Not all males have better visuospatial ability than all females—the substantial overlap indicates that, although the average score of males is higher, many females outperform most males on such tasks.

virtually disappeared, but that the math and visuospatial differences still favored males (Voyer, Voyer, & Bryden, 1995).

Some experts in the gender area, such as Janet Shibley Hyde (1993), believe the cognitive differences between females and males have been exaggerated. For example, she argues that there is considerable overlap in the distributions of female and male scores on math and visuospatial tasks. Figure 13.5 shows that although the average score for males is higher than the average score for females, female and male scores overlap substantially. Many females have higher scores on visuospatial tasks than most males do. Statements like "Males outperform females in math" should not be read as making the claim that all males outperform all females in mathematics. Rather, such a statement means that the average math achievement score for males is higher than the average math achievement score for females (Hyde & Plant, 1995).

Socioemotional

Most males are more active and aggressive than most females (Fabes, Knight, & Higgins, 1995; Maccoby, 1987; Maccoby & Jacklin, 1974). The consistent difference in aggression often appears in children's development as early as 2 years of age.

Females and males also differ in their social connectedness. Boys often define themselves apart from caregivers and peers, while girls emphasize their social ties. As adults, females often become more caring, supporting, and empathic, while males become more independent, self-reliant, and unexpressive. To further evaluate the nature of gender, turn to Critical Thinking About Children's Development.

Rethinking the Words We Use in Discussing Gender

Several decades ago the word *dependency* was used to describe the relational orientation of femininity. Dependency had negative connotations for females—that families can't take care of themselves and males can. In the 1990s, the term *dependency* is being replaced by the term *relational abilities*, which has much more positive connotations (Caplan & Caplan, 1994). Rather than being thought of as dependent, women are now described more often as skilled in forming and maintaining relationships. Make up a list of words that you associate with masculinity and a list of those that you associate with femininity. Evaluate the words in terms of whether they have any negative connotations for males or females. For the words that do have negative connotations, think about replacements that have more positive connotations. By rethinking the words we use to describe males and females, you are learning to think critically about development by *making accurate observations and descriptions*.

What about gender and emotion—do females and males differ in their emotional makeup? Unless you have been living in isolation, away from people, television, magazines, and newspapers, you probably know the master stereotype: *She is emotional, he is not.* This stereotype is powerful and pervasive in our culture (Shields, 1991).

Is this stereotype confirmed when researchers study the nature of emotional experiences in females and males? Researchers have found that females and males are often more alike in the way they experience emotion than the master stereotype would lead us to believe. Females and males often use the same facial expressions, adopt the same language, and describe their emotional experiences similarly when they keep diaries about their life experiences. Thus, the master stereotype about females being emotional and males not is simply that—a stereotype. Given the complexity and vast territory of emotion, we should not be surprised that this stereotype is not supported when actual emotional experiences are examined. Thus, for many emotional experiences, researchers do not find differences between females and males—both sexes are equally likely to feel love, jealousy, anxiety in new social situations, anger when they are insulted, grief when close relationships end, and embarrassment when they make mistakes in public (Tavris & Wade, 1984).

And what about gender and achievement—do females and males differ in achievement? For some areas of achievement, gender differences are so large they can best be described as nonoverlapping. For example, no major league baseball players are female, and 96 percent of all registered nurses are female. In contrast, many measures of achievement-related behaviors do not reveal gender differences. For example, girls show just as much persistence at tasks. The question of whether males and females differ in their expectations for success at various achievement tasks is not yet settled.

Gender Controversey

Not all psychologists agree that sex differences between females and males are rare or small. Alice Eagly (1995, 1996) stated that the belief that such differences are rare or small is due to a feminist commitment to gender similarity as a route to political equality and arose from piecemeal and inadequate interpretations of relevant empirical research. Many feminists express a fear that differences will be interpreted as deficiencies on the part of females, and as biologically based, which could revive traditional stereotypes that women are innately inferior to men (Unger & Crawford, 1996). Eagly (1995, 1996) argues that contemporary psychology has produced a large body of research revealing that behavior is sex differentiated to varying extents.

Evolutionary psychologist David Buss (1995) argues that men and women differ in some psychological domains—specifically, those domains in which they have faced different adaptive problems across their evolutionary history. In all other domains, predicts Buss, the sexes are psychologically similar. He cites a sex difference in the cognitive domain that favors males—spatial rotation. This ability is essential for hunting, in which the trajectory of a projectile must anticipate the trajectory of a prey animal as each moves through space and time. Buss also cites a sex difference in casual sex, with men engaging in this behavior more often than women. In one study, men said that ideally they would like to have more than 18 sex partners in their lifetime, whereas women stated that ideally they would like to have only 4 or 5 (Buss & Schmitt, 1993). In another study, 75 percent of the men but none of the women approached by an attractive stranger of the opposite sex consented to a request for sex (Clark & Hatfield, 1989). Such sex differences, says Buss, are exactly the type predicted by evolutionary psychology.

How does context influence gender? For example, how does the context influence the nature of helping in females and males? Emotion?

likely to show anger toward strangers, especially male strangers, when they feel that they have been challenged. Males also are more likely than females to turn their anger into aggressive action (Travis & Wade, 1984). Emotional differences between females and males are most common in contexts that highlight social roles and relationships. For example, females are more likely than males to discuss emotions in terms of interpersonal relationships (Saarni, 1988). And they are more likely than males to express fear and sadness, especially when communicating with their friends and family.

At this point we have discussed a number of ideas about what gender is, biological, social, and cognitive influences on gender, and gender stereotypes, similarities, and differences. A summary of these ideas is presented in concept table 13.1.

GENDER-ROLE CLASSIFICATION

How were gender roles classified in the past? What is androgyny? Is a strong masculine orientation related to problem behaviors in adolescent males? What is gender-role transcendence?

In sum, there is great controversy over whether sex differences are rare and small or common and large (Derry, 1996; Maracek, 1995). The controversy is evidence that negotiating the science and politics of gender is not an easy task (Eagly, 1995).

Gender in Context

When thinking about gender similarities and differences, keep in mind that the contexts in which females and males are thinking, feeling, and acting should be taken into account (Harter, Waters, & Whitesell, 1996). To see the importance of context, let's explore helping behavior and emotion in relation to gender.

Males are more likely to help in situations in which a perceived danger is present and in which males feel most competent to help (Eagly & Crowley, 1986). For example, males are more likely than females to help a person who is stranded by the roadside with a flat tire, because automobile problems are a context in which many males feel a sense of competence. In contrast, if the context involves volunteering time to help a child with a personal problem, females are more likely to help because there is little danger present and females feel more competent at nurturing. In many cultures, girls show more caregiving behavior than boys do (Blakemore, 1993). However, in the few cultures where boys and girls both care for younger siblings on a regular basis, boys and girls have similar tendencies to nurture (Whiting, 1989).

For both males and females, the display of emotion also depends upon context (Anderson & Leaper, 1996; Shields, 1991). Consider anger. Males are more

The Past

At a point not too long ago, it was accepted that boys should grow up to be masculine and that girls should grow up to be feminine, that boys are made of frogs and snails and puppy dogs' tails, and that girls are made of sugar and spice and all that's nice. Today, diversity characterizes gender roles and the feedback individuals receive from their culture. A girl's mother might promote femininity, the girl might be close friends with a tomboy, and the girl's teachers at school might encourage her assertiveness.

In the past, the well-adjusted male was expected to be independent, aggressive, and power oriented. The well-adjusted female was expected to be dependent, nurturant, and uninterested in power. Further, masculine characteristics were considered to be healthy and good by society; female characteristics were considered to be undesirable. A classic study in the early 1970s summarized the traits and behaviors that college students believed were characteristic of males and those they believed were characteristic of females (Broverman & others, 1972). The traits were clustered into two groups that were labeled "instrumental" and "expressive." The instrumental traits paralleled the male's purposeful, competent entry into the outside world to gain goods for his family; the expressive traits paralleled the female's responsibility to be warm and emotional in the home. Such stereotypes are more harmful to females than to males because the characteristics assigned to males are more valued than those assigned to females. The beliefs and stereotypes have led to the negative treatment of females because of their sex, or what is called *sexism*. Females

The Nature of Gender, Biological, Social, and Cognitive Influences on Gender, and Gender Stereotypes, Similarities, and Differences

Concept	Processes/Related Ideas	Characteristics/Description
What Is Gender?	Its nature	*Gender* refers to the social dimension of being male or female. A gender role is a set of expectations that prescribes how females or males should think, act, and feel.
Biological, Social, and Cognitive Influences	Biological influences	Freud's and Erikson's theories promote the idea that anatomy is destiny. Hermaphrodites are individuals whose genitals become intermediate between male and female because of a hormonal imbalance. Today's child developmentalists are all interactionists when biological and environmental influences on gender are considered. However, interaction means different things to different people.
	Social influences	Both identification theory and social learning theory emphasize the adoption of parents' gender characteristics. Peers are especially adept at rewarding gender-apropriate behavior. There is still concern about gender inequity in education. A special concern is that middle schools are better suited to males because their environment promotes impersonality and independence. Despite improvements, TV still portrays males as more competent than females.
	Cognitive influences	Both cognitive developmental and gender schema theories emphasize the role of cognition in gender development. Gender is present in the language children use and encounter. The language children hear most of the time is sexist.
Gender Stereotypes, Similarities and Differences	Stereotypes	Gender stereotypes are widespread around the world, especially emphasizing the male's power and the female's nurturance.
	Similarities and differences	A number of physical and biological differences exist between females and males. Some experts, such as Hyde, argue that cognitive differences between males and females have been exaggerated. In terms of socioemotional development, males are more aggressive and active than females, while females emphasize social ties.
	Gender controversy	There is great controversy over how similar or different males and females are in a number of areas.
	Gender in context	An important dimension of understanding gender is to consider the context that is involved.

receive less attention in schools, are less visible in leading roles on television, are rarely depicted as competent, dominant characters in children's books, are paid less than males even when they have more education, and are underrepresented in decision-making roles throughout our society, from corporate executive suites to Congress.

Androgyny

In the 1970s, as both males and females became dissatisfied with the burdens imposed by their strictly stereotyped roles, alternatives to "masculinity" and "femininity" were explored. Instead of thinking of masculinity and femininity as a continuum, with more of one meaning less of the other, it was proposed that individuals could show both expressive *and* instrumental traits. This thinking

led to the development of the concept of **androgyny,** *the presence of desirable masculine and feminine characteristics in the same individual* (Bem, 1977; Spence & Helmreich, 1978). The androgynous individual might be a male who is assertive (masculine) and nurturant (feminine), or a female who is dominant (masculine) and sensitive to others' feelings (feminine).

Measures have been developed to assess androgyny. One of the most widely used gender measures, the Bem Sex-Role Inventory, was constructed by a leading early proponent of androgyny, Sandra Bem. To see what the items on Bem's measure are like, see table 13.1. Based on their responses to the items in the Bem Sex-Role Inventory, individuals are classified as having one of four gender-role orientations: masculine, feminine, androgynous, or undifferentiated (see figure 13.6). The androgynous

TABLE 13.1

The Bem Sex-Role Inventory: Are You Androgynous?

The following items are from the Bem Sex-Role Inventory. To find out whether you score as androgynous, first rate yourself on each item, on a scale from 1 (never or almost never true) to 7 (always or almost always true).

1. self-reliant	17. loyal	32. compassionate	47. gullible
2. yielding	18. unpredictable	33. sincere	48. inefficient
3. helpful	19. forceful	34. self-sufficient	49. acts as a leader
4. defends own beliefs	20. feminine	35. eager to soothe hurt	50. childlike
5. cheerful	21. reliable	feelings	51. adaptable
6. moody	22. analytical	36. conceited	52. individualistic
7. independent	23. sympathetic	37. dominant	53. does not use harsh
8. shy	24. jealous	38. soft-spoken	language
9. conscientious	25. has leadership abilities	39. likable	54. unsystematic
10. athletic	26. sensitive to the needs of	40. masculine	55. competitive
11. affectionate	others	41. warm	56. loves children
12. theatrical	27. truthful	42. solemn	57. tactful
13. assertive	28. willing to take risks	43. willing to take a stand	58. ambitious
14. flatterable	29. understanding	44. tender	59. gentle
15. happy	30. secretive	45. friendly	60. conventional
16. strong personality	31. makes decisions easily	46. aggressive	

SCORING
(a) Add up your ratings for items 1, 4, 7, 10, 13, 16, 19, 22, 25, 28, 31, 34, 37, 40, 43, 46, 49, 55, and 58. Divide the total by 20. That is your masculinity score.
(b) Add up your ratings for items 2, 5, 8, 11, 14, 17, 20, 23, 26, 29, 32, 35, 38, 41, 44, 47, 50, 53, 56, and 59. Divide the total by 20. That is your femininity score.
(c) If your masculinity score is above 4.9 (the approximate median for the masculinity scale) and your femininity score is above 4.9 (the approximate femininity median) then you would be classified as androgynous on Bem's scale.

From Janet S. Hyde, *Half the Human Experience: The Psychology of Women,* 3d ed. Copyright © 1985 D. C. Heath and Company, Lexington, MA. Reprinted by permission.

individual is simply a female or a male who has a high degree of both feminine (expressive) and masculine (instrumental) traits. No new characteristics are used to describe the androgynous individual. A feminine individual is high on feminine (expressive) traits and low on masculine (instrumental) traits; a masculine individual shows the reverse of these traits. An undifferentiated person is not high on feminine or masculine traits.

Androgynous individuals are described as more flexible and more mentally healthy than either masculine or feminine individuals. Individuals who are undifferentiated are the least competent. To some degree, though, the context influences which gender type is most adaptive. In close relationships, femininity or androgyny might be more desirable because of the expressive nature of close relationships. However, masculinity or androgyny might be more desirable in academic and work settings because of the instrumental nature of these settings. To further evaluate gender roles, turn to Critical Thinking About Children's Development.

The culture in which individuals live also plays an important role in determining what is adaptive. On the one hand, increasing numbers of children in the United States and other modernized countries, such as Sweden, are being raised to behave in androgynous ways. On the other hand, traditional gender roles continue to dominate the cultures of many countries around the world. To

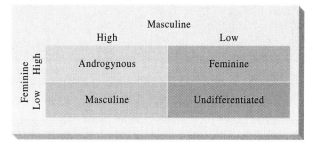

Figure~13.6

Gender-Role Classification

read about traditional gender-role practices in Egypt, as well as the nature of gender roles in China, turn to Sociocultural Worlds of Children.

Traditional Masculinity and Problem Behaviors in Males

As females and males experience many physical and social changes during early adolescence, they have to come to terms with new definitions of their gender roles. During early adolescence, individuals develop the adult, physical aspects of their gender. Some theorists and researchers have proposed that, with the onset of puberty, girls and boys experience an intensification in gender-related

CRITICAL THINKING ABOUT CHILDREN'S DEVELOPMENT

Gender Roles, Parenting, and the Future

In the last two decades, dramatic changes in gender roles have taken place in the United States. How much change have you personally experienced? How do you think gender roles will be different in the twenty-first century? Or do you believe that gender roles will stay about the way they are now?

There is a practical side to considering such questions. How will you raise your children, in terms of gender matters? Will gender neutrality be your goal? Will you encourage more traditional gender distinctions? By evaluating the nature of gender roles, parenting, and the future, *you are learning to think critically by applying developmental concepts to enhance personal adaptation.*

The gender intensification hypothesis states that psychological and behavioral differences between boys and girls become greater during early adolescence because of increased socialization, pressures to conform to traditional masculine and feminine gender roles. Puberty's role in gender intensification may involve a signaling to socializing others—parents, peers, and teachers, for example—that the adolescent is beginning to approach adulthood and, therefore, should begin to act in ways that resemble the stereotypical female or male adult.

expectations. The **gender intensification hypothesis** *states that psychological and behavioral differences between boys and girls become greater during early adolescence because of increased socialization pressures to conform to traditional masculine and feminine gender roles* (Hill & Lynch, 1983; Lynch, 1991). Puberty's role in gender intensification may involve a signaling to socializing others—parents, peers, and teachers, for example—that the adolescent is beginning to approach adulthood and therefore should begin to act more in ways that resemble stereotypical female or male adult behavior. In one recent study, sex differences in gender-role attitudes increased across the early adolescent years (Galambos, Almeida, & Petersen, in press). Gender-role attitudes were measured by the Attitudes Toward Women Scale (Galambos & others, 1985), which assesses the extent to which adolescents approve of gender-based division of roles. For example, the adolescent is asked such questions as whether girls should have the same freedom as boys. Other researchers also have reported evidence of gender intensification in early adolescence (Hill & Lynch, 1983).

There is a special concern about adolescent boys who adopt a strong masculine role in adolescence, because this is increasingly being found to be associated with problem behaviors. Joseph Pleck (Pleck, 1983, 1995) believes that what defines traditional masculinity in many Western cultures includes behaviors that do not have social approval but nonetheless validate the adolescent boy's masculinity. That is, in the male adolescent culture, male adolescents perceive that they will be perceived as more masculine if they engage in premarital sex, drink alcohol and take drugs, and participate in illegal delinquent activities.

The idea that male problem behaviors have something to do with "masculinity" has gotten the attention of policymakers. U.S. Department of Health and Human Services Secretary Louis Sullivan (1991) called for action to address a generation for whom a male's manhood is measured by the caliber of gun he carries or the number of children he has fathered. In a similar vein, Virginia Governor Douglas Wilder (1991) urged policymakers to get across the message that, contrary to what many of today's youth think, making babies is no act of manhood. Addressing and challenging traditional beliefs about masculinity in adolescent males may have the positive outcome of helping to reduce their problem behaviors.

Gender-Role Transcendence

Although the concept of androgyny was an improvement over exclusive notions of femininity and masculinity, it has turned out to be less of a panacea than many of its early proponents envisioned (Paludi, 1995). Some theorists, such as Pleck (1983), believe that the idea of androgyny

SOCIOCULTURAL WORLDS OF CHILDREN

Gender Roles in Egypt and China

In recent decades, roles assumed by males and females in the United States have become increasingly similar—that is, androgynous. In many countries, though, gender roles have remained more gender-specific. For example, in Egypt, the division of labor between Egyptian males and females is dramatic: Egyptian males are socialized to work in the public sphere, females in the private world of home and child rearing. The Islamic religion dictates that the man's duty is to provide for his family, the woman's to care for her family and household (Dickerscheid & others, 1988). Any deviations from this traditional gender-role orientation are severely disapproved of.

Egypt is not the only country in which males and females are socialized to behave, think, and feel in strongly gender-specific ways. Kenya and Nepal are two other cultures in which children are brought up under very strict gender-specific guidelines (Munroe, Himmin, & Munroe, 1984). In the People's Republic of China, the female's status has historically been lower than the male's. The teachings of the fifth-century B.C. Chinese philosopher Confucius were used to reinforce the concept of the female as an inferior being. Beginning with the 1949 revolution in China, women began to achieve more economic freedom and more-equal status in marital relationships. However, even with the sanctions of a socialist government, the old patriarchal traditions of male supremacy in China have not been completely uprooted. Chinese women still make considerably less money than Chinese men in comparable positions, and in rural China a tradition of male supremacy still governs many women's lives.

Thus, while in China, females have made considerable strides, complete equality remains a distant objective. And in many cultures, such as Egypt and other countries where the Muslim religion predominates, gender-specific behavior is pronounced, and females are not given access to high-status positions.

In Egypt, near the Aswan Dam, women are returning from the Nile river, where they have filled their water jugs. How might gender-role socialization for girls in Egypt compare to that in the United States?

In China, females and males are usually socialized to behave, feel, and think differently. The old patriarchal traditions of male supremacy have not been completely uprooted. Chinese women still make considerably less money than Chinese men do, and, in rural China (such as here in the Lixian Village of Sichuan, male supremacy still governs many women's lives.

should be replaced with the idea of **gender-role transcendence,** *the belief that, when an individual's competence is at issue, it should be conceptualized not on the basis of masculinity, femininity, or androgyny, but rather on a personal basis.* Thus, rather than merging gender roles or stereotyping people as "masculine" or "feminine," Pleck believes we should begin to think about people as people. However, the concepts of androgyny and gender-role transcendence draw attention away from women's unique needs and the power imbalance between women and men in most cultures (Hare-Muston & Maracek, 1988).

> *To be meek, patient, tactful, modest, honorable, brave, is not to be either manly or womanly; it is to be humane.*
>
> —Jane Harrison

DEVELOPMENTAL WINDOWS OF GENDER OPPORTUNITY AND ASYMMETRIC GENDER SOCIALIZATION

Are children more prone to forming gender roles at some points in development than at others? Are the amount, timing, and intensity of gender socialization different for girls and boys?

Developmental Windows of Gender Opportunity

Do gender lessons have to be hammered into children's heads year after year? Apparently not, according to gender expert Carol Beal (1994). Instead, what girls and boys learn about gender seems to be learned quickly at certain points in development, especially when new abilities first emerge. For example, considerable gender learning occurs during the toddler years, when children first make bids for autonomy and begin to talk. Children form many ideas about what the sexes are like during the toddler years from about 1½ to 3 years of age. Many parents don't really start to think about gender issues involving their child until preschool or kindergarten, but at that point children have already altered their gender behavior and learned to think of themselves as a girl or a boy. Few parents have to tell their little boys not to wear pink pants to the first grade!

Early adolescence is another transitional point that seems to be especially important in gender development. Young adolescents have to cope with the enormous changes of puberty, changes that are intensified by their expanding cognitive abilities that make them acutely aware of how they appear to others. Relations with others change extensively as dating relationships begin and sexuality is experienced. Adolescents often cope with the stress of these changes by becoming more conservative

and traditional in their gender thinking and behavior, a tendency that is enhanced by media stereotypes of females and males.

Asymmetric Gender Socialization

The amount, timing, and intensity of gender socialization is different for girls and boys (Beal, 1994). Boys receive earlier and more intense gender socialization than girls do. The social cost of deviating from the expected male role is higher for boys than is the cost for girls of deviating from the expected female role, in terms of peer rejection and parental disapproval. Imagine a girl who is wearing a toy holster, bandanna, and cowboy hat, running around in the backyard pretending to herd cattle. Now imagine a boy who is wearing a flowered hat, ropes of pearls, and lipstick, pretending to cook dinner on a toy stove. Which of these do you have a stronger reaction to—the girl's behavior or the boy's? Probably the boy's. Researchers have found that "effeminate" behavior in boys elicits much more negative reactions than does "masculine" behavior in girls (Feinman, 1981; Martin, 1990).

Boys might have a more difficult time learning the masculine gender role, because male models are less accessible to young children and messages from adults about the male role are not always consistent. For example, most mothers and teachers would like for boys to behave in masculine ways, but also to be neat, well-mannered, and considerate. However, fathers and peers usually want boys to behave in another way—independent and engaging in rough-and-tumble play. The mixed messages make it difficult for boys to figure out which gender role they should follow. According to Beal (1994), although gender roles have become more flexible in recent years, the flexibility has occurred more for girls than for boys. Girls can now safely be ambitious, competitive, and interested in sports, but relatively few adults are equally supportive of boys' being gentle, interested in fashion, and motivated to sign up for ballet classes.

WOMEN'S AND MEN'S ISSUES

Feminist scholars are developing new perspectives that focus on girls' and women's experiences and development. What is the nature of these women's issues? And what men's issues are involved in adolescent development?

Women's Issues

Many feminist scholars believe that, historically, psychology has portrayed human behavior with a "male dominant theme" (Paludi, 1995). They also believe that sexism is still rampant in society. As leading feminist scholar Jean Baker Miller (1986) wrote in *Toward a New Psychology of Women,*

> In the last decade it has become clearer that if women are trying to define and create a full personhood, we

are engaged in a huge undertaking. We see that this attempt means building a new way of living which encompasses all realms of life, from global economic, social and political levels to the most intimate personal relationships. (p. xi)

Feminist scholars are putting greater emphasis on women's life experiences and development, including girls and women as authorities about their own experiences or, as Harvard psychologist Carol Gilligan (1992) advocates, listening to women's voices.

> *We need every human gift and cannot afford to neglect any gift because of artificial barriers of sex or race or class or national origin.*
>
> —**Margaret Mead,** *Male and Female*

Miller (1986) has been an important voice in stimulating the examination of psychological issues from a female perspective. She believes that the study of women's psychological development opens up paths to a better understanding of all psychological development, male or female. She also concludes that, when researchers examine what women have been doing in life, they find that a large part of it is active participation in the development of others. In Miller's view, women often try to interact with others in ways that foster the others' development along many dimensions—emotionally, intellectually, and socially.

Many feminist thinkers believe that it is important for women not only to maintain their competency in relationships but to be self-motivated too. Miller believes that, through increased self-determination and already developed relationship skills, many women will gain greater power in the American culture. As feminist scholar Harriet Lerner (1989) concludes in her book *The Dance of Intimacy,* it is important for women to bring to their relationships nothing less than a strong, assertive, independent, and authentic self. She believes that competent relationships are those in which the separate "I-ness" of both persons can be appreciated and enhanced while the persons stay emotionally connected to each other.

Not only is a distinct female voice an important dimension of the feminist perspective on gender, but so is the effort to reduce and eventually end prejudice and discrimination against females (Paludi, 1995). Although females have broken through many male bastions in the past several decades, feminists argue that much work is left to be done. Feminists today believe that too many people passively accept traditional gender roles and believe that discrimination no longer exists in politics, work, the family, and education. They encourage individuals to question these assumptions, and especially strive to get females to evaluate the gender circumstances of their lives. For example, if you are a female, you may remember situations in which you were discriminated against because of your sex. If derogatory comments are made to you because you are a female, you might ask yourself why you have allowed these comments to go unchallenged or why they made you so angry. Feminists hope that, if you are a male, you will become more conscious of gender issues, of female and male roles, and of fairness and sensitivity interactions and relationships between females and males.

Men's Issues

The male of the species—what is he really like? What does he really want? As a result of the women's movement and its attack on society's male bias and discrimination against women, men have developed their own movement (Pollack, 1995). The men's movement has not been as political or as activist as the women's movement. Rather, it has been more an emotional, spiritual movement that reasserts the importance of masculinity and urges men to resist women's efforts to turn them into "soft" males. Or it has been a psychological movement that recognizes men's need to be less violent and more nurturant but still retain much of their masculine identity. Many of the men's movement disciples argue that society's changing gender arena has led many men to question what being a man really means.

Herbert Goldberg (1980) became a central figure in the early development of the men's movement in the 1970s and early 1980s, mainly as a result of his writings about men's rights in *The Hazards of Being Male* and *The New Male.* Goldberg argues that a critical difference between men and women creates a precipitous gulf between them. That difference: Women can sense and articulate their feelings and problems; men, because of their masculine conditioning, can't. The result is an armor of masculinity that is defensive and powerful in maintaining self-destructive patterns. Goldberg says that most men have been effective work machines and performers but that most else in their lives suffers. Men live about 8 years less than women, on the average, have higher hospitalization rates, and show more behavioral problems. In a word, Goldberg believes, millions of men are killing themselves by striving to be "true" men, a heavy price to pay for masculine "privilege" and power.

How can men solve their dilemma and live more physically and psychologically healthy lives? Goldberg argues that men need to get in touch with their emotions and their bodies. They can't do this by just piggybacking on the changes that are occurring in women's attitudes, he says. Rather, men need to develop their own realization of what is critical for their survival and well-being. Goldberg especially encourages men to do the following:

- Recognize the suicidal "success" syndrome and avoid it
- Understand that occasional impotence is nothing serious

- Become aware of their real needs and desires and get in touch with their own bodies
- Elude the binds of masculine role-playing
- Relate to liberated women as their equal rather than serving as their guilty servant or hostile enemy
- Develop male friendships

Goldberg's messages to men that they need to become more attuned to their inner self and emotional makeup and work on developing more positive close relationships are important ones. Other gender specialists echo Goldberg's belief that males need to improve the quality of their close relationships (Bergman, 1995; Pleck, 1995).

One author who helped to usher in a renewed interest in the men's movement in the 1990s is Robert Bly (1990), a poet, storyteller, translator, and best-selling author who is a disciple of Carl Jung's ideas. In *Iron John*, Bly says we live in a society that hasn't had fathers around since the Industrial Revolution. With no viable rituals for introducing young boys to manhood, today's men are left confused. Bly thinks that too many of today's males are "soft," having bonded with their mothers because their fathers were unavailable. These "soft" males know how to follow instead of lead, how to be vulnerable, and how to go with the flow, says Bly. He believes that they don't know what it's like to have a deep masculine identity. Iron John, a hairy mythological creature, has a deep masculine identity. He is spontaneous and sexual, an action taker, a boundary definer, and an earth preserver. He has untamed impulses and thoughtful self-discipline.

Bly not only writes poetry and books. He and his associates conduct 5-week gatherings and weekend workshops for men. At these gatherings, the participants try to capture what it is like to be a true man by engaging in such rituals as drum beating and naming ceremonies.

Many critics do not like Bly's strong insistence on the separateness of the sexes. Only masculine men and feminine women populate Bly's world. Feminist critics deplore Bly's approach, saying it is a regression to the old macho model of masculinity. Not everyone applauds Bly's belief that men can learn to become true men by going off into the woods to beat drums, dance around the fire, and bare their souls.

ETHNICITY AND GENDER

Are gender-related attitudes and behavior similar across different ethnic groups? All ethnic minority females are females, and all ethnic minority males are males, so there are many similarities in the gender-related attitudes of females across different ethnic minority groups and of males across different ethnic minority groups. Nevertheless, the different ethnic and cultural experiences of African American, Latino, Asian American, and Native American females and males need to be considered in understanding their gender-related attitudes and behavior,

Once a year, the giant wooden phallus made during one of Robert Bly's male retreats is raised and used as a centerpiece for a naming ceremony at the Mendocino's Men's Conference in California.

because in some instances even small differences can be important (Ballou, 1996; Jordan, 1997). For example, the socialization of males and females in other cultures who subsequently migrate to America often reflects a stronger gap between the status of males and females than is experienced in America. Keeping in mind that there are many similarities between females in all ethnic minority groups and between males in all ethnic minority groups, we examine, first, information about females from specific ethnic minority groups, followed by a discussion of males from specific ethnic minority groups.

Ethnic Minority Females

Let's now consider the behavior and psychological orientations of females from specific ethnic minority groups, beginning with African American females, and then in turn, study Asian American females, Mexican American females, and Native American females.

> *In the end, antiblack, antifemale, and all forms of discrimination are equivalent to the same thing—antihumanism.*
>
> —**Shirley Chisholm, Unbought and Unbossed**

Researchers in psychology have only begun to focus on the behavior of African American females. For too long, African American females only served as a comparison group for White females on selected psychological dimensions, or they served as the subjects in studies in which the primary research interest related to poverty, unwed motherhood, and so on (Hall, Evans, & Selice,

1989). This narrow research approach could be viewed as attributing no personal characteristics to African American females beyond the labels given to them by society.

The nature and focus of psychological research on African American females has begun to change—to some extent paralleling societal changes (Hall, Evans, & Selice, 1989). In the last decade, more individualized, positive dimensions of African American females are being studied, such as self-esteem, identity achievement, motivation, and self-control (Swanson, 1997). In the 1980s, psychological studies of African American females began to shift away from studies focused only on the problems of African American females and toward research on the positive aspects of African American females in a pluralistic society.

African American females, as well as other ethnic minority females, have experienced the double jeopardy of racism and sexism. The ingenuity and perseverance shown by ethnic minority females as they have survived and grown against the odds is remarkable. For example, 499 African American women earned doctoral degrees in 1986. This represents only 2 percent of the Ph.D.'s awarded (in comparison, 6.4 percent of the general population are African American females). However, the positive side of these figures is that the Ph.D.'s earned by African American women in 1986 represented an almost 16 percent increase over the number earned in 1977. Despite such gains, our society needs to make a strong commitment to providing African American, and other ethnic minority, females with the opportunities they deserve (Young, 1993).

Asian females are often expected to carry on domestic duties, to marry, to become obedient helpers of their mother-in-law, and to bear children, especially males (Nishio & Bilmes, 1993). In China, the mother's responsibility for the emotional nurturance and well-being of the family, and for raising children, derives from Confucian ethics. However, as China has become modernized, these roles have become less rigid. Similarly, in acculturated Chinese families in the United States, only derivatives of these rigidly defined roles remain. For example, Chinese American females are not entirely relegated to subservient roles.

Traditionally in Mexican American families, women assume the expressive role of homemaker and caretaker of children. This continues to be the norm, although less so than in the past (Chow, Wilkinson, & Baca Zinn, 1996; Comas-Diaz, 1993). Historically, the Mexican American female's role has been one of self-denial, and her needs were considered to be subordinate to those of other family members. Joint decision making and greater equality of males' and females' roles are becoming more characteristic of Mexican American families. Of special significance is the increased frequency of Mexican American women's employment outside the home, which in many instances has enhanced a wife's status in the family and in decision making (Espin, 1993).

For Native Americans, the amount of social and governing control exhibited by women or men depends on the tribe (LaFromboise, 1993; LaFromboise & Trimble, 1996). For example, in the traditional matriarchal Navajo family, an older woman might live with her husband, her unmarried children, her married daughter, and the daughter's husband and children. In patriarchal tribes, women function as the central "core" of the family, maintaining primary responsibility for the welfare of children. Grandmothers and aunts often provide child care. As with other ethnic minority females, Native American females who have moved to urban areas experience the cultural conflict between traditional ethnic values and the values of the American society.

Ethnic Minority Males

Just as ethnic minority females have experienced considerable discrimination and have had to develop coping strategies in the face of adversity, so have ethnic minority males (Coleman, 1996; Parham, 1996). As with ethnic minority females our order of discussion will be African American males, Asian American males, Mexican American males, and Native American males.

Some statistics provide a portrayal of the difficulties many African American males have faced (Parham & McDavis, 1993). African American males of all ages are three times as likely as White males to live below the poverty line. African American males aged 20 to 44 are twice as likely to die as White males. African American male heads of household earn 70 percent of the income of their White male counterparts. Although they make up only 6.3 percent of the U.S. population, African American males comprise 42 percent of jail inmates and more than 50 percent of men executed for any reason in the last 50 years! Murder by gun is the leading cause of death among African American males aged 15 to 19, and these rates are getting worse. From 1979 to 1989, the death rate by guns among this age group of African American males increased 71 percent. In one recent study, the problem of inadequate male role models in African American boys' development surfaced (Browne & others, 1993).

Statistics sometimes do not tell the complete story (Evans & Whitfield, 1988). The sociocultural aspects of historical discrimination against an ethnic minority group must be taken into account to understand these statistics (Neighbors & Jackson, 1996). Just as with African American females, researchers are beginning to focus on some of the more positive dimensions of African American males. For example, researchers are finding that African American males are especially efficient at the use of body language in communication, decoding nonverbal cues, multilingual/multicultural expression, and improvised problem solving.

Asian cultural values are reflected in traditional patriarchal Chinese and Japanese families (Copeland, Hwang,

& Brody, 1996; Leong, 1996; Sue & Sue, 1993). The father's behavior in relation to other family members is generally dignified, authoritative, remote, and aloof. Sons are generally valued over daughters. Firstborn sons have an especially high status. As with Asian American females, the acculturation experienced by Asian American males has eroded some of the rigid gender roles that characterized Asian families in the past. Fathers still are often the figurative heads of families, especially when dealing with the public, but in private they have relinquished some of their decision-making powers to their wives.

In Mexican American families, men traditionally assume the instrumental role of provider and protector of the family (Ramirez, 1989). The concept of machismo—being a macho man—continues to influence the role of the male and the patriarchal orientation of Mexican American families, though less so than in the past. Traditionally, this orientation required men to be forceful and strong, and also to withhold affectionate emotions. Ideally, it involved a strong sense of personal honor, family, loyalty, and care for children. However, it also has involved exaggerated masculinity and aggression. The concepts of machismo and absolute patriarchy are currently diminishing in influence among Mexican Americans, although adolescent males are still given much more freedom than adolescent females are in Mexican American families (Arrendondo, 1996).

Some Native American tribes are also patriarchal, with the male being the head of the family and primary decision maker. In some tribes, though, child care is shared by men. For example, Mescalero Apache men take responsibility for children when not working away from the family. Autonomy is highly valued among the male children in many Native American tribes, with the males operating semi-independently at an early age (LaFromboise, 1993). As with Native American females, increased movement to urban areas has led to modifications in the values and traditions of some Native American males.

At this point, we have discussed a number of ideas about gender-role classification; the feminist perspective on gender; and ethnicity and gender. A summary of these ideas is presented in concept table 13.2.

CONCEPT TABLE 13.2

Gender-Role Classification, Windows of Opportunity and Asymmetry, Women's and Men's Issues, and Ethnicity and Gender

Concept	Processes/Related Ideas	Characteristics/Description
How Can Gender Roles Be Classified?	The past	In the past, a well-adjusted male was supposed to show instrumental traits, a well-adjusted female expressive traits. Masculine traits were more valued by society. Sexism was widespread.
	Androgyny	In the 1970s, alternatives to traditional masculinity and femininity were explored. It was proposed that individuals could show both expressive and instrumental traits. This thinking led to the development of the concept of androgyny, the presence of desirable masculine and feminine traits in one individual. Gender-role measures often categorize individuals as masculine, feminine, androgynous, or undifferentiated. Androgynous individuals are often flexible and mentally healthy, although the particular context and the individual's culture also determine the adaptiveness of a gender-role orientation.
	Traditional masculinity and problem behaviors in males	As males and females experience many physical and social changes during adolescence, they must come to terms with a new definition of their gender roles. Some experts on adolescence believe that gender-role intensification occurs in early adolescence because of increased social pressures to conform to traditional masculine and feminine roles. Researchers have found that problem behaviors in adolescent males are associated with their having traditional beliefs about masculinity.
	Gender-role transcendence	One alternative to androgyny is gender-role transcendence, but like androgyny, it draws attention away from the imbalance of power between males and females.
Developmental Windows of Gender Opportunity and Asymmetric Gender Socialization	Developmental windows of gender opportunity	Two especially important transition points in learning gender roles are the toddler years and early adolescence.
	Asymmetric gender socialization	The amount, timing, and intensity of gender socialization are different for girls and boys. Boys receive earlier and more intense gender socialization than girls do. Boys also often have a more difficult time learning the masculine gender role, because male models are less accessible to boys than female models are to girls, and because the messages from adults about the male role are not always consistent.
Women's and Men's Issues	Women's issues	Feminist scholars are developing new perspectives that focus on girls' and women's experiences and development. Emphases include connectedness and self-determination as contributors to women's well-being. The feminist perspective stresses the importance of reducing and eventually ending prejudice and discrimination against females.
	Men's issues	As a result of the women's movement, men have developed their own movement. Herb Goldberg was a central figure in the men's movement. A special concern is the self-destructive behavior patterns of males that involve low interest in the inner self and a lack of connectedness to others.
Ethnicity and Gender	Similarities and differences	There are many similarities among the females in various ethnic minority groups and among the males in different ethnic minority groups, but even small differences can sometimes be important.
	Ethnic minority females	Researchers in psychology have only begun to focus on female behavior in specific ethnic groups in a positive way. Many ethnic minority females have experienced the double jeopardy of racism and sexism.
	Ethnic minority males	Just as ethnic minority females have experienced considerable discrimination and have had to develop coping strategies in the face of adversity, so have ethnic minority males. Just as with African American females, researchers are beginning to focus more on the positive dimensions of African American males.

This chapter has been about gender, our social worlds as females and males. Nowhere in children's development have there been more sweeping changes and more controversial issues than in gender. Few aspects of life are more central to children's identity than gender.

We began this chapter by contemplating tomorrow's gender worlds of today's children, and then defined what gender is. We studied biological, social, and cognitive influences and charted the nature of gender stereotypes, similarities and differences, gender controversy, and gender in context. Our examination of gender-role classification focused on the past, androgyny, gender-role intensification and problem behaviors in adolescent males, and gender-role transcendence. We discussed developmental windows of gender opportunity and asymmetric gender socialization. We also explored men's and women's issues, as well as ethnicity and gender.

Don't forget that you can obtain an overall summary of the chapter by again studying the two concept tables on pages 418 and 427. In the next chapter, we will turn our attention to another important facet of children's development—their moral development. In our discussion of moral development, we will study in greater detail Carol Gilligan's ideas on connectedness and relationships.

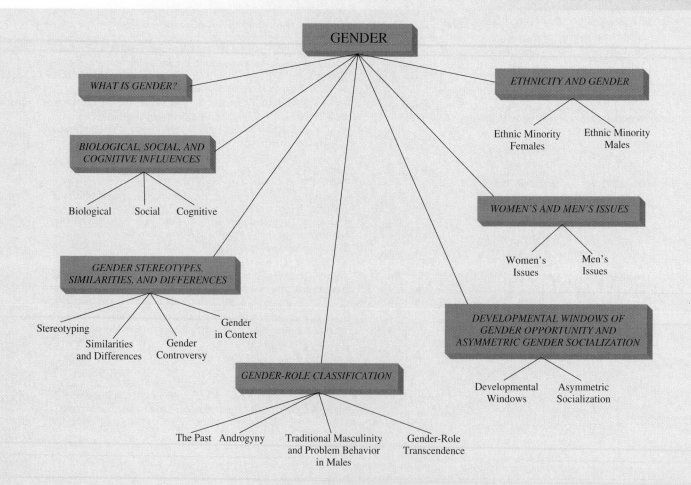

PRACTICAL KNOWLEDGE ABOUT CHILDREN

Alike and Different

(1992) edited by Bonnie Neugebauer, Washington, DC: National Association for the Education of Young Children.

This collection of practical essays addresses the many complex issues involved in educating young children from diverse ethnic backgrounds, as well as those with special needs. Special attention is given to nonsexist child-rearing curricula. The essays describe many useful activities that promote an antibias atmosphere in early childhood education, and they cover criteria for selecting antibiased books and materials, resources for diversity, and the interface between families and schools. A variety of excellent multicultural programs are outlined.

The Mismeasure of Woman

(1992) by Carol Tavris, New York: Simon & Schuster.

Tavris believes that no matter how hard women try, they can't measure up. They are criticized for being too female or not female enough, but they are always judged and mismeasured by how well they fit into a male world. *The Mismeasure of Woman* contains a thorough review of research studies that document how females are ignored, misrepresented, or even harmed by the still male-dominated health professions, which base their standards of normalcy on male anatomy, physiology, and psychology.

This is an excellent book on gender stereotyping, similarities and differences between the sexes, and how females should be measured by their own standards, not males'. It is well documented and captivating in presenting a witty portrayal of women's issues and dilemmas, and what can be done about them.

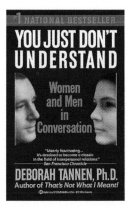

You Just Don't Understand

(1990) by Deborah Tannen, New York: Ballantine.

The subtitle of this book is "Women and Men in Conversation." This is a book about how women and men communicate—or all too often miscommunicate—with each other. *You Just Don't Understand* reached the status of number one on best-sellers lists, Tannen shows that friction between women and men in conversation often develops because boys and girls were brought up in two virtually distinct cultures. Tannen believes that the two gender cultures are distinguished by rapport talk (women) and report talk (men).

Tannen's book has especially connected with many females, who after reading it have wanted their husband or boyfriend to read it. The book is well written, well researched, and entertaining. Tannen has a keen sense for pinpointing ways in which talk gets us into trouble as females and males.

To further explore the nature of child development, we will examine a research study on family context and gender intensification, and we will discuss parenting, gender, achievement, and careers.

RESEARCH IN CHILD DEVELOPMENT

Family Context and Gender Intensification

Featured Study

Crouter, A. C., Manke, B. A., and McHale, S. M. (1995). The family context of gender intensification in early adolescence. *Child Development*, 66, 317–329.

Researchers have noted that during early adolescence boys and girls increasingly diverge in several areas of development, such as attitudes about gender roles and math. The explanation for this increasing divergence has usually been the belief that during adolescence there is increased socialization pressure to conform to traditional masculine and feminine roles. In this study, it was hypothesized that gender-differential socialization would increase early in adolescence, but that the family context would mediate gender intensification in early adolescence. More specifically, it was predicted that gender intensification would be strongest in families in which

(a) parents maintained a traditional division of labor, and (b) there was an opposite-sex younger sibling in the family.

Method

The study was longitudinal in nature, focusing on 144 youth who were 9 to 11 years of age when initially assessed (152 adolescents were initially assessed at time 1; 144 of them remained in the study at the second assessment 1 year later). The families were intact (stepfamilies and divorced families were not included). The father was employed full-time; the mother's work hours varied.

At both assessments, families participated in two types of data collection: home interviews and a series of telephone interviews. The measures included the following: (1) Background characteristics, such as parents' educational levels, work hours, and incomes. These were obtained during home interviews. (2) Adolescents' participation in household tasks. In telephone interviews, adolescents reported whether they had performed each of twelve household tasks, such as making beds, clean-

ing, and doing outdoor work. (3) Parent-child joint activities. The adolescent was interviewed to determine the extent to which parents and adolescents engaged in activities together, such as going to religious services, watching television, and playing a video game. (4) Parental monitoring. This was based on a set of questions asked of parents and adolescents about such areas as where and with whom the adolescent spent time that day. (5) Parental division of labor. This was based on husbands' and wives' reports of their involvement in each of eleven household tasks, such as cooking and gardening.

Results and Discussion

Based on longitudinal analyses of adolescents' participation in "feminine" and "masculine" household chores, adolescents' involvement in dyadic activities with mothers and fathers, and parental monitoring, gender intensification was apparent for some activities but not others. When gender intensification was apparent, it usually emerged in some family contexts but not others. Only dyadic parent-adolescent involvement was characterized by an overall pattern of gender intensification in which girls became increasingly involved with their mothers and boys with their fathers; this pattern was strongest in families in which the adolescent had a younger, opposite-sex sibling. Results of this study underscore the important point made earlier in this chapter—the context of gender is a key aspect for understanding gender's effects on children's development.

IMPROVING THE LIVES OF CHILDREN

Parenting, Gender, Achievement, and Careers

How much influence do parents have on their daughters' and sons' achievement and career orientation? Developmental psychologist Jacqueline Eccles and her colleagues (Eccles, 1993; Eccles & Harold, 1991; Harold & Eccles, 1990) believe the influence is substantial. In one recent study, 1,500 mothers and their daughters and sons were studied to determine the role of maternal expectations, advice, and provision of opportunities in their sons' and daughters' occupational aspirations. Mothers were more likely to encourage their sons to consider the military, to expect their sons to go into the military right after high school, and to discuss with their sons the education needed for, and likely income of, various jobs. Expecting marriage right after high school and discussing the problems of combining work and family were more common to their behavior toward their daughters. Also, mothers were more worried that their daughters would not have a happy marriage, and they were more likely to want their sons to have a job that would support a family. Further, mothers worked more with their sons on computers, and also more often provided them with computers, software, and programs. The mothers also bought more math or science books and games for the boys and more often enrolled them in computer classes. The sons were provided more sports opportunities, while girls were given more opportunities in music, art, and dance. The mothers said their sons had more talent in math and were better suited for careers in math, although they believed their daughters had more talent in English and were better suited for English-related careers.

The maternal advice, provision of opportunities, expectations, and ability assessments were associated with adolescents' occupational aspirations in the previous study. More often, these mothers tended to provide math or science books to daughters who aspired to male-typed occupations (nontraditional girls) than to daughters who aspired to female-typed jobs (traditional girls). The mothers talked about the importance of looking good more to their daughters who aspired to female-typed occupations than to their daughters who aspired to male-typed jobs. They also expected their daughters who aspired to female-typed occupations to be more likely to get married right after high school than their nontraditional counterparts. Further, several of the mothers' and adolescent daughters' family/work role values were related. For example, the mothers' belief that it was better for a man to be a breadwinner and a woman to take care of the family was related to the adolescents' belief. The mothers' belief that working mothers can establish just as warm and secure a relationship with their children as nonworking mothers was related to their adolescents' belief that it is all right for mothers to have full-time careers. The nontraditional girls were more likely to endorse the belief that women are better wives and mothers if they have paid jobs. In sum, this research study documented that parental socialization practices in the form of provision of opportunities, expectations, and beliefs are important sources of daughters' and sons' occupational aspirations (Eccles, 1993; Eccles & Wigfield, 1997; Harold & Eccles, 1990).

Pablo Picasso
Les Tuileries detail

Chapter

14

Moral Development

Chapter Outline

Chapter Boxes

IMAGES OF CHILDREN

Children's Perceptions of Morals on the Make-Believe Planet of Pax

PREVIEW

In this chapter we will explore such matters as equitable sharing, helping, rules and regulations, moral dilemmas, values, and self-control. Among the questions we will attempt to answer are these: What is moral development? What is the nature of children's moral thoughts, moral behavior, moral feelings, and altruism? Should children be morally educated, and if so, what should that education be like? And what is the nature of juvenile delinquency?

Can children understand such concepts as discrimination, economic inequality, affirmative action, and comparable worth? Probably not, if we use those terms, but might we be able to construct circumstances involving those concepts that they are able to understand? Phyllis Katz (1987) asked elementary-school-age children to pretend that they had taken a long ride on a spaceship to a make-believe planet called Pax. She asked for their opinions about various situations in which they found themselves. The situations involved conflict, socioeconomic inequality, and civil-political rights. For example, included in the conflict items was the question of what a teacher should do when two students were tied for a prize or when they have been fighting. The economic equality dilemmas included a proposed field trip that not all students could afford, a comparable-worth situation in which janitors were paid more than teachers, and an employment situation that discriminated against those with dots on their noses instead of stripes. The rights items dealt with minority rights and freedom of the press.

The elementary school children did indeed recognize injustice and often came up with interesting solutions to problems. For example, all but two children believed that teachers should earn as much as janitors—the holdouts said teachers should make less because they stay in one room or because cleaning toilets is more disgusting and therefore deserves higher wages. Children were especially responsive to the economic inequality items. All but one thought that not giving a job to a qualified applicant who had different physical characteristics (a dotted rather than a striped nose) was unfair. The majority recommended an affirmative action solution—giving the job to the one from the discriminated-against minority. None of the children verbalized the concept of freedom of the press or seemed to understand that a newspaper has the right to criticize a mayor in print without being punished. What are our schools teaching children about democracy? Some of the courses of action suggested were intriguing. Several argued that the reporters should be jailed. One child said that, if she were the mayor being criticized, she would worry, make speeches, and say, "I didn't do anything wrong," not unlike what American presidents have done in recent years. Another said that the mayor should not put the newspaper people out of work, because that might make them print more bad things. "Make them write comics instead," he said. The children believed that poverty exists on Earth but mainly in Africa, big cities, or Vietnam. War was mentioned as the biggest problem on Earth, although children were not certain whether it is presently occurring. Other problems mentioned were crime, hatred, school, smog, and meanness. Overall, the types of rules the children believed a society should abide by were quite sensible—almost all included the need for equitable sharing of resources and work and prohibitions against aggression.

WHAT IS MORAL DEVELOPMENT?

Moral development is one of the oldest topics of interest to those who are curious about human nature. In prescientific periods, philosophers and theologians heatedly debated children's moral status at birth, which they felt had important implications for how children should be reared. Today, people are hardly neutral about moral development; most have very strong opinions about acceptable and unacceptable behavior, ethical and unethical conduct, and the ways in which acceptable and ethical behaviors are to be fostered in children.

Moral development *concerns rules and conventions about what people should do in their interactions with other people.* In studying these rules, developmentalists examine three domains. First, how do children *reason or think* about rules for ethical conduct? For example, consider cheating. A child can be presented with a story in which someone has a conflict about whether or not to cheat in a particular situation, such as when taking a test in school. The child is asked to decide what is appropriate for the character to do and why. The focus is placed on the reasoning children use to justify their moral decisions.

Second, how do children actually *behave* in moral circumstances? In our example of cheating, emphasis is on observing the child's cheating and the environmental circumstances that produced and maintain the cheating. Children might be presented with some toys and asked to select which one they believe is the most attractive. Then, the experimenter tells the young child that the particular toy selected is someone else's and is not to be played with. Observations of different conditions under which the child deviates from the prohibition or resists temptation are conducted.

Third, how does the child *feel* about the moral matters? In the example of cheating, does the child feel enough guilt to resist temptation? If children cheat, do feelings of guilt after the transgression keep them from cheating the next time they face temptation?

It is important to note that moral development involves both *interpersonal* dimensions (involving others' rights and well-being) and *intrapersonal* dimensions (involving an individual's own basic values and sense of self) (Walker, 1996; Walker & Hennig, in press). The interpersonal dimension of moral development regulates people's social interactions and arbitrates conflicts. The intrapersonal dimension prescribes people's activities when they are not engaged in social interaction. In sum, moral development is a multifaceted concept.

MORAL THOUGHTS

How do children think about the standards of right and wrong? Piaget had some thoughts about this question, and so did Lawrence Kohlberg.

Piaget's Theory

Interest in how children think about moral issues was stimulated by Piaget (1932), who extensively observed and interviewed children from the ages of 4 through 12. Piaget watched children play marbles to learn how they used and thought about the game's rules. He also asked children questions about ethical issues—theft, lies, punishment, and justice, for example. Piaget concluded that children think in two distinct ways about morality, depending on their developmental maturity. **Heteronomous morality** is *the first stage of moral development in Piaget's theory, occurring from 4 to 7 years of age. Justice and rules are conceived of as unchangeable properties of the world, removed from the control of people.* **Autonomous morality** is *the second stage of moral development in Piaget's theory, displayed by older children (about 10 years of age and older). The child becomes aware that rules and laws are created by people and that, in judging an action, one should consider the actor's intentions as well as the consequences.* Children 7 to 10 years of age are in a transition between the two stages, evidencing some features of both.

Let's consider Piaget's two stages of moral development further. A heteronomous thinker judges the rightness or goodness of behavior by considering the consequences of the behavior, not the intentions of the actor. For example, the heteronomous thinker says that breaking 12 cups accidentally is worse than breaking 1 cup intentionally while trying to steal a cookie. For the moral autonomist, the reverse is true. The actor's intentions assume paramount importance. The heteronomous thinker also believes that rules are unchangeable and are handed down by all-powerful authorities. When Piaget suggested to a group of young children that new rules be introduced into the game of marbles, they resisted. They insisted that the rules had always been the same and could not be altered. In contrast, older children—who are moral autonomists—accept change and recognize that rules are merely convenient, socially agreed-upon conventions, subject to change by consensus.

The heteronomous thinker also believes in **immanent justice,** *the concept that, if a rule is broken, punishment will be meted out immediately.* The young child somehow believes that the violation is connected automatically to the punishment. Thus, young children often look around worriedly after committing a transgression, expecting inevitable punishment. Immanent justice also implies that if something unfortunate happens to someone it must be because the person had transgressed earlier. Older children, who are moral autonomists, recognize that punishment is socially mediated and occurs only if a relevant person witnesses the wrongdoing and that, even then, punishment is not inevitable.

Piaget argued that, as children develop, they become more sophisticated in thinking about social matters, especially about the possibilities and conditions of cooperation. Piaget believed that this social understanding comes about through the mutual give-and-take of peer relations. In the child's peer group, where others have power and status similar to the child's, plans are negotiated and coordinated, and disagreements are reasoned about and eventually settled. Parent-child relations, in which parents have the power and children do not, are less likely to advance moral reasoning, because rules are often handed down in an authoritarian way.

Remember that Piaget believed that adolescents usually become formal operational thinkers. Thus, they are no longer tied to immediate and concrete phenomena but are more logical, abstract, and deductive reasoners. Formal operational thinkers frequently compare the real to the ideal; create contrary-to-fact propositions; are cognitively capable of relating the distant past to the present; understand their roles in society, in history, and in the universe; and can conceptualize their own thoughts and think about their mental constructs as objects. For example, it usually is not until about the age of 11 or 12 that boys and girls spontaneously introduce concepts of belief, intelligence, and faith into their definitions of their religious identities.

Kohlberg's Theory

The most provocative view of moral development in recent years was crafted by Lawrence Kohlberg (Kohlberg, 1958, 1976, 1986). We will explore Kohlberg's concept of moral stages, influences on the Kohlberg stages, and Kohlberg's critics.

Kohlberg's Stages

Kohlberg believed that moral development is primarily based on moral reasoning and unfolds in a series of stages. He arrived at his view after extensively interviewing children about moral dilemmas. In the interview, children are presented with a series of stories in which characters face moral dilemmas. The following is the most popular of the Kohlberg dilemmas:

> In Europe a woman was near death from a special kind of cancer. There was one drug that the doctors thought might save her. It was a form of radium that a druggist in the same town had recently discovered. The drug was expensive to make, but the druggist was charging ten times what the drug cost him to make. He paid $200 for the radium and charged $2,000 for a small dose of the drug. The sick woman's husband, Heinz, went to everyone he knew to borrow the money, but he could only get together $1,000, which is half of what it cost. He told the druggist that his wife was dying and asked him to sell it cheaper or let him pay later. But the druggist said, "No, I discovered the drug, and I am going to make money from it." So Heinz got desperate and broke into the man's store to steal the drug for his wife. (Kohlberg, 1969, p. 379)

This story is one of eleven Kohlberg devised to investigate the nature of moral thought. After reading the story, interviewees answer a series of questions about the moral dilemma. Should Heinz have stolen the drug? Was stealing it right or wrong? Why? Is it a husband's duty to steal the drug for his wife if he can get it no other way? Would a good husband steal? Did the druggist have the right to charge that much when there was no law setting a limit on the price? Why?

Based on the answers interviewees gave for this and other moral dilemmas, Kohlberg concluded that three levels of moral development exist, each of which is characterized by two stages. A key concept in understanding moral development, especially for Kohlberg's theory, is **internalization,** *the developmental change from behavior that is externally controlled to behavior that is controlled by internal, self-generated standards and principles.* As children develop, their moral thoughts become more internalized. Let's look further at Kohlberg's three levels of development.

1. Kohlberg's Level 1: preconventional reasoning. **Preconventional reasoning** *is the lowest level in Kohlberg's theory of moral development. At this level, the child shows no internalization of moral values—moral reasoning is controlled by external rewards and punishments.*
    - Stage 1. **Punishment and obedience orientation** *is the first stage in Kohlberg's theory of moral development. At this stage, moral thinking is based on punishment.* Children obey because adults tell them to obey.
    - Stage 2. **Individualism and purpose** *is the second stage in Kohlberg's theory of moral development. At this stage, moral thinking is based on rewards and self-interest.* Children obey when they want to obey and when it is in their best interest to obey. What is right is what feels good and what is rewarding.

2. Kohlberg's Level 2: conventional reasoning. **Conventional reasoning** *is the second, or intermediate, level in Kohlberg's theory of moral development. At this level, children's internalization is intermediate. The child abides by certain standards (internal), but they are the standards of others (external), such as parents or the laws of society.*
    - Stage 3. **Interpersonal norms** *is the third stage in Kohlberg's theory of moral development. At this stage, children value trust, caring, and loyalty to others as the basis of moral judgments.* Children often adopt their parents' moral standards at this stage, seeking to be thought of by their parents as a "good girl" or a "good boy."
    - Stage 4. **Social system morality** *is the fourth stage in Kohlberg's theory of moral development. At this stage, moral judgments are based on*

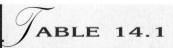

TABLE 14.1

Moral Reasoning at Kohlberg's Stages in Response to the "Heinz and the Druggist" Story

Stage Description	Examples of Moral Reasoning That Support Heinz's Theft of the Drug	Examples of Moral Reasoning That Indicate Heinz Should Not Steal the Drug
Preconventional Reasoning		
Stage 1: Avoid punishment	Heinz should not let his wife die; if he does, he will be in big trouble.	Heinz might get caught and sent to jail.
Stage 2: Seek rewards	If Heinz gets caught, he could give the drug back and maybe they would not give him a long jail sentence.	The druggist is a businessman and needs to make money.
Conventional Reasoning		
Stage 3: Gain approval/avoid disapproval especially with family	Heinz was only doing something that a good husband would do; it shows how much he loves his wife.	If his wife dies, he can't be blamed for it; it is the druggist's fault. He is the selfish one.
Stage 4: Conformity to society's rules	If you did nothing, you would be letting your wife die; it is your responsibility if she dies. You have to steal it with the idea of paying the druggist later.	It is always wrong to steal; Heinz will always feel guilty if he steals the drug.
Postconventional Reasoning		
Stage 5: Principles accepted by the community	The law was not set up for these circumstances; taking the drug is not really right, but Heinz is justified in doing it.	You can't really blame someone for stealing, but extreme circumstances don't really justify taking the law into your own hands. You might lose respect for yourself if you let your emotions take over; you have to think about the long term.
Stage 6: Individualized conscience	By stealing the drug, you would have lived up to society's rules, but you would have let down your conscience.	Heinz is faced with the decision of whether to consider other people who need the drug as badly as his wife. He needs to act by considering the value of all the lives involved.

understanding the social order, law, justice, duty. For example, an individual might say that it is always wrong to steal because laws that have been developed are for the good of society.

3. Kohlberg's Level 3: postconventional reasoning. **Postconventional reasoning** *is the highest level in Kohlberg's theory of moral development. At this level, morality is completely internalized and not based on others' standards.* The person recognizes alternative moral courses, explores the options, and then decides on a personal moral code.

- Stage 5. **Community rights versus individual rights** *is the fifth stage in Kohlberg's theory of moral development. At this stage, the person understands that values and laws are relative and that standards may vary from one person to another.* The person recognizes that laws are

important for society but knows that laws can be changed. The person believes that some values, such as liberty, are more important than the law.

- Stage 6. **Universal ethical principles** *is the sixth and highest stage in Kohlberg's theory of moral development. At this stage, one has developed a moral standard based on universal human rights.* When faced with a conflict between law and conscience, the person will follow conscience, even though the decision might involve personal risk.

Some of the responses to the dilemma of Heinz and the druggist are given in table 14.1, which should provide you with a better understanding of the reasoning that occurs at the six stages in Kohlberg's theory.

Notice that whether Heinz steals the drug is not the important issue in Kohlberg's cognitive developmental theory. What is crucial is how the person reasons about the moral dilemma.

Kohlberg believed that these levels and stages occur in a sequence and are age related: Before age 9, most children reason about moral dilemmas in a preconventional way; by early adolescence, they reason in more conventional ways; and, by early adulthood, a small number of people reason in postconventional ways. In a 20-year longitudinal investigation, the uses of stages 1 and 2 decreased. Stage 4, which did not appear at all in the moral reasoning of the 10-year-olds, was reflected in the moral thinking of 62 percent of the 36-year-olds. Stage 5 did not appear until the age of 20 to 22 and never characterized more than 10 percent of the individuals. Thus, the moral stages appeared somewhat later than Kohlberg initially envisioned, and the higher stages, especially stage 6, were extremely elusive (Colby & others, 1983). Recently, stage 6 was removed from the Kohlberg scoring manual but is still considered to be theoretically important in the Kohlberg scheme of moral development.

Influences on the Kohlberg Stages

Kohlberg believed that children's moral orientation unfolds as a consequence of their cognitive development. Children construct their moral thoughts as they pass from one stage to the next rather than passively accepting a cultural norm of morality. Investigators have sought to understand the factors that influence children's movement through the moral stages, among them modeling, cognitive conflict, peer relations, and perspective-taking opportunities (Turiel, 1997).

Several investigators have attempted to advance individuals' levels of moral development by having a model present arguments that reflect moral thinking one stage above the individuals' established levels. These studies are based on the cognitive developmental concepts of equilibrium and conflict. By presenting moral information slightly beyond the children's cognitive level, a disequilibrium is created that motivates them to restructure their moral thought. The resolution of the disequilibrium and conflict should be toward increased competence, but the data are mixed. In one of the pioneer studies on this topic, Eliot Turiel (1966) discovered that children prefer a moral judgment stage one stage above their current stage over two stages above it. However, in the study, they chose one stage below their stage more often than one stage above it. Apparently, the children were motivated more by security needs than by the need to reorganize their thought to a higher level. Other studies indicate children prefer a more advanced stage over a less advanced stage (Rest, Turiel, & Kohlberg, 1969).

Since the early studies of stage modeling, a number of investigations have attempted to determine more precisely the effectiveness of various forms of stage modeling

Both Piaget and Kohlberg believed that peer relations are a critical part of the social stimulation that challenges children to advance their moral reasoning. The mutual give-and-take of peer relations provides children with role-taking opportunities that give them a sense that rules are generated democratically.

and argument (Lapsley & Quintana, 1985). The upshot of these studies is that virtually any plus-stage discussion format, for any length of time, seems to promote more advanced moral reasoning. For example, in one investigation (Walker, 1982), exposure to plus-two-stage reasoning (arguments two stages above the child's current stage of moral thought) was just as effective in advancing moral thought as plus-one-stage reasoning. Exposure to plus-two-stage reasoning did not produce more plus-two-stage reasoning but rather, like exposure to plus-one-stage reasoning, increased reasoning at one stage above the current stage. Other research has found that exposure to reasoning only one third of a stage higher than the individual's current level of moral thought advances that person's moral thought (Berkowitz & Gibbs, 1983). In sum, current research on modeling and cognitive conflict reveals that moral thought can be moved to a higher level through exposure to models or discussion that is more advanced than the child's level.

Kohlberg believed that peer interaction is a critical part of the social stimulation that challenges children to change their moral orientation. Whereas adults characteristically impose rules and regulations on children, the mutual give-and-take in peer interaction provides children with an opportunity to take the perspective of another person and to generate rules democratically. Kohlberg stressed that perspective-taking opportunities can, in principle, be engendered by any peer group encounter. Although Kohlberg believed that such perspective-taking opportunities are ideal for moral development, he also believed that certain types of parent-child experiences can induce the child to think at more advanced levels of moral thinking. In particular, parents who allow or encourage conversation about value-laden issues promote more advanced moral thought in their children; however, many parents do not systematically provide their children with such perspective-taking opportunities. Nonetheless, in one recent study, children's moral development was related to their parents' discussion style, which involved questioning and supportive interaction (Walker & Taylor, 1991). There is an increasing emphasis on the role of parenting in moral development (Eisenberg & Murphy, 1995).

Kohlberg's Critics

Kohlberg's provocative theory of moral development has not gone unchallenged (Lapsley, 1996; Puka, 1991). The criticisms involve the link between moral thought and moral behavior, the quality of the research, inadequate consideration of culture's role in moral development, and underestimation of the care perspective.

Moral Thought and Moral Behavior   Kohlberg's theory has been criticized for placing too much emphasis on moral thought and not enough emphasis on moral behavior. Moral reasons can sometimes be a shelter for immoral behavior. Bank embezzlers and presidents endorse the loftiest of moral virtues when commenting about moral dilemmas, but their own behavior may be immoral. No one wants a nation of cheaters and thieves who can reason at the postconventional level. The cheaters and thieves may know what is right, yet still do what is wrong.

In evaluating the relation between moral thought and moral behavior, consider the corrupting power of rationalizations and other defenses that disengage us from self-blame; these include reconstrual of the situation, euphemistic labeling, and attribution of blame to authorities, circumstances, or victims (Bandura, 1991).

Assessment of Moral Reasoning   Some developmentalists fault the quality of Kohlberg's research and believe that more attention should be paid to the way moral development is assessed (Boyes, Giordano, & Galperyn, 1993). For example, James Rest (1986) argued that alternative methods should be used to collect information about moral thinking instead of relying on a single method that requires individuals to reason about hypothetical moral dilemmas. Rest also said that Kohlberg's stories are extremely difficult to score. To help remedy this problem, Rest developed his own measure of moral development, called the Defining Issues Test (DIT).

The DIT attempts to determine which moral issues individuals feel are more crucial in a given situation by presenting them with a series of dilemmas and a list of definitions of the major issues involved (Kohlberg's procedure does not make use of such a list). In the dilemma of Heinz and the druggist, individuals might be asked whether a community's laws should be upheld or whether Heinz should be willing to risk being injured or caught as a burglar. They might also be asked to list the most

important values that govern human interaction. They are given six stories and asked to rate the importance of each issue involved in deciding what ought to be done. Then they are asked to list what they believe are the four most important issues. Rest argued that this method provides a more valid and reliable way to assess moral thinking than Kohlberg's method.

Researchers also have found that the hypothetical moral dilemmas posed in Kohlberg's stories do not match the moral dilemmas many children and adults face in their everyday lives (Walker, de Vries, & Trevethan, 1987). Most of Kohlberg's stories focus on the family and authority. However, when one researcher invited adolescents to write stories about their own moral dilemmas, the adolescents generated dilemmas that were broader in scope, focusing on friends, acquaintances, and other issues, as well as family and authority (Yussen, 1977). The adolescents' moral dilemmas also were analyzed in terms of their content. As shown in figure 14.1, the moral issue that concerned adolescents more than any other was interpersonal relationships.

Some moral development researchers believe that a valuable method is to have research participants recall and discuss real-life dilemmas from their own experience (Walker & others, 1987). This strategy can provide a valid assessment not only of their moral stage but also of how they interpret moral situations that are relevant to them.

Culture and Moral Development   Yet another criticism of Kohlberg's view is that it is culturally biased (Banks, 1993; Jensen, 1995; Miller, 1991, 1995). A review of research on moral development in twenty-seven countries concluded that moral reasoning is more culture-specific than Kohlberg envisioned and that Kohlberg's scoring system does not recognize higher-level moral reasoning in certain cultural groups (Snarey, 1987). Examples of higher-level moral reasoning that would not be scored as such by Kohlberg's system are values related to communal equity and collective happiness in Israel, the unity and sacredness of all life-forms in India, and the relation of the individual to the community in New Guinea. These examples of moral reasoning would not be scored at the highest level in Kohlberg's system because they do not emphasize the individual's rights and abstract principles of justice. One study assessed the moral development of twenty adolescent male Buddhist monks in Nepal (Huebner & Garrod, 1993). The issue of justice, a basic theme in Kohlberg's theory, was not of paramount importance in the monks' moral views, and their concerns about prevention of suffering and the role of compassion are not captured by Kohlberg's theory. More about cultural variations in adolescents' moral thought appears in Sociocultural Worlds of Children. In sum, although Kohlberg's approach does capture much of the moral reasoning voiced in various cultures around the world, as we

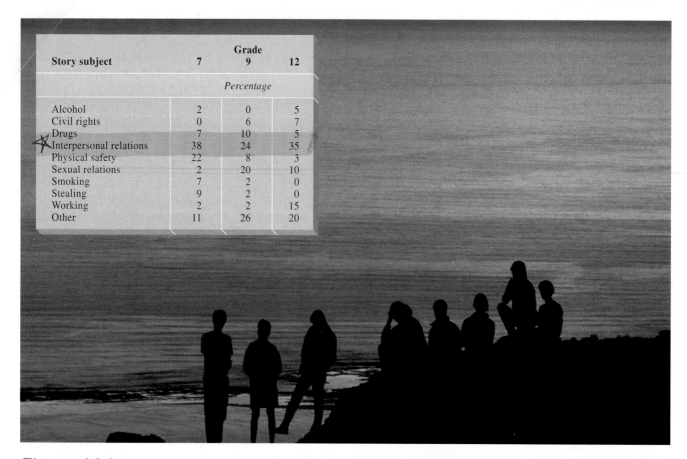

Story subject	Grade		
	7	9	12
	Percentage		
Alcohol	2	0	5
Civil rights	0	6	7
Drugs	7	10	5
Interpersonal relations	38	24	35
Physical safety	22	8	3
Sexual relations	2	20	10
Smoking	7	2	0
Stealing	9	2	0
Working	2	2	15
Other	11	26	20

Figure~14.1

Actual Moral Dilemmas Generated by Adolescents

have just seen, there are some important moral concepts in particular cultures that his approach misses or miscontrues (Haidt, 1997; Walker, 1996).

Gender and the Care Perspective

In chapter 13, we discussed Carol Gilligan's view that relationships and connections to others are critical aspects of female development. Gilligan (1982, 1992, 1996) also has criticized Kohlberg's theory of moral development. She believes that his theory does not adequately reflect relationships and concern for others. The **justice perspective** *is a moral perspective that focuses on the rights of the individual; individuals stand alone and independently make moral decisions. Kohlberg's theory is a justice perspective.* By contrast, the **care perspective** *is a moral perspective that views people in terms of their connectedness with others and emphasizes interpersonal communication, relationships with others, and concern for others. Gilligan's theory is a care perspective.* According to Gilligan, Kohlberg greatly underplayed the care perspective in moral development. She believes that this may have happened because he was a male, because most of his research was with males rather than females, and because he used male responses as a model for his theory.

In extensive interviews with girls from 6 to 18 years of age, Gilligan and her colleagues found that girls consistently interpret moral dilemmas in terms of human relationships and base these interpretations on listening and watching other people (Gilligan, 1992, 1996; Gilligan, Brown, & Rogers, 1990). According to Gilligan, girls have the ability to sensitively pick up different rhythms in relationships and often are able to follow the pathways of feelings. Gilligan believes that girls reach a critical juncture in their development when they reach adolescence. Usually around 11 to 12 years of age, girls become aware that their intense interest in intimacy is not prized by the male-dominated culture, even though society values women as caring and altruistic. The dilemma is that girls are presented with a choice that makes them look either selfish or selfless. Gilligan believes that, as adolescent girls experience this dilemma, they increasingly silence their "distinctive voice."

Contextual variations influence whether adolescent girls silence their "voice." In one recent study, Susan Harter and her colleagues (1996) found evidence for a refinement of Gilligan's position in that feminine girls reported lower levels of voice in public contexts (at school with teachers and classmates) but not in more private

SOCIOCULTURAL WORLDS OF CHILDREN

Children's Moral Reasoning in the United States and India

Cultural meaning systems vary around the world, and these systems shape children's morality (Miller & Bersoff, 1993). Consider a comparison of American and Indian Hindu Brahman children (Shweder, Mahapatra, & Miller, 1987). Like people in many other non-Western societies, Indians view moral rules as part of the natural world order. This means that Indians do not distinguish between physical, moral, and social regulation, as Americans do. For example, in India, violations of food taboos and marital restrictions can be just as serious as acts intended to cause harm to others. In India, social rules are seen as inevitable, much like the law of gravity.

As shown in figure 14.A, there is some, but not much, overlap in the moral concerns of children in Indian and American cultures. For Americans accustomed to viewing morality as a freely chosen social contract, Indian beliefs pose a different worldview, one that is not easy to reconcile with such treasured ideas as the autonomy of an individualized conscience. The interviews conducted by Richard Shweder and his colleagues (Shweder, Mahapatra, & Miller, 1987) with Indian and American children revealed sharp cultural differences in what people judge to be right and wrong. For example, Indian and American children disagree about eating beef. On the other hand, there are areas of overlap between the two cultures. For example, both think that breaking promises and ignoring beggars is wrong.

According to William Damon (1988), where culturally specific practices take on profound moral and religious significance, as in India, the moral development of children focuses extensively on their adherence to custom and convention. In contrast, Western moral doctrine tends to elevate abstract principles, such as justice and welfare, to a higher moral status than customs or conventions. As in India, socialization practices in many Third World countries actively instill in children a great respect for their culture's traditional codes and practices (Edwards, 1987).

Figure~14.A

Agreements/Disagreements Between American and Indian Hindu Brahman Children About Right and Wrong

Disagreement: Brahman children think it is right; American children think it is wrong.

—Hitting an errant child with a cane
—Eating with one's hands
—Father opening a son's letter

Disagreement: Brahman children think it is wrong; American children think it is right.

—Addressing one's father by his first name
—Eating beef
—Cutting one's hair and eating chicken after father's death

Agreement: Brahman and American children think it is wrong.

—Ignoring a beggar
—Destroying another's picture
—Kicking a harmless animal
—Stealing flowers

Agreement: Brahman and American children think it is right.

—Men holding hands

Carol Gilligan (*center*) is shown with some of the students she has interviewed about the importance of relationships in a female's development. According to Gilligan, the sense of relationships and connectedness is at the heart of female development.

interpersonal relationships with close friends and parents. However, androgynous girls reported a strong voice in all contexts. Harter and her colleagues also found that adolescent girls who buy into societal messages that females should be seen and not heard are at most risk in their development of a self. The greatest liabilities occurred for females who not only lacked a "voice" but emphasized the importance of appearance. In focusing on their outer selves, these girls face formidable challenges in meeting the punishing cultural standards of attractiveness.

Researchers have found support for Gilligan's claim that females' and males' moral reasoning often centers around different concerns and issues (Galotti, Kozberg, & Appleman, in press; Garmon, Basinger, & Gibbs, 1995; Wark & Krebs, 1996). However, one of Gilligan's initial claims—that traditional Kohlbergian measures of moral development are biased against females—has been extensively disputed. For example, most research studies using the Kohlberg stories and scoring system do not find sex differences (Walker, 1984). Thus, the strongest support for Gilligan's claims comes from studies that focus on items and scoring systems pertaining to close relationships, pathways of feelings, sensitive listening, and the rhythm of interpersonal behavior (Galotti, Kozberg, & Farmer, 1990).

While females often articulate a care perspective and males a justice perspective, the gender difference is not absolute, and the two orientations are not mutually exclusive (Lyons, 1990; Rothbart, Hanley, & Albert, 1986). For example, in one study, 53 of 80 females and males showed either a care or a justice perspective, but 27 subjects used both orientations, with neither predominating (Gilligan & Attanucci, 1988). To further evaluate the justice and care perspectives, turn to Critical Thinking About Children's Development.

MORAL BEHAVIOR

What are the basic processes that behaviorists believe are responsible for children's moral behavior? What is the nature of resistance to temptation and self-control? How do cognitive social learning theorists view children's moral development? We will explore each of these questions in turn.

Reinforcement, Punishment, Imitation, and Situational Variations

The study of moral behavior has been influenced primarily by social learning theory. The familiar processes of reinforcement, punishment, and imitation have been invoked to explain how and why children learn certain responses and why their responses differ from one another; the general conclusions to be drawn are the same as elsewhere. When children are reinforced for behavior that is consistent with laws and social conventions, they are likely to repeat that behavior. When provided with models who behave "morally," children are likely to adopt their actions. Finally, when children are punished for "immoral" or unacceptable behaviors, those behaviors can be eliminated, but at the expense of sanctioning punishment by its very use and of causing emotional side effects for the child.

To these general conclusions are added some qualifiers. The effectiveness of reward and punishment depends on the consistency with which they are administered and the schedule (for example, continuous or partial) that is adopted. The effectiveness of modeling depends on the characteristics of the model (such as esteem or power) and the presence of symbolic codes to enhance retention of the modeled behavior.

What kind of adult moral models are children being exposed to in our society? Do such models usually do what they say? There is evidence that the adult models children are exposed to often display a double standard, with their moral thinking not always corresponding to their actions. A poll of 24,000 Americans sampled their views on a wide variety of moral issues. Eight detailed scenarios of everyday moral problems were developed to test moral decision making. A summary of the responses to these moral dilemmas is shown in table 14.2. Consider the example of whether the person queried would knowingly buy a stolen color television set. More than 20 percent of the respondents said they would, even though 87 percent said that such an act is probably morally wrong. Further, approximately 31 percent of the adults said that, if they knew they would not get caught, they would be more likely to buy the stolen television. Although moral thought is a very important dimension of moral development, these data glaringly point out that what people believe about right and wrong does not always predict how they will act in moral situations.

In addition to emphasizing the role of reinforcement, punishment, and imitation in determining moral behavior, behaviorists make a strong claim that moral behavior is situationally dependent. That is, from the behavioral perspective, children do not consistently display moral behavior in different situations. In a classic investigation of moral behavior, one of the most extensive ever conducted, Hugh Hartshorne and Mark May (1928–1930) observed the moral responses of 11,000 children who were given the opportunity to lie, cheat, and steal in a variety of circumstances—at home, at school, at social events, and in athletics. A completely honest or a completely dishonest child was difficult to find. Situation-specific behavior was the rule. Children were more likely to cheat when their friends put pressure on them to do so and when the chance of being caught was slim. Other analyses of the consistency of moral behavior suggest that, although moral behavior is influenced by situational determinants, some children are more likely than others to cheat, lie, and steal (Burton, 1984).

Resistance to Temptation and Self-Control

A key ingredient of moral development from the social learning perspective is a child's ability to resist temptation and to develop self-control (Bandura, 1986; Mischel, 1987). When pressures mount for children to cheat, lie, or steal, it is important to ask whether they have developed the ability to control themselves and to resist such temptations.

Developmentalists have invented a number of ways to investigate such temptations. In one procedure, children are shown attractive toys and told that the toys belong to someone else, who has requested that they not be touched. Children then experience social influence, perhaps in the form of a discussion of virtues about respecting other people's property or in the form of a model resisting or giving in to the temptation to play with prohibited objects. Children are left alone in the room to amuse themselves when the experimenter departs (under a pretext), announcing that he or she will return in 10 to 15 minutes. The experimenter then watches through a one-way mirror to see whether children resist or give in to the temptation to play with the toys.

There has been considerable interest in examining the effects of punishment on children's ability to resist temptation (Parke, 1972, 1977). For the most part, offering

TABLE 14.2

The Hypocrisy of Adult Moral Models

Would You:	Percent Who Said Yes, or Probably:	Percent Who Said It Is, or Probably Is, Unethical:	Percent Who Would, or Probably Would, Be More Likely to If Sure They Would Not Get Caught:
Drive away after scratching a car without telling the owner?	44%	89%	52%
Cover for a friend's secret affair?	41	66	33
Cheat on your spouse?	37	68	42
Keep $10 extra change at a local supermarket?	26	85	33
Knowingly buy a stolen color television set?	22	87	31
Try to keep your neighborhood segregated?	13	81	8
Drive while drunk?	11	90	24
Accept praise for another's work?	4	96	8

Reprinted with permission from *Psychology Today* magazine. Copyright © 1993 (Sussex Publishers, Inc.).

children cognitive rationales enhances most forms of punishment, such as reasons why a child should not play with a forbidden toy. Cognitive rationales have been more effective in getting children to resist temptation over a period of time than have strategies that do not use reasoning, such as when parents place children in their rooms without explaining the consequences for others of the children's deviant behavior.

The ability to resist temptation is closely tied to delay of gratification. Self-control is involved in both the ability to resist temptation and the ability to delay gratification. In the case of resisting temptation, children must overcome their impulses to get something that is desired but is known to be prohibited. Similarly, children must show a sense of patience and self-control in delaying gratification for a desirable future reward rather than succumbing to the immediate pressure of pursuing a smaller reward.

Considerable research has been conducted on children's self-control. Walter Mischel (1974) believes that self-control is strongly influenced by cognitive factors. Researchers have shown that children can instruct themselves to be more patient and, in the process, show more self-control. In one investigation, preschool children were asked to perform a very dull task (Mischel & Patterson, 1976). Close by was a very enticing talking

mechanical clown that tried to persuade the children to play with it. The children who had been trained to say to themselves, "I'm not going to look at Mr. Clown when Mr. Clown says to look at him" were more likely to control their behavior and continue working on the dull task than were children who were not given the self-instructional strategy.

Interest in the cognitive factors in resistance to temptation, delay of gratification, and self-control reflects the increasing interest among social learning theorists in the ways in which such cognitions mediate the link between environmental experiences and moral behavior. Next, we will examine a view that captures this cognitive trend.

Cognitive Social Learning Theory

The **cognitive social learning theory of morality** *emphasizes a distinction between a child's* moral competence *(the ability to produce moral behaviors) and* moral performance *(those behaviors in specific situations)* (Mischel & Mischel, 1975). Moral competence, or acquisition of moral knowledge, depends primarily on cognitive-sensory processes; it is the outgrowth of these processes. Competencies include what children are capable of doing, what they know, their skills, their awareness of moral rules and regulations, and their cognitive ability to construct behaviors. Children's moral performance, or behavior, however, is determined by their motivation and the rewards and incentives to act in a specific moral way. Albert Bandura (1991) also believes that moral development is best understood by considering a combination of social and cognitive factors, especially those involving self-control.

In general, social learning theorists have been critical of Kohlberg's theory of moral development. Among other reasons, they believe he placed too little emphasis on moral behavior and the situational determinants of morality. However, although Kohlberg argued that moral judgment is an important determinant of moral behavior, he, like the Mischels, stressed that an individual's interpretation of both the moral and the factual aspects of a situation leads to a moral decision (Kohlberg & Candee, 1979). For example, Kohlberg mentioned that "extramoral" factors, such as the desire to avoid embarrassment, may cause children to avoid doing what they believe to be morally right. In sum, according to both the Mischels and Kohlberg, moral action is influenced by complex factors. Overall, the findings are mixed with regard to the association of moral thought and behavior (Arnold, 1989), although in one investigation with college students, individuals with both highly principled moral reasoning and high ego strength were less likely to cheat in a resistance-to-temptation situation than were their low-principled and low-ego-strength counterparts (Hess, Lonky, & Roodin, 1985).

At this point, we have discussed a number of ideas about what moral development is, moral thoughts, and moral behavior. A summary of these ideas is presented in concept table 14.1. In the next section, we will turn our attention to moral feelings.

MORAL FEELINGS, ALTRUISM, AND PARENTING

In addition to moral thought and moral behavior, moral development also involves moral feelings. Sometimes those moral feelings involve the positive side of moral development—altruism. An increasing interest in children's moral development is the role that parents play.

Moral Feelings

Think about when you do something you sense is wrong—does it affect you emotionally? Maybe you get a twinge of guilt. And when you give someone a gift, a feeling of joy might emerge. Let's further explore the nature of moral feelings.

Psychoanalytic Theory

In chapter 2, we discussed Sigmund Freud's psychoanalytic theory, which describes the *superego* as one of the three main structures of personality (the id and ego are the other two). In Freud's classical psychoanalytic theory,

a child's superego—the moral branch of personality—develops as the child resolves the Oedipus conflict and identifies with the same-sex parent in the early childhood years. One reason children resolve the Oedipus conflict is to alleviate the fears of losing their parents' love and of being punished for their unacceptable sexual wishes toward the opposite-sex parent. To reduce anxiety, avoid punishment, and maintain parental affection, children form a superego by identifying with the same-sex parent. Through this identification, children internalize the parent's standards of right and wrong that reflect societal prohibitions. Also, the child turns inward the hostility that was previously aimed externally at the same-sex parent. This inwardly directed hostility is then experienced self-punitively (and unconsciously) as guilt. In the psychoanalytic account of moral development, self-punitiveness of guilt keeps children from committing transgressions. That is, children conform to societal standards to avoid guilt.

> *What is moral is what you feel good after and what is immoral is what you feel bad after.*
>
> —**Ernest Hemingway**

In Freud's view, the superego consists of two main components, the ego-ideal and conscience, which promote children's development of moral feelings. The **ego-ideal** *is the component of the superego that involves ideal standards approved of by parents,* whereas **conscience** *is the component of the superego that involves behaviors disapproved of by parents.* A child's ego-ideal rewards the child by conveying a sense of pride and personal value when the child acts according to moral standards. The conscience punishes the child for acting immorally by making the child feel guilty and worthless. In this way, self-control replaces parental control.

Empathy

Positive feelings, such as empathy, contribute to the child's moral development. Feeling **empathy** *means reacting to another's feelings with an emotional response that is similar to the other's feelings* (Damon, 1988). Although empathy is experienced as an emotional state, it often has a cognitive component—the ability to discern another's inner psychological states, or what we have previously called *perspective taking* (Eisenberg & others, 1991). Infants have the capacity for some purely empathic responses, but, for effective moral action, children need to learn to identify a wide range of emotional states in others and to anticipate what kinds of action will improve another person's emotional state.

What are the main milestones in children's development of empathy? According to an analysis by child developmentalist William Damon (1988), changes in empathy take place in early infancy, at 1 to 2 years in age,

The Nature of Moral Development, Moral Thoughts, and Moral Behavior

Concept	Processes/ Related Ideas	Characteristics/Description
What Is Moral Development?	Its nature	Moral development concerns rules and regulations about what people should do in their interactions with others. Developmentalists study how children think, behave, and feel about such rules and regulations.
Moral Thoughts	Piaget's theory	It distinguishes between the heteronomous morality of younger children and the autonomous morality of older children. Piaget's ideas on formal operational thought have implications for understanding adolescents' moral development.
	Kohlberg's theory	Kohlberg developed a provocative view of the development of moral reasoning. He argued that moral development consists of three levels—preconventional, conventional, and postconventional—and six stages (two at each level). Increased internalization characterizes movement to levels 2 and 3. Kohlberg's longitudinal data show a relation of the stages to age, although the highest two stages, especially stage 6, rarely appear. Influences on the Kohlberg stages incude cognitive development, imitation and cognitive conflict, peer relations, and perspective taking. Criticisms of Kohlberg's theory involve an overemphasis on cognitive factors and inadequate attention to behavior, the quality of the research, inadequate consideration of the care perspective, and an underestimation of the role of culture. Carol Gilligan advocates a stronger care perspective (which views people in terms of their connectedness to others and interpersonal communication). Gilligan also believes that early adolescence is a critical juncture in the development of a moral voice for females. Researchers have found support for Gilligan's claim that females' and males' moral reasoning often center on different concerns, although gender differences in Kohlberg's stages have not been found consistently. Studies that focus more extensively on the items pertaining to close relationships, and use of scoring systems that emphasize connectedness, support Gilligan's claims.
Moral Behavior	Reinforcement, punishment, imitation, and situational variations	Behaviorists argue that children's moral behavior is determined by the processes of reinforcement, punishment, and imitation. Situational variability in morality is stressed.
	Resistance to temptation and self-control	Behaviorists who study children's moral behavior often examine resistance to temptation and the development of self-control. The use of cognitive rationales has improved children's ability to resist temptation. Children's self-control is also influenced by cognitive factors, such as self-instruction.
	Cognitive social learning theory	It emphasizes a distinction between moral competence (the ability to produce moral behaviors) and moral performance (those behaviors in specific situations). In general, social learning theorists have been critical of Kohlberg's theory, believing he placed too little emphasis on moral behavior and its situational variability.

in early childhood, and at 10 to 12 years of age. **Global empathy** *is the young infant's empathic response in which clear boundaries between the feelings and needs of the self and those of another have not yet been established.* For example, one 11-month-old infant fought off her own tears, sucked her thumb, and buried her head in her mother's lap after she had seen another child fall and hurt himself. Not all infants cry every time someone else is hurt, though. Many times, an infant will stare at another's pain with curiosity. Although global empathy is observed in some infants, it does not consistently characterize all infants' behavior.

Between 1 and 2 years of age, the infant's undifferentiated feelings of discomfort at another's distress grow into more genuine feelings of concern. The infant realizes that others are independent persons in their own right, with their own unhappy feelings. The infant may sense that these unhappy feelings in others need attention and relief, but the infant cannot translate this realization into effective behavior. For example, toddlers may offer a beloved blanket or doll for comfort to an unhappy-looking adult. In one study, empathy appeared more regularly after 18 months (Lamb, 1993).

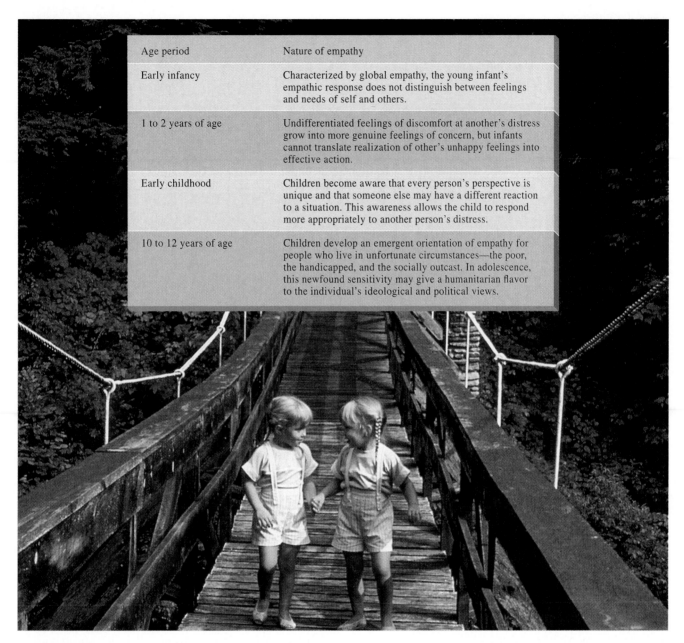

Age period	Nature of empathy
Early infancy	Characterized by global empathy, the young infant's empathic response does not distinguish between feelings and needs of self and others.
1 to 2 years of age	Undifferentiated feelings of discomfort at another's distress grow into more genuine feelings of concern, but infants cannot translate realization of other's unhappy feelings into effective action.
Early childhood	Children become aware that every person's perspective is unique and that someone else may have a different reaction to a situation. This awareness allows the child to respond more appropriately to another person's distress.
10 to 12 years of age	Children develop an emergent orientation of empathy for people who live in unfortunate circumstances—the poor, the handicapped, and the socially outcast. In adolescence, this newfound sensitivity may give a humanitarian flavor to the individual's ideological and political views.

Figure~14.2

Damon's Description of Developmental Changes in Empathy

In the early childhood years, children become aware that every person's perspective is unique and that someone else may have a reaction to a situation that is different from their own. Such awareness permits the child to respond more appropriately to another's distress. For example, at the age of 6, a child may realize that, in some instances, an unhappy person may best be left alone rather than helped, or the child may learn to wait for just the right time to give comfort. In sum, at this point, children make more objective assessments of others' distress and needs.

Toward the end of the elementary school years, at about 10 to 12 years of age, children develop empathy for people who live in unfortunate circumstances. Children's concerns are no longer limited to the feelings of particular persons in situations the child observes directly (Shorr & Shorr, 1995). Instead, children expand their concerns to the general problems of people in unfortunate situations—the poor, the handicapped, and the socially outcast, for example. This newfound sensitivity may lead to altruistic behavior by the older elementary school child and later, in adolescence, give a humanitarian flavor to the adolescent's development of ideological and political views. A summary of Damon's description of empathy development is shown in figure 14.2.

Although everyone may be capable of responding with empathy, not all individuals do. There is considerable

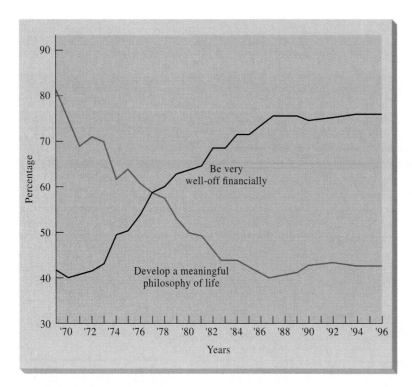

Figure~14.3

Changing Freshman Life Goals, 1970–1994
The percentages indicated are in response to the question of identifying a life goal as "essential" or "very important." There has been a significant reversal in freshman life goals in the last two decades, with a far greater percentage of today's college freshmen stating that a "very important" life goal is to be well-off financially, and far fewer stating that developing a meaningful philosophy of life is a "very important" life goal.

variation in individual empathic behavior. For example, in older children and adolescents, empathic dysfunctions can contribute to antisocial behavior. Some delinquents convicted of violent crimes show a lack of feeling for their victims' distress. A 13-year-old boy convicted of violently mugging a number of elderly people, when asked about the pain he had caused for one blind woman, said, "What do I care? I'm not her" (Damon, 1988).

Not only is there individual variation in adolescents' empathy and concern about the welfare of others, but sociohistorical influences also may be involved. Over the past two decades, adolescents have shown an increased concern for personal well-being and a decreased concern for the welfare of others, especially for the disadvantaged. As shown in figure 14.3, today's college freshmen are more strongly motivated to be well-off financially and less motivated to develop a meaningful philosophy of life than were their counterparts 20 or even 10 years ago (Astin & others, 1997). Among high school seniors, increasing numbers are motivated by the opportunity to make a considerable amount of money (Bachman, Johnston, & O'Malley, 1987).

However, two values that increased during the 1960s continue to be important to today's youth: self-fulfillment and self-expression (Conger, 1988). As part of their motivation for self-fulfillment, many adolescents show great interest in their physical health and well-being. Greater self-fulfillment and self-expression can be laudable goals, but if they become the only goals, self-destruction, loneliness, or alienation may result. Young people also need to develop a corresponding sense of commitment to others' welfare (Yates, 1996). Encouraging adolescents to have a strong commitment to others, in concert with an interest in self-fulfillment, is a major task for our nation at the close of the twentieth century. To further evaluate values, see Critical Thinking About Children's Development.

The Contemporary Perspective on the Role of Emotions in Moral Development

We have seen that classical psychoanalytic theory emphasizes the power of unconscious guilt in moral development but that other theorists, such as Hoffman and Damon, emphasize the role of empathy. Today, many child developmentalists believe that both positive feelings, such as empathy, sympathy, admiration, and self-esteem, and negative feelings, such as anger, outrage, shame, and guilt, contribute to children's moral development (Damon, 1988; Eisenberg & Fabes, 1997; Roberts & Strayer, 1996). When strongly experienced, these

CRITICAL THINKING ABOUT CHILDREN'S DEVELOPMENT

Values Billboards

Over the last two decades or so, Americans have adopted a popular dress code that provides an opportunity for interpreting the values that individuals hold: decorated T-shirts. By observing and interpreting adolescents' T-shirts, you might be able to determine the identity of their favorite musical groups, their allegiance to sports teams, the colleges they aspire to attend, and a host of other information. In addition, these data can imply values. For example, if you encounter an adolescent with a T-shirt that proclaims recent participation in a bowling tournament, you may reasonably infer that the adolescent values competition.

Carefully observe the next ten adolescents with decorated T-shirts that you encounter. What do you observe about the preferences they are displaying? What can you infer about the wearers' values from the identities they promote? How confident are you regarding your interpretations? By observing and interpreting adolescents' T-shirts, you are learning to think critically by *making accurate observations, descriptions, and inferences about children's development.*

emotions influence children to act in accord with standards of right and wrong. Such emotions as empathy, shame, guilt, and anxiety over other people's violations of standards are present early in development and undergo developmental change throughout childhood and beyond (Damon, 1988). These emotions provide a natural base for children's acquisition of moral values, both orienting children toward moral events and motivating them to pay close attention to such events. However, moral emotions do not operate in a vacuum to build a child's moral awareness, and they are not sufficient in themselves to generate moral responsivity. They do not give the "substance" of moral regulation—the rules, values, and standards of behavior that children need to understand and act on. Moral emotions are inextricably interwoven with the cognitive and social aspects of children's development.

In a recent study of fifth-, eighth-, and eleventh-graders, parents were the individuals most likely to evoke guilt (Williams & Bybee, 1994). With development, guilt evoked by family members was less prevalent, but guilt engendered by girlfriends or boyfriends was more frequent. At the higher grade levels, the percentage of students reporting guilt about aggressive, externalizing behaviors declined, whereas those mentioning guilt over internal thoughts and inconsiderateness increased. Males were more likely to report guilt over externalizing behaviors, while females reported more guilt over violating norms of compassion and trust.

The web of feeling, cognition, and social behavior is also experienced in altruism—the aspect of children's moral development we will discuss next.

Altruism

Altruism *is an unselfish interest in helping another person.* Human acts of altruism are plentiful—the hardworking laborer who places $5 in a Salvation Army kettle; rock concerts to feed the hungry, help farmers, and fund AIDS research; and the child who takes in a wounded cat and cares for it. How do psychologists account for such acts of altruism?

> *But you cannot give to people what they are incapable of receiving.*
>
> —**Agatha Christie, *Funerals Are Fatal* (1953)**

göra en gentjänst / besvara

Reciprocity and exchange are involved in altruism. Reciprocity is found throughout the human world. Not only is it the highest moral principle in Christianity, but it is also present in every widely practiced religion in the world—Judaism, Hinduism, Buddhism, and Islam. Reciprocity encourages children to do unto others as they would have others do unto them. Human sentiments are *känslor, åsikter* wrapped up in this reciprocity. Trust is probably the most important principle, over the long run, in altruism. Guilt surfaces if the child does not reciprocate, and anger may result if someone else does not reciprocate. Not all altruism is motivated by reciprocity and exchange, but self-other interactions and relationships help us understand altruism's nature. The circumstances most likely to involve altruism are empathic emotion for an individual in need or a close relationship between benefactor and recipient (Batson, 1989).

In addition to presenting a developmental sequence of children's empathy, which we discussed earlier, Damon (1988) has also described a developmental sequence of children's altruism, especially of sharing. Most sharing during the first 3 years of life is done for nonempathic reasons, such as for the fun of the social play ritual or out of mere imitation. Then, at about 4 years of age, a combination of empathic awareness and adult encouragement produces a sense of obligation on the part of the child to share with others. This obligation forces the child to share, even though the child may not perceive this as the best way to have fun. Most 4-year-olds are not selfless saints, however. Children believe they have an obligation to share but do not necessarily think they should be as generous to others as they are to themselves. Neither do their actions always support their beliefs, especially when the object of contention is coveted. What is important developmentally is that the child has developed an internal belief that sharing is an obligatory part of a social relationship and that this involves a question of right and wrong. However, a preschool child's sense of reciprocity does not constitute a moral duty but, rather, is a pragmatic means of getting one's way. Despite their shortcomings, these ideas about justice formed in early childhood set the stage for giant strides that children make in the years that follow.

> *Every man takes care that his neighbor shall not cheat him. But a day comes when he begins to care that he does not cheat his neighbor. Then all goes well.*
>
> —Ralph Waldo Emerson

By the start of the elementary school years, children genuinely begin to express more objective ideas about fairness. These notions about fairness have been used throughout history to distribute goods and to resolve conflicts. They involve the principles of equality, merit, and benevolence. *Equality* means that everyone is treated the same. *Merit* means giving extra rewards for hard work, a talented performance, or other laudatory behavior. *Benevolence* means giving special consideration to individuals in a disadvantaged condition. Equality is the first of these principles used regularly by elementary school children. It is common to hear 6-year-old children use the word *fair* as synonymous with *equal* or *same*. By the mid to late elementary school years, children also believe that equity means special treatment for those who deserve it—the principles of merit and benevolence.

Missing from the factors that guide children's altruism is one that many adults might expect to be the most influential of all: the motivation to obey adult authority figures. Surprisingly, a number of studies have shown that adult authority has only a small influence on children's sharing. For example, when Nancy Eisenberg (1982) asked children to explain their own altruistic acts, they mainly gave empathic and pragmatic reasons for their spontaneous acts of sharing. Not one of the children referred to the demands of adult authority. Parental advice and prodding certainly foster standards of sharing, but the give-and-take of peer requests and arguments provide the most immediate stimulation of sharing. Parents can set examples that children carry into peer interac-

tion and communication, but parents are not present during all of their children's peer exchanges. The day-to-day construction of fairness standards is done by children in collaboration and negotiation with each other. Over the course of many years and thousands of encounters, children's understanding of altruism deepens. With this conceptual elaboration that involves such notions as equality, merit, benevolence, and compromise come a greater consistency and generosity in children's sharing behavior (Damon, 1988).

> *Without civic morality communities perish; without personal morality their survival has no value.*
>
> —Bertrand Russell

Parenting and Children's Moral Development

Both Piaget and Kohlberg held that parents do not provide any unique or essential inputs to children's moral development. They do believe that parents are responsible for providing general role-taking opportunities and cognitive conflict, but they reserve the primary role in moral development for peers (Walker, 1996).

Parental Discipline

In Freud's psychoanalytic theory, the aspects of child rearing that encourage moral development are practices that instill the fears of punishment and of losing parental love. Child developmentalists who have studied child-rearing techniques and moral development have focused on parents' discipline techniques. These include love withdrawal, power assertion, and induction (Hoffman, 1970). Love withdrawal comes closest to the psychoanalytic emphasis on fear of punishment and of losing parental love. **Love withdrawal** *is a discipline technique in which a parent withholds attention or love from the child,* as when the parent refuses to talk to the child or states a dislike for the child. For example, the parent might say, "I'm going to leave you if you do that again," or "I don't like you when you do that." **Power assertion** *is a discipline technique in which a parent attempts to gain control over the child or the child's resources.* Examples include spanking, threatening, or removing privileges. **Induction** *is the discipline technique in which a parent uses reason and explanation of the consequences for others of the child's actions.* Examples of induction include, "Don't hit him. He was only trying to help" and "Why are you yelling at her? She didn't mean to trip you."

Moral development theorist and researcher Martin Hoffman (1970) believes that any discipline produces arousal on the child's part. Love withdrawal and power assertion are likely to evoke a very high level of arousal, with love withdrawal generating considerable anxiety and power assertion considerable hostility. Induction is more likely to produce a moderate level of arousal in children, a level that permits them to attend to the cognitive rationales parents offer. When a parent uses power assertion and love withdrawal, the child may be so aroused that, even if the parent gives accompanying explanations about the consequences for others of the child's actions, the child may not attend to them. Power assertion presents parents as weak models of self-control—as individuals who cannot control their feelings. Accordingly, children may imitate this model of poor self-control when they face stressful circumstances. The use of induction, however, focuses the child's attention on the action's consequences for others, not on the child's own shortcomings. For these reasons, Hoffman (1988) believes that parents should use induction to encourage children's moral development. In research on parenting techniques, induction is more positively related to moral development than is love withdrawal or power assertion, although the findings vary according to children's developmental level and socioeconomic status. Induction works better with elementary-school-age children than with preschool children (Brody & Shaffer, 1982) and better with middle-class than with lower-class children (Hoffman, 1970). Older children are probably better able to understand the reasons given to them and are better at perspective taking. Some theorists believe that the internalization of society's moral standards is more likely among middle-class than among lower-class individuals, because internalization is more rewarding in the middle-class culture (Kohn, 1977).

Some Conclusions About Parenting and Children's Moral Development

Parental discipline does contribute to children's moral development, but there are other aspects of parenting that also play an important role, such as providing opportunities for perspective taking and modeling moral behavior and thinking. Nancy Eisenberg and Bridget Murphy (1995) recently summarized the findings from the research literature on ways in which parenting can influence children's moral development. They concluded that, in general, moral children tend to have parents who

- Are warm and supportive rather than punitive
- Use inductive discipline
- Provide opportunities for the children to learn about others' perspectives and feelings
- Involve children in family decision making and in the process of thinking about moral decisions
- Model moral behaviors and thinking themselves and provide opportunities for their children to model such moral behaviors and thinking

Parents who show this configuration of behaviors likely foster the development of concern and caring about others in their children, and create a positive parent-child relationship. These parents also provide information about what behaviors are expected of the child and why, and promote an internal rather than an external sense of morality.

MORAL EDUCATION

The moral education of children has become a widely discussed topic. Many parents worry that their children are growing up without traditional values. Teachers complain that many of their students are unethical. Among the questions about moral education we will examine are the following: What is the hidden curriculum? What is the nature of direct moral education versus indirect moral education? What is values clarification? What is cognitive moral education?

The Hidden Curriculum

The **hidden curriculum** *is the pervasive moral atmosphere of a school. This atmosphere includes school and classroom rules, attitudes toward academics and extracurricular activities, the moral orientation of teachers and school administrators, and text materials.* More than half a century ago, educator John Dewey (1933) recognized that, whether or not they offer specific programs in moral education, schools provide moral education through the hidden curriculum. Schools, like families, are settings for moral development. Teachers serve as models of ethical or unethical behavior. Classroom rules and peer relations at school transmit attitudes about cheating, lying, stealing, and consideration of others, and the school administration, through its rules and regulations, represents a value system to children.

Direct and Indirect Moral Education

Approaches to moral education can be classified as either direct or indirect (Benninga, 1988). **Direct moral education** *involves either emphasizing values or character traits during specified time slots or integrating these values or traits throughout the curriculum.* **Indirect moral education** *involves encouraging adolescents to define their own and others' moral values and helping them define the moral perspectives that support those values.*

Direct Moral Education (Character Education)

In the direct moral education approach, instruction in specified moral concepts can assume the form of example and definition, class discussions and role-playing, or rewarding students for proper behavior. The use of McGuffey Readers during the early part of the twentieth century exemplifies the direct approach. The stories and poems in the readers taught moral behavior and character in addition to academics.

Many of the current character education approaches advocate the development of a "basic moral literacy" to prevent youth from engaging in immoral behavior and doing harm to others and themselves. Many of the character education interventions are at the level of the elementary school. Recent books that advocate this character education approach include *The Book of Virtues* (Bennett, 1991), *Educating for Moral Character* (Lickona, 1991), *Reclaiming Our Schools* (Wynne & Ryan, 1993), and *Greater Expectations* (Damon, 1995).

Political campaigns now emphasize such concepts as "the moral crisis," "the breakdown of family values," "America's moral decline," "moral illiteracy," and "the values crisis." Movements include the New Character Education partnership, the Character Education Network, the Aspen Declaration on Character Education, and the publicity campaign "Character Counts."

Former U.S. secretary of Education William Bennett (1986) wrote:

> If college is really interested in teaching its students a clear lesson in moral responsibility, it should tell the truth about drugs in a straightforward way. This summer our college presidents should send every student a letter saying they will not tolerate drugs on campus—period. The letter should then spell out precisely what the college's policy will be toward students who use drugs. Being simple and straightforward about moral responsibility is not the same as being simplistic and unsophisticated.

Bennett also believes that every elementary and secondary school should have a discipline code, making clear to adolescents and parents what the school expects of them. Then the school should enforce the code.

Indirect Moral Education

The most widely adopted indirect approaches to moral education are values clarification and cognitive moral education.

Values Clarification   **Values clarification** *is an indirect moral education approach that focuses on helping students clarify what their lives are for and what is worth working for.* In values clarification, students are asked questions or presented with dilemmas and expected to respond, either individually or in small groups. The intent is to help students define their own values and to become aware of others' values (Nucci & Weber, 1991).

In the following example of values clarification, students are asked to select from among 10 people the 6 who will be admitted to a fallout shelter during World War III:

> Suppose you are a government decision maker in Washington, D.C., when World War III breaks out. A fallout shelter under your administration in a remote Montana highland contains only enough space, air, food, and water for 6 people for 3 months, but 10 people wish to be admitted. The 10 have agreed by radio contact that, for the survival of the human race,

you must decide which 6 of them shall be saved. You have exactly 30 minutes to make up your mind before Washington goes up in smoke. These are your choices:

1. A 16-year-old girl of questionable IQ, who is a high school dropout and pregnant
2. A policeman with a gun (which cannot be taken from him), thrown off the force recently for brutality
3. A clergyman, 75
4. A woman physician, 36, known to be a confirmed racist
5. A male violinist, 46, who served 7 years for pushing narcotics
6. A 20-year-old Black militant with no special skills
7. A former prostitute, female, 39
8. An architect who is a male homosexual
9. A 26-year-old law student
10. The law student's 25-year-old wife, who spent the past 9 months in a mental hospital and is still heavily sedated; they refuse to be separated

In this exercise, no answers are considered right or wrong. The clarification of values is left up to individual students. Advocates of the values clarification approach argue that it is value free, but critics argue that, because of its controversial content, it offends community standards (Eger, 1981). Critics also say that, because of its relativistic nature, values clarification undermines accepted values and fails to stress truth and right behavior (Oser, 1986).

Cognitive Moral Education   Like values clarification, cognitive moral education also challenges direct moral instruction. **Cognitive moral education** *is an indirect moral education approach that emphasizes that children adopt such values as democracy and justice as their moral reasoning is developed.* In this approach, students' moral standards are allowed to develop through their attention to environmental settings and exercises that encourage more advanced moral thinking. Thus, in contrast to values clarification, cognitive moral education is not value free. Such values as democracy and justice are emphasized. The advocates of cognitive moral education argue that when moral standards are imposed—as in the direct instruction approach—children can never completely integrate and fully understand moral principles. Only through participation and discussion can children learn to apply the rules and principles of cooperation, trust, community, and self-reliance.

Lawrence Kohlberg's theory of moral development has extensively influenced the cognitive moral education approach. Contrary to what some critics say, Kohlberg's theory is not completely relativistic and it is not completely morally neutral. It treats higher-level moral thinking as better than lower-level moral thinking, and it stresses that higher-level thinking can be stimulated through focused discussion of moral dilemmas (Higgins, 1991; Power, 1991). Also, in the 1980s, Kohlberg (1981, 1986) revised his views on moral education by placing more emphasis on the school's moral atmosphere, as John Dewey did many years ago.

Rheta DeVries and her colleagues (DeVries & Zan, 1995; DeVries, Haney, & Zan, 1991; DeVries & Zan, 1994) argue that children's sociomoral attitudes develop very early. Their research has found that children in early childhood classrooms characterized by a constructivist sociomoral atmosphere (Kohlberg's approach) are more advanced in moral development, resolve more of their conflicts, and enjoy more friendly interaction with their peers than do children educated in more authoritarian classroom atmospheres.

Damon's Comprehensive Approach

William Damon (1988) believes that moral education should follow from what we know about the nature of children's moral development. Based on scientific studies and observations of children's moral development, Damon believes that the following six principles should serve as a foundation for the development of moral education programs:

1. Children experience classic moral issues facing humans everywhere simply by participating in social relationships: issues of fairness, honesty, responsibility, kindness, and obedience, for example. Thus, children's moral awareness develops within their normal social experiences. Their moral awareness may need to be guided, informed, and enhanced, but it does not need to be imposed directly in a punitive, authoritarian manner.

2. Children's moral awareness is shaped and supported by natural emotional reactions to observations and events, which begin as early as infancy. Such emotional reactions as empathy support moral compassion and altruism. Such reactions as shame, guilt, and fear support obedience and rule adoption. Children's love and attachment feelings for parents provide an affective foundation for children's developing respect for authority.

3. Interactions with parents, teachers, and other adults introduce children to important social standards and rules. These interactions produce knowledge and respect for the social order, including its principles of organization and legitimate authority. Authoritative adult-child (for example, parent-child or teacher-child) relationships, in which extensive verbal give-and-take and nonpunitive adult control that

justifies demands are present, yield the most positive results for children's moral judgment and behavior.

4. Peer relations introduce children to the norms of direct reciprocity and to the standards for sharing, cooperation, and fairness. Through peer relations, children learn about mutuality, equality, and perspective taking, which promote the development of altruism.

5. Broad variations in social experiences can produce broad differences in moral orientation among children. One such variation is the different roles and expectations that girls and boys experience, especially in traditional social environments. As we learned earlier in our discussion of Carol Gilligan's ideas, the moral development of girls is oriented more toward relationships and care, whereas the moral development of boys is oriented more toward the individual and justice. There is reason to believe that such orientations can be socially transformed as cultures change. According to Damon, there should be an increased emphasis on learning the principles of care and justice by both boys and girls.

6. Moral development in schools is determined by the same cognitive and social processes that apply to moral development in other settings. This means that children acquire moral values by actively participating in adult-child and peer relationships that support, enhance, and guide their natural moral tendencies. According to Damon, children's morality is not enhanced by lessons or lectures in which children are passive recipients of information or, even worse, are captive and recalcitrant audiences. Further, the quality of social interaction in a school setting communicates a moral message that is more enduring than direct, declarative statements and lectures by teachers. To receive a competent moral education in a democratic society, children need to experience egalitarian interactions that reflect democratic values—among them, equality, fairness, and responsibility.

Damon (1988) argues that, for teachers and parents to contribute positively to a child's moral development, they need to practice respectful engagement with the child. Children need adult guidance, but, for the guidance to register, children need to be productively engaged and their own initiatives and reactions must be respected.

Damon recognizes that parents alone, or schools alone, are not completely responsible for children's moral development. Children's moral education occurs both in and out of school through their interactions with parents, peers, and teachers, and through their experiences with society's standards. These interactions are not value

Social Contexts of Development

It is not enough for parents to understand children. They must also accord children the privilege of understanding them.

—Milton Saperstein

Parents cradle children's lives, but children's growth is also shaped by successive choirs of siblings, peers, friends, and teachers. Children's small worlds widen as they discover new refuges and new people. In the end there are but two lasting bequests that parents can leave children: one being roots, the other wings. In this section, we will study four chapters: "Families" (chapter 15), "Peers, Play, and the Media" (chapter 16), "Schools and Achievement" (chapter 17), and "Culture, Poverty, and Ethnicity" (chapter 18).

Edouard Vuillard
Femme Et Enfant Au Jardin detail

Chapter

15

Families

*T*here's no vocabulary for love within a family, love that's lived in but not looked at, love within the light of which all else is seen, the love within which all other love finds speech. This love is silent.

—T. S. Eliot

Chapter Boxes

*We never know the love of
our parents until we have
become parents.*

—Henry Ward Beecher, 1887

The Diversity of Families and Parenting

PREVIEW

$\mathscr{T}$he two children you will read about in Images of Children are growing up in very different family atmospheres. In this chapter, we will explore the many and diverse worlds of families. We will examine the parenting role and parenting styles, effects of divorce, stepfamilies, working parents, culture and ethnicity, and gender. But to begin with, we will study some basic ideas about the nature of family processes.

Children grow up in a diversity of families. Some children live in families that have never experienced divorce, some live virtually their entire childhood in single-parent families, and yet others live in stepfamilies. Some children live in poverty, others in economically advantaged families. Some children's mothers are employed full-time outside the home and place their children in day care, while other mothers stay home with their children. Some children grow up in an Anglo-American culture, others in ethnic minority cultures. Some children have siblings, others don't. Some children have parents who treat them harshly and abuse them; other children have parents who nurture and support them.

In thinking about the diversity of families and parenting, consider the following two circumstances and predict how they might influence the child's development. First consider the children in the following circumstance:

A mother is holding an infant in her arms and is trying to keep track of two boys walking behind her. The younger boy, who is about 3, clutches an umbrella but seems to be having trouble with it. He drags its curved handle along the ground, and that irritates his mother. She tells him to carry the umbrella right or she will knock the (expletive) out of him. "Carry it right, I said," she says,

and then she slaps him in the face, knocking him off balance. She rarely nurtures her son and has beaten him so hard that at times he has bruises that don't go away for days. The mother lives in the poverty of an inner city and she is unemployed. She is unaware of how her own life stress affects her parenting behavior.

Now consider another child who is growing up in a very different family environment:

A mother is walking along the street with her 4-year-old daughter. They are having a conversation about her daughter's preschool. As the conversation continues, they smile back and forth several times as the daughter describes some activities she did. As they reach home, the mother tells her daughter that she loves her and gives her a big hug. This mother also lives in a poverty-stricken area. She has received considerable support from her extended family in raising her daughter, and the preschool her daughter attends has high ratings. The mother reports that she sincerely enjoys being with her daughter and loves to plan enjoyable things for her to do.

THE NATURE OF FAMILY PROCESSES

Among the important considerations in studying children and their families are reciprocal socialization, synchrony, and the family system; how children construct relationships and how such relationships influence the development of social maturity; adapting parenting to developmental changes in the child; the family life cycle; and social and historical influences on the family.

Reciprocal Socialization and the Family as a System

For many years, socialization between parents and children was viewed as a one-way process: Children were considered to be the products of their parents' socialization techniques. Today, however, we view parent-child interaction as reciprocal (Schaffer, 1996). **Reciprocal socialization** *is socialization that is bidirectional; children socialize parents just as parents socialize children.* For example, the interaction of mothers and their infants is sometimes symbolized as a dance or dialogue in which successive actions of the partners are closely coordinated. This coordinated dance or dialogue can assume the form of mutual synchrony (each person's behavior depending on the partner's previous behavior), or it can be reciprocal in a more precise sense; the actions of the partners can be matched, as when one partner imitates the other or when there is mutual smiling (Cohn & Tronick, 1988).

When reciprocal socialization has been investigated in infancy, mutual gaze or eye contact has been found to play an important role in early social interaction (Fogel, Toda, & Kawai, 1988). In one investigation, the mother and infant engaged in a variety of behaviors while they looked at each other; by contrast, when they looked away from each other, the rate of such behaviors dropped considerably (Stern & others, 1977). In sum, the behaviors of mothers and infants involve substantial interconnection and synchronization. And in one investigation, synchrony in parent-child relationships was positively related to children's social competence (Harrist, 1993).

Scaffolding *refers to parental behavior that serves to support children's efforts, allowing them to be more skillful than they would be if they relied only on their own abilities.* Parents' efforts to time interactions in such a way that the infant experiences turn-taking with the parent illustrates an early parental scaffolding behavior. For example, in the game peek-a-boo, mothers initially cover their babies, then remove the covering, and finally register "surprise" at the reappearance. As infants become more skilled at peek-a-boo, they do the covering and uncovering. In addition to peek-a-boo, pat-a-cake and so-big are other caregiver games that exemplify scaffolding and turn-taking sequences. In one investigation, infants who had more-extensive scaffolding experiences with their parents, especially in the form of turn taking, were more likely to engage in turn taking as they interacted with their peers (Vandell & Wilson, 1988). Scaffolding is not just confined to parent-infant interaction but can be used by parents to support children's efforts at any age (Stringer & Neal, 1993). For example, parents can support children's achievement-related efforts in school by modifying the amount and type of support they provide to best suit the child's level of development.

As a social system, the family can be thought of as a constellation of subsystems defined in terms of generation, gender, and role (Davis, 1996). Divisions of labor among family members define particular subunits, and attachments define others. Each family member is a participant in several subsystems—some dyadic (involving two people), some polyadic (involving more than two people). The father and child represent one dyadic subsystem, the mother and father another; the mother-father-child represent one polyadic subsystem, the mother and two siblings another (Piotrowski, 1997).

An organizational scheme that highlights the reciprocal influences of family members and family subsystems is shown in figure 15.1 (Belsky, 1981). As the arrows in the figure show, marital relations, parenting, and infant/child behavior can have both direct and indirect effects on each other. For example, in one study, when marriages were less intimate and more distant during prenatal development, mothers were less sensitive, and fathers invested less time in parenting, when the infants were 3 months old (Cox & others, 1989).

The Developmental Construction of Relationships

Developmentalists have shown an increased interest in understanding how we construct relationships as we grow up (Costanzo & Dunsmore, 1993; Shaver, 1993). Psychoanalytic theorists have always been interested in how this process works in families. However, the current explanations of how relationships are constructed is virtually stripped of Freud's psychosexual stage terminology and also is not always confined to the first 5 years of life, as has been the case in classical psychoanalytic theory. Today's **developmental construction views** *share the belief that as individuals grow up they acquire modes of relating to others. There are two main variations within this view, one of which emphasizes continuity and stability in relationships through the life span and one of which emphasizes discontinuity and change in relationships through the life span.*

The Continuity View

The **continuity view** *emphasizes the role that early parent-child relationships play in constructing a basic way of relating to people throughout the life span.* These early parent-child relationships are carried forward to later points in development to influence all subsequent relationships (with peers, with friends, with teachers, and with romantic

Figure~15.1

Interaction Between Children and Their Parents: Direct and Indirect Effects

partners, for example) (Ainsworth, 1979; Bowlby, 1989; Ostoja & others, 1995; Sroufe, 1985; Waters & others, 1995). In its extreme form, this view states that the basic components of social relationships are laid down and shaped by the security or insecurity of parent-infant attachment relationships in the first year or two of the infant's life (remember our discussion of attachment in chapter 11).

Close relationships with parents also are important in the child's development, because these relationships function as models or templates that are carried forward over time to influence the construction of new relationships. Clearly, close relationships do not repeat themselves in an endless fashion over the course of the child's development. And the quality of any relationship depends to some degree on the specific individual with whom the relationship is formed. However, the nature of earlier relationships that are developed over many years often can be detected in later relationships, both with those same individuals and in the formation of relationships with others at a later point in time (Gjerde, Block, & Block, 1991). Thus, the nature of parent-adolescent relationships does not depend only on what happens in the relationship during adolescence. Relationships with parents over the long course of childhood are carried forward to influence, at least to some degree, the nature of parent-adolescent relationships. And the long course of parent-child relationships also could be expected to influence, again at least to some degree, the fabric of the adolescent's peer relationships, friendships, and dating relationships.

The Discontinuity View

The **discontinuity view** *emphasizes change and growth in relationships over time.* As people grow up, they develop many different types of relationships (with parents, with peers, with teachers, and with romantic partners, for example). Each of these relationships is structurally different. With each new type of relationship, individuals encounter new modes of relating (Buhrmester & Furman, 1987; Piaget, 1932; Sullivan, 1953; Youniss, 1980). For example, Piaget (1932) argued that parent-child relationships are strikingly different from children's peer relationships. Parent-child relationships, he said, are more likely to consist of parents' having unilateral authority over children. By contrast, peer relationships are more likely to consist of participants who relate to each other on a much more equal basis. In parent-child relationships, since parents have greater knowledge and authority, their children often must learn how to conform to rules and regulations laid down by parents. In this view, we use the parental-child mode when relating to authority figures (such as with teachers and experts) and when we act as authority figures (when we become parents, teachers, and experts).

By contrast, relationships with peers have a different structure and require a different mode of relating to others. This more egalitarian mode is later called upon in relationships with romantic partners, friends, and coworkers. Because two peers possess relatively equal knowledge and authority (their relationship is reciprocal and symmetrical), children learn a democratic mode of relating that is based on mutual influence. With peers, children learn to formulate and assert their own opinions, appreciate the perspectives of peers, cooperatively negotiate solutions to disagreements, and evolve standards for conduct that are mutually acceptable. Because peer relationships are voluntary (rather than obligatory, as in the family), children and adolescents who fail to become skillful in the symmetrical, mutual, egalitarian, reciprocal mode of relating have difficulty being accepted by peers.

Calvin and Hobbes

by Bill Watterson

WHAT ASSURANCE DO I HAVE THAT YOUR PARENTING ISN'T SCREWING ME UP?

While the change-and-growth variation of the developmental construction view does not deny that prior close relationships (such as with parents) are carried forward to influence later relationships, it does stress that each new type of relationship that children and adolescents encounter (such as with peers, with friends, and with romantic partners) requires the construction of different and ever more sophisticated modes of relating to others. Further, in the change-and-growth version, each period of development uniquely contributes to the construction of relationship knowledge; development across the life span is not solely determined by a sensitive or critical period during infancy.

Adapting Parenting to Developmental Changes in the Child

Children change as they grow from infancy to early childhood and on through middle and late childhood and adolescence. Being a competent parent involves adapting to the child's developmental changes. Parents should not treat a 5-year-old the same as a 2-year-old. The 5-year-old and 2-year-old have different needs and abilities. In the first year, parent-child interaction moves from a heavy focus on routine caretaking—feeding, changing diapers, bathing, and soothing—to later include more noncaretaking activities, such as play and visual-vocal exchanges. During the child's second and third years, parents often handle disciplinary matters by physical manipulation: They carry the child away from a mischievous activity to the place they want the child to go to; they put fragile and dangerous objects out of reach; they sometimes spank. As the child grows older, however, parents increasingly turn to reasoning, moral exhortation, and giving or withholding special privileges. As children move toward the elementary school years, parents show them less physical affection (Maccoby, 1984).

Parent-child interactions during early childhood focus on such matters as modesty, bedtime regularities, control of temper, fighting with siblings and peers, eating behavior and manners, autonomy in dressing, and attention seeking. Although some of these issues—fighting and reaction to discipline, for example—are carried forward into the elementary school years, many new issues appear by the age of 7 (Maccoby, 1984). These include whether children should be made to perform chores and, if so, whether they should be paid for them, how to help children learn to entertain themselves rather than relying on parents for everything, and how to monitor children's lives outside the family in school and peer settings.

As children move into the middle and late childhood years, parents spend considerably less time with them. In one investigation, parents spent less than half as much time with their children aged 5 to 12 in caregiving, instruction, reading, talking, and playing as when the children were young (Hill & Stafford, 1980). This drop in parent-child interaction may be even more extensive in families with little parental education. Although parents spend less time with their children in middle and late childhood than in early childhood, parents continue to be extremely important socializing agents in their children's lives (Collins, Harris, & Susman, 1995). Children also must learn to relate to adults outside the family on a regular basis—adults who interact with the child much differently than parents do. During middle and late childhood, interactions with adults outside the family involve more formal control and achievement orientation.

Discipline during middle and late childhood is often easier for parents than it was during early childhood; it may also be easier than during adolescence. In middle and late childhood, children's cognitive development has matured to the point where it is possible for parents to reason with them about resisting deviation and controlling their behavior. By adolescence, children's reasoning has become more sophisticated, and they may be less likely to accept parental discipline. Adolescents also push more strongly for independence, which contributes to parenting difficulties. Parents of elementary school children use less physical discipline than do parents of preschool children. By contrast, parents of elementary school children are more likely to use deprivation of privileges, appeals directed at the child's self-esteem, comments designed to increase the child's sense of guilt, and statements indicating to the child that she is responsible for her actions.

During middle and late childhood, some control is transferred from parent to child, although the process is gradual and involves *coregulation* rather than control by either the child or the parent alone (Maccoby, 1984). The major shift to autonomy does not occur until about the age of 12 or later. During middle and late childhood, parents continue to exercise general supervision and exert control while children are allowed to engage in moment-to-moment self-regulation. This coregulation process is a transition period between the strong parental control of early childhood and the increased relinquishment of general supervision of adolescence.

During this coregulation, parents should

- monitor, guide, and support children at a distance;
- effectively use the times when they have direct contact with the child; and
- strengthen in their children the ability to monitor their own behavior, to adopt appropriate standards of conduct, to avoid hazardous risks, and to sense when parental support and contact are appropriate.

To be a competent parent, further adaptation is required as children become adolescents, which will be discussed later in the chapter. As we will see next, however, other important aspects of understanding parenting involve the family life cycle.

The Family Life Cycle

As we go through life, we are at different points in the family life cycle. The stages of the family life cycle include leaving home and becoming a single adult; the joining of families through marriage—the new couple; becoming parents and families with children; families with adolescents; families at midlife; and the family in later life. A summary of these stages in the family life cycle are shown in figure 15.2, along with key aspects of emotional processes involved in the transition from one stage to the next, and changes in family status required for developmental change to take place (Carter & McGoldrick, 1989).

Leaving Home and Becoming a Single Adult

Leaving home and becoming a single adult *is the first stage in the family life cycle and involves the concept of launching.* **Launching** *is the process in which the youth moves into adulthood and exits his or her family of origin.* Adequate completion of launching requires that the young adult separate from the family of origin without cutting off ties completely or fleeing in a reactive way to find some form of substitute emotional refuge. The launching period is a time for the youth and young adult to formulate personal life goals, to develop an identity, and to become more independent before joining with another person to form a new family. This is a time for young people to sort out emotionally what they will take along from the family of origin, what they will leave behind, and what they will create themselves.

Complete cutoffs from parents rarely, or never, resolve emotional problems. The shift to adult-to-adult status between parents and children requires a mutually respectful and personal form of relating, in which young adults can appreciate parents as they are, needing neither to make them into what they are not nor to blame them for what they could not be. Neither do young adults need to comply with parental expectations and wishes at their own expense.

The Joining of Families Through Marriage: The New Couple

The new couple *is the second stage in the family life cycle, in which two individuals from separate families of origin unite to form a new family system.* This stage involves not only the development of a new marital system but also a realignment with extended families and friends to include the spouse. Women's changing roles, the increasingly frequent marriage of partners from divergent cultural backgrounds, and the increasing physical distances between family members are placing a much stronger burden on couples to define their relationship for themselves than was true in the past. Marriage is usually described as the union of two individuals, but in reality it is the union of two entire family systems and the development of a new, third system. Some experts on marriage and the family believe that marriage represents such different phenomena for women and men that we need to speak of "her" marriage and "his" marriage. In American society, women have anticipated marriage with greater enthusiasm and more positive expectations than men have, although statistically it has not been a very healthy system for them.

Becoming Parents and Families with Children

Becoming parents and families with children *is the third stage in the family life cycle. Entering this stage requires that adults now move up a generation and become caregivers to*

Family Life-Cycle Stage	Emotional Process of Transition: Key Principles	Changes in Family Status Required to Proceed Developmentally
1. Leaving home: Single young adults	Accepting emotional and financial responsibility for self	a. Differentiation of self in relation to family of origin b. Development of intimate peer relationships c. Establishment of self in relation to work and financial independence
2. The joining of families through marriage: The new couple	Commitment to new system	a. Formation of marital system b. Realignment of relationships with extended families and friends to include spouse
3. Becoming parents and families with children	Accepting new members into the system	a. Adjusting marital system to make space for child(ren) b. Joining in child-rearing, financial, and household tasks c. Realignment of relationships with extended family to include parenting and grandparenting roles
4. Families with adolescents	Increasing flexibility of family boundaries to include children's independence and grandparents' frailties	a. Shifting of parent-child relationships to permit adolescent to move in and out of system b. Refocus on midlife marital and career issues c. Beginning shift toward joint caring for older generation
5. Midlife families	Accepting a multitude of exits from and entries into the family system	a. Renegotiation of marital system as a dyad b. Development of adult-to-adult relationships between grown children and their parents c. Realignment of relationships to include in-laws and grandchildren d. Dealing with disabilities and death of parents (grandparents)
6. Families in later life	Accepting the shifting of generational roles	a. Maintaining own and/or couple functioning and interests in face of physiological decline; exploration of new familial and social role options b. Support for a more central role of middle generation c. Making room in the system for the wisdom and experience of the elderly, supporting the older generation without overfunctioning for them d. Dealing with loss of spouse, siblings, and other peers and preparation for own death; life review and integration

Figure~15.2

The Stages of the Family Life Cycle

From Betty Carter and Monica McGoldrick, The Changing Family Life Cycle: A Framework for Family Therapy 2/E.Copyright ©1989 by Allyn and Bacon. Reprinted by permission.

the younger generation. Moving through the lengthy stage successfully requires a commitment of time as a parent, understanding the roles of parents, and adapting to developmental changes in children. Problems that emerge when a couple first assumes the parental role are struggles with each other about taking responsibility, as well as refusal or inability to function as competent parents to children.

When people become parents through pregnancy, adoption, or stepparenting, they face disequilibrium and must adapt. Parents want to develop a strong attachment to their infant, but they still want to maintain strong attachments to their spouse and friends, and possibly continue their careers. Parents ask themselves how this new being will change their lives. A baby places new restrictions on partners; no longer will they be able to rush out to a movie on a moment's notice, and money will not be readily available for vacations and other luxuries. Dual-career parents ask, "Will it harm the baby to place her in day care? Will we be able to find responsible baby-sitters?"

The excitement and joy that accompany the birth of a healthy baby are often followed by "postpartum blues" in mothers—a depressed state that lasts as long as 9 months into the infant's first year (Field, 1995). The early months of the baby's physical demands may bring not only the joy of intimacy but also the sorrow of exhaustion. Pregnancy and childbirth are demanding physical events that require recovery time for the mother.

Many fathers are not sensitive to these extreme demands placed on the mother. Busy trying to make enough money to pay the bills, fathers may not be at home much of the time. A father's ability to sense and adapt to the stress placed on his wife during the first year of the infant's life has important implications for the success of the marriage and the family.

Becoming a father is both wonderful *and* stressful. In a longitudinal investigation of couples from late pregnancy until 3½ years after the baby was born, Carolyn and Phillip Cowan (Cowan & others, 1991) found that the couples enjoyed more positive marital relations before the baby was born than after. Still, almost one-third showed an increase in marital satisfaction. Some couples said that the baby had brought them closer together *and* moved them farther apart. They commented that being parents enhanced their sense of themselves and gave them a new, more stable identity as a couple. Babies opened men up to a concern with intimate relationships, and the demands of juggling work and family roles stimulated women to manage family tasks more efficiently and pay attention to their personal growth.

At some point during the early years of the child's life, parents do face the difficult task of juggling their roles as parents and as self-actualizing adults. Until recently in our culture, nurturing our children and having a career were thought to be incompatible. Fortunately, we have come to recognize that the balance between caring and achieving, nurturing and working—although difficult to manage—can be accomplished.

The Family with Adolescents

The **family with adolescents** *is the fourth stage of the family life cycle. Adolescence is a period of development in which individuals push for autonomy and seek to develop their own identity.* The development of mature autonomy and identity is a lengthy process, transpiring over at least 10 to 15 years. Compliant children become noncompliant adolescents. Parents need to adopt one of two strategies to handle noncompliance—either clamping down and putting more pressure on the adolescent to conform to parental values or becoming more permissive and letting the adolescent have extensive freedom. Neither is a wise overall strategy; rather, a more flexible, adaptive approach is best. Later in the chapter we will explore the family worlds of adolescents and their parents in greater detail.

Midlife Families

The **family at midlife** *is the fifth stage in the family life cycle. It is a time of launching children, playing an important role in linking generations, and adapting to midlife changes in development.* Until about a generation ago, most families were involved in raising their children for much of their adult lives until old age. Because of the lower birth rate and the longer life of most adults, parents now launch their children about 20 years before retirement, which frees many midlife parents to pursue other activities.

> *The generations of living things pass in a short time, and like runners hand on the torch of life.*
>
> —**Lucretius, 1st Century B.C.**

For the most part, family members maintain considerable contact across generations. Parent-child similarity is most noticeable in religious and political areas, least in gender roles, lifestyle, and work orientation. Gender differences also characterize intergenerational relationships (Nydegger & Mitteness, 1991). In one investigation, mothers and their daughters had much closer relationships during their adult years than did mothers and sons, fathers and daughters, and fathers and sons (Rossi, 1989). Also, in this same investigation, married men were more involved with their wives' kin than with their own. These findings underscore the significance of the woman's role as mother in monitoring access to and feelings toward kin.

The Family in Later Life

The **family in later life** *is the sixth and final stage in the family life cycle. Retirement alters a couple's lifestyle, requiring adaptation. Grandparenting also characterizes many families in this period.* The greatest changes occur in the traditional family, in which the husband works and the wife is a homemaker. The husband might not know what to do with his time, and the wife might feel uneasy having him around the house all of the time. In traditional families, both partners may need to move toward more expressive roles. The husband must adjust from being the good provider to being a helper around the house; the wife must change from being only a good homemaker to being even more loving and understanding. Marital happiness as an older adult is also affected by each partner's ability to deal with personal conflicts, including aging, illness, and eventual death (Zarit & Eggebeen, 1995).

> *G*row old with me!
> The best is yet to be,
> The last of life,
> For which the first was made.
>
> **—Browning**

Individuals who are married in late adulthood are usually happier than those who are single (Lee, 1978). Marital satisfaction is greater for women than for men, possibly because women place more emphasis on attaining satisfaction through marriage than men do. However, as more women develop careers, this gender difference might not continue.

About three of every four adults over the age of 65 have at least one living grandchild, and most grandparents have some regular contact with their grandchildren (Smith, 1995). About 80 percent of grandparents say they are happy in their relationships with their grandchildren, and a majority of grandparents say that grandparenting is easier than parenthood and that they enjoy it more than parenthood (Brubaker, 1985). In one investigation, grandfathers were less satisfied with grandparenthood than grandmothers were, and middle-aged grandparents (aged 45–60) were more willing to give advice and to assume responsibility for watching and disciplining grandchildren than were older grandparents (aged 60 and older) (Thomas, 1986). Also, maternal grandparents often interact more with their grandchildren than paternal grandparents do (Bahr, 1989).

Sociocultural and Historical Changes

Family development does not occur in a social vacuum. Important sociocultural and historical influences affect family processes (Parke, 1993; Parke & Buriel, 1997). Family changes may be due to great upheavals in a nation, such as war, famine, or mass immigration. Or they may be due more to subtle transitions in ways of life. The Great Depression in the early 1930s had some negative effects on families. During its height, the Depression produced economic deprivation, adult discontent, depression about living conditions, marital conflict, inconsistent child rearing, and unhealthy lifestyles—heavy drinking, demoralized attitudes, and health disabilities—especially in fathers (Elder, 1980). Subtle changes in a culture that have significant influences on the family were described by the famous anthropologist Margaret Mead (1978). The changes focus on the longevity of the elderly and the role of the elderly in the family, the urban and suburban orientation of families and their mobility, television, and a general dissatisfaction and restlessness.

Fifty years ago, the older people who survived were usually hearty and still closely linked to the family, often helping to maintain the family's existence. Today, older people live longer, which means that their middle-aged children are often pressed into a caretaking role for their parents or the elderly parents may be placed in a nursing home. Elderly parents may have lost some of their socializing role in the family during the twentieth century as many of their children moved great distances away.

Many of these family moves were away from farms and small towns to urban and suburban settings. In the small towns and farms, individuals were surrounded by life-long neighbors, relatives, and friends. Today, neighborhood and extended-family support systems are not nearly as prevalent. Families now move all over the country, often uprooting the child from a school and peer group he or she has known for a considerable length of time. And for many families, this type of move occurs every year or two, as one or both parents are transferred from job to job.

Television also plays a major role in the changing family. Many children who watch television find that parents are too busy working to share this experience with them. Children increasingly experience a world their parents are not a part of. Instead of participating in neighborhood peer groups, children come home after school and plop down in front of the television set. And television allows children and their families to see new ways of life. Lower-class families can look into the family lives of the middle class by simply pushing a button.

Another subtle change in families has been an increase in general dissatisfaction and restlessness. Women have become increasingly dissatisfied with their way of life, which has resulted in great strain in many marriages. With fewer elders and long-term friends close by to help and advise young people during the initial difficult years of marriage and childbearing, marriages begin to fracture at the first signs of disagreement. Divorce has become epidemic in our culture. As women move into the labor market, men simultaneously become restless and look for stimulation outside of family life. The result of such restlessness and the tendency to divorce and remarry has been a hodgepodge of family structures, with far greater numbers of single-parent and stepparent families than ever before in history. Later in the chapter, we discuss such aspects of the changing social world of the child and the family in greater detail.

THE PARENTAL ROLE AND PARENTING STYLES

What is the nature of the parental role? What parenting techniques and styles do parents use with children?

The Parental Role

For many adults, the parental role is well planned and coordinated with other roles in life and is developed with the

CHEEVERWOOD © 1986 Michael Fry.

individual's economic situation in mind. For others, the discovery that they are about to become parents is a startling surprise. In either event, the prospective parents may have mixed emotions and romantic illusions about having a child. Parenting consists of a number of interpersonal skills and emotional demands, yet there is little in the way of formal education for this task. Most parents learn parenting practices from their own parents—some of these practices they accept, some they discard. Husbands and wives may bring different viewpoints of parenting practices to the marriage. Unfortunately, when methods of parents are passed on from one generation to the next, both desirable and undesirable practices are perpetuated.

> *For years we have given scientific attention to the care and rearing of plants and animals, but we have allowed babies to be raised chiefly by tradition.*
>
> **—Edith Belle Lowry, *False Modesty* (1912)**

The needs and expectations of parents have stimulated many myths about parenting (Okun & Rappaport, 1980):

- The birth of a child will save a failing marriage
- As a possession or extension of the parent, the child will think, feel, and behave like the parents did in their childhood
- Children will take care of parents in old age
- Parents can expect respect and get obedience from their children
- Having a child means that the parents will always have someone who loves them and is their best friend
- Having a child gives the parents a "second chance" to achieve what they should have achieved
- If parents learn the right techniques, they can mold their children into what they want

- It's the parents fault when children fail
- Mothers are naturally better parents than fathers
- Parenting is an instinct and requires no training

Parenting Styles

Parents want their children to grow into socially mature individuals, and they may feel frustrated in trying to discover the best way to accomplish this. Developmentalists have long searched for the ingredients of parenting that promote competent social development in children. For example, in the 1930s, John Watson argued that parents were too affectionate with their children. In the 1950s, a distinction was made between physical and psychological discipline, with psychological discipline, especially reasoning, emphasized as the best way to rear a child. In the 1970s and beyond, the dimensions of competent parenting have become more precise.

Especially widespread is the view of Diana Baumrind (1971), who believes parents should be neither punitive nor aloof, but should instead develop rules for their children and be affectionate with them. She emphasizes three types of parenting that are associated with different aspects of the child's social behavior: authoritarian, authoritative, and laissez-faire (permissive). More recently, developmentalists have argued that permissive parenting comes in two different forms: neglectful and indulgent. What are these forms of parenting like?

> *I looked on child rearing not only as a work of love and duty but as a profession that was fully as interesting and challenging as any honorable profession in the world and one that demanded the best that I could bring to it.*
>
> **—Rose Kennedy**

Authoritarian parenting *is a restrictive, punitive style in which the parents* exhort *the child to follow their directions and to respect work and effort. The authoritarian parent places firm limits and controls on the child and allows little verbal exchange. Authoritarian parenting is associated with children's social incompetence.* For example, an authoritarian parent might say, "You do it my way or else. There will be no discussion!" Children of authoritarian parents are often anxious about social comparison, fail to initiate activity, and have poor communication skills. And in a study, early harsh discipline was associated with child aggression (Weiss & others, 1992).

Authoritative parenting *is a style in which the parents encourage children to be independent but still place limits and controls on their actions. Extensive verbal give-and-take is allowed and parents are warm and nurturant toward the child. Authoritative parenting is associated with children's social competence.* An authoritative parent might put his arm around the child in a comforting way and say, "You know you should not have done that; let's talk about how you can handle the situation better next time." Children whose parents are authoritative are socially competent, self-reliant, and socially responsible.

Permissive parenting comes in two forms: neglectful and indulgent (Maccoby & Martin, 1983). **Neglectful parenting** *is a style in which the parent is very uninvolved in the child's life; it is associated with children's social incompetence, especially a lack of self-control.* This parent cannot answer the question, "It is 10 P.M. Do you know where your child is?" Children have a strong need for their parents to care about them; children whose parents are permissive-indifferent develop the sense that other aspects of the parents' lives are more important than they are. Children whose parents are neglectful are socially incompetent—they show poor self-control and do not handle independence well.

Indulgent parenting *is a style of parenting in which parents are highly involved with their children but place few demands or controls on them. Indulgent parenting is associated with children's social incompetence, especially a lack of self-control.* They let their children do what they want, and the result is the children never learn to control their own behavior and always expect to get their way. Some parents deliberately rear their children in this way because they believe the combination of warm involvement with few restraints will produce a creative, confident child. One boy I knew whose parents deliberately reared him in an indulgent manner moved his parents out of their bedroom suite and took it over for himself. He is now 18 years old and has not learned to control his behavior; when he can't get something he wants, he still throws temper tantrums. As you might expect, he is not very popular with his peers. Children whose parents are indulgent rarely learn respect for others and have difficulty controlling their behavior.

The four classifications of parenting just discussed involve combinations of acceptance and responsiveness on the one hand, and demand and control on the other. How these dimensions combine to produce authoritarian, authoritative, neglectful, and indulgent parenting is shown in figure 15.3. To further evaluate parenting styles, turn to Critical Thinking About Children's Development.

> *Parenting is a very important profession, but no test of fitness for it is ever imposed in the interest of children.*
>
> —George Bernard Shaw,
> **Everybody's Political About What, 1944**

Child Abuse

Unfortunately, parental hostility toward children in some families escalates to the point where one or both parents abuse the children. Child abuse is an increasing problem in the United States. Estimates of its incidence vary, but some authorities say that as many as 500,000 children are physically abused every year. Laws in many states now require doctors and teachers to report suspected cases of child abuse, yet many cases go unreported, especially those of battered infants.

Child abuse is such a disturbing circumstance that many people have difficulty understanding or sympathizing with parents who abuse or neglect their children (Crittenden, 1988). Our response is often outrage and anger directed at the parent. This outrage focuses our attention on parents as bad, sick, monstrous, sadistic individuals who cause their children to suffer. Experts on child abuse believe that this view is too simple and deflects attention away from the social context of the abuse and parents' coping skills. It is especially important to recognize that child abuse is a diverse condition, that it is usually mild to moderate in severity, and that it is only partially caused by individual personality characteristics of parents (Emery, 1989).

The Multifaceted Nature of Child Maltreatment

Whereas the public and many professionals use the term *child abuse* to refer to both abuse and neglect, developmentalists increasingly are using the term *child maltreatment* (Manly, 1995). This term reduces the emotional impact of the term *abuse* and acknowledges that maltreatment includes several different conditions. Among the different types of maltreatment are physical and sexual abuse; fostering delinquency; lack of supervision; medical, educational, and nutritional neglect; and drug or alcohol abuse (Barnett & McGee, 1993). In one large survey, approximately 20 percent of the reported cases involved abuse alone, 46 percent neglect alone, 23

Figure~15.3

Classification of Parenting Styles
The four types of parenting styles (authoritative, authoritarian, permissive-indulgent, and permissive-neglectful) involve the dimensions of acceptance and responsiveness, on the one hand, and demandingness and control on the other.

percent both abuse and neglect, and 11 percent sexual abuse (American Association for Protecting Children, 1986).

Severity of Abuse

The concern about child abuse began with the identification of the "battered child syndrome" and has retained the characteristics of severe, brutal injury for several reasons. First, the media tend to underscore the most bizarre and vicious incidents. Second, much of the funding for child-abuse prevention, identification, and treatment depends on the public's perception of the horror of child abuse and the medical profession's lobby for funds to investigate and treat abused children and their parents. The emphasis is often on the worst cases. These horrific cases do exist, and are indeed terrible, but they make up only a small minority of abused children.

Less than 1 percent of abused children die, and another 11 percent suffer life-threatening, disabling injuries (American Association for Protecting Children, 1986). By contrast, almost 90 percent suffer temporary physical injuries. These milder injuries, though, are likely to be experienced repeatedly in the context of daily hostile family exchanges. Similarly, neglected children, who suffer no physical injuries, often experience extensive, long-term psychological harm (Paget & Abramczyk, 1993).

The Cultural Context of Maltreatment

The extensive violence that takes place in the American culture is reflected in the occurrence of violence in the family (Gelles & Conte, 1990). A regular diet of violence appears on television screens, and parents often resort to power assertion as a disciplinary technique. In

Evaluating the Parenting Styles of Both Parents

In our discussion of parenting styles, authoritative parenting was associated with social competence in children. In some cases, though, one parent engages in one parenting style and the other parent in another style. Consider all four styles of parenting—authoritarian, authoritative, neglectful, and indulgent. The best case is when both parents are authoritative. What might the effects on the child be, though, if the father is authoritarian and the mother is indulgent, the father is authoritarian and the mother is authoritative, and so on? Is it best for the child for the parents to be consistent, even if both are authoritarian, both are indulgent, or both are neglectful? Or is it best for the child to have at least one authoritative parent when the other parent is authoritarian, indulgent, or neglectful?

In thinking about parenting styles, consider also what style or styles your father and mother used in rearing you. Were they both authoritative? Was one authoritarian, the other indulgent? And so on. What effects do you think their parenting styles had on your development?

By evaluating the nature of parenting styles on the part of both parents, you are learning to think critically by *applying developmental concepts to enhance personal adaptation.*

China, where physical punishment is rarely used to discipline children, the incidence of child abuse is reported to be very low. In the United States, many abusing parents report that they do not have sufficient resources or help from others. This may be a realistic evaluation of the situation experienced by many low-income families, who do not have adequate preventive and supportive services (Rodriguez-Haynes & Crittenden, 1988).

Community support systems are especially important in alleviating stressful family situations, thereby preventing child abuse. An investigation of the support systems in 58 counties in New York State revealed a relation between the incidence of child abuse and the absence of support systems available to the family (Garbarino, 1976). Both family resources—relatives and friends, for example—and such formal community support systems as crisis centers and child-abuse counseling were associated with a reduction in child abuse.

Family Influences

To understand abuse in the family, the interaction of all family members needs to be considered, regardless of who actually performs the violent acts against the child (Daro, 1988). For example, even though the father may be the one who physically abuses the child, contributions by the mother, the child, and siblings also should be evaluated. Many parents who abuse their children come from families in which physical punishment was used. These parents view physical punishment as a legitimate way of controlling the child's behavior, and physical punishment might be a part of this sanctioning. Characteristics of the children themselves might contribute to child abuse. An unattractive child might receive more physical punishment than an attractive child, and a child from an unwanted pregnancy may be especially vulnerable to abuse (Harter, Alexander, & Neimeyer, 1988). Husband-wife violence and financial problems can result in displaced aggression toward a defenseless child. Displaced aggression is commonly involved in child abuse.

Developmental Consequences of Child Maltreatment

The developmental consequences of child maltreatment include poor emotion regulation, attachment problems, problems in peer relations, difficulty in adapting to school, and other psychological problems (Rogosch & others, 1995).

Emotion Regulation   Difficulties in initiating and modulating positive and negative affect have been observed in maltreated infants (Cicchetti, Ganiban, & Barnett, 1991). Maltreated infants also might show excessive negative affect or blunted positive affect.

Attachment   Not only do maltreated infants show insecure patterns of attachment, they also might show a form of attachment not often found in normal samples of children. Maltreated children tend to display an inconsistent attachment pattern referred to as *disorganized*, which involves high avoidance and high resistance (Main & Solomon, 1990). In one study, the disorganized attachment pattern was found in 80 percent of the maltreated infants observed (Carlson & others, 1989).

Peer Relations   Maltreated children appear to be poorly equipped to develop successful peer relations, due to their aggressiveness, avoidance, and aberrant responses to both distress and positive approaches from peers (Mueller & Silverman, 1989). Two patterns of social behavior are common in maltreated children: excessive physical and verbal aggression, and avoidance. These patterns have been described in terms of "fight or flight."

Adaptation to School Maltreated children's difficulties in establishing effective relationships can show up in their interactions with teachers. Maltreated children might expect teachers to be unresponsive or unavailable, based on their relationships with their parents. In the lives of maltreated children, dealing with fears of abuse and searching for security in relationships with adults can take precedence over performing competently at academic tasks.

Psychopathology Being physically abused has been linked with children's anxiety, personality problems, depression, conduct disorder, and delinquency (Toth, Manley, & Cicchetti, 1992). Later, during the adult years, maltreated children show increased violence toward other adults, dating partners, and marital partners, as well as increased substance abuse, anxiety, and depression (Malinosky-Rummell & Hansen, 1993). In sum, child maltreatment places children at risk for the development of a wide range of problems and disorders.

A Model of Intervention

Dante Cicchetti and his colleagues (Cicchetti & Toth, 1997; Rogosch & others, 1995) have developed a model of intervention with maltreated children that is receiving increased attention. The model is used at the Mount Hope Family Center of the University of Rochester. Intervention with maltreating families is difficult because of the multiple risk factors involved and the difficulty in getting such families to deal with the chaos in their lives. Poverty, intellectual and educational limitations, social isolation, and mental disorders are but a few of the factors that make it difficult to involve these families in effective treatment. A multidisciplinary approach uses the expertise of social workers, special educators, speech therapists, and psychologists to address the complexities associated with child maltreatment. Therapeutic preschool services are provided for children 3 to 5 years of age, individual and group psychotherapy are offered to children and parents, and families also participate in a home-based component. Therapists assist families in modifying their caregiving style, provide support in times of crisis, and encourage them to develop supportive social networks.

Both after-school and summer camps are available at Mount Hope Family Center. One of the main goals of the after-school program is to provide maltreated children with some positive relationships. Because many of these children's past caregivers were inconsistent, unavailable, and lacking in warmth toward the children, the program attempts to provide the children with stable supportive relationships with counselors and peers. Much

Dante Cicchetti has significantly advanced our knowledge of maltreated children. He and his colleagues at Mount Hope Family Center in Rochester, New York, have developed a model of intervention with maltreated children that is receiving increased attention.

of the relationship-building occurs in the context of recreational games and activities. Parenting groups also are part of the after-school program. Because many of the families involved are on welfare and do not have the means to send their children to a summer camp, the camp is free of charge. Children are invited to attend the camp annually to encourage reliability and consistency in relationships.

SIBLING RELATIONSHIPS AND BIRTH ORDER

Our coverage of siblings focuses on the nature of sibling relationships, sibling interaction and socialization, and birth order.

The Nature of Sibling Relationships

Sandra describes to her mother what happened in a conflict with her sister:

> We had just come home from the ball game. I sat down on the sofa next to the light so I could read. Sally (the

sister) said, "Get up, I was sitting there first. I just got up for a second to get a drink." I told her I was not going to get up and that I didn't see her name on the chair. I got mad and started pushing her. Her drink spilled all over her. Then she got really mad; she shoved me against the wall, hitting and clawing at me. I managed to grab a handful of hair.

At this point, Sally comes into the room and begins to tell her side of the story. Sandra interrupts, "Mother, you always take her side." Sound familiar? Any of you who have grown up with siblings probably have a rich memory of aggressive, hostile interchanges; but sibling relationships have many pleasant, caring moments as well. Children's sibling relationships include helping, sharing, teaching, fighting, and playing. Children can act as emotional supports, rivals, and communication partners (Carlson, 1995; Cicirelli, 1994). More than 80 percent of American children have one or more siblings (brothers or sisters). Because there are so many possible sibling combinations, it is difficult to generalize about sibling influences. Among the factors to be considered are the number of siblings, age of siblings, birth order, age spacing, sex of siblings, and whether sibling relationships are different from parent-child relationships.

Sibling Interaction and Socialization

Is sibling interaction different than parent-child interaction? There is some evidence that it is. Observations indicate that children interact more positively and in more varied ways with their parents than with their siblings (Baskett & Johnson, 1982). Children also follow their parents' dictates more than those of their siblings, and they behave more negatively and punitively with their siblings than with their parents.

In some instances, siblings may be stronger socializing influences on the child than parents are (Cicirelli, 1977). Someone close in age to the child—such as a sibling—may be able to understand the child's problems and be able to communicate more effectively than parents can. In dealing with peers, coping with difficult teachers, and discussing taboo subjects such as sex, siblings may be more influential in the socialization process than parents.

Is sibling interaction the same around the world? In industrialized societies like the United States, delegation of responsibility for younger siblings to older siblings tends to be carried out informally by parents, primarily to give the parent freedom to pursue other activities. However, in nonindustrialized countries, such as Kenya in Africa, a much greater degree of importance is attached to the older sibling's role as a caregiver to younger siblings. In industrialized countries, the older sibling's caregiving role is often discretionary; in nonindustrialized countries it is more obligatory (Cicirelli, 1994).

What socializing role do siblings play in children's development?

Birth Order

Birth order is a special interest of sibling researchers. When differences in behavior are found to correlate with birth order, they usually are explained by variations in interactions with parents and siblings associated with the unique experiences of being in a particular position in the family. This is especially true in the case of the firstborn child (Murphy, 1993; Teti & others, 1993). The oldest child is the only one who does not have to share parental love and affection with other siblings—until another sibling comes along. An infant requires more attention than an older child; this means that the firstborn sibling now gets less attention than before the newborn arrived. Does this result in conflict between parents and the firstborn? In one research study, mothers became more negative, coercive, and restraining, and played less, with the firstborn following the birth of a second child (Dunn & Kendrick, 1982). Even though a new infant requires more attention from parents than does an older child, an especially intense relationship is often maintained between parents and firstborns throughout the life cycle. Parents have higher expectations for, put more pressure for achievement and responsibility on, and interfere more with the activities of firstborn children as compared to later-born children (Furman, 1995).

Birth order is also associated with variations in sibling relationships. The oldest sibling is expected to

The one-child family is becoming much more common in China because of the strong motivation to limit the population growth in the People's Republic of China. The policy is still new, and its effects on children have not been fully examined.

exercise self-control and show responsibility in interacting with younger siblings. When the oldest sibling is jealous or hostile, parents often protect the younger sibling. The oldest sibling is more dominant, competent, and powerful than the younger siblings; the oldest sibling is also expected to assist and teach younger siblings. Indeed, researchers have shown that older siblings are both more antagonistic—hitting, kicking, and biting—and more nurturant toward their younger siblings than vice versa (Abramovitch & others, 1986). There is also something unique about same-sex sibling relationships. Aggression and dominance occur more in same-sex relationships than in opposite-sex sibling relationships (Minnett, Vandell, & Santrock, 1983).

Given the differences in family dynamics involved in birth order, it is not surprising that firstborns and later-borns have different characteristics. Firstborn children are more adult oriented, helpful, conforming, anxious, self-controlled, and less aggressive than their siblings. Parents give more attention to firstborns, and this is related to firstborns' nurturant behavior (Stanhope & Corter, 1993). Parental demands and high standards established for firstborns result in these children excelling in academic and professional endeavors. Firstborns are over-represented in *Who's Who* and Rhodes scholars, for example. However, some of the same pressures placed on firstborns for high achievement may be the reason they also have more guilt, anxiety, difficulty in coping with stressful situations, and higher admission to child guidance clinics.

What is the only child like? The popular conception of the only child is a "spoiled brat" with such undesirable characteristics as dependency, lack of self-control, and self-centered behavior. But researchers present a more positive portrayal of the only child, who often is achievement oriented and displays a desirable personality, especially in comparison to later-borns and children from large families (Falbo & Poston, 1993; Jiao, Ji, & Jing, 1996; Thomas, Coffman, & Kipp, 1993).

So far our consideration of birth-order effects suggests that birth order might be a strong predictor of behavior. However, an increasing number of family researchers believe that birth order has been overdramatized and overemphasized. The critics argue that, when all of the factors that influence behavior are considered, birth order itself shows limited ability to predict behavior. Consider just sibling relationships alone. They not only vary in birth order but also in number of siblings, age of siblings, age spacing of siblings, and sex of siblings.

Consider also the temperament of siblings. Researchers have found that siblings' temperamental traits (such as "easy" and "difficult," for example), as well as differential treatment of siblings by parents, influence how siblings get along (Stocker & Dunn, 1991). Siblings with "easy" temperaments who are treated in relatively equal ways by parents tend to get along with each other the best, whereas siblings with "difficult" temperaments, or who are treated unequally by their parents, get along the worst.

Beyond temperament and differential treatment of siblings by parents, think about some of the other important factors in children's lives that influence their behavior beyond birth order. They include heredity, models of competency or incompetency that parents present to children on a daily basis, peer influences, school influences, socioeconomic factors, sociohistorical factors, cultural variations, and so on. When someone says firstborns are always like this, but lastborns are always like that, you now know that they are making overly simplistic statements that do not adequately take into account the complexity of influences on a child's behavior. Keep in mind, though, that, while birth order itself may not be a good predictor of children's behavior, sibling relationships and interaction are important dimensions of family processes.

FAMILY PROCESSES IN ADOLESCENCE

What are some of the most important issues and questions that need to be raised about family relationships in adolescence? They include: What is the nature of autonomy and attachment in adolescence? How extensive is parent-adolescent conflict, and how does it influence the adolescent's development?

Autonomy and Attachment

The adolescent's push for autonomy and a sense of responsibility puzzles and angers many parents. Parents see their teenager slipping from their grasp. They may have an urge to take stronger control as the adolescent seeks autonomy and responsibility. Heated emotional exchanges may ensue, with either side calling names, making threats, and doing whatever seems necessary to gain control. Parents may seem frustrated because they *expect* their teenager to heed their advice, to want to spend time with the family, and to grow up to do what is right (Collins & Luebker, 1993). Most parents anticipate that their teenager will have some difficulty adjusting to the changes that adolescence brings, but few parents can imagine and predict just how strong an adolescent's desires will be to spend time with peers or how much adolescents will want to show that it is they—not their parents—who are responsible for their successes and failures.

The ability to attain autonomy and gain control over one's behavior in adolescence is acquired through appropriate adult reactions to the adolescent's desire for control (Keener & Boykin, 1996; Urberg & Wolowicz, 1996). At the onset of adolescence, the average individual does not have the knowledge to make appropriate or mature decisions in all areas of life. As the adolescent pushes for autonomy, the wise adult relinquishes control in those areas where the adolescent can make reasonable decisions but continues to guide the adolescent to make reasonable decisions in areas where the adolescent's knowledge is more limited. Gradually, adolescents acquire the ability to make mature decisions on their own.

But adolescents do not simply move away from parental influence into a decision-making process all their own. There is continued connectedness to parents as adolescents move toward and gain autonomy (Juang & Nguyen, 1997). In the last decade, developmentalists have begun to explore the role of secure attachment, and related concepts such as connectedness to parents, in adolescent development. They believe that attachment to parents in adolescence may facilitate the adolescent's social competence and well-being, as reflected in such characteristics as self-esteem, emotional adjustment, and physical health (Allen & Kuperminc, 1995; Black & Mc-Cartney, 1995; Kobak & others, 1993). For example, adolescents who have secure relationships with their parents have higher self-esteem and better emotional well-being (Armsden & Greenberg, 1987). In contrast, emotional detachment from parents is associated with greater feelings of parental rejection and a lower sense of one's own social and romantic attractiveness (Ryan & Lynch, 1989). Thus, attachment to parents during adolescence may serve the adaptive function of providing a secure base from which adolescents can explore and master new environments and a widening social world in a psychologically healthy manner (Allen & Bell, 1995; Bell, 1995). Secure attachment to parents may buffer adolescents from the anxiety and potential feelings of depression or emotional distress associated with the transition from childhood to adulthood.

Secure attachment or connectedness to parents promotes competent peer relations and positive close relationships outside of the family. In one investigation, attachment to parents and peers was assessed (Armsden & Greenberg, 1984). Adolescents who were securely attached to parents were also securely attached to peers; those who were insecurely attached to parents were also more likely to be insecurely attached to peers. In another investigation, college students who were securely attached to their parents as young children were more likely to have securely attached relationships with friends, dates, and spouses than their insecurely attached counterparts (Hazen & Shaver, 1987). And in yet another investigation, older adolescents who had an ambivalent attachment history with their parents reported greater jealousy, conflict, and dependency along with less satisfaction in their relationship with their best friend than their securely attached counterparts (Fisher, 1990). There are times when adolescents reject closeness, connection, and attachment to their parents as they assert their ability to make decisions and to develop an identity. But for the most part, the worlds of parents and peers are coordinated and connected, not uncoordinated and disconnected (Haynie & McLellan, 1992).

Parent-Adolescent Conflict

While attachment and connectedness to parents remains strong during adolescence, the attachment and connectedness is not always smooth (Grotevant, 1997). Early adolescence is a time when conflict with parents escalates beyond childhood levels (Steinberg, 1991). This increase may be due to a number of factors: the biological changes of puberty, cognitive changes involving increased idealism and logical reasoning, social changes focused on independence and identity, maturational changes in parents, and violated expectations on the part of parents and adolescents. The adolescent compares her parents to an ideal standard and then criticizes the flaws. A 13-year-old girl tells her mother, "That is the tackiest-looking dress I have ever seen. Nobody would be caught dead wearing that." The adolescent demands logical explanations for comments and discipline. A 14-year-old boy tells his mother, "What do you mean I have to be home at 10 P.M. because it's the way we do things around here? Why do we do things around here that way? It doesn't make sense to me."

Communicating with Children About Divorce

If parents decide to obtain a divorce, how should they communicate with their children about the divorce? For one thing, they should explain the separation as soon as daily activities in the home make it obvious that one parent is leaving. If possible, both parents should be present when the children are told about the separation. Children also should be told that any time they want to talk about the separation, they should come to the parents. It is healthy for children to get their pent-up emotions out in the open in discussions with their parents and to learn that their parents are willing to listen to their feelings and fears. Can you think of other stategies divorcing parents can use effectively to communicate with their children? By evaluating ways to communicate with children about divorce, you are learning to think critically by *using knowledge about development to improve human welfare*.

families, in which a woman has custody of children from a previous marriage, make up 70 percent of stepfamilies. Stepmother families make up almost 20 percent of stepfamilies, and a small minority are blended with both partners bringing children from a previous marriage. A substantial percentage of stepfamilies produce children of their own.

Like divorce, remarriage has also become commonplace in American society. The United States has the highest remarriage rate in the world, and Americans tend to remarry soon after divorce. Younger women remarry more quickly than older women, and childless women, divorced prior to the age of 25, have higher remarriage rates than women with children. The more money a divorced male has, the more likely he is to remarry, but for women the opposite is true. Remarriage satisfaction, similar to satisfaction in first marriages, appears to decrease over time (Guisinger, Cowan, & Schuldberg, 1989). In fact, few differences have been found between the factors that predict marital satisfaction in first marriages and remarriage (Coleman & Ganong, 1990).

Just like couples who are first married, remarried individuals often have unrealistic expectations about their stepfamily. Thus, an important adjustment for remarried persons is to develop realistic expectations. Money and the complexities of family structure in the remarried family often contribute to marital conflict.

Many variations in remarriage have the potential for what is called **boundary ambiguity**—*the uncertainty in stepfamilies about who is in or out of the family and who is performing or responsible for certain tasks in the family system*. The uncertainty of boundaries likely increases stress for the family system and the probability of behavior problems in children.

Research on stepfamilies has lagged behind research on divorced families, but a number of investigators have turned their attention to this increasingly common family structure (Hetherington, 1995; Hetherington & Clingempeel, 1992; Insabella, 1995; Jodl, 1995; Santrock, Sitterle, & Warshak, 1988). Following remarriage of their parents, children of all ages show a rise resurgence of behavior problems (Freeman, 1993). Younger children seem to eventually form an attachment to a stepparent and accept the stepparenting role. However, the developmental tasks facing adolescents make them especially vulnerable to the entrance of a stepparent. At the time they are searching for an identity and exploring sexual and other close relationships outside the family, a nonbiological parent may increase the stress associated with these important tasks. In one recent study, entrance of a stepfather when children were 9 years or older was associated with more problems than when the stepfather family was formed earlier (Hetherington, 1995).

Following the remarriage of the custodial parent, an emotional demonstration upheaval usually occurs in girls, and problems in boys often intensify (Henderson & others, 1996). Over time, preadolescent boys seem to improve more than girls in stepfather families. Sons who frequently are involved in conflicted or coercive relations with their custodial mothers probably have much to gain from living with a warm, supportive stepfather. In contrast, daughters who have a close relationship with their custodial mothers and considerable independence frequently find a stepfather both disruptive and constraining.

Children's relationships with their biological parents are more positive than with their stepparents, regardless of whether a stepmother or stepfather family is involved (Henderson, 1995; Santrock & Sitterle, 1987). However, stepfathers are often distant and disengaged from their stepchildren. As a rule, the more complex the stepfamily, the more difficult the child's adjustment. Families in which both parents bring children from a previous marriage have the highest level of behavioral problems.

In an investigation by E. Mavis Hetherington (1995), both parenting techniques and the school environment were associated with whether children coped effectively with living in a divorced family and a stepfamily. From the first grade on, an authoritative environment (an organized, predictable environment with clearly defined standards, and a responsive, nurturant environment) was linked with greater achievement and fewer problems in children than three other environments—authoritarian (coercive, power assertive, punitive, more criticism than praise, little responsiveness to individual children's needs, and low nurturance), permissive (low structure, disorganized, and high warmth), and chaotic/neglecting (disorganized, ineffective, erratic though usually harsh control, unstructured, low expectations, and hostile relationships). In divorced families, when only one parent was authoritative, or when neither parent was authoritative, an authoritative school improved the child's adjustment. A chaotic/neglecting school environment had the most adverse effects on children, which were most marked when there was no authoritative parent in the home.

Working Parents

Interest in the effects of parental work on children has increased in recent years. Our examination of parental work focuses on the following issues: the role of working mothers, the adjustment of latchkey children, the effects of relocation, and the influence of unemployment.

Working Mothers

Because household operations have become more efficient and family size has decreased in America, it is not certain that children with mothers working outside the home actually receive less attention than children in the past whose mothers were not employed. Outside employment—at least for mothers with school-age children—may simply be filling time previously taken up by added household burdens and more children. It also cannot be assumed that, if the mother did not go to work, the child would benefit from the time freed by streamlined household operations and smaller families. Mothering does not always have a positive effect on the child. The educated, nonworking mother may overinvest her energies in her children, fostering an excess of worry and discouraging the child's independence. In such situations, the mother may inject more parenting than the child can profitably handle. Also, the mother's employment might serve to alleviate financial strains in the family and increase the family's resources.

As Lois Hoffman (1989) comments, maternal employment is a part of modern life. It is not an aberrant aspect of it, but a response to other social changes that meets the needs that cannot be met by the previous family ideal of a full-time mother and homemaker. Not only does it meet the parent's needs, but in many ways it

What issues do women face as they combine a career and family? What are the effects of mothers' working on children's development?

may be a pattern better suited to socializing children for the adult roles they will occupy. This is especially true for daughters, but it is also true for sons. The broader range of emotions and skills that each parent presents is more consistent with this adult role. Just as his father shares the breadwinning role and the child-rearing role with his mother, so the son, too, will be more likely to share these roles. The rigid gender-role stereotyping perpetuated by the divisions of labor in the traditional family is not appropriate for the demands children of either sex will have made on them as adults. The needs of the growing child require the mother to loosen her hold on the child, and this task may be easier for the working woman whose job is an additional source of identity and self-esteem. Overall, researchers have found no detrimental effects of maternal employment on children's development (Gottfried, Gottfried, & Bathurst, 1995; Richards & Duckett, 1994). Working and nonworking mothers have similar attitudes toward parenting (O'Brien, 1993).

A common experience of working mothers (and working fathers) is feeling guilty about being away from their children. The guilt may be triggered by parents missing their child, worrying that their child is missing them, being concerned about the implications of working (such as whether the child is receiving good child care), and worrying about the long-term effects of working (such as having anxiety about jeopardizing the child's future). To reduce guilt, the guilt needs to be acknowledged. Pediatrician T. Berry Brazelton (1983) believes that parents respond to guilt either by admitting it and working through it or by denying it and rationalizing it away. The latter tendency is not recommended. Working parents' guilt can also be reduced if they begin paying closer attention to how their children are doing.

Latchkey Children

While the mother's working is not associated with negative outcomes for children, a certain set of children from working-mother families bears further scrutiny—those called latchkey children. Latchkey children typically do not see their parents from the time they leave for school in the morning until about 6 or 7 P.M. They are called latchkey children because they often are given the key to their home, take the key to school, and let themselves into the home while their parents are still at work. Many latchkey children are largely unsupervised for 2 to 4 hours a day during each school week, or for entire days, 5 days a week, during the summer months.

Thomas and Lynette Long (1983) interviewed more than 1,500 latchkey children. They concluded that a slight majority of these children had negative latchkey experiences. Some latchkey children may grow up too fast, hurried by the responsibility placed on them (Elkind, 1981). How do latchkey children handle the lack of limits and structure during the latchkey hours? Without limits and parental supervision, it becomes easier for latchkey children to find their way into trouble—possibly abusing a sibling, stealing, or vandalizing. The Longs found that 90 percent of the adjudicated juvenile delinquents in Montgomery County, Maryland, were from latchkey families. In another investigation of more than 4,900 eighth-graders in Los Angeles and San Diego, those who cared for themselves 11 or more hours a week were twice as likely to have abused alcohol and other drugs than were their counterparts who were supervised before and after school (Richardson & others, 1989). Adolescent expert Joan Lipsitz (1983), testifying before the Select Committee on Children, Youth, and Families, called the lack of adult supervision of children and adolescents in the after-school hours one of the nation's major problems. Lipsitz called it the "3:00 to 6:00 P.M. problem" because it was during this time frame that the Center for Early Adolescence in North Carolina, where she was director, experienced a peak of adolescent referrals for clinical help.

But while latchkey children may be vulnerable to problems, keep in mind that the experiences of latchkey children vary enormously, just as do the experiences of all children with working mothers (McCartney & others, 1997; Pettit, 1997). Parents need to give special attention to the ways their latchkey children's lives can be monitored effectively. Variations in latchkey experiences suggest that parental monitoring and authoritative parenting help the children to cope more effectively with latchkey experiences, especially in resisting peer pressure (Steinberg, 1986). In one recent study, attending a formal after-school program that included academic, recreational, and remedial activities was associated with better academic achievement and social adjustment in comparison to other types of after-school care (such as informal adult supervision or self-care) (Posner & Vandell, 1994). The degree to which latchkey children are at developmental risk remains unsettled. A positive sign is that researchers are beginning to conduct more precise analysis of latchkey experiences in an effort to determine which aspects of latchkey circumstances are the most detrimental and which aspects foster better adaptation.

Relocation

Geographical moves or relocations are a fact of life for many American families. The U.S. Census Bureau estimates that 17 percent of the population changes residences on a yearly basis (U.S. Bureau of the Census, 1986). This figure does not include multiple moves within the same year, so it may even underestimate the mobility of the U.S. population. The majority of these moves are made because of job demands. Moving can be especially stressful for children, disrupting friendship ties and activities (Brown & Orthner, 1990). The sources of support to which children and their parents turn, such as extended-family members and friends, are often unavailable to recently moved families.

While relocations are often stressful for all individuals involved, they may be especially stressful for adolescents because of their developing sense of identity and the importance of peer relations in their lives. In one study, geographical relocation was detrimental to the well-being of 12- to 14-year-old females but not their male counterparts (Brown & Orthner, 1990). The adolescent girls' life satisfaction was negatively related to both recent moves and to a high number of moves in their history, and a history of frequent moves was also associated with the girls' depression. However, the immediate negative effects on the girls disappeared over time. The researchers concluded that female adolescents may require more time to adapt to family relocations. Male adolescents may use sports and other activities in their new locale to ease the effects of relocation.

Unemployment

Unemployment rates and economic distress in the last decade reached levels unknown since the Great Depression. Plant closings, layoffs, and demotions are facts of life for many contemporary parents. What effects do they have on families and children's development? During the Great Depression, unemployment dramatically increased parental stress and undermined the school achievement and health of children (Elder, 1974).

In one investigation, the effects of changes in parental work status on young adolescents' school adjustment were explored (Flanagan & Eccles, 1993). Four groups were compared. *Deprived* families reported a layoff or demotion at time 1 but no recovery 2 years later. *Declining* families experienced a layoff or demotion between times 1 and 2. *Recovery* families reported similar losses at time 1 but reemployment 2 years later. *Stable* families reported no layoffs or demotions between times 1 and 2. Adolescents in deprived and declining families showed less competent peer interaction, and adolescents in deprived families were the most disruptive in school. The transition to adolescence was especially difficult for children whose parents were coping with changes in their work status. Other researchers have also recently found that economic downturn and joblessness can have negative effects on the child's development (Conger, 1997; Gomel, Tinsley, & Clark, 1995; Wilson, 1997).

Culture and Ethnicity

Cultures vary on a number of issues involving families, such as what the father's role in the family should be, the extent to which support systems are available to families, and how children should be disciplined (Harkness & Super, 1995). Although there are cross-cultural variations in parenting, in one study of parenting behavior in 186 cultures around the world, the most common pattern was a warm and controlling style, one that was neither permissive nor restrictive (Rohner & Rohner, 1981). The investigators commented that the majority of cultures have discovered, over many centuries, a "truth" that only recently emerged in the Western world—namely, that children's and adolescents' healthy social development is most effectively promoted by love and at least some moderate parental control.

Ethnic minority families differ from White American families in their size, structure and composition, reliance on kinship networks, and level of income and education (Coll, Meyer, & Brillion, 1995; Zambrana, 1995). Large and extended families are more common among ethnic minority groups than among White Americans (Wilson, 1989). For example, more than 30 percent of Latino families consists of five or more individuals. African American and Latino children interact more with grandparents, aunts, uncles, cousins, and more distant relatives than do White American children.

Single-parent families are more common among African Americans and Latinos than among White Americans. In comparison with two-parent households, single parents often have more limited resources of time, money, and energy. This shortage of resources may prompt them to encourage early autonomy among their children. Also, ethnic minority parents are less well educated and engage in less joint decision making than White American parents. And ethnic minority children are more likely to come from low-income families than are White American children. Although impoverished families often raise competent youth, poor parents may have a diminished capacity for supportive and involved parenting (McLoyd, 1990).

Some aspects of home life can help to protect ethnic minority children from social patterns of injustice (Spencer & Dornbusch, 1990). The community and family can filter out destructive racist messages, parents can provide alternate frames of reference than those presented by the majority, and parents can also provide competent role models and encouragement. And the extended-family system in many ethnic minority families provides an important buffer to stress (Lomnitz, 1997; Wakschlag, Chase-Lansdale, & Brooks-Gunn, 1996). To read further about the extended-family system in African American and Latino families, turn to Sociocultural Worlds of Children.

Gender and Parenting

What is the mother's role in the family? the father's role? How can mothers and fathers become cooperative, effective partners in parenting?

The Mother's Role

What do you think of when you hear the word *motherhood*? If you are like most people, you associate motherhood with a number of positive images, such as warm, selfless, dutiful, and tolerant (Matlin, 1993). And while most women expect that motherhood will be happy and fulfilling, the reality is that motherhood has been accorded relatively low prestige in our society. When stacked up against money, power, and achievement, motherhood unfortunately doesn't fare too well, and mothers rarely receive the appreciation they warrant. When children don't succeed or develop problems, our society has had a tendency to attribute the lack of success or the development of problems to a single source—mothers. One of psychology's most important lessons is that behavior is multiply determined. So it is with children's development—when development goes awry, mothers are not the single cause of the problems even though our society stereotypes them in this way.

The reality of motherhood in the 1990s is that while fathers have increased their child-rearing responsibilities somewhat, the main responsibility for children still falls on the mother's shoulders (Barnard & Martell, 1995). Mothers do far more family work than fathers do—two to three times more (Thompson & Walker, 1989). A few "exceptional" men do as much family work as their wives; in one study the figure was 10 percent of the men (Berk, 1985). Not only do women do more family work than men, the family work most women do is unrelenting, repetitive, and routine, often involving cleaning, cooking, child care, shopping, laundry, and straightening up. The family work most men do is infrequent, irregular, and nonroutine, often involving household repairs, taking out the garbage, and yard work. Women report that they often have to do several tasks at once, which helps to explain why they find domestic work less relaxing and more stressful than men do (Shaw, 1988).

African American and Latino Families

According to the Children's Defense Fund, African American children were three times as likely as White children to (Edelman, 1996):

- Be poor.
- Live with a parent who was separated from a spouse.
- Die of child abuse.

They are five times as likely to:

- Be dependent on welfare.

And they are twelve times as likely to:

- Live with a parent who never married.

Nonetheless, it is important to keep in mind that millions of African American families are not on welfare, have children who stay in school and out of trouble, and find ways to cope with and overcome problems they experience during difficult times. In 1967, Martin Luther King reflected on the African American family and gave the following caution: "As public awareness of the predicament of the Black family increases, there will be danger and opportunity. The opportunity will be to deal fully rather than haphazardly with the problem as a whole, as a social catastrophe brought on by many years of oppression. The danger is that the problems will be attributed to innate Black weaknesses and used to justify further neglect and to rationalize continued oppression." In today's world, Dr. King's words still ring true.

The African American cultural tradition of an extended-family household—in which one or several grandparents, uncles, aunts, siblings, or cousins either live together or provide support—has helped many African American parents cope with adverse social conditions such as economic stress (Taylor, 1997). Researchers have found that the extended African American family helps to reduce the stress of poverty and single parenting through emotional support, sharing income and economic responsibility, and surrogate parenting (Taylor & others, 1990). The presence of grandmothers in the households of many African American adolescents and their infants has been an important support system for both the teenage mother and the infant (Stevens, 1984). Active and involved extended family support systems also help a parent or parents from other ethnic minority groups cope with poverty and its related stress. In one recent study of African American families, mothers whose interactions with their own mothers were open,

Although African American children are more likely than White children to be poor and live with a parent who has been separated from a spouse, it is important to keep in mind that millions of African American families are not on welfare, have considerable family support, and find ways to effectively cope with stress. The extended family, especially grandmothers, plays an important role in African American children's development.

flexible, and autonomous were able to provide similarly appropriate parenting to their young children (Wakschlag, Chase-Lansdale, & Brooks-Gunn, 1996).

A basic value in Mexico is represented by the saying "As long as our family stays together, we are strong." Mexican children are brought up to stay close to their family, often playing with siblings rather than with schoolmates or neighborhood children, as American children usually do. Unlike the father in many American families, the Mexican father is the undisputed authority on all family matters and is usually obeyed without question. The mother is revered as the primary source of affection and care. This emphasis on family attachment leads the Mexican to say, "I will achieve mainly because of my family, and for my family, rather than myself." By contrast, the self-reliant American would say, "I will achieve mainly because of my ability and initiative and for myself rather than for my family." Unlike most Americans, families in Mexico tend to stretch out in a network of relatives that often runs to scores of individuals.

Children can significantly benefit from interaction with a caring, accessible, and dependable father who fosters a sense of trust and confidence.

Because family work is intertwined with love and embedded in family relations, it has complex and contradictory meanings (Villani, 1997). Many women feel that family tasks are mindless but essential. They usually enjoy tending to the needs of their loved ones and keeping the family going, even if they do not find the activities themselves enjoyable and fulfilling. Family work is both positive and negative for women. They are unsupervised and rarely criticized, they plan and control their own work, and they have only their own standards to meet. However, women's family work is often worrisome, tiresome, menial, repetitive, isolating, unfinished, inescapable, and often unappreciated. It is not surprising that men report that they are more satisfied with their marriage than women do.

In sum, the role of the mother brings with it benefits as well as limitations. Although motherhood is not enough to fill most women's entire lives, for most mothers, it is one of the most meaningful experiences in their lives (Hoffnung, 1984).

The Father's Role

The father's role has undergone major changes (Lamb, 1997; Lambert, 1997). During the colonial period in America, fathers were primarily responsible for moral teaching. Fathers provided guidance and values, especially through religion. With the Industrial Revolution, the father's role changed; he gained the responsibility as the breadwinner, a role that continued through the Great Depression. By the end of World War II, another role for fathers emerged, that of being a gender-role model. Although being a breadwinner and moral guardian continued to be important father roles, attention shifted to his role as a male, especially for sons. Then, in the 1970s, the current interest in the father as an active, nurturant, caregiving parent emerged. Rather than being responsible only for the discipline and control of older children and for providing the family's economic base, the father now is being evaluated in terms of his active, nurturant involvement with his children (McBride, 1991).

How actively involved are today's fathers with their children? Fathers in two-parent families typically spend about one-fourth to one-third as much time with young children as do mothers, although in the past decade fathers have slightly increased their participation (Biller, 1993). Having a father at home is no guarantee of meaningful parental involvement with the child. While some fathers are exceptionally committed parents, other fathers are virtual strangers to their children even though they reside in the same household.

Children's social development can significantly benefit from interaction with a caring, accessible, and dependable father who fosters a sense of trust and confidence (Burton & Snyder, 1997; Davis-Kean, 1997; Palmer & Bridges, 1995). The father's positive family involvement assumes special importance in developing children's social competence because he is often the only male the child encounters on a regular day-to-day basis.

The father's role in China has been slow to change, but it is changing. Traditionally in China, the father has been expected to be strict, the mother kind. The father is characterized as a stern disciplinarian; the child is expected to fear the father. The notion of the strict father has ancient roots. The Chinese character for father *(fu)* evolved from a primitive character representing a hand holding a cane, which symbolizes authority. However, the twentieth century has witnessed a decline in the father's authority. Younger fathers are more inclined to allow children to express their opinions and be more independent. Influenced to a degree by the increased employment of mothers, Chinese fathers are becoming more involved in caring for their children. In some instances, intergenerational tension has developed between fathers and sons, as younger generations behave in less traditional ways.

In one investigation, Frank Furstenberg and Kathleen Harris (1992) documented how nurturant fathering can overcome children's difficult life circumstances. In low-income African American families, children who reported close attachments and feelings of identification with their fathers during adolescence were twice as likely as young adults to have found a stable job or to have entered college, and were 75 percent less likely to have become unwed parents, 80 percent less likely to have been in jail, and 50 percent less likely to have developed depression. Unfortunately, however, only 10 percent of the economically disadvantaged children they studied experienced a stable, close relationship with their father during childhood and adolescence. In two other studies, college females and males reported better personal and social adjustment when they had grown up in a home with a nurturant, involved father rather than a negligent or rejecting father (Fish & Biller, 1973; Reuter & Biller, 1973).

Partners in Parenting

When parents show cooperation, mutual respect, balanced communication, and attunement to each other's needs, this helps the adolescent develop positive attitudes toward both males and females (Biller, 1993). It is much easier for working parents to cope with changing family circumstances when the father and mother equitably share child-rearing responsibilities. Mothers feel less stress and have more positive attitudes toward their husbands when the husband is a supportive partner. Researchers have found that egalitarian marital relationships have positive effects on adolescent development, fostering their trust and encouraging communication (Yang & others, 1996).

At this point we have discussed a number of ideas about the effects of divorce on children, stepfamilies, working parents, culture and ethnicity, and gender and parenting. A summary of these ideas is expressed in concept table 15.2.

The Effects of Divorce on Children, Stepfamilies, Working Parents, Culture and Ethnicity, and Gender and Parenting

Concept	Processes/Related Ideas	Characteristics/Description
The Effects of Divorce on Children	Their nature	Two main models of divorce effects have been proposed: the family structure model and the multiple-factor model. The family structure model is overly simplistic. The contemporary multiple-factor model takes into account the complexity of the divorce context, including conflict and postdivorce family functioning. Among the important factors in understanding the effects of divorce on children are age and developmental changes, conflict, sex of the child, the nature of custody, and income and economic stress. In recent years, developmentalists have moved away from the model of single parents as atypical or pathological, focusing more on the diversity of children's responses to divorce and the factors that facilitate or disrupt the adjustment of children in these family circumstances.
Stepfamilies	Their effects	Just as divorce produces disequilibrium and stress for children, so does remarriage. Over time, preadolescent boys seem to improve more than girls in stepfather families. Adolescence is an especially difficult time for adjustment to the entrance of a stepparent. Children's relationships with biological parents are consistently better than with stepparents, and children's adjustment is adversely affected the more complex the stepfamily becomes. An authoritative environment at home and at school helps children adjust to living in a divorced or stepparent family.
Working Parents	Nature of their effects on children	Overall, the mother's working outside the home does not have an adverse effect on the child's development. Latchkey experiences do not have a uniformly negative influence on children's development. Parental monitoring and participation in structured activities with competent supervision are important influences on latchkey children's adjustment. Relocation may have a more adverse effect on adolescents than children, but research on this issue is sparse. Unemployment of parents has a detrimental effect on children's development.
Culture and Ethnicity	Nature of their effects	Authoritative parenting is the most common child-rearing pattern around the world. Ethnic minority families differ from White American families in their size, structure, and composition; their reliance on kinship networks; and their levels of income and education.
Gender and Parenting	The mother's role	Most people associate motherhood with a number of positive images, but the reality is that motherhood is accorded a relatively low status in our society. Unfortunately, when children's development goes awry, mothers are more often labeled as the single cause of the problem. Mothers do far more family work than fathers do. Despite its stressful aspects, for most mothers, motherhood is one of the most meaningful experiences in their lives.
	The father's role	Over time, the father's role in the child's development has evolved from moral teacher to breadwinner to gender-role model to nurturant caregiver. Fathers are much less involved in child rearing than mothers are. Children's social development can significantly benefit from interaction with a caring, accessible, and dependable father who fosters trust and confidence.
	Partners in parenting	Father-mother cooperation and mutual respect help the child to develop positive attitudes toward both males and females. Mothers feel less stress and have more positive attitudes toward their husband when he is a supportive partner.

SUMMARY

Parents cradle children's lives. For most children, parents are the critical caregivers.

We began this chapter by describing the diversity of families and parenting. Then, we examined the nature of some important family processes—reciprocal socialization and the family as a system, the developmental construction of relationships, adapting parenting to developmental changes in the child,

the family life cycle, and sociocultural and historical changes. We read about the parental role and parenting styles, sibling relationships and birth order, and family processes in adolescence. We also explored the effects of divorce on children, stepfamilies, working parents, culture and ethnicity, and gender and parenting, especially focusing on the mother's role, the father's role, and the importance of being partners in parenting.

Remember that you can obtain a summary of the chapter by again studying the two concept tables on pages 488 and 497. In the next chapter, we will turn our attention to the roles of peers, play, and the media in children's development. You will discover that the worlds of families and peers are more connected than once was believed.

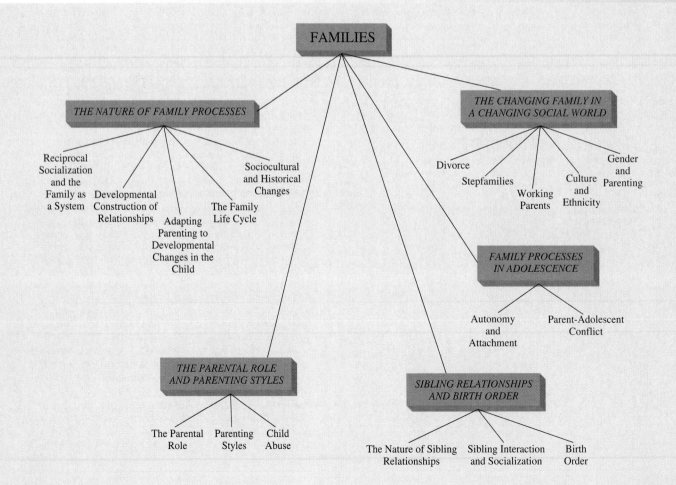

PRACTICAL KNOWLEDGE ABOUT CHILDREN

Children: The Challenge
(1964) by Rudolph Dreikurs, New York: Hawthorn Books.

Children: The Challenge tells parents how to discipline their children more effectively. Author Rudolph Dreikurs was a Viennese psychiatrist who collaborated with famous psychoanalyst Alfred Adler in conducting child guidance clinics. Dreikurs came to the United States in 1937 and soon became a highly respected authority on child rearing. Dreikurs teaches parents how to understand their children and meet their needs. He stresses that the main reason for children's misbehavior is discouragement. Discouraged children often demand undue attention, he says. Parents usually respond to this negative attention-seeking behavior by trying to impose their will on the child, who in turn keeps misbehaving. Dreikurs says that parents who get caught up in this cycle are actually rewarding their children for misbehavior. He counsels parents on how to instead become calm and pleasant when disciplining the child. Dreikurs especially recommends family discussion for solving family problems.

Children: The Challenge is easy to read, and the examples are clear and plentiful. The author discusses a wide range of situations in which discipline is called for. Although it was written three decades ago, this book is still one of the books on parental discipline most widely recommended by mental health professionals.

Raising Black Children
(1992) by James P. Comer and Alvin E. Poussaint, New York: Plume.

Raising Black Children is written by two of the most highly respected experts on African American children—James Comer and Alvin Poussaint, professors of psychiatry at Yale and Harvard, respectively. Comer and Poussaint argue that African American parents face additional difficulties in raising emotionally healthy African American children because of race and income problems. Comer and Poussaint's guide contains almost a thousand child-rearing questions they have repeatedly heard from African American parents across the income spectrum. The issues they advise parents on include how to improve the African American child's self-esteem and identity, how to confront racism, how to teach their children to handle anger, conflict, and frustration, and how to deal with the mainstream culture and retain an African American identity. This is an excellent book for African American parents that includes wise suggestions that are not in most child-rearing books (almost all others are written for middle-class White parents and do not deal with special problems faced by ethnic minority parents or parents from low-income backgrounds).

EXPLORATIONS IN CHILD DEVELOPMENT

To further explore the nature of child development, we will examine a research study on African American single mothers and adolescent socioemotional functioning, and then we will discuss the goals of caregiving.

RESEARCH IN CHILD DEVELOPMENT

African American Single Mothers and Adolescent Socioemotional Functioning

Featured Study

McLoyd, V. C., Jayaratne, T., Ceballo, R., Borquez, J. (1994). Unemployment and work interruption among African American single mothers: Effects on parenting and adolescent socioemotional functioning. *Child Development, 65,* 562–589.

This study was designed to assess the role of maternal psychological functioning and parenting in linking unemployment and work interruption to socioemotional functioning in adolescents. The study focused on a subgroup that lies at one of the intersections of gender, ethnicity, and marital status: single African American women and their children.

Method

The participants in the study were 241 single African American mothers and their seventh- and eighth-grade children. They lived in predominantly lower- and working-class neighborhoods with a high rate of unemployment. The mothers and their children were interviewed in their homes.

The interviews focused on economic factors—past work interruption, current employment status, and financial strain; maternal factors—depressive symptoms, negative perception of maternal role, availability of support, and maternal punishment; adolescent factors—the adolescent's perception of negative relations with the mother, the adolescent's perception of the family's economic hardship, cognitive distress, depressive symptomatology, general anxiety, and self-esteem.

Results and Discussion

In general, the economic stressors of maternal unemployment and work interruption affected adolescent socioemotional functioning indirectly rather than directly, through their impact on the mother's psychological functioning and, in turn, on her parenting behavior and maternal-child relations. Current unemployment, but not past work interruption, had a direct effect on depressive symptomatology in mothers. As expected, depressive symptomatology in mothers predicted more frequent maternal punishment of adolescents, and this relation was linked with the mother's negative perception of the maternal role. More frequent maternal punishment was associated with increased cognitive distress and depressive symptoms in adolescents. Increased availability of support predicted fewer depressive symptoms in mothers, less punishment of adolescents, and less negativity about the maternal role. Adolescents who perceived their families as experiencing more severe economic hardship reported higher anxiety, more cognitive distress, and lower self-esteem.

The Goals of Caregiving

Are there some overarching goals that caregivers should set in their effort to take responsibility for the development of infants? Infant researcher and parent educator Burton White (1990) believes there are three basic general goals that caregivers should pursue:

- To give the infant a sense of being loved and cared for
- To help the infant to develop specific skills
- To encourage the infant's interest in the outside world

Giving the Infant a Sense of Being Loved and Cared For

In the first 2 years of life, all infants and toddlers have a strong need to establish an attachment to one or more older humans. In the process of developing this attachment they begin their long road to being socialized and socializing others. As we have seen, Erikson (1968) believes the central goal of the first year of life is the development of a sense of trust rather than mistrust on the part of the infant. This is in keeping with White's perspective as well as the perspective of this text. The frequency and degree of discomfort and distress babies feel depends in large part on the kind of treatment they experience. There is no way to prevent a fair amount of unhappiness from such factors as hunger, indigestion, teething, and a cold diaper. However, such unhappiness can be prolonged and allowed to escalate if the avoidable discomfort and distress are not responded to promptly.

Caregivers who respond to infants with loving care and attention make strong contributions to the development of competence in the infant. As White indicates, no requirement of good caregiving is more natural or more rewarding than tending to the baby in a loving and attentive way.

Helping the Infant to Develop Specific Skills

Over the course of the first 2 years of life, an infant develops from being a creature who cannot think, use language, socialize with a human being, run, walk, or even deliberately move around, into a socialized individual who has accumulated a number of specific skills. Good child rearing in the first 2 years of an infant's life includes knowing the normal pattern of emerging skills and facilitating their emergence and development. Most of these skills evolve unaided under average rearing circumstances, but good parenting ensures the optimal development of these skills. Throughout the three chapters on infant development, we have specified the normal patterns of development of physical, cognitive, and social skills during the infant years and how caregivers can interact with infants in developmentally appropriate ways to enhance these skills. Facilitating the development of the infant's specific skills is tied to White's third general goal of caregiving competence.

Encouraging the Infant's Interest in the Outside World

Whether an infant first learns to reach for objects at 3 months or at 5 months is probably of less consequence than seeing that the babies are regularly involved in activities that interest them. Instead of trying to push infants to develop skills beyond their current level (and become a "superbaby"), it is more important for parents to interact with the infant in ways that keep the infant interested, cheerful, and alert. After the first several months, infants should be actively enjoying themselves at least some of the time.

Winslow Homer
Three Boys and a Kitten detail

Chapter

16

Peers, Play, and the Media

*T*he little ones leaped, and shouted, and
laugh'd and all the hills echoed.

—William Blake

You are troubled at seeing him spend his early years in doing nothing. What! Is it nothing to be happy? Is it nothing to skip, to play, to run about all day long? Never in his life will he be so busy as now.

—Jean-Jacques Rousseau

PREVIEW

*C*hildren's growth is shaped by successive waves of peers and friends, and play is their work. This chapter focuses on the following important dimensions of children's lives: Peers, play, and the media.

IMAGES OF CHILDREN

The Importance of Friends

Think back over your childhood and adolescent years for a moment. Who were your best friends? Why were they important to you? Consider the important role that friendship plays in this 13-year-old girl's life:

> My best friend is nice. She is honest, and I can trust her. I can tell her my innermost secrets and know that nobody else will find out about them. I have other friends, too, but she is my best friend. We consider each other's feelings and don't want to hurt each other. We help each other when we have problems. We have most of our classes together at school and we often do our homework together. We make up funny names for people and laugh ourselves silly. We make lists of which boys are the sexiest and which are the ugliest. My best friend means a lot to me. I don't know what I would do without her.

Researchers have found that friendships play an important role in children's development. One aspect of children's de-velopment that friendship influences is school behavior. In one study, children with many friends at the time they entered kindergarten developed more positive perceptions of school than did children with fewer friends (Ladd, 1990). And children who maintained these friendships also liked school better as the school year progressed. Making new friends in the classroom also predicted gains in school performance over the year, while being disliked by other children forecast unfavorable school attitudes and performance.

Friendships also can help ease the stressful transition from elementary school to middle or junior high school. In one study, as children moved from an elementary school through the first year of junior high school, those who reported more contact with their friends and higher-quality friendships had more positive perceptions of themselves and of their junior high school than did their low-friendship counterparts (Berndt, Hawkins, & Hoyle, 1986).

PEERS

As children grow older, peer relations consume increasing amounts of their time. What is the function of a child's peer group? Although children spend increasingly more time with peers as they become older, are there ways in which family and peer relations are coordinated? What is the developmental course of peer relations in childhood? Why are some children popular, rejected, or neglected? What is the role of cognition in peer relations? What is the nature of friendship and of peer relations in adolescence?

Peer Group Functions

Peers *are children of about the same age or maturity level.* Same-age peer interaction fills a unique role in our culture (Hartup, 1976). Age grading would occur even if schools were not age graded and children were left alone to determine the composition of their own societies. One of the most important functions of the peer group is to provide a source of information and comparison about the world outside the family. Children receive feedback about their abilities from their peer group. Children evaluate what they do in terms of whether it is better than, as good as, or worse than what other children do. It is hard to do this at home because siblings are usually older or younger.

Are peers necessary for development? When peer monkeys who have been reared together are separated, they become depressed and regress socially (Suomi, Harlow, & Domek, 1970). The human development literature contains a classic example of the importance of peers in social development. Anna Freud (Freud & Dann, 1951) studied six children from different families who banded together after their parents were killed in World War II. Intensive peer attachment was observed; the children formed a tightly knit group, dependent on one another and aloof with outsiders. Even though deprived of parental care, they became neither delinquent nor psychotic.

Thus, good peer relations may be necessary for normal social development. Social isolation, or the inability to "plug in" to a social network, is linked with many problems and disorders ranging from delinquency and problem drinking to depression (Hops & others, 1997; Kupersmidt & Coie, 1990; Prinstein, Fetter, & LaGreca, 1996; Ryan & Patrick, 1996; Simons, Conger, & Wu, 1992). In one investigation, poor peer relations in childhood was associated with a tendency to drop out of school and delinquent behavior in adolescence (Roff, Sells, & Golden, 1972). In another investigation, harmonious peer relations in adolescence were related to positive mental health at midlife (Hightower, 1990).

As you might have detected from our discussion of peer relations thus far, peer influences can be both positive and negative (Rubin, Bukowski, & Parker, 1997). Both Jean Piaget (1932) and Harry Stack Sullivan (1953) were influential theorists who stressed that it is through peer interaction that children and adolescents learn the symmetrical reciprocity mode of relationships discussed in chapter 15. Children explore the principles of fairness and justice by working through disagreements with peers. They also learn to be keen observers of peers' interests and perspectives in order to smoothly integrate themselves into ongoing peer activities. In addition, Sullivan argued that adolescents learn to be skilled and sensitive partners in intimate relationships by forging close friendships with selected peers. These intimacy skills are carried forward to help form the foundation of later dating and marital relationships, according to Sullivan (Buhrmester, 1996).

By contrast, some theorists have emphasized the negative influences of peers on children's and adolescents' development. Being rejected or overlooked by peers leads some children to feel lonely or hostile. Further, such rejection and neglect by peers are related to an individual's subsequent mental health and criminal problems. Some theorists have also described the children's peer culture as a corrupt influence that undermines parental values and control. Further, peers can introduce adolescents to alcohol, drugs, delinquency, and other forms of behavior that adults view as maladaptive.

The Distinct but Coordinated Worlds of Parent-Child and Peer Relations

What are some of the similarities and differences between peer and parent-child relationships? Children touch, smile, frown, and vocalize when they interact with both parents and peers. However, rough-and-tumble play occurs mainly with other children, not with adults, and, in times of stress, children often move toward their parents rather than toward their peers.

In addition to evaluating whether children engage in similar or dissimilar behaviors when interacting with parents and peers, it is also important to examine whether children's peer relations develop independently of parent-child relationships or are wedded to them. Recall our discussion of the developmental construction of relationships in chapter 15, which consists of two different views. In the continuity view, early parent-child relationships strongly influence children's subsequent peer relations and friendships. By contrast, in the discontinuity view, peer relations and friendships have a more independent developmental path.

A number of theorists and researchers argue that parent-child relationships serve as emotional bases for exploring and enjoying peer relations (Crockenberg & Lourie, 1993; Mize, Petit, & Brown, 1995; Posada, Lord, & Waters, 1995). In one study, the relationship history of each peer helped to predict the nature of peer interaction (Olweus, 1980) (see figure 16.1). Some boys were highly aggressive ("bullies") and other boys were the recipients of aggression ("whipping boys") throughout their preschool years. The bullies and the whipping boys had distinctive relationship histories. The bullies' parents frequently rejected them, were authoritarian, and were permissive about their sons' aggression, and the bullies' families were characterized by discord. By contrast, the whipping boys' parents were anxious and overprotective, taking special care to have their sons avoid aggression. The well-adjusted boys in the study were much less likely to be involved in aggressive peer interchanges than were the bullies and whipping boys. Their parents did not sanction aggression, and their responsive involvement with their sons promoted the development of self-assertion rather than aggression or wimpish behavior.

Figure~16.1

Peer Aggression
Children's behavior is influenced by their relationship histories.

Parents also may model or coach their children in the ways of relating to peers. In one investigation, parents indicated they recommended specific strategies to their children regarding peer relations (Rubin & Sloman, 1984). For example, parents told their children how to mediate disputes or how to become less shy with others. They also encouraged them to be tolerant and to resist peer pressure. In another study, parents who frequently indicated peer contacts for their preschool children had children who were more accepted by their peers and higher levels of prosocial behavior (Ladd & Hart, 1992).

A key aspect of peer relations can be traced to basic lifestyle decisions by parents (Cooper & Ayers-Lopez, 1985). Parents' choices of neighborhoods, churches, schools, and their own friends influence the pool from which their children might select possible friends. For example, the chosen schools can lead to specific grouping policies, as well as particular academic and extracurricular activities. In turn, such facts affect which students their children meet, their purpose in interacting, and eventually who become friends. For example, classrooms in which teachers encourage more cooperative peer interchanges have fewer isolates.

In sum, parent-child and peer worlds are coordinated and connected (Brown & Huang, 1995; Ladd & Le Sieur, 1995; Maccoby, 1996; Silbereisen, 1995). But they also are distinct. Earlier we indicated that rough-and-tumble play occurs mainly with other children, not in parent-child interaction. And, in times of stress, children often turn to parents, not peers, for support. Peer relations also are more likely to consist of interaction on a much more equal basis than parent-child relations. In parent-child relations, since parents have greater knowledge and authority, their children must often learn how to conform to rules and regulations laid down by parents. With peers, children learn to formulate and assert their own opinions, appreciate the perspective of peers, cooperatively negotiate solutions to disagreements, and evolve standards of conduct that are mutually acceptable. To further evaluate parent-peer linkages, see Critical Thinking About Children's Development.

The Developmental Course of Peer Relations in Childhood

Although we generally think of peer relations as assuming an important role in early childhood, some researchers believe that the quality of peer interaction in infancy provides valuable information about social development (Vandell, 1985). For example, in one investigation, positive affect in infant peer relations was related to easy access to peer play groups and to peer popularity in early childhood (Howes, 1985). As increasing numbers of children attend day care, peer interaction in infancy takes on a more important developmental role.

Parent-Peer Linkages in Your Adolescence

Think back to your middle school/junior high and high school years. What was your relationship with your parents like? Were you securely attached or insecurely attached to them? How do you think your relationship with your parents affected your friendship and peer relations in adolescence? Consider also dating and romantic relationships. How do adolescents' observations of their parents' marital lives and their own relationships with their parents influence their dating and romantic relationships? By exploring your relationships with your parents in adolescence and how they might have influenced your dating and romantic relationships, you are learning to think critically by *creating arguments based on developmental concepts.*

The frequency of peer interaction, both positive and negative, picks up considerably during early childhood (Hartup, 1983). Although aggressive interaction and rough-and-tumble play increase, the *proportion* of aggressive exchanges, compared to friendly exchanges, decreases. Children tend to abandon their immature and inefficient social exchanges with age and acquire more mature ways of relating to peers.

Children spend an increasing amount of time in peer interaction during middle and late childhood and adolescence. In one investigation, children interacted with peers 10 percent of their day at age 2, 20 percent at age 4, and more than 40 percent between the ages of 7 and 11. In a typical school day, episodes with peers totaled 299 times per day (Barker & Wright, 1951).

Peer Statuses

Children often think, "What can I do to get all of the kids at school to like me?" or "What's wrong with me? Something must be wrong or I would be more popular." What makes a child popular with peers? **Popular children** *are frequently nominated as a best friend and are rarely disliked by their peers.* Researchers have found that popular children give out reinforcements, listen carefully, maintain open lines of communication with peers, are happy, act like themselves, show enthusiasm and concern for others, and are self-confident without being conceited (Hartup, 1983).

Developmentalists have distinguished three types of children who have a different peer status than popular children: those who are neglected, those who are rejected, and those who are controversial (Wentzal & Asher, 1995). **Neglected children** *are infrequently nominated as a best friend but are not disliked by their peers.* **Rejected children** *are infrequently nominated as someone's best friend and are actively disliked by their peers.* **Controversial children** *are frequently nominated both as someone's best friend and as being disliked.*

The controversial peer status had not been studied until recently. In one study, girls who had a controversial peer status in the fourth grade were more likely to become adolescent mothers than were girls of other peer statuses (Underwood, Kupersmidt, & Coie, 1996). Also, aggressive girls had more children than nonaggressive girls.

Rejected children often have more serious adjustment problems than those who are neglected (Dishion & Spacklen, 1996; Kupersmidt & Patterson, 1993; Parker & Asher, 1987). For example, in one study, 112 fifth-grade boys were evaluated over a period of 7 years until the end of high school (Kupersmidt & Coie, 1990). The key factor in predicting whether rejected children would engage in delinquent behavior or drop out of school later during adolescence was their aggression toward peers in elementary school.

Not all rejected children are aggressive (Bierman, Smoot, & Aumiller, 1993). While aggression and its related characteristics of impulsiveness and disruptiveness underlie rejection about half the time, approximately 10 to 20 percent of rejected children are shy (Cillessen & others, 1992).

An important question to ask is, How can neglected children and rejected children be trained to interact more effectively with their peers? (Coie & Dodge, 1997). The goal of training programs with neglected children is often to help them attract attention from their peers in positive ways and to hold their attention by asking questions, by listening in a warm and friendly way, and by saying things about themselves that relate to the peers' interests. They also are taught to enter groups more effectively (Duck, 1988).

The goal of training programs with rejected children is often to help them listen to peers and "hear what they say" instead of trying to dominate peer interactions. Rejected children are trained to join peers without trying to change what is taking place in the peer group.

Children may need to be persuaded or motivated that these strategies work effectively and are satisfying.

In some programs, children are shown videotapes of appropriate peer interaction; then they are asked to comment on them and to draw lessons from what they have seen. In other training programs, popular children are taught to be more accepting of neglected or rejected peers.

One issue that has recently been raised about improving the peer relations of rejected children is whether the focus should be on improving their prosocial skills (better empathy, careful listening, improved communication skills, and so on) or on reducing their aggressive, disruptive behavior and improving their self-control (Coie & Koeppl, 1990). In one recent study, socially rejected young adolescents were coached on the importance of showing behaviors that would improve their chance of being liked by others (Murphy & Schneider, 1994). The intervention was successful in improving the friendships of the socially rejected youth. Improving the prosocial skills of rejected children, though, does not automatically eliminate their aggressive or disruptive behavior. Aggression often leads to reinforcement because peers give in to aggressive children's demands. Thus, in addition to teaching better prosocial skills to rejected children, direct steps must also be taken to eliminate their aggressive actions. Further, acquiring positive status with peers may take time to achieve because it is hard for peers to change their opinions if children frequently engage in aggressive conduct. Next, we turn our attention to the role of social cognition in understanding peer relations. Part of this discussion further considers ideas about reducing the aggression of children in their peer encounters.

Social Cognition

How might children's thoughts contribute to their peer relations? Three possibilities are through their perspective-taking ability, social information-processing skills, and social knowledge.

Perspective taking *involves taking another's point of view.* As children enter the elementary school years, both their peer interaction and their perspective-taking ability increase. Reciprocity—playing games, functioning in groups, and cultivating friendships, for example—is especially important in peer interchanges at this point in development. One of the important skills that help elementary school children improve their peer relations is communication effectiveness. In one investigation, the communication exchanges among peers at kindergarten, first-, third-, and fifth-grade levels were evaluated (Krauss & Glucksberg, 1969). Children were asked to tell a peer about a new set of block designs. The peer sat behind a screen with blocks similar to those the subject communicated to her (see figure 16.2). The kindergarten children made numerous errors in telling the peer how to duplicate the novel block stack. The older children were much more efficient in communicating to a peer how to construct the novel block stack, especially the fifth-graders. They were sensitive to the communication demands of the task and

were far superior at perspective taking and figuring out how they had to talk for the peer to understand them. In elementary school, children also become more efficient at understanding complex messages, so the listening skills of the peer in this experiment probably helped the communicating peer as well. Other researchers have documented the link between perspective-taking skills and the quality of peer relations, especially in the elementary school years (LeMare & Rubin, 1987).

Of special interest is how children process information about peer relations (Dodge, 1993; Quiggle & others, 1992). For example, a boy accidentally trips and knocks a peer's soft drink out of his hand. The peer misinterprets the encounter as hostile, which leads him to retaliate aggressively against the boy. Through repeated encounters of this kind, other peers come to perceive the aggressive boys as habitually acting inappropriately. Peer relations researcher Kenneth Dodge (1983) argues that children go through five steps in processing information about their social world: decoding social cues, interpreting, searching for a response, selecting an optimal response, and enacting it. Dodge has found that aggressive boys are more likely to perceive another child's actions as hostile when the child's intention is ambiguous, and when aggressive boys search for clues to determine a peer's intention, they respond more rapidly, less efficiently, and less reflectively than nonaggressive children. These are among the social cognitive factors believed to be involved in the nature of children's conflicts (Dodge & Feldman, 1990; Shantz, 1988).

Social knowledge also is involved in children's ability to get along with peers. An important part of children's social life involves choosing which goals to pursue in poorly defined or ambiguous situations. Social relationship goals are also important, such as how to initiate and maintain a social bond. Children need to know what scripts to follow to get children to be their friends. For example, as part of the script for getting friends, it helps to know that saying nice things, regardless of what the peer does or says, will make the peer like the child more.

From a social cognitive perspective, children who are maladjusted do not have adequate social cognitive skills to interact skillfully with others (Rabiner & others, 1991). One investigation explored the possibility that maladjusted children do not have the social cognitive skills necessary for positive social interaction (Asarnow & Callan, 1985). Boys with and without peer adjustment difficulties were identified, and their social cognitive skills were assessed. Boys without peer adjustment problems generated more alternative solutions to problems, proposed more assertive and mature solutions, gave less-intense aggressive solutions, showed more adaptive planning, and evaluated physically aggressive responses less positively than did the boys with peer adjustment problems.

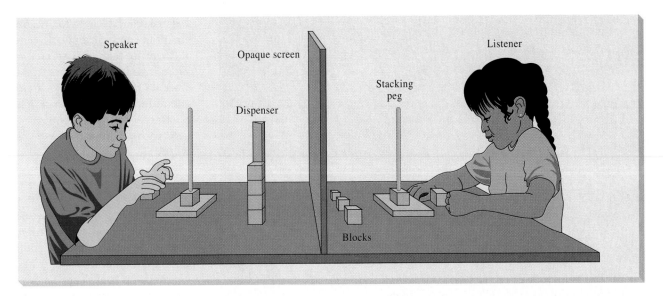

Figure~16.2

The Development of Communication Skills
This is an experimental arrangement of speaker and listener in the investigation of the development of communication skills.

The world of peers is one of varying acquaintances; children interact with some children they barely know, and with others they know well, for hours every day. It is to the latter type—friends—that we now turn.

Friendships

At the beginning of the chapter, we learned that friendships play an important role in helping children adapt to school. Let's now explore the world of children's friendships in more detail, examining the importance of friendships, Sullivan's ideas on friendships, and intimacy and similarity in friendships.

The Importance of Friendships

Friendships serve six functions (Gottman & Parker, 1987) (see figure 16.3):

1. *Companionship.* Friendship provides children with a familiar partner, someone who is willing to spend time with them and join in collaborative activities.

2. *Stimulation.* Friendship provides adolescents with interesting information, excitement, and amusement.

3. *Physical support.* Friendship provides time, resources, and assistance.

4. *Ego support.* Friendship provides the expectation of support, encouragement, and feedback that helps children to maintain an impression of themselves as competent, attractive, and worthwhile individuals.

5. *Social comparison.* Friendship provides information about where children stand vis-à-vis others and whether children are doing okay.

6. *Intimacy/affection.* Friendship provides children with a warm, close, trusting relationship with another individual, a relationship that involves self-disclosure.

> *Each friend represents a world in us, a world possibly not born until they arrive, and it is only by this meeting that a new world is born.*
>
> **—Anaïs Nin**

Sullivan's Ideas on Friendships

Harry Stack Sullivan (1953) was the most influential theorist to discuss the importance of friendships. He argued that there is a dramatic increase in the psychological importance and intimacy of close friends during early adolescence. In contrast to other psychoanalytic theorists' narrow emphasis on the importance of parent-child relationships, Sullivan contended that friends also play important roles in shaping children's and adolescents' well-being and development. In terms of well-being, he argued that all people have a number of basic social needs, including the need for tenderness (secure attachment), playful companionship, social acceptance, intimacy, and sexual relations. Whether or not these needs are fulfilled largely determines our emotional well-being. For example, if the need for playful companionship goes unmet, then we become bored and depressed; if the need for social acceptance is not met, we suffer a lowered sense of self-worth. Developmentally, friends become increasingly depended upon to satisfy these needs during adolescence, and thus the ups and downs of experiences with friends increasingly shape adolescents' state of well-being. In particular, Sullivan

Hartam

| Companionship | Stimulation | Physical support |
| Ego support | Social comparison | Intimacy/affection |

Figure~16.3

The Functions of Friendships

believed that the need for intimacy intensifies during early adolescence, motivating teenagers to seek out close friends. He felt that, if adolescents failed to forge such close friendships, they would experience painful feelings of loneliness coupled with a reduced sense of self-worth.

Research findings support many of Sullivan's ideas. For example, adolescents report more often disclosing intimate and personal information to their friends than do younger children (Buhrmester & Furman, 1987). Adolescents also say they depend more on friends than parents to satisfy needs for companionship, reassurance of worth, and intimacy (Furman & Buhrmester, 1992). In one study, daily interviews with 13- to 16-year-old adolescents over a 5-day period were conducted to find out how much time they spent engaged in meaningful interactions with friends and parents (Carbery & Buhrmester, 1993). Adolescents spent an average of 103 minutes per day in meaningful interactions with friends, compared to just 28 minutes per day with parents. In addition, the quality of friendship is more strongly linked to feelings of well-being during adolescence than during childhood. Teenagers with superficial friendships, or no close friendships at all, report feeling lonelier and more depressed and anxious, and they have a lower sense of self-esteem than teenagers with intimate friendships (Buhrmester, 1990).

A man's growth is seen in the successive choirs of his friends.

—**Ralph Waldo Emerson**

The increased closeness and importance of friendship challenges adolescents to master ever more sophisticated social competencies. Viewed from the developmental constructionist perspective described in chapter 15, adolescent friendship represents a new mode of relating to others that is best described as a *symmetrical intimate mode*. During childhood, being a good friend involves being a good playmate: Children must know how to play cooperatively and must be skilled at smoothly entering ongoing games on the playground (Putallaz, 1983; Taylor & Machida, 1993). By contrast, the greater intimacy of adolescent friendships demands that teenagers learn a number of close relationship competencies, including knowing how to self-disclose appropriately, being able to provide emotional support to friends, and managing disagreements in ways that do not undermine the intimacy of the friendship (Buhrmester, 1990). These competencies require more sophisticated skills in perspective taking, empathy, and social problem solving than were involved in childhood playmate competencies (Selman, 1980).

In addition to the role they play in the socialization of social competence, friendship relationships are often important sources of support. Sullivan described how friends support one another's sense of personal worth. When close friends disclose their mutual insecurities and fears about themselves, they discover that they are not "abnormal" and that they have nothing to be ashamed of. Friends also act as important confidants that help children and adolescents work through upsetting problems (such as difficulties with parents or the breakup of romance) by providing both emotional support and informational advice (Savin-Williams & Berndt, 1990). Friends can also protect "at risk" children from peer victimization (Bukowski, Sippola, & Boivin, 1995). In addition, friends can become active partners in building a sense of identity. During countless hours of conversation, friends act as sounding boards as teenagers explore issues ranging from future plans to stances on religious and moral issues.

Willard Hartup (1996), who has studied peer relations across four decades, recently concluded that children often use friends as cognitive and social resources on a regular basis. Hartup also commented that normative transitions, such as moving from elementary to middle school, are negotiated more competently by children who have friends than by those who don't. The quality of friendship is also important to consider. Supportive friendships between socially skilled individuals are developmentally advantageous, whereas coercive and conflict-ridden friendships are not. Friendship and its developmental significance also can vary from one child to another. Children's characteristics, such as temperament ("easy" versus "difficult," for example), likely influence the nature of their friendships.

Intimacy and Similarity in Friendships

In the context of friendship, *intimacy* has been defined in different ways. For example, it has been defined broadly

Without question, one of the most important dimensions of friendships is intimacy. Children want to be able to share problems with a friend, have their friend understand them, and listen when they talk about their own thoughts and feelings. Girls are more likely to describe their best friend with greater intimacy than boys are.

to include everything in a relationship that makes the relationship seem close or intense. In most research studies, though, **intimacy in friendship** *is defined narrowly as self-disclosure and the sharing of private thoughts.* Private or personal knowledge about a friend also has been used as an index of intimacy (Selman, 1980; Sullivan, 1953).

The most consistent finding in the last two decades of research on friendships is that intimacy is an important feature of friendship (Berndt & Perry, 1990; Rotenberg, 1993). When individuals are asked what they want from a friend or how they can tell someone is their best friend, they frequently say that a best friend will share problems with them, understand them, and listen when they talk about their own thoughts or feelings. When young children talk about their friendships, comments about intimate self-disclosure or mutual understanding are rare. In one investigation, friendship intimacy was more prominent in 13- to 16-year-olds than in 10- to 13-year-olds (Buhrmester, 1989).

Are the friendships of girls more intimate than the friendships of boys? When asked to describe their best friends, girls refer to intimate conversations and faithfulness more than boys do. For example, girls are more likely to describe their best friend as "sensitive just like me" or "trustworthy just like me" (Duck, 1975). The assumption behind this gender difference is that girls are more oriented toward interpersonal relationships. Boys may discourage one another from openly disclosing their problems as part of their masculine, competitive nature (Maccoby, 1995). Boys make themselves vulnerable to being called "wimps" if they can't handle their own problems and insecurities.

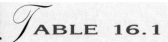

TABLE 16.1

Appropriate and Inappropriate Strategies for Making Friends at School

Category	Examples
Strategies Appropriate for Making Friends	
Initiate interaction	Learn about friend: ask for their name, age, favorite activities. Prosocial overtures: introduce self, start a conversation, invite them to do things.
Be nice	Be nice, kind, considerate.
Prosocial behavior	Honesty and trustworthiness: tell the truth, keep promises. Be generous, sharing, cooperative.
Respect for self and others	Respect others, have good manners: be polite, courteous, listen to what others say. Have a positive attitude and personality: be open to others, be friendly, be funny. Be yourself. Enhance your own reputation: be clean, dress neatly, be on best behavior.
Provide social support	Be supportive: help, give advice, show you care. Engage in activities together: study or play, sit next to one another, be in same group. Enhance others: compliment them.
Strategies Inappropriate for Making Friends	
Psychological aggression	Show disrespect, bad manners: be prejudiced, inconsiderate, use others, curse, be rude. Be exclusive, uncooperative: don't invite them to do things, ignore them, isolate them, don't share or help them. Hurt their reputation or feelings: gossip, spread rumors, embarrass them, criticize them.
Negative self-presentation	Be self-centered: be snobby, conceited, jealous, show off, care only about yourself. Have bad attitude or affect: be mean, cruel, hostile, a grouch, angry all the time. Hurt own reputation: be a slob, act stupid, throw temper tantrums, start trouble, be a sissy.
Antisocial behavior	Physical aggression: fight, trip, spit, cause physical harm. Verbal aggression or control: yell at others, pick on them, make fun of them, call them names, be bossy. Dishonesty, disloyalty: tell lies, steal, cheat, tell secrets, break promises. Break school rules: skip school, drink alcohol, use drugs.

Adolescents also regard loyalty or faithfulness as more critical in friendships than children do (Berndt & Perry, 1990). When talking about their best friend, adolescents frequently refer to the friend's willingness to stand up for them when around other people. Typical comments are: "Bob will stick up for me in a fight," "Sally won't talk about me behind my back," or "Jennifer wouldn't leave me for somebody else." In these descriptions, adolescents underscore the obligations of a friend in the larger peer group.

Another predominant characteristic of friendship is that, throughout the childhood and adolescent years, friends are generally similar—in terms of age, sex, ethnicity, and many other factors (Berndt, 1996; Lempers & Clark-Lempers, 1993; Luo, Fang, & Aro, 1995). Friends often have similar attitudes toward school, similar educational aspirations, and closely aligned achievement orientations. Friends like the same music, wear the same kind of clothes, and prefer the same leisure activities (Berndt, 1982). If friends have different attitudes about schools, one of them may want to play basketball or go shopping rather than do homework. If one friend insists on completing homework while the other insists on playing basketball, the conflict might weaken the friendship, and the two might drift apart. Table 16.1 describes appropriate and inappropriate strategies for making friends at school.

In one recent study of adolescent peer networks in sixth grade through twelfth grade, older adolescents were more selective in naming friends (Urberg & others, 1995). In twelfth grade, they made and received fewer friendship choices and had fewer mutual friends than in early adolescence. This increased selectivity might be due to increased social cognitive skills that allow older adolescents to make more accurate inferences about who likes them. Female students were more integrated into school social networks than males were. Girls were also more likely than boys to have a best friend and to be a clique member. Let's further explore the nature of peer relations in adolescence.

Peer Relations in Adolescence

Imagine you are back in junior or senior high school, especially during one of your good times. Peers, friends, cliques, dates, parties, and clubs probably come to mind. Adolescents spend huge chunks of time with peers, more than in middle and late childhood. Among the important issues and questions to be asked about peer relations in adolescence are the following: What is the nature of peer pressure and conformity? How important are cliques in adolescence? How do children and adolescent groups differ? What is the nature of dating in adolescence?

Peer Pressure and Conformity

Consider the following statement made by an adolescent girl:

> Peer pressure is extremely influential in my life. I have never had very many friends, and I spend quite a bit of time alone. The friends I have are older. . . . The closest friend I have had is a lot like me in that we are both sad and depressed a lot. I began to act even more depressed than before when I was with her. I would call her up and try to act even more depressed than I was because that is what I thought she liked. In that relationship, I felt pressure to be like her.

Conformity to peer pressure in adolescence can be positive or negative (Wall, 1993). Teenagers engage in all sorts of negative conformity behavior—for instance, they use seedy language, steal, vandalize, and make fun of parents and teachers. However, a great deal of peer conformity, such as dressing like one's friends and wanting to spend huge chunks of time with members of a clique, is not negative and consists of the desire to be involved in the peer world.

> *Each of you, individually; walkest with the tread of a fox, but collectively ye are geese.*
>
> **—Solon, Ancient Greece**

During adolescence, especially early adolescence, we conformed more to peer standards than we did in childhood. Investigators have found that, around the eighth and ninth grades, conformity to peers—especially to their antisocial standards—peaks (Berndt, 1979; Leventhal, 1994). At this point in development, an adolescent is most likely to go along with a peer to steal hubcaps off a car, draw graffiti on a wall, or steal cosmetics from a store counter.

Cliques and Crowds

Most peer group relationships in adolescence can be categorized in one of three ways: the crowd, the clique, or individual friendships. The **crowd** *is the largest and least personal of adolescent groups.* Members of the crowd meet because of their mutual interest in activities, not because they are mutually attracted to each other. **Cliques** *are smaller, involve greater intimacy among members, and have more group cohesion than crowds.*

Allegiance to cliques, clubs, organizations, and teams exerts powerful control over the lives of many adolescents (McLellan, Haynie, & Strouse, 1993; Tapper, 1996). Group identity often overrides personal identity. The leader of a group might place a group member in a position of considerable moral conflict by asking, in effect, "What's more important, our code or your parents'?" or "Are you looking out for yourself, or the members of the group?" Such labels as *brother* and *sister* sometimes are adopted and used

Most adolescents conform to the mainstream standards of their peers. However, the rebellious or anticonformist adolescent reacts counter to the mainstream peer group's expectations, deliberately moving away from the actions or beliefs this group advocates.

in the members' conversations with each other. These labels symbolize the bond between the members and suggest the high status of group membership.

One of the most widely cited studies of adolescent cliques and crowds is that of James Coleman (1961). Students from 10 high schools were asked to identify the leading crowds in their schools. They also were asked to identify the students who were the most outstanding in athletics, popularity, and various school activities. Regardless of the school sampled, the leading crowds were composed of athletes and popular girls. Much less power in the leading crowd was attributed to bright students.

Think about your high school years. What were the cliques, and which one were you in? Although the names of cliques change, we could go to almost any high school in the United States and find three to six well-defined cliques or crowds. In one investigation, six peer group structures emerged: populars, unpopulars, jocks, brains, druggies, and average students (Brown & Mounts, 1989). The proportion of students placed in these cliques was much lower in multiethnic schools because of the additional existence of ethnically based crowds.

In one study, clique membership was associated with the adolescent's self-esteem (Brown & Lohr, 1987). Cliques included jocks (athletically oriented), populars (well-known students who lead social activities), normals (middle-of-the-road students who make up the masses), druggies or toughs (known for illicit drug use or other delinquent activities), and nobodies (low in social skills or intellectual abilities). The self-esteem of the jocks and the populars was highest, whereas that of the nobodies

Artist unknown
Khamseh

Chapter 17

Schools and Achievement

The world rests on the breath of the children in the schoolhouse.

—The Talmud

Chapter Outline

Chapter Boxes

> *Children have to be educated, but they also have to be left to educate themselves.*
>
> —Ernest Dimnet

PREVIEW

In school, children spend many years as members of a small society that exerts tremendous influence on who they will become. In addition to teaching children to write and read, schools help children develop the fundamental aspects of their personality, such as identity and standards of right and wrong. Schools also help children understand how social systems outside the family function. Our coverage of schools explores the following questions: What is the nature of children's schooling? What is early childhood education like? How do children experience the transition to elementary school? How do various characteristics of classrooms and teachers influence children's development? What roles do social class and ethnicity play in schooling? What are schools for adolescents like? How should children with special needs be educated? In this chapter, we also explore the nature of children's achievement.

Some schools are ineffective, others effective, as revealed in the following excerpts (Lipsitz, 1984):

> A teacher in a social studies class squelches several imaginative questions, exclaiming, "You're always asking 'what if' questions. Stop asking 'what if.' " When a visitor asks who will become president if the president-elect dies before the electoral college meets, the teacher explodes, "You're as bad as they are! That's another 'what if' question!"
>
> A teacher drills students for a seemingly endless amount of time on prime numbers. After the lesson, not one student can say why it is important to learn prime numbers.
>
> A visitor asks a teacher if hers is an eighth-grade class. "It's called eighth grade," the teacher answers archly, "but we know it's really kindergarten, right class?"
>
> In a predominantly Latino school, only the one adult hired as a bilingual teacher speaks Spanish.
>
> In a biracial school, the principal and the guidance counselor cite test scores with pride. They are asked if the difference between the test scores of black and white students is narrowing: "Oh, that's an interesting question!" says the guidance counselor with surprise. The principal agrees. It has never been asked by or of them before.

The preceding vignettes are from schools where life seems to be difficult and unhappy for students. By contrast, consider the following circumstances in effective schools (Lipsitz, 1984):

> Everything is peaceful. There are open cubbies instead of locked lockers. There is no theft. Students walk quietly in the corridors. "Why?" they are asked. "So as not to disturb the media center," they answer, which is self-evident to them, but not the visitor, who is left wondering. . . . When asked, "Do you like this school?" (They) answer, "No, we don't like it. We love it!"
>
> When asked how the school feels, one student answered, "It feels smart. We're smart. Look at our test scores." Comments from one of the parents of a student at the school are

revealing: "My child would have been a dropout. In elementary school, his teacher said to me, 'That child isn't going to give you anything but heartaches.' He had perfect attendance here. He didn't want to miss a day. Summer vacation was too long and boring. Now he's majoring in communications at the University of Texas. He got here and all of a sudden, someone cared for him. I had been getting notes about Roger every other day, with threats about exclusion. Here, the first note said, 'It's just a joy to have him in the classroom.' "

> The humane environment that encourages teachers' growth . . . is translated by the teachers . . . into a humane environment that encourages students' growth. The school feels cold when one first enters. It has the institutional feeling of any large school building with metal lockers and impersonal halls. Then one opens the door to a team area, and it is filled with energy, movement, productivity, doing. There is a lot of informal relating among students and between students and teachers. Visible from one vantage point are students working on written projects, putting the last touches on posters, watching a film, and working independently from reading kits. . . . Most know what they are doing, can say why it is important, and go back to work immediately after being interrupted.

> Authors' Week is a special activity built into the school's curriculum that entices students to consider themselves in relation to the rich variety of making and doing in people's lives. Based on student interest, availability, and diversity, authors are invited . . . to discuss their craft. Students sign up to meet with individual authors. They must have read one individual book by the author. . . . Students prepare questions for their sessions with the authors. . . . Sometimes, an author stays several days to work with a group of students on his or her manuscript.

The Nature of Children's Schooling

Two important issues that pertain to the nature of children's schooling are these: What is the function of schools? What is the nature of changing social developmental contexts in schools?

Functions of Children's Schools

What should the function of schools be? Let's explore the controversies involved in the back-to-basics versus comprehensive training debate and the knowledge versus process debate.

Back-to-Basics Versus Comprehensive Training

In the 1980s, the back-to-basics movement gained momentum. The **back-to-basics movement** *stresses that the main function of schools should be the rigorous training of intellectual skills through such subjects as English, math, and science.* Advocates of the back-to-basics movement argue that there is excessive fluff in elementary and secondary school curricula, with too many alternative subjects that do not give students a basic education in intellectual subjects. Back-to-basics advocates believe that schools should be in the business of imparting knowledge to children and should not be as concerned about their socioemotional lives. The back-to-basics advocates want students to have more homework, more tests, and more discipline. They say that children should usually be seated at their desks and not roaming around the room. Teachers should be at the head of the classroom, drilling knowledge into children's minds. Some back-to-basics supporters also think that the school day should be longer and that the school year should be extended through the summer months.

By contrast, some education experts argue that the function of education should involve more comprehensive training that emphasizes both cognitive and socio-emotional processes. They also believe that education should involve more "hands-on" instruction—in which children are more actively involved in discovering knowledge rather than having it drilled into them. As we see next, a close parallel to the back-to-basics versus comprehensive education debate is found in the knowledge versus process debate.

Knowledge Versus Process

Should schools be imparting knowledge to children? Or should they be teaching them how to think? This is the key issue in the knowledge versus process debate in children's education. The current debate is nowhere more clear than in the views of two leading educators—E. D. Hirsch and Theodore Sizer. Hirsch (1987, 1996) is on the knowledge side, Sizer (1996) is on the process side.

For Hirsch, *what* students learn is important. Knowledge is the cornerstone of education. The types of classroom activities advocated by Hirsch for knowledge-building include many old-fashioned ideas: a rigorous course of study, book learning, recitation, in-charge teaching, and lots of testing.

For Sizer, *how* students learn is the key to education. Education should stress thinking skills. Students should learn how to think independently and critically. In-depth projects should replace standardized testing. Teachers should act as "coaches" in helping students with hands-on projects. Single-subject teaching should be abandoned in favor of interdisciplinary study.

Sizer criticizes the "lecture-drill-and-test systems" of many schools. He believes that, instead, schools should encourage children to ask inquiring questions and use knowledge in thoughtful ways. Critical to such

The back-to-basics movement stresses the importance of rigorous training. It also advocates that schools should impart knowledge to children and not be as concerned about their socioemotional lives.

Advocates of comprehensive training believe that both cognitive and socioemotional aspects of children's lives should be addressed in schools. In Theodore Sizer's process approach, *how* students learn is the key to education.

who insists on giving the farm animals a bath. The children recite the whimsical lines, clearly enjoying one of their favorite stories. The hallway outside the kindergarten is lined with drawings depicting the children's own interpretation of the book. After the first reading, volunteers act out various parts of the book. There is not one bored face in the room (Kantrowitz & Wingert, 1989).

This is not reading, writing, and arithmetic the way most individuals remember it. A growing number of educators and psychologists believe that preschool and young elementary school children learn best through active, hands-on teaching methods like games and dramatic play. They know that children develop at varying rates and that schools need to allow for these individual differences. They also believe that schools should focus on improving children's social development as well as their cognitive development. Educators refer to this type of schooling as **developmentally appropriate practice**, *which is based upon knowledge of the typical development of children within an age span (age appropriateness) as well as the uniqueness of the child (individual appropriateness)*. Developmentally appropriate practice contrasts with developmentally inappropriate practice, which ignores the concrete, hands-on approach to learning. Direct teaching largely through abstract, paper-and-pencil activities presented to large groups of young children is believed to be developmentally inappropriate.

One of the most comprehensive documents addressing the issue of developmentally appropriate practice in early childhood programs is the position statement by the NAEYC (National Association for the Education of Young Children) in 1986 (Bredekamp, 1987). This document represents the expertise of many of the foremost experts in the field of early childhood education. By turning to figure 17.1, you can examine some of the NAEYC recommendations for developmentally appropriate practice. In one study, children who attended developmentally appropriate kindergartens displayed more appropriate classroom behavior, had better conduct records, and better work-study habits in the first grade than children who attended developmentally inappropriate kindergartens (Hart & others, 1993).

A special worry of early childhood educators is that the back-to-basics movement that has recently characterized educational reform is filtering down to kindergarten. Another worry is that many parents want their children to go to school earlier than kindergarten for the purpose of getting a "head start" in achievement.

Does It Really Matter If Children Attend Preschool Before Kindergarten?

According to child developmentalist David Elkind (1987), parents who are exceptionally competent and dedicated and who have both the time and the energy can provide the basic ingredients of early childhood education in their home. If parents have the competence and resources to provide young children with a variety of learning experiences and exposure to other children and adults (possibly through neighborhood play groups), along with opportunities for extensive play, then home schooling may sufficiently educate young children. However, if parents do not have the commitment, the time, the energy, and the resources to provide young children with an environment that approximates a good early childhood program, then it *does* matter whether a child attends preschool. In this case, the issue is not whether preschool is important, but whether home schooling can closely duplicate what a competent preschool program can offer (Beardslee & Richmond, 1992).

We should always keep in mind that the view of early childhood education as an early start to ensure that participants will finish early or on top in an educational race is an unfortunate one. Elkind (1988) points out that perhaps the choice of the phrase "head start" for the education of disadvantaged children was a mistake. "Head Start" does not imply a race. Not surprisingly, when middle-class parents heard that low-income children were getting a "head start," they wanted a "head start" for their own young children. In some instances, starting children in formal academic training too early can produce more harm than good. In Denmark, where reading instruction follows a language experience approach and formal instruction is delayed until the age of 7, illiteracy is virtually nonexistent. By contrast, in France, where state-mandated formal instruction in reading begins at age 5, 30 percent of the children have reading problems. Education should not be stressful for young children. Early childhood education should not be solely an academic prep school.

Preschool is rapidly becoming a norm in early childhood education. Twenty-three states already have legislation pending to provide schooling for 4-year-old children, and there are already many private preschool programs. The increase in public preschools underscores the growing belief that early childhood education should be a legitimate component of public education. There are dangers, though. According to David Elkind (1988), early childhood education is often not well understood at higher levels of education. The danger is that public preschool education for 4-year-old children will become little more than a downward extension of traditional elementary education. This is already occurring in preschool programs in which testing, workbooks, and group drill are imposed on 4- and 5-year-old children.

Elkind believes that early childhood education should become a part of public education but on its own terms. Early childhood should have its own curriculum, its own methods of evaluation and classroom management, and its own teacher-training programs. Although there may be some overlap with the curriculum, evaluation, classroom management, and teacher training at the upper levels of

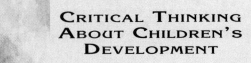

CRITICAL THINKING ABOUT CHILDREN'S DEVELOPMENT

Observing Children in Preschool and Kindergarten

To learn about children, there is no substitute for interacting with them and observing them. Try to visit at least one preschool and one kindergarten. When I (your author) was trying to develop a meaningful idea for a master's thesis some years ago, my advisor suggested that I spend several weeks at a variety of

Head Start programs in Miami, Florida. The experience was invaluable and contributed significantly to my further pursuing a career in the field of child development.

When you conduct your observations, consider whether the programs meet the criteria of developmentally appropriate education. Are the programs play- and child-centered or academics-centered? By visiting early childhood education programs and evaluating whether they are developmentally appropriate, you are learning to think critically by *making accurate observations, descriptions, and inferences about children's development.*

schooling, they certainly should not be identical. To further evaluate the nature of preschools and kindergartens, turn to Critical Thinking About Children's Development.

Researchers are already beginning to document some of the stress that increased academic pressure can bring to young children (Greenberg, 1992). In one investigation, Diane Burts and her colleagues (1989) compared the frequencies of stress-related behaviors observed in young children in classrooms with developmentally appropriate and developmentally inappropriate instructional practices. They found that children in the developmentally inappropriate classrooms exhibited more stress-related behaviors than children in the developmentally appropriate classrooms did. In another investigation, children in a high academically oriented early childhood education program were compared with children in a low academically oriented early childhood education program (Hirsch-Pasek & others, 1989). No benefits appeared for children in the high academically oriented early childhood education program, but some possible harmful effects were noted. Higher test anxiety, less creativity, and a less positive attitude toward school characterized the children who attended the high academic program more than the low academic program.

One of the concerns of Americans is that our school children fare poorly when their achievement test scores in math and science are compared with the test scores of school children from many other industrialized nations, especially such Asian nations as Japan and China (McKnight & others, 1987). Many Americans attribute the differences in achievement scores to a rigid system that sets young children in a lockstep march from cradle to college. In fact, the early years of Japanese schooling are anything but a boot camp. To read further about the nature of early childhood education in Japan, turn to Sociocultural Worlds of Children.

The Effects of Early Childhood Education

Because kindergarten and preschool programs are so diverse, it is difficult to make overall conclusions about their effects on children's development. Nonetheless, in one review of early childhood education's influence (Clarke-Stewart & Fein, 1983), it was concluded that children who attend preschool or kindergarten

- Interact more with peers, both positively and negatively
- Are less cooperative with and responsive to adults than home-reared children
- Are more socially competent and mature in that they are more confident, extraverted, assertive, self-sufficient, independent, verbally expressive, knowledgeable about the social world, comfortable in social and stressful circumstances, and better adjusted when they go to school (exhibiting more task persistence, leadership, and goal direction, for example)
- Are less socially competent in that they are less polite, less compliant to teacher demands, louder, and more aggressive and bossy, especially if the school or family supports such behavior

In sum, early childhood education generally has a positive effect on children's development, since the behaviors just mentioned—while at times negative—seem to be in the direction of developmental maturity in that they increase as the child ages through the preschool years.

Education for Disadvantaged Children

For many years, children from low-income families did not receive any education before they entered the first grade. In the 1960s, an effort was made to try to break the

Component	Appropriate practice	Inappropriate practice
Curriculum goals	Experiences are provided in all developmental areas—physical, cognitive, social, and emotional.	Experiences are narrowly focused on cognitive development without recognition that all areas of the child's development are interrelated.
	Individual differences are expected, accepted, and used to design appropriate activities.	Children are evaluated only against group norms, and all are expected to perform the same tasks and achieve the same narrowly defined skills.
	Interactions and activities are designed to develop children's self-esteem and positive feelings toward learning.	Children's worth is measured by how well they conform to rigid expectations and perform on standardized tests.
Teaching strategies	Teachers prepare the environment for children to learn through active exploration and interaction with adults, other children, and materials.	Teachers use highly structured, teacher-directed lessons almost exclusively.
	Children select many of their own activities from among a variety the teacher prepares.	The teacher directs all activity, deciding what children will do and when.
	Children are expected to be mentally and physically active.	Children are expected to sit down, be quiet, and listen, or do paper-and-pencil tasks for long periods of time. A major portion of time is spent passively sitting, watching, and listening.
Guidance of socioemotional development	Teachers enhance children's self-control by using positive guidance techniques such as modeling and encouraging expected behavior, redirecting children to a more acceptable activity, and setting clear limits.	Teachers spend considerable time enforcing rules, punishing unacceptable behavior, demeaning children who misbehave, making children sit and be quiet, or refereeing disagreements.
	Children are provided many opportunities to develop social skills such as cooperating, helping, negotiating, and talking with the person involved to solve interpersonal problems.	Children work individually at desks and tables most of the time and listen to the teacher's directions to the total group.

Figure~17.1

Developmentally Appropriate and Inappropriate Practice in Early Childhood Education: NAEYC Recommendations

Santrock: Child Development

Component	Appropriate practice	Inappropriate practice
Language development, literacy, and cognitive development	Children are provided many opportunities to see how reading and writing are useful before they are instructed in letter names, sounds, and word identification. Basic skills develop when they are meaningful to children. An abundance of these activities is provided to develop language and literacy: listening to and reading stories and poems, taking field trips, dictating stories, participating in dramatic play; talking informally with other children and adults; and experimenting with writing.	Reading and writing instruction stresses isolated skill development, such as recognizing single letters, reading the alphabet, singing the alphabet song, coloring within predefined lines, or being instructed in correct formation of letters on a printed line.
	Children develop an understanding of concepts about themselves, others, and the world around them through observation, interacting with people and real objects, and seeking solutions to concrete problems. Learning about math, science, social studies, health, and other content areas is integrated through meaningful activities.	Instruction stresses isolated skill development through memorization. Children's cognitive development is seen as fragmented in content areas such as math or science, and times are set aside for each of these.
Physical development	Children have daily opportunities to use large muscles, including running, jumping, and balancing. Outdoor activity is planned daily so children can freely express themselves.	Opportunity for large muscle activity is limited. Outdoor time is limited because it is viewed as interfering with instructional time, rather than as an integral part of the children's learning environment.
	Children have daily opportunities to develop small muscle skills through play activities, such as puzzles, painting, cutting, and similar activities.	Small motor activity is limited to writing with pencils, coloring predrawn forms, or engaging in similar structured lessons.
Aesthetic development and motivation	Children have daily opportunities for aesthetic expression and appreciation through art and music. A variety of art media is available.	Art and music are given limited attention. Art consists of coloring predrawn forms or following adult-prescribed directions.
	Children's natural curiosity and desire to make sense of their world are used to motivate them to become involved in learning.	Children are required to participate in all activities to obtain the teacher's approval, to obtain extrinsic rewards like stickers or privileges, or to avoid punishment.

Early Childhood Education in Japan

In the midst of low academic achievement by children in the United States, many Americans are turning to Japan, a country of high academic achievement and economic success, for possible answers. However, the answers provided by Japanese preschools are not the ones Americans expected to find. In most Japanese preschools, surprisingly little emphasis is put on academic instruction. In one investigation, 300 Japanese and 210 American preschool teachers, child development specialists, and parents were asked about various aspects of early childhood education (Tobin, Wu, & Davidson, 1989). Only 2 percent of the Japanese respondents listed "to give children a good start academically" as one of their top three reasons for a society to have preschools. In contrast, over half the American respondents chose this as one of their top three choices. To prepare children for successful careers in first grade and beyond, Japanese schools do not teach reading, writing, and mathematics but rather skills, such as persistence, concentration, and the ability to function as a member of a group. The vast majority of young Japanese children are taught to read at home by their parents.

In the comparison of Japanese and American preschool education, 91 percent of Japanese respondents chose providing children with a group experience as one of their top three reasons for a society to have preschools (Tobin, Wu, & Davidson, 1989). Sixty-two percent of the most individually oriented Americans listed group experience as one of their top three choices. An emphasis on the importance of the group seen in Japanese early childhood education continues into elementary school education.

Lessons in living and working together grow naturally out of the Japanese culture. In many Japanese kindergartens, children wear the same uniforms, including caps, which are of different colors to indicate the classrooms to which they belong. They have identical sets of equipment, kept in identical drawers and shelves. This is not intended to turn the young children into robots, as some Americans have observed, but to impress on them that other people, just like themselves, have needs and desires that are equally important (Hendry, 1986).

Like in America, there is diversity in Japanese early childhood education. Some Japanese kindergartens have specific aims, such as early musical training or the practice of Montessori aims (Hendry, 1986). In large cities, some kindergartens are attached to universities that have elementary and secondary schools. Some Japanese parents believe that, if their young children attend a university-based program, it will increase the children's chances of eventually being admitted to top-rated schools and universities. Several more progressive programs have introduced free play as an antidote for the heavy intellectualizing in some Japanese kindergartens.

In Japan, learning how to cooperate and participating in group experiences are viewed as extremely important reasons for the existence of early childhood education.

cycle of poverty and poor education for young children in the United States through compensatory education. **Project Head Start** *is a compensatory education program designed to provide children from low-income families the opportunity to acquire the skills and experiences important for success in school.* Project Head Start began in the summer of 1965, funded by the Economic Opportunity Act, and it continues to serve disadvantaged children today. In 1990, the Head Start program was reauthorized at its highest funding level ever with the hope that it would serve all eligible 3- to 5-year-olds through 1994 (National Association for the Education of Young Children, 1991; *Report on Preschool Programs*, 1992).

Initially, Project Head Start consisted of many different types of preschool programs in different parts of the country. Little effort was made to find out whether some programs worked better than others, but it became apparent that some programs did work better than others. **Project Follow Through** *was implemented in 1967 as an adjunct to Project Head Start. In Project Follow Through, different types of educational programs were devised to determine which programs were the most effective. In the Follow Through programs, the enriched programs were carried through the first few years of elementary school.*

Were some Follow Through programs more effective than others? Many of the different variations were able to produce the desired effects on children. For example, children in academically oriented, direct-instruction learning environments did better on achievement tests and were more persistent on tasks than were children in the other approaches. Children in affective education approaches were absent from school less often and showed more independence than children taught under other approaches. Thus, Project Follow Through was important in demonstrating that variations in early childhood education do have significant effects in a wide range of social and cognitive areas (Stallings, 1975).

The effects of early childhood compensatory education continue to be studied, and recent evaluations support the positive influence on both the cognitive and social worlds of disadvantaged young children (Gaines, Blair, & Cluett, 1995; Klein & Starkey, 1995). Of special interest are the long-term effects such intervention might produce. Model preschool programs lead to lower rates of placement in special education, dropping out of school, grade retention, delinquency, and use of welfare programs. Such programs might also lead to higher rates

These preschool children are attending a Head Start program, a national effort to provide children from low-income families the opportunity to experience an enriched environment.

of high school graduation and employment. For every dollar invested in high-quality, model preschool programs, taxpayers receive about $1.50 in return by the time the participants reach the age of 20 (Haskins, 1989). The benefits include savings on public school education (such as special education services), tax payments on additional earnings, reduced welfare payments, and savings in juvenile justice system costs. Predicted benefits over a lifetime are much greater to the taxpayer, a return of $5.73 on every dollar invested.

One long-term investigation of early childhood education was conducted by Irving Lazar, Richard Darlington, and their colleagues (1982). They pooled their resources into what they called a consortium for longitudinal studies, developed to share information about the long-term effects of preschool programs so that better designs and methods could be created. At the time the data from the eleven different early education studies were analyzed together, the children ranged in age from 9 to 19 years. The early education models varied substantially, but all were carefully planned and executed by experts in early childhood education. Outcome measures included indicators of school competence (such as special education and grade retention), abilities (as measured by standardized intelligence and achievement tests), attitudes and values, and impact on the family. The results indicated substantial benefits of competent preschool education with low-income children on all four dimensions investigated. In sum, ample evidence indicates that well-designed and well-implemented early childhood education programs with low-income children are successful (Robinson & Redden, 1997).

While educational intervention in impoverished young children's lives is important, not all Head Start programs are created equal. Edward Zigler and Susan Muenchow (1992) concluded that 40 percent of the 1,400 Head Start programs are of questionable quality. More attention needs to be given to developing consistently high-quality Head Start programs (Bronfenbrenner, 1995; Parker & others, 1995; Powell, 1995; Susman & Adams, 1995). One high-quality early childhood education program is the Perry Preschool program in Ypsilanti, Michigan, which was designed by David Weikart (1982, 1993). The Perry Preschool program is a 2-year preschool program that includes weekly home visits from program personnel. In a recent analysis of the long-term effects of the program, as young adults the Perry Preschool children had higher high school graduation rates, more are in the workforce, fewer need welfare, crime rates are lower among them, and fewer had teen pregnancies, compared to a control group from the same background who did not get the enriched early childhood education experience (Weikart, 1993).

Nonsexist Early Childhood Education

An important goal of nonsexist early childhood education is to free children from constraining stereotypes of gender roles so that no aspect of their development will be closed off because of the child's sex. Another important goal is to promote equality for both sexes by facilitating each child's participation in activities necessary for optimal cognitive and socioemotional development. Yet another important goal is to help children develop skills that will enable them to challenge sexist stereotypes and behaviors.

Young children's awareness of equitable gender roles can be expanded by having them participate in a number of activities, such as these (Derman-Sparks & the ABC Task Force, 1989):

- Reading books about girls and boys that contradict gender stereotypes. Examples of such books are *William's Doll* (Zolotow, 1972), *Stephanie and the Coyote* (Crowder, 1969), and *Everybody Knows That* (Pearson, 1978).
- Getting children to find and cut out magazine pictures of girls and boys, women and men, with a diversity of looks, dress, activities, and emotions.
- Creating a display of photographs and pictures of women and men performing the same kind of tasks in the home and in the world of work. The display can be used to talk with children about the tasks that family members do and what kinds of tasks the children will do when they grow up.
- Being a nonsexist role model as a teacher, helping children learn new skills, and sharing tasks in a nonsexist manner.

- Inviting members of children's families (including extended-family relatives) who have nontraditional jobs (such as a male flight attendant, nurse, or secretary; a female construction worker, engineer, or doctor) to come and talk with the class about their work.
- Supporting children's dramatic play that involves nontraditional gender roles.
- Telling stories about nonstereotyped dolls that support nontraditional behaviors and describing the conflicts they sometimes have when acting in ways that challenge stereotypical gender roles.

School Readiness

Educational reform has prompted considerable concern about children's readiness to enter kindergarten and first grade. The issue gained national attention when the president and the nation's governors adopted school readiness as a national educational goal, vowing that by the year 2000 all children will start to school ready to learn. The concept of school readiness is based on the assumption that all children need to possess a predetermined set of capabilities before they enter school. Thus, any discussions of school readiness should consider three important factors:

- The diversity and inequity of children's early life experiences
- The wide range of variation in young children's development and learning
- The degree to which school expectations for children entering kindergarten are reasonable, appropriate, and supportive of individual differences in children

The National Association for the Education of Young Children (1990; Willer & Bredekamp, 1990) stresses that government officials and educators who promote universal school readiness should commit to the following:

- Addressing the inequities in early life experiences so that all children have access to the opportunities that promote success in school
- Recognizing and supporting individual differences in children
- Establishing reasonable and appropriate expectations for children's capabilities upon school entry

The NAEYC believes that every child, except in the most severe instances of abuse, neglect, or disability, enters school ready to learn. However, not all children succeed in school. Inadequate health care and economic difficulties place many children at risk for academic failure before they enter school. Families who lack emotional resources and support also are not always capable of preparing their children to meet school expectations.

Therefore, according to the NAEYC, it is important to provide families with access to the services and support necessary to prepare children to succeed in school. Such services include basic health care, economic support, basic nutrition, adequate housing, family support services, and high-quality early-childhood education programs.

Expectations for young children's skills and abilities need to be based on knowledge of child development and how children learn. A basic principle of child development is that there is tremendous normal variability both among children of the same chronological age and within an individual child. Children's social skills, physical skills, cognitive skills, and emotional adjustment are equally important areas of development, and each contributes to how well children do in school. Within any group of children, one child may possess advanced language and cognitive skills, but show poor social skills and emotional adjustment; another child may have advanced social skills, be well adjusted emotionally, and have good physical skills, but have poor language skills, and so on. Readiness expectations should not be based on a narrow checklist focusing on only one or two dimensions of development. Such a narrow focus—only considering language or cognitive skills, for example—ignores the complexity and multidimensionality of children's development.

Wide variability also occurs in the rate of children's development (Dickinson, 1995). The precise time at which children will achieve a certain level of development or acquire specific skills is difficult to predict. Learning and development often do not occur in rigid, uniform ways. Thus, raising the legal entry age for school or holding a child out of school for a year may not be wise, but could be misdirected efforts that only serve to impose a rigid schedule on the child's development despite their normal differences from other children (Spitzer & Dicker, 1993).

At this point, we have discussed a number of ideas about children's education and early childhood education. Next, we will turn our attention to the transition to elementary school.

The Transition to Elementary School

For most children, entering the first grade signals a change from being a "homechild" to being a "schoolchild" in which

As children make the transition to elementary school, they interact and develop relationships with new and significant others. School provides them with a rich source of new ideas to shape their sense of self.

new roles and obligations are experienced. Children take up a new role (being a student), interact and develop relationships with new significant others, adopt new reference groups, and develop new standards by which to judge themselves. School provides children with a rich source of new ideas to shape their sense of self (Stipek, 1992).

Knowledge which is acquired under compulsion obtains no hold on the mind.

—**Plato**

A special concern about children's early school experiences is emerging. Evidence is mounting that early schooling proceeds mainly on the basis of negative feedback. For example, children's self-esteem in the latter part of elementary school is lower than it is in the earlier part, and older children rate themselves as less smart, less good, and less hardworking than do younger ones (Blumenfeld & others, 1981). In one investigation, the first year of school was identified as a period of considerable importance in shaping achievement, especially for ethnic minority children (Alexander & Entwisle, 1988). African American and White children began school with similar achievement test scores but, by the end of the first year, African American children's performance lagged noticeably behind that of the White children, and the gap widened over the second year of schooling. The grades teachers gave to African American children in the first two grades of school also were lower than those they gave to White children.

In school, as well as out of school, children's learning, like children's development, is *integrated* (NAEYC, 1988). One of the main pressures on elementary teachers has been the need to "cover the curriculum." Frequently, teachers have tried to do so by tightly scheduling discrete time segments for each subject. This approach ignores the fact that children often do not need to distinguish learning by subject area. For example, they advance their knowledge or reading and writing when they work on social studies projects; they learn mathematical concepts through music and physical education (Katz & Chard, 1989; Van Deusen-Henkel & Argondizza, 1987). A curriculum can be facilitated by providing learning areas in which children plan and select their activities. For example, the classroom may include a fully equipped publishing center, complete with materials for writing, illustrating, typing, and binding student-made books; a science area with animals and plants for observation and books to study; and other similar areas (Van Deusen-Henkel & Argondizza, 1987). In this type of classroom, children learn reading as they discover information about science; they learn writing as they work together on interesting projects. Such classrooms also provide opportunities for spontaneous play, recognizing that elementary school children continue to learn in all areas through unstructured play, either alone or with other children.

Education experts Lillian Katz and Sylvia Chard (1989) recently described two elementary school classrooms. In one, children spent an entire morning making identical pictures of traffic lights. The teacher made no attempt to get the children to relate the pictures to anything else the class was doing. In the other class, children were investigating a school bus. They wrote to the district's school superintendent and asked if they could have a bus parked at their school for a few days. They studied the bus, discovered the functions of its parts, and discussed traffic rules. Then, in the classroom, they built their own bus out of cardboard. The children had fun, but they also practiced writing, problem solving, and even some arithmetic. When the class had their parents' night, the teacher was ready with reports on how each child was doing. However, all the parents wanted to see was the bus, because their children had been coming home and talking about it for weeks. Many contemporary education experts believe that this is the kind of education all children deserve. That is, they believe that children should be taught through concrete, hands-on experience.

The Nature of Adolescents' Schooling

Among the special concerns about adolescents' schooling are the transition to middle or junior high school, what makes an effective school for young adolescents, and high school dropouts.

The Transition to Middle or Junior High School

The emergence of junior high schools in the 1920s and 1930s was justified on the basis of physical, cognitive, and social changes that characterize early adolescence, as well as the need for more schools for the growing student population. Old high schools became junior high schools and new regional high schools were built. In most systems, the ninth grade remained a part of the high school in content, although physically separated from it in a 6-3-3 system. Gradually, the ninth grade has been restored to the high school as many school systems have developed middle schools that include the seventh and eighth grades, or sixth, seventh, and eighth grades. The creation of middle schools has been influenced by the earlier onset of puberty in recent decades.

> *In youth we learn, in age we understand.*
> —Marie Ebner von Eschenbach

One worry of educators and psychologists is that junior high and middle schools have simply become watered-down versions of high schools, mimicking their curricular and extracurricular schedules. The critics argue that unique curricular and extracurricular activities reflecting a wide range of individual differences in biological and psychological development in early adolescence should be incorporated into our junior high and middle schools. The critics also stress that many high schools foster passivity rather than autonomy, and that schools should create a variety of pathways for students to achieve an identity.

The transition to middle school or junior high school from elementary school interests developmentalists because, even though it is a normative experience for virtually all children, the transition can be stressful. Why? Because the transition takes place at a time when many changes—in the individual, in the family, and in school—are taking place simultaneously (Simmons & Blyth, 1987). These changes include puberty and related concerns about body image; the emergence of at least some aspects of formal operational thought, including accompanying changes in social cognition; increased responsibility and independence in association with decreased dependency on parents; change from a small, contained classroom structure to a larger, more impersonal school structure; change from one teacher to many teachers and a small, homogeneous set of peers to a larger, more heterogeneous

The transition from elementary to middle or junior high school occurs at the same time a number of other changes take place in development. Biological, cognitive, and social changes converge with this schooling transition to make it a time of considerable adaptation.

set of peers; and increased focus on achievement and performance, and their assessment. This list includes a number of negative, stressful features, but there can be positive aspects to the transition. Students are more likely to feel grown up, have more subjects from which to select, have more opportunities to spend time with peers and to locate compatible friends, enjoy increased independence from direct parental monitoring, and may be more challenged intellectually by academic work.

When students make the transition from elementary school to middle or junior high school, they experience the **top-dog phenomenon,** *the circumstance of moving from the top position (in elementary school, the oldest, biggest, and most powerful students in the school) to the lowest position (in middle or junior high school, the youngest, smallest, and least powerful students in the school).* Researchers who have charted the transition from elementary to middle or junior high school find that the first year of middle or junior high school can be difficult for many students (Eccles & Midgely, 1990). For example, in one investigation of the transition from sixth grade in an elementary

school to the seventh grade in a junior high school, adolescents' perceptions of the quality of their school life plunged in the seventh grade (Hirsch & Rapkin, 1987). In the seventh grade, the students were less satisfied with school, were less committed to school, and liked their teachers less. The drop in school satisfaction occurred regardless of how academically successful the students were.

The transition to middle school or junior high school and the mismatch between the young adolescent and the school can be especially problematic for poor urban youth in resource-poor schools. In one recent study of such poor urban youth, the transition from elementary school to middle or junior high school was characterized by increasing disengagement from school (a decline in extracurricular participation, a decline in perception of support by school personnel, an increase in daily hassles at school, and decreased hassles with peers whose values the young adolescents saw as being increasingly antisocial) (Seidman & others, 1994). Such findings underscore the importance of the recommendation by the Carnegie Council on Adolescent Development (1989) to create small communities of learning where stable, close, mutually respectful relationships with adults and peers enhance intellectual and socioemotional development.

Effective Schools for Young Adolescents

What makes a successful middle school? Joan Lipsitz (1984) and her colleagues searched the nation for the best middle schools. Extensive contacts and observations were made. Based on the recommendations of education experts and observations in schools in different parts of the United States, four middle schools were chosen for their outstanding ability to educate young adolescents. What were these middle schools like? The most striking feature was their willingness and ability to adapt all school practices to the individual differences in physical, cognitive, and social development of their students. The schools took seriously the knowledge we have developed about young adolescents. This seriousness was reflected in the decisions about different aspects of school life. For example, one middle school fought to keep its schedule of minicourses on Friday so that every student could be with friends and pursue personal interests. Two other middle schools expended considerable energy on a complex school organization so that small groups of students worked with small groups of teachers who could vary the tone and pace of the school day, depending on the students' needs. Another middle school developed an advisory scheme so that each student had daily contact with an adult who was willing to listen, explain, comfort, and prod the adolescent. Such school policies reflect thoughtfulness and personal concern about individuals who have compelling developmental needs.

Another aspect of the effective middle schools was that early in their existence—the first year in three of

Joan Lipsitz (shown here talking with young adolescents) has been an important spokesperson for the needs of adolescents. Former director of the Center for Early Adolescence at the University of North Carolina, she wrote the widely acclaimed book *Successful Schools for Young Adolescents*.

the schools and the second year in the fourth school—they emphasized the importance of creating an environment that was positive for the adolescent's social and emotional development. This goal was established not only because such environments contribute to academic excellence, but also because social and emotional development are valued as intrinsically important in adolescents' schooling.

Recognizing that the vast majority of middle schools do not have the qualities of the excellent schools described by Joan Lipsitz (1984), in 1989 the Carnegie Council on Adolescent Development issued an extremely negative evaluation of our nation's middle schools. In the report, *Turning Points: Preparing American Youth for the 21st Century*, the conclusion was put forth that most young adolescents attend massive, impersonal schools, learn from seemingly irrelevant curricula, trust few adults in school, and lack access to health care and counseling. The Carnegie report (1989) recommended the following:

- Develop smaller "communities" or "houses" to lessen the impersonal nature of large middle schools
- Lower student-to-counselor ratios from several hundred-to-1 to 10-to-1
- Involve parents and community leaders in schools
- Develop curricula that produce students who are literate, understand the sciences, and have a sense of health, ethics, and citizenship
- Have teachers team teach in more flexibly designed curriculum blocks that integrate several disciplines instead of presenting students with disconnected, rigidly separated 50-minute segments
- Boost students' health and fitness with more in-school programs and help students who need public health care to get it

Many of these recommendations were echoed in a report from the National Governor's Association (*America in Transition*, 1989), which stated that the very structure of middle school education in America neglects the basic developmental needs of young adolescents. Many educators and psychologists strongly support these recommendations (Entwisle, 1990; MacIver & others, 1992; Wigfield & Eccles, 1994, 1995). The Edna McConnell Clark Foundation's Program for Disadvantaged Youth is an example of a multiyear, multisite effort designed to implement many of the proposals for middle school improvement. The foundation has engaged the Center for Early Adolescence at the University of North Carolina to guide five urban school districts in their middle school reform (Scales, 1990). In sum, middle schools throughout the nation need a major redesign if they are to be effective in educating adolescents for becoming competent adults in the twenty-first century (Urdan, Midgley, & Wood, 1995).

Through its Middle Grade School State Policy Initiative, the Carnegie Foundation of New York is implementing the *Turning Points* recommendations in nearly 100 schools and 15 states nationwide. A national evaluation of this initiative is currently under way. Data from the state of Illinois already show that in 42 schools participating in at least 1 year of the study since 1991, enactment of the *Turning Points* recommendations was associated with significant improvements in students' reading, math, and language arts achievement. In 31 schools with several years of data, the same pattern of positive results was found *within* schools over time. That is, as schools continued to implement the *Turning Points* recommendations, students' achievement continued to improve (Carnegie Council on Adolescent Development, 1995).

High School Dropouts

For many decades, dropping out of high school has been viewed as a serious educational and societal problem. By leaving high school before graduating, many dropouts take with them educational deficiencies that severely diminish their economic and social well-being throughout their adult lives (Cohen, 1994; Rumberger, 1987). We will study the scope of the problem, the causes of dropping out, and ways to reduce dropout rates. While dropping out of high school often has negative consequences for youth, the picture is not entirely bleak (William T. Grant Foundation Commission on Work, Family, and Citizenship, 1988). Over the last 40 years, the proportion of adolescents who have not finished high school has decreased considerably. In 1940, more than 60 percent of all individuals 25 to 29 years of age had not completed high school. By 1986, this proportion had dropped to less than 14 percent. From 1973 to 1983, the annual dropout rate nationwide fell by almost 20 percent, from 6.3 to 5.2 percent.

Despite the decline in overall high school dropout rates, a major concern is the higher dropout rate of minority group and low-income students, especially in large cities (Evans & others, 1995). While the student dropout rates of most minority groups have been declining, they remain substantially above those of White adolescents. The proportion of Latino youth who finish high school is not keeping pace with the gains by African American and other minority groups. High school completion rates for Latino youth dropped from 63 percent in 1985 to 56 percent in 1989; the completion rate was 52 percent in 1972. In contrast to the pattern among Latino youth, the high school graduation rate for African American youth increased from 67 percent in 1972 to 76 percent in 1989. The comparable rates for White youth remained the same—82 percent in both 1972 and 1989.

Dropout rates are also high for Native Americans (fewer than 10 percent graduate from high school) (LaFromboise & Low, 1989). In some inner-city areas the dropout rate for ethnic minority students is especially high, reaching more than 50 percent in Chicago, for example (Hahn, 1987).

Students drop out of schools for many reasons (Jacobs, Garnier, & Weisner, 1996; McDougall, Schonert-Reichel, & Hymel, 1996). In one investigation, almost 50 percent of the dropouts cited school-related reasons for leaving school, such as not liking school or being expelled or suspended (Rumberger, 1983). Twenty percent of the dropouts (but 40 percent of the Latino students) cited economic reasons for leaving school. One-third of the female students dropped out for personal reasons, such as pregnancy or marriage.

Most research on dropouts has focused on high school students. One recent study focused on middle school dropouts (Rumberger, 1995). The observed differences in dropout rates among ethnic groups were related to differences in family background—especially socioeconomic status. Lack of parental academic support, low parental supervision, and low parental expectations for their adolescents were also related to dropping out of middle school.

The I Have a Dream (IHAD) Program is a comprehensive, long-term dropout prevention program administered by the National "I Have a Dream" Foundation in New York. Local IHAD projects around the country "adopt" entire grades (usually the third or fourth) from public elementary schools, or corresponding age-cohorts from public housing developments. These children—"Dreamers"—are then provided with a program of academic, social, cultural, and recreational activities throughout their elementary, middle school, and high school years. An important part of this program is that it is personal rather than institutional: IHAD sponsors and staff develop close long-term relationships with the children. When participants complete high school, IHAD provides the tuition assistance necessary for them to attend a state or local college or vocational school.

These adolescents participate in the "I Have a Dream" program, a comprehensive, long-term dropout prevention program that has been very successful.

The IHAD Program was created in 1981, when philanthropist Eugene Lang made an impromptu offer of college tuition to a class of graduating sixth-graders at P.S. 121 in East Harlem. Statistically, 75 percent of the students should have dropped out of school; instead, 90 percent graduated and 60 percent went on to college. Since the National IHAD Foundation was created in 1986, it has grown to number over 150 Projects in 57 cities and 28 states, serving some 12,000 children.

To help reduce the dropout rate, community institutions, especially schools, need to break down the barriers between work and school. Many youth step off the education ladder long before reaching the level needed for a professional career, often with nowhere to step next, and left to their own devices to search for work. These youth need more assistance than they are now receiving. Among the approaches worth considering are these (William T. Grant Foundation on Work, Family, and Citizenship, 1988):

- Monitored work experiences, such as through cooperative education, apprenticeships, internships, pre-employment training, and youth-operated enterprises
- Community and neighborhood services, including voluntary and youth-guided services
- Redirected vocational education, the principal thrust of which should not be preparation for specific jobs but acquisition of basic skills needed for a wide range of jobs
- Guarantees of continuing education, employment, or training, especially in conjunction with mentor programs

- Career information and counseling to expose youth to job opportunities and career options as well as to successful role models
- School volunteer programs, not only for tutoring but also for providing access to adult friends and mentors

Cross-Cultural Comparisons of Secondary Schools

Secondary schools in different countries share a number of features, but differ on others (Thomas, 1988). Let's explore the similarities and differences in secondary schools in six countries: Australia, Brazil, Germany, Japan, Russia, and the United States.

Most countries mandate that children begin school at 6 to 7 years of age and stay in school until they are 14 to 17 years of age. Brazil requires students to go to school only until they are 14 years of age, while Russia mandates that students stay in school until they are 17. Germany, Japan, Australia, and the United States require school attendance until ages 15 to 16.

Most secondary schools around the world are divided into two or more levels, such as middle school (or junior high school) and high school. However, Germany's schools are divided according to three educational ability tracks: (1) The *main school* provides a basic level of education, (2) the *middle school* gives students a more advanced education, and (3) the *academic school* prepares students for entrance to a university. German schools, like most European schools, offer a classical education, which includes courses in Latin and Greek.

Japanese secondary schools have an entrance exam, but secondary schools in the other five countries do not. Only Australia and Germany have comprehensive exit exams.

The United States is the only country in the world in which sports are an integral part of the public school system. Only a few private schools in other countries have their own sports teams, sports facilities, and highly organized sports events.

The nature of the curriculum is often similar in secondary schools in different countries, although there are some differences in content and philosophy. For example, at least until recently, the secondary schools in Russia have emphasized the preparation of students for work. The "labor education program," which is part of the secondary school curriculum, includes vocational training and on-the-job experience. The idea is to instill in youth a love for manual work and a positive attitude about industrial and work organizations. Russian students who are especially gifted—academically, artistically, or athletically—attend special schools where the students are encouraged to develop their talents and are trained to be the very best in their vocation. With the breakup of the Soviet Union, it will be interesting to follow what changes in education take place in Russia.

In Brazil, students are required to take Portuguese (the native language) and four foreign languages (Latin,

The juku, or "cramming school," is available to Japanese children and adolescents in the summertime and after school. It provides coaching to help them improve their grades and their entrance exam scores for high schools and universities. The Japanese practice of requiring an entrance exam for high school is a rarity among the nations of the world.

French, English, and Spanish). Brazil requires these languages because of the country's international character and emphasis on trade and commerce. Seventh-grade students in Australia take courses in sheep husbandry and weaving, two areas of economic and cultural interest in the country. In Japan, students take a number of Western courses in addition to their basic Japanese courses; these courses include Western literature and languages (in addition to Japanese literature and language), Western physical education (in addition to Japanese martial arts classes), and Western sculpture and handicrafts (in addition to Japanese calligraphy). The Japanese school year is also much longer than that of other countries (225 days versus 180 days in the United States, for example).

At this point we have discussed a number of ideas about the nature of children's schooling, early childhood education, the transition to elementary school, and the nature of adolescents' schooling. A summary of these ideas is presented in concept table 17.1. Next, we will turn our attention to schools, classrooms, and teachers.

SCHOOLS, CLASSROOMS, AND TEACHERS

Schools, classrooms, and teachers vary on many dimensions, among them school size and classroom size, classroom structure and climate, and teacher traits.

School Size and Classroom Size

A number of factors led to the increased size of schools in the United States: increasing urban enrollments, decreasing budgets, and an educational rationale of increased academic stimulation in consolidated institutions (Minuchin & Shapiro, 1983). However, is bigger really better?

CONCEPT TABLE 17.1

The Nature of Children's Schooling and Children's Developmental Status

Concept	Processes/Related Ideas	Characteristics/Description
The Nature of Children's Schooling	Functions of children's schools	Educators debate what the function of schools should be. Arguments often focus on (1) the back-to-basics movement versus a more comprehensive focus that includes socioemotional development, and (2) knowledge versus process.
	Schools' changing social developmental contexts	Social contexts differ at the preschool, elementary, and secondary levels, becoming much more expansive for adolescents.
Early Childhood Education	Variations	Variations include child-centered kindergarten, the Montessori approach, the Reggio Emilia approach, and developmentally appropriate and inappropriate education.
	Does it matter if children attend preschool before kindergarten?	There is a special concern about preschool programs that are academically oriented because researchers have found them to be too stressful for young children.
	The effects of early childhood education	It is difficult to evaluate the effects of early childhood education, but the effects overall seem positive.
	Education for disadvantaged children	Compensatory education has tried to break through the poverty cycle with such programs as Head Start and Follow Through. Long-term studies reveal that model preschool programs have positive effects on development.
	Nonsexist early childhood education	An important goal is to free children from constraining stereotypes of gender roles so that no aspect of their development will be closed off because of the child's sex.
	School readiness	Many early childhood education experts believe current school readiness guidelines are not developmentally appropriate.
The Transition to Elementary School	Its nature	A special concern is that early elementary school education proceeds mainly on the basis of negative feedback to children. The curriculum in elementary schools should be integrated. Many educators and psychologists believe that children should be taught through concrete, hands-on experience in the early elementary school years.
The Nature of Adolescents' Schooling	The transition to middle or junior high school	The emergence of junior highs in the 1920s and 1930s was justified on the basis of physical, cognitive, and social changes in early adolescence and the need for more schools in response to a growing student population. Middle schools have become more popular in recent years and coincide with puberty's earlier arrival. The transition to middle or junior high school coincides with many social, familial, and individual changes in the adolescent's life. The transition involves moving from the top-dog to the lowest position.
	Effective schools for young adolescents	Successful schools for young adolescents take individual differences in development seriously, show a deep concern for what is known about early adolescence, and emphasize social and emotional development as much as intellectual development. In 1989, the Carnegie Corporation recommended a major redesign of middle schools.
	High school dropouts	Dropping out has been a serious problem for decades. Many dropouts have educational deficiencies that curtail their economic and social well-being for much of their adult life. Some progress has been made in that dropout rates for most ethnic minority groups have declined in recent decades, although dropout rates for inner-city, low-income minorities, Latinos, and Native Americans are still precariously high. Dropping out of school is associated with demographic, family-related, peer-related, school-related, economic, and individual factors.
	Cross-cultural comparisons of secondary schools	There are a number of similarities and differences in secondary schools around the world.

No systematic relation between school size and academic achievement has been found, but more prosocial behavior and possibly less antisocial behavior take place in small schools (Rutter & others, 1979). For secondary schools, the upper limit has been set at various levels between 500 and 1,000 students (Garbarino, 1980). Large schools may not provide a personalized climate that allows for an effective system of social control. Students might feel alienated and might not take responsibility for their conduct. This may be especially true for unsuccessful students who do not identify with their school and who become members of oppositional peer groups. The responsiveness of the school may mediate the impact of school size on adolescent behavior. For example, in one investigation, low-responsive schools (that is, schools that offer few rewards for desirable behavior) had higher crime rates than did high-responsive schools (McPartland & McDill, 1976). Even though school responsiveness may mediate conduct, small schools may be more flexible and responsive than larger schools.

Besides the belief that smaller schools provide children and adolescents with a better eduction, there also is a belief that smaller classes are better than larger classes. Traditional schools in the United States have about 30 to 35 students. An analysis of a large number of investigations revealed that, as class size increases, achievement decreases (Glass & Smith, 1978). The researchers conclude that a pupil who would score at about the 63rd percentile on a national test when taught individually would score at about the 37th percentile when taught in a class of 40 students. They also concluded that being taught in a class of 20 students rather than in a class of 40 students is an advantage of about 10 percentile points on national achievement tests. These researchers also found that the greatest gains in achievement occurred among students who were taught in classes of 15 or fewer students. In classes of 20 to 40 students, class size had a less dramatic influence on students' achievement. Although this research has been criticized on methodological grounds, other researchers have reanalyzed the data using different techniques and have arrived at the same conclusions (Hedges & Stock, 1983).

Unfortunately, to maximize each child's learning potential, classes must be so small that few schools can afford to staff and house them (Klein, 1985; Slavin, 1989). Although a class size of 15 or fewer students is not feasible for all subjects, one alternative is to allocate a larger portion of resources to the grade levels or subjects that seem the most critical. For example, some schools are beginning to reduce class size in core academic subjects, such as math, English, and science, while increasing class size in elective subjects.

Classroom Structure and Climate

The most widely debated issue in classroom structure and climate in recent years has focused on open versus traditional classrooms. The open versus traditional classroom concept is multidimensional. Open classrooms, or open schools, have such characteristics as the following:

- Free choice by students of activities they will participate in
- Space flexibility
- Varied, enriched learning materials
- Emphasis on individual and small-group instruction
- The teacher is more a facilitator than a director of learning
- Students learn to assume responsibility for their learning
- Multi-age grouping of children
- Team teaching
- Classrooms without walls in which the physical nature of the school is more open

Overall, researchers have found that open classrooms are associated with lower language achievement but improved attitudes toward school (Giaconia & Hedges, 1982).

Beyond the overall effects of open versus traditional classrooms, it is important to evaluate how specific dimensions of open classrooms are related to specific dimensions of a child's development. In this regard, researchers have found that individualized instruction (adjusting rate, methods, materials, small-group methods) and the role of the child (the degree of activity in learning) are associated with positive effects on the child's self-concept (Giaconia & Hedges, 1982).

Teachers

Almost everyone's life is affected in one way or another by teachers. You were probably influenced by teachers as you grew up; you may become a teacher yourself or work with teachers through counseling or psychological services; and you may one day have children whose education will be guided by many teachers through the years. You can probably remember several of your teachers vividly. Perhaps one never smiled, another required you to memorize everything in sight, and yet another always appeared happy and vibrant and encouraged verbal interaction. Psychologists and educators have tried to create a profile of a good teacher's personality traits, but the complexity of personality, education, learning, and individual differences makes the task difficult (Sadker & Sadker, 1991). Nonetheless, some teacher traits are associated with positive student outcomes more than others; enthusiasm, ability to plan, poise, adaptability, warmth, flexibility, and awareness of individual differences are a few (Gage, 1965). In one study, teacher support had a strong influence on students' achievement (Goodenow, 1993). And in another recent study, aspects of the teacher-child relationship (such as intimacy) were related to the kindergarten child's adjustment (Birch, 1995).

Erik Erikson (1968) believed that good teachers should be able to produce a sense of industry, rather than inferiority, in their students. Good teachers are trusted and respected by the community and know how to alternate work and play, study and games, said Erikson. They know how to recognize special efforts and to encourage special abilities. They also know how to create a setting in which children feel good about themselves and how to handle children to whom school is not important. In Erikson's (1968) words, children should be "mildly but firmly coerced into the adventure of finding out that one can learn to accomplish things which one would never have thought of by oneself" (p.127).

Person-Environment Fit and Aptitude-Treatment Interaction

Some of the negative psychological changes associated with development might result from a mismatch between the needs of developing adolescents and the opportunities afforded them by the schools they attend. Jacqueline Eccles and her colleagues (1993) described ways in which developmentally appropriate school environments can be created that match up better with adolescents' needs. Their recommendations are based on a large-scale study of 1,500 young adolescents in middle-income communities in Michigan. They were studied as they made the change from the sixth grade in an elementary school to the seventh grade in a junior high school.

Both the early adolescents and their teachers reported less opportunity for adolescent participation in classroom decision making in the seventh grade than in the sixth grade. By contrast, the students wanted to participate more in classroom decision making in the seventh grade than in the sixth grade. According to Eccles and her colleagues, such findings represent a person-environment mismatch that harms adolescent development.

As we have just seen, the characteristics and motivation of the child or adolescent need to be considered in determining what their developmentally appropriate education should be. In education, this match is usually referred to as **aptitude-treatment interaction (ATI),** *which stresses the importance of both children's characteristics and motivation and the treatment or experiences they receive in schools. Aptitude refers to such characteristics as the academic potential and personality characteristics on which students differ; treatment refers to educational techniques, such as structured versus flexible classrooms* (Cronbach & Snow, 1977). Researchers have found that children's achievement level (aptitude) interacts with classroom structure (treatment) to produce the best learning (Peterson, 1977).

For example, students who are highly achievement-oriented usually do well in a flexible classroom and enjoy it; low achievement-oriented students usually fare worse and dislike such flexibility. The reverse often appears in structured classrooms.

SOCIAL CLASS AND ETHNICITY IN SCHOOLS

It has been argued that schools do a much better job of educating White, middle-class children than children from ethnic minority, low-income backgrounds. The critics point out that schools have not effectively educated low-income, ethnic minority children to overcome the barriers that block their advancement (Jackson, 1997; Scott-Jones, 1996).

Children from low-income and ethnic minority backgrounds do have more difficulties in school than their middle-class, White counterparts (Fenzel & Magaleta, 1993). In his famous "I Have a Dream" speech, Martin Luther King, Jr., said, "I have a dream that my four little children will one day live in a nation where they will not be judged by the color of their skin but by the content of their character."

One of the largest efforts to study ethnicity in schools has focused on desegregation through busing (Bell, 1980). Desegregation attempts to make the proportions of minority-group and White student populations in schools more equal. Efforts to improve this ratio have often involved busing students, usually minority-group students, from their home neighborhoods to more distant schools. The underlying belief is that bringing different groups together will reduce stereotyped attitudes and improve intergroup relations. However, busing tells us nothing about what goes on inside the school once students get there. Minority-group children bused to a predominantly White school are often resegregated in the classroom through seating patterns, ability grouping, and tracking systems. Overall, the findings pertaining to desegregation through busing have shown dismal results (Minuchin & Shapiro, 1983).

School segregation is still a factor in the education of African American and Latino children and adolescents (Simons, Finlay, & Yang, 1991). Almost one-third of African American and Latino students attend schools in which 90 percent or more of the students are from ethnic minority groups. In the last two decades, the proportion of Latino children who attend predominantly minority schools has increased, while the proportion of African American children in this type of schooling has decreased somewhat.

Improvements in interracial relations among children in schools depend on what happens after students arrive at the school. In one comprehensive national investigation of factors that contribute to positive interracial relations, more than 5,000 fifth-grade students and more than 400 tenth-grade students were evaluated (Forehand, Ragosta, & Rock, 1976). Multiethnic curricula, projects focused on ethnic issues, mixed work groups, and supportive teachers and principals led to improved interethnic relations.

When the schools of Austin, Texas, were desegregated through extensive busing, the outcome was increased ethnic tension among African Americans, Mexican Americans, and Whites, producing violence in the schools. The superintendent consulted with Eliot Aronson, a prominent social psychologist who was at the University of Texas at Austin at the time. Aronson thought it was more important to prevent ethnic hostility than to control it. This led him to observe a number of elementary school classrooms in Austin. What he saw was fierce competition between persons of unequal status.

Aronson stressed that the reward structure of elementary school classrooms needed to be changed from a setting of unequal competition to one of cooperation among equals, without making any curriculum changes. To accomplish this, he put together the *jigsaw classroom*, a form of cooperative learning. How might this work? Consider a class of 30 students, some White, some African American, some Latino. The lesson to be learned in the class focuses on the life of Joseph Pulitzer. The class might be broken up into five groups of six students each, with the groups being as equal as possible in terms of ethnic composition and academic achievement level. The lesson about Pulitzer's life could be divided into six parts, with one part given to each member of each six-person group. The parts might be paragraphs from Pulitzer's biography, such as how the Pulitzer family came to the United States, Pulitzer's childhood, his early work, and so on. The components are like parts of a jigsaw puzzle. They have to be put together to form the complete puzzle.

All students in each group are given an allotted time to study their parts. Then the groups meet and each member tries to teach a part to her group. After an hour or so, each member is tested on the entire life of Pulitzer, with each member receiving an individual rather than a group score. Each student, therefore, must learn the entire lesson; learning depends on the cooperation and effort of the other members. Aronson (1986) believes that this type of learning increases the students' interdependence through cooperatively reaching the same goal.

The school experiences of children and adolescents from different ethnic groups vary considerably (DeBlasie & DeBlasie, 1996; Mare, 1996). African American and Latino students are much less likely than White or Asian students to be enrolled in academic, college preparatory programs, and much more likely to be enrolled in remedial and special education programs. African American children are twice as likely as children from other ethnic groups to be enrolled in educable mentally retarded programs. Asian children are the least likely of any ethnic group to be in any special education program for students with disabilities. Asian students are much more likely than any other ethnic group to take advanced math and science courses in high school. Almost 25 percent of all Asian students take advanced-placement calculus, compared with less than 3 percent of all other students, and Asian students are three times as likely as students in any other ethnic groups to take advanced-placement chemistry or physics. African Americans are twice as likely as Latinos, Native Americans, or Whites to be suspended from school or to be corporally punished.

American anthropologist John Ogbu (1974, 1986, 1989) proposed a controversial view that ethnic minority children are placed in a position of subordination and exploitation in the American educational system. He believes that ethnic minority children, especially African American and Latinos, have inferior educational opportunities, are exposed to teachers and administrators who have low academic expectations for them, and encounter negative stereotypes about ethnic minority groups. Ogbu states that ethnic minority opposition to the middle-class White educational system stems from a lack of trust because of years of discrimination and oppression. Says Ogbu, it makes little sense to do well academically if occupational opportunities are often closed to ethnic minority youth.

Completing high school, or even college, does not always bring the same job opportunities for many ethnic minority youth as for White youth (Entwistle, 1990). In terms of earnings and employment rates, African American high school graduates do not do as well as their White counterparts. Giving up in school because of a perceived lack of reward with regard to future job opportunities characterizes many Latino youth as well.

According to American educational psychologist Margaret Beale Spencer and sociologist Sanford Dornbusch (1990), a form of institutional racism prevails in many American schools. That is, well-meaning teachers, acting out of misguided liberalism, often fail to challenge ethnic minority students. Knowing the handicaps these children face, some teachers accept a low level of performance from them, substituting warmth and affection for academic challenge and high standards of performance. Ethnic minority students, like their White counterparts, learn best when teachers combine warmth with challenging standards.

One person who is trying to do something about the poor quality of education for inner-city children is African American psychiatrist James Comer (1988). He has devised an intervention model that is based on a simple principle: Everyone with a stake in a school should have a say

James Comer (*left*) is shown with some of the inner-city African American children who attend a school that became a better learning environment because of Comer's intervention. Comer is convinced that a strong, familylike atmosphere is a key to improving the quality of inner-city schools.

in how it's run. Comer's model calls for forming a school-governance team, made up of the principal, psychologists, and even cafeteria workers. The team develops a comprehensive plan for operating the school, including a calendar of academic and social events that encourage parents to come to school as often as possible. Comer is convinced that a strong family orientation is a key to educational success, so he tries to create a familylike environment in schools and also makes parents feel comfortable in coming to their children's school. Among the reasons for Comer's concern about the lack of parental involvement in African American and Latino children's education is the high rate of single-parent families in these ethnic minority groups. A special concern is that 70 percent of the African American and Latino single-parent families headed by mothers are in poverty (McLoyd & Ceballo, 1995). Poor school performance among many ethnic minority children is related to this pattern of single-parenting and poverty (Dornbusch & others, 1985).

The social and academic development of children from low-income and ethnic minority backgrounds benefits when schools have positive, strong expectations for achievement, teachers are sensitive to sociocultural diversity, there are positive links between the school and the community, and when low-income, ethnic minority

parents have high expectations for achievement and encourage education. Children from low-income, ethnic minority backgrounds do not benefit from schools characterized by chaotic classrooms and violence or punitive discipline. Firm but considerate rules and regulations are needed for schools to function effectively in educating children. Children also do not benefit when their parents fail to encourage and support educational accomplishments or when community-school ties are weak (Honig, 1996; Luster & McAdoo, 1996).

CHILDREN WITH A DISABILITY

Children with a disability are especially sensitive about their differentness and how it is perceived by others. Life is not always fair for children with a disability. Adjusting to school and to peers is often difficult for them.

Scope and Education

An estimated 10 to 15 percent of the U.S. population of children between the ages of 5 and 18 are classified as children with a disability. Table 17.1 shows the percentages of children who have various disabilities—ranging from 3 to 4 percent of children with a speech disability to 0.1 percent with a visual impairment.

TABLE 17.1

Estimates of the Percentage and Number of Children with a Disability in the United States

Handicap	% of Population	Number of Children, Ages 5 to 18
Visual impairment (includes blindness)	0.1	55,000
Hearing impairment (includes deafness)	0.5–0.7	275,000–385,000
Speech handicap	3.0–4.0	1,650,000–2,200,000
Orthopedic and health impairments	0.5	275,000
Emotional disorders	2.0–3.0	1,100,000–1,650,000
Mental retardation (both educable and trainable)	2.0–3.0	1,100,000–1,650,000
Learning disabilities	2.0–3.0	1,100,000–1,650,000
Multiple handicaps	0.5–0.7	275,000–385,000
Total	**10.6–15.0**	**5,830,000–8,250,000**

The Exceptional Student in the Regular Classroom 6/E by Gearheart/Weishahn, © 1996. Adapted by permission of Prentice-Hall, Inc., Upper Saddle River, NJ.

Public Law 94-142 *is the federal government's mandate to provide a free and appropriate education for all children. A key provision of the bill is the development of individualized education programs for children with a disability.* The individualized plan should meet with the approval of the child's parents, counselors, educational authorities, and, when feasible, the children themselves.

Many children with a disability are taught in the regular classroom today. This used to be called "mainstreaming," but today this term is being replaced with the term **inclusion,** *which refers to educating children in their natural environment, such as in typical elementary school classrooms.* More than a decade ago it was considered appropriate to educate children with a disability outside of the regular classroom. The trend today, though, is to fully include all students with a disability in the regular classroom (Sigel, 1997).

Some of the education of students with a disability also might take place in a resource room in addition to the regular classroom. The resource room is an instructional classroom for students with a disability and the professionals who work with them. The resource professional has training in working with students who have a disability. To further evaluate children with a disability, turn to Critical Thinking About Children's Development.

Learning Disabilities

Paula does not like kindergarten and can't seem to remember the names of her teacher and classmates. Bobby's third-grade teacher complains that his spelling is awful and that he is always reversing his letters. Eleven-year-old Tim hates to read. He says it is too hard for him and that the words just don't make any sense. Each of these children is learning disabled. Children with a **learning disability** *(1) are of normal intelligence or above, (2) have difficulties in several academic areas but usually do not show deficiencies in others, and (3) are not suffering from any other conditions or disorders that could explain their learning problems.* The wide range of learning disabilities has generated controversy about just what learning disabilities are.

The global concept of learning disabilities includes problems in listening, thinking, memory, reading, writing, spelling, and much more (Spear-Swerling & Sternberg, 1994). Attention deficits involving the inability to sit still, pay attention, and concentrate are also often classified under learning disabilities. The U.S. Department of Education puts the number of identified children with a learning disability between the ages of 3 and 21 at about 2 million.

Improvements in the lives of children with a learning disability will come through (1) recognizing the complex, multifaceted nature of learning disabilities (biological, cognitive, and socioemotional dimensions of learning disabilities need to be considered, for example); and (2) becoming more precise in our analysis of the learning environments in which these children participate (Gerber, Reiff, & Ginsberg, 1996; Rosenshine, 1997; Stevens & Salisbury, 1997). The following discussion of one type of learning disability, attention-deficit hyperactivity disorder, exemplifies this complexity and preciseness.

Attention-Deficit Hyperactivity Disorder

Matthew's handwriting is messy. Matthew has trouble attending to the teacher's instructions. He is always in motion; he can't sit still for more than a few minutes at

Working with Children with a Disability

Get together with some other students and visit several public schools to learn how they are providing individualized and appropriate programs for children with a disability. Do they have a resource room for children with a disability? Also think about what special skills are needed to work with a child with a disability. Would you want to become a teacher of children with a disability? By evaluating different dimensions of educating children with a disability, you are learning to think critically by *making accurate observations, descriptions, and inferences about development.*

Public Law 94-142 mandates free, appropriate education for all children. A key provision of the bill was the development of an individualized education program for each identified child with a disability. Among the important issues involved in the education of children with a disability are mainstreaming and labeling.

a time. His mother describes him as very fidgety. Matthew has **attention-deficit hyperactivity disorder,** *the technical term for what is commonly called hyperactivity. This disorder is characterized by a short attention span, distractibility, and high levels of physical activity.* In short, these children do not pay attention and have difficulty concentrating on what they are doing (Wodrich, 1994). Estimates of the percentage of children with attention-deficit hyperactivity disorder vary from less than 1 percent to 5 percent. Although young children and even infants can show characteristics of this disorder, the vast majority of hyperactive children are identified in the first three grades of elementary school when teachers recognize they have considerable difficulty paying attention, sitting still, and concentrating on their schoolwork.

What makes Jimmy so impulsive, Sandy so distractible, and Harvey so excitable? Possible causes include heredity, prenatal damage, diet, family dynamics, and the physical environment (O'Connell, 1996). As we saw in chapter 3, the influence of heredity on temperament is increasingly considered, with activity level being one aspect of temperament that differentiates one child from another very early in development. Approximately four times as many boys as girls are hyperactive. This sex difference may be due to differences in the brains of boys and girls determined by genes on the Y chromosome. The prenatal hazards we discussed in chapter 4 may also produce hyperactive behavior. Excessive drinking by women during pregnancy is associated with poor attention and concentration by their offspring at 4 years of age, for example (Streissguth & others, 1984). With regard to diet, severe vitamin deficiencies can lead to attentional problems. Vitamin B deficiencies are of special concern. Caffeine and sugar may also contribute to attentional problems.

A wide range of psychotherapies and drug therapies have been used to improve the lives of hyperactive children (Rapport, 1997). For unknown reasons, some drugs that stimulate the brains and behaviors of adults have a quieting effect on the brains and behaviors of children. The drugs most widely prescribed for hyperactive children are amphetamines, especially Ritalin. Amphetamines work effectively for some hyperactive children, but not all. As many as 20 percent of hyperactive children treated with Ritalin do not respond to it. Even when Ritalin works, it is also important to consider the social world of the hyperactive child. The teacher is especially important in this social world, helping to monitor the child's academic and social behavior to determine whether the drug works and whether the prescribed dosage is correct.

Attention-deficit hyperactivity disorder has received far less attention in adolescents than in children (Faigel & others, 1995). In many individuals, this disorder does not disappear at puberty, and it can play a critical role in the academic and social lives of adolescents. Estimates suggest that attention-deficit hyperactivity disorder decreases in only about one-third of affected adolescents (Fischer & others, 1990).

ACHIEVEMENT

We are a species motivated to do well at what we attempt, to gain mastery over the world in which we live, to explore with enthusiasm and curiosity unknown environments, and to achieve the heights of success. We live in an achievement-oriented world with standards that tell children success is important. The standards suggest that success requires a competitive spirit, a desire to win, a motivation to do well, and the wherewithal to cope with adversity and persist until an objective is reached. Some developmentalists, though, believe that we are becoming a nation of hurried, "wired" people who are raising our children to become the same way—uptight about success and failure and far too worried about what we accomplish in comparison to others (Elkind, 1981). It was in the 1950s that an interest in achievement began to flourish. The interest initially focused on the need for achievement.

Need for Achievement

Think about yourself and your friends for a moment. Are you more achievement oriented than they are, or are you less so? If we asked you and your friends to tell stories about achievement-related themes, could we accurately determine which of you is the most achievement oriented?

Some individuals are highly motivated to succeed and they expend a lot of effort striving to excel. Other individuals are not as motivated to succeed and don't work as hard to achieve. These two types of individuals vary in their **achievement motivation (need for achievement),** *the desire to accomplish something, to reach a standard of excellence, and to expend effort to excel.* Borrowing from Henry Murray's (1938) theory and measurement of personality, psychologist David McClelland (1955) assessed achievement by showing individuals ambiguous pictures that were likely to stimulate achievement-related responses. The individuals were asked to tell a story about the picture, and their comments were scored according to how strongly they reflected achievement.

A host of studies have correlated achievement-related responses with different aspects of the individual's experiences and behavior. The findings are diverse, but they do suggest that achievement-oriented individuals have a stronger hope for success than fear of failure, are moderate rather than high or low risk-takers, and persist for appropriate lengths of time in solving difficult problems (Atkinson & Raynor, 1974). Early research indicated that independence training by parents promoted children's achievement, but more-recent research reveals that parents, to increase achievement, need to set high standards for achievement, model achievement-oriented behavior, and reward their children for their achievements (Huston-Stein & Higgens-Trenk, 1978). And in one recent study, middle school students had the highest grades when their parents, teachers, and school were authoritative (Paulson, Marchant, & Rothlisberg, 1995).

Intrinsic and Extrinsic Motivation

Our achievement motivation—whether in school, at work, or in sports—can be divided into two main types: **intrinsic motivation,** *the internal desire to be competent and to do something for its own sake;* and **extrinsic motivation,** *being influenced by external rewards and punishments.* If you work hard in college because a personal standard of excellence is important to you, intrinsic motivation is involved. But if you work hard in college because you know it will bring you a higher-paying job when you graduate, extrinsic motivation is at work.

An important consideration when motivating a child to do something is whether or not to offer an incentive (Ames & Ames, 1989; Gottfried, Gottfried, & Bathurst, 1988; Rotter, 1989). If a child is not doing competent work, is bored, or has a negative attitude, it may be worthwhile to consider incentives to improve motivation. However, there are times when external rewards can get in the way of motivation. In one investigation of children with a strong interest in art, those who expected no reward spent more time in a drawing activity than did their counterparts who knew that they would be rewarded for it (Lepper, Greene, & Nisbett, 1973).

Intrinsic motivation implies that internal motivation should be promoted and external factors deemphasized. In this way, children learn to attribute to themselves the cause of their success and failure, and especially how much effort they expend. But in reality, achievement is motivated by both internal and external factors; children are never divorced from their external environment. Some of the most achievement-oriented children are those who have a high personal standard for achievement and are also highly competitive. In one investigation, low-achieving boys and girls who engaged in individual goal setting (intrinsic motivation) and were given comparative information about peers (extrinsic motivation) worked more math problems and got more of them correct than did their counterparts who experienced either condition alone (Schunk, 1983). Other research suggests that social comparison by itself is not a wise strategy (Nicholls, 1984). The argument is that social comparison puts the child in an ego-involved, threatening, self-focused state rather than in a task-involved, effortful, strategy-focused state.

Another important consideration is the role of the child's home environment in promoting internal motivation. In a recent investigation, Adele and Allen Gottfried (1989) found that greater variety of home experiences, parental encouragement of competence and curiosity, and home emphasis on academically related behaviors are related to children's internal motivation for achievement.

An extremely important aspect of internal causes of achievement is *effort*. Unlike many causes of success, effort is under the child's control and is amenable to change (Schunk, 1990). The importance of effort in achievement is recognized by most children. In one study, third- through sixth-grade students felt that effort was the most effective strategy for good school performance (Skinner, Wellborn, & Connell, 1990).

Mastery Orientation Versus Helpless and Performance Orientations

Closely related to an emphasis on intrinsic motivation, attributions of internal causes of behavior, and the importance of effort in achievement is a mastery orientation. Developmental psychologists Valanne Henderson and Carol Dweck (1990) have found that children and adolescents show two distinct responses to difficult or challenging circumstances: The **helpless orientation** *is the orientation of children who seem trapped by the experience of difficulty. They attribute their difficulty to a lack of ability.* They frequently say things like, "I'm not very good at this," even though they may have earlier demonstrated their ability through numerous successes. And once they view their behavior as failure, they often feel anxious about the situation, and their performance worsens even further. The **mastery orientation** *is the orientation of children who are task oriented. Instead of focusing on their ability, they become concerned about their learning strategies.* Mastery-oriented children often instruct themselves to pay attention, to think carefully, and to remember strategies that have worked for them in previous situations. They frequently report feeling challenged and excited by difficult tasks rather than being threatened by them (Anderman, Maehr, & Midgley, 1996). In one recent study, the use of task-focused policies and practices in middle school environments was linked with positive motivational shifts in early adolescence (Anderman, Maehr, & Midgley, 1996).

Another issue in motivation involves whether to adopt a mastery or a performance orientation. We have already described what a mastery orientation is like. A **performance orientation** *involves being concerned with the achievement outcome rather than the achievement process. Winning is what matters, and happiness is thought to result from winning.*

What sustains mastery-oriented individuals is the self-efficacy and satisfaction they feel from effectively dealing with the world in which they live. In contrast, what sustains performance-oriented individuals is winnings. Although skills can be and often are involved in winning, performance-oriented individuals often do not view themselves as necessarily having skills. Rather, they see themselves as using tactics, such as undermining others, to get what they want.

Does all of this mean that mastery-oriented individuals do not like to win and that performance-oriented individuals are not motivated to experience the self-efficacy that comes from being able to take credit for one's behavior? No. A matter of emphasis or degree is involved, though. For mastery-oriented individuals, winning isn't everything. For performance-oriented individuals, skill development and self-efficacy take a back seat to winning.

In summary, we have seen that a number of psychological and motivational factors influence children's achievement. Especially important in the child's ability to adapt to new academic and social pressures are achievement motivation, internal attributions of effort, intrinsic motivation, and a mastery achievement orientation. Next, we examine the role of ethnicity in achievement.

Achievement in Ethnic Minority Children

Too often, the findings of research on minority groups are presented in terms of "deficits" by middle-class, White standards. Rather than characterizing individuals as *culturally different*, many conclusions unfortunately characterize the cultural distinctiveness of African Americans, Latinos, and other minority groups as deficient in some way.

Much of the research on minority-group children is plagued by a failure to consider socioeconomic status (determined by some combination of education, occupation, and income). In many instances, when ethnicity and socioeconomic status (also called social class) are investigated in the same study, social class is a far better predictor of achievement orientation than ethnicity is. Middle-class individuals fare better than do their lower-class counterparts in a variety of achievement-oriented circumstances—expectations for success, achievement aspirations, and recognition of importance of effort, for example (McAdoo & McAdoo, 1985).

Educational psychologist Sandra Graham has conducted a number of investigations that reveal not only stronger social class than ethnic group differences but also the importance of studying minority-group motivation in the context of general motivational theory (Graham, 1986, 1987, 1990). Her inquiries focus on the reasons

African Americans give for their achievement orientation—why they succeed or fail, for example. She is struck by how consistently middle-class African Americans do not fit our stereotypes of either deviant or special populations. They, like their middle-class White counterparts, have high expectations and understand that failure is often due to lack of effort rather than to luck.

It is always important to keep in mind the diversity that exists within an ethnic group (Fletcher, 1995; Slaughter-DeFoe & others, 1990; Swanson, 1995). Consider Asian American children. Many Asian American children fit the "whiz kid, superachiever" image, but there are still many Asian American children who are struggling just to learn English. The "whiz kid" image fits many of the children of Asian immigrant families who arrived in the United States in the late 1960s and early 1970s. Many of these immigrants came from Hong Kong, South Korea, India, and the Philippines. The image also fits many of the more than 100,000 Indochinese (primarily Vietnamese) immigrants who arrived in the United States after the end of the Vietnam War in 1975. Both groups included mostly middle- to upper-income professional people who were reasonably well educated and who passed along a strong interest in education and a strong work ethic to their children. For thousands of other Asian Americans, including a high percentage of the 600,000 Indochinese refugees who fled Vietnam, Laos, and Cambodia in the late 1970s, the problems are legion. Many in this wave of refugees lived in poor surroundings in their homelands. They came to the United States with few skills and little education. They speak little English and have a difficult time finding a decent job. They often share housing with relatives. Adjusting to school is difficult for their children; some drop out and some are attracted to gangs and drugs. Better school systems use a variety of techniques to help these Asian Americans, including English as a second language class, as well as a range of social services.

At this point we have discussed a number of ideas about schools, classrooms, and teachers, social class and ethnicity in schools, the education of children with special needs, and achievement. A summary of these ideas is presented in concept table 17.2.

CONCEPT TABLE 17.2

Schools, Classrooms, and Teachers; Social Class and Ethnicity in Schools; Children with a Disability; and Achievement

Concept	Processes/ Related Ideas	Characteristics/Description
Schools, Classrooms, and Teachers	School size and classroom size	Smaller is usually better when school size and classroom size are at issue.
	Classroom structure and climate	The open classroom concept is multidimensional. Person-environment fit and aptitude-treatment interaction are important aspects of understanding classroom structure and climate.
	Teachers	Teacher characteristics involve many different dimensions; arriving at a profile of competent teacher traits is difficult.
	Person-environment fit and aptitude-treatment interaction	Some of the negative psychological changes associated with development might result from a mismatch between the needs of the developing child or adolescent and the opportunities afforded by the schools they attend. One mismatch is between adolescents' desire for increased decision making and the decrease in the amount of decision making they get to do in schools. Closely related to concerns about person-environment fit is aptitude-treatment interaction.
Social Class and Ethnicity in Schools	Issues and effects	Criticisms have been leveled that schools do a much better job of educating middle-class, White students than low-income, ethnic minority students. Improvements in interethnic relations among students depend on what happens after students arrive. Cooperative learning benefits interethnic relations. Ogbu proposed a controversial view that ethnic minority children are placed in a position of vulnerability in American schools. The social and academic development of children from low-income, ethnic minority backgrounds benefits when schools have positive strong expectations for achievement, teachers are sensitive to sociocultural diversity, there are positive links between the school and the community, and parents have high expectations for achievement and encourage education.
Children with a Disability	Scope and education	An estimated 10 to 15 percent of the U.S. population of children from 5 to 18 years of age are classified as children with a disability. Public Law 94-182 mandates a free and appropriate education for all children. A key provision for children with a disability is an individualized education program. The term *inclusion,* which refers to educating children in their natural environment, is now being used instead of the term *mainstreaming.*
	Learning disabilities	Children with a learning disability have normal or above-normal intelligence, have difficulties in some areas but not others, and do not suffer from some other disorder that could explain their learning problems. Learning disabilities are complex.
	Attention-deficit hyperactivity disorder	This is the technical term for what is commonly called "hyperactivity." This disorder is characterized by a short attention span, distractibility, and high levels of physical activity.
Achievement	Need for achievement	Achievement motivation (or need for achievement) is the desire to accomplish something, to reach a standard of excellence, and to expend effort to excel.
	Intrinsic and extrinsic motivation	Intrinsic motivation is the internal desire to be competent and do something for its own sake. Extrinsic motivation is influenced by external rewards and punishment. Children's intrinsic motivation is related to higher school achievement, although achievement is determined by both internal and external factors.
	Mastery orientation versus helpless and performance orientations	Children with a mastery orientation are task oriented and concerned with learning strategies rather than ability. Experts recommend a mastery orientation rather than a helpless orientation (feeling trapped by the experience of difficulty and attributing problems to a lack of ability) or a performance orientation (feeling that winning is what matters).
	Ethnic minority children	Too often, ethnic differences are interpreted as deficits by middle-class White standards. It is always important to distinguish ethnic and social class influences. Middle-class children fare better than their lower-class counterparts on many achievement dimensions. Asian American children often have a strong achievement motivation, but it is always important to recognize diversity within any ethnic group.

Children spend many hours in school, where there are tasks to be accomplished, people to socialize with and be socialized by, and competencies to be developed.

We began this chapter by exploring several effective and ineffective kinds of schools, as well as the nature of schooling, studying the function of schools and the changing social developmental contexts in schools. Our coverage of schools and developmental status focused on early childhood education, the transition to elementary school, and schools for adolescents. We also read about schools, classrooms, and teachers, evaluating school and classroom size, structure and climate, teachers, and person-environment fit and aptitude-treatment interaction. We discussed social class and ethnicity in schools, and we learned about children with a disability, examining scope and education, children with a learning disability, and attention-deficit hyperactivity disorder. And we studied achievement—the need for achievement, intrinsic/extrinsic motivation, mastery versus helpless and performance orientations, and ethnicity.

Don't forget that you can obtain an overall summary of the chapter by again studying the two concept tables on pages 555 and 565. In this chapter we explored schools and achievement. In the next chapter, we will explore culture, poverty, and ethnicity in relation to children's development.

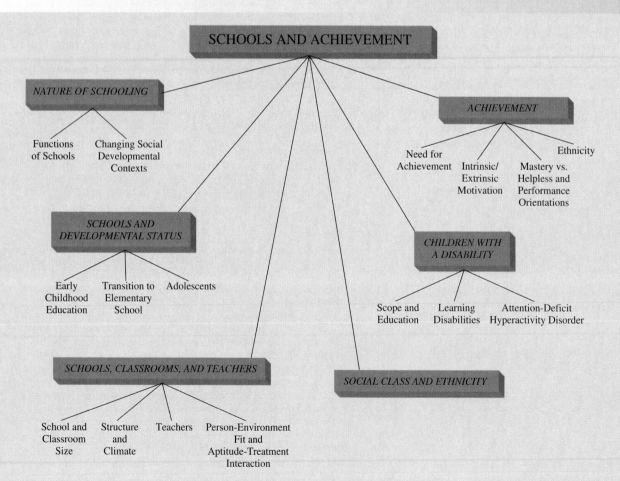

PRACTICAL KNOWLEDGE ABOUT CHILDREN

Reaching Potentials: Appropriate Curriculum and Assessment for Young Children (Vol. 1)

(1992) edited by Sue Bredekamp and Teresa Rosegrant, Washington, DC: National Association for the Education of Young Children.

This is an excellent book on how to help young children reach their full potential—not only academically and vocationally, but as healthy, sensitive, caring, and contributing members of society. The authors argue that curriculum, assessment, and teaching practices help to determine whether these potentials are reached. The book closely follows the guidelines for appropriate curriculum content and assessment developed by the National Association for the Education of Young Children (NAEYC), a highly respected organization of early childhood educators. Bredekamp is the editor of NAEYC's position statements on accreditation, developmentally appropriate education, and standardized testing.

Smart Schools, Smart Kids

(1992) by Edward Fiske, New York: Touchstone.

This book tours dozens of pioneering schools in the United States and describes how successful programs work, problems they have encountered, and the results they have achieved. Fiske says that too many of America's schools are put together on the outdated nineteenth-century factory model of schools. He addresses how to develop learning communities, incorporate new technologies into classrooms, and go beyond testing. The book also tackles the learning crisis in children's education, providing many vivid examples of the tragedies of poor schools and the victories of competent schools.

EXPLORATIONS IN CHILD DEVELOPMENT

To further explore the nature of child development, we will examine a research study on cooperative learning, and we will discuss the role of parenting in young children's learning and education.

RESEARCH IN CHILD DEVELOPMENT

Cooperative Learning

Featured Study

Stevens, R. J., & Slavin, R. E. (1995). The cooperative elementary school: Effects on students' achievement, attitudes, and social relations. *American Educational Research Journal, 32*, 321–351.

Cooperative learning methods have been studied for more than two decades and have been increasingly used in elementary and secondary schools. Most applications of cooperative learning have been implemented teacher by teacher, usually one subject at a time, and few studies have involved durations of more than one semester. Could cooperative learning be used on a broad scale in many subjects and over extended time frames to basically change the organization of schools and classrooms? This was one of main questions addressed in this study.

The components of the cooperative learning model were these: using cooperative learning across a variety of content areas, full-scale inclusion of academically disabled students in regular classrooms, peer coaching, teachers planning cooperatively, and parent involvement in the school.

Method

The subjects were 1,012 second- to sixth-grade students in a suburban Maryland school district. Twenty-one classes in the two treatment schools were matched with 24 classes in the three comparison schools on the basis of achievement test scores in a number of areas. The schools were located in predominantly working-class neighborhoods. Slightly less than 10 percent of the students were learning disabled.

Each component of the cooperative learning program was gradually phased in during the first year. Prior to implementation of the component, the faculty were given training on its use. During the school year, members of the research staff observed classes, met with teachers, and observed steering committee meetings to facilitate the implementation of the cooperative learning program.

Assessment of the program's results was conducted over a 2-year period. In the spring of the first and second years of the study, teachers administered the California Achievement Test. Both pre- and posttest, students' attitudes toward, and their perceived ability, in various school subjects were evaluated, and students' social relations also were assessed by asking the students to name their friends in the class.

Results

After the first year of the program's implementation, students in the cooperative schools had higher achievement in reading vocabulary than the students in the regular schools. After the second year, students in the cooperative school had higher achievement in reading vocabulary, reading comprehension, language expression, and math computation than their regular-classroom counterparts. After 2 years, the academically disabled students in the cooperative schools had higher achievement in a wide variety of academic subjects than their peers in the regular schools. The social relations of students in the cooperative schools also were better.

Discussion

Because the experimental cooperative learning program had so many components, it is difficult to determine which components made the program a success. Nonetheless, the results support the belief that cooperative learning can be applied across many subject domains. Future research should disentangle which of the components give cooperative learning an advantage.

The Role of Parenting in Young Children's Learning and Education

Mothers and fathers play important roles in the development of young children's positive attitudes toward learning and education (Cowan, Heming, & Schuck, 1993). In one investigation, mothers and their preschool children were evaluated and then the children's academic competence was assessed when they were in sixth grade (Hess & others, 1984). Maternal behavior in the preschool years was related to the children's academic competence in sixth grade. The best predictors of academic competence in sixth grade were the following maternal behaviors shown during the preschool years: effective communication with the child, a warm relationship with the child, positive expectations for achievement, use of rule-based rather than authority-based discipline, and not believing that success in school was based on luck.

The father's involvement with the child can also help to build positive attitudes toward school and learning. Competent fathers of preschool children set aside regular time to be with the child, listen to the child and respond to questions, become involved in the child's play, and show an interest in the child's preschool and kindergarten activities. Fathers can help with the young child's schooling in the following ways (Swick & Manning, 1983):

- Supporting their children's efforts in school and their children's unique characteristics
- Helping children with their problems when the children seek advice
- Communicating regularly with teachers
- Participating in school functions

The relationship between the school and the parents of children is an important aspect of education (Helling, 1993; Innocenti & Huh, 1993; Marcon, 1993; McAdoo, Luster, & Perkins, 1993). Schools and parents can cooperate to provide young children with the best possible educational experience, and a positive orientation toward learning. In one investigation, the most important factor in contributing to the success of the preschool program was the positive involvement of the parents in their young children's learning and education (Lally, Mangione, & Honig, 1987).

William H. Johnson
Girl in Green Dress

Chapter

18

Culture, Poverty, and Ethnicity

---

*O*ur most basic common link is that we all inhabit this planet. We all breathe the same air. We all cherish our children's future.

—John F. Kennedy, address, The American University, 1963

Chapter Outline

Chapter Boxes

EPILOGUE
Children: The Future of Society

In the end the power behind development is life.
—Erik Erikson

As the twenty-first century approaches, the well-being of children is one of our most important concerns. We all cherish the future of our children, for they are the future of any society. Children who do not reach their full potential, who are destined to make fewer contributions to society than society needs, and who do not take their place as productive adults diminish the power of that society's future. In this epilogue, we will summarize some of the most important concepts and issues that have been discussed in this book and present a montage of thoughts that convey the power, beauty, and complexity of children's development.

Our journey through childhood has been long and complex, and you have read about many different facets of children's lives. This is a good time to stand back and ask yourself what you have learned. What theories, studies, and ideas struck you as more important than others? What did you learn about your own development as an infant, a child, and an adolescent? Did anything you learn stimulate you to rethink how children develop? How you developed into the person you are today?

THEMES IN CHILDREN'S DEVELOPMENT

As we look back across the chapters of *Child Development*, some common themes emerge. Let's explore some of these main themes.

Knowledge About Children's Development Has Benefited from a Diversity of Theories and an Extensive Research Enterprise

A number of theories have made important contributions to our understanding of children's development. From the biological theory of ethology to the cognitive theories of Piaget and Vygotsky to the social theories of Erikson and Bronfenbrenner, each has contributed an important piece of the developmental puzzle. However, no single theory is capable of predicting, explaining, and organizing the rich, complex, multifaceted landscape of the child's developmental journey. The inability of a single theory to explain all of children's development should not be viewed as a shortcoming of a theory. Any theory that attempts to explain all of children's development is too general. The field of child development has been moved forward by theories that are precise and zero in on key aspects of one or two dimensions of children's lives rather than by theories that try to do everything.

Knowledge about children's development has also benefited from a research effort that has greatly expanded over the last several decades. The science of child development has become a highly sophisticated field in which collecting evidence about children is based on well-defined rules, exemplary practices, mathematical procedures for handling the evidence, and drawing inferences from what has been found.

Children Benefit from Both Basic Research and Applied Research

Across the eighteen chapters of *Child Development*, we have discussed both basic research and applied research. Basic research, sometimes called pure research, is the study of issues to obtain knowledge for its own sake rather than for practical application. By contrast, applied research is the study of issues that have direct practical significance, often with the intent of changing human behavior. Social policy research is applied research rather than basic research.

A developmentalist who conducts basic research might ask: How is the cognitive development of children different from adolescents? By contrast, a developmentalist who conducts applied research might ask: How can knowledge about children's and adolescents' cognitive development be used to educate them more effectively or to help them cope more effectively with stress? A basic researcher might also ask: Can a nonhuman primate, such as a chimpanzee, learn to use sign language? An applied researcher might ask: Can strategies used to teach language to chimpanzees be applied to improve the language abilities of retarded children who do not speak?

Most developmentalists believe that both basic and applied research contribute to improving children's lives. Although basic research sometimes produces information that can be applied to improve the welfare of children, it does not guarantee this application. By contrast, insisting that research always be relevant is like trying to grow flowers by focusing only on the blossoms and not tending to the roots (Walker, 1970). Basic research is root research. Without the discovery of basic principles, we would have little information to apply (Wade & Tavris, 1993).

Children's Development Is Influenced by an Interaction of Heredity and Environment

Both heredity and environment are necessary even for children to exist. Heredity and environment operate together—or cooperate—to produce a child's height and weight, ability to shoot a basketball, intelligence, reading skills, temperament, and all other dimensions of the child's development.

In chapter 1, we discussed the nature-nurture controversy, the debate about whether development is primarily influenced by heredity and maturation (nature) or by environment and experience (nurture). The debate shows no signs of subsiding, but for now virtually all developmentalists are interactionists, accepting that children's development is determined by both heredity and environment. Behavior geneticists continue to specify more precisely the nature of heredity-environment interaction through such concepts as those of passive, evocative, and active genotype/environment interactions and shared and nonshared environmental influences.

Children's Development Involves Both Continuity and Discontinuity

Some developmentalists emphasize the continuity of development, the view that development involves gradual, cumulative change from conception to death. Others stress the discontinuity of development, the view that development consists of distinct stages in the life span.

Development involves both continuity and discontinuity. For example, while Piaget's stages reflect discontinuity in that they portray children as making a distinct change from preoperational to concrete operational thinking, researchers recently have found that young children's intelligence shows more continuity than was once believed. Who is right? Probably both. As Piaget envisioned, most preschool children are egocentric and center on the obvious physical characteristics of stimuli. Most concrete operational children do not think hypothetically and don't solve problems in a scientific manner. In these ways, children's development is stagelike, as Piaget proposed. However, as information-processing oriented researchers believe, children's thinking is not as stagelike as Piaget thought.

Children's Development Is Determined by Both Early and Later Experiences

While children's development is influenced by both early and later experiences, developmentalists still debate how strong the contributions of each type of experience are. The early-experience advocates argue that early experiences, especially in infancy, are more important than later experiences. They believe, for example, that warm, nurturant, sensitive caregiving in the first year of life is necessary for optimal later development. Later experiences are not as important in shaping the child's developmental path, they say.

By contrast, other developmentalists stress that later experiences are just as important as early experiences in children's development. That is, warm, nurturant, sensitive parenting is just as important in the elementary school years in shaping children's development as it is in infancy. People in Western cultures are stronger advocates of early experiences, those in Eastern cultures of later experiences. The debate goes on.

Children's Development Is Determined by an Interaction of Biological, Cognitive, and Social Processes

Biological processes involve changes in a child's physical nature, such as genes inherited from parents, development of the brain, prenatal and pubertal hormonal changes, and the development of motor skills. Cognitive processes involve changes in the child's thought, intelligence, and language, such as developing symbols for objects, memorizing a poem, solving a math problem, and putting together a sentence. Socioemotional processes involve changes in the child's relationships with other people, emotions, and personality, such as an infant's smile in response to her mother's touch, the intimate conversation of two friends, and a girl's development of assertiveness.

In many parts of the book, you read about how biological, cognitive, and socioemotional processes are intricately interwoven. For example, biology plays an important role in children's temperament, especially influencing how shy or gregarious children are. Inadequate parenting early in children's development can seriously undermine their intelligence. Cognitive changes substantially alter how children think about their parents and peers. Both theory and research involving children's development are becoming more integrated and less compartmentalized as links across different domains of development are sought.

Children's Development Involves Both Communalities with Other Children and Individual Variation

Every child develops in certain ways like all other children. Every child, unless afflicted by a serious handicap, walks by the age of 1 to 1½ years, talks by the age of 2 or 2½ years, engages in fantasy play in early childhood, is reared by adult caregivers who have more power and control than the child does, engages in mutual give-and-take in peer relations, goes to school, and becomes more independent and searches for an identity as an adolescent.

But children are not just like collections of geese; they are also unique, each child writing an individual history. One child may grow up in the well-groomed lawns of suburbia, another in the confines of an inner-city ghetto. One child may be short, another tall. One child may be a genius, another mentally retarded. One child may be abused, another lavished with love. And one child may be highly motivated to learn, another couldn't care less.

Children's Behavior Is Multiply Determined

An important aspect of thinking about the behavior of any child is that the child's behavior is multiply determined. When we think about what causes a child's behavior, we often lean toward explaining it in terms of a single cause. Consider a 7-year-old boy named Bobby. His teacher says that he is having trouble in school because he is from a father-absent home. The implication is that not having a father present in the home causes Bobby's poor academic performance. Not having a father might be one factor in Bobby's poor performance in school, but many others also influence his behavior. These factors include his genetic heritage and a host of environmental and sociocultural experiences, both in the past and the present. On closer inspection of Bobby's circumstances, we learn that not only has he been father-absent all of his life, never knowing his father, but that his extended-family support system has also been weak. We also learn that he lives in a low-income area with little community support for recreation, libraries, and child services. The school system Bobby is enrolled in has a poor record of helping low-achieving children and has little interest in developing programs for children from disadvantaged circumstances. We could find other factors that help explain Bobby's poor school achievement, but these examples illustrate the importance of going beyond accepting a single cause as *the* reason for a child's behavior. As with each of us, Bobby's behavior is multiply determined.

Children's Development Is Determined by Internal/External and Self/Other Influences

Controversy still surrounds whether children are architects of their own development (internal, self-determined) or whether their development is primarily orchestrated by the external forces of others. However, most experts on children recognize that development is not entirely internal and self-generated and, likewise, not entirely external and other-determined. Trying to tease apart internal/external and self/other influences is extraordinarily difficult because the child is always embedded in a social context with others. To be certain, children are not buffeted about helplessly by their environment. Children bring developmental capacities to any situation and act on the situation. At the same time, however, they interact with others who offer their own versions of the world, which children sometimes learn from and adopt for themselves. At times, children are solitary young scientists, crafting their own book of dreams and reality, as Piaget envisioned; at others, they are socially intertwined with skilled teachers and peers, as Vygotsky conceived.

America, especially male America, has had a history of underscoring the importance of self-determination and individualism. Recently, however, females have challenged the status of self-determination as a more important human value than being connected to others and competent at relationships. And as psychologists have become more interested in cultures around the world, they have begun to recognize that many cultures, especially Eastern cultures, promote values that emphasize concern for others, interdependence, and harmonious relationships. It is important for us to raise a nation of children who not only value a separate "I"-ness, uniqueness, and self-determination but who also value connectedness with others, concern for others, and harmony in relationships.

We Need to Dramatically Reduce the Number of Children at Risk of Not Reaching Their Full Potential

Far too many children in America are not reaching their full potential because they are not being adequately reared by caregivers, adequately instructed in school, or adequately supported by society. Children who do reach their full potential and grow up to make competent contributions to their world invariably have been given considerable individual attention and support as they were growing up. Children need parents who are extensively involved with them, are sensitive to their needs, and have a sound understanding of their own and their children's development.

We also need schools that place a greater emphasis on a curriculum that is developmentally appropriate. This needs to be accomplished at all levels of education, especially in early childhood education, elementary school education, and middle school education. And we need to give more attention to our nation's social policy, especially in terms of ways to break through the poverty cycle that enshrouds more than 25 percent of the children in the United States. Our nation's political values need to reflect greater concern for the inadequate conditions in which far too many children live. And, to reduce the number of children at risk for not reaching their potential, we should focus our attention on the prevention of problems or early intervention in the problems.

Children Will Benefit from an Interdisciplinary Approach to Their Development

Some of you taking this class in child development are being taught by a child psychologist, others by someone who specialized in human development or family relationships, others by an educational psychologist or professor in an education department, others by a nurse or pediatrician, and yet others by professors from different disciplines. The field of child development has become more interdisciplinary. Our knowledge about children, and how to improve children's lives, has benefited, and will continue to benefit, from the contributions of scholars and professionals from a number of different disciplines, including developmental psychology, education and educational psychology, pediatrics and nursing, child clinical psychology and child psychiatry, sociology, anthropology, and law. The collaboration between child developmentalists and pediatricians/nurses is one example of this interdisciplinary cooperation, with the emerging area of how development influences children's health reflecting this cross-disciplinary trend. Another example is the interest in children's eyewitness testimony that links the fields of child development and law.

Children's Development Is Embedded in Sociocultural, Historical Circumstances

Throughout this book we have emphasized the importance of considering the contexts in which the child develops. Context refers to the setting in which development occurs, a setting that is influenced by historical, economic, social, and cultural factors. These contexts or settings include homes, schools, peer groups, churches, cities, neighborhoods, communities, university laboratories, the United States, Russia, France, Japan, Egypt, and many others—each with meaningful historical, economic, social, and cultural legacies.

In the twentieth century alone in the United States, successive waves of children have witnessed dramatic historical changes, including two world wars and their violence, the Great Depression and its economic woes, the advent of television and computers, increased levels of education, and altered gender roles. And as new generations of babies have been born, they have increasingly been babies with an ethnic minority heritage.

THE JOURNEY OF CHILDHOOD

I hope you can look back and say that you have learned a lot in this course about children, not only other children, but yourself as a child and how your childhood contributed to who you are today. The insightful words of philosopher Søren Kierkegaard capture the importance of looking back to understand ourselves: "Life is lived forward but understood backwards." I also hope that those of you who become the parents of children or who work with children in some capacity—whether as teacher, as counselor, or as community leader—feel that you now have a better grasp of what children's development is all about.

Future generations depend on our ability to face our children. At some point in our adult lives, each one of us needs to examine the shape of our life and ask whether we have met the responsibility of competently and caringly carving out a better world for our children. Twenty-one centuries ago, Roman poet and philosopher Lucretius described one of adult life's richest meanings: grasping that the generations of living things pass in a short while and, like runners, pass on the torch of life. More than twenty centuries later, American writer James Agee captured yet another of life's richest meanings: In every child who is born, the potentiality of the human species is born again.

As we come to the end of this book, I leave you with the following montage of thoughts and images that convey the beauty and complexity of children's development.

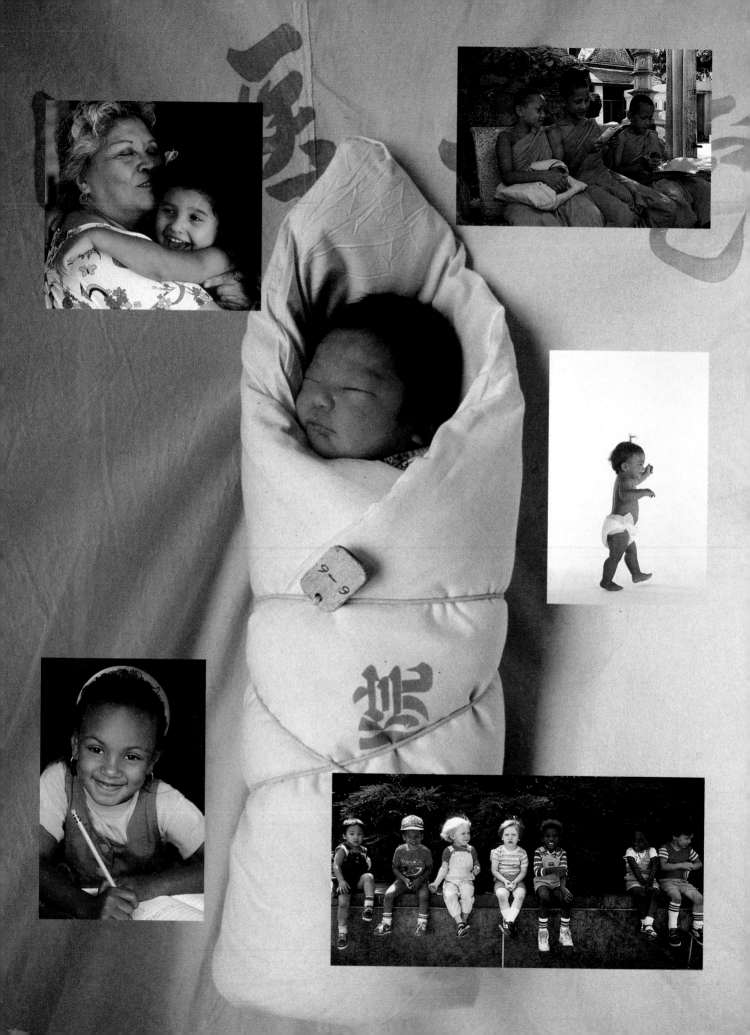

The rhythm and meaning of human development involve beginnings, when questions of whence and whither, when and how are asked. How from so simple a beginning do endless forms develop and grow and mature? What was this organism, what is it now, and what will it become? Birth's fragile moment arrives, when the newborn is on a threshold between two worlds.

As newborns, we were not empty-headed organisms. We cried, kicked, coughed, sucked, saw, heard, and tasted. We slept a lot and occasionally we smiled, although the meaning of our first smiles was not entirely clear. We crawled and then we walked, a journey of a thousand miles beginning with a single step. With each forward step we left some ghost of ourselves behind. Sometimes we conformed, sometimes others conformed to us. Our development was a continuous creation of more-complex forms and our helpless kind demanded the "meeting eyes of love." We split the universe into two halves: "me" and "not me." And we juggled the need to curb our own will with becoming what we could will freely.

In early childhood, our greatest untold poem was being only 4 years old. We skipped, played, and ran all the day long, never again in our lives to be so busy, busy becoming something we had not quite grasped yet. Who knew our thoughts, which we worked up into small mythologies all our own? While our thoughts and feelings took wings, the blossoms of our heart no wind could touch. Our small world widened as we discovered new refuges and new people. When we said "I," we meant something totally unique, not to be confused with any other.

In middle and late childhood, we were on a different plane, belonging to a generation and feeling properly our own. It is the wisdom of human development that at no other time are we more ready to learn than at the end of early childhood's period of expansive imagination. Our thirst was to know and to understand. Our parents continued to cradle our lives, but our growth was also being shaped by successive choirs of friends. We did not think much about the future or the past, but enjoyed the present.

In no order of things was adolescence the simple time of life for us. We clothed ourselves with rainbows and went "brave as the zodiac," flashing from one end of the world to the other. We tried on one face after another, searching for a face of our own. We wanted our parents to understand us and hoped they would give us the privilege of understanding them. We wanted to fly but found that first we had to learn to stand and walk and climb and dance. In our most pimply and awkward moments we became acquainted with sex. We played furiously at adult games but were confined to a society of our own peers. Our generation was the fragile cable by which the best and the worst of our parents' generation were transmitted to the present. In the end, there were but two lasting bequests our parents could leave us—one being roots, the other wings.

GLOSSARY

AB̄ error   The Piagetian object-permanence concept in which an infant progressing into substage 4 makes frequent mistakes, selecting the familiar hiding place (A) rather than the new hiding place (B̄).   217

accommodation   Piagetian concept of adjustment to new information.   213

acculturation   Cultural change that results from continuous, firsthand contact between two distinctive cultural groups.   368, 578

achievement motivation (need for achievement)   The desire to accomplish something, to reach a standard of excellence, and to expend effort to excel.   562

active (niche-picking) genotype-environment interactions   The type of interactions that occur when children seek out environments they find compatible and stimulating.   95

activity level   The tempo and vigor of movement.   357

adaptive behavior   In evolutionary conceptions of psychology, behavior that promotes the organism's survival in its natural habitat.   77

adolescence   The developmental period of transition from childhood to early adulthood, entered at approximately 10 to 12 years of age and ending at 18 to 22 years of age.   18

adolescent egocentrism   A characteristic of adolescence, consisting of an imaginary audience and a personal fable.   228

adoption study   A study in which investigators seek to discover whether, in behavior and psychological characteristics, adopted children are more like their adoptive parents, who provided a home environment, or more like their biological parents, who contributed their heredity. Another form of the adoption study is to compare adoptive and biological siblings.   93

affordances   The opportunities for interaction that an object offers us, allowing us to perform functional activities.   156

afterbirth   The third birth stage, when the placenta, umbilical cord, and other membranes are detached and expelled.   121

agency   The idea that people cause events to happen through motivation that is entirely internal.   258

AIDS (Acquired Immune Deficiency Syndrome)   A disease caused by a virus (HIV) that destroys the body's immune system. Consequently, germs that usually do not harm someone with a normal immune system produce devastating results and death.   192

allocentric representations   All relations among the entities within a space.   261

alternation   A model that assumes that it is possible for an individual to know and understand two different cultures, and that individuals can alter their behavior to fit a particular social context.   578

altruism   An unselfish interest in helping another person.   449

amniocentesis   A prenatal medical procedure in which a sample of amniotic fluid is withdrawn by syringe and tested to discover if the fetus is suffering from any chromosomal or metabolic disorders. It is performed between the 12th and 16th weeks of pregnancy.   87

amnion   A bag or envelope that contains a clear fluid in which the developing embryo floats. The amnion is an important life-support system. It provides an environment that is temperature and humidity controlled, as well as shockproof.   108

anal stage   The second Freudian stage of development, occurring between 1½ and 3 years of age, in which the child's greatest pleasure involves the anus or the eliminative functions associated with it.   37

androgen   The main class of male sex hormones.   407

androgyny   The presence of desirable masculine and feminine characteristics in one individual.   418

anger cry   A variation of the basic cry in which more excess air is forced through the vocal cords.   362

animism   A facet of preoperational thought, the belief that inanimate objects have "lifelike" qualities and are capable of action.   220

anorexia nervosa   An eating disorder that involves the relentless pursuit of thinness through starvation.   198

anoxia   The insufficient supply of oxygen to the infant.   121

Apgar scale   A widely used method to assess the health of newborns at 1 to 5 minutes after birth. The Apgar scale evaluates infants' heart rate, respiratory effort, muscle tone, body color, and reflex irritability.   127

aphasia   A language disorder, resulting from brain damage, that involves a loss of the ability to articulate and/or comprehend ideas.   321

aptitude-treatment interaction (ATI)   ATI stresses the importance of both children's characteristics and motivation and the treatment or experience they are given in the classroom. Aptitude refers to such characteristics as the academic potential and personality characteristics on which students differ; treatment refers to educational techniques, such as structured versus flexible classrooms.   557

assimilation   The absorption of ethnic minority groups into the dominant group, which often means the loss of some, or virtually all, of the behavior and values of the ethnic minority group; Piagetian concept of the incorporation of new information into existing knowledge.   213, 578

associative play   Play that involves social interaction, with little or no organization.   518

attachment   A close emotional bond between an infant and a caregiver.   349

attention   Concentration and focusing of mental resources.   250

attention-deficit hyperactivity disorder   Hyperactivity, characterized by a short attention span, distractibility, and high levels of physical activity.   561

authoritarian parenting   A restrictive, punitive style in which the parents exhort child to follow the directions and to respect work and effort. Firm limits and controls are placed on a child, and their little verbal exchange allows. This style is associated with children's social incompetence.   479

authoritative parenting   A parenting style in which the parents encourage children to be independent but still place limits and controls on their actions. Extensive give-and-take is allowed, and parents are warm and nurturant toward the child. This style is associated with children's social competence.   479

automaticity The ability to process information with little or no effort. 250

autonomous morality The second stage of moral development in Piaget's theory, displayed by older children (about 10 years of age and older). The child becomes aware that rules and laws are created by people and that, in judging an action, one should consider the actor's intentions as well as the consequences. 435

autonomy versus shame and doubt Erikson's second stage of development, occurring in late infancy and toddlerhood (1–3 years of age). After gaining trust in their caregivers, infants begin to discover that their behavior is their own. They start to assert their sense of independence or autonomy. 39

axon The part of the neuron that carries information away from the cell body to other cells. 146

back-to-basics movement The idea that the function of schools should be the rigorous training of intellectual skills through such subjects as English, math, and science. 539

basic cry A rhythmic pattern that usually consists of a cry, followed by a briefer silence, then a shorter inspiratory whistle that is of somewhat higher pitch than the main cry, then a brief rest before the next cry. 362

basic-skills-and-phonetics approach The view that reading instruction should stress phonetics and its basic rules for translating written symbols into sounds. Early reading instruction should involve simplified materials. 334

Bayley Scales of Infant Development An instrument, developed by Nancy Bayley, to be used in the assessment of infant development. The current version has three components: a Mental Scale, a Motor Scale, and an Infant Behavior Profile. 294

becoming parents and families with children The third stage in the family life cycle, which requires that adults now move up a generation and become caregivers to the younger generation. 474

behavior genetics The study of the degree and nature of behavior's hereditary basis. 92

behaviorism A view that emphasizes the scientific study of observable behavioral responses and their environmental determinants. 46

bilingual education Programs for students with limited proficiency in English that instruct students in their own language part of the time while they learn English. 337

biological processes Changes in an individual's physical nature. 16

blastocyst The inner layer of cells that develops during the germinal period. These cells later develop into the embryo. 107

bonding Close contact, especially physical, between parents and their newborn in the period shortly after birth. 130

boundary ambiguity The uncertainty in stepfamilies about who is in or out of the family and who is performing or responsible for certain tasks in the family system. 490

Brazelton Neonatal Behavioral Assessment Scale A test, given hours after birth, to assess newborns' neurological development, reflexes, and reactions to people. 127

breech position The baby's position in the uterus that causes the buttocks to be the first part to emerge from the vagina. 121

brightness constancy The recognition that an object retains the same degree of brightness even though different amounts of light fall on it. 159

Broca's area The area of the left frontal lobe of the brain that directs the muscle movements involved in speech production. 321

bulimia An eating disorder that involves a binge-and-purge sequence on a regular basis. 198

canalization The process by which characteristics take a narrow path or developmental course. Apparently, preservative forces help to protect or buffer a person from environmental extremes. 92

cardinality Absolute numerical size. 262

care perspective The moral perspective of Carol Gilligan, that views people in terms of their connectedness to others and focuses on interpersonal communication, relationships with others, and concern for others. Gilligan's perspective. 440

case study An in-depth look at an individual, used mainly by clinical psychologists when the unique aspects of a person's life cannot be duplicated, for either practical or ethical reasons. 57

centration The focusing of attention on one characteristic to the exclusion of all others. 222

cephalocaudal pattern The sequence in which the greatest growth occurs at the top—the head—with physical growth in size, weight, and feature differentiation gradually working from top to bottom. 141

cesarean section The surgical removal of the baby from the uterus. 121

child-centered kindergarten The education of the whole child, including concern for the child's physical, cognitive, and social development. Instruction is organized around the child's needs, interests, and learning styles. The process of learning, rather than the finished product, is emphasized. 540

chlamydia A sexually transmitted disease named for the bacteria that cause it. 191

chorionic villus test A prenatal medical procedure in which a small sample of the placenta is removed at a certain point in the pregnancy from the 8th through the 11th week. 87

chromosomes Threadlike structures that come in 23 pairs, one member of each pair coming from each parent. Chromosomes contain the genetic substance DNA. 82

chronosystem The system involving the patterning of environmental events and transitions over the life course and sociohistorical circumstances. 50

classical conditioning A form of learning in which a neutral stimulus acquires the ability to produce a response originally produced by another stimulus. 44

clinical depression Depression diagnosed as experiencing major depressive disorder (MDD) or dysthymic disorder. 365

cliques Small adolescent groups that involve greater intimacy among members and more group cohesion than crowds. 513

cognitive appraisal Lazarus's term for individuals' interpretation of events in their lives as harmful, threatening, or challenging, and their determination of whether they have the resources to cope effectively with the event. 367

cognitive developmental theory of gender The view that children's gender typing occurs after they have developed a concept of gender. Once they begin to consistently conceive of themselves as male or female, children often organize their world on the basis of gender. 409

cognitive monitoring The process of taking stock of what you are currently doing, what you will do next, and how effectively the mental activity is unfolding. 274

cognitive moral education An indirect moral education approach that emphasizes that children adopt such values as democracy and justice as their moral reasoning is developed. 452

cognitive processes Changes in an individual's thought, intelligence, and language. 16

cognitive social learning theory of morality The theory that distinguishes between a child's moral competence (the ability to produce moral behaviors) and moral performance (those behaviors in specific situations). 444

cohort effects   Effects due to an individual's time of birth or generation that have nothing to do with the individual's actual age.   62

collectivism   Emphasizing values that serve the group by subordinating personal goals to reserve group integrity, interdependence of members, and harmonious relationships.   576

commitment   The part of identity development in which adolescents show a personal investment in what they are going to do.   394

community rights versus individual rights   The fifth stage in Kohlberg's theory of moral development. At this stage, children understand that values and laws are relative and that standards vary from one person to another.   437

computer-assisted instruction   A method of education that uses the computer as a tutor to individualize instruction: to present information, give students practice, assess their level of understanding, and provide additional instruction if needed.   527

concrete operational stage   Piaget's third developmental stage which lasts from approximately 7 to 11 years of age. Children can now perform operations, and logical reasoning replaces intuitive thought as long as reasoning can be applied to specific or concrete examples.   42

conditioned response (CR)   The learned response to the conditioned stimulus that occurs after CS-US pairing.   45

conditioned stimulus (CS)   A previously neutral stimulus that eventually elicits the conditioned response after being paired with the US.   45

conduct disorder   The psychiatric diagnostic category used when multiple behaviors, such as running away, setting fires, cruelty to animals, and truancy, occur over a 6-month period. When three or more of these behaviors co-occur before the age of 15 and the child or adolescent is considered unmanageable or out of control, the clinical diagnosis is conduct disorder.   455

connectedness   An important element in adolescent identity development. It consists of two dimensions: mutuality (sensitivity to and respect for others' views) and permeability (openness to others' views).   396

conscience   The component of the superego that involves behaviors disapproved of by parents.   445

conservation   The idea that an amount stays the same regardless of how its container changes.   222

constructive play   Play that combines sensorimotor and practice repetitive activity with the symbolic representation of ideas. Constructive play occurs when children engage in self-regulated creation or construction of a product or problem solution.   521

constructivist view   Advocated by Piaget and the information processing psychologists, states that perception is a cognitive construction based on sensory input plus information retrieved from memory. In this view, perception is a kind of representation of the world that builds up as the infant constructs an image of experiences.   155

content validity   A test's ability to test a broad range of the content that is to be measured.   288

context   The settings in which development occurs. These settings are influenced by historical, economic, social, and cultural factors.   9

continuity of development   The view that development involves gradual, cumulative change from conception to death.   19

continuity view   The view that emphasizes the role that early parent-child relationships play in constructing a basic way of relating to others throughout the life span.   471

controversial children   Children who are frequently nominated as someone's best friend and as being disliked.   507

conventional reasoning   The second, or intermediate, level in Kohlberg's theory of moral development. Children's internalization is intermediate. They abide by certain standards (internal), but they are the standards of others (external), such as parents or the laws of society.   436

convergent thinking   Thinking that produces one correct answer and is characteristic of the kind of thinking required on standardized intelligence tests.   307

cooperative play   Play that involves social interaction in a group, with a sense of group identity and organized activity.   518

coordination of secondary circular reactions   Piaget's fourth sensorimotor substage, which develops between 8 and 12 months of age. In this substage, several significant changes take place involving the coordination of schemes and intentionality.   216

correlational coefficient   A number based on statistical analysis that is used to describe the degree of association between two variables.   60

correlational strategy   A strategy in which the goal is to describe the strength of the relation between two or more events or characteristics.   60

counterconditioning   A classical conditioning procedure for weakening a CR by associating the stimuli with a new response incompatible with the CR.   46

creativity   The ability to think about something in a novel and unusual way and to come up with unique solutions to problems.   307

crisis   A period of identity development during which the adolescent is choosing among meaningful alternatives.   394

criterion validity   A test's ability to predict an individual's performance when measured by other measures, or criteria, of an attribute.   288

critical period   A fixed time period very early in development during which certain behaviors optimally emerge.   49

critical thinking   Grasping the deeper meaning of problems, keeping an open mind about different approaches and perspectives, not accepting on faith what other people and books tell you, and thinking reflectively rather than accepting the first idea that comes to mind.   273

cross-cultural studies   Studies that compare two or more cultures. Such studies provide information about the degree to which children's development is similar, or universal, across cultures and about the degree to which it is culture-specific.   9, 575

cross-sectional approach   A research strategy in which individuals of different ages are compared all at one time.   61

crowd   The largest and least personal adolescent group.   513

cultural-familial retardation   Mental retardation in which there is no evidence of organic brain damage; individuals' IQs range from 55 to 70.   305

culture   The behavior, patterns, beliefs, and all other products of a particular group of people that are passed on from generation to generation.   9, 573

culture-fair tests   Intelligence tests that are intended to not be culturally biased.   301

dating scripts   The cognitive models that adolescents and adults use to guide and evaluate dating interactions.   516

defense mechanisms   The psychoanalytic term for unconscious methods used by the ego to distort reality in order to protect itself from anxiety.   36

dendrite   The receiving part of the neuron, collecting information and routing it to the cell body.   146

dependent variable   The factor that is measured in an experiment; it may change because of the manipulation of the independent variable.   61

depressed mood Periods of sadness or unhappy mood that can last for a brief or an extended period of time. They may occur as a result of the loss of a significant relationship or failure on an important task. 365

depressive syndromes A cluster of behaviors and emotions that include feeling lonely, crying, fear of doing bad things, feeling the need to be perfect, feeling unloved, feeling worthless, nervous, guilty, or sad, and worrying. 365

deprivation dwarfism A type of growth retardation caused by emotional deprivation; when children are deprived of affection, they experience stress, which alters the release of hormones by the pituitary gland. 174

development The pattern of change that begins at conception and continues through the life span. 16

developmental biodynamics The new perspective on motor development in infancy that seeks to explain how motor behaviors are assembled for perceiving and acting. 153

developmental construction view The belief that as individuals grow up they acquire modes of relating to others. Of the two main variations of this view, one emphasizes continuity and stability in relationships throughout the life span, and the other emphasizes discontinuity and change in relationships throughout the life span. 471

developmentally appropriate practice Education based on knowledge of the typical development of children within an age span (age appropriateness) and the uniqueness of each child (individual appropriateness). 542

developmental quotient (DQ) An overall developmental score that combines subscores in the motor, language, adaptive, and personal-social domains in the Gesell assessment of infants. 294

difficult child A child who tends to react negatively and cry frequently, who engages in irregular daily routines, and who is slow to accept new experiences. 357

direct moral education An educational approach that involves either emphasizing values or character traits during specified time slots or integrating those values or traits throughout the curriculum. 451

discontinuity of development The view that development involves distinct stages in the life span. 19

discontinuity view The view that emphasizes change and growth in relationships over time. 472

dishabituation Renewed interest in a stimulus. 249

displacement The use of language to communicate information about another place and time. 317

divergent thinking Thinking that produces many answers to a question and is characteristic of creativity. 307

DNA A complex molecule that contains genetic information. 82

dominant-recessive genes principle The principle that if one gene of a pair is dominant and one is recessive, the dominant gene exerts its effect, overriding the potential influence of the recessive gene. A recessive gene exerts its influence only if both genes in a pair are recessive. 90

doula A caregiver who provides continuous physical, emotional, and educational support to the mother before, during, and just after childbirth. 123

Down syndrome A common genetically transmitted form of mental retardation, caused by the presence of an extra (47th) chromosome. 85

dysthymic disorder A period of at least 1 year in which the person has shown depressed or irritable mood every day without more than 2 symptom-free months. Further, dysthymic disorder requires the presence of at least two of the following symptoms: eating problems, sleeping problems, lack of energy, low self-esteem, reduced concentration or decision-making ability, and feelings of hopelessness. 365

early childhood The developmental period that extends from the end of infancy to about 5 or 6 years of age; sometimes called the preschool years. 17

early-later experience issue An issue focusing on the degree to which early experiences (especially in infancy) or later experiences are the key determinants of the child's development. 19

easy child A child who is generally in a positive mood, who quickly establishes regular routines in infancy, and who adapts easily to new experiences. 357

echoing Repeating what someone says, especially if it is an incomplete phrase or sentence. 324

eclectic theoretical orientation The approach that uses whatever is considered the best in each theory. 53

ecological theory A theory that emphasizes the role of social contexts in development. 49

ecological view The view, advocated by the Gibsons, that perception has the functional purposes of bringing the organism into contact with the environment and increasing its adaptation. 156

ectoderm The outer layer of cells, which becomes the nervous system, sensory receptors (ears, nose, and eyes, for example), and skin parts (hair and nails, for example). 107

ego The Freudian structure of personality that deals with the demands of reality. 36

egocentrism A salient feature of preoperational thought, the inability to distinguish between one's own and someone else's perspective. 220

ego-ideal The component of the superego that involves ideal standards approved of by parents. 445

elaboration A process of going beyond the information given to make information more memorable. 252

embryonic period The period of prenatal development that occurs 2 to 8 weeks after conception. During the embryonic period, the rate of cell differentiation intensifies, support systems for the cells form, and organs appear. 107

emergent literacy Children's beginning to construct knowledge about the uses and nature of written language long before they begin decoding familiar words and writing in conventional ways. 336

emic approach An approach in which the goal is to describe behavior in one culture or ethnic group in terms that are meaningful and important to the people in that group, without regard to other cultures or ethnic groups; culture-specific. 58

emotion Feeling or affect that involves a mixture of physiological arousal (fast heartbeat, for example) and overt behavior (a smile or grimace, for example). 360

emotionality The tendency to be distressed. 357

empathy Reacting to another's feelings with an emotional response that is similar to the other's feelings. 445

endoderm The inner layer of cells, which develops into digestive and respiratory systems. 107

equilibration A mechanism in Piaget's theory invoked to explain how children shift from one stage of thought to the next. The shift occurs as children experience cognitive conflict or disequilibrium in trying to understand the world. Eventually, they resolve the conflict and reach equilibrium of thought. 214

erogenous zones Freud's concept of the parts of the body that have especially strong pleasure-giving qualities at each stage of development.   37

estradiol A hormone associated in girls with breast, uterine, and skeletal development.   185

estrogen The main class of female sex hormones.   407

ethnic gloss The use of an ethnic label, such as *African American, Latino, Asian,* or *Native American,* in a superficial way that makes an ethnic group seem more homogeneous than it actually is.   59

ethnic identity An individual's sense of membership in an ethnic group based upon shared language, religion, customs, values, history, and race.   10

ethnicity A dimension of culture based on cultural heritage, nationality characteristics, race, religion, and language; *ethnicity* is derived from the Greek word for "nation."   10, 584

ethnocentrism A tendency to favor one's own group over other groups.   389

ethology The theory that behavior is strongly influenced by biology, is tied to evolution, and is characterized by critical or sensitive periods.   48

etic approach An approach in which the goal is to describe behavior so that generalizations can be made across cultures; culture-universal.   58

evocative genotype-environment interactions The type of interactions that occur when the child's genotype elicits certain types of physical and social environments.   95

evolutionary psychology A contemporary approach that emphasizes that behavior is a function of mechanisms, requires input for activation, and ultimately is related to survival and reproduction.   79

exosystem The system involved when experiences in another social setting—in which the individual does not have an active role—influence what the individual experiences in an immediate context.   50

expanding Restating, in a linguistically sophisticated form, what a child has said.   324

experimental strategy A strategy that allows investigators to precisely determine behavior's causes by performing an experiment in a precisely regulated setting in which one or more of the factors believed to influence the behavior being studied is manipulated and all others are held constant.   60

extrinsic motivation The influence of external rewards and punishments on behavior.   562

family at midlife The fifth stage in the family life cycle, a time of launching children, playing an important role in linking generations, and adapting to midlife changes in development.   476

family in later life The sixth and final stage in the family life cycle, when retirement alters a couple's lifestyle. Grandparenting also characterizes many families in later life.   476

family structure model of divorce effects A model according to which any differences in children are due to family structure variations, such as divorce, death, or having a father present.   487

family with adolescents The fourth stage in the family life cycle, during which parents cope with the adolescent who is seeking autonomy and her or his own identity.   476

feminization of poverty The fact that far more women than men live in poverty. Women's low income, divorce, and inadequate alimony awards and child-support enforcement, which leave women with less money than they and their children need to adequately function, are the likely causes.   584

fetal alcohol syndrome (FAS) A cluster of abnormalities that appears in the offspring of mothers who drink alcohol heavily during pregnancy.   116

fetal period The prenatal period of development that begins 2 months after conception and lasts for 7 months on the average.   109

fine motor skills Motor skills that involve more finely tuned movements, such as finger dexterity.   151

first habits and primary circular reactions Piaget's second sensorimotor substage, which develops between 1 and 4 months of age. Infants learn to coordinate sensation and types of schemes or structures—that is, habits and primary circular reactions.   215

forebrain An area of the brain consisting of a number of structures, including the cerebrum, the most recently evolved portion of the brain. The cerebrum makes up 80 percent of the brain's volume and covers the lower portions of the brain like a large cap. The cerebrum plays important roles in language, thinking, and intelligence.   145

formal operational stage Piaget's fourth and final developmental stage which appears between the ages of 11 and 15. Individuals move beyond the world of concrete experiences and think in abstract and more logical terms.   42

fraternal twins Twins who develop from separate eggs and separate sperm, making them genetically no more similar than ordinary siblings.   93

frontal lobe The portion of the cerebrum involved in the control of voluntary muscles and intelligence.   145

fusion model A model that reflects the assumptions behind the melting-pot theory, which implies that cultures sharing economic, political, or geographical boundaries will fuse together until they are indistinguishable and form a new culture.   578

games Activities engaged in for pleasure that include rules and often competition.   522

gametes Human reproduction cells created in the testes of males and the ovaries of females.   82

gender The sociocultural dimension of being male or female.   10, 407

gender identity The sense of being male or female, which most children acquire by the time they are 3 years old.   407

gender intensification hypothesis The hypothesis that psychological and behavioral differences between boys and girls become greater during adolescence because of increased socialization pressures to conform to traditional masculine and feminine gender roles.   420

gender role A set of expectations that prescribes how females and males should think, act, and feel.   407

gender-role transcendence The belief that, when an individual's competence is at issue, it should be conceptualized not on the basis of masculinity, femininity, or androgyny, but rather on a personal basis.   422

gender schema A cognitive structure that organizes the world in terms of female and male.   413

gender schema theory The theory that an individual's attention and behavior are guided by an internal motivation to conform to gender-based sociocultural standards and stereotypes.   413

gender stereotypes Broad categories that reflect our impressions and beliefs about what behavior is appropriate for females and males.   414

generativity versus stagnation Erikson's seventh developmental stage, occurring during middle adulthood. A chief concern is to assist the younger generation in developing and leading useful lives.   39

genes Units of hereditary information composed of DNA. Genes act as a blueprint for cells to reproduce themselves and manufacture the proteins that maintain life. 82

genetic epistemology The study of how children's knowledge changes over the course of their development. 13

genital stage The fifth and final Freudian stage of development, occurring from puberty on. This stage is one of sexual reawakening; the source of sexual pleasure now becomes someone outside of the family. 38

genotype A person's genetic heritage; the actual genetic material. 91

germinal period The period of prenatal development that takes place in the first 2 weeks after conception. It includes the creation of the zygote, continued cell division, and the attachment of the zygote to the uterine wall. 107

gifted Having above-average intelligence (an IQ of 120 or higher), a superior talent for something, or both. 305

global empathy A young infant's empathic response in which clear boundaries between the feelings and needs of the self and those of another have not yet been established. 446

grasping reflex A neonatal reflex that occurs when something touches the infant's palms. The infant responds by grasping tightly. 148

gross motor skills Motor skills that involve large muscle activities, such as walking. 151

habituation The repeated presentation of a stimulus that causes reduced attention to the stimulus. 249

helpless orientation Attributing difficulty to lack of ability. Children with this orientation seem to be trapped by the experience of difficulty. 563

herpes simplex virus II A virus that causes a sexually transmitted disease whose symptoms include irregular cycles of sores and blisters in the genital area. 191

heteronomous morality The first stage of moral development in Piaget's theory, occurring from 4 to 7 years of age. Justice and rules are conceived of as unchangeable properties of the world, removed from the control of people. 435

hidden curriculum The pervasive moral atmosphere of a school. This atmosphere includes school and classroom rules, attitudes toward academics and extracurricular activities, the moral orientation of teachers and school administrators, and the text materials. 451

hindbrain The lowest portion of the brain, located at the rear of the skull. One of the hindbrain's structures is the cerebellum, which plays an important role in motor development and control. 144

holophrase hypothesis The theory that infants use a single word to imply a complete sentence and that this is characteristic of an infant's first words. 328

horizontal décalage Piaget's concept that similar abilities do not appear at the same time within a stage of development. 224

hypotheses Assumptions that can be tested to determine their accuracy. 35

hypothetical-deductive reasoning Piaget's formal operational concept that adolescents have the cognitive ability to develop hypotheses about ways to solve problems and can systematically deduce which is the best path to follow in solving the problem. 228

id The Freudian structure of personality that consists of instincts, which are an individual's reservoir of psychic energy. 36

identical twins Twins who develop from a single fertilized egg that splits into two genetically identical replicas, each of which becomes a person. 93

identification theory A theory that stems from Freud's view that preschool children develop a sexual attraction to the opposite-sex parent, then at 5 to 6 years of age renounce the attraction because of anxious feelings, subsequently identifying with the same-sex parent and unconsciously adopting the same-sex parent's characteristics. 408

identity achievement Marcia's term for an adolescent's having undergone a crisis and having made a commitment. 395

identity diffusion Marcia's term for the state adolescents are in when they have not yet experienced a crisis (that is, they have not yet explored meaningful alternatives) or made any commitments. 394

identity foreclosure Marcia's term for the state adolescents are in when they have made a commitment but have not experienced a crisis. 394

identity moratorium Marcia's term for the state of adolescents who are in the midst of a crisis but whose commitments either are absent or are only vaguely defined. 395

identity versus identity confusion Erikson's fifth developmental stage, which individuals experience during the adolescent years. At this time, individuals are faced with finding out who they are, what they are all about, and where they are going in life. 39, 393

idiographic needs Needs that are important to the individual, not to the group. 65

imagery Sensations without the presence of corresponding external stimuli. A strategy that helps individuals improve their memory. 253

imaginary audience An adolescent's belief that others are as preoccupied with her as she is. 228

immanent justice According to Piaget, the concept that, if a rule is broken, punishment will be meted out immediately. 435

implantation The attachment of the zygote to the uterine wall, which takes place about 10 days after conception. 107

imprinting The ethological concept of rapid, innate learning within a limited critical period of time that involves attachment to the first moving object seen. 48

impulsivity A cognitive style in which individuals act before they think. 255

inclusion Educating children in their natural environment, such as typical elementary school classrooms. 560

independent variable The manipulated, influential, experimental factor in the experiment. 61

index offenses Criminal acts, whether they are committed by juveniles or adults, such as robbery, aggravated assault, rape, and homicide. 455

indirect moral education An educational approach that involves encouraging children to define their own and others' values and helping them define the moral perspectives that support those values. 451

individual differences The stable, consistent ways in which people are different from each other. 287

individualism Giving priority to personal goals rather than to group goals; emphasizing values that serve the self, such as feeling good, personal distinction and achievement, and independence. 576

individualism and purpose The second stage in Kohlberg's theory of moral development. Moral thinking is based on rewards and self-interest. 436

individuality An important element in adolescent identity development. It consists of two dimensions: self-assertion (the ability to have and communicate a point of view) and separateness (the use of communication patterns to express how one is different from others). 396

induction A discipline technique in which a parent uses reason and explanation of the consequences for others of a child's actions. 450

indulgent parenting A style of parenting in which parents are highly involved with their children but place few demands or controls on them. Indulgent parenting is associated with children's social incompetence, especially a lack of self-control.   479

industry versus inferiority Erikson's fourth developmental stage, occurring approximately in the elementary school years. Children's initiative brings them into contact with a wealth of new experiences. As they move into middle and late childhood, they direct their energy toward mastering knowledge and intellectual skills.   39

infancy The developmental period that begins at birth and ends at about 18 to 24 months.   17

infinite generativity An individual's ability to generate an infinite number of meaningful sentences using a finite set of words and rules, which makes language a highly creative enterprise.   317

information processing A model of cognition concerned with how individuals process information about their world—how information enters the mind, how it is stored and transformed, and how it is retrieved to perform such complex activities as problem solving and reasoning.   43

information-processing approach An approach to understanding thinking that emphasizes that thinking is information processing, stresses the processes involved in thinking (such as memory, concept formation, and problem solving in particular contexts), focuses on precise analysis of change mechanisms, and advocates careful task analyses.   245

initiative versus guilt Erikson's third stage of development, occurring during the preschool years. As preschool children encounter a widening social world, they are challenged more than they were as infants. Active, purposeful behavior is needed to cope with these challenges.   39

innate goodness view The idea, presented by Swiss-born philosopher Jean-Jacques Rousseau, that children are inherently good.   11

integration A model that includes both the maintenance of cultural integrity and movement to become an integral part of the larger culture.   578

integrity versus despair Erikson's eighth and final developmental stage, occurring in late adulthood. In the later years of life, we look back and evaluate what we have done with our lives.   39

intelligence Verbal ability, problem-solving skills, and the ability to learn from and adapt to the experiences of everyday life.   287

intelligence quotient (IQ) Devised in 1912 by William Stern, IQ consists of mental age divided by chronological age, multiplied by 100.   289

intermodal perception The ability to relate and integrate information from two or more sensory modalities, such as vision and hearing.   164

internalization The developmental change from behavior that is externally controlled to behavior that is controlled by internal, self-generated standards and principles.   436

internalization of schemes Piaget's sixth sensorimotor substage, which develops between 18 and 24 months of age. In this substage, infants' mental functioning shifts from a purely sensorimotor plane to a symbolic plane, and they develop the ability to use primitive symbols.   216

interpersonal norms The third stage in Kohlberg's theory of moral development. Children value trust, caring, and loyalty to others as the basis of moral judgments.   436

intimacy in friendship Self-disclosure and the sharing of private thoughts.   511

intimacy versus isolation Erikson's sixth developmental stage, which individuals experience during the early adulthood years. At this time, individuals face the developmental task of forming intimate relationships with others.   39

intrinsic motivation The internal desire to be competent and to do something for its own sake.   562

intuitive thought substage The second substage of preoperational thought, occurring approximately between 4 and 7 years of age. Children begin to use primitive reasoning and want to know the answers to all sorts of questions.   221

in vitro fertilization Conception outside the body.   83

involution The process by which the uterus returns to its prepregnant size 5 or 6 weeks after birth.   129

justice perspective A moral perspective that focuses on the rights of the individual; individuals stand alone and independently make moral decisions. Kohlberg's perspective.   440

juvenile delinquency A broad range of behaviors, from socially unacceptable behavior to status offenses to criminal acts.   455

keyword method An imagery strategy that uses vivid imagery of important words, or keywords, to improve memory.   253

Klinefelter syndrome A genetic disorder in which males have an extra X chromosome, making them XXY instead of XY.   87

labeling Identifying the names of objects.   324

laboratory A controlled setting in which many of the complex factors of the "real world" are removed.   56

Lamaze method A form of prepared childbirth developed by Fernand Lamaze, a pioneering French obstetrician. Widely accepted in the medical profession, it involves helping pregnant women cope actively with the pain of childbirth and to avoid or reduce medication.   123

language A system of symbols, or word sequences, used to communicate with others, that involves infinite generativity, displacement, signal simultaneity and overlap, and rule systems.   317

language acquisition device (LAD) A biological prewiring that enables children to detect certain language categories, such as phonology, syntax, and semantics. Chomsky proposes that the LAD is an innate grammatical ability that underlies all human languages.   324

latency stage The fourth Freudian stage of development, which occurs between approximately 6 years of age and puberty; the child represses all interest in sexuality and develops social and intellectual skills.   38

launching The process in which the youth moves into adulthood and exits his/her family of origin.   474

learned helplessness A feeling of helplessness that arises in individuals who have been exposed to negative experiences, such as prolonged stress or pain, over which they have no control. Seligman suggests that depression is learned helplessness.   365

learning disability Difficulties in several academic areas for children of normal or higher intelligence who usually do not show deficits in other areas and are not suffering from other conditions or disorders that could explain their learning problems.   560

leaving home and becoming a single adult The first stage in the family life cycle, involving launching.   474

Leboyer method A birth process developed by French obstetrician Frederick Leboyer that tends to make birth less stressful for infants. The procedure is referred to as "birth without violence."   122

life course theory Glenn Elder's view that the human life span can be best understood by considering human lives in historical time and place, the timing of lives, linked or interdependent lives, and human agency and social constraints. 51

life-history records Records that present a chronology of activities and events of a person's lifetime. Such records can include data records on education, work, family, and residence. 59

literacy The ability to read and write. 336

longitudinal approach A research strategy in which the same individuals are studied over a period of time, usually several years or more. 62

long-term memory A relatively permanent type of memory that holds huge amounts of information for a long period of time. 247

love withdrawal A discipline technique in which a parent withholds attention or love from a child. 450

low-birthweight infants Infants born after a regular period of gestation (the length of time between conception and birth) of 38 to 42 weeks, but who weigh less than 5½ pounds. 125

M

macrosystem The system consisting in the culture in which individuals live. *Culture* refers to behavior patterns, beliefs, and all other products of a particular group of people that are passed on from generation to generation. 50

major depressive disorder A disorder present when the adolescent has experienced five or more of the following symptoms for at least a 2-week period at a level that differs from previous functioning: depressed mood or irritable most of the day; decreased interest in pleasurable activities; changes in weight or failure to make necessary weight gains in adolescence; sleep problems; psychomotor agitation or retardation; fatigue or loss of energy; feelings of worthlessness or abnormal amounts of guilt; reduced concentration and decision-making ability; and repeated suicide ideation, suicide attempts, or plans of suicide. 365

marasmus A wasting away of the body's tissues in an infant's first year, caused by a severe deficiency of protein and calories. 144

marginalization The process in which groups are put out of cultural and psychological contact with both their traditional culture and the larger, dominant culture. 578

mastery orientation Task orientation. Children with this orientation are concerned about their learning strategies and do not focus on their abilities. 563

maternal blood test A prenatal diagnostic technique that is used to assess blood alphaprotein level, which is associated with neural-tube defects. This technique is also called alpha-fetoprotein test (AFP). 87

maturation The orderly sequence of changes dictated by a genetic blueprint. 18

Maximally Discriminative Facial Movement Coding System (MAX) Izard's system of coding infants' facial expressions related to emotions. Using MAX, coders watch slow-motion and stop-action videotapes of infants' facial reactions to stimuli. 362

mean length of utterance (MLU) An index of language development based on the number of morphemes per sentence a child produces in a sample of about 50 to 100 sentences. 330

means-ends analysis Examining one's current situation, as well as one's current goal, and how to get from the current situation to the goal. 266

meiosis The process of cell doubling and separation of chromosomes in which each pair of chromosomes in a cell separates, with one member of each pair going into each gamete. 82

memory The retention of information over time. Memory is central to information processing. 246

menarche First menstruation. 183

mental age (MA) A child's level of mental development relative to others. 289

mental retardation A condition of limited mental ability in which individuals have a low IQ, usually below 70 on a traditional test of intelligence, have difficulty adapting to everyday life, and have an onset of these characteristics during the so-called developmental period—before age 18. 304

mesoderm The middle layer of cells, which becomes the circulatory system, bones, muscles, excretory system, and reproductive system. 107

mesosystem The system involving relationships between microsystems or connections between contexts, such as the connection between family experience and the school experience. 50

metacognitive knowledge Knowledge about how the human mind works. 253

microsystem In Bronfenbrenner's ecological theory, the setting in which an individual lives. This context includes the person's family, peers, school, and neighborhood. The most direct interactions with social agents occur in the microsystem. 50

midbrain Located between the hindbrain and the forebrain, this is where many fibers ascend and descend, connecting higher and lower portions of the brain. 144

middle and late childhood The developmental period that extends from about 6 to 11 years of age, approximately corresponding to the elementary school years; sometimes called the elementary school years. 18

Montessori approach A philosophy of education in which chidren are given considerable freedom in choosing activities and are allowed to move about the room as they desire. The teacher is a facilitator rather than a director of learning. 541

moral character Having the strength of your convictions, persisting, and overcoming distractions and obstacles. 454

moral development Development regarding rules and conventions about what people should do in their interactions with other people. 435

moral judgment Making decisions about which actions are right and which are wrong. 454

moral motivation Giving moral values a higher priority than other personal vaues. 454

moral sensitivity The interpretation of situations with an awareness of how our actions affect other people. 454

Moro reflex A neonatal startle response that occurs in reaction to a sudden, intense noise or movement. When startled, the newborn arches it back, throws its head back, and flings out its arms and legs. Then the newborn rapidly closes its arms and legs to the center of the body. 147

morphology The rules for combining morphemes; morphemes are the smallest meaningful units of language. 319

motherese Talk to babies using a higher-than-normal pitch, more extreme intonation contours, simpler, more repetitive vocabulary, shorter utterances, and concentration on "here and now" communication. 324

multicultural model A model that promotes a pluralistic approach to understanding two or more cultures. This model argues that people can maintain their distinct identities while working with others from different cultures to meet common national or economic needs. 578

multiple-factor model of divorce effects   A model that takes into account the complexity of the divorce context and examines a number of influences on the child's development, including not only family structure, but also the strengths and weaknesses of the child prior to the divorce, the nature of the events surrounding the divorce itself, the type of custody involved, and visitation patterns. 487

multiple-factor theory   Thurstone's theory that intelligence consists of seven primary abilities: verbal comprehension, number ability, word fluency, spatial visualization, associative memory, reasoning, and perceptual speed.   291

myelination   A process in which nerve cells are insulated with a layer of fat cells, which increases the speed at which information travels through the nervous system.   174

myelin sheath   A layer of fat cells that encases most axons. The myelin sheath insulates the nerve cells and helps nerve impulses travel faster.   146

naturalistic observation   A method in which scientists observe behavior in real-world settings and make no effort to manipulate or control the situation.   56

natural selection   The evolutionary process that favors individuals of a species that are best adapted to survive and reproduce.   77

nature-nurture controversy   *Nature* refers to an organism's biological inheritance, *nurture* to environmental experience. The "nature" proponents claim that biological inheritance is the most important influence on development; the "nurture" proponents claim that environmental experiences are the most important.   19

negative affectivity (NA)   Emotions that are negatively toned, such as anxiety, anger, guilt, and sadness.   360

neglected children   Children who are infrequently nominated as a best friend but are not disliked by their peers.   507

neglectful parenting   A parenting style in which the parent is very uninvolved in the child's life; it is associated with children's social incompetence, especially a lack of self-control.   479

neo-Piagetians   Developmentalists who have elaborated on Piaget's theory, believing that children's cognitive development is more specific in many respects than he thought.   233

neurons   Nerve cells that handle information processing at the cellular level.   145

new couple, the   The second stage in the family life cycle, in which two individuals from separate families of origin unite to form a new family system.   474

nomothetic research   Research conducted at the group level in which individual variation is not a major focus.   64

nonnutritive sucking   Sucking behavior, unrelated to the infant's feeding, that is the primary response measure used to assess infant attention and learning.   148

nonshared environmental experiences   The child's own unique experiences, both within the family and outside the family, that are not shared by another sibling. Thus, experiences occurring within the family can be part of the "nonshared environment."   96

normal distribution   A symmetrical configuration of scores, with a majority of cases falling in the middle of the possible range of scores and few scores appearing toward the extremes of the range.   290

norms   Established standards of performance for a test.   289

obesity   Weighing 20 percent or more above the ideal weight for a particular age, taking both height and sex into account.   181

object permanence   The Piagetian term for one of an infant's most important accomplishments: understanding that objects and events continue to exist even when they cannot directly be seen, heard, or touched.   216

occipital lobe   The portion of the cerebrum involved in vision.   145

Oedipus complex   The Freudian concept that young children develop an intense desire to replace the parent of the same sex and enjoy the affections of the opposite-sex parent.   37

onlooker play   Play that occurs when a child watches other children play.   518

operant conditioning   Also called instrumental conditioning; a form of learning that occurs when the consequences of behavior produce changes in the probability that the behavior will occur.   46

operations   Internalized sets of actions that allow children to do mentally what before they had done physically.   219

oral rehydration therapy (ORT)   A treatment involving a range of techniques designed to prevent dehydration during episodes of diarrhea by giving children fluids by mouth.   180

oral stage   The first Freudian stage of development, occurring during the first 18 months of life, in which the infant's pleasure centers around the mouth.   37

ordinality   The property of numerical relation. Ordinal properties are numerical relations among things.   262

organic retardation   Mental retardation caused by a genetic disorder or brain damage; *organic* refers to the tissue or organs of the body, so there is some physical damage in organic retardation.   304

organization   Piaget's concept of grouping isolated behaviors into a higher-order, more smoothly functioning cognitive system; the grouping or arranging of items into categories. The use of organization improves long-term memory.   214, 252

organogenesis   The process of organ formation that takes place during the first 2 months of prenatal development.   109

original sin view   The idea, especially advocated during the Middle Ages, that children are basically born into the world as evil beings.   11

overextension   Children's tendency to misuse words by extending one word's meaning to include objects that are not related to, or are inappropriate for, the word's meaning.   328

oxytocin   A hormone that stimulates and regulates the rhythmicity of uterine contractions. It has been widely used as a drug to speed delivery. Controversy surrounds its use.   121

pain cry   A sudden appearance of loud crying without preliminary moaning and a long initial cry followed by an extended period of breath holding.   363

parallel play   Play that occurs separately from other children, but with toys like those the others are using or in a manner that mimics their play.   518

parietal lobe   The portion of the cerebrum involved in processing bodily sensations, such as touch.   145

passive genotype-environment interactions   The type of interactions that occur when the biological parents, who are genetically related to the child, provide a rearing environment for the child.   95

peers   Children of about the same age or maturity level.   505

perception   The interpretation of what is sensed.   155

performance orientation   Being concerned with the achievement outcome rather than the achievement process. Winning is what matters, and happiness is thought to result from winning.   563

personal fable An adolescent's sense of personal uniqueness and indestructibility. 228

perspective taking Taking another's point of view. 508

phallic stage The third Freudian stage of development, which occurs between the ages of 3 and 6; its name comes from the Latin word *phallus*, which means "penis." During this stage, the child's pleasure focuses on the genitals, and the child discovers that self-manipulation is enjoyable. 37

phenotype The way an individual's genotype is expressed in observed and measurable characteristics. 91

phenylketonuria (PKU) A genetic disorder in which an individual cannot properly metabolize an amino acid. PKU is now easily detected but, if left untreated, results in mental retardation and hyperactivity. 85

phobias Irrational fears. 45

phonology The study of a language's sound system. 317

phonotactics Allowable sound sequences; that is, certain sounds cannot appear in certain sequences within words or in certain positions within words. 317

placenta A life-support system that consists of a disk-shaped group of tissues in which small blood vessels from the mother and offspring intertwine but do not join. 107

play Pleasurable activity engaged in for its own sake. 516

play therapy Therapy that allows children to work off frustrations and is a medium through which therapists can analyze children's conflicts and ways of coping with them. Children may feel less threatened, and be more likely to express their true feelings, in the context of play. 518

pluralism The coexistence of distinct ethnic and cultural groups in the same society. 588

polygenic inheritance A genetic principle that the effects of many genes combine to produce a particular characteristic. 91

popular children Children who are frequently nominated as a best friend and are rarely disliked by their peers. 507

positive affectivity (PA) The range of positive emotions from high energy, enthusiasm, and excitement, to calm, quiet, and withdrawn. Joy, happiness, and laughter may involve PA. 360

possible self What individuals might become, what they would like to become, and what they are afraid of becoming. 384

postconventional reasoning The highest level in Kohlberg's theory of moral development. Morality is completely internalized. 437

postpartum period The period after childbirth or delivery. It is a time when the woman's body adjusts, both physically and psychologically, to having completed the process of childbearing. It lasts for about 6 weeks or until the body has completed its adjustment and has returned to a near prepregnant state. 127

power assertion A discipline technique in which a parent attempts to gain control over a child or a child's resources. 450

practice play Play that involves the repetition of behavior when new skills are being learned or when physical or mental mastery and coordination of skills are required for sports. 519

pragmatics The use of appropriate conversation and knowledge underlying the use of language in context. 320

precipitate delivery A delivery that takes place too rapidly; the baby squeezes through the birth canal in less than 10 minutes. 121

preconventional reasoning The lowest level in Kohlberg's theory of moral development. The child shows no internalization of moral values—moral reasoning is controlled by external rewards and punishments. 436

prejudice An unjustified negative attitude toward an individual because of that person's membership in a group. 389, 587

prenatal period The time from conception to birth. 17

preoperational stage The second Piagetian developmental stage, which lasts from about 2 to 7 years of age. Children begin to represent the world with words, images, and drawings. 42

prepared, or natural, childbirth A childbirth strategy that includes being informed about what will happen during the procedure, knowing about comfort measures for childbirth, anticipating that little or no medication will be used, and if complications arise, expecting to participate in decisions made to resolve the problems. 122

pretend/symbolic play Play that occurs when a child transforms the physical environment into a symbol. 520

preterm infant An infant born prior to 38 weeks after conception. 125

primary appraisal Children's interpretation of whether an event involves harm or loss that has already occurred, a threat to some future danger, or a challenge to be overcome. 367

primary circular reactions Schemes based on the infant's attempt to reproduce an interesting or pleasurable event that initially occurred by chance. 215

problem solving An attempt to find an appropriate way of attaining a goal when barriers prevent its immediate attainment. 263

Project Follow Through A program implemented in 1967 as an adjunct to Project Head Start. In the Follow Through programs, the enriched planned variation was carried through the first few years of elementary school. 547

Project Head Start A compensatory education program designed to give children from low-income families the opportunity to acquire the skills and experiences important for success in school. 547

proximodistal pattern The sequence in which growth starts at the center of the body and moves toward the extremities. 141

psychometrics The field that involves the assessment of individual differences. 287

psychosocial moratorium Erikson's term for the long gap between childhood security and adult autonomy that adolescents experience as part of their identity exploration. 393

puberty A period of rapid skeletal and sexual maturation that occurs mainly in early adolescence. 183

Public Law 94-142 The federal government's mandate to all states to provide a free, appropriate education for all children. A key provision of the bill is the development of individual education programs for children with a disability. 560

punishment A consequence that decreases the probability that a behavior will occur. 46

punishment and obedience orientation The first stage in Kohlberg's theory of moral development. Moral thinking is based on punishment. 436

questionnaire Similar to a highly structured interview except that respondents read the questions and mark their answers on paper rather than respond verbally to the interviewer. 57

race The term for a system for classifying plants and animals into subcategories according to specific physical and structural characteristics. 80

random assignment The assignment of subjects to experimental and control conditions by chance, which reduces the likelihood that the results of the experiment will be due to preexisting differences in the two groups. 60

reaction range The range of possible phenotypes for each genotype, suggesting the importance of an environment's restrictiveness or enrichment. 91

recasting Phrasing the same or a similar meaning of a sentence in a different way, perhaps turning it into a question. 324

reciprocal socialization Bidirectional socialization: Children socialize parents just as parents socialize them. 471

reflection A cognitive style in which individuals think before they act, usually scanning information carefully and slowly. 275

reflexes Automatic stimulus-response connections. 44

reflexive smile A smile that does not occur in response to external stimuli. It happens during the first month after birth, usually during irregular patterns of sleep, not when the infant is in an alert state. 363

Reggio Emilia An approach to early childhood education that views young children as competent, encourages them to learn by investigating and exploring topics that interest them, and uses a wide range of stimulating media and materials. 541

rehearsal Extended repetition of material after it has been presented. 251

reinforcement Also called reward; a consequence that increases the probability that a behavior will occur. 46

rejected children Children who are infrequently nominated as a best friend and are openly disliked by their peers. 507

reliability The extent to which a test yields a consistent, reproducible measure of performance. 287

REM (rapid eye movement) sleep A recurring sleep stage during which vivid dreams occur. 142

repression The most powerful and pervasive defense mechanism. It pushes unacceptable id impulses out of awareness and back into the unconscious mind. 36

reproduction The process that occurs when a female gamete (ovum) is fertilized by a male gamete (sperm). 82

rites of passage Ceremonies or rituals that mark an individual's transition from one status to another, especially into adulthood. 577

rooting reflex A newborn's built-in reaction that occurs when the infant's cheek is stroked or the side of the mouth is touched. In response, the infant turns its head toward the side that was touched, in an apparent effort to find something to suck. 147

scaffolding Parental behavior that supports children's efforts, allowing children to be more skillful than they would be if they relied only on their own abilities. 471

schema A cognitive structure, or network of associations, that organizes and guides an individual's perceptions; concepts and knowledge about events that influence how an individual interprets new information. 247, 413

scheme The basic unit of an organized pattern of sensorimotor functioning. 214

scientific method An approach that can be used to discover accurate information about behavior and development that includes the following steps: identify and analyze the problem, collect data, draw conclusions, and revise theories. 35

script A schema that focuses on the order of a predictable series of events. 248

secondary appraisal Children's evaluation of their resources and determination of how effectively they can cope with the event. 367

secondary circular reactions Piaget's third sensorimotor substage, which develops between 4 and 8 months of age. Infants become more object oriented or focused on the world, moving beyond preoccupation with the self in sensorimotor interactions. 215

secure attachment The infant uses a caregiver as a secure base from which to explore the environment. Ainsworth believes that secure attachment in the first year of life provides an important foundation for psychological development later in life. 350

selective attention The ability to focus mental effort on the stimuli that are important in a particular situation while ignoring other stimuli. 250

self-concept Domain-specific evaluations of the self. 388

self-esteem The global evaluative dimension of the self; also referred to as self-worth or self-image. 387

self-understanding The child's cognitive representation of the self; the substance and content of the child's self-conceptions. 381

semantic network The network of relations among key concepts in an individual's representation of a domain of knowledge. 257

semantics The meanings of words and sentences. 320

sensation The interaction of information with the sensory receptors—the eyes, ears, tongue, nostrils, and skin. 155

sensorimotor play Behavior engaged in by infants to derive pleasure from exercising their sensorimotor schemas. 519

sensorimotor stage The first of Piaget's developmental stages, which lasts from birth to about 2 years of age. Infants construct an understanding of the world by coordinating sensory experiences (such as seeing and hearing) with physical, motoric actions. 42

sensory memory Memory that holds information from the world in its original sensory form for not much longer than the brief instant of exposure to the visual, auditory, and other sensory stimuli. 246

separation Self-imposed withdrawal from the larger culture. 578

set point The weight one maintains when one makes no effort to gain or lose weight. 181

sexual script A stereotyped pattern of role prescriptions for how individuals should behave sexually. 190

shape constancy The recognition that an object remains the same shape even though its orientation to us changes. 158

shared environmental experiences Children's common environmental experiences that are shared with their siblings, such as their parents' personalities and intellectual orientation, the family's social class, and the neighborhood in which they live. 96

sickle-cell anemia A genetic disorder that affects the red blood cells and occurs most often in individuals of African descent. 86

simple reflexes Piaget's first sensorimotor substage, which corresponds to the first month after birth. The basic means of coordinating sensation and action is through reflexive behaviors, such as rooting and sucking, which infants have at birth. 215

size constancy The recognition that an object remains the same size even though the retinal image of the object changes. 158

slow-to-warm-up child A child who has a low activity level, is somewhat negative, shows low adaptability, and displays a low intensity of mood. 357

sociability The tendency to prefer the company of others to being alone. 357

social class A grouping of people with similar occupational, educational, and economic characteristics. Also called socioeconomic status, or SES. 580

social identity theory Social psychologist Henry Tajfel's theory that, when individuals are assigned to a group, they invariably think of that group as an in-group for them, because individuals want to have a positive self-image. 388

social learning theory A view that emphasizes behavior, environment, and cognition as the key factors in development. 47

social learning theory of gender The theory that children's gender development occurs through observation and imitation of gender behavior, as well as through the rewards and punishments they experience for gender-appropriate and gender-inappropriate behavior. 409

social play Play that involves social interaction with peers. 521

social policy A national government's course of action designed to influence the welfare of its citizens. 13

social smile A smile in response to an external stimulus. Early in development, it typically is in response to a face. 363

social system morality The fourth stage in Kohlberg's theory of moral development. Moral judgments are based on understanding the social order, law, justice, and duty. 436

sociobiology A view that relies on the principles of evolutionary biology to explain behavior. 78

socioemotional processes Changes in an individual's relationships with other people, emotions, and personality. 16

solitary play Play when a child is alone. 518

standardization The development of uniform procedures for administering and scoring a test. It also involves the development of norms for the test. 289

standardized tests Tests requiring an individual to answer a series of written or oral questions. They have two distinct features. First, psychologists usually total an individual's score to yield a single score, or set of scores, that reflects something about the individual. Second, psychologists compare the individual's score to the scores of a large group of similar people to determine how the individual responded relative to others. 57

status offenses Acts that, when committed by youth under a specified age, classify those children as juvenile delinquents. Included are such acts as running away, truancy, underage drinking, and sexual promiscuity. 455

stereotype A broad category that reflects our impressions and beliefs about people. All stereotypes involve an image of what the typical member of a particular group is like. 200

Strange Situation An observational measure of infant attachment that requires the infant to move through a series of introductions, separations, and reunions with the caregiver and an adult stranger in a prescribed order. 351

strategies Cognitive processes that do not occur automatically but require effort and work. 251

stress This is the response of individuals to the circumstances and events, called stressors, that threaten them and tax their coping abilities. 367

sucking reflex A newborn's built-in reaction of automatically sucking an object placed in its mouth. The sucking reflex enables the infant to get nourishment before it has associated a nipple with food. 147

sudden infant death syndrome (SIDS) A condition in which an infant stops breathing, usually during the night, and suddenly dies without an apparent cause. 142

superego The Freudian structure of personality that is the moral branch. The branch that takes into account whether something is right or wrong. 36

symbolic function substage The first substage of preoperational thought, occurring roughly between the ages of 2 and 4. In this substage, the young child gains the ability to represent mentally an object that is not present. 219

syntax The way words are combined to form acceptable phrases and sentences. 319

tabula rasa view The idea, proposed by John Locke, that children are not innately bad but instead are like a "blank tablet." 11

telegraphic speech The use of short, precise words to communicate; it is characteristic of young children's two-word utterances. 330

temperament An individual's behavioral style and characteristic way of responding. 356

temporal lobe The portion of the cerebrum involved in hearing. 145

teratogen From the Greek word *tera* meaning "monster"; any agent that causes a birth defect. The field of study that investigates the causes of birth defects is called teratology. 114

tertiary circular reactions Schemes in which the infant purposely explores new possibilities with objects, continually changing what is done to them and exploring the results. 216

tertiary circular reactions, novelty, and curiosity Piaget's fifth sensorimotor substage, which develops between 12 and 18 months of age. Infants become intrigued by the variety of properties that objects possess and by the multiplicity of things they can make happen to objects. 216

testosterone A hormone associated in boys with the development of genitals, an increase in height, and a change in voice. 185

test-retest reliability The extent to which a test yields the same measure of performance when an individual is given the same test on two different occasions. 287

theory A coherent set of ideas that helps explain data and make predictions. 35

top-dog phenomenon The circumstance of moving from the top position (in elementary school, the oldest, biggest, and most powerful students in the school) to the lowest position (in middle or junior high school, the youngest, smallest, and least powerful students in the school). 551

toxoplasmosis A mild infection that causes coldlike symptoms or no apparent illness in adults; a potential teratogen for the unborn baby, possibly causing eye defects, brain defects, and premature birth. 119

triarchic theory Sternberg's theory that intelligence consists of componential intelligence, experiential intelligence, and contextual intelligence. 292

trophoblast The outer layer of cells that develops during the germinal period. These cells provide nutrition and support for the embryo. 107

trust versus mistrust Erikson's first psychosocial stage, which is experienced in the first year of life. A sense of trust requires a feeling of physical comfort and a minimal amount of fear and apprehension about the future. 39

Turner syndrome A genetic disorder in which females are missing an X chromosome, making them XO instead of XX. 87

twin study A study in which the behavioral similarity of identical twins is compared with the behavioral similarity of fraternal twins. 93

two-factor theory Spearman's theory that children have both general intelligence, called g, and a number of specific types of intelligence, called s. 290

type A babies Infants who exhibit insecurity by avoiding a caregiver—for example, by failing to seek proximity. 350

type B babies Infants who use a caregiver as a secure base from which to explore the environment. 350

type C babies Infants who exhibit insecurity by resisting a caregiver—for example, by clinging but at the same time fighting against closeness. 350

ultrasound sonography A prenatal medical procedure in which high-frequency sound waves are directed into the pregnant woman's abdomen. 87

umbilical cord A life-support system, containing two arteries and one vein, that connects the baby to the placenta. 107

unconditioned response (UR) An unlearned response that is automatically associated with the US. 44

unconditioned stimulus (US) A stimulus that produces a response without prior learning. 44

underextension Children's tendency to extend the use of a noun to other events or objects it applies to. 328

universal ethical principles The sixth and highest stage in Kohlberg's theory of moral development. Individuals develop a moral standard based on universal human rights. 437

unoccupied play Play that occurs when a child is not engaging in play as it is commonly understood; the child may stand in one spot, look around the room, or perform random movements that do not seem to have a goal. 518

validity The extent to which a test measures what it is intended to measure. 288

values clarification An indirect moral education approach that focuses on helping students clarify what their lives are for and what is worth working for. 452

Wernicke's area An area of the brain's left hemisphere involved in language comprehension. 321

whole-language approach The view that reading instruction should parallel children's natural language learning, and that reading materials should be whole and meaningful. 334

wisdom Expert knowledge about the practical aspects of life. 232

working memory (short-term memory) A limited-capacity memory system in which information is retained for as long as 30 seconds unless it is rehearsed, in which case it can be retained longer. 247

XYY syndrome A genetic disorder in which males have an extra Y chromosome. 87

zone of proximal development (ZPD) Vygotsky's term for the range of tasks that are too difficult for children to master alone but that can be mastered with the guidance and assistance of adults or more highly skilled children. 234

zygote A single cell formed through fertilization. 82

REFERENCES

Aber, J. L. (1993, March). *Poverty and child development: The policy implications of understanding causal mechanisms.* Paper presented at the biennial meeting of the Society for Research in Child Development, New Orleans.

Aboud, F., & Skerry, S. (1983). Self and ethnic concepts in relation to ethnic constancy. *Canadian Journal of Behavioral Science, 15,* 3–34.

Abramovitch, R., Corter, C., Pepler, D. J., & Stanhope, L. (1986). Sibling and peer interaction: A final follow-up and comparison. *Child Development, 47,* 217–229.

Abramson, L. Y., Metalsky, G. I., & Alloy, L. B. (1989). Hopelessness depression: A theory-based subtype of depression. *Psychological Bulletin, 96,* 358–372.

Achenbach, T. M. (1991). *Integrative guide for the 1991 CBCL/4-18, YSR, and TRF Profiles.* Burlington: University of Vermont, Department of Psychiatry.

Achenbach, T. M., Phares, V., Howell, V. A., Rauh, V. A., & Nurcombe, B. (1990). Seven-year outcome of the Vermont Intervention Program for Low-Birthweight Infants. *Child Development, 61,* 1672–1681.

Ackerman, B. P. (1988). Thematic influences on children's judgments about story accuracy. *Child Development, 59,* 918–938.

Acredolo, L. P. (1978). The development of spatial orientation in infancy. *Developmental Psychology, 14,* 224–234.

Acredolo, L. P., Adams, A., & Goodwyn, S. W. (1984). The role of self-produced movement and visual tracking in infant spatial orientation. *Journal of Experimental Child Psychology, 38,* 312–327.

Acredolo, L. P., & Hake, J. L. (1982). Infant perception. In B. B. Wolman (Ed.), *Handbook of developmental psychology.* Englewood Cliffs, NJ: Prentice Hall.

Adams, M. J., Treiman, R., & Pressley, M. (1997). Reading, writing, and literacy. In I. E. Sigel & K. A. Renninger (Eds.), *Handbook of child psychology* (5th Ed., Vol. IV). New York: Wiley.

Adams, R. J. (1989). Newborns' discrimination among mid- and long-wavelength stimuli. *Journal of Experimental Child Psychology, 47,* 130–141.

Adato, A. (1995, April). Living legacy? Is heredity destiny? *Life,* pp. 60–68.

Adler, T. (1991, January). Seeing double? Controversial twins study is widely reported, debated. *APA Monitor, 22,* 1, 8.

Ainsworth, M. D. S. (1967). Infancy in Uganda: Infant care and the growth of love. In B. M. Caldwell & H. N. Riccuiti (Eds.), *Review of child development research* (Vol. 3). Chicago: University of Chicago Press.

Ainsworth, M. D. S. (1979). Infant-mother attachment. *American Psychologist, 34,* 932–937.

Alan Guttmacher Institute. (1990). *Adolescence sexuality.* New York: Author.

Albro, E. R. (1993, March). *The development of a story concept.* Paper presented at the biennial meeting of the Society for Research in Child Development, New Orleans.

Alexander, G. R., & Korenbrot, C. C. (1995). The role of prenatal care in preventing low birth weight. *The Future of Children, 5*(1), 103–120.

Alexander, K. L., & Entwisle, D. R. (1988). Achievement in the first two years of school: Patterns and processes. *Monographs of the Society for Research in Child Development, 53* (2, Serial No. 218).

Al-Issa, I., & Tousignant, M. (1997). *Ethnicity, immigration, and psychopathology.* New York: Plenum.

Allen, J. P., & Bell, K. L. (1995, March). *Attachment and communication with parent and peers in adolescence.* Paper presented at the meeting of the Society for Research in Child Development, Indianapolis.

Allen, J. P., & Kuperminc, G. P. (1995, March). *Adolescent attachment, social competence, and problematic behavior.* Paper presented at the meeting of the Society for Research in Child Development, Indianapolis.

Allen, L., & Majidi-Ahi, S. (1989). Black American children. In J. T. Gibbs & L. N. Huang (Eds.), *Children of color.* San Francisco: Jossey-Bass.

Amabile, T. M., & Hennessey, B. A. (1988). The motivation for creativity in children. In A. K. Boggiano & T. Pittman (Eds.), *Achievement motivation: A social-developmental perspective.* New York: Cambridge University Press.

America in Transition. (1989). Washington, DC: National Governors' Association Task Force on Children.

American Association for Protecting Children. (1986). *Highlights of official child neglect and abuse reporting: 1984.* Denver: American Humane Association.

American College Health Association. (1989, May). *Survey of AIDS on American college and university campuses.* Washington, DC: American College Health Association.

Ames, C., & Ames, R. (Eds.). (1989). *Research on motivation in education: Vol. 3. Goals and cognitions.* San Diego: Academic Press.

Amsterdam, B. K. (1968). *Mirror behavior in children under two years of age.* Unpublished doctoral dissertation, University of North Carolina, Chapel Hill.

Anastasi, A. (1988). *Psychological testing* (6th ed.). New York: Macmillan.

Anderman, E. M., Maehr, M. L., & Midgley, C. (1996). *Declining motivation after the transition to middle school: Schools can make a difference.* Unpublished manuscript, University of Kentucky, Lexington.

Anderson, D. R., Lorch, E., Field, D., Collins, P., & Nathan, J. (1986). Television viewing at home: Age trends in visual attention and time with TV. *Child Development, 52,* 151–157.

Anderson, K. J., & Leaper, C. (1996, March). *The social construction of emotion and gender between friends.* Paper presented at the meeting of the Society for Research on Adolescence, Boston.

Anderson, L. D. (1939). The predictive value of infant tests in relation to intelligence at 5 years. *Child Development, 10,* 202–212.

Anderson, N. (1996, June). *Socio-economic status and health.* Paper presented at the meeting of the American Psychological Society, San Francisco.

Antell, S. E., & Keating, D. P. (1983). Perception of numerical invariance in neonates. *Child Development, 54,* 695–701.

Archer, S. L. (1989). The status of identity: Reflections on the need for intervention. *Journal of Adolescence, 12,* 345–359.

Archer, S. L. (Ed.). (1994). *Intervention for adolescent identity development.* Newbury Park, CA: Sage.

Archer, S. L., & Waterman, A. S. (1994). Adolescent identity development: Contextual perspectives. In C. Fisher & R. Lerner (Eds.), *Applied developmental psychology.* New York: McGraw-Hill.

Arehart, D. M., & Smith, P. H. (1990). Identity in adolescence: Influences on dysfunction and psychosocial task issues. *Journal of Youth and Adolescence, 19,* 63–72.

Ariès, P. (1962). *Centuries of childhood* (R. Baldrick, Trans.). New York: Knopf.

Armsden, G., & Greenberg, M. T. (1984). *The inventory of parent and peer attachment: Individual differences and their relationship to psychological well-being in adolescence.* Unpublished manuscript, University of Washington.

Armsden, G., & Greenberg, M. T. (1987). The inventory of parent and peer attachment: Individual differences and their relationship to psychological well-being in adolescence. *Journal of Youth and Adolescence, 16,* 427–454.

Arnold, M. L. (1989, April). *Moral cognition and conduct: A quantitative review of the literature.* Paper presented at the Society for Research in Child Development meeting, Kansas City.

Aronson, E. (1986, August). *Teaching students things they think they already know about: The case of prejudice and desegregation.* Paper presented at the meeting of the American Psychological Association, Washington, DC.

Arrendondo, P. (1996). Multicultural counseling theory and Latino/Hispanic-American populations. In D. W. Sue (Ed.), *Theory of multicultural counseling and therapy.* Pacific Grove, CA: Brooks/Cole.

Arroyo, C. G., & Sternberg, R. J. (1993). *Against all odds: A view of the gifted disadvantaged.* New Haven, CT: Yale University, Department of Psychology.

Asarnow, J. R., & Callan, J. W. (1985). Boys with peer adjustment problems: Social cognitive processes. *Journal of Consulting and Clinical Psychology, 53,* 80–87.

Asian Week. (1990, June 29). Poll finds racial tension decreasing, p. 4.

Aslin, R. N., Jusczyk, P., & Pisoni, D. B. (1997). Speech and auditory processing during infancy. In D. Kuhn & R. S. Siegel (Eds.), *Handbook of child psychology* (5th Ed., Vol. II). New York: Wiley.

Astin, A. W., Korn, W. S., Sax, L. J., & Mahoney, K. M. (1994). *The American freshman.* Los Angeles: UCLA, Higher Education Research Institute.

Astin, A. W., Parrott, S. A., Korn, W. S., & Sax, L. J. (1997). *The American freshman: Thirty year trends.* Los Angeles, CA: Higher Education Research Institute, UCLA.

Atkinson, J. W., & Raynor, I. O. (1974). *Motivation and achievement.* Washington, DC: V. H. Winston & Sons.

Ayman-Nolley, S., & Church, R. B. (1993, March). *Social and cognitive mechanisms of learning through interaction with peers.* Paper presented at the biennial meeting of the Society for Research in Child Development, New Orleans.

Bachman, J. G., Johnston, L. P., & O'Malley, P. M. (1987). *Monitoring the future.* Ann Arbor: University of Michigan, Institute of Social Research.

Bacon, M. K., Child, I. L., & Barry, H. (1963). A cross-cultural study of correlates of crime. *Journal of Abnormal and Social Psychology, 66,* 291–300.

Bahr, S. J. (1989). Prologue: A developmental overview of the aging family. In S. J. Bahr & E. T. Peterson (Eds.), *Aging and the family.* Lexington, MA: Lexington Books.

Baillargeon, R. (1986). Representing the existence and the location of hidden objects: Object permanence in 6- and 8-month-old infants. *Cognition, 23,* 21–41.

Baillargeon, R. (1987). Object permanence in 3 1/2 and 4 1/2 month old infants. *Developmental Psychology, 23,* 655–664.

Baillargeon, R. (1995). The object concept revisited: New directions in the investigation of infants' physical knowledge. In C. E. Granrud (Ed.), *Visual perception and cognition in infancy.* Hillsdale, NJ: Erlbaum.

Baillargeon, R., DeVos, J., & Graber, M. (1989). Location memory in 8-month-old infants in a nonsearch AB task: Further evidence. *Cognitive Development, 4,* 345–367.

Bakeman, R., & Brown, J. V. (1980). Early interaction: Consequences for social and mental development at three years. *Child Development, 51,* 437–447.

Baker, L., & Brown, A. L. (1984). Metacognitive skills and reading. In P. D. Pearson (Ed.), *Handbook of reading research* (Part 2). New York: Longman.

Ballenger, M. (1983). Reading in the kindergarten: Comment. *Childhood Education, 59,* 187.

Ballou, M. (1996). Multicultural counseling theory and women. In D. W. Sue (Ed.), *Theory of multicultural counseling and therapy.* Pacific Grove, CA: Brooks/Cole.

Baltes, P. B. (1997, February). Interview. *APA Monitor, 28,* pp. 1, 9.

Baltes, P. B. (in press). On the incomplete architecture of human ontogeny. *American Psychologist.*

Baltes, P. B., Lindenberger, U., & Staudinger, U. M. (1997). Life-span theory in developmental psychology. In R. M. Lerner (Ed.), *Handbook of child psychology* (5th Ed., Vol. 1). New York: Wiley.

Baltes, P. B., Staudinger, U. M., Maercker, A., & Smith, J. (1995). People nominated as wise: A comparative study of wisdom-related knowledge. *Psychology and Aging, 10,* 155–166.

Bancroft, J. (1990). The impact of sociocultural influences on adolescent development: Further considerations. In J. Bancroft & J. Reinisch (Eds.), *Adolescence and puberty.* New York: Plenum.

Bandura, A. (1965). Influence of models' reinforcement contingencies on the acquisition of imitative responses. *Journal of Personality and Social Psychology, 1,* 589–595.

Bandura, A. (1977). *Social learning theory.* Englewood Cliffs, NJ: Prentice Hall.

Bandura, A. (1986). *Social foundations of thought and action: A social cognitive theory.* Englewood Cliffs, NJ: Prentice Hall.

Bandura, A. (1991). Social cognitive theory of moral thought and action. In W. M. Kurtines & J. Gewirtz (Eds.), *Handbook of moral behavior and development* (Vol. 1). Hillsdale, NJ: Erlbaum.

Bandura, A. (1997). *Self-efficacy: The exercise of self-control.* New York: W. H. Freeman.

Banks, E. C. (1993, March). *Moral education curriculum in a multicultural context: The Malaysian primary curriculum.* Paper presented at the biennial meeting of the Society for Research in Child Development, New Orleans.

Banks, M. S., & Salapatek, P. (1983). Infant visual perception. In P. H. Mussen (Ed.), *Handbook of child psychology* (4th ed., Vol. 2). New York: Wiley.

Barber, B. L., Clark, J. J., Clossick, M. L., & Wamboldt, P. (1992, March). *The effects of parent-adolescent communication on adjustment: Variations across divorced and intact families.* Paper presented at the meeting of the Society for Research on Adolescence, Washington, DC.

Barker, R., & Wright, H. F. (1951). *One boy's day.* New York: Harper & Row.

Barkow, J., Cosmides, L., & Tooby, J. (Eds.). (1992). *The adapted mind.* New York: Oxford University Press.

Barnard, K. E., & Martell, L. K. (1995). Mothering. In M. H. Bornstein (Ed.), *Handbook of parenting* (Vol. 3). Hillsdale, NJ: Erlbaum.

Barnett, D., & McGee, R. (1993, March). *Advances in the operationalization and quantification of child maltreatment: Implications for developmental theory, research, and social policy.* Paper presented at the biennial meeting of the Society for Research in Child Development, New Orleans.

Baron, N. S. (1992). *Growing up with language*. Reading, MA: Addison-Wesley.

Barr, R. G., Desilets, J., & Rotman, A. (1991, April). *Parsing the normal crying curve. Is it really the evening fussing curve?* Paper presented at the biennial meeting of the Society for Research in Child Development, Seattle.

Barrett, D. E., Radke-Yarrow, M., & Klein, R. E. (1982). Chronic malnutrition and child behavior: Effects of calorie supplementation on social and emotional functioning at school age. *Developmental Psychology, 18,* 541–556.

Barrett, K. C. (1995, March). *Functionalism, contextualism, and emotional development.* Paper presented at the meeting of the Society for Research in Child Development, Indianapolis.

Barron, F. (1989, April). The birth of a notion: Exercises to tap your creative potential. *Omni,* pp. 112–119.

Baskett, L. M., & Johnston, S. M. (1982). The young child's interaction with parents versus siblings. *Child Development, 53,* 643–650.

Bat-Chava, Y., Allen, L., Aber, J. L., & Seidman, E. (1997, April). *Racial and ethnic identity and the contexts of development.* Paper presented at the meeting of the Society for Research in Child Development, Washington, DC.

Bates, A. S., Fitzgerald, J. F., Dittus, R. S., & Wollinsky, F. D. (1994). Risk factors for underimmunization in poor urban infants. *Journal of the American Medical Association, 272,* 1105–1109.

Bates, E., & Thal, D. (1991). Associations and dissociations in language development. In J. Millder (Ed.), *Research on language disorders: A decade of progress.* Austin: Pro-Ed.

Batson, C. D. (1989). Personal values, moral principles, and the three path model of prosocial motivation. In N. Eisenberg & J. Reykowski (Eds.), *Social and moral values.* Hillsdale, NJ: Erlbaum.

Bauer, P. J. (1996). What do infants recall of their lives? *American Psychologist, 51,* 29–41.

Bauer, P. J., & Dow, G. A. A. (1994). Episodic memory in 16- and 20-month-old children: Specifics are generalized. *Developmental Psychology, 30,* 403–417.

Bauer, P. J., & Hertsgaard, L. A. (1993). Increasing steps in recall of events: Factors facilitating immediate and long-term memory in 13.5- and 16.5-month-old children. *Child Development, 64,* 1204–1223.

Baumrind, D. (1971). Current patterns of parental authority. *Developmental Psychology Monographs, 4* (1, Pt. 2).

Baumrind, D. (1989, April). *Sex-differentiated socialization effects in childhood and adolescence.* Paper presented at the biennial meeting of the Society for Research in Child Development, Kansas City.

Baumrind, D. (1993). The average expectable environment is not good enough: A response to Scarr. *Child Development, 64,* 1299–1317.

Baydar, N., Brooks-Gunn, J., & Warren, M. P. (1992). *Changes in depressive symptoms in adolescent girls over four years: The effects of pubertal maturation and life events.* Unpublished manuscript, Department of Psychology, Columbia University, New York.

Bayley, N. (1943). Mental growth during the first three years. In R. G. Barker, J. S. Kounin, & H. F. Wright (Eds.), *Child behavior and development.* New York: McGraw-Hill.

Bayley, N. (1969). *Manual for the Bayley Scales of infant development.* New York: Psychological Corp.

Bayley, N. (1970). Development of mental abilities. In P. H. Mussen (Ed.), *Manual of child psychology* (3rd ed., Vol. 1). New York: Wiley.

Beagles-Roos, J., & Gat, I. (1983). Specific impact of radio and television in children's story comprehension. *Journal of Educational Psychology, 75,* 128–137.

Beal, C. R. (1990). The development of text evaluation and revision skills. *Child Development, 61,* 247–258.

Beal, C. R. (1994). *Boys and girls: The development of gender roles.* New York: McGraw-Hill.

Bean, C. R. (1990). *Methods of childbirth* (rev. ed.). New York: Quill.

Beardslee, W. R., & Richmond, J. B. (1992). Day care and preschool programs. In R. A. Hoekelman, S. B. Friedman, N. M. Nelson, & S. H. Seidel (Eds.), *Primary pediatric care* (2nd ed.). St. Louis: Mosby Yearbook.

Bechtold, A. G., Busnell, E. W., & Salapatek, P. (1979, April.) *Infants' visual localization of visual and auditory targets.* Paper presented at the meeting of the Society for Research in Child Development, San Francisco.

Beck, A. T. (1973). *The diagnosis and management of depression.* Philadelphia: University of Pennsylvania Press.

Beck, I. L., & McKeown, M. G. (1984). Application of theories of reading to instruction. *American Journal of Education, 93,* 61–81.

Becker, H. J., & Sterling, C. W. (1987). Equity in school computer use: National data and neglected considerations. *Journal of Educational Computing Research, 3,* 289–311.

Bednar, R. L., Wells, M. G., & Peterson, S. R. (1995). *Self-esteem* (2nd ed.). Washington, DC: American Psychological Association.

Bell, A. P., Weinberg, M. S., & Mammersmith, S. K. (1981). *Sexual preference: Its development in men and women.* New York: Simon & Schuster.

Bell, D. (Ed.). (1980). *Shades of brown: New perspectives on school desegregation.* New York: Teachers College Press.

Bell, K. L. (1995, March). *Attachment and flexibility at self-presentation during the transition to adulthood.* Paper presented at the meeting of the Society for Research in Child Development, Indianapolis.

Bell, S. M., & Ainsworth, M. D. S. (1972). Infant crying and maternal responsiveness. *Child Development, 43,* 1171–1190.

Bell-Scott, P., & Taylor, R. L. (1989). Introduction: The multiple ecologies of black adolescent development. *Journal of Adolescent Research, 4,* 117–118.

Bellinger, D., Leviton, A., Waternaux, C., Needleman, H., & Rabinowitz, M. (1987). Longitudinal analysis of prenatal and postnatal lead exposure and early cognitive development. *New England Journal of Medicine, 316,* 1037–1043.

Belsky, J. (1981). Early human experience: A family perspective. *Developmental Psychology, 17,* 3–23.

Belsky, J. (1989). Infant-parent attachment and day care: In defense of the strange situation. In J. S. Lande, S. Scarr, & N. Gunzenhauser (Eds.), *Caring for children: Challenge to America.* Hillsdale, NJ: Erlbaum.

Belsky, J. (1992). Consequences of child care for children's development: A deconstructionist view. In A. Booth (Ed.), *Child care in the 1990s.* Hillsdale, NJ: Erlbaum.

Belson, W. (1978). *Television violence and the adolescent boy.* London: Saxon House.

Bem, S. L. (1977). On the utility of alternative procedures for assessing psychological androgyny. *Journal of Consulting and Clinical Psychology, 45,* 196–205.

Bem, S. L. (1981). Gender schema theory: A cognitive account of sex-typing. *Psychological Review, 88,* 354–364.

Bennett, W. J. (1986). *First lessons: A report on elementary education in America.* Washington, DC: U.S. Government Printing Office.

Bennett, W. J. (1991). *The book of virtues.* New York: HarperCollins.

Benninga, J. S. (1988, February). An emerging synthesis in moral education. *Phi Delta Kappan*, pp. 415–418.

Benson, P. (1993). *The troubled journey: A portrait of 6th–12th grade youth.* Minneapolis: Search Institute.

Berg, C. A., & Sansone, C. (1991, April). *To plan or not to plan? Paper presented at the Society for Research in Child Development meeting, Seattle.*

Bergen, D. (1988). Stages of play development. In D. Bergen (Ed.), *Play as a medium for learning and development.* Portsmouth, NH: Heinemann.

Bergman, S. J. (1995). Men's psychology development: A relational perspective. In R. F. Levant & W. S. Pollack (Eds.), *A new psychology of men.* New York: Basic Books.

Berk, S. F. (1985). *The gender factory: The apportionment of work in American households.* New York: Plenum.

Berko, J. (1958). The child's learning of English morphology. *Word, 14,* 150–177.

Berkowitz, M., & Gibbs, J. (1983). Measuring the developmental features of moral discussion. *Merrill-Palmer Quarterly, 29,* 399–410.

Berlin, L. (1993, March). *Attachment and emotions in preschool children.* Paper presented at the biennial meeting of the Society for Research in Child Development, New Orleans.

Berlyne, D. E. (1960). *Conflict, arousal, and curiosity.* New York: McGraw-Hill.

Berndt, T. J. (1979). Developmental changes in conformity to peers and parents. *Developmental Psychology, 15,* 608–616.

Berndt, T. J. (1982). The features and effects of friendships in early adolescence. *Child Development, 53,* 1447–1460.

Berndt, T. J. (1996). Transitions in friendships and friends' influence. In J. A. Graber, J. Brooks-Gunn, & A. C. Petersen (Eds.), *Transitions through adolescence.* Hillsdale, NJ: Erlbaum.

Berndt, T. J., Hawkins, J. A., & Hoyle, S. G. (1986). Changes in friendship during a school year: Effects on children's and adolescents' impressions of friendship and sharing with friends. *Child Development, 57,* 1284–1297.

Berndt, T. J., & Perry, T. B. (1990). Distinctive features and effects of early adolescent friendships. In R. Montemayor (Ed.), *Advances in adolescent research.* Greenwich, CT: JAI Press.

Berrueta-Clement, J., Schweinhart, L., Barnett, W., & Weikart, D. (1986). The effects of early educational intervention on crime and delinquency in adolescence and early adulthood. In J. Burchard & S. Burchard (Eds.), *Prevention of delinquent behavior.* Newbury Park, CA: Sage.

Berry, J. W. (1971). Ecological and cultural factors in spatial perceptual development. *Canadian Journal of Behavioral Science, 3,* 324–336.

Berry, J. W. (1983). Textured contexts: Systems and situations in cross-cultural psychology. In S. H. Irvine & J. W. Berry (Eds.), *Human assessment and cultural factors.* New York: Plenum.

Berry, J. W. (1990). Psychology of acculturation: Understanding individuals moving between cultures. In R. W. Brislin (Ed.), *Applied cross-cultural psychology.* Newbury Park, CA: Sage.

Bertenthal, B., & Clifton, R. K. (1997). Perception and action. In D. Kuhn & R. S. Siegler (Eds.), *Handbook of child psychology* (5th Ed., Vol. II). New York: Wiley.

Bertenthal, B. I. (1993). Infants' perception of biomechanical motions: Intrinsic image and knowledge-based constraints. In C. E. Granrud (Ed.), *Visual perception and cognition in infancy.* Hillsdale, NJ: Erlbaum.

Bertenthal, B. I., Campos, J. J., & Barrett, K. C. (1984). Self-produced locomotion: An organizer of emotional, cognitive, and social development in infancy. In R. Emde and R. Harmon (Eds.), *Continuities and discontinuities in development.* New York: Plenum.

Bierman, K. L., Smoot, D. L., & Aumiller, K. (1993). Characteristics of aggressive-rejected, aggressive (nonrejected), and rejected (nonaggressive) boys. *Child Development, 64,* 139–151.

Bigler, R. S., & Liben, L. S. (in press). Cognitive mechanisms in children's gender stereotyping: Theoretical and educational implications of a cognitive-based intervention. *Child Development.*

Bigler, R. S., Liben, L. S., & Yekel, C. A. (1992, August). *Developmental patterns of gender-related beliefs: Beyond unitary constructs and measures.* Paper presented at the meeting of the American Psychological Association, Washington, DC.

Biller, H. B. (1993). *Fathers and families: Paternal factors in child development.* Westport, CT: Auburn House.

Birch, S. H. (1995, March). *The teacher-child relationship and children's early school adjustment.* Paper presented at the meeting of the Society for Research in Child Development, Indianapolis.

Bjorklund, D. F.(1997). In search of a metatheory for cognitive development (or, Piaget is dead and I don't feel so good myself). *Child Development, 68,* 144-148.

Bjorklund, D. F., & Harnishfeger, K. K. (1987). Developmental differences in the mental effort requirements for the use of an organizational strategy in free recall. *Journal of Experimental Child Psychology, 44,* 109–125.

Black, A. E., & Pedro-Carroll, J. L. (1993, March). *The long-term effects of interpersonal conflict and parental divorce among late adolescents.* Paper presented at the biennial meeting of the Society for Research in Child Development, New Orleans.

Black, K. A., & McCartney, K. (1995, March). *Associations between adolescent attachment to parents and peer interactions.* Paper presented at the meeting of the Society for Research in Child Development, Indianapolis.

Blair, C., & Ramey, C. (1996). Early intervention with low birth weight infants: The path to second generation research. In M. J. Guralnick (Ed.), *The effectiveness of early intervention.* Baltimore: Paul H. Brookes.

Blakemore, J. E. O. (1993, March). *Preschool children's interest in babies: Observations in naturally occurring situations.* Paper presented at the biennial meeting of the Society for Research in Child Development, New Orleans.

Blash, R., & Unger, D. G. (1992, March). *Cultural factors and the self-esteem and aspirations of African-American adolescent males.* Paper presented at the meeting of the Society for Research on Adolescence, Washington, DC.

Blasi, A. (1988). Identity and the development of the self. In D. Lapsley & F. C. Power (Eds.), *Self, ego, and identity: Integrative approaches.* New York: Springer-Verlag.

Bloom, L. (1997). Language acquisition in developmental contexts. In D. Kuhn & R. S. Siegler (Eds.), *Handbook of child psychology* (5th Ed., Vol. II). New York: Wiley.

Blos, P. (1989). The inner world of the adolescent. In A. H. Esman (Ed.), *International annals of adolescent psychiatry* (Vol. 1). Chicago: University of Chicago Press.

Blumenfeld, P. C., Pintrich, P. R., Wessles, K., & Meece, J. (1981, April). *Age and sex differences in the impact of classroom experiences on self-perceptions.* Paper presented at the biennial meeting of the Society for Research in Child Development, Boston.

Bly, R. (1990). *Iron John.* New York: Vintage Books.

Bonvillian, J. D., Orlansky, M. D., & Novack, L. L. (1983). Developmental milestones: Sign language and motor development. *Child Development, 54,* 1435–1445.

Booth, A., & Dunn, J. F. (Eds.). (1996). The effectiveness of providing social support for families of children at risk. In M. J. Guralnick (Ed.), *The effectiveness of early intervention.* Baltimore: Paul Brookes.

Bordelon, K. W. (1985). Sexism in reading materials. *Reading Teacher, 38,* 792–797.

Boring, E. G. (1950). *A history of experimental psychology.* New York: Appleton-Century-Crofts.

Bornstein, M. H. (1989). Stability in early mental development. In M. H. Bornstein & N. A. Krasnegor (Eds.), *Stability and continuity in mental development.* Hillsdale, NJ: Erlbaum.

Bornstein, M. H., & Krasnegor, N. A. (1989). *Stability and continuity in mental development.* Hillsdale, NJ: Erlbaum.

Bornstein, M. H., & Sigman, M. D. (1986). Continuity in mental development from infancy. *Child Development, 57,* 251–274.

Bouchard, T. J., Lykken, D. T., McGue, M., Segal, N. L., & Tellegen, A. (1990). Source of human psychological differences: The Minnesota Study of Twins Reared Apart. *Science, 250,* 223–228.

Bouchard, T. J., Lykken, D. T., Tellegen, A., & McGue, M. (1996). Genes, drives, environment, and experience. In D. Lubinski & C. Benbow (Eds.), *Psychometrics and social issues concerning intellectual talent.* Baltimore: Johns Hopkins University Press.

Bower, B. (1985). The left hand of math and verbal talent. *Science News, 127,* 263.

Bower, T. G. R. (1966). Slant perception and shape constancy in infants. *Science, 151,* 832–834.

Bower, T. G. R. (1977). *A primer of infant development.* New York: W. H. Freeman.

Bower, T. G. R. (1989). *The rational infant.* San Francisco: W. H. Freeman.

Bower, T. G. R. (1996, January). Personal communication. Program in Psychology and Human Development, University of Texas at Dallas, Richardson, TX.

Bowlby, J. (1969). *Attachment and loss* (Vol. 1). London: Hogarth Press.

Bowlby, J. (1989). *Secure and insecure attachment.* New York: Basic Books.

Bowser, B. P., & Hunt, R. G. (Eds.). (1996). *Impacts of racism on White Americans.* Newbury Park, CA: Sage.

Boyes, M. C., Giordano, R., & Galperyn, K. (1993, March). *Moral orientation and interpretive contexts of moral deliberation.* Paper presented at the biennial meeting of the Society for Research in Child Development, New Orleans.

Brackbill, Y. (1979). Obstetric medication and infant behavior. In J. D. Osofsky (Ed.), *Handbook of infant development.* New York: Wiley.

Bracken, M. B., Eskenazi, B., Sachse, K., McSharry, J., Hellenbrand, K., & Leo-Summers, L. (1990). Association of cocaine use with sperm concentration, motility, and morphology. *Fertility and Sterility, 53,* 315–322.

Braham, P., Rattansi, A., & Skellington, R. (Eds.). (1992). *Racism and anti-racism.* Newbury Park, CA: Sage.

Braungart, J. M., Plomin, R., Defries, J. C., & Fulker, D. W. (1992). Genetic influence on tester-rated infant temperament as assessed by Bayley's Infant Behavior Record: Nonadoptive and adoptive siblings and twins. *Developmental Psychology, 28,* 40–47.

Brazelton, T. B. (1956). Sucking in infancy. *Pediatrics, 17,* 400–404.

Brazelton, T. B. (1973). *Neonatal behavioral assessment scale.* London: Heinemann Medical Books.

Brazelton, T. B. (1983). *Infants and mothers: Differences in development.* New York: Delta.

Brazelton, T. B., Nugent, J. K., & Lester, B. M. (1987). Neonatal Behavioral Assessment Scale. In J. D. Osofsky (Ed.), *Handbook of infant development* (2nd ed.). New York: Wiley.

Bredekamp, S. (1987). *Developmentally appropriate practice in early childhood programs serving children from birth through age 8.* Washington, DC: National Association for the Education of Young Children.

Bredekamp, S. (1993). Reflections on Reggio Emilia. *Young Children, 49,* 13–16.

Bredekamp, S., & Shepard, L. (1989). How to best protect children from inappropriate school expectations, practices, and policies. *Young Children, 44,* 14–24.

Bretherton, I. (1996). Attachment theory and research in historical and personal context. *Contemporary Psychology, 41,* 236–237.

Bretherton, I., Fritz, J., Zahn-Waxler, C., & Ridgeway, D. (1986). Learning to talk about emotions. *Child Development, 57,* 529–548.

Brewer, M. B., & Campbell, D. T. (1976). *Ethnocentrism and intergroup attitudes.* New York: Wiley.

Bridgman, A. (1997, April). *The board on children, youth, and families: Dissemination and communication activities.* Paper presented at the meeting of the Society for Research in Child Development, Washington, DC.

Brislin, R. (1993). *Culture's influence on behavior.* Fort Worth, TX: Harcourt Brace.

Brislin, R. (1993). *Understanding culture's influence on behavior.* Fort Worth, TX: Harcourt Brace.

Brislin, R. W. (1990). Applied cross-cultural psychology: An introduction. In R. W. Brislin (Ed.), *Applied cross-cultural psychology.* Newbury Park, CA: Sage.

Brody, G. H., & Shaffer, D. R. (1982). Contributions of parents and peers to children's moral socialization. *Developmental Review, 2,* 31–75.

Brody, G. H., Stoneman, Z., Flor, D., McCrary, C., Hastings, L., & Conyers, O. (1994). Functional resources, parent psychological functioning, parent co-caregiving, and early adolescent competence in rural two-parent African-American families. *Child Development, 65,* 590–605.

Brodzinsky, D. M., Lang, R., & Smith, D. W. (1995). Parenting adopted children. In M. H. Bornstein (Ed.), *Handbook of parenting* (Vol. 3). Hillsdale, NJ: Erlbaum.

Brodzinsky, D. M., Schechter, D. E., Braff, A. M., & Singer, L. M. (1984). Psychological and academic adjustment in adopted children. *Journal of Consulting and Clinical Psychology, 52,* 582–590.

Bronfenbrenner, U. (1986). Ecology of the family as a context for human development: Research perspectives. *Developmental Psychology, 22,* 723–742.

Bronfenbrenner, U. (1995). Developmental ecology through space and time: A future perspective. In P. Moen, G. H. Elder, & K. Luscher (Eds.), *Examining lives in context.* Washington, DC: American Psychological Association.

Bronfenbrenner, U. (1995). The bioecological model from a life course perspective. In P. Moen, G. H. Elder, & K. Luscher (Eds.), *Examining lives in context.* Washington, DC: American Psychological Association.

Bronfenbrenner, U. (1995, March). *The role research has played in Head Start.* Paper presented at the meeting of the Society for Research in Child Development, Indianapolis.

Bronfenbrenner, U., & Morris, P. A. (1997). The ecology of developmental processes. In R. M. Lerner (Ed.), *Handbook of child psychology* (5th Ed., Vol. 1). New York: Wiley.

Bronstein, P., Stoll, M. F., Clausen, J., & Abrams, C. L. (1994). *Fathering after separation or divorce: Which dads make a difference?* Unpublished manuscript, Department of Psychology, University of Vermont, Burlington.

Brooks-Gunn, J. (1991). Maturational timing variations in adolescent girls, antecedents of. In R. M. Lerner, A. C. Petersen, & J. Brooks-Gunn (Eds.), *Encyclopedia of adolescence* (Vol. 2). New York: Garland.

Brooks-Gunn, J., & Chase-Lansdale, P. L. (1995). Adolescent parenthood. In M. H. Bornstein (Ed.), *Children and parenting* (Vol. 3). Hillsdale, NJ: Erlbaum.

Brooks-Gunn, J., Graber, J. A., & Paikoff, R. L. (1994). Studying links between hormones and negative affect: Models and measures. *Journal of Research on Adolescence, 4*, 469–486.

Brooks-Gunn, J., Klebanov, P. K., & Duncan, G. J. (1996). Ethnic differences in children's intelligence test scores: Role of economic deprivation, home environment, and maternal characteristics. *Child Development, 67*, 396–408.

Brooks-Gunn, J., Klebanov, P. K., & McCarton, C. (1997, April). *Neighborhood and family risk factors: Links to development in the first three years of life.* Paper presented at the meeting of the Society for Research in Child Development, Washington, DC.

Brooks-Gunn, J., & Matthews, W. S. (1979). *He and she: How children develop their sex role identity.* Englewood Cliffs, NJ: Prentice Hall.

Brooks-Gunn, J., McCarton, C., & Tonascia, J. (1992, May). *Enhancing the development of LBW, premature infants: Defining risk and targeting subgroups in the Infant Health and Development Program.* Paper presented at the International Conference on Infant Studies, Miami Beach.

Brooks-Gunn, J., & Paikoff, R. (in press). Sexuality and developmental transitions during adolescence. In J. Schulenberg, J. Maggs, & K. Hurrelmann (Eds.), *Health risks and developmental transitions during adolescence.* New York: Cambridge University Press.

Brooks-Gunn, J., & Paikoff, R. L. (1993). "Sex is a gamble, kissing is a game": Adolescent sexuality and health promotion. In S. G. Millstein, A. C. Petersen, & E. O. Nightingale (Eds.), *Promoting the health of adolescents.* New York: Oxford University Press.

Brooks-Gunn, J., & Warren, M. P. (1989, April). *How important are pubertal and social events for different problem behaviors and contexts?* Paper presented at the biennial meeting of the Society for Research in Child Development, Kansas City.

Broughton, J. M. (1978). Development of concepts of self, mind, reality, and knowledge. In W. Damon (Ed.), *Social cognition.* San Francisco: Jossey-Bass.

Broughton, J. M. (1983). The cognitive developmental theory of self and identity. In B. Lee & G. Noam (Eds.), *Developmental approaches to self.* New York: Plenum.

Broverman, I., Vogel, S., Broverman, D., Clarkson, F., & Rosenkranz, P. (1972). Sex-role stereotypes: A current appraisal. *Journal of Social Issues, 28*, 59–78.

Brower, A. V. Z. (1996). Parallel race formation and the evolution of mimicry in *Heliconius* butterflies: A phylogenetic hypothesis from mitochondrial DNA sequences. *Evolution, 50*, 195–221.

Brown, A. C., & Orthner, D. K. (1990). Relocation and personal well-being among early adolescents. *Journal of Early Adolescence, 10*, 366–381.

Brown, A. L. (1990). Domain-specific principles affect learning and transfer in children. *Cognitive Science, 14*, 107–133.

Brown, A. L., & DeLoache, J. S. (1978). Skills, plans, and self-regulation. In R. S. Siegler (Ed.), *Children's thinking: What develops?* Hillsdale, NJ: Erlbaum.

Brown, A. L., Kane, M. J., & Echols, K. (1986). Young children's mental models determine analogical transfer across problems with a common goal structure. *Cognitive Development, 1*, 103–122.

Brown, A. L., & Palincsar, A. M. (1984). Reciprocal teaching of comprehension-fostering and monitoring activities. *Cognition and Instruction, 1*, 175–177.

Brown, A. L., & Palincsar, A. M. (1989). Guided, cooperative learning and individual knowledge acquisition. In L. G. Resnick (Ed.), *Knowing and learning: Essays in honor of Robert Glaser.* Hillsdale, NJ: Erlbaum.

Brown, B. B., Dolcini, M. M., & Leventhal, A. (1995, March). *The emergence of peer crowds: Friend or foe to adolescent health?* Paper presented at the meeting of the Society for Research in Child Development, Indianapolis.

Brown, B. B., & Huang, B.-H. (1995). Examining parenting practices in different peer contexts: Implications for adolescent trajectories. In L. J. Crockett & A. C. Crouter (Eds.), *Pathways through adolescence.* Hillsdale, NJ: Erlbaum.

Brown, B. B., & Lohr, M. J. (1987). Peer group affiliation and adolescent self-esteem: An integration of ego identity and symbolic interaction theories. *Journal of Personality and Social Psychology, 52*, 47–55.

Brown, B. B., Mory, M., & Kinney, D. A. (1994). Casting adolescent crowds in relational perspective: Caricature, channel, and context. In R. Montemayor, G. R. Adams, & T. P. Gulotta (Eds.), *Advances in adolescent development: Vol. 6. Personal relationships during adolescence.* Newbury Park, CA: Sage.

Brown, B. B., & Mounts, N. S. (1989, April). *Peer group structures in single versus multiethnic high schools.* Paper presented at the meeting of the Society for Research in Child Development, Kansas City.

Brown, B. B., Steinberg, L., Mounts, N., & Philipp, M. (1990, March). *The comparative influence of peers and parents on high school achievement: Ethnic differences.* Paper presented at the meeting of the Society for Research on Adolescence, Atlanta.

Brown, B. B., & Theobald, W. (1996, March). *Is teenage romance hazardous to adolescent health?* Paper presented at the meeting of the Society for Research on Adolescence, Boston.

Brown, J. S., & Burton, R. B. (1978). Diagnostic models for procedural bugs in basic mathematical skills. *Cognitive Science, 2*, 155–192.

Brown, R. (1973). *A first language: The early stages.* Cambridge, MA: Harvard University Press.

Brown, R. (1986). *Social psychology* (2nd ed.). New York: Free Press.

Browne, C. R., Brown, J. V., Blumenthal, J., Anderson, L., & Johnson, P. (1993, March). *African-American fathering: The perception of mothers and sons.* Paper presented at the biennial meeting of the Society for Research in Child Development, New Orleans.

Brownell, K. D. (1990, August). *Dieting, weight, and body image: Where culture and physiology collide.* Paper presented at the meeting of the American Psychological Association, Boston.

Brubaker, T. H. (1985). *Later life families.* Newbury Park, CA: Sage.

Bruner, J. (1997, April). Discussant on symposium, *Social foundations of language development.* Society for Research in Child Development, Washington, DC.

Bruner, J. S. (1983). *Child talk.* New York: W. W. Norton.

Bruner, J. S. (1989, April). *The state of developmental psychology.* Paper presented at the meeting of the Society for Research in Child Development, Kansas City.

Bryne, R. (1997). Evolution and sociobiology. In P. Scott & C. Spencer (Eds.), *Psychology.* Cambridge, MA: Blackwell.

Brynes, J. P. (1993). Analyzing perspectives on rationality and critical thinking: A commentary on the *Merrill-Palmer Quarterly* invitational issue. *Merrill-Palmer Quarterly, 39*, 159–171.

Bryon, Y. J., Pang, S., Wei, L. S., Dickover, R., Diange, A., and Chen, I. S. Y. (1995). Clearance of HIV infection in a perinatally infected infant. *New England Journal of Medicine, 332*, 833–838.

Buchanan, C. M., Maccoby, E. E., & Dornbusch, S. M. (1992). Adolescents and their families after divorce: Three residential arrangements compared. *Journal of Research in Adolescence, 2*(3), 261–291.

Budwig, N. (1993). *A developmental functionalist approach to child language.* Hillsdale, NJ: Erlbaum.

Buhrmester, D. (1989). *Changes in friendship, interpersonal competence, and social adaptation during early adolescence.* Unpublished manuscript, Department of Psychology, UCLA, Los Angeles.

Buhrmester, D. (1990). Friendship, interpersonal competence, and adjustment in preadolescence and adolescence. *Child Development, 61,* 1101–1111.

Buhrmester, D. (1993, March). *Adolescent friendship and the socialization of gender differences in social interaction styles.* Paper presented at the biennial meeting of the Society for Research in Child Development, New Orleans.

Buhrmester, D. (1996, January). Personal communication, Program in Psychology, University of Texas at Dallas, Richardson, TX.

Buhrmester, D., & Furman, W. (1987). The development of companionship and intimacy. *Child Development, 58,* 1101–1113.

Bukowski, W. M., Sippola, L. K., & Boivin, M. (1995, March). *Friendship protects "at risk" children from victimization by peers.* Paper presented at the meeting of the Society for Research in Child Development, Indianapolis.

Burchinal, M. R., Roberts, J. E., Nabors, L. A., & Bryant, D. M. (1996). Quality of center child care and infant cognitive and language development. *Child Development, 67,* 606–620.

Burton, L. M., & Synder, A. R. (1997). The invisible man revisited. In A. Booth & A. C. Crouter (Eds.), *Men in families.* Mahwah, NJ: Erlbaum.

Burton, R. V. (1984). A paradox in theories and research in moral development. In W. M. Kurtines & J. L. Gewirtz (Eds.), *Morality, moral behavior, and moral development.* New York: Wiley.

Burts, D. C., Hart, C. H., Charlesworth, R., Hernandez, S., Kirk, L., & Mosley, J. (1989, March). *A comparison of the frequencies of stress behaviors observed in kindergarten children in classrooms with developmentally appropriate vs. developmentally inappropriate instructional practices.* Paper presented at the annual meeting of the American Educational Research Association, San Francisco.

Buss, A. H., & Plomin, R. (1984). *A temperament theory of personality development.* New York: Wiley-Interscience.

Buss, A. H., & Plomin, R. (1987). Commentary. In H. H. Goldsmith, A. H. Buss, R. Plomin, M. K. Rothbart, A. Thomas, A. Chess, R. R. Hinde, & R. B. McCall (Eds.), Roundtable: What is temperament? Four approaches. *Child Development, 58,* 505–529.

Buss, D. M. (1994). *The evolution of desire.* New York: Basic Books.

Buss, D. M. (1995). Evolutionary psychology: A new paradigm for psychological science. *Psychological Inquiry, 6,* 1–30.

Buss, D. M. (1995). Psychological sex differences: Origins through sexual selection. *American Psychologist, 50,* 164–168.

Buss, D. M., & Malamauth, N. (Eds.). (1996). *Sex, power, and conflict.* New York: Oxford University Press.

Buss, D. M., & Schmitt, D. P. (1993). Sexual strategies theory: An evolutionary perspective on human mating. *Psychological Review, 100,* 204–232.

Cairns, R. B. (1983). The emergence of developmental psychology. In P. H. Mussen (Ed.), *Handbook of child psychology* (4th ed., Vol. 1). New York: Wiley.

Cairns, R. B. (1997). The making of developmental psychology. In R. M. Lerner (Ed.), *Handbook of child psychology* (5th Ed., Vol. I). New York: Wiley.

Caldwell, M. B., & Rogers, M. F. (1991). Epidemiology of pediatric HIV infection. *Pediatric Clinics of North America, 38,* 1–16.

Calkins, S. D., & Fox, N. A. (1992). The relations among infant temperament, security of attachment, and behavioral inhibition at twenty-four months. *Child Development, 63,* 1456–1472.

Call, J. (1955, March). *Imitative learning as a problem-solving strategy in Orangutans (pono pygmaeus) and three- and four-year-old human children.* Paper presented at the meeting of the Society for Research in Child Development, Indianapolis.

Camara, K. A., & Resnick, G. (1988). Interparental conflict and cooperation: Factors moderating children's postdivorce adjustment. In E. M. Hetherington & J. D. Arasteh (Eds.), *Impact of divorce, single parenting, and stepparenting on children.* Hillsdale, NJ: Erlbaum.

Cameron, D. (1988, February). Soviet schools. *NEA Today,* p. 15.

Cameron, J. R., Hansen, R., & Rosen, D. (1989). Preventing behavioral problems in infancy through temperament assessment and parental support programs. In W. B. Carey & S. C. McDevitt (Eds.), *Clinical and education applications of temperament research.* Amsterdam: Swets & Zeitlinger.

Campbell, C. Y. (1988, August 24). Group raps depiction of teenagers. *Boston Globe,* p. 44.

Campbell, D. T., & LeVine, R. A. (1968). Ethnocentrism and intergroup relations. In R. Abelson & others (Eds.), *Theories and cognitive consistency: A sourcebook.* Chicago: Rand-McNally.

Campbell, F. A., & Ramey, C. T. (1994). Effects of early intervention on intellectual and academic achievement: A follow-up study of children from low-income families. *Child Development, 65,* 684–698.

Campbell, S. B., Cohn, J. F., & Meyers, T. (1995). Depression in first-time mothers: Mother-infant interaction and depression chronicity. *Developmental Psychology, 31,* 349–357.

Campos, J. (1994, spring). The new functionalism in emotions. *SRCD Newsletter,* pp. 1, 7, 9–11, 14.

Campos, J. J. (1997, April). *What develops in emotional development?* Paper presented at the meeting of the Society For Research in Child Development, Washington, DC.

Campos, J. J., Langer, A., & Krowitz, A. (1970). Cardiac responses on the visual cliff in prelocomotor human infants. *Science, 170,* 196–197.

Canfield, R. L., & Haith, M. M. (1991). Young infants' visual expectations for symmetric and asymmetric stimulus sequences. *Developmental Psychology, 27,* 198–208.

Caplan, P. J., & Caplan, J. B. (1994). *Thinking critically about research on sex and gender.* New York: Harper Collins.

Carbery, J., & Buhrmester, D. (1993, March). *The need-fulfilling roles of friendship during three young adults' phases.* Paper presented at the biennial meeting of the Society for Research in Child Development, New Orleans.

Carey, S. (1977). The child as word learner. In M. Halle, J. Bresman, & G. Miller (Eds.), *Linguistic theory and psychological reality.* Cambridge, MA: MIT Press.

Carey, S. (1988). Are children fundamentally different kinds of thinkers and learners than adults? In K. Richardson & S. Sheldon (Eds.), *Cognitive development to adolescence.* Hillsdale, NJ: Erlbaum.

Carey, S., & Gelman, R. (1991). *The epigenesis of mind.* Hillsdale, NJ: Erlbaum.

Carlson, K. S. (1995, March). *Attachment in sibling relationships during adolescence: Links to other familial and peer relationships.* Paper presented at the meeting of the Society for Research in Child Development, Indianapolis.

Carlson, V., Cicchetti, D., Barnett, D., & Braunwald, K. (1989). Disorganized/disoriented attachment relationships in maltreated infants. *Developmental Psychology, 25,* 525–531.

Carnegie Council on Adolescent Development. (1989). *Turning points: Preparing youth for the 21st century.* New York: Carnegie Corporation.

Carnegie Council on Adolescent Development. (1995). *Great transitions.* New York: Carnegie Foundation.

Carraher, T. H., & Carraher, D. W. (1981). Do Piagetian stages describe the reasoning of the unschooled adults? *Quarterly Newsletter of the Laboratory of Comparative Human Cognition, 3,* 61–68.

Carter, B., & McGoldrick, M. (1989). Overview: The changing family life cycle–A framework for family therapy. In B. Carter & M. McGoldrick (Eds.), *The changing family life cycle* (2nd ed.). Boston: Allyn & Bacon.

Carter, D. B., & Levy, G. D. (1988). Cognitive aspects of children's early sex-role development: The influence of gender schemas on preschoolers' memories and preference for sex-typed toys and activities. *Child Development, 59,* 782–793.

Case, R. (1985). *Intellectual development: A systematic reinterpretation.* New York: Academic Press.

Case, R. (1985). *Intellectual development: Birth to adulthood.* New York: Aca-demic Press.

Case, R. (Ed.). (1992). *The mind's staircase: Exploring the conceptual underpinnings of children's thought and knowledge.* Hillsdale, NJ: Erlbaum.

Case, R. (1996). Introduction: Reconceptualizing the nature of children's conceptual structures and their development in middle childhood. In R. Case & Y. Okamoto, (Eds.), The role of central conceptual structures in the development of children's thought. *Monographs of the Society for Research in Child Development, 61,* 1–26.

Case, R. (1997). The develpment of conceptual structures. In D. Kuhn & R. S. Siegler (Eds.), *Handbook of child psychology* (5th Ed., Vol. II). New York: Wiley.

Case, R., Kurland, D. M., & Goldberg, J. (1982). Operational efficiency and the growth of short-term memory span. *Journal of Experimental Child Psychology, 33,* 386–404.

Case, R., & Okamoto, Y. (Eds.), (1996). The role of central conceptual structures in the development of children's thought. *Monographs of the Society for Research in Child Development, 61,.*1–26.

Caspi, A., Henry, B., McGee, R. O., Moffitt, T. E., & Silva, P. A. (1995). Temperamental origins of child and adolescent behavior problems: From age three to age fifteen. *Child Development, 66,* 55–68.

Cassell, C. (1984). *Swept away: Why women fear their own sexuality.* New York: Simon & Schuster.

Cassidy, J. (1994). Emotion regulation: Influences of attachment relationships. In N. Fox (Ed.), The development of emotion regulation. *Monographs of the Society for Research in Child Development,* Serial no. 240, Vol. 59, Nos. 2–3.

Ceballo, R., & Olson, S. L. (1993, March). *The role of alternative caregivers in the lives of children from poor, single-parent families.* Paper presented at the biennial meeting of the Society for Research in Child Development, New Orleans.

Ceci, S. (1990). *On intelligence . . . more or less: A bioecological treatise.* Englewood Cliffs, NJ: Prentice Hall.

Ceci, S. J. (1996). Unpublished review of *Child Development* (8th ed.) by J. W. Santrock. Dubuque, IA: Brown & Benchmark.

Ceci, S. J. & Barnett, S. M. (1997, April). *Convergence or divergence in intelligence?* Paper presented at the meeting of the Society for Research in Child Development, Washington, DC.

Ceci, S. J., & Bruck, M. (1993, fall). Child witnesses: Translating research into policy. *Social Report, Society for Research in Child Development, 7* (3), 1–31.

Ceci, S. J., & Bruck, M. (1997). Children's testimony. In I. E. Siegel & K. A. Renninger (Eds.), *Handbook of child psychology* (5th Ed., Vol. IV). New York: Wiley.

Chall, J. S. (1979). The great debate: Ten years later, with a modest proposal for reading stages. In L. B. Resnick & P. A. Weaver (Eds.), *Theory and practice of early reading.* Hillsdale, NJ: Erlbaum.

Chamberlin, P., & Patterson, G. R. (1995). Discipline and child compliance in parenting. In M. H. Bornstein (Ed.), *Handbook of parenting* (Vol. 4). Hillsdale, NJ: Erlbaum.

Charlesworth, R. (1987). *Understanding child development* (2nd ed.). Albany, NY: Delmar.

Charlesworth, R. (1989). "Behind" before the start? *Young Children, 44,* 5–13.

Charlesworth, W. R. (1992). Commentary: Can biology explain human development? *Human Development, 35,* 9–11.

Chase-Lansdale, P. L. (1996, June). *Effects of divorce on mental health through the life span.* Informal talk at the Family Research Summer Consortium, San Diego.

Chase-Lansdale, P. L., & Brooks-Gunn, J. (Eds.). (1996). *Escape from poverty.* New York: Cambridge University Press.

Chase-Lansdale, P. S., & Brooks-Gunn, J. (1994). Correlates of adolescent pregnancy. In C. B. Fisher & R. M. Lerner (Eds.), *Applied developmental psychology.* New York: McGraw-Hill.

Chasnoff, I. J., Griffith, D. R., Freier, C., & Murray, J. (1992). Cocaine/polydrug use in pregnancy: Two-year follow-up. *Pediatrics, 89,* 284–289.

Chattin-McNichols, J. (1992). *The Montessori controversy.* Albany, NY: Delmar.

Chemitz, V. R., Cheung, L. W. Y., & Lieberman, E. (1995, spring). The role of lifestyle in preventing low birth weight. *The Future of Children, 5*(1), 121–138.

Chen, C. (1997, April). *Acculturation of values and attitudes: A study of Chinese early and late adolescents.* Paper presented at the meeting of the Society for Research in Child Development, Washington, DC.

Chen, L. A., & Yu, P. P. H. (1997, April). *Parental ethnic socialization in Chinese American families.* Paper presented at the meeting of the Society for Research in Child Development, Washington, DC.

Chesney-Lind, M. (1989). Girls' crime and woman's place: Toward a feminist model of female delinquency. *Crime and Delinquency, 35,* 5–30.

Chess, S., & Thomas, A. (1977). Temperamental individuality from childhood to adolescence. *Journal of Child Psychiatry, 16,* 218–226.

Chi, M. T. H. (1978). Knowledge structures and memory development. In R. S. Siegler (Ed.), *Children's thinking: What develops?* Hillsdale, NJ: Erlbaum.

Chi, M. T. H., Bassok, M., Lewis, M., Reimann, P., & Glaser, R. (1989). Self-explanations: How students study and use examples in learning to solve problems. *Cognitive Science, 13,* 145–182.

Chi, M. T. H., & Koeske, R. D. (1983). Network representation of a child's dinosaur knowledge. *Developmental Psychology, 19,* 29–39.

Chi, M. T. H., Slotta, J. D., & de Leeuw, N. (1994). From things to processes: A theory of conceptual change for learning science concepts [Special issue of conceptual change] *Learning and Instruction: The Journal of the European Association for Research on Learning and Instruction.*

Child Trends. (1996). *Facts at a glance.* Washington, DC: Child Trends.

Children's Defense Fund. (1992). *The state of America' children, 1992.* Washington, DC: Author.

Chodorow, N. J. (1989). *Feminism and psychoanalytic theory.* New Haven, CT: Yale University Press.

Chomsky, N. (1957). *Syntactic structures.* The Hague: Mouton.

Chow, E. N., Wilkinson, D., & Baca Zinn, M. (1996). *Common bonds, different voices.* Newbury Park, CA: Sage.

Cicchetti, D., Ganiban, J., & Barnett, D. (1991). Contributions from the study of high risk populations to understanding the development of emotion regulation. In J. Garber & K. Dodge (Eds.), *The development of emotion regulation and dysregulation*. New York: Cambridge University Press.

Cicchetti, D., & Toth, S. (1997). Perspectives on research and practice in developmental psychopathology. In I. E. Sigel & K. A. Renninger (Eds.), *Handbook of child psychology* (5th Ed., Vol. IV). New York: Wiley.

Cicirelli, V. (1977). Family structure and interaction: Sibling effects on socialization. In M. McMillan & M. Sergio (Eds.), *Child psychiatry: Treatment and research*. New York: Brunner/Mazel.

Cicirelli, V. G. (1994). Sibling relationships in cross-cultural perspective. *Journal of Marriage and the Family, 56*, 7–20.

Cillessen, A. H. N., Van Ijzendoorn, H. W., Van Lieshout, C. F. M., & Hartup, W. W. (1992). Heterogeneity among peer-rejected boys: Subtypes and stabilities. *Child Development, 63*, 893–905.

Clark, E. V. (1983). Meanings and concepts. In P. H. Mussen (Ed.), *Handbook of child psychology* (4th ed., Vol. 4). New York: Wiley.

Clark, K. B., & Clark, M. P. (1939). The development of self and the emergence of racial identification in Negro preschool children. *Journal of Social Psychology, 10*, 591–599.

Clark, R. D., & Hatfield, E. (1989). Gender differences in receptivity to sexual offers. *Journal of Psychology and Human Sexuality, 2*, 39–55.

Clark, S. D., Zabin, L. S., & Hardy, J. B. (1984). Sex, contraception, and parenthood: Experience and attitudes among urban black young men. *Family Planning Perspectives, 16*, 77–82.

Clarke-Stewart, K. A., Allhusen, V. D., & Clements, D. C. (1995). Nonparental caregiving. In M. H. Bornstein (Ed.), *Handbook of parenting* (Vol. 3). Hillsdale, NJ: Erlbaum.

Clarke-Stewart, K. A., & Fein, G. G. (1983). Early childhood programs. In P. H. Mussen (Ed.), *Handbook of child psychology* (4th ed., Vol. 2). New York: Wiley.

Clausen, J. A. (1993). *American lives*. New York: Free Press.

Clement, J., Lockhead, J., & Soloway, E. (1979, March). *Translation between symbol systems: Isolating a common difficulty in solving algebra word problems*. COINS technical report No. 79-19. Amherst: University of Massachusetts, Department of Computer and Information Sciences.

Clifford, B. R., Gunter, B., & McAleer, J. L. (1995). *Television and children*. Hillsdale, NJ: Erlbaum.

Clifton, R. K., Morrongiello, B. A., Kulig, J. W., & Dowd, J. M. (1981). Developmental changes in auditory localization in infancy. In R. N. Aslin, J. R. Alberts, & M. R. Petersen (Eds.), *Development of perception* (Vol. 1). Orlando FL: Academic Press.

Clifton, R. K., Muir, D. W., Ashmead, D. H., & Clarkson, M. G. (1993). Is visually guided reaching in early infancy a myth? *Child Development, 64*, 1099–1110.

Clinchy, B. M., Mansfield, A. F., & Schott, J. L. (1995, March). *Development of narrative and scientific modes of thought in middle childhood*. Paper presented at the meeting of the Society for Research in Child Development, Indianapolis.

Cloninger, S. C. (1996). *Theories of personality* (2nd ed.). Upper Saddle River, NJ: Prentice Hall.

Coffman, S., Levitt, M. J., & Guacci-Franco, N. (1996). Infant-mother attachment: Relationships to maternal responsiveness and infant temperament. *Journal of Pediatric Nursing, 10*, 9–18.

Cohen, H. J., Grosz, J., Ayooh, K., & Schoen, S. (1996). Early intervention for children with HIV infections. In M. J. Guralnick (Ed.), *The effectiveness of early intervention*. Baltimore: Paul H. Brookes.

Cohen, R. J., Swerdlik, M. E., & Phillips, S. M. (1996). *Psychological testing and assessment* (3rd. ed.). Mountain View, CA: Mayfield.

Cohen, S. E. (1994, February). *High school dropouts*. Paper presented at the meeting of the Society for Research on Adolescence, San Diego.

Cohn, J. F., & Tronick, E. Z. (1988). Mother-infant face-to-face interaction. Influence is bidirectional and unrelated to periodic cycles in either partner's behavior. *Developmental Psychology, 24*, 396–397.

Coie, J. D., & Dodge, K. A. (1997). Aggression and antisocial behavior. In N. Eisenberg (Ed.), *Handbook of child psychology* (5th Ed., Vol. III). New York: Wiley.

Coie, J. D., & Koeppl, G. K. (1990). Adapting intervention to the problems of aggressive and disruptive rejected children. In S. R. Asher & J. D. Coie (Eds.), *Peer rejection in childhood*. New York: Cambridge University Press.

Colby, A., Kohlberg, L., Gibbs, J., & Lieberman, M. (1983). A longitudinal study of moral judgment. *Monographs of the Society for Research in Child Development* (Serial No. 201).

Cole, C. F., & Richman, B. A. (1997, April). A world of Sesame Street. Paper presented at the meeting of the Society for Research in Child Development, Washington, DC.

Cole, M. (1997). *Cultural psychology*. Cambridge, MA: Harvard U. Press.

Cole, M., & Cole, S. R. (1993). *The development of children* (2nd ed.). New York: W. H. Freeman.

Coleman, J. S. (1961). *The adolescent society*. New York: Free Press.

Coleman, L. (1996, March). *What does it mean to be a Black man or a Black woman?* Paper presented at the meeting of the Society for Research on Adolescence, Boston.

Coles, R. (1970). *Erik H. Erikson: The growth of his work*. Boston: Little, Brown.

Coll, C. T. G., Erkut, S., Alarcon, O., Garcia, H. A. V., & Tropp, L. (1995, March). *Puerto Rican adolescents and families: Lessons in construct and instrument development*. Paper presented at the meeting of the Society for Research in Child Development, Indianapolis.

Coll, C. T. G., Meyer, E. C., & Brillion, L. (1995). Ethnic and minority parenting. In M. H. Bornstein (Ed.), *Children and parenting* (Vol. 2). Hillsdale, NJ: Erlbaum.

Collins, W. A. (1990). Parent-child relationships in the transition to adolescence: Continuity and change in interaction, affect, and cognition. In R. Montemayor, G. R. Adams, & T. P. Gulotta (Eds.), *From childhood to adolescence: A transitional period?* Newbury Park, CA: Sage.

Collins, W. A., Harris, M., & Susman, A. (1995, March). Parenting during middle childhood. In M. H. Bornstein (Ed.), *Handbook of parenting* (Vol. 1). Hillsdale, NJ: Erlbaum.

Collins, W. A., & Luebker, C. (1993, March). *Parental behavior during adolescence: Individual and relational significance*. Paper presented at the biennial meeting of the Society for Research in Child Development, New Orleans.

Comas-Diaz, L. (1993). Hispanic/Latino communities: Psychological implications. In D. R. Atkinson, G. Morten, & D. W. Sue (Eds.), *Counseling American minorities*. Dubuque, IA: Brown & Benchmark.

Comer, J. P. (1988). Educating poor minority children. *Scientific American, 259*, 42–48.

Compas, B. (1989, April). *Vulnerability and stress in childhood and adolescence.* Paper presented at the biennial meeting of the Society for Research in Child Development, Kansas City.

Compas, B. E., & Grant, K. E. (1993, March). *Stress and adolescent depressive symptoms: Underlying mechanisms and processes.* Paper presented at the biennial meeting of the Society for Research in Child Development, New Orleans.

Conger, R. (1997, April). *Family resilience and vulnerability to economic adversity.* Paper presented at the meeting of the Society for Research in Child Development, Washington, DC.

Conger, R. D., Ge, X., Elder, G. H., Lorenz, F. O., & Simons, R. L. (1994). Economic stress, coercive family process, and developmental problems of adolescents. *Child Development, 65,* 541–561.

Connell, J. P., Spencer, M. B., & Aber, J. L. (1994). Educational risk and resilience in African-American youth: Context, self, action, and outcomes in school. *Child Development, 65,* 493–506.

Cook, M., & Birch, R. (1984). Infant perception of the shapes of tilted plane forms. *Infant Behavior and Development, 7,* 389–402.

Cooper, C., Lopez, E., Dunbar, N., & Figuera, J. (1996, March). *Identity, relationships, and opportunity structures: African-American and Latino youth in university academic outreach programs.* Paper presented at the meeting of the Society for Research on Adolescence, Boston.

Cooper, C. R., & Ayers-Lopez, S. (1985). Family and peer systems in early adolescence: New models of the role of relationships in development. *Journal of Early Adolescence, 5,* 9–22.

Cooper, C. R., & Grotevant, H. D. (1989, April). *Individuality and connectedness in the family and adolescents' self and relational competence.* Paper presented at the meeting of the Society for Research in Child Development, Kansas City.

Cooper, C. R., Grotevant, H. D., Moore, M. S., & Condon, S. M. (1982, August). *Family support and conflict: Both foster adolescent identity and role taking.* Paper presented at the meeting of the American Psychological Association, Washington, DC.

Coopersmith, S. (1967). *The antecedents of self-esteem.* San Francisco: W. H. Freeman.

Copeland, A. P., Hwang, H., & Brody, L. R. (1996, March). *Asian-American adolescents: Caught between cultures?* Paper presented at the meeting of the Society for Research on Adolescence, Boston.

Corrigan, R. (1981). The effects of task and practice on search for invisibly displaced objects. *Developmental Review, 1,* 1–17.

Costanzo, P. R., & Dunsmore, J. (1993, March). *The impact of parental values on children's developing moral thought.* Paper presented at the biennial meeting of the Society for Research in Child Development, New Orleans.

Cote, J. E., & Levine, C. (1988). A critical examination of the ego identity status paradigm. *Developmental Review, 8,* 147–184.

Coulton, C. J., & Korbin, J. E. (1995, March). *How do measures of community organization differ in African-American and European-American neighborhoods?* Paper presented at the meeting of the Society for Research in Child Development, Indianapolis.

Cowan, C. P., Cowan, P. A., Heming, G., & Miller, N. (1991). Becoming a family: Marriage, parenting, and child development. In P. A. Cowan & E. M. Hetherington (Eds.), *Family transitions.* Hillsdale, NJ: Erlbaum.

Cowan, C. P., Heming, G. A., & Shuck, E. L. (1993, March). *The impact of interventions with parents of preschoolers on the children's adaptation to kindergarten.* Paper presented at the biennial meeting of the Society for Research in Child Development, New Orleans.

Cox, F. D. (1994). *The AIDs booklet* (3rd ed.). Dubuque, IA: Brown & Benchmark.

Cox, M. J., Owen, M. T., Lewis, J. M., & Henderson, V. K. (1989). Marriage, adult adjustment, and early parenting. *Child Development, 60,* 1015–1024.

Crawford, C. (1987). Sociobiology: Of what value to psychology? In C. Crawford, M. Smith, & D. Krebs (Eds.), *Sociobiology and psychology.* Hillsdale, NJ: Erlbaum.

Creasy, G. L., Mitts, N., Catanzaro, L. E., & Lustig, K. (1993, March). *Associations among daily hassles, coping, and behavior problems among kindergartners.* Paper presented at the biennial meeting of the Society for Research in Child Development, New Orleans.

Crick, M. (1977). *Explorations in language and meaning: Toward a scientific anthropology.* New York: Halstead.

Crittenden, P. (1988). Relationships at risk. In J. Belsky & T. Nezworski (Eds.), *The clinical implications for attachment.* Hillsdale, NJ: Erlbaum.

Crnic, K. (1996). *Children, families, and stress.* Cambridge, MA: Blackwell.

Crockenberg, S., & Lourie, A. (1993, March). *Conflict strategies: Parents with children and children with peers.* Paper presented at the biennial meeting of the Society for Research in Child Development, New Orleans.

Crockenberg, S. B. (1986). Are temperamental differences in babies associated with predictable differences in caregiving? In J. V. Lerner & R. M. Lerner (Eds.), *Temperament and social interaction during infancy and childhood.* San Francisco: Jossey-Bass.

Crockett, L. J., & Chopak, J. S. (1993). Pregnancy prevention in early adolescence. In R. M. Lerner (Ed.), *Early adolescence: Perspectives on research, policy, and intervention.* Hillsdale, NJ: Erlbaum.

Cromer, R. (1987). Receptive language in the mentally retarded: Processes and diagnostic distinctions. In R. Schiefelbusch & L. Lloyd (Eds.), *Language perspectives: Acquisition, retardation, and intervention.* Baltimore: University Park Press.

Cronbach, L. J., & Snow, R. E. (1977). *Aptitudes and instructional methods.* New York: Irvington.

Cross, K. P. (1984, November). The rising tide of school reform reports. *Phi Delta Kappan,* pp. 167–172.

Crouter, A. C., Manke, B. A., & McHale, S. M. (1995). The family context of gender intensification in early adolescence. *Child Development, 66,* 317–329.

Crowder, J. (1969). *Stephanie and the coyote.* Upper Strata, Box 278, Bernalillo, NM 87004.

Crump, A. D., Haynie, D., Aarons, S., & Adair, E. (1996, March). *African American teenagers' norms, expectations, and motivations regarding sex, contraception, and pregnancy.* Paper presented at the meeting of the Society for Research on Adolescence, Boston.

Culbertson, F. M. (1997). Depression and gender. *American Psychologist, 52,* 25–31.

Cummings, E. M. (1987). Coping with background anger in early childhood. *Child Development, 58,* 976–984.

Cummings, L. M., Rebello, P. M., & Gardinier, M. (1995, March). *The UN convention on the rights of the child: A call to child development professionals around the world.* Paper presented at the meeting of the Society for Research in Child Development, Indianapolis.

Curran, J. M. (1997, April). *Creativity across the life-span.* Paper presented at the meeting of the Society for Research in Child Development, Washington, DC.

Curry, N. E. (1971). Consideration of current basic issues in play. In N. E. Curry & S. Arnaud (Eds.), *Play: The child strives toward self-regulation.* Washington, DC: National Association for the Education of Young Children.

Curtis H., & Barnes, N. S. (1989). *Biology* (5th ed.). New York: Worth.

Curtiss, S. (1977). *Genie.* New York: Academic Press.

Cushner, K., & Brislin, R. W. (Eds.) (1997). *Improving cultural interactions*. Thousand Oaks, CA: Sage.

D'Angelo, D. A., & Adler, C. R. (1991). A catalyst for improving parent involvement. *Phi Delta Kappan*, pp. 350–354.

Daly, M., & Wilson, M. (1995). Evolutionary psychology: Adaptationist, selectionist, and comparative. *Psychological Inquiry, 6*, 34–38.

Damon, W. (1988). *The moral child*. New York: Free Press.

Damon, W. (1991). Self-concept, adolescent. In R. M. Lerner, A. C. Petersen, & J. Brooks-Gunn (Eds.), *Encyclopedia of adolescence* (Vol. 2). New York: Garland.

Damon, W. (1995). *Greater expectations*. New York: Free Press.

Damon, W., & Hart, D. (1988). *Self-understanding in childhood and adolescence*. New York: Cambridge University Press.

Dannemiller, J. L. (1985). The early phase of dark adaptation in human infants. *Vision Research, 25*, 207–212.

Darling, C. A., Kallen, D. J., & VanDusen, J. E. (1984). Sex in transition, 1900–1984. *Journal of Youth and Adolescence, 13*, 385–399.

Daro, D. (1988). *Confronting child abuse*. New York: Free Press.

Darwin, C. (1859). *On the origin of species*. London: John Murray.

Dasen, P. R. (1977). Are cognitive processes universal? A contribution to cross-cultural Piagetian psychology. In N. Warran (Ed.), *Studies in cross-cultural psychology* (Vol. 1). London: Academic Press.

Dasen, P. R., Ngini, L., & Lavalée, M. (1979). Cross-cultural training studies of concrete operations. In L. H. Eckenberger, W. J. Lonner, & Y. H. Poortinga (Eds.), *Cross-cultural contributions to psychology*. Boston: Allyn & Bacon.

Davis, K. (1996). *Families*. Pacific Grove, CA: Brooks/Cole.

Davis-Kean, P. E. (1997, April). *The role of fathers in the family process*. Paper presented at the meeting of the Society for Research in Child Development, Washington, DC.

Day, R. H. (1987). Visual size constancy in infancy. In B. E. McKenzie and R. H. Day (Eds.), *Perceptual development in early infancy: Problems and issues*. Hillsdale, NJ: Erlbaum.

Day, R. H., & McKenzie, B. E. (1973). Perceptual shape constancy in early infancy. *Perception, 2*, 315–320.

Dazinger, S., & Dazinger, S. (1993). Child poverty and public policy: Toward a comprehensive antipoverty agenda. *Daedalus: America's Childhood, 122*, 57–84.

DeBlassie, A. M., & DeBlassie, R. R. (1996). Education of Hispanic youth: A cultural lag. *Adolescence, 121*, 205–214.

DeCasper, A. J., & Spence, M. J. (1986). Prenatal maternal speech influences newborn's perception of speech sounds. *Infant Behavior and Development, 9*, 133–150.

Degirmencioglu, S. M., Saltz, E., & Ager, J. W. (1995, March). *Early dating and "going steady": A retrospective and prospective look*. Paper presented at the meeting of the Society for Research in Child Development, Indianapolis.

DelCielo, D., Castaneda, M., Hui, J., & Frye, D. (1993, March). *Is theory of mind related to categorization?* Paper presented at the biennial meeting of the Society for Research in Child Development, New Orleans.

DeLoache, J. S. (1984). Oh where, oh where: Memory-based searching by very young children. In C. Sophian (Ed.), *Origins of cognitive skills*. Hillsdale, NJ: Erlbaum.

DeLoache, J. S. (1989). The development of representation in young children. In H. W. Reese (Ed.), *Advances in child development and behavior* (Vol. 22, pp. 1–39). New York: Academic Press.

DeLoache, J. S., Cassidy, D. J., & Brown, A. L. (1985). Precursors of mnemonic strategies in very young children's memory. *Child Development, 56*, 125–137.

DeLoache, J. S., Cassidy, D. J., & Carpenter, C. J. (1987). The Three Bears are all boys: Mothers' gender labeling of neutral picture book characters. *Sex Roles, 17*, 163–178.

DeLoache. J. S., Miller, K. F., & Pierroutsakos, S. L. (1997). Reasoning and problem solving. In D. Kuhn & R. S. Siegler (Eds.), *Handbook of child psychology* (5th Ed., Vol. II). New York: Wiley.

DeMarie-Dreblow, D., & Miller, P. H. (1988). The development of children's strategies for selective attention: Evidence for a transitional period. *Child Development, 59*, 1504–1513.

Dempster, F. N. (1981). Memory span: Sources of individual and developmental differences. *Psychological Bulletin, 89*, 63–100.

Denmark, F. L., Russo, N. F., Frieze, I., II, & Sechzur, J. (1988). Guidelines for avoiding sexism in psychological research: A report of the Ad Hoc Committee on Nonsexist Research. *American Psychologist, 43*, 582–585.

Derman-Sparks, L., and the ABC Task Force. (1989). *Anti-bias curriculum*. Washington, DC: National Association for the Education of Young Children.

Derry, P. S. (1996). Buss and sexual selection: The issue of culture. *American Psychologist, 51*, 159–160.

Deutsch, M. (Ed.). (1967). *The disadvantaged child: Selected papers of Martin Deutsch and his associates*. New York: Basic Books.

DeVet, K. A., Brodsky, A. E., & Ialongo, N. S. (1997, April). *Parent monitoring in dangerous neighborhoods*. Paper presented at the meeting of the Society for Research in Child Development, Washington, DC.

de Villiers, J. (1996). Towards a rational empiricism: Why interactionism isn't behaviorism any more than biology is genetics. In M. Rice (Ed.), *Towards a genetics of language*. Hillsdale, NJ: Erlbaum.

DeVries, R., Haney, J., & Zan, B. (1991). Sociomoral atmosphere in direct-instruction, eclectic, and constructivist kindergartens: A study of teachers' enacted interpersonal understanding. *Early Childhood Research Quarterly, 6*, 473–517.

DeVries, R., & Zan, B. (1994). *Moral classrooms, moral children: Creating a constructivist atmosphere in early education*. New York: Teachers College Press.

DeVries, R., & Zan, B. (1995). Creating a constructivist classroom atmosphere. *Young Children, 51*, 4–13.

Dewey, J. (1933). *How we think: A restatement of the relation of reflective thinking to the educative process*. Lexington, MA: D. C. Heath.

Diamond, A., & Goldman-Rakic, P. S. (1989). Comparison of human infants and rhesus monkeys on Piaget's AB search task: Evidence for dependence on dorsolateral prefrontal cortex. *Experimental Brain Research, 74*, 24–40.

Diamond, A. D. (1955, March). *Exciting new findings in development cognitive neuroscience*. Paper presented at the meeting of the Society for Research in Child Development, Indianapolis.

Diamond, A. D. (1985). Development of the ability to use recall to guide action, as indicated by infants' performance on AB. *Child Development, 56*, 868–883.

Diaz, R. (1983). Thought and two languages: The impact of bilingualism on cognitive development. *Review of Research in Education, 10*, 23–54.

DiBiase, R. (1993, March). *Attachment, temperament, and ego development in adolescence*. Paper presented at the biennial meeting of the Society for Research in Child Development, New Orleans.

Dickerscheid, J. D., Schwarz, P. M., Noir, S., & El-Taliawy, T. (1988). Gender concept development of preschool-aged children in the United States and Egypt. *Sex Roles, 18,* 669–677.

Dickinson, D. K. (1995, March). *Readiness: According to whom and what?* Paper presented at the meeting of the Society for Research in Child Development, Indianapolis.

Didow, S. M. (1993, March). *Language and action: Toddlers' coordinated talk with a partner.* Paper presented at the meeting of the Society for Research in Child Development, New Orleans.

DiPardo, A. (1966). Review of *Writers in the Zone of Proximal Development* by Petrick-Steward. *Contemporary Psychology, 41,* 51–52.

Dishion, T. J., Andrews, D. W., & Crosby, L. (1995). Antisocial boys and their friends in early adolescence: Relationship characteristics, quality, and interactional process. *Child Development, 66,* 139–151.

Dishion, T. J., & Spacklen, K. M. (1996, March). *Childhood peer rejection in the development of adolescent substance abuse.* Paper presented at the meeting of the Society for Research on Adolescence, Boston.

Dodge, K. A. (1993). Social cognitive mechanisms in the development of conduct disorder and depression. *Annual Review of Psychology, 44,* 559–584.

Dodge, K. A. (1993, March). *Social information processing and peer rejection factors in the development of behavior problems in children.* Paper presented at the biennial meeting of the Society for Research in Child Development, New Orleans.

Dodge, K. A., & Feldman, E. (1990). Issues in social cognition and sociometric status. In S. R. Asher & J. D. Coie (Eds.), *Peer rejection in childhood.* New York: Cambridge University Press.

Dolgin, K. G., & Behrend, D. A. (1984). Children's knowledge about animates and inanimates. *Child Development, 55,* 1646–1650.

Dorn, L. D., & Lucas, F. L. (1995, March). *Do hormone-behavior relations vary depending upon the endocrine and psychological status of the adolescent?* Paper presented at the meeting of the Society for Research in Child Development, Indianapolis.

Dornbusch, S. M., Carlsmith, J. M., Bushwall, S. J., Ritter, P. I., Leidman, P. H., Hastorf, A. H., & Gross, R. T. (1985). Single parents, extended households, and the control of adolescents. *Child Development, 56,* 326–341.

Doubleday, C. N., & Droege, K. L. (1993). Cognitive developmental influences on children's understanding of television. In G. L. Berry & J. K. Asamen (Eds.), *Children and television.* Newbury Park, CA: Sage.

Douvan, E., & Adelson, J. (1996). *The adolescent experience.* New York: Wiley.

Dowdy, B. B., & Kliewer, W. (1996, March). *Dating, parent-adolescent conflict, and autonomy.* Paper presented at the meeting of the Society for Research on Adolescence, Boston.

Dow-Edwards, D. L. (1995). Developmental toxicity of cocaine: Mechanisms of action. In M. Lewis & M. Bendersky (Eds.), *Mothers, babies, and cocaine.* Hillsdale, NJ: Erlbaum.

Downey, G., & Bonica, C. A. (1997, April). *Characteristics of early adolescent dating relationships.* Paper presented at the meeting of the Society for Research in Child Development, Washington, DC.

Downey, G., & Coyne, J. C. (1990). Children of depressed parents: An integrative review. *Psychological Bulletin, 108,* 50–76.

Doyle, A., Doehring, P., Tessier, O., de Lorimier, S., & Shapiro, S. (1992). Transitions in children's play: A sequential analysis of states preceding and following social pretense. *Developmental Psychology, 28,* 137–144.

Draper, T. W., Larsen, J. M., Haupt, J. H., Robinson, C. C., & Hart, C. (1993, March). *Family emotional climate as a mediating variable between parent education and child social competence in an advantaged subculture.* Paper presented at the biennial meeting of the Society for Research in Child Development, New Orleans.

Dreman, S. (1997). *The family of the 21st century.* Mahwah, NJ: Erlbaum.

Dreyer, P. H., Jennings, T., Johnson, L., & Evans, D. (1994, February). *Culture and personality in urban schools: Identity status, self-concept, and locus of control among high school students in monolingual and bilingual homes.* Paper presented at the meeting of the Society for Research on Adolescence, San Diego.

Drickamer, L. C., Vessey, S. H., & Miekle, D. (1996). *Animal behavior* (4th ed.). Dubuque, IA: Wm. C. Brown.

Dryfoos, J. G. (1990). *Adolescents at risk: Prevalence and prevention.* New York: Oxford University Press.

DuBois, D. L., Felner, R. D., & Brand, S. (1997, April). *Self-esteem profiles and adjustment in early adolescence: A two-year longitudinal study.* Paper presented at the meeting of the Society for Research in Child Development, Washington, DC.

DuBois, D. L., & Hirsch, B. J. (1990). School and neighborhood friendship patterns of Blacks and Whites in early adolescence. *Child Development, 61,* 524–536.

Duck, S. W. (1975). Personality similarity and friendship choices by adolescents. *European Journal of Social Psychology, 5,* 351–365.

Duck, S. W. (1988). Child adolescent friendships. In P. Marsh (Ed.), *Eye to eye: How people interact.* Topsfield, MA: Salem House.

Duckett, R. H. (1997, July). *Strengthening families/building communities.* Paper presented at the conference on Working with America's Youth, Pittsburgh, PA.

Duke, D. L., & Canady, R. L. (1991). *School policy.* New York: McGraw-Hill.

Duncan, G. J., Brooks-Gunn, J., & Klebanov, P. K. (1994). Economic deprivation and early childhood development. *Child Development, 65,* 296–318.

Duncker, K. (1945). On problem solving. *Psychological Monographs, 58* (Whole No. 270).

Dunn, J., & Kendrick, C. (1982). *Siblings.* Cambridge, MA: Harvard University Press.

Dunphy, D. C. (1963). The social structure of urban adolescent peer groups. *Society, 26,* 230–246.

Durkin, K. (1985). Television and sex-role acquisition: 1. Content. *British Journal of Social Psychology, 24,* 101–113.

Durkin, K., & Hutchins, G. (1984). Challenging traditional sex role stereotypes via career education broadcasts: The reactions of young secondary school pupils. *Journal of Educational Television, 10,* 25–33.

Eagly, A. H. (1995). The science and politics of comparing men and women. *American Psychologist, 50,* 145–158.

Eagly, A. H. (1996). Differences between women and men. *American Psychologist, 51,* 158–159.

Eagly, A. H., & Crowley, M. (1986). Gender and helping behavior: A meta-analytic review of the social psychological literature. *Psychological Bulletin, 100,* 283–308.

Early Childhood and Literacy Development Committee of the International Reading Association. (1986). Literacy development and pre-first grade. *Young Children, 41,* 10–13.

East, P., & Felice, M. E. (1996). *Adolescent pregnancy and parenting.* Hillsdale, NJ: Erlbaum.

Eccles, J. S. (1993, March). *Parents as gender-role socializers during middle childhood and adolescence*. Paper presented at the biennial meeting of the Society for Research in Child Development, New Orleans.

Eccles, J. S., & Harold, R. D. (1991, April). *Influences on, and consequences of, parents' beliefs regarding their children's abilities and interests*. Paper presented at the meeting of the Society for Research in Child Development, Seattle.

Eccles, J. S., & Midgley, C. (1990). Changes in academic motivation and self-perception during early adolescence. In R. Montemayor, G. R. Adams, & T. P. Gullotta (Eds.), *From childhood to adolescence: A transitional period?* Newbury Park, CA: Sage.

Eccles, J. S., Midgley, C., Wigfield, A., Buchanan, C. M., Reuman, D., Flanagan, C., & MacIver, D. (1993). Development during adolescence: The impact of stage-environment fit on adolescents' experiences in schools and families. *American Psychologist, 48*, 90–101.

Eccles, J. S., Wigfield, A., & Schiefele, U. (1997). Motivation to succeed. In N. Eisenberg (Ed.), *Handbook of child psychology* (5th Ed., Vol. III). New York: Wiley.

Eccles, J. S., & Wigfield, A. L. (1997, April). *Gendered values and attitudes: Developmental, historical, and cultural changes*. Paper presented at the meeting of the Society for Research in Child Development, Washington, DC.

Edelman, M. W. (1992). *The state of America's children, 1992*. Washington, DC: Children's Defense Fund.

Edelman, M. W. (1996). *The state of America's children*. Washington, DC: Children's Defense Fund.

Edelman, M. W. (1997, April). *Children, families and social policy*. Paper presented at the meeting of the Society for Research in Child Development, Washington, DC.

Educational Testing Service. (1992). [Cross-national comparison of children's learning and achievement.] Unpublished data, Educational Testing Service, Princeton, NJ.

Edwards, C. P. (1987). Culture and the construction of moral values. In J. Kagan & S. Lamb (Eds.), *The emergence of morality in young children*. Chicago: University of Chicago Press.

Egeland, B. (1989, January). *Secure attachment in infancy and competence in the third grade*. Paper presented at the meeting of the American Association for the Advancement of Science, San Francisco.

Eger, M. (1981). The conflict in moral education: An informal case study. *Public Interest, 63*, 62–80.

Ehrhardt, A. A. (1987). A transactional perspective on the development of gender differences. In J. M. Reinisch, L. A. Rosenblum, & S. A. Sanders (Eds.), *Masculinity/femininity: Basic perspectives*. New York: Oxford University Press.

Eiferman, R. R. (1971). Social play in childhood. In R. Herron & B. Sutton-Smith (Eds.), *Child's play*. New York: Wiley.

Eiger, M. S. (1992). The feeding of infants and children. In R. A. Hoekelman, S. B. Friedman, N. M. Nelson, & H. M. Seidel (Eds.), *Primary pediatric care* (2nd ed.). St. Louis: Mosby Yearbook.

Eimas, P. (1995). The perception of representation of speech by infants. In J. L. Morgan & K. Demuth (Eds.), *Signal to syntax*. Hillsdale, NJ: Erlbaum.

Eisenberg, A., Murkoff, H., & Hathaway, S. (1988). *What to expect when you're expecting*. New York: Workman.

Eisenberg, N. (Ed.). (1982). *The development of prosocial behavior*. New York: Wiley.

Eisenberg, N. (1992, fall). Social development. Current trends and future possibilities. *SRCD Newsletter*, pp. 1, 10–11.

Eisenberg, N., & Fabes, R. A. (1997). Prosocial development. In N. Eisenberg (Ed.), *Handbook of child psychology* (5th Ed., Vol. III). New York,: Wiley.

Eisenberg, N., & Murphy, B. (1995). Parenting and children's moral development. In M. H. Bornstein (Ed.), *Children and parenting* (Vol. 4). Hillsdale, NJ: Erlbaum.

Eisenberg, N., Shea, C. I., Carolo, G., & Knight, G. P. (1991). Empathy-related responding and cognition: A chicken and egg dilemma. In W. M. Kurtines & J. Gewirtz (Eds.), *Moral behavior and development* (Vol. 2). Hillsdale, NJ: Erlbaum.

Elder, G. (in press). The life course and human development. In W. Damon (Ed.), *Handbook of child psychology*. New York: Wiley.

Elder, G. H. (1974). *Children of the Great Depression*. Chicago: University of Chicago Press.

Elder, G. H. (1979). Historical change in life patterns and personality. In P. B. Baltes & O. G. Brim (Eds.), *Life-span development and behavior*. New York: Academic Press.

Elder, G. H. (1980). Adolescence in historical perspective. In J. Adelson (Ed.), *Handbook of adolescent psychology*. New York: Wiley.

Elder, G. H. (1995). Human lives in changing societies: Life course and developmental insights. In R. B. Cairns, G. H. Elder, & E. J. Costello (Eds.), *Developmental science*. New York: Cambridge.

Elder, G. H., Modell, J., & Parke, R. D. (Eds.). (1993). *Children in time and place: Developmental and historical insights*. New York: Cambridge University Press.

Elkind, D. (1961). Quantity conceptions in junior and senior high school students. *Child Development, 32*, 551–560.

Elkind, D. (1976). *Child development and education*. New York: Oxford University Press.

Elkind, D. (1978). Understanding the young adolescent. *Adolescence, 13*, 127–134.

Elkind, D. (1981). *The hurried child*. Reading, MA: Addison-Wesley.

Elkind, D. (1987). *Miseducation: Preschoolers at risk*. New York: Knopf.

Elkind, D. (1988, January). Educating the very young: A call for clear thinking. *NEA Today*, pp. 22–27.

Ellis, H. C. (1987). Recent developments in human memory. In V. P. Makosky (Ed.), *The G. Stanley Hall lecture series*. Washington, DC: American Psychological Association.

Ellis, L., & Ames, M. A. (1987). Neurohormonal functioning and sexual orientation: A theory of homosexuality-heterosexuality. *Psychological Bulletin, 101*, 233–258.

Ellis, N. C., & Laporte, N. (1997). Contexts of acquisition effects, In A. M. B. de Groot & J. F. Knoll (Eds.), *Tutorials in bilingualism*. Mahwah, NJ: Erlbaum.

Emde, R. N., Gaensbauer, T. G., & Harmon, R. J. (1976). Emotional expression in infancy: A biobehavioral study. *Psychological Issues: Monograph Series, 10* (37).

Emery, R. E. (1989). Family violence. *American Psychologist, 44*, 321–328.

Emlen, S. T. (1984). Cooperative breeding in birds and mammals. In J. R. Krebs & N. B. Davies (Eds.), *Behavioral ecology: An evolutionary approach* (2nd ed.). Oxford: Blackwell Scientific.

Enger, E. D., Kormelink, R., Ross, F. C., & Otto, R. (1996). *Diversity of life*. Dubuque, IA: Wm. C. Brown.

Enright, R. D., Lapsley, D. K., Dricas, A. S., & Fehr, L. A. (1980). Parental influence on the development of adolescent autonomy and identity. *Journal of Youth and Adolescence, 9*, 529–546.

Entwisle, D. R. (1990). Schools and the adolescent. In S. S. Feldman & G. R. Elliott (Eds.), *At the threshold: The developing adolescent*. Cambridge, MA: Harvard University Press.

Epstein, J. (1990). School and family connections: Theory, research, and implications for integrating sociologies of education and family. In D. G. Unger & M. B. Sussman (Eds.), *Families in community settings*. New York: Haworth Press.

Epstein, J. L. (1992). School and family partnerships. *Encyclopedia of educational research* (6th ed.). New York: Macmillan.

Erikson, E. H. (1950). *Childhood and society*. New York: W. W. Norton.

Erikson, E. H. (1962). *Young man Luther*. New York: W. W. Norton.

Erikson, E. H. (1968). *Identity: Youth and crisis*. New York: W. W. Norton.

Erikson, E. H. (1969). *Gandhi's truth*. New York: W. W. Norton.

Erlick, A. C., & Starry, A. R. (1973, June). *Sources of information for career decisions*. Report of Poll No. 98, Purdue Opinion Panel.

Erwin, E. J. (Ed.). (1996). *Putting children first*. Baltimore: Paul H. Brookes.

Espin, O. M. (1993). Psychological impact of migration on Latinos. In D. R. Atkinson, G. Morten, & D. W. Sue (Eds.), *Counseling American minorities*. Dubuque, IA: Brown & Benchmark.

Etzel, R. (1988, October). *Children of smokers*. Paper presented at the meeting of the American Academy of Pediatrics New Orleans.

Evans, B. J., & Whitfield, J. R. (Eds.). (1988). *Black males in the United States: An annotated bibliography from 1967 to 1987*. Washington, DC: American Psychological Association.

Evans, I. M., Cicchelli, T., Cohen, M., & Shapiro, N. (1995). *Staying in school*. Baltimore: Paul H. Brookes.

Eyler, F. D., Behnke, M. L., & Stewart, N. J. (1990). *Issues in identification and follow-up of cocaine-exposed neonates*. Unpublished manuscript, University of Florida, Gainesville.

Eyler, J., & Giles, D. (1997). The importance of program quality in service-learning. In A. S. Waterman (Ed.), *Service-learning*. Mahwah, NJ: Erlbaum.

Fabes, R. A., Knight, G. P., & Higgins, D. A. (1995, March). *Gender differences in aggression: A meta-analytic reexamination of time and age effects*. Paper presented at the meeting of the Society for Research in Child Development, Indianapolis.

Fabricius, W. V., & Hagen, J. W. (1984). Use of causal attributions about recall performance to assess metamemory and predict strategic memory behavior in young children. *Developmental Psychology, 20*, 975–987.

Fagot, B. I. (1995). Parenting boys and girls. In M. H. Bornstein (Ed.), *Handbook of parenting* (Vol. 1). Hillsdale, NJ: Erlbaum.

Faigel, H. C., Sznajderman, S., Tishy, O., Turel, M., & Pinus, U. (1995). Attention deficit disorder during adolescence: A review. *Journal of Adolescent Health, 16*, 174–184.

Falbo, T., & Poston, D. L. (1993). The academic, personality, and physical outcomes of only children in China. *Child Development, 64*, 18–35.

Fantz, R. L. (1963). Pattern vision in newborn infants. *Science, 140*, 296–297.

Farmer, J. E., Peterson, L., & Kashani, J. H. (1989, April). *Injury risk, parent and child psychopathology*. Paper presented at the biennial meeting of the Society for Research in Child Development, Kansas City.

Fasick, F. (1988). Patterns of formal education in high school as rites of passage. *Adolescence, 23*, 457–468.

Fein, G. G. (1986). Pretend play. In D. Görlitz & J. F. Wohlwill (Eds.), *Curiosity, imagination, and play*. Hillsdale, NJ: Erlbaum.

Feinman, S. (1981). Why is cross-sex-role behavior more approved for girls than for boys? A status characteristic approach. *Sex Roles, 7*, 289–299.

Feiring, C. (1992, March). *Concepts of romance in mid-adolescence*. Paper presented at the meeting of the Society for Research on Adolescence, Washington, DC.

Feiring, C. (1994, February). *Concepts of romance and sexuality in middle adolescence*. Paper presented at the meeting of the Society for Research on Adolescence, San Diego.

Feiring, C. (1995, March). *The development of romance from 15 to 18 years*. Paper presented at the meeting of the Society for Research in Child Development, Indianapolis.

Feiring, C. (1996). Concepts of romance in 15-year-old adolescents. *Journal of Research on Adolescence, 6*, 181–200.

Feiring, C. (1997, April). *Gender identity and the development of adolescent romance*. Paper presented at the meeting of the Society for Resesarch in Child Development, Washington, DC.

Feldman, D. H., & Piirto, J. (1995). Parenting talented children. In M. H. Bornstein (Ed.), *Handbook of parenting* (Vol. 1). Hillsdale, NJ: Erlbaum.

Feldman, M. A. (1996). The effectiveness of early intervention for children of parents with mental retardation. In M. J. Guralnick (Ed.), *The effectiveness of early intervention*. Baltimore: Paul H. Brookes.

Feldman, S. S., & Elliott, G. R. (1990). Progress and promise of research on normal adolescent development. In S. S. Feldman & G. Elliott (Eds.), *At the threshold: The developing adolescent*. Cambridge, MA: Harvard University Press.

Fenson, L., Dale, P. S., Reznick, S. J., Bates, E., Thal, D. J., & Pethick, S. (1994). Variability in early communicative development. *Monographs of the Society for Research in Child Development*, Serial No. 242, Vol. 60, No. 5.

Fenzel, L. M., & Magaletta, P. R. (1993, March). *Predicting intrinsic motivation of Black early adolescents: The roles of school strain, academic competence, and self-esteem*. Paper presented at the biennial meeting of the Society for Research in Child Development, New Orleans.

Ferguson, D. M., Harwood, L. J., & Shannon, F. T. (1987). Breastfeeding and subsequent social adjustment in 6- to 8-year-old children. *Journal of Child Psychology and Psychiatry, 28*, 378–386.

Ferrari, M., & Sternberg, R. J. (1997). The development of mental abilities. In D. Kuhn & R. S. Siegler (Eds.), *Handbook of child psychology* (5th Ed., Vol. II). New York: Wiley.

Field, T. (1990). *Infancy*. Cambridge, MA: Harvard University Press.

Field, T. (1992, September). Stroking babies helps growth, reduces stress. *Brown University Child and Adolescent Behavior Letter*, pp. 1, 6.

Field, T. (1995). Psychologically depressed parents. In M. H. Bornstein (Ed.), *Handbook of parenting* (Vol. 4). Hillsdale, NJ: Erlbaum.

Field, T., Sandberg, D., Quetel, T. A., Garcia, R., & Rosario, M. (1985). Effects of ultrasound feedback on pregnancy anxiety, fetal activity, and neonatal outcomes. *Obstetrics and Gynecology, 66*, 525–528.

Field, T., Scafidi, F., & Schanberg, S. (1987). Massage of preterm newborns to improve growth and development. *Pediatric Nursing, 13*, 385–387.

Field, T. M. (Ed.). (1995). *Touch in early development*. Hillsdale, NJ: Erlbaum.

Field, T. M., Grizzle, N., Scafidi, F., Abrams, S., & Richardson, S. (in press). Massage therapy for infants of depressed mothers. *Infant Behavior and Development*.

Field, T. M., Woodson, R., Greenberg, R., & Cohen, D. (1982). Discrimination and imitation of facial expressions by neonates. *Science, 218*, 179–181.

Finn-Stevenson, M. F., & Chung, D. (1995). *Evaluation of the School of the 21st Century: Preliminary findings*. New Haven, CT: Yale Bush Center.

Fischer, K. W., & Bidell, T. (1997). Dynamic development of psychological structures in action. In R. M. Lerner (Ed.), *Handbook of child psychology* (5th Ed., Vol. I). New York: Wiley.

Fischer, M., Barkley, R. A., Edelbrock, C. S., & Smallish, L. (1990). The adolescent outcome of hyperactive children diagnosed by research criteria: II. Academic, attentional, and neuropsychological status. *Journal of Consulting and Clinical Psychology, 58,* 550–558.

Fish, K. D., & Biller, H. B. (1973). Perceived childhood paternal relationships and college females' personal adjustment. *Adolescence, 8,* 415–420.

Fisher, C. B., Jackson, J. F., & Villarruel, F. A. (1997). The study of African-American and Latin-American children and youth. In R. M. Lerner (Ed.), *Handbook of child psychology* (5th Ed., Vol. I). New York: Wiley.

Fisher, D. (1990, March). *Effects of attachment of adolescents' friendships.* Paper presented at the meeting of the Society for Research in Adolescence, Atlanta.

Fisher-Thompson, D., Polinski, L., Eaton, M., & Hefferman, K. (1993, March). *Sex-role orientation of children and their parents: Relationship to the sex-typing of Christmas toys.* Paper presented at the biennial meeting of the Society for Research in Child Development, New Orleans.

Fivush, R. (1995, March). *The development of narrative remembering: Implications for the recovered memory debate.* Paper presented at the meeting of the Society for Research in Child Development, Indianapolis.

Flanagan, C. A., & Eccles, J. S. (1993). Changes in parents' work status and adolescents' adjustment at school. *Child Development, 64,* 246–257.

Flavell, J. H. (1980, fall). A tribute to Piaget. *Society for Research in Child Development Newsletter,* p. 1.

Flavell, J. H. (1992). Cognitive development: Past, present, and future. *Developmental Psychology, 28,* 998–1005.

Flavell, J. H., Beach, D. R., & Chinksy, J. M. (1966). Spontaneous verbal rehearsal in a memory task as a function of age. *Child Development, 37,* 283–289.

Flavell, J. H., Flavell, E. R., & Green, F. L. (1983). Development of the appearance-reality distinction. *Cognitive Psychology, 15,* 95–120.

Flavell, J. H., Green, F. L., & Flavell, E. R. (1995). Young children's knowledge about thinking. *Monographs of the Society for Research in Child Development, 60*(1).

Fletcher, A. (1995, March). *Parental and peer influences on academic achievement in African-American girls.* Paper presented at the meeting of the Society for Research in Child Development, Indianapolis.

Fogel, A., Toda, S., & Kawai, M. (1988). Mother-infant face-to-face interaction in Japan and the United States: A laboratory comparison using 3-month-old infants. *Developmental Psychology, 24,* 398–406.

Folkman, S., & Lazarus, R. (1991). Coping and emotion. In N. Stein, B. L. Leventhal, & T. Trabasso (Eds.), *Psychological and biological approaches to emotion.* Hillsdale, NJ: Erlbaum.

Fordham, S., & Ogbu, J. U. (1986). Black students' school success: Coping with the burden of "acting white." *Urban Review, 18,* 176–206.

Forehand, G., Ragosta, J., & Rock, D. (1976). Conditions and processes of effective school desegregation. Princeton, NJ: Educational Testing Service.

Forgatch, M. S., Patterson, G. R., & Ray, J. A. (1996). Divorce and boys' adjustment problems: Two paths with a single model. In E. M. Hetherington & E. A. Blechman (Eds.), *Stress, coping, and resilience in children and families.* Hillsdale, NJ: Erlbaum.

Forrest, J. D. (1990). Cultural influences on adolescents' reproductive behavior. In J. Bancroft & J. M. Reinisch (Eds.), *Adolescence and puberty.* New York: Oxford University Press.

Forshaun, S. (1996, March). *Attributions concerning adolescent suicide: The impact of gender, method, and outcome.* Paper presented at the meeting of the Society for Research on Adolescence, Boston.

Fox, N. (Ed.). (in press). The development of emotion regulation: Biological and behavioral considerations. *Monographs of the Society for Research in Child Development.*

Fraiberg, S. (1959). *The magic years.* New York: Charles Scribner's Sons.

Francis, J., Fraser, G., & Marcia, J. (1989). *Cognitive and experimental factors in moratorium-achievement (MAMA) cycles.* Unpublished manuscript. Department of Psychology, Simon Fraser University, Burnaby, British Columbia.

Fraser, S. (Ed.). (1995). *The bell curve wars: Race, intelligence, and the future of America.* New York: Basic Books.

Freedman, D. G., & Freedman, N. (1969). Behavioral differences between Chinese-American and European-American newborns. *Nature, 224,* 1127.

Freedman, J. L. (1984). Effects of television violence on aggressiveness. *Psychological Bulletin, 96,* 227–246.

Freeman, D. (1983). *Margaret Mead and Samoa.* Cambridge, MA: Harvard University Press.

Freeman, K. E., & Gehl, K. S. (1995, March). *Beginnings, middles, and ends: 24-month-olds' understanding of analogy.* Paper presented at the meeting of the Society for Research in Child Development, Indianapolis.

Freud, A., & Dann, S. (1951). Instinctual anxiety during puberty. In A. Freud (Ed.), *The ego and its mechanisms of defense.* New York: International Universities Press.

Freud, S. (1917). *A general introduction to psychoanalysis.* New York: Washington Square Press.

Fried, P. A., & Watkinson, B. (1990). 36- and 48-month neurobehavioral follow-up of children prenatally exposed to marijuana, cigarettes, and alcohol. *Developmental and Behavioral Pediatrics, 11,* 49–58.

Friedman, H. S., Tucker, J. S., Schwartz, J. E., Tomlinson-Keasy, C., Martin, L. R., Wingard, D. L., & Criqui, M. H. (1995). Psychosocial and behavioral predictors of longevity: The aging and death of the "Termites." *American Psychologist, 50,* 69–78.

Friedman, W. J. (1991). *About time: Inventing the fourth dimension.* Cambridge, MA: MIT Press.

Friedrich, L. K., & Stein, A. H. (1973). Aggressive and prosocial TV programs and the natural behavior of preschool children. *Monographs of the Society for Research in Child Development, 38* (4, Serial No. 151).

Frost, J. L., & Wortham, S. C. (1988, July). The evolution of American playgrounds. *Young Children,* 19–28.

Frye, D., Zelazo, P. D., Brooks, P. J., & Samuels, M. C. (1996). Inference and action in early causal reasoning. *Developmental Psychology, 32,* 120–131.

Fuller, M. (1984). Black girls in a London comprehensive school. In M. Hammersley & P. Woods (Eds.), *Life in school: The sociology of pop culture.* New York: Open University Press.

Furman, W. (1995). Parenting siblings. In M. H. Bornstein (Ed.), *Handbook of parenting* (Vol. 1). Hillsdale, NJ: Erlbaum.

Furman, W., & Buhrmester, D. (1992). Age and sex differences in perceptions of networks of personal relationships. *Child Development, 63,* 103–115.

Furstenberg, F. F. (1988). Child care after divorce and remarriage. In E. M. Hetherington & J. D. Arasteh (Eds.), *Impact of divorce, single parenting, and stepparenting on children.* Hillsdale, NJ: Erlbaum.

Furstenberg, F. F., Brooks-Gunn, J., & Chase-Lansdale, L. (1989). Teenage pregnancy and childbearing. *American Psychologist, 44,* 313–320.

Furstenberg, F. F., Jr., & Harris, K. T. (1992). When fathers matter/why fathers matter: The impact of paternal involvement on the offspring of adolescent mothers. In R. Lerman and T. Ooms (Eds.), *Young unwed fathers.* Philadelphia: Temple University Press.

Furth, H. G. (1973). *Deafness and learning: A psychosocial approach.* Belmont, CA: Wadsworth.

Furth, H. G., & Wachs, H. (1975). *Thinking goes to school.* New York: Oxford University Press.

Gadpaille, W. J. (1996). *Adolescent suicide.* Washington, DC: American Psychological Association.

Gage, N. L. (1965). Desirable behaviors of teachers. *Urban Education, 1,* 85–96.

Gaines, K. R. E., Blair, C. B., & Cluett, S. E. (1995, March). *Family environments, cultural diversity, and Head Start: Policy implications.* Paper presented at the meeting of the Society for Research in Child Development, Indianapolis.

Galambos, N. L., Almeida, D. M., & Petersen, A. C. (in press). Masculinity, femininity, and sex role attitudes in early adolescence: Exploring gender intensification. *Child Development.*

Galambos, N. L., Petersen, A. C., Richards, M., & Gitleson, I. B. (1985). The Attitudes toward Women Scale for Adolescents (AWSA): A study of reliability and validity. *Sex Roles, 13,* 343–356.

Galambos, N. L., & Sears, H. A. (1995, March). *Depressive symptoms in adolescents: Examining family matters.* Paper presented at the meeting of the Society for Research in Child Development, Indianapolis.

Galambos, N. L., & Tilton-Weaver, L. (1996, March). *The adultoid adolescent: Too much, too soon.* Paper presented at the meeting of the Society for Research on Adolescence, Boston.

Galambos, N. L., & Turner, P. K. (1997, April). *Shaping parent-adolescent relations: Examining the goodness-of-fit in parent and adolescent temperaments.* Paper presented at the meeting of the Society for Research in Child Development, Washington, DC.

Galotti, K. M. (1989). Approaches to studying formal and everyday reasoning. *Psychological Bulletin, 105,* 331–351.

Galotti, K. M., Kozberg, S. F., & Appleman, D. (in press). Younger and older adolescents' thinking about commitments. *Journal of Experimental Child Psychology.*

Gandini, L. (1993). Fundamentals of the Reggio Emilia approach to early childhood education. *Young Children, 49,* 4–8.

Gangestad, S. W. (1995). The new evolutionary psychology: Prospects and challenges. *Psychological Inquiry, 6,* 38–41.

Garbarino, J. (1976). The ecological correlates of child abuse: The impact of socioeconomic stress on mothers. *Child Development, 47,* 178–185.

Garbarino, J. (1980). Some thoughts on school size and its effects on adolescent development. *Journal of Youth and Adolescence, 9,* 19–31.

Garbarino, J. (1980). The issue is human quality: In praise of children. *Children and Youth Services Review, 1,* 353–377.

Garbarino, J., & Asp, C. E. (1981). *Successful schools and competent students.* Lexington, MA: Lexington Books.

Garcia, J. G., & Zea, M. C. (1997). *Psychological interventions and research with Latino populations.* Needham Heights, MA: Allyn, & Bacon.

Garcia, L., Hart, D., & Johnson-Ray, R. (in press). What do children and adolescents think about themselves? A developmental account of self-concept development. In S. Hala, (Ed.), *The development of social cognition.* London: University College of London Press.

Gardner, B. T., & Gardner, R. A. (1971). Two-way communication with an infant chimpanzee. In A. Schrier & F. Stollnitz (Eds.), *Behavior of nonhuman primates* (Vol. 4). New York: Academic Press.

Gardner, H. (1938). *Frames of mind.* New York: Basic Books.

Gardner, H. (1989). Beyond a modular view of mind. In W. Damon (Ed.), *Child development today and tomorrow.* San Francisco: Jossey-Bass.

Gardner, L. I. (1972). Deprivation dwarfism. *Scieentific American, 227,* 76–82.

Garmezy, N. (1985). Stress-resistant children: The search for protective factors. In J. E. Stevenson (Ed.), *Recent Research in Developmental Psychopathology: Journal of Child Psychology and Psychiatry Book Supplement, 4,* 213–233.

Garmezy, N. (1993). Children in poverty: Resilience despite risk. *Psychiatry, 56,* 127–136.

Garner, D. M., & Garfinkel, P. E. (1997). *Handbook of treatment for eating disorders.* New York: Plenum.

Garrett, P., Ng'andu, N., & Ferron, J. (1994). Poverty experiences of young children and the quality of their home environments. *Child Development, 65,* 331–345.

Garvey, C. (1977). *Play.* Cambridge, MA: Harvard University Press.

Garwood, S. G., Phillips, D., Hartman, A., & Zigler, E. F. (1989). As the pendulum swings: Federal agency programs for children. *American Psychologist, 44,* 434–440.

Gauvain, M. (1995). Thinking in niches: Sociocultural influences on cognitive development. *Human Development, 38,* 25–45.

Gazzaniga, M. S. (1986). *The social brain.* New York: Plenum.

Geary, D. C., Fan, L., Bow-Thomas, C. C., & Siegler, R. S. (1993). Even before formal instruction Chinese children outperform American children in mental addition. *Cognitive Development, 8,* 517–529.

Gelfand, D. M., Teti, D. M., & Fox, C. E. R. (1992). Sources of parenting stress for depressed and nondepressed mothers of infants. *Journal of Clinical Child Psychology, 21,* 262–272.

Gelles, R. J., & Conte, J. R. (1990). Domestic violence and sexual abuse of children: A review of research in the eighties. *Journal of Marriage and the Family, 52,* 1045–1058.

Gelman, R. (1969). Conservation acquisition: A problem of learning to attend to relevant attributes. *Journal of Experimental Child Psychology, 7,* 67–87.

Gelman, R., & Au, T. K. (Eds.). (1996). *Perceptual and cognitive development* (2nd ed.). San Diego: Academic Press.

Gelman, R., & Baillargeon, R. (1983). A review of some Piagetian concepts. In P. H. Mussen (Ed.), *Handbook of child psychology* (4th ed., Vol. 3). New York: Wiley.

Gelman, R., & Gallistel, C. R. (1978). *The child's understanding of numbers.* Cambridge, MA: Harvard University Press.

Gelman, R., & Williams, E. M. (1997). Enabling constraints for cognitive development and learning. In D. Kuhn & R. S. Siegler (Eds.), *Handbook of child psychology* (5th Ed., Vol. II). New York: Wiley.

Gelman, S. A., & Markman, E. (1987). Young children's inductions from natural kinds: The role of categories and appearances. *Child Development, 58,* 1532–1541.

George, C. M. (1996, March). *Gene-environment interactions: Testing the bioecological model during adolescence.* Paper presented at the meeting of the Society for Research on Adolescence, Boston.

Gerber, P. J., Reiff, H. B., & Ginsberg, R. (1996). Reframing the learning disabilities experience. *Journal of Learning Disabilities, 18,* 98–101.

Gerry, M. (1997, April). *Policies on universal health and child care.* Paper presented at the meeting of the Society for Research in Child Development, Washington, DC.

Gesell, A. L. (1928). *Infancy and human growth.* New York: Macmillan.

Gesell, A. L. (1934). *Infancy and human growth.* New York: Macmillan.

Gesell, A. L. (1934). *An atlas of infant behavior.* New Haven, CT: Yale University Press.

Gewirtz, J. (1977). Maternal responding and the conditioning of infant crying: Directions of influence within the attachment-acquisition process. In B. C. Etzel, J. M. LeBlanc, & D. M. Baer (Eds.), *New developments in behavioral research.* Hillsdale, NJ: Erlbaum.

Giaconia, R. M., & Hedges, L. V. (1982). Identifying features of effective open education. *Review of Educational Research, 52,* 579–602.

Gibbs, J. T., & Huang, L. N. (1989). A conceptual framework for assessing and treating minority youth. In J. T. Gibbs & L. N. Huang (Eds.), *Children of color.* San Francisco: Jossey-Bass.

Gibson, E. G. (1969). *The principles of perceptual learning and development.* New York: Appleton-Century-Crofts.

Gibson, E. J. (1982). The concept of affordances in development: The renaissance of functionalism. In W. A. Collins (Ed.), *Minnesota Symposium on Child Psychology* (Vol. 15). Hillsdale, NJ: Erlbaum.

Gibson, E. J. (1989). Exploratory behavior in the development of perceiving, acting, and the acquiring of knowledge. *Annual Review of Psychology, 39.* Palo Alto, CA: Annual Reviews.

Gibson, E. J. (1989). Exploratory behavior in the development of perceiving, acting, and the acquiring of knowledge. *Annual Review of Psychology, 39.*

Gibson, E. J., Riccio, G., Schmuckler, M. A., Stoffregen, T. A., Rosenberg, D., & Taormina, J. (1987). Detection of the traversibility of surfaces by crawling and walking infants. *Journal of Experimental Psychology: Human Perception and Performance, 13,* 533–544.

Gibson, E. J., & Walk, R. D. (1960). The "visual cliff." *Scientific American, 202,* 64–71.

Gibson, J. J. (1966). *The senses considered as perceptual systems.* Boston: Houghton Mifflin.

Gibson, J. J. (1979). *The ecological approach to visual perception.* Boston: Houghton Mifflin.

Gilligan, C. (1982). *In a different voice.* Cambridge, MA: Harvard University Press.

Gilligan, C. (1990). Teaching Shakespeare's sister. In C. Gilligan, N. Lyons, & T. Hammer (Eds.), *Making connections: The relational worlds of adolescent girls at the Emma Willard School.* Cambridge, MA: Harvard University Press.

Gilligan, C. (1992, May.) *Joining the resistance: Girls' development in adolescence.* Paper presented at the Symposium on Development and Vulnerability in Close Relationships, Montreal.

Gilligan, C. (1996). The centrality of relationships in psychological development: A puzzle, some evidence, and a theory. In G. G. Noam & K. W. Fischer (Eds.), *Development and vulnerability in close relationships.* Hillsdale, NJ: Erlbaum.

Gilligan, C., & Attanucci, J. (1988). Two moral orientations. In C. Gilligan, J. V. Ward, J. M. Taylor, & B. Bardige (Eds.), *Mapping the moral domain.* Cambridge, MA: Harvard University Press.

Gilligan, C., Brown, L. M., & Rogers, A. G. (1990). Psyche embedded: A place for body, relationships, and culture in personality theory. In A. I. Rabin, R. A. Zucker, R. A. Emmons, & S. Frank (Eds.), *Studying persons and lives.* New York: Springer.

Ginsburg, H. P., Klein, A., & Starkey, P. (1997). The development of children's mathematical thinking. In I. E. Sigel & K. A. Renninger (Eds.), *Handbook of child psychology* (5th Ed., Vol. IV). New York: Wiley.

Gjerde, P. F., Block, J., & Block, J. H. (1991). The preschool family context of 18-year-olds with depressive symptoms: A prospective study. *Journal of Research on Adolescence, 1,* 63–92.

Glass, G. V., & Smith, M. L. (1978, September). *Meta-analysis of research on the relationship of class size and achievement.* San Francisco: Far West Educational Laboratory.

Glassman, M. J. (1995, March). *Vygotsky's times: Their times, his times, our times.* Paper presented at the meeting of the Society for Research in Child Development, Indianapolis.

Glick, J. (1975). Cognitive development in cross-cultural perspective. In F. Horowitz (Ed.), *Review of child development research* (Vol. 4). Chicago: University of Chicago Press.

Glueck, S., & Glueck, E. (1950). *Unraveling juvenile delinquency.* Cambridge, MA: Harvard University Press.

Glueck, S., & Glueck, E. (1950). *Unraveling juvenile delinquency.* New York: Commonwealth Fund.

Gold, M., & Petronio, R. J. (1980). Delinquent behavior in adolescence. In J. Adelson (Ed.), *Handbook of adolescent psychology.* New York: Wiley.

Goldberg, H. (1980). *The new male.* New York: Signet.

Goldfield, E. C., Kay, B. A., & Warren, W. H. (1993). Infant bouncing: The assembly and tuning of action systems. *Child Development, 64,* 1128–1142.

Goldin-Meadow, S. (1977). The development of language-like communication without a language model. *Science, 197,* 401–403.

Goldscheider, F. C. (1997). Family relationships and life course strategies for the 21st century. In S. Dreman (Ed.), *The family on the threshold of the 21st century.* Mahwah, NJ: Erlbaum.

Goldsmith, H. H. (1988, August). *Does early temperament predict late development?* Paper presented at the meeting of the American Psychological Association, Atlanta.

Goldsmith, H. H., & Gottesman, I. I. (1981). Origins of variation in behavioral style: A longitudinal study of temperament in young twins. *Child Development, 52,* 91–103.

Goldstein, A. P., & Conoley, J. C. (1997). *School violence intervention.* New York: Guilford.

Golombok, S., Cook, R., Bish, A., & Murray, C. (1995). Families created by the new reproductive technologies: Quality of parenting and social and emotional development of the children. *Child Development, 66,* 285–298.

Golombok, S., & Tasker, F. (1996). Do parents influence the sexual orientation of their children? Findings from a longitudinal study of lesbian families. *Child Development, 32,* 3–11.

Gomel, J. N., Tinsley, B. J., & Clark, K. (1995, March). *Family stress and coping during times of economic hardship: A multiethnic perspective.* Paper presented at the meeting of the Society for Research in Child Development, Indianapolis.

Gomez, R., & Thompson, L. (1993, March). *How children organize their knowledge of everyday events: Exploring the generality of event representations.* Paper presented at the biennial meeting of the Society for Research in Child Development, New Orleans.

Goodenow, C. (1993, March). *Friends, classmates, and teachers as influences on the academic motivation of early adolescent students.* Paper presented at the biennial meeting of the Society for Research in Child Development, New Orleans.

Goodnow, J. J. (1995, March). *Incorporating "culture" into accounts of development.* Paper presented at the meeting of the Society for Research in Child Development, Indianapolis.

Gopnik, A. (1997, April). *How the child's theory of mind changes.* Paper presented at the meeting of the Society for Research in Child Development, Washington, DC.

Gordon, I. (1978, June). *What does research say about the effects of parent involvement on schooling?* Paper presented at the meeting of the Association for Supervision and Curriculum Development, Washington, DC.

Gottfried, A. E., & Gottfried, A. W. (1989, April). *Home environment and children's academic intrinsic motivation: A longitudinal study.* Paper presented at the biennial meeting of the Society for Research in Child Development, Kansas City.

Gottfried, A. E., Gottfried, A. W., & Bathurst, K. (1988). Maternal employment, family environment, and children's development: Infancy through the school years. In A. E. Gottfried & A. W. Gottfried (Eds.), *Maternal employment and children's development: Longitudinal research.* New York: Plenum.

Gottfried, A. E., Gottfried, A. W., & Bathurst, K. (1995). Maternal and dual-earner employment status and parenting. In M. H. Bornstein (Ed.), *Handbook of parenting* (Vol. 3). Hillsdale, NJ: Erlbaum.

Gottfried, A. W., & Lussier, C. M. (1993, March). *Continuity, stability, and change in temperament: A 10-year longitudinal investigation from infancy through adolescence.* Paper presented at the biennial meeting of the Society for Research in Child Development, New Orleans.

Gottlieb, G. (1997). *Synthesizing nature-nurture.* Mahwah, NJ: Erlbaum.

Gottlieb, G., Wahlsten, D., & Lickliter, R. (1997). The significance of biology for human development. In R. M. Lerner (Ed.), *Handbook of child psychology* (5th Ed., Vol. I). New York: Wiley.

Gottman, J. M., & Parker, J. G. (Eds.). (1987). *Conversations of friends.* New York: Cambridge University Press.

Gould, S. J. (1981). *The mismeasure of man.* New York: W. W. Norton.

Gounin-Decarie, T. (1996). Revisiting Piaget, or the vulnerability of Piaget's infancy theory in the nineties. In G. G. Noam & K. W. Fischer (Eds.), *Development and vulnerability in close relationships.* Hillsdale, NJ: Erlbaum.

Graber, J. A., Brooks-Gunn, J., Paikoff, R. L., & Warren, M. P. (1994). Prediction of eating problems: An eight-year study of adolescent girls. *Developmental Psychology, 30* (6), 823–834.

Graber, J. A., Brooks-Gunn, J., & Warren, M. P. (1995). The antecedents of menarcheal age: Heredity, family environment, and stressful life events. *Child Development, 66,* 346–359.

Graber, J. A., Petersen, A. C., & Brooks-Gunn, J. (1996). Pubertal processes: Methods, measures, and models. In J. A. Graber, J. Brooks-Gunn, & A. E. Petersen (Eds.), *Transitions through adolescence.* Hillsdale, NJ: Erlbaum.

Graham, S. (1986, August). *Can attribution theory tell us something about motivation in blacks?* Paper presented at the meeting of the American Psychological Association, Washington, DC.

Graham, S. (1987, August). *Developing relations between attributions affect and intended social behavior.* Paper presented at the meeting of the American Psychological Association, New York.

Graham, S. (1990). Motivation in Afro-Americans. In G. L. Berry & J. K. Asamen (Eds.), *Black students: Psychosocial issues and academic achievement.* Newbury Park, CA: Sage.

Grant, J. P. (1996). *The state of the world's children.* New York: UNICEF and Oxford University Press.

Grantham-McGregor, S. M. (1995, March). *Studies of the effects of nutrition and stimulation on children's behavioral development in Jamaica.* Paper presented at the meeting of the Society for Research in Child Development, Indianapolis.

Graziano, W. J. (1955). Evolutionary psychology: Old music, but now on CDs? *Psychological Inquiry, 6,* 31–34.

Green, P. (1995, March). *Sesame Street: More than a television show.* Paper presented at the meeting of the Society for Research in Child Development, Indianapolis.

Greenberg, P. (1992). Why not academic preschool? Part 2. Autocracy or democracy in the early years. *Young Children, 47,* 54–64.

Greenfield, P. M. (1966). On culture and conservation. In J. S. Bruner, R. P. Oliver, & P. M. Greenfield (Eds.), *Studies in cognitive growth.* New York: Wiley.

Greenfield, P. M., & Suzuki, L. K. (1997). Culture and human development. In I. E. Sigel & K. A. Renninger (Eds.), *Handbook of child psychology* (5th Ed., Vol. IV). New York: Wiley.

Grotevant, H. D. (1997). Adolescent development in family contexts. In N. Eisenberg (Ed.), *Handbook of child psychology* (5th Ed., Vol. III). New York: Wiley.

Grotevant, H. D., & Cooper, C. R. (in press). Individuality and connectedness in adolescent development: Review and prospects for research on identity, relationships, and context. In E. Skoe & A. von der Lippe (Eds.), *Personality development in adolescence: A cross-national and life-span perspective.* London: Routledge.

Grotevant, H. D., & McRoy, R. G. (1990). Adopted adolescents in residential treatment: The role of the family. In D. M. Brodzinsky & M. D. Schechter (Eds.), *The psychology of adoption.* New York: Oxford University Press.

Gruskin, E. (1994, February). *A review of research on self-identified gay, lesbian, and bisexual youth from 1970–1993.* Paper presented at the meeting of the Society for Research on Adolescence, San Diego.

Gruys, A. (1993, March). *Security of attachment and its relation to quantitative and qualitative aspects of friendship.* Paper presented at the biennial meeting of the Society for Research in Child Development, New Orleans.

Guilford, J. P. (1967). *The structure of intellect.* New York: McGraw-Hill.

Gunnar, M. R., Malone, S., & Fisch, R. O. (1987). The psychobiology of stress and coping in the human neonate: Studies of the adrenocortical activity in response to stress in the first week of life. In T. Field, P. McCabe, & N. Scheiderman (Eds.), *Stress and coping.* Hillsdale, NJ: Erlbaum.

Gunter, B. (1994). The question of media violence. In J. Bryant & D. Zillman (Eds.), *Media effects.* Hillsdale, NJ: Erlbaum.

Gur, R. C., Mozley, L. H., Mozley, P. D., Resnick, S. M., Karp, J. S., Alavi, A., Arnold, S. E., & Gur, R. E. (1995). Sex differences in regional cerebral glucose metabolism during a resting state. *Science, 267,* 528–531.

Gustafson, G. E., Green, J. A., & Kalinowski, L. L. (1993, March). *The development of communicative skills: Infants' cries and vocalizations in social context.* Paper presented at the biennial meeting of the Society for Research in Child Development, New Orleans.

Hack, M. H., Klein, N. K., & Taylor, H. G. (1995, spring). Long-term developmental outcomes of low birth weight infants. *The Future of Children, 5*(1), 176–196.

Hahn, A. (1987, December). Reaching out to America's dropouts: What to do? *Phi Delta Kappan,* pp. 256–263.

Haidt, J. D. (1997, April). *Cultural and class variations in the domain of morality and the morality of conventions.* Paper presented at the meeting of the Society for Research in Child Development, Washington, DC.

Haight, W. L., & Miller, P. J. (1993). *Pretending at home.* Albany: State University of New York Press.

Haith, M. H. (1991, April). *Setting a path for the '90s: Some goals and challenges in infant sensory and perceptual development.* Paper presented at the meeting of the Society for Research in Child Development, Seattle.

Haith, M. M., Hazen, C., & Goodman, G. S. (1988). Expectation and anticipation of dynamic visual events by 3.5 month old babies. *Child Development, 59,* 467–479.

Hakim-Larson, J. A. (1995, March). *Affective defaults: Temperament, goals, rules, and values.* Paper presented at the meeting of the Society for Research in Child Development, Indianapolis.

Hakuta, K., & Garcia, E. E. (1989). Bilingualism and education. *American Psychologist, 44*, 374–379.

Hale, S. (1990). A global developmental trend in cognitive processing speed. *Child Development, 61*, 653–663.

Hall, C. C. I., Evans, B. J., & Selice, S. (Eds.). (1989). *Black females in the United States*. Washington, DC: American Psychological Association.

Hall, G. S. (1904). *Adolescence* (Vols. 1 & 2). Englewood Cliffs, NJ: Prentice Hall.

Halonen, J. (1995). Demystifying critical thinking. *Teaching of Psychology, 22*, 75–81.

Hamilton, M. C. (1991). *Preference for sons or daughters and the sex role characteristics of potential parents*. Paper presented at the meeting of the Association for Women in Psychology, Hartford, CT.

Hammen, C. (1993, March). *Risk and resilience in children and their depressed mothers*. Paper presented at the biennial meeting of the Society for Research in Child Development, New Orleans.

Hammond, W. R. (1993, August). Participant in open forum with the APA Commission on Youth and Violence, meeting of the American Psychological Association, Washington, DC.

Hans, S. (1989, April). *Infant behavioral effects of prenatal exposure to methadone*. Paper presented at the biennial meeting of the Society for Research in Child Development, Kansas City.

Hare, B. R., & Castenell, L. A. (1985). No place to run, no place to hide: Comparative status and future prospects of black boys. In M. B. Spencer, G. K. Brookins, & W. R. Allen (Eds.), *Beginnings: The social and affective development of black children*. Hillsdale, NJ: Erlbaum.

Hare-Muston, R., & Maracek, J. (1988). The meaning of difference: Gender theory, postmodernism, and psychology. *American Psychologist, 43*, 455–464.

Harkness, S., & Super, C. M. (1995). Culture and parenting. In M. H. Bornstein (Ed.), *Children and parenting* (Vol. 2). Hillsdale, NJ: Erlbaum.

Harlow, H. F., & Zimmerman, R. R. (1959). Affectional responses in the infant monkey. *Science, 130*, 421–432.

Harold, R. D., & Eccles, J. S. (1990, March). *Maternal expectations, advice, and provision of opportunities: Their relationships to boys' and girls' occupational aspirations*. Paper presented at the meeting of the Society for Research in Adolescence, Atlanta.

Harris, G., Thomas, A., & Booth, D. A. (1990). Development of salt taste in infancy. *Developmental Psychology, 26*, 534–538.

Harris, P. L. (1989). *Children and emotion*. London: Basil Blackwell.

Harrist, A. W. (1993, March). *Family interaction styles as predictors of children's competence: The role of synchrony and nonsynchrony*. Paper presented at the biennial meeting of the Society for Research in Child Development, New Orleans.

Hart, B., & Risley, T. R. (1955). *Meaningful differences*. Baltimore: Paul H. Brookes.

Hart, C. H., Charlesworth, R., Burts, D. C., & DeWolf, M. (1993, March). *The relationship of attendance in developmentally appropriate or inappropriate kindergarten classrooms to first-grade behavior*. Paper presented at the biennial meeting of the Society for Research in Child Development, New Orleans.

Hart, D. (1996). Unpublished review of *Child Development* (8th ed.) by J. W. Santrock. Dubuque, IA: Brown & Benchmark.

Hart, D., & Fegley, S. (1995). Prosocial behavior and caring in adolescence: Relations to self-understanding and social judgment. *Child Development, 66*, 1346–1359.

Hart, D., Field, N., Garfinkle, J., & Singer, J. (in press). Representations of self and other: A semantic space model. *Journal of Personality*.

Hart, D., & Karmel, M. P. (1996). Self-awareness and self-knowledge in humans, great apes, and monkeys. In A. Russon, K. Bard, & S. Parker (Eds.), *Reaching into thought*. New York: Cambridge University Press.

Harter, S. (1982). The Perceived Competence Scale for Children. *Child Development, 53*, 87–97.

Harter, S. (1985). *Self-Perception Profile for Children*. Denver: University of Denver, Department of Psychology.

Harter, S. (1986). Processes underlying the construction, maintenance, and enhancement of the self-concept of children. In J. Suls & A. Greenwald (Eds.), *Psychological perspective on the self* (Vol. 3). Hillsdale, NJ: Erlbaum.

Harter, S. (1989). *Self-Perception Profile for Adolescents*. Denver: University of Denver, Department of Psychology.

Harter, S. (1990a). Processes underlying adolescent self-concept formation. In R. Montemayor, G. R. Adams, & T. P. Gulotta (Eds.), *From childhood to adolescence: A transitional period?* Newbury Park, CA: Sage.

Harter, S. (1990b). Self and identity development. In S. S. Feldman & G. R. Elliott (Eds.), *At the threshold: The developing adolescent*. Cambridge, MA: Harvard University Press.

Harter, S. (1997). The development of self-representations. In N. Eisenberg (Ed.), *Handbook of child psychology* (5th Ed., Vol. III). New York: Wiley.

Harter, S., Alexander, P. C., & Neimeyer, R. A. (1988). Long-term effects of incestuous child abuse in college women. Social adjustment, social cognition, and family characteristics. *Journal of Consulting and Clinical Psychology, 56*, 5–8.

Harter, S., & Lee, L. (1989). *Manifestations of true and false selves in adolescence*. Paper presented at the meeting of the Society for Research in Child Development, Kansas City.

Harter, S., & Marold, D. B. (1992). Psychological risk factors contributing to adolescent suicide ideation. In G. Noam & S. Borst (Eds.), *Child and adolescent suicide*. San Francisco: Jossey Bass.

Harter, S., Marold, D. B., Whitesell, N. R., & Cobbs, G. (in press). A model of the effects of perceived parent and peer support on adolescent false self behavior. *Child Development*.

Harter, S., & Monsour, A. (1992). Developmental analysis of conflict caused by opposing attributes in the adolescent self-portrait. *Developmental Psychology, 28*, 251–260.

Harter, S., Waters, P., & Whitesell, N. (1996, March). *False self behavior and lack of voice among adolescent males and females*. Paper presented at the meeting of the Society for Research on Adolescence, Boston.

Hartshorne, H., & May, M. S. (1928–1930). *Moral studies in the nature of character: Vol. 1. Studies in deceit. Vol. 2. Studies in self-control. Vol. 3. Studies in the organization of character*. New York: Macmillan.

Hartup, W. W. (1976). Peer interaction and the development of the individual child. In E. Schopler & R. J. Reichler (Eds.), *Psychopathology and child development*. New York: Plenum.

Hartup, W. W. (1983). The peer system. In P. H. Mussen (Ed.), *Handbook of child psychology* (4th ed., Vol. 4). New York: Wiley.

Hartup, W. W. (1996). The company they keep: Friendships and their developmental significance. *Child Development, 67*, 1–13.

Haskins, R. (1989). Beyond metaphor: The efficacy of early childhood education. *American Psychologist, 44*, 274–282.

Hatano, G., Siegler, R. S., Richards, D. D., Inagaki, K., Stavy, R., & Wax, N. (1993). The development of biological knowledge: A multi-national study. *Cognitive Development, 8*, 47–62.

Hatkoff, A., & Klopp, K. (1992). *How to save the children*. New York: Simon & Schuster.

Havighurst, R. J. (1976). A cross-cultural view. In J. F. Adams (Ed.), *Understanding adolescence*. Boston: Allyn & Bacon.

Hayden-Thomson, L., Rubin, K. M., & Hymel, S. (1987). Sex preferences in sociometric choices. *Developmental Psychology, 23*, 558–562.

Haynie, D., & McLellan, J. (1992, March). *Continuity in parent and peer relationships.* Paper presented at the meeting of the Society for Research on Adolescence, Washington, DC.

Hazen, C., & Shaver, P. (1987). Romantic love conceptualized as an attachment process. *Journal of Personality and Social Psychology, 51*, 511–524.

Heath, S. B. (1983). *Ways with words.* Cambridge, England: Cambridge University Press.

Heath, S. B. (1989). Oral and literate traditions among Black Americans living in poverty. *American Psychologist, 44*, 367–373.

Heath, S. B., & McLaughlin, M. W. (Eds.). (1993). *Identity and inner-city youth.* New York: Teachers College Press.

Hedges, L. V., & Stock, W. (1983, spring). The effects of class size: An examination of rival hypotheses. *American Education Research Journal*, 63–85.

Hellige, J. B. (1990). Hemispheric asymmetry. *Annual Review of Psychology, 41.*

Helling, M. K. (1993, March). *Relations among information received from the school and parental behaviors.* Paper presented at the biennial meeting of the Society for Research in Child Development, New Orleans.

Helson, R. M. (1993, August). *Issues of change and stability in creative lives.* Paper presented at the meeting of the American Psychological Association, Toronto.

Henderson, S. D. (1995, March). *Parent-child relationships in nondivorced, simple-step, and complex-step families.* Paper presented at the meeting of the Society for Research in Child Development, Indianapolis.

Henderson, S. H., Hetherington, E. M., Mekos, D., & Reiss, D. (1996). Stress, parenting, and adolescent psychopathology in nondivorced and stepfamilies: A within-family perspective. In E. M. Hetherington & E. A. Blechman (Eds.), *Stress, coping, and resiliency in children and families.* Hillsdale, NJ: Erlbaum.

Henderson, V. L., & Dweck, C. S. (1990). Motivation and achievement. In S. S. Feldman & G. R. Elliott (Eds.), *At the threshold: The developing adolescent.* Cambridge, MA: Harvard University Press.

Hendry, J. (1986). *Becoming Japanese: The world of the preschool child.* Honolulu: University of Hawaii Press.

Herdt, G. H. (1988, August). *Coming out processes as an anthropological rite of passage.* Paper presented at the meeting of the American Psychological Association, Atlanta.

Hernandez, D. J. (1997). Child development and the social demography of childhood. *Child Development, 68*, 149–169.

Hernstein, R. J., & Murray, C. (1994). *The bell curve: Intelligence and class structure in modern life.* New York: Free Press.

Hess, L., Lonky, E., & Roodin, P. A. (1985, April). *The relationship of moral reasoning and ego strength to cheating behavior.* Paper presented at the meeting of the Society for Research in Child Development, Toronto.

Hess, R. D., Holloway, S. D., Dickson, W. P., & Price, G. G. (1984). Maternal variables as predictors of children's school readiness and later achievement in vocabulary and mathematics in the sixth grade. *Child Development, 55*, 1902–1912.

Hetherington, E. M. (1995, March). *The changing American family and the well-being of children.* Paper presented at the meeting of the Society for Research in Child Development, Indianapolis.

Hetherington, E. M., & Clingempeel, W. G. (1992). Coping with marital transition. *Monographs of the Society for Research in Child Development.* Serial no. 227, Vol. 57.

Hetherington, E. M., Cox, M., & Cox, R. (1982). Effects of divorce on children and parents. In M. E. Lamb (Ed.), *Nontraditional families.* Hillsdale, NJ: Erlbaum.

Hetherington, E. M., & Stanley-Hagan, M. M. (1995). Parenting in divorced and remarried families. In M. H. Bornstein (Ed.), *Children and parenting* (Vol. 4). Hillsdale, NJ: Erlbaum.

Hiester, M., Carlson, E., & Sroufe, L. A. (1993, March). *The evolution of friendships in preschool, middle childhood, and adolescence: Origins in attachment history.* Paper presented at the biennial meeting of the Society for Research in Child Development, New Orleans.

Higgins, A. (1991). Lawrence Kohlberg: The vocation of an educator, part II. In W. M. Kurtines & J. Gewirtz (Eds.), *Moral behavior and development* (Vol. 1). Hillsdale, NJ: Erlbaum.

Hightower, E. (1990). Adolescent interpersonal and familial precursors of positive mental health at midlife. *Journal of Youth and Adolescence, 19*, 257–275.

Hill, C. R., & Stafford, F. P. (1980). Parental care of children: Time diary estimate of quantity, predictability, and variety. *Journal of Human Resources, 15*, 219–239.

Hill, H., Soriano, F. I., Chen, A., & LaFromboise, T. (1994). Sociocultural factors in the etiology and prevention of violence among ethnic minority youth. In L. Eron, J. H. Gentry, & P. Schlegel (Eds.), *Reason to hope.* Washington, DC: American Psychological Association.

Hill, J. P. (1983, April). *Early adolescence: A research agenda.* Paper presented at the meeting of the Society for Research in Child Development, Detroit.

Hill, J. P., & Lynch, M. E. (1983). The intensification of gender-related role expectations during early adolescence. In J. Brooks-Gunn & A. C. Petersen (Eds.), *Girls at puberty.* New York: Plenum.

Hinde, R. A. (1992). Developmental psychology in the context of other behavioral sciences. *Developmental Psychology, 28*, 1018–1029.

Hines, M. (1982). Prenatal gonadal hormones and sex differences in human behavior. *Psychological Bulletin, 92*, 56–80.

Hiraga, Y., Cauce, A. M., Mason, C., & Ordonez, N. (1993, March). *Ethnic identity and the social adjustment of biracial youth.* Paper presented at the biennial meeting of the Society for Research in Child Development, New Orleans.

Hirsch, B. J., & Rapkin, B. D. (1987). The transition to junior high school: A longitudinal study of self-esteem, psychological symptomatology, school life, and social support. *Child Development, 58*, 1235–1243.

Hirsch, E. D. (1987). *Cultural literacy.* Boston: Houghton Mifflin.

Hirsch, E. D. (1996). *The schools we need and why we don't have them.* Boston: Houghton Mifflin.

Hirsch-Pasek, K., Hyson, M., Rescorla, L., & Cone, J. (1989, April). *Hurrying children: How does it affect their aca-demic, social, creative, and emotional development?* Paper presented at the Society for Research in Child Development meeting, Kansas City.

Ho, D. Y. F. (1987). Fatherhood in Chinese culture. In M. E. Lamb (Ed.), *The father's role: Cross-cultural perspectives.* Hillsdale, NJ: Erlbaum.

Hoagwood, K., Jensen, P., & Fisher, C. (Eds.). (1996). *Ethical issues in mental health research with children and adolescents.* Hillsdale, NJ: Erlbaum.

Hofer, B. K., Carlson, D. M., & Stevenson, H. W. (1996, March). *Gender differences in attitudes and beliefs about mathematics: Correlates of achievement in six countries.* Paper presented at the meeting of the Society for Research on Adolescence, Boston.

Hoff-Ginsberg, E., & Tardif, T. (1995). Socioeconomic status and parenting. In M. H. Bornstein (Ed.), *Children and parenting* (Vol. 2). Hillsdale, NJ: Erlbaum.

Hoffman, L. W. (1989). Effects of maternal employment in the two-parent family. *American Psychologist, 44,* 283–292.

Hoffman, M. L. (1970). Moral development. In P. H. Mussen (Ed.), *Manual of child psychology* (3rd ed., Vol. 2). New York: Wiley.

Hoffman, M. L. (1988). Moral development. In M. H. Bornstein & E. Lamb (Eds.), *Developmental psychology: An advanced textbook* (2nd ed.). Hillsdale, NJ: Erlbaum.

Hoffman, M. L. (1993). Empathy, social cognition, and moral education. In A. Garrod (Ed.), *Approaches to moral development.* New York: Teachers College Press.

Hoffnung, M. (1984). Motherhood: Contemporary conflict for women. In J. Freeman (Ed.), *Women: A feminist perspective* (3rd ed.). Palo Alto, CA: Mayfield.

Hofstede, G. (1980). *Culture's consequences: International differences in work-related values.* Newbury Park, CA: Sage.

Holmbeck, G. N. (1996). A model of family relational transformations during the transition to adolescence: Parent-adolescent conflict and adaptation. In J. A. Graber, J. Brooks-Gunn, & A. C. Petersen (Eds.), *Transitions through adolescence.* Hillsdale, NJ: Erlbaum.

Holmbeck, G. N., Paikoff, R. L., & Brooks-Gunn, J. (1995). Parenting adolescents. In M. H. Bornstein (Ed.), *Children and parenting* (Vol. 1). Hillsdale, NJ: Erlbaum.

Holmes, L. B. (1992). General clinical principles in genetic disorders. In R. E. Behrman (Ed.), *Nelson textbook of pediatrics* (14th ed.). Philadelphia: Saunders.

Holmes, L. D. (1987). *Quest for the real Samoa: The Mead-Freeman controversy and beyond.* South Hadley, MA: Bergin & Garvey.

Holt, S. A., & Fogel, A. (1993, March). *Emotions as components of dynamic systems.* Paper presented at the biennial meeting of the Society for Research in Child Development, New Orleans.

Holtzmann, W. (1982). Cross-cultural comparisons of personality development in Mexico and the United States. In D. Wagner & H. W. Stevenson (Eds.), *Cultural perspectives on child development.* San Francisco: W. H. Freeman.

Hommerding, K. D., & Kriger, M. (1993, March). *Stability and change in infant-mother attachment: A study of low-income families.* Paper presented at the biennial meeting of the Society for Research in Child Development, New Orleans.

Honig, A. (1996, April). Unpublished review of *Child Development* (8th ed.) by J. W. Santrock. Dubuque, IA: Brown & Benchmark.

Honing, A. S. (1995). Choosing childcare for young children. In M. H. Bornstein (Ed.), *Handbook of parenting* (Vol. 4). Hillsdale, NJ: Erlbaum.

Honzik, M. P., MacFarlane, J. W., & Allen, L. (1948). The stability of mental test performance between two and eighteen years. *Journal of Experimental Education, 17,* 309–324.

Hops, H., Davis, B., Alpert, A., & Longoria, N. (1997, April). *Adolescent peer relations and depressive symptomatology.* Paper presented at the meeting of the Society for Research in Child Development, Washington, DC.

Horney, K. (1967). *Feminine psychology.* New York: W. W. Norton.

Horowitz, F. D., & O'Brien, M. (1980). In the interest of the nation: A reflective essay on the state of knowledge and the challenges before us. *American Psychologist, 44,* 441–445.

Hort, B. E., & Leinbach, M. D. (1993, March). *Children's use of metaphorical cues in gender-typing of objects.* Paper presented at the biennial meeting of the Society for Research in Child Development, New Orleans.

Hoving, K. L., Spender, T., Robb, K. Y., & Schulte, D. (1978). Developmental changes in visual information processing. In P. A. Ornstein (Ed.), *Memory development in children.* Hillsdale, NJ: Erlbaum.

Howe, M. L. (1995, March). *Early memory development and the emergence of autobiographical memory.* Paper presented at the meeting of the Society for Research in Child Development, Indianapolis.

Howes, C. (1985, April). *Predicting preschool sociometric status from toddler peer interaction.* Paper presented at the meeting of the Society for Research in Child Development, Toronto.

Howes, C. (1988, April). *Can the age of entry and the quality of infant child care predict behaviors in kindergarten?* Paper presented at the International Conference on Infant Studies, Washington, DC.

Howes, C. (1992). *The collaborative construction of pretend: Social pretend play functions.* Albany: State University of New York Press.

Howes, C., & Hamilton, C. E. (1992). Children's relationships with caregivers: Mothers and child care teachers. *Child Development, 63,* 859–866.

Huang, L. N., & Gibbs, J. T. (1989). Future directions: Implications for research training, and practice. In J. T. Gibbs & L. N. Huang (Eds.), *Children of color.* San Francisco: Jossey-Bass.

Huang, L. N., & Ying, Y. (1989). Chinese American children and adolescents. In J. T. Gibbs & L. N. Huang (Eds.), *Children of color.* San Francisco: Jossey-Bass.

Hudson, L. M., Forman, E. R., & Brion-Meisels, S. (1982). Role-taking as a predictor of prosocial behavior in cross-age tutors. *Child Development, 53,* 1320–1329.

Huebner, A. M., & Garrod, A. C. (1993). Moral reasoning among Tibetan monks: A study of Buddhist adolescents and young adults in Nepal. *Journal of Cross-Cultural Psychology, 24,* 167–185.

Huebner, A. M., Garrod, A. C., & Snarey, J. (1990, March). *Moral development in Tibetan Buddhist monks: A cross-cultural study of adolescents and young adults in Nepal.* Paper presented at the meeting of the Society for Research in Adolescence, Atlanta.

Huesmann, L. R. (1986). Psychological processes promoting the relation between exposure to media violence and aggressive behavior by the viewer. *Journal of Social Issues, 42,* 125–139.

Huesmann, L. R., Eron, L. D., Klein, R., Brice, P., & Fischer, P. (1983). Mitigating the imitation of aggressive behaviors by changing children's attitudes about media violence. *Journal of Personality and Social Psychology, 44,* 899–910.

Huff, C. R. (Ed.). (1990). *Gangs in America.* Newbury Park, CA: Sage.

Huston, A. C. (1983). Sex-typing. In P. H. Mussen (Ed.), *Handbook of child psychology* (4th ed., Vol. 4). New York: Wiley.

Huston, A. C., McLoyd, V. C., & McColl, C. G. (1994). Children and poverty: Issues in contemporary research. *Child Development, 65,* 275–282.

Huston, A. C., Seigle, J., & Bremer, M. (1983, April). *Family environment and television use by preschool children.* Paper presented at the meeting of the Society for Research in Child Development, Detroit.

Huston, A. C., Watkins, B. A., & Kunkel, D. (1989). Public policy and children's television. *American Psychologist, 44,* 424–433.

Huston, A. C., & Wright, J. C. (1997). Mass media and children's development. In I. E. Siegel, & K. A. Renninger (Eds.), *Handbook of child psychology* (5th Ed., Vol. IV). New York: Wiley.

Huston-Stein, A., & Higgens-Trenk, A. (1978). Development of females from childhood through adulthood: Career and feminine role orientations. In P. Baltes (Ed.), *Life-span development and behavior* (Vol. 1). New York: Aca-demic Press.

Huttenlocher, J., & Newcombe, N. (1984). The child's representation of information about location. In C. Sophian (Ed.), *Origins of cognitive skills.* Hillsdale, NJ: Erlbaum.

Hyde, J. S. (1993). Meta-analysis and the psychology of women. In F. L. Denmark and M. A. Paludi (Eds.), *Handbook on the psychology of women*. Westport, CT: Greenwood.

Hyde, J. S., & Plant, E. A. (1995). Magnitude of psychological gender differences: Another side of the story. *American Psychologist, 50,* 159–161.

I

Inagaki, K. (1995, March). *Young children's personifying and vitalistic biology*. Paper presented at the meeting of the Society for Research in Child Development, Indianapolis.

Innocenti, M., & Huh, K. (1993, March). *A comparative study of the child and family effects of adding parent involvement program to an existing early intervention program*. Paper presented at the biennial meeting of the Society for Research in Child Development, New Orleans.

Inoff-Germain, G., Arnold, G. S., Nottelmann, E. D., Susman, E. J., Cutler, G. B., & Chrousos, G. P. (1988). Relations between hormone levels and observational measures of aggressive behavior of young adolescents in family interactions. *Developmental Psychology, 24,* 129–139.

Insabella, G. M. (1995, March). *Varying levels of exposure to marital conflict: Prediction of adolescent adjustment across intact families and stepfamilies*. Paper presented at the meeting of the Society for Research in Child Development, Indianapolis.

Intons-Peterson, M. (1996). Memory aids. In D. Hermann, C. McEvoy, C. Hertog, P. Hertel, & M. Johnson (Eds.), *Basic and applied memory research* (Vol. 2). Hillsdale, NJ: Erlbaum.

Izard, C. E. (1982). *Measuring emotions in infants and young children*. New York: Cambridge University Press.

J

Jackson, J. F. (1993). Human behavioral genetics, Scarr's theory, and her views on interventions: A critical review and commentary on their implications for African American children. *Child Development, 64,* 1318–1332.

Jacobs, J. K., Garnier, H. E., & Weisner, T. (1996, March). *The impact of family life on the process of dropping out of high school*. Paper presented at the meeting of the Society for Research on Adolescence, Boston.

Jacobsen, R. H., Lahey, B. B., & Strauss, C. C. (1983). Correlates of depressed mood in normal children. *Journal of Abnormal Child Psychology, 11,* 29–39.

Jacobson, J. L., Jacobson, S. W., Fein, G. G., Schwartz, P. M., & Dowler, J. K. (1984). Prenatal exposure to an environmental toxin: A test of the multiple-effects model. *Developmental Psychology, 20,* 523–532.

Jacobson, J. L., Jacobson, S. W., Padgett, R. J., Brumitt, G. A., & Billings, R. L. (1992). Effects of prenatal PCB exposure on cognitive processing efficiency and sustained attention. *Developmental Psychology, 28,* 297–306.

Jackson, J. F. (1997, April). *Primary grade public schooling: A risk factor for African-American children?* Paper presented at the meeting of the Society for Research in Child Development, Washington, DC.

Jadack, R. A., Hyde, J. S., Moore, C. F., & Keller, M. L. (1995). Moral reasoning about sexually transmitted diseases. *Child Development, 66,* 167–177.

James, W. (1890/1950). *The principles of psychology*. New York: Dover.

Janz, N. K., Zimmerman, M. A., Wren, P. A., Israel, B. A., Freudenberg, N., & Carter, R. J. (1996). Evaluation of 37 AIDS prevention projects: Successful approaches and barriers to program effectiveness. *Health Education Quarterly, 23,* 80–97.

Janzen, L., & Nanson, J. (1993, March). *Neuropsychological evaluation of preschoolers with fetal alcohol syndrome*. Paper presented at the biennial meeting of the Society for Research in Child Development, New Orleans.

Jarrett, R. L. (1995). Growing up poor: The family experiences of socially mobile youth in low-income African-American neighborhoods. *Journal of Adolescent Research, 10,* 111–135.

Jeans, P. C., Smith, M. B., & Stearns, G. (1955). Incidence of prematurity in relation to maternal nutrition. *Journal of the American Dietary Association, 31,* 576–581.

Jenkins, E. J., & Bell, C. C. (1992). Adolescent violence: Can it be curbed? *Adolescent Medicine, 3,* 71–86.

Jensen, A. R. (1969). How much can we boost IQ and scholastic achievement? *Harvard Educational Review, 39,* 1–123.

Jensen, L. A. (1995, March). *The moral reasoning of orthodox and progressivist Indians and Americans*. Paper presented at the meeting of the Society for Research in Child Development, Indianapolis.

Jensen, R. A. (1969). How much can we boost IQ and scholastic achievement? *Harvard Educational Review, 39,* 1–123.

Jiao, S., Ji, G., & Jing, Q. (1996). Cognitive development of Chinese urban only children and children with siblings. *Child Development, 67,* 387–395.

Jodl, K. M. (1995, March). *Modeling the relationship between distal stress, proximal stress, and competence in adolescents growing up in stepfamilies*. Paper presented at the meeting of the Society for Research in Child Development, Indianapolis.

Johnson, D. D. L., Swank, P., Howie, V. M., Baldwin, C., & Owen, M. (1993, March). *Tobacco smoke in the home and child intelligence*. Paper presented at the meeting of the Society for Research in Child Development, New Orleans.

Johnson, J. E., Christie, J. F., & Yawkey, T. D. (1987). *Play and early childhood development*. Glenview, IL: Scott, Foresman.

Johnston, J., Etteman, J., & Davidson. (1980). *An evaluation of Freestyle: A television series to reduce sex-role stereotypes*. Ann Arbor: University of Michigan, Institute of Social Research.

Johnston, L., Bachman, J., & O'Malley, P. (1994, January 31). *Drug use rises among American teenagers*. News release, Institute of Social Research, University of Michigan, Ann Arbor.

Johnston, L., O'Malley, P., & Bachman, G. (1993, March). *Drug use rises among the nation's eighth-grade students*. Ann Arbor: University of Michigan, Institute of Social Research.

Johnston, L. D., O'Malley, P., & Bachman, G. (1996). *The monitoring the future study*. Ann Arbor, MI: Institute of Social Research, U. of Michigan.

Johnston, M. H. (1997). The neural basis of cognitive development. In D. Kuhn & R. S. Siegler (Eds.), *Handbook of child psychology* (5th Ed., Vol. II). New York: Wiley.

Jones, D. C., & Costin, S. E. (1997, April). *The friendships of African-American and European-American adolescents*. Paper presented at the meeting of the Society for Research in Child Development, Washington, DC.

Jones, E. R., Forrest, J. D., Goldman, N., Henshaw, S. K., Lincoln, R., Rosoff, J. I., Westoff, C. G., & Wulf, D. (1985). Teenage pregnancy in developed countries: Determinants and policy implications. *Family Planning Perspectives, 17,* 53–63.

Jones, J. M. (1993, August). *Racism and civil rights: Right problem, wrong solution*. Paper presented at the meeting of the American Psychological Association, Toronto, Canada.

Jones, J. M. (1994). The African American: A duality dilemma? In W. J. Lonner & R. Malpass (Eds.), *Psychology and culture*. Needham Heights, MA: Allyn & Bacon.

Jones, L. (1996). *HIV/AIDS: What to do about it*. Pacific Grove, CA: Brooks/Cole.

Jones, M. C. (1924). A laboratory study of fear: The case of Peter. *Journal of Genetic Psychology, 31,* 308–315.

Jones, M. C. (1965). Psychological correlates of somatic development. *Child Development, 36*, 899–911.

Jordan, J. V. (1997). *Women's growth in diversity*. New York: Guilford.

Joseph, C. L. M. (1989). Identification of factors associated with delayed antenatal care. *Journal of the American Medical Association, 81*, 57–63.

Josselson, R. (1994). Identity and relatedness in the life cycle. In H. A. Bosma, T. L. G., Graafsma, H. D. Grotevant, & D. J. De Levita (Eds.), *Identity and development*. Newbury Park, CA: Sage.

Juang, L. P., & Nguyen, H. H. (1997, April). *Autonomy and connectedness: Predictors of adjustment in Vietnamese adolescents*. Paper presented at the meeting of the Society for Research in Child Development, Washington, DC.

Kagan, J. (1965). Impulsive and reflective children: Significance of conceptual tempo. In J. D. Krumboltz (Ed.), *Learning and the educational process*. Chicago: Rand McNally.

Kagan, J. (1984). *The nature of the child*. New York: Basic Books.

Kagan, J. (1987). Perspectives on infancy. In J. D. Osofsky (Ed.), *Handbook on infant development* (2nd ed.). New York.

Kagan, J. (1989). *Unstable ideas: Temperament, cognition, and self*. Cambridge, MA: Harvard University Press.

Kagan, J. (1992). Yesterday's premises, tomorrow's premises. *Developmental Psychology, 28*, 990–997.

Kagan, J. (1995, August). *Temperament and development*. Paper presented at the meeting of the American Psychological Association, New York City.

Kagan, J., Kearsley, R. B., & Zelazo, P. R. (1978). *Infancy*. Cambridge, MA: Harvard University Press.

Kagan, S., & Madsen, M. C. (1972). Experimental analysis of cooperation and competition of Anglo-American and Mexican children. *Developmental Psychology, 6*, 49–59.

Kagitcibasi, C. (1988). Diversity of socialization and social change. In P. R. Dasen, J. W. Berry, & N. Sartorious (Eds.), *Health and cross-cultural psychology: Toward applications*. Newbury Park, CA: Sage.

Kagitcibasi, C. (1995). Is psychology relevant to global human development issues? Experience from Turkey. *American Psychologist, 50*, 293–300.

Kagitcibasi, C. (1996). *Human development across cultures*. Hillsdale, NJ: Erlbaum.

Kail, R. (1993, March). *The nature of global developmental change in processing time*. Paper presented at the biennial meeting of the Society for Research in Child Development, New Orleans.

Kail, R., & Pellegrino, J. W. (1985). *Human intelligence*. New York: W. H. Freeman.

Kalichman, S. C. (1996). *Answering your questions about AIDS*. Washington, DC: American Psychological Association.

Kamerman, S. B. (1989). Child care, women, work, and the family: An international overview of child care services and related policies. In J. S. Lande, S. Scarr, & N. Gunzenhauser (Eds.), *Caring for children: Challenge to America*. Hillsdale, NJ: Erlbaum.

Kamerman, S. B., & Kahn, A. J. (1988). Social policy and children in the United States and Europe. In J. L. Palmer, T. Smeeding, & B. B. Torrey (Eds.), *The vulnerable America's young and old in the industrialized world*. Washington, DC: Urban Institute.

Kantrowitz, B., & Wingert, P. (1989, April 17). How kids learn. *Newsweek*, pp. 4–10.

Katz, L., & Chard, S. (1989). *Engaging the minds of young children: The project approach*. Norwood, NJ: Ablex.

Katz, P. A. (1987, August). *Children and social issues*. Paper presented at the meeting of the American Psychological Association, New York.

Kaufman, A. S., & Kaufman, N. L. (1983). *Kaufman Assessment Battery for Children*. Circle Pines, MN: American Guidance Service.

Kearins, J. M. (1981). Visual spatial memory in Australian aboriginal children of desert regions. *Cognitive Psychology, 13*, 434–460.

Keating, D. P. (1990). Adolescent thinking. In S. S. Feldman & G. R. Elliott (Eds.), *At the threshold: The developing adolescent*. Cambridge, MA: Harvard University Press.

Keating, D. P. (1997, April). Discussant, symposium on intelligence. Society for Research in Child Development, Washington, DC.

Keating, D. P. (in press, a). Understanding human intelligence: Toward a developmental synthesis. In C. Benbow & D. Lubinsky (Eds.), *From psychometrics to giftedness: Essays in honor of Julian Stanley*. Baltimore: Johns Hopkins University Press.

Keating, D. P. (in press, b). Habits of mind: Developmental diversity in competence and coping. In D. K. Detterman (Ed.), *Current topics in human intelligence*. Norwood, NJ: Ablex.

Kee, D. W., & Howell, S. (1988, April). *Mental effort and memory development*. Paper presented at the meeting of the American Educational Research Association, New Orleans.

Keeney, T. J., Cannizzo, S. R., & Flavell, J. H. (1967). Spontaneous and induced verbal rehearsal in a recall task. *Child Development, 38*, 953–966.

Keil, F. C. (1989). *Concepts, kinds, and cognitive development*. Cambridge, MA: MIT Press.

Keller, A., Ford, L., & Meacham, J. (1978). Dimensions of self-concept in preschool children. *Developmental Psychology, 14*, 483–489.

Kellman, P. J. & Banks, M. S. (1997). Infant visual perception. In D. Kuhn & R. S. Siegler (Eds.), *Handbook of child psychology* (5th Ed., Vol. II). New York: Wiley.

Kendler, K. S. (1996). Parenting: A genetic-epidemiologic perspective. *American Journal of Psychiatry, 153*, 11–20.

Kenney, A. M. (1987, June). Teen pregnancy: An issue for schools. *Phi Delta Kappan*, pp. 728–736.

Kerkman, D. D., & Siegler, R. S. (1993). Individual differences and adaptive flexibility in lower-income children's strategy choices. *Learning and Individual Differences, 5*, 113–136.

Kermoian, R., & Campos, J. J. (1988). Locomotor experience: A facilitator of spatial cognitive development. *Child Development, 59*, 908–917.

Kessen, W., Haith, M. M., & Salapatek, P. (1970). Human infancy. In P. H. Mussen (Ed.), *Manual of child psychology* (3rd ed., Vol. 1). New York: Wiley.

Kimmel, A. (1996). *Ethical issues in behavioral research*. Cambridge, MA: Blackwell.

King, N. (1982). School uses of material traditionally associated with children's play. *Theory and Research in Social Education, 10*, 17–27.

Kinman, J. R., & Henderson, D. L. (1985). An analysis of sexism in Newberry Award books from 1977 to 1984. *Reading Teacher, 38*, 885–889.

Kisilevsky, B. S. (1995). The influence stimulus and subject variables on human fetal responses to sound and vibration. In J-P Lecanuet, W. P. Fifer, M. A. Krasnegor, & W. P. Smotherman (Eds.), *Fetal development*. Hillsdale, NJ: Erlbaum.

Klahr, D., & MacWhinney, B. (1997). Information processing. In D. Kuhn & R. S. Siegler (Eds.), *Handbook of child psychology* (5th Ed., Vol. II). New York: Wiley.

Klaus, M., & Kennell, H. H. (1976). *Maternal-infant bonding*. St. Louis: Mosby.

Klaus, M. H., Kennell, J. H., & Klaus, P. H. (1993). *Mothering the mother*. Reading, MA: Addison-Wesley.

Klein, A. S., & Starkey, P. (1995, March). *Preparing for the transition to school mathematics: The Head Start family math project*. Paper presented at the meeting of the Society for Research in Child Development, Indianapolis.

Klein, K. (1985, April). The research on class size. *Phi Delta Kappan*, pp. 578–580.

Klonoff-Cohen, H. S., Edelstein, S. L., Lefkowitz, E. S., Srinivasan, I. P., Kaegi, D., Chang, J. C., and Wiley, K. J. (1995). The effect of passive smoke and tobacco exposure through breast milk on sudden infant death syndrome. *Journal of the American Medical Association, 293,* 795–798.

Kobak, R. R., Cole, H. E., Ferenz-Gillies, R., & Fleming, W. S. (1993). Attachment and emotional regulation during mother-teen problem-solving: A control theory analysis. *Child Development, 64,* 231–245.

Kobasigawa, A., Ransom, C. C., & Holland, C. (1980). Children's knowledge about skimming. *Alberta Journal of Educational Research, 26,* 169–182.

Koenig, W. D., Mumme, R. L., & Pitelka, F. A. (1984). The breeding system of the acorn woodpecker in central coastal California. *Z. Tierpsychol., 65,* 289–308.

Kohlberg, L. (1958). *The development of modes of moral thinking and choice in the years 10 to 16.* Unpublished doctoral dissertation, University of Chicago.

Kohlberg, L. (1966). A cognitive-developmental analysis of children's sex-role concepts and attitudes. In E. E. Maccoby (Ed.), *The development of sex differences.* Palo Alto, CA: Stanford University Press.

Kohlberg, L. (1969). Stage and sequence: The cognitive-developmental approach to socialization. In D. A. Goslin (Ed.), *Handbook of socialization theory and research.* Chicago: Rand McNally.

Kohlberg, L. (1976). Moral stages and moralization: The cognitive-developmental approach. In T. Lickona (Ed.), *Moral development and behavior.* New York: Holt, Rinehart & Winston.

Kohlberg, L. (1981). *The philosophy of moral development.* New York: Harper & Row.

Kohlberg, L. (1986). A current statement on some theoretical issues. In S. Modgil & C. Modgil (Eds.), *Lawrence Kohlberg.* Philadelphia: Falmer.

Kohlberg, L., & Candee, D. (1979). *Relationships between moral judgment and moral action.* Unpublished manuscript, Harvard University.

Kohn, M. L. (1977). *Class and conformity* (2nd ed.). Homewood, IL: Dorsey.

Kohn, M. L. (1977). *Class and conformity: A study in values* (2nd ed.). Chicago: University of Chicago Press.

Kopp, C. B. (1983). Risk factors in development. In P. H. Mussen (Ed.), *Handbook of child psychology* (4th ed., Vol. 2). New York: Wiley.

Kortenhaus, C. M., & Demarest, J. (1993). Gender role stereotyping in children's literature: An update. *Sex Roles, 28,* 219–230.

Kostelecky, K. L. (1997, April). *Stressful life events, relationships, and distress during late adolescence.* Paper presented at the meeting of the Society for Research in Child Development, Washington, DC.

Krauss, R. A., & Glucksberg, S. (1969). The development of communication: Competence as a function of age. *Child Development, 40,* 255–266.

Kuhl, P. K. (1993a). Infant speech perception: A window on psycholinguistic development. *International Journal of Psycholinguistics, 9,* 33–56.

Kuhl, P. K. (1993b). Early linguistic experience and phonetic perception: Implications for theories of developmental speech perception. *Journal of Phonetics, 21,* 125–139.

Kuhn, D. (1995). Microgenetic study of change: What has it told us? *Psychological Science, 3,* 133–139.

Kuhn, D., Amsel, E., & O'Laughlin, M. (1988). *The development of scientific thinking skills.* Orlando, FL: Academic Press.

Kuhn, D., Schauble, L., & Garcia-Mila, M. (1992). Cross-domain development of scientific reasoning. *Cognition and Instruction, 9,* 285–327.

Kupersmidt, J. B., & Coie, J. D. (1990). Preadolescent peer status, aggression, and school adjustment as predictors of externalizing problems in adolescence. *Child Development, 61,* 1350–1363.

Kupersmidt, J. B., & Patterson, C. (1993, March). *Developmental patterns of peer relations and aggression in the prediction of externalizing behavior problems.* Paper presented at the biennial meeting of the Society for Research in Child Development, New Orleans.

Kurdek, L. A., & Krile, D. (1982). A developmental analysis of the relation between peer acceptance and both interpersonal understanding and perceived social self-competence. *Child Development, 53,* 1485–1491.

Kurtz, D. A., Cantu, C. L., & Phinney, J. S. (1996, March). *Group identities as predictors of self-esteem among African American, Latino, and White adolescents.* Paper presented at the meeting of the Society for Research on Adolescence, Boston.

Labouvie-Vief, G. (1982). Dynamic development and mature autonomy: A theoretical prologue. *Human Development, 25,* 161–191.

Labouvie-Vief, G. (1986, August). *Modes of knowing and life-span cognition.* Paper presented at the meeting of the American Psychological Association, Washington, DC.

Ladd, G., & Hart, C. H. (1992). Creating informal play opportunities: Are parents' and preschoolers' initiations related to children's competence with peers? *Cognitive Psychology, 28,* 1179–1187.

Ladd, G. W. (1990). Having friends, keeping friends, making friends, and being liked by peers in the classroom: Predictors of children's early school adjustment. *Child Development, 61,* 1081–1100.

Ladd, G. W., & Le Sieur, K. D. (1995). Parents and children's peer relationships. In M. H. Bornstein (Ed.), *Children and parenting* (Vol. 4). Hillsdale, NJ: Erlbaum.

LaFromboise, T., Coleman, H. L. K., & Gerton, J. (1993). Psychological impact of biculturalism: Evidence and theory. *Psychological Bulletin, 114,* 395–412.

LaFromboise, T., & Trimble, J. (1996). Multicultural counseling theory and American-Indian populations. In D. W. Sue (Ed.), *Theory of multicultural counseling and therapy.* Pacific Grove, CA: Brooks/Cole.

LaFromboise, T. D. (1993). American Indian mental health policy. In D. R. Atkinson, G. Morten, & D. W. Sue (Eds.), *Counseling American minorities.* Dubuque, IA: Brown & Benchmark.

LaFromboise, T. D., & Low, K. G. (1989). American Indian children and adolescents. In J. T. Gibbs & L. N. Huang (Eds.), *Children of color.* San Francisco: Jossey-Bass.

Lally, J. R., Mangione, P., & Honig, S. (1987). *The Syracuse University family development research program.* Unpublished manuscript, Syracuse University, Syracuse, NY.

Lamb, M. (1994). Infant care practices and the application of knowledge. In C. B. Fisher & R. M. Lerner (Eds.), *Applied developmental psychology.* New York: McGraw-Hill.

Lamb, M. E. (1977). The development of mother-infant and father-infant attachments in the second year of life. *Developmental Psychology, 13,* 637–648.

Lamb, M. E. (1986). *The father's role: Applied perspectives.* New York: Wiley.

Lamb, M. E. (1994). Infant care practices and the application of knowledge. In C. B. Fisher & R. M. Lerner (Eds.), *Applied developmental psychology.* New York: McGraw-Hill.

Lamb, M. E. (1997). Fatherhood then and now. In A. Booth & A. C. Crouter (Eds.), *Men in families.* Mahwah, NJ: Erlbaum.

Lamb, M. E. (1997). Nonparental child care. in I. E. Sigel & K. A. Renninger (Eds.), *Handbook of child psychology* (5th Ed., Vol. IV). New York: Wiley.

Lamb, M. E., Frodi, A. M., Hwant, C. P., Frodi, M., & Steinberg, J. (1982). Mother- and father-infant interaction involving play and holding in traditional and nontraditional Swedish families. *Developmental Psychology, 18,* 215–221.

Lamb, M. E., & Sternberg, K. J. (1992). Sociocultural perspectives on nonparental child care. In M. E. Lamb, K. J. Sternberg, C. Hwang, & A. G. Broberg (Eds.), *Child care in context.* Hillsdale, NJ: Erlbaum.

Lamb, S. (1993). The beginnings of morality. In A. Garrod (Ed.), *Approaches to moral development.* New York: Teachers College Press.

Lambert, J. D. (1997, April). *Fathers as developing individuals: Investigating contemporary father-child relationships.* Paper presented at the meeting of the Society for Research in Child Development, Washington, DC.

Landau, B., Spelke, E. S., & Gleitman, H. (1984). Spatial knowledge in a young blind child. *Cognition, 16,* 225–260.

Landesman-Dwyer, S., & Sackett, G. P. (1983, April). *Prenatal nicotine exposure and sleep-wake patterns in infancy.* Paper presented at the biennial meeting of the Society for Research in Child Development, Detroit.

Lane, H. (1976). *The wild boy of Aveyron.* Cambridge, MA: Harvard University Press.

Lang, E., & Rivera, J. (1987). In Harlem: Millionaire's promise still inspires. *New York Times,* June 20, 53.

Lapsley, D. K. (1989). Continuity and discontinuity in adolescent social cognitive development. In R. Montemayor, G. Adams, & T. Gullota (Eds.), *Advances in adolescence research* (Vol. 2). Orlando, FL: Academic Press.

Lapsley, D. K. (1996). *Moral psychology.* Boulder, CO: Westview Press.

Lapsley, D. K., & Murphy, M. N. (1985). Another look at the theoretical assumptions of adolescent egocentrism. *Developmental Review, 5,* 201–217.

Lapsley, D. K., & Power, F. C. (Eds.). (1988). *Self, ego, and identity.* New York: Springer-Verlag.

Lapsley, D. K., & Quintana, S. M. (1985). Recent approaches in children's elementary moral and social education. *Elementary School Guidance and Counseling Journal, 19,* 246–251.

Larson, R., & Richards, M. H. (1994). *Emergent realities.* New York: Basic Books.

Lasko, D. S., Field, T. M., Gonzalez, K. P., Harding, J., Yando, R., & Bendell, D. (1996). Adolescent depressed mood and parental unhappiness. *Adolescence, 121,* 49–58.

LaVoie, J. (1976). Ego identity formation in middle adolescence. *Journal of Youth and Adolescence, 5,* 371–385.

Lay, K., Waters, E., & Park, K. A. (1989). Maternal responsiveness and child compliance: The role of mood as a mediator. *Child Development, 60,* 1405–1411.

Lazar, L., Darlington, R., & Collaborators. (1982). Lasting effects of early education: A report from the consortium for longitudinal studies. *Monographs of the Society for Research in Child Development, 47.*

Lazarus, R. S. (1990, August). *Progress on a cognitive-motivational-relational theory of emotion.* Paper presented at the meeting of the American Psychological Association, Boston.

Lazarus, R. S. (1996). *Psychological stress and the coping process.* New York: McGraw-Hill.

Leboyer, F. (1975). *Birth without violence.* New York: Knopf.

Lecaunet, J-P, Graneir-Deferre, C., & Busnel, M-C. (1995). Human fetal auditory perception. In J-P Lecaunet, W. P. Fifer, N. A. Krasnegor, and W. P. Smotherman (Eds.), *Fetal development.* Hillsdale, NJ: Erlbaum.

Lee, G. R. (1978). Marriage and morale in late life. *Journal of Marriage and the Family, 40,* 131–139.

Lehrer, R. (1992). Authors of knowledge: Patterns of hypermedia design. In S. Lajoie and S. Derry (Eds.), *Computers as cognitive tools.* Hillsdale, NJ: Erlbaum.

Lehrer, R., & Littlefield, J. (1991). Misconceptions and errors in LOGO: The role of instruction. *Journal of Educational Psychology, 83,* 124–133.

Leifer, A. D. (1973). *Television and the development of social behavior.* Paper presented at the meeting of the International Society for the Study of Behavioral Development, Ann Arbor, MI.

LeMare, L. J., & Rubin, K. H. (1987). Perspective taking and peer interaction: Structural and developmental analyses. *Child Development, 58,* 306–315.

Lempers, J. D., & Clark-Lempers, D. S. (1993, March). *Adolescents' perceptions of their same-sex and opposite-sex friends: A longitudinal look.* Paper presented at the biennial meeting of the Society for Research in Child Development, New Orleans.

Lempers, J. D., Flavell, E. R., & Flavell, J. H. (1977). The development in very young children of tacit knowledge concerning visual perception. *Genetic Psychology Monographs, 95,* 3–53.

Lenneberg, E. (1967). *The biological foundations of language.* New York: Wiley.

Lenneberg, E. H., Rebelsky, F. G., & Nichols, I. A. (1965). The vocalization of infants born to deaf and hearing parents. *Human Development, 8,* 23–37.

Leong, F. (1996). Multicultural counseling theory and Asian-American populations. In D. W. Sue (Ed.), *Theory of multicultural counseling and therapy.* Pacific Grove, CA: Brooks/Cole.

Lepper, M., Greene, D., & Nisbett, R. R. (1973). Undermining children's intrinsic interest with extrinsic rewards. *Journal of Personality and Social Psychology, 28,* 129–137.

Lepper, M. R. (1985). Microcomputers in education: Motivational and social issues. *American Psychologist, 40,* 1–18.

Lepper, M. R., & Gurtner, J. (1989). Children and computers: Approaching the twenty-first century. *American Psychologist, 44,* 170–178.

Lerner, H. G. (1989). *The dance of intimacy.* New York: Harper & Row.

Lerner, R. M., & Karabenick, S. A. (1974). Physical attractiveness, body attitudes, and self-concept in late adolescence. *Journal of Youth and Adolescence, 3,* 307–316.

Lester, B. M., Freier, K., & LcGasse, K. (1995). Prenatal cocaine exposure and child outcome: How much do we really know? In M. Lewis & M. Bendersky (Eds.), *Mothers, babies, and cocaine.* Hillsdale, NJ: Erlbaum.

Leventhal, A. (1994, February). *Peer conformity during adolescence: An integration of developmental, situational, and individual characteristics.* Paper presented at the meeting of the Society for Research on Adolescence, San Diego.

Levin, J. (1980). *The mnemonic '80s: Keywords in the classroom.* Theoretical paper No. 86. Wisconsin Research and Development Center for Individualized Schooling, Madison.

Levy, G. D., & Carter, D. B. (1989). Gender schema, gender constancy, and gender-role knowledge: The roles of cognitive factors in preschoolers' gender-role stereotype attributions. *Developmental Psychology, 25,* 444–449.

Levy, G. D., & Katz, P. A. (1993, March). *Differences in preschoolers' race schemas: Relations among schematization, race-based peer preferences, and memory for race-based stereotyped portrayals.* Paper presented at the biennial meeting of the Society for Research in Child Development, New Orleans.

Lewinsohn, P. M., Seeley, J. R., Rohde, P., Gotlib, I. H., & Hops, H. (1993). *Adolescent depression: II. Psychosocial risk factors.* Unpublished manuscript, Oregon Research Institute, University of Oregon, Eugene.

Lewis, M., & Brooks-Gunn, J. (1979). *Social cognition and the acquisition of the self.* New York: Plenum.

Lewis, M., Sullivan, M. W., Sanger, C., & Weiss, M. (1989). Self-development and self-conscious emotions. *Child Development, 60,* 146–156.

Liben, L. S., & Signorella, M. L. (1993). Gender-schematic processing in children: The role of initial presentation of stimuli. *Developmental Psychology, 29,* 141–149.

Lickona, T. (1993). *Education for moral character.* New York: Bantam Books.

Lifshitz, F., Pugliese, M. T., Moses, N., & Weyman-Daum, M. (1987). Parental health beliefs as a cause of nonorganic failure to thrive. *Pediatrics, 80,* 175–182.

Light, P., & Butterworth, G. (Eds.). (1993). *Context and cognition.* Hillsdale, NJ: Erlbaum.

Lipsitz, J. (1983, October). *Making it the hard way: Adolescents in the 1980s.* Testimony presented at the Crisis Intervention Task Force, House Select Committee on Children, Youth, and Families. Washington, DC.

Lipsitz, J. (1984). *Successful schools for young adolescents.* New Brunswick, NJ: Transaction.

Lively, W., & Bromley, D. (1973). *Person perception in childhood and adolescence.* New York: Wiley.

Locke, J. L. (1993). *The child's path to spoken language.* Cambridge, MA: Harvard University Press.

Locke, J. L., Bekken, K. E., Wein, D., & Ruzecki, V. (1991, April). *Neuropsychology of babbling: Laterality effects in the production of rhythmic manual activity.* Paper presented at the meeting of the Society for Research in Child Development, Seattle.

Lockman, J. J., & Pick, H. L. (1984). Problems of scale in spatial development. In C. Sophian (Ed.), *Origins of cognitive skills.* Hillsdale, NJ: Erlbaum.

Lockman, J. J., & Thelen, E. (1993). Developmental biodynamics: Brain, body, behavior connections. *Child Development, 64,* 953–959.

Loftus, E. F. (1993). The reality of repressed memories. *American Psychologist, 48,* 518–537.

Lomnitz, L. (1997). Family, networks, and survival on the threshold of the 21st century in urban Mexico. In S. Dreman (Ed.), *The family on the threshold of the 21st century.* Mahwah, NJ: Erlbaum.

Long, T., & Long, L. (1983). *Latchkey children.* New York: Penguin.

Lonner, W. J. (1988, October). *The introductory psychology text and cross-cultural psychology: A survey of cross-cultural psychologists.* Bellingham: Western Washington University, Center for Cross-cultural Research.

Lonner, W. J. (1990). An overview of cross-cultural testing and assessment. In R. W. Brislin (Ed.), *Applied cross-cultural psychology.* Newbury Park, CA: Sage.

Lorch, E. P. (1995, March). *Young children's perception of importance in televised stories.* Paper presented at the meeting of the Society for Research in Child Development, Indianapolis.

Lorenz, K. Z. (1965). *Evolution and the modification of behavior.* Chicago: University of Chicago Press.

Lourenco, O., & Machado, A. (1996). In defense of Piaget's theory: A reply to 10 common criticisms. *Psychological Review, 103,* 143–164.

Louv, R. (1990). *Childhood's future.* Boston: Houghton Mifflin.

Luo, Q., Fang, X., & Aro, P. (1995, March). *Selection of best friends by Chinese adolescents.* Paper presented at the meeting of the Society for Research in Child Development, Indianapolis.

Luria, A., & Herzog, E. (1985, April). *Gender segregation across and within settings.* Paper presented at the biennial meeting of the Society for Research in Child Development, Toronto.

Luster, T., & McAdoo, H. (1996). Family and child influences on educational attainment: A secondary analysis of the High/Scope Perry data. *Developmental Psychology, 32,* 26–39.

Luster, T. J., Perlstadt, H., McKinney, M. H., & Sims, K. E. (1995, March). *Factors related to the quality of the home environment adolescents provide for their infants.* Paper presented at the meeting of the Society for Research in Child Development, Indianapolis.

Lyle, J., & Hoffman, H. R. (1972). Children's use of television and other media. In E. A. Rubenstein, G. A. Comstock, & J. P. Murray (Eds.), *Television and social behavior* (Vol. 4). Washington, DC: U.S. Government Printing Office.

Lynch, M. E. (1991). Gender intensification. In R. M. Lerner, A. C. Petersen, & J. Brooks-Gunn (Eds.), *Encyclopedia of adolescence* (Vol. 1). New York: Garland.

Lyons, N. P. (1990). Listening to voices we have not heard. In C. Gilligan, N. P. Lyons, & T. J. Hammer (Eds.), *Making connections.* Cambridge, MA: Harvard University Press.

Lytton, H. (1995, March). *Child and family predictors of conduct disorders and criminality.* Paper presented at the meeting of the Society for Research in Child Development, Indianapolis.

Mac Iver, D., Urdan, T., Beck, J., Midgley, C., Reuman, D., Tasko, A., Fenzel, L. M., Arhar, J., & Kramer, L. (1992, March). *Changing schools and classrooms in the middle grades: Research on new partnerships, processes, practices, and programs.* Paper presented at the meeting of the Society for Research on Adolescence, Washington, DC.

Maccoby, E. E. (1980). *Social development.* San Diego: Harcourt Brace Jovanovich.

Maccoby, E. E. (1984). Middle childhood in the context of the family. In *Development during middle childhood.* Washington, DC: National Academy Press.

Maccoby, E. E. (1987, November). Interview with Elizabeth Hall: All in the family. *Psychology Today,* pp. 54–60.

Maccoby, E. E. (1992). The role of parents in the socialization of children: An historical overview. *Developmental Psychology, 28,* 1006–1018.

Maccoby, E. E. (1992). Trends in the study of socialization: Is there a Lewinian heritage? *Journal of Social Issues, 48,* 171–185.

Maccoby, E. E. (1993, March). *Trends and issues in the study of gender role development.* Paper presented at the biennial meeting of the Society for Research in Child Development, New Orleans.

Maccoby, E. E. (1995). The two sexes and their social systems. In P. Moen, G. H. Elder, & K. Luscher (Eds.), *Examining lives in context.* Washington, DC: American Psychological Association.

Maccoby, E. E. (1996). Peer conflict and intrafamily conflict: Are there conceptual bridges? *Merrill-Palmer Quarterly, 42,* 165–176.

Maccoby E. E. (1997, April). Discussant on symposium, *Missing pieces in the puzzle: biological contributions to gender development.* Society for Research in Child Development, Washington, DC.

Maccoby, E. E., & Jacklin, C. N. (1974). *The psychology of sex differences.* Palo Alto, CA: Stanford University Press.

Maccoby, E. E., & Martin, J. A. (1983). Socialization in the context of the family: Parent-child interaction. In P. H. Mussen (Ed.), *Handbook of child psychology* (4th ed., Vol. 4). New York: Wiley.

MacDonald, K. (1992). Warmth as a developmental construct: An evolutionary analysis. *Child Development, 63,* 753–773.

MacDonald, K. (1996). *Evolution and development.* Unpublished manuscript, California State University, Long Beach.

MacFarlane, J. A. (1975). Olfaction in the development of social preferences in the human neonate. In *Parent-infant interaction.* Ciba Foundation Symposium No. 33. Amsterdam: Elsevier.

Maddux, J. E., Roberts, M. C., Sledden, E. A., & Wright, L. (1986). Developmental issues in child health psychology. *American Psychologist, 41,* 24–34.

Mader, S. (1996). *Biology* (5th ed.). Dubuque, IA: Wm. C. Brown.

Magai, C., & McFadden, S. H. (1995). *The role of emotions in social and personality development.* New York: Plenum Press.

Magnusson, D., Stattin, H., & Allen, V. L. (1985). Biological maturation and social development: A longitudinal study of some adjustment processes from mid-adolescence to adulthood. *Journal of Youth and Adolescence, 14*, 267–283.

Main, M., & Solomon, J. (1990). Procedures for identifying infants as disorganized/disoriented during the Ainsworth Strange Situation. In M. Greenberg, D. Cicchetti, & E. M. Cummings (Eds.), *Attachment during the preschool years.* Chicago: University of Chicago Press.

Malcom, S. M. (1988). Technology in 2020: Educating a diverse population. In R. S. Nickerson & P. P. Zodhiates (Eds.), *Technology in education: Looking toward 2020.* Hillsdale, NJ: Erlbaum.

Malinosky-Rummell, R., & Hansen, D. J. (1993). Long-term consequences of childhood physical abuse. *Psychological Bulletin, 114*, 68–79.

Malinowski, B. (1927). *Sex and repression in savage society.* New York: Humanities Press.

Mandler, J. (1997). Representation. In D. Kuhn & R. S. Siegler (Eds.), *Handbook of child psychology* (5th Ed., Vol. II). New York: Wiley.

Mandler, J. M. (1990). A new perspective on cognitive development in infancy. *American Scientist, 78*, 236–243.

Manly, J. R. (1995, March.) *Definition of child maltreatment: The relations between maltreatment dimensions and child outcomes.* Paper presented at the meeting of the Society for Research in Child Development, Indianapolis.

Maracek, J. (1995). Gender, politics, and psychology's ways of knowing. *American Psychologist, 50*, 162–163.

Maratsos, M. (1997). The acquisition of grammar. In D. Kuhn & R. S. Siegler (Eds.), *Handbook of child psychology* (5th Ed., Vol. II). New York: Wiley.

Maratsos, M. P. (1989). Innateness and plasticity in language acquisition. In M. L. Rice and R. L. Schiefelbusch (Eds.), *The teachability of language.* Baltimore: Paul H. Brookes.

Marcia, J. (1996). Unpublished review of *Adolescence* (7th ed.) by J. W. Santrock. Dubuque, IA: Brown & Benchmark.

Marcia, J. E. (1980). Identity in adolescence. In J. Adelson (Ed.), *Handbook of adolescent psychology.* New York: Wiley.

Marcia, J. E. (1987). The identity status approach to the study of ego identity development. In T. Honess & K. Yardley (Eds.), *Self and identity: Perspectives across the lifespan.* London: Routledge & Kegan Paul.

Marcia, J. E. (1994). The empirical study of ego identity. In H. A. Bosma, T. L. G. Graafsma, H. D. Grotevant, & D. J. De Levita (Eds.), *Identity and development.* Newbury Park, CA: Sage.

Maris, R. W., Silverman, M., & Canetto, S. S. (1997). *Review of suicidology, 1997.* New York: Guilford.

Marcon, R. A. (1993, March). *Parental involvement and early school success following the 'class of 2000' at year five.* Paper presented at the biennial meeting of the Society for Research in Child Development, New Orleans.

Marks, I. M. (1987). *Fears, phobias, and rituals.* New York: Oxford University Press.

Markstrom, C. A., & Tryon, R. J. (1997, April). *Resiliency, social support, and coping among poor African-American and European-American Appalachian adolescents.* Paper presented at the meeting of the Society for Research in Child Development, Washington, DC.

Markstrom-Adams, C., & Spencer, M. B. (1994). A model for identity intervention with minority adolescents. In S. A. Archer (Ed.), *Intervention for adolescent identity development.* Newbury Park, CA: Sage.

Markus, H., & Nurius, P. (1986). Possible selves. *American Psychologist, 41*, 954–969.

Marr, D. (1982). *Vision.* New York: W. H. Freeman.

Marten, L. A., & Matlin, M. W. (1976). Does sexism in elementary readers still exist? *Reading Teacher, 29*, 764–767.

Martin, C. L. (1990). Attitudes and expectations about children with nontraditional traditional gender roles. *Sex Roles, 22*, 151–165.

Martin, D. W. (1996). *Doing psychology experiments* (4th ed.). Pacific Grove, CA: Brooks/Cole.

Martin, N. C. (1997, April). *Adolescents' possible selves and the transition to adulthood.* Paper presented at the meeting of the Society for Research in Child Development, Washington, DC.

Martorano, S. (1977). A developmental analysis of performance on Piaget's formal operations tasks. *Developmental Psychology, 13*, 666–672.

Mason, C. A., & Cauce, A. M. (1991, August). *An ecological model of adjustment in African American adolescents.* Paper presented at the meeting of the American Psychological Association, San Francisco.

Masten, A. S., & Hubbard, J. J. (1995, March). *Resilient adolescents: Do they differ from competent peers unchallenged by adversity?* Paper presented at the meeting of the Society for Research in Child Development, Indianapolis.

Matas, L., Arend, R. A., & Sroufe, L. A. (1978). Continuity in adaptation: Quality of attachment and later competence. *Child Development, 49*, 547–556.

Matlin, M. W. (1993). *The psychology of women* (2nd ed.). San Diego: Harcourt Brace Jovanovich.

Matsumoto, D. (1997). *Culture and modern life.* Pacific Grove, CA: Belmont.

Maurer, D., & Salapatek, P. (1976). Developmental changes in the scanning of faces by young infants. *Child Development, 47*, 523–527.

Mayer, F. S., & Sutton, K. (1996). *Personality.* Upper Saddle River, NJ: Prentice Hall.

Mayes, L. C., & Bornstein, M. (1995). Developmental dilemmas to cocaine-abusing parents and their children. In M. Lewis & M. Bendersky (Eds.), *Mothers, babies, and cocaine.* Hillsdale, NJ: Erlbaum.

McAdoo, H. P., Luster, T., & Perkins, D. (1993, March). *Family factors related to success among African-American adults: A secondary analysis of the Perry Preschool data.* Paper presented at the biennial meeting of the Society for Research in Child Development, New Orleans.

McAdoo, H. P., & McAdoo, J. L. (Eds.). (1985). *Black children: Social, educational, and parental environments.* Beverly Hills, CA: Sage.

McBride, B. A. (1991, April). *Variations in father involvement with preschool-aged children.* Paper presented at the biennial meeting of the Society for Research in Child Development, Seattle.

McCall, R. B., Applebaum, M. I., & Hogarty, P. S. (1973). Developmental changes in mental performance. *Monographs of the Society for Research in Child Development, 38* (Serial No. 150).

McCartney, K., Marshall, N. L., Marx, F., Ruh, J. L., & Keefe, N. (1997, April). *The impact of urban children's after-school time and their emotional well-being.* Paper presented at the meeting of the Society for Research in Child Development, Washington, DC.

McClelland, D. C. (1955). Some social consequences of achievement motivation. In M. R. Jones (Ed.), *The Nebraska Symposium on Motivation.* Lincoln: University of Nebraska Press.

McCord, J. (1990). Problem behaviors. In S. S. Feldman & G. R. Elliott (Eds.) *At the threshold: The developing adolescent.* Cambridge, MA: Harvard University Press.

McDaniel, M. A., & Pressley, M. (1987). *Imagery and related mnemonic process.* New York: Springer-Verlag.

McDougall, P., Schonert-Reichel, K., & Hymel, S. (1996, March). *Adolescents at risk for high school dropout: The role of social factors.* Paper presented at the meeting of the Society for Research on Adolescence, Boston.

McFarlane, J., Parker, B., & Soeken, K. (1996). Abuse during pregnancy: Associations with maternal health and infant birth weight. *Nursing Research, 45*, 37–47.

McGue, M., & Carmichael, C. M. (1995). Life-span developmental psychology: A behavioral genetic perspective. In L. F. Dilalla & S. M. C. Dollinger (Eds.), *Assessment of biological mechanisms across the life span*. Hillsdale, NJ: Erlbaum.

McHale, J. L., Frosch, C. A., Greene, C. A., & Ferry, K. S. (1995, March). *Correlates of maternal and paternal behavior*. Paper presented at the meeting of the Society for Research in Child Development, Indianapolis.

McHale, S. M. (1995). Lessons about adolescent development from the study of African-American youth. In L. J. Crockett & A. C. Crouter (Eds.), *Pathways through adolescence*. Hillsdale, NJ: Erlbaum.

McKnight, C. C., Crosswhite, F. J., Dossey, J. A., Kifer, E., Swafford, J. O., Travers, K. J., & Cooney, T. J. (1987). *The underachieving curriculum: Assessing U.S. school mathematics from an international perspective*. Champaign, IL: Stipes.

McLellan, J. A., Haynie, D., & Strouse, D. (1993, March). *Membership of high school crowd clusters and relationships with family and friends*. Paper presented at the biennial meeting of the Society for Research in Child Development, New Orleans.

McLoyd, V. (1990). Minority children: An introduction to the special issue. *Child Development, 61*, 263–266.

McLoyd, V. (1993, March). *Direct and indirect effects of economic hardship on socioemotional functioning in African-American adolescents*. Paper presented at the biennial meeting of the Society for Research in Child Development, New Orleans.

McLoyd, V. C. (1982). Social class differences in sociodramatic play: A critical review. *Developmental Review, 2*, 1–30.

McLoyd, V. C. (1993, March). *Sizing up the future: Economic stress, expectations, and adolescents' achievement motivation*. Paper presented at the biennial meeting of the Society for Research in Child Development, New Orleans.

McLoyd, V. (1997, April). *Reducing stressors, increasing supports in the lives of ethnic minority children in America: Social policy issues*. Paper presented at the meeting of the Society for Research in Child Development, Washington, DC.

McLoyd, V. C. (1997). Children in poverty. In I. E. Siegel & K. A. Renninger (Eds.), *Handbook of child psychology* (5th Ed., Vol. IV). New York: Wiley.

McLoyd, V. C., & Ceballo, R. (1995, March). *Conceptualizing economic context*. Paper presented at the meeting of the Society for Research in Child Development, Indianapolis.

McLoyd, V. C., Jayaratne, T. E., Ceballo, R., & Borquez, J. (1994). Unemployment and work interruption among African American single mothers: Effects on parenting and adolescent socioemotional functioning. *Child Development, 65*, 562–589.

McPartland, J. M., & McDill, E. L. (1976). *The unique role of schools in the causes of youthful crime*. Baltimore: Johns Hopkins University Press.

McWhirter, D. P., Reinisch, J. M., & Sanders, S. A. (1990). *Homosexuality/heterosexuality*. New York: Oxford University Press.

Mead, M. (1928). *Coming of age in Samoa*. New York: Morrow.

Meadowcraft, J., & Reeves, B. (1989). Influence of story schema development on children's attention to television. *Communication Research, 16*, 352–374.

Meehl, P. (1990). Why summaries of research on a psychological theory are often uninterpretable. In R. E. Snow & D. E. Wiley (Eds.), *Improving inquiry in social science*. Hillsdale, NJ: Erlbaum.

Mehegany, D. V. (1992). The relation of temperament and behavior disorders in a preschool clinical sample. *Child Psychiatry and Human Development, 22*, 129–136.

Mehler, J., Jusczyk, P. W., Lambertz, G., Halsted, N., Bertoncini, J., & Amiel-Tison, C. (1988). A precursor of language acquisition in young infants. *Cognition, 29*, 132–178.

Meichenbaum, D. H., & Goodman, J. (1971). Training impulsive children to talk to themselves: A means of developing self-control. *Journal of Abnormal Psychology, 77*, 115–126.

Meltzoff, A. N. (1988). Infant imitation and memory: Nine-month-old infants in immediate and deferred tests. *Child Development, 59*, 217–225.

Meltzoff, A. N. (1990, June). *Infant imitation*. Invited address at the University of Texas at Dallas.

Mercer, J. R., & Lewis, J. F. (1978). *System of multicultural pluralistic assessment*. New York: Psychological Corp.

Meredith, H. (1978). Research between 1960 and 1970 on the standing height of young children in different parts of the world. In H. W. Reece & L. P. Lipsitt (Eds.), *Advances in child development and behavior* (Vol. 12). New York: Academic Press.

Michael, R., Gagnon, J., Laumann, E., & Kolata, G. (1994). *Sex in America*. Boston: Little, Brown.

Michel, G. L. (1981). Right-handedness: A consequence of infant supine head-orientation preference? *Science, 212*, 685–687.

Miller, B. C., Christopherson, C. R., & King., P. K. (1993). Sexual behavior in adolescence. In T. P. Gullotta, G. R. Adams, & R. Montemayor (Eds.), *Adolescent sexuality*. Newbury Park, CA: Sage.

Miller, G. A. (1981). *Language and speech*. New York: W. H. Freeman.

Miller, J. B. (1986). *Toward a new psychology of women* (2nd ed.). Boston: Beacon Press.

Miller, J. G. (1991). A cultural perspective on the morality of beneficence and interpersonal responsibility. In S. Ting-Toomey & F. Korzenny (Eds.), *International and intercultural communication annual* (Vol. 15). Newbury Park, CA: Sage.

Miller, J. G. (1995, March). *Culture, context, and personal agency: The cultural grounding of self and morality*. Paper presented at the meeting of the Society for Research in Child Development, Indianapolis.

Miller, J. G., & Bersoff, D. M. (1993, March). *Culture and affective closeness in the morality of caring*. Paper presented at the biennial meeting of the Society for Research in Child Development, New Orleans.

Miller, M. E. (1992). Genetic disease. In R. A. Hoekelman (Ed.), *Primary pediatric care* (2nd ed.). St. Louis: Mosby Yearbook.

Miller, S. A., & Harley, J. P. (1996). *Zoology* (3rd ed.). Dubuque, IA: Wm. C. Brown.

Miller, W. B. (1958). Lower-class culture as a generating milieu of gang delinquency. *Journal of Social Issues, 14*, 5–19.

Miller-Jones, D. (1989). Culture and testing. *American Psychologist, 44*, 360–366.

Minnett, A. M., Vandell, D. L., & Santrock, J. W. (1983). The effects of sibling status on sibling interaction: Influence of birth order, age spacing, sex of the child, and sex of the sibling. *Child Development, 54*, 1064–1072.

Minuchin, P. P., & Shapiro, E. K. (1983). The school as a context for social development. In P. H. Mussen (Ed.), *Handbook of child psychology* (4th ed., Vol. 4). New York: Wiley.

Mischel, W. (1973). Toward a cognitive social learning reconceptualization of personality. *Psychological Review, 80*, 252–283.

Mischel, W. (1974). Process in delay of gratification. In L. Berkowitz (Ed.), *Advances in experimental social psychology* (Vol. 7). New York: Academic Press.

Mischel, W. (1987). *Personality* (4th ed.). New York: Holt, Rinehart & Winston.

Mischel, W. (1994, August.) *From good intentions to willpower*. Paper presented at the meeting of the American Psychological Association, Los Angeles.

Mischel, W., & Mischel, H. (1975, April). *A cognitive social-learning analysis of moral development*. Paper presented at the meeting of the Society for Research in Child Development, Denver.

Mischel, W., & Patterson, C. J. (1976). Substantive and structural elements of effective plans for self-control. *Journal of Social and Personality Psychology, 34,* 942–950.

Mize, J., Petit, G. S., & Brown, E. G. (1995). Mothers' supervision of their children's play: Relations with beliefs, perceptions, and knowledge. *Developmental Psychology, 31,* 311–321.

Moely, B. E., Olson, F. A., Halwes, T. G., & Flavell, J. H. (1969). Production deficiency in young children's clustered recall. *Developmental Psychology, 1,* 26–34.

Montemayor, R. (1982). The relationship between parent-adolescent conflict and the amount of time adolescents spend with parents, peers, and alone. *Child Development, 53,* 1512–1519.

Morelli, G. A., Rogoff, B., & Angelillo, C. (1992). *Cultural variation in young children's opportunities for involvement in adult activities*. Poster presented at the meeting of the American Anthropological Association, San Francisco.

Morgan, J. L., & Demuth, K. (Eds.). (1995). *Signal to syntax*. Hillsdale, NJ: Erlbaum.

Morrison, F. J., Holmes, D. L., & Haith, D. L. (1974). A developmental study of the effects of familiarity on short-term visual memory. *Journal of Experimental Child Psychology, 18,* 412–425.

Morrison, G. S. (1995). *Early childhood education today* (6th ed.). Columbus, OH: Merrill.

Morrongiello, B. A., Fenwick, K. D., & Chance, G. (1990). Sound localization acuity in very young infants: An observer-based testing procedure. *Developmental Psychology, 26,* 75–84.

Morrow, L. (1988, August 8). Through the eyes of children. *Time,* pp. 32–33.

Mortimer, E. A. (1992). Child health in the developing world. In R. E. Behrman, R. M. Kliegman, W. E. Nelson, & V. C. Vaughan (Eds.), *Nelson textbook of pediatrics* (14th ed.).

Moshman, D. (1997). Cognitive development beyond childhood. In D. Kuhn & R. S. Siegler (Eds.), *Handbook of child psychology* (5th Ed., Vol. II). New York: Wiley.

Mott, F. L., & Marsiglio, W. (1985, September–October). Early childbearing and completion of high school. *Family Planning Perspectives,* p. 234.

Muecke, L., Simons-Morton, B., Huang, I. W., & Parcel, G. (1992). Is childhood obesity associated with high-fat foods and low physical activity? *Journal of School Health, 62,* 19–23.

Mueller, N., & Silverman, N. (1989). Peer relations in maltreated children. In D. Cicchetti & V. Carlson (Eds.), *Child maltreatment*. New York: Cambridge University Press.

Mundy, P., Seibert, J., & Hogan, A. (1984). Relationship between sensorimotor and early communication abilities in developmentally delayed children. *Merrill-Palmer Quarterly, 30,* 33–48.

Munroe, R. H., Himmin, H. S., & Munroe, R. L. (1984). Gender understanding and sex role preference in four cultures. *Developmental Psychology, 20,* 673–682.

Murphy, K., & Schneider, B. (1994). Coaching socially rejected early adolescents regarding behaviors used by peers to infer liking: A dyad-specific intervention. *Journal of Early Adolescence, 14,* 83–95.

Murphy, S. O. (1993, March). *The family context and the transition to siblinghood: Strategies parents use to influence sibling-infant relationships*. Paper presented at the biennial meeting of the Society for Research in Child Development, New Orleans.

Murray, H. A. (1938). *Explorations in personality*. New York: Oxford University Press.

Murray, V. M. (1996, March). *Sexual and motherhood statuses*. Paper presented at the meeting of the Society for Research on Adolescence, Boston.

Myers, M., & Paris, S. G. (1978). Children's metacognitive knowledge about reading. *Journal of Educational Psychology, 70,* 680–690.

Nagata, D. K. (1989). Japanese American children and adolescents. In J. T. Gibbs & L. N. Huang (Eds.), *Children of color*. San Francisco: Jossey-Bass.

National Advisory Council on Economic Opportunity. (1980). *Critical choices for the 80s*. Washington, DC: U.S. Government Printing Office.

National and Community Service Coalition. (1995). *Youth volunteerism: Here's what the surveys say*. Washington, DC: Author.

National Association for the Education of Young Children. (1986). *How to choose a good early childhood program*. Washington, DC: Author.

National Association for the Education of Young Children. (1988). NAEYC position statement on developmentally appropriate practices in the primary grades, serving 5- through 8-year-olds. *Young Children, 43,* 64–83.

National Association for the Education of Young Children. (1990). NAEYC position statement on school readiness. *Young Children, 46,* 21–28.

National Association for the Education of Young Children. (1991). Public policy report (101st Congress): The children's congress. *Young Children, 47,* 78–80.

National Association for the Education of Young Children. (1996). NAEYC position statement: Responding to linguistic and cultural diversity—recommendations for effective early childhood education. *Young Children, 51,* 4–12.

Neighbors, H. W., & Jackson, J. S. (Eds.). (1996). *Mental health in Black America*. Newbury Park, CA: Sage.

Neimark, E. D. (1982). Adolescent thought: Transition to formal operations. In B. B. Wolman (Ed.), *Handbook of developmental psychology*. Englewood Cliffs, NJ: Prentice Hall.

Neisser, U., Boodoo, G., Bouchard, T. J., Boykin, A. W., Brody, N., Ceci, S. J., Halpern, D. F., Loehlin, J. C., Perloff, R., Sternberg, R. J., & Urbina, S. (1996). Intelligence: Knowns and unknowns. *American Psychologist, 51,* 77–101.

Nelson, K. (1997, April). *Social foundations of lexical development*. Paper presented at the meeting of the Society for Research in Child Development, Washington, DC.

Nelson, K. E., & Réger, Z. (Eds.). (1995). *Children's language* (Vol. 8). Hillsdale, NJ: Erlbaum.

Nevid, J. S., & Gottfried, F. (1995). *Choices: Sex in the age of STDs*. Boston: Allyn & Bacon.

Newman, D. L., & Caspi, A. (1996, March). *Temperament styles observed at age 3 predict interpersonal functioning in the transition to adulthood*. Paper presented at the meeting of the Society for Research on Adolescence, Boston.

Newman, J. (1995). How breast milk protects newborns. *Scientific American, 273*(6), 76–80.

NICHD Early Child Care Research Network. (1996, April 20). *Infant child care and attachment security: Results of the NICHD Study of Early Child Care*. Paper presented at the International Conference on Infant Studies, Providence, RI.

Nicholls, J. G. (1984). Conceptions of ability and achievement motivation. In R. E. Ames & C. Ames (Eds.), *Motivation in education*. New York: Academic Press.

Ninio, A., & Snow, C. E. (1996). *Pragmatic development*. Boulder, CO: Westview Press.

Nishio, K., Bilmes, M. (1993). Psychotherapy with Southeast Asian clients. In D. R. Atkinson, G. Morten, & D. W. Sue (Eds.), *Counseling American minorities*. Dubuque, IA: Brown & Benchmark.

Nolen-Hoeksema, S., Girgus, J. S., & Seligman, M. E. P. (1991). Sex differences in depression and explanatory style in children. *Journal of Youth and Adolescence, 20*, 233–246.

Nottlemann, E. D., Susman, E. J., Blue, J. H., Inoff-Germain, G., Dorn, L. D., Loriaux, D. L., Cutler, G. B., & Chrousos, G. P. (1987). Gonadal and adrenal hormone correlates of adjustment in early adolescence. In R. M. Lerner & T. T. Foch (Eds.), *Biological-psychological interactions in early adolescence*. Hillsdale, NJ: Erlbaum.

Nucci, L., & Weber, E. K. (1991). The domain approach to values education: From theory to practice. In W. M. Kurtines & J. Gewirtz (Eds.), *Moral behavior and development* (Vol. 3). Hillsdale, NJ: Erlbaum.

Nydegger, C. N., & Mitteness, L. S. (1991). Fathers and their adult sons and daughters. *Marriage and Family Review, 16*, 249–266.

Nyiti, R. M. (1982). The validity of "cultural differences explanations" for cross-cultural variation in the rate of Piagetian cognitive development. In D. Wagner & H. Stevenson (Eds.), *Cultural perspectives on child development*. New York: W. H. Freeman.

O

O'Brien, M. (1993, March). *Are working mothers different? Attitudes toward parenthood in employed and nonemployed mothers of infants and toddlers*. Paper presented at the biennial meeting of the Society for Research in Child Development, New Orleans.

O'Connell, K. L. (1996). Attention deficit hyperactivity disorder. *Pediatric Nursing, 22*, 30–33.

O'Conner, T. G. (1997, April). *Cognitive gains in adoptees exposed to severe deprivation*. Paper presented at the meeting of the Society for Research in Child Development, Washington, DC.

Obeidallah, D. (1994, February). *Gender and depression in young adolescents: Links with parental style and marital roles*. Paper presented at the meeting of the Society for Research on Adolescence, San Diego.

Obler, L. K. (1993). Language beyond childhood. In J. B. Gleason (Ed.), *The development of language* (3rd ed.). New York: Macmillan.

Offer, D., Ostrov, E., Howard, K. I., & Atkinson, R. (1988). *The teenage world: Adolescents' self-image in ten countries*. New York: Plenum.

Ogbu, J. U. (1974). *The next generation: An ethnography of education in an urban neighborhood*. New York: Academic Press.

Ogbu, J. U. (1986). The consequences of the American caste system. In U. Neisser (Ed.), *The school achievement of minority children: New perspectives*. Hillsdale, NJ: Erlbaum.

Ogbu, J. U. (1989, April). *Academic socialization of Black children: An inoculation against future failure?* Paper presented at the biennial meeting of the Society for Research in Child Development, Kansas City.

Okun, B. F., & Rappaport, L. J. (1980). *Woring with families*. North Scituate, MA: Duxbury Press.

Oller, D. K. (1995, February). *Early speech and word learning in bilingual and monolingual children: Advantages of early bilingualism*. Paper presented at the meeting of the American Association for the Advancement of Science, Atlanta.

Olson, H. C., & Burgess, D. M. (1996). Early intervention with children prenatally exposed to alcohol and other drugs. In M. J. Guralnick (Ed.), *The effectiveness of early intervention*. Baltimore: Paul H. Brookes.

Olvera-Ezzell, N., Power, T. G., Cousins, J. H., Guerra, A. M., & Trujillo, M. (1994). The development of health knowledge in low-income Mexican American children. *Child Development, 65*, 416–427.

Olweus, D. (1980). Bullying among schoolboys. In R. Barnen (Ed.), *Children and violence*. Stockholm: Acaemic Litteratur.

Olweus, D., Matteson, A., Schalling, D., & Low, H. (1988). Circulating testosterone levels and aggression in adolescent males: A causal analysis. *Psychosomatic Medicine, 50*, 261–272.

Ornstein, P. A. (1955, March). *Remembering the distant past: Implications of research on children's memory for the recovered memory debate*. Introduction to symposium at the Society for Research in Child Development, Indianapolis.

Oser, F. K. (1986). Moral education and values education: The discourse perspective. In M. C. Wittrock (Ed.), *Handbook of research on teaching*. New York: Macmillan.

Ostoja, E., McCrone, E., Lehn, L., Reed, T., & Sroufe, L. A. (1995, March). *Representations of close relationships in adolescence: Longitudinal antecedents from infancy through childhood*. Paper presented at the meeting of the Society for Research in Child Development, Indianapolis.

Paget, K. D., & Abramczyk, L. W. (1993, March). *Family functioning and child neglect: The contribution of maternal and child perceptions*. Paper presented at the biennial meeting of the Society for Research in Child Development, New Orleans.

Paikoff, R. L., Brooks-Gunn, J., & Warren, M. P. (1991). Effects of girls' hormonal status on depressive and aggressive symptoms over the course of one year. *Journal of Youth and Adolescence, 20*, 191–215.

Palmer, S. A., & Bridges, L. J. (1995, March). *Paternal characteristics and father involvement*. Paper presented at the meeting of the Society for Research in Child Development, Indianapolis.

Paludi, M. A. (1955). *The psychology of women* (2nd ed.). Madison, WI: Brown & Benchmark.

Paneth, N. S. (1995, spring). The problem of low birth weight. *The Future of Children, 5*(1), 19–34.

Papert, S. (1980). *Mindstorms: Children, computers, and powerful ideas*. New York: Basic Books.

Parcel, G. S., Simons-Morton, G. G., O'Hara, N. M., Baranowski, T., Kolbe, L. J., & Bee, D. E. (1987). School promotion of healthful diet and exercise behavior: An integration of organizational change and social learning theory interventions. *Journal of School Health, 57*, 150–156.

Parcel, G. S., Tiernan, K., Nadar, P. R., & Gottlob, D. (1979). Health education and kindergarten children. *Journal of School Health, 49*, 129–131.

Parham, T. (1996). Multicultural counseling theory and African-American populations. In D. W. Sue (Ed.), *Theory of multicultural counseling and therapy*. Pacific Grove, CA: Brooks/Cole.

Parham, T. A., & McDavis, R. J. (1993). Black men, an endangered species: Who's really pulling the trigger? In D. R. Atkinson, G. Morten, & D. W. Sue (Eds.), *Counseling American minorities*. Dubuque, IA: Brown & Benchmark.

Paris, S. G., & Lindauer, B. K. (1982). The development of cognitive skills during childhood. In B. B. Wolman (Ed.), *Handbook of developmental psychology*. Englewood Cliffs, NJ: Prentice Hall.

Park, K. J., & Honig, A. S. (1991, August). *Infant child care patterns and later ratings of preschool behaviors*. Paper presented at the meeting of the American Psychological Association, San Francisco.

Parke, R. D. (1972). Some effects of punishment on children's behavior. In W. W. Hartup (Ed.), *The young child* (Vol. 2.). Washington, DC: National Association for the Education of Young Children.

Parke, R. D. (1977). Some effects of punishment on children's behavior—Revisited. In E. M. Hetherington & R. D. Parke (Eds.), *Readings in contemporary child psychology*. New York: McGraw-Hill.

Parke, R. D. (1993, March). *Family research in the 1990s.* Paper presented at the biennial meeting of the Society for Research in Child Development, New Orleans.

Parke, R. D., & Buriel, R. (1997). Socialization in the family. In N. Eisenberg (Ed.), *Handbook of child psychology* (5th Ed., Vol. III). New York: Wiley.

Parke, R. D., & Sawin, D. B. (1980). The family in early infancy. In F. Pedersen (Ed.), *The father-infant relationship: Observational studies in family context.* New York: Praeger.

Parker, F. L., Abdul-Kabir, S., Stevenson, H. G., & Garrett, B. (1995, March). *Partnerships between researchers and the community in Head Start.* Paper presented at the meeting of the Society for Research in Child Development, Indianapolis.

Parker, J. G., & Asher, S. R. (1987). Peer relations and later personal adjustment: Are low accepted children at risk? *Psychological Bulletin, 102,* 357–389.

Parmalee, A. H. (1986). Children's illnesses: Their beneficial effects on behavioral development. *Child Development, 57,* 1–10.

Parten, M. (1932). Social play among preschool children. *Journal of Abnormal Social Psychology, 27,* 243–269.

Pascual-Leone, J. (1987). Organismic processes for Neo-Piagetian theories: A dilectical causal account of cognitive development. *International Journal of Psychology, 22,* 531–570.

Pascual-Leone, J., & Shafrir, U. (1991, April). *The development of post-failure reflectivity.* Paper presented at the Society for Child Development meeting, Seattle.

Patterson, C. J. (1995). Lesbian and gay parenthood. In M. H. Bornstein (Ed.), *Handbook of parenting* (Vol. 3). Hillsdale, NJ: Erlbaum.

Patterson, G. R., Capaldi, D., & Bank, L. (1991). An early starter model for predicting delinquency. In D. Pepler & K. Rubin (Eds.), *The development and treatment of childhood aggression.* Hillsdale, NJ: Erlbaum.

Patterson, G. R., DeBaryshe, B. D., & Ramsey, E. (1989). A developmental perspective on antisocial behavior. *American Psychologist, 44,* 329–355.

Patterson, G. R., & Stouthamer-Loeber, M. (1984). The correlation of family management practices and delinquency. *Child Development, 55,* 1299–1307.

Patterson, S. J., Sochting, I., & Marcia, J. E. (1992). The inner space and beyond: Women and identity. In G. R. Adams, T. P. Gullotta, & R. Montemayor (Eds.), *Adolescent identity formation.* Newbury Park, CA: Sage.

Paulson, S. E., Marchant, G. J., & Rothlisberg, B. (1995, March). *Relations among parent, teacher, and school factors: Implications for achievement outcome in middle grade students.* Paper presented at the meeting of the Society for Research in Child Development, Indianapolis.

Pavlov, I. P. (1927). In G. V. Anrep (Trans.), *Conditioned reflexes.* London: Oxford University Press.

Pearson, S. (1978). *Everybody knows that.* New York: Dial.

Pederson, D. R., Moran, G., Sitko, C., Campbell, K., Ghesquire, K., & Acton, H. (1989, April). *Maternal sensitivity and the security of infant-mother attachment.* Paper presented at the meeting of the Society for Research in Child Development, Kansas City.

Pellegrini, A. D. (1996). *Observing children in their natural worlds.* Hillsdale, NJ: Erlbaum.

Pennebaker, J. (1995). Commentary for *Psychology: The science of mind and behavior* (4th ed) by John W. Santrock. Dubuque, IA: Brown & Benchmark.

Penner, S. G. (1987). Parental responses to grammatical and ungrammatical child utterances. *Child Development, 58,* 376–384.

Perfetti, C. A. (1984). *Reading ability.* New York: Oxford University Press.

Perfetti, C. A. (1992). The representation problem in reading acquisition. In P. B. Gouth, L. C. Ehri, & R. Treiman (Eds.), *Reading acquisition.* Hillsdale, NJ: Erlbaum.

Perkins, D. N. (1984, September). Creativity by design. *Educational Leadership,* pp. 18–25.

Perry, W. G. (1981). Cognitive and ethical growth. The making of meaning. In A. W. Chickering (Ed.), *The modern American college: Responding to the new realities of diverse students and a changing society.* San Francisco: Jossey-Bass.

Peskin, H. (1967). Pubertal onset and ego functioning. *Journal of Abnormal Psychology, 72,* 1–15.

Petersen, A. C. (1979, January). Can puberty come any faster? *Psychology Today,* pp. 45–56.

Petersen, A. C. (1993). Creating adolescents: The role of context and process in developmental trajectories. *Journal of Research on Adolescence, 3,* 1–18.

Petersen, A. C. (1997, April). *National Science and Technology Council's children's initiative.* Paper presented at the meeting of the Society for Research in Child Development, Washington, DC.

Petersen, A. C., & Ding, S. (1994, February). *Depression and body image disorders in adolescence.* Paper presented at the meeting of the Society for Research on Adolescence, San Diego.

Petersen, A. C., Leffert, N., & Miller, K. (1993, March). *The role of interpersonal relationships in the development of depressed affect and depression in adolescence.* Paper presented at the biennial meeting of the Society for Research in Child Development, New Orleans.

Petersen, A. C., Sarigiani, P. A., & Kennedy, R. E. (1991). Adolescent depression: Why more girls? *Journal of Youth and Adolescence, 20,* 147–271.

Petersen, A. C., Sarigiani, P. A., & Kennedy, R. E. (1991). Coping with adolescence. In M. E. Colte & S. Gore (Eds.), *Adolescent stress: Causes and consequences.* New York: Aldine de Gruyter.

Peterson, C. C., & Peterson, J. L. (1973). Preference for sex of offspring as a measure of change in sex attitudes. *Psychology, 10,* 3–5.

Peterson, P. L. (1977). Interactive effects of student anxiety, achievement orientation, and teacher behavior on student achievement and attitude. *Journal of Educational Psychology, 69,* 779–792.

Pfeffer, C. R. (1996). *Severe stress and mental disturbance in children.* Washington, DC: American Psychiatric Press.

Phillips, D. A., Voran, K., Kisker, E., Howes, C., & Whitebook, M. (1994). Child care for children in poverty: Opportunity or inequity? *Child Development, 65,* 472–492.

Phillips, R. (1997, July). *Strengthening school and community partnerships: Prevention that works!* Paper presented at the conference on Working with America's Youth, Pittsburgh, PA.

Phinney, J. S. (1989). Stages of ethnic identity development in minority group adolescents. *Journal of Early Adolescence, 9,* 34–49.

Phinney, J. S., & Alipura, L. L. (1990). Ethnic identity in college students from four ethnic groups. *Journal of Adolescence, 13,* 171–183.

Phinney, J. S., & Cobb, N. J. (1993, March). *Adolescents' reasoning about discrimination: Ethnic and attitudinal predictors*. Paper presented at the biennial meeting of the Society for Research in Child Development, New Orleans.

Phinney, J. S., Dupont, S., Landin, J., & Onwughalu, M. (1994, February). *Social identity orientation, bicultural conflict, and coping strategies among minority adolescents*. Paper presented at the meeting of the Society for Research on Adolescence, San Diego.

Piaget, J. (1932). *The moral judgment of the child*. New York: Harcourt Brace Jovanovich.

Piaget, J. (1952). *The origins of intelligence in children*. (M. Cook, Trans.). New York: International Universities Press.

Piaget, J. (1952a). Jean Piaget. In C. A. Murchison (Ed.), *A history of psychology in autobiography* (Vol. 4). Worcester, MA: Clark University Press.

Piaget, J. (1954). *The construction of reality in the child*. New York: Basic Books.

Piaget, J. (1962). *Play, dreams, and imitation in childhood*. New York: W. W. Norton.

Piaget, J. (1967). The mental development of the child. In D. Elkind (Ed.), *Six psychological studies by Piaget*. New York: Random House.

Piaget, J. (1970). Piaget's theory. In P. H. Mussen (Ed.), *Manual of child psychology* (3rd ed., Vol. 1). New York: Wiley.

Piaget, J. (1971). *The construction of reality in the child*. New York: Ballantine.

Piaget, J. (1972). Intellectual evolution from adolescence to adulthood. *Human Development, 15*, 1–12.

Piaget, J., & Inhelder, B. (1969). *The child's conception of space* (F. J. Langdon & J. L. Lunzer, Trans.). New York: W. W. Norton. (Original work published 1948)

Pickens, J. (1994). Perception of auditory-visual distance relations by 5-month-olds. *Developmental Psychology, 30*, 537–544.

Picó, I. (1983). *Machismo y educación in Puerto Rico* (2nd ed.). Rio Piedras: Universidad de Puerto Rico.

Pillow, B. H. (1988). Young children's understanding of attentional limits. *Child Development, 49*, 38–46.

Pillow, D. R., Zautra, A. J., & Sandler, I. (1996). Major life events and minor stressors: Identifying mediational links in the stress process. *Journal of Personality and Social Psychology, 70*, 381–394.

Piotrowski, C. C. (1997, April). *Mother and sibling triads in conflict: Linking conflict style and the quality of sibling relationships*. Paper presented at the meeting of the Society for Research in Child Development, Washington, DC.

Pipes, P. (1988). Nutrition in childhood. In S. R. Williams & B. S. Worthington-Roberts (Eds.), *Nutrition throughout the life cycle*. St. Louis: Times Mirror/Mosby.

Pleck, J. H. (1983). The theory of male sex role identity: Its rise and fall, 1936–present. In M. Levin (Ed.), *In the shadow of the past: Psychology portrays the sexes*. New York: Columbia University Press.

Pleck, J. H. (1995). The gender role strain paradigm: An update. In R. F. Levant & W. S. Pollack (Eds.), *A new psychology of men*. New York: Basic Books.

Plomin, R. (1993, March). *Human behavioral genetics and development: An overview and update*. Paper presented at the biennial meeting of the Society for Research in Child Development, New Orleans.

Plomin, R. (1996, August). *Nature and nurture together*. Paper presented at the meeting of the American Psychological Association, Toronto.

Plomin, R., DeFries, J. C., & McClearn, G. E. (1990). *Behavioral genetics: A primer*. New York: W. H. Freeman.

Plomin, R., DeFries, J. C., McClearn, G. E., & Rutter, M. (1997). *Behavioral genetics* (3rd. Ed.), New York: W. H. Freeman.

Poest, C. A., Williams, J. R., Witt, D. D., & Atwood, M. E. (1990). Challenge me to move: Large muscle development in young children. *Young Children, 45*, 4–10.

Pollack, W. S. (1995). No man is an island: Toward a new psychoanalytic psychology of men. In R. F. Levant & W. S. Pollack (Eds.), *A new psychology of men*. New York: Basic Books.

Pollitt, E. P., Gorman, K. S., Engle, P. L., Martorell, R., & Rivera, J. (1993). Early supplementary feeding and cognition. *Monographs of the Society for Research in Child Development, 58* (7, Serial No. 235).

Pomeroy, C. (1996). Anorexia nervosa, bulimia nervosa, and binge eating disorder. In J. K. Thompson (Ed.), *Body image, eating disorders, and obesity*. Washington, DC: American Psychological Association.

Posada, G., Lord, C., & Waters, E. (1995, March). *Secure base behavior and children's misbehavior in three different contexts: Home, neighbors, and school*. Paper presented at the meeting of the Society for Research in Child Development, Indianapolis.

Posner, J. K., & Vandell, D. L. (1994). Low-income children's after-care: Are there benefits of after-school programs? *Child Development, 65*, 440–456.

Posner, M., & Rothbart, M. (1989, August). *Attention: Normal and pathological development*. Paper presented at the meeting of the Society for Research in Child Development, New Orleans.

Poulin-Doubois, D., & Shultz, T. R. (1988). The development of the understanding of human behavior: From agency to intentionality. In J. Astington, P. Harris, & D. Olson (Eds.), *Developing theories of mind*. Cambridge, MA: Cambridge University Press.

Powell, G. (1995, March). *Research initiatives in Head Start*. Paper presented at the meeting of the Society for Research in Child Development, Indianapolis.

Powell, G. J., & Fuller, M. (1972). The variables for positive self-concept among young Southern Black adolescents. *Journal of the National Medical Association, 43*, 72–79.

Power, C. (1991). Lawrence Kohlberg: The vocation of an educator, part I. In W. M. Kurtines & J. Gewirtz (Eds.), *Moral behavior and development* (Vol. 1). Hillsdale, NJ: Erlbaum.

Premack, D. (1986). *Gavagai! The future history of the ape language controversy*. Cambridge, MA: MIT Press.

Pressley, M., & Schneider, W. (1997). *Introduction to memory development during childhood and adolescence*. Mahwah, NJ: Erlbaum.

Presson, C. G., & Ihrig, L. H. (1982). Using matter as a spatial landmark: Evidence against egocentric coding in infancy. *Developmental Psychology, 18*, 699–703.

Prinstein, M. M., Fetter, M. D., & La Greca, A. M. (1996, March). *Can you judge adolescents by the company they keep?: Peer group membership, substance abuse, and risk-taking behaviors*. Paper presented at the meeting of the Society for Research on Adolescence, Boston.

Puka, B. (1991). Toward the redevelopment of Kohlberg's theory: Preserving essential structure, removing controversial content. In W. M. Kurtines & J. Gewirtz (Eds.), *Moral behavior and development: Advances in theory, research, and application*. Hillsdale, NJ: Erlbaum.

Putallaz, M. (1983). Predicting children's sociometric status from their behavior. *Child Development, 54*, 1417–1426.

Quiggle, N. L., Garber, J., Panak, W. F., & Dodge, K. A. (1992). Social information processing in aggressive and depressed children. *Child Development, 63*, 1305–1320.

Rabin, B. E., & Dorr, A. (1995, March). *Children's understanding of emotional events on family television series.* Paper presented at the meeting of the Society for Research in Child Development, Indianapolis.

Rabiner, D. L., Gordon, L., Klumb, D., & Thompson, L. B. (1991, April). *Social problem solving deficiencies in rejected children: Motivational factors and skill deficits.* Paper presented at the meeting of the Society for Research in Child Development, Seattle.

Rabrenovic, G., & Kelleher, M. E. (1995, March). *Neighborhood problems, resources, and child well-being.* Paper presented at the meeting of the Society for Research in Child Development, Indianapolis.

Radke-Yarrow, M., Nottlemann, E., Martinez, P., Fox, M. B., & Belmont, B. (1992). Young children of affectively ill parents: A longitudinal study of psychosocial development. *Journal of the Academy of Child and Adolescent Psychiatry, 31,* 68–77.

Ramirez, O. (1989). Mexican American children and adolescents. In J. T. Gibbs & L. N. Huang (Eds.), *Children of color.* San Francisco: Jossey-Bass.

Rapport, M. D. (1997). Attention-deficit hyperactivity disorder. In V. B. Van Hasselt & M. Hersen (Eds.), *Handbook of psychological treatment protocols for children and adolescents.* Mahwah, NJ: Erlbaum.

Ratner, N. (1996). Unpublished review of *Child Development* (8th ed.) by J. W. Santrock. Madison, WI: Brown & Benchmark.

Ratner, N. B. (1993a). Atypical language development. In J. B. Gleason (Ed.), *The development of language* (3rd ed.). New York: Macmillan.

Ratner, N. B. (1993b). Learning to speak. *Science, 262,* 260.

Reilly, R. (1988, August 15). Here no one is spared. *Sports Illustrated,* pp. 70–77.

Reinherz, H. Z., Giaconia, R. M., Silverman, A. B., & Friedman, A. C. (1994, February). *Early psychosocial risks for adolescent suicide ideation and attempts.* Paper presented at the meeting of the Society for Research on Adolescence, San Diego.

Report on Preschool Programs. (1992, February 26). Head Start, psychologists launch new mental health initiatives (p. 42). Arlington, VA: Capital.

Resnick, L. B. (1987). *Education and learning to think.* Washington, DC: National Academy Press.

Rest, J. (1995). *Concerns for the social-psychological development of youth and educational strategies: Report for the Kaufmann Foundation.* Minneapolis: University of Minnesota, Department of Educational Psychology.

Rest, J. (1996, January). Unpublished review of *Adolescence* (7th ed.) by J. W. Santrock. Dubuque, IA: Brown & Benchmark.

Rest, J. R. (1986). *Moral development: Advances in theory, research, and application.* New York: Praeger.

Rest, J. R., Turiel, E., & Kohlberg, L. (1969). Relations between level of moral judgment and preference and comprehension of the moral judgments of others. *Journal of Personality, 37,* 225–252.

Reuter, M. W., & Biller, H. B. (1973). Perceived paternal nurturance-availability and personality adjustment among college males. *Journal of Consulting and Clinical Psychology, 40,* 339–342.

Reynolds, C. R., & Kamphaus, R. W. (Eds.). (1990). *Handbook of psychological and educational assessment of children: Intelligence and achievement.* New York: Guilford.

Rice, M. (Ed.). (1996). *Toward a genetics of language.* Hillsdale, NJ: Erlbaum.

Rice, M. L. (1989). Children's language acquisition. *American Psychologist, 44,* 149–156.

Richards, M. H., & Duckett, E. (1994). The relationship of maternal employment to early adolescent daily experiences with and without parents. *Child Development, 65,* 225–236.

Richards, M., Sulieman, L., Sims, B., & Sedeno, A. (1994, February). *Experiences of ethnically diverse young adolescents growing up in poverty.* Paper presented at the meeting of the Society for Research on Adolescence, San Diego.

Richardson, J. L., Dwyer, K., McGrugan, K., Hansen, W. B., Dent, C., Johnson, C. A., Sussman, S. Y., Brannon, B., & Glay, B. (1989). Substance use among eighth-grade students who take care of themselves after school. *Pediatrics, 84,* 556–566.

Rieser, J. (1979). Spatial orientation of six-month-old infants. *Child Development, 50,* 1078–1087.

Rieser, J. J., Hill, E. W., Taylor, C. A., Bradfield, A., & Rosen, R. (1989, April). *The perception of locomotion and the role of visual experience in the development of spatial knowledge.* Paper presented at the meeting of the Society for Research in Child Development, Kansas City.

Ritblatt, S. N. (1995, March). *Theory of mind in preschoolers: False beliefs, deception, and pretend play.* Paper presented at the meeting of the Society for Research in Child Development, Indianapolis.

Roberts, D., Jacobson, L., & Taylor, R. D. (1996, March). *Neighborhood characteristics, stressful life events, and African-American adolescents' adjustment.* Paper presented at the meeting of the Society for Research on Adolescence, Boston.

Roberts, W., & Strayer, J. (1996). Empathy, emotional expressiveness, and prosocial behavior. *Child Development, 67,* 471–489.

Robinson, D. P., & Greene, J. W. (1988). The adolescent alcohol and drug problem: A practical approach. *Pediatric Nursing, 14,* 305–310.

Robinson, N. M., & Redden, D. (1997, April) *Factors associated with high academic achievement in former Head Start students.* Paper presented at the meeting of the Society for Research in Child Development, Washington, DC.

Robinson, N. S. (1995). Evaluating the nature of perceived support and its relation to perceived self-worth in adolescents. *Journal of Research on Adolescence, 5,* 253–280.

Rodin, J. (1984, December). Interview: A sense of control. *Psychology Today,* pp. 38–45.

Rodin, J. (1992). *Body traps.* New York: William Morrow.

Rodriguez-Haynes, M., & Crittenden, P. M. (1988). *Ethnic differences among abusing, neglecting, and nonmaltreating families.* Paper presented at the Southeastern Conference on Human Development, Charleston, SC.

Roff, M., Sells, S. B., & Golden, M. W. (1972). *Social adjustment and personality development in children.* Minneapolis: University of Minnesota Press.

Rogers, A. (1987). *Questions of gender differences: Ego development and moral voice in adolescence.* Unpublished manuscript, Department of Education, Harvard University.

Rogers, C. R. (1950). The significance of the self regarding attitudes and perceptions. In M. L. Reymart (Ed.), *Feelings and emotions.* New York: McGraw-Hill.

Rogers, C. S., & Sawyers, J. K. (1988). *Play in the lives of children.* Washington, DC: National Association for the Education of Young Children.

Rogoff, B. (1990). *Apprenticeship in thinking.* New York: Oxford University Press.

Rogoff, B. (1997). Cognition as a collaborative process. In D. Kuhn & R. S. Siegler (Eds.), *Handbook of child psychology* (5th Ed., Vol. II). New York: Wiley.

Rogoff, B., & Morelli, G. (1989). Perspectives on children's development from cultural psychology. *American Psychologist, 44*, 343–348.

Rohner, R. P., & Rohner, E. C. (1981). Parental acceptance-rejection and parental control: Cross-cultural codes. *Ethnology, 20*, 245–260.

Root, M. P. (Ed.). (1992). *Racially mixed people in America.* Newbury Park, CA: Sage.

Rose, H. A. (1997, April). *Bringing biology back in: A biopsychosocial model of gender development.* Paper presented at the meeting of the Society for Research in Child Development, Washington, DC.

Rose, H. A., & Martin, C. L. (1993, March). *Children's gender-based inferences about others' activities, emotions, and occupations.* Paper presented at the biennial meeting of the Society for Research in Child Development, New Orleans.

Rose, S., & Frieze, I. R. (1993). Young singles' contemporary dating scripts. *Sex Roles, 28*, 499–509.

Rose, S. A., Feldman, J. F., McCarton, C. M., & Wolfson, J. (1988). Information processing in seven-month-old infants as a function of risk status. *Child Development, 59*, 489–603.

Rose, S. A., Feldman, J. F., & Wallace, I. F. (1992). Infant information processing in relation to six-year cognitive outcomes. *Child Development, 63*, 1126–1141.

Rose, S. A., & Ruff, H. A. (1987). Cross-modal abilities in human infants. In J. D. Osofsky (Ed.), *Handbook of infant development* (2nd ed.). New York: Wiley.

Rosenberg, M. (1965). *Society and the adolescent self-image.* Princeton, NJ: Princeton University Press.

Rosenberg, M. (1979). *Conceiving the self.* New York: Basic Books.

Rosenberg, M. (1986). Self-concept from middle childhood through adolescence. In J. Suls & A. G. Greenwald (Eds.), *Psychological perspectives on the self* (Vol. 3). Hillsdale, NJ: Erlbaum.

Rosenblith, J. F. (1992). *In the beginning* (2nd ed.). Newbury Park, CA: Sage.

Rosenshine, B. (1997). Advances in research on instruction. In J. W. Lloyd, E. J. Kameenui, & D. Chard (Eds.), *Issues in educating students with disabilities.* Hillsdale, NJ: Erlbaum.

Rosenstein, D., & Oster, H. (1988). Differential facial responses to four basic tastes in newborns. *Child Development, 59*, 1555–1568.

Rosenthal, D. M., & Sawyers, J. Y. (1996). Building successful home/school partnerships: Strategies for parent support and involvement. *Childhood Education, 72*, 194–200.

Rosenthal, R., & Jacobsen, L. (1968). *Pygmalian in the classroom.* New York: Holt, Rinehart & Winston.

Rosnow, R. L., & Rosenthal, R. (1996). *Beginning behavioral research* (2nd ed.). Upper Saddle River, NJ: Prentice Hall.

Rosnow, R. L., & Rosenthal, R. (1997). *People studying people: Artifacts and ethics in behavioral research.* New York: W. H. Freeman.

Rossi, A. S. (1989). A life-course approach to gender, aging, and intergenerational relations. In K. W. Schaie & C. Schooler (Eds.), *Social structure and aging.* Hillsdale, NJ: Erlbaum.

Rotenberg, K. J. (1993, March). *Development of restrictive disclosure to friends.* Paper presented at the biennial meeting of the Society for Research in Child Development, New Orleans.

Rothbart, M. K. (1997, April). Discussant on symposium, *Continuity and change in temperament from infancy to childhood and adolescence.* Society for Research in Child Development, Washington, DC.

Rothbart, M. K., Hanley, D., & Albert, M. (1986). Gender differences in moral reasoning. *Sex Roles, 15*, 645–653.

Rotter, J. B. (1989, August). *Internal versus external locus of control of reinforcement: A case history of a variable.* Paper presented at the meeting of the American Psychological Association, New Orleans.

Rovee-Collier, C. (1987). Learning and memory in children. In J. D. Osofsky (Ed.), *Handbook of infant development* (2nd ed.). New York: Wiley.

Rubenstein, J., Heeren, T., Houseman, D., Rubin, C., & Stechler, G. (1989). Suicidal behavior in "normal" adolescents: Risk and protective factors. *American Journal of Orthopsychiatry, 59*, 59–71.

Rubert, M. L., & Rubovits, D. S. (1997, April). *A history of adolescent pregnancy programs in the 20th century.* Paper presented at the meeting of the Society for Research in Child Development, Washington, DC.

Rubin, K. H., Bukowski, W., & Parker, J. G. (1997). Peer interactions, relationships, and groups. In N. Eisenberg (Ed.), *Handbook of child psychology* (5th Ed., Vol. III). New York: Wiley.

Rubin, K. H., Maioni, T. L., & Hornung, M. (1976). Free play behaviors in middle and lower social class preschoolers: Parten and Piaget revisited. *Child Development, 47*, 414–419.

Rubin, K. N., Fein, G. G., & Vandenberg, B. (1983). Play. In P. H. Mussen (Ed.), *Handbook of child psychology* (4th ed., Vol. 4). New York: Wiley.

Rubin, Z., & Sloman, J. (1984). How parents influence their children's friendships. In M. Lewis (Ed.), *Beyond the dyad.* New York: Plenum.

Ruble, D. (1983). The development of social comparison processes and their role in achievement-related self-socialization. In E. Higgins, D. Ruble, & W. Hartup (Eds.), *Social cognitive development: A social-cultural perspective.* New York: Cambridge University Press.

Ruble, D. N., Boggiano, A. K., Feldman, N. S., & Loebl, J. H. (1980). Developmental analysis of the role of social comparison in self-evaluation. *Developmental Psychology, 16*, 105–115.

Ruble, D. N., & Martin, C. L. (1997). Gender development. In N. Eisenberg (Ed.,), *Handbook of child psychology* (5th Ed. Vol III). New York: Wiley.

Ruff, H. A., & Lawson, K. R. (1990). Development of sustained, focused attention in young children during free play. *Developmental Psychology, 26*, 85–93.

Rumbaugh, D. M., & Rumbaugh, E. (1990, June). *Chimpanzees: Language, speech, counting and video tasks.* Paper presented at the meeting of the American Psychological Association, Dallas.

Rumberger, R. W. (1983). Dropping out of high school: The influence of race, sex, and family background. *American Educational Research Journal, 20*, 199–220.

Rumberger, R. W. (1987). High school dropouts: A review of the issues and evidence. *Review of Educational Research, 57*, 101–121.

Rumberger, R. W. (1995). Dropping out of middle school: A multilevel analysis of students and schools. *American Educational Research Journal, 3*, 583–625.

Rushton, J. P. (1988). Race differences in behavior: A review and evolutionary analysis. *Journal of Personality and Individual Differences, 9*, 1035–1040.

Russo, N. F. (1990). Overview: Forging research priorities for women's mental health. *American Psychologist, 45*, 368–374.

Rutter, M., & Garmezy, N. (1983). Developmental psychopathology. In P.H. Mussen (Eds.), *Handbook of child psychology* (4th ed., Vol. 4). New York: Wesley.

Rutter, M., Maughan, B., Mortimore, P., & Ouston, J. (1979). *Fifteen thousand hours: Secondary schools and their effects on children.* Cambridge, MA: Harvard University Press.

Ryan, A. M., & Patrick, H. (1992, March). *Positive peer relationships and psychosocial adjustment during adolescence.* Paper presented at the meeting of the Society for Research on Adolescence, Boston.

Ryan, R. M., & Lynch, J. H. (1989). Emotional autonomy versus detachment: Revisiting the vicissitudes of adolescence and young adulthood. *Child Development, 60,* 340–356.

Ryan-Finn, K. D., Cauce, A. M., & Grove, K. (1995, March). *Children and adolescents of color: Where are you? Selection, recruitment, and retention in developmental research.* Paper presented at the meeting of the Society for Research in Child Development, Indianapolis.

Rymer, R. (1992). *Genie.* New York: Harper Collins.

S

Saarni, C. (1988). Children's understanding of the interpersonal consequences of dissemblance of nonverbal emotional-expressive behavior. *Journal of Nonverbal Behavior, 12,* 275–294.

Sachs, J. (1993). The emergence of intentional communication. In J. B. Gleason (Ed.), *The development of language* (3rd ed.). New York: Macmillan.

Sadker, M., & Sadker, D. (1986, March). Sexism in the classroom: From grade school to graduate school. *Phi Delta Kappan,* pp. 512–515.

Sadker, M., & Sadker, D. (1994). *Failing at fairness.* New York: Touchstone.

Sadker, M. P., & Sadker, D. M. (1991). *Teachers, schools, and society* (2nd ed.). New York: McGraw-Hill.

Sagan, C. (1977). *The dragons of Eden.* New York: Random House.

Sallade, J. B. (1973). A comparison of the psychological adjustment of obese versus non-obese children. *Journal of Psychosomatic Research, 17,* 89–96.

Samaras, A. P. (1996). Children's computers. *Childhood Education, 72,* 133–136.

Sameroff, A. J., & Bartko, W. T. (1997, April). *Neighborhood as a contributor to multiple risk scores for predicting adolescent competence.* Paper presented at the meeting of the Society for Research in Child Development, Washington, DC.

Sampson, R. J., & Earls, F. (1995, April). *Community social organization in the urban mosaic: Project on human development in Chicago neighborhoods.* Paper presented at the meeting of the Society for Research in Child Development, Indianapolis.

Sampson, R. J., & Laub, J. H. (1994). Urban poverty and the family context of delinquency: A new look at structure and process in a classic study. *Child Development, 65,* 523–540.

Sanson, A., & Rothbart, M. K. (1995). Child temperament and parenting. In M. H. Bornstein (Ed.), *Handbook of parenting* (Vol. 4). Hillsdale, NJ: Erlbaum.

Santrock, J. W. (1997). *Life-span development* (6th ed.). Madison, WI: Brown & Benchmark.

Santrock, J. W., & Sitterle, K. A. (1987). Parent-child relationships in stepmother families. In K. Pasley & M. Ihinger-Tallman (Eds.), *Remarriage and stepparenting.* New York: Guilford.

Santrock, J. W., Sitterle, K. A., & Warshak, R. A. (1988). Parent-child relationships in stepfather families. In P. Bronstein & C. P. Cowan (Eds.), *Fatherhood today.* New York: Wiley.

Santrock, J. W., & Warshak, R. A. (1986). Development, relationships, and legal/clinical considerations in father-custody families. In M. E. Lamb (Ed.), *The father's role: Applied perspectives.* New York: Wiley.

Sattler, J. (1988). *Assessment of children.* (3rd ed.). San Diego: Jerome Sattler.

Saudino, K. J. (1997, April). *Genetic and environmental contributions to continuity and change in temperament.* Paper presented at the meeting of the Society for Research in Child Development, Washington, DC.

Savin-Williams, R., & Rodriguez, R. G. (1993). A developmental clinical perspective on lesbian, gay male, and bisexual youths. In T. P. Gullottas, G. R. Adams, & R. Montemayor (Eds.), *Adolescent sexuality.* Newbury Park, CA: Sage.

Savin-Williams, R. C., & Berndt, T. J. (1990). Friendship and peer relations. In S. S. Feldman & G. R. Elliot (Eds.), *At the threshold: The developing adolescent.* Cambridge, MA: Harvard University Press.

Savin-Williams, R. C., & Demo, D. H. (1983). Conceiving or misconceiving the self: Issues in adolescent self-esteem. *Journal of Early Adolescence, 3,* 121–140.

Sax, G. (1989). *Principles of educational and psychology measurement* (3rd ed.). Belmont, CA: Wadsworth.

Saxe, G. B. (1981). Body parts as numerals: A developmental analysis of numeration among the Oksapmin in Papua, New Guinea. *Child Development, 52,* 306–316.

Scales, P. (1990). Developing capable young people: An alternative strategy for prevention programs. *Journal of Early Adolescence, 10,* 420–438.

Scarr, S. (1984, May). Interview. *Psychology Today,* pp. 59–63.

Scarr, S. (1989, April). *Transracial adoption.* Discussion at the meeting of the Society for Research in Child Development, Kansas City.

Scarr, S. (1993). Biological and cultural diversity: The legacy of Darwin for development. *Child Development, 64,* 1333–1353.

Scarr, S. (1996). Best of human genetics. *Contemporary Psychology, 41,* 149–150.

Scarr, S., & Kidd, K. K. (1983). Developmental behavior genetics. In P. H. Mussen (Ed.), *Handbook of child psychology* (4th ed., Vol. 2). New York: Wiley.

Scarr, S., Lande, J., & McCartney, K. (1989). Child care and the family: Complements and interactions. In J. Lande, S. Scarr, & N. Gunzenhauser (Eds.), *Caring for children: Challenge to America.* Hillsdale, NJ: Erlbaum.

Scarr, S., & Weinberg, R. A. (1976). IQ test performance of black children adopted by white families. *American Psychologist, 31,* 726–739.

Scarr, S., & Weinberg, R. A. (1983). The Minnesota adoption studies: Genetic differences and malleability. *Child Development, 54,* 253–259.

Schaff, E. A. (1992). Abortion. In R. A. Hoekleman, S. B. Friedman, N. M. Nelson, & H. M. Seidel (Eds.), *Primary pediatric care* (2nd ed.). St. Louis: Mosby Yearbook.

Schaffer, H. R. (1996). *Social development.* Cambridge, MA: Blackwell.

Schaie, K. W. (1994). Developmental designs revisited. In S. H. Cohen & H. W. Reese (Eds.), *Life-span developmental psychology: Methodological contributions.* Hillsdale, NJ: Erlbaum.

Schatz, M., & Gelman, R. (1973). The development of communication skills: Modifications in the speech of young children as a function of the listener. *Monographs of the Society for Research in Child Development, 38* (Serial No. 152).

Schauble, L. (1990). Belief revision in children: The role of prior knowledge and strategies for generating evidence. *Journal of Experimental Child Psychology, 49,* 31–57.

Schauble, L. (1996). The development of scientific reasoning in knowledge-rich contexts. *Developmental Psychology, 32,* 102–119.

Schlicker, S. A., Borra, S. T., & Regan, C. (1994). The weight and fitness status of United States children. *Nutrition Reviews, 52,* 11–17.

Schmitz, S., Saudino, K. J., Plomin, R., Fulker, D. W., & DeFries, J. C. (1996). Genetic and environmental influences on temperament in middle childhood: Analyses of teacher and tester ratings. *Child Development, 67,* 409–422.

Schneider, W., & Bjorklund, D. F. (1997). Memory. In D. Kuhn & R. S. Siegler (Eds.), *Handbook of child psychology* (5th Ed., Vol. II). New York: Wiley.

Schneider, W., Korkel, J., & Weinart, F. E. (1989). Domain-specific knowledge and memory performance: A comparison of high- and low-aptitude children. *Journal of Educational Psychology, 81,* 306–312.

Schneider, W., & Pressley, M. (1989). *Memory development between 2 and 20.* New York: Springer-Verlag.

Schneidman, E. S. (1971). Suicide among the gifted. *Suicide and life-threatening behavior, 1,* 23–45.

Schnorr, T. M., & others. (1991). Videodisplay terminals and the risk of spontaneous abortion. *New England Journal of Medicine, 324,* 727–733.

Schoendorf, K. C., & Kiely, J. L. (1992). Relationship of sudden infant death syndrome to maternal smoking during and after pregnancy. *Pediatrics, 90,* 905–908.

Schrag, S. G., & Dixon, R. L. (1985). Occupational exposure associated with male reproductive dysfunction. *Annual Review of Pharmacology and Toxicology, 25,* 467–592.

Schunk, D. H. (1983). Developing children's self-efficacy and skills: The roles of social comparative information and goal-setting. *Contemporary Educational Psychology, 8,* 76–86.

Schunk, D. H. (1990). Introduction to the special section on motivation and efficacy. *Journal of Educational Psychology, 82,* 3–6.

Schwartz, D., & Mayaux, M. J. (1982). Female fecundity as a function of age: Results of artificial insemination in nullparous women with azoospermic husbands. *New England Journal of Medicine, 306,* 304–406.

Scott, P. (1997). Language. In P. Scott & C. Spencer (Eds.), *Psychology.* Cambridge, MA: Blackwell.

Scott-Jones, D. (1995, March). *Incorporating ethnicity and socioeconomic status in research with children.* Paper presented at the meeting of the Society for Research in Child Development, Indianapolis.

Scott-Jones, D. (1996). Toward a balanced view of family change. In A. Booth & J. F. Dunn (Eds.), *Family-school links.* Hillsdale, NJ: Erlbaum.

Scott-Jones, D. (1997). Editorial. *Journal of Research on Adolescence, 7,* 1–2.

Segalowitz, N. (1997). Individual differences in second language acquisition. In A.M.B. de Groot & J. F. Knoll (Eds.), *Tutorials in bilingualism.* Mahwah, NJ: Erlbaum.

Seidman, E., Allen, L., Aber, J. L., Mitchell, C., & Feinman, J. (1994). The impact of school transitions in early adolescence on the self-system and perceived social context of poor urban youth. *Child Development, 65,* 507–522.

Seligman, M. E. P. (1975). *Learned helplessness.* San Francisco: W. H. Freeman.

Seligman, M. E. P. (1995). *The optimistic child.* Boston: Houghton Mifflin.

Selman, R. L. (1976). Social-cognitive understanding. In T. Lickona (Ed.), *Moral development and behavior.* New York: Holt, Rinehart & Winston.

Selman, R. L. (1980). *The growth of interpersonal understanding.* New York: Academic Press.

Selman, R. L., Newberger, C. M., & Jacquette, D. (1977, April). *Observing interpersonal reasoning in a clinic/educational setting: Toward the integration of developmental and clinical child psychology.* Paper presented at the meeting of the Society for Research in Child Development, New Orleans.

Semaj, L. T. (1985). Afrikanity, cognition, and extended self-identity. In M. B. Spencer, G. K. Brookins, & W. R. Allen (Eds.), *Beginnings: The social and affective development of black children.* Hillsdale, NJ: Erlbaum.

Serbin, L. A., & Sprafkin, C. (1986). The salience of gender: The process of sex-typing in three- to seven-year-old children. *Child Development, 57,* 1188–1209.

Serdula, M., Williamson, D. F., Kendrick, J. S., Anda, R. F., & Byers, T. (1991). Trends in alcohol consumption by pregnant women: 1985 through 1988. *Journal of the American Medical Association, 265,* 876–879.

Shade, B. J., Kelly, C., & Oberg, M. (1997). *Creating culturally-responsive schools.* Washington, DC: American Psychological Association.

Shagle, S. C., & Barber, B. K. (1994, February). *Effects of parenting variables, self-derogation, and depression on adolescent suicide ideation.* Paper presented at the meeting of the Society for Research on Adolescence, San Diego.

Shantz, C. O. (1988). Conflicts between children. *Child Development, 59,* 283–305.

Sharma, A. R., McGue, M. K., & Benson, P. L. (1996, March). *The emotional and behavioral adjustment of United States adopted adolescents.* Paper presented at the meeting of the Society for Research on Adolescent Development, Boston.

Shaver, P. R. (1993, March). *Where do adult romantic attachment patterns come from?* Paper presented at the biennial meeting of the Society for Research in Child Development, New Orleans.

Shaw, S. M. (1988). Gender differences in the definition and perception of household labor. *Family Relations, 37,* 333–337.

Sheeber, L., Hops, H., Andrews, J. A., & Davis, B. (1997, April). *Family support and conflict: Prospective relation to adolescent depression.* Paper presented at the meeting of the Society for Research in Child Development, Washington, DC.

Shields, S. A. (1991, August). *Doing emotion/doing gender.* Paper presented at the annual meeting of the American Psychological Association, San Francisco.

Shiono, P. H., & Behrman, R. E. (1995, spring). Low birth weight: Analysis and recommendations. *The Future of Children, 5(1),* 4–18.

Shirley, M. M. (1933). *The first two years.* Minneapolis: University of Minnesota Press.

Shorr, D. N., & Schorr, C. J. (1995, March). *Children's perceptions of kindness and anonymity in others' helping.* Paper presented at the meeting of the Society for Research in Child Development, Indianapolis.

Short, R. J., & Talley, R. C. (1997). Rethinking psychology and the schools. *American Psychologist, 52,* 234–240.

Shultz, T. R., Fisher, G. W., Pratt, C. C., & Rulf, S. (1986). Selection of causal rules. *Child Development, 57,* 143–152.

Shweder, R., Mahapatra, M., & Miller, J. (1987). Culture and moral development. In J. Kagan & S. Lamb (Eds.), *The emergence of morality in young children.* Chicago: University of Chicago Press.

Shweder, R. A., Goodnow, J., Hatano, G., LeVine, R. A., Markus, H., & Miller, P. (1997). The cultural psychology of development. In R. M. Lerner (Ed.), *Handbook of Psychology* (5th Ed., Vol. I).

Siegel, L. S., & Wiener, J. (1993, spring). *Canadian special education policies: Children with disabilities in a bilingual and multicultural society.* Social Policy Report, Society for Research in Child Development, Vol. 7, pp. 1–16.

Siegler, R. S. (1976). Three aspects of cognitive development. *Cognitive Psychology, 8,* 481–520.

Siegler, R. S. (1988). Individual differences in strategy choices: Good students, not-so-good students, and perfectionists. *Child Development, 59,* 833–851.

Siegler, R. S. (1991). *Children's thinking* (2nd ed.). Englewood Cliffs, NJ: Prentice Hall.

Siegler, R. S. (1995, March). *Nothing is; everything becomes.* Paper presented at the meeting of the Society for Research in Child Development, Indianapolis.

Siegler, R. S. (1996). A grand theory of development. *Monographs of the Society for Research in Child Development, 61,* 266–275.

Siegler, R. S., & Campbell, J. (1989). Individual differences in children's strategy choices. In P. L. Ackerman, R. J. Sternberg, and R. Glaser (Eds.), *Learning and individual differences: Advances in theory and research.* New York: W. H. Freeman.

Siegler, R. S., & Robinson, M. (1982). The development of numerical understandings. In H. W. Reese & L. P. Litsitt (Eds.), *Advances in child development and behavior* (Vol. 12). New York: Academic Press.

Sigel, B. (1997, April). *Developmental and social policy issues and the practice of educational mainstreaming and full inclusion.* Paper presented at the meeting of the Society for Research in Child Development, Washington, DC.

Silbereisen, R. K. (1995). How parenting styles and crowd contexts interact in actualizing potentials for development: Commentary. In L. J. Crockett & A. C. Crouter (Eds.), *Pathways through adolescence.* Hillsdale, NJ: Erlbaum.

Silberg, J. L., & Rutter, M. L. (1997, April). *Pubertal status, life stress, and depression in juvenile twins.* Paper presented at the meeting of the Society for Research in Child Development, Washington, DC.

Simmons, R. G., & Blyth, D. A. (1987). *Moving into adolescence.* Hawthorne, NY: Aldine.

Simon, H. A. (1981). *The sciences of the artificial.* Cambridge, MA: MIT Press.

Simons, J., Finlay, B., & Yang, A. (1991). *The adolescent and young adult fact book.* Washington, DC: Children's Defense Fund.

Simons, R., Conger, R., & Wu, C. (1992, March). *Peer group as amplifier/moderator of the stability of adolescent antisocial behavior.* Paper presented at the meeting of the Society for Research on Adolescence, Washington, DC.

Sims, R. (1983). Strong Black girls. *Journal of Research and Development in Education, 16,* 21–28.

Singer, J. L., & Singer, D. G. (1988). Imaginative play and human development: Schemas, scripts, and possibilities. In D. Bergen (Ed.), *Play as a medium for learning and development.* Portsmouth, NH: Heinemann.

Sizer, T. (1996). *Horace's hope: What works for the American high school.* Boston: Houghton Mifflin.

Skinner, B. F. (1938). *The behavior of organisms: An experimental analysis.* New York: Appleton-Century-Crofts.

Skinner, B. F. (1957). *Verbal behavior.* New York: Appleton-Century-Crofts.

Skinner, E. A., Wellborn, J. G., & Connell, J. P. (1990). What it takes to do well in school and whether I've got it: A process model of perceived control and children's engagement and achievement in school. *Journal of Educational Psychology, 82,* 22–32.

Skoe, E. E., & Marcia, J. E. (1988). *Ego identity and care-based moral reasoning in college women.* Unpublished manuscript, Acadia University.

Slaughter, V. P. (1995, March). *Conceptual coherence in a child's theory of mind: Training children to understand belief.* Paper presented at the meeting of the Society for Research in Child Development, Indianapolis.

Slaughter-Defoe, D. T., Nakagawa, K., Takanishi, R., & Johnson, D. J. (1990). Toward cultural/ecological perspectives on schooling and achievement in African- and Asian-American children. *Child Development, 61,* 363–383.

Slavin, R. E. (1988). *Educational psychology* (2nd ed.). Englewood Cliffs, NJ: Prentice Hall.

Slavin, R. E. (1989). Achievement effects of substantial reductions in class size. In R. E. Slavin (Ed.), *School and classroom organization.* Hillsdale, NJ: Erlbaum.

Slawinski, J., & Best, D. L. (1995, March). *Effects of metamemory instruction on children's predictions of recall.* Paper presented at the meeting of the Society for Research in Child Development, Indianapolis.

Slobin, D. (1972, July). Children and language: They learn the same all around the world. *Psychology Today,* pp. 71–76.

Smith, J., & Baltes, P. B. (in press). A study of wisdom-related knowledge: Age-cohort differences in responses to life-planning problems. *Developmental Psychology.*

Smith, L., Ulvund, S. E., & Lindemann, R. (1994). Very low birth weight infants at double risk. *Journal of Developmental and Behavioral Pediatrics, 15,* 7–13.

Smith, P. K. (1995). Grandparenthood. In M. H. Bornstein (Ed.), *Handbook of parenting* (Vol. 3). Hillsdale, NJ: Erlbaum.

Snarey, J. (1987, June). A question of morality. *Psychology Today,* pp. 6–8.

Snow, C. E. (1996). Interactionist account of language acquisition. In M. Rice (Ed.), *Toward a genetics of language.* Hillsdale, NJ: Erlbaum.

Snow, C. E. (1997, April). *Cross-domain connections and social class defferences: Two challenges to nonenvironmentalists.* Paper presented at the meeting of the Society for Research in Child Development, Washington, DC.

Sommer, B. B. (1978). *Puberty and adolescence.* New York: Oxford University Press.

Sophian, C. (1985). Perseveration and infants' search: A comparison of two- and three-location tasks. *Developmental Psychology, 21,* 187–194.

Sophian, C., Wood, A., & Vong, K. (1995, March). Making numbers count: The early development of numerical inferences. *Developmental Psychology, 31,* 263–273.

Sorensen, E. S. (1993). *Children's stress and coping.* New York: Guilford.

Spade, J. Z., & Reese, C. A. (1991). We've come a long way, maybe: College students' plans for work and family. *Sex Roles, 24,* 309–321.

Spear-Swerling, L., & Sternberg, R. J. (1994). The road not taken: An integrative theoretical model of reading disability. *Journal of Learning Disabilities, 27*(2), 91–103.

Spearman, C. E. (1927). *The abilities of man.* New York: Macmillan.

Spelke, E. J. (1987). The development of intermodal perception. In P. Salapatek & L. Cohen (Eds.), *Handbook of infant perception* (Vol. 2). Orlando, FL: Academic Press.

Spelke, E. S. (1979). Perceiving bimodally specified events in infancy. *Developmental Psychology, 5,* 626–636.

Spelke, E. S. (1988). The origins of physical knowledge. In L. Weiskrantz (Ed.), *Thought without language.* New York: Oxford University Press.

Spelke, E. S. (1991). Physical knowledge in infancy: Reflections on Piaget's theory. In S. Carey & R. Gellman (Eds.), *The epigenesis of mind: Essays on biology and cognition.* Hillsdale, NJ: Erlbaum.

Spelke, E. S. (1997, April). *Nativism, empiricism, and the origins of knowledge.* Paper presented at the meeting of the Society for Research in Child Development, Washington, DC.

Spelke, E. S., Breinlinger, K., Macomber, J., & Jacobson, K. (1992). Origins of knowledge. *Psychological Review, 99,* 605–632.

Spelke, E. S., & Owsley, C. J. (1979). Intermodal exploration and knowledge in infancy. *Infant Behavior and Development, 2,* 13–28.

Spence, J. T., & Helmreich, R. (1978). *Masculinity and femininity: Their psychological dimensions.* Austin: University of Texas Press.

Spence, M. J., & DeCasper, A. J. (1987). Prenatal experience with low-frequency maternal voice sounds influences neonatal perception of maternal voice samples. *Infant Behavior and Development, 10,* 133–142.

Spencer, M. B., & Dornbusch, S. M. (1990). Challenges in studying minority youth. In S. S. Feldman & G. R. Elliott (Eds.), *At the threshold: The developing adolescent.* Cambridge, MA: Harvard University Press.

Spitzer, S., & Dicker, S. G. (1993, March). *School entrance age and social acceptance in kindergarten: Social policy implications.* Paper presented at the biennial meeting of the Society for Research in Child Development, New Orleans.

Springer, K., & Keil, F. C. (1991). Early differentiation of causal mechanisms appropriate to biological and nonbiological kinds. *Child Development, 4,* 767–781.

Sroufe, L. A. (1985). Attachment classification from the perspective of infant-caregiver relationships and infant temperament. *Child Development, 56,* 1–14.

Sroufe, L. A. (1996). *Emotional development.* New York: Cambridge University Press.

Sroufe, L. A., & Waters, E. (1976). The ontogenesis of smiling and laughter: A perspective on the organization of development in infancy. *Psychological Review, 83,* 173–198.

Stallings, J. (1975). Implementation and child effects of teaching practices in Follow Through classrooms. *Monographs of the Society for Research in Child Development, 40* (Serial No. 163).

Stanhope, L., & Corter, C. (1993, March). *The mother's role in the transition to siblinghood.* Paper presented at the biennial meeting of the Society for Research in Child Development, New Orleans.

Stanley, K., Soule, B., & Copans, S. A. (1979). Dimensions of prenatal anxiety and their influence on pregnancy outcome. *American Journal of Obstetrics and Gynecology, 135,* 333–348.

Stanton-Salazar, R. D., & Dornbusch, S. M. (in press). Social capital and the social reproduction of inequality: Information networks among Mexican-origin high school students. *Sociology of Education.*

Stapp, J., Tucker, A. M., & VandenBos, G. R. (1985). Census of psychological personnel, 1983. *American Psychologist, 40,* 1317–1351.

Stattin, H., & Magnusson, D. (1990). *Pubertal maturation in female development: Paths through life* (Vol. 2). Hillsdale, NJ: Erlbaum.

Staub, E. (1996). Cultural-societal roots of violence. *American Psychologist, 51,* 117–132.

Staub, E. (in press). Altruism and aggression in children and youth: Origins and cures. In R. Feldman (Ed.), *The psychology of adversity.* Amherst: University of Massachusetts Press.

Staub, E., & Rosenthal, L. (1994). Mob violence: Social-cultural influences, group processes and participants. In L. Eron, J. H. Gentry, & P. Schlegel (Eds.), *Reason to hope.* Washington, DC: American Psychological Association.

Stechler, G., & Halton, A. (1982). Prenatal influences on human development. In B. B. Wolman (Ed.), *Handbook of developmental psychology.* Englewood Cliffs, NJ: Prentice Hall.

Stein, N. L. (1995, March). *Understanding and remembering emotional events.* Paper presented at the meeting of the Society for Research in Child Development, Indianapolis.

Steinberg, E. R. (1990). *Computer-assisted instruction.* Hillsdale, NJ: Erlbaum.

Steinberg, L. (1991). Parent-adolescent relations. In R. M. Lerner, A. C. Petersen, & J. Brooks-Gunn (Eds.), *Encyclopedia of adolescence* (Vol. 2). New York: Garland.

Steinberg, L. D. (1986). Latchkey children and susceptibility to peer pressure: An ecological analysis. *Developmental Psychology, 22,* 433–439.

Steiner, J. E. (1979). Human facial expressions in response to taste and smell stimulation. In H. Reese & L. Lipsitt (Eds.), *Advances in child development and behavior* (Vol. 13). New York: Academic Press.

Stenhouse, G. (1996). *Practical parenting.* New York: Oxford University Press.

Stern, D. N., Beebe, B., Jaffe, J., & Bennett, S. L. (1977). The infant's stimulus world during social interaction: A study of caregiver behaviors with particular reference to repetition and timing. In H. R. Schaffer (Ed.), *Studies in mother-infant interaction.* London: Academic Press.

Sternberg, R. J. (1986). *Intelligence applied.* San Diego: Harcourt Brace Jovanovich.

Sternberg, R. J. (1987). Teaching intelligence: The application of cognitive psychology of intellectual skills. In J. B. Baron & R. J. Sternberg (Eds.), *Teaching thinking skills: Theory and practice.* New York: W. H. Freeman.

Sternberg, R. J. (1990, April). *Academic and practical cognition as different aspects of intelligence.* Paper presented at the 12th West Virginia conference on life-span developmental psychology, Morgantown.

Sternberg, R. J. (1994, December). Commentary. *APA Monitor,* p. 22.

Sternberg, R. J. (1997, April). *Practical intelligence differs from academic intelligence.* Paper presented at the meeting of the Society for Research in Child Development, Washington, DC.

Sternglanz, S. H., & Serbin, L. A. (1974). Sex-role stereotyping in children's television programming. *Developmental Psychology, 10,* 710–715.

Steur, F. B., Applefield, J. M., & Smith, R. (1971). Televised aggression and interpersonal aggression of preschool children. *Journal of Experimental Child Psychology, 11,* 442–447.

Stevens, J. H. (1984). Black grandmothers' and black adolescents mothers' knowledge about parenting. *Developmental Psychology, 20,* 1017–1025.

Stevens, R. J., & Salisbury, J. D. (1997). Accommodating student heterogeneity in mainstreamed classrooms through cooperative learning. In J. W. Lloyd, E. J. Kameenui, & D. Chard (Eds.), *Issues in educating students with disabilities.* Mahwah, NJ: Erlbaum.

Stevens, R. J., & Slavin, R. E. (1995). The cooperative elementary school: Effects on students' achievement, attitudes, and social relations. *American Educational Research Journal, 32,* 321–351.

Stevenson, H. G. (1995, March). *Missing data: On the forgotten substance of race, ethnicity, and socioeconomic classifications.* Paper presented at the meeting of the Society for Research in Child Development, Indianapolis.

Stevenson, H. W. (1992, December). Learning from Asian schools. *Scientific American, 267*(6), 70–76.

Stevenson, H. W. (1995). Mathematics achievement of American students: First in the world by the year 2000? In C. A. Nelson (Ed.), *Basic and applied perspectives on learning, cognition, and development.* Minneapolis: University of Minnesota Press.

Stevenson, H. W., Chen, C., & Lee, S. Y. (1993). Mathematics achievement of Chinese, Japanese & American children: ten years later. *Science, 259,* 53–58.

Stevenson, H. W., & Stigler, J. W. (1992). *The learning gap: Why our schools are failing and what we can learn from Japanese and Chinese education.* New York: Summit.

Stevenson, M. R., & Black, K. N. (1996). *How divorce affects offspring.* Boulder, CO: Westview Press.

Steward, P. (1955). *Beginning writers in the zone of proximal development.* Hillsdale, NJ: Erlbaum.

Stigler, J. W. (1984). "Mental abacus": The effect of abacus training on Chinese children's mental calculation. *Cognitive Psychology, 16,* 145–176.

Stigler, J. W., Nusbaum, H. C., & Chalip, L. (1988). Developmental changes in speed of processing: Central limiting mechanism or skill transfer. *Child Development, 59,* 1144–1153.

Stipek, D. (1992). The child at school. In M. H. Bornstein & M. E. Lamb (Eds.), *Developmental psychology: An advanced textbook* (3rd ed.). Hillsdale, NJ: Erlbaum.

Stocker, C., & Dunn, J. (1991). Sibling relationships in adolescence. In R. M. Lerner, A. C. Petersen, & J. Brooks-Gunn (Eds.), *Encyclopedia of adolescence* (Vol. 2). New York: Garland.

Stormer, S. M., & Thompson, J. K. (1996). Explanations of body image disturbance: A test of maturational status, negative verbal commentary, social comparison, and sociocultural hypotheses. *International Journal of Eating Disorders, 19,* 193–199.

Strachen, A., & Jones, D. (1982). Changes in identification during adolescence: A personal construct theory approach. *Journal of Personality Assessment, 46,* 139–148.

Strahan, D. B. (1983). The emergence of formal operations in adolescence. *Transcendence, 11,* 7–14.

Strahan, D. B. (1987). A developmental analysis of formal reasoning in the middle grades. *Journal of Instructional Psychology, 14,* 67–73.

Strasburger, V. C. (1995). *Adolescents and the media.* Newbury Park, CA: Sage.

Strauss, M. S., & Curtis, L. E. (1984). Development of numerical concepts in infancy. In C. Sophian (Ed.), *The origins of cognitive skills.* Hillsdale, NJ: Erlbaum.

Streissguth, A. P., Martin, D. C., Barr, H. M., Sandman, B. M., Kirshner, G. L., & Darby, B. L. (1984). Intrauterine alcohol and nicotine exposure: Attention and reaction time in 4-year-old children. *Developmental Psychology, 20,* 533–541.

Streissguth, A. P., Martin, D. C., Sandman, B. M., Kirchner, G. L., & Darby, B. L. (1984). Intrauterine alcohol and nicotine exposure: Attention and reaction time in four-year-old children. *Developmental Psychology, 20,* 533–543.

Streri, A., & Pecheux, M. G. (1986). Vision to touch and touch to vision transfer of form in 5-month-old infants. *British Journal of Developmental Psychology, 4,* 161–167.

Striegel-Moore, R., Pike, K., Rodin, J., Schreiber, G., & Wilfley, D. (1993, March). *Predictors and correlates of drive for thinness.* Paper presented at the meeting of the Society for Research in Child Development, New Orleans.

Stringer, S., & Neal, C. (1993, March). *Scaffolding as a tool for assessing sensitive and contingent teaching: A comparison between high- and low-risk mothers.* Paper presented at the biennial meeting of the Society for Research in Child Development.

Stunkard, A. J. (1987). The regulation of body weight and the treatment of obesity. In H. Weiner & A. Baum (Eds.), *Eating regulation and discontrol.* Hillsdale, NJ: Erlbaum.

Sue, D., & Sue, D. W. (1993). Ethnic identity: Cultural factors in the psychological development of Asians in America. In D. R. Atkinson, G. Morten, & D. W. Sue (Eds.), *Counseling American minorities.* Dubuque, IA: Brown & Benchmark.

Sue, S. (1990, August). *Ethnicity and culture in psychological research and practice.* Paper presented at the meeting of the American Psychological Association, Boston.

Sullivan, H. S. (1953). *The interpersonal theory of psychiatry.* New York: W. W. Norton.

Sullivan, K., & Sullivan, A. (1980). Adolescent-parent separation. *Developmental Psychology, 16,* 93–99.

Sullivan, L. (1991, May 25). US secretary urges TV to restrict "irresponsible sex and reckless violence." *Boston Globe,* p. A1.

Suomi, S. J., Harlow, H. F., & Domek, C. J. (1970). Effect of repetitive infant-infant separations of young monkeys. *Journal of Abnormal Psychology, 76,* 161–172.

Super, C. M. (1980). Cross-cultural research on infancy. In H. C. Triandis & A. Heron (Eds.), *Handbook of cross-cultural psychology, development psychology* (Vol. 4). Boston: Allyn & Bacon.

Susman, A. R., & Adam, E. K. (1995, March). *Poverty and educational outcomes: Contexts, diversity, and change.* Paper presented at the meeting of the Society for Research in Child Development, Indianapolis.

Susman, E. J., Inoff-Germain, G. E., Nottelmann, E. D., Cutler, G. B., Loriaux, D. L., & Chrousos, G. P. (1987). Hormones, emotional dispositions, and aggressive attributes in early adolescents. *Child Development, 58,* 1114–1134.

Susman, E. J., Murowchick, E., Worrall, B. K., & Murray, D. A. (1995, March). *Emotionality, adrenal hormones, and context interactions during puberty and pregnancy.* Paper presented at the meeting of the Society for Research in Child Development, Indianapolis.

Sutton-Smith, B. (1985, October). The child at play. *Psychology Today,* pp. 64–65.

Swanson, D. P. (1995, March). *The effects of racial identity and socioeconomic status on academic outcomes for adolescents.* Paper presented at the meeting of the Society for Research in Child Development, Indianapolis.

Swanson, D. P. (1997, April). *Identity and coping styles among African American females.* Paper presented at the meeting of the Society for Research in Child Development, Washington, DC.

Swick, K. J., & Manning, M. L. (1983). Father involvement in home and school settings. *Childhood Education, 60,* 128–134.

Switzer, G. E., & Dew, M. A. (1995, March). *Political socialization as a function of volunteerism.* Paper presented at the meeting of the Society for Research in Child Development, Indianapolis.

Tager-Flusberg, H. (Ed.). (1994). *Constraints on language acquisition.* Hillsdale, NJ: Erlbaum.

Tajfel, H. (1978). The achievement of group differentiation. In H. Tajfel (Ed.), *Differentiation between social groups: Studies in the social psychology of intergroup relations.* London: Aca-demic Press.

Takanishi, R. (1993). The opportunities of adolescence—research, interventions, and policy. *American Psychologist, 48,* 85–87.

Takanishi, R., & DeLeon, P. H. (1994). A Head Start for the 21st century. *American Psychologist, 49,* 120–122.

Tamarin, R. (1996). *Principles of genetics* (5th ed.). Dubuque, IA: Wm. C. Brown.

Tanner, J. M. (1978). *Fetus into man: Physical growth from conception into maturity.* Cambridge, MA: Harvard University Press.

Tapper, J. (1996, March). *Values, lifestyles, and crowd identification in adolescence.* Paper presented at the meeting of the Society for Research on Adolescence, Boston.

Tappero, E. (1996). Making choices to ease the stress. *Journal of Neonatal Nursing, 15,* 5–6.

Tavris, C., & Wade, C. (1984). *The longest war: Sex differences in perspective* (2nd ed.). San Diego: Harcourt Brace Jovanovich.

Taylor, A., & Machida, S. (1993, March). *Effects of parent involvement and teacher support on school progress of Head Start children.* Paper presented at the biennial meeting of the Society for Research in Child Development, New Orleans.

Taylor, H. G., Klein, N., & Hack, M. (1994). Academic functioning in <750 gm birthweight children who have normal cognitive abilities: Evidence for specific learning disabilities. *Pediatric Research 35,* 289A.

Taylor, R. D. (1997). The effects of economic and social stressors on parenting and adolescent adjustment in African-American families. In R. D. Taylor & M. C. Wang (Eds.), *Social and emotional adjustment and family relations in ethnic minority families.* Mahwah, NJ: Erlbaum.

Taylor, R. J., Chatters, L., Tucker, M. B., & Lewis, E. (1990). Developments in research on black families: A decade review. *Journal of Marriage and the Family, 52,* 993–1014.

Terman, L. (1925). *Genetic studies of genius: Vol. 1. Mental and physical traits of a thousand gifted children.* Stanford, CA: Stanford University Press.

Terman, L. H., & Oden, M. H. (1959). *Genetic studies of genius: Vol. 5. The gifted group at mid-life.* Stanford, CA: Stanford University Press.

Zarit, S. H., & Eggebeen, D. J. (1995). Parent-child relationships in adulthood and old age. In M. H. Bornstein (Ed.), *Handbook of parenting* (Vol. 1). Hillsdale, NJ: Erlbaum.

Zeskind, P. S., Klein, L., & Marshall, T. R. (1992). Adults' perceptions of experimental modifications of durations and expiratory sounds in infant crying. *Developmental Psychology, 28,* 1153–1162.

Zigler, E. (1987, April). *Child care for parents who work outside the home: Problems and solutions.* Paper presented at the biennial meeting of the Society for Research in Child Development, Baltimore.

Zigler, E., & Muenchow, S. (1992). *Head Start.* New York: Basic Books.

Zigler, E. F., & Finn-Stevenson, M. F. (1955, August). *The child care crisis: Implications for the growth and development of the nation's children.* Paper presented at the meeting of the American Psychological Association, New York City.

Zigler, E. F. (1997, April). Discussant on symposium, *Communities as ecologies of risk and opportunity.* Society for Research in Child Development, Washington, DC.

Zolotow, C. (1972). *William's doll.* New York: Harper & Row.

Zubay, G. L. (1996). *Origins of life on the earth and in the cosmos.* Dubuque, IA: Wm. C. Brown.

Zuckerman, M. (1979). *Sensation seeking: Beyond the optimal level of arousal.* Hillsdale, NJ: Erlbaum.

CREDITS

Photographs

Prologue

Opener: © Si Chi Ko

Section Openers

1: © Walter Imber; 2: © Lennart Nilsson/A Child is Born; 3: © D.Lisl/Image Bank; 4: © David Burnett/Contact Press; 5: © John Kelly/Image Bank

Chapter 1

Opener: © 1997/Estate of Pablo Picasso/ARS; **1.1:** © Courtesy of Nancy Agostini; **p. 11 (top):** © M. Richards/Photo Edit; **p. 11 (middle):** © Image Works/Fujiphotos; **p. 11 (bottom):** © Joseph Nettis/Photo Researchers; **1.2:** Erich Lessing/Art Resource, NY; **1.2 (inset):** Scala/Art Resource, New York; **1.3:** Archives of the History of American Psychology, Louise Bates Ames Gift; **1.4a (middle):** © Michael Melford/Image Bank–Chicago; **1.4b (top left):** © Michael Melford/Image Bank–Chicago; **1.4c (top right):** © Mark Walker/Picture Cube; **p. 16:** Courtesy of Marian Wright Edelman; **1.6 (top to bottom):** © James Shaffer; © Michael Salas/Image Bank–Chicago, © Chromosohm Media/Image Works, Courtesy of John Santrock, © L. Shettles; **p. 20:** © Duka/Photo Network; **p. 24 (left):** The Institute of Texan Cultures, San Antonio, Texas; **p. 24 (right):** Courtesy of Kenneth Clark; **1.8:** © Superstock; **p. 27:** © 1997 Estate of Pablo Picasso/ARS, New York.

Chapter 2

Opener: Courtesy of James R. Bakker Antiques and Melvin Holmes; **p. 35:** Sharon Beals/CP "Insight Magazine"; **p. 37:** © Bettmann Newsphotos; **p. 38 (top):** © Shooting Star; **p. 38 (bottom):** © Stock Montage; **p. 40 (top):** © Robin Smith/Superstock; **p. 40 (bottom left):** The Bettmann Archive; **p. 40 (bottom right):** Courtesy of Nancy Chodorow; **p. 39:** © Sarah Putnam/Picture Cube; **p. 41 (top to bottom):** © William Hopkins, © Suzanne Szasz/Photo Researchers, © Suzanne Szasz/Photo Researchers, © Mel Digiacomo/Image Bank; **p. 42 (top to bottom):** © Sam Zarember/ The Image Bank–Tx, © Brett Froomer/The Image Bank–Tx; © Alan Carey/The Image Works, © Art Kane/The Image Bank–Tx; **p. 43:** © Yves DeBraine/Black Star; **2.4:** The Bettmann Archive; © Whitney Lane/The Image Bank–Texas; **2.5:** Courtesy of Professor Benjamin Harris, University of Wisconsin; **p. 47 (left):** © Bettmann Archive; **p. 47 (right):** Courtesy of Albert Bandura; **2.7:** Photo by Nina Leen/Time/Life Magazine, © Time Inc.; **2.8:** © David Austen/Stock Boston; **p. 50 (left):** Courtesy of Urie Bronfenbrenner; **p. 50 (right):** Courtesy of Glen Elder; **p. 52 (left):** Tony Stone; **p. 52 (right):** After: Carter, B., McGoldrick, M. Overview: The changing life cycle–a framework for family therapy. In: B. Carter & M. McGoldrick (Eds.) The Changing Family Life Cycle 2/e, 1989 Allyn & Bacon: Boston; **2.9a:** © Jerry Alexander/Tony Stone Worldwide;

2.9b: © James Rowan/Tony Stone Worldwide; **2.9c:** © Jacques Jangoux/Tony Stone Worldwide; **2.10:** A. Bandura/Stanford University; **p. 56:** © Ray Stott/Image Works; **p. 58:** © Ed Tronick/Anthro Photo; **2.11:** © Jeff Hunter/The Image Bank–Chicago; **2.12:** © Gary Chapman/ The Image Bank–Texas; **p. 63:** Courtesy of Dr. Florence L. Denmark/Photo by Robert Wesner; **p. 68:** Courtesy of James R. Bakker Antiques and Melvin Holmes.

Chapter 3

Opener: © Mills College Art Gallery, Gift of A.S. Lauenson through A.M. Bender; **p. 76:** © Enrico Ferorelli; **3.1a:** © John P. Kelly/The Image Bank; **3.1b (inset):** © Michael P. Gadomski/Photo Researchers, Inc.; **p. 78:** © Gabe Palmer/The Stock Market; **p. 81:** Courtesy of United Nations; **p. 81 (top left):** Courtesy of United Nations; **p. 81:(top right):** © David Hartman/The Image Bank–Texas; **p. 81 (middle):** © Elaine Sulle/The Image Bank–Chicago; **p. 81 (bottom left):** © Janeart/Image Bank–Chicago; **p. 81 (bottom right):** © Harvey Lloyd/The Stock Market; **3.2:** Regents of the University of California; **3.3b (top):** © R. Heinzen/Superstock; **3.3c (bottom):** © Elyse Lewin/The Image Bank–Texas; **3.4:** © Sundstroem/Gamma Liaison; **3.5:** © Alexandria Tsiaras/Photo Researchers; **p. 84:** © Kelly Wilkinson/Indianapolis Star; **3.6a:** © Andrew Eccles/Outline; **3.6b:** © Andrew Eccles/Outline; **3.7:** © Will and Deni McIntyre/Photo Researchers Inc.; **3.8:** © J. Pavlovsky/Sygma; **3.9:** © Grant A. Hall/Unicorn Stock Photos; **3.10a (top):** © Tim Davis/ Photo Researchers, Inc.; **3.10b (bottom):** © Sandy Roessler/The Stock Market; **p. 93:** © Myrleen Ferguson/Photo Edit; **p. 96:** Courtesy of Sandra Scarr; **p. 99:** © Mills College Art Gallery, Gift of A.S. Lavenson through A.M. Bender; **p. 103:** ©Andrew Eccles/Outline.

Chapter 4

Opener: Scala/Art Resource; **4.1:** © Russ Kinne/Comstock; **p. 110 (all):** © Lennart Nilsson; **pp. 112–113, 4.4b:** © Petit Format/Nestle Science Source/Photo Researchers, Inc.; **p. 113 (top) 4.4c:** © Lennart Nilsson; **p. 113 (middle) 4.4d:** © Nestle/Photo Researchers; **p. 113 (bottom) 4.4e:** © Nestle/Photo Researchers, Inc.; **p. 116:** © Richard Cash/PhotoEdit; **4.6:** © Will, Deni McIntyre/Photo Researchers; **p. 118:** © Chas Cancellare/Picture Group; **p. 119:** © Charles Gupton/Stock Boston; **p. 121:** © Erika Stone; **p. 124:** © Charles Gupton/Tony Stone; **p. 126 (top left):** © Steven McBrady/PhotoEdit; **p. 126 (top right):** © David Brownell/Image Bank–Chicago; **p. 126 (bottom):** © Charles Gupton/Stock Boston; **p. 130:** © Michael Newman/PhotoEdit; **p. 133:** Scala/Art Resource; **p. 137:** Courtesy of Dr. Tiffany Fields.

Chapter 5

Opener: John May Whitey Collection, National Gallery of Art, Wash., D.C.; **p. 143:** © Bruce

McAllister/The Image Works; **p. 145:** © C. Vergara/Photo Researchers; **5.2:** © Hank Morgan/Photo Researchers; **5.4:** © Lennart Nilsson; **5.5:** © Lennart Nilsson; **5.7b (left):** © Elizabeth Crews/The Image Works; **5.7c (middle):** © James G. White Photography; **5.7d (right):** © Petit Format/Photo Researchers Inc.; **5.10:** © Judith Canty/Stock Boston; **p. 153:** Courtesy of Esther Thelen; **5.11:** © Betts Anderson/Unicorn; **p. 162:** © Myrleen Ferguson/PhotoEdit; **5.12:** Courtesy of Dr. Charles Nelson; **5.13b:** © David Linton; **5.15:** © Enrico Ferorelli; **5.16:** © Joe McNally/SYGMA; **5.17a:** © Michael Siluk; **5.17b:** © Dr. Melanie Spence, University of Texas; **5.18:** © Jean Guichard/SYGMA; **5.19:** Rosenstein, D., & Oster. H. (1988), Child Development, 59, pp. 1561–1563.; **p. 166:** John May Whitey Collection, National Gallery of Art, Wash., D.C.; **p. 169:** © George Goodwin/Monkmeyer.

Chapter 6

Opener: © Superstock; **p. 172:** © Joe McNally; **6.1:** © FPG; **6.3:** Adapted from Schirmer, G. J. (Ed), 1974. Performance Objectives for Preschool Children, pp. 69–72: Adapt Press; **p. 177 (top):** © Marc Romanelli/The Image Bank–Chicago; **6.4:** Adapted from Schirmer, G. J. (Ed), 1974. Performance Objectives for Preschool Children, pp. 74–75, Adapt Press; **p. 177 (bottom):** © Bob Daemmrich/The Image Works; **p. 180:** © Les Stone/Sygma; **p. 182:** © David Young Wolff/Photo Edit; **p. 183:** © Alan Carey/Image Works; **6.6:** © Luis Villota/The Stock Market; **p. 185:** © Guiseppe Molteni/The Image Bank–Chicago; **6.7:** © Alan Carey/The Image Works; **p. 190:** © Lawrence Migdale/Stock Boston; **p. 192:** Courtesy of the New York Dept. of Health; **6.11:** © William Hopkins Photography; **p. 194:** © Robert Llewellyn/Superstock; **p. 196:** © Alan Carey/The Image Works; **p. 198:** © George Zimbel/Monkmeyer Press; **p. 200:** © Carl Purcell, 1989; **p. 220 (inset):** © Alan Odie/Photo Edit; **p. 201:** © David R. Frazier/Photo Researchers, Inc.; **p. 203:** © Superstock; **p. 207:** Courtesy of Ruby Takanishi; © Benjamin Tice Smith.

Chapter 7

Opener: © Superstock; **p. 213:** © Yves DeBraine/Black Star; **7.1 (top to bottom):** © Laura Dwight/Peter Arnold, Inc., © C & W Shields, © Gabor Demjen/Stock Boston, © Joel Gordon, © Nancy Sheehan/Photo Edit, © Eric Wheater; **7.2a:** © D. Goodman/Monkmeyer Press; **7.2b:** © D. Goodman/Monkmeyer Press; **7.3:** © Denise Marcotte/The Picture Cube; **7.7:** © Owen Franken/Stock Boston; **7.9:** © Paul Fusco/Magnum Photos, Inc.; **p. 226:** UNICEF/Photo by Sean Sprague; **7.11:** © Richard Hutchings/Photo Researchers, Inc.; **7.12:** © Paul Conklin; **p. 231 (top):** © Ellis Herwig/Spencer Grant/Stock Boston; **p. 231 (middle):** © Stacy Pick/Jim Pickerell/Stock Boston; **p. 231 (bottom):** © Elizabeth Crews/Image Works; **p. 233:** © Yves DeBraine/Black Star; **p. 234:** © M & E Bernheim/Woodfin Camp and Assoc.;

p. 235: © James Wertsch/Washington University; 7.13: © Alan Becker/The Image Bank–Chicago; p. 238: © Superstock; p. 241: © 1990 Barbara Rogoff/Apprenticeship in Thinking (Oxford University Press).

Chapter 8

Opener: © Musée du Louvre, Bridgeman Art Library/Superstock; p. 248: © Suzanne Szasz/Photo Researchers, Inc.; 8.4: Courtesy of Rovee Collier; 8.5: © Joe McNally/SYGMA, p. 252: Courtesy of John Flavell; p. 255 (top): © Superstock, Inc.; p. 255 (bottom): © Tony Freeman/PhotoEdit; p. 259: Courtesy of Henry Wellman; p. 262: © Joe McNally/SYGMA; p. 264: © Margaret Peterson/Image Bank–Chicago; 8.10: © Enrico Ferorelli; p. 269: Courtesy of Judy DeLoache; 8.A: © David Gillison/Peter Arnold; p. 278: © Eiji Miyazawa/Black Star; p. 280: Musée du Louvre, Bridgeman Art Library/Superstock.

Chapter 9

Opener: Bequest of Marion Koogler McNay, collection of the McNay Art Museum; 9.1a: © Mark Antman/The Image Works; 9.1b: © Dr. Rose Gantner/Comstock; 9.1c: © Meike Mass/The Image Bank, Dallas; p. 292: © Rick Friedman/Black Star; 9.5a: © David Austen/Stock Boston; 9.5b: © Ben Simmons/Stock Market; 9.7: © Jill Cannefax/EKM Nepenthe; p. 306: © Bettmann; p. 309: Bequest of Marion Koogler McNay, collection of the McNay Art Museum.

Chapter 10

Opener: Courtesy of Daniel B. Grossman Gallery, New York; 10.1: © H. Anders/The Image Bank–Chicago; 10.2 left: LIFE Magazine July 1993 pg 52; 10.2 right: LIFE Magazine July 1993 pg 52; 10.4: © Enrico Ferorelli; 10.5: From The New Yorker, April 13, 1992, page 41; p. 326: © Katrina Thomas/Photo Researchers; 10.6: © James L. Shaffer; p. 330: ©Anthony Bannister/Earth Scenes/Animals Animals; 10.8: Courtesy of Roger Brown; p. 334 (left): © Brett Froomer/The Image Bank–Chicago; p. 334 (right): © Doug Menuez/Stock Boston; 10.10b: © Richard Howard; p. 338: © Lawrence Migdale/Photo Researchers, Inc.; p. 340: Courtesy of Daniel B. Grossman Gallery, New York; p. 443: © John Carter/ Photo Researchers.

Chapter 11

Opener: © Superstock; p. 348a: © Leonard Lee Rue/Photo Researchers, Inc.; p. 348b: © Mitch Reardon/Photo Researchers, Inc.; p. 348c: © Anthony Boccaccio/The Image Bank–Chicago; 11.1: © Martin Rogers/Stock Boston; p. 350: Courtesy of Dr. Mary Ainsworth; p. 351a: © David Young–Wolff/PhotoEdit; p. 351b: © Kathleen Loewenberg; 352: © Penny Tweedie/Tony Stone Worldwide; p. 353: © Myrleen Cate/PhotoEdit; p. 355: © Cesar Lucas/The Image Bank–Chicago; p. 359: © Alan Oddie/Photo Edit; 11.4: © Joe McNally/SYGMA; p. 366: © J. Gerard Smith/Monkmeyer; p. 369 (background): © David Young–Wolff/Photo Edit; p. 369 (top left): © Luis Villota/Stock Market; p. 369 (top right): © Catherine Gehm; p. 370 (left): © Olivier Rebbot/Woodfin Camp; p. 370 (right): Courtesy of Deborah Belle; p. 371: Courtesy of Madeline Cartwright; p. 373: © Gallery of Modern Art/ET Archive, London/Superstock.

Chapter 12

Opener: © Thomas Nygard Inc.; 12.1: © Dennis Cox; 12.2: © Michael Melford/The Image Bank–Texas; 12.4: © Eddie Adams/Time Magazine; p. 393: © Paul Popper, Ltd.; p. 395: Courtesy of James Marcia; 12.5: © Jeff Persons/Stock Boston; p. 397 (left): Courtesy of Margaret Beale Spencer; p. 397 (right): © Bob Daemmrich/The Image Works; p. 400: © Thomas Nygard; p. 403 (left): © 1988 by Warner Bros. Inc., Photo by Tony Friedkin; p. 403 (right): © Joan Marcus.

Chapter 13

Opener: Daniel Garber/TANIS 1915 The Warner Collection of the Gulf States Paper Corporation; 13.1: © Digital Stock/Babies and Children; 13.2: © Larry Voight/Photo Researchers; p. 410 (left): © Suzanne Szasz/Photo Researchers, Inc.; p. 410 (right): Courtesy of Eleanor Maccoby; p. 411: © The Everett Collection; 13.4: © Ken Gaghan/Jeroboam; p. 417: © Sumo/The Image Bank–Chicago; p. 421 (left): © Bernard Pierre Wolff/Photo Researchers, Inc.; p. 421 (right): © Catherine Gehm; 420: © Tony Freeman/PhotoEdit; p. 424: ©Robert Potter; p. 428: Daniel Garber/TANIS 1915 The Warner Collection of the Gulf States Paper Corporation; p. 429 (top): Bonnie Nevgebauer ALIKE AND DIFFERENT 1992 Washington, D.C. National Association for the Education of Young Children.

Chapter 14

Opener: © Superstock; p. 438: © Joan Bushno/Unicorn Stock Photos; 14.1: © Janeart Ltd./The Image Bank; 14.A: © David R. Frazier Photolibrary; p. 442: © Keith Carter Photography; 14.2: © Barbara Feigles/Stock Boston; 14.3: © D.W. Productions/The Image Bank–Chicago; p. 457: © Edward Lettau/Photo Researchers, Inc; p. 458: © Andrew Sacks/Time; p. 461: © Christie's Images/Superstock.

Chapter 15

Opener: © Superstock; 15.1: © David De Lossy/The Image Bank–Chicago; 15.2 (top to bottom): ©Tony Freeman/Photo Edit; ©Alan Oddie/Photo Edit; © John Carter/Photo Researchers; © Llewellyn/Superstock; © K. Kasmauski/Woodfin Camp; After: Carter, B., McGoldrick, M. Overview: The changing life cycle–a framework for family therapy. In: B. Carter & M. McGoldrick (Eds.) The Changing Family Life Cycle, 2/e, 1989 Allyn & Bacon: Boston p.15; 15.3: © Eri Heller/The Picture Group; p. 482: Courtesy of Dr. Dante Cicchetti; p. 483: © Amy C. Etra/PhotoEdit; p. 484: © Jim Richardson/West Light; 15.4: © Michael Melford/Image Bank; p. 491: © Kenneth Jarecke/Contact Press; p. 494: © Karen Kasmauski/Woodfin Camp; p. 495: © Tim Bieber/Image Bank–Chicago; p. 496: © Kathy Tarantola Photography; p. 498: © Christie's Images/Superstock; p. 499B: James P. Comer and Alvin F. Poussaint, Raising Black Children New York: Plume.

Chapter 16

Opener: © Worcester Art Museum, Worcester, MA, sustaining membership; 16.1: © Erik Anderson/Stock Boston; p. 511: © Erika Stone; p. 513: © Tony Freeman/Photo Edit; 16.4 (top to bottom): © Mary Kate Denny/PhotoEdit; © Jean Claude Lejeune; © Peter Vandermark/Stock Boston; © David De Lossy/The Image Bank–Chicago; © Myrleen Cate/PhotoEdit; p. 515:

© Jan Doyle; p. 519: © Richard Hutchings/PhotoEdit; 16.5 (main photo): © Explorer/Schuster/Photo Researchers, Inc.; 16.5A: © Superstock; 16.5B: © Comstock; 16.5C: © Stephen Marks/The Image Bank–Texas; 16.5D: © Elizabeth Crews/Image Works; 16.5E: © Patrick Watson/Image Works; p. 522 (left): Rosanne Olson/Tony Stone Images; p. 522 (right): © Bryan Peterson; 523A: © Pieter Breughel/Kunsthistorisches Museum; p. 523B: © Bob Daemmrich/The Image Works; p. 528: Courtesy of IBM; p. 529: © Bob Daemmrich/Stock Boston; p. 531: © Worcester Art Museum, Worcester, MA, Sustaining membership.

Chapter 17

Opener: Scala/Art Resource, New York; p. 539 (left): © Don Klumpp/The Image Bank–Chicago; p. 539 (right): © John Ficara/Woodfin Camp; p. 541: © Bettmann; 17.1: © Jake Rajs/Image Bank–Texas; p. 546: © Robert Wallis/SIPA Press; p. 547: © R. Knowles/Black Star; p. 549: © David DeLossy/Image Bank–Texas; p. 551: © Bob Daemmrich/The Image Works; p. 552: Courtesy of Joan Lipsitz; p. 553: Courtesy of I Have A Dream Program; p. 554: © H. Yamaguchi/Gamma Liaison; p. 559: © John S. Abbott; p. 561 (top): © Will McIntyre/Photo Researchers, Inc.; p. 561 (bottom): © Richard Hutchings/Photo Researchers, Inc.; p. 566: Scala/Art Resource, New York.

Chapter 18

Opener: © National Museum of American Art, Washington D.C./Art Resource, N.Y.; p. 574 (top left): © Phil Borges/Tony Stone Images; p. 574 (top right): © Connie Coleman/Allstock/ Tony Stone Images; p. 574 (bottom left): © David Frazier Photolibrary; p. 574 (middle): © Marvin E. Newman/The Image Bank; p. 574 (bottom right): © Carlos Navajas/The Image Bank; p. 575: Courtesy of the Institute for Intercultural Studies, Inc. New York; p. 576: ©Marjorie Shostak/Anthro Photo; p. 577: © Daniel Laine; p. 581: © R. Mayer/Armstrong Roberts; 18.3: © Marc Po Kempner/Tony Stone Worldwide; p. 585 (left): © Olivier Rebbot/Woodfin Camp; p. 585 (right): Courtesy of Dr. Vonnie McLoyd; p. 586 (all): AP/Wide World Photos; p. 587 (top): © Michael Newman/PhotoEdit; p. 587 (main): © Scott Thode/International Stock Photo; p. 587 (middle): © Tony Freeman/PhotoEdit; p. 587 (bottom): © David Hartman/The Image Bank–Texas; p. 592: © National Museum of American Art, Washington, D.C./Art Resource, N.Y.; 18.A (top to bottom): © FPG; ©Peter Turnley/Black Star; © Kevin Horan/Picture Group; Alan Stuart Frank/Photo Researchers; © Joseph Rodriquez/Black Star.

Epilogue

Opener: © T. Rosenthal/Superstock; p. 602 (middle): © Kelsh Marr Studios; p. 602 (top right): © Cammermann Int'l; p. 602 (middle right): © Elyse Lewin/The Image Bank–Chicago; p. 602 (bottom right): © Owen Franklin/Stock Boston; p. 602 (bottom left): © Elyse Lewin/The Image Bank–Chicago; p. 602 (top left): © Elyse Lewin/Image Bank–Chicago; p. 603: © Lennart Nilsson; p. 604: © Niki Mareschal/Image Bank–Texas; p. 605: © Barbara Feigles/Stock Boston; p. 606: © Comstock; p. 607: © J. Devenney/The Image Bank.

Line Art, Excerpts, Poems, Text

Prologue

Poem, p. 1: By Gwendolyn Brooks © 1991. From *BLACKS*, by Gwendolyn Brooks, and published by Third World Press, Chicago, 1991. Reprinted by permission.

Chapter 1

Fig. 1.4: Data from the Children's Defense Fund, 1994; **p. 25:** From Marian Wright Edelman, *The Measure of Our Success: A Letter to My Children and Yours.* Copyright © 1992 Harper Perennial, a division of HarperCollins Publishers, New York, NY. Reprinted by permission; **p. 29:** Reprinted with the permission of Simon & Schuster from *Familyhood* by Dr. Lee Salk; **Fig. 2.1:** From *Psychology: A Scientific Study of Human Behavior* by L. S. Wrightsman, C. K. Sigelman, and F. H. Sanford. Copyright © 1979, 1975, 1970, 1965, 1961 Brooks/Cole Publishing Company, Pacific Grove, CA 93950, a division of International Thomson Publishing Inc. By permission of the publisher.

Chapter 2

Poem, p. 37: From *The Poetry of Robert Frost*, edited by Edward Connery Lathem. Copyright 1936 by Robert Frost. © 1964 by Lesley Ballantine Frost. © 1969 Henry Holt & Co., Inc. Reprinted by permission of Henry Holt & Co., Inc.; **Fig. 2.8,** C B Kopp/J B Krakow, *Child Development in the Social Context*, (page 648), © 1982 by Addison-Wesley Publishing Company, Inc. Reprinted by permission of Addison-Wesley Longman Inc.; **Excerpt pp. 63–64:** From Florence Denmark, et al., "Guidelines for Avoiding Sexism in Psychological Research: A Report of the Ad Hoc Committee on Nonsexist Research" in *American Psychologist*, 43:582–585. Copyright 1988 by the American Psychological Association. Reprinted with permission; **p. 69:** From Erik H. Erikson, *Identity: Youth and Crisis.* Copyright © 1968 W. W. Norton & Company, Inc., New York, NY. Reprinted by permission; **p. 69** From Phillis Moen, et al. (eds.), *Examining Lives in Context: Perspectives on the Ecology of Human Development.* Copyright © by the American Psychological Association. Reprinted with permission; **Poem, p. 82:** From *Verses From 1929 On* by Ogden Nash. Copyright 1940 by Ogden Nash. By permission of Little, Brown and Company; **Fig. 3.11,** From I. Gottesman, "Genetic Aspects of Intellectual Behavior" in *"Handbook of Mental Deficiency,"* Norman R. Ellis (ed.). Copyright © 1963 McGraw-Hill, Inc., New York, NY. Reprinted by permission of Norman R. Ellis; **p. 100:** From *Being Adopted* (jacket cover) by Dr. David Brodzinsky, M. Schechter & R. Henig. Used by permission of Doubleday, a division of Bantam Doubleday Dell Publishing Group, Inc. **p. 101:** Cover from *Prenatal Tests* by Robin J. R. Blatt. Copyright © 1988 Vintage Books, a division of Random House, Inc. Reprinted by permission; **p. 101:** Reprinted with the permission of Simon & Schuster from *How Healthy is Your Family Tree?* by Carol Krause.

Chapter 4

Fig. 4.2, From Charles Carroll and Dean Miller, *Health: The Science of Human Adaption*, 5th ed. Copyright © 1991 Times Mirror Higher Education Group, Inc., Dubuque, Iowa. All Rights Reserved. Reprinted by permission; **Fig. 4.4,** Reproduced from *Pregnancy, Childbirth and the Newborn* by Simkin, P., Whalley, J., and Keppler, A. With permission from the Childbirth Education Association of Seattle and Meadowbrook Press; **Fig. 4.5,** From K. L. Moore, *The Developing Human: Clinically Oriented Embryology*, 4th ed. Copyright © 1988 W. B. Saunders Co., Philadelphia, PA. Reprinted by permission; **p. 134** *What to Expect When You're Expecting* by Arlene Eisenberg, Heidi E. Murkoff, and Sandee E. Hathaway © 1984, 1988, 1991. Cover reprinted by permission of Workman Publishing Company, Inc. All rights reserved; **p. 135:** R S Abrams, *Will It Hurt the Baby?* © 1990 Richard S. Abrams. Reprinted by permission of Addison-Wesley Longman Inc.; **p. 135:** Cover of *Methods of Childbirth* by Constance A. Bean. By permission of William Morrow & Company, Inc.

Chapter 5

Figure 5.6: From *Postnatal Development of the Human Cerebral Cortex*, Volumes I–VI, by J. L. Conel, Cambridge, Mass.: Harvard University Press, Copyright © 1939, 1941, 1947, 1951, 1955, 1959 by the President and Fellows of Harvard College; **Figure 5.8:** From E. Thelen, "Rhythmical Behavior in Infancy: An Ethological Perspective" in *Developmental Psychology*, 17:237-257. Copyright 1981 by the American Psychological Association. Reprinted with permission; **Figure 5.9:** From W. K. Frankenburg and J. B. Dodds, "The Denver Development Screening Test" in *Journal of Pediatrics*, 71:181–192. Copyright © 1967 Mosby-Year Book, Inc., St. Louis, MO. Reprinted by permission; **Figure 5.10:** Source: Data from R. Charlesworth, *Understanding Child Development*, 2d ed, Delmar, Albany, NY, 1987; and G. J. Schirmer (ed.), *Performance Objectives for Preschool Children*, Adapt Press, Sioux Falls, SD, 1974; **p.167:** From *Baby Steps* by Kopp. Copyright © 1994 by W. H. Freeman and Company. Used with permission; **p. 167:** The cover of *Infancy*, by Tiffany Field, Cambridge, Mass.: Harvard University Press, Copyright © 1990 by the President and Fellows of Harvard College.

Chapter 6

Figure 6.1: Source: National Center for Health Statistics, NCHS Growth Charts, *Monthly Vital Statistics Report*, 25(3); **Figure 6.2:** From Albert Damon, *Human Biology and Ecology*. Copyright © 1977 W. W. Norton & Company, Inc., New York, NY. Reprinted by permission; **Figure 6.3:** Source: Data from G. J. Schirmer, *Performance Objectives for Preschool Children*, Adapt Press, Sioux Falls, SD, 1974; **Figure 6.4:** Source: Data from G. J. Schirmer, *Performance Objectives for Preschool Children*, Adapt Press, Sioux Falls, SD, 1974; **Figure 6.5:** From *The Process of Human Development*, 2d ed, by Clara Shaw Schuster and Shirley Smith Ashburn, HarperCollins Publishers. Copyright © 1986 by Clara Shaw Schuster and Shirley Smith Ashburn. Reprinted by permission; **Figure 6.6:** © The Society for Research in Child Development, Inc. Reprinted by permission; **Figure 6.7** From J. M. Tanner, R. H. Whitehouse, and M. Takaishi, "Standards from Birth to Maturity for Height, Weight, Height Velocity, and Weight Velocity: British Children, 1965" in *Archives of Diseases in Childhood*, 41. Copyright © 1966 British Medical Association, London, England. Reprinted by permission; **Figure 6.9:** Source: Data from J. Brooks-Gunn, et al., *Journal of Research on Adolescence*, 4:469–486, 1994; **Figure 6.10:** Source: Data from The Guttmacher Institute, 1988; **Figure 6.11:** Source: Data from *Child Trends*. Child Trends, Washington, DC, 1996; **p. 204:** Hornick/Rivlin. Reprinted by permission; **p. 205:** From *Kid Fitness* (jacket cover) by Kenneth H. Cooper. Used by permission of Bantam Books, a division of Bantam Doubleday Dell Publishing Group, Inc.; **p. 205:** *Great Transitions: Preparing Adolescents for a New Century*, Carnegie Council on Adolescent Development, Carnegie Corporation of New York, October 1995.

Chapter 7

Figure 7.4 left: Dennis Palmer Wolf/Project PACE; **Figure 7.4 right:** Courtesy of Dr. Ellen Winner, Project Zero; **p. 239:** D Elkind, *The Hurried Child*. © 1988 by David Elkind. Reprinted by permission of Addison-Wesley Longman Inc.; **Figure 7.14:** Reprinted from Baillargeon, *Cognition*, 1986, page 27, with kind permission from Elsevier Science - NL, Sara Burgerhartstraat 25, 1055 KV Amsterdam, The Netherlands.

Chapter 8

Figure 8.3: From Steve Yussen, et al., "The Robustness and Temporal Cause of the Story Schemas Influence on Recall" in *Journal of Experimental Psychology: Learning, Memory, and Cognition*, 14:173–179. Copyright 1988 by the American Psychological Association. Reprinted with permission; **Figure 8.6:** From Joel Levin, et al., "The Keyword Method in the Classroom" in *Elementary School Journal*, 80:4. Copyright © 1980 University of Chicago Press. Reprinted by permission; **Figure 8.7:** From M. T. H. Chi and R. D. Koeske, "Network Representation of a Child's Dinosaur Knowledge" in *Developmental Psychology*, 19:29–39. Copyright 1983 by the American Psychological Association. Reprinted with permission; **Figure 8.9:** From Robert S. Siegler, *Four Rules for Solving the Balance Scale Task*. Copyright © Robert S. Siegler. Reprinted by permission; **Figure 8.11:** From Klahr and Robinson (1981), "Formal Assessment of Problem Solving and Planning Processes in Preschool Children." *Cognitive Psychology*, 13:113–148. Copyright © Academic Press. Reprinted by permission; **Figure 8.12:** From J. Kagan, et al., "Conceptual Impulsivity and Inductive Reasoning" in *Child Development*, 37:585. Copyright © 1966 The Society for Research in Child Development, Inc. Reprinted by permission; **Figure 8.A** © The Society for Research in Child Development, Inc. Reprinted by permission; **p. 218:** Cover copyright © Lundgren Graphics, New York, NY. Reprinted by permission.

Chapter 9

Figure 9.4: Courtesy of John W. Berry; **Figure 9.6:** Item A5 from Raven's *Standard Progressive Matrices*. Reprinted by permission of J. C. Raven Limited; **p. 310:** From Testing and Your Child by Virginia E. McCullough. Used by permission of Dutton Signet, a division of Penguin Books USA; **p. 311:** From Howard Gardner, *Creating Minds*. Copyright © 1993 Basic Books, a division of HarperCollins Publishers, New York, NY.

Reprinted by permission; **p. 311:** From Ellen Winner, *Gifted Children.* Copyright © 1996 HarperCollins Publishers. Reprinted by permission.

Chapter 10

Figure 10.7: From "Recognize Language Development and Delay in Early Childhood" by J. U. Dumtschin, 1988, *Young Children,* 43(3), p. 19. Copyright 1988 by the National Association for the Education of Young Children. Used by permission; **Figure 10.8** From Roger Brown, et al., "The Child's Grammar from I to III" in John P. Hill (ed.), *Minnesota Symposia on Child Psychology,* Vol. 2. Copyright © 1969 University of Minnesota Press, Minneapolis, MN. Reprinted by permission; **Figure 10.9:** From Berko, *Word,* 14:361. Copyright © 1958 International Linguistic Association, New York, NY. Reprinted by permission; **Figure 10.10:** Source: Data from Spear-Swirling and Sternberg, 1994; **Figure 10.11:** From Dickinson, Wolf, and Stotsky, *The Development of Language,* 3d ed, Jean Berko Gleason (ed.). Copyright © 1993 by Allyn and Bacon. Reprinted by permission; **p. 341:** From Naomi S. Baron, *Growing Up with Language,* 1992. Design copyright © Stephen Gleason. Photo © Elizabeth Hathon. Reprinted by permission.

Chpater 11

P. 341: From Eden Lipson, *The New York Times Parents' Guide to the Best Books for Children.* Copyright © 1991 Random House, Inc. Reprinted by permission of Random House, Inc., and Gloria Adelson/LuLu Graphics, New York, NY; **Figure 11.2:** From M. D. Ainsworth, "The Development of Infant Mother Attachment" in *Review of Child Development Research,* Vol. 3, B. Caldwell and H. Ricciut (eds.). Copyright © The Society for Research in Child Development. Reprinted by permission; **Figure 11.5:** Excerpts from *The Optimistic Child.* Copyright © 1995 by Martin E. P. Seligman, Ph.D., Karen Reivich, M.A., Lisa Jaycox, Ph.D., and Jane Gillham, Ph.D. Reprinted by permission of Houghton Mifflin Company. All rights reserved; **p. 374:** The cover of *Daycare,* by Alison Clarke-Stewart, Cambridge, Mass.: Harvard University Press, Copyright © 1982, 1993 by Kathleen Alison Clarke-Stewart; **p. 375:** © 1990 Hornick/Rivlin; **p. 375:** Cover from *The Optimistic Child.* Copyright © 1995 by Martin E. P. Seligman, Ph.D., Karen Reivich, M.A., Lisa Jaycox, Ph.D., and Jane Gillham, Ph.D. Reprinted by permission of Houghton Mifflin Company. All rights reserved.

Chapter 12

Excerpt, p. 380: From S. Shirley Feldman and Glen R. Elliott, *At the Threshold: The Developing Adolescent,* 1990. Reprinted by permission; **Figure 12.1:** From M. Lewis and J. Brooks-Gunn, *Social Cognition and the Acquisition of the Self.* Copyright © 1979 Plenum Publishing Corporation. Reprinted by permission; **Figure 12.3** From R. C. Savin-Williams and D. H. Demo, "Conceiving or Misconceiving the Self: Issues in Adolescent Self-Esteem" in *Journal of Early Adolescence,* 3:121–140. Copyright © 1983 by H.E.L.P. Books, Inc., Tucson, AZ. Reprinted by permission of Sage Publications, Inc.; **p. 401:** Reprinted with the permission of

Simon & Schuster from *The Road Less Traveled* by M. Scott Peck. Copyright © 1978 by Simon and Schuster, Inc.; **p. 401:** D Elkind, *All Grown Up and No Place to Go,* © 1984 David Elkind. Reprinted by permission of Addison-Wesley Longman Inc.

Chapter 13

Figure 13.3: Illustration by Carole Byard reprinted by permission of Coward, McCann & Geoghegan, Inc. from *Cornrows* by Camille Yarbrough, illustrations copyright © 1979 by Carole Byard; **Figure 13.5:** From Janet S. Hyde, et al., "Gender Differences in Mathematics Performance" in *Psychological Bulletin,* 107:139–155. Copyright 1990 by the American Psychological Association. Reprinted with permission; **p. 429:** Reprinted with the permission of Simon & Schuster from *Mismeasure of Woman* by Carol Tavris; **p. 429:** Cover from *You Just Don't Understand* by Deborah Tannen. Copyright © 1990 Ballantine Books, a division of Random House, Inc. Reprinted by permission; **p. 429:** From Bonnie Neugebauer (ed.), *Alike and Different.* Copyright © 1992 National Association for the Education of Young Children. Reprinted by permission.

Chapter 14

Figure 14.1: From Steve Yussen, "Characteristics of Moral Dilemmas Written by Adolescents" in *Developmental Psychology,* 13:162–163. Copyright 1977 by the American Psychological Association. Reprinted with permission; **Figure 14.A:** From R. Shweder, et al., "Culture and Moral Development" in J. Kagan and S. Lamb (eds.), *The Emergence of Morality in Young Children.* Copyright © 1987 University of Chicago Press. Reprinted by permission; **Excerpt, p. 443:** Source: *Making Connections: The Relational Worlds of Adolescent Girls at Emma Willard School,* Carol Gilligan, Nona P. Lyons, and Trudy J. Hanmer (eds.), Harvard University Press, 1990; **Figure 14.3:** Source: Data from E. L. Dey, et al., *The American Freshman: Twenty-Five-Year Trends,* 1991; A. W. Astin, et al., *The American Freshman: National Norms for Fall,* 1991, 1993, 1994; and E. L. Dey, et al., *The American Freshman: National Norms for Fall,* 1992; Higher Education Research Institute, UCLA; **Figure 14.5:** From *Adolescents at Risk: Prevalence and Prevention* by Joy G. Dryfoos. Copyright © 1991 by Joy G. Dryfoos. Used by permission of Oxford University Press, Inc.; **p. 463:** Reprinted with the permission of Simon & Schuster from *How to Save the Children* by Amy Hatkoff and Karen Klopp.

Chapter 15

Figure 15.16: From Jay Belsky, "Early Human Experiences: A Family Perspective" in *Developmental Psychology,* 17:3–23. Copyright © 1981 by the American Psychological Association. Reprinted with permission; **Figure 15.5:** Source: F. Hobbs, "Child's Well-Being: An International Comparison," U.S. Department of Commerce: Bureau of the Census, 1990; **p. 499:** From *Children: The Challenge* by Rudolf Dreikurs, M.D., with Vickie Soltz, R.N., Copyright 1964 by Rudolf Dreikurs, M.D. Used by permission of Dutton Signet, a division of Penguin Books USA Inc.;

p. 499: From *Raising Black Children* by James P. Comer and Alvin F. Poussaint. Copyright 1975, 1992 by James P. Comer and Alvin F. Poussaint. Used by permission of Dutton Signet, a division of Penguin Books USA Inc.

Chapter 16

Figure 16.4: Source: Data from Dexter C. Dunphy, "The Social Structure of Urban Adolescent Peer Groups" in *Sociometry,* Vol. 26, American Sociological Association, 1963; **p. 533:** P. Zimbardo, *Shyness,* © Phillip Zimbardo, Inc. Reprinted by permission of Addison-Wesley Longman Inc. Illustration © 1989 by Bart Goldman. Reprinted by permission; **p. 533:** From Lillian Rubin, *Just Friends.* Copyright © 1985 HarperCollins Publishers. Reprinted by permission; **p. 538:** Reprinted by permission of Transaction Publishers. *Successful Schools for Young Adults* by Joan Lipsitz. Copyright © 1984 by Transaction Publishers, Rutgers–the State University of New Jersey; all rights reserved.

Chapter 17

Figure 17.1: Excerpted from *Developmentally Appropriate Practice* (pp. 54–56), S. Bredekamp, ed., 1987, Washington, DC: the National Association for the Education of Young Children. Copyright © 1987 by NAEYC. Used by permission; **p. 567:** From Sue Bredekamp and Teresa Rosegrant (eds.), *Reaching Potentials: Appropriate Curriculum and Assessment for Young Children,* Vol. I. Copyright © National Association for the Education of Young Children. Reprinted by permission; **p. 567:** Reprinted with the permission of Simon & Schuster from *Smart Schools, Smart Kids* by Edward Fiske.

Chapter 18

Poem, p. 572: Reprinted by permission from *Selections from the Writings of 'Abdu'l-Baha.* Copyright © 1978 by the Universal House of Justice; **Figure 18.1:** From Harry C. Triandis, "Making Basic Texts in Psychology More Culture-Inclusive and Culture-Sensitive." Reprinted by permission; **Figure 18.2:** Source: Data from A. C. Erlick and A. R. Starry, "Sources of Information for Career Decisions" in *Report of Poll No. 98,* Purdue Opinion panel, June 1973, by Purdue Research Foundation, West Lafayette, IN; **Figure 18.3:** Source: Data from *The State of America's Children,* The Children's Defense Fund, Washington, DC, 1992; **p. 593:** From Janet Simons, Belva Finlay, and Alice Yang, *The Adolescent & Young Adult Fact Book.* Copyright © 1993 Children's Defense Fund, Washington, DC. Reprinted by permission; **p. 593:** From Jewelle Taylor Gibbs and Lake Nahme Huang and Associates, *Children of Color.* Copyright © Jossey-Bass, Inc., Publishers. Reprinted by permission of Willi K. Baum; **p. 593:** From Walter J. Lonner and Roy Malpass (eds.), *Psychology and Culture.* Copyright © 1994 Allyn and Bacon. Reprinted by permission.

NAME INDEX

Miller, J., 9, 441
Miller, J. B., 422, 423
Miller, J. G., 439, 441
Miller, K. F., 66, 269, 365
Miller, M. E., 85
Miller, N., 476
Miller, P., 9
Miller, P. H., 252
Miller, P. J., 520
Miller, S. A., 82
Miller, S. I., 116
Miller, W. B., 457
Miller-Jones, D., 300
Minnett, A. M., 484
Minuchin, P. P., 540, 554, 557
Mischel, H., 444
Mischel, W., 47, 443, 444
Mitchell, C., 551
Mitteness, L. S., 476
Mitts, N., 368
Mize, J., 505
Modell, J., 52
Moely, B. E., 252
Moffitt, T. E., 357
Molmes, D. L., 246
Monsour, A., 383
Montemayor, R., 486
Moore, C. F., 464
Moore, M. S., 244, 395, 486
Moran, G., 350
Morelli, G. A., 234, 241
Morgan, J. L., 318
Morris, P. A., 51
Morrison, F. J., 246
Morrison, G. S., 528
Morrongiello, B. A., 161, 164
Morrow, L., 6
Mortimer, E. A., 144
Mortimore, P., 556
Mory, M., 514
Moses, N., 142
Moshman, D., 232
Mosley, J., 543
Mott, F. L., 194
Mounts, N. S., 513, 515
Mozley, L. H., 415
Muecke, L., 181
Muehchow, S., 548
Mueller, N., 482
Muir, D. W., 153
Mumme, R. L., 79
Mundy, P., 327
Munroe, R. H., 421
Munroe, R. L., 421
Murkoff, H., 106
Murowchick, E., 59, 185
Murphy, B., 439, 451
Murphy, K., 508
Murphy, M. N., 228
Murphy, S. O., 483
Murray, C., 84, 94, 102
Murray, D. A., 59, 185
Murray, H. A., 562
Murray, J., 116
Murray, V. M., 194
Myers, M., 335

Nabors, L. A., 354
Nadar, P. R., 179
Nagata, D. K., 572
Nakagawa, K., 564
Nanson, J., 116
Nathan, J., 527
National Academy of Medicine, 143
National Advisory Council on
    Economic Opportunity, 369
National and Community Service
    Coalition, 465
National Association for the Education
    of Young Children, 337, 338,
    356, 526, 542, 547, 548, 550
Neal, C., 471
Neckerman, K. M., 369
Needleman, H., 118
Neighbors, H. W., 425
Neimark, E. D., 229
Neimeyer, R. A., 481
Neisser, U., 298, 302, 303
Nelson, K. E., 325, 327
Nevid, J. S., 191
Newberger, C. M., 535
Newcombe, N., 261
Newman, D. L., 357
Newman, J., 143
New Yorker, 20
Ng'andu, N., 582
Ngini, L., 226
Nguyen, H. H., 485
NICHD Early Child Care Research
    Network, 355
Nicholls, J. G., 563
Ninio, A., 332
Nisbett, R. R., 562
Nishio, K., 425
Noir, S., 421
Nolen-Hoeksema, S., 366
Nottlemann, E. D., 185, 188, 365
Novack, L. L., 218
Nucci, L., 452
Nugent, J. K., 127
Nurcombe, B., 136
Nurius, P., 384
Nusbaum, H. C., 247
Nydegger, C. N., 476
Nyiti, R. M., 226

Obeidallah, D., 366
Oberg, M., 581
Obler, L. K., 322, 323
O'Brien, M., 15, 491
O'Connell, K. L., 561
Oden, M. H., 306
Offer, D., 200
Ogbu, J. U., 307, 396, 515, 558, 565
O'Hara, N. M., 182
Okamoto, Y., 234
Okun, B. F., 478
O'Laughlin, M., 268
Oller, D. K., 337
Olson, F. A., 252

Olson, H. C., 116
Olson, S. L., 369
Olweus, D., 188, 505
O'Malley, P. M., 195, 196, 448
Onwughalu, M., 396
Ordonez, N., 397
Orlansky, M. D., 218
Ornstein, P. A., 283
Orthner, D. K., 492
Ortmann, J., 197
Orwell, G., 172
Oser, F. K., 452
Oster, H., 163
Ostoja, E., 351, 472
Ostrov, E., 200
Otto, R., 77
Ouston, J., 556
Overa-Ezzell, N., 180
Owen, D. R., 87
Owen, M. T., 116, 471
Owsley, C. J., 164

Padgett, R. J., 118
Paget, K. D., 480
Paikoff, R. L., 187, 188, 486
Palincsar, A. M., 274
Palmer, S. A., 495
Paludi, M. A., 63, 79, 420, 422, 423
Panak, W. F., 365, 508
Paneth, N. S., 125
Pang, S., 115
Papert, S., 528
Parcel, G. S., 179, 181, 182
Parham, T. A., 425
Paris, S. G., 251, 335
Park, K. A., 362
Park, K. J., 355
Parke, R. D., 52, 352, 443, 477
Parker, B., 114
Parker, F. L., 548
Parker, J. G., 505, 507, 509
Parmalee, A. H., 180
Parrott, S. A., 448
Partanen, T., 362
Parten, M., 518
Pascual-Leone, J., 233, 275
Patrick, H., 505
Patterson, C., 507
Patterson, C. J., 191, 444
Patterson, G. R., 35, 456, 457, 487
Patterson, S. J., 398
Paulson, S. E., 562
Pavlov, I. P., 43–46, 55, 68
Pearson, S., 548
Pecheux, M. G., 164
Pederson, D. R., 350
Pedro-Carroll, J. L., 489
Pellegrini, A. D., 57
Pellegrino, J. W., 286, 293
Pennebaker, J., 360
Penner, S. G., 326
Pepler, D. J., 484
Perfetti, C. A., 335
Perkins, D. N., 313, 569
Perloff, R., 298, 302, 303

$\mathscr{S}$UBJECT INDEX

Bell curve concept
    criticisms of, 95
    intelligence, 94–95
Bem Sex-Role Inventory, 418, 419
Bilingualism, 337–38
    bilingual education, 337, 338
    effects of, 337–38
Binet intelligence test, 12, 289
Biological concepts, children's
    understanding of, 260
Biological processes
    and development, 16
    evolutionary theory, 77–80
    and gender development, 407
    heredity, 82–95
    and reproduction, 82–83
Birth order, 483–84
    characteristics of
        firstborns/laterborns/only
        children, 484
Birth process. *See* Childbirth
Blastocyst, 107
Blinking reflex, 150
Bonding, mother-infant, 129–30
Boundary ambiguity, stepfamilies, 490
Brain
    development of, 146–47
    in early childhood, 174
    in infancy, 144, 146–47
    language areas, 321
    structures of, 144–45
Brazelton Neonatal Behavioral
    Assessment Scale, 127, 129
Breast-feeding, versus bottle-
    feeding, 143
Breech position, 121
Brightness constancy, 159
Broca's area, 321
Bulimia, 198

C

Canada, cultures of, 589
Canalization, 92
Cardinality, of number, 262, 263
Careers in child development, 21,
    22–23
Care perspective, moral development,
    440, 442
Carolina Abecedarian Project, 298
Case studies, 57
Centration, Piaget's theory, 222
Cephalocaudal growth, 141
Cesarean section, 121
Character education, 451–52
Child abuse, 479–82
    cultural context of, 480–81
    developmental consequences of, 481–82
    intervention for, 482
    severe abuse, effects of, 480
Childbirth
    complications of, 121
    doula, 123
    drugs in childbirth, 121–22
    father's participation, 124
    infant assessment measures, 127
    Lamaze method, 123
    Leboyer method, 122
    low-birthweight infants, 125–26
    postpartum period, 127, 129–31

prepared (natural) childbirth, 122–23
    preterm infants, 125
    sibling preparation, 124–25
    stages of, 120–21
    standard childbirth, 122
    trends related to, 123–24
Child care policy, sociocultural
    view, 354
Child-centered kindergarten, 540
Child development
    careers in, 21, 22–23
    ethnic minorities in field of, 24
    historical view of study, 10–12
    modern study of, 12–13
    rationale for study of, 7
    and social policy, 13, 15
    themes related to, 597–600
Child development issues
    education, 7–8
    family, 7
    sociocultural issues, 8–10
Child development theories
    behaviorism, 43–47
    eclectic theoretical orientation, 53–54
    ecological theory, 49–51
    Erikson's theory, 38–41
    ethological theories, 48–49
    Freud's theory, 36–38
    information processing, 43
    life course theory, 51–52
    Piaget's theory, 41–42
    social learning theory, 47–48
Child maltreatment, use of term,
    481–82
Children's Defense Fund, 15
Chlamydia, 191
Chorionic villus test, 87
Chromosomes, 82
    and sex-determination, 83, 90, 407
Chronosystem, 50–51
Cigarette smoking, and prenatal
    development, 116
Classical conditioning, 44–46
    counterconditioning, 46
    Pavlov's experiment, 44–45
    of phobias, 44–45
    stimulus/response concept in, 44–45
Classification, Piaget's theory, 224, 226
Clinical depression, 365
Cliques, 513–14
    functions in adolescence, 513–514
Cocaine
    adolescents' use of, 196
    and prenatal development, 116–17
Cognitive appraisal, 367
Cognitive development
    information processing, 43
    and language development, 327
    Piaget's theory, 41–42
    Vygotsky's theory, 234–36
Cognitive developmental theory,
    gender development, 417–18
Cognitive monitoring, 274–75
    definition of, 274
    instructional methods for, 274–75
Cognitive moral education, 452–53
Cognitive processes, and
    development, 16
Cognitive social learning theory, moral
    behavior, 444–45

Cognitive styles, 275–76
    impulsivity, 275
    and problem solving, 275–76
    reflection, 275
Cognitive theories
    of depression, 365
    of stress, 367
Cohort effects, nature of, 62
Collectivism, characteristics of, 576
Color vision, 157
Commitment, and identity
    development, 394
Common Cents, 465
Community, and juvenile
    delinquency, 457
Compact Youth Incentive Program,
    402–3
Comprehensive Child Care Bill, 15
Computers, 527–29
    computer-assisted instruction, 527–28
    negative effects of, 529
    positive effects of, 527–28
Concept development, 257–63
    of biological concepts, 260
    concept of mind, 258–60
    concepts as implicit theories, 257–58
    of physical concepts, 260–63
    and semantic network, 257
Concepts, in infancy, 218–19
Concrete operational stage
    classification, 224, 226
    conservation, 224
    horizontal décalage, 224
    nature of, 42, 223–27
Conditioned response (CR), 45
Conditioned stimulus (CS), 45
Conduct disorders, 455
Conformity, and peer pressure, 513
Connectedness, meaning of, 396
Conscience, 445
Conservation
    Piaget's theory, 222, 224
    sociocultural view, 226
Constructive play, 521–22
Constructivist view, perceptual
    development, 155
Content knowledge, 254–56
    novices and experts, 255
Content validity, 288
Context, meaning of, 9
Continuity of development, 598
    meaning of, 19
Continuity view, relationships, 471–72
Controversial children, 507
Conventional reasoning, moral
    development, 436–37
Convergent thinking, 307
Cooperative learning, 568
Cooperative play, 518
Correlational research, 60, 61
Correlation coefficient, 60
Counterconditioning, process of, 46
Counting, 263
Creativity, 307–8
    definition of, 307
    and divergent thinking, 307
    snowflake model, 313
    and television viewing, 527
Crisis, and identity development, 394
Criterion validity, 288–89

Emotionality, 357
Emotions, 360–62
    definition of, 360
    functions of, 361–62
    gender differences, 416
    and moral development, 448–49
    new functionalist approach, 363–64
    parent/child affective
        communication, 362
    positive and negative affectivity, 360–61
Empathy, 445–48
    global empathy, 446
Endoderm, 107
Environmental hazards, and prenatal
    development, 117–19
Equilibration, Piaget's theory, 214
Erikson, Erik, biographical
    information, 34
Erikson's theory, 38–41
    of attachment, 349–50
    basis of, 38–39
    identity development, 393–94
    play, 518
    stages in, 39, 41
Erogenous zones, 37
Estradiol, 185
Estrogen, 407, 415
Ethics, and child development
    research, 63
Ethnic gloss, and cross-cultural
    research, 59
Ethnic identity, meaning of, 10
Ethnicity
    compared to race, 80
    emphasis on differences, 585–86
    meaning of, 10, 584
    and pluralism, 588–89
    world conflicts related to, 584
Ethnic minorities
    and acculturative stress, 368–69
    and achievement, 563–64, 575–76
    diversity within groups, 8–9, 564,
        586–87
    and family, 493, 494
    in field of child development, 24
    and gender roles, 424–26
    growth of population, 8
    and high school dropouts, 553
    and identity development, 396–98
    and peers, 515
    and poverty, 582
    and prejudice, 587–88
    and schools, 557–59
    and self-esteem, 390
    and social class, 582, 584–85
Ethnocentrism, 573
    and self-esteem, 389
Ethological theories, 48–49
    of attachment, 349–50
    critical period in, 49
    imprinting, 48
Ethology, meaning of, 48
Etic approach, cross-cultural
    research, 58
Evocative genotype-environment
    interactions, 95
Evolutionary psychology, 79–80
    applied to child development, 79–80
    basic principles of, 79
    criticism of, 80
    sex differences, view of, 416

Evolutionary theory, 77–80
    adaptive behavior, 77
    evolutionary psychology, 79–80
    language development, 321
    natural selection, 77
    sociobiology, 78–79
Exercise, 181–82
    deficiency for children, 181–82
    healthy forms of, 182
Exosystem, 50
Expanding, 324
Experimental research, 60–61
    random assignment in, 60–61
    variables in, 61
Experts, 255
Extrinsic motivation, 562

F

Faces, infant recognition of, 157–58
Family
    and adolescents, 485–86
    child abuse, 479–82
    contemporary issues related to, 7
    divorce, 487–89
    and ethnic minorities, 493, 494
    and exercise participation, 182
    father's role, 495, 496
    historical view, 477
    life cycle of, 474–77
    mother's role, 493, 495
    scaffolding behavior, 471
    siblings, 482–83
    and socialization, 471–73
    stepfamilies, 489–91
    and unemployment, 492–93
    working parents, 491–93, 494
    See also Parenting
Family services, pyramid concept,
    594–95
Family structure model, of divorce
    effects, 487
Fathers
    caregiving and attachment, 352–53
    participation in birth process, 124
    role in family, 495, 496
    and schooling of child, 569
    See also Family; Parenting
Feminization of poverty, 584
Fetal alcohol syndrome (FAS), 116
Fetal period, 109
Fine motor skills
    in early childhood, 175–76
    handedness, 176–77
    in infancy, 153
    in middle/late childhood, 178–79
Forebrain, 145
Formal operational stage, 227–32
    abstract thought, 228
    adolescent egocentrism, 228
    compared to young adult thinking, 232
    early/late phases of, 229
    hypothetical-deductive reasoning,
        228, 229
    imaginary audience, 228
    individual variations in, 229, 231
    nature of, 42
    personal fable, 228
Fraternal twins, 93
Freud's theory, 13, 36–38
    of attachment, 349
    criticisms of, 40

    defense mechanisms, 36–37
    ego-ideal, 445
    erogenous zones, 37
    id/ego/superego, 36
    latency/genital stage, 38
    moral feelings, 445
    Oedipus complex, 37–38
    oral/anal/phallic stage, 37
    play, 518
Friendships, 509–12
    functions of, 509–11
    gender differences, 511–12
    importance of, 509
    and intimacy, 511–12
    and similarity, 512
    Sullivan's view of, 509–11
Frontal lobe, 145
Fusion model, cultural change, 578

G

Games, 522
Gametes, 82
Gangs, violent youth, 458
Gender, meaning of, 10, 407
Gender development
    biological influences, 407
    cognitive developmental theory, 417–18
    gender schema theory, 413
    hormonal influences, 407
    identification theory, 408–9
    and language, 414
    and parenting, 409–10
    peer influences, 410
    school/teacher influences, 410–11
    social influences, 407–8
    social learning theory, 409
Gender differences
    aggression, 415, 417
    biological differences, 415
    and context, 417
    emotions, 416
    friendships, 511–12
    identity development, 398
    issues related to, 416–17
    mathematics ability, 415
    moral development, 440, 442
    social connectedness, 415
    verbal ability, 415
Gender identity, meaning of, 407
Gender intensification hypothesis, 420
Gender roles
    androgyny, 418–19
    and asymmetric gender socialization, 422
    and ethnic minorities, 424–26
    gender intensification hypothesis,
        420, 430
    gender-role transcendence, 420, 422
    instrumental/expressive traits, 417
    meaning of, 407
    men's issues, 423–24
    past view of, 417–18
    sociocultural view, 421
    transitional points in development, 422
    women's issues, 422–23
Gender schema, 413
Gender schema theory, gender
    development, 413
Gender stereotypes
    forms of, 414
    meaning of, 414
    and media, 411–12
    sociocultural view, 414

Generativity versus stagnation, 39, 41
Genes, 82
Genetic abnormalities, 85–87
  anencephaly, 88
  cystic fibrosis, 88
  Down syndrome, 85–86, 88
  hemophilia, 88
  incidence of, 87
  Klinefelter's syndrome, 87, 88
  phenylketonuria (PKU), 85, 88
  pyloric stenosis, 88
  sickle-cell anemia, 86, 88
  spina bifida, 88
  Tay-Sachs disease, 88
  thalassemia, 88
  Turner's syndrome, 87, 88
  XYY syndrome, 87
Genetic counseling, process of, 103
Genetic epistemology, meaning of,
    13–14
Genetic principles, 87, 90–92
  canalization, 92
  dominant-recessive genes principle, 90
  genotype and phenotype, 91, 92
  polygenic inheritance, 91
  reaction range, 91
Genetic testing
  amniocentesis, 87
  chorionic villus test, 87
  maternal blood test, 87
  ultrasound sonography, 87
Genital herpes, and prenatal
    development, 114
Genital stage, 38
Genotype, 91, 92
Germinal period, 107
Gesell measure, of infant
    intelligence, 294
Giftedness, 305–7
  characteristics of, 306
  gifted disadvantaged children, 307
  and IQ score, 305
  Terman study, 306–7
Global empathy, 446
Grammar, language development, 333–34
Grandparenting, 476–77
Grasping reflex, 148, 150
Gross motor skills
  in early childhood, 175
  in infancy, 151–52
  in middle/late childhood, 178
Guilt, 445, 449

ℋ

Habituation, in infancy, 249, 250, 295
Handedness, 176–77
  development of, 177
  left-handedness, 176–77
Health
  exercise, 181–82
  obesity problem, 181
  and poverty, 180
  and young children, 179
Health education programs, 179
Hearing, development in infants, 160–61
Height
  early childhood, 173–74
  infancy, 141
  middle/late childhood, 178
  and puberty, 186

Helpless orientation, and motivation,
    563
Hemophilia, 88
Heredity, 82–95
  behavior genetics, 92–93
  genes, 82
  genetic abnormalities, 85–87
  genetic principles, 87, 90–92
  genetic testing, 87
  influence on development, 93–95
  and reproduction, 82–84
Heredity-environment controversy
  intelligence, 93–95, 297–98
  nature of, 96–97
Heredity-environment interaction,
    95–97, 598
  active (niche-picking) genotype-
    environment interactions, 95
  evocative genotype-environment
    interactions, 95
  passive genotype-environment
    interactions, 95
  shared and nonshared environmental
    experiences, 96
Heroin, and prenatal development, 116
Herpes simplex virus II, 191
Heteronomous morality, 435
Hidden curriculum, 451
High school dropouts, 552–54
  and ethnic minorities, 553
  intervention for, 553–54
  statistics about, 552
Hindbrain, 144
Historical influences, in life course,
    51–52
History of child development study
  behavioral approach, 13
  early research centers, 12
  Freud's view, 13
  genetic epistemology view, 13–14
  Gesell's study, 12–13
  Hall's study, 12, 13
  innate goodness view, 11
  original sin view, 11
  Piaget in, 13
  tabula rasa view, 11
Holophrase hypothesis, 328
Homosexuality, 190–91
  views of causation, 190–91
Horizontal décalage, Piaget's
    theory, 224
Hormones
  and gender development, 407
  and puberty, 185–86, 188
Hypotheses, definition of, 35
Hypothetical-deductive reasoning,
    228, 229

ℐ

Id, 36
Identical twins, 93
Identification theory, gender
    development, 408–9
Identity achievement, 395
Identity development
  components of, 394
  and developmental changes, 395
  and education/work programs, 402–3
  Erikson's theory, 393–94
  and ethnic minorities, 396–98
  gender differences, 398

identity statuses in, 394–95
  and juvenile delinquency, 456
  and parenting, 395–96
  and role experimentation, 393–94
Identity diffusion, 394
Identity foreclosure, 394–95
Identity moratorium, 395
Identity versus identity confusion, 39,
    41, 393
Idiographic needs, 65
I Have a Dream (IHAD) Program, 553
Illness
  early childhood, 179–80
  global view, 180–81
Imagery, memory strategy, 253
Imaginary audience, 228
Imitation
  by infants, 265–66
  and problem solving, 265–66
Immanent justice, 435–36
Implantation, in fertilization, 107
Imprinting, 48
Impulsivity, cognitive style, 275
Inclusion, 560
Independent variable, 61
Index offenses, 455
Indirect moral education, 452
Individual differences
  assessment of, 287
  in cognitive style, 275–76
  intelligence, 287
Individualism, characteristics of, 576
Individuality, meaning of, 396
Induction, discipline method, 450, 451
Indulgent parenting, 479
Industry versus inferiority, 39, 41
Infancy
  brain, development of, 144, 146–47
  emotions in, 362–63
  infant states, 141–42
  language development, 328, 330, 342–43
  memory in, 249
  motor development, 147–55
  nutrition, 142–44
  perceptual development, 155–64
  physical growth, 141–42
  self-understanding, 381
  time span of, 17
  toilet training, 144
Infant assessment measures
  Apgar scale, 127
  Brazelton Neonatal Behavioral
    Assessment Scale, 127, 129
Infant intelligence tests, 294–95
  Bayley Scales of Infant Development,
    294–95
  Gesell measure, 294
Infant states, 141–42
Infertility
  and adoption, 84–85
  incidence of, 84
  in vitro fertilization, 83–84
Infinite generativity, of language, 317
Information processing
  academic skills, 270–73
  attention, 250–51
  automaticity, 250
  basis of theory, 43
  characteristics of approach, 245
  cognitive monitoring, 274–75
  compared to Piagetian approach, 245–46

concept development, 257–63
content knowledge, 254–55
critical thinking, 273–74
cultural differences, 276–79
and depression, 365
habituation/dishabituation, 249
individual differences, 275–76
memory, 246–49
memory strategies, 251–53
metacognitive knowledge, 253–54
perceptual development, 155
problem solving, 263–70
and reading, 334–36
Initiative versus guilt, 39, 41
Innate goodness, 11
Insecure attachment, 350
Integration, cultural change, 578
Integrity versus despair, 39, 41
Intelligence
adoption studies, 93
bell curve concept, 94–95
contextual views, 298–300
and creativity, 307–8
cultural/ethnic comparisons, 298–300
definitional disagreements, 293–94
definition of, 287
early intervention, effects of, 298, 312
giftedness, 305–7
heredity-environment controversy,
93–95, 297–98
individual differences, 287
mental retardation, 304–5
multiple-factor theory, 291
prediction in childhood, 295
seven intelligences theory, 291–92
stability of, 295
triarchic theory, 292–93
twin studies, 94, 297
two-factor theory, 290
Intelligence quotient (IQ)
formula for, 289
meaning of, 289
Intelligence tests
Binet test, 289
cultural bias, 95, 300–301
culture fair tests, 301–2
infant intelligence tests, 294–95
norms, 289
reliability, 287
standardization, 289
Stanford-Binet intelligence test, 289–90
use and misuse of, 302–3
validity of, 288–89
Wechsler scales, 290
Interactionist view, language
development, 326–27
Intermodal perception, 163–64, 218
auditory-visual intermodal perception,
164, 168
haptic-visual intermodal perception, 164
meaning of, 164
Internalization, moral
development, 436
Internalization of schemes, 216
Interpersonal norms, 436
Interviews, research-oriented, 57
Intimacy, and friendships, 511–12
Intimacy versus isolation, 39, 41
Intrinsic motivation, 562
Intuitive thought substage, 220–22
In vitro fertilization, 83–84
Involution, 129

J

Journals
child development, types of, 70
format of articles, 70–71
Junior high school. *See* Middle school
Justice perspective, moral
development, 440
Juvenile delinquency, 455–59
and community, 457
conduct disorders, 455
and identity development, 456
index offenses, 455
and parenting, 456–57
prevention/intervention, 458–59
and social class, 457
status offenses, 455
violent youth, 457–58

K

Kaufman Assessment Battery for
Children, 302
Keyword method, memory strategy, 253
Klinefelter's syndrome, 87, 88
Kohlberg's moral development theory,
436–40
criticisms of, 439–40
influences on, 438–39
levels of moral development, 436–38

L

Labeling, 324
Laboratory observation, 56
Lamaze method, 123
Landmark-based representations, of
physical concepts, 261
Language
characteristics of, 317
definition of, 317
and gender development, 414
Language acquisition device (LAD), 324
Language acquisition support system
(LASS), 327
Language development
animals and language learning, 321–22
behavioral view, 325–26
bilingualism, 337–38
and biological evolution, 321
and brain, 321
and cognition, 327
critical period, 322–23
early childhood, 330–33, 343
grammar, 333–34
infancy, 328, 330, 342–43
interactionist view, 326–27
language acquisition device (LAD), 324
language acquisition support system
(LASS), 327
mean length of utterance (MLU), 330
middle/late childhood, 333–37
motherese in, 324
parental activities for promotion of, 326,
342–43
reading, 334–37
and rules of language, 331–33
and social class, 580–81
social supports for, 324–25
sociocultural view, 324, 325
telegraphic speech, 330
and thought, 236
vocabulary, increases in, 333

Language rules
developmental view of learning of,
331–33
morphology, 319
phonology, 317–19
pragmatics, 320
semantics, 320
syntax, 319–20
Latchkey children, 492
Late childhood. *See* Middle/late
childhood
Latency stage, 38
Latinos
diversity within groups, 586
family system of, 494
female gender role, 425
identity development, 397–98
male gender role, 426
and poverty, 582
and schools/education, 557–59
self-esteem, 390
single-parent families, 493
Launching, family life cycle, 474
Learned helplessness, and
depression, 365
Learning disability
educational interventions, 560
nature of, 560
Leboyer method, 122
Life course theory, 51–52
historical influences, 51–52
linked lives, 52
planful competence, 52
social timing of lives, 52
Life events, and stress, 367
Life-history records, 59
Literacy, 336–37
definition of, 336
emergent literacy, 336
literacy programs, 336–37
Longitudinal research, 62
Long-term memory, 247
Love withdrawal, discipline
method, 450
Low-birth-weight infants, 125–26
cross-cultural view, 128
intervention programs for, 127, 136
and later development, 126–27
size of, 125

M

Macrosystem, 50
Major depressive disorder, 365
Malnutrition
in America, 145
in infancy, 144
Manville School, 535
Marasmus, 144
Marginalization, cultural change, 578
Marijuana, and prenatal development,
116
Masculinity, male problem behaviors,
420
Massage
of preterm babies, 136–37
therapeutic use with children, 137
Mastery orientation, and motivation,
563
Maternal age, and prenatal
development, 111

secondary circular reactions, 215–16
  simple reflexes, 215
  tertiary circular reactions, 216
  time span of, 214
Sensory memory, 246–47
Separation, cultural change, 578
Set point, and body weight, 181
Seven intelligences theory, 291–92
Sex, meaning of, 10
Sex-determination, and chromosomes, 83, 90, 407
Sex education, sociocultural view, 194
Sexist research, 63–64
  guidelines for nonsexist research, 63–64
Sexuality, 188–91
  adolescent behaviors, 189–90
  homosexuality, 190–91
  sexual scripts, 190
Sexually abused children, repressed memories of, 283
Sexually transmitted diseases, 191–93
  AIDS, 192–93
  chlamydia, 191
  herpes simplex virus II, 191
  moral reasoning about, 464
  syphilis, 191–92
Shape constancy, 158–59
Shared environmental experiences, 96
Short-term memory, 247
Siblings, 482–83
  birth order, 483–84
  preparation for new baby, 124–25
  and socialization, 483
  sociocultural view, 483
  temperament, effects of, 484
Sickle-cell anemia, 86, 88
Size constancy, 158
Sleep
  infancy, 141–42
  REM (rapid eye movement) sleep, 142
Slow-to-warm-up child, 357
Smell, infant sensation of, 162–63
Smiling, infancy, 363
Snowflake model, creativity, 313
Sociability, 357
Social class
  and child rearing, 580
  elements of, 580
  and ethnic minorities, 584–85
  and juvenile delinquency, 457
  and language development, 580–81
  and neighborhood schools, 581
  poverty, 581–84
  and psychological problems, 581
Social cognition, and peer relations, 508–9
Social comparisons, and self, 384
Social connectedness, gender differences, 415
Social identity theory, self-esteem, 388–89
Social isolation
  and language development, 323, 324
  problems of, 505
Socialization, 471–73
  reciprocal socialization, 471
  and siblings, 483
Social learning theory, 47–48
  gender development, 409
  moral behavior, 444–45
  observational learning, 47–48

Social play, 521
Social policy
  and child development, 13, 15
  and teenage pregnancy, 194–95
Social smile, 363
Social system morality, 436–37
Sociobiology, 78–79
  basis of, 78–79
  criticism of, 79
Sociocultural context, 8–10
  context in, 9
  culture in, 9
  ethnicity in, 10
  gender in, 10
Sociocultural view
  achievement, 276–79
  child care policy, 354
  conservation (Piagetian), 226
  culture-making and people, 78
  early childhood education, 546
  gender roles, 421
  gender stereotypes, 414
  intelligence, 298–300
  language development, 324, 325
  mathematics learning, 276–78
  moral development, 441
  play, 522–23
  prenatal care, 128
  problem solving, 269–70
  rites of passage, 577–78
  secondary schools, 554
  self-esteem, 389, 390
  sex education, 194
  sports training for children, 172
  temperament, 358–59
Socioemotional development
  attachment, 349–56
  emotional development, 362–64
  emotions, 360–62
  temperament, 356–60
Socioemotional processes, and development, 16
Solitary play, 518
Spina bifida, 88
Sports participation
  competitive pressures of, 182, 183
  positive/negative aspects, 183
Standardization of test, 289
Standardized tests, 57–58
Stanford-Binet intelligence test, 289–90
Status offenses, 455
Stepfamilies, 489–91
  and coping, 491
  problems of, 490–91
Stepping reflex, 150
Stereotypes
  of adolescents, 200–201
  gender and media, 411–12
  meaning of, 200
Strange Situation, 351, 352
Stress, 366–71
  acculturative stress, 368–69
  cognitive view, 367
  and daily hassles, 368
  definition of, 367
  and life events, 367
  maternal, and prenatal development, 111
  and optimism/pessimism, 367, 368
  and poverty, 369–70
  and resilience, 370–71
Sucking reflex, 147, 148, 150

Sudden infant death syndrome (SIDS), 142
Suicide
  and adolescents, 196–97
  causes of, 197
  steps to take, 197
Superego, 36, 445
Swimming, for infants, 152
Swimming reflex, 150
Symbolic function substage, 219–20
Syntax
  and language development, 332
  nature of, 319–20
Syphilis, 191–92
  and prenatal development, 114
System of Multicultural Pluralistic Assessment (SOMPA), 301–2

T

Tabula rasa, 11
Taste, infant sensation of, 163
Tay-Sachs disease, 88
Teachers, 556–57
  traits of effective teachers, 556–57
Telegraphic speech, 330
Television, 524–27
  and aggression, 525–26
  amount watched by children, 525
  and changing family, 477
  and cognitive development, 526–27
  multiple-roles of, 524
  and overweight, 182
  and prosocial behavior, 525–26
Temperament, 356–60
  activity level, 357
  definition of, 356
  difficult child, 357, 360
  easy child, 357
  emotionality, 357
  and parenting, 359–60
  and siblings, 484
  slow-to-warm-up child, 357
  sociability, 357
  sociocultural view, 358–59
  stability/consistence of, 358
Temporal lobe, 145
Teratogens, and prenatal development, 114
Terman study, giftedness, 306–7
Tertiary circular reactions, 216
Testosterone, 185, 415
Test-retest reliability, 287–88
Thalassemia, 88
Thalidomide, and prenatal development, 115
Theories of development. *See* Child development theories
Theory, definition of, 35
Toilet training, 144
Tonic neck reflex, 150
Top-dog phenomenon, 551
Touch, infant sensation of, 161
Toxoplasmosis, and prenatal development, 119
Triarchic theory, intelligence, 292–93
Trophoblast, 107
Trust versus mistrust, 39, 41, 349–50
Turner's syndrome, 87, 88
Twins, identical and fraternal, 93